*The
Negotiator's
Fieldbook*

Published by the American Bar Association, Section of Dispute Resolution

ABA Section of Dispute Resolution
740 15th St. NW, Washington, DC 20005
(202) 662-1680
Fax (202) 662-1683
dispute@abanet.org
www.abanet.org/dispute

Section Director: Ellen M. Miller
Staff Editors: Gina Viola Brown, Stephen Kotev and Ellen Miller
Managing Editor: Carrie Kratochvil

Cites were checked by Laurie Best, Angie Hanneman, Kristi Henkelman, Teresa Kern, Anson Kuri-akose, Brett Larson, Kyle Lindsey, Mat Pauley, Michael Rust, and Andrea Will, and Stacey Meyer performed a final full check. The index is by Robert Elwood.

Library of Congress Cataloging-in-Publication Data
The negotiator's fieldbook / Andrea Kupfer Schneider, Christopher Honeyman, editors.–1st ed.
p. cm.
Includes index.
ISBN 1-59031-545-6
1. Dispute resolution (Law)–United States. 2. Negotiation in business–United States.
I. Schneider, Andrea Kupfer. II. Honeyman, Christopher. III. American Bar Association. Section of Dispute Resolution.
KF9084.Z9N436 2006
347.73'9–dc22
2006021678

The Negotiator's Fieldbook

Andrea Kupfer Schneider
Christopher Honeyman

Editors

AMERICAN BAR ASSOCIATION
SECTION OF DISPUTE RESOLUTION
WASHINGTON, DC

SUMMARY OF CONTENTS

ANNOTATED TABLE OF CONTENTS

Mnookin's on the principles of "not negotiating," and to Morash's, whose discussion of "nonevents" is one form of the systemic chilling that Bingham discusses here.

What do you do when you think something should be discussed, but others don't seem to recognize there's an issue? This essay uses specific examples from health care to make a larger point. Health care professionals often choose not to view supposedly-minor errors and "incidents" as triggering a need for a discussion with a patient. By taking this view, of course, they set themselves up for a confrontation later, when and if the patient finds out anyway. Do similar assumptions limit discussion with your kinds of clients? What are the consequences?

"How can I shake them out of their complacency?" Hawkins, Hyman & Honeyman use three different examples to discuss the first step of a negotiation—getting the other side even to recognize that you might have something worthwhile to add. Linked to the chapters on avoiding negotiation and "nonevents," this chapter addresses the problems and tactics of getting your counterpart to recognize that there is a negotiation table, and that they will be better off if they meet you around it.

How do you know when it's time to get serious about negotiating? When is a deal ready to be made? In the settlement of civil disputes, we often see parties expensively delaying negotiations, even waiting for mediation till they're on the proverbial courthouse steps. Is there a science to this? From the perspective of international relations, Zartman analyzes the issue of ripeness and demonstrates when it's time to settle.

Does how we negotiate reflect or shape our character, or both? Does choosing to negotiate have moral implications? What are the ethical and moral implications of making the assumption that negotiation is inappropriate? Here, Menkel-Meadow notes that not all negotiation is based in the idea of compromise, and discusses the ethical and moral underpinnings of our choices in negotiation—choices we can ignore we are making, but cannot avoid making.

In all of negotiation there is no bigger trap than "fairness." Welsh explains why: among multiple models of fairness, people tend to believe that the one that applies *here* is the one that happens to favor *them*. This often creates a bitter element in negotiation, as each party proceeds from the unexamined assumption that its standpoint is the truly fair one. Welsh argues that for a negotiation to end well, it is imperative for both parties to assess the fairness of their own proposals from multiple points of view, not just their instinctive one—and to consider the fairness of their procedures as well as of their substantive proposals (in which respect this chapter should be read in conjunction with Putnam on Communication).

Your dilemmas as a negotiator fall into two basic sets, "what's possible?" and "what's right?" The first is treated by many chapters in this book. Here, from his philosopher's background, Gibson writes about the influence of morality on negotiations, and how we can think more clearly about what's the right thing to do.

This chapter should be read in conjunction with Menkel-Meadow and with Ryan on Rawls; for the rebound effects, you might turn next to Tinsley et al., Reputations.

        How far can you go in extolling the virtues of your widgets without crossing the line to fraud? Other chapters (on trust, reputation, ethics) consider the morality and the implications of negotiation behavior. This chapter focuses on the legal limits of negotiation: sometimes, you or your counterparts have employees with children to feed, and somebody *will* go to the limit of what is legally permissible. Every negotiator needs to know where that limit actually is and how it's influenced by the context.

        Can you both trust and distrust the other side? In fact, we often do exactly that. Lewicki provides practical advice on dealing with trust and distrust in each interaction. Of particular importance to negotiators facing troubled relationships, this chapter shows how distrust is not merely a mirror image of trust: it actually works quite differently. Effective negotiators must learn both to build trust *and* to manage distrust. This chapter should be read in conjunction with Tinsley et al., Reputations.

        Time was when a Formica plaque could often be found on the desk of a certain type of negotiator. It said "Yea, when I walk through the Valley of the Shadow of Death I shall fear no evil, for I am the meanest son of a bitch in the valley." Is it really to your advantage to have a reputation as one of the junkyard dogs of negotiation? The authors approach the question from three very different starting points. Tinsley summarizes the research on reputation in controlled settings. Schneider turns to real-life reputations of lawyers in action. Finally, Cambria shows how the life-and-death negotiations which characterize the work of the New York Police Department's Hostage Negotiation Team have led to a new understanding of reputation. This chapter should be read in conjunction with Lewicki on Trust.

        Most discussions of negotiation tacitly assume that self-interest is the predominant, or even the only, basis for what is going on. Discussing the fascinating research on altruism in negotiation, Wade-Benzoni explains that many negotiations actually include an element of "negotiating with the future"—and that in these settings, negotiators may act in unexpected and pro-social ways. This chapter should be read in conjunction with Welsh on Fairness.

III. The People on All Sides   224
A. Who Are You?

        How can you expect to get good results in a negotiation if you give little thought to who you really are, and to who your counterpart is? Shapiro analyzes the research on identity, showing how you can predict the likely reactions of your counterpart to some kinds of proposals—as well as your own propensity to avoid some kinds of proposals that might be to your advantage. This chapter should be read in close conjunction with the chapters on internal conflict, psychology and perceptions.

        Have you ever been in a negotiation where you (or the other side) seem to be acting instinctively, but perhaps not helpfully? Have you wondered what was going on inside your counterpart? Deutsch summarizes how psychological theory applies to basic negotiation, and explains how negotiators' internal conflicts affect them and everybody else in the room.

for you. Using e-mail, it turns out, can distort what you're trying to say, and may also affect your perception of what *they* are trying to say.

chapters on team negotiations, particularly Bellman's on internal discord within a team.

negotiators can miss their own team's internal signals has implications for your negotiations too. What can you do, the next time you are working with a team under high pressure and with high stakes, to improve your own communication?

       The third chapter in our trilogy on teams discusses how, as negotiator or mediator, you may find yourself in a complex dispute in which one of the parties appears to have substantial conflicts within its team. Bellman shows why these conflicts, when they are not amenable to the same techniques the mediator would use for inter-party conflicts, may be resolved by developing an internal mediator within the conflicted team.

       When setting up for a negotiation, let alone actually in one, it's all too easy to focus on the numerous tasks immediately in front of you. Docherty argues that for many negotiations, the key to unlocking the potential is to think more broadly about how to achieve the *overall* objectives. What tools are available to supplement the obvious one of sitting down with your counterparts? Should some of these, perhaps, come first? Should some be used simultaneously with negotiation? And should you plan to use still other "away from the table" tools to sustain your agreement?

       How's your negotiation going? Is it possible you need a mediator? This chapter, the first of our mediation trilogy, uses three different case studies to show why and when mediation can help negotiators reach an agreement. It explains the different types of mediation goals, and how each of those goals can affect the process. This should be read in conjunction with Honeyman on Understanding Mediators and Abramson on the Culturally Suitable Mediator.

       Perhaps you've reached the point in the negotiation where it's time to bring in a third party. This chapter, the second in our mediation trilogy, helps you make wise choices about whom to hire as a mediator. It's designed to help the negotiator understand how mediators actually operate, and to be aware of the skill set and biases within which any given mediator must operate.

       Often overlooked in the search for a mediator is the need for one whose competence includes cultural awareness. Any ordinary negotiator is more likely than ever before to find herself in a negotiation with a party from another country, or a different culture within the same country. This chapter discusses the most common culture-based differences in mediation styles, and when each might be appropriate. It should be read in conjunction not only with the other chapters on mediation but also with the chapters by Kelly and Goh on negotiating in other cultures.

       In a thought-provoking book, Mayer analyzed new roles that experienced mediators and other neutrals might play. Here, he takes the other side of the coin, and discusses how negotiators could enlist skilled neutrals as allies instead. This could help you to get a complex negotiation framed properly or to approach the other side in ways that will put them in the right frame of mind.

ACKNOWLEDGEMENTS

We owe thanks to a long list of people who made this book possible. We'd like to detail their exact contributions; but we would also like you to be able to fit this book on your bookshelf! So we have to be brief. We first thank our authors, who are the backbone of this effort. We thank them not only for the quality of their contributions (which the reader can see for herself) but beyond that, for two things that are not so obvious: their frequently rather quick turn-around time, and their universal graciousness throughout the long and involved editing process.

Three institutional players have underpinned this undertaking. We thank the William and Flora Hewlett Foundation, a longtime supporter of Chris, as well as Marquette University, for their financial support and encouragement, and not only throughout the initiative that led to this book. As explained in the Introduction and Appendix, this book is actually the culmination of a long line of projects that Hewlett and Marquette have supported. We are both very grateful for the opportunities these projects have created, but in particular, for their making this book possible. And our publisher, the ABA's Section of Dispute Resolution, deserves our warm thanks, particularly Ellen Miller and Gina Viola Brown, for their untiring support of this risk-taking project as well as for their wise suggestions along the way.

A team at Marquette Law School has had a less obvious, but indispensable role. We particularly appreciate the extraordinary amount and care of the work Andrea's assistant Carrie Kratochvil put into this book; she became invaluable to the ABA as well as to the editors. Andrea's small army of students, meanwhile, dispatched with aplomb a remarkable amount of interdisciplinary cite-checking, and double-checking. Our thanks go to Laurie Best, Angie Hanneman, Kristi Henkelman, Teresa Kern, Anson Kuriakose, Brett Larson, Kyle Lindsey, Mat Pauley, Michael Rust, and Andrea Will for their conscientiousness, as well as for devoting more time to this project than any of them expected. Thanks go also to Stacey Meyer for her final "please nitpick" read, delivered in amazingly quick fashion.

Most of all, we thank our families, who not only have supplied lots of our own stories about conflict and its resolution, but more importantly, inspire us both to continue to work for the next generation. This book is dedicated, in order of increasing experience with the world's need for better negotiation, to Zachary, Noah, Joshua, Catie, Ian, Rodd and Elaine.

I. Why Even the Best Get Stuck

☙ 1 ❧

Introduction: A "Canon of Negotiation" Begins to Emerge

Christopher Honeyman & Andrea Kupfer Schneider

The White Rabbit put on his spectacles.
"Where shall I begin, please your Majesty?" he asked.

"Begin at the beginning," the King said gravely,
"and go on till you come to the end: then stop."

Lewis Carroll, Alice's Adventures in Wonderland, 1865

Perhaps concerned about falling down the White Rabbit's proverbial hole, most readers tend to apply the King's advice to themselves, and to treat books as a straight-line proposition. This book, however, is designed to reward different ways of approaching it, depending on who you are.

If much of your everyday work is negotiation or mediation and you're faced with an all-too-real negotiating problem every week, we believe you will find here the most comprehensive available reference work on negotiation. This book is a working tool that can help you figure out quickly what went wrong in yesterday's meeting, and how to fix it in tomorrow's follow-up. And if you see your needs primarily in those terms, you will be in good company. The wisest and most experienced of negotiators will often admit that at certain critical moments, they simply do not know what to do.

And negotiation skills are clearly needed more broadly than just by working professionals, in a world in which small manufacturers find their customers and their suppliers on the far side of the globe; in a world in which lifetime stability of employment has been replaced by successive negotiation for new jobs; and in a world in which prenuptial agreements and mediated divorces flank a noticeable percentage of marriages. On a larger level, those who advance concepts of peacebuilding, as a matter of morality or as a matter of political will that "peace must be waged," increasingly recognize that the work of peacemaking requires negotiation at many levels. In many other settings, there is growing understanding that negotiation can help achieve the maximum results with the minimum long-term cost.[1] Readers with any of these interests might also logically see this book primarily as a reference work, and one to keep close at hand.

Meanwhile, the intellectual basis of the field is now wide, multidisciplinary, and deep. The diversity of sources and of uses, however, has created a trap. No one, literally *not one* negotiator or scholar of the field, has truly been able to keep up with all the new knowledge, while the drive to establish negotiation as an essential practice in law, in business, in planning and in other professional practices has created an impetus toward using and highlighting the discoveries invented in each respective discipline. The result is fractionation, the opposite of what is so desperately needed: continuous improvement in everyday understanding of what different disciplines have to contribute to each other's conceptions and to practical skills in negotiation. We believe that challenging ourselves to rethink our field and our supposed "truths" at recurrent intervals is the only way to reverse that fractionation, or even to keep it from becoming much worse.

So if you are a negotiation professor or a scholar in any of a variety of professional disciplines, you will find here chapters that summarize ideas and research from a multitude of perspectives. This book stands as an assertion that in the future, *all* relevant disciplines must be included in negotiation textbooks and courses offered—regardless of the discipline you actually teach.

The fact that so many different perspectives are included is, of course, what leads to the length of this book. As you can read in more detail in the Appendix, when we started thinking about a negotiation canon—i.e. the things that should be considered for inclusion in every course regardless of discipline—the *current* "taught everywhere" list was remarkably small: it appeared that only six topics were taught consistently in negotiation classes across disciplines. Our first effort at expanding this list was published in the MARQUETTE LAW REVIEW in Spring 2004. It included an additional 25 topics. Two years later, we have arrived at 80.

The Structure of This Book

Perhaps the easiest way to think about the collection of materials here is in three different areas. First are the topics that a knowledgeable reader might *expect* to find in an up-to-date book on negotiation, and the authors one might expect to find writing them. Yet those expectations are, of course, formed by your particular field and experience, because of the current fractionation of the field discussed above. Thus no matter what discipline you work in, a quick review of the *Contributors* section at the back of the book will probably reveal not only some names you know well, but some others who seem equally famous, and are nevertheless new to you.

Lawyers, for an obvious example, would probably expect chapters on building skills, managing fairness and power, understanding the other side, cultural differences and the like. Less familiar to lawyers, perhaps, are topics like aspirations, decision-making, creativity, and apology. These have been of great interest to negotiation scholars for some time, but are still relatively new to the textbooks. One step further from lawyers' standard expectations are some topics from non-law disciplines that are starting to be introduced to new audiences. For example, certain concepts from psychology, particularly barriers such as loss aversion, the endowment effect, and anchoring, have started to migrate rather consistently into law school classes in negotiation, though not yet into practice manuals for those long past law school. In this book, we have tried to take the same logic further, including chapters from related disciplines in social psychology and positive psychology, disciplines with other kinds of links, such as international relations and economics, and disciplines previously regarded as totally unrelated to law, such as the arts and neurobiology.

There are also topics in this book that are relatively specialized, and yet crucial if you find yourself in the particular situation each one addresses. For example, Sanda Kaufman's chapter on the use of interpreters in negotiation is a completely new concept for many of us (including these editors); but the day you find yourself in an international negotiation, we predict you are going to need that chapter. Similarly, few of us, other than hostage negotiators, have thought in any disciplined way about the challenges of negotiating with disordered or mentally ill people, and how their illnesses might affect the negotiation. Yet the percentage of the population that has a diagnosable mental illness at one time or another is strikingly large. So it is likely that every professional will face this often bewildering situation more than once during a career, and we concluded the subject was essential to include in a reference work.

Finally, we found experienced practitioners who could directly relate theory to practice. The most perceptive practitioners are often good at demonstrating how openness to multiple sources of influence and learning has enriched their practice and sharpened their practical skills. So, interspersed with more theoretical pieces, we have included chapters that show how some of the best negotiators and mediators working today have integrated their hard-won knowledge into practical multidisciplinary skills.

Because of this multiplicity of approaches, we recognize that no two readers are likely to see these offerings in quite the same way. Some will find one chapter too academic, some will find another too practical. Certain chapters may seem difficult, or strange. We hope you will try them out anyway—they may be the ones that years from now you most remember, as having provided you with a whole new way of looking at an issue.

With our multiple purposes in mind, we have opted for something of a "scaled" approach to the order of chapters, starting with concepts that affect large numbers of participants in settings that transcend single negotiation "cases," and working toward more individual concerns.[2] Thus, following the three context-setting chapters in the introductory section is a series of chapters built around how people tend to frame negotiation. This discussion proceeds to when a negotiation is really what's needed, along with underlying concepts of morality and fairness. The subject then shifts successively to the people on all sides; strategies and tactics for a particular case; enlisting help of various kinds; and finally, what it takes to become *really* good at negotiation.

Several people[3] suggested that a single, conventional table of contents cannot do justice to the variety of potential reader interests here. We agree. Accordingly, we have put one alternate table of contents on the Web,[4] and will consider making others available to serve the interests of different "idea markets." We invite suggestions.

We should also note that many chapters relate to other chapters in the book that are not contiguous. We have tried to highlight this in two ways. The editors' note at the beginning of each chapter points to related chapters. And rather than putting references to other chapters in endnotes, we have kept such "internal" references within the text, signified by square brackets with the author and abbreviated title of the referenced chapter. For example, an internal reference to this Introduction would show as [Honeyman & Schneider, *Introduction*]. We hope this helps you find your own best order of chapters.

This Book and Existing Texts

As we've indicated above, we hope teachers of negotiation and students will see this volume as a potential textbook for a course that is badly needed, but as yet barely exists anywhere—a truly cross-disciplinary advanced course in negotiation.

At one level, courses in negotiation have already become a staple of higher education in many kinds of schools. In parallel, a number of negotiation texts have been developed. Those works, however, tend to fall into one of three patterns. In the existing market, a book on negotiation is typically intended either as (1) a mass-market primer; (2) a text for a basic course; or (3) a specialized work intended to develop further skills and/or understanding, but within a single discipline. The result is that no previous work has attempted to articulate the basis for an advanced course in negotiation in its entirety, i.e. one that truly draws from the many fields which have contributed to our collective understanding of negotiation. We should offer students a corresponding caution, though. *If you have never taken a course in negotiation or looked at one of the basic texts in the field, this book may not be for you; at least, not as your first reading.* We have, in fact, made every effort to avoid including material which is effectively shared across fields in textbooks already in use.

What's Next?

As we have not tried to write a formal conclusion to the book, this seems a good moment to articulate a few goals that have been implicit in this and in predecessor projects. (For the context, please see the book's Appendix.) We know, of course, that no two people could possibly come up with a full-scale plan for achieving these goals. The most we can do is to commit to working toward them; but articulating them clearly for your consideration is an element of that commitment.

Where do we go from here? To begin with, we believe the "A" in "ADR" must be put to rest as a core concept of the field. Dispute resolution as we know it and teach it is not at all *alternative*, it is increasingly the norm. For example, relatively few people outside law schools or law practice know that the likelihood, when someone "makes a Federal case" out of something, that it will actually go to trial is now all of 1.8%. (That is not a misprint, and the recent numbers for state courts show a similar trend.[5]) Many more people have a general sense that what was once "alternative" is now increasingly "accepted." Some programs have already updated their "A" to "appropriate;" true integration of the field into daily life will be achieved when the "A" is eliminated completely.

Within law schools, business and planning schools and other professional programs, we need to see to it that equal or greater resources are devoted to training in dispute resolution as to other skills. Until our students are actually trained in the skills necessary to implement the ideas in this book and elsewhere—perhaps via new material under the existing headings of interviewing, counseling, negotiating, decision-making, team management and more—this will remain theory, not fully available in actual practice to clients, business colleagues, and citizens.

Universities must promote interdisciplinary connections in a meaningful way. It's time to demand that universities move toward incorporation of interdisciplinary work requirements in hiring, tenure and promotion processes, perhaps using questions such as "Whom have you been working with outside this field? What have you produced together? What additional fields do you think you need to work with next?" Of course, the cross-disciplinary workshops, networks, and publications also need to be encouraged and rewarded. A sign that "we're getting there" will be when we see dispute resolution skills taught in ways that show that teachers understand the value of disciplines that are not their own, and integrate their learnings into curricula for all levels of education. In parallel, schools will move beyond peer mediation programs, recognizing the life skills that can be taught. In turn, critically important institutions such as the military and police will come to recognize these as core competencies, so that they as well as other kinds of employers will increasingly hire and promote based on them.

We will know we've had success in negotiation skill-building when enough of us are good enough at resolving conflicts, once they arise, that we find ourselves able to focus more energy on preventive diplomacy in all areas, developing theories of what kinds of interventions and actions prevent or mitigate disputes in the first place along with practical skills to match. We will also focus more on implementation after agreements are reached, so that "resolution" is recognized as involving the ongoing management of conflict.

Finally, the conclusive sign of success of the dispute resolution field will be a visible sea change in how our culture characterizes disputes. Rather than the "argument culture" of Deborah Tannen,[6] we look forward to popular authors writing about our "culture of negotiation." Lawyers and other agents will someday be portrayed in film and on television as possessing problem-solving skills, serving their clients with an accurate perception of the client's real needs, more than with zealous pit-bull advocacy. So we need to find ways to help popular culture absorb and reflect the "new advocacy" as described in this book by Julie Macfarlane.

"No news is good news" works in reverse too, so it's not clear that good news about successful resolution of disputes will ever become celebrated. But an equivalent might be to see metaphors of creativity and cross-cultural understanding supplanting the tired metaphors of the past drawn mostly from war and sports.

Conclusion: a Limitation and a Warning

Two forms of modesty are essential in a book that attempts to cover such broad conceptual territory. The first is cultural. The co-editors of this book are all too aware that we are both Westerners. Although we are fortunate to have a few contributors whose starting points are far from typical Western perspectives, we acknowledge that the overall approach we take and the subjects we consider relevant are controlled by forces we only imperfectly understand. Simply put, we don't know what we don't know.

Second, like the reader, the co-editors of this book are grounded in specific experience; we must admit that each of us operates from a knowledge base that is, at best, partial. Assembling this volume has been an enlightening but also a humbling experience. The sources of wisdom in our "composite field" are so diverse and fast-moving that an effort like this can succeed only if it thoroughly enlists criticism and amendment. The Appendix describes our efforts in that direction so far. But our field's capacity to surprise and to innovate will certainly continue. We look forward to the discoveries yet to be made as well as to the enlightenment that will come from critiques of this work.

In the meantime, we hope you will find the writings in this volume to be wise, and that, whatever immediate concern impelled you to pick this book up, the book will help you in your upcoming negotiation tomorrow.

Endnotes

[1] For example, the U.S. Air Force has won awards for its dispute resolution program, initially in the area of military contracting, where its previous methods had resulted in significant public black eyes. A major reason for the change in methods was the realization that there were so few potential bidders for increasingly high-tech contracts that the Air Force had *no choice* but to teach the companies that compete with each other for its prime contracts to cooperate with each other as well. When the prime contract is awarded, it is now routine for the winning bidder to find it must immediately subcontract large parts of the job to its competitor, just to get the job done on time and to the exacting specification. *See* "The Air Force's Alternative Dispute Resolution Program Was Honored As The Best In The Federal Government At A White House Ceremony" (Air Force Acquisition Newsletter, April-May 2002, *available at* https://www.safaq.hq.af.mil/news/aprilmay02/adr_award.cfm (last visited Feb. 26, 2006). Subsequently, the Air Force has expanded its understanding of uses of negotiation into "deployed settings"—*e.g.* Iraq. C.J. Dunlap, Jr. and P.B. McCarron, *Negotiation in the Trenches*, DISPUTE RESOLUTION MAGAZINE, Fall 2003, at 4-7.

[2] We would like to acknowledge our debt to another field—architecture—which has encountered a similar problem. In particular, a remarkable book compiled by six architects, *A Pattern Language*, showed us the value of the "scaled" approach to ordering disparate information, thus proving useful beyond its original domain—itself a telling exemplar of the principles behind this book. This book was an extraordinary effort to compile aspects of town planning, design of individual buildings, and details of those buildings which have survived through hundreds of years, remaining responsive to human needs across radical changes in society. CHRISTOPHER ALEXANDER, ET AL., A PATTERN LANGUAGE (1968).

[3] We are indebted, in particular, to audience members at our presentations to the Wisconsin Association of Mediators, Madison, Wisconsin and the Program on Negotiation/ESSEC conference on negotiation teaching, Cergy, France, for their suggestions.

[4] A permanent Web page address (URL) has not been established at the time of printing. A search on *negotiator's fieldbook alternate contents* or similar terms, using any standard Internet search engine, should locate it.

[5] *See*, for instance, Marc Galanter, *A World Without Trials?* JOURNAL OF DISPUTE RESOLUTION (forthcoming 2006) and also the various commenting articles in that issue.

[6] Deborah Tannen, THE ARGUMENT CULTURE: MOVING FROM DEBATE TO DIALOGUE (1999).

❧ 2 ❧

The Unstated Models in Our Minds

Jayne Seminare Docherty

Editors' Note: *You're an experienced negotiator. But when was the last time you examined your own pattern of thinking? And is your pattern the same as your counterpart's? This chapter helps you work out what's going on under the surface, and leads onward to chapters about framing, internal conflict of the negotiator, and the characteristic problems of teams. It also suggests which chapters in this book best address your real-world negotiation problems, and how to get the most out of negotiation research.*

In 2003 Christopher Honeyman and Andrea Schneider convened a working conference of faculty members who teach negotiation in various disciplines. We were asked "to begin a conversation about creating a canon of negotiation" and then write papers collaboratively that would be published in the *Marquette Law Review*. The hope was that after struggling and wrestling to reach consensus about what should be taught in a negotiation course regardless of the discipline, we would at least begin to identify a "canon of negotiation" skills and theories.

In reality, we skipped much of the struggling and wrestling. We identified some important topics and we wrote papers together, but I'm not sure we did the hardest part. To illustrate with my own experience, a law school professor and I agreed that we would write a paper on the problem of agency (i.e., what happens in negotiation when the parties work through representatives) and structure (which it turned out we defined differently). I sketched out some of the main ideas that are contained in the paper that is now co-authored with Marcia Caton Campbell. [Docherty & Caton Campbell, *Agency*] My would-be co-author scratched his head—or at least I think he did since we were negotiating our writing assignment via e-mail—and said something that I heard as, "What are you talking about? This is not what I thought we were writing about, but it is interesting. Why don't you go ahead and write this?" [Bhappu & Barsness, *E-mail*] Meanwhile Marcia, whose work in multi-party, public negotiations is similar to my work in strategic peace building,[1] "got it" immediately and we agreed to finish the paper together. All of which is to say that I'm not sure that all of our papers are the cross-disciplinary products we envisioned. The same difficulty attends the chapters in this book, as well as practical negotiations that must draw from more than one field: we start in different mental spaces, and it is all too easy to end up there, with fundamental questions unrecognized, much less addressed.

One rarely addressed but fundamental question is: how much does the *context* in which we are negotiating influence the way we negotiate and the way we teach negotiation?[2] Nor do we grapple easily with questions such as: do professional disciplines make different underlying assumptions about human nature and social relationships? If yes, how do those assumptions influence the way negotiation is practiced and taught in each profession? How do they reshape basic concepts such as power and decision-making? And, how do they influence the ways we talk about timing, moves, tactics, strategies, and a host of other aspects of negotiation?

Truthfully, just uncovering all of the underlying assumptions would have required years, not months of exploration and discussion. And doing so would have delayed what many see as a very interesting collection of ideas, first in the *Marquette Law Review* and now in much expanded form in this volume. But for those of us who are still interested in the deeper conversation about hidden assumptions behind various approaches to negotiation, where do we begin? I would say: this volume is not a bad place to start, as long as we approach the chapters with some basic questions. First, what is similar about the way these writers approach human interactions—specifically, human interactions in which the participants communicate with one another in order to promote shared understandings, overcome differences, reach compromises, or make mutually beneficial tradeoffs? Second, what accounts for their differences?

This chapter is a first cut at identifying important similarities and differences that might be used to cluster the chapters in this book and other negotiation literature in useful ways. I think we can end up with something better than the disciplinary tower of Babel that we started with; but we will probably never develop a fully generic approach to negotiation. This chapter is very much intended as a conversation starter, not a definitive treatise, and I look forward to further discussions and debates on this issue.

What Do We Have in Common?

Barry Johnson has made a career out of studying "polarities" in human organizations, in order to help individuals and groups identify and manage "unsolvable problems." Johnson argues that many polarities in the workplace are incorrectly framed as either/or propositions of opposites, or as problems to be solved. Is a good leader conservative to support stability or is she revolutionary to encourage change? Does an organization need to be centralized to enhance coordination or decentralized to encourage initiative? Should an organization reward team development or individual achievement? None of the above is a problem that can be solved by choosing one option and neglecting the other. "They are what we call polarities (dilemmas, paradoxes) which are inherently unavoidable and unsolvable. The on-going, natural tension between the poles can be destructive and debilitating or the tension can be *managed*, and channeled into a creative synergy that leads to superior outcomes."[3]

Social theorists have long struggled with a polarity that is particularly relevant to the applied fields of conflict resolution including negotiation, mediation, facilitation, and strategic peace building. Do human beings shape their own lives and destinies or are human beings shaped by the structures in which they live? In other words, do human beings have agency, which "refers to the *actors' characteristics and capabilities* in perceiving, interpreting, analyzing, evaluating, and acting as well as affecting the world around them?"[4] Or are human beings 'subjects' existing within structures that shape their choices at an unconscious as well as a conscious level, force compliance through the use of power, and/or induce compliance through the allocation of material and non-material rewards?

Anthony Giddens argues that this agency-or-structure dilemma should actually be considered a duality, not unlike Johnson's concept of polarity. According to Giddens, social structures both *constrain and enable* the choices and behaviors of human actors, but social structures only exist because human actors reproduce them through their interactions, particularly through their routinized interactions. Structure is both the medium and the outcome of the human conduct it recursively organizes.[5] Or, put another way, "social activity does not take place prior to or outside of social structure. Social agents may modify or transform structures or create entirely new structures, but they do this within given social (and material) conditions."[6]

Familiar styles and forms of conduct are the glue that sustains social structures and organizations, precisely by shaping the choices of human beings, allowing them to do some things easily while making other possible actions considerably more difficult to conceive and to enact. At the same time, human beings are actors with agency—in other words with free will. They have a drive to make their lives meaningful and coherent. They also have the ability to make strategic decisions about their interactions with others, and the ability to make changes in structures by 'playing with' and modifying the routine scripts of social life.[7] Structures are written into and enacted in social organizations and written into the unconscious mind and the routinized interactions of human beings. But structures are also created, recreated and modified by human actors who can become conscious, and who can choose to act in ways that contradict routinized activities and thereby rewrite the 'code' or the rule sets[8] for social structures. [Abramson, *Cross-cultural Mediation*; Goh, *Errors*; Peppet & Moffitt, *How to Learn*]

When we talk about negotiation, we are inclined to look at the problem solving and creativity that go into crafting an agreement. In other words, most people studying negotiation tend to favor the human agency side of the agency-structure duality. This, as much as anything else, holds the negotiation literature together. We all believe that human beings are agents and we all are interested in how those human agents are able to negotiate with one another in order to manage problems and conflicts.

What Separates Us?

In spite of this shared approach to human interactions, there are still undeniable differences in basic points of view among the chapters in this book and the papers in the *Marquette Law Review* special issue. I would suggest that sorting these chapters according to the way they answer three basic questions would reveal a great deal about patterns of similarities and differences in negotiation research, teaching, and practice.[9]

- First, is the author primarily interested in the immediate negotiation, or is she also interested in the ways negotiation can be used to assist larger social (structural) change processes?
- Second, does the author assume that the context or social structures surrounding a negotiation are stable, or unstable?
- Third, how does the author describe human decision-making in negotiation?

Is Negotiation Connected to Structural Change Issues?

A number of chapters in this volume examine the pressures on negotiators and the ways that negotiators draw on cultural knowledge [Abramson, *Cross-cultural Mediation*; Goh, *Errors*; Welsh, *Fairness*] and institutional rules and resources [Mayer, *Allies*; Menkel-Meadow, *Ethics*; Shapiro, *Identity*] during negotiation. I suspect Giddens would be pleased to see negotiation scholars moving beyond a tendency to focus almost exclusively on the actions, interactions and goal-directed choices of the negotiators. He would like the fact that these authors are concentrating upon "how actors reflexively monitor what they do" and "how actors draw upon rules and resources in the constitution of interaction."[10]

However, this approach does not fully embrace the reality that negotiations (and negotiators) can help reproduce *or* they can help modify social structures. Sometimes the renegotiation of social structures is an unintended consequence of our negotiation of a particular problem.

For example, faculty members in a graduate program in conflict resolution negotiate to open and staff a Practice Institute. The Practice Institute garners several million dollars in program grants within the first year of operation. Three years later, the faculty members find themselves negotiating with the Practice Institute staff about balancing power between the Practice Institute and the graduate program and integrating the practice activities more effectively into the teaching program. The result is likely to be a significant transformation in the identity, structures, cultural norms, and daily practices of the graduate program. None of these changes was intended by any of the negotiators (Practice Institute staff or faculty) when the Practice Institute was created.

At other times, one or more of the parties in the negotiation is consciously attempting to renegotiate social structures. For example, parties with low social power may want to use negotiation to change their status, while their negotiating partners, who benefit from the current social order, want to solve a specific problem without altering the overall social order. One is trying to renegotiate the social order and one is trying to avoid renegotiating the social order. Here, it is important to recognize that seeing negotiation as a mechanism for assisting in larger change processes does not always mean disrupting the status quo or challenging established rules. In some highly chaotic contexts, a larger change process involves establishing shared norms and rule sets to govern community life, and negotiations can help with this stabilization or they can hinder it.[11]

In spite of these realities, negotiation scholars are not typically inclined to examine whether or how the negotiators are modifying or sustaining the institutions in which they operate.[12] It would be interesting to discuss which authors in this book do look at this problem—even indirectly—and which ones do not address it at all. Personally, I see the issue of how negotiating specific problems shapes and reshapes the social order as a cutting-edge problem for our field, and I hope that simply pointing to the relative lack of attention it has received will spark some interesting discussion and research.

Is the Context Seen as Stable or Unstable?

But if we want to engage the issue of the way negotiations sustain or modify social structures, we must first give serious consideration to the *context of negotiation*. We must ask: what are the larger institutional or structural pressures on negotiators and how do those pressures manifest in the negotiation process? Does the *structural context* in which negotiators encounter one another profoundly affect the ways they negotiate?

When we gathered for our first meeting in late 2003, we tended to focus on our disciplinary contexts—law, business, psychology, conflict resolution or trans-formation, public policy, etc.—as a variable that might explain why we saw things differently. I would suggest, however, that the contexts in which we work are not identical to our disciplines. We can, in fact, identify features of our contexts that make some disciplines more similar than others.

For example, I think I see some patterns of differences between those au-thors/participants who work in settings that I would define as "relatively highly structured" and those who work in settings that I would define as "turbulent or more tenuously structured."[13] Highly structured environments include those where the parties, issues, rules (formal and informal) of interaction, and modes of decision-making are clear, stable, widely accepted, and routinized. Legal and labor relations settings are classic examples. But sometimes even the law and relations between economic classes are up for grabs. Labor negotiations after a corporate merger followed by downsizing differ significantly from labor negotiations in more stable settings, particularly when those negotiations occur in a global context that makes the relocation of corporate enterprises a realistic option.[14] In turbulent or more tenuously structured environments, uncertainty and instability can enter the negotiations in a number of different ways. The parties that need to be involved in the negotiation may not be clearly identified, parties may emerge or disappear during the middle of negotiation, and parties may be subject to complicated inter-nal pressures that make them operate in ways that are difficult to predict. In unstructured contexts, the issues under negotiation are highly contested and the process for defining the issues is subject to unpredictable outside pressures. The rules of interaction (formal and informal) are often contested and may be the sub-ject of negotiation in their own right. The modes of decision-making are not routinized and may differ among parties.

Some hypothetical examples may help illustrate these differences. Two attor-neys negotiating a contract on behalf of their clients may encounter complications in their negotiation. The issues may be highly technical and complex. Difficulties between the agents and their respective principals may complicate the negotiation. There may be significant disagreement between the attorneys about which laws apply and which precedents will hold sway in this particular case. But, in the end, the legal context narrows the range of issues and solution options. The attorneys succeed or fail based on their ability to understand and apply a limited array of 'rules' to this particular case. There is certainly creativity, but it is creativity held in check by rule sets that have legitimacy for the parties and for the wider society in which the parties are operating.

On the other hand, when negotiating a peace agreement in a country beset by civil violence, there are few precedents and rules to help bound the negotiation process. The parties build the negotiation 'venue' even as they negotiate the issues, and they negotiate the rule sets for their decision-making as they proceed. Which parties are allowed at the negotiation table is also unclear. There is a tendency in many cases to restrict the parties at the table to the combatants, but this has often led to unsuccessful outcomes, so that now there are significant pressures to in-clude civil society organizations, women, and victims of the fighting in the peace negotiation process.[15] Unlike the attorneys in a contract negotiation, these negotia-tors cannot rely on a stable set of institutions to enforce their agreements, so they spend significant amounts of time negotiating the rules of law that will hold sway after the violence ends. In the absence of stable structures, the negotiators can (and usually do) draw on competing norms and rule sets to justify their positions, and ultimately they must reach agreement on structures as well as issues.

In reality, "highly structured" and "unstructured" contexts are not dichotomous categories, but rather points on a continuum. Many negotiations occur in situations that are structured in some respects and unstructured in others.

For example, suppose the two attorneys mentioned above are negotiating a divorce agreement on behalf of their respective clients. The law constrains their negotiations related to property settlement, child custody, support, and other issues in which the state takes an interest. But the negotiation of ongoing shared parenting relationships and other "soft" issues is typically not structured by the legal context. It is up to the attorneys and their clients to work out the details of their agreement *and* the norms and unspoken rules that will govern the negotiation of these issues, including the ways the parties will renegotiate these issues in the future. Because the rule sets provided by the legal context are of little or no use for this type of negotiation, the clients may turn to a counselor or other professional for assistance. Lack of coordination between the legal negotiation of divorce settlements and the renegotiation of relationship norms and behaviors has led some attorney mediators to work more closely with counselors, and it has also given rise to the "collaborative divorce" movement.[16] In other words, some attorneys have become involved in efforts to restructure divorce processes in order to work with a broader range of issues than the legal context normally addresses.

In our other hypothetical case, the negotiators trying to end a civil conflict are often constrained by outside forces. These outside forces can include powerful parties that have a vested interest in the outcome of their negotiations. Threats of military action or promises of funds for reconstruction and development projects are among the tools used by outside parties to influence the negotiators. The negotiators may also be constrained by existing laws such as the codes of the International Criminal Court or the previously mentioned UN requirements to include women in the negotiation process. While it is clear that they are operating in a less structured context and they must create structures as part of their negotiation, their scope of creativity is not unlimited.

So what? Why should we bother thinking about whether a chapter in this book or any other literature on negotiation is treating the context of negotiation as relatively stable or relatively unstable? I think considering this issue helps us with several tasks. First, we can begin to track and explain differences in negotiation literature that are not strictly tied to academic or practice disciplines. We can, for example, begin to understand why not all law-related authors in this volume seem to be taking the same approach to negotiation. Some are looking at problems in turbulent settings while others are looking at problems in more stable settings. Or perhaps some are *assuming* stability and others are *assuming* turbulence and it is up to us, the readers, to decide which assumptions better match reality.

Second, I think that if we begin talking about the context in which we operate, we will also set the stage for some ethical discussions about larger social issues.[17] Many of us work as agents for clients [Nolan-Haley, *Informed Consent*] or we assist parties in negotiations [Mayer, *Allies*] where we may not have a direct stake in the outcome. Some of us work in settings where the effects of our negotiation (negative as well as positive) will be carried by other people for a very long time, and I am not only thinking about negotiating major social issues like ending civil conflict. Even routine divorce negotiations and business negotiations have spillover effects that can do good or cause harm to persons not at the table. I hope that focusing on the context question will lead us to discuss whether our goal as negotiators is primarily about getting the best deal within the current context for the parties at the table, or also includes using negotiation to create more just and equitable social structures.

How Does the Author Describe Human Decision-Making?

Shifting gears (temporarily) from issues of context, I think it is also useful to ask how an author describes human decision-making processes as they manifest in negotiation. Tom R. Burns notes that even when we begin with a shared assumption about the importance of human agency, we can still differ greatly in the way we understand human decision-making. Burns identifies two models of decision-making—rational choice theory (RCT) and social game theory (SGT), which both give priority to human agency while also exhibiting "substantially different conceptions of human agency and its realization in action and interaction."[18] He summarizes their differences as follows:

- *On the nature of the human agent:*
  RCT "assumes an *asocial* (or trans-social) *being* oriented to the consequences of action for self (and only for self)." Actors are extracted from their historical and social relationships, shared meanings, and cultural forms. This contrasts markedly with SGT which assumes *socially constructed agency* [Shapiro, *Identity*] and "rejects the notion of a single, universal, utilitarian type of agent" in favor of actors who are shaped (constrained and enabled) by their "different roles, relationships, institutional settings, and cultural frameworks."[19]

- *On the normative and moral aspects of human agency:*
  "In RCT norms and ethical considerations are not part of the conception of human agency." Interests are paramount and questions of ethics or of moral sentiments are not discussed explicitly although they may be incorporated into an actor's preference structure. In SGT, however, human agents are seen as fundamentally moral creatures whose moral sentiments—shaped by their relationships and roles—enter into their judgment and action processes.[20]

- *On the human agent's power to reshape social structures:*
  "RCT presumes a type of agent who makes choices according to a single principle (maximization of utility) *within* a given situation." This type of agent draws on and uses the established rules and resources and does not "*deviate* from the given principle or action conditions; she does not transform conditions...." This contrasts with SGT, which assumes "that human actors have a creative/destructive capability." Through innovation and creativity, agents can "structure and restructure preferences, sets of options, and outcome structures, indeed entire decision and game systems in which they and others participate."[21]

Perhaps the most striking differences among chapters in this book as well as other negotiation publications stem from differences in assumptions about whether the decision makers are operating primarily from an RCT framework or an SGT framework. Yet, we rarely name the question that clearly. Instead, we talk about differences between negotiators from individualist cultures and collectivist cultures or we talk about personality characteristics or emotional states that influence decision-making. In some cases, there is an assumption that culture, personalities, or emotional states are "getting in the way of" rationality. This assumption privileges RCT-style rationality over SGT-style rationality without any critical examination of that privileging.

We might make more headway in our effort to distill some cross-disciplinary assumptions about negotiation if we convene a discussion about our unspoken assumptions about human nature, decision-making and the role of human agents in sustaining or changing the social order. Sorting out RCT and SGT assumptions is a start. However, I would caution against turning these into rigid categories. Many of us probably operate with assumptions that mix RCT and SGT principles. We see negotiators as RCT actors in some settings and as SGT actors in other settings. And, even in the SGT framework we might identify different types of logic or different rationalities at work in the actors, depending on the context and the predisposition of the negotiator. Elsewhere, I have used Weber's observation about four types of social action to offer greater nuance to our discussions about what constitutes rationality.[22] These can be used to further refine our conversation about decision-making. This allows us to ask something other than "is the author a lawyer or a business negotiator or a psychologist?" Instead, we can ask "how does this author conceptualize human rationality and decision-making and *why* does she think about rationality in this particular way?

I said earlier that I was only leaving the issue of context temporarily. I would suggest that how we think about human decision-making in negotiation may actually be tied in some respects to whether we work in stable or unstable settings. Or more accurately, our approach may be more tied to whether we *think* about our setting as stable or unstable. In stable settings, established rule sets and norms create the basis for a shared interaction logic which masks some of the cultural and socially grounded aspects of decision-making. Unstable settings or situations of crisis and emerging problems call forth the creativity of human agents and in negotiations reveal competing or contrasting judgment systems, rule sets and logics.

Conclusion: Suggestions for Reading (Using) this Book

Keeping in mind that this book is supposed to be for practitioners as well as academics and is intended as a field guide, what use is this excursion into discussing structure and agency, decision-making models or paradigms, and social change? Well, a field guide—particularly one of this size and offering this variety of papers—is only useful if the reader can *find* the material most useful to his problem. To make the hunt for relevant papers easier and more fruitful, I suggest the following approach for readers and users of this book.

First, think about your particular case and ask yourself: am I trying to figure out how my work is connected to a social change process (desired or undesired)? Are the conditions in which I am operating stable or unstable? Are the parties striving for purely rational choice decision-making or do they see themselves as tied to other actors and social pressures? In other words, first know yourself and know your own problem. Then as you read the various chapters that you think might be helpful, ask whether the author is actually addressing the problems you are facing. Or, is the author making some assumptions that don't match your reality? Even if the author's assumptions don't fully match your reality, or your reality as you perceive it, that does not mean you can't use any of the material in that chapter. It just means you need to use it with caution and perhaps with adaptations.

Speaking from my own experience, I am always more wary of claims made by authors working in my own field when they transfer assumptions about negotiation from more stable settings into peace negotiations or conflict transformation processes without considering the effects of an unstable context. It is not that I reject what they are saying out of hand, but I use their work cautiously. For example, I think that it is easier to think of negotiators as rational choice theory decision makers when you are working in a stable setting with a bounded rule set to guide choices. Since I work in unstable settings, I see the persons I am working with as more oriented to a social game theory style of decision-making. They have constituencies pressuring them; they are embedded in roles that limit their range of actions; they carry (and often openly discuss) ethical limitations on their choices. Research that focuses entirely on a rational choice theory paradigm of decision-making can seem irrelevant to my work. Yet, I have found great benefit in reading negotiation materials on rational choice theory and decision-making. They remind me that even actors who see themselves as socially embedded decision makers do make cost-benefit calculations. And, if I can help them lay out the social and ethical factors they want to include in their cost-benefit matrix, they can make better decisions.

In closing, I hope that some day we might convene a discussion in the field about our unspoken assumptions and how they influence the ways we approach negotiation. The models we carry in our heads are as important for understanding why we do our work in similar or different ways as the differences in our academic disciplines or our practice arenas.

Endnotes

[1] *See* LISA SCHIRCH, THE LITTLE BOOK OF STRATEGIC PEACEBUILDING (2005), which defines strategic peacebuilding as "an interdisciplinary, coordinated approach to building a sustainable *justpeace*—a peace with justice" (6) and lays out a framework for understanding the many activities (including negotiation) involved in strategic peacebuilding.

[2] *See* MICHAEL L. SPANGLE & MYRA WARREN ISENHART, NEGOTIATION: COMMUNICATION FOR DIVERSE SETTINGS (2003), for a book that addresses the context issue in explicit terms.

[3] *Polarity Management: A Concept Whose Time Has Come*, Polarity Management Associates, *at* http://www.polaritymanagement.com (last visited Mar. 8, 2006); *see also*, BARRY JOHNSON, POLARITY MANAGEMENT: IDENTIFYING AND MANAGING UNSOLVABLE PROBLEMS (1992, 1996).

[4] Tom R. Burns, *Two Conceptions of Human Agency: Rational Choice Theory and the Social Theory of Action*, *in* AGENCY AND STRUCTURE: REORIENTING SOCIAL THEORY 202 (Piotr Sztompka ed., 1994).

[5] *See* ANTHONY GIDDENS, THE CONSTITUTION OF SOCIETY: OUTLINE OF THE THEORY OF STRUCTURATION 281-372 (1984).

[6] Burns, *supra* note 4 at 209.

[7] A script is "a commonly assumed temporal ordering for some kind of event, for example, 'a meal in a restaurant', 'trip to the beach.'" *See* ROGER C. SCHANK & ROBERT P. ABELSON, SCRIPTS, PLANS, GOALS AND UNDERSTANDING: AN INQUIRY INTO HUMAN KNOWLEDGE STRUCTURES (1977). Negotiations are deeply influenced by the unspoken scripts of the negotiators. *See* Jayne Seminare Docherty, *Culture and Negotiation: Symmetrical Anthropology for Negotiators*, 87 MARQUETTE LAW REVIEW 711 (2004). I am also indebted to Carol J. Gowler and Tamara Mihalic for insightful discussions about the role of scripts in peace building practice and complex negotiations.

[8] In this chapter, I am following THOMAS P. M. BARNETT, THE PENTAGON'S NEW MAP: WAR AND PEACE IN THE TWENTY-FIRST CENTURY 9 (2004), in using the term rule sets to refer to "a collection of rules that delineates how some activity normally unfolds." Rule sets are a combination of explicitly stated and referenced rules that are enforced by authorities and unconscious norms and expectations that are enforced by the tacit agreement of those who participate in a given activity.

[9] It is important to recognize that many chapters will not answer these questions directly. But the answers can be derived from critical reading of the texts. An author may never mention the context of a negotiation, but her *assumption* of stability in the context will be apparent in the absence of any reference to outside forces that might disrupt the negotiation.

[10] GIDDENS, *supra* note 5 at 373.

[11] For a case in which negotiating specific problems such as disarmament of a rebel group relates to renegotiating the rules that hold together social structures, *see* Jacqueline Nolan-Haley, *Agents and Informed Consent*, Chapter 58 in this volume.

[12] For resources that do take this approach, *see* PETER M. KELLETT & DIANA G. DALTON, MANAGING CONFLICT IN A NEGOTIATED WORLD: A NARRATIVE APPROACH TO ACHIEVING DIALOGUE AND CHANGE (2001); *see also*, Carrie Menkel-Meadow, *The Ethics of Compromise*, Chapter 18 in this volume for some discussion of the larger social implications of negotiation; *see also*, JAYNE SEMINARE DOCHERTY, THE LITTLE BOOK OF STRATEGIC NEGOTIATION: NEGOTIATING DURING TURBULENT TIMES (2005).

[13] *See* DOCHERTY, *supra* note 12 at 9-11.

[14] *See* RICHARD E. WALTON, JOEL CUTCHER-GERSHENFELD & ROBERT B. MCKERSIE, STRATEGIC NEGOTIATIONS: A THEORY OF CHANGE IN LABOR-MANAGEMENT RELATIONS (1994) and JOEL CUTCHER-GERSHENFELD, ROBERT B. MCKERSIE & RICHARD E. WALTON, PATHWAYS TO CHANGE: CASE STUDIES OF STRATEGIC NEGOTIATIONS (1995).

[15] *See* MARI FITZDUFF AND CHEYANNE CHURCH, NGOS AT THE TABLE: STRATEGIES FOR INFLUENCING POLICIES IN AREAS OF CONFLICT (2004). *See also* Inventory of United Nations Resources on Women, Peace, and Security, *available at*
http://www.un.org/womenwatch/osagi/resources/wps/Inventory-11Oct2004.pdf
(last visited Mar. 8, 2006) for a summary of various United Nations efforts to ensure that women are involved in peace negotiations, peacekeeping, and peace building initiatives.

[16] Collaborative law "engages in informal discussions and conferences to settle all issues" (http://www.collaborativedivorce.com/info.html). Collaborative divorce is a subset of the collaborative law approach focused specifically on divorce. It involves a team of professionals—attorneys, coaches/counselors, child specialists, and financial analysts—working together to help a couple (family) through the process of divorce using collaborative approaches to problem solving (http://www.collaborativedivorce.com/cdteam.html). For a discussion of the potential role of collaborative divorce initiatives in changing the legal system, *see* Jayne Seminare Docherty and David Anderson Hooker, *Evaluation Report: Collaborative Divorce Project Rapides Parish* (Sept. 2005) (unpublished evaluation report) (on file with authors).

[17] *See, e.g.,* Carrie Menkel-Meadow, *Correspondences and Contradictions in International and Domestic Conflict Resolution: Lessons from General Theory and Varied Contexts*, 2003 JOURNAL OF DISPUTE RESOLUTION 319.

[18] Burns, *supra* note 4, at 202-03.

[19] *Id.*

[20] *Id.*

[21] *Id.* at 203-204.

[22] JAYNE SEMINARE DOCHERTY, LEARNING LESSONS FROM WACO: WHEN THE PARTIES BRING THEIR GODS TO THE NEGOTIATION TABLE 167-71 (2001). Weber identifies four forms of social action: goal-rational action, value-rational action, affectual (relational) action, and traditional action. Each one contains its own internal logic or rationality and actors can operate from a mixed set of social actions or logics. Instrumental rationality most coincides with RCT. The other three are all different versions of SGT rationality. MAX WEBER, THE THEORY OF SOCIAL AND ECONOMIC ORGANIZATION 88 (A.M. Henderson & Talcott Parsons trans., 1947) (1964).

ༀ 3 ༁

Protean Negotiation

Peter S. Adler

Editors' Note: *What does it take to be really proficient as a negotiator? Adler argues that negotiators routinely allow themselves to be trapped by their own mental frameworks, unnecessarily restricting their own conceptions of what is desirable, or even possible. He suggests that you cannot do your best work as a negotiator till you absorb all of the often-competing theories that follow in this book, and develop a working competence at selecting which theory applies when.*

Being also some Ruminations and Speculations on Evolutionary Impulses, a Minor Greek God, the Literatures of Negotiation and Mediation, Cooperation and Competition, Morality and Pragmatism, Paradox and Dilemma, the Bushmen of the Kalahari, Sun Tzu's Strategy, and the Management of Four Contradictory Imperatives, All of Which and Each of Which are Perfectly Correct Things to Do.

Ancient Imperatives

Around the world, in classrooms, board rooms, and airport waiting rooms, the theory and practice of negotiation is awash with advice. Much of it is simplistic and some of it contradictory. One writer implores us to know our bottom line. Another urges us to ignore it and focus on needs. A third says to wait until the last moment to do a deal when the situation is ripe. A fourth counsels us to get in early. At best, the many lists of "dos" and "don'ts" serve as reference points and modest road maps for certain situations. At worst, they misdirect us into thinking there is some grand unified field theory or universal paradigm that, if we master it, will carry us seamlessly through every deal and dispute.

More worrisome among the fashions of the moment is the trend towards fundamentalism in the practice of mediation and facilitation which is closely allied with negotiation theory. While there are many different styles, schools, and brands with names like "collaborative law," "extreme facilitation," and "transformative mediation," most of these seem to devolve to four basic schools of thinking about how humans behave in the face of real or imagined conflict, how they negotiate, and how we might help them. One presupposes that all of us are fundamentally competitive. A second assumes we are, at core, cooperative. A third takes for granted that all of us will seek to do what is morally correct. A fourth assumes we are rational and pragmatic.

These four impulses—pursuing your own fair share, uniting with others to achieve a common end, insisting on doing what is right, and using logic and reasoning to solve practical problems—seem to have evolutionary roots that date back to our origins on the African savannah.[1] [Yarn & Jones, *Biology*] The impulses also lead to different theories of conflict and ideologies of negotiation and mediation that descend from, embody, and personify these impulses. But there is also a fifth way, one that acknowledges the universality and importance of all of them but is not explicitly and strictly any of them. It too has ancient roots. Let's call it "Protean Negotiation."

Rumble in the Jungle[2]

Imagine you are a senior official at Pulsar Pharmaceuticals International ("PPI"), a mid-sized drug manufacturer that is seeking bio-prospecting rights in the central Brazilian rainforest. PPI has a standing corporate pledge to "create enterprise that is socially desirable, economically profitable, and ecologically sustainable." Pulsar has several Brazil-originated medicines it seeks to develop: an extract from the trauma leaf which could treat degenerative arthritis; a slime mold which may yield new therapies for allergies; and the root of the muirapuama, considered an aphrodisiac by certain tribal healers and known locally as "Amazon Viagra."

In the last six months, however, your job has become more complicated. You have learned that you closest competitor, Amalgamated Biological Sciences ("ABS"), is pursuing the same three drugs. Brazil's Ministry of Trade has recently proposed new regulations and royalty rates that could add huge risks to Pulsar's investment. The government sees pharmaceuticals as a logical part of its economic strategy and wants to control and profit from them. They are also sensitive to bio-piracy from foreign countries. The Amazonian tribes and their "shaman knowledge" are another potentially volatile issue. They have been the subject of United Nations inquiries into human rights abuses, are an increasingly important cultural icon for South America's tourism industry, have the sympathies of many urban voters, and control large tracts of land in the interior, some of which government would like to see opened for logging and farming.

You undertake a series of exploratory discussions beginning with the Minister of Trade, Carlos Mendoza. In public pronouncements, Mendoza has let it be known that the government favors a centralized permitting system and a data bank that will store the knowledge accumulated by "traditional scientists," as the shamans are called. Prospecting rights will then be licensed to accredited drug manufacturers. Privately, Mendoza says he is looking for a reputable pharmaceutical manufacturer to help set up Brazil's system and hints that whoever undertakes this will have an inside track on early and perhaps discounted permit applications. He also lets you know that he is talking with your competitor, ABS.

You are also in contact with Arturo Terena, one of several elder leaders of the Council of Amazon Tribes. Terena says his people would prefer to set up their own system of patents, permits, and royalties and wants PPI to support their effort and help them form a corporation. They have little regard for the Brazilian government and would much prefer to maintain dominion over their own lands. Terena says that Brazil has committed many historical atrocities against the people of the forests and owes them this last chance at preserving their culture and heritage and benefiting from it in a modern world.

Not long after and over a dinner in Rio de Janeiro, you talk with John Henderson, your counterpart at ABS. The two of you have known each other for many years. You exchange family news, swap stories about baseball and politics, and then the talk turns to bio-prospecting in South America and the challenges of working with the government on one hand and the tribes on the other. In discreet terms, Henderson telegraphs signals that ABS might be willing to explore some kind of joint venture to help both companies deal with the situation. You thank him for a nice evening and tell him you will raise it with your people.

Back in your office, you comb through your books on negotiation. The problem seems to come down to a series of not very clear-cut strategic choices. Assuming the numbers pencil out, do you trust ABS enough to join forces for what could be a complex and long-term set of challenges with unclear payoffs? Can PPI cooperate on this venture but compete in other places? Would the strains turn the relationship toxic? Either way, and regardless of whether you do or don't join forces, should you pursue the inside track with Mendoza? Can the government really be trusted? Might they use you to help set up their management system and then have contracts awarded elsewhere? And what about Terena? You know that the tribes have been treated badly but can you and should you ally yourself with them? Is a company that prides itself on "creating enterprise that is socially desirable, economically profitable, and ecologically sustainable" obligated to do so? What would be the impacts on relations with the government of Brazil, and on ABS if you are competing with them?

Four Pathways to Problem Solving
The literatures on negotiation, including those in this volume, suggest other considerations. For PPI to engage the challenge of discovering new products and bringing them to market, it might want to examine various cultural factors, [Avruch, *Buyer—Seller*] keep an eye on escalation dynamics, [Zartman, *Ripeness*; Coleman, et al., *Dynamical*] have a passing knowledge of the complexity and chaos concepts, understand agency [Docherty & Caton Campbell, *Agency*] and representation, [Nolan-Haley, *Informed Consent*] hone its skills at in-team bargaining, [Bellman, *Team Conflicts*] manage the perpetual tides of emotion and affect, [Shapiro, *Emotions*] and have a good grasp of the slightly different challenges of negotiated dispute resolution (untangling the past) versus negotiated deal-making (crafting the future). Directly in the telescope of this negotiation, however, are some major collisions between the cooperative, competitive, moral, and pragmatic imperatives. The crosshairs look like this:

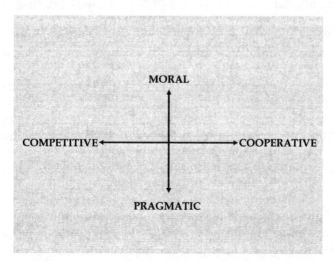

Played out in the realm of negotiation, each of these imperatives has its own logic, its own bargaining pattern, its own outlook and style, its own assumptions about human nature, its own explanation of conflict, its own theoreticians, and its own zealots. Each also stands in tension with one or more of the others.

In popular writing, competitive negotiation is often considered a natural extension of sport, warfare, Darwinism, and the long and sometimes gruesome struggles between individuals and individuals and groups and groups. In his book *Rules for Radicals*, for example, Saul Alinsky, a community organizer and champion of underdogs, argued that power derives from money, position, and privilege and since poor people have little of any of these, they must band together and push their way in. [Korobkin, *Power*] His negotiation advice included formulating a clear enemy, causing confusion, fear, and retreat, making the enemy live up to their own espoused book of rules, and infuriating the opposition through strategic ridicule.[3] As different as they may be substantively, Alinsky is not that far away procedurally and psychologically from his counterparts in the business world, someone like Donald Trump, who says: "I don't do it for the money. I've got enough, much more than I'll ever need. I do it to do it. Deals are my art form."[4]

In scholarly and professional literatures, Alinsky's rules are a colorful variation of distributive bargaining which focuses on allocating the value at play and maximizing one's own gains. The themes of distributive bargaining deal with target and resistance points, the dance of demands and offers, the role of position-taking and concession-making, and the use of tactics such as low-balls, nibbles, bogeys, good guys/bad guys working in tandem, and many more. Distributive negotiation tends to be about hard bargaining and substantive winners and losers.[5]

In these same professional and popular literatures, cooperative negotiation is often pejoratively thought of (and criticized by competitors) as "soft" bargaining. More accurately, it is called integrative bargaining and focuses in great part on the quest for relatedness in ways that are jointly affirming of the interests that often underlie competitive position taking.[6] Lewicki, Raiffa, and others describe some of integrative bargaining's themes as mutuality, reciprocity, communication, and the free exchange of information. Where distrust is the assumed condition of competitive bargaining, the creation and maintenance of trust is the bedrock of cooperative negotiation. "Negotiators create a communication system," says Bernard Mayer. "It may be carried over from previous exchanges, or it may be freshly created, and its nature strongly affects how the negotiation proceeds."[7] Cooperative negotiation is predicated on the search for common ground. It seeks reciprocity, mutuality, and the avoidance of breakdowns because of relationship problems.

Closely allied to cooperation is a third negotiating philosophy which begins with a moral or ethical proposition and builds to what one set of writers has called the creation of "higher ground."[8] To accomplish this, moral suasion in negotiation takes a fact pattern, invokes a set of principles, builds logic around them, applies them to the facts, and works to bring others to the same conclusions. [Welsh, *Fairness*] Many negotiations over larger or smaller matters, especially those that are aimed at disentangling a grievance, begin with one side or the other saying "it's the principle of it." Third parties who work from this same premise often prefer the term "peacemaking" to "mediation" because it implies something greater than making a deal or restoring a relationship. "The moral imagination," as John Paul Lederach calls it, "has a quality of transcendence. It breaks out of what appear to be narrow, shortsighted, or structurally determined dead ends."[9]

Finally, and in counterpoint to the moral impulse in negotiation, is a philosophy of pragmatism and rational problem-solving. Much of the literature on interest-based negotiation might be thought of in this vein. It assumes that people know and understand their needs, that interests can rationally and dispassionately analyzed, and that elegant if not super-optimum solutions can be found. Fisher and Ury's famous dictums of separating the people from the problem, focusing on interests, generating possibilities, and insisting on objective criteria are an attempt to create a rational, if not quasi-scientific critical inquiry process that leads to a more easily negotiated result.[10]

Even more expressive of rationalistic negotiation is the work of Brams and Taylor, who have developed clever numeric formulas that overcome the problem of envy and successfully divide everything from goods and services, to marriages and whole businesses, to the borders and territories of feuding countries. "The problem of fair division," they write, "is old as the hills, but our approach to this problem is new. It involves setting forth explicit criteria, or properties, that characterize different notions of fairness; providing step-by-step procedures, or algorithms, for obtaining a fair division of goods, or alternatively, preferred positions on a set of issues in negotiations; and illustrating these algorithms with applications to real life situations."[11]

By itself, each of these negotiating imperatives—pursuing a fair if not favorable share, uniting with others to make common purpose, insisting on doing what is right, and using logic and reasoning to solve problems—has a particular clarity and utility in the moment of certain facts and circumstances. Yet, taken to excess or transformed into orthodoxy, each runs the risk of instability and destructiveness. The more attached we become to the impulse and the more extreme we become in its use, the greater the danger. Saul Alinsky and Donald Trump are tough, competitive, goal-oriented poker players accustomed to pushing, pulling, probing, bluffing, feinting, and bullying. So was Slobodan Milosevic, who evolved into a consummate warrior, a political monster, and a war criminal obsessed with his intergenerational blood-feud. At the farthest boundary of competitive bargaining lies the seduction of ruthlessness, retaliation, and predation.

Cooperative approaches are also vulnerable. If everyone is trusting, it is easy to be cheated by competitors disguised as cooperators, or duped by "free riders." Neville Chamberlain fell into this trap in his negotiations with Adolph Hitler before Germany invaded Poland. Similarly, a sole and persistent absorption with the moral dimension is no more immune than other strategies taken to excess. Unbridled moral preoccupation easily transforms to smugness, sanctimony, and fanaticism. There is a line, not always distinguishable at first, between the purity of a moral high ground and the fervor of an Osama Bin Laden who would like to eliminate all non-believers. Finally, unchecked rationality and hyper-pragmatism eventually overwhelms the collective humanity that links all of us through our hopes, fears, hurts, joys and curiosities. A sole focus on rationality makes us cold. In the extreme, when science goes completely mad, it takes us to the strange banality of an Adolph Eichmann whose highest accomplishment in life was making death efficient and systematic.

When individuals and groups bargain with each other, the four imperatives play out in complex and nuanced ways, and with unpredictable emotional intensities. As the impulses come to control our behavior and as the behaviors amplify, they become more risky, exposed, and dangerous. Fortunately, most of us do not operate from a single value premise. Values compete within us, seeking attention. Though we may all yearn for the clarity that would come from a single gospel of negotiation, the popular and scholarly literatures don't really tell us how to reconcile them. So most of us, most of the time, do what we always do. In the words of Robert Frost, "We dance around a ring and suppose, but the secret sits in the middle and knows." We muddle along until we succeed or fail, never quite knowing why either of those happened.

Polarity and Paradox

It doesn't matter if you are a tenant talking to your landlord, an ambassador pressing for security measures on the Indian and Pakistani border, or Amalgamated and Pulsar testing the waters for a joint venture in Brazil: competition and cooperation form a paradox. So too do the pressures of acting ethically and pragmatically. Not every negotiation embodies every tension, nor are these four the only predicaments that come up when people struggle to reconcile different ideas. Nonetheless, inconsistency and contradiction create paradox, and paradox fosters what Todd Bryan calls a "strange loop that cannot be resolved to our satisfaction."[12]

Confronted by the ambiguity and inconsistency of countervailing imperatives, the human mind seeks the purity of "one" or the "other." We veer away from the discomfort of being or doing "both," split the differing injunctions apart, and resolve the contradictions by insisting that life is one or the other. We are competitive or cooperative, moral or pragmatic, emotional or intellectual, expressive or bureaucratic, open or closed, aggressive or passive. Yet conflict inevitably brings these paradoxes back to the fore. It forces us to confront what is incongruous and requires us to take some kind of action.

This is not a new problem. Between 480 and 221 B.C., for example, during what is now called the Warring States Period of the Chou Dynasty, a general who would later be given the honorific name of Sun Tzu wrote a short treatise on how to triumph in warfare. Sun Tzu's advice was simple and tough. He believed in estimating costs, making plans, positioning oneself for success, maneuvering for advantage, gathering intelligence, staying calm under fire, and wherever possible avoiding unnecessary confrontation. Those sound like the traits of a good negotiator, no less than a good general. And if Leonard Lira is correct, the two are intimately connected. [Lira, *Military*]

At core, said Sun Tzu, conflict is not just *in* the nature of things, it *is* the nature of things. Conflict is as sure a thing as sickness and health, day and night, joy and sadness, risk and opportunity. The paradoxical nature of conflict is thus something to be mastered and used. He said: "To act on an entire organization is ideal; to break an organization is inferior. To act on an entire corps is ideal; to break a corps is inferior." In sum, he opined, "Those who win one hundred triumphs in one hundred conflicts do not have supreme skill. Those who have supreme skill use strategy to bend others without coming to conflict."[13] All of this may sound like New Age hocus-pocus, but it is also the common sense of a veteran military leader who needs to achieve an overall objective at the lowest possible cost.

Negotiation is filled with detailed strategic and tactical paradoxes of just this type. All of them require attention and action.[14] If I am Pulsar, do I disclose information to ABS or withhold it? If I am the ambassador, do I make a first move or wait for theirs? If I am the tenant, do I come on tough or open friendly to the landlord? And more generically, should I meet in their office or insist that they come to me? Do I try to do a fast deal or wait for a better one? Do I come right to the point and start with an offer or demand or establish atmospherics and context first? All of these decisions represent choices in time and each choice potentially has cascading effects, not all of which can be predicted, all of which must be made with imperfect knowledge, and any or all of which could reverberate back negatively as revenge effects.[15]

Ultimately, managing paradox requires us to embrace both ends of the dilemma (because both ends have validity), then to find a comfortable place with the uncertainty that sits between them, and to apply that uncertainty to the negotiation at hand. In negotiations, there are specific things to be done. We can make the dilemmas that usually stay unspoken explicit by giving voice to them. We can seek to define and clarify them to make sure everyone understands them. We can map them by describing the polarities, examine their attributes carefully, and review the strengths, weaknesses, threats, and opportunities that attend each.[16]

Finally, we can use both ends of a paradox to help reframe the opposites into questions that can be answered through negotiation.

The affinity, ability, and tolerance for doing these things are the essence of "Protean" negotiation.

The Elusive God of Negotiation

Amidst the incessant feuding and dysfunctional love lives of the Greek gods, Proteus was an enigma. A minor actor at best, he was one of Poseidon's less known children, and certainly not the most important. In fact, he resided by himself on an island called Pharos off the coast of the Nile delta, his day job being the tending of his father's seal herds. As such, he was more of a servant than a political player. Yet Proteus had unique qualities. He was a shapeshifter and a much sought after mystic who could peer into the future and answer the most difficult questions posed to him with great prescience and clairvoyance. Other gods would try to capture him and force answers from him. Proteus would wiggle away from their grasp by changing shapes. It was his way of avoiding the uncomfortable task of telling others what they ought to do, and perhaps of being wrong.

In the late 1960s, psychiatrist and historian Robert Jay Lifton picked up on this notion of psychological shapeshifting, in a series of talks he gave for the Canadian Broadcasting System. In his radio essays, Lifton ruminated on some of the cases he had been dealing with, among them, survivors of Hiroshima, victims of brainwashing in China, and young radicals in both Asia and America who found their traditional sensibilities collapsing about them. In the context of great institutional upheavals and rapid social changes, Lifton found some common threads among his disparate patients: a deep loneliness; restlessness and constant flux; a persistent feeling of isolation and disconnection; and a constant and sometimes all-consuming search for authenticity. Paradoxically, he also found great strengths: an intellectual, emotional, and spiritual rejection of orthodoxy; resilience and an often fluid ability to reinvent oneself; and a sense of inner "many-sidedness" that created a certain gift of empathy and tolerance.

A deeply reflective man and a skillful writer, Lifton synthesized his observations and tried to place them in a larger context. He saw a connection between the dislocations of his patients and the historical dislocations of the times. In so doing, he talked about a new and distinctly "Protean Style" of identity that he was finding in different cultures and countries. Lifton speculated that it might be part of a more universal response to what we now know as globalization, the unprecedented flooding of images and ideas across borders, the meltdown of the traditional anchors of family and place, and a reaction to our permanently altered notions of nature and culture.

"The Protean style of self-process," he said, "is characterized by an interminable series of experiments and explorations, some shallow, some profound, each of which can readily be abandoned in favor of still new psychological quests." [17] Like that ancient son of Poseidon sitting alone with his seals and visions, modern humans are, for the first time in history and on a scale unimagined, becoming shapeshifters, able to adjust and adapt, able to manage contrary imperatives, able to succeed in the midst of complexity and chaos. Foreshadowing some of the ideas of Thomas Friedman three decades later, Lifton contrasted this new Protean style of identity with an older more fundamentalist self-conception that he found rigid, unyielding, fearful of breakdown, obsessed with chaos, wary of loss of control, and absolutely self-certain. [18]

"An effective negotiator," says Robert Benjamin "requires a thinking frame that is adaptive, dynamic, fluid, and shifting and a model of negotiation that can house a variety of negotiation rituals."[19] As the following schematic suggests, the Protean negotiator is not a polymath but more of a dancer.

He or she can dance the competitor's jitterbug, the collaborator's tango, the moralist's waltz, and the pragmatist's four step. One dance may be more comfortable than the others, and the dances can be sequenced, but they are all in the repertoire. The Protean negotiator adapts.

Like Proteus, skilled negotiators seem to be able to reconcile the tensions of inconsistent and confusing impulses that may attend cooperative, competitive, moral, or pragmatic approaches to negotiation. They have agile minds and ecumenical temperaments. In an instant, they can undertake some kind of emotional and intellectual diagnostic, recalibrate expectations, and reflexively adjust their approach. Paradox is neither distasteful nor uncomfortable for these people. In fact, the ambiguity and tension created by paradox becomes the spawning ground of artistry. Malcolm Gladwell calls this "thin slicing," a form of rapid cognition and sometimes subliminal conclusion-making of the sort that artists, emergency room physicians, athletes, policemen, and many others use to great effect in everyday life.[20]

Negotiation is an all-too-human business, a strange and challenging alchemy of difficult choices. It reflects, says Susan Podziba, "a chaotic mix of passions, values, interests, emotions, self interest, and altruism."[21] Negotiation is filled with contradictions, some of obvious magnitude and importance, others seemingly small and almost insignificant but which can amplify as a negotiation proceeds. It is the job of the Protean negotiator to manage all of these with the highest degree of elegance and intelligence possible. It is also the job of the Protean mediator to help other negotiators turbo-charge their efforts and make them as humane and productive as possible.

Ancient Imperatives—Revisited

In 1950 John Marshall, an anthropologist and film maker, received funding from the Smithsonian Institution and Harvard University to study one of the last migratory bands of the Kung people, also known as the Bushmen or San People. Living in small groups in Namibia on the edge of the Kalahari Desert, these people were, and remain, one of the last true hunting and gathering peoples left on the planet. Though few in numbers, they are, even today, what we all were like 2,000 generations back.

The result of Marshall's work was a film called "The Hunters." It was, among

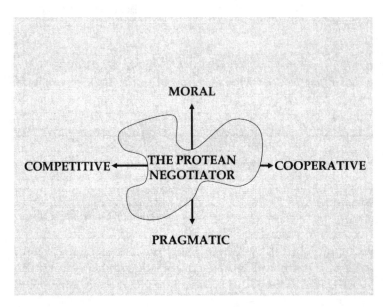

other triumphs, the first use of color film in ethnographic cinematography. The film, which I first saw as a graduate student, is remarkable for more substantive reasons as well. In a slow but mounting drama, it chronicles the story of a hunting expedition by four men from a particular band who have set off to find large game at a time when the group desperately needs a major infusion of protein. The band is small, four or five extended families, with a total population of about 30, and they exist on the thin margin of hunger, which is a vicious cycle. Without fresh food, elders and babies will soon die and able-bodied men and women and men will eventually lack the strength to gather and hunt.

So the men depart. Over the next several days, in fits and starts, they spot and track various animals without much luck. They sneak up on a kudu, try to get close, and inadvertently spook the animal just as they are about to loose their arrows. They find some porcupines and eat their meager flesh themselves. They spot other animals but are unsuccessful in bringing them down. Finally, they encounter a small herd of giraffes and succeed: after many complications, they manage to lodge a single arrow tipped with poison into one of them. For the next few days we follow them as they track the creature over hard terrain, nearly losing it in the surrounding hills and scrub. Finally, they find the animal in a stand of trees, weakened and abandoned by the rest of the herd. With arrows and spears they battle the still dangerous giraffe and bring it down, butcher and dry the meat, and begin the journey home.

Seeing this film again after many years, I now looked at it through the lens of a professional career layered with the dilemmas of hundreds of disputes, deals, and conflicts. I hazily recalled the four hunters as short, tough, skilled men working in tandem to accomplish their objectives. I remembered the dry and torturous terrain and the sense of urgency I felt for them to find food. But this time, I saw something else: their individuality and uniqueness; their quarrels, irritations, and teasings; their moments of stress; their constant and small presence in a large and dangerous landscape. And rising above these moments, I saw four men, each different; four functions in the group, each different; four skills and preoccupations, each different.

Although all of them hunt, one man among them is more skilled than the others. He is strong and highly competitive, able to pick up scents and follow trails when the others seem baffled. In these moments, the others cede leadership to his knowledge and prowess. The second is a craftsman. He is the technician, the one who fashions the small, intricate, and lethal poison-tipped arrows they use, the one who repairs spears and belts and bows. At certain moments, others cede leadership to his knowledge and skill. The third is the shaman, the man who performs small ceremonies along the way and who reminds the others of the rituals that must be done if harmony in the world is to be maintained. At key moments, he leads. And the last is the headman, the man who insists on cooperation when the others are quarreling, the one who wears the weight of their many failures on his shoulder, the one who urges them to work together until their goal is accomplished.

Four men, four styles of leadership, four approaches to the negotiation of their work, four ancient imperatives that permeate our work as problem solvers in dimly understood ways.[22]

In an essay celebrating Marshall's 1950 ethnography, William Irwin Thompson[23] writes about the historic clash of values that each of these men represent. "The model of four seems to be a persistent one," he writes; "it recalls the rule of four in the Indian caste system, Plato, Vico, Blake, Marx, Jung, and McLuhan." Perhaps that same rule is at play now in Pulsar's negotiations in Brazil, in the tenant's urgings to her landlord, in the secret ambassadorial talks that are inevitably

going on along some border. Says Thompson: "we may never know if this structure of four exists in reality or is simply a convenient artifice that we have
concocted to try to explain our crude fumblings when we attack difficult problems."

Either way, Marshall's film hints at something older and more mysterious that
permeates the negotiations we are all engaged in. If there is a deep imperative
here, perhaps it is a constant reminder that negotiation is an all too human craft
and that like so many other human endeavors, our greatest individual and collective strengths, taken to excess, inevitably become our greatest weaknesses.

The chapters that follow offer a rich tapestry of models, theories, and ideas to
test this notion. Collectively, they won't resolve the deep-running, perhaps even
hard-wired tensions between cooperation, competition, morality, and pragmatism.
They may, however, foster a few new insights and judgments that allow us to
manage the tensions with a greater measure of grace.

Endnotes

My thanks to friends and colleagues Bob Benjamin, David Newton, Ann Gosline, Clare
Colburn, and Doug Thompson who helped refine the ideas in this chapter.

[1] See MATT RIDLEY, ORIGINS OF VIRTUE (1996); RICHARD DAWKINS, THE SELFISH GENE (1976); ROBERT ARDREY, AFRICAN GENESIS (1961).
[2] This problem is adapted from Larry Rohter, *Brazil Moves to Protect Jungle Plants From Foreign Biopiracy*, N.Y. TIMES, Dec. 23, 2001, at A4.
[3] SAUL ALINSKY, RULES FOR RADICALS (1971). For other iconic popular examples, *see* DONALD TRUMP, THE ART OF THE DEAL (1987); ROBERT RINGER, WINNING THROUGH INTIMIDATION (1973); LEONARD KOREN & PETER GOODMAN, THE HAGGLER'S HANDBOOK (1991); MICHAEL SCHATZKI, NEGOTIATION: THE ART OF GETTING WHAT YOU WANT (1981).
[4] TRUMP, *supra* note 3, at 3.
[5] See ROY LEWICKI ET AL., NEGOTIATION (2d ed. 1982); HOWARD RAIFFA, THE ART AND SCIENCE OF NEGOTIATION (1982).
[6] See ROGER BARUCH BUSH & JOSEPH FOLGER, THE PROMISE OF MEDIATION (1994).
[7] BERNARD MAYER, DYNAMICS OF CONFLICT RESOLUTION 152 (2000).
[8] See E. FRANKLIN DUKES ET AL., REACHING FOR HIGHER GROUND IN CONFLICT RESOLUTION (2000).
[9] JOHN PAUL LEDERACH, THE MORAL IMAGINATION: THE ART AND SOUL OF BUILDING PEACE 27 (2005).
[10] ROGER FISHER, ET AL., GETTING TO YES: NEGOTIATING AGREEMENT WITHOUT GIVING IN (2d ed. 1991).
[11] STEVEN BRAMS & ALAN TAYLOR, FAIR DIVISION: FROM CAKE-CUTTING TO DISPUTE RESOLUTION 1 (1996).
[12] Todd Bryan, *Tragedy Averted: The Promise of Collaboration*, 17 SOCIETY & NATURAL RESOURCES 881, 886 (2004).
[13] R.L. WING, THE ART OF STRATEGY: A NEW TRANSLATION OF SUN TZU'S CLASSIC 45 (1988).
[14] An interesting and perhaps analogous maxim used by chess players is to play tactically when you know what to do, and strategically when you don't.
[15] See EDWARD TENNER, WHY THINGS BITE BACK: TECHNOLOGY AND THE REVENGE OF UNINTENDED CONSEQUENCES (1997).
[16] See BARRY JOHNSON, POLARITY MANAGEMENT: IDENTIFYING AND MANAGING UNSOLVABLE PROBLEMS (1992).
[17] ROBERT LIFTON, BOUNDARIES: PSYCHOLOGICAL MAN IN REVOLUTION 4 (1967).
[18] THOMAS FRIEDMAN, THE LEXUS AND THE OLIVE TREE: UNDERSTANDING GLOBALIZATION (2000).
[19] Robert Benjamin, *The Protean Sensibility: Recommending Approaches to Leadership and Negotiation* (2004) (unpublished paper) (on file with author).
[20] MALCOLM GLADWELL, BLINK: THE POWER OF THINKING WITHOUT THINKING (2005).
[21] Susan Podziba, *The Human Side of Complex Public Policy Mediation*, 19 NEGOTIATION JOURNAL 285 (2003).

[22] Of course, the story also describes a classically variegated team, in which the strengths and weaknesses of any one individual, if replicated across the entire team, would lead to failure. *See* David Sally & Kathleen O'Connor, *Negotiating in Teams*, Chapter 62 in this volume.

[23] WILLIAM IRWIN THOMPSON, AT THE EDGE OF HISTORY 109 (1971).

☙ 4 ❧

The Road to Hell is Paved with Metaphors

Howard Gadlin, Andrea Kupfer Schneider & Christopher Honeyman

Editors' Note: *Metaphors are so deeply embedded in our minds that they are, to a large extent, how we think. This creates an enormous trap for negotiators, as negotiators not only tend to start out with metaphors for conflict handling that derive from war, but tend not to notice their assumptions. Yet metaphors can be the key to a solution, as well as the central problem.*

When one talks about meaning in human communication, inevitably one must talk about metaphor. In the past few years, students of negotiation and mediation looking to understand better what conflicts are really about have discovered the importance of metaphor.[1] Much of this work has been inspired by the research and writings of George Lakoff[2] and his colleagues, who have demonstrated that much of abstract thinking is dependent upon metaphor, and that we can more fully grasp how someone understands a matter, and the emotions associated with that understanding, through a careful examination of the metaphors by which they describe it. Even on the most bare-bones practical level, it turns out, an awareness of metaphor is important to any negotiator or mediator who hopes to jog someone out of an unproductive pattern of thinking.

The interest in metaphors parallels in some respects the interest in framing; both are concerned to explicate how disputants understand their own disputes, how they see those with whom they are in dispute, and how they experience the dispute resolution processes through which they address the disputes. [Caton Campbell & Docherty, *Framing*] This interest is, again, more than academic; people who work regularly with people in conflict learn very quickly that there is typically much more to a conflict than there appears to be at first. Of course there are many reasons that the stories parties tell might not reveal everything that is important about a dispute—concerns about confidentiality, questions of trust regarding the mediator and/or the other party, embarrassment about some of the facts in or aspects of the dispute, along with the to-be-expected hope to elicit sympathy from a mediator and the desire to position oneself well in relation to an adversary. But even after taking these factors into account, after trust is built, embarrassment overcome, confidentiality concerns addressed, a mediator, and sometimes the parties too, must recognize that much more is involved than has been identified by the parties. Metaphor becomes important because often it is at the heart of the most elusive aspects of the dispute. Metaphor is also one of the key reasons parties often need a mediator: since we all think *in* metaphors, a dispassionate and skilled third party may have no greater service to offer the parties than the ability to help them get outside the metaphors that may be limiting the solutions they can currently see. For these reasons, much of what follows is in the voice of a mediator.

Metaphor as Reflecting Emotion

Jayne Docherty eloquently states the opportunity that attending to metaphor provides us: "We can train ourselves to hear their metaphors and stories and to probe them in order to learn more about how they are framing the conflict and the negotiation process, and this in turn opens options for reframing both the conflict and the process we are using to manage it."[3]

Although metaphor can help us recognize factors that might make people reluctant to tell a full story, it is especially useful in orienting us toward two features of people's thinking that we often confront when working with conflict. The first is succinctly described by Jones and Hughes: "humans are feeling beings with thoughts and not thinking beings with feelings." Every negotiator or mediator has had the experience of realizing how thoroughly the issues in a dispute are infused with emotions, sometime even while the parties deny that this is the case. The second is that much of our cognitive process proceeds outside of our conscious awareness. Note that in speaking about thought processes as "unconscious" we are using the term in a somewhat different way than did Freud, who was referring to what we think of as "irrational" aspects of thinking. [Deutsch, *Internal Conflict*] The "unconscious" thinking that Lakoff and others examine is what we ordinarily think of as "rational."

Every negotiator faces two realities about what they hear: people don't always mean what they say; people don't always say what they mean. Perhaps paradoxically, the astute negotiator is able to recognize this while still finding a way to take people at their word; or at least, to understand them *from* their words. We attend to metaphors in communication because they provide some link to understanding in two ways. First, metaphors reflect the feelings that are a part of how people think about the dispute and, second, they provide a way to go from what people say to what they mean to say.

In part because of these realities, in recent years conceptions of mediation have expanded beyond the notion of the self-centered, rational pursuit of self-interest through distributive bargaining. The ideal of the rational actor has been challenged both by the recognition that emotions are intrinsically tied up with thoughts and by the realization that much thinking goes on outside the scope of conscious awareness. This recognition also has opened up ideas about the negotiation process. We are now alert to the fact that negotiations are *always* about more than the pursuit of interests; they are also about identity and about relationships. The key to understanding these dimensions of what a negotiation is "really" about resides in the stories that people tell about the conflicts or issues that bring them into the negotiation as well as how they describe the negotiation process itself. [Heen & Stone, *Perceptions*]

There are two major ways in which negotiators or mediators can benefit from understanding and attending to metaphor. One has to do with how we interpret what we hear; the other has to do with how we intervene. While using a person's metaphors as a means to interpret where the person is coming from is obviously very important, the question of what one does with what one learns from the metaphor is not straightforward. As Jones and Hughes make clear, metaphors help us see and feel both what a party feels about something and how the party thinks about it, and that how they feel and how they think are intrinsically interwoven. The old advice of separating the feelings from the issues, if it ever was believed, is clearly off base. If we follow Jones and Hughes, the feeling cannot be separated from the "thinking about" because the thinking contains the feelings within it.[4]

Metaphors can be used to help a party express directly what is only being expressed indirectly. One of the authors, for instance, worked for some time with a deeply disturbed person who was experiencing a wide range of workplace performance and relationship problems. In every one of the mediating conversations, while her words were about work-related matters, the metaphors were about neglect and abuse. It was not until these metaphors were brought to her attention that she was able to move toward a framing of the various issues in ways that were amenable to being addressed successfully.

Metaphor as a Reflection of Relationship

The disputing parties' use of metaphor can help us better appreciate how they understand and experience the negotiation/mediation process, as well as how they understand and experience the conflict and their relationship with their counterpart. If, in talking about the conflict, they are using words with combat connotations, it suggests that perhaps the parties see all interactions with the other person as acts of war. Most likely this means they see the negotiation in terms of winning and losing. If they see it in terms of winning and losing they are likely to be on the lookout for dirty tactics ("All's fair in love and war") and highly suspicious of communications from the other person. Of course the person who sees a negotiation as war might also justify withholding crucial information and disguising their true intent. (Consider how many stories from war glorify deception tactics—from the Trojan Horse to D-Day. In a war metaphor, deception is not unethical, it is accepted practice.)

The war metaphor also alerts us to the fact that the conflict has very high stakes; people may feel that their very identity is at stake. For the negotiator or mediator this is a sign that she must carefully explore, through questioning, what the conflict means to the disputants. On the other hand, if the war metaphors have emerged only in their discussion of the mediation process and not in their accounts of the reasons they have come to mediation, the mediator can take the war metaphor as an indicator of apprehension about the process of mediation.

Recognizing the metaphor that is guiding the parties' orientation toward the negotiation or mediation process always presents the negotiator or mediator with a tactical decision point—whether to work with the parties' metaphors, or to introduce a different metaphor that might help re-orient one or both parties toward their own dispute. When working with people who are divided by deep enmity and longstanding rivalry, one of the authors often talks early on (but after they have described their conflict and its history) about establishing the terms of a cease-fire or a truce. Doing this honors their war metaphor, but orients them towards a different outcome than the one with which they arrived, i.e. win/lose. At other times, a metaphorical expression that introduces a greater transformation than in the example above might be used, one that helps to reframe the conflict itself and not just the negotiation process. For example, when people describe how they are always fighting at work and are unable to cooperate, it may become appropriate to comment on how *well choreographed* their conflict appears. In this case the dance metaphor, by referring to the synchronization of movements that choreography produces, points directly to the sort of "cooperation" that is required between people who sustain a conflict over time—and undermines the idea that they are unable to cooperate.

The judicious use of a new metaphor can also allow the mediator to articulate what the disputants may not be able to state directly. Sometimes when participants in a failed collaboration are exchanging accusations of blame and describing each other's inability to change, one can ask whether they have ever thought about divorce. Introducing a marriage metaphor in a workplace dispute can give permission for the disputants to discuss their problems in a new way. With parties who have not been able to articulate the depths of their enmity and the breadth of their incompatibility, such a framing is often a relief, both because it acknowledges dimensions of the conflict they have only alluded to and because it undermines the fear that working with an institutionally "centrist" player—such as, at NIH, the ombudsman's office—means they are going to have to become friends.

Metaphor as a Reflection of the Rules

Sometimes metaphors can reflect the underlying assumptions that the parties are making about the negotiation process. As mentioned above, the war metaphor seems to imply no limit on tactics. When, for example, a negotiator talks about negotiation as poker, it seems to imply that bluffing will be part of that negotiator's repertoire *and that we, the other side, ought to know that*. Bluffing is, after all, acceptable and expected in the game of poker. Since not every negotiator assumes that those are the rules of the game, unpacking this metaphor and realizing its ramifications can be crucial if you were expecting a more candid exchange.

Another common metaphor for negotiation is sports or games. In sports, we assume that the teams are relatively equal, that the score starts at 0-0, and that, even after a loss, the score starts the next day again at 0-0. We can draw the metaphor out even further talking about "an even playing field" and how any team can win on "any given day." It is unclear that these assumptions apply to most negotiations where the parties are not balanced and are unable to start each negotiation, regardless of how the last interaction went, at a new starting place. Yet if the negotiator on the other side seems to be talking about her "team" and the game of negotiation, that will reflect some important values about negotiation that would be good for us to know.

What about mountain climbing as a metaphor? Well, that one is not usually a good sign. Parties "ratchet" themselves upwards to a "precipice" from which they need help "climbing down." (Of course, you could always jump!)

Other metaphors for negotiation are less combative (a war metaphor itself). Sometimes we say that we are "working through" the problem, or building a bridge to the other side, almost invoking an engineering or production-management view of the world. If we are "hammering out our differences," it connotes that we are in the mechanic's shop trying to find ways of "repair," but working together. (The phrase is metaphorically distinguished from another use of similar language, in which the parties are hammering each other—or in which even mediators have been known to refer to hammering a party.) Each of these metaphors, and many others, helps clarify the assumptions that each party has about the "rules of the game" and the negotiation interaction.

Among the other metaphors are some that are quite specialized, and to be used only sparingly. One of the authors, for instance, used to spend a great deal of time mediating between extremely liberal public-sector unions and thoroughly conservative rural county and school boards. The boards were dominated by farmers, who tended toward metaphors of individualism and self-reliance. This had its comic aspect, to anyone with a smattering of knowledge about the complicated government farm price support system, from which many farmers suffer while some do rather well. More than once, a particularly recalcitrant board member who enjoyed membership in the latter camp would find the mediator making an apparently offhand remark, usually to someone else entirely, about "farming the federal government." But those occasions had to be very selectively chosen.

Recognizing Our Own Metaphors

It is important to note here that negotiators and mediators must at least try to be aware of the metaphors that reflect and inform their own understanding of the mediation. [Riskin, *Mindfulness*] We must recognize that the very language that is used to describe the negotiation or mediation process can frame and shape the interaction and substantive content of the negotiation between the parties. A mediator who is using a dance metaphor might herself be "out of step" with the disputing parties. Dance often has connotations of intimacy, and the parties might find such a framing inappropriate for their situation, especially if lack of trust is a major issue. Sometimes a mediator is able to help the parties adopt his governing metaphor for the process, but there are circumstances where metaphor mismatch is partly responsible for failure of the process.

One can easily imagine an introduction to the mediation process in which a mediator and the parties "negotiate," implicitly or explicitly, which metaphor will govern the mediation process. One of the authors recently conducted a mediation session in which one party began by asking that his concerns about possible retaliation by his supervisor be addressed before we discussed substantive matters, while the supervisor asserted that it was critically important for him that the other party affirm his trust in him so that they could be partners in problem solving. The employee was very uncertain of his ability to stand up to the supervisor. Clearly, the mediation meant something different, and raised different issues, for the two parties. They were not able to make any progress until, in a private caucus, the mediator talked with the supervisor about coaching the employee about how to help the employee be stronger in his dealings with the supervisor. The concept of "coach" changes the underlying metaphor from "hierarchy" (boss/underling) to "team." In this metaphor, a player can be a star. But because a coach still tells a player what to do, this metaphor is also widely accepted in management. It was, indeed, readily adopted, and as the supervisor changed his stance from boss to coach, the interactions between the two were transformed.

Of course, there is no reason to assume that there will only be one governing metaphor—interactions can go from dancing to warfare and back and forth many times. In one such mediation, one of the authors gave a fairly standard interest-based negotiation introduction at the outset of the mediation to four scientists involved in a complex dispute concerning, among other things, the use of space and facilities in a shared laboratory. They had brought the dispute to an ombudsman because it had become a battle that was quite personal and was undermining their ability to do their scientific work. Recognizing how suspicious they had become of one another, the ombudsman suggested that as scientists, they might think of taking a stance of curiosity toward each other's statements and positions, rather than the adversarial stance they had assumed in their daily interactions. One of the scientists promptly brightened, looking as if he had been freed from himself, and said "Curiosity? I can do that." Science as metaphor was introduced, in this case, as a deliberate attempt to move them away from their description of a battle over space, not by challenging their battle metaphor but by substituting curiosity for opposition and tapping into the one passion that was certain to re-orient them toward what they all wanted—to "do science." But the session proceeded under the orientation provided by the guidance of *two* governing metaphors, scientific inquiry and interest-based bargaining. Instead of attacking each other's statements they began to ask questions of one another. While it was not a love-fest, they were able to work out a quite satisfactory arrangement, one that has held for three years.

It is important to recognize that metaphorical communication need not be verbal. One of the authors was once working with the new director of a small biomedical research program that had been fraught with conflict since the departure of the former director (a man highly revered by all). The departure of the former director had meant not just the loss of a leader, but also the diminution of the importance of the program—its resources were cut and its importance in the overall research program of this particular institute had been similarly reduced. The new director, a thoughtful, intellectual and culturally refined man, was one of those scientists who is not especially tuned in to the fine points of human interaction, and was not able to describe in useful detail the nature of the problems being experienced within his group. Earlier conversations with him, however, had revealed his deep appreciation and knowledge of classical music. In our caucus, while haltingly discussing the situation in his group and the impact of losing their leader, the mediator suggested that perhaps Mozart's requiem would be an appropriate piece to capture the feeling of the group. Almost instantly the scientist replied no; the Mozart would not be appropriate; but the Haydn requiem would be. He then proceeded to explain what it was about that piece of music that more accurately reflected the sense of mourning he experienced with his group than did the Mozart. That was exactly the breakthrough needed to develop a plan for intervention with his team.

Metaphor as Tool

This story illustrates how a mediator can use metaphor not only as a tool to understand a situation but also to intervene in it. The use of metaphors that differ from those employed by the disputants can help to reorient the parties toward the negotiation/mediation process and help reframe the parties' understanding of the conflict and the issues in dispute. This is an especially important point because the terms by which disputants describe their conflicts raise complex challenges to mediator neutrality. Among the guiding principles of mediation is the belief that parties to a dispute ought to be able to speak for themselves and play an active role in deciding what would be an acceptable resolution of a dispute. In a negotiation, what people say is the primary raw material with which negotiators work. On the one hand it is crucially important for mediators to understand how the disputants understand a conflict. On the other hand, we know that we cannot take literally the stories disputants tell us about their conflicts.

Working effectively requires some degree of interpretation, and metaphor provides one of the most reliable pathways to interpretations that can be helpful to the participants, because we are working with their own words even as we move beyond their stated understanding of the situation. If we were to understand the conflict in the same terms as the disputants do, even if they agree with each other, then we would become, to some degree, co-participants in the conflict rather than independent interveners. Neutrality and fairness *require* that we understand the dispute in terms other than those stated by the disputants, while still being anchored in their understandings. Identifying and understanding the metaphors

used by the disputants is the single most important step we can take toward helping the disputants reframe the dispute in ways that are true to the full meaning of
the dispute to them.

Of course this forces us to confront the fact that mediators *are* interveners,
with the active rather than passive metaphors that term embodies. All mediators
intervene in disputes by attempting, at various times, to influence (or help) people
to alter the way they interact and speak with each other, the ways they understand and feel about the issues in a dispute, and the possible solutions they can
imagine. Even the "transformative" mediators, who assert that the mediator
should not "try to influence how problems are defined and how solutions are chosen," discuss the value of a party realizing better what matters to her, being able to
listen and communicate better, being able to see a situation differently. The trick is
to find a use of language that accurately reflects what the parties are experiencing
(as you understand it from how they have described it to you, and recognizing the
paradox created by this if you are trying to avoid excessively influencing them) but
at the same time introduces enough of a different perspective that it allows the
parties to go beyond their initial descriptions and positions. The beauty of a creative use of metaphor as intervention is in its ability to stay true enough to the
disputants' metaphors that they still recognize what you are talking about, while
introducing something novel enough to allow them to reconfigure their own feelings and thinking into a new framework.

At the least, the current attention to metaphor is part of the natural expansion
of the repertoire of conceptual tools by which negotiations can be understood and
directed. This expansion, in turn, reflects an increase in the degree to which negotiators and mediators are incorporating into their work conceptual approaches and
methods of intervention developed in other areas of research and professional
practice. This shift has been described as "process pluralism,"[5] the recognition that
different varieties of conflict require different conceptual frameworks and different modes of intervention.

It might also be that these developments reflect a fundamental shift in the
way we think about conflict, negotiation and mediation, a movement away from
reductionist conceptualizations toward a more holistic approach. [Docherty, *Many
Tools*] From this perspective it becomes easier to recognize that the dynamics of
conflict can only be understood within the context of the disputants' lives—the
multiplicity of identities that define them, the full range of their relationships, and
the institutions within which they are embedded. With more attention to and
greater skill with metaphor, we have better tools to appreciate the motivating factors behind the verbiage, and will be in a better position to help people negotiate
effectively—or to negotiate with them more effectively ourselves.

Endnotes

[1] Jayne Docherty, *Narratives, Metaphors, and Negotiation*, 87 MARQUETTE LAW REVIEW 847
(2004); Wendell Jones & Scott Hughes, *Complexity, Conflict Resolution, and How the Mind
Works*, 20 CONFLICT RESOLUTION QUARTERLY 485 (2003); Jonathan Cohen, *Adversaries? Parties?
How about Counterparts? On Metaphors in the Practice and teaching of Negotiation and Dispute Resolution* 20 CONFLICT RESOLUTION QUARTERLY 433 (2003).
[2] GEORGE LAKOFF & MARK JOHNSON, PHILOSOPHY IN THE FLESH (1999).
[3] Docherty, *supra* note 1.
[4] Jones & Hughes, *supra* note 1.
[5] CARRIE MENKEL-MEADOW, LELA LOVE, ANDREA SCHNEIDER & JEAN STERNLIGHT, DISPUTE
RESOLUTION: BEYOND THE ADVERSARIAL MODEL 4 (2005).

❧ 5 ☙

What's in a Frame?

Marcia Caton Campbell & Jayne Seminare Docherty

Editors' Note: How you conceive what your negotiation is all about, and how the other side perceives it, can be a complete mismatch resulting in mutual frustration. Here, Caton Campbell and Docherty address the all-important question of framing, providing a set of ways to think through your assumptions and those of the other side. You may want to read this chapter in close conjunction with those by Heen & Stone and Ricigliano.

In most large-scale multi-party disputes, such as those characteristic of public policy and environmental conflicts, third-party intervenors make detailed conflict assessments before beginning facilitated or mediated processes.[1] Fundamental to these assessments is identifying and unpacking the multiple frames disputants hold, to get a clearer picture of the conflict's drivers.[2] Frames are perceptions that the parties hold about what defines the conflict, who is involved in it, how issues are presented, what the expected outcomes might be, and how outcomes will be reached and evaluated.[3] Frames structure disputants' conceptions of the conflict and exert profound influences on their behavior, strategizing, and choice of negotiating tactics. Frames can be malleable, although some are essentially immutable.[4] At times, disputants will cling to particular conflict frames that stymie negotiations and push conflicts into intractability. Thus, if left unexamined, frames can limit the range of possible solutions the disputing parties can envision.

This essay presents an entrenched, large-scale, multi-party conflict as the basis for a brief discussion of frames and framing dynamics. Its focus is on macro-level frames that determine the parties' approach to the conflict, including their perceptions of negotiation as a conflict resolution process, rather than on micro-level moves and countermoves among the parties while they are negotiating. Macro-level conflict frames structure the possibilities for resolution while micro-level frames shape the nature of party interactions at the table. Macro-level frames are important tools for understanding the long-term, strategic negotiation goals of a party, which may or may not be identical to the party's tactical goals in the negotiation itself.[5] In some cases, reframing can enhance the prospects for negotiation or conflict transformation, leading to resolution; however, in others, reframing is less plausible.[6] Although empirical research on multi-party dispute framing is a relatively recent development, frame analysis has quickly become a central part of the conflict assessment pedagogical canon and the public sector dispute resolver's tool kit. Frame analysis can hold utility for lawyers and other representatives as well, as they seek to understand what motivates the strategic choices made by their clients and by those who sit across the negotiating table.

Highway Through a Monument: A "Road to Nowhere"?[7]

In the desert Southwest stretches a 17-mile-long mesa of black volcanic rocks covered with over 15,000 ancient carvings, some of which may date back 2,000 years or more. This boulder field is a sacred shrine for a Native American tribe, and draws other tribes from across the southwestern states for religious practices. Designated a national monument by the National Park Service over a decade ago, the 7,000-acre park lies directly west of a rapidly growing city of 700,000 residents. This sprawling city is landlocked by a forest to the north, a mountain range and a Native American reservation to the east, and an Air Force Base to the south. The city's planners project population growth of fifty percent over the next twenty-five years, to more than one million people, and expect most of the residential development accommodating the growth to occur west of the city. Housing prices in subdivisions on the city's west side are substantially more affordable than in the rest of the metropolitan area, but the monument is a physical barrier between the city and the undeveloped land to the west.

Three years after the monument's designation, developers and their political allies proposed a six-lane highway extension through the monument to connect future residential development with the existing highway that runs across the northern part of the city. Approximately one-quarter mile of the highway extension would cut through the national monument and require moving about a dozen of the ancient petroglyphs and the loss of 8.5 acres of the park for the highway corridor.[8] The tribe, which holds creation beliefs that their ancestors emerged from the earth, considers the monument an organic whole that links its people with the spirit world in the afterlife. As a result, the tribe also finds abhorrent options such as tunneling under the monument or building a bridge over it. For religious reasons, the tribe would even prefer that the ancient carvings were destroyed than relocated to another part of the park. The Native Americans vehemently oppose the road—in any form—as a desecration of sacred tribal lands.

The highway extension is backed by the City Council, most of the state's Congressional delegation, and the local business community. Voters' polls yield conflicting results: one poll conducted by a local newspaper shows that a slight majority of the respondents favor the extension through the monument, while another poll shows that a majority of the city's residents prefer an alternate route. (Voters rejected a previous referendum for the highway extension because the proposed location necessitated destroying several holes of a local golf course, causing tribal members to question what non-Natives consider truly sacred.)

During this time, as development begins to encroach on the monument, the debate surrounding the highway proposal turns vociferous and bitter. Critics of the monument and proponents of the road publicly question the legitimacy of the Native Americans' religious practices and the monument's importance to them. They contend that few in the area considered the monument sacred prior to its designation by the National Park Service, and that the tribes are being obstructionist about the city's future development. The tribes counter that because the religious rituals performed have always been kept secret, the monument's cultural and religious significance has not been fully appreciated by people outside the tribes. Not only that, they fear that if the monument is desecrated by the road's development, this will set a precedent that opens the way for similar destruction of other sacred Native American sites elsewhere.

The city's recently elected mayor was the sole candidate, in a field of seven, who opposed the highway extension; however, he was elected to office by just twenty-nine percent of the electorate. In addition to a five-tribe coalition and the mayor, other opposition to the proposed highway extension comes from preservationists, environmentalists, the state's smart-growth anti-sprawl organization, the National Parks and Conservation Association, and the National Park Service itself. Besides their opposition to cutting through the monument, these groups point out that the highway extension has negative environmental consequences as well—there simply is not enough water available in the desert region to support the residential growth that the road would make possible.

Over a several-year period, discussions about the highway extension became extremely contentious, polarizing the many stakeholders involved. The state's Congressional delegation introduced bills in the U.S. House and Senate to remove the proposed 8.5-acre highway corridor from the national park and decertify the corridor from protected status. Native Americans held public protests against the proposed road. The parties were deadlocked and held rigidly to their positions. The city's growth is inevitable, but where and how it is accommodated is open to negotiation. Other aspects of this conflict may not be negotiable. How can we tell which are which? Frame analysis helps pinpoint where the conflict's tensions and intractability lie; it can guide strategic and tactical moves during negotiation, and it also reveals potential areas of agreement or opportunities for conflict transformation.

Generic Frames (Frames as Categories of Experience)

Researchers in communications,[9] and more recently in environmental conflict resolution,[10] have identified broad categories of frames known as generic frames or categories of experience. Parties in conflict do not necessarily use each one of these frames equally. Some frames may predominate, while others may not come into play at all. In still other instances, parties may have clashing versions of the same type of frame (a form of cognitive dissonance), or their frames may undergo shifts related to information learned during the course of negotiating a specific issue or problem. This chapter describes different types of frames and some of the ways frame analysis can help negotiators.

Worldmaking Stories

Even before parties encounter one another in a conflict, they hold large cognitive frames that can usefully be thought of as worldmaking stories.[11] Worldmaking stories are narratives that are told and retold by many people; they become symbolic focal points around which organizations, communities, and civilizations shape their collective lives. Each worldmaking story expresses the authoritative claims of the community that validates it, and every worldmaking story contains implicit, if not explicit, patterns of compulsions and permissions to act in certain ways and prohibitions against acting in other ways.[12] Some worldmaking stories are blatantly sacred; the worldmaking story of the Native American party in our case study would fall into this category. Other worldmaking stories are ostensibly secular, but they function as a sacred narrative because they, too, contain claims about ultimate truth or authority, and they contain action imperatives and prohibitions. Many of the non-Native parties in this case are likely to bring a secular worldmaking story into this encounter—a narrative that assumes that human beings have the right to reshape the natural world and that the instrumental needs of the many outweigh the religious rights of the few. Some non-Native parties—possibly environmentalist and preservationist groups—may hold secular worldmaking stories that are akin to the Native American stories in their willingness to place non-instrumental factors above such things as growth and development.

Whole Story

Also known as substantive frames, whole story frames are the basic nutshell stories parties offer when asked, "What is this conflict about?" Parties use whole story frames to guide their behavior in negotiations. In the case described above, for example, proponents of the highway extension are likely to describe the conflict as being about the need to accommodate future urban growth. Environmental and anti-sprawl groups may describe the conflict as being about the physical and environmental limits to growth, while the tribes will likely describe the conflict as being about the desecration of sacred tribal lands. Early in the negotiation process, however, mediators can sometimes help parties jointly reframe their substantive frames into a single whole story frame more amenable to resolution. The extent to which this is possible can depend on the influence of other frames held by the parties. If less malleable frames dominate negotiations, as is likely in the case described here (see discussion below), a shared, whole story frame may not be achievable.

Since mediators also carry worldmaking stories with them, there is a significant risk that they will favor one whole story over another. For example, collaborative planning processes used to address environmental conflicts often use a narrative about stakeholders and interest-based parties. This worldmaking narrative recognizes actors who hold discrete, quantifiable, instrumental interests. It has a difficult time accommodating parties who make values-based claims about sacred space or the world as a sacred, living being.[13] The Native American parties in our case study may find it difficult to speak their truth into the negotiation arena; they may have to twist what they want to say to make it fit into a secular worldmaking story.[14]

Identity

One of the least malleable frames over time and a major contributor to dispute intractability,[15] identity frames describe how parties view themselves, both as individuals and as members of a group. They answer the question: "Who are we in this conflict?" Identity frames are also closely tied to worldmaking stories, particularly through the action imperatives and prohibitions contained in every worldmaking story. We are a people, because we do X, and we do not do Y; we believe A and we reject B. Identity frames are typically positive in tone and are based on parties' demographic characteristics, place or location, roles they play, interests they hold, and institutions with which they are affiliated. Because identity frames are fundamental to parties' self-conceptualizations, threats to either self-identity or group identity can cause conflicts to escalate rapidly.[16]

In the monument/highway conflict above, the tribe has a distinct, well-defined identity and culture (described here in its creation beliefs), which is being threatened not only by the proposed location of the highway, but also by the highway's proponents casting aspersions on the validity of tribal religious practices. In addition, the potential exists for threats to Native American culture and identity more broadly if the door is opened to threatening the protected status of sites sacred to other tribes. Meanwhile, as is typical in development scenarios, the City Council and development community probably hold an identity frame constructed around their roles as protectors of the city's future and advocates of "progress." Given the checkered history between U.S. government at all levels (federal, state, and local) and Native American tribes as sovereign nations, interactions that question tribal identity are likely to cause this conflict to spiral rapidly upward.

Power

Recent research on intractable environmental disputes identifies nine categories of power frames: authority/positional (based on traditional sources such as role, job title, or institutional status), access to resources (money, staff, time), expertise, interpersonal style, coalitional/relational (group affiliation), sympathy/vulnerability (role as victim), force/threat (of legal action, coercion, or BATNA use), moral/righteous, and voice (participation at the table).[17] In our case, both the City Council and the mayor have power based on their authority as government officials, although the mayor's mandate is relatively weak because he did not carry a majority of the voters with him. They and the development community have power based on access to resources, expertise, and voice. The tribes have power based on moral (religious) grounds, although it may not be fully recognized by secular interests until the tribes exercise power through force or threat of legal action. They may also garner some power from a sympathy/vulnerability frame, given the history of federal government mistreatment of tribes. The tribes' ability to exercise power based on participation at the table (a voice frame) may be constrained by the sacred worldmaking story that they hold.

The same dispute can be variously framed based on interests, rights, or power, with different outcomes as a result. Disputes framed on the basis of parties' interests are more resolvable, while disputes based on rights (particularly when rights are in question) and power can be more polarizing.[18] In the monument/highway case, the Congressional delegation has clearly framed the dispute as one of power: the tribe's unwillingness to concede what in the legislators' view is a small percentage of the monument's acreage has led them to try to resolve the dispute by decertifying the land at issue (an exercise of legislative authority and power). The tribe, however, has framed the dispute as one of sacred rights to land of critical cultural and religious significance. Any third party intervenor walking into this situation should not assume from the outset that the conflict can be reframed as a dispute based on interests.

Conflict Management or Process

Conflict management or process frames encompass the parties' preferences for particular ways of dealing with a conflict. These range from passive strategies, such as avoidance, to increasingly more active strategies, such as fact-finding, joint problem solving, decisions based on expertise, appeals to political action, or direct action such as struggle, sabotage, or violence.[19] When the parties encounter each other in a stable negotiation context—based on established relationships and a stable sense of reality that exist within recognized social structures—mechanisms exist to support the negotiation process, such as mutually accepted norms about behavior and what is considered fair, some certainty that the parties have a shared future, and formal or informal institutions that can enforce the resultant negotiated agreements. In other instances, parties must negotiate in a less stable context, in which their future together is uncertain; behavioral and fairness norms are unclear, disputed, or contested; and mechanisms and institutions to support negotiated agreements are controversial, fragile, or non-existent.[20] The stability of the negotiating context will influence the conflict management frames that parties adopt, with direct effects on the potential for conflict resolution.

One factor likely to contribute to a conflict escalation in this case is the clash between an overtly sacred worldmaking story and a secular worldmaking story. When a place is deemed sacred by some people and viewed as malleable and instrumental by others, we have a recipe for potential violence. This is particularly true when there is a great power differential between the group espousing a religious view and a dominant secular view that is being enforced by powerful authorities.[21]

Looking at nonviolent options, preference for particular process frames may hinge on parties' perceptions of their BATNAs (Best Alternative to a Negotiated Agreement). In a stable climate,[22] the City Council and Congressional delegation will fall back on conflict management processes rooted in technical expertise, adjudication, and political action, as indicated by the City's use of road-siting referenda and the Congressional delegation's introduction of legislation to decertify 8.5 acres of the monument for the road. The tribal consortium, on the other hand, has already demonstrated its preference for direct action through public protests. Other options available to highway opponents include simply delaying action until a threat is clearly felt (in the example, we are still at the "proposal" stage), and then taking legal action based on the National Parks Act, the National Environmental Policy Act, historic preservation law, or constitutional or legislative protections of religious freedoms.

Finally, powerful parties may lurk in the "shadows" of the conflict. While not directly at the negotiating table, these parties have the ability to influence the central conflict's outcome. If the negotiating parties directly at the table are to negotiate effectively, they must be aware of the existence of these powerful, but tangential actors. In some instances, the parties at the table may be able to influence the behavior of these actors; in other instances, they may not.[23]

Characterization

Characterization frames represent how parties view the "other." Although they may be positive in tone, they are more likely to consist of negative, often stereotyped attributions of blame (often captured in blaming stories[24]) or causality in the conflict. Characterization frames can be closely linked to identity in framing dynamics, since strong group identity can contribute to conflict escalation by fueling a party's negative characterizations of other parties.[25] For example, in the case at hand, the environmental and anti-sprawl groups opposing the road will likely characterize the City Council and development community as seeing no limits to growth. Road proponents have already pronounced the tribal consortium "obstructionist" and questioned the validity of their religious practices. This type of frame is more mutable, however, if a skilled intervenor can get parties to recognize each other's positive characteristics during negotiations.[26]

Risk and Gain vs. Loss

Risk frames come into play in environmental disputes when health and human safety are threatened by environmental hazards. Local governments, government agencies, and business interests will assess the potential risk of different outcomes using cost-benefit or contingent valuation analyses.[27] These rubrics do not incorporate the non-quantifiable concerns about risk that parties representing the public or special groups may have. They most clearly do not incorporate a religiously motivated party's sense of "spiritual risk." If a party sees itself as mandated to protect something sacred, it may endure bodily harm, severe hardships, or even death rather than "risk" failing in its duty to an authority that supercedes secular authorities.[28] Risk frames influence how parties perceive potential gains or losses in negotiations. Thus, parties that have borne disproportionate levels of environmental or social harm in the past may find what seems to some a small amount of harm, such as the destruction of a dozen of over 15,000 petroglyphs, to be completely unacceptable.

Frames as Issue Development

Another approach to framing not detailed here involves tracking frame shifts as the conflict unfolds over time. Aspects of this approach include an emphasis on negotiation context, particularly the history of relations between the parties, including the standard issues that are raised between them; issue shaping and conceptualization, or, how the interaction between parties shapes the issues under discussion and the frames in use; and, reframing or problem transformation, in which parties' conceptions of the conflict undergo substantive changes as a function of their interactions.[29] The primary tool for analyzing frames as issue development is linguistic discourse analysis, usually of transcripts from negotiation sessions.[30]

Strategies for Reframing and Transforming Conflict

Reframing and conflict transformation depend upon parties' willingness and ability to comprehend the views of the "other," by stepping outside their own cognitive frames and adopting a different perspective. Both substantive and procedural reframing are possible. Substantive reframing can involve the movement from frames based on power or rights to frames based on interests, as discussed above. It can also be based on a search for common ground on substantive issues.[31] Apology, conciliation, and reparations also play important roles in opening parties up to conflict transformation. [Brown & Robbennolt, *Apology*; Waldman & Luskin, *Anger & Forgiveness*]

Another helpful approach is to recognize that not all issues on the table are the same, and not all of the parties sort the issues into the same categories. One party may see everything on the table as subject to interest-based bargaining, while another party sees some things as bargainable and others as sacred. From outside that party's worldmaking story, the bargainable and the sacred may look very similar. The common error is to accuse this party of bargaining in bad faith or betraying the negotiation process. It is important for negotiators and third-party intervenors to learn how to "hear" a party's worldmaking story, so that they can recognize when and why some things are tradable and other things are not.[32] It is equally critical for negotiators to understand the role of principal-agent relationships and the effects these relationships can have on the time it takes to negotiate or mediate, particularly in an unstable negotiating context.[33] [Docherty & Caton Campbell, *Agency*]

Sometimes it is even possible to reach agreement and take joint action without reconciling frame differences. The parties can coordinate their frames rather than changing them.[34] [Docherty & Caton Campbell, *Agency*] This is particularly useful when working across a secular/religious worldview divide, like the one described in our case, so long as the negotiators recognize that they do not share frames. Otherwise, they are likely to assume they have reconciled their worldmaking stories when they have not.

In terms of process, reframing that promotes dispute tractability includes acknowledging the existence of underlying identity issues, such as the tribal concerns here, and reducing the negative characterizations that parties use to describe each other. Controlling the number and size of issues on the table can also help transform entrenched conflicts such as this one. Having multiple issues on the agenda can obscure the core issue in the dispute; thus, an essential part of conflict transformation may involve the stripping away of peripheral or "overlay" issues that may be of concern, but are not central to the conflict.[35] In addition, construction of shared place-based identity frames, a common conflict management frame, and mutually agreed-upon methods of risk assessment can enhance negotiations, as can agreeing upon the forum in which the decision will be made.[36] In long-term conflicts that have been intractable, it may be necessary to see a particular negotiation as only one small part of a process for transforming the conflict. Parties may agree to negotiate a few issues, but prefer to use other approaches to address different aspects of their conflict. For example, the tribes in our case may be more willing to negotiate about this site if the issue is framed as how to protect the site during development, not how much of the site can be damaged during development. They may also be more willing to negotiate if the negotiation is preceded by or coincides with a process of truth-telling about relations between Native Americans and European settlers in New Mexico.

Even in cases where fundamental differences between parties make a dispute quite difficult to resolve, intervenors are on occasion able to move parties away from a focus on the immutable, such as identity or worldview, to focus on other, practical aspects of the dispute that are open to reframing, such as conflict management process and aspiration frames. There are cases, though, in which a focus on the immutable—worldmaking stories, values, and rights—is precisely what the parties need. In these cases, disputes should be "resolved" through mechanisms other than negotiations.[37]

Conclusion

Whether parties are explicitly aware of them or not, frames and framing dynamics play a critical role in determining how they view each other, which tactics they choose, how they strategize in disputing contexts, and how the conflict management process unfolds. Negotiators who develop the capacity for paying attention to worldmaking stories (including their own!) will be more effective and creative when it comes to framing and reframing a dispute for negotiation.[38] As negotiators or third-party intervenors, we must train ourselves to listen for indicators of frame differences during a negotiation session; this involves honing our skills of "on the fly" discourse and rhetorical analysis, and learning when we need to ask for help from others who can serve as "worldview translators" when we do not understand the worldmaking story or frames of another party.[39]

Endnotes

[1] See Lawrence Susskind & Jennifer Thomas-Larmer, Conducting a Conflict Assessment, in THE CONSENSUS BUILDING HANDBOOK 99 (Lawrence Susskind, et al. eds., 1999); Marcia Caton Campbell, Intractability in Environmental Disputes: Exploring a Complex Construct, 17 JOURNAL OF PLANNING LITERATURE 12 (2003); see also, Deborah Shmueli, Conflict Assessment, available at http://www.beyondintractability.org/m/conflict_assessment.jsp (Oct. 2003) (last visited Mar. 9, 2006).

[2] "Causes" and "drivers" are two different things. It is risky to claim causality in conflict assessment (though perhaps that is a result of our training in philosophy). "Drivers," however, calls for "a clearer picture of what drives the conflict," and it is entirely appropriate to seek these. We can likely identify what is currently driving the conflict at the time of an assessment, which may be entirely different from what any initial "causes" might have been (if the parties can even agree on what those might be—and they have been known to get bogged down in that for a long, long time).

[3] ROY J. LEWICKI, ET AL., ESSENTIALS OF NEGOTIATION 31 (3d ed. 2001).

[4] *Id.; see also*, JAYNE SEMINARE DOCHERTY, LEARNING LESSONS FROM WACO: WHEN PARTIES BRING THEIR GODS TO THE NEGOTIATION TABLE (2001); Barbara Gray, *Framing of Environmental Disputes, in* MAKING SENSE OF INTRACTABLE ENVIRONMENTAL CONFLICTS: CONCEPTS AND CASES 23 (Roy J. Lewicki, et al. eds., 2003).

[5] Broadly speaking, parties' strategic goals relate to their long-term preference related to changing (or not changing) the relationships and power balance among parties in the conflict and remaking (or not remaking) social structures and established systems that govern their interactions. Tactical goals relate to the way parties attempt to shape the negotiation table and exert control over interactions at the table. For a more detailed discussion of strategic versus tactical negotiation, *see* JAYNE SEMINARE DOCHERTY, THE LITTLE BOOK OF STRATEGIC NEGOTIATION: NEGOTIATING DURING TURBULENT TIMES 5-15 (2005). For more on the relationship between larger conflict dynamics and negotiation, *see also* Caton Campbell, *supra* note 1.

[6] On the potential for reframing, *see generally* Michael Elliott, et al., *Lessons Learned about the Framing and Reframing of Intractable Environmental Conflicts, in* MAKING SENSE *supra* note 4; Linda L. Putnam & Majia Holmer, *Framing, Reframing, and Issue Development, in* COMMUNICATION AND NEGOTIATION 128 (Linda L. Putnam & Michael E. Roloff, eds. 1992); Gray, *supra* note 4, at 11-34. On conflict transformation, *see* E. FRANKLIN DUKES, RESOLVING PUBLIC CONFLICT: TRANSFORMING COMMUNITY AND GOVERNANCE (1996); DOCHERTY, *supra* note 4; Heidi Burgess & Guy Burgess, *Constructive Confrontation: A Transformative Approach to Intractable Conflicts,* 13 MEDIATION Quarterly 305 (1996).

[7] This case is adapted from James Brooke, *Sprawling Albuquerque Hopes to Cut through Monument,* N.Y. TIMES, Jan. 25, 1998, at 12; John McQuaid, *Standing Their Ground: Unwelcome Neighbors: How the Poor Bear the Burdens of America's Pollution,* NEW ORLEANS TIMES-PICAYUNE, May 24, 2000, at A6; *Highway Plan Through N.M. Petroglyph Memorial Rocks Community,* WASH. POST, Mar. 23, 1998, at A5.

[8] Brooke, *supra* note 7.

[9] Putnam & Holmer, *supra* note 6, at 128-55.

[10] Gray, *supra* note 4.

[11] DOCHERTY, *supra* note 4, at 61-62.

[12] W. BARNETT PEARCE & STEPHEN W. LITTLEJOHN, MORAL CONFLICT: WHEN SOCIAL WORLDS COLLIDE 54 (1997); DOCHERTY, *supra* note 4.

[13] DOCHERTY, *supra* note 4, at 66-67.

[14] In her dissertation, How Our Values Shape Our Practices: Exploding the Myth of Neutrality (unpublished Ph.D. dissertation, Syracuse University) (on file with author), Rachel Miriam Goldberg documents a case in which Native American negotiators struggling to achieve permanent resident status on their traditional homeland found themselves in the position of negotiating for permanent homes, because the agency they were dealing with (and some of the third party intervenors) assumed that permanent residency required a permanent home. The conflict became heated, and many would say intractable, until a culturally savvy mediator asked the tribe to clarify what they meant by permanent residency. It turned out that the tribe never lived there permanently and did not want to live in permanent houses on the land now. They wanted the right to build temporary camps on the land during a specific season of the year, but the dominant cultural frame (worldmaking story) "forced" them to take a position they did not even hold.

[15] Gray, *supra* note 4, at 23.

[16] *Id.; see alsoi,* Caton Campbell, *supra* note 1, at 12-23.

[17] Gray, *supra* note 4, at 29-30.

[18] WILLIAM L. URY, ET AL., GETTING DISPUTES RESOLVED: DESIGNING SYSTEMS TO CUT THE COSTS OF CONFLICT 3-19 (1988).

[19] DOCHERTY, *supra* note 4, at 25-26.

[20] DOCHERTY, *supra* note 5, at 7-15.

[21] *See* CATHERINE WESSINGER, MILLENNIALISM, PERSECUTION, AND VIOLENCE: HISTORICAL CASES 3-39 (2000), for a discussion of internal and external factors that promote or mitigate violence in encounters between minority religious groups and secular authorities, *also see* James T. Richardson, *Minority Religions and the Context of Violence: A Conflict/Interactionist Perspective* 13 TERRORISM & POLITICAL VIOLENCE 103 (2001). In some cases the religious groups turn violence outward against authorities, but in many cases they turn violence inward against themselves. In the case described herein, the tribe's espoused willingness to destroy their own sacred site rather than see it moved or partially damaged should be explored carefully since it might be a form of symbolic violence turned inward on the community out of despair.

[22] DOCHERTY, *supra* note 5, at 7.

[23] *Id.* at 14-15. In the case under discussion, a powerful external actor—the New Mexico state legislature—had a direct and unfortunate (for the tribes) effect on the outcome of the highway conflict, exercising its legislative power to appropriate funds for the construction of the highway.

[24] DOCHERTY, *supra* note 4, at 63.

[25] Gray, *supra* note 4, at 24.

[26] There is some evidence that a secular/sacred divide between the parties may make it more difficult to get parties to recognize each other's positive characteristics. Insofar as the "religious" party's identity frame is tied to a worldmaking story about sacred space and "secular" parties treat that sacred space as instrumental, malleable, and subject to bargaining, the secular parties attack the identity of the religious party simply by stating their own preferred outcome. Insofar as the secular party shows a willingness to desecrate sacred space, they affirm the religious party's assumption that they are apostates, unbelievers, and possibly beyond redemption. *See* DOCHERTY, *supra* note 4, at 189-224.

[27] Gray, *supra* note 4, at 31.

[28] DOCHERTY, *supra* note 4, at 176-77.

[29] LEWICKI ET AL., *supra* note 3, at 38-40; *see also*, PEARCE & LITTLEJOHN, *supra* note 12; DOCHERTY, *supra* note 4.

[30] *See* Jayne Seminare Docherty, *Culture and Negotiation: Symmetrical Anthropology for Negotiators*, 87 MARQUETTE LAW REVIEW 711 (2004) (describing skills that let us hear the linguistic indicators of frames and changes in frames during a negotiation).

[31] *See e.g.*, John Forester, *Dealing with Deep Value Differences, in* THE CONSENSUS BUILDING HANDBOOK: A COMPREHENSIVE GUIDE TO REACHING AGREEMENT 463 (Lawrence Susskind, et al., eds. 1999) (discussing the Colorado State Health Department's process of priority setting regarding federal funding for HIV and AIDS treatment); *see also*, DUKES, *supra* note 6; Linda L. Putnam & Julia M. Wondolleck, *Intractability: Definitions, Dimensions, and Distinctions, in* MAKING SENSE, *supra* note 4; Jennifer Gerarda Brown, Marcia Caton Campbell, Jayne Seminare Docherty, & Nancy Welsh, *Negotiation as One Among Many Tools*, 87 MARQUETTE LAW REVIEW 853 (2004).

[32] DOCHERTY, *supra* note 4, at 154-88.

[33] DOCHERTY, *supra* note 5, at 49-56.

[34] DOCHERTY, *supra* note 4, at 170, 175-76.

[35] Burgess & Burgess, *supra* note 6.

[36] Elliott, et al., *supra* note 6, at 419.

[37] Caton Campbell, *supra* note 1, at 12-23; DOCHERTY, *supra* note 5.

[38] DOCHERTY, *supra* note 4, at 280-82.

[39] *Id.* at 290-99; *see also*, Karen Umemoto, *Walking in Another's Shoes: Epistemological Challenges in Participatory Planning*, 21 JOURNAL OF PLANNING, EDUCATION AND RESEARCH 17 (2001) (on the importance of cultural translators to facilitation in cross-cultural contexts).

◌ 6 ◌

When the Play's in the Wrong Theater

Gale Miller & Robert Dingwall

Editors' Note: *Before metaphor, underneath framing, lies the structure in which you find yourself negotiating. Because the structural elements are often buried, they can go unremarked. But many times, there is a choice of structure, or dispute domain, within which you may be able to place your negotiation. The authors use one particular type of negotiation to explain how this works and how you might foresee a need to switch to another process.*

As sociologists have recognized for more than a century, conflict is a fundamental form of social relationship. Writing before World War I, the great German sociologist, Georg Simmel showed that conflict linked at least two parties together through their mutual opposition.[1] This often led into quite stable and predictable patterns of interaction that are shaped by the parties' orientations both towards each other and towards their preferred and acceptable resolutions. As social relationships, however, conflicts are embedded in social contexts, what Miller and Holstein have called *dispute domains*, whose organization constrains the possibilities for the conduct of disputes and for the negotiation of their resolution.[2] Many negotiators tend to emphasize the need to understand and work with the positions of the parties: this chapter will focus on the additional need to understand the features of the domains within which the conflict is being conducted, and the ways in which these may narrow or enlarge the possibilities for resolution beyond those offered by a strict focus on the parties themselves.

Simmel notes the complex ways in which conflict relationships combine both negative (divisive) and positive (solutions) elements.[3] This reminds us that conflict resolution involves much more than eliminating issues of disagreement. It is a process in which past assumptions and interaction patterns are replaced by new ones. Conflict negotiation and resolution interactions necessarily orient to the divisions between conflicting parties and their preferred resolutions, although different approaches may involve differing emphases on divisions or resolutions. However, these interactions do not take place in isolation. Negotiations are also influenced by the degree to which there is an environmental requirement to orient to institutional resolutions (such as legal and organizational responses) versus facilitating resolutions constructed by the parties in the conflict. The environment may also promote the engagement of other parties, whether third party interveners or agents such as lawyers. This difference is significant because, as Simmel notes, the possibility of conspiracy always arises when three participants are in-volved so that two may, consciously or unconsciously, align against the third.[4] The impact of these environmental variations is captured by the notion of a dispute domain, whose social organization may facilitate some strategies, roles and actors and militate against others.

Dispute Domains

Miller and Holstein use the term *dispute domain* to identify the ways in which con-flicts are differently organized within diverse conflict negotiation and resolution settings.[5] Dispute domains consist of the dominant orientations to the conflict issues at hand in different settings, the conflict resolution options that partici-pants see as available in the settings, and the typical ways that participants interact with each other. Dispute domains range from angry—and seemingly un-organized—exchanges between neighbors, spouses, workers or strangers on the street to highly structured and institutionalized interactions, such as the question-answer sequences that organize legal proceedings. They differ in the parties in-volved in conflict negotiations and their roles, and in the parties' orientations to the moral issues at stake and the relevance of legal standards in assigning culpa-bility to disputants and determining appropriate redress.

Mediation and similar contexts for conflict negotiation and resolution exist as dispute domains between the domains of everyday personal conflicts and the in-stitutionalized domains of law and courts. While conflicts often evolve and change as they are moved from one dispute domain to another (such as backyard argu-ments that are taken to mediation and then to small claims court), each dispute domain may be analyzed as a distinctive site for negotiation that is organized to make some outcomes more likely than others. Dispute domains are not neutral locales in which any and all issues are treated as relevant, where anyone can say whatever they want or where all potential conflict resolutions are treated equally.

Consider, for example, the social organization of conflict in a work-to-welfare program known as WIN.[6] WIN's objective was to implement rules requiring desig-nated welfare recipients to look for jobs with the assistance of program staff. The staff assumed that many clients would try to avoid the program's job seeking re-quirements. Thus, they watched for signs of uncooperativeness and responded quickly to clients assessed as actually or potentially resistant, by insisting on their obligations to WIN. We see the staff's sensitivity to the potential for client resis-tance and conflict in the following staff member response to a new client who asked, "What will I have to do here?" The staff member began by describing the purposes of WIN and then he turned to the staff's obligation to make certain that clients met their WIN obligations. He concluded, "I'll be on your ass is what I'll be. I'll be on your ass to get a job ... that's my job to be on your ass all the time to find a job."[7]

We see the three elements of a dispute domain in this exchange and its con-text. First, while the meaning of the client's question might be interpreted in several different ways, the staff member treats it as a potential sign of uncoopera-tiveness, not only by reviewing the WIN mandate and the client's obligations in the program, but by casting his role as being "on your ass to get a job." For the staff member, this is the central issue at stake in the interaction. His choice of lan-guage might also be seen as defining staff-client relations as conflicts of interest and as creating a potential self-fulfilling prophecy. That is, because staff members expect clients to be uncooperative, they are more likely to see and define clients' behavior as oppositional. Second, the staff member's response points to the institutionally preferred resolution to staff-client conflict in WIN; that is, clients must cooperate by acquiescing to the staff's directives.

Finally, the exchange emerged in the context of a typical staff-client interaction concerned with registering new clients in WIN. The interactions included staff members reviewing the forms previously completed by new clients, explaining WIN expectations and procedures, informing clients of their initial WIN assignments, and answering clients' questions about the program. Staff members oriented to similar concerns in their subsequent meetings with clients. In these regularly scheduled meetings, clients reported on their efforts to fulfill their WIN assignments (usually looking for jobs).

The above statement was a typical WIN staff member response to clients assessed as potentially uncooperative. When statements like this failed to obtain the desired results, staff members turned to more formal dispute domains available within WIN. Their first response was to call "pattern of behavior" meetings by sending written notices to clients' homes. The notices required clients to appear at the WIN office at designated times to discuss their participation in the program. Pattern of behavior meetings began with staff members voicing specific complaints about clients' failure to meet their WIN obligations. Staff members also insisted that the clients agree to cooperate in the future and noted that they might eventually be terminated from WIN (thus, losing some or all of their welfare benefits) if their uncooperative behavior continued.

The pattern of behavior dispute domain differed from routine staff-client interactions in several ways. Pattern of behavior meetings focused only on staff members' complaints about clients' behavior, not the wider range of issues considered in other interactions. Pattern of behavior meetings could be called to discuss any client transgression of WIN procedures and assignments, but the vast majority dealt with clients' failure to keep their regularly scheduled meetings with WIN staff and to keep written records of where and when they had sought jobs. The meetings also transformed the previously defined generalized conflict of interest between staff and clients into conflicts between specific staff members and specific clients. While the preferred conflict resolution response in pattern of behavior meetings continued to be client acquiescence, staff also raised the possibility that clients might be terminated from the program if they continued to act in uncooperative ways. The interactional organization and tone of pattern of behavior meetings were also distinctive because staff made accusations against clients and demanded that clients account for their behavior.

Clients' opportunities to speak in pattern of behavior meetings were limited to addressing staff concerns. Clients who stated that they did not understand, or asked for clarification of WIN rules and expectations, were told that this information had previously been provided to them and that it was their responsibility to remember it. Staff members then re-provided the requested information. Clients usually responded by explaining, apologizing, and promising to cooperate in the future. Staff members treated these statements as sufficient for the resolution of the immediate conflict and often told clients that they would forgive some or all of the rule violations. Forgiveness was, however, contingent on clients fulfilling their WIN obligations in the future. If clients failed to do this, staff members referred them for "conciliation meetings."

WIN conciliation further formalized the conflict and escalated the severity of the charges against clients. Conciliation meetings were conducted by conciliation officers (also members of the local WIN office staff) and, in addition to the complaining staff members and accused clients, included representatives from local welfare offices. Conciliation officers and complaining staff members usually met prior to the conciliation meetings to review the cases against the clients, discuss the most effective strategies for documenting the staff members' charges, and develop agreements about preferred resolutions. As Simmel observed, conflict negotiations involving three or more parties can develop into conspiracies, in this case with the conciliation officers and staff members using the pre-conciliation meetings to define their shared interests in cases in opposition to clients' interests.[8]

Staff members sometimes informed welfare officials of the agreements and sought their support immediately prior to conciliation meetings with clients. The inclusion of welfare officials could expand the scope of complaints against clients (both WIN and the welfare department had grievances against them) and the opportunity for conspiracy. It also signaled the possibility that clients might be removed from WIN and have their welfare benefits cut or eliminated completely. Clients removed from WIN could be readmitted to the program only after a designated time period (usually 30 days).

Thus, the issues at stake in the conciliation meetings were different from those in routine staff-client interactions and pattern of behavior meetings, which included discussions of what *might happen* if clients continued to violate WIN rules. Conciliation meetings were about what *will happen* if such behavior continues. There was now little room for forgiving clients' past actions, since the preferred resolution was that clients would promise to cooperate in the future while clearly understanding that even a single future violation would result in their immediate termination from WIN. When clients refused to promise to cooperate, they were terminated from WIN.

The interaction patterns of conciliation meetings also differed from other WIN dispute domains. The meetings began with formal accusations against clients by conciliation officers, who then asked complaining WIN staff members to present the cases. They did so by reading entries in WIN files reporting on the times when clients had failed to fulfill their WIN assignments or were openly hostile to the staff. Clients often responded by offering explanations that were usually accepted in prior dispute domains, such as "I forgot about my WIN appointments," "I did not realize that I was supposed to keep track of my job contacts," and "I am experiencing family or personal problems that keep me from fulfilling my WIN assignments." In conciliation meetings, though, these statements were treated, by both WIN and welfare officials, as excuses, attempts by clients to avoid responsibility for their actions. The officials' responses emphasized that the clients had no alternative but to cooperate with WIN staff if they wished to remain in the program.

In sum, what began as a social relationship based on a generalized conflict of interest between staff and clients in routine staff-client meetings was transformed as it moved through a series of dispute domains into a formalized conflict relationship pitting clients against WIN and the welfare department in conciliation meetings. This transformation had implications both for what staff members and clients could talk about and in the opportunities available to them to speak. The changes were particularly constraining for clients who found that they were allowed fewer opportunities to speak in pattern of behavior and conciliation meetings than in routine staff-client interactions. Clients also discovered that staff members were less likely to listen to their concerns or to accept their explanations for failing to meet WIN requirements as the conflict negotiations moved across the dispute domains. The constraints were most severe in conciliation meetings where virtually all client attempts to explain their circumstances were dismissed as excuses by staff members.

Who and What Are Marginalized in Dispute Domains?

Observing interaction patterns in diverse dispute domains is helpful in identifying what might be called the *unintended conspiracies* in conflict negotiations, conspiracies that cannot be seen by looking only at their outcomes. Consider, for example, Greatbatch and Dingwall's analysis of "The Marginalization of Domestic Violence in Divorce Mediation,"[9] which deals with social interactions in a dispute domain that is intended to give equal treatment to all parties in conflict. Greatbatch and Dingwall show, however, that potential accusations of domestic abuse (which are most likely to be voiced by the female partner) are likely to be marginalized in the dispute domain of divorce mediation. We use the term "potential accusations" because the speakers' claims were never treated as full-fledged charges or accusations in this domain.[10]

The marginalization process involves both the ways in which the potential accusers voice their concerns and in which others respond to them. Specifically, Greatbatch and Dingwall point out that the issue of domestic violence was raised as one of several topics in extended disagreements.[11] It was introduced after other grievances had been voiced, and the speakers sometimes downplayed its significance by, for example, prefacing its entry into the mediation by saying, "another point." Another speaker raised the issue by noting her concerns for her safety, but then qualified the statement by adding "really" at the end. Such interactional moves are significant because they allow others in the conflict negotiations wide latitude in interpreting and responding to the issue. It is perhaps not surprising that opposed parties in the interactions directly and forcefully denied the potential accusations. But the mediators also responded in marginalizing ways, by stressing the importance within this domain of focusing on the present and future (not the past) and by changing the direction of the interaction.

Greatbatch and Dingwall are not blaming the victims of domestic abuse for their marginalization.[12] Nor are they saying that mediators are intentionally biased against victims of domestic abuse, although the social organization of this dispute domain might be said to be biased against them. Greatbatch and Dingwall address the "bias"[13] of the dispute domain in making several concrete suggestions for how conflicting parties can be better prepared for voicing their concerns in mediation, such as by informing them "of the importance of raising allegations early and assertively if they are to be treated as a serious part of the agenda." Greatbatch and Dingwall also suggest that mediators be informed about research showing that people often raise "delicate" issues with professionals in indirect and provisional ways. There is a sense in which the initial statements are "tests" of mediators. Speakers use mediators' responses to assess how seriously more comprehensive and assertive claims will be received.

These are issues that conflict negotiators should consider in reflecting on their own practices, and should take into account in deciding whether to refer clients to mediation. They should also consider how cultural differences may enter into dispute domains and shape conflict negotiations. For example, Welsh and Lewis note that while Cambodian-Americans are positively oriented to mediation, they often orient to the mediations differently than other Americans.[14] Specifically, the Cambodian-Americans in this study preferred mediators of higher social standing than the disputants and mediators who evaluated the claims of disputants (rather than facilitating negotiations). Welsh and Lewis conclude their study by recommending some ways in which typical mediation practices might be modified, in effect to create a form of dispute domain better able to address the distinctive concerns and preferences of Cambodian-Americans. [Abramson, *Cross-cultural Mediation*]

What Resolutions Are Available in What Dispute Domains?

Just as different dispute domains are organized to take some conflict issues more seriously than others, so they orient to conflict resolution differently. We see this in WIN where the types of possible conflict resolutions available to staff and clients changed as the conflicts moved across the dispute domains. Staff members' initial willingness to treat clients' questions and failure to fulfill their WIN assignments as matters of client misunderstanding was replaced in pattern of behavior and, especially, in conciliation meetings with an emphasis on holding clients accountable for their transgressions. Miller and Holstein analyze conflict resolution in WIN as a narrowing process, because staff members' and clients' conflict resolution options were reduced as the conflicts were considered in pattern of behavior and conciliation meetings.[15]

The social organization of conflict resolution in WIN draws attention to the practical impact of referring conflicts from one dispute domain to another. The referrals may have profound implications for the options and resources available to conflicting parties and negotiators. A fundamental question that negotiators should ask in making referrals involves whether they wish to narrow or widen the context for resolution. In WIN, for example, the only option available to clients terminated from the program was to request WIN hearings. This action added yet another party to the conflict relationship (a hearings officer associated with state government) and raised a new issue for conflict resolution (whether staff members' termination of clients from WIN was legally justifiable). It further narrowed the resources available to staff and clients in "telling their stories" and pressing their interests in WIN hearings. Issues unrelated to the legal appropriateness of the terminations were dismissed and ignored by the hearings officers.

The interactional format of WIN hearings also required staff and clients to present their arguments within question-answer sequences comparable to those in legal proceedings and through the submission of documentary evidence. At the end of the presentations, hearings officers often raised the possibility of staff and clients resolving their differences outside the hearings process. This option was overwhelmingly refused by one or both of the conflicting parties, obliging the hearings officers to render binding decisions about the legal justifiability of staff members' actions. These decisions created a win-lose resolution because the hearings officers could only find that the staff members acted properly or improperly.

It is useful to consider how these conflicts might have evolved had clients had other options for appeal available to them, or had staff and clients responded to the hearings officers' invitations to take up their differences in another dispute domain. One such dispute domain is mediation, a social setting designed to consider a variety of conflict resolution options that are not available in legal settings. For example, what if the conflict negotiation had been referred to mediators using negotiating techniques adapted from solution-focused therapy?[16] Solution-focused mediators seek to widen conflict resolution possibilities by asking conflicting parties to discuss the most recent times when they have successfully resolved other disagreements. The mediators build on the parties' answers by asking them to describe in detail the personal strengths and resources that they drew upon in managing these potentially intractable situations. The parties' answers provide the mediators and conflicting parties with beginning points for talking about how the strengths, resources and lessons learned from past successful negotiations might be used to resolve the conflicts at hand.

Solution-focused mediators also ask conflicting parties to imagine and describe how their lives will be different (improved) after the conflicts at hand have been resolved. Solution-focused mediators use conflicting parties' answers to invite them to discuss what steps they might take—starting today—to begin moving toward their desired future lives. The mediators also ask their clients to describe what they consider to be observable signs of positive change and to suggest that they begin to look for the signs in their daily lives. Thus, in asking conflicting parties to reflect on their past, present and future lives, solution-focused mediators assist conflicting parties in widening available resolutions by identifying and negotiating conflict resolutions that they have overlooked in the past.

What Hasn't Been Addressed in Previous Dispute Domains?

So far, we have focused on how conflict issues and resolutions are affected when the conflicts move from one dispute domain to another. This question reminds us to also notice how negotiation and resolution within a dispute domain may be affected by prior negotiations in other dispute domains. Specifically, the question asks negotiators to consider how issues that are unresolved in prior dispute domains may re-emerge in later dispute domains. Again, it is useful to look at conflict negotiation and resolution in WIN, particularly at how client concerns raised in prior dispute domains were sometimes introduced in WIN conciliation meetings and hearings. The lingering issue most frequently raised by WIN clients involved their relationships with staff members. Clients complained that staff members were overly concerned that clients fulfill their WIN obligations and paid too little attention to clients' needs and desires. Staff members often responded to such complaints in routine staff-client interactions and pattern of behavior meetings by explaining that their seeming inattentiveness to clients' concerns was not personal. Rather, it was an important part of their jobs.

The contexts for interpreting and responding to clients' complaints were quite different in conciliation meetings and WIN hearings, however. In conciliation meetings, staff members responded by casting clients' complaints as excuses and as evidence of their refusal to take their WIN obligations seriously. Rather than addressing clients' concerns and complaints, staff members left them to linger on, perhaps to re-emerge in the narrowed context of WIN hearings. Hearings officers responded to clients' complaints by asking them to show how the complaints were relevant to whether staff members had acted appropriately in terminating them from WIN. Virtually no clients had prepared an answer to this question. Thus, clients' dissatisfactions were left unaddressed until they re-enrolled in WIN and the cycle began anew.

Dismissing conflicting parties' lingering concerns is not always as easy as in WIN, however. For example, sociologist Joseph Hopper's interviews with divorced couples and the attorneys who represented them suggest that attorneys sometimes create future impediments to conflict resolution by insisting that clients conform to the attorneys' preferred orientation.[17] Hopper reports that the women and men in his study constructed their divorces within a moral dispute domain concerned with assessing the divorcing parties' moral culpability for the failure of their marriages. Their attorneys, on the other hand, organized the negotiations within a "no fault" dispute domain focused on helping their clients "get on with their lives" by negotiating agreements that would make going to trial unnecessary. The attorneys emphasized that they were seeking to protect their clients from the financial and emotional costs of adversarial proceedings.

Nonetheless, the issue of finding fault remained a lingering issue in many divorces. Several attorneys in Hopper's study noted that the issue of fault often re-emerged in the form of disagreements about child custody, a dispute domain that allows for the assessment of the moral character of the divorcing parties. A major difference between this dispute domain and prior ones was that the couples' children were now part of the conflict relationships (even if the children did not know it). The issue was no longer about who is to blame for the divorce but, "Is one of the parties unfit to have custody of the children and perhaps to see them in unsupervised situations?" The attorneys also stated that if the issue of fault could somehow be addressed earlier in the divorce process, then divorcing parents would be less likely to draw their children into their conflicts with each other. This might involve divorce attorneys modifying how they orient to divorce processes or, perhaps, including other conflict negotiators in the process, such as professionals trained to address the moral and emotional implications of divorce.

Conclusion

In this essay, we have used the concept of dispute domain to examine the interactional underpinnings of conflict negotiations. The concept reminds us of how conflict negotiations are influenced by contextual and interaction factors that are often unnoticed by negotiating parties. The factors include taken-for-granted rules and expectations about the purposes of different kinds of conflict negotiations, participants' roles within the negotiations, and how speaker turns are arranged within conflict negotiations. The factors also influence what issues will be taken seriously and what issues will be marginalized in the negotiations, as well as what counts as acceptable resolutions to the conflicts at hand.

Following Simmel's lead, we have analyzed different conflict negotiating strategies and settings as offering distinctive opportunities for conflict resolution and as sources of constraint on both conflicting parties and negotiators. We have also stressed how conflict relationships and opportunities for resolution evolve and change (sometimes to the benefit of some disputing parties over others) as they move from one dispute domain to another. Finally, our analysis points to some of the ways in which conflict negotiators might serve their clients by assessing which available dispute domains best address their clients' distinctive circumstances, needs and desires.

Endnotes

[1] GEORG SIMMEL, CONFLICT (1955).
[2] GALE MILLER & JAMES A. HOLSTEIN, DISPUTE DOMAINS AND WELFARE CLAIMS: CONFLICT AND LAW IN PUBLIC BUREAUCRACIES (1996).
[3] SIMMEL, *supra* note 1.
[4] GEORG SIMMEL, THE SOCIOLOGY OF GEORG SIMMEL (1950).
[5] MILLER & HOLSTEIN, *supra* note 2.
[6] GALE MILLER, ENFORCING THE WORK ETHIC: RHETORIC AND EVERYDAY LIFE IN A WORK INCENTIVE PROGRAM (1991).
[7] *Id.* at 106.
[8] SIMMEL, *supra* note 4.
[9] David Greatbatch & Robert Dingwall, *The Marginalization of Domestic Violence in Divorce Mediation*, 13 INTERNATIONAL JOURNAL OF LAW, POLICY & THE FAMILY 147 (1999).
[10] *Id.*
[11] *Id.*
[12] *Id.*
[13] *Id.* at 187.
[14] Nancy A. Welsh & Debra Lewis, *Adaptations to the Civil Mediation Model: Suggestions from Research into the Twin Cities Cambodian Community*, 15 MEDIATION QUARTERLY 345 (1998).
[15] MILLER & HOLSTEIN, *supra* note 2.
[16] Robert Dingwall & Gale Miller, *Lessons from Brief Therapy? Some Interactional Suggestions for Family Mediators*, 19 CONFLICT RESOLUTION QUARTERLY 269 (2002).
[17] Joseph Hopper, *Contested Selves in Divorce Proceedings*, in INSTITUTIONAL SELVES: TROUBLED IDENTITIES IN A POSTMODERN WORLD 127-41 (2001).

❧ 7 ❧

A Three-Dimensional Analysis of Negotiation

Robert Ricigliano

Editors' Note: Docherty's introductory chapter on Models shows why people faced with intractable conflict can often feel completely at sea. Here, Ricigliano uses experience of years of field work, on conflicts from Georgia to Baghdad to Congo, to frame a three-part structure—transaction, context and time—for understanding intractable conflict.

Theoretical physics and developing a negotiation canon have more in common than you might think. One current debate in physics, put simply, is whether the universe is more like a series of strings or more like an Oreo cookie.[1] Without getting into the specifics of this debate, what is clear is that images—strings and Oreo cookies—have led to powerful insights into how our universe works. In his chapter, Kevin Avruch [Avruch, *Buyer—Seller*] poses a powerful question about whether we will be able to develop a canon of negotiation if we are not able to move past the buyer-seller heuristic—the image of two parties bargaining over some problem of mutual concern. The thesis of this response chapter is that a canon of negotiation has to take a three-dimensional view of negotiation; one that encompasses the *transaction* (whether between a buyer-seller, president and rebel leader, or victim-offender), the *context* within which that transaction takes place, and how that transaction and the context evolve together over *time*.

The "existing common core" of negotiation as defined by Andrea Kupfer Schneider and Chris Honeyman contains key six parts, which comprise the basic building blocks of negotiation theory.[2] This developing canon is an attempt to describe and codify knowledge about the transactional component of negotiation—knowledge about how the individual negotiators interact with each other to achieve a desired outcome. But, as Avruch writes, this canon, based on the transactional, buyer-seller heuristic, does not satisfactorily explain the dynamics of identity and value-based conflicts. Similarly, the chapters by Charles Hauss, [Hauss, *Captive Audience*] on the work of Search for Common Ground, John McDonald, [McDonald, *Kashmir*] on the Institute for Multi-Track Diplomacy's work in Kashmir, and Peter Coleman, et al., [Coleman, et al., *Dynamical*] on Dynamical Systems, describe initiatives and methodologies that address protracted, identity/values based conflicts and that go well beyond the transactional level of negotiation.

Does this mean, as Avruch laments, that the negotiation canon, as currently articulated, is of limited usefulness? It is not that the canon is of limited usefulness, rather that it is less descriptive of the richness of negotiation, in the way that a one-dimensional photo of the Grand Canyon is less impressive than the breathtaking, three-dimensional scenic vista one takes in when standing on the rim of the Grand Canyon. A negotiation canon that can help explain the management of complex conflicts, such as those described in the Hauss, McDonald, and Coleman chapters, has to put the transactional dimension of negotiation in relationship with the context and time dimensions in order to produce a robust model of how negotiation dynamics play out in conflicts beyond the basic buyer-seller model.

Considering Context and Time

As Avruch and others note, the transitional, rational actor paradigm of negotiation does not adequately address conflicts that have basic needs and values at their core. Avruch points out that needs and values cannot be thought of as just deeper levels of interests, nor can issues like identity be traded off in same way as dollars or health benefits. Avruch concludes that this inability of the buyer-seller model to account for needs and values means that the "old" canon of negotiation, based on this model, is critically limited. However, the problem is not that the existing negotiation canon is invalid, but that needs and values cannot, for the most part, be satisfied at the transactional level alone. Rather, value and need-based conflicts are often addressed through the interplay over *time* of progress at the *transactional* level (e.g. specific negotiated outcomes) with changes that occur at the *contextual* level. Before looking further at the interplay of these three dimensions, it will be helpful to elaborate on the context and time dimensions.

Conflicts that involve issues of identity, fundamental values, and/or basic human needs require consideration of two critical contextual elements: structures and social relations between groups in society. Structures refer to the systems and institutions in society that are designed to meet people's basic human needs for identity, security, vitality, and community. These systems and institutions include governance, security, rule of law/human rights, social services (education, healthcare), environment/natural resources, and media and civil society. Social relations refers to the state of relations between groups in the society, be they based on ethnicity, race, religion, class, clan, etc. It refers to the levels of trust between groups, the level of inter-group tensions, inter-group perceptions, and the various dynamic interactions between groups (e.g. victim-oppressor, relative deprivation, etc.). Often, the deeper roots of protracted conflicts are in the contextual dimension. For example, breakdowns in structures (e.g. as in failed states such as Somalia) mean that people's basic human needs are systematically not being met. Likewise, breakdowns in social relations between groups often reflect a society that at least one group feels does not represent important values, such as perceived injustice, relative economic deprivation, and intolerance inflicted on one social group at the hands of another (e.g. as in pre-genocide Rwanda).

Often in the buyer-seller model, you don't have fundamental disagreements over structural or social issues. Buyers and sellers have differences over price, timing, financing, and other such issues. But, in the typical buyer-seller scenario, there are not major disputes over the underlying structural elements, such as the system of property rights, the legality of banks charging interest on loans, or the legitimacy of housing codes. In addition, most transactions are not viewed as extensions of conflict between the social group affiliations of the participants. And, when a buyer-seller transaction fails due to social (inter-group) issues, such as in cases of racially discriminatory housing practices, there are systems (courts) for handling this conflict. Thus, it is not surprising that in most buyer-seller transactions, contextual factors such as structural and social issues are mostly overlooked.

The dimension of time does not need elaboration (or if it does, then you need to turn back to the quantum physicists and their theories of strings versus Oreos). Time comes in because structures and inter-group social relationships do not change quickly. While a long transactional process can take a few years (and most take considerably less time), building structures in a society can take a generation, and social changes can take even longer. Thus, if values and needs are best addressed at the contextual level, then you have to consider the dimension of time.

Time, Context and Transaction as a Dynamic System

Transactions (negotiated agreements) affect the underlying context and are affected by it. When you look at this relationship over time, you get what Coleman et al. describe as a "Dynamical System." If the system, over time, heads toward a more peaceful state, we see what Hauss describes as conflict transformation. If the system heads toward a more violent state we see conflict escalation. The key is that for values and needs to be addressed, there needs to be a process of transactions spurring contextual change over time, and contextual change providing the impetus for more (and more successful) transactions. In systems terms, this produces a "virtuous cycle." On the other hand, deteriorating social relationships or structures might make it more difficult to negotiate transactions, and lead to a downward spiral.

For example, take the conflict in the Democratic Republic of Congo (DRC), which saw two wars and over 3.5 million deaths between 1996 and 2003. The second Congolese war (1998-2003) featured three main Congolese combatant groups and saw seven foreign armies fighting in the DRC. The three main Congolese combatant groups were the DRC Government in Kinshasa (which was formerly the Rwandan-backed rebel group that overthrew the government of Mobutu Sese Seko in 1997), the Movement for the Liberation of the Congo (MLC) backed by Uganda, and the Congolese Rally for Democracy (RCD) backed by Rwanda.

The conflict is incredibly complex but the three dimensional model of time, context & transactions can help explain, in a very general way, what happened in the Congolese peace process. The inability of the combatants to negotiate effectively was one of the factors that contributed to outbreaks of armed conflict. But the real roots of the conflict are in severe structural failures in the DRC; the crumbling of the country's infrastructure, a failed health system and rampant (often preventable) disease, severe lack of physical security in many areas, breakdowns of law and governance structures, etc. Further, there are social tensions among the many tribes and ethnic groups in the DRC, especially between the Tutsi and non-Tutsi populations in eastern DRC (which were exacerbated by the genocides in Congo's neighbors to the east—Rwanda and Burundi—involving Hutus and Tutsis).

The conflict in the DRC contained both issues of conflicting interests (e.g. who would be the head of a transitional government? How would a national army be created? etc.), basic human needs (security, identity, etc.), and values (justice, equality, opportunity). While the three dimensional model does not explain why the process happened as it did, the DRC peace process does demonstrate the three dimensional model in action. The peace process cannot be understood by only looking at the transactions, or negotiations that took place. However, negotiated outcomes did provide an environment for structural and social change, and vice versa. The formal transactional process sputtered from 1999 until 2002 until a series of agreements resulted in the withdrawal of the Ugandan and Rwandan armies from Congo. These agreements, and their implementation, helped improve the security situation (structural change) which in turn helped create the conditions for a comprehensive peace agreement between the internal combatants. This, in turn, led to the further improvement of the security situation (in many parts of the country), paved the way for resumption of international aid for reconstruction (economic, natural resource and social service systems), and began the process of preparing for local and national elections (governance system). Also, the presence of a prominent Tutsi rebel leader as a vice-president in the transitional government was an important symbol that had an impact on relations between Tutsis and non-Tutsis. Further, against the backdrop of slow contextual change, the power-sharing government produced more transactions that in turn affected (again) the basic context. Unfortunately, the lack of an effective government has also led to a backsliding toward violence in parts of the country.

The situation in Congo remains precarious, two years into the transitional government, and life on the ground has not improved greatly since the official end of the war. But it does illustrate the interaction of three dimensions of time, transaction, and context. The 'People's Bus" example provided by Ambassador McDonald and the description of the events in Poland in the late 1980s provided by Coleman et al. can also be put in terms of the three dimensional model. In the Kashmir example, Ambassador McDonald describes a series of transactions that led to a structural change (a transportation link between the two Kashmirs). The people-to-people exchange also began affecting social attitudes about the conflict and may, based on initial accounts, help lay the foundation for a reduction in tensions and further progress in the official negotiations between India and Pakistan over Kashmir. In their chapter, Coleman et al. attribute the break in the deadlock that existed between pro and anti-government forces in Poland to the creation of a transactional process (the Round Table negotiations), that provided "solutions" to several structural problems, such as "education, industry, health, economic issues, and so forth." These structural changes in the Polish context led to changes in social relations as the Round Table negotiations and outcomes led people to think in new ways about each other and the conflict.

Resolving the Values-Needs-Interests Debate

The three dimensional model of negotiation also helps resolve the question of whether values and needs are merely more fundamental extensions of interests, or not. It is important to note that interests are often described as being satisfied and temporally bounded (e.g. a union's interest in better health benefits is met by a new insurance plan). Needs are less often seen in such a time bounded way (e.g. my need for security does not go away if I am secure today). Values are even less often viewed in this way (e.g. satisfying one's sense of justice in one case does not mean that justice is no longer an important concern). In this sense, addressing needs and values requires a dynamic process over time. Put another way, a negotiated agreement is seen as resolving a set of interests, while needs and values are not addressed (or not only addressed) by static solutions but by the process of working together to address basic needs and realize core values.

For example, take Avruch's "two-religions heuristic" which represents a conflict of fundamental values about what religion a child should be raised in when the child's parents come from two different religions. Addressing the underlying values in this situation is not about the outcome in terms of what religion the child is raised in, but is more about whether the parents deal with this issue (e.g. their "transactions") over time in a way that is consistent with their values (e.g. the interaction is loving, respectful, fair, etc.). Also, the three dimensional model also implies that interests, values, and needs are each independent and significant in their own right. They are neither subsets of each other, nor is it a question of priority (e.g. values being more important than needs which are more important than interests). In the DRC case, the RCD rebel movement had interests (the ministries they would control in a power sharing government, security for their representatives in the capital city, how the army was to be reformed, etc.), needs (e.g. the broader need for security for themselves and the people they purported to represent, etc.), and values (e.g. acceptance of Congolese Tutsis, etc.). All three—interests, needs and values—provide motivations for the RCD, as well as the other parties, during the peace process. But while interests can be said to be satisfied in the context of a transaction, needs and values have to be pursued over time. Furthermore, it is the resultant changes in the underlying context in which the participants interact that marks whether needs are being met and values are being realized.

Moving from Description to Prescription

Accurately describing and understanding the dynamics of complex negotiations is the first step toward developing better prescriptive theory. In this sense, a major implication of the three dimensional model of negotiation is that effective negotiation training cannot only describe the transactional dimension of negotiation. Describing the interaction of transactions and context over time may not be necessary for many basic (buyer-seller) type negotiations, but no picture of negotiation, or of the role and importance of negotiation skills, is complete without painting the three dimensional model of negotiation.

Without considering the dimensions of time and context, the transactional component of negotiations is often given undue importance, especially in the international conflict field. "Negotiate a peace agreement" is often the prescription to complex conflicts, and once an agreement is reached there tends to be a dropoff in international aid and attention. This distorted importance given to the negotiation process can have disastrous results. In 1993-1994 a peace deal was negotiated in Rwanda between the Hutu-controlled government and the Tutsi-led rebel army, know as the Rwandan Patriotic Front. Ironically, this agreement is seen by many as one of the prime contributing factors in the assassination of the Hutu President of Rwanda and the launching of one of the deadliest genocides in history. Philip Gourevitch, author of *We Wish To Inform You That Tomorrow We Will Be Killed With Our Families*, a seminal book on the Rwandan Genocide, explains that it was the pressure on then-Rwandan President Juvénal Habyarimana to implement the peace deal (calling for a Hutu-Tutsi power-sharing government) which led to President Habyarimana's own assassination and the subsequent genocide.[3] The small UN peacekeeping force in Rwanda that was sent there to help implement the peace agreement was overwhelmed by the pace of the genocide and the international community moved quickly to remove them from harm's way. While the genocide in Rwanda has complex and deep rooted causes, one of the precipitating factors was the failure of the international community to appreciate the impact on the Rwandan context (structurally and socially) of a peace agreement, and to either change their negotiation process or intervene effectively to assist the implementation of the agreement.[4]

The Rwandan example, and others like it, are stark reminders of the importance of considering the transactional dimension of negotiation alongside the contextual dimensions of structural and social factors. The "old" negotiation canon is a good example of how to understand and prescribe best practices at the transactional level. Indeed that at-best-partial canon, and newer works such as this book, capture the wealth of theoretical and practical work being done on negotiation and negotiation training. This knowledge needs to be blended with the volumes of work in the development and social psychological fields that go to defining best practices in the contextual fields of structural and social change. In complex conflicts, how are negotiations at the transactional level impacted by context? How do transactions impact structures and social attitudes and relationships over time in the midst of a peace process? Are there predictable patterns and best practices?

There are some works that are beginning to take up this challenge. The piece by Coleman, et al., is a great example, as they suggest a theory to explain and predict how transactions can be used to spur positive contextual change and vice versa. Their concepts of "attractors" and the need to restore multi-dimensionality to a system, provide a theory of how negotiated transactions can be used to change the contextual dynamics in a conflict situation. In addition to this, and other systems approaches, Anderson and Olsen in their book *Confronting War,* and the work of the Reflecting on Peace Practice Project, offer a model for effective peace work that moves from affecting "Key People" (through transactions) to affecting "More People" (social change) and from affecting people at the individual level to affecting the society at the socio-political level.[5] In addition, "Networks of Effective Action" is an approach that advocates for a process approach to implementing a holistic, systems strategy for peacebuilding.[6]

The development and elaboration of this "next generation" negotiation canon is a hopeful sign that as a discipline, the field of negotiation is advancing toward the development of sound foundational theory that can be used to improve training new generations of practitioners and academics in the field. It also provides a stepping stone for the field to improve understanding of how the process of negotiation can best integrate with long-term change processes, and how the context within which negotiation happens impacts on the process itself. The three-dimensional model of negotiation and the connection to systems thinking that it occasions represent perhaps the next important frontier, for the development of a *third* generation of the negotiation canon.

Endnotes

[1] *See* Dennis Overbye, *Lisa Randall; On Gravity, Oreos, and the Theory of Everything,* N.Y. TIMES, Nov. 1, 2005, at F1.
[2] The canon includes 6 topics: "(1) the idea of personal style or strategy in a negotiation (including the concepts of competitive or adversarial v. interests-based or principled or problem-solving); (2) the use of communication skills—both listening and talking in negotiation; (3) the concept of integrative v. distributive negotiations; (4) the concept of a "bargaining zone" between the parties as well as the concepts of BATNA and reservation price; (5) the use of brainstorming and option creation in negotiation; and (6) the importance of preparation to negotiation." Chris Honeyman & Andrea K. Schneider, *Keeping Up with the Major-General: the Need for a "Canon of Negotiation,"* 87 MARQUETTE LAW REVIEW 637, 643-44 (2004).
[3] *Frontline: The Triumph of Evil* (PBS television broadcast, Jan. 26, 1999), interview *available at* http://www.pbs.org/wgbh/pages/frontline/shows/evil/interviews/gourevitch.html.
> Gourevitch explains:
> What's most clear is that the circumstantial evidence points to the fact that it was actually the extremists in the president's own entourage, who had often predicted that if he didn't comply with them and complied instead with the peace deal, he would be meeting his maker. They staged a coup within half an hour. Essentially, the government now became a government of unabashed Hutu extremists.

See also, Treaty of Peace at Versailles, June 28, 1919 which has been cited as one of the contributing factors to World War II.
[4] In fact, the then head of UN Peacekeeping operations, Kofi Annan, refused a request from the peacekeepers in Rwanda to act on an informant's tip that extremists were storing arms for the purposes of exterminating Tutsis.
[5] *See* MARY ANDERSON & LARA OLSEN, CONFRONTING WAR: CRITICAL LESSONS FOR PEACE PRACTITIONERS (2002), *available at* http://www.cdainc.com/publications/rpp/confrontingwar/ConfrontingWar.pdf.
[6] *See* Robert Ricigliano, *Networks of Effective Action: Implementing an Integrated Approach Peacebuilding,* 34 SECURITY DIALOGUE 445 (2003).

Protracted Conflicts as Dynamical Systems

Peter T. Coleman, Lan Bui-Wrzosinska, Robin R. Vallacher & Andrzej Nowak

Editors' Note: Are you involved in a conflict which, no matter what anyone does, always seems to go on and on and get worse? This chapter can explain why. Moreover, if you are determined to do something about the situation, it will give you clues as to where to put your effort. Fair warning: if you're not a trained social psychologist, this is not easy material. But if you find the practicalities daunting, you might find encouragement by reading this side by side with Ambassador John McDonald's chapter on the Kashmir conflict.

Most conflict negotiations are fairly straightforward, at least from a technical point of view; they involve information processing, decision-making and influence, and occur in a normative context where roles, regulations, and relationships shape and constrain the parties' choices of strategies and tactics. But when conflicts persist and escalate, the feelings, issues, parties, and alliances associated with them can change, multiply, and intensify, often repeatedly, resulting in a continual need to reorient and renegotiate. Conflicts that reach high levels of destructiveness, volatility, and complexity can be particularly difficult to manage, and often become unresponsive to traditional methods of conflict resolution (negotiation, mediation, diplomacy, etc.). Such conflicts, often labeled intractable, take on a unique, self-sustaining character, where strong patterns of internal dynamics make them more and more resistant to outside intervention.[1] These conflicts can instill a basic sense of hopelessness among stakeholders and outside interveners alike. However, recent research on "dynamical" systems (systems that change and evolve over time) provides frame-breaking insights into the nature of such patterns, and thus can offer new tools to move them beyond intractability.

This chapter presents a brief, practical overview of a dynamical systems approach to addressing protracted conflicts. We begin by comparing this approach with a problem-solving model of conflict intervention, and then outline the implications of the dynamical systems framework for comprehending protracted conflict systems. The primary emphasis of this chapter will be an elaboration of the guidelines and methods that the dynamical perspective offers for working in a unique way with enduring social conflicts.

Conflicts as Dynamical Systems

Dynamical systems theory (DST) is an increasingly influential paradigm in many areas of science,[2] which offers an innovative set of ideas and methods for conceptualizing and addressing conflict. A dynamical system is defined as a set of interconnected elements (such as beliefs, feelings, and behaviors) that change and evolve in time. A change in each element depends on influences from other elements. Due to these mutual influences, the system as a whole evolves in time. Thus, changes in any element of a marital relationship (such as level of trust) depend on influences of various other elements (each partner's motives, attitudes, actions, etc.), which evolve over time to affect the general pattern of interactions (positive or negative) of the couple. The principles defining the evolution of dynamical systems have wide generality and have been employed to conceptualize and investigate a highly diverse set of conflict-related phenomena (emotion, stereotyping, attitude change, cooperation versus competition in social dilemmas, etc.).

Table 1: Comparison of Traditional and Dynamical Models of Conflict Intervention

Problem-solving model:	Dynamical systems model:

• Assumptions
  - Externally-determined, linear change processes
  - Static targets of action (insight, behavior change, agreement)
	• Assumptions
	  - Non-linear, internal/external dynamics
	  - Dynamic targets of change (patterns of thinking, feeling, acting)

• Orientation
  - Identify presenting conflict issues & relations
  - Focus on dyads and multiparty stakeholders
	• Orientation
	  - Identify manifest & latent attractor landscape
	  - Focus on multiple, interdependent roles

• Objective
  - Satisfy needs, resolve conflict
	• Objective
	  - Reconfigure attractor landscape

• Approach
  - Conflict analysis & intervention
	• Approach
	  - Case study (loop analysis), computer simulation, intervention & feedback

• Tools
  - Problem-solving, compensation, log-rolling, pressure, coercion
	• Tools
	  - Restore multidimensionality; isolate issues and individuals; restore balance; decouple positive feedback loops, introduce negative feedback loops; incrementally establish constructive attractors

Table 1 provides a simplified comparison of a dynamical systems approach to conflict with a more common problem-solving method.[3] The starting point for a dynamical analysis of conflict is the recognition that conflicts are inherently dynamic; they escalate and deescalate, change form, spread into new groups, and can be passed from generation to generation. This has two major implications. First, conflict dynamics are often significantly influenced by the *internal dynamics* of the various elements which constitute the conflict. Therefore, when external agents or third parties intervene in a conflict, they are not directly inducing change (as is assumed in some models), but are instead perturbing a system that has its own, often quite strong dynamics. In this context, the conflict may respond to external intervention by (1) completely resisting the intervention and maintaining the status quo; (2) showing an exaggerated response to a seemingly insignificant intervention, though in the desired direction; (3) evolving in a completely unpredictable direction independent of the intervention; or (4) responding in a manner proportional to the actions and plans undertaken by the intervener. Any of these responses are possible outcome states, depending on the initial conditions of the system at the time of intervention, the type and level of intervention, and the amount of time required for a given outcome state to result.

The second implication of a dynamical approach to conflict is that because change evolves through the complex interactions of both internal and external elements, specific outcomes are always unpredictable. That is because conflict systems can respond to specific changes (such as the signing of a peace treaty) in an almost infinite number of ways. However, every conflict system—be it a marriage or a labor-management relationship or an ethnically divided community—will evidence *general patterns* of interactions between the parties, which are more predictable and stable. From this perspective, interveners working with protracted conflicts should be less concerned with bringing about specific outcomes in a conflict (particular insights, agreements, behavior change, etc.), but rather altering the general patterns of interactions of the parties in a more constructive direction. This requires a substantial frame change of interveners—away from a focus on the most salient presenting issues of dyads and stakeholders, toward a view of the evolution of the system-as-a-whole; toward an understanding of the multiple interdependent elements affecting change; and toward a sense that there are both latent and manifest patterns unfolding in the system. We will elaborate on these ideas in the following sections.

Protracted Conflicts as Strong Attractors

We have proposed a dynamical model of protracted social conflict, which offers a unique perspective on the phenomenon of intractability for conflicts at all levels.[4] This dynamical model emphasizes the following processes underlying enduring conflicts.

Qualitative Changes

As some conflicts escalate, there occur changes in key psychological, social, and community-based factors, and changes in the way in which these factors are interlinked, resulting in dramatic, qualitative changes in the character of the conflicts.[5] In other words, as the forces promoting conflict grow (and the forces restraining conflict diminish), the intensity of the conflict increases at a gradual, incremental rate until it reaches a threshold, after which the intensity shows a catastrophic increase. For example, this type of qualitative shift was observed in the dramatic outbreak of genocidal violence that occurred in Rwanda in the 1990s (where almost one million were killed in 100 days), which followed years of more gradual increases in inter-ethnic hostilities between Tutsis and Hutus. Once conflict has reached such an extreme level of intensity, decreasing the forces that drive it will not reduce the intensity to its original level—until another threshold is reached that represents a considerably lower level of forces. Thus, in Rwanda it has taken over a decade of intervention including military actions, legislation, criminal tribunals, and local truth and reconciliation processes (the Gacaca courts) among other initiatives to begin to reduce trauma, suspiciousness and interethnic hostility to pre-conflict levels.

A Loss of Balanced Feedback

Effective conflict-regulation involves both positive and negative feedback loops. A positive feedback loop (where one element stimulates another along its current trajectory) is instrumental in bringing together the mechanisms necessary to generate and maintain an action (such as when a series of negative encounters with someone leads to an explicit expression of conflict). A negative feedback loop (where one element constrains another), on the other hand, is necessary for terminating action once a threshold is reached that suggests the action is sufficient or extreme (such as when a parent steps in to stop a fight between siblings that is about to become physical). As long as a system is characterized by negative feedback loops, control mechanisms can be used in order to mitigate or terminate conflict, allowing situations of conflict to be temporary and constructive rather than destructive. We suggest that conflict escalates to uncontrolled (and often unwanted) levels when positive feedback increases and negative feedback recedes, thus disengaging or reversing this natural self-regulatory tendency.

For instance, our internal moral sense typically acts as a source of negative feedback for us, restraining our overly aggressive impulses and reactions against our opponents in conflict. However, as other parties begin to employ more aggressive or even "immoral" tactics against us in conflict, the constraining influence of our moral guides diminishes or becomes reversed. When the actions of other parties crosses our moral boundaries (they behave in ways we consider to be morally reprehensible), then the very moral sense that had discouraged our aggression may begin to demand it, as we feel an increased sense of responsibility to right a moral wrong. Thus, a negative feedback loop becomes a source of positive feedback, thereby further escalating the conflict. In this instance, even an action by the other that is perceived by outsiders as a slight provocation may result in full retaliation.

Positive Feedback Between Levels

The escalation and maintenance of conflict can be manifest at various levels of psychological and social reality: the thoughts, feelings, and actions of specific individuals, the dynamics of interpersonal relations, and the relations, norms and institutions within and between social groups and nations. Moreover, in intractable conflicts, these levels tend to become interlinked, so that mechanisms at one level stimulate conflict at other levels. The structure of conflict is thus maintained not only by positive feedback loops among features at a given level, but also by positive feedback between levels. This means that conflict launched at one level is likely to recruit other levels as well. Conflict that began at an inter-group level, for instance, is likely to spawn and maintain the beliefs, emotions, and actions of individuals in their interpersonal relations. The reciprocal feedback loops among levels are in large part responsible for the intractable nature of certain conflicts. Even if the conflict at one level is fully understood and resolvable in principle, the links to other levels can reinstate the conflict.

A Collapse of Multidimensionality

In any healthy relationship—whether between individuals, groups, or nations—there are likely to be many distinct issues and dimensions along which the relationship can be defined (e.g. my friend is chronically late and tends to exaggerate the truth, but is generally well-intentioned, bright and kind). Such multidimensionality and complexity in relationships mitigates against malignant social relations. For instance, if my friend harms me, our common goals and bonds should buffer my experience of the harm and constrain any overly aggressive response. Under these conditions, I will typically be able to maintain a nuanced understanding of my friend (her strengths and weaknesses), the act (situational and personal attributions of responsibility), and even myself (my role and responsibility in bringing about the act). However, as conflicts escalate and persist, we often see the character of the relations between distinct psychological elements (i.e. my beliefs, attitudes, and feelings toward my friend) and distinct social elements (group memberships, bonds, goals) becoming more aligned and positively correlated so that they begin to trigger and mutually reinforce one another. This convergence is made easier by a natural tendency towards coherence in psychological and social systems.[6] This reduction of multidimensionality (in our sense of the other, the relationship, the problem, and our self) fosters a more homogenous view of the ingroup and outgroups in conflict, increased polarization, and the increase in positive feedback described above.

The Emergence of Strong Attractors

Once a conflict has crossed its destructive threshold, is governed by perceptions and relationships with low levels of dimensionality, and becomes sustained primarily by positive feedback loops within and across levels, we see the emergence of strong, stable *attractors* (patterns of thinking, feeling, and acting). These attractors pull all thoughts, feelings, actions, norms, even institutions, toward a negative, destructive state that becomes self-organizing and self-perpetuating. In other words, they begin to feed off of their own strong, internal dynamics. Such attractors may be particularly influenced by key elements (such as identities; strongly identifying with being anti-Israeli or anti-Palestinian), but because of the tightly-coupled nature of multiple elements in the system, constructive changes in any element are hard to bring about, and even if they occur, can be inconsequential to the general patterns of the conflict. This results in malignant social processes that the disputants see as irreversible and within which they feel entrapped. In this state, many of the constructive forces and connections which are inherent to any social system (networks of effective action) become taxed, obstructed, or destroyed, constraining their capacities to ameliorate the conflict. *This culminates in a pattern we define as intractable.*

When strong, negative attractors develop in a conflict system, the resolution of specific issues or the satisfaction of particular needs are unlikely to terminate or even dampen the conflict. Isolated approaches aimed at finding resolution to incompatible activities may be successful for more benign conflicts, but such approaches are likely to fail in cases of intractable conflict. A permanent solution to intractable conflict requires changing the system's dynamics and hence the attractor structure of the personal and social systems involved. The question thus becomes *how to change the dynamics of the system.* The general answer is to increase the multi-dimensionality of the situation, block the positive feedback loops that maintain the conflict at multiple levels, introduce negative feedback loops that de-escalate the conflict once it reaches a certain threshold, create the conditions for alternative, constructive attractors to emerge, and work actively to disassemble strong negative attractors. Translating these general recommendations into practice, however, is hardly a trivial matter. The remainder of this paper specifies these recommendations in more detail.

Guidelines and Methods For Intervention

In this section, we will use the case of the protracted conflict over democracy that occurred in Poland in the 1980s to illustrate some of the dynamical strategies and mechanisms that contributed to the transformation of the conflict and to the transition of the country to a democratic system.

Communism and Democracy in Poland

The events in Poland in the late 1980s provide a prototypical (and hopeful) example of how complexity and pluralism can be reinstated after a prolonged period of polarization and strong autocratic control (i.e., by the Communist party). Attempts by the Communists to stabilize the political system in Poland by suppressing dissent, often by the use of violence, resulted in a heightened state of conflict. As long as the political situation was defined in pro- versus anti-government terms, there was essentially a political deadlock in the society. The government was unable to suppress dissent and the people could not overthrow the government (in part because of its support by the former Soviet Union). This conflict between the Communist regime and the opposition in Poland remained intractable for years. The deadlock was broken by the implementation of the Round Table negotiations.

In February 1989, after a series of informal meetings, delegates from the opposition and leaders from the Communist party sat down together at "The Round Table" and began official talks. At that point, legalization of the opposition's organization, "Solidarity", and a new democratic order were negotiated. The symbolic, ceremonial opening Round Table Negotiations were followed by a variety of "sub-table" talks focusing on specific elements of the negotiated new system such as education, unions, the media, political institutions, the economy and healthcare. These negotiations initiated the first free elections in Poland since World War II, the implementation of a new democratic system and the collapse of the Communist regime. Such a peaceful revolution was made possible by the transformation of the previous system where intractability over political rule was at a stalemate, to a new system where in-depth discussions over the multitude of issues concerning the nation could be addressed. Significantly, this change did much to eliminate the conflict that had defined the political situation in Poland for almost half a century. Nevertheless, it is important to emphasize that the negotiated collapse of the Communist regime did not resolve all the conflicts that divided the society, and perhaps it even fostered the manifestation of other deep social divides. But it also enabled a transition from a protracted, violent conflict to a democratic process where social problems could be expressed and addressed constructively. Thus, it constitutes a promising example of how a seemingly intractable conflict over ideology and power was transformed to a more tractable set of public disputes.

A Change of Frame

A dynamical systems approach to addressing protracted conflicts orients us toward new aspects of a conflict system, and thus toward new priorities in conflict resolution. Thus, applying the approach to actual events requires a significant change of frame for most interveners trained in conflict resolution. Although it can be viewed as complementary with other approaches to conflict, it emphasizes unfamiliar elements and processes, and is based on an alternative set of assumptions about intervention and change (see Table 1). Systems thinking in general represents a radical shift in the worldview of social scientists from the atomistic-mechanistic, linear view of the world championed by Descartes and Newton, toward a more holistic-ecological and dynamic point-of-view.[7] Thus, an effective application of the principles of dynamical systems to conflict requires a temporary suspension of our often deeply ingrained modes of thinking and action.

Case Study and Loop Analysis

The first step in approaching a case like that in Poland is to understand the dynamical system defining the conflict. What are the relevant elements, and what is the nature of the linkage among these elements? What are the significant feedback loops defining the patterns of the system? Are there primary subsystems or clusters of loops that hang together? Are the destructive patterns stable or oscillating between low and high intensity? Once these characteristics are identified, the initial task is to disrupt the most important linkages and thereby decouple the elements. This allows us to begin to destabilize the current system and disassemble the destructive attractor. The complexity of all the elements, and the mechanisms by which they influence each other, are likely to vary a great deal from one instance to another and thus require a careful *case study*. This type of analysis often occurs in the context of mediation and problem-solving workshops, although typically with a narrower focus on key issues and causes. Here, the analysis emphasizes the dynamical structure of positive and negative feedback, with an eye to those mechanisms which stimulate and/or fail to constrain escalatory patterns.

A methodology for mapping the landscape of positive and negative feedback loops to comprehend the structure of evolving phenomena has been developed by Maruyama[8] and applied by Weick[9] and Morgan.[10] Figure 1 presents a partial mapping of the elements and feedback loops that contributed to years of political stalemate in Poland. Here we see a preponderance of positive feedback loops (solid lines) which fed the escalatory patterns of the conflict and kept it in a state of high intensity. The escalation of the conflict was not always "transparent": power imbalances between the parties, censorship, repression, and propaganda contributed to a concealed economic crisis and to the development of an underground opposition movement. Over time, the support of the opposition by Polish society, the Polish Diaspora, the international community and the Catholic Church contributed to a rise of power of "Solidarity," and to a deeper division between the regime and the society. Moreover, the Communist propaganda did not allow for negative feedback or regulation of the economic situation in the country, which led to a heightened crisis. Thus, as the power of the opposition rose and the power of the regime diminished, the conflict became redefined by a system sustained primarily by positive feedback loops of escalation and retaliation between the parties, where the system's self-regulatory mechanisms were blocked and so corrections in the system had little chance to occur.

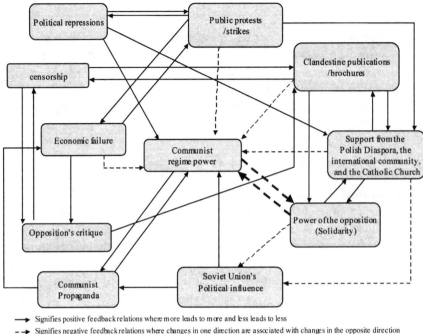

Signifies positive feedback relations where more leads to more and less leads to less
Signifies negative feedback relations where changes in one direction are associated with changes in the opposite direction

Figure 1: Feedback Loop Analysis of Case in Poland

Through the use of computer simulation technology, case-specific models such as this can be constructed, which allow for the testing of intervention targets and strategies prior to their use in actual situations. For example, one could test the effects of a substantial increase in support from the Polish Diaspora (such as through funding or military hardware) to determine the overall effects on the balance of power and the intensity of the conflict that emerges over time. Modeling can help us better comprehend the trade-offs and unintended consequences of different types and levels of intervention in a system determined by strong internal dynamics.[11]

Reorienting from Outcomes to Patterns

From a dynamical point of view, it is important to distinguish between short-term and sustained changes in the dynamics of a conflict. Short-lived oscillations in conflict intensity are likely to be observed in any relationship characterized by attractor dynamics. Such short-term changes can provide a misleading sense of the state of the conflict. Although it may be natural to experience hope and despair in response to changes in conflict intensity, they are not indicative of lasting changes as long as the underlying structure of the system remains stable. For lasting change to occur, the structure of the system must be modified in such a way that the attractor landscape is reconfigured. Such reconfiguration, in turn, requires changing the relations among system variables in a way that restores complexity.

For example, prior to the round table agreements, Poland experienced many cycles of escalation and de-escalation of the conflict as workers organized strikes against nationalized industries, which were always met with a strong retaliation from the Communist party. The strikes in June 1956 in Poznan, the Hungarian revolution in October 1956, student protests in 1968, the strikes in Gdansk in 1970, and the strikes in Radom in 1976 were all followed by a strong retaliation from the party with many strikers killed or imprisoned. The culmination of the military response of the Communist party to civil disobedience was the introduction of martial law in 1981 to put down the growing Solidarity movement. As long as the society was divided between the party and the opposition, a state of intractability persisted and resulted in ongoing cycles of violence and containment.

Reconfiguring Landscapes: Addressing <u>Both</u> Manifest and Latent Attractors

The essence of the attractor concept and the relevance of attractors for conflict can be captured in a simple metaphor. Figure 2 portrays a ball on a hilly landscape. The ball represents the current state of the system and the valley represents the system's attractor. The ball will roll down the hill and come to rest at the bottom of a valley in Figure 2.

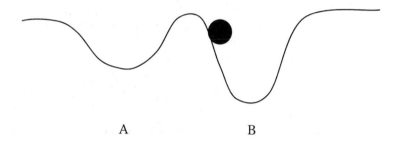

A   B

Figure 2: A dynamical system with two attractors (A and B)

A system may have more than one attractor. Figure 2 portrays a system with two attractors (A and B). Each attractor has its own a basin of attraction—that is, a set of states that will evolve toward the attractor. Attractors may differ in the width of their respective basins of attraction. In the figure, the basin of attraction for Attractor A is somewhat wider than the basin of attraction for Attractor B. This means that a wider variety of states will evolve toward Attractor A than toward Attractor B. Attractors can also vary in their respective strength, which is depicted as the relative depth of the two valleys in Figure 2. Attractor B, then, is stronger than Attractor A. This means that once a system is at Attractor B, it is more difficult for it to be dislodged by external influence.

Some changes in a system's dynamical properties can be easily observed because they affect the current state of the system (illustrated by the ball). Other changes, however, may affect the ensemble of *possible* states of the system and thus may not be immediately apparent (the landscape). Such changes may remain latent for extended periods of time, but can be manifested in a relatively short period of time in response to external influences and events that seem relatively minor. The concept of attractors provides a way to characterize both the current and potential states of a social system.

For example, it is important to understand that the seemingly overnight effectiveness of the Round Table negotiations actually represented a "tipping point"[12] in a process that had been underway for several years. The efficacy of this process was occluded from public awareness by the strong attractor provided by the martial law imposed by the Polish government. Pressure from the opposition on specific issues, as well as talks among the conflicting parties concerning these issues, created a multitude of latent attractors, each of which corresponded to new ways to think about a specific subset of issues. Because these latent attractors defined new possible states of the system that had been unimaginable during the height of the Cold War, the Round Table negotiations made the transition to these states possible.

Nonetheless, the situation in Poland was delicate. On one hand, you had the intelligentsia working to establish a new structure to help sustain democracy (such as new laws, economic reforms, educational institutions, a free press, etc.—the A valley in Figure 2). But the impact of these structures remained latent until the old system was destabilized through initiatives such as the strikes and other sources of influence (such as pressure from the international community).

However, premature, radical steps from the opposition party, when the landscape for democracy was not yet sufficiently developed, led to the contrary reaction of the system: stronger responses from the communist party in reaction to the strikes (the ball was pushed uphill, but was not displaced from the attractor, and therefore fell back to the original basin of attraction). Latent attractors become visible and define the intrinsic tendencies of the system once the current activities of the system fall within their basins of attraction. The creation and destruction of latent attractors may thus be critical in shaping how the system will respond to events and conditions that have yet to take place. Such changes are occluded from the vantage point of both participants and observers who know only the current state of the system.

Recognition of latent attractors is not only critical to characterizing the current state of the system, but also for understanding (and implementing) plausible scenarios of change. Although movement between attractors is likely to be rapid and abrupt, the change of attractors themselves is likely to be far slower and more gradual. When a specific policy or intervention does not produce a visible effect, this does not mean that it is doomed to futility. Rather, such an event may be creating, deepening, or destroying a latent attractor for the system. In other words, it may affect the range of possible states rather than the current state. The Solidarity movement is a good example of this. For years, their actions had no visible impact on the system. But the Round Table agreements would not have been possible without the years of opposition activity that preceded the negotiations.

This may be the case for both negative (undesirable) and positive (desirable) attractors in a social system. Genocides, for example, usually are initiated in a very rapid fashion, but are invariably preceded by a period of a series of changes in inter-group attitudes and behaviors such as the humiliation of group members, stereotyping, and denial of rights (such as seen in pre-genocide Rwanda). Since these changes are not necessarily dramatic by themselves, public opposition to them (negative feedback) may be fairly minimal and contained. Each change, however, first creates and then deepens a latent attractor that will subsequently determine the fate of inter-group relations. Once an attractor for destructive conflict has been established, relatively small provocations may move the system into the basin of this attractor, thereby dragging the whole system into full-blown conflict. More generally, even a seemingly minor event may function as a "tipping point" if it moves the system into the basin of attraction of a different attractor.

By the same token, many positive acts by one group toward another group may be rejected at face value and thus not have an immediate effect. Nonetheless, such acts may pave the way for a sudden escape from a negative attractor by building a positive attractor to which the system can move. For example, during the recent Orange revolution in Ukraine, the relations between Poland and Ukraine changed rapidly from fairly negative to very positive. Although the observable change took place in a matter of weeks, it would not have occurred if not for the groundwork established by positive interactions and exchanges between

various groups of people that took place years before the Orange revolution. Another example is the rapid repair in relations between the U.S. and the USSR after
decades of the Cold War, which as some have argued, was fostered by a series of
low-profile citizen exchanges, such as the Dartmouth conferences that occurred in
the years leading up to Perestroika.[13]

It is important to remember, however, that latent attractors not only provide a
foundation for conflict resolution, but also pose a risk of a rapid return to hostile
feelings and actions. The resolution of a conflict, then, does not necessarily mean
that no further efforts are required. As long as the attractor of conflict remains, it
holds potential for recapturing the dynamics of the system. Currently, Pol-
ish/Ukrainian relations are at a tentative threshold, so one must be aware of how
certain symbolic issues and interactions could return the system to the latent, destructive attractor.

Thus, the detection and disassembly of latent negative attractors should be the
aim of both conflict prevention and intervention. Early warning systems that report on the number and intensity of inflammatory media broadcasts, hate crimes,
human rights violations, and other elements which constitute destructive attractors can increase the salience of and attention to such emerging patterns. Short-
term or emergency programs should focus on the elimination of the triggers that
fuel catastrophic changes in the state of the system. In situations of instability
they could be crucial, because once the state of the system jumps into a new attractor, the way back is much harder. However, these types of initiatives are
insufficient and ultimately ineffective if they are not supported by long-term, incremental work on latent attractors.

From the dynamical perspective, then, important and lasting changes in a social system correspond to *changes in the attractor landscape of the system*. Although a
change within a basin of attraction is likely to be short-lived and resisted by the
system, a change in the attractors themselves reconfigures the ensemble of likely
states that can be adopted and alters the forces operating within the system.
Changes in the attractor landscape can bring about changes in system behavior
that are not only lasting but also self-sustaining and self-enhancing over time.

Restoring Multidimensionality and Balance to the System

Changing the structure of attractors is equivalent to changing properties of the
system's dynamics. This occurs when there is a change in the relationship among
variables in the system. If variables defining the conflict are strongly interlinked
by positive feedback loops, then activation of a single variable will feed into the
activation of other variables, and the system will evolve toward a coherent but
negative state. Positive feedback among variables producing conflict, then, results
in the creation of an attractor for destructive conflict. A complex and multidimensional system, on the other hand, is likely to be characterized by multiple
weak attractors. The factors that promote a collapse of complexity and a reduction
of dimensionality are likely to enhance the escalation of conflict, whereas factors
that untangle issues and individuate members of the outgroup are likely to promote de-escalation of conflict.

There are many routes to increased complexity in a conflictful relationship.
The Polish example illustrates one such route: the transformation of a unidimensional conflict over power into a multitude of small issue-specific conflicts.
Another plausible scenario centers on restoring the complexity associated with
perception of outgroup members. Research has shown, for example, that showing
positive examples of specific outgroup members, or fostering interactions with

outgroup members that prove to be unambiguously positive, can prevent the development of malignant ingroup-outgroup conflict.[14] Under certain conditions (e.g., equal status), contacts between ingroup and outgroup members should result in increased complexity of the perception of outgroup members. However, because of coherence mechanisms in social judgment,[15] the differentiation in outgroup perception may not be sustainable. A durable breakdown in outgroup homogeneity may occur in response to social interaction, but only if the ingroup and outgroup are interdependent on important issues that require coordination, accommodation or other forms of cooperation.[16] If members of two conflictful groups must cooperate and share resources in order to meet a common threat, for example, it is difficult to maintain a coherent negative view of the individuals in the opposing group. These effects on perceptions of outgroup members have been found to occur during problem-solving workshops,[17] and reportedly occurred during the Round Table negotiations as well. Another tack is to increase ingroup complexity by locating an important (e.g., high status, charismatic) ingroup member who doesn't share the ingroup's view of the conflict. If this person is sufficiently central that he or she cannot be marginalized within the group, the homogeneity of the ingroup's perspective will be destabilized. Such was the role of Adam Michnik, one of the central leaders of the opposition in Poland. He describes how his personal background, coming form a Communist family, predestined him to think about the enemy as human beings, and potential partners for dialogue. As one of the most active and repeatedly imprisoned leaders of the movement, he had a strong need to propagate his perception of the enemy within his group.

Another common scenario involves the break-up of the outgroup into two (or more) subgroups, with the negative feelings attached to only one subgroup. When this occurs, a negative behavior by a member of the disliked subgroup will not generalize to other subgroups. For instance, soon after the death of Yasser Arafat in 2004, there was a terrorist attack in Israel. For the first time in several years, however, this attack did not result in immediate Israeli retaliation against the Palestinians. Instead, this attack was interpreted as an isolated act of an extreme Palestinian group. From the Israeli point of view, the homogeneity of hostile intentions on the part of Palestinians was broken and replaced by a distinction between vicious extremist groups and the larger population seeking means of achieving peace. A similar process may have been at play when extremists from both parties were excluded from the Round Table negotiations in Poland.

Conclusion

The principles of dynamical systems theory offer the field of conflict studies a unique frame through which to comprehend the basic structural dynamics which give rise to enduring, destructive conflict. From the dynamical perspective, conflict intervention in cases of protracted conflict must go beyond agreements and attempts to change the current state of the system, to changing the ensemble of possible and achievable states of the system. Changing the state of the system, whether in a positive or a negative direction, is easily observable and, depending on the direction, often dramatic or spectacular. Changing the attractors of the system, in contrast, is more likely to be a gradual and far less visible process. Paradoxically, one could argue that when these efforts involve disassembly of the negative attractor, their effects will never be visible. This is because the success of the process is defined in terms of the non-occurrence of the negative transformation. Nevertheless, such efforts may be critical for avoiding malignant conflict in the long run. Although the creation of positive latent attractors, if successful, will be visible, conflict resolution *per se* is likely to be attributed to observable and dramatic actions preceding the transition from conflict to peace rather than to the much slower and less spectacular groundwork that paved the way for the transition to occur.

Endnotes

[1] *See* Peter Coleman, *Characteristics of Protracted, Intractable Conflict: Towards the Development of a Meta-Framework*, 9 PEACE & CONFLICT: JOURNAL OF PEACE PSYCHOLOGY 1 (2003); Louis Kriesberg, *Intractable Conflict*, *in* THE HANDBOOK OF INTERETHNIC COEXISTENCE 332 (Eugene Wiener ed., 1998); Louis Kriesberg, *Nature, Dynamics, and Phases of Intractability*, *in* CHESTER CROCKER, GRASPING THE NETTLE: ANALYZING CASES OF INTRACTABLE CONFLICT (2005).

[2] *Cf.* STEVEN JOHNSON, EMERGENCE: THE CONNECTED LIVES OF ANTS, BRAINS, CITIES, AND SOFTWARE (2001); ANDRZEJ NOWAK & ROBIN VALLACHER, DYNAMICAL SOCIAL PSYCHOLOGY (1998); HEINZ G. SCHUSTER, DETERMINISTIC CHAOS: AN INTRODUCTION (1998); STEVEN STROGATZ, SYNC: THE EMERGING SCIENCE OF SPONTANEOUS ORDER (2003); GERARD WEISBUCH, COMPLEX SYSTEMS DYNAMICS (1991); Robin Vallacher, et al., *Special Issue: The Dynamical Perspective in Personality and Social Psychology*, 6 PERSONALITY & SOCIAL PSYCHOLOGY REVIEW 264 (2002).

[3] Problem-solving and dynamical approaches to conflict are conceptually distinct, but should be seen as mutually complementary methods for addressing conflict.

[4] From interpersonal to international. *See* Peter Coleman, et al., Intractable Conflict as an Attractor (unpublished manuscript on file with author); Robin Vallacher, et al., *Attracted to Conflict: a Dynamical Perspective on Malignant Social Relations*, *in* UNDERSTANDING SOCIAL CHANGE: POLITICAL PSYCHOLOGY IN POLAND (Agnieszka Golec & Krystyna Skarzynska eds, forthcoming).

[5] *See* DEAN PRUITT, ET AL., SOCIAL CONFLICT: ESCALATION, STALEMATE, AND SETTLEMENT (3d ed., 2004); Lan Bui-Wrzosinska, The Dynamics of Conflict in a School Setting (2005) (unpublished Masters thesis, Warsaw School for Social Psychology) (on file with author).

[6] *Cf.* FRITZ HEIDER, THE PSYCHOLOGY OF INTERPERSONAL RELATIONS (1958); PAUL THAGARD, COHERENCE IN THOUGHT AND ACTION (2000); Robin Vallacher & Andrzej Nowak, *Dynamical Social Psychology: Toward Coherence in Human Experience and Scientific Theory*, *in* SOCIAL PSYCHOLOGY: HANDBOOK OF BASIC PRINCIPLES (E. Tory Higgins & Arie Kruglanski eds., 2d ed. in press).

[7] *See* Wendell Jones & Scott Hughes, *Complexity, Conflict Resolution and How the Mind Works*, 20 CONFLICT RESOLUTION QUARTERLY 4 (2003).

[8] *See* Magorah Maruyama, The Second Cybernetics: Deviation Amplifying Mutual Causal Processes 51 AMERICAN SCIENTIST 164 (1963); Magorah Maruyama, *Mindscapes, Management, Business Policy, and Public Policy*, 7 ACADEMY OF MANAGEMENT REVIEW 612 (1982).

[9] *See* KARL WEICK, THE SOCIAL PSYCHOLOGY OF ORGANIZING (1979).

[10] *See* GARETH MORGAN, IMAGES OF ORGANIZATION (1997); Gareth Morgan, *The Schismatic Metaphor and Its Implication for Organizational Analysis*, 2 ORGANIZATION STUDIES 23 (1981).

[11] *See* DIETRICH DORNER, THE LOGIC OF FAILURE: WHY THINGS GO WRONG AND WHAT WE CAN DO TO MAKE THEM RIGHT (Rita Kimber & Robert Kimber trans., 1996).

[12] *Cf.* MALCOLM GLADWELL, THE TIPPING POINT: HOW LITTLE THINGS CAN MAKE A BIG DIFFERENCE (2000).

[13] *See* HAROLD SAUNDERS, A PUBLIC PEACE PROCESS: SUSTAINED DIALOGUE TO TRANSFORM RACIAL AND ETHNIC CONFLICTS (1999).

[14] *See* GEORGE A. Quattrone, *On the Perception of a Group's Variability*, *in* PSYCHOLOGY OF INTERGROUP RELATIONS (Stephen Worchel & William Austin eds., 1986); Miles Hewstone, *Contact and Categorization: Social Psychological Interventions to Change Intergroup Relations*, *in* FOUNDATIONS OF STEREOTYPES AND STEREOTYPING 323 (C. Neil Mactrae, et al., eds., 1996).

[15] *Cf.* THAGARD, *supra* note 6; NOWAK & VALLACHER, *supra*, note 2.

[16] *Cf.* SHERIF MUZAFER, ET AL., INTERGROUP CONFLICT AND COOPERATION: THE ROBBERS CAVE EXPERIMENT (1961).

[17] *See* Herbert Kelmen, *Reconciliation as Identity Change: A Social-Psychological Perspective*, *in* FROM CONFLICT RESOLUTION TO RECONCILIATION 111 (Yaacov Y. Bar-Siman-Tov ed., 2004), *available at* http://www.wcfia.harvard.edu/faculty/hckelman/papers/hck_Reconciliation.pdf.

❧ 9 ❧

Rawls on Negotiating Justice

Cheyney Ryan

Editors' Note: *What does the philosophical concept of justice have to do with ordinary negotiations? Does John Rawls deserve a place at the table? Ryan explains what we negotiators can learn from political philosophy's debates on fairness—and what political philosophers should take from us. This chapter should be read in conjunction with Welsh on Fairness and both of the chapters on ethics.*

For several decades political philosophy has been centered around the discussion of justice begun by John Rawls, the leading English-speaking philosopher of the second half of the 20th century. This essay discusses some of the interesting ways that Rawls' reflections on justice and the study of negotiation can enrich one another. But my larger aim is to argue that philosophy and the study of negotiation have much to learn from one another. Let me begin with this general point and then turn to Rawls and justice.

One way to relate philosophy and negotiation is to consider how philosophical ideas can illuminate specific practices of negotiation and our understanding of those practices. For example, philosophers have a good deal to say about the different types of ethical reasoning, or the tensions between ethics and more personal claims, or the general relation between ethics and self-interest. A philosophy of negotiation can relate philosophy's ongoing discussion of these matters to the ethical concerns that arise in negotiation. Philosophy can also shed light on the nature of the "self" in negotiation. A popular idea in approaching negotiation is the value of "separating people from the problem" as a means of focusing on the substantive issues at hand and developing a more impartial perspective towards things. In specific contexts this is a valuable tool, but a philosopher will wonder if the picture of the "self" it presumes is always a tenable one. What if the self is *defined* by its problems, as certain sociological views would suggest? Indeed, what if my sense of who I am is defined by those commitments that I regard as non-negotiable: what do I do when they come into conflict with the concerns of others?[1] Asking me to separate myself from these matters may be akin to asking me to become another person.

One final example from philosophy concerns the role of hope and optimism in negotiation. In difficult negotiations an important premium attaches to being creative, especially when an impasse reflects the fact that the parties have lost hope of any meaningful alternatives being found. A lot of what goes on in difficult negotiations involves sustaining hope, in part because hope is so intimately connected to trust. But what, precisely, is "hope"? There is an extraordinarily rich philosophical literature on this that engages lots of fascinating issues (like the distinction between "hope" and "optimism").[2] We all have a working gut understanding of these notions, but we all can benefit from engaging the philosophical reflections on them.

In these and other instances the philosophy of negotiation *begins* with philosophy, and asks how negotiation's problems and strategies are engaged by it. But the philosophy of negotiation can proceed in the other direction as well, by asking how the practices of negotiation can illuminate and even inform our most basic philosophical ideas—like truth or justice. The work of John Rawls provides a significant case in point of how philosophy and negotiation can learn from one another.

As noted, Rawls is the most important political philosopher of our time, and part of his greatness lay in his willingness to modify his views in the face of objections. Rawls' thinking changed substantially from his earlier *A Theory of Justice* to his later work on what he termed "political liberalism."[3] Issues of negotiation became increasingly central to his basic project. But a weakness of his work has been its failure to engage negotiation as it is actually practiced and discussed. He and his followers have continued to rely on abstract, if not other-worldly conceptions of these matters. Their views could benefit profoundly from exploring the lessons of negotiation as an ongoing practical field.

From the start Rawls asked us to think of justice as a matter of *agreement*. He suggested that we think of the principles guiding a just society as the ones that individuals would agree to—with the crucial proviso that they do not know where they themselves would end up in society, on the top or the bottom. They would thus act from behind a "veil of ignorance" in Rawls' words. Given this constraint, no individual could tailor the principles of justice to his or her special talents or circumstances, which is why Rawls called this approach "justice as fairness." Rawls suggested that the principles that would be agreed to would be ones that were deeply committed to basic human rights and had a strong presumption in favor of economic equality. Inequalities would only be tolerated if they most greatly benefited the least well off; this is Rawls' "difference principle."

But how should the "agreement" that leads to such principles be conceived?

The first incarnation of Rawls' theory conceived the process of agreement in an extremely idealized, rationalistic way. Rawls employed the highly formalized tools of game theory and social choice theory to describe the process as akin to how the abstract "consumers" of neoclassical economics hypothetically agree to a set of prices. Hence the agreement did not involve any real *negotiation*, just a "rational calculation" on each person's part of how to "maximize" his or her own situation.

Turning justice into a formal bargaining game was what lots of economists and political scientists initially liked about Rawls' theory. But this was also what many others *dis*liked about it. The idea that "justice" was not some Platonic form hanging in the sky but was grounded in the fair agreements of people seemed true and important. But as Rawls developed it, much of that apparent truth and importance seemed to disappear into the clouds of hyper-rationalistic economic theory. What relevance could talk of such agreement have if real people were left out?

If Rawls' thinking had stopped there, his theory might by now be relegated to those obscure corners of social science where professors noodle on their mathematical models for their own amusement. But his thinking did not stop there.

The turn in Rawls' thinking can be described by introducing a distinction he draws on heavily in his later work, between the *rational* and the *reasonable*.[4] The distinction is fascinating in its own right, plus it is a useful one for thinking about practical issues in negotiation.

At first their meanings might seem quite similar; but let's reflect on what is involved in characterizing individuals as "rational" in contrast to characterizing them as "reasonable". A rational person would seem to be someone who is effective at pursuing his or her own interests. When I say to someone "You're not being rational" what I often mean is that given your goals, you have not chosen an effective means to achieve them. If my goal were only to make the highest possible salary, for example, it would be irrational for me to continue teaching in a philosophy department rather than seeking a job in a law school. Rationality can sometimes involve revising one's goals, though only when experience shows that one's current goals are unachievable in some sense; so we tinker with our goals to make them more achievable.

Rationality of this sort can be evidenced in complete *isolation* from other people. Thus, Robinson Crusoe was its model (forgetting about his servant "Friday" of course): one could speak of him as being less rational in how he went about providing for his wants, alone on his desert island. Sometimes rationality puts us in need of other people, though; and when it does, our actions towards one another reduce to strategies for mutual advantage. The upshot of rational agents entering into commercial contracts may be the benefit of both parties, but this mutual benefit is just the side effect of each angling for his or her own benefit. (The philosopher Immanuel Kant once characterized marriage in this way as a contract for the exclusive use of each other's sex organs!)

Rationality of this sort is an essential aspect of any negotiation relationship. If parties did not have goals that they are trying to pursue effectively, then there would be nothing to negotiate about. At the same time the fact that negotiation is required in the first place suggests that each side's rational search for its advantage does not automatically generate a "solution."

This is where being *reasonable* comes in. Reasonableness is a more complex and open-textured notion than rationality. But following Rawls, we might identify it with a number of qualities, all of which derive from the notion that a reasonable person is someone who takes *other* people into account. I may suggest to my wife Sandy that we spend all day Saturday watching the Master's. That may be a rational thing for me to wish, given my interest in golf, but a totally *un*reasonable thing to suggest to her, given that she hates golf. Reasonableness involves attending to what other people can accept, on the assumption that sharing agreements and the relations they sustain are valuable in themselves, over and above their promoting my particular interests. A totally *un*reasonable person—and some of us have had colleagues like this—is blind to what other people can accept, because the *mutual* acceptance of goals or policies is of absolutely no interest to them. Rationality is something you can evidence on a desert island; reasonableness pertains to dealings with other people.

Rationality is a kind of "capacity" that persons possess. Reasonableness, on the other hand, is more a kind of "virtue" that people can have to varying degrees, and that can be cultivated. This brief description should suggest how reasonableness is an absolutely central virtue for negotiation, perhaps *the* central virtue, and how much of what we worry about in facilitating negotiation pertains to the cultivation of reasonableness. The parties in negotiation must be *both* rational and reasonable: they must have goals that they seek to pursue effectively, but in doing so they must be open to the interests of others in ways that value the mutual acceptance of the agreements reached. [Rose, *Ulysses*]

This distinction leads to some interesting questions about *reciprocity* that have substantial bearing on our understanding of negotiation. Reciprocity is a very great social value, and one that would seem essential to a successful negotiation. A fair agreement would seem to be one that instantiates the value of reciprocity.[Welsh, *Fairness*] Reflection on the distinction between the rational and the reasonable compels us to see that there are different notions of reciprocity, and that people can disagree about which model is appropriate in different situations. Kant's picture of marriage embodies a weird, exclusively economic kind of reciprocity; truly loving relations involve a quite different kind, less redolent of mutual exploitation; other types of relations fall somewhere in between. Maybe an issue in negotiation is determining which kind of reciprocity is relevant.

To return to Rawls' project: Rawls' earlier thinking regarded the process leading to agreement as one of rationality alone.[5] The bargaining that generated the principles of justice was conceived as a search for mutual advantage of his hypothetical choosers; hence, the appeal to game theory and the like. But over time he concluded that the problem of justice was better conceived as one of reasonableness. The question to ask of principles of justice was, what were the most *reasonable* ones for people to agree to given the nature of our society and the nature of who we are? Justice, thus reconceived, lost the harsh individualism that Rawls' earlier theory seemed to possess. The stress on reasonableness meant that people taking others into account was an *essential* part of what justice was all about. His theory also moved away from his earlier hyper-abstraction, insofar as talk of what is "reasonable" invariably refers not to some hypothetical persons with hypothetical aims but to real people—in this case, us, here and now.

The turn to *reasonableness* as the reference point in philosophy is one we see in a great many areas these days.[6] In Anglo-American philosophy it was anticipated by the work of the great classical pragmatists; John Dewey's focus on "intelligence" is not that different from a focus on reasonableness.[7] Intelligence, for Dewey, is not something rooted in the "head" but is part of the larger social process of inquiry by which a community employs shared methods to arrive at common solutions to problems; hence intelligence, like reasonableness, orients us to ongoing dialogue with others. In general the privileging of reasonableness seems to follow from the almost universal rejection of metaphysical foundations in ethics and epistemology. Jurgen Habermas's discourse theory, for example, suggests that what counts as true both factually and normatively is what reasonable persons would agree to, given certain processes of deliberation and reflection.[8] Habermas's stress on the non-coercive nature of these processes would seem to be implicit in the notion that a reasonable agreement is one that all affected persons can share without being forced.

Where real life negotiation and reflection on its practice come in is that, despite all the stress on reasonable processes of agreement in current philosophy, the received discussion still remains very abstract and hypothetical. There is no attention to what the study of negotiation can reveal about the nature of rationality, reasonableness, and reciprocity. It is as if philosophers want to replace the rational by the reasonable, but don't want to complete the turn to the real world that this involves. This is a criticism that Habermas has made of others, but I would suggest it holds for him as well. If reasonableness is the central virtue of negotiation then its character will best reveal itself in the actual practice of negotiation, including the strategies for making it better. A lot of the questions that still remain about Rawls' theory, for example, involve whether his notion of being reasonable still presumes too much that persons abstract themselves and their concerns from their own contingent circumstances. Whether or not reasonableness requires this would seem to be a question about what is required for reaching mutually accepted agreements. Answering this would seem to involve us in attending to real-life practices of reaching such agreements.

I've suggested that the philosophy of negotiation can proceed from two rather different directions. But the upshot is that their relation might be best thought of as one of *mutual containment*, to borrow a term from W. V. Quine. Philosophers have things to say about justice that can be brought to bear on the concerns of negotiation by invoking issues of fairness; thus the move from philosophy to negotiation. But the discussion of Rawls suggests that *what* philosophers say about justice may ultimately draw on what they learn *from* negotiation about the virtues of reasonable persons; thus the move from negotiation to philosophy. Negotiation, as concerned with the resolution of differences through such truly human practices as dialogue and sharing, thus takes its place at the center of a truly human philosophy.

Endnotes

[1] *See* HARRY FRANKFURT, THE IMPORTANCE OF WHAT WE CARE ABOUT: PHILOSOPHICAL ESSAYS (1988).

[2] The starting point for a discussion of hope is GABRIEL MARCEL, HOMO VIATOR: INTRODUCTION TO A METAPHYSICS OF HOPE (Emma Craufurd trans., 1978). This usage is distinguished from a more economic usage, as in Jennifer G. Brown, *The Role of Hope in Negotiation*, 44 UCLA LAW REVIEW 1661 (1997).

[3] The key texts of Rawls' are A THEORY OF JUSTICE (1971); POLITICAL LIBERALISM (1993); and JUSTICE AS FAIRNESS: A RESTATEMENT (Erin Kelly ed., 2001) (representing his later views).

[4] The distinction is addressed in RAWLS, POLITICAL LIBERALISM and JUSTICE AS FAIRNESS, *supra* note 3.

[5] Rawls himself might question this stark contrast, but I think it captures the basic shift in his views.

[6] *See, e.g.*, THOMAS SCANLON, WHAT WE OWE TO EACH OTHER (1998) (employing the notion to develop an account of morality as a whole).

[7] *See, e.g.*, JOHN DEWEY, EXPERIENCE AND NATURE (1929).

[8] *See* JURGEN HABERMAS, MORAL CONSCIOUSNESS AND COMMUNICATIVE ACTION (Christian Lenhardt & Shierry Nicholsen trans., 1990); JURGEN HABERMAS, THE THEORY OF COMMUNICATIVE ACTION (Thomas McCarthy trans., 1984).

❧ 10 ❧

The Poverty of Buyer and Seller

Kevin Avruch

Editors' Note: *In a world in which negotiating can implicate your most important values, Avruch points out that the most common mental model of negotiators is that of buyer and seller. Yet both our most intimate and our greatest negotiations have little to do with the whole basis of buyer-and-seller ideas. Avruch offers a way at least to begin to rethink, to find our way out of this trap.*

My goal in this essay is to examine the question of whether negotiation theory and practice is of much use in social conflicts involving deeply rooted disputes over values. I proceed first by examining critically the foundational heuristic of what I call canonical or first-generation negotiation theory: the *buyer-seller* heuristic.[1] I then propose, and critically examine, another heuristic.

The First Generation Heuristic: Rational Choice and the Buyer-Seller

Almost every formal academic treatment of negotiation, and quite a few informal ones as well, reveals its basis in the larger theory of rational choice (or rational decision-making) and the key heuristic of the buyer-seller encounter.[2] Buyers meet sellers in different sorts of markets all the time and everywhere, and although the nature of these markets is hardly the same, the essential roles are remarkably constant and recognizable.[3] The two—the theory and the heuristic—are of course inextricably entangled in neo-classical economics: rational choice as its conceptual foundation and the buyer-seller transaction as its paradigmatic praxis. No one can deny the rigor, parsimony, and productiveness of the rational choice paradigm even if, as one commentator notes, the model is not without flaws, "not least through the real world's bloody-minded obstinacy in simply not conforming to theory."[4] The obvious and frequent disconnect between actors' behavior as "predicted" by the paradigm and their actual behavior has long been noted by scholars, both those working within the paradigm and those critics outside it. Perhaps the explanation for the disconnect that is most friendly to the theory involves information. Rational choice requires actors to possess rigorously valid and reliable information about many variables to arrive at a decision. In the "real world" such information is very often partial or imperfect and hence, expectedly, decisions are far from optimally rational.[5]

A more serious critique raises the possibility that the human cognizing apparatus charged with effecting rational choice decision-making calculi is itself intrinsically to blame: it is not up to the task. This can result from structural limitations in the capacity of the cognitive apparatus to store, retrieve, or process information, or from a range of other distortion-causing mechanisms, many supported by the apparent organismic requirement for "cognitive miserliness" (or risk aversion), resulting in such framing biases as attribution errors, just-world thinking, mirror imaging, illusory correlations, reactive devaluation, etc.[6] More recently, that most important distinction in the theory of mind assumed by rational choice theory—a bifurcation, actually—between "cognition" on the one hand and "emotion" on the other has been questioned. Affect and cognition appear to interpenetrate one another all the time in our thinking.[7] And if our conception of thinking—of cognition—no longer allows the partitioning away of (messy, irrational) emotion, then how can we assume that rational choice theory "predicts" any actor's behavior any time?

These are some of the critiques that have emerged from within cognitive psychology itself, at the foundation of rational choice theorizing. I will not engage here two other important sources of critique. The first has to do with the problem of how one gets from the behavior of an individual rational actor to the behavior of the collective—a problem that has engaged some of the best minds in a variety of the social sciences.[8] The second is basically a cultural critique, questioning the assumption of the universality of utilities divorced from their encompassing contexts of meaning and valuation.[9] The adequacy of such a concept of utility for understanding other cultures has long been questioned,[10] but the questions become harder if one imagines trying to "transact" (say, negotiate) *across* different "utility universes." For even if we assume that a behavioral theory of utility maximizing holds across all cultures, if we admit that the nature of utilities varies cross-culturally, then, to imagine intercultural "rational" transactions we would also have to assume that culturally-specific utilities are everywhere essentially fungible.[11] But for the purposes of this essay I want to hold cultural variability constant, and redirect our analysis of utility to the related notion, so important in contemporary negotiation theory and practice, that of "interest."

In what one might legitimately call the first "Copernican revolution" of negotiation theory and practice, the idea was put forward that if individuals could be shown that most unproductive and inefficient negotiation involves arguments around surface demands or "positions," then the act of having parties move beyond positions to analyze their underlying interests would free them to engage in a whole range of creative problem-solving activities. Put more formally, one could in many (though certainly not all) situations move from distributive (fixed-pie, zero-sum) bargaining toward problem solving and integrative (expanded-pie, positive-sum) solutions, toward the famous "win-win" agreement.[12] The question which some within our field have asked is whether anything (capable of motivating behavior or social action) lay "beneath" interests. This is the crucial question if one wants to assess the relevance of negotiation for conflicts around issues involving ideology, identity, or values.

Values-Based Conflicts, Interests, Rights, and Power

Several major theorists have identified a "bedrock" level of motivators beneath mere interests; these are often called "basic human needs."[13] Sandwiched between the presumed universal comparability of utilities, opening the way for creative problem solving at the level of interests, and the bedrock universality of basic human needs, lies the layer Warfield calls "values."[14] Inculcated in individuals through socialization and enculturation, "values" in this scheme cover a wide range of notions, including such ideas as ideology, beliefs, or worldview, which are not at all identical. So the term is being used here, imperfectly, as a kind of shorthand.[15] Instead of being linked, through the notion of utility, to what is useful, desired, or preferred, values are linked (through a different calculus?) to what is deemed good and true. Warfield also argues that at this level some sort of "non-rational choice paradigm" is the appropriate one for understanding social transactions—conflict or its resolution, for example. At the least, values-based conflicts may resist the sort of rational, problem solving negotiation practices that often and demonstrably work well to address conflicts involving competing interests. In the past, many such values-based conflicts have been labeled as "intractable," especially if they involve basic incompatibilies between the parties at the deepest levels of worldview, or perceived threats to personal or group identity.[16]

A first step in addressing value conflicts requires perhaps the formulation of a different heuristic for orienting oneself to these sorts of conflicts, different, that is, from the *buyer-seller* metaphor that is central to interest-based negotiation theory, research, and practice. The metaphor/heuristic of *buyer-seller* is hardly in itself "value-neutral" in this regard. Consider, for example, how it orients us to the notion of "trust" in negotiation. [Lewicki, *Trust*] Discussing the concept of "reservation point"—essentially the quantification of one's BATNA—Leigh Thompson assesses the wisdom of one party revealing her reservation point to the other, in part thereby demonstrating "good faith and trust" in the other party. Thompson writes, prescriptively: "Negotiation is not an issue of trust; it is an issue of strategy. The purpose of negotiation is to maximize your surplus, so why create a conflict of interest with the other party by 'trusting' them with your reservation point?"[17] Given the underlying and orienting heuristic, this seems a perfectly reasonable, indeed rational way to structure a buyer-seller relationship and approach negotiation within one.[18] But if one is negotiating with another in the context of a values-based conflict, ought the matter of "trust" be dismissed so emphatically? If one thinks not, then what sort of heuristic can move us away from thinking of negotiation in a "maximize your surplus," buyer-seller modality?

Before suggesting such a heuristic, it is worthwhile briefly to examine how rational choice and interest-based negotiation theorists have themselves addressed values-based conflicts. The two main ways pull in rather different directions.

First, one can simply deny that any significantly different sorts of "motivators" underlie interests. This is the tack taken by Dean Pruitt and Sung Hee Kim, who see "interests underlying interests," although they do agree that interests cluster into "hierarchical trees," the deepest or most "basic" level of which consist of such Burtonian basic human needs as identity, security, justice, or self-esteem. However, they do not agree with needs theorists "about the need to draw a sharp distinction between interest-based conflicts and needs-based" ones.[19]

The second tack is very different. Agreeing that values-based conflicts are rarely if ever amenable to interest-based negotiations, these analysts suggest that two other modes of settlement or resolution may be called for, one based upon power, the other upon rights.[20] Both may be deployed in the framework of a "negotiation," although such negotiations rarely present the same opportunities as interest-based ones, i.e. for creative or "pie-expanding" problem solving. Power implies coercion of one sort or another, whether deployed as threat or exercised in some sort of contest—the outer limits of "negotiation." Rights refer to standards of legitimacy, justice or fairness, whether formally codified in a contract or generally understood in some cultural context. Rights may be generally socially accepted, but they are as often as not contested as well, frequently looping us back to power.

When faced with values-based conflicts, then, the choice with regard to negotiation at present seems to be between presuming that such conflicts are not qualitatively different from other sorts of interest-based conflicts; or presuming that the notion of interests no longer productively applies, and negotiation itself constricts to power-plays or rights contests. And what about rights? If one thinks of such commonly conceived rights as fairness, equity, or justice, it seems as if we are very close to the domain of "values" as this is commonly conceived as well. Can we imagine an expanded canon of negotiation capable of addressing these sorts of conflicts? If so, I think we have to begin by conceptualizing a heuristic for negotiation different from that of *buyer-seller*.

A New Heuristic for Negotiation

If one thinks about a deep values conflict in our contemporary society then something like abortion or capital punishment is immediately suggested. But if we want a heuristic similar in type to *buyer-seller*, focused (microsociologically) on dyadic actors in a specified and delimited decision-making situation, consider the following:

A couple, each deeply religious but coming from very different religious traditions, has a child. Religion is extremely important to both of them, and while each "respects" the tradition of the other, a decision must be made as to which tradition the child will be affiliated with and raised in. How do they go about "negotiating" this?

Perhaps the first thing to note about this—let us call it the *two-religions*—heuristic is how, by its own limitations, it highlights the robustness and appeal of *buyer-seller*. For one thing, *buyer-seller* has wide, virtually universal, applicability as an example of a decision-making situation. In stark contrast, the *two-religions* heuristic is only *imaginable* in an essentially liberal society in which religion is culturally constituted as a matter of individual "conscience," privatized and free of coercive pressures from larger social groups—at least larger than each of the couple's immediate family.[21] In many of the world's societies, today and historically, this scenario would make no sense. It is, compared to *buyer-seller*, narrowly historically and culturally contingent.

What would a "rights" paradigm bring to this decision? In an explicit patriarchy, of course, the "right" to specify the religion of the child would reside with husband/father; we're back to culture again (which in effect constitutes "rights"), and also, of course, to power. But in our own society—not *normatively* patriarchal—rights won't get us very far.

It's also difficult to imagine a "power" process being applied to this decision without great damage to the relationship, and perhaps eventually to the child as well. However, if power is conceived beyond the bonds of the dyadic relationship and generalized to society, then one can imagine a rational decision being made to raise the child in the tradition that is more closely identified with the power structure of the society, for the future advancement and "benefit" of the child. In fact, under some circumstances values do get treated like interests and negotiated as one would negotiate interests. This happens in the U.S. Congress or parliaments or in democratic electoral politics generally—not to mention in labor-management relations—more often than not. But if we insist on preserving the genuine and deeply held values—the non-utilitarian—nature of the couples' thinking (and *feeling*) as they make their decision, then choosing on the basis of secular, "profane," and interest-based advantage should be offensive to both parties.[22]

Is this decision *negotiable* at all?

Conclusion: A New Canon for a New Heuristic?

I do not, in fact, have a very decisive or satisfying answer to this question. But the raising of it brings us back to the starting-point of the essay, the call for a new, expanded canon of negotiation theory, research, and practice. I do think the *two-religions* heuristic demonstrates the limitations of the older canon, based on rational choice and buyer-seller, in approaching these sorts of conflicts. I can see that based upon the older canon of negotiation we might well call this conflict fully "intractable" and non-negotiable. The advice of a third party to this couple might then be to forego bringing children into their relationship entirely—or rethink the sustainability, if not the value, of the relationship. Hardly win-win.

But if new heuristics guide or orient our thinking about problems in new ways, then what might the *two-religions* heuristic suggest? The list of topics for a new "common core" in an expanded canon of negotiation suggested by many of the authors in the *Marquette Law Review* (and now addressed in this volume) include subjects under apology, culture, emotions, ethics, identity, power (beyond coercion), narrative, and metaphor.[23] If the older canon seems too restricted to imagine negotiating the *two-religions* conflict under it, it is equally difficult to imagine a negotiation—were one possible—that did not include recourse to some of the subjects listed above. But how?

One important question raised here is under what circumstances does the interest-based paradigm work or fail when confronted by values-based conflicts: when are values reducible or irreducible to interests? I think we need a more nuanced—procedural and dynamical—way of describing negotiations in values-based conflict. Wallace Warfield, for example, suggests that we shouldn't so much see interests and values in a hierarchical relationship where one "trumps" the other—my earlier game metaphor—as understand the ability of oppositional parties in negotiations of various dimensions to engage in what he describes as "rapid shifting" between "negotiable interests and so-called non-negotiable values." Reflecting on his own conflict resolution training and workshop practice in postgenocide Rwanda, Warfield writes: "Thus Rwandans (Hutus and Tutsis) were able to negotiate around interests in a scenario that dealt with organizational conflict, because organizational structure and culture provided negotiators a bridge. Whereas, those same parties, when it came to fundamental issues of genocide and forgiveness, struggled to find a common ground." He suggests the need for heuristics and models that depict not static layers, but "shifting … boundaries driven by situation and perhaps other characteristics."[24]

The really hard work, not even attempted in this essay, is not to devise a new heuristic, but having proposed one, to develop it in order to imagine the possibility for *negotiation* of values-based conflicts now deemed intractable, beyond the sometimes uncertain remedies of rights and power. The *two-religions* heuristic, given its limitations, may in the end serve only to remind us that these sorts of deeply embedded conflicts demand, on the part of theorists and practitioners alike, greater attention to understanding the dynamics of values-based negotiations (in the area of practice), and for theorists, greater attention to axiology in general and the nexus between values and identity—in the end hinted at but unexplored here—in particular.

Endnotes

A version of this essay was presented at the annual meeting of the International Association for Conflict Management on June 6-9, 2004 in Pittsburgh, PA. I thank co-panelist Linda Putnam and organizers Christopher Honeyman and Andrea Schneider. In subsequent drafts, Evans Mandes helped with additional sources in cognitive psychology. My colleagues Marc Gopin, Christopher Honeyman, Dan Rothbart, Richard Rubenstein, Andrea Schneider, and Wallace Warfield all read earlier drafts closely and critically. Having satisfied none of them entirely, I thank them wholeheartedly.

[1] I borrow the notion of a negotiation 'canon' from Christopher Honeyman and Andrea Schneider. *See* the special issue they edited of the *Marquette Law Review: The Emerging Interdisciplinary Canon of Negotiation*, 87 MARQUETTE LAW REVIEW (2004).

[2] *See, e.g.*, HOWARD RAIFFA, THE ART AND SCIENCE OF NEGOTIATION (1982); RICHARD E. WALTON & ROBERT B. MCKERSIE, A BEHAVIORAL THEORY OF LABOR NEGOTIATIONS (1965); ROGER FISHER & WILLIAM URY, GETTING TO YES: NEGOTIATING AGREEMENT WITHOUT GIVING IN (1981).

[3] 'Recognizable' but not necessarily 'identical.' Other markets in other places ('cultures') provide evidence of this. *See* Clifford Geertz, *Suq: The Bazaar Economy in Sefrou, in* MEANING AND ORDER IN MOROCCAN SOCIETY 222 (Clifford Geertz, et al., eds., 1979). Among other things—*pace* Leigh Thompson on 'trust'—Geertz writes of buyer-seller interaction in the suq: 'Bargaining does not operate in purely pragmatic, utilitarian terms, but is hedged in by deeply felt rules of etiquette, tradition, and moral expectation.' *Id.*

[4] Jocelyn Evans, *Fitting Extremism into the Rational Choice Paradigm*, 39 GOVERNMENT AND OPPOSITION 110 (2004).

[5] HERBET A. SIMON, MODELS OF BOUNDED RATIONALITY (1982).

[6] For a discussion of such regular distortions found in international negotiation at the state level, *see* ROBERT JERVIS, PERCEPTION AND MISPERCEPTION IN INTERNATIONAL POLITICS (1976). An early insight in this direction, deeply connected to peace studies and coming from a polymath and perennially former-economist is KENNETH BOULDING, THE IMAGE: KNOWLEDGE OF LIFE AND SOCIETY (1956).

[7] A sample of recent works in this vein—JOSEPH FORGAS, FEELING AND THINKING: THE ROLE OF AFFECT IN SOCIAL COGNITION (2001); ERIC EICH, COGNITION AND EMOTION (2000); EMOTIONS AND BELIEFS: HOW FEELINGS INFLUENCE THOUGHT (Nico H. Fridja, et al., eds., 2000).

[8] On the 'tragedy of the commons,' start with this classic work: Garrett Hardin, *The Tragedy of the Commons*, SCIENCE, Dec. 13, 1968, at 1243-48. An economist proposes an 'impossibility theorem' in KENNETH ARROW, SOCIAL CHOICE AND INDIVIDUAL VALUES (1963). For skepticism directed at a sociological 'invisible hand' capable of maximally organizing social collectivities, *see* MICHAEL HECHTER, PRINCIPLES OF GROUP SOLIDARITY (1987). I have hardly scratched the surface of this literature in rational choice and exchange theory, ranging from ecology and economics to sociology and political science.

[9] KEVIN AVRUCH, CULTURE AND CONFLICT RESOLUTION (1998).

[10] Start with MARSHALL D. SAHLINS, CULTURE AND PRACTICAL REASON (1976).

[11] *See* Aaron Wildavsky, *Choosing Preference by Constructing Institutions: A Cultural Theory of Preference Formation*, 81 AMERICAN POLITICAL SCIENCE REVIEW 3 (1987) (arguing against the universality and for the cultural variability of 'preferences' [utilities]).

[12] Outside of the more formal negotiation literature the *locus classicus* of this argument is Fisher and Ury's GETTING TO YES, *supra* note 2 (*but see* the book's second edition, 1991). Although I have critiqued this book from a cultural perspective in the past, it is mildly distressing to see 'win-win' turned so decisively into a cliché. I have been in the field long enough to remember first encountering the phrase 'win-win' as a genuine and thought-provoking insight. Now one can hear it used routinely by Pentagon spokespersons, or on unwary consumers in the finance departments of Ford dealerships all over the country.

[13] John W. Burton has been the most forceful advocate of such a theory; *see, e.g.*, JOHN W. BURTON, CONFLICT: RESOLUTION AND PREVENTION (1990).

[14] Wallace Warfield, *Public Policy Conflict Resolution: The Nexus Between Culture and Process, in* CONFLICT RESOLUTION THEORY AND PRACTICE (Dennis Sandole & Hugo van der Merwe eds., 1993).

[15] Values are connected closely to matters of ideology and identity, and therefore values-based conflicts to ideological and identity conflicts. However, to keep the discussion that follows relatively simple I will focus on values only, and leave the nature of their connection to the latter two unspecified.

[16] *See* INTRACTABLE CONFLICTS AND THEIR TRANSFORMATION (Louis Kriesberg, et al., eds., 1989) (especially chapters by John Agnew, Susan Hunter, and Terrell Northrup).

[17] LEIGH L. THOMPSON, THE MIND AND HEART OF THE NEGOTIATOR 43 (2d ed. 2001).

[18] Granted, though I suspect that another reason for this assertion, regarding trust in general, if not disclosing one's BATNA, has to do with the presumption (particularly in simulation or experimentalist settings) that buyer-seller negotiations are one-off, 'cash-and-carry,' non-repetitive encounters. If one assumes a continuing relationship, even in strictly surplus-maximizing, cost-benefit encounters, then perhaps the notion of trust looms larger—it becomes another utility? The one-off nature of the buyer-seller heuristic is of course not a necessary element, but a commonly assumed one. More broadly, Thompson is forgetting that even the most coldly rational or economistic negotiation between buyer and seller depends upon the existence of some shared norms, for example a consensual legal framework that valorizes contracts. In this sense one might assume there is a basic level of trust in 'the system' if not in the (other) individual. Finally, markets in other cultures may well parse trust in different ways; *See* Geertz, *supra* note 3.

[19] DEAN PRUITT & SUNG HEE KIM, SOCIAL CONFLICT: ESCALATION, STALEMATE, AND SETTLEMENT 199-200 (3d ed. 2004).

[20] *See* WILLIAM URY, ET AL., GETTING DISPUTES RESOLVED: DESIGNING SYSTEMS TO CUT THE COSTS OF CONFLICT (1988).

[21] Other features of this social setting may include notions of gender equality (for heterosexual couples), egalitarianism, the absence of an official state-sponsored religion or at least the effective legal separation of 'church' and state.

[22] Among my (American) colleagues who read and responded critically to this essay, it was the colleague who is most committed to his faith and cultural/ethnic identity who was the most unhappy with the *two-religions* scenario as a basis for much of anything.

[23] *Supra* note 2.

[24] Wallace Warfield, personal e-mail communication (June 30, 2004) (on file with author).

∝ 11 ∞

Game Theory Behaves

David F. Sally & Gregory Todd Jones

Editors' Note: *Almost everybody who has taken a basic course in negotiation in the last 20 years has encountered basic game theory, at least to the extent of the widely used "prisoner's dilemma" games. But game theoreticians have been hard at work, and have come up with some disturbing findings that go way beyond the simple strategic calculations in the prisoner's dilemma game and its equivalents. Sally and Jones analyze what has been discovered, and what it means for negotiators who need to think at least one step ahead of their counterpart and one step beyond their own biases. And if you're a real negotiator, you're tough enough not to be scared off by a mere equation or two.*

Half a century ago, bargaining was central to the maturation of game theory, a field that uses mathematical theories and laboratory experiments to study strategic interaction. John Nash developed his beautiful bargaining solution by making "certain idealizations" about negotiations, namely, "that the two individuals are highly rational, that each can accurately compare his desires for various things, that they are equal in bargaining skill, and that each has full knowledge of the tastes and preferences of the other."[1] Nash translated these idealizations into simple mathematics. First, accurate comparison of desires allows each bargainer's preferences to be represented by a utility function, u_1 or u_2, respectively. Second, each bargainer has a threat point, the outcome if no deal occurs—in current negotiation parlance, the best alternative to a negotiated agreement, $BATNA_1$ and $BATNA_2$. The solution to the negotiation is the contract that maximizes the following multiplicative quantity: $(u_1 - BATNA_1) \cdot (u_2 - BATNA_2)$.

More important, Nash demonstrated that his idealizations could produce a solution in not just the bargaining game but all other games as well.[2] The Nash equilibrium is a pair of strategies in a two-player game that are the best possible responses to each other. For example, there is one Nash equilibrium in the matching pennies game. Two players have a penny and must decide which face to show. One player wins if the same face (head or tail) is shown; the other wins if there is a mismatch. The stable pair of strategies consists of each player flipping his or her coin so that the presented face is chosen randomly.

Of course, Nash understood how important his idealized assumptions were to his proof. With respect to whether his model matched the reality of the bargaining game, he wrote, "The usual haggling process is based on imperfect information, the hagglers trying to propagandize each other into misconceptions of the utilities involved. Our assumption of complete information makes such an attempt meaningless."[3] A greater part of the history of game theory over the last half century involves the analysis of whether hagglers, or just perfect players, will arrive at Nash's solution. It happened that many players in laboratories or real markets chose the strategic equivalent of "tails" when Nash's solution predicted "heads." Such mismatching has led to the rise of behavioral game theory, which assumes haggling and other player imperfections are meaningful.

The purpose of this essay is to review several of the new matches between theory and reality that behavioral game theory has been responsible for in the last decade, especially those concurrences that have relevance to those who teach, study and practice the bargaining game. One historical mismatch that we assume most readers are familiar with occurred in the testing of the prisoners' dilemma.[4] This game has served as an exemplar of the tension between cooperation and competition, between self-interest and joint maximization. Since this game and, to a lesser extent, the ultimatum game have been widely discussed and employed in the negotiation literature, we will focus on games that are not as widely known and on newly identified motives for cooperative or fair behavior.

New Games, New Motives

Strategic Sophistication

One of the primary pieces of advice offered to negotiators is to prepare, prepare, prepare, just like the Boy Scouts, only more. The negotiator is told to consider not only her own interests and issues, but also those of her opponent. Yet, there is a basic question that is almost never addressed: should I prepare for a prepared opponent or an unprepared opponent? This question and its more complicated variants (prepare for a prepared opponent who knows I am preparing?) involve the issue of strategic sophistication. A high degree of strategic sophistication was inherent in Nash's idealizations: his equilibrium arises from two very rational players who choose strategies that are reciprocally best responses to each other. However, if one player is boundedly rational and not really thinking things through, the other's best response to this naïvete might be quite different from the Nash equilibrium strategy.

A clever new guessing game that can diagnose strategic sophistication was introduced in 1995.[5] The standard numerical guessing game involves a group of players trying to come closest to a target integer between zero and one hundred that someone has picked. This someone might be, for example, a third grade teacher deciding which student gets to take the class bunny home and care for it over vacation week. Here, in Nagel's version, the target number is generated by the players themselves—it is some positive fraction, greater than zero and less than one, of the average of all of their guesses. The person closest to this shared mean wins a prize. Players need to anticipate where the average guess will be and then adjust downward, a cognitive process that depends on making some assumptions about the other players, their understandings of the game and the numbers they are likely to advance.

As a numerical example, suppose there are ten players whose guesses are equally spaced between 0 and 90, i.e., 0, 10, 20, 30, etc. Suppose, also, that the target is ½ of the mean. Then, the average guess is 45, the target is 22½, and the person who guessed 20 would win. Note that the person who guessed 90 is not even close. If you held everybody else's guesses fixed, then she would much prefer to change her guess to 19.[6] Now, the person guessing 80 would like to slash her guess, and so on. It turns out that the only Nash equilibria consist of each player guessing 1 or each guessing 0.

Because of the structure of the game, a player's guess reveals how sophisticated she believes the other players are. Assume, for the moment, that all the players except for one are not even bothering to think through the game. We can call them zero-step players because they refuse to enter into the strategic domain, foregoing any consideration of what might be the best move. If our tenth player was strategic, she would choose the best response to her naïve co-participants. This one-step player would select 24,[7] and would win the game if her prediction about the other players comes true. A two-step player would make a best response to opponents who are all one-step players—a guess of 11.[8] Three-step players would assume that all others are two-step and would choose the corresponding strategy. The process continues and converges on Nash's idealized players who are infinitely sophisticated and choose 0 or 1. Note that this progression makes the number line diagnostic, as only zero-step players will make guesses significantly greater than 25, one-step players will be around 25, two-step players will cluster around 11, etc.

Experimental tests have revealed how far real players are from Nash's archetypes: the strong majority of participants are either one-step or two-step players.[9] The remainder are more likely to be zero-step than three-step or more. Other games and experimental technologies have confirmed this finding of modest strategic sophistication.[10] The best place to be in these games, all else being equal, is close to the two-step players, adjusting upward if the game is complicated and more zero-step players are anticipated, or downward if more two-step players are forecasted. In the example game above, that position might be a guess of 13 or 14.

These behavioral game theory results provide a foundation for training in negotiation. Many bargainers are one-step strategists, worried only about their own interests and outcomes and incurious about those of the other side. Much of the knowledge imparted in the classroom is designed to make students be two-step strategists. The prescriptive rule is that you want to be one degree more strategically sophisticated than your counterparts, for it can be just as costly to over-think a negotiation as to under-think it (5 is as bad a guess in the example game as 25 is). "Plan, plan, plan" may be too much; "plan plus one," i.e., go one step further than your opponent, may be just right. In addition, there is a good chance that your counterpart is a one-step player, and therefore, you will need to directly educate him or her about your interests and issues. The counterpart's reticence and lack of inquiry may be due to ineptitude rather than strategy.

Learning

As one might imagine, if these guessing games are repeated with the same players, all the guesses drop pretty quickly to the Nash equilibria.[11] Players are effective and quick learners in this type of game, but there are others in which the players never quite figure things out. Learning, both the speed and process of knowledge acquisition and its strategic implementation, has been a very active topic in game theory. Theories and experiments investigate whether players use history to alter their assumption about other players and then optimally respond to these changed expectations, or use it simply to mimic strategies that won in earlier rounds.[12] Note that the first approach, "fictitious play," takes more cognitive effort than the second, "reinforcement." A hybrid model that allowed for both learning approaches depending on the characteristics of the individual and the game was able to explain the evolution of strategic choices by many players in a wide range of repeated games.[13]

This hybrid model was predictive in part because it allowed sophisticated players both to learn and to anticipate that others were learning as well.[14] Consider the guessing game for a last time, and suppose the target (½ of the mean) for the first round turned out to be 13. Pure reinforcement learners might choose 13, naïve fictitious play learners would choose 6 or 7, but more sophisticated learners would anticipate the learning of the other players and adjust their strategy accordingly. Camerer writes, "[A]s players gain experience with the game, the degree of sophistication rises—they learn that others (like themselves) are learning."[15]

Negotiation scholars, because of their familiarity with the prisoners' dilemma, are well versed in the effects of repetition on creating value and encouraging cooperation. They are less attuned to the learning that takes place across repetitions. Simply put, experienced negotiators themselves and the learning processes they employ have been ignored. [Peppet & Moffitt, *How to Learn*] On the experimental side, the reason for this is due to the pools of the usual subjects—students enrolled in a negotiation class, and those from the larger campus. The former are rarely, if ever, confronted with the same negotiation from an earlier week, and the latter are generally quite inexperienced negotiators.

Negotiation should follow the lead of game theory and place learning near the top of its research agenda. The relationship between learning and complexity and the relative importance of reinforcement and fictitious play lead to many fascinating questions that could be studied more rigorously and are quite relevant for the practice of negotiations:

- If a negotiator has success with a particular tactic, how likely is she to use that tactic in the next negotiation? Conversely, if a counterpart has succeeded with a tactic, under what conditions are you likely to trot out the same tactic, or, go one step deeper and introduce a counter-tactic?
- What is the most effective way to teach key principles such as interest-based bargaining? Is there a path or process that is clearly to be preferred?
- Does the Nash bargaining solution appear more frequently when negotiations are recurring? Does this kind of convergence cut the costs of bargaining?
- How much is experience worth? What is the relative cost in the short run and the return on the investment in the long run of sending a neophyte negotiator to the bargaining table?

Social Preferences

A basic principle of negotiation, one that is learned through both reinforcement and the negative effects of its absence, is trust. The trust game was developed in the last ten years and has been employed as another tool to examine the factors of cooperation, reciprocity, fairness, and generosity that the prisoners' dilemma and ultimatum games have traditionally illuminated.[16] The trust game is a two-person bargaining game that is played as follows: player P is given a certain amount of money, say, $10. P may give some portion of the endowment to the other player, the receiver, R. Every dollar that P sends to R is doubled or tripled. R, then, makes another allocation decision—how much of the newly augmented pot will be remanded to P. (This basic game is varied by constraining the options for the amounts offered to R and back to P). As is true in its companion games, the trust game rarely results in the uncooperative, untrusting Nash equilibrium of no money being sent in either direction. Rather, positive amounts are usually sent and reciprocated, with the mean and median being around half of the total.[17]

The unmistakable implication of these results to behavioral economists has been that individuals are endowed with social preferences, not with the atomistic, self-concerned preferences traditionally assumed in economics.[18] "Full knowledge of the tastes and preferences of the other" reveals that the other places some weight on the utility of the self (and vice versa). Nash's bargaining solution is transformed: $(u_1 + \lambda_{12}u_2 - \text{BATNA}_1) \cdot (u_2 + \lambda_{21}u_1 - \text{BATNA}_2)$, with λ_{ij} representing the weight player i places on player j's utility. Although such weights are an idea with deep roots in economics going back to Adam Smith and Alfred Marshall, it is only recently that formal other-concern has moved from the margins to a central object of study.[19]

Behavioral game theorists have rediscovered the importance and malleability of intentions. A willingness to trust the other party and the evaluation of an offer as fair depend critically on our perception of the other's intentions.[20] In the trust game, for example, if player P publicly forgoes a lucrative option, such as a free agent contract with another employer, receiver R is much more likely to be generous than if P had no choice.[21] The reason, of course, is that R credits P with good intentions in the first case but not in the second. In general, the utility weight, λ_{ij}, is negative if player j has bad intentions and deserves to be punished, but it is positive if player j is credited with good intentions and deserves to be rewarded.

The perception of intentions, like all perceptions, is ultimately subjective. It is influenced by the personality of the perceiver, the particulars of the social interaction, and the norms and rules of the greater society. One measure of personality is social values orientation, which is disclosed through a series of outcome choices involving various payoffs for self and other.[22] Those who are identified as "prosocial" in this test tend to be more cooperative in a variety of games and are more productive in integrative negotiations.[23] More importantly, if the players are physically or psychologically close, prosocial behavior is much more likely.[24] The chance to make eye contact, co-presence in a room, shared opinions and attitudes, similarity of appearance and tastes, positive mood and affection all make trust more likely and reliably boost the utility weight of working with the other side (λ_{ij}).[25]

One study of the trust game allowed participants to meet each other and identify commonalities before choosing, and these participants sent significantly larger offers than did the anonymous, distant subjects of other experiments.[26] [Bhappu & Barsness, *E-mail*] Finally, the norms of society serve as a basis for the perception of intentions and the appropriate ways to react to benign or malign intent. For example, a trust game played across segments of Israeli society discovered that all segments were equally unlikely to trust a receiver whose family emigrated from Africa or Asia (Sephardic Jews).[27] Despite the fact that these Israelis remitted as large a proportion as did those whose families originated in America or Europe (Ashkenazi Jews), they were entrusted with, on average, only half of the amount that the "Western" Israelis were, and far more "Easterners" than "Westerners" were given nothing at all. The most parsimonious explanation is that the norm or cultural bias in Israel considers "Easterners," wrongly, to be unreliable and ungenerous.

That economists have finally recognized social preferences may be greeted by negotiation researchers with a chorus of "it's about time" and "so what?" Nevertheless, this belated "discovery" does present some challenges and opportunities, if only to respond to economists' innate desire to model and measure as much as they can. Clearly, the process of negotiation may alter social preferences and raise or lower the utility weight (λ_{ij}): the questions are, how much? how often? at what cost? For example, schmoozing can be thought of as the exchange of trivial personal information with the goal to find salient and public similarities that, in turn, will foster trust, e.g., "you were in Des Moines last week? Oh, my cousin's best friend's mother is from there." How much value is there in schmoozing, physical co-presence, familiarity, and other factors that narrow social distance?

Because we actively, and sometimes unconsciously, participate in the preservation of our perceptions and preferences, situations of great conflict and social distance are especially troublesome. We perceive our enemies to be evil, distant, strange, unapproachable, unfamiliar, distasteful, and unknowable.[28] Moreover, we actively resist any evidence to the contrary. Hence, productive negotiations must take a great deal of time, and the process will necessarily have to decrease social distance slowly and imperceptibly.

Finally, there is renewed emphasis on the active management and manipulation of intentions. The following tactics are examples: letting the other side know that a valuable option was foresworn in order to bargain, demonstrating good faith by sharing information early on, apologizing [Brown & Robbennolt, *Apology*] for any wrongs perceived as intentional or excusing them as inadvertent errors, and watching your wallet when someone is overaggressive about narrowing social distance.

The Value of Information

Also inherent in Nash's idealizations was complete, or perfect, information about the taste and preferences of the bargainer on the other side of the table. As noted earlier, Nash acknowledged that the "usual haggling process"[29] was mired in imperfect information, producing an informational asymmetry that has been the focus of a great deal of experimental game theory.[30] The mismatch between the perfect predictions of formal models and the imperfectness of actual bargaining interactions has produced a prescription that recommends identification and clarification of relevant party interests (i.e., $u_2 + \lambda_{21}u_1$) and improved estimates of other parties' alternatives to a negotiated agreement (i.e., $BATNA_2$). To the extent that a party falls short of Nash's perfect ideal, one would think that they would surely place value on the means to improve their knowledge (even if they decide to apply it in an unsophisticated way as discussed above).

These means are varied and could include additional research effort, external consultants, or "neutral" third parties engaged to guide the negotiation process, offering reality checks where unrealistic party expectations warrant and providing a form of social lubricant to counteract the informational friction that threatens to preserve asymmetry. While there has been significant debate about the extent to which third parties should implicitly or explicitly act to address such imbalances,[31] it seems clear that if third parties were not able to shift either the utility function or the BATNA of at least one party, then they could have no effect on the outcome of the negotiation.[32]

If information is power, if parties inevitably fall short of the Nash idealization of complete information, and if a source exists than can move one closer to the ideal, then how might one put a value on this supplier of advantage? One strategy would be to consider the value of theoretically perfect information—information in fact so probative that the negotiator can proceed with certainty.[33] Knowing the precise interests of the other party, the value of their threat point, or BATNA, and consequently their reservation price, such an omniscient negotiator would be able to maximize value in the negotiation and then claim the maximum share of this value, that share that just meets the other party's reservation and prevents them from walking away from the table. While such perfect information is rarely available in practice, it turns out that this theoretical benchmark, known as the expected value of perfect information,[34] is fairly straightforward to compute.

Again, however, real parties fall short of even this patched up version of Nash's beautiful bargaining solution. Under experimental conditions, not only do parties suffer the consequences of imperfect information, but they demonstrate a robust tendency to undervalue opportunities to improve (e.g., by participating in a third-party-guided process).[35] Indeed, even when uncertainty regarding information sources is incorporated into the model (the expected value of *im*perfect information), parties still dramatically underestimate the value of these sources.[36] And the news gets worse.

Once parties have invested in knowledge that is at least more complete, for example by buying research, hiring consultants, [Wade, *Experts*] or by engaging in a third-party process, the information provided by these sources is poorly utilized. When compared to the rational, Nash-idealization-like, benchmark for information integration, Bayes' theorem,[37] parties under experimental conditions are significantly anchored by their initial subjective expectations and are unwilling to modify these expectations, even in the face of reliable information to the contrary.[38] Third parties, research and other information sources are both undervalued and underutilized.

Conclusion

So it appears that reality is a bit more complicated than Nash's idealizations might have suggested. Here we have shown the difficulties of accounting for the strategic sophistication in the course of preparation; the challenges inherent in not only learning in repeated play, but in learning that your opponents are learning as well; the complexities of transforming Nash's bargaining solution to include social preferences as well as self-interest; and the tendency to undervalue alternative sources of information once shortfalls from the perfect ideal are recognized. At first this may seem disappointing, and the departures from idealization overwhelming. However, in our view, behavioral game theory offers good news. Many behavioral effects are being replicated in vastly different experimental settings, across gender, culture, and geographical boundaries. Robust effects offer prescriptions, and prescriptions offer tangible improvements for those that teach, study and practice the bargaining game. Game theory works best when game theory behaves.

Endnotes

[1] John Nash, *The Bargaining Problem*, 18 ECONOMETRICA 155 (1950).

[2] *See* John Nash, *Two-Person Cooperative Games*, 21 ECONOMETRICA 128 (1953).

[3] *Id.* at 138.

[4] For a review of experimental results, *see* David Sally, *Conversation and Cooperation in Social Dilemmas: A Meta-Analysis of Experiments from 1958 to 1992*, 7 RATIONALITY & SOCIETY 58 (1995).

[5] *See* Rosemarie Nagel, *Unraveling in Guessing Games: an Experimental Study*, 85 AMERICAN ECONOMIC REVIEW 313 (1995).

[6] The solution to the equation that sets one half of the new mean equal to her guess, x: 1/2 *(360+x)/10=x.

[7] Because the nine zero-step players would be choosing randomly, the expected total of their guesses is 450. The one-step player solves the following equation to determine her best guess, x: 1/2 *(450+x)/10=x.

[8] The solution to 1/2 *(216+x)/10=x.

[9] *See* Nagel, *supra*, note 5; Teck-Hua Ho, et al., *Iterated Dominance and Iterated Best Response in Experimental "p-Beauty Contests"*, 88 AMERICAN ECONOMIC REVIEW 947 (1998).

[10] *See* Miguel Costa-Gomes, et al., *Cognition and Behavior in Normal-form Games: An Experimental Study*, 69 ECONOMETRICA 1193 (2001); Trey Hedden & Jun Zhang, *What Do You Think I Think You Think? Strategic Reasoning in Matrix Games*, 85 COGNITION 1 (2002); Dale O. Stahl & Paul Wilson, *On Players' Models of Other Players: Theory and Experimental Evidence*, 10 GAMES & ECONOMIC BEHAVIOR 218 (1995).

[11] *See* Ho, et al., *supra* note 9.

[12] *See* Yin-Wong Cheung & Daniel Friedman, *Individual Learning in Normal Form Games: Some Laboratory Results*, 19 GAMES & ECONOMIC BEHAVIOR 46 (1997); Ido Erev & Alvin Roth, *Predicting How People Play Games: Reinforcement Learning in Experimental Games with Unique, Mixed-Strategy Equilibria*, 88 AMERICAN ECONOMIC REVIEW 848 (1998).

[13] *See* Colin Camerer & Teck-Hua Ho, *Experience-Weighted Attraction Learning in Normal Form Games*, 67 ECONOMETRICA 827 (1999).

[14] *See* Colin Camerer, et al., *Sophisticated Experience-Weighted Attraction Learning and Strategic Teaching in Repeated Games*, 104 JOURNAL OF ECONOMIC THEORY 137 (2002).

[15] Colin Camerer, *Behavioral Studies of Strategic Thinking in Games*, 7 TRENDS IN COGNITIVE SCIENCE 225, 227 (2003).

[16] *See* Joyce Berg, et al., *Trust, Reciprocity and Social History*, 10 GAMES & ECONOMIC BEHAVIOR 122 (1995).

[17] *Id.*; *See* Kevin McCabe, et al., *Reciprocity, Trust and Payoff Privacy in Extensive Form Bargaining*, 24 GAMES & ECONOMIC BEHAVIOR 10 (1998); Andreas Ortmann, et al., *Trust, Reciprocity and Social History: a Re-examination*, 3 EXPERIMENTAL ECONOMICS 81 (2000).

[18] *See* David Sally, *A General Theory of Sympathy, Mind-Reading, and Social Interaction with an Application to the Prisoners' Dilemma*, 39 SOCIAL SCIENCE INFORMATION 567 (2000); Gary Charness & Matthew Rabin, *Understanding Social Preferences with Simple Tests*, 117 QUARTERLY JOURNAL OF ECONOMICS 817 (2002).

[19] *See* ADAM SMITH, THEORY OF MORAL SENTIMENTS (1790); ALFRED MARSHALL, THE EARLY ECONOMIC WRITINGS OF ALFRED MARSHALL, 1867-1890, VOL. 2 (John K. Whitaker ed., 1975). *See also*, Sally, *supra* note 18, for a review of the history.

[20] *See* Sally, *supra* note 18; Matthew Rabin, *Incorporating Fairness into Game Theory and Economics*, 83 AMERICAN ECONOMIC REVIEW 1281 (1993).

[21] *See* Kevin McCabe, et al., *Positive Reciprocity and Intentions in Trust Games*, 52 JOURNAL OF ECONOMIC BEHAVIOR & ORGANIZATION 267 (2003).

[22] *See* David Messick & Charles McClintock, *Motivational Basis of Choice in Experimental Games*, 4 JOURNAL OF EXPERIMENTAL SOCIAL PSYCHOLOGY 1 (1968).

[23] *See* Carsten De Dreu, et al., *Influence of Social Motives on Integrative Negotiations: a Meta-Analytic Review and Test of Two Theories*, 78 JOURNAL OF PERSONALITY & SOCIAL PSYCHOLOGY 889 (2000).

[24] *See* Sally, *supra* note 18; Elizabeth Hoffman, et al., *Social Distance and Other-Regarding Behavior in Dictator Games*, 86 AMERICAN ECONOMIC REVIEW 653 (1996).

[25] The complete argument including connections to the literature in social and cognitive psychology is contained in Sally, *supra* note 18.

[26] *See* Edward Glaeser, et al., *Measuring Trust*, 115 Q. J. ECON. 811 (2000).

[27] *See* Chaim Fershtman & Uri Geezy, *Discrimination in a Segmented Society: An Experimental Approach*, 116 QUARTERLY JOURNAL OF ECONOMICS 351 (2001).

[28] *See* David Sally, *Into the Looking Glass: Discerning the Social Mind Through the Mindblind*, 18 ADVANCES IN GROUP PROCESSES 99 (2001).

[29] *See* Nash, *supra* note 1.

[30] *See* Camerer, *supra* note 15.

[31] A debate that will not be revisited here. For a complete coverage of concerns on both sides of the issue, *see* Gregory Jones & Douglas Yarn, *Evaluative Dispute Resolution Under Uncertainty: an Empirical Look at Bayes' Theorem and the Expected Value of Perfect Information*, 2003 JOURNAL ON DISPUTE RESOLUTION 427 (2003).

[32] Many forms of alternative dispute resolution "share the feature that a third party is involved who offers an opinion or communicates information about the dispute to the disputants"—information that should cause the parties to modify their subjective expectations regarding possible outcomes. *See* Steven Shavell, *Alternative Dispute Resolution: an Economic Analysis*, 24 JOURNAL OF LEGAL STUDIES 1 (1995); *see also*, Gregory Jones, et al., *Evaluative Dispute Resolution Under Uncertainty: Framing, Confirmatory Evidence Bias, and the Expected Value of Imperfect Information* (unpublished working paper) (on file with author).

[33] *See* Jones, *supra* note 32.

[34] For a thorough, but accessible, treatment of the mathematics, *see* ROBERT CLEMEN, MAKING HARD DECISIONS: AN INTRODUCTION TO DECISION ANALYSIS (1991).

[35] *See* Jones, *supra* note 32.

[36] *Id.*

[37] *Id.*

[38] *Id.*

Ꮃ 12 Ꮗ

Process and Stages

I. William Zartman

Editors' Note: *Every negotiation has a rhythm to it—whether lyrical, musical or mechanical. The rhythm regulates a progression which, once understood, can help you realize where you stand at any given moment. Here, Zartman outlines the process and the typical steps that negotiations must work through.*

When Egypt's President Anwar al-Sadat and Israel's Prime Minister Menachem Begin negotiated at Camp David, Sadat talked about broad principles of agreement while Begin, uninterested, was haggling over details. Thanks to the integrating efforts of the mediator, US President Jimmy Carter, they reached some sort of agreement, but their progress was greatly hampered by the fact that the two protagonists were not just demanding different things but were operating in different phases of the negotiating process, and therefore made little sense to each other.

Negotiation is a process, and its outcome can only be explained by process analysis: where you get is a function of how you get there.[1] Pioneering work by economists introduced process analysis in the early twentieth century, but, while theoretically elegant, it was hampered by two assumptions: fixed initial positions and constant concession rates.[2] Camp David, for example, cannot be understood by analyzing the parties' movement from given numbers of settlements or predetermined definitions of autonomy to a compromise figure somewhere in the middle. Present-day understanding of process is in terms of stages, which gains in realism by overcoming the two limiting assumptions at the cost of quantitative theoretical elegance.[3]

Like the earlier economic work, the notion of a staged process came from an attempt to capture the flow of labor-management negotiations. Early attempts focused on the notion of a bargaining range (often called a Zone of Possible Agreement, ZOPA), to be achieved through 3 stages: establishing the range, reconnoitering the range, and precipitating the decision crisis;[4] or the notion of problem-solving, to be achieved through a different 3-stage process: problem identification, alternate solution search, solution selection.[5] An anthropological model of information exchange and learning extends to 8 stages: searching for an arena, defining issues, limiting issues, narrowing differences, bargaining preliminaries, bargaining finalities, ritual affirmation, and executing agreement;[6] a social psychological model reduces these to 4: agenda debate, search for principles, issue definition, concession exchange and implementing details.[7] Common to these attempts to grasp the essential process of negotiation are a sequential progression, both procedurally and substantively, allowing for overlapping and even backtracking; alternating antagonistic and coordinating behavior; variable concession or conciliation rates; increasing specification of positions; and synchronization problems for the bargainers.[8]

At the core of such attempts lies a three-stage process, containing essential differences in behavior and implications for expectations. The first stage in the process is that of *diagnosis*; it is sometimes termed pre-negotiation because it takes place before the parties meet at the "green table" and so is often forgotten in the analysis of negotiation. Yet negotiators often declare that as much as 75% of their time is spent in diagnosing the situation in preparation for their formal meetings, and negotiations often collapse, drag on interminably, or leave unclaimed potential gains on the table because the parties have not prepared sufficiently ahead of time. Diagnosis requires each party to ask a number of questions, first about itself and then about the other, and to fill a number of functions. Questions include: what is the conflict/problem about? What other conflicts/problems is it like? What are the precedents for their solutions? What are the real interests (as opposed to the positions) involved? Once these questions are answered from the asking party's point of view, it needs to find out the opposing party's answers to the same questions and compare the results.[9] This part of diagnosis is generally unilateral, but it is also a time when the parties signal to each other their interests and positions, making sure that the other party understands them well.

Diagnosis also involves a number of items to be decided before actual negotiations can begin.[10] This part of diagnosis involves the sides' working together, at least tacitly. They must consider and specify the persons to be included in the negotiations as representatives of the two (or more) sides who will make a deal with each other. They must also consider and specify the issues to be covered, separating those that can be negotiated from those that can or must be left out. The parties must communicate requitement (their willingness to reciprocate concessions), which is the basis of the negotiation process, and the meaning of "fair play." They need to clarify the costs and risks involved in beginning negotiations to have an assurance that the other party is not leading them into unbearable burdens. At home, they must also assure themselves of support for engaging in negotiations, including a willingness to make a deal based on less than the whole loaf and to replace conflict (violent or political) with some form of cooperation. And they need to begin building bridges and making pre-negotiation contacts, so that the first meeting will not be such a shock as to be unproductive. Like the diagnostic questions, these functions will need to be established before real bargaining can begin, and if this is not done before the first formal meeting, it will have to occupy the first few—or more—formal sessions.

Once this basis for bi- or multilateral exchanges is begun, the parties meet a Turning Point of Seriousness, where they each have and convey to the other the sense that they can arrive at an outcome, without yet defining what it is. At this point phase 2 or *Formulation* begins, although it should be remembered that parties can always backtrack to the previous phase; in any case, they continue to check their diagnosis throughout the process.[11] Phase 2 involves a search for a Formula, defined as either a common understanding of the problems and its (type of) solution, an identification of the terms of trade, or a shared sense of justice.

The notion of Formula is crucial, because it indicates that the parties do not begin making concessions and bargaining details without having first established a principled basis of their search for a joint solution. Again, they may do this inductively, but if they do so, it will constitute a wasteful process and produce a less coherent result. They may also appear to skip the phase because the formula is already established (as in most collective bargaining where the formula is simply wages-for-productivity, or in rug buying where the formula is money-for-rug, no matter how many cups of tea are drunk). It took the parties and mediators two decades to arrive at the formula of UNSC resolution 242 of 1968, "Territory for Security," in the Arab-Israeli dispute, used subsequently as the basis for the disengagement agreements of 1973-74, the Camp David Agreement and Washington Treaty of 1978-79, and the Oslo Agreements of 1993. Of the many ways of looking at the problem/conflict, the parties need to harmonize their views of what they are solving and hence of the appropriate type of solution. They need to indicate what will be used to buy each other's agreement, since negotiations are giving something to get something. And of the many understandings of justice—equality, equity, compensation, principled (i.e. legal), procedural—they need to decide, by negotiation, which understanding will govern their exchange.[12] [Welsh, *Fairness*]

That exchange can take place in one of three ways: by concession, by compensation, or by construction. Concession means each side giving in a bit on the same item until they meet near the middle or somewhere between the two total positions; it is, by its nature, a zero-sum process. Compensation is a positive-sum process of paying for one item with another, the equivalence to be negotiated, and it follows Homans' Maxim: "The more the items at stake can be divided into goods valued more by one party than they cost to the other and goods valued more by the other party than they cost to the first, the greater the chances of a successful outcome."[13] Assistant Secretary of State Chester Crocker broke a ten-year logjam in the Namibian negotiations by obtaining the withdrawal of 50,000 Cuban troops from Angola to compensate South Africa for the withdrawal of its 50,000 troops from Namibia (and thus achieving Namibian independence); each side received 100% of its demands in exchange for 100% of the other party's demands. Construction is also positive-sum and depends on reframing the conflict/problem in new terms so that both parties can achieve a large portion of their interests without its being at the expense of the other. By reframing the border issue between Ecuador and Peru as one of development rather than competing legal claims, mediators were able to achieve an agreement in 1999 redefined in terms that benefited both sides.

But all this is still on the level of principles and parameters. The third phase takes the negotiations into *specification* of the details of the agreement—sometimes termed the lawyers' phase, but in fact also the work of the diplomats and politicians. It is at this point that negotiators can turn to a translation of the formula into detailed terms, specifying for example how much of one term of trade will buy how much of the other, or how the agreed sense of justice governs the items being discussed. The stalemate in Israeli-Syrian negotiations hangs on major disagreement on details: whereas one side wants total return of the Golan Heights in exchange for minimal relations, the other side wants partial return of the Syrian territory in exchange for total security and full recognition and relations.

An understanding of the process phases is not only a guide for appropriate negotiating behavior but also provides a basis for expectations that reduce surprises.[14] In dealing with the basic underlying Toughness Dilemma that all negotiators face ("Should I be tough and raise the chances of a favorable agreement but reduce the chance of any agreement at all, or soft and raise the chances of an agreement but lower the chances of a favorable one?"), the phases give some guidance. In diagnosis, parties are expected to act tough to get their message across, so we should not be surprised if they behave up through the first meeting with posturing and blustering. In formulation or in setting up their ZOPA, they are expected to act soft, cooperating to find a mutually satisfactory formula and, as Jean Monnet put it, "put[ting] the problem before them on the other side of the table rather than put[ting] the adversary across the table." And in specification, they are expected to act tough, making sure the details fit the formula and the formula translates into acceptable details, trying to win back on details what they have lost in the formula, and even—at a moment known as the Crest—trying to get in one last concession with the argument that the other party would not want to upset the whole agreement so nicely worked out for "just one little matter." [Wade, *Last Gap*]

The three-phase understanding process captures the essence of negotiation as it is done when it is done well, and other aspects of the process find their place in the general pattern. Of course it can be done otherwise, but at the cost of coherence and efficiency.

Endnotes

[1] Paraphrase attributed to Henry Kissinger.

[2] FRANCIS YSIDRO EDGEWORTH, MATHEMATICAL PSYCHICS (1881); FREDERIK ZEUTHEN, PROBLEM OF MONOPOLY AND ECONOMIC WARFARE (1930); *see also*, OREN YOUNG, BARGAINING: FORMAL THEORIES OF NEGOTIATION (1975).

[3] INTERNATIONAL NEGOTIATION: APPROACHES, ANALYSIS, ISSUES (Victor A. Kremenyuk ed., 2003).

[4] Ann Douglas, *The Peaceful Settlement of Industrial and Intergroup Disputes*, 1 JOURNAL OF CONFLICT RESOLUTION 69 (1957).

[5] RICHARD WALTON & ROBERT MCKERSIE, A BEHAVIORAL THEORY OF LABOR NEGOTIATIONS (1965).

[6] P.H. GULLIVER, DISPUTES AND NEGOTIATIONS: A CROSS CULTURAL PERSPECTIVE (1979).

[7] Daniel Druckman, *Social Psychology and International Negotiations: Processes and Influences, in* ADVANCES IN APPLIED SOCIAL PSYCHOLOGY 2 (Robert F. Kidd and Michael Saks eds., 1983).

[8] Daniel Druckman, *Negotiation, in* PEACEMAKING IN INTERNATIONAL CONFLICT (I. William Zartman ed., 2005).

[9] I. WILLIAM ZARTMAN & MAUREEN BERMAN, THE PRACTICAL NEGOTIATOR (1982).

[10] JANICE STEIN, GETTING TO THE TABLE (1989).

[11] ZARTMAN & BERMAN, *supra* note 9; P. TERRENCE HOPMANN, THE NEGOTIATION PROCESS AND THE RESOLUTION OF INTERNATIONAL CONFLICTS (1996).

[12] I. William Zartman, et al., *Negotiation as a Search for Justice, in* INTERNATIONAL NEGOTIATION 79 (1996).

[13] CHARLES HOMANS, SOCIAL BEHAVIOR (1961); HOWARD RAIFFA, ET AL., NEGOTIATION ANALYSIS (2002).

[14] ZARTMAN & BERMAN, *supra* note 9; PAUL PILLAR, NEGOTIATING PEACE (1983); DAVID LAX & JAMES SEBENIUS, THE MANAGER AS NEGOTIATOR (1986).

‿ 13 ‿

When *Not* to Negotiate

Gabriella Blum & Robert H. Mnookin

Editors' Note: *"I shouldn't enter into negotiations at all" is an instinctive reaction of many disputants. Mnookin and Blum provide a useful theoretical framework to demonstrate what a party should consider before making this decision. While they suggest that sometimes it can be entirely rational to refuse to negotiate, their framework shows how disputants may often make distorted assessments, exaggerating the costs and underestimating the benefits of entering into negotiations. Their theoretical contribution is nicely complemented by Lisa Bingham's highly pragmatic treatment of related issues in the chapter that follows.*

The negotiation canon largely focuses on the benefits of the process, particularly when compared to more coercive means of dispute resolution. While conflicts characteristically involve distributive dimensions, negotiation—in contrast to litigation or warfare—provides value-creating, pie-expanding opportunities. Accordingly, negotiation scholars, drawing from a variety of disciplines, have set out to identify and offer prescriptive advice to overcome various barriers to the negotiated resolution of disputes.

We certainly agree that there are a variety of potential benefits that parties can only achieve if they enter into negotiations. The most conspicuous potential benefit is a resolution of the conflict that serves the interest of both parties to better their alternatives. Moreover, even if an agreement is not reached, the parties may through negotiation reduce the total costs of resolution, learn valuable information, sharpen their understanding of their own interests as well as those of their counterpart, and even improve their relationship. At the same time, however, we feel that the literature has often ignored the possible *costs* of entering into and conducting negotiations. Indeed, the negotiation process itself is not costless and it often entails risks. This inevitably raises the question that we wish to address in this chapter: how should a party to conflict decide whether the benefits of negotiation outweigh the costs? Sometimes these potential costs outweigh the potential benefits. In such circumstances, a rational party should refuse to negotiate, and instead, pursue a unilateral alternative.

Our goal here is to offer a decision-making framework that exposes the relevant considerations, both benefits and costs, that a party should appropriately take into account in thinking whether or not to enter a negotiation process. We then wish to use the same framework to expose the risk that parties to a conflict may too often go through the calculus in a biased way and refuse to negotiate in circumstances when in fact it might well make sense. Finally, we will show how the design of institutional arrangements may affect the relative costs and benefits of a refusal to negotiate, thus influencing parties' decision about whether to negotiate.

The focus of this chapter is on the decision whether or not to enter into a negotiation in the first place, and not decisions about the scope of a negotiation (what issues are "on the table" and what other issues are "non-negotiable"), or tactics within a negotiation that involve claims that one will negotiate no further.[1] For purposes of this current work, we define negotiation as a *joint decision-making process* involving *interactive communication* in which parties *lack identical interests but attempt to reach agreement.*[2] This definition requires active communication, as well as a mixed-motive game, in which not all interests are aligned.

A Framework for Decision-Making

While negotiation involves *joint decision-making*, the decision whether to enter into negotiation or instead pursue some other alternative can be framed in terms of decision analysis, [Senger, *Risk*] in which a decision-maker *independently* assesses the expected costs and benefits of negotiation and its alternatives. As we noted above, many negotiation scholars have emphasized the potential benefits of negotiation, without due regard to its potential costs.

At the outset we wish to acknowledge that performing the cost-benefit analysis of entering into a negotiation is a challenging task for three reasons: (1) The consequences of different actions are inevitably marked by *uncertainty*: there is always some uncertainty surrounding the estimation of short and long-term costs and benefits of negotiation, as well as the potential costs and benefits of the disputant's alternatives to negotiation. Uncertainty also underlies predictions about the various parties' interests, possible negotiated outcomes, and their future implementation. (2) As both negotiation and its alternatives—whether litigation or war—occur in the context of strategic interaction, the probability of any particular outcome as well as its potential costs or benefits depends on the counterpart's actions (and reactions) no less than one's own.[3] Moreover, while the decision whether or not to negotiate is unilateral, it takes place in a context of strategic interaction. The consequences of that decision are thus not independent of the other party's strategies. (3) The decision whether to negotiate may implicate difficult value choices. Assessing benefits and costs—which involves the use of a utilitarian or consequentialist frame—may be especially difficult when issues of morality or ethics must be weighed.

Our framework poses six questions that should be addressed. Four of these draw from negotiation analysis and ask about interests, alternatives, possible negotiated outcomes and the feasibility of reliable commitments. These same considerations are equally valid in informing an individual's decision whether one should enter into a negotiation. In addition, in making this decision one must also consider the expected costs—both direct and indirect—of engaging in the negotiation process, as well as issues of legitimacy and morality with regard to each possible course of action.

Interests: What Are my Interests? What Are my Counterpart's Interests?

Analysis begins by identifying one's own interests: long-term as well as short-term, intangible as well as tangible, indirect as well as direct, etc. Interests should also be prioritized, from the very crucial ("deal-breakers") to the less important ("nice to have"). One should then proceed to perform the same identification and assessment, given the available information, of the interests of the other parties.

Negotiation theory teaches, among other things, that it is necessary to probe beneath stated demands and positions and ask, what is actually important to the other side and what do they value.

It is in light of these interests that an analyst can assess possible negotiated outcomes, as well as the benefits and costs of alternative courses of actions.

Alternatives: What Are my Alternatives to Negotiation? What Are my Counterpart's?

The second set of questions concerns alternative strategies and outcomes to negotiation. In deciding whether to negotiate, it obviously makes sense to consider one's legitimate alternatives to negotiation, and assess how well those alternatives serve one's own interests. It is also important to try and assess the counterparts' alternatives, and the potential effects of those alternatives on one's self.

One alternative might be to do nothing—walk away from the deal, ignore the conflict, etc.. Another alternative might be to engage in self-help or a unilateral action. Every bigger child who snatches a toy from a smaller one understands the potential superiority of a self-help strategy over negotiation. But it also suggests the need to consider the legitimacy of a self-help alternative, especially when it involves the use of force.

In some contexts, a party can initiate an institutional process that can coercively—and legitimately—impose an outcome. For example, when a party has a legal claim, an alternative might be to bring a lawsuit, which if successful, will require the other party to do or abstain from doing certain things.

An important point here is that when an alternative strategy is implemented, there may be a broad range of possible outcomes. It is not enough, for example, to consider the best outcome of litigation; you must consider the full range of possible outcomes, and assess the expected value of each, i.e., the value (positive or negative) of a certain outcome multiplied by the probability of that outcome occurring. If one is risk neutral, the expected value of the litigation, not the best outcome, would be the yardstick for litigation. But if one is risk averse, the "WATNA" (Worst Alternative to a Negotiated Agreement) may be more determinative.

Negotiated Outcomes: Are There Potential Negotiated Outcomes That Can Satisfy my Interests and Those of the Other Party Better Than Our Respective Alternatives?

The third question requires an assessment of possible negotiated agreements that might serve each party better than that party's alternatives. If a party has an alternative that is clearly superior in terms of its expected value to any possible negotiated agreement, it typically would not make sense to negotiate, although there may be cases in which a decision-maker would find it beneficial to negotiate, even if conscious of the low-probability of a better negotiated outcome, in order to appease constituencies or to prove that all "peaceful" methods have been exhausted prior to using coercive means.

Implementation: Could a Deal be Struck? If So, Would it be Implemented?

In thinking about possible negotiated outcomes, a party must consider not only whether a certain arrangement would be acceptable for the other side, but also whether that party itself could in fact implement the agreed arrangement: practical considerations, constituency pressures, or institutional constraints may all impede the possibility of implementing certain negotiated outcomes, rendering them irrelevant for purposes of analysis.

It would equally make no sense to initiate negotiations if one believes that a deal could never be made, or if made—implemented, due to a lack of will or of capacity on the part of the adversary. If one believes the other party would never uphold its end of the bargain and that there is no effective mechanism for enforcing the negotiated deal, there is no point in negotiating.

In some instances, it may simply be a matter of personal trust. Past behavior may be an indication of future trustworthiness or one that warrants suspicion. Thus, President Bush's refusal to negotiate with the Taliban regime after 9/11 was due, in part, to the futility of previous negotiations with the regime, following the 1998 bombings of the U.S. embassies in Dar-A-Salaam and Nairobi.

In others, there may be a real inability by the counterpart to implement a deal. In some cases, there may be problems of representation, authority and accountability of the negotiator on the other side: if the negotiator is not empowered or is otherwise ineffective in binding her senders in a deal, negotiation is futile. Representation problems may also occur where a counterpart is actually a diverse set of stakeholders, lacking agreement among them, where such an agreement is essential for the deal.

In assessing whether a negotiated deal would in fact be implemented, one must also consider that often deals must be implemented over time; important issues of sequencing may arise and incentives to defect might appear. Commercial lawyers who participate in deal-making often put a great deal of effort into creating incentives to prevent one's counterpart from defecting later. In many commercial deals, one can create legally binding contracts which provide some opportunities to subsequent third-party enforcement, if and when the counterpart proves unreliable.

In the international sphere, things may prove even more complicated, as there is often no third-party effective enforcement, and one must instead rely on a system of monitoring, deterrence, self-regulation and "soft-enforcement". Where effective mechanisms to ensure compliance are nonexistent, the assessment of future implementation of a negotiated deal becomes inevitably more difficult and at the same time more crucial.

Costs: What Are the Expected Costs, Direct and Indirect, of Negotiation?

A rational decision obviously requires a consideration of costs. Beyond the clear benefits arising from negotiating, there are also costs involved in the process. These costs are incurred by the negotiation process itself, regardless of whether a deal is ultimately made, and even if the deal, if made, may subsume some of them. For an informed decision to be made about negotiating, these costs must be weighed in advance by the decision-maker.

We have divided the type of costs into "direct" and "indirect"; this division, as well as the subcategories we enumerate within each one, is of course not clear-cut, and some of the examples we offer involve more than one type of costs.

Direct Transaction Costs

Whether one is making a deal or resolving a conflict, the process of negotiation imposes *transaction costs* on the parties, who must invest time, money, manpower, and other resources.[4] Negotiation can absorb the attention and energy of persons whose time is valuable.

In some instances, transaction costs may make negotiation an economically inefficient process. In general, this would be true for any business that performs a large volume of transactions with a large number of parties, such as restaurants, large stores, theatres, museums, etc. For example, Macy's in Herald Square, New York, receives about 30,000 visitors a day. If, on average, one of three visitors purchases one item, then there are about 10,000 transactions a day at the store. Now, imagine the store willing to negotiate the price of each purchase. The transaction costs involving the hiring and training of additional employees, the devising of complicated employment compensation schemes with incentives for "good negotiators," coupled with concerns regarding possible damages to reputation and branding, would probably outweigh any potential benefit. In fact, many of the large stores aim at cutting transaction time as much as possible, negotiation being the opposite of an effective strategy.

The transaction costs of participating in a negotiation may, in some instances, be so high as to make it altogether impossible for parties to even participate effectively in a negotiation process, even though they may have a real stake in the process. Indeed, protest by developing countries against their lack of voice in multilateral trade negotiations has led to international assistance programs directed at providing technical assistance and funding to developing countries' missions to subsequent rounds of negotiations.[5]

Beyond the immediate transaction costs, direct costs also involve the *disclosure of information*, which may be exploited by the counterpart in future actions, regardless of whether an agreement is achieved in the first instance. This is of course the counter effect of the benefit of gaining information through the negotiation process. Exposing intelligence-gathering capabilities, a company's vulnerabilities, or even personal desires may prove detrimental in future interactions with the same party.

Indirect or Spillover Costs

Apart from the direct transaction costs, there may be a variety of indirect or spillover costs. First, entering into a negotiation may affect a party's *reputation*: people's instincts may tell them that if someone is willing to settle, there must be something to the claims against them. Thus, even if a physician can settle a meritless malpractice claim for less than the expected litigation costs, she may prefer pursuing the litigation to avoid any implication that she was at any way at fault. In a similar vein, the mere willingness on the part of a defendant to negotiate a plea bargain with the District Attorney might be perceived as an admission of guilt.

Reputation is somewhat related to another type of spillover costs. Even if negotiating a resolution of this single dispute may make sense in light of the immediate cost savings, the *precedent* of a negotiated settlement here may bring a flood of similar claims later. An employer may refuse to negotiate with unlawfully striking workers if the employer believes that negotiation may only encourage future employees to go on strike. For example, in 1981 when 11,400 air traffic controllers went on strike for higher wages and better working conditions, President Ronald Reagan and the Federal Aviation Administration (FAA) refused to negotiate, fired the striking controllers, hired replacements, and barred the strikers from ever being re-employed by the FAA.[6]

In a different context, numerous countries around the globe, including the U.S., Britain, France, Italy, Germany, Israel, the Philippines, Guatemala, Peru, and Russia have a declared policy of refusing to negotiate with terrorists. This refusal, as we shall later show, is no doubt driven by additional considerations, but it is also intended to avoid providing incentives for further extortions by future terrorists.

Beyond the costs associated with the parties "at the table", there are also spill-over costs "behind the table" relating to one's *constituents* or *coalitions*.[7] The decision to enter into negotiations may have an adverse effect on those whom you will need to rally to your cause in the event negotiations fail. Constituents might believe your ineffective negotiation has been the cause of failure, or question the justifications for taking extreme measures against someone with whom an agreed deal had almost been struck.

A dramatic example with respect to constituents relates to Sir Winston Churchill's refusal to accept an invitation to begin negotiations directly with Mussolini—and indirectly with Hitler—in May of 1940. Churchill had just become Prime Minister, France had very nearly been overrun, and tens of thousands of British troops appeared to be trapped around Dunkirk. The Battle of Britain had just begun, and German bombers had launched their attack. While Churchill's refusal to negotiate reflected a number of considerations, one of which was his skepticism that Hitler would abide by any deal that might be at all acceptable to his government, a primary reason for Churchill's refusal related to his concern that the act of negotiating with the Axis would have a devastating impact on the morale of his constituents and their ability to make the sacrifices necessary if negotiations failed.[8]

Apart from one's own constituents, there can also be effects on coalitions—those whom one may need as allies if negotiations fail. A decision by one member to negotiate separately may also have a devastating effect on the viability of a previously effective coalition. Liggett's decision to negotiate with a plaintiff in a tobacco suit generated a flood of lawsuits and settlements across the country because of its destructive impact on the previously effective coalition among all the major tobacco companies, which for years had insisted on litigating to the end all tort claims.

A final cost consideration relates to the opportunities that must be foregone if one chooses to negotiate with a particular party at a particular time. In circumstances where it is impossible to negotiate simultaneously with more than one party, choosing to negotiate with one may preclude the opportunity to negotiate with another. The basic idea here relates to the straightforward economic concept of "opportunity costs". Because resources are always constrained, devoting resources to negotiation precludes using them somewhere else.

Legitimacy and Morality: What Considerations of Legitimacy and Morality Should be Taken Into Account?

In considering the benefits and costs of the decision whether to negotiate, there is no avoiding questions of legitimacy, morality and ethics. One aspect of such considerations was mentioned earlier: when thinking about alternatives to negotiation, one must consider the legitimacy of those alternatives. A bigger child may have the power to grab the toy of a younger and smaller sibling, but most parents would prefer that the child not exercise that alternative but instead ask to use the toy. A self-help alternative to negotiation may not be considered legitimate, at least without some institutional approval. Few doubted the capacity of the U.S. to bring about a regime change in Iraq, but many have questioned the legitimacy of the American resort to force in the absence of explicit U.N. Security Council authorization.

Considerations of legitimacy and morality underlie decisions to negotiate, especially in conflict situations. The mere process of negotiation with a counterpart is perceived as conferring some *recognition* and *legitimacy* on them. Providing a counterpart with "a place at the table" acknowledges their existence, actions, and (to some degree) the validity of their interests and claims. To avoid such valida-tion, countries have often refused to negotiate with rebels or insurgent groups, denying them any recognition or legitimacy. Thus, for decades, Israel refused to formally negotiate with the Palestinian Liberation Organization, Britain denied any status to the Irish Republican Army, the Spanish would not negotiate with the Basque separatist rebels, Peru would not engage in a dialogue with the Tupac Amaru, and Russia announced an absolute policy of not negotiating with the Che-chen rebels. The interest of denying recognition and legitimacy is also apparent in the interstate sphere, and largely determines the relationships between Israel and some Arab countries, between China and Taiwan, and between the European Un-ion and the Turkish Republic of Northern Cyprus.

The policy of refusing to negotiate with terrorists and insurgent groups derives not only from the fear of conferring legitimacy or recognition, but also from aver-sion to *rewarding past bad behavior*. When previous interactions have failed to satisfy the claims of a party, satisfying its claims under the pressure of violence implies that violence was indeed worthwhile. This consideration, of course, is problematic. Although most of the national liberation movements around the world have em-ployed violence in their struggle to gain independence or self-determination (among very few Gandhi-like exceptions), once violence is employed it usually entrenches political rivals, at least in the short term following violence.

Beyond these considerations, a party may refuse to negotiate with a certain counterpart for reasons of deep moral aversion. Perhaps the most renowned ex-ample of a refusal to negotiate for moral convictions is the earlier mentioned refusal by Churchill to negotiate directly or indirectly with Adolf Hitler in May of 1940. For Churchill, the refusal derived not only from the questionable effective-ness of such negotiations, or the potential effects of failed negotiations on his fellow citizens, but also from a strong moral aversion to *"doing business with the devil."* Churchill truly believed that Britain had a deep moral obligation, on behalf of itself as well as the rest of the world, to fight Nazi Germany. In relation to Brit-ish advocates of appeasement, he said: "An appeaser is one who feeds a crocodile—hoping it will eat him last."[9] More recently, Iraqi officials have ex-pressed an outright refusal to negotiate with insurgents in Iraq, arguing that "[t]hese groups have no religion and no limits."[10]

On the domestic front, the dealing-with-the-devil consideration often fuels debates over plea-bargains made between prosecutors and suspected criminals, in which sentences are mitigated in exchange for confessions and trial-avoidance. Although such bargains are intended to make the justice system more cost-efficient, opponents argue that the moral price associated with such bargains is just too high.[11]

As we have indicated earlier, adding considerations of morality, legitimacy or ethics into the calculus of whether or not to negotiate necessarily complicates the decision-making analysis, not only because such considerations are impossible to quantify and incorporate into a simple cost-benefit analysis, but also because par-ties in conflict, as we shall show, tend to exaggerate these considerations and turn them essentially into trump cards.

The Limitations of the Rational Decision-Making Framework

Our suggested framework demonstrates that it would be unwise to believe that it always makes sense to negotiate. It shows that a party must assess a variety of considerations, including the costs of negotiation, before deciding whether to ne-gotiate. In this section, we will apply our own framework, to real people, *in situations of conflict*, recognizing that real people may too frequently make biased assessments that lead them to erroneously refuse to negotiate. Especially in conflict situations, human emotions, implications for identity, as well as common cognitive biases may cloud and distort judgment. We illustrate this theme by revisiting the elements of the general framework, and demonstrating possible distortions in their application in situations of conflict.

Interests

The rational analytic model implicitly assumes that parties' interests and preferences are exogenous, fixed, and well understood. But as any experienced mediator can report, many parties to a conflict have a very difficult time articulating, much less prioritizing, their own interests. Indeed, negotiation analysts have demonstrated that parties often fall prey to the zero-sum, or fixed-pie fallacy—the assumption that a conflict is purely distributive, and that any gain by one necessarily poses a loss to the other.

To complicate things further, in particularly bitter and protracted conflicts, a party may believe that they have an important interest in punishing, harming, taking revenge, or even destroying their opponent. Recognizing that no one would ever rationally consent to their own destruction, they may conclude that negotiation makes no sense

While unattractive, we do not believe that this kind of interest is necessarily irrational. Instead, our concern is more fundamental: we believe that through the process of negotiation people's priorities and interests can sometimes change and evolve. In thinking about whether to negotiate, a party to conflict may too readily assume that their interests and priorities are fixed. They might attach exaggerated importance to some interests, and be ready to forgo the achievement of others, where a process of negotiation might have altered this. This is not to say that negotiation would always succeed, or to deny that the process itself may inflame conflict; it is only to suggest that at times, the negotiation process itself may be transformative, and that *ex ante*, people may overlook or underestimate this possibility.

However difficult it is for a party to assess their own interests, these problems are obviously compounded when assessing those of someone you define as "your enemy". Problems of negative attributions—assuming the worst about the rival's motives, interests, and wishes (often believing their main preoccupation is with harming you)—or of projections of a party's own negative feelings onto the rival, often mark the bilateral dealing in situations of deep-rooted conflict. [Coleman, et al., *Dynamical*]

ATNAs

With respect to alternatives to negotiated outcomes (ATNAs), the risk is that in deciding whether to negotiate, a party to a conflict may exaggerate the expected value of their unilateral alternatives. If litigation is the alternative, parties may systematically overestimate the probability that the judge would rule in their favor. This is because they would have spent a good deal of time thinking about their own arguments and the justness of their own cause, and may not have fully assessed the countervailing arguments, factual, legal or normative.[12] [Korobkin & Guthrie, *Heuristics*] Even where such assessment has been made, parties tend to view their own positions as more justifiable. Daniel Kahneman and Amos Tversky's research shows that parties systematically underestimate the risks of extreme adverse outcomes, and tend to be overconfident and optimistic about their ability to succeed.[13]

Potential Negotiated Outcomes

In addition to the problems associated with the zero-sum mindset, and the consequential limitations in imagining value-creating possibilities, there is a more general problem: parties to a conflict may be prone to having a very constricted and constipated view of what might be possible. Negotiation analysts often encourage a process of "brainstorming," in which parties are encouraged to think about the unthinkable and to be creative in terms of option-generation. The risk is that *ex ante*, a party to a conflict may systematically have too narrow a view of potential outcomes, not taking into account the possibility of generating new options through direct interaction with the rival.

Implementation and the Reliability of the Counterpart

Parties to a conflict are often quite distrustful of each other. The relationship is often marked by deep suspicion and one or both parties may believe that they have been betrayed by the other in the past. [Lewicki, *Trust*] The risk here is that a party may, based on their past experience, simply assume that their counterpart will betray them in the future, and underestimate the extent to which the other party would actually want to abide by a negotiated agreement in the future. Even more basically a party may underestimate the possibility that through a combination of incentives, monitoring, and potential sanctions, future behavior might be constrained.

Costs

Of the various types of costs we have outlined in our model, it can be predicted that while the direct transaction costs could normally be objectively evaluated even in times of conflict, some of the costs that we have labeled as "indirect" or "spillover" might be exaggerated. A party may tend to exaggerate the degree to which a reputation may be harmed—especially in the longer term—by entering into a negotiation with a rival as well as the degree to which a current precedent would prove constraining in the future. Parties to a conflict may also tend to overlook the fact that reputations can recover from a short-term hit, and that in the future, precedents can always be distinguished.

Similarly, a leader may be exquisitely attuned to the objections of parts of her constituents to entering into negotiation, but may underestimate the possibility that she could in fact manage or contain these behind-the-table conflicts, or rally the necessary support of the constituents if and when negotiations fail. [Wade, *Tribe*]

We are reasonably confident that the magnitude of these indirect costs is a function of the intensity of the conflict. We also believe that conflicts exacerbate a short-term perspective: a decision-maker may see these costs as immediate and salient, while the benefits of negotiating remain speculative.

Legitimacy and Morality

A core tenet of social psychology has been the "fundamental attribution error."[14] This relates to the human tendency, when evaluating the conduct of others, to exaggerate the importance of character and to underestimate the influence of context. For example, when we observe someone engaging in inappropriate behavior we tend to attribute that to the person's bad character and not take into account the contextual pressures that may have in fact influenced the behavior. Interestingly, in assessing our own behavior, there is a human tendency to have quite the opposite reaction: we tend to justify our own bad behavior on the grounds that there were special circumstances that put us under unusual pressure.

This social science finding has obvious relevance in terms of assessing legitimacy and morality in dealing with an adversary. Because of past behavior, we may tend to characterize our "enemy" as being evil, akin to the devil. This may make us extremely reluctant to confer any recognition and legitimacy on the adversary.

We have often observed a tendency by parties to a conflict to place undue emphasis on the moral dimensions of the conflict while underestimating the importance of more tangible interests. This occurs both with respect to themselves and to the other party. The rivalry will tend to be framed almost exclusively in terms of good vs. evil, truth vs. falsehood, justice vs. wrongfulness. In judging others, character may be emphasized at the expense of context. There may be a reluctance to acknowledge the degree to which material and tangible interests (as opposed to "morality" or character) are determining the behavior of both sides.

When a conflict implicates issues of identity, which is often true, for example, in ethnic disputes, there may be a greater tendency towards framing issues in moral terms. We also think that the converse is true: once a dispute is framed in moral terms, identity is often defined in opposition to "the other." Making a concession—even in the form of entering into a negotiation—may be seen not only as a moral concession, but even as a potential threat to one's identity.

We are not claiming that the tendency to accentuate issues of morality or legitimacy is necessarily wrong, irrational, or "biased," although our intuition is that often disputants have not carefully considered alternative ways of framing their conflicts or the issues at hand. Our own anecdotal experience suggests that this may well be the case. When conflicts are resolved through negotiation, parties after the fact often express regret that it took them so long to get to the bargaining table.

Our suggestion that parties to conflict may tend to underestimate the potential benefits and exaggerate the potential costs of entering into negotiations is necessarily tentative and speculative, unsupported by systematic empirical evidence. We do believe, however, that on average parties too often refuse to enter into negotiations where it would make sense. To the extent we are correct, it would suggest that in situations of conflict, parties should begin their decision-making process from a presumption—rebuttable to be sure—in favor of entering into negotiations. One possible way to make such a presumption operational would be to urge disputants to seek the advice of more dispassionate third parties who might be less subject to biased assessments.

Another possibility, discussed below, might involve the careful design of institutions to affect the assessment of the costs and benefits of negotiation. Some institutional arrangements, by raising the costs of a refusal to negotiate, may create a de-facto presumption in favor of negotiation.

Institutional Design Implications

Institutional structures can affect both the costs and benefits of negotiation. In many contexts, the existence of an institutional hierarchy may make negotiation unnecessary because one party can impose its will very effectively by fiat or command. In an army, a superior can order a subordinate to undertake some task and reasonably expect his command to be followed. Parents are often advised not to negotiate bedtime with their young children. And a teacher in school would most often impose on the students the date and time of the final exam.

Rules and procedures that are established to *inhibit* negotiations are not unique to hierarchical institutions. Thus, although customers and dealers typically haggle over the price of a new car, at least one new brand—Saturn—has made part of its marketing strategy that at their dealers, the price will be fixed and there will be no haggling. In this way, the manufacture has gone to great length to ensure that local dealers and their salespeople have no discretion with respect to price. This marketing strategy in effect precludes negotiation.

Another example comes from the academic world: Harvard University has a rule that no Harvard professor may simultaneously be on the faculty of another university. Realizing that a valued faculty member might have more leverage to negotiate such an arrangement with his or her Dean, the rule explicitly provides that neither the Dean, nor the President of the University can make an exception to the case. In fact, the only authorized body to make such an exception is the Harvard Corporation—a seven person governing board. The purpose of this rule is obviously to make the question non-negotiable, and signal to even powerful faculty that neither the Dean nor the President has the power to negotiate.

Equally interesting are situations where an institution is designed to *encourage* or even *require* negotiation as a prerequisite to some other method of dispute resolution. In the family law area, for example, several states require mediation—in which a neutral facilitates negotiation—as a condition precedent to the adjudication of child custody disputes.[15] In California, for instance, a judge would not hear a child custody dispute until after the parents have tried to work out a negotiated resolution. Similarly, in various kinds of civil disputes, federal district courts have implemented a variety of schemes to encourage early negotiated resolutions. Similarly, a number of state courts either allow or require judges to order mediation before a trial can begin.

Nongovernmental institutions have also acted to lower the costs of negotiation in commercial conflicts: the International Institute for Conflict Prevention and Resolution is an organization composed of major corporations and law firms. Its corporate members are encouraged to sign a "pledge," which commits their corporation to entering into negotiation before suit is filed, whenever it is in conflict with another CPR member.[16] The same logic operates in the international arena: the World Trade Organization's Dispute Settlement Understanding calls on member states to initiate a consultation process with a view to attempting to reach agreement over trade disputes, before asking for the establishment of a formal dispute settlement panel.[17]

Although some analysts claim that mandatory mediation is an oxymoron—how do you make a party who does not think negotiation is helpful, engage in good faith in the negotiation process?—empirical research suggests that requiring negotiation in fact leads to many settlements that might not otherwise occur. This evidence, to some degree, confirms the analysis offered in the previous section, for it indicates that some parties who would never voluntarily enter into negotiation would in fact find the process beneficial.[18]

This also means that institutional designs may make the rebuttable presumption in favor of negotiation, as we have argued for in situations of conflict, operational: by raising the costs of the refusal to negotiate, parties in conflict would have to add these costs to their calculus of whether they should abstain from negotiation, and only if willing to bear these costs, adhere to their refusal to negotiate.

Conclusion

This chapter is a preliminary foray into an important set of intellectual and practical questions relating to negotiation: how should a party rationally decide about entering into negotiation? What social, cognitive or perhaps cultural biases may make rational analysis more difficult? And by what means can institutional mechanisms influence the decision?

While much theoretical and empirical work remains to be done, we offer several preliminary conclusions:

First, it is wrong to assume that entering into negotiation is always the right thing to do. The model of rational decision-making that we lay out plainly shows that there will be cases where the costs of entering the negotiation plainly outweigh the potential benefits.

Our second conclusion is in some ways more troubling: it is that parties engaged in conflict often tend to make distorted assessments, in which the costs of entering into negotiation may be exaggerated and the potential benefits may be underestimated. This analysis indicates that the negotiation imperialists may be intuitively correct in assuming that negotiation is under-utilized, especially in conflict situations. For this reason, we recommend that individuals in conflict be aware of such biases and operate with a rebuttable presumption that favors the use of negotiation as means for the conflict's resolution.

Finally, we demonstrate how various institutional arrangements can affect the costs and benefits of the negotiation process, and consequently, the individual decision about whether to enter into the process. Institutional design could thus be used, at least in some contexts, to effect the rebuttable presumption in favor of negotiation. Viewing institutional design through the prism of its effects on the costs and benefits of negotiation may offer important insights with respect to a variety of possible policy alternatives.

Endnotes

This chapter draws on and extends earlier work, a portion of which was previously published as Robert H. Mnookin, *When Not to Negotiate: A Negotiation Imperialist Reflects on Appropriate Limits*, 74 UNIVERSITY OF COLORADO LAW REVIEW 1077 (2003).

[1] Refusals to negotiate can often simply be a tactic that is used as part of the negotiation process. *See id.* at 1081-82.
[2] The term "negotiation" is hardly self-defining. Negotiation scholars have defined "negotiation" in a variety of ways. *See id.* at 1079-80 for a discussion of the definitional issues.
[3] Parties typically have access to different information. Predicting another party's reaction is especially difficult in the context of informational asymmetries.
[4] ROBERT H. MNOOKIN, ET AL., BEYOND WINNING: NEGOTIATING TO CREATE VALUE IN DEALS AND DISPUTES 104-05 (2000).
[5] *See* Global Trade Negotiations Home Page—Development Summary, *at* http://www.cid.harvard.edu/cidtrade/issues/development.html (last visited Dec. 20, 2005).
[6] *See Postal Service Said to Beckon to Ex-Air Controllers*, N.Y. TIMES, Aug. 20, 1982, at A17.
[7] MNOOKIN, ET AL., *supra* note 4 at 303-06.
[8] *See generally* JOHN LUKACS, FIVE DAYS IN LONDON: MAY 1940 (1999).
[9] Tom Kuntz, *Aftermath*, N.Y. TIMES, Sept. 23, 2001, §4 at 3.
[10] AMER OAULI, *IRAQ'S UNIVERSITIES FACE CATASTROPHE*, MIDDLE EAST ONLINE (Sept. 16, 2004), *at* http://www.middle-east-online.com/english/culture/?id=11281.
[11] In some cultures, this may take the form of denial that such negotiations take place at all, despite vanishingly small trial rates. *See* Alexander Hawkins, Chris Stern Hyman and Christopher Honeyman, *Negotiating Access*, Chapter 16 in this volume.
[12] *See* Daniel Kahneman & Amos Tversky, *Conflict Resolution: A Cognitive Perspective*, 45, 46 *in* BARRIERS TO CONFLICT RESOLUTION (Kenneth Arrow, et al., eds., 1995).
[13] *Id.* at 46-50.
[14] Lee Ross, *The Intuitive Psychologist and His Shortcomings: Distortions in the Attribution Process*, *in* ADVANCES IN EXPERIMENTAL SOCIAL PSYCHOLOGY (Leonard Bekowitz ed., 1977).
[15] California is one example. *See* ELEANOR E. MACCOBY & ROBERT H. MNOOKIN, DIVIDING THE CHILD: SOCIAL AND LEGAL DILEMMAS OF CUSTODY (1994).
[16] *See International Institute for Conflict Prevention & Resolution*, The Pledge, *at* http://www.cpradr.org/CMSdisp.asp?page=CPRPledgeIntro&M=11.1 (visitedMar.14, 2006).
[17] Article 4 of the Understanding on Rules and Procedures Governing the Settlement of Disputes, Annex 2 to Marrakesh Agreement Establishing the World Trade Organization, Apr. 15, 1994, *in* WORLD TRADE ORGANIZATION, THE LEGAL TEXTS: THE RESULTS OF THE URUGUAY ROUND OF MULTILATERAL TRADE NEGOTIATIONS 357-58 (1999).
[18] *See e.g.*, Craig A. McEwen & Thomas W. Milburn, *Explaining a Paradox of Mediation*, 9 NEGOTIATION JOURNAL 23 (1993).

❧ 14 ❧

Avoiding Negotiating: Strategy and Practice

Lisa Blomgren Bingham

Editors' Note: *Should you even negotiate over this issue? With this party? Now? Bingham presents a pragmatic overview of when negotiation might logically be avoided, and when, particularly in multiparty or dispute systems design, you might need to think strategically about unintended "chilling." This essay is closely linked to Blum's & Mnookin's on the principles of "not negotiating" and to Morash's, whose discussion of "nonevents" is one form of the systemic chilling that Bingham discusses here.*

Sometimes, people don't want to negotiate. Sometimes, people don't need to negotiate. And sometimes, it is just plain smarter not to negotiate. This chapter reviews some of the circumstances that call for not approaching the negotiating table or walking away from it. Specifically, it examines strategies including avoidance of conflict, yielding to the other (giving up or giving in), and deploying one's best alternative to a negotiated agreement (BATNA) or walking away. In addition, it examines how dispute system and multi-party group designs may deter negotiation, by causing parties not to participate in a group process or creating a chilling or a narcotic effect that suppresses negotiation.

Not Negotiating—At Least For Now and On This

The focus of this chapter is a long-term absence from negotiation, not a temporary one. There are many circumstances in which a brief hiatus, or not negotiating for a short period of time, can actually advance the negotiation process over the long haul. Examples include delaying coming to the table to investigate facts and prepare for negotiation, not coming to the table until you have all the right people (those with authority and who can make a settlement happen or can sabotage it), taking a break from the negotiation if things escalate and you are tempted to make a precipitous decision, or having a cooling off period to allow tempers to calm and minds to clear. It may make sense to have a period of rescission after an agreement, particularly in circumstances of power imbalance at the table, so that if people have second thoughts, they can call it off. All of these periods of not negotiating are necessary and customary stages of the larger negotiation process. The focus here is rather on not negotiating at all or bringing negotiations to a close without an agreement.

Avoidance

Avoidance is not participating in negotiation. How many of us have decided not to pursue a claim to redress some wrong or chosen not to stand up for ourselves in the face of another's assertiveness? Naming and blaming come before claiming; even people who have identified both a perceived injury and the person responsible for it may nevertheless knowingly choose to do nothing.[1]

Scholars have created several taxonomies to categorize people's basic responses to conflict. The dual concerns model[2] suggests that people will respond with inaction or avoid conflict when they have little concern about either their own outcomes or whether the other side gets what they want. "Inaction is often synonymous with withdrawal or passivity; the party prefers to retreat, be silent, or do nothing."[3] This approach is appropriate when the issue is trivial, the dysfunctional effect of confronting the other outweighs any gain, or cooling off is desirable.[4] It is certainly advisable if you are not prepared to negotiate or if you stand to lose more than you may gain. However, it is unwise when the issue is important, you have responsibility to decide a dispute, people want a decision, or time is of the essence.

For example, one form of avoidance is exit from the workplace. There is substantial research on exit, voice, and loyalty: the dynamic in which an employee decides whether to file a grievance and attempt to resolve a dispute within the workplace, or simply to leave. Victims of sexual harassment often find it more desirable to leave the workplace rather than confront the harasser. While many would say this approach is not appropriate because the issue is important not only for the victim, but for others, the victim may feel intimidated and be unwilling to pay the emotional price of confrontation. Victims of discrimination on the basis of race, sex, sexual orientation, or other protected categories may chose not to pursue a claim for fear that this will hinder their ability to obtain a new job; they do not want to be labeled as a "trouble-maker." Again, the dysfunctional effect of confrontation on employability may outweigh the gain at that workplace. In contrast, avoidance is a wholly inappropriate strategy for the managers who are supposed to be supervising both victims and alleged wrong-doers; they have a responsibility not only to address the particular case, but to ensure that there is no recurrence or pattern of harassment or discrimination. Failure to do so may result in liability in the next case. This dynamic is present in many workplace disputes involving individual employees.

The dynamic is somewhat different in the context of collective bargaining. The union may raise issues on behalf of all similarly situated employees, and indeed, may have a responsibility to do so because it has a duty of fair representation to all employees in the unit. It cannot exit, nor does it want to. However, it may choose to avoid conflict when it feels that it has bigger fish to fry. Specifically, some issues or grievances may be so trivial that the union feels it will lose credibility with management if it chooses to pursue them—even if the union feels that the grievance is justified. For example, many contracts require consultation of various kinds before management takes action. Management may fail to consult, or fail to consult early enough. Management may blow deadlines in the grievance procedure. Rather than pursue a grievance over these technical failures, the union may avoid this conflict in favor of more substantive issues.

Yielding

Yielding is giving in quickly during negotiation. You don't negotiate; you just give up. People may have process and relationship goals that are more important than prevailing in negotiation on the immediate substantive issue. In the dual concerns model, they have low concern for their own outcomes but high concern for the outcomes of the other.[5] In such circumstances, they may fold, yield, or oblige.

Yielding may be as effective as the blade of grass that bends and survives. Yielding may be as destructive as appeasing the aggressor to avoid war. This strategy makes sense if you may be wrong, if you are in a weak position, if you want something in the future, and if you want to preserve the relationship.[6] However, it may be a mistake if you believe you are right, the issue is important, and the other is unethical.

The classic dysfunctional example of yielding is the emotionally or physically abusive interpersonal relationship involving spouses or partners. Typically, such relationships begin with efforts by the abuser to control the other partner on matters involving the shared environment, such as ways to organize the home or schedule. If the other yields, then the abuser controls access to the outside environment by asserting that the other ought not to socialize with or see certain people and ought not to go out. There is an effort to isolate the victim socially. Initially, the other again may yield in the interest of preserving the relationship. Motivations for yielding may change as the abuser escalates to threats. The victim of abuse may feel that they are in a weak position. For example, women in situations involving domestic violence may be economically dependent; they may have concerns about their ability to support children. They may be trying to shield the children from becoming the object of violence.

Yielding can also be constructive. The willingness to admit you were wrong, to apologize, and take responsibility for the wrongdoing may greatly enhance your credibility in the future. For example, supervisors who admit they were wrong to employees may build significant loyalty. A service provider who yields on a claim regarding the quality of service may preserve a client relationship and generate repeat business. Yielding may turn into logrolling, in which negotiating partners trade agreements on minor issues to build momentum in negotiation.

In labor relations, yielding reflects an interest in picking and choosing your battles. Yielding may build goodwill or simply preserve resources for more significant disputes. The union or management may prefer to yield on a grievance rather than pay the costs of arbitrating it. This may build credibility in the long term by signaling that if the party is pursuing the dispute to arbitration, they must feel strongly that they are right. In contrast, some lawyers counsel essentially a scorched-earth response to all claims; litigate them to the bitter end to deter anyone from filing in the first place. Some non-union employers adopt this approach to individual employee claims.

Walking Away

You may just need to walk away from the negotiating table and stop the communication process that is negotiation. The other side may drive you to it, as for example when the other negotiator engages in unethical or hard bargaining tactics,[7] or will only claim but not help create value.[8] Hard bargaining tactics may include public commitments, locking in a position, stonewalling, personal slurs, reneging on earlier concessions, and taking extreme positions. The other party may engage in unethical conduct by lying or providing misleading or incomplete information. In between, there are hard bargaining tactics that are marginally ethical, such as using emotional manipulation by faking anger, fear, elation, or other emotions, attacking your reputation with peers, getting information by bribery or spying, and bluffing.[9] The other side may engage in criminal conduct such as fraud or try to get others to engage in it. The other party may be untrustworthy to implement a deal.

In these circumstances, it may make more sense simply to 'deploy your BATNA' and walk away. The BATNA is a source of power [Korobkin, *Power*] and leverage in any negotiation, and a key concept. It is not static, but can evolve if you take steps to explore other alternatives and develop your choices. The other side may hear information about your BATNA as a threat. Ury suggests this as a last resort and only after a period of reality testing with the other side, in which the negotiator agrees where possible, explains the reasons for negotiating, engages in a discussion about principled bargaining in lieu of whatever tactic is in use, tries to make agreement desirable to the other party, and identifies clearly what will happen when negotiations end.[10]

Walking away may also happen after a period of good faith negotiation if a party hits their reservation price. The reservation price differs from a mere resistance point. Although authors differ in their use of these terms,[11] the reservation price is that point in the settlement range below which it is more desirable or economically rational to resort to the BATNA. A resistance point occurs at an earlier stage in discussions; it is not typically a walk-away event, but rather a temporary halt in the progress of negotiation based on behavioral, emotional, or value-driven factors such as a need for recognition. The classic example is when venting and apology are necessary before meaningful progress.

Walking away is not simply taking a break or invoking a cooling off period; it is a permanent, not a temporary, cessation in talks. There is also a difference between a bluff and true willingness to walk away. The former is risky; the latter is important leverage. By definition, when both parties stop negotiating after a period of engaging in the process, they are at impasse. Walking away is different from yielding. In yielding, there is a quick agreement to the other's position. In walking away, there is no agreement. Walking away is also different from avoidance. In avoidance, there is never any negotiation. In walking away, there is negotiation that ends without an agreement.

For example, a contested divorce is a form of walking away from the long-term negotiation that is marriage. Litigation or grievance arbitration of an employment claim is a way to deploy your BATNA rather than negotiate terms. In a business negotiation, you may walk away because you realize you can get a better deal with a different supplier. You may start negotiating with a local car dealer, only to break off discussions when you find what you want on the Web.

Walking away from the table may have positive long-term effects on your negotiating relationship by establishing credibility; the other side learns it should not assume you are bluffing. For example, consider a public sector labor negotiation in which both parties have a long-term bargaining relationship and the same BATNA, i.e. last best offer issue-by-issue binding interest arbitration. This is a process in which, for each disputed issue in the contract, the parties make a final offer, and an arbitrator is empowered to select one party's offer on that issue. The arbitrator can build a package by letting each party win on some of the issues. The challenge for negotiators is to predict a reasonable package and try to make a reasonable offer on each issue, while anticipating that they will need to lose on some. It is a strategy game like playing bridge (lose your losers first) or chess (sacrifice the pawn to save the rook).

In labor negotiation, one party may be obdurate on an important issue, creating an impasse. For example, in a poor school district, teachers want a raise the school board can't afford. There are two elements to this issue: the amount of the raise and how the money is distributed among junior and senior teachers. Typically, senior teachers dominate on negotiating committees. The board makes a reasonable offer and distributes the salary the way the union wants by rewarding senior teachers over junior ones. The board's interest is in raising starting salaries to be more competitive hiring new teachers. However, the board is willing to distribute the raise the way the union wants as a compromise for agreement on a contract. The union rejects the offer. At impasse in interest arbitration, the board submits the same amount of money it offered at the table, but distributes it the way it wants, raising salaries more for junior teachers than senior ones. The board wins; as a result, the union may be more receptive to compromise the next time they negotiate a new contract. The board has deployed its BATNA in a way that may have positive long-term effects on the negotiating relationship.

Multi-Party Negotiations—When You Don't Negotiate, But The Rest of Them Do

Often, a problem involves many people or organizations, such as environmental conflict with multiple stakeholders. The negotiation process then presents special concerns about how to get people to the table and keep them there, and engaged in a productive discussion. Failure to manage a group process effectively may end up disenfranchising the minority voices, causing them never to reach the table or to walk away from it and a possible integrative consensus.[12] When a group is formed, it is important for them to understand the consequences of failure[13] and the various alternatives or BATNAs available to each of the various members.[14] If you choose not to or are not permitted to participate, can they achieve their goals without you? Who are the spoilers who can block a deal or sabotage it?

In a well-designed multiparty process with a professional mediator or facilitator, the first step is the conflict assessment, in which the third party neutral attempts to identify the people who need to be at the table. One method for doing this is essentially snowball sampling; you ask each party who else should be at the table until you keep getting all the same names. Nevertheless, it is possible to miss a relevant stakeholder. Sometimes, the omitted stakeholder is discovered before a settlement is reached, and joins the process late. This presents problems of resistance to whatever progress has been made in their absence.

If stakeholders are entirely cut out of the process, they are essentially forced to deploy their BATNA when they learn of a settlement in which they did not participate. This generally entails political action in the form of organized protests to the elected officials responsible for implementing the settlement, followed by litigation challenging it if protests are unsuccessful. Moreover, the resulting agreement may have flaws, because the absent voices have critical information. For example, one negotiated rulemaking process over the transportation of honeybees from Florida to the blueberry farms of the north ran into trouble, because the convenor failed to invite both highbush and lowbush blueberry growers to the table, and their concerns were not the same.

Stakeholders may actively refuse to participate if they feel they have nothing to gain from an agreement. For example, the City of New Bedford, Massachusetts most literally faced a downstream environmental dispute arising from significant contamination of its harbor by polychlorinated biphenyls (PCBs), produced by factories upstream along the Acushnet River over a period of 30 years.[15] An original EPA disposal plan called for dredging the harbor and incinerating the contaminated material at a location near the city. Citizen groups and environmentalists protested, and the conflict threatened to erupt. The Massachusetts Office of Dispute Resolution convened a 25-member representative stakeholder group and provided mediation services. During the four-year mediation process, citizens learned about other technologies to address the contamination, identified promising alternatives, built trust, and learned to work together. However, one group of citizens refused to participate in this process—specifically, those living next to the proposed disposal site. As the other parties approached consensus, the non-participants' concerns and political action doomed the plan for on-site treatment. The non-participants eventually prevailed and achieved an alternative off-site landfill plan.

Group members may not walk away, but quietly give in or yield by ceasing to participate actively in the discussion.[16] Circumstances that lead to this failure to negotiate include a sense that one's voice is neither useful nor valued because there are experts, others making compelling arguments, pressure from others to conform, or weak group leadership. This is essentially a kind of group process fatigue. Activist groups have criticized consensus-building processes for this reason. They argue that participation in these processes strains their resources and results in a kind of cooptation that dilutes their political voice. Essentially, they stop negotiating effectively by participating in a prolonged group process.

However, choosing not to participate in a group negotiation poses significant risks. The others will negotiate without you; they likely will reach agreement. The words of the agreement are shaped by the voices at the table. If your BATNA is weak or if you are not in a position to block or veto the multiparty agreement, it is likely your interests will not be adequately addressed. If you fail to participate, you may be stuck with their deal. For example, in Superfund cases in which parties are jointly and severally liable for the cleanup, one group of potentially responsible parties may cut a deal for their share, and you may be left holding the bag for the remainder. A group may negotiate agreement on consultants and scientific information related to an environmental dispute. If you are not there, you may be stuck with their evidence. As a general matter, it is probably wiser to be at the table than to boycott it. You can always walk away later if your BATNA is strong.

The Chilling and Narcotic Effects

Sometimes a dispute system design creates a disincentive to negotiate. In other words, given the rules of the game, parties decide they are better off either not coming to the table at all or stonewalling once there. Parties may decide not to come to the negotiating table either in designs that require them to signal weakness or lose face in order to participate, or that create new deadlines that alter the natural progress of negotiation in a case, or in voluntary designs that have the appearance of bias. Once at the table, parties may stonewall in designs that penalize them for flexibility by using intransigence to anchor the range of an award, or, in designs that allow the parties to duck responsibility for a politically undesirable result, may simply not negotiate in good faith.

For example, the accepted wisdom in litigation is that there are four common points of settlement in the life of a case: immediately before a complaint is filed, immediately after a complaint is filed, after the conclusion of discovery, and on the eve of trial. In one court-annexed arbitration system in New Jersey, researchers found that the existence of a fixed date for the arbitration hearing, for example six months after the date of filing the complaint, had a chilling effect on the willingness of counsel to engage in bilateral settlement negotiations.[17] The lawyers delayed negotiating in favor of waiting for the pressure created by the arbitration deadline. One explanation is that the date altered the common points of settlement, moving up the eve of trial point, but making it so close to the point of filing and discovery that it was easier simply to wait than settle. The overall effect was to slow down, rather than speed up, progress on the court's docket.

Another example has to do with willingness to mediate, a form of assisted negotiation. Some designs rely on the parties to request mediation. The parties, however, may be unwilling to signal weakness or willingness to settle by making the request. These models produce lower participation rates. In contrast, an 'opt out' design, in which all cases are referred to mediation automatically unless the parties affirmatively opt out, allows them to save face and come to the negotiating table. Some studies in the federal court system have found that opt out models have participation rates almost as high as mandatory mediation designs.

Dispute system designs can chill negotiation by appearing biased. For example, if an employer designs a mediation program in which it selects, trains, pays, and appoints the mediators to cases, this may raise suspicion about the independence of the mediators. In the United States Postal Service, the vast majority of discrimination complaints involve issues that do not constitute provable, prohibited discrimination. If mediators were permitted to evaluate cases on the merits, in the great majority of cases they would explain that there was no chance for recovering damages; this would exacerbate the appearance of bias. By law, federal employee participation in mediation is voluntary. It is likely that an evaluative mediation system design would deter participation and hence chill negotiation. For this reason, the USPS chose a model of mediation that does not permit evaluation, specifically, transformative mediation.[18] It has a voluntary participation rate of over 75%.[19]

Early research on public sector labor relations examined whether the availability of later mediation, fact-finding, and binding interest arbitration had an effect on the willingness of labor and management to engage in serious negotiations and compromise.[20] Researchers found a chilling effect, defined as a tendency not to compromise in anticipation of binding interest arbitration, perhaps because parties thought the arbitrator would split the baby and they were trying to anchor the range.[21]

There is also evidence of a narcotic effect from binding interest arbitration.[22] For example, public sector labor contracts have a direct impact on the local government tax burden. There is a political price when an elected official urges approval of a collective bargaining agreement that will require a tax increase to implement. Similarly, a union representative who urges compromise pays a political price with his or her constituency. Members may wonder whether this union is doing the best job advocating for them. This may create an incentive for negotiators to stonewall and grandstand instead of focusing on interests earlier in the negotiation. By stonewalling, negotiators can avoid the political responsibility for the compromises necessary to reach a negotiated settlement.

Third party interventions that take decision-making power away from the parties as a last resort in case of impasse may paradoxically create more impasses. Both union and management can avoid responsibility and blame for the settlement by leaving it up to the binding interest arbitration panel. Once parties become accustomed to the arbitration process, instead of providing an incentive for serious negotiation, it may provide an easy way out. Moreover, sometimes arbitrators are easy to blame in the public sector because they are outsiders and political appointees. There is no clear process for removing them. They do not have the market discipline of having to ensure the parties are willing to select them again—the repeat play of grievance arbitration in which the parties select the arbitrator mutually. At least in grievance arbitration, the parties have some responsibility for the award because they picked the arbitrator.

Those in a position to design dispute systems should think carefully about how the system will appear to potential users. As a general rule, early mediation in 'opt out' programs produces better systemic results than later, voluntary mediation. Arbitration in which parties have to bear some responsibility for a poor result is better than arbitration where they can easily blame it on an outsider. For example, some nonbinding court annexed programs penalize parties who recover less in litigation than they were awarded in earlier nonbinding arbitration; this creates an incentive to negotiate. The negotiation process is dynamic and human; people very quickly learn the rules of the game and how to game a particular system. Dispute system designers need to anticipate these behaviors.

Conclusion

Sometimes, not negotiating is the right choice. However, you may be losing a unique opportunity to identify, explore, and combine your interests with those of another in a way that creates something new and better for both of you. Do not forego or leave the negotiating table lightly. You may be leaving something of value behind.

Endnotes

[1] *See* William L. F. Felstiner, et al., *The Emergence and Transformation of Disputes: Naming, Blaming, and Claiming*, 15 LAW & SOCIOLOGY REVIEW 631 (1981).

[2] ROY J. LEWICKI, ET AL., NEGOTIATION 22 (4th ed. 2003).

[3] *Id.* at 23.

[4] *See* LEWICKI, ET AL., *supra* note 2, at 24 reproducing AFZUAL M. RAHIM, RAHIM ORGANIZATIONAL CONFLICT INVENTORY: PROFESSIONAL MANUAL (1990).

[5] LEWICKI, ET AL., *supra* note 2.

[6] *See* LEWICKI, ET AL., *supra* note 2.

[7] *See* WILLIAM URY, ET AL., GETTING PAST NO: NEGOTIATING WITH DIFFICULT PEOPLE (1991).

[8] *See* DAVID LAX & JAMES SEBENIUS, THE MANAGER AS NEGOTIATOR: BARGAINING FOR COOPERATION AND COMPETITIVE GAIN (1986).

[9] LEWICKI ET AL., *supra* note 2, at 250.

[10] *See* URY, *supra* note 7.

[11] LEWICKI, ET AL., *supra* note 2, at 75-77.

[12] *Id.* at 186.

[13] Jeanne Brett, *Negotiating Group Decisions*, 7 NEGOTIATION JOURNAL 291 (1991).

[14] LEWICKI, ET AL., *supra* note 2, at 350.

[15] State DR Office/Community Group, *Dealing With PCBs in the New Bedford, MA Harbor* (1998), *at* http://www.policyconsensus.org/casestudies/environment.html (last visited dec. 20, 2005).

[16] LEWICKI, ET AL., *supra* note 2, at 354.

[17] *See* ROBERT J. MACCOUN, *Unintended Consequences of Court Arbitration: A Cautionary Tale From New Jersey*, 14 JUSTICE SYSTEM JOURNAL 229 (1991).

[18] ROBERT A. BARUCH BUSH & JOSEPH FOLGER, THE PROMISE OF MEDIATION 228-31 (2d ed. 2004).

[19] *See* LISA B. BINGHAM, MEDIATION AT WORK: TRANSFORMING WORKPLACE CONFLICT AT THE UNITED STATES POSTAL SERVICE (2003).

[20] THOMAS A. KOCHAN, COLLECTIVE BARGAINING AND INDUSTRIAL RELATIONS 272 (1980).

[21] LEWICKI, ET AL., *supra* note 2, at 471.

[22] LEWICKI, ET AL, *supra* note 2, at 472.

∽ 15 ∾

Nonevents and Avoiding Reality

Susan K. Morash

Editors' Note: *What do you do when you think something should be discussed, but others don't seem to recognize there's an issue? This essay uses specific examples from health care to make a larger point. Health care professionals often choose not to view supposedly-minor errors and "incidents" as triggering a need for a discussion with a patient. By taking this view, of course, they set themselves up for a confrontation later, when and if the patient finds out anyway. Do similar assumptions limit discussion with your kinds of clients? What are the consequences?*

Much of the literature on negotiation, especially outside the spheres of international and race relations disputes, begins with an implicit assumption that the parties know when they are parties, and that the existence of a "negotiable event" is on the table for discussion by then, even if the merits are questioned. But there are situations where the knowledge that might give rise to the negotiation—or if there is no negotiation, perhaps, to a much more contentious dispute later—is in the possession of only the potentially "responding" party or person. How they react to this power, perhaps a very temporary power, has moral and often legal as well as practical implications. Health care practice abounds in these moments and is an excellent place to study them. This chapter will focus on health care settings, in order to permit a factually rich inquiry; but the reader is invited to assess whether she knows of similar problems and situations in her own field.

Background

"Error ... A commission or an omission with potentially negative consequences for the patient that would have been judged wrong by skilled and knowledgeable peers at the time it occurred, independent of whether there were any negative consequences." [1]

In the 1990's some highly publicized cases of serious malpractice, including a lethal overdose of chemotherapy to a prominent health reporter of a Boston newspaper, and the amputation of the wrong leg of a patient in a Florida hospital, came to the public's attention. "These, and other sentinel events, were the impetus for the Institute of Medicine [IOM] Report, To Err is Human." [2] Data from this 2000 report indicate that the rate of adverse events in a hospital ranges from 2.9% to 3.7% of hospitalizations. The report also estimated that as many as 98,000 people die every year in the U.S. because of mistakes by medical professionals in hospitals.[3] These shocking figures called for attention and immediate action concerning the problem of medical errors and adverse events occurring in our hospitals.

Talking about errors in practice is not easy for anyone, especially those who work in health care. Unfortunately, mistakes by health care workers happen with alarming frequency and are a common "shock and awe" event seen on nightly television news broadcasts and news magazine programs. These stories commonly describe extremely serious mistakes or even events that result in a patient's death, and highlight a patient's vulnerability when they are ill and under the care of medical personnel.

It is painful for anyone to admit their own error, especially to those patients who have been harmed by them. "Nevertheless, offering an apology for harming a patient should be considered to be one of the ethical responsibilities of the profession of medicine. Full and honest disclosure of errors is most consistent with the mutual respect and trust patients expect from their doctors."[4]

New Standards of Care

The IOM's report prompted calls for immediate changes in how mistakes are documented and reported to patients. In July 2001, the Joint Commission on Accreditation of Health Care Organizations (JCAHO) responded by introducing new patient safety standards, including a requirement that all unanticipated outcomes of care be disclosed (JCAHO Standard RI.1.2.2).[5] This standard clearly indicates that in addition to the documentation that an error has occurred, accredited organizations must tell patients when harm occurs to them in the course of their treatment. [6]

A 2002 survey of risk managers in a nationally representative sample of hospitals done by Lamb, et al. gave the authors some cause for optimism regarding compliance to the new JCAHO standard for the disclosure of medical errors to patients.

> the vast majority [of risk managers] reported that their hospital's practice was to disclose harm at least some of the time, although only one-third of the hospitals actually had board-approved policies in place. More than half of respondents reported that they would always disclose a death or serious injury, but when presented with actual clinical scenarios, respondents were much less likely to disclose preventable harms than to disclose non-preventable harms of comparable severity.[7]

A Call for Further Examination

The survey, done by Lamb, et al., contains findings that require further analysis. The phrase in the survey results "…their hospital's practice was to disclose harm at least *some* of the time" is significant. It seems to reveal both a lack of full compliance with the spirit of the JCAHO standard and a suggestion that subjectivity on the part of medical personnel is a big factor when determining what constitutes harm, in the context of a medical mistake.

The intent of this chapter is to review briefly the reporting and disclosure of adverse events policies that several academic medical centers have implemented secondary to the JCAHO's standards for accreditation, and through informal interviews of a modest cross-section of nurses (25), examine how nursing practice conforms to these policies. These incidents are commonly referred to in hospital policies as: *reportable incidents, medical accidents, medical errors,* or *adverse patient events*.

Several hospital policies will describe how these events are expected to be managed by staff, but the focus of this work is mainly on how nurses react to and manage these events. During the interview, two hypothetical adverse patient events were depicted, and nurses were asked to describe how they would manage the event. The nurses' reported actions in connection with these events as well as the rationale for their actions were also explored.

An additional goal of this survey was to explore the possible motives behind practices that in reality often differ from what many in the public desire, that is, full disclosure of medical errors. Between the planned objective to achieve an atmosphere of trust and a culture of openness about accidents and safety, and the actual culture that still exists in many of our hospitals today, lies some considerable distance.

This project mimics to some extent a 2003 study published in the Journal of the American Medical Association (JAMA) that examined patients' and physicians' attitudes about error disclosure.[8] In that study, physicians were given hypothetical situations involving medication errors and were then asked whether, or how the described medical errors should be disclosed to patients. In this study "[p]hysicians agreed in principle that patients should be told about any error that caused harm, and many said that such disclosure was ethically imperative".[9] However, they also identified situations in which they might not disclose an error, even if it caused harm to a patient. Reasons not to disclose included feelings that the event was too trivial to mention, belief that some patients would prefer not to be told, and worry that informing patients of the event would lead to a diminished trust in their physician.

Defining Adverse Events

The academic medical centers referred to in this project define a reportable event in similar ways but with subtle differences [see definitions below]. They all appear to be consistent with the intent of the JCAHO standard, to identify unanticipated outcomes of care

In all cases, a sentinel event is a category of medical accidents of an extreme nature (accidental death, suicide, surgery on the wrong body part, etc.). These events are strictly defined, and require immediate notification to the appropriate authorities. It is the less dramatic events, however, that are of particular interest here.

Academic Medical Center #1

Error: An event or act or commission or omission with unintended, potentially negative consequences for the patient, independent of whether there were any negative consequences. This includes:
- System error (latent error or failure) that reaches the patient
- Unintended individual error
- Events or acts with either actual or potential negative consequences
- Errors of judgment and errors of action

Academic Medical Center #2

Adverse patient event: an unexpected, unintended occurrence that results in injury to the patient or has the potential for causing injury.
Medical Error: an adverse event that is caused by unintended action or mistake and results in patient injury.

Examples of adverse events: events that require additional treatment, increased monitoring, delay in discharge, or transfer to an intensive care unit.

Academic Medical Center #3

Reportable incident: any occurrence or issue inconsistent with quality care or the routine operations of the hospital. A report should be completed whenever there is an injury *or potential injury* to a patient, visitor, or staff member. Any condition, which might be hazardous, should be reported.

This policy also further describes the importance of the inclusion of any event that may have led to patient injury, or for which evaluation may lead to improvement in care. These include:

- A patient fall
- Medication error
- Incident involving a medical device or equipment
- Adverse drug reaction
- Unintentional retention of a foreign body
- Unexpected death (including suicide) or serious injury

Management of an Adverse Event

The overall management of adverse events should include four components: treat, report, document, and disclose. The practice for the initial management of an adverse event is consistent in all the institutions in this project. All agree that the first concern is for the well being of the patient and support of their family. This includes care of the patient with immediate diagnosis, stabilization, treatment, and prevention of further injury.

The intended goals for the management of an adverse event, in addition to the ethical necessity to be honest to patient regarding their care, are to:

- Identify, report and investigate all events inconsistent with optimum care of patients or routine operations of the hospital
- Strengthen institutional efforts to improve patient safety through the identification of system vulnerability to future events
- Restore patient confidence that systems are in place to prevent future events from affecting other patients
- Maximize patient safety by reducing patient mortality and morbidity.
- Support staff that has been involved in an adverse event
- Identify "near miss" incidents caused by system inadequacies
- Meet all outside regulatory requirements related to reporting defined events to oversight agencies

The committees that wrote these policies intended them to encourage an environment that empowered staff to identify system issues and follow through with a full review and analysis.

Management of events in all the facilities in this project includes objective documentation in the medical record, avoiding speculation and blame, as well as timely notification of patients. Academic Medical Center #3 also describes the ethical obligation to inform patients about events that caused significant injuries that led to change in course of treatment or outcome of care. The policy also goes on to specify, "if the event is of a serious nature, it should be reported immediately."

Academic Medical Center #1's policy regarding disclosure states that patients or their family representatives must be fully informed of errors that reach patients under the following circumstances: (1) when there is clear or potential clinical significance; (2) when some unintended act or substance reaches the patient resulting in harm. The policy goes on to give examples of errors that need to be disclosed: "errors resulting in the need for additional treatment, increased monitoring, or transfer to an intensive care unit."

The policies of these three academic medical centers all require the completion of a safety report or an incident report to be filed, as well as objective documentation of the event in the patient's medical record. The information in the safety/incident report in these facilities is for the sole purpose of an internal evaluation of these events and is treated as a confidential and privileged process, and protected as peer-reviewed information. The data and the conclusions from these reports are not disclosed to anyone outside of the facility.

There appears to be room for interpretation by an individual practitioner in all of these cited institutions' policies. This carries with it some risk. A 2002 report by Health Care Risk Control (HRC) System warns,

> Any disclosure policy should include an explanation of exactly what is expected to be disclosed. A policy without clear and concise guidance in this regard will allow too much latitude and individual interpretation of whether the occurrence is reportable. Adverse outcomes, unanticipated outcomes, medical misadventure, medical error, and events are all terms that may vary significantly in meaning to different health care professionals.[10]

All of the hospital policies examined in this project have a goal to achieve a culture of openness regarding medical errors. However, as stated by Thomas Gallagher and his co-authors, "An important component of the response to an error is deciding whether and how to tell the patient what happened. Disclosing medical errors respects patient autonomy and truth-telling, is desired by patients, and has been endorsed by multiple ethicists and professional organizations."[11]

But, *does this actually happen*?

Perceptions and Practice: Reporting and Disclosing of Adverse Events Survey Results

Twenty-five nurses were informally surveyed about adverse events. They were given two hypothetical events and asked to comment on how they would manage these events, their understanding of the hospital's expected reporting practice, and how they believe these situations are commonly handled on their units. A discussion followed about their feeling about errors in general and the actions nurses take when adverse events occur.

Situation #1

You hear a patient call out for help. When you enter the patient's room they are on the floor. You help them to the chair and ask the patient what occurred and they state, "I just felt weak so I just slid myself down to the floor." They report no injuries. What do you do next? How would you report this incident?

All the nurses reported that they would immediately help the patient off the floor, place the patient in a secure position, assess vital signs and look for possible injuries. Their reporting methods are noted below. The action reports what the nurses would do in this event. [Note: nurses can take/select more than one action]. Their rationale describes their personal beliefs about why they feel they, or their peers take that action.

Results Situation #1 Patient Found on the Floor

ACTION	# Nurses	(Typical) Rationale
File an incident report	22	"It's the policy for slips and falls" "Our nurse manager would kill us if we didn't" "The incident report protects you if the patient later sues the hospital" "Fill one out just to be on the safe side"
Notify the physician	22	"It is expected for a nurse to call the MD in this situation" "Reporting it to the MD covers you [nurse]"
Document in the patient's medical record	6	"It's an event that happened to your patient on your shift"
No documentation in record	19	"I made out an incident report, I think that's enough"
Do nothing	3	"The patient told you that they just sat down and they state they aren't hurt" "The patient says he's OK. If I file an incident report it just leaves me open to someone looking at it and questioning my assessment of the patient for risk for a fall" "The patient isn't hurt, and I'm too busy to make out an incident report if the patient says he's OK" "The incident report tracks the event back to you". "Some patients fall all the time, if you made out an incident report every time you'd go crazy" (If patient is not injured)

In this scenario, most nurses responded appropriately and identified this as an event requiring an incident report and physician notification. However, most nurses did not identify or understand the need to document the event in the patient record. Those that "did nothing" as a response to this event described fears of retribution by hospital administration, or a lack of time as the major causes for their decision-making. The majority of the nurses felt that slips and falls are fairly common and for the most part an unavoidable event in the hospital, and that management of such an incident is straightforward.

Situation #2

At the start of the shift you check your patient's Heparin infusion.[12] *The patient is ordered for Heparin 1000 Units per hour. You note on the infusion pump that the patient is receiving 1200 Units of Heparin per hour. What are your next actions?*

Results: Situation # 2 Heparin Error

Action	# Nurses	Rationale
Notify the Physician	15	"Depends if the patient is having symptoms" "Depends on why your patient was getting Heparin. In some patients even this small discrepancy could be problematic"
File an incident report	12	"If the MD told me to" "If the MD was notified you should" "Depends on your unit culture" "It's a med error" "Only if the MD thinks it's a problem. They'll just tell you to check the blood level, and if it's OK they won't care about the difference"
Document in the patient's medical record	8	"Only the amount the patient received; not the discrepancy" "Write only objective information about the event and place no blame"
No documentation in record	17	"That would get you subpoenaed" "Never document in the record, that's what incident reports are for" "That would put yourself right out there" "Never in the record" "Only document in the chart if there is some type of medical intervention" "We were taught never to document that kind of thing in the record"
Believe the event would be disclosed to patient (By a Physician)	2	"Unless the patient received a massive overdose or was bleeding, they wouldn't be told." "Some people are lawsuit crazy and this would make them look into everything" "This might cause them to say that now they believe they are sick because of the discrepancy" "Would upset some patients to learn this" "The patients wouldn't trust us anymore"
Do nothing *(other than to correct the IV rate)*	10	"This is a very small discrepancy. I would follow the policy if it were a large overdose or if the patient was having symptoms" "Heparin has a range of being therapeutic, this small amount wouldn't probably matter" "You'd get your peer in trouble" "This happens fairly frequently. It's not a big deal. I would tell the MD if it was 5,000 units over, instead of just 200 units over"

After giving their comments to this hypothetical scenario, staff asked what the correct response should be to this error with the Heparin infusion. We discussed one of the hospital policies that stated, *"A report should be completed whenever there is an injury or potential injury to the patient, or any occurrence inconsistent with quality care"* as well as the policy to document adverse events in the patient's medical record. This sparked a lively discussion about what constitutes harm or injury to a patient, as it related to the Heparin error and medication errors in general. The nurses' responses were on a continuum from voicing the opinion that this patient was most certainly harmed, to the belief that there was no harm in this scenario. Nurses that felt that the patient was harmed were adamant that this was a medication error and should be treated as such. They stated that when the physician is notified of such an error, she would minimally want an additional blood sample to be taken from the patient to check the drug level. This action alone was considered by many of the nurses in the survey to be an additional invasive procedure, and thus a source of harm to the patient. Those that felt the patient was unharmed countered this opinion by stating that patients get blood drawn all the time. "It's part of the routine of being in a hospital."

The discussion was expanded to include the question, "What would you tell the patient if they asked why they were having an additional blood sample taken"? The group of nurses that felt this to be a minor incident stated it would be simple to explain to the patient that the MD ordered an additional sample today, and few patients would question it further. The RN's that felt an error had occurred stated that they would disclose the Heparin discrepancy themselves at this point. They would not mislead the patient in any way. The debate then shifted to include the monetary effect this could have on the patient's hospitalization (charge for the added blood work), and did this constitute, "harm"? The nurses that felt that this event was minor responded to that question by stating, "their insurance covers that, and the patient isn't directly charged." Others disagreed with this rationalization.

It is important to understand in this scenario or with other adverse events in the hospital, the practitioner must first identify the event as adverse before they move to the next step: management. In many hospital policies, these definitions are vague enough to allow for interpretation, and thus for management of the event to vary. In fact, two of the academic medical centers' policies state, *"consideration should be given to disclosing errors that reach patients and do not result in harm. The decision to disclose will depend on the circumstances of the event."* The important variable seems to be, what is considered harm to one health care professional may not be to another. The hospital policies may in some way give support to the nurses' rationalizations not to disclose in situation #2, the Heparin scenario.

Reluctance to Report and Disclose

Are nurses and physicians reporting and disclosing adverse events as required by the JCAHO and hospital policy? If they are not, what are the barriers to compliance? The first question is more complex than at first glance. As indicated earlier, the definitions and policies are somewhat ambiguous, and health care professionals may for different reasons choose to interpret the policy in a manner that they believe protects themselves, their colleagues and even the patient. In the case of a near miss (adverse outcome that almost happened), what should the patient be told? Though there "is no legal obligation to disclose negligence that didn't cause an injury, [even] risk managers disagree over what doctors should say in these situations ... and these incidents need to be decided case by case."[13]

When the IOM published its blunt assessment of the large numbers of medical errors in today's hospitals it caused the health care industry to take a closer look at both reporting practices and the inadequate information patients often received if they were the victim of a medical mistake. The results of this survey show that some errors are being reported to the safety office through incident reports. This finding coincides with statistics cited in the Boston Globe. The newspaper reports, "in the latest period measured by state researchers, stretching from July 1, 2002 through June 30, 2003 hospitals reported 757 errors that resulted in injury to patients, including 65 deaths. That compares with 574 mistakes in 2000."[14] Some believe that this increase in error reports reflects greater vigilance by medical centers in reporting their mistakes, rather than a true spike in errors.[15]

The barriers to reporting are well known. The greatest barrier to reporting and disclosing events identified in this small survey and other similar surveys of nurses and physicians is fear of litigation. Nurses and physicians fear that increased documentation and reporting will just increase the interest of lawyers in finding these errors and bringing lawsuits. All of the nurses in this survey, even those that felt that the Heparin discrepancy in the hypothetical situation was a true error and needed to be reported and disclosed, remarked on the fear nurses have of both litigation and reprisal by hospital administration if they are involved in an adverse event. When nurses in the survey commented on the "Patient Fall" scenario, those that responded that they would "no nothing" [action] spoke of fears that nursing administration would be apt to question their assessment skills regarding the patient's risk for falls, and fault them for not preventing the situation in the first place.

Many of the nurses in this survey commented on the infamous "Betsy Lehman Case" at the Dana Farber Institute in Boston and how the fallout from that case still influences nurses' attitudes on reporting errors. Despite the fact that the American Nurses Association (ANA) and the Massachusetts Nurses Association (MNA) supported the nurses involved in the fatal chemotherapy error to Ms. Lehman, citing a hospital system failure,[16] the Massachusetts Board of Nursing (BORN) leveled formal reprimands to those nurses and mandated them to participate in both retraining and re-certification. The Dana Farber Institute and the Department of Public Health (DPH) in this case did not hold the nurses accountable for the error, yet the nurses were at the mercy of the BORN for nearly five years until they rendered their decision. MNA member Judith Shindul-Rothchild, PhD, RN, CS told the Boston Globe "...the proposed new regulations [BORN's power to summarily suspend a nurse's license] present grave problems around holding individual nurses accountable for systems failures."[17] The ANA has stressed that a non-punitive culture is needed to support and enhance the reporting of adverse events to relevant oversight bodies, both to learn from these errors and to change systems to prevent future events in the future.[18] The nurses in this survey shared the opinion that at this point, they do not trust that they will be supported by hospital administration if they are involved in an adverse event. They worry about losing their jobs and fear loss of their license to practice nursing as well.

Nurses' attitudes toward disclosure are complex. Nurses do not normally disclose an adverse event to the patient. That job normally belongs to the physician responsible for the patient's care, but the nurses in the survey had strong opinions about this practice. Overwhelmingly, the nurses in this survey stated that patients should always be informed when a medical error has caused them serious harm. In the hypothetical Heparin error, even those nurses that would not have reported the error, stated that if the Heparin was overdosed by enough to cause abnormal or obvious bleeding, or underdosed by enough to cause a clot to form, all reporting and disclosure to the patient should take place. The biggest barrier to disclosure they identified, again, was fear of litigation. The second reason they identified not to disclose was the potentially negative reaction by the patient to the event. Some voiced concern that the disclosure of even a small error, or one that caused no harm, would be upsetting to many patients. Some nurses stated that many patients would not understand that the discrepancy in the Heparin amount was quite minor, and could lead them to imagine unrealistic consequences to their condition, causing undue worry. This could ultimately lead to distrust of all their caregivers. The overwhelming majority (23 out of 25 nurses in the survey) unequivocally stated that the Heparin error in Situation # 2 would "never be disclosed to a patient."

Ironically, many patients echo the nurses' attitudes in this survey concerning disclosure. In the similar survey of physicians and patients done by Gallagher, et al., "patients wanted disclosure of all harmful errors and sought information about what happened, why the error happened, how the error's consequences will be mitigated and how recurrences will be prevented."[19] In the case of near misses (errors that are discovered before they reach or harm the patient), though, patients had mixed opinions about whether they should be told. Some patients described that hearing about a near miss could potentially alert them to what errors they should look for and would reassure them that the systems in place to prevent errors were working. Other patients thought that hearing about a near miss would be upsetting.[20] In this same survey, the authors ventured an opinion that medical errors are an unfortunate and usually unavoidable part of medical practice. Despite the IOM report, and new JCAHO standards, debate about what or when to disclose continues.

Conclusion

This project raises additional questions and areas for continued discussion about reporting and disclosing adverse events. It must be mentioned that in this survey of nurses, nearly all of the participants were unaware of either the IOM's report on medical errors or the subsequent changes in JCAHO standards. Ignorance of this information appears to be a significant factor for many in their responses to the hypothetical situations in the survey.

The finding that many nurses are not comfortable reporting errors is not surprising. The more perplexing fact revealed was the high number of nurses that could deny that "harm" had occurred in the Heparin error scenario, and then rationalize their opinion whether an error had indeed occurred in this case. At what point do health care workers feel that a patient is owed details of an error? One explanation for this high number of "non-reporters" may be found early on in this chapter. The definitions and policies surrounding the reporting of adverse events appear somewhat ambiguous, and thus open to subjective interpretation to whether an "event" is deemed harmful or not. Another explanation is a desire to hide errors to avoid possible retribution.

When faced with the commission of an error and possible harm to the patient, most nurses describe becoming panicked at the possible repercussions. However, all of the nurses that participated in this small survey expressed the opinion that if there is obvious, or serious harm to a patient, all reporting and documentation must take place, and the patient informed. The major issue, again, seems to be that what is interpreted as harm by one nurse may not be interpreted as harm by another.

The information obtained in the interviews with the nurses suggests that nurses want to do the right thing. Nurses, however, overwhelmingly still feel that reporting and disclosing errors carries with it the risk of retribution by hospital administration, and probable legal consequences. Nurses need to become more comfortable with reporting, and also understand that reporting even relatively minor errors can identify systems' problems and possibly prevent future errors. They need to feel confident that the key to reducing errors is to focus on systems to improve care, not to place blame on individuals.

There are potential health care-specific remedies for most of these issues. But of greater relevance in the context of this book, none of the issues will get addressed as long as the underlying failure to disclose is considered tenable by large numbers of the professionals involved. How many other professional fields, and potential discussion/negotiation settings, could say the same?

The only honest answer is, no one knows. But most of the motives found in this survey have their counterparts in situations far removed from health care. This chapter is thus offered as a modest hint of the possible extent of the problem of unilateral, self-interested and short-sighted decision-making as to what should even be "put on the table" for discussion.

Many hospitals are working hard to create a safer, "blame-free environment." There is a beginning understanding for some in health care of the need to have frank discussions with patients about adverse events, as well an enlightenment among some in the health care field about the potential opportunity that this new environment presents to partner with patients in an honest dialogue when less than optimal care occurs during their hospitalization. Clearly, more education is needed in this area. Today, episodes of harm or potential harm are analyzed in an increasingly open fashion, both to determine how human factors or systems may have contributed to the event, and to assist the evaluation of new technologies to streamline the reporting and the analysis of the adverse event. Health care workers may not yet realize the potential benefits of disclosing these potentially "negotiable events", but they are beginning to understand the need as well as the moral urgency to be forthcoming when these events occur.

Endnotes

[1] Albert W. Wu, et al., *To Tell the Truth: Ethical and Practical Issues in Disclosing Medical Mistakes to Patients*, 12 JOURNAL OF GENERAL INTERNAL MEDICINE 770, 770-75 (1997).

[2] Natalia G. Correia, DO, *Adverse Events: Reducing the Risk of Litigation*, 69 CLEVELAND CLINIC JOURNAL OF MEDICINE 16 (2002).

[3] INSTITUTE OF MEDICINE, TO ERR IS HUMAN: BUILDING A SAFER HEALTH SYSTEM (Janet Corrigan, et al., eds. 2000).

[4] S.P. Kalantri, *Medical Errors and Ethics*, 47 INDIAN JOURNAL OF ANAESTHESIA 175 (2003).

[5] JOINT COMMISSION ON ACCREDITATION OF HEALTHCARE ORGANIZATIONS, *Patient safety and Medical/Health Care Error Reduction Standard* (hospital accreditation standard) (2001).

[6] Rae M. Lamb, et al., *Hospital Disclosure Practices: Results of a National Survey*, 22 HEALTH AFFAIRS 73, 74 (2003).

[7] *Id.* at 73.

[8] Thomas H. Gallagher, et al., *Patients' and Physicians' Attitudes Regarding the Disclosure of Medical Errors*, 289 Journal of the American Medical Association 1001 (2003).

[9] *Id.*

[10] *Disclosure of Unanticipated Outcomes*, HEALTHCARE RISK CONTROL (HRC), (ECRI, Plymouth Meeting, PA) (2002).

[11] Gallagher, et al., *supra* note 8.

[12] Heparin is an anticoagulant given intravenously to prevent potentially lethal clots from forming and migrating to sites in the body, such as the lungs or brain. The drug level is checked daily to see that the patient is receiving a therapeutic dose of the drug (too much can cause unwanted bleeding, and too little can result in blood clots). This drug is not particularly sensitive to exact dosages, compared to some other drugs—which is the reason it was chosen for this exercise.

[13] Mark Crane, *What to Say if You Made a Mistake*, 8 MEDICAL ECONOMICS 27 (2001).

[14] Stephen Smith, *Hospitals Report Increase in Errors Leading Causes: Falls and Surgical Blunders*, BOSTON GLOBE, Oct. 29, 2003, at B1.

[15] *Id.*

[16] Susan Trossman, *ANA, MNA Support Dana-Farber Nurses Facing Disciplinary Action*, NURSING WORLD (Mar./Apr. 1999).

[17] *Massachusetts Board Reprimands Dana-Farber Nurse*, THE AMERICAN NURSE, *at* http:www.nursingworld.org/tan/99sptoct/farber.htm (last visited Mar. 15, 2006).

[18] Gallagher, et al., *supra* note 8.

[19] *Id.*

[20] *Id.*

❦ 16 ❧

Negotiating Access

Alexander Hawkins, Chris Stern Hyman
& Christopher Honeyman

Editors' Note: *"How can I shake them out of their complacency?" Hawkins,*
Hyman & Honeyman use three different examples to discuss the first step of a nego-
tiation—getting the other side even to recognize that you might have something
worthwhile to add. Linked to the chapters on avoiding negotiation and "nonevents,"
this chapter addresses the problems and tactics of getting your counterpart to recog-
nize that there is a negotiation table, and that they will be better off if they meet you
around it.

Negotiating access to a situation or group is a basic problem which occurs in many
guises. To experienced negotiators and mediators, who have encountered it in
many forms, it is so *obviously* a problem that they may think the solutions are also
obvious. But the widespread failure of intelligent people to obtain access to situations in which, from an observer's point of view, their contributions could have
been helpful demonstrates that this is not so. This chapter will illustrate the problem using three brief case studies and will venture some preliminary conclusions.
Our three selected examples deliberately invoke a range of kinds of access problem: beginning with the difficulty of a researcher negotiating access to
information held by practitioners, we continue with a third-party mediator's problem of access to potential case streams, and to close the circle, an example which
involved a practitioner negotiating access to scholars.

Recognizing the existence of something is a good (if again deceptively obvious-
sounding) place to start a discussion. In particular, if the practical field of negotiation is to prosper in the long term, it is important for educational institutions to
acknowledge negotiation as a phenomenon for study. To American readers, this
may appear a trifling point; in the U.S., teaching programs in negotiation (including courses under banners such as "Alternative Dispute Resolution") are now
commonplace. Yet in the United Kingdom and elsewhere, the same cannot yet be
said.[1] A recent law undergraduate at Cambridge University, for instance, did not
even hear the word "negotiation" in a three-year law program, perhaps excepting
some obvious usages in the teaching of contract law.[2]

But even when negotiation is recognized as an area worthy of attention, actual
study may require a level of access to data that proves elusive. Plea bargaining in
the UK provides an excellent example.

Case Study #1: Researcher to Practitioners

The plea bargaining literature, like so many others, has several "streams": lawyers have their own discussions, as do sociologists, philosophers, anthropologists, and so on (with economists plowing an even more solitary furrow). Yet each of these disciplines is concerned with the same basic fact situation of negotiation and almost certainly therefore has insights to share with the next. Whilst plea bargaining is very obviously a process of negotiation, for instance, it is rarely analyzed as such.[3]

Exploring interdisciplinary perspectives, then, is likely to be one way to further and develop learning about negotiation. But there remains another significant problem, of access to understandings and data as between the academy and the profession that actually does the bargaining. One reason is that in the UK, at least, the professionals in question do not like to admit that they bargain in the first place. In fact, there is a more or less open hostility to the idea that negotiation takes place at all. The reasons seem to center on the traditional liberal-legalist picture of the law. In that frame, negotiation of a core set of "rights" is regarded as deeply subversive. Negotiation is then caricatured as a crude bartering process, and those who do not balk at putting a price on justice usually agree with Kant that to do so is conceptually impossible. Not even the best lawyers the UK has to offer possess the sleight of hand to hide the high incidence of guilty pleas; but that such pleas might be negotiated is something of a guarded secret.

How subversive the concept of "Negotiated Justice" is can perhaps best be illustrated with reference to the saga (almost folkloric among socio-legal researchers in the UK) of the Baldwin and McConville book of that name.[4] That work was the first book-length investigation into plea bargaining carried out in the UK and, as such, was bound to surprise people who still hewed to the textbook picture of the criminal process. What was not so obvious was that smears on the integrity of the researchers, along with concerted efforts to suppress publication of the book, would come from the very top of both wings of the legal profession (events documented in an article by the authors).[5] The legal establishment thus adopted a "siege mentality" toward investigation of the practice.

To this day, research on plea bargaining in the UK remains extremely thin on the ground, especially when compared to the literature of the United States. Similarly, the number of reported cases is minimal. In an organizational climate such as this, sharing of learning between the legal profession and the academy is fraught with difficulty. Data collection, for example, becomes a highly sensitive issue. In some situations, academics may even begin to question their own enterprise. In one student's first year of doctoral research, there was a potentially unnerving experience with a very senior local Crown Prosecution Service official. They were talking together at an informal gathering of lawyers, after it became clear that they were the only ones at the meeting with any substantial interest in the criminal law and its processes. The prosecutor discovered that the student was just beginning some research. And what, more precisely, was that research about?

"Plea bargaining."

At which the prosecutor looked at once puzzled, apologetic, and slightly stern:

"Well, of course, you do realize that it doesn't exist, don't you?"

In a slightly conciliatory way, the prosecutor then reassured the student that it indeed happened in America (and maybe he could investigate it there); but it just wasn't the English way. (This conversation took place more than 25 years after the Baldwin and McConville book cited above.)

The problem of access in this specific situation has not been solved, and stands as a continuing challenge to the sophistication and determination of the negotiation field. We know that criminal lawyers indeed do negotiate, but at the same time we know they do not want to be seen as a professional group to be negotiating the disposition of their cases. Yet negotiating these cases is part of their inherent promise of service to their clients.[6] Furthermore, how is the public to assess whether the manner, means and results of the unadmitted practice serve or harm its interests?

The remainder of this chapter will discuss some ways of addressing this state of affairs. First, a summary of our chosen "problem situation":

- Access is a particular problem where (for whatever reason) the existence or empirical extent of the negotiation processes which would benefit from shared learning is denied or obscured. In fact, access is doubly awkward as a result of this: in the given example, scholars and practitioners first need to be convinced to talk about negotiation among their own peers; and second, the academy and the profession need to be convinced to talk about it to each other.

- The legal profession is one whose professionals almost exclusively have academic training in the form of a university degree. This "history" provides certain opportunities for fostering dialogue between professionals and academics.

- Improving access to education about negotiation (through introducing it onto curricula, and through intra- and interdisciplinary cooperation) may well affect the nature of the profession. Conversely, attitudes of the law profession towards academia (whether positive or negative in any given jurisdiction) can affect the shape and product of academic institutions.

Case Study #2: Practitioner to Potential Clients

Incorporating relevant new participants into an existing process, even when it is conspicuously not working well, may be essential to the future vitality of that process. Yet it may be frequently sabotaged by barriers that include resistance toward the unknown, skepticism about effectiveness, and concerns about wasting time and money. Identifying some variables that determine success or failure in negotiating access to potential participants could be instructive. The following two examples—one a failure and one a success—identify a few of them. Both are drawn from health care, an environment replete with both admitted and unadmitted conflict. [Morash, *Nonevents*]

First, let's discuss a failure. Bill collection for hospitals seeking payment from self-pay patients in the United States is tricky. It typically involves hiring collection agencies that hound the former patients, usually people with limited financial resources, for payment and if necessary then sue them for breach of contract. One of the authors had served as a mediator in such lawsuits, and to her, the advantages of a negotiated settlement to both the plaintiff and the defendant were clear. The mediations created durable agreements, in contrast to court orders, where there is often a default with additional litigation then required to enforce the judgment. In one of the mediations, the collection agency's attorney attributed the durable agreements in this type of case to two factors: the defendant feels she has a stake in an agreement she helped craft, and the payment schedule is realistic.

Based on some such successes, the author and several colleagues approached a community hospital that had approximately $19 million in "delinquent patient receivables." They suggested that the hospital consider a pilot mediation project for a specified category of the receivables—$5000 and above for in-patient hospital stays of self-pay patients—and offer mediation before those cases were sent to a collection agency. The potential benefits, as they saw it, might include retention rather than alienation of a former patient, increased likelihood that the hospital would recover a portion of the money owed, and financial savings, due to lower transaction costs of mediation versus litigation. They developed the forms and the details of how the project would work and how data could be collected for evaluation. Over months of negotiation, they met with the chairman of the board of trustees and administrative officers, including the vice-president for finance and the chief financial officer, but they were ultimately unsuccessful. They attributed this defeat, at the time, to several factors: the stranglehold of the status quo; the difficulty of convincingly describing a process which may need to be experienced in order to understand its benefits fully; and the absence of empirical data to prove mediation's efficacy. But comparison to the other case studies here suggests there may be a more "granular" way to analyze the contributing factors.

Now the success story. In 2002 a colleague and one of the authors were principal investigators of the Demonstration Mediation and ADR Project ("Demonstration Project"), part of the Project on Medical Liability in Pennsylvania.[7] Just as the project began, Pennsylvania enacted a statute as part of a tort reform package that required hospital administrators to send written notice to patients, and under some circumstances their families, within seven days of a "serious event."[8] In this environment, assessing and improving communication between physicians and patients suddenly jumped to the top of hospital administrators' (and some physicians') to-do lists. In order to reduce the possibility of a lawsuit, the administrators immediately understood that a conversation disclosing the serious event must precede receipt of the written notification from the hospital. The Demonstration Project was working closely with three Pennsylvania hospitals/health care systems, and offered each three initiatives that might be helpful in responding to the new disclosure requirement and in resolving malpractice claims that had been filed against them. One initiative chosen by all three was training of physicians and other health care professionals in communication skills.

Negotiation with the hospitals centered on the amount of time for the training and which staff would attend. Of particular interest were the meetings with key administrators—the chief of medicine, the patient safety officer, the chief executive officer, and the chief operating officer—of one of the participating hospitals, a suburban community teaching hospital with approximately 500 beds. The principal investigators reviewed with them the research showing that ineffective communication between physicians and patients is the critical factor in predicting why physicians are sued.[9] It seemed obvious to the investigators that the training of physicians should be several days of interactive exercises. (Their frame of reference was the 40 hour training for mediators who are taught the same communication skills.) But the hospital's representatives told the investigators that *90 minutes* was the maximum amount of time available to train its physicians—though with the possibility of additional "advanced" training for some!

The investigators' initial (private) reaction was that 90 minute training sessions would be of limited lasting value, at best. However, in the course of talking with the hospital, they became more aware of time as a scarce commodity for health care providers, particularly physicians. Even 90 minute training sessions impinge on their intensely scheduled days; for many, adding one more such obligation would require a choice between a remunerative activity versus attending training on a topic that many did not yet appreciate as having any importance in their professional practice. For the hospital, scarcity had a different meaning. The administrators recognized that the training being offered was not only timely, in light of the written notification statutory requirement, but cost effective—because the grant funded Demonstration Project would provide it at no cost.[10] [Guthrie, *Compliance*]

Several additional factors influenced the negotiation, including this hospital's reputation for commitment to improving patient safety. From the principal investigators' perspective, training the physicians to appreciate how communicating more effectively with patients and their families was beneficial, ethical and could improve patient safety was a prerequisite for the hospital to be able to achieve its goal. The investigators were impressed by the positive reactions expressed in the meetings, and wanted to collaborate with the physicians. Ultimately they reconciled themselves to 90 minute trainings (some of which were conducted at 6:45 a.m. to accommodate physicians' schedules). They conducted three 90 minute training sessions and one four-hour "advanced" training session under the grant. (They were subsequently invited back to present at "Grand Rounds," a teaching forum held weekly in academic medical centers to review general topics and update hospital staff and attending physicians on current and emerging issues in medicine, and to conduct another 90 minute training, this time for a fee.)

Agreeing to the 90 minute training sessions caused the investigators to rethink their preconceptions of the goals of the training. Their primary adjustment was to distinguish between training that produces *mastery* of skills and training that introduces the *complexity* of skills—along with the benefits of consulting with colleagues who are experts and have mastered the skills. They realized that physicians will only experience a disclosure conversation with a patient or family as a result of a "serious event" once or twice in their professional lives, and therefore will not have occasion to maintain their skills. Appreciating the complexity of the disclosure process and the difficulty of doing it well, a physician is more likely to consult an expert on staff about planning and conducting the conversation.

The accommodation and collaboration achieved in the negotiation provided benefits for both parties that were unanticipated at the beginning of the process. The goal changed from training physicians to master the skills, to recommending that hospitals create a communication consultation service, which physicians could consult in planning a disclosure conversation.[11] The physicians, too, seem to have learned something: anecdotally, their awareness of communication skills broadened, and at least some ventured that "times have changed" and that they should pay more attention to how they speak to, and whether they listen to, their patients.

Case Study #3: Practitioner to Scholars

By now it should be evident that while the situations that require negotiating for access are extremely varied, they have one thing in common: the party seeking access, by definition, perceives the situation as one that calls for negotiation, while the other party, at least initially, does not. Often, this is an artifact of a recognized difference between the two in power or status. [Morash, *Nonevents*] That certainly was the case in our third example. In that situation, a working mediator/arbitrator from an ordinary environment sought, and obtained, access on something like equal terms to a distinguished group of academics.

Background

One of the authors of this chapter had been engaged in independent research and development ("R&D") work in conflict resolution, particularly in mediation, for about twelve years, in addition to full-time practice work as a mediator, arbitrator and in other neutral roles. The R&D work, more than the practice work, had brought him to the attention of a major foundation that had already underwritten research and theory-building in conflict resolution for a number of years. The foundation had recently commissioned an outside evaluation of the corpus of work produced to date in its conflict resolution program—an evaluation that strongly affirmed the overall value of the work, but made some criticisms. A signal area of criticism was consistent with a simultaneous report to the foundation, on a related matter, by the practitioner in question. Both reports suggested that despite an extraordinary rate of development of new ideas, there was relatively little evidence of actual adoption of those ideas in existing practice, and there was correspondingly little evidence that theory-building or research designs were generally informed by a reliable feedback loop from practical experience. The practitioner proposed to the foundation a plan to investigate the causes, and if feasible, to enact a plan of action.

Some months of relative inaction ensued, during which it became evident that program staff at the foundation were tempted by the idea of an explicit "theory to practice" R&D program but were hesitant to invite a full-scale proposal. The reasons were not clearly stated. Instead, months went by in which sporadic discussion did not produce a clear result.

The practitioner knew the program staff well enough to know that this was not a matter of personal or institutional indecisiveness. As the discussion developed over months, the reasons for hesitancy seemed rather to center on doubt over how such an initiative might be perceived by the often high-status scholars funded by the foundation. A further complication was the number of academic institutions involved that tended to perceive each other only partly as colleagues, and partly as rivals. Clearly, a delicate set of relationships had to be addressed.

The practitioner had three existing sources of potential acceptability among the scholars involved. One was a track record of writing a number of articles in one of their journals, a distinctive act for a practitioner as practice experience was underrepresented in that venue. Another was that he had worked successfully with some of the scholars involved on another project he had managed, and was therefore not a total unknown. The third was that he had engaged with the full group of scholars at one of the annual meetings convened by the group when it was, at that time, extremely unusual for a practitioner to take part. In a mutual effort to break the logjam, program staff agreed to a suggestion that the practitioner be invited to another such meeting—and that this time, he would arrive armed with an exercise to test whether his proposal could be accepted by the scholars present.

The practitioner then designed a survey that could be administered to those present in 60 seconds, which (he hoped) would reveal patterns of behavior that would demonstrate to all concerned the value of the proposed project. The survey queried the scholars' (asserted) depth, but also their sources, of knowledge of a subset of supposedly influential books in the field—works which casual auditing of scholars' conversation might convince one they had all read in depth. The practitioner suspected otherwise, having turned a mediator's ear to numerous conversations over the years that appeared syntactically constructed, consciously or unconsciously, to allow two highly educated and highly intelligent scholars to conduct an amiable conversation without either having to admit that he had not read the other's most important book and was not about to.

The responses to this survey have been previously published.[12] What is important for the present purpose is that the survey demonstrated to those present that contrary to their own self-impression in a number of cases, they were mostly not, in fact, in-depth readers of each other's most cherished material. This was a blatant challenge to the system of distribution of new findings that they had believed in. Furthermore, while the survey indicated a significant level of knowledge about the underlying material in the books selected, it also showed that the scholars had often acquired that knowledge not by "study" as generally defined, but by informal contacts, by oral presentations in meetings, and by reading terse or secondary-source summaries—all of which placed them on a footing closer to that of practitioners than they had perceived. Several of the scholars later remarked that they had felt somewhat insulted when they first saw the survey—a feeling that dissipated only when they realized what the results meant.

The practitioner also took pains to frame the contemplated project as a kind of large-scale mediation "case" between "parties" consisting of theorists, researchers and practitioners. This kept the project in a space separate from the scholars' own projects (thus also keeping it from directly vying with any of theirs for scarce funds). That, however, would probably not have been enough to put the proposal "over the top" without an act of generosity by one of the scholars. A long-time friend and colleague of the practitioner, who was present to represent a particularly high-status institution, virtually ordered the practitioner to a walk in the garden immediately after his presentation—a moment when, providentially, there was a break in the proceedings. Out of earshot of the group, the scholar, who was scheduled to speak immediately after the break, announced, "I've been watching their reaction to that, and they're going to try to duck the implications. And I'm not going to let them." Following the break, the scholar—to the visible surprise of the others—announced that since her institution's productivity was on record and since she believed the group needed to process what had just been put on the table, she would turn in three-quarters of her designated speaking time for that purpose.

This, of course, not only sent up a flag to others that the subject was being taken seriously by at least one high-level scholar, but put them on notice that she expected them in turn to confront the issues dead-on. Helpfully, the foundation program officer took the opportunity to suggest that each person in the room comment in turn—a tactic that not only left no place to hide, but flagged his own interest in taking the proposal seriously. Thus emboldened, "closet supporters" began to speak up. By the time the circuit had been completed, it was clear that a substantial majority, if not universally looking forward to what was likely to be a somewhat uncomfortable inquiry, had at least resigned themselves to the notion that something new seemed to be needed. Their reactions also generally signaled that the idea specifically on the table seemed supportable. Thus it became evident to the foundation that a key "market" for the idea in question would, at least, not oppose it. Support from the foundation—generous support—was thereafter obtained for an initial foray. (That became the beginning of a nine-year series of activities, of which this book is the culmination.)

Some Preliminary Conclusions

Our three selected case studies are all modest in scale, and they are quite different in circumstances, in setting, and in results. What, if anything, do they indicate in common?

We believe our three examples show several commonalities, suggesting (along with, of course, many other experiences not reported here) that there may be a number of quite commonsensical characteristics of negotiation over access. We will attempt here to summarize a few of the most salient:

- Such a negotiation has multiple stages. Especially if a group is involved, the approach is highly unlikely to be successful without recognition that the process has phases.

- In the first phase, an open admission by the other side that there should even be a serious discussion is improbable. What you are negotiating for, at least the first time around, is more an admission that the other party even has an issue or a problem. This is perhaps summarized as, "We admit we have a problem, which you are not obviously disqualified from helping with." In this construct, the difference between our first case study and our third is stark: in the third case, there was already a report from a distinguished scholar—not just one from the practitioner—supporting the notion that *scholars* should recognize there was a problem. In the first case study, by contrast, no statement by anyone *within* the legal system was already available to support the concept that continued denial of the existence of plea bargaining in any way harmed the interests of the legal professionals able to block such discussion.

- The low level of problem admission possible in the first phase means that a low level of commitment of time or any other resource by the other party seems appropriate. Pressing for more is likely to be counterproductive. This creates an imbalance, in which significant time and resources may have to be invested on your part in the pursuit of what is admittedly a somewhat one-sided initiative aimed at bolstering the other side's perception of a need to engage seriously with you in the first place.

- When the moment comes to engage with more than one potential "early adopter," that moment needs to be chosen and structured as carefully as possible, and it should be expected that everyone else in the room assumes that you are wasting their time, until you prove otherwise.

- Although it is not always essential to have a high-status existing supporter already among the other party, it is a great help. This too raises the ante for the would-be negotiator, as the process of developing familiarity with a potential supporter is likely to be time intensive. Perhaps another implication of this is that small-scale work is the best way to begin in a new area. Aiming high might lead one to attempt to enter into dialogue with a much more faceless entity (e.g., "the state"). Aiming low (e.g., the local prosecution office) may, in some situations, yield a greater chance of success (i.e., bottom-up, rather than top-down, influence).

- There is no good reason to expect the other party to be flexible, regardless of the possibility that their situation may be about to become untenable without the intervention you propose. If you need to negotiate for access at all, that means there are powerful reasons in play why the other party does not want to talk to you. [Bernard, *Powerlessness*] Effectiveness requires recognizing the power of those reasons, picking them apart, and designing an approach that will lead to a perhaps only modestly successful but definitely low-cost intervention (in time as well as resources) from *their* point of view. With at least a little success to show, you can then build on that for a greater commitment. This staged approach requires great flexibility on your part to rethink the nature of what is being proposed immediately, because most people who have recognized an emergent need are more inclined to try to "teach" their proposed counterparts about this need than to redesign their approaches until they come up with one that fits within a limited framework of possible acceptability from the other side's point of view. Thus, accepting that the apparently absurd proposition of a 90 minute training was actually a sizable step from the point of view of the other party opened the possibility of the health care team making at least some inroads. Beyond that, (talent assumed) there is another day possible and a little more acceptance next time.

- Risk aversion is not *always* a good orientation to this kind of work—but you have to pick your moment. The third case study suggests that a willingness to take a chance may—if you've prepared the ground well—draw an "early adopter" or two among the other party to reciprocate. Because your counterparts, with the possible exception of a few "early adopters," have good reasons from their point of view not to engage with you, it may be necessary to dramatize—at some point. But such a dramatization, which in a sense describes the 60-second survey above, is a high-wire act, prone to fail suddenly and calamitously. In particular, it is very easy to appear to exaggerate or overstate your case. So "drama" is probably most effective when you are otherwise known for a relatively low-key, logical approach—and have your ducks in a row already so that some "research basis" for the drama is apparent.

- Despite all of the preparation and strategy that the above implies, it remains important to recognize that there is an element of timing and an element of luck in this endeavor. By its nature, luck is not under the control of the actor, and under many circumstances, the timing may not be either.

Negotiating access, it turns out, is a three-level kind of negotiation. The protagonist seeks first, to develop recognition of negotiation as valuable to the other party (i.e., "How do we convince them they, not just we, have a problem?"); second, "negotiating about negotiating" (i.e., "How do we convince them to think seriously about the negotiation, instead of fobbing it off with platitudes?"); and only third, "actual" negotiating (i.e., "How do we address the underlying problem?").

But the very fact that we must be concerned with how to negotiate about negotiation shows the pervasiveness, usefulness, and reflexivity of the practice.

Endnotes

[1] This is not to say that negotiation training is non-existent for those whose university education does not include it. For example, negotiation forms part of the professional training that aspiring legal practitioners must undertake if they are to enter the profession. As such, however, it is treated as a vocational skill rather than something for critical academic scrutiny. Moreover, this training is often said by those who undertake it to be geared towards commercial transactions, to the neglect of other types of negotiations.
[2] Indeed, teaching on "law in action" in any sense was, with a couple of exceptions, almost invisible.

[3] *See, e.g.,* Rebecca Hollander-Blumoff, *Getting to "Guilty": Plea Bargaining as Negotiation,* 2 HARVARD NEGOTIATION LAW REVIEW 115 (1997).

[4] JOHN BALDWIN & MICHAEL MCCONVILLE, NEGOTIATED JUSTICE: PRESSURES TO PLEAD GUILTY (1977).

[5] John Baldwin & Michael McConville, *Plea Bargaining: Legal Carve-up and Legal Cover-up,* 5 BRITISH JOURNAL OF LAW & SOCIOLOGY 228 (1978).

[6] Although we have called them criminal lawyers rather than professional negotiators here, the job description "professional negotiator" is of course not empirically inaccurate.

[7] Carol B. Liebman & Chris Stern Hyman, *Medical Error Disclosure, Mediation Skills, and Malpractice Litigation: A Demonstration Project in Pennsylvania,* THE PROJECT ON MEDICAL LIABILITY IN PENNSYLVANIA (2005), *available at*
http://medliabilitypa.org/research/liebman0305/LiebmanReport.pdf.

[8] Medical Care Availability and Reduction of Error Act, 40 PA. STAT. ANN. §§ 1303.302-308 (WEST 2005). Subsection 308 contains the written notification requirement and subsection 302 defines "serious event" as "an event, occurrence or situation involving the clinical care of a patient in a medical facility that results in death or comprises patient safety and results in an unanticipated injury requiring the delivery of additional health care services to the patient."

[9] Wendy Levinson, et al., *Physician-Patient Communication: The Relationship with Malpractice Claims among Primary Care Physicians and Surgeons,* 277 JOURNAL OF THE AMERICAN MEDICAL ASSOCIATION 553 (1997); Gerald B. Hickson, et al., *Factors that Prompted Families to File Medical Malpractice Claims Following Perinatal Injuries,* 267 JOURNAL OF THE AMERICAN MEDICAL ASSOCIATION 1359 (1992).

[10] Robert Cialdini's sixth principle of influence "scarcity" appears applicable to both sides in different ways in this negotiation for access. ROBERT B. CIALDINI, INFLUENCE: SCIENCE AN PRACTICE 203 (4th ed. 2001).

[11] Carol B. Liebman & Chris Stern Hyman, *A Mediation Skills Model to Manage Disclosure of Errors and Adverse Events to Patients,* 23 HEALTH AFFAIRS 22 (2004).

[12] Christopher Honeyman, et al., *Here There Be Monsters: At the Edge of the Map of Conflict Resolution,* THE CONFLICT RESOLUTION PRACTITIONER (2001), *available at*
http://www.convenor.com/madison/monsters.htm.

❧ 17 ❦

Timing and Ripeness

I. William Zartman

Editors' Note: *How do you know when it's time to get serious about negotiating? When is a deal ready to be made? In the settlement of civil disputes, we often see parties expensively delaying negotiation, even waiting for mediation till they're on the proverbial courthouse steps. Is there a science to this? From the perspective of international relations, Zartman analyzes the issue of ripeness and demonstrates when it's time to settle.*

After chronicling a series of failed initiatives to mediate a peace in El Salvador, Alvaro de Soto, UN Assistant Secretary General for Political Affairs, points to the turning point of the FMLN's major November 1989 offensive, which penetrated the main cities including the capital but failed to dislodge the government.

> The silver lining was that it was, almost literally, a defining moment—the point at which it became possible to seriously envisage a negotiation. The offensive showed the FMLN that they could not spark a popular uprising,.... The offensive also showed the rightist elements in government, and elites in general, that the armed forces could not defend them, let alone crush the insurgents.... As the dust settled, the notion that the conflict could not be solved by military means, and that its persistence was causing pain that could no longer be endured, began to take shape. The offensive codified the existence of a mutually hurting stalemate. The conflict was ripe for a negotiated solution.[1]

Joe Slovo, head of the South African Communist Party, expressed a similar view, "Neither side won the war. The National Party couldn't rule any longer, and we (the African National Congress) couldn't seize power by force. So that means both sides have to compromise. That's the reality."[2]

While most studies on peaceful settlement of disputes see the substance of the proposals for a solution as the key to a successful resolution of conflict, a growing focus of attention shows that a second and equally necessary key lies in the timing of efforts for resolution.[3] Parties resolve their conflict only when they are ready to do so—that is, when alternative, unilateral means of achieving a satisfactory result are blocked and the parties feel that they are in a painful and costly predicament. At that ripe moment, they grab on to proposals that usually have been in the air for a long time and that only now appear attractive: they are pushed by the pain into seeking resolution. Labor economists have long used this situation for their theories; when the threat of a strike does not portend sufficient pain, the threat is executed and the parties then calculate their costs in lost sales against warchests until their strike costs mount higher than the costs of concessions and they begin bargaining on an equilibrium point for an agreement.[4] Sometimes this can take a long time, as the 2004-2005 hockey players' season showed. In this analysis I will use imagery drawn from international negotiations, including the prospect of violence; but the underlying principles are just as applicable in domestic and lower-stakes negotiations.

The Push Factor

The concept of a ripe moment involves two subjective elements.[5] One is the parties' perception of a Mutually Hurting Stalemate (MHS).[6] When the parties find themselves locked in a conflict from which they cannot escalate to victory and this deadlock is painful to both of them (although not necessarily in equal degree or for the same reasons), they seek an alternative policy or a bi-/multilateral way out of the pain and hence out of the conflict or problem. If the parties were not stalemated and pained, they would simply continue to live with the problem or wage the war. An MHS is often associated with an impending, past or recently avoided catastrophe that provides a deadline or a lesson that pain can be sharply increased if something is not done about it now; catastrophe is a useful, imaged extension of MHS but is not necessary either to its definition or to its existence. Using different images, the stalemate has been termed the Plateau, a flat, unending terrain without relief, and the catastrophe, the Precipice, the point where things suddenly and predictably get worse. If the notion of mutual blockage is too static to be realistic, the concept may be stated dynamically as a moment when the upper hand slips and the lower hand rises, both parties moving toward equality, with both movements portending cost for the parties.

Chester A. Crocker, US Assistant Secretary of State for Africa between 1981 and 1989, patiently mediated an agreement for the withdrawal of Cuban troops from Angola and of South African troops from Namibia, then to become independent. For years a mutual hurting stalemate, and hence productive negotiations, had eluded the parties. "The second half of 1987 was ... the moment when the situation 'ripened.'"[7] After a major offensive, South African troops and Cuban troops were unable to dislodge each other from their bases in southern Angola, white body bags were beginning to return to South Africa, and Cuba doubled its troops and threatened hot pursuit into South African territory in Namibia, but at the same time let it be known that it wanted to go home. In his conclusion, Crocker identifies specific signs of ripeness, while qualifying that "correct timing is a matter of feel and instinct."[8] The American mediation involved building diplomatic moves that paralleled the growing awareness of the parties, observed by the mediator, of the hurting stalemate in which they found themselves.

The mutually hurting stalemate is grounded in cost-benefit analysis, fully consistent with public choice notions of rationality,[9] and public choice studies of war termination and negotiation,[10] that assume that a party will pick its preferred alternative, and that a decision to change is induced by increasing pain associated with the present (conflicted) course. In game theory terms, it marks the transformation of the situation in the parties' perception from a prisoners' dilemma game (PDG) into a chicken dilemma game (CDG).[11] Or, in other terms, the realization that the status quo or no negotiation is a negative-sum situation, and that to avoid the zero-sum outcomes now considered impossible the positive-sum outcome must be explored. The idea is also related to prospect theory, which indicates that parties are more responsive to losses than to gains and will try to prevent them more readily than they will try to attain new benefits.[12] [Korobkin & Guthrie, *Heuristics*]

Ripeness is necessarily a perceptual event, but, as with any subjective perception, it is likely to be related to objective referents. These can be resisted so long as the conflicting party refuses or is otherwise able to block out their perception. But it is the perception of the objective condition, not the condition itself, that makes for a MHS. If the parties do not recognize "clear evidence" (in someone else's view) that they are in an impasse, a Mutually Hurting Stalemate has not (yet) occurred, and if they do perceive themselves to be in such a situation, no matter how flimsy the "evidence," the MHS is present.

An MHS is the necessary but not sufficient condition for initiating negotiations. It is insufficient to pull the negotiations to a successful conclusion, but it needs to continue to be felt throughout the negotiations, lest the parties reevaluate their positions and drop out, in the revived hope of being able to find a unilateral solution through escalation. The MHS is the basis of the parties' security points, the value of the outcome to be obtained in the absence of negotiations, against which the parties judge the current offers. If the hurt or the prospect of it fades during negotiations, a party will adopt a tougher position, raising its demands and losing its interest in a successful outcome. Bosnian President Alija Izetbegovic accepted the Vance-Owen Plan for his country in early 1993, under the pressure of rising violence, but then reneged when he felt that the violence was sustainable and the U.S.—opposed to Vance-Owen—would offer better terms if the Bosnians would hold out. It is therefore important that constraints or "pain" imposed by the unresolved problem continue to be present and felt, with the problem occasionally reminding the parties of its presence or the conflicting party "brandishing a little violence" or a strike threat from time to time, to keep the MHS alive. For the most part, the supply of pain is latent and contingent (as is the other side's supply of concessions, as in any negotiation, until the deal is closed), as a threat to be used if negotiations break down.[13] However, exogenous inputs such as unexpected catastrophes and new information have been seen to spark negotiations and by extension promote progress in negotiations already underway, as they heighten the sense of an MHS.[14] Chernobyl, Exxon Valdez, and fish depletion information have all been exogenous inputs that have convinced interested parties that they are stalemated before a problem and must concert to overcome it.

As in any bargaining problem, the agreement is determined by the intersection of supply and demand, so the supply of real or potential constraints and violence must be high enough to cover the demands or the demands must be lowered to correspond to the available threats and dangers. The demanders make demands, and they supply armed conflict; in the negotiations, they trade off the abstention from violence against the satisfactions of their demands. Violence is the only money of exchange that they have, and they are not going to give it up until they have bought the concessions they need. Its cessation is almost always the major demand of the government side. It is obvious therefore that ceasefires will not be granted on mere faith, but will be part of the concluding elements of the bargain, because ceasing fire means ending the MHS that brought about the negotiations. In interstate conflicts over cooperation or problem-solving, the pressure of the constraint comes from outside the parties and acts on them, even if to varying degrees, but the notion of the MHS still obtains: the parties are stalemated in their individual attempts to deal with the problem and are hurting as a result, and need to cooperate.

In Yugoslavia, Secretary of State James Baker looked for a ripe moment during his quick trip to Belgrade in June 1991 and reported the same day to President George Bush that he did not find it: "My gut feeling is that we won't produce a serious dialogue on the future of Yugoslavia until all the parties have a greater sense of urgency and danger;"[15] Richard Holbrooke called this "a crucial misreading."[16] Holbrooke had his own image of the MHS (or the upper hand slipping and the underdog rising): "The best time to hit a serve is when the ball is suspended in the air, neither rising nor falling. We felt this equilibrium had arrived, or was about to, on the battlefield [in October 1995]," and he tried to instill a perception of a ripe moment in the mind of Bosnian President Izetbegovic.[17] A State Department official stated, "Events on the ground have made it propitious to try again to get the negotiations started. The Serbs are on the run a bit. That won't last forever. So we are taking the obvious major step...."[18]

As the notion of ripeness implies, MHS can be a very fleeting opportunity, a moment to be seized lest it pass, or it can be of a long duration, waiting to be noticed and acted upon by mediators. In fact, failure to seize the moment often hastens its passing, as parties lose faith in the possibility of a negotiated solution or regain hope in the possibility of unilateral escalation; parties frequently fall back on their previous perceptions that the other side will never be ready and the only course left is to hope and fight for a total realization of one's goals, no matter how long it takes. Israel's reluctance to implement the agreed steps of the Oslo Agreement, especially after Netanyahu's election as prime minister, led many Palestinian's to think that no agreement would be honored by Israel and so total resistance was the only course open, a conclusion which then convinced many Israelis that the Palestinians would never agree to share the land of Palestine and so a military policy was the only course open. By the same token, the possibility of long duration often dulls the urgency of rapid seizure, and parties fall into an S^5 situation (a soft, stable, self-serving stalemate) with no incentive to negotiate their way out of it.

The Pull Factor

The other element necessary for a ripe moment is also perceptional: a Way Out (WO). Parties have to be able to sense that a negotiated solution is possible for the searching and that the other party shares that sense and the willingness to search too. The negotiators must provide or be provided prospects for a more attractive future to pull them out of their problem or conflict, once an MHS has pushed them into negotiations. That is the function of the Mutually Enticing Opportunity (MEO).[19] The seeds of the pull factor begin with the Way Out that the parties vaguely perceive as part of the initial ripeness, but that general sense of possibility needs to be developed and fleshed out into the vehicle for an agreement, a formula for settlement and a prospect of reconciliation that the negotiating parties design during negotiations. The negotiators' challenge is to turn the initial sense of a Way Out into a satisfying MEO.

Without the pull of a Way Out, the push associated with the MHS would leave the parties with nowhere to go; they need to devise something to impel them through their negotiations and into an agreement.[20] When an MEO is not developed in the negotiations, they remain truncated and unstable, even if they reach a conflict management agreement to suspend violence.[21] The 1994 ceasefire in Nagorno-Karabagh has never been complemented by a resolution of the area's territorial status, keeping the conflict alive and the truce unstable; the 1984 Lusaka and Nkomati agreements that South Africa negotiated to bring ceasefires to its conflicts with Angola and Mozambique suspended the fighting but provided no solution to the two conflicts, and so soon fell apart.

Like the MHS, the WO/MEO is a figment of perception, a subjective appreciation of objective elements, but unlike the MHS, it is an invention of the parties (and their mediator) internal to the negotiation process, not a result of an objective external situation. It must be produced by the parties, using their analysis of the conflict and its causes, their appreciation of their interests and needs, and their creativity in crafting a mutually attractive solution. It resolves the conflict and is perceived to contain elements that continue to carry the resolution process into the future. An MEO contains forward-looking provisions to deal with the basic problem or dispute, with unresolved leftovers of the conflict and its possible reemergence, and with new relations of interdependence between the conflicting parties.

In judging the attractiveness of any posited formula, or in proposing one, conflicting parties compare the value of the proposed solution to the value of the status quo (their security point or reservation price.[22]) The S^5 Situation is a condition not conducive to solution but in potentially cooperative cases, it is the normal condition, and this again is why attempts at cooperative agreement so often fail.[23] Unless a non-solution is actually painful, it may constitute a viable alternative that leaves the future open, creates no pressure for a search for a solution, and requires no risky decision. The decision to seize a negotiating opportunity and turn it into a search for a solution depends not merely on a judgment of how well that or any solution meets the parties' needs and interests or objectively solves the problem or resolves the conflict, but an estimation of how its uncertainty compares with the better known value of the status quo.[24] These calculations will be determinant in deciding whether any proposed resolving formula will or can constitute an MEO. Thus an MEO is a resolving formula that is seen by the parties as meeting their needs better than the status quo.

Whether, in either situation, a particular resolving formula is enticing to the parties or not is for them to perceive and decide; the best an external analyst or practitioner can say is whether the formula fits the past and future extensions of the problem or conflict, that is, whether the parties "should" see their interest in taking it, but not whether they will. A resolving formula is the objectively necessary, if insufficient, condition for durable agreements; subjectively, the parties need to see it as such for it to constitute an opportunity that will pull them out of the conflict or problem and into new, positive relations. While external parties can do much to create a resolving formula and bring the parties to accept it, the outcome is ultimately in the hands of the parties themselves, as it should be.

In cases of interstate cooperation, involving problem-solving rather than conflict resolution in usual terms (although in fact each involves the other), there are important differences in the same categories of variables. The constraints are not violent and the source of the constraints is external—the pain of the situation, the externalities of non-cooperation. There is no demander among the parties, no one to bargain on behalf of the problem to be overcome, which in itself also explains the difficulties of arriving at a high level of cooperation, as opposed to a lowest common denominator agreement. The closest thing to a demander is a particularly affected party among the others who presses for a high-level solution. However, this means that there is nothing for a party to use to purchase agreement other than positive inducements;[25] the situation, not any party, has control of the constraints or negative inducements, and it is for the parties together—who feel the pain differently—to bargain a solution to control them.

Ripeness in Practice

While ripeness has not always been seized upon to open negotiations, there have been occasions when it has come into play, as identified by both analysts and practitioners. Touval's work on the Middle East was particularly important in launching the idea.[26] A number of studies beyond the original examination[27] have used and tested the notion of ripeness in regard to negotiations in Zimbabwe, Namibia and Angola, Eritrea, South Africa, Philippines, Cyprus, Iran-Iraq, Israel and Mozambique, among others.[28] In general, these studies have found the concept applicable and useful as an explanation for the successful initiation of negotiations or their failure, while in some cases proposing refinements to the concept.

Some practitioners have given a more nuanced endorsement of the concept, although not all have read the conceptual fine print carefully. Itamar Rabinovich, the careful historian and skillful ambassador in the failed negotiations between Israel and Syria, terms the concept "a very useful analytical tool ... but ... less valuable as an operational tool," but he expects that "ripeness will account for the success of negotiations" rather than simply provide a necessary but insufficient condition for their initiation. [29]

Implications

There are intriguing problems raised by ripeness theory. One complication arises when increased pain increases resistance rather than reducing it (it must be remembered that while ripeness is a necessary precondition for negotiation, not all ripeness leads to negotiation.) The imposition of pain to a present course in conflict is not likely to lead to a search for alternative measures without first being tested. Although this may be considered "bad," irrational or even adolescent behavior, it is a common reaction and one that may be natural and functional. Reinforcement is the normal response to opposition: "don't give up without a fight," "no gain without pain," "hold the course, whatever the cost," "when the going gets tough, the tough get going," and "if at first you don't succeed, try, try again." The theory itself takes this into account by focusing on the parties' perception that they cannot escalate their way out of their stalemate, implying efforts to break out before giving in (without being able to predict when the shift will take place).

In addition to increased means and efforts, escalation also refers to the image of the party in conflict, a natural tendency which justifies resistance and so also lessens chances of reconciliation,[30] but which has the functional advantage to the parties of strengthening their resolve. Particular types of adversaries such as "true believers," "warriors" or "hardliners" are unlikely to be led to compromise by increased pain; instead, pain is likely to justify renewed struggle.[31] Justified struggles call for greater sacrifices, which absorb increased pain and strengthen determination. The cycle is functional and self-protecting. To this type of reaction, it is the release of pain or an admission of pain on the other side which justifies relaxation; when the opponent admits the error of its ways, the true believer can claim the vindication of its efforts which permits a management of the conflict.[32]

Ripeness is only a condition, necessary but not sufficient for the initiation of negotiations. It is not self-fulfilling or self-implementing. It must be seized, either directly by the parties or, if not, through the persuasion of a mediator. Thus, it is not identical with its results, which are not part of its definition, and is therefore not tautological. Not all ripe moments are so seized and turned into negotiations. Although ripeness theory is not predictive in the sense that it can tell when a given situation will become ripe or turn into negotiations, it is predictive in the sense of identifying the elements necessary (even if not sufficient) for the productive inauguration of negotiations. This type of analytical prediction is the best that can be obtained in social science, where stronger predictions could only be ventured by eliminating free choice (including the human possibility of creativity, blindness and mistakes). As such it is of great prescriptive value to policymakers seeking to know when and how to begin a peace process.

Finding a ripe moment requires research and intelligence studies to identify the objective and subjective elements. Subjective expressions of pain, impasse, and inability to bear the cost of further escalation, related to objective evidence of stalemate, data on numbers and nature of casualties and material costs, and/or other such indicators of MHS, along with expressions of a sense of a Way Out, can be researched on a regular basis in a conflict to establish whether ripeness exists. Researchers would look for evidence, for example, whether the fluid military balance in conflict has given rise at any time to a perception of MHS by the parties, and to a sense by authoritative spokespersons for each side that the other is ready to seek a solution to the conflict, or, to the contrary, whether it has reinforced the conclusion that any mediation is bound to fail because one or both parties believes in the possibility or necessity of escalating out of the current impasse to achieve a decisive military victory.[33]

In his parting report as Under-Secretary-General of the United Nations, Marrack Goulding,[34] specifically cited the literature on ripeness in discussing the selection of conflicts to be handled by an overburdened UN. "Not all conflicts are 'ripe' for action by the United Nations (or any other third party).... It therefore behooves the Secretary-General to be selective and to recommend action only in situations where he judges that the investment of scarce resources is likely to produce a good return (in terms of preventing, managing and resolving conflict.)" Similarly, research would indicate that there was no chance of mediating a settlement in the Ethiopia-Eritrean conflict in the early 1980s and the early 1990s, or in the Southern Sudan conflict in the 1990s, the skills of President Carter notwithstanding, because the components of ripeness were not present.[35]

Unripeness should not constitute an excuse for inaction, even if one or both of the conflicting parties are mired in their hopes of escalation and victory. Crocker states very forcefully (in boldface in the original) that "the absence of 'ripeness' does not tell us to walk away and do nothing. Rather, it helps us to identify obstacles and suggests ways of handling them and managing the problem until resolution becomes possible."[36] Crocker's own experience indicates, before and above all, the importance of being present and available to the contestants helping the moment to ripen, so as to be able to seize it when it occurs. Two strategies are available: either to ripen or to position.[37] Ripening involves convincing the parties that escalation and unilateral victory are impossible or too costly, that there is an acceptable diplomatic Way Out, and that the other party can be made to share this perception. For a third party, giving the others fresh ideas; building basic principles; identifying the parties necessary to a settlement and the issues to be resolved, and separating out issues not resolvable in the conflict; airing alternatives to the current conflict course; clarifying costs and risks involved in seeking settlement; and working to assure support for a settlement policy within each party's domestic constituency are all tactics for the ripening. It may also require concrete measures to block escalation and attempts at unilateral solutions or to keep the weaker party in the conflict or problem.

Positioning means being there for when the parties finally feel a need. Tactics can include becoming an indispensable channel for contacts and such low-intensity or specialized negotiation between the parties as may be happening while the "big table" is empty; tending trust with the conflicting parties or those affected by the problem, and building a reputation among them for fairness and reliability; establishing basic principles to form building blocks of a settlement; and establishing an acceptable mechanism for negotiation and for registering an agreement.

Most of the work on negotiation—including most of the contributions in this book—has concentrated on ways of bringing the conflicting parties together to resolve their problems, but recognizing the necessity of ripeness is crucial to the success of these efforts. If parties do not feel they have to seek a settlement with their opponents or their problem because the status quo does not hurt or they feel they can escape it on their own, they simply will not negotiate. Parties who want to get their adversary or their problem to the table, or mediators who want to help produce a settlement among the parties, must recognize that first the status quo must be painful to the parties. If it is not, the parties must be convinced of their predicament before they will want to look for a way out.

Endnotes

[1] Alvaro DeSoto, *Multiparty Mediation: El Salvador, in* HERDING CATS: MULTIPARTY MEDIATION IN A COMPLEX WORLD 7, 7-8 (Chester A. Crocker, et al., eds., 1999).

[2] *Quoted in* Paul Taylor, *South African Communist Sparks an Explosive Debate*, WASHINGTON POST, Nov. 22, 1992, at A32.

[3] I. WILLIAM ZARTMAN, RIPENESS: THE HURTING STALEMATE AND BEYOND, IN INTERNATIONAL CONFLICT RESOLUTION AFTER THE COLD WAR (Paul Stern & Daniel Druckman eds., 2000).

[4] FRANCIS Y. EDGEWORTH, MATHEMATICAL PHYSICS (1881); FREDERIK ZEUTHEN, PROBLEMS OF MONOPOLY AND ECONOMIC WARFARE (1930); *see also*, BARGAINING: FORMAL THEORIES OF NEGOTIATION (Young Oran ed., 1975).

[5] The original formulation of the theory added a third element to the definition of ripeness, the presence of a Valid Spokesman for each side. As a structural element it is of a different order than the other two defining perceptual elements. Nonetheless, it remains of some importance, as Stedman and Lieberfield have pointed out. The presence of strong leadership recognized as representative of each party and able to deliver compliance to the agreement is a necessary (while alone insufficient) condition for productive negotiations to begin, or indeed to end successfully. Daniel Lieberfield, *Conflict 'Ripeness' Revisited: South African and Israeli/Palestinian Cases*, 15 NEGOTIATION JOURNAL 63, 63-82 (1999); DANIEL LIEBERFIELD, TALKING WITH THE ENEMY: NEGOTIATION AND THREAT PERCEPTION IN SOUTH AFRICA AND ISRAEL/PALESTINE (1999); STEPHEN JOHN STEDMAN, PEACEMAKING IN CIVIL WAR: INTERNATIONAL MEDIATION IN ZIMBABWE (1991).

[6] I. WILLIAM ZARTMAN & MAUREEN BERMAN, THE PRACTICAL NEGOTIATOR 66-78 (1982); SAADIA TOUVAL, THE PEACE BROKERS (1982); William I. Zartman, *The Strategy of Preventive Diplomacy in Third World Conflicts, in* MANAGING U.S.-SOVIET RIVALRY (Alexander L. George ed., 1983); INTERNATIONAL MEDIATION IN THEORY AND PRACTICE 11, 258-60 (Saadia Touval & I. William Zartman eds., 1985); I. WILLIAM ZARTMAN, RIPE FOR RESOLUTION: CONFLICT AND INTERVENTION IN AFRICA (1985).

[7] CHESTER A. CROCKER, HIGH NOON IN SOUTHERN AFRICA: MAKING PEACE IN A ROUGH NEIGHBORHOOD 363 (1992).

[8] *Id.* at 481.

[9] AMARTYA SEN, COLLECTIVE CHOICE AND SOCIAL WELFARE (1970); KENNETH ARROW, SOCIAL CHOICE AND INDIVIDUAL VALUES (1963); OLSON MANCUR, JR., THE LOGIC OF COLLECTIVE ACTION: PUBLIC GOODS AND THE THEORY OF GROUPS (rev ed. 1971) (1965).

[10] STEVEN J. BRAMS, NEGOTIATION GAMES (1990); STEVEN J. BRAMS, THEORY OF MOVES (1994); Quincy Wright, *The Escalation of International Conflicts*, 9 JOURNAL OF CONFLICT RESOLUTION 4, 434-49 (1965).

[11] Joshua Goldstein, The Game of Chicken in International Relations: An Underappreciated Model, American University School of International Service (1998) (unpublished paper, on file with author).

[12] Daniel Kahneman & Amos Tversky, *Prospect Theory: An Analysis of Decisions Under Risk*, 47 ECONOMETRICA 2, 263-92 (1979); CHOOSING TO COOPERATE: HOW STATES AVOID LOSS (Janice Stein & Louis Pauly eds., 1992); Christopher Mitchell, Cutting Losses (George Mason University Institute for Conflict Analysis & Resolution, Working Paper No. 9, 1995); ESCALATION AND NEGOTIATION (I. William Zartman & Guy Olivier Faure eds., 2005).

[13] THOMAS C. SCHELLING, STRATEGY OF CONFLICT (1960).

[14] INTERNATIONAL ENVIRONMENTAL NEGOTIATIONS (Gunnar Sjöstedt ed., 1994); GETTING IT DONE: POSTAGREEMENT NEGOTIATIONS (Bertram Spector & I. William Zartman eds., 2004).

[15] JAMES BAKER & THOMAS DEFRANK, THE POLITICS OF DIPLOMACY (1995).

[16] RICHARD HOLBROOKE, TO END A WAR 27, 73 (1998).

[17] *Id.* at 193.

[18] R. W. Apple, Jr., *Clinton Sending 2 Foreign Policy Advisors to Europe with new Proposals on Balkans*, N. Y. TIMES, Aug. 9, 1995, at A7.

[19] Thomas Olson, Power Politics and Peace Politics (Uppsala University Department of Peace and Conflict Research, Working Paper No. 9, 1998); Dean G. Pruitt & Paul V. Olczak, *Approaches to Resolving Seemingly Intractable Conflict*, in CONFLICT, COOPERATION AND JUSTICE (Barbara Bunker & Jeffrey Rubin eds., 1995).

[20] I. William Zartman & Johannes Aurik, *Power Strategies in De-escalation*, in TIMING THE DE-ESCALATION OF INTERNATIONAL CONFLICTS (Louis Kriesberg & Stuart Thorson eds., 1991).

[21] ZARTMAN, RIPE FOR RESOLUTION, *supra* note 6; Moorad Mooradian & Daniel Druckman, *Hurting Stalemate or Mediation? The Conflict over Nagorno-Karabakh, 1990-95*, 36 JOURNAL OF PEACE RESEARCH 6, 709 (1999).

[22] HOWARD RAIFFA, NEGOTIATION ANALYSIS: THE ART AND SCIENCE OF COLLABORATIVE DECISION-MAKING (John Richardson & David Metcalfe eds., 2002).

[23] ELUSIVE PEACE: NEGOTIATING AN END TO CIVIL WARS (I. William Zartman ed., 1995); RETHINKING THE ECONOMICS OF WAR: THE INTERSECTION OF NEED, CREED AND GREED (Cynthia Arnson & I. William Zartman eds., 2005).

[24] ZARTMAN, *supra* note 3.

[25] SCOTT BARRETT, ENVIRONMENT AND STATECRAFT: THE STRATEGY OF ENVIRONMENTAL TREATY-MAKING (2003).

[26] TOUVAL, *supra* note 6, at 228-32, 328.

[27] ZARTMAN & BERMAN, *supra* note 6; Zartman, *The Strategy of Preventive Diplomacy in Third World Conflicts*, *supra* note 6; Touval & Zartman, *supra* note 6; I. William Zartman, *Ripening Conflict, Ripe Moment, Formula and Mediation*, in PERSPECTIVES ON NEGOTIATION (Diane Bendahmane & John McDonald eds., 1986); ZARTMAN, RIPE FOR RESOLUTION, *supra* note 6; Zartman & Aurik, *supra* note 20.

[28] TOUVAL, *supra* note 6; RICHARD HAAS, CONFLICTS UNENDING (1985); STEDMAN, *supra* note 5; Kriesberg & Thorson, *supra* note 20; TIMOTHY SISK, DEMOCRATIZATION IN SOUTH AFRICA: THE ELUSIVE SOCIAL CONTRACT (1995); Daniel Druckman & Justin Green, *Playing Two Games*, in Zartman, *supra* note 23; ZARTMAN, ELUSIVE PEACE, *supra* note 23; TOVE NORLEN, A STUDY OF THE RIPE MOMENT FOR CONFLICT RESOLUTION AND ITS APPLICABILITY TO TWO PERIODS IN THE ISRAELI-PALESTINIAN CONFLICT (1995); James Goodby, *When War Won Out: Bosnian Peace Plans Before Dayton*, 1 INTERNATIONAL NEGOTIATION 3, 501-23 (1996); FEN OSLER HAMPSON, NURTURING PEACE (1996); Michael Salla, *Creating the 'Ripe Moment' in The East Timor Conflict*, 34 JOURNAL OF PEACE RESEARCH 4, 449-66 (1997); CIVIL WARS IN AFRICA: ROOTS AND RESOLUTION (Taisier Ali & Robert Matthews, eds., 1999); Mooradian & Druckman, *supra* note 21; THE OSLO NEGOTIATIONS, IN INTERNATIONAL NEGOTIATION (Dean G. Pruitt ed. 1997); Karin Aggestam & Christer Jönson, *(Un)ending Conflict*, 36 MILLENNIUM 3, 771-94 (1997).

[29] ITAMAR RABINOVICH, THE BRINK OF PEACE: THE ISRAELI-SYRIAN NEGOTIATIONS 251 (1998).

[30] DEAN G. PRUITT & SUNG-HEE KIM, SOCIAL CONFLICT (2004).

[31] ERIC HOFFER, THE TRUE BELIEVER (1951); HAROLD NICOLSON, DIPLOMACY (1960); GLENN SNYDER & PAUL DIESING, CONFLICT AMONG NATIONS (1977).

[32] RUSSELL LEIGH MOSES, FREEING THE HOSTAGES (1996).

[33] Mooradian & Druckman, *supra* note 21.

[34] Marrack Goulding, *Enhancing the United Nations' Effectiveness in Peace and Security* 20 (United Nations: Report to the Secretary General, June 30, 1997).

[35] Marina Ottaway, *Eritrea and Ethiopia: Negotiations in a Transitional Conflict, in* ELUSIVE PEACE: NEGOTIATING AN END TO CIVIL WARS (I. William Zartman ed., 1995); Francis Deng, *Negotiating a Hidden Agenda: Sudan's Conflict of Identities, in* ELUSIVE PEACE: NEGOTIATING AN END TO CIVIL WARS (I. William Zartman ed., 1995).

[36] CROCKER, *supra* note 7, at 471-72; *see also*, HAAS, *supra* note 27; Goulding, *supra* note 34.

[37] CROCKER, *supra* note 7.

❧ 18 ❧

The Ethics of Compromise

Carrie Menkel-Meadow

Editors' Note: Does how we negotiate reflect or shape our character, or both? Does choosing to negotiate have moral implications? What are the ethical and moral implications of making the assumption that negotiation is inappropriate? Here, Menkel-Meadow notes that not all negotiation is based in the idea of compromise, and discusses the ethical and moral underpinnings of our choices in negotiation—choices we can ignore we are making, but cannot avoid making.

If you negotiate…you treat your principles as mere interests
and emerge compromised.
David Luban, Bargaining and Compromise, at 411 (1985)

Parties might settle while leaving justice undone.
Owen Fiss, Against Settlement, at 1085 (1984)

The compromise process is a conscious process in which
there is a degree of moral acknowledgment of the other party.
Martin P. Golding, The Nature of Compromise, at 16 (1979)

Criticisms of Negotiation as a Process

Most discussions of negotiation, including virtually everything in this book, begin with the assumption that negotiation is not only necessary to order our modern lives, but probably desirable as well. Negotiation is assumed to be a productive human process because it greases the social wheels of agreements and transactions to be made, disputes and conflicts to be avoided or settled, and relationships to be formed or made better.

But, in many circles of political philosophy and even some in law, negotiation is not a good thing at all—being morally defective because of its use of bargaining, traded preferences, and the presumed compromise of important principles.[1] In addition, many have criticized the "privatization" of justice that ensues when parties and their lawyers remove cases from courts, settle for money or other relief, and add insult to injury by signing secrecy agreements.[2] When this happens we lose our ability to have a public conversation about important social and legal values, we lose the stuff of which social norms are created (fact and law intensive cases producing richly reasoned precedents) and we diminish our polity by reducing what is (or should be[3]) debated in the public and transparent sphere. Others would add we are unable to determine, in private negotiations, whether justice has been done, both for the parties who negotiate, and for or "to" others who might be affected by the negotiation process or its outcome.[4] Most recently, in the face of terrorism and "viral" warfare, some have suggested that there are circumstances in which it is wrong (morally and instrumentally) to negotiate with some other parties whom we cannot trust (such as terrorists or certain nation-states, e.g. North Korea) because to do so would grant them legitimacy they should not have.[5] [Blum & Mnookin, *Not Negotiating*] Others have suggested that we should always leave negotiation open as an option, especially where violence and war are possible, or where trust may never be fully forthcoming (consider the purchase of used goods or one-shot negotiations, as in a flea market).

Negotiation as a Morally Preferable Process

In this essay I argue the case, as I have before,[6] that negotiation is a moral and ethical process, worthy of deep philosophical, political, legal and human respect. While most who write about negotiation ethics focus on what I have called the "micro-ethics" of negotiation[7] (how to behave inside a negotiation, e.g. whether and when it is permissible to be less than fully candid in negotiation, or what "tactics" might be appropriate), here I want to focus on the "macro-ethics" of negotiation—the justification of negotiation as an often morally preferable way of ordering human affairs.

Both I and others have argued the case for the instrumental (Pareto) superiority of negotiation processes, when conducted from a problem-solving, interests-based, or principled conception. There, the argument rests on the notion that well-planned and executed deliberations about true needs and interests of the parties will result in opportunities to "create value," expand the available resources at issue, and/or solve human and legal problems, as well as create new relationships, entities or transactions.[8]

Here I want to reaffirm that when negotiation is conducted with these goals in mind it is not only instrumentally better (and justified by principles of utilitarianism) but morally superior to other forms of conflict resolution, for intrinsic or deontological reasons: serious problem-solving negotiation means we treat the Others in negotiation as morally constituted equals, or Ends not Means, in the negotiation.[9] In addition, processes that seek peace, as well as a consensual form of justice, are, I suggest, morally superior to processes that encourage unproductive adversarial argument and continued strife (and perhaps violence). This means that even much criticized compromises[10] may be morally superior, in some instances, to more so-called "principled" resolutions of problems that leave some parties looking for appeal, excuse, or worse, revenge. Of course, much of what I say here should be subjected to closer contextual analysis. Not all negotiations are created equal. Settlement of lawsuits is not the same as peace treaties after war or international treaties about trade or environmental conditions, but in general, I am prepared to say, as others have before me, "as long as the parties keep talking, they are not killing each other."[11]

Relation of Ends to Means: Negotiation as Ethical Choices

Of course, as part of this argument about the importance of negotiation as a violence-reducing, peace-making, and justice-seeking process, *how* one actually

negotiates matters a great deal. But like others,[12] I suggest here that *how* we negotiate is more than the sum of our behavioral parts. The stance, purpose or mindset about what we hope to accomplish in a negotiation is an ethical and moral
matter, long before we choose any particular behavior.[13] Thus, whether one
chooses an adversarial or competitive stance to "defeat the other side" (perhaps
because of assumptions about the empirical world of assumed scarce or contested
resources) or a problem-solving orientation that at least hopes that negotiation
will make all the parties *better off as a result of the negotiation than they would have been
without the negotiation* (and assumes that at least some joint gain is possible) is itself an ethical choice.

Here I am using "ethical choice" in the way at least some philosophers would.
Simon Blackwell suggests that we create "ethical environments" by creating and
choosing "the climate of ideas about how to live."[14] Choosing or elaborating models of negotiation, as well as the choice to negotiate, rather than to use some other
process, like fighting, litigation or withdrawal, are ethical choices.

In my view, the choice to negotiate is ethical and moral (that is true, right and
good) when it treats the Other (or counterpart[15]) as an End, not as a Means, in the
Kantian sense. To negotiate is to acknowledge that one cannot accomplish one's
own ends alone—one needs others (even if one needs others to apologize, correct,
or compensate for a wrong committed). Next, one makes ethical choices when
deciding whether to maximize individual gain (often, but not always, at the expense of others) or whether to offer or look for mutually advantageous ways for
two or more parties to act together (variously called interest-based, mutual gains
or integrative bargaining).

The objective of a negotiation is ethically chosen—it is based, in Blackwell's
terms, on our "ideas about how to live" (I would add, "with others.") Lawyers, as
agents, may think they have to maximize their client's gain as "zealous" advocates, although so might real estate brokers, sports and entertainment agents, and
others, who think the objectives are for principals-clients to determine.[16] The location of legal negotiations within the cultural and legal norms of both 1) the
adversary system and 2) the "agency" of legal representation may make ethical
choices in legal negotiations seem somewhat constrained.[17]

Those who make choices about objectives in negotiation often assume that a
limited array of outcomes is possible. So those who see a negotiation as an opportunity to "win" or maximize one "side's" gain assume scarce resources which
must be allocated. More often, especially in litigation settings, sophisticated lawyers now make economic assessments about the expected value of their case (a
probabilistic statement of the hoped for legal result weighed by the probabilities,
best, worst or most likely outcome, before judge or jury[18]) minus the transaction
costs of trial as compared to the transaction costs of negotiation and settlement,
sometimes purely on the basis of transaction costs or "nuisance value." Many critics have decried this form of "settlement without the merits"[19] as being a non-law
enforcing crass monetary alternative to formal justice. For those who think that
negotiated justice should track legal justice this is a bad, some would say immoral,
result.

But even if legal justice were achieved in other settings like full trial (and I am
quite doubtful about how often that happens), negotiated justice may be better
than legal justice in many, if not all, cases. To negotiate is to find out what someone else might need or want out of a situation in order to grant you what you
want or need. It necessarily involves inquiry, discussion, and (even if conducted as
argument for persuasion), engagement with our fellow human beings, assuming,

for purposes of the special discussion that negotiation is, that the parties are free to work with each other to seek a solution to a mutual problem that would put them in a better position than they would be in without the discussion.

Of course, there are potential problems with many negotiation structures and dynamics—one party may have more power, money, or better lawyers and so the negotiation may not be of actual equals. [Bernard, *Powerlessness*] This can lead to distortions, of potentially serious magnitude, in the negotiation process and the outcome it produces. But certainly the "power imbalance" problem, as it is known to dispute resolution professionals, is present in all other forms of dispute resolution—litigation, arbitration, mediation and certainly, withdrawal or avoidance.

When negotiators seek to explore possibilities for the creation of new entities or transactions, or to resolve disputes in any kind of negotiation, they must take account of the "other" side in a direct and engaged way. This is often more humanely "ethical" than the stylized miscommunication of other forms of dispute resolution.

Solved Problems, Peace, and Yes, Even Compromise

Even when outcomes of "compromise" or "peace" are sought, as opposed to that desideratum of problem-solving or principled negotiation—the pareto optimal solution—such outcomes may be more "ethical" than the binary or draconian solutions of other settings. Consider first that compromise may not be necessary for a successful bargain to be reached—the principled negotiation of Fisher and Ury[20] or the problem-solving negotiation suggested by Menkel-Meadow[21] ask the parties to hold constant their own needs and interests and seek how they may both be satisfied, often by using the Homans principle of "complementary, not conflicting" needs and interests.[22] This is negotiation as traded preferences or utilities (I get the icing, you get the cake.) Or, taking Fisher & Ury's exhortation to use "objective criteria," the parties might actually use reasoned argument to persuade each other of just, fair, legally required, or factually correct allocations.[23] Or, the parties may use their feelings, emotions, religious or ethical values to make the other side feel guilty or wrong, or kind and charitable, in order to get their way. Here the parties are using a third level of discourse—affective, emotional or value-based claims.[24] All of these forms of negotiation involve engaged discourse and interaction with others, assuming that the other party is similarly engaged (whether for instrumental or ethical reasons).

But even that most feared outcome of negotiation—compromise itself—can be thought of as moral or ethical. In many kinds of negotiations there may be no principled reason for allocation—think of child custody in a non-contested divorce with parents having equal parenting skills, or situations where right is either on both sides or on neither. Many years ago, legal scholar John Coons pointed out that "precise" justice sometimes requires solutions that meet in the middle or at least do not allocate everything to one party.[25] In many legal (and human and political) cases there will be inevitable indeterminacy of facts or law that may require even that most dreaded of negotiated outcomes—the 50/50 or "split the difference" solution. For, as Coons argues, where there is not a clear principle for allocation, or knowledge of crucial information for proper allocation, it may be most just to split the proceeds between those in dispute. This principled argument for compromise is deeply ethical on at least two levels: (1) it says that where there is no just reason for allocation, the parties should share *equally* in the uncertainty and (2) it is better to resolve a dispute or allocation problem *peacefully* by some method than not to resolve it all.

In the second sense of compromise suggested here, negotiation, even when it leads to compromise, is a moral process—it produces peace, resolution, and its own form of justness (justice) and fairness, especially when legal principles cannot be or should not be controlling. Compromise, bargaining, and negotiation produce resolutions and outcomes and have other moral qualities. They assume (and some would say wrongly) that all who participate live in a shared community and have equal rights to claim something and seek outcomes. Thus, bargaining legitimates the agency of those who seek to negotiate. This can be generalized to see negotiation as a democratic process—it encourages, indeed demands, participation and it cannot succeed, by definition, without "consent of the governed."

The Politics of Negotiation

Furthermore, compromise, bargaining and negotiation are socially necessary for people to accomplish things, whether they are the unprincipled log-rolling of the traded-for legislative process,[26] the hard-bargained-for, split-the-difference solution between equipoised or exhausted and unresolved claims of rights or interests, or the recognition of mutual interest and cooperation (I will let you have some of what you want, if I can have some of what I want). While many have criticized those who compromise, especially "unprincipled" politicians, Machiavelli, at least, has argued that the leader sometimes must compromise, or at least, have no principles of his own, if he is to hold the whole (and conflicting) polity together.[27] And Edmund Burke, consummate politician, observed that "all government...every virtue and every prudent act is founded on compromise and barter."[28] By finding "golden means" or agreeable, if not optimal, solutions to contested problems, politicians, like negotiators, make things happen, keep the peace, and often also keep some rough accounting of just deserts for the next time around. And in better case scenarios, negotiators can actually solve problems and get parties just what they need.[29]

Thus, the solutions that bargaining and negotiation produce, through a process of engagement, consent, and decision, by giving something to everyone, may have greater participation, legitimacy and longevity than other ways of doing business. Jon Elster, in a study of comparative constitutional processes, has noted that the "second best" form of secret, committee-based, bargaining that produced the American constitution, filled with compromises, has been more robust than the more open, principled, and plenary forms of decision-making that formed the first French constitution.[30] In these observations the instrumental (robustness) may become its own form of moral justification (despite the injustice of slavery and the lost lives of the Civil War, the United States has had a more robust form of government and peacefulness than many other countries). The brilliance of our Framers then, was not only in the substance of their constitutive documents, but in the processes they selected to create them.[31]

Not all legal disputes are constitutional conventions, but neither are all legal disputes simple cases between a single plaintiff and defendant. If there is an ethical justification for self-determination and participation in dispute processes, then negotiated processes may have a higher claim on modern complex, multi-partied, multi-issue disputes than traditional forms of litigation.[32] As the new field of multi-party negotiation and consensus building has demonstrated,[33] the complexity of managing multiple stakeholders, with some conflicting and some complementary interests, requires processes that allow trades, joint fact finding, contingent agreements, coalition building and simultaneous participation. Although freighted with its own ethical dilemmas (side-deals, hold-outs, enforcement of commitments, deception, and use cf caucuses and separate meet-ings[34]) the negotiation of multi-party disputes permits both instrumentally satisfying and more ethical processes and outcomes to be utilized. More people participate, and instead of looking for majority votes, or "lowest common denomi-nator" solutions, parties seek solutions that satisfy as many needs as possible, without making any party necessarily worse off. This facilitated negotiation, or "consensus building" is intended to improve on what conventional processes of voting and strategic behavior usually produce. Often enough, it does.

Means: Choosing and Doing

Chosen objectives in negotiation (whether to seek joint or individual gain), in turn, often mold the behavioral choices negotiators make. Professional agents, like lawyers, are probably most likely (despite professional ethics rules which require consultation[35]) to choose their own means. The relationship of means to ends in negotiation remains one of assumption and prescription, with little actual empiri-cal verification and description. While many negotiators believe it is to their advantage to lie, cheat, steal, dissemble, or simply to deflect inquires about bottom lines, preferences and reservation prices,[36] we actually don't know how effective these tactics are in achieving the ends of their deployers.[37] We do know, however, that those lawyers who are perceived as unethical are also perceived as ineffective. [Tinsley, et al., *Reputations*] We do know that these behavioral choices can get their users into legal, and occasionally, ethical trouble. Fraud, mutual or even unilateral mistake, some omissions or failures to correct bad information[38] or even negligent misrepresentations may, under state law (and some specialized federal laws, like securities laws[39]) void agreements made and cause liability to be assessed against their perpetrators. And, although rare, some of the most adversarial behaviors may run afoul of lawyers' ethics rules that may result in professional discipline, such as violations of Model Rule 3.3 (Candor to Tribunals); Rule 4.1 (Truthfulness in Statements to Others[40]) and Rule 8.4 (Misconduct).

The dictates of these rules and laws are far from clear, however, and so nego-tiation practices vary a great deal.[41] The question of what factors influence choices about practice and behaviors continues to be studied and debated—whether pro-fessional socialization and culture,[42] gender[43] or ethnicity[44] or nationality in both domestic and international contexts.[45]

When agreements are breached or push comes to shove, the parties may liti-gate about what standards should govern their behavior, and with what results. Thus, many who choose particular behaviors because they believe, perhaps wrongly, such behaviors will permit them to "win"[46] at negotiation may be com-mitting triple errors of judgment: (1) assumptions that "tough tactics" will be effective for individual gain maximization; (2) exposure to potential legal and other liability for formal rule or law violations and; (3) misconceptions about the effectiveness of objectives chosen (perhaps attempting to achieve joint gain would be more likely to ensure that each negotiator actually gets what he wants).[47]

Thus, "bad" ethical choices about ends and means can lead to instrumentally suspect outcomes—ineffective, unenforceable or regretted outcomes—not to men-tion the "economic waste" of not seeing if joint gain or resource enhancement is possible. But such choices are more than instrumentally problematic.

If negotiators, especially legal negotiators, persist in assumptions of resource scarcity or individual gain maximization, the behaviors they choose will perpetu-ate the myths or assumptions of adversarialism as well as our short and brutish lives. Thus, the ethical environment we create, in Blackwell's sense, is comprised not only by the ideas we have about how we should live, but by the behaviors we choose to live with. If the theory of conflict resolution has taught us anything, empirically, it is that escalation of conflict begets more conflict and it is harder (though not impossible) to de-escalate,[48] And more conflict, producing even shorter and more brutish lives, will clearly prevent our achieving good or at least better solutions to our many problems.

So, to conclude, how we choose to negotiate (whether to negotiate at all, how we make our choices about what we are trying to accomplish, and what behaviors we choose to accomplish those objectives) is an ethical matter. By choosing different negotiation models or behaviors we are choosing the "ideas" by which we live, and as I have suggested here, some ideas are morally superior to others.

Endnotes

[1] *See e.g.*, David Luban, *Bargaining and Compromise: Recent Work on Negotiation and Informal Justice*, 14 PHILOSOPHY & PUBLIC AFFAIRS 397 (1985) and Jules Coleman & Charles Silver, *Justice in Settlements*, 4 SOCIAL PHILOSOPHY & POLICY 102 (1986).

[2] *See e.g.* Owen Fiss, *Against Settlement*, 93 YALE LAW JOURNAL 1073 (1984); David Luban, *Settlements and the Erosion of the Public Realm*, 83 GEORGETOWN LAW JOURNAL 2619 (1995); Susan Koniak, and George M. Cohen, *Under Cloak of Settlement*, 82 VIRGINIA LAW REVIEW 1051 (1996); Carrie Menkel-Meadow, *Public Access to Private Settlements: Conflicting Legal Policies*, 11 (6) ALTERNATIVES TO HIGH COST OF LITIGATION 85 (June, 1993).

[3] Hannah Arendt, among other political philosophers, has written eloquently on the need for "public conversations" about public matters, *see e.g.*, HANNAH ARENDT, THE HUMAN CONDITION 22-78 (1958). David Luban has called this the "public life conception" of political decision-making.

[4] The question of the effects of negotiation processes and outcomes on others who do not participate in the negotiation is an important question, receiving insufficient attention in our literature. For some useful exceptions to this see Lawrence Susskind, *Environmental Mediation and the Accountability Problem*, 6 VERMONT LAW REVIEW 1 (1981); CARRIE MENKEL-MEADOW & MICHAEL WHEELER, WHAT'S FAIR: ETHICS FOR NEGOTIATORS (2004). Dispute resolution professionals call this the problem of "generations" (as in environmental mediation) or stakeholders (those with an interest in a negotiated matter). Economists call this the problem of ethical "externalities"—those who are outside a bargaining process but will be affected by it.

[5] *See e.g.* Robert Mnookin, *When Not to Negotiate: A Negotiation Imperialist Reflects on Appropriate Limits*, 74 UNIVERSITY OF COLORADO LAW REVIEW 1077 (2003). This argument usually focuses on Chamberlain's ill-fated negotiations with the Nazi regime at Munich. It was also made during the Viet Nam peace talks (the shape of the table negotiations originally excluded the Viet Cong) and again during Israeli peace talks when the participation of the Palestinian Liberation Organization was at issue because of the fear of "legitimation" of an organization of "terrorism."

[6] Carrie Menkel-Meadow, *Whose Dispute Is It Anyway?: A Philosophical and Democratic Defense of Settlement (in Some Cases)*, 83 GEORGETOWN LAW JOURNAL 2663 (1995); Carrie Menkel-Meadow, *Toward Another View of Legal Negotiation: The Structure of Problem Solving*, 31 UCLA LAW REVIEW 754 (1984) [hereinafter *Toward Another View*].

[7] Carrie Menkel-Meadow, *Ethics, Morality and Professional Responsibility in Negotiation*, in DISPUTE RESOLUTION ETHICS (Phyllis Bernard & Bryant Garth eds., 2002).

[8] The classics in this literature are ROGER FISHER, ET AL., GETTING TO YES, (2d ed. 1991); HOWARD RAIFFA, THE ART AND SCIENCE OF NEGOTIATION (1982); DAVID LAX AND JAMES SEBENIUS, THE MANAGER AS NEGOTIATOR (1986), and *Toward Another View, supra* note 6, all written within a few years of each other. Much of the work here was based on the earlier path-breaking work of Mary Parker Follett, especially her "Constructive Conflict" essay, now available in, MARY PARKER FOLLETT—PROPHET OF MANAGEMENT: A CELEBRATION OF WRITINGS FROM THE 1920s (Pauline Graham ed., 1995).

[9] Jonathan Cohen, *When People are the Means: Negotiating with Respect*, 14 THE GEORGETOWN JOURNAL OF LEGAL ETHICS 739 (2001).

[10] The philosophical, sociological and political study of compromise is attracting scholastic attention again in Europe, if not in the United States, see special issue, *Compromis/Compromise*, 43 INFORMATION SUR LES SCIENCES SOCIALES 131-305 (2004). *See also*, MARTIN BENJAMIN, SPLITTING THE DIFFERENCE: COMPROMISE AND INTEGRITY IN ETHICS AND POLITICS (1990) and NOMOS: COMPROMISE IN ETHICS, LAW AND POLITICS, (J. Roland Pennock & John W. Chapman eds., 1979) [hereinafter, COMPROMISE].

[11] "Keep the parties talking" may be one of those close-to-universal rules in negotiation, whether in international negotiations or hostage negotiations. "One of the things we adopted early on was the motto "Talk to Me"—it's not "Listen to Me, I know better than you do"—it's "TALK to Me." Often times by setting up this dialogue, and allowing this person to tell us what was wrong, we found out that many of the things that we thought were problems just weren't." See Jack Cambria, et al., *Negotiation Under Extreme Pressure: The Mouth Marines and the Hostage Takers*, 18 NEGOTIATION JOURNAL 331, 334 (2002). Of course, it is essential to be sure the parties are not doing other nasty things while talking—that's why the U.S. wanted (and needed) verification during the nuclear disarmament talks. And constant talking and no decision can, of course, harm some parties more than others (plaintiffs for example, who may need the money for which they are suing).

[12] *See, e.g.,* G. RICHARD SHELL, BARGAINING FOR ADVANTAGE: NEGOTIATION STRATEGIES FOR REASONABLE PEOPLE, 201-33 (1999); HOWARD RAIFFA, THE ART AND SCIENCE OF NEGOTIATION 344-55 (1982); HOWARD RAIFFA, WITH JOHN RICHARDSON AND DAVID METCALFE, NEGOTIATION ANALYSIS: THE SCIENCE AND ART OF COLLABORATIVE DECISION MAKING 507-22 (2002).

[13] As I discussed in *Toward Another View, supra* note 6, the purpose, goal, mind-set or "orientation" toward a negotiation problem or one's negotiation counterpart precedes in analysis any actual behavioral choice, see *Toward Another View, supra* note 6, at 759-62. This means that when we choose to use negotiation as a process we are making a choice about what we want to accomplish ("solve a problem" or "beat the other side") that then influences what behaviors we choose (collaborative or competitive) which we think will have an influence on the outcome achieved. (The links between these choices and their actual affects is, in fact, an empirical question, and we have precious little data to support whether anyone's assumptions in these choices are actually right.) But, the point here is, the choice of how to orient one's self in a negotiation—that is how to conceptualize the problem at hand—is, in my view, an ethical one.

[14] SIMON BLACKWELL, BEING GOOD: A SHORT INTRODUCTION TO ETHICS 1 (2001).

[15] Jonathan Cohen has recently offered an important ethical intervention in our negotiation discourse, suggesting that how we "label" or name the Other in negotiation is also a moral choice, which reflects the orientation, mind-set or sensibilities with which we approach others, *see* Jonathan Cohen, *Adversaries? Partners? How About Counterparts? On Metaphors in the Practice and Teaching of Negotiation and Dispute Resolution*, 20 CONFLICT RESOLUTION QUARTERLY 433 (2003). *See also*, Elizabeth Thornburg, *Metaphors Matter: How Images of Battles, Sports and Sex Shape the Adversary System*, 10 WISCONSIN WOMEN'S LAW JOURNAL 225 (1995).

[16] This would be consistent with a reading of Model Rule of Professional Conduct, Rule 1.2, which states that "a lawyer shall abide by a client's decisions concerning the objectives of representation and ... shall consult with the client as to the means by which they are to be pursued."

[17] But some lawyers have recently chosen to take themselves out of those constraints by limiting what they will do in negotiation or litigation, calling themselves, "Collaborative lawyers," *see, e.g.,* PHYLLIS TESLER, COLLABORATIVE LAW: ACHIEVING EFFECTIVE RESOLUTION IN DIVORCE WITHOUT LITIGATION (2001). Of course, whether lawyers can limit their representation, by contract or otherwise, is also a legal and ethical question; John Lande, *Possibilities for Collaborative Law: Ethics and Practice of Lawyer Disqualification and Process Control in a New Model of Lawyering*, 64 OHIO STATE LAW JOURNAL 1315 (2003).

[18] *See e.g.* Marjorie Corman Aaron & David Hoffer, *Decision Analysis as a Method of Evaluating the Trial Alternative, in* MEDIATING LEGAL DISPUTES (Dwight Golann ed. 1996).

[19] Janet Cooper Alexander, *Do the Merits Matter? A Study of Settlements in Securities Class Actions,* 43 STANFORD LAW REVIEW 497 (1991).

[20] FISHER, ET AL., *supra* note 8.

[21] *Toward Another View, supra* note 6.

[22] GEORGE HOMANS, SOCIAL BEHAVIOR (1961).

[23] In one of the earliest articles on legal negotiation Melvin Eisenberg argued that negotiations, in both disputes and deals, were "norm" based with various forms of reasoned elaboration characterizing what occurred in a wide variety of settings, *see* Melvin Eisenberg, *Private Ordering Through Negotiation: Dispute-Settlement and Rulemaking,* 89 HARVARD LAW REVIEW 637 (1976).

[24] I have recently suggested that conflict resolution engages in three different kinds of discourse, reasoned argument, traded preferences (bargaining) and affective and value-based claims, for which different kinds of processes might be appropriate, *see* Carrie Menkel-Meadow, *The Lawyer's Role(s) in Deliberative Democracy,* 5 NEVADA LAW REVIEW 347 (2004).

[25] John E. Coons, *Compromise as Precise Justice, in* COMPROMISE IN ETHICS, LAW AND POLITICS (J. Roland Pennock & John W. Chapman eds., 1979).

[26] *See, e.g.,* Martin Golding, *The Nature of Compromise: A Preliminary Inquiry, in* COMPROMISE, *supra* note 10, at 14; Joseph H. Carens, *Compromise in Politics, in* COMPROMISE, *surpa* note 10, at 123.

[27] MACHIAVELLI, THE PRINCE 68-70 (Harvey Mansfield trans., 2d ed. 1998).

[28] Edmund Burke, *On Conciliation with the Colonies, in* SPEECHES AND LETTERS ON AMERICAN AFFAIRS 130-31 (Ernest Rhys ed., 1942) (1977).

[29] Or, as those great philosophers, the Rolling Stones, have said: "You can't always get what you want, but if you try, sometimes, you can get what you need" YOU CAN'T ALWAYS GET WHAT YOU WANT (ABKCO 1969).

[30] Jon Elster, *Strategic Uses of Argument, in* BARRIERS TO CONFLICT RESOLUTION (Kenneth Arrow, et al. eds., 1995).

[31] Dana Lansky, *Proceeding to a Constitution: A Multi-Party Negotiation Analysis of the Constitutional Convention of 1787,* 5 HARVARD NEGOTIATION LAW REVIEW 279 (2000); Jack Rakove, *The Great Compromise: Ideas, Interests and Politics of Constitution Making,* 44 WILLIAM & MARY LAW REVIEW 424 (1987).

[32] *See* Carrie Menkel-Meadow, *The Trouble with the Adversary System in a Post-Modern, Multi-Cultural World,* 38 WILLIAM & MARY LAW REVIEW 5 (1996).

[33] Lawrence Susskind, et al., *What We Have Learned About Teaching Multiparty Negotiation,* 21 NEGOTIATION JOURNAL 395 (2005); LAWRENCE SUSSKIND, ET AL., THE CONSENSUS BUILDING HANDBOOK (1999).

[34] *See, e.g.,* Carrie Menkel-Meadow, *The Lawyer as Consensus Builder: Ethics for a New Practice,* 70 TENNESSEE LAW REVIEW 63 (2002); JOHN FORESTER, THE DELIBERATIVE PRACTITIONER: ENCOURAGING PARTICIPATORY PLANNING PROCESSES (1999).

[35] *See* Model Rules of Professional Conduct, Rules 1.2, 1.4 and cmt.

[36] For the classic index of competitive ploys to use in a position-maximizing legal negotiation, *see* Michael Meltsner & Philip Schrag, *Negotiating Tactics for Legal Services Lawyers,* 7 CLEARINGHOUSE REVIEW 259 (1973). For more general advice about how to attempt to take advantage of others *see* HERB COHEN, YOU CAN NEGOTIATE ANYTHING (1982): HERB COHEN, NEGOTIATE THIS! BY CARING, BUT NOT T-H-A-T MUCH (2003); JIM CAMP, START WITH NO (2002).

[37] For one attempt to get at some empirical measurement of negotiation behaviors, even if only second-hand reports of others' behaviors, *see* Andrea Kupfer Schneider, *Shattering Negotiation Myths: Empirical Evidence on the Effectiveness of Negotiation Style,* 7 HARVARD NEGOTIATION LAW REVIEW 143 (2002).

[38] *See, e.g.*, Stare v. Tate, 21 Cal. App. 3d 432 (1971) (valuation error made by one spouse and taken advantage of by other spouse's knowing professionals in divorce proceeding caused agreement to be rescinded and reformed!)

[39] Donald Langevoort, *Half-Truths: Protecting Mistaken Inferences By Investors and Others*, 52 STANFORD LAW REVIEW 87 (1999).

[40] "A lawyer shall not make a false statement of material fact or law to a third person; or fail to disclose a material fact to a third person when the disclosure is necessary to avoid assisting a criminal or fraudulent act by a client...." MPRC Rule 4.1 (2005).

[41] *See, e.g.*, Schneider, *supra* note 37.

[42] *See, id.* Michael Wheeler and I have been studying lawyers, law students, business students and business people in their "Negotiation Choices" about representations made in the sale of property and have so far discovered differences in the professions—lawyers and law students are more likely to take advantage of unsuspecting partners with respect to market price but are more likely to disclose possible environmental defects (the influence of knowledge of the law of real estate disclosures?). And law students and lawyers are also slightly more likely to do what their superiors tell them to do. *See also*, JAMES FREUND, SMART NEGOTIATING: HOW TO MAKE GOOD DEALS IN THE REAL WORLD (1992) for an inside view of large law firm negotiation practice and ethics.

[43] The debate about whether women negotiate differently and more "ethically" continues apace, still, in my scholarly opinion, unresolved, *see* CAROL GILLIGAN, IN A DIFFERENT VOICE: PSYCHOLOGICAL THEORY AND WOMEN'S DEVELOPMENT (1982); RAND JACK AND DANA CROWLEY JACK, MORAL VISION AND PROFESSIONAL DECISIONS: THE CHANGING ROLE OF WOMEN AND MEN LAWYERS (1989); Carrie Menkel-Meadow, *Portia Redux: Another Look at Gender, Feminism and Legal Ethics*, 2 VIRGINIA JOURNAL OF SOCIAL POLICY & LAW 75 (1994); DEBORAH KOLB & JUDITH WILLIAMS, EVERYDAY NEGOTIATIONS: NAVIGATING THE HIDDEN AGENDAS IN BARGAINING (2003); LINDA BABCOCK & SARA LASCHEVER, WOMEN DON'T ASK: NEGOTIATION AND THE GENDER DIVIDE (2003).

[44] *See, e.g.*, Ian Ayres, *Fair Driving: Gender and Race Discrimination in Retail Car Negotiations*, 104 HARVARD LAW REVIEW 817 (1991); Ian Ayres, *Further Evidence of Discrimination in New Car Negotiations and Estimates of its Cause*, 94 MICHIGAN LAW REVIEW 109 (1995).

[45] *See, e.g.*, FRANK L. ACUFF, HOW TO NEGOTIATE ANYTHING WITH ANYONE AROUND THE WORLD (1997); JEANNE BRETT, NEGOTIATING GLOBALLY: HOW TO NEGOTIATE DEALS, RESOLVE DISPUTES AND MAKE DECISIONS ACROSS CULTURAL BOUNDARIES (2001); Jeffrey Z. Rubin and Frank Sander, *Culture, Negotiation, and the Eye of the Beholder*, 7 NEGOTIATION JOURNAL 249 (1991).

[46] It is common in the popular literature on negotiation to hear the phrase "win-win negotiation" as the alternative to binary, competitive negotiations in which one side "bests" the other in some way. I prefer to avoid this term. Most negotiations are not "win-win" in the sense that both parties win what they want. A good negotiation is one in which each party does better than it might have done without the negotiation taking place (such as losing litigation or failing to establish a new transaction)—but seldom will both sides actually "win" everything they want. *See* Carrie Menkel-Meadow, *When Winning Isn't Everything: The Lawyer as Problem Solver*, 28 HOFSTRA LAW REVIEW 905 (2000).

[47] Even if competitive maximizers were successful in "winning," their victory over another negotiator may cause anger, resentment, and a regret factor so strong that the defeated party will seek revenge, or at least fail to comply with the agreement, causing additional hardship and expense in enforcement of an agreement, that may be voidable.

[48] DEAN PRUITT & JEFFREY Z. RUBIN, SOCIAL CONFLICT, ESCALATION, STALEMATE AND SETTLEMENT (1986); ROBERT AXELROD, THE EVOLUTION OF COOPERATION (1984); ROBERT AXELROD, THE COMPLEXITY OF COOPERATION (1997).

❧ 19 ❦

Perceptions of Fairness

Nancy A. Welsh

Editors' Note: *In all of negotiation there is no bigger trap than "fairness." Welsh explains why: among multiple models of fairness, people tend to believe that the one that applies here is the one that happens to favor them. This often creates a bitter element in negotiation, as each party proceeds from the unexamined assumption that its standpoint is the truly fair one. Welsh argues that for a negotiation to end well, it is imperative for both parties to assess the fairness of their own proposals from multiple points of view, not just their instinctive one—and to consider the fairness of their procedures as well as of their substantive proposals (in which respect this chapter should be read in conjunction with Putnam on Communication).*

Generally, when people negotiate, they prefer to win. At the very least, they work to achieve outcomes they can call "fair," and particularly, "fair enough to *me*!" This concern for fairness can lead to apparently irrational behaviors in negotiation. We all know people (including ourselves) who have offered more than was necessary or rejected offers even though they made economic sense. Such actions, which have been replicated by researchers in experiments involving "ultimatum games,"[1] can be explained by examining perceptions of fairness. Negotiators rely upon their assessments of distributive and procedural fairness in making offers and demands, reacting to the offers and demands of others, and deciding whether to reach an agreement or end negotiations. Because fairness perceptions are so significant in understanding people's negotiating behaviors, this essay will examine briefly the criteria that undergird differing fairness judgments—both distributive and procedural—and the social, psychological and cognitive variables that influence people's perceptions of fairness.

Distributive Fairness Perceptions

The concept of distributive fairness focuses on the criteria that people use (often quite unconsciously) to judge whether they have received their "fair share"—i.e., that the outcome of a negotiation or other decision-making process is fair. People often disagree regarding the most appropriate criteria to be applied in determining whether an outcome is fair. As is obvious from reading judicial opinions in appellate cases, even impartial and educated people can review the identical record and reach widely disparate yet equally principled conclusions regarding what constitutes a fair result. The definition of distributive fairness is, therefore, inevitably influenced by subjectivity. This realization leads to the following questions: what is the range of criteria that people—including negotiators—use to guide their judgments regarding distributive fairness? What variables influence people's selection among the different criteria? Last, why do people find it difficult to reach agreement even when they agree that they should use the principle of equitable distribution to arrive at an outcome?

Competing Criteria for Judging Distributive Fairness

The various criteria for judging distributive (or outcome) fairness can be distilled into four basic, competing principles or rules—equality, need, generosity, and equity. The *equality principle* provides that everyone in a group should share its benefits equally. According to the *need principle*, "those who need more of a benefit should get more than those who need it less."[2] The *generosity principle* decrees that one person's outcome should not exceed the outcomes achieved by others. Finally, the *equity principle* ties the distribution of benefits to people's relative contribution. Those who have contributed more should receive more than those who have contributed less. The closer that the actual outcome of a negotiation is to the outcome a negotiator anticipated based on the application of her favored principle, the greater the likelihood that the negotiator will perceive the outcome as fair.[3]

Imagine the application of the four principles described above to a negotiation between two individuals who are establishing a joint venture and negotiating the distribution of income. The first negotiator, who has little capital, is contributing the idea and the time and energy to implement the idea. The other negotiator is supplying the needed funds for the development and marketing of the idea. If these individuals are guided by the equality principle, they will distribute the income from the joint venture equally. If they use the need principle, the poorer negotiator who is contributing "sweat equity" will receive a greater share of the income. Under the generosity principle, neither negotiator would want his income to exceed the income of the other. Last, and perhaps most difficult, is the application of the equity principle. Both contributions are needed. Whose is more valuable? The negotiators' assessments regarding the relative value of their contributions are likely to be affected by many factors that this essay will examine in more detail below.

Variables Affecting Negotiators' Selection Among Competing Fair Allocation Principles

Research has shown that several variables influence negotiators' selection among equality, need, generosity or equity to guide their assessment of fairness in a particular negotiation. These variables include self-interest, social relationships, and the interaction between cultural norms and situational needs.

The Influence of Self-Interest and Relationships Between Negotiators

The relationship between negotiators—or the lack of a relationship—matters very much in negotiators' definitions of fair outcomes. If *no* relationship exists between negotiators, self-interest will guide their choice of the appropriate allocation principle to use in negotiation. In other words, a negotiator who does not expect future interactions with the other person will use whatever principle—need, generosity, equality, or equity—produces the best result for her. When a negotiator has a *negative* relationship with her counterpart, she will define her desired outcome in relative terms—i.e., she must do *better* than the other negotiator—and she will even undertake a risky strategy to achieve this goal. She certainly will not worry about achieving an outcome that is fair for that other, despised negotiator.

On the other hand, the existence of a *positive* relationship with another negotiator makes the attainment of a mutually fair outcome relevant. Positive social relationships also influence negotiators' selection of the particular fair allocation principle that will anchor their negotiations. If a negotiator is dividing a resource with someone else and expects future, positive interactions with that person, the negotiator tends to use the equality principle to define distributive fairness. However, the strength of the relationship matters. People who place primary value upon the continuation of their relationship—e.g., romantically involved negotiators—have lower aspirations and reach less Pareto-efficient outcomes. In contrast, negotiators who are friends or colleagues often benefit from the combination of a valued long-term relationship and high individual aspirations, making the achievement of a Pareto-optimal outcome more likely. This social dynamic may help to explain why experienced lawyer-negotiators often concentrate on case analysis to justify their differing valuations of a case (thus primarily relying on the equity principle) for most of their negotiations with each other, but may then revert to "splitting the difference" (thus invoking the equality principle) in order to reach a final settlement.

The Influence of Situational Needs and Cultural Norms

As commerce has become increasingly global, cross-cultural negotiation has also become more commonplace. Some cultures are known for placing greater emphasis upon maintaining social relationships than attaining individual objectives. Many believe, therefore, that the cultural dimension of collectivism-individualism should have great salience in the negotiation context. Simply, "individualism refers to a tendency to put a stronger emphasis on one's personal interest and goals, whereas collectivism refers to a stronger emphasis on the interests and goals of one's in-group members."[4] Collectivist negotiators ought to be more likely than individualists to choose harmony-enhancing principles for the distribution of benefits (e.g., equality, need, or generosity principles).

Research indicates, however, that negotiators' choices among the various allocation principles are not so predictable. First, and consistent with the importance of relationships noted above, it is only when collectivists are negotiating with other in-group members that they are more likely to use a harmony-enhancing principle. If they are not closely related to the other negotiators, collectivists behave like individualists and tie fair allocation to contribution, thus leading to their use of the equity principle. Second, collectivists' choice among allocation principles depends upon the extent to which they anticipate receiving some portion of the benefits being allocated. If a collectivist will not be a recipient (e.g., a supervisor allocating rewards to employees), the collectivist is less likely to be concerned about fostering harmony and more likely to use the equity principle that will best enhance productivity. Last, negotiators in collectivist cultures will be influenced by situational needs. As previously noted, the supervisor managing a work group in a collectivist culture is likely to make allocations that will enhance productivity rather than harmony. Collectivist negotiators who are acutely aware of resource scarcity may choose to allocate resources based on the need principle, in recognition of the greater interest in ensuring basic survival rather than harmony. The existence of an overarching collectivist culture is certainly relevant to negotiators' definitions of distributive fairness, but the impact of this culture depends very much on the particular context within which a negotiation occurs.

Variables Affecting Negotiators' Application of the Equity Principle

Even if negotiators share a preference for use of the equity principle, they are nonetheless likely to find it difficult to reach an agreement in a difficult dispute. Self-interest, negative relationships between negotiators, and the dynamics of the negotiation interaction itself can help to explain this tension.

The Influence of Self-Interest

Even when negotiators express a desire to be fair and to allocate resources in a manner that is equitable, their definitions of "equitable outcomes" are almost inevitably affected by self-interest or an "egocentric bias."[5] People value their own contributions much more highly than they value the identical contributions of others. In one research project, for example, when people were asked to determine what amount should be paid for accomplishing a particular task, they expected to be paid substantially more for their own work than they were willing to pay to someone else.[6]

Another interesting study simulated the impact of the egocentric bias in the litigation context.[7] The subjects in the research project learned all the facts involved in a personal injury accident in which a motorcyclist was hit by a car and injured. They then determined what they thought would be a fair settlement to compensate the motorcyclist for his injuries. After this, the researchers assigned the subjects to play the role of either the motorcyclist or the driver of the car and to negotiate a settlement. Settlements were reached in nearly every case. The researchers then worked with another set of subjects but, this time, began by assigning them to the roles of the motorcyclist and the driver. While playing their roles, the subjects learned the facts, calculated a "fair" settlement, and tried to negotiate a settlement. These subjects had a very difficult time reaching a settlement. Their perceptions of fairness were affected by the roles they were playing. The motorcyclists' pre-negotiation judgments of a fair settlement generally involved a large damage award, while the drivers were much more likely to assess a small damage award. Not coincidentally, these assessments worked to their own favor. The further apart the pre-negotiation judgments regarding fair outcomes, the more likely the negotiations were to end in impasse. Equitable distribution, it seems, is in the eyes of the self-interested beholder.

The Influence of Negative Relationships

In negotiation, the messenger is very much a part of the message. The perceived equitable fairness of an outcome is influenced by who offers it. A solution that appears fair—even attractive—often loses its luster as soon as the *other negotiator* puts it on the table. Several cognitive and psychological processes explain this effect, which has been labeled "reactive devaluation."[8] When negotiators are adversaries or have a negative relationship, they are likely to view each other's offers with even greater suspicion. Indeed, research has demonstrated that while people will react positively to a solution when it is proposed by someone they view as an ally or neutral, they will reject precisely the same solution as insufficient when it is suggested by their adversary.[9]

The Influence of the Negotiation Interaction

A significant body of research has also found that people's perceptions of outcome fairness are influenced by how they felt they were treated during a dispute resolution or decision-making process. If they perceived themselves as treated in a procedurally fair manner, they are more likely to judge the outcome of that process as fair, even if the outcome is unfavorable. Most of this research focuses on the manner in which a third-party decision-maker treats the disputants, but more recent research indicates that in consensual processes such as mediation and negotiation, the disputants may also be influenced by their interactions with each other.[10] This research suggests that many negotiators' perceptions of sufficiently equitable arrangements will be influenced by how they were treated during the negotiation process. If a negotiator perceives that the other negotiator gave her sufficient opportunity to speak, tried to be open-minded in considering what she had to say, and treated her with respect, she is more likely to view the outcome of the negotiation as fair, even if that outcome is not all that she hoped it would be. These interactional elements—which signal procedural fairness—will be examined in greater detail below.

The Influence of Contextual Distributive Justice Norms

Thus far, this essay has focused on social and psychological variables that influence negotiators' perceptions regarding equitable distributions. There are also rational variables that can mitigate the influence of social and psychological factors. For example, within the legal context, experienced lawyers' susceptibility to the egocentric bias is likely to be tempered by their knowledge of the applicable law and legal standards. These lawyers' negotiations are and should be conducted within the "shadow of the law."[11] Experienced lawyers also possess the knowledge to apply a rational, expected financial value analysis to determine whether a proposed settlement is sufficiently consistent with the trial and settlement outcomes in similar cases.[12] Clients can turn to these sophisticated agents[13] to gain outcomes that are more likely to be consistent with the equitable norms that apply within the legal context and, at the very least, are no worse than those received by other similarly-situated litigants.[14] At the same time, lawyers are not immune from the effects of social and psychological influences. Indeed, lawyers' increasing reliance upon mediators for second opinions suggests a certain awareness of the difficulties created by the egocentric, availability, and other biases.[15]

Procedural Fairness Perceptions

Criteria for Judging Procedural Fairness

Procedural fairness is concerned with people's perceptions of the fairness of the procedures or processes used to arrive at outcomes. In contrast to the earlier discussion of competing criteria for judging distributive fairness, researchers have discovered a striking consistency in the criteria that people use to judge whether a dispute resolution or decision-making process was fair.[16] People in a variety of settings (e.g., workplace, contacts with police, litigation) and from different countries and cultures agree on four process characteristics as significant in signaling procedural fairness. First, people are more likely to judge a process as fair if they are given a meaningful opportunity to tell their story (i.e., an opportunity for voice). Second, in a process that feels fair, people receive assurance that the decision-maker has listened to them and understood and cared about what they had to say. Third, people watch for signs that the decision-maker is trying to treat them in an even-handed and fair manner. Finally, people value a process that accords them dignity and respect.

Effects of Procedural Fairness and Theories Regarding Its Impact

Researchers have found that people's perceptions of procedural justice can have profound effects. First, people who believe that they have been treated in a procedurally fair manner are more likely to conclude that the resulting outcome is substantively fair, even if that outcome is unfavorable. This effect may be particularly strong when available outcome information (e.g., comparative data) is ambiguous. In effect, a person's perception of procedural fairness anchors general fairness impressions. Second, people who believe that they were treated fairly in a dispute resolution or decision-making procedure are more likely to comply with the outcome of the procedure. This effect will occur even if the outcomes are not favorable or produce unhappiness. Last, people's perceptions of the procedural fairness provided by a decision-maker affect the respect, loyalty and trust accorded to that decision-maker. Perhaps surprisingly, perceptions of distributive justice generally have a much more modest impact than perceptions of procedural justice.

The impact of procedural fairness perceptions upon distributive fairness perceptions is so intriguing that this connection merits a bit more exploration. Two theories help to explain this effect of procedural fairness. The first theory, which takes an instrumentalist approach, urges that people value the opportunity for voice because it permits them to influence the final outcome of dispute resolution or decision-making processes.[17] Because they have been invited to express their views, people can be more confident that the final decision will be fully informed and substantively fair. This theory is quite rational, but it was revealed as an incomplete explanation when researchers discovered that the opportunity for voice led to perceptions of procedural justice even when people knew that their views would not and could not influence the final outcome.[18]

Scholars today theorize that perceptions of procedural fairness actually represent a heuristic, or mental shortcut, for assessments of distributive fairness.[19] In addition, however, researchers also have found empirical support for a second theory, called the group value theory, which provides that procedures themselves communicate whether people are viewed as valuable members of the relevant group.[20] The opportunity for voice, consideration, and dignified, even-handed treatment send powerful messages to people regarding their social status, which then "validates their self-identity, self-esteem, and self-respect."[21] Recognition as a member of the favored "in-group" suggests other benefits as well. If people can infer that the decision-maker is "trustworthy and benevolently disposed"[22] toward them, "they can trust that in the long run the authority with whom they are dealing will work to serve their interests."[23] Perhaps in recognition of the potential for manipulation of process signals, however, people are quite alert for signs that an apparently just process is, in actuality, a sham.[24]

Procedural Fairness in Negotiation and Mediation

Importantly, most of the research that has been done regarding procedural justice has focused on people's interactions with third-party authorities, like judges, police and managers. Recently, however, researchers have begun to examine procedural justice perceptions in the interactions between negotiators and the participants in mediation sessions. These studies indicate that people notice whether they were treated in a procedurally just manner by the other negotiator— or by the other participant in a mediation session. For example, in a study of a transformative mediation program involving disputes between managers and employees, researchers found that the mediation participants' procedural fairness perceptions were based very much upon the dynamics of their interaction with each other, much more than their interaction with the mediator.[25] This research and other studies described *infra* are beginning to confirm directly that perceptions of process fairness are relevant in negotiation[26] and will often impact both negotiators' perceptions of each other and proposed outcomes' fairness. Indeed, Tom Tyler has suggested that the importance of dignified treatment parallels a finding in the negotiation literature that "issues of 'face saving' often overwhelm bargainers, leading them to make choices not in their economic self-interest."[27]

Researchers have also found, however, that procedural justice has a greater impact on some negotiators than on others. Consistent with the group value theory, negotiators who define and evaluate themselves based on their relationships with others, or believe that social interactions should affirm basic moral values, will react more strongly to the procedural fairness (or unfairness) exhibited by their negotiating counterparts.[28] Individualistic negotiators' attitudes and behaviors are less affected by process fairness. Negotiators' relative status in the group also helps to determine the influence of procedural fairness upon their attitudes and behaviors. In a negotiation between two individuals who perceive themselves to be of uneven status, the lower status negotiator is more likely to be satisfied with an unfavorable outcome, as long as she is treated in a procedurally just manner by the higher status negotiator.[29] The higher status negotiator, in contrast, is less likely to allow process fairness to soften the blow of an unfavorable outcome. In fact, for the higher status negotiator, procedural fairness contributes significantly to her satisfaction only if the outcome is also favorable. People become especially aware of procedural fairness in settings in which status differences are made salient (e.g., a negotiation between a manager and employee at work; a negotiation between a struggling solo practitioner and a senior partner at a leading law firm, especially if the negotiation occurs in the firm's impressive board room).[30]

Ultimately, the procedural justice literature indicates that negotiators need to consider *how* they will communicate with each other just as seriously as *what* they will communicate. [Putnam, *Communication*]

Conclusion

All negotiators, including lawyers and clients, rely upon their assessments of fairness to make all sorts of decisions during negotiation: what offer shall we make? How should we respond to the other side's demand? Should we settle or make a counteroffer? Is the other side being so ridiculous that it is time to call an impasse?

Each one of these questions requires consideration of fairness, and it should now be quite clear that fairness—whether distributive or procedural—is largely a matter of perception. Perhaps what is most interesting about the research that has been done regarding fairness perceptions is the extent to which it undermines the iconic image of two rational stranger-negotiators locked in a battle of logic, economics, and will. Rather, the research reveals that negotiators' aspirations and moves will be significantly influenced by the culture and context within which they are negotiating, their own self-interest, and most intriguing of all, their social connection to each other. Ironically, as negotiations become increasingly global and virtual, it may be the development of old-fashioned relationships that will be found to matter most of all.

Endnotes

[1] In these games, Player 1 is given a fixed sum of money and instructed to divide the money in any way he chooses with Player 2. If Player 2 accepts the offer, both players will receive their designated allocations. If Player 2 rejects the offer, neither player will receive anything. Economic models indicate that Player 1 should offer only slightly more than zero to Player 2, and Player 2 should accept this amount as an improvement on his *status quo*. Instead, Player 1 generally offers 30-50% of the sum to Player 2. Twenty percent of those playing Player 2, meanwhile, reject profitable offers to take zero instead. *See* Max H. Bazerman & Margaret A. Neale, *The Role of Fairness Considerations and Relationships in a Judgmental Perspective of Negotiation, in* BARRIERS TO CONFLICT RESOLUTION 90-91 (Kenneth Arrow, et al. eds., 1995). Some commentators argue that negotiators are motivated less by a desire to be fair than by self-interest or a strong aversion to being disadvantaged themselves. Madan M. Pilluta & J. Keith Murnighan, *Fairness in Bargaining*, 16 SOCIAL JUSTICE RESEARCH 241 (2003) (arguing, based on a review of empirical research, that negotiators' behaviors that produce fair results are motivated less by a commitment to fairness than by self-interest and considerations of social utility); *see* E. Fehr & S. Gachter, *Altruistic Punishment in Humans*, 415 NATURE 137 (2002); Andrew Oswald & Daniel Zizzo, *Are People Willing to Pay to Reduce Others' Incomes?*, ANNALES D'ECONOMIE ET DE STATISTIQUE, July/Dec. 2001, at 39. Apparently, the aversion to being disadvantaged (or "envy principle") affects other animal species as well. *See* Sarah F. Brosnan & Frans B.M. de Waal, *Monkeys Reject Unequal Pay*, 425 NATURE 297 (2003) (reporting that high percentages of capuchin monkeys rejected the opportunity to trade rocks for cucumber slices when they saw other monkeys receiving grapes—which were perceived as more desirable—either in exchange for their rocks or without being required to exchange anything).

[2] Morton Deutsch, *Justice and Conflict, in* THE HANDBOOK OF CONFLICT RESOLUTION 42 (Morton Deutsch & Peter Coleman eds., 2000).

[3] *See* E. ALLAN LIND, ET AL., THE PERCEPTION OF JUSTICE: TORT LITIGANTS' VIEWS OF TRIALS, COURT-ANNEXED ARBITRATION, AND JUDICIAL SETTLEMENT CONFERENCES 59 (1989) (noting that litigants perceived procedures to be more fair and were more satisfied with their outcomes and with the courts when their outcomes exceeded their subjective expectations); Bazerman & Neale, *supra* note 1, at 90 ("[O]ptimal decision making requires consideration of the expectations and standards of the other parties with whom one is transacting business."); Chris Guthrie & James Levin, *A "Party Satisfaction" Perspective on a Comprehensive Mediation Statute*, 13 OHIO STATE JOURNAL ON DISPUTE RESOLUTION 885, 888-89 (1998) (describing the impact of parties' expectations upon their satisfaction with the mediation process); Roselle L. Wissler, *Mediation and Adjudication in Small Claims Court: The Effects of Process and Case Characteristics*, 29 LAW & SOCIOLOGICAL REVIEW 323, 346-47 (1995) (reporting that disputants' satisfaction with outcomes was influenced primarily by outcome measures and to a lesser but significant degree, by process evaluations; noting that these results are "consistent with theories that maintain that outcome satisfaction is influenced more by one's assessment of the outcome compared with expectations or with others' outcomes than by the absolute outcome received").

[4] Kwok Leung & Michael W. Morris, *Justice Through the Lens of Culture and Ethnicity, in* HANDBOOK OF JUSTICE RESEARCH IN LAW 348 (Joseph Sanders & V. Lee Hamilton eds., 2001).

[5] *See* Linda Babcock, et al., *Biased Judgment of Fairness in Bargaining*, 85 AMERICAN ECONOMIC REVIEW 1337 (1995); *see also,* Leigh Thompson & Janice Nadler, *Judgmental Biases in Conflict Resolution and How to Overcome Them, in* HANDBOOK OF CONFLICT RESOLUTION, *supra* note 2, at 219 (summarizing research regarding egocentric judgment).

[6] *See* Thompson & Nadler, *supra* note 5, at 224-25.

[7] *See id.* at 225.

[8] Such cognitive and psychological processes "range from the perfectly rational tendency for negotiators to view an adversary's willingness to offer rather than withhold a given concession as informative of that concession's *value*, to the motivational bias that frequently makes people devalue whatever is at hand or readily available relative to whatever is unavailable or withheld." Robert M. Mnookin & Lee Ross, *Introduction, in* BARRIERS TO CONFLICT RESOLUTION, *supra* note 1, at 15.

[9] *See id.*; Lee Ross, *Reactive Devaluation in Negotiation and Conflict Resolution, in* BARRIERS TO CONFLICT RESOLUTION, *supra* note 1, at 29, 41-42.

[10] *See* Tina Nabatchi & Lisa Bingham, *Expanding Our Models of Justice in Dispute Resolution: A*

Field Test of the Contribution of Interactional Justice (June 12-15, 2005) (paper presented at conference of the International Association for Conflict Management) (finding that disputants' satisfaction with mediation in the REDRESS program was best explained by their perceptions of their interactions with each other—and particularly, being empowered (or exercising control over process) and receiving recognition (or receiving respectful treatment) from each other).

[11] *See* Robert Mnookin & Lewis Kornhauser, *Bargaining in the Shadow of the Law: The Case of Divorce*, 88 YALE LAW JOURNAL 950, 959-66, 968 (1979) (discussing how the "shadow of the law" affects the negotiation of disputes).

[12] Russell Korobkin & Chris Guthrie, *Psychology, Economics and Settlement: A New Look at the Role of the Lawyer*, 76 TEXAS LAW REVIEW 77, 122 (1997). But this does not mean they always do so, in practice; *see generally*, Richard Birke & Craig R Fox, *Psychological Principles in Negotiating Civil Settlements*, 4 HARVARD NEGOTIATION LAW REVIEW 1 (1999) (discussing the considerations that influence attorneys' settlement decisions); Jeffrey M. Senger & Christopher Honeyman, *Cracking the Hard-Boiled Student: Some Ways to Turn Research Findings into Effective Training Exercises*, in THE CONFLICT RESOLUTION PRACTITIONER: A MONOGRAPH BRIDGING THEORY AND PRACTICE 190 (Shinji Morokuma ed., 2001).

[13] *See* ROBERT H. MNOOKIN, ET AL., BEYOND WINNING: NEGOTIATING TO CREATE VALUE IN DEALS AND DISPUTES 93-96 (2000) (describing the benefits of using attorneys as agents); Jeffrey Z. Rubin & Frank E.A. Sander, *When Should We Use Agents? Direct vs. Representative Negotiation*, in NEGOTIATION THEORY AND PRACTICE 81, 81-87 (J. William Breslin & Jeffrey Rubin eds., 1991) (describing the potential advantages and disadvantages of using agents in negotiation).

[14] Thus, attorneys can help their clients avoid perceiving themselves as the victims of comparative imbalance. According to the theory of relative deprivation, people care very much about whether their results are at least comparable to those received by similarly-situated others. The sense of being deprived occurs if there is a perceived discrepancy between what a person obtains, of what she wants, and what she believes she is entitled to obtain. The deprivation is relative because one's sense of deprivation is largely determined by past and current comparisons with others as well as by future expectations. Deutsch, *supra* note 2, at 44.

[15] *See* Nancy A. Welsh, *Making Deals in Court-Connected Mediation: What's Justice Got To Do With It?*, 79 WASHINGTON UNIVERSITY LAW QUARTERLY 787, 807-09 (2001) (examining lawyers' preference for mediators who engage in evaluative interventions).

[16] There is a significant body of research regarding procedural justice. *See, e.g.,* E. ALLAN LIND & TOM R. TYLER, THE SOCIAL PSYCHOLOGY OF PROCEDURAL JUSTICE 211-12 (1988); TOM TYLER, WHY PEOPLE OBEY THE LAW (1990); Stephen LaTour, et al., *Procedure: Transnational Perspectives and Preferences*, 86 YALE LAW JOURNAL 258 (1976); E. Allan Lind, et al., *Reactions to Procedural Models for Adjudicative Conflict Resolution: A Cross-National Study*, 22 JOURNAL OF CONFLICT RESOLUTION 318 (1978); Craig A. McEwen & Richard J. Maiman, *Mediation in Small Claims Court: Achieving Compliance Through Consent*, 18 LAW & SOCIETY REVIEW 11, 37 (1984); Tom R. Tyler, *Conditions Leading to Value-Expressive Effects in Judgments of Procedural Justice: A Test of Four Models*, 52 JOURNAL OF PERSONALITY & SOCIAL PSYCHOLOGY 333, 337 (1987); Tom R. Tyler, *The Psychology of Procedural Justice: A Test of the Group-Value Model*, 57 JOURNAL OF PERSONALITY & SOCIAL PSYCHOLOGY 830, 834 (1989); E. Allan Lind, et al., *In the Eye of the Beholder: Tort Litigants' Evaluations of Their Experiences in the Civil Justice System*, 24 LAW & SOCIETY REVIEW 953, 958 (1990); E. Allan Lind, et al., *Individual and Corporate Dispute Resolution: Using Procedural Fairness as a Decision Heuristic*, 38 ADMINISTRATIVE SCIENCE QUARTERLY, 224, 225 (1993).

[17] *See* E. Allan Lind, *Procedural Justice, Disputing, and Reactions to Legal Authorities*, in EVERYDAY PRACTICES AND TROUBLE CASES 177, 179 (Austin Sarat, et al. eds., 1998) [hereinafter Lind, *Procedural Justice, Disputing, and Reactions to Legal Authorities*].

[18] *See, e.g.,* E. Allan Lind, et al., *Voice, Control, and Procedural Justice: Instrumental and Noninstrumental Concerns in Fairness Judgments*, 59 JOURNAL OF PERSONALITY & SOCIAL PSYCHOLOGY 952, 957 (1990) (finding that people's fairness judgments are enhanced by the opportunity to voice their opinions even when this opportunity does not occur until after a decision has been made; having a "voice *with* the possibility of influence ... leads to even greater perceived fairness"); Tom R. Tyler, et al., *Influence of Voice on Satisfaction with Leaders: Exploring the Meaning of Process Control*, 48 JOURNAL OF PERSONALITY & SOCIAL PSYCHOLOGY 72, 80 (1985) [hereinafter Tyler, et al., *Influence of Voice*] (based on one field study and two laboratory studies, researchers concluded that voice heightens procedural justice judgments and lead-

ership endorsement even when disputants perceive that they have little control over the decision); *see also* Lind & Tyler, *supra* note 16, at 215. Some studies reveal that variations in decision control either have no influence on satisfaction or judgment of procedural justice or have a smaller influence than the effects of control over voice. *Id.* Growing evidence suggests that control over the process or having a voice "enhances judgments of procedural fairness because it is instrumental in assuring fair outcomes." *Id.* It is important to point out, however, that disputants' perceptions of procedural justice are affected by whether or not they perceive that the decision-maker has considered what they said. *See* Lind, *Procedural Justice, Disputing, and Reactions to Legal Authorities, supra* note 17, at 183; Donald E. Conlon, et al., *Nonlinear and Nonmonotonic Effects of Outcome on Procedural and Distributive Fairness Judgments,* 19 JOURNAL OF APPLIED SOCIAL PSYCHOLOGY 1085, 1095 (1989); Debra L. Shapiro & Jeanne M. Brett, *Comparing Three Processes Underlying Judgments of Procedural Justice: A Field Study of Mediation and Arbitration,* 65 JOURNAL OF PERSONALITY & SOCIAL PSYCHOLOGY. 1167, 1173 (1993). In addition, studies have found that under certain conditions, voice without decision control heightens feelings of procedural injustice and dissatisfaction with leaders, a result described as the "frustration effect." *See* Tyler, et al., *Influence of Voice, supra* note 18, at 74.

[19] *See* Lind, *Procedural Justice, Disputing, and Reactions to Legal Authorities, supra* note 17, at 177, 185.

[20] *Id.* at 182.

[21] Tom R. Tyler, *Psychological Models of the Justice Motive: Antecedents of Distributive and Procedural Justice,* 67 JOURNAL OF PERSONALITY & SOCIAL PSYCHOLOGY 850, 852 (1994).

[22] Lind, *Procedural Justice, Disputing, and Reactions to Legal Authorities, supra* note 17, at 182.

[23] Tyler, *supra* note 21, at 854.

[24] According to the procedural justice literature, citizens are aware of their vulnerability to intentional and unintentional manipulation and, if they perceive any evidence of unfair treatment or perceive "false representations of fair treatment," they respond with "extremely negative reactions." Lind, *Procedural Justice, Disputing, and Reactions to Legal Authorities, supra* note 17, at 187.

[25] *See* Nabatchi & Bingham, *supra* note 10.

[26] It should be noted, however, that recent research also suggests that the bare exchange of offers and counter-offers, which might be viewed as the opportunity for the expression of "voice," does not increase perceptions of fairness. Rather, this sort of negotiation "serve[s] to heighten the salience of conflict between the actors, trigger[s] self-serving attributions that lead actors to perceive others' motives and traits unfavorably, and increase[s] perceptions that the other is unfair." Linda Molm, et al., *In the Eye of the Beholder: Procedural Justice in Social Exchange,* 68 AMERICAN SOCIOLOGICAL REVIEW 128 (2003).

[27] Tom R. Tyler, *The Psychology of Disputants' Concerns in Mediation,* 3 NEGOTIATION JOURNAL 367, 371 (1987).

[28] Joel Brockerner, et al., *The Influence of Interdependent Self-Construal on Procedural Fairness Effects,* 96 ORGANIZATIONAL BEHAVIOR AND HUMAN DECISION PROCESSES 155 (2005). *See also* David De Cremer & Tom Tyler, *Managing Group Behavior: The Interplay Between Procedural Justice, Sense of Self, and Cooperation, in* ADVANCES IN EXPERIMENTAL SOCIAL PSYCHOLOGY (M. Zanna ed., 2005) (describing impact of procedural fairness on persons with a high need for belongingness).

[29] Ya-Ru Chen, et al., *When Is It "A Pleasure To Do Business With You?" The Effects of Relative Status, Outcome Favorability, and Procedural Fairness,* 92 ORGANIZATIONAL BEHAVIOR AND HUMAN DECISION PROCESSES 1 (2003). It is interesting to consider the interaction that may exist between perceptions of procedural fairness, negotiators' substantive expectations and the theory of relative deprivation. *See supra* notes 3 and 14.

[30] Jan-Willem van Prooijen, et al., *Procedural Justice and Status Salience as Antecedent of Procedural Fairness Effects,* 83 JOURNAL OF PERSONALITY AND SOCIAL PSYCHOLOGY 1353, 1359 (2002). *See* JANE W. ADLER, ET AL., SIMPLE JUSTICE: HOW LITIGANTS FARE IN THE PITTSBURGH COURT ARBITRATION PROGRAM 76, 83 (1983) (Unlike unsophisticated individual litigants, institutional litigants who made extensive use of the arbitration program appeared to care little about "qualitative aspects of the hearing process. They judge arbitration primarily on the basis of the outcomes it delivers.")

❧ 20 ❧

Ethics and Morality In Negotiation

Kevin Gibson

Editors' Note: *Your dilemmas as a negotiator fall into two basic sets, "what's possible?" and "what's right?" The first is treated by many chapters in this book. Here, from his philosopher's background, Gibson writes about the influence of morality on negotiations, and how we can think more clearly about what's the right thing to do. This chapter should be read in conjunction with Menkel-Meadow and with Ryan on Rawls; for the ongoing effects of morality, you might turn next to Tinsley, et al., Reputations.*

The Moral Backdrop

Negotiation is a value-based enterprise, and hence studying negotiation will also involve questions about the nature of our personal values. Negotiators necessarily make decisions about the process they will use and the posture they will adopt to satisfy their needs, and those decisions will reflect personal values involving moral issues such as fairness, rights and justice. Parties rarely have full information about each other, and so they may be in a position to take advantage of a perceived deficiency or present information that may not be true. [Korobkin, et al., *Law of Bargaining*] They may also agree to a settlement that affects third parties—for example, they could externalize costs by putting them on some entity not present at the negotiation. [Wade-Benzoni, *Future*] There may be obvious opportunities to exploit someone's ignorance or lack of power. [Bernard, *Powerlessness*] We have a background set of values that will mean that we choose to highlight some issues and ignore others, or forgo material gains for peace of mind. Even those who treat negotiation as an amoral game not subject to ordinary moral constraints have *chosen* to act that way, which is in itself an ethical choice. Ethical issues are not always clear and distinct at a conscious level in negotiation, either. Sometimes ethical issues arise quickly and we have to resolve them without being able to reflect quietly or at leisure. Thus, there are a number of reasons we should consider our moral stance prior to sitting down at the negotiating table and look at ethics construed much more broadly that it traditionally has been.

This chapter gives an outline of some of the major ways that we can think about the morality of negotiation, and how it may develop in the future. The field has matured sufficiently that ethical discussions should encompass three major elements: first, the moral stance of the parties themselves; second, issues such as trust, disclosure or beneficence which arise from their perspective of negotiation as a competition or alternatively mutual problem-solving. Finally, we should also recognize that private deal making is sanctioned against a societal backdrop that currently gives a lot of latitude to agreements as long as they are not unconscionable. Hence, we ought to be aware of the way negotiation fits into the wider political context of justice, rights, equality or welfare. [Welsh, *Fairness*]

Initially we should consider the language involved. "Ethics" is typically used in two different senses, first as a set of rules in a limited domain and second as a frame for discussing value judgments of right and wrong, good and bad, as well as fairness, justice and rights. In the first sense, it would be appropriate to say there is an ethics of poker, where those playing the game acknowledge the specific rules and behavior involved. Thus lying may be routine and expected, and the aim is to win out over your opponents. At the same time, though, it is unacceptable to play with marked cards or a confederate. In this sense we can talk about "the ethics of the mob" where reporting illegal acts to the police may result in retribution from colleagues, although ordinarily we might consider such a report as the decent and legal thing to do.

The view of ethics as providing rules has some important implications. It will appeal to those who have a strong sense of role morality, that is, those who believe that there are different sets of behavior that apply when we undertake distinct functions. Role morality may constrain a lawyer from disclosing information about the whereabouts of a murder victim's body to grieving relatives because of the primacy of lawyer/client confidentiality.[1] In the case of negotiation, it will serve those who believe that negotiation is a competitive amoral game where success can be achieved by any legal means and it is measured by substantive gains alone.[2] Some writers, such as James White, have advocated that the only constraint on behavior in negotiation should be its legality, since the duty of an attorney in negotiation is to maximize gains for his or her client by whatever legal means are available. He says: "The negotiator's role is at least passively to mislead his opponent about his settling point while at the same time to engage in ethical behavior."[3] In essence, he takes the legal threshold as the benchmark of ethical behavior. There are a number of problems associated with this view: the law is largely a reactive instrument that responds to challenges, and this means it does not legislate everything—new and different issues not covered by settled law have no moral anchor. [Korobkin, et al., *Law of Bargaining*] Furthermore, we could imagine a world where this is the prevailing attitude. In it, all human interaction would be governed by reference to a legal code, and thus we would need armies of monitors, jurists and enforcers. A more practical approach is to reward trust and good reputation. In contrast to the poker model our everyday lives are, in fact, marked by a background condition of trust that makes sharp dealing conspicuous and jarring. [Lewicki, *Trust*]

The second sense of role morality suggests that human conduct cannot be compartmentalized into distinct spheres and that a similar notion of, say, justice will apply in all of our activities. Here ethics is used as talk about values, and prohibitions against immoral activities such as lying will be just as applicable to negotiation as they would be in any other interaction. Viewed in this way, the legal and ethical spheres may often overlap, but what is right is gauged by reference to personal morality rather than a legal code.[4]

Another way we can describe this central difference in approach is to use the terms "intrinsic" and "instrumental." Some traditions believe that we should always do the right thing for the sake of goodness alone, without regard for any potential reward.[5] Thus, promises should be kept and obligations met merely because they are duties, which should not be compromised because of inconvenience or greater benefits elsewhere. These are known generally as deontological views, and emphasize the importance of assessing motives, securing rights and respecting individuals as ends-in-themselves rather than as a means to some end.

Other approaches stress the consequences of an action, and seek to maximize the benefits from a particular decision. Some of this family are instrumental views that acknowledge that we are largely motivated by self-interest and are likely to act accordingly.[6] They might interpret apparent altruistic acts, say, donating blood, in terms of greater psychological welfare for the donors, or as strategic self-interest, because they are contributing to an institution that they may ultimately benefit from.

We can use the case of lying in negotiation as a simple example: some people will hold truth telling so inviolate that they would never give a false answer to a direct question; others might do so if the reward was sufficiently tempting, and others would have few qualms about making false statements. It is often difficult to assess motives, of course, and a sufficiently sophisticated instrumental negotiator may tell the truth as a strategy because he or she realizes that there are personal benefits in the long run by maintaining a reputation for honesty.

Thus, individuals come to negotiation with significantly different views about the nature of ethics and how it applies to negotiation. Nevertheless, there are several key elements that may substantially enhance our understanding of the way that values play into our bargaining behavior.

Ethics Education in Negotiation

"The law," it is often asserted, provides a clear threshold of unacceptable activity. However, leaving aside the question of whether this is true in any beyond the most general sense, there is considerable latitude for discretionary behavior. So, for example, under Federal Rule of Evidence 408, settlement discussions may not be used in future litigation. At the same time, participants may not have to tell the truth in those discussions or even bargain in good faith.[7]

Individuals will come to a negotiation with differing views about the nature of the process, and these are reflected in the various ways it has been defined.[8] A worthwhile starting point in discussions about negotiation is to discover what individuals believe the aim of negotiation is and what they consider the proper way to achieve it. Some may feel that negotiation is a zero-sum game where the object is to win at the expense of another, and any notion of compromise would be unacceptable. Others might align more closely with the belief that each party will naturally seek mutually beneficial outcomes, and these values will steer the way they negotiate.

Some exercises in negotiation force participants to confront their personal ethics. For instance, in iterated prisoner dilemma games it is often profitable for parties to lie or betray each other. Empirical work shows that some participants will prefer to retain a sense of ethical self-worth rather than compromise their values for instant gain.[9] Others will not feel constrained by concerns about lying or defection. Empirical testing based on personality types found that cooperative people believe there are cooperative, neutral and competitive people in the world; people with a more neutral disposition felt there were neutral and competitive sorts; and competitive individuals felt that everyone was exclusively competitive too.[10] Our approach to negotiation involved an assessment of the party across the bargaining table, and unrealistically imputing values to others meant that the style of bargaining was unnecessarily limited and opportunities for settlement were lost. Competitive behavior in these tests was associated with selective misrepresentation and willingness to renege on agreements. Professor Gerry Williams would characterize such behavior in role as "aggressive."[11] In contrast to the cooperative negotiator, the aggressor will push the other side as far as it will go, in the belief that the opponent will stop them if they go over the boundary of moral acceptability. In that sense, they do not self-monitor their behavior, but rather rely on their opponents to restrain them, a stance that may leave other parties feeling "steamrollered."[12] Some negotiation exercises may foster self-consciousness about our individual approach to negotiation and our perceptions of others, and reassessing our personal values is useful in developing a greater repertoire of potential actions and responses.

There is a considerable literature that treats negotiation as an amoral game, where ethical concerns do not stand in the way of substantive gains.[13] For example, Herb Cohen's bestselling book *You Can Negotiate Anything* advocates the so-called floor model technique that involves walking up to a refrigerator you are considering purchasing in a store and muttering to the sales clerk that you notice a blemish. "What if there are no multiple blemi [sic] on the refrigerator?" Cohen asks rhetorically, "You can always make blemi."[14] Given the prevalence of such approaches it is worthwhile to be aware of the nature of the techniques involved and the dynamics they set up. Clearly, the aim in most of these "tricks of the trade" is to give one party an advantage in bargaining. The practical difficulty with employing these tactics is that they often put one's credibility at risk, and once that is compromised then there is little prospect of future interaction.[15] Although the aggression and competition of gamesmanship may lead to short-term gains, it risks reputation.[16] [Tinsely, et al., *Reputations*] The evidence is that any immediate benefit will typically be negated by the inefficiencies imposed by distrust and the opportunity costs of foregone future transactions.[17] Because withholding information and staking out positions effectively narrows the positive bargaining zone and limits the possibilities for settlement, much of the current focus has moved to the greater potential of integrative interest-based bargaining.

Interest-Based Bargaining and Ethics

Interest-based bargaining is a form of negotiation that promotes mutual problem-solving in order to maximize the welfare of all parties to a negotiation.[18] It expands the analysis of an individual's interests from the substantive outcome to include psychological and process needs. Hence, a person who does not haggle may still get a good deal in that she is satisfied with the outcome. The approach suggests that we look at negotiation as mutual problem-solving, where negotiators often have overlapping desires that could be integrated if there was more open disclosure and greater trust, in contrast to the adversarial posture of traditional positional bargaining. But we are often wedded to the way we have always dealt with things, and as Michael Watkins suggests, "truth telling, fairness, and balanced representation of parties absent from the table present the biggest challenges."[19]

Empirical work in sociobiology [Yarn & Jones, *Biology*] and game theory indicates that cooperative approaches are optimal when there are repeated encounters.[20] Doing good by not lying, building a reputation and cooperating may, in fact, lead to doing well. Developing effective relationships for optimal settlements may involve initially risky moves, such as promoting trust or conciliatory initiatives, but can eventually lead to more mutually satisfactory outcomes.[21] [Tinsley, et al., *Reputations*]

Following Fisher and Ury, some forms of integrative bargaining are referred to as "principled bargaining" since agreement is based on an appeal to an independent principle or criterion. These principles will often be value-laden; for example they propose among others moral standards, tradition, and equal treatment.[22] Typically, there will also be a justification given for acceding to the criteria, such as custom, law, precedent or some conception of fairness. However, under Fisher's definition at least, as long as the disputants are content with the criteria, they will qualify as objective. They do not have to be "fair" and "just" in any sense other than that the parties are able to muster some argument to that effect. Consider an example: a student and teacher are disputing a grade. They might agree to settle based on an average of all other work submitted over the term, on an average of best and worst grades, or on the class average, all of which are independent criteria, in that they might be suggested by an impartial third party and could be defended in terms of being just and unprejudiced. We should note that they are not, and need not, be defended in terms of some conception of *truth*. Indeed, although the criteria may have a justification of reasonableness, the disputants may even select an arbitrary criterion as one that they can both agree to as an independent standard. This is often done to break an impasse. Thus, if the only way to break a deadlock between student and teacher is to resort to some arbitrary device, they may use a random mechanical means like tossing a coin to come to some resolution. This will fulfill Fisher's conditions, (both can agree on it and it has some 'reasoned basis')—yet it is a far cry from pure objectivity, and may not represent common sense notions of fairness or justice.

Present Directions in Ethics

The emergence of ethics awareness and training might be considered an expanding circle, where originally it dealt mainly with compliance and avoiding sanctions, but now has moved to looking at issues in a far wider and more comprehensive context.[23] One manifestation of the wider realm of moral concern is the more frequent use of stakeholder analysis. Stakeholders are people or institutions that will be helped or harmed in some way by change, and perhaps ought to be considered at the bargaining table even if they are not represented.[24] Communitarian theorists also believe that we need to move from thinking of individuals in the world as disconnected atomic units toward instead seeing them as part of a connected web of interactions. This contrasts to the traditional enlightenment liberal notion where the individual is sovereign, and his or her duty is to maximize personal welfare.[25]

The expansion of ethical consideration has also been referred to as plus-one staging.[26] Lawrence Kohlberg developed a well-known set of moral levels. They move from the pre-conventional, where moral reasoning revolves around the physical consequences of action in terms of punishment and reward, to the conventional level where conformity to social order takes priority and we want to fit in with prevailing norms. He then describes the post-conventional that focuses on principled reasoning where the subject is motivated by moral values and principles with a concern for universality and consistency.[27] Kohlberg's research suggests that most people are in the conventional level, and plus-one staging challenges individuals to assess their own moral development and think at higher levels with a wider perspective about what they should do. In negotiation theory we often begin by making sure that a participant's actions will not lead to punishment by poor performance or breaching the law, and then move on to exploring how we think an ideal negotiator might behave. Using the Kohlberg model, some negotiation trainers encourage personal reflection and moral development.

Kohlberg's work has been supplemented by insights by Carol Gilligan.[28] Gilligan noted that oftentimes when women were confronted with moral dilemmas, they thought about them differently from the men—roughly, they were more concerned about relationships between individuals and about why the dilemma arose in the first place. It is not surprising, then, that women (in general) may deal with moral concerns, conflict, and negotiation in ways that have not traditionally been explored in the classroom. There is growing literature both in ethical theory and negotiation that challenges the established (male) template of correct action.[29] [Kolb & Putnam, *Gender*]

Another movement in ethics is to closely examine the language we use and its moral implications. Negotiators are aware of so-called "framing effects," a broad term that covers the ways that different articulations of the same facts may affect the way people will react. For example, if an issue is perceived as foregoing a gain, individuals will be less concerned than if they believe they are taking a loss—even if the net result is the same.[30] [Korobkin & Guthrie, *Heuristics*] Post-modernist writers view this kind of dynamic in a more radical way with deeper moral implications. They have proposed that we need to look at the world as a set of perceived narratives, and, consequently, that we should see negotiation not so much as an exposition of positions and interests, but also as a question of which story comes to dominate the discourse.[31] Research indicates when inexperienced or untrained individuals negotiate, settlements emerge out of the initial narrative almost eighty percent of the time, which means there is immense power to being the first to make a case. As Cobb and Rifkin note, justice issues will be more than substantive or procedural guidelines and spill over into "a question of access, of participation in the construction of dominant descriptions and stories."[32] The upshot is that ethics in negotiation involves not only the process of negotiation and the participant's behavior, but might be expanded significantly to consider the whole context in which the negotiation is set and the way the parties' interpretations are presented, contested, transformed and finally settled upon in terms of what would be most just, fair or appropriate. For example, two insurance adjusters may share the same worldview and agree on the terms of negotiation, whereas if we think of a struggling tenant and landlord, the difference is not just one of positions and interests, but the very way in which they see and make sense of the world.

Conclusion

Morality is a matter of our values. Some values are trivial, some can be traded, and some we use to identify who we are in the world—and compromising those may be, in some cases, literally more than our life is worth. We can also see the power of a moral appeal in the early claims of children that something is "just not fair." One of the elements that makes negotiation so complex and not just a mechanical procedure is that we are dealing with individuals who have psychological and emotional needs that are intimately linked with their value systems. Thus, asking someone to make a commitment to a settlement that is perceived as unfair or unjust is likely to tap into our core philosophical approach to who we are and how we relate to others. This means that while we may accept or reject the value systems that others have, any serious examination of negotiation cannot afford to ignore their effects. Ethical issues in negotiation may be approached in a narrow sense that looks at the minimally acceptable levels of bargaining behavior. However, we have seen that the current movement is to think seriously about the fundamental issues of justice and fairness in a much wider perspective. Essentially this will provide us with a much more comprehensive and useful way to analyze and make recommendations for the field of negotiation as a whole.

Endnotes

[1] *See, e.g.*, DAVID LUBAN, LAWYERS AND JUSTICE (1988).
[2] *See, e.g.*, G. RICHARD SHELL, BARGAINING FOR ADVANTAGE: NEGOTIATION STRATEGIES FOR REASONABLE PEOPLE 201-34 (1999) (contrasting deception to integrity). *See generally* Murray L. Schwartz, *The Professionalism and Accountability of Lawyers*, 66 CALIFORNIA LAW REVIEW 669 (1978); Walter W. Steele, Jr., *Deceptive Negotiating and High-Toned Morality*, 39 VANDERBILT LAW REVIEW 1387 (1986); Charles B. Craver, *Negotiation Ethics: How to be Deceptive Without Being Dishonest/How to be Assertive Without Being Offensive*, 38 SOUTH TEXAS LAW REVIEW 713

(1997); *see also* MONROE H. FREEDMAN, LAWYERS' ETHICS IN AN ADVERSARY SYSTEM 9 (1975) ("Let justice be done—that is, for my client let justice be done—though the heavens fall."). Note that legality remains the benchmark of acceptable behavior, and thus reliance on misrepresented information, for instance, would still be actionable.

[3] James J. White, *The Pros and Cons of "Getting to Yes"*, 34 JOURNAL OF LEGAL EDUCATION 115, 118 (1984).

[4] *See generally* DAVID LYONS, ETHICS AND THE RULE OF LAW (1984); LON L. FULLER, THE MORALITY OF LAW, (rev. ed. 1965); MORTON R. KADISH & SANFORD H. KADISH, DISCRETION TO DISOBEY (1973).

[5] ROGER FISHER, ET AL., BEYOND MACHIAVELLI: TOOLS FOR COPING WITH CONFLICT 108-13 (1994).

[6] This is not to say that individuals cannot combine both intrinsic and instrumental approaches.

[7] FEDERAL RULE OF EVIDENCE 408.

[8] To negotiate is defined by the OXFORD ENGLISH DICTIONARY as "to confer with another with a view to compromise or agreement" Chris Moore says it is "a problem-solving process in which two or more people voluntarily discuss their differences and attempt to reach a joint decision on their common concerns." CHRISTOPHER MOORE, DECISION MAKING AND CONFLICT MANAGEMENT (1987). For additional definitions of negotiation *see* JEFFREY RUBIN & BERT BROWN, SOCIAL PSYCHOLOGY OF BARGAINING AND NEGOTIATION (1975).

[9] *See generally* J. KEITH MURNIGHAN, BARGAINING GAMES (1992).

[10] H. Kelly & A. Stahelski, *Social Interaction Basis of Cooperators and Competitor's Beliefs About Others*, JOURNAL OF PERSONALITY & SOCIAL PSYCHOLOGY 66, 66-91 (1970).

[11] Gerald R. Williams, *Style and Effectiveness in Negotiation, in* NEGOTIATION: STRATEGIES FOR MUTUAL GAIN 172-74 (Lavinia Hall ed., 1993). Phyllis Beck Kritek makes the point well when she says that negotiators need to be aware of their own core values but ought not to try to impose them on others lest they are rejected by the other bargainers and the dynamic in the negotiation changes to a power struggle over the acceptability of that particular set of values. PHYLLIS BECK KRITEK, NEGOTIATING AT AN UNEVEN TABLE 215 (2002).

[12] Kelly & Stahelski, *supra* note 10.

[13] There is a considerable literature on the ploys of so-called 'hard' bargaining. *See generally* MICHAEL SCHARTZKI & WAYNE R. COFFEY, NEGOTIATION: THE ART OF GETTING WHAT YOU WANT (1981); ROBERT J. RINGER, WINNING THROUGH INTIMIDATION (1974); VICTOR GOTBAUM, NEGOTIATING IN THE REAL WORLD: GETTING THE DEAL YOU WANT (1999).

[14] HERB COHEN, YOU CAN NEGOTIATE ANYTHING 33-34 (1980) (emphasis omitted).

[15] In iterated prisoner's dilemmas where one side has defected following a period of cooperation, a voluntary working relationship can be reestablished, but typically the injured party demands considerable penance; that is, there are costs to the defecting party if it wants to interact again with the same partner. *See* Kevin Gibson, et al., *Once Bitten: Defection and Reconciliation in a Cooperative Enterprise*, 9 BUSINESS ETHICS QUARTERLY 69, 75-85 (1999)

[16] Akerlof makes the point that if it is known that there is a percentage of duds in a given market (e.g., 10% of cars are lemons) then customers will discount what they are prepared to pay to compensate for the risk of ending up with one of the duds. This implies that parties in a negotiation will lower their substantive offers in relation to the possibility of getting taken. Similarly, they will pay more for what they perceive as a straight deal. Thus the overall effect of sharp practice is to lower the gains of those involved. *See* George A. Akerlof, *The Market for Lemons: Quality Uncertainty and the Market Mechanism*, 84 QUARTERLY JOURNAL OF ECONOMICS 488, 488-500 (1970).

[17] *See generally* LEIGH THOMPSON, THE MIND AND HEART OF THE NEGOTIATOR (2005). A recent study at the University of Michigan demonstrated that a good reputation for seller on E-bay led to a twelve percent increase in profits. Catherine Dupree, *Integrity has its Price*, HARVARD MAGAZINE July-Aug. 2003, *available at* http://www.harvardmagazine.com/on-line/070378.html (last visited Mar. 17, 2006).

[18] ROGER FISHER & WILLIAM URY, GETTING TO YES (1981).

[19] MICHAEL WATKINS, BREAKTHROUGH BUSINESS NEGOTIATION: A TOOLBOX FOR MANAGERS 111 (2002).

[20] *See* Elizabeth Mannix, Catherine Tinsley & Max Bazerman, *Negotiation Over Time: Impediments to Integrative Solutions*, 62 ORGANIZATIONAL BEHAVIOR AND HUMAN DECISION PROCESSES 241, 241-51 (1995); FRANS DE WAAL, PEACEMAKING AMONG PRIMATES (1989); ANDREW COLMAN, COOPERATION AND COMPETITION IN HUMANS AND ANIMALS (Andrew M. Colman ed., 1982).

[21] Dean G. Pruitt, *Strategy in Negotiation*, *in* INTERNATIONAL NEGOTIATION 78 (Victor A. Kremenyuk ed., 1991).

[22] FISHER & URY, *supra* note 18 at 89.

[23] *See* PETER SINGER, THE EXPANDING CIRCLE: ETHICS AND SCOIOBIOLOGY (1981).

[24] There is extensive literature on stakeholder theory in business ethics. *See* R. Edward Freeman & John McVea, *A Stakeholder Approach to Strategic Management*, *in* THE BLACKWELL HANDBOOK OF STRATEGIC MANAGEMENT 189 (Michael A. Hitt, et al. eds., 2001).

[25] *See, e.g.*, AMITAI ETZIONI, THE NEW GOLDEN RULE: COMMUNITY AND MORALITY IN A DEMOCRATIC SOCIETY (1996); MARKATE DALY, COMMUNITARIANISM: A NEW PUBLIC ETHICS (1994).

[26] Janet A. Schmidt & Mark Davison, *Helping Students Think*, 61 PERSONNEL GUIDANCE JOURNAL 563, 563-69 (1983).

[27] Lawrence Kohlberg & Richard Kramer, *Continuities and Discontinuities in Childhood and Adult Moral Development*, 12 HUMAN DEVELOPMENT 93 (1969).

[28] CAROL GILLIGAN, IN A DIFFERENT VOICE: PSYCHOLOGICAL THEORY AND WOMEN'S DEVELOPMENT (1982).

[29] *See, e.g.*, DEBORAH KOLB & JUDITH WILLIAMS, EVERYDAY NEGOTIATION: NAVIGATING THE HIDDEN AGENDAS IN BARGAINING (2003); DEBORAH KOLB & JUDITH WILLIAMS, THE SHADOW NEGOTIATION: HOW WOMEN CAN MASTER THE HIDDEN AGENDAS THAT DETERMINE BARGAINING SUCCESS (2000); LINDA BABCOCK & SARA LASCHEVER, WOMEN DON'T ASK: NEGOTIATION AND THE GENDER DIVIDE (2003). *See generally* ALISON M. JAGGAR & IRIS MARION YOUNG, A COMPANION TO FEMINIST PHILOSOPHY (1998); MARILYN PEARSAL, WOMEN AND VALUES: READINGS IN RECENT FEMINIST PHILOSOPHY (1993).

[30] Max H. Bazerman, *The Relevance of Kahneman and Tversky's Concept of Framing to Organizational Behavior*, 10 JOURNAL OF MANAGEMENT, 333, 333-43 (1984).

[31] For an overview, *see* Sara Cobb & Janet Rifkin, *Practice and Paradox: Deconstructing Neutrality in Mediation*, 16 LAW & SOCIAL INQUIRY 36 (1991).

[32] *Id.* at 62.

❦ 21 ❧

The Law of Bargaining

Russell Korobkin, Michael L. Moffitt & Nancy A. Welsh

Editors' Note: How far can you go in extolling the virtues of your widgets without crossing the line to fraud? Other chapters (on trust, reputation, ethics) consider the morality and the implications of negotiation behavior. This chapter focuses on the legal limits of negotiation: sometimes, you or your counterparts have employees with children to feed, and somebody will go to the limit of what is legally permissible. Every negotiator needs to know where that limit actually is and how it's influenced by the context.

Negotiation is sometimes compared to poker. Though imperfect, this analogy is apt in two related respects. First, poker players and negotiators both sometimes perceive opportunities to deceive or exploit their counterparts in ways that produce a distributive advantage. Lies, bluffs, false signals, covert manipulation and outright coercion occupy a significant place in the repertoires of some negotiators. Second, the ability of both negotiators and poker players to deceive and exploit is constrained by a pre-established set of rules governing behavior. This brief chapter surveys the ways in which law constrains negotiators' behavior.

At least three categories of rules comprise the law of bargaining. First, common law limitations govern virtually all negotiators: the doctrines of fraud and misrepresentation limit the extent to which negotiators may deceive, and the doctrine of duress limits the extent to which bargainers can use superior bargaining power to coerce agreement. Second, context-specific laws sometimes circumscribe negotiating behavior in specific settings when general rules are less restrictive. Third, the conduct of certain negotiators is constrained by professional or organizational regulations inapplicable to the general public. These categories are discussed in turn. The final section of this essay reflects on constraints on negotiator behavior in the absence of law.

Common Law Limits on Bargaining Behavior

Deceit

When a negotiated agreement results from false statements made during the bargaining process, the common law of tort and contract sometimes holds negotiators liable for damages or makes their resulting agreements subject to rescission.[1] The common law does not, however, amount to a blanket prohibition on all lying. Instead, the common law principles are subject to the caveats that false statements must be material, the opposing negotiator must rely on the false statements, and such reliance must be justified. Whether reliance is justified depends on the type of statement at issue and the statement's specificity. A seller's specific false claim ("this car gets 80 miles per gallon gas mileage") is actionable, but his more general claim ("this car gets good gas mileage") is probably not, because the latter statement is acknowledged as the type of "puffing" or "sales talk" on which no reasonable buyer would rely.

While it is often said that misrepresentations of fact are actionable but misrepresentations of opinion are not, this statement is not strictly accurate. Statements of opinions can be false, either because the speaker does not actually have the claimed opinion ("I think this Hyundai is the best car built in the world today") or because the statement implies knowledge of facts that are, in fact, untrue ("I think this Hyundai gets the best gas mileage of any car"). But statements of opinion are less likely to induce justified reliance than are statements of specific facts, especially when they are very general, such as a claim that an item is one of "good quality."[2] Thus, a plaintiff attempting to negotiate the settlement of a lawsuit may not, within the bounds of the law, falsely tell the defendant that he believes he broke five ribs in his collision with the defendant's car, but a statement that he suffered a "painful injury" in the collision would not be actionable, even if the plaintiff subjectively felt little pain. In one recent example of this distinction, a court ruled that a defendant's claim that the poultry breeding stock sold to the plaintiff had "very high productive traits" was mere "commercial puffery" that could not form the basis of a fraud claim because it did "not set forth a concrete representation."[3]

Whether reliance on a statement of fact or opinion is justified depends significantly on the context of the negotiation and whether the speaker has access to information that the recipient does not have. A seller "aggressively" promoting his product, whose stated opinions imply facts that are not true, is less likely to find himself in legal difficulty if the veracity of his claims are easily investigated by an equally-knowledgeable buyer than if his customer is a consumer unable to evaluate the factual basis of the claims.[4] The case for liability is stronger, however, when the negotiator holds himself out as being particularly knowledgeable about the subject matter that the expressed opinion concerns.[5] Whether a false statement can be insulated from liability by a subsequent disclaimer depends on the strength and clarity of the disclaimer, as well as on the nature of the false statement. Again, the standard is whether the reasonable recipient of the information in total would rely on the statement at issue when deciding whether to enter into an agreement.[6]

While the law frowns on false statements about the qualities of goods or services that are the subject matter of a negotiation, it is universally recognized that a negotiator's false statements concerning how valuable an agreement is to her or the maximum she is willing to give up or exchange in order to seal an agreement (the negotiator's "reservation point," or "bottom line") are not actionable, again on the ground that such false statements are common and no reasonable negotiator would rely upon them. So, to take one example, an insurance adjuster who claimed that $900 was "all he could pay" to settle a claim is not liable for fraud, even if the statement was false.[7]

The law is less settled regarding the status of false statements concerning the existence of outside alternatives for a negotiator. A false claim of an offer from a third-party is relevant because it implies a strong reservation point, so a negotiator might logically argue that such a claim is no more actionable than a claim as to the reservation point itself. Courts, however, have occasionally ruled that false claims of a specific third-party offer are actionable, on the ground that they are material to the negotiation and that the speaker has access to information that cannot be easily verified by the listener's independent investigation.[8]

The most inscrutable area of the law of deception concerns when a negotiator may be held legally liable for failing to disclose information that might weaken his bargaining position (rather than affirmatively asserting a false claim). The traditional laissez-faire rule that affirmative disclosures are not necessary—traceable to Chief Justice John Marshall's 1817 decision in *Laidlaw v. Organ* that a tobacco purchaser buying on the cheap had no obligation to inform a seller that the War of 1812 had ended, and with it the British naval blockade that had depressed crop prices[9]—eroded somewhat in the twentieth century, with courts placing greater disclosure responsibility on negotiators. It is clear that any affirmative action taken to conceal a fact, including the statement of a "half-truth" that implies a false fact, will be treated as if it were an affirmative false statement. Thus, in one well-known case, a seller who advertised that her residential dwelling could be rented as apartments was found liable for misrepresentation because she failed to disclose that the use of the property in this way violated local zoning regulations that prohibited multi-family uses. Her representation, the court ruled, implied that the proposed use was legal, even though it did not explicitly include such a statement.[10] Beyond this point, however, the law becomes murky. Although the general rule is probably still that negotiators have no general disclosure obligation, some courts require bargainers (especially sellers) to disclose known material facts not easily discovered by the other party.[11]

Coercion

Just as the law places some limits on the use of deceptive behavior to seal a bargain, so too does it place some limits upon negotiators' ability to use threats to coerce acquiescence with their demands. Courts can invoke the doctrine of duress to protect parties who are both the victims of a threat that is "improper" and have "no reasonable alternative" but to acquiesce to the other party's demand that is backed by the threat.[12]

A prototypical example of duress is when a mobster procures a business owner's consent to an agreement to provide garbage collection services at an inflated price by threatening to have the citizen's kneecaps broken if he declines. The threat is clearly improper because the threatened action, if carried out, would be a crime. The citizen does have an alternative to acquiescing—he could suffer the injury, notify the police and bring a civil suit for damages—but this will not restore his health, so it seems unreasonable to expect him to follow this course of action.

On the other hand, negotiators may procure a more favorable deal by threatening to take other types of actions to the detriment of a counterpart who will not agree to their demands. The purveyor of sanitation services may threaten to let the citizen's garbage rot on the curbside unless the citizen agrees to pay the exorbitant price that she wishes to charge for garbage collection. Such threats are routinely implied—if not explicitly asserted—in negotiating encounters, of course, and the ability to make such a threat *credibly* (the threat is useless if the citizen believes the garbage collector will pick up the garbage in any event) is often considered an important source of bargaining power.[13] What is perceived as coercion in the eyes of a negotiator on one side of the table is often considered mere leverage or "hard

bargaining" by the negotiator on the other side and by a court reviewing the behavior.

The linguistic touchstones of the duress doctrine, "improper" threats and the
lack of "reasonable" alternatives, are indeterminate, and published judicial opinions also fail to delineate clearly when a negotiator's threat to carry out an act or
omission that will cause harm to his negotiating counterpart is so coercive that it
meets the legal requirements of duress. A few principles may be inferred from the
case law, however.

First, if a negotiator owes a fiduciary or quasi-fiduciary duty to his negotiation
counterpart and threatens an action of questionable legal right, courts often find
the threat improper—even when the action would not clearly meet the definition
of a tort or a crime. In this situation, courts also will often adopt a loose interpretation of the requirement that the victim has "no reasonable alternative" but to
acquiesce. So, for example, one court found a plaintiff stated a claim for duress
when an insurance company threatened to stop her ongoing disability payments if
she would not agree to a lump sum settlement,[14] and another upheld a claim for
duress when a lawyer threatened not to return important client documents
(needed in order to consummate a pending deal in which time was of the essence)
until a fee dispute was settled.[15]

Second, a negotiator's threat to breach an agreement if its contractual partner
will not agree to the negotiator's demands can constitute duress when the original
contract made the victim particularly vulnerable to the later threat. In the landmark case of *Austin Instruments v. Loral Corp.*,[16] the New York Court of Appeals
found duress when a supplier used the threat of breach of its contract with a defense contractor to force concessions and the contractor's reputation with the
military would have suffered had it refused to agree to the supplier's demands and
consequently failed to meet its production obligations.

In addition to the doctrine of duress, courts may invoke other contract defenses to remedy exploitation when the bargaining parties' relationship is not
arms-length or is markedly one-sided. For example, the common law provides the
defense of undue influence to negotiators who can show that they were dependent upon and thus vulnerable to the other, dominant negotiator.[17] A dramatically
dominant party who uses high-pressure tactics and thus secures a patently unreasonable deal may find the agreement crumbling in response to a charge of
substantive and procedural unconscionability.[18] Finally, some negotiators (most
notably minors) belong to a sort of "protected class" whose exercise of "free will"
in entering into a negotiated agreement can never be assumed.[19]

Context-Specific Regulation of Negotiators' Behavior

Beyond the broad set of common law constraints on negotiators' behavior, the law
imposes particularized parameters on bargainers engaged in negotiations in some
specific contexts.

In some areas of practice, the bargaining process itself is highly formalized and
constrained. For example, compared with their counterparts in non-unionized
settings, employers, employees, and their representatives involved in collective
bargaining all have considerable limits on their ability to adopt certain approaches
to negotiating the terms and conditions of employment. Federal and state laws
proscribe a range of behaviors in collective bargaining contexts. The most vivid
encapsulation of these requirements is the duty imposed on both sides by the National Labor Relations Act to bargain in "good faith."[20] The concept of "good faith"
bargaining lacks clear parameters, but courts measure each side's behaviors

against a "totality of conduct" standard.[21] Over the several decades since the Supreme Court first articulated this test, courts have also identified an increasing list of specifically proscribed behaviors. Negotiators acting in other contexts are free to give each other take-it-or-leave-it offers. They can set up meetings whenever they choose, and can freely choose not to attend unless a court has required attendance. Negotiators in many contexts outside of labor can engage in tactics designed to delay the negotiations; they can send representatives without authority; and they can withdraw their assent to provisions to which they had previously tentatively agreed. In labor negotiations, however, each of these behaviors can form the basis of an actionable claim that the negotiator breached its duty to bargain in "good faith."[22] The bargaining process, and the behaviors of the individuals engaged in bargaining, is therefore constrained.

In other contexts, the law imposes affirmative duties of disclosure rather than attempting to define broader parameters of negotiation behavior. For example, in residential real estate transactions in many states, sellers have a legal obligation to disclose a range of information even if the buyer does not request it.[23] Supplanting the baseline principle of *caveat emptor*, many states have judged that real estate transactions require different foundational principles. Similarly, in negotiations between spouses contemplating the terms of a divorce agreement, each spouse is held to be in a confidential, fiduciary relationship with the other, provided that the negotiations are not being conducted through attorneys or other agents. And with that status attaches a set of duties to disclose a broader range of information than would be the case in negotiations conducted at arm's length.[24]

In certain bargaining contexts that seem unusually prone to exploitation, the law provides paternalistic protection for potential victims—those who because of relatively lower power or information might be unacceptably exploited by their negotiating counterparts. One category of such protections includes judicial supervision of the terms of negotiated agreements. In most negotiations, parties may enter binding agreements without the "approval" of any external body. In certain contexts, however, the court becomes involved in reviewing the terms of an agreement before it is finalized. For example, certain legal disputes involving seamen (this term is regarded as gender neutral both in the relevant statute and by the Navy) on the high seas and their employers require judicial approval, because of the perceived power imbalance between seamen and ship owners.[25] Similarly, most jurisdictions require court ratification of divorce and custody agreements.[26] To protect principal parties with little ability to monitor their agents, settlements of class action[27] and shareholder derivative suits[28] also require a judicial finding of fairness.

The second category of paternalistic protections provides potential victims with easier means of extracting themselves from unfavorable agreements after-the-fact. For example, many jurisdictions give consumers in certain vulnerable contexts the self-help remedy of unilaterally rescinding an agreement within several days of acceptance, such as when they accept a bargain proposed by telemarketers or door-to-door salespersons.[29] The law also sometimes establishes dispute resolution mechanisms for contexts frequently characterized by dissatisfaction with negotiated agreements. For example, lemon laws anticipate that some percentage of negotiations over new car purchases will result in unhappy consumers. In states with lemon laws, consumers who are dissatisfied with their purchase because of a nonconformity with the manufacturer's warranty need not establish one of the traditional bases for rescinding a contract or ceasing performance (for example fraud, duress, or material breach). Instead, consumers have a streamlined system for demonstrating eligibility for the laws' protections after the fact.[30]

Professional and Organizational Constraints on Bargaining Behavior

Some negotiators operate not only within the legal constraints applicable to the general public, but also within the parameters of professional or organizational codes of conduct. These parameters can provide another layer of substantive constraints on negotiating behavior (in addition to those provided by generally applicable law), additional or enhanced enforcement mechanisms, or both.

As an example, attorneys are subject not only to generally applicable legal constraints on negotiating behavior but also to the administrative regulations of their state bar associations, which generally reflect the American Bar Association's Model Rules of Professional Conduct. Model Rule 4.1(a) provides that "[i]n the course of representing a client a lawyer shall not knowingly ... make a false statement of material fact or law to a third person."[31] The commentary to the rule suggests that the scope of the rule roughly parallels the common law. For example, estimates of "price or value" are not considered material,[32] thus permitting lawyers in general to "puff" as well as lie outright about their reservation prices. One important difference, however, between the administrative rules governing lawyer-negotiators and the common law governing all bargainers is the absence of the requirements of reliance and damages in the regulatory context. To sustain a tort or contract action, the victim must actually suffer harm. Although punishment for transgressions in bargaining outside of the doors of the courthouse is a relatively rare occurrence, in theory lawyers can face disciplinary action for making material misrepresentations even if no legally cognizable damage results.[33]

Lawyers, like other professionals, may also enter into voluntary or contractual relationships that constrain their ability to engage in the full range of behaviors the common law permits. For example, an increasing number of lawyers engaged in the practice of family law have opted to join the "collaborative law" movement. The centerpiece of collaborative law is an agreement between collaborative lawyers and their clients, in which the lawyer pre-commits to withdraw from representing the client in the event that settlement discussions fail and the case proceeds to litigation. This aspect of the agreement is not, technically, an agreement to collaborate. It is merely an agreement not to participate in any litigation efforts subsequent to negotiation. Collaborative lawyers in some jurisdictions, however, also affirmatively commit to greater restrictions on their behavior. For example, some commit that they will "provide good faith responses to any good faith questions and requests" during the course of their negotiations—a commitment far greater than those imposed by ordinary common law obligations.[34] In this way, lawyers or other negotiators may constrain their own negotiating behavior voluntarily and publicly, in advance of a given negotiation.

Negotiations Beyond the Law's Reach

Not all negotiations take place in a context in which legal structures can constrain the behavior of negotiators. Some negotiations are conducted in such a private forum that law serves at most a minimal function. Spouses' negotiations about the division of household tasks, child rearing philosophies, and appropriate toilet seat protocols may take place largely beyond the reach of the law. The law has only minimal impact on other negotiations because of unlikely enforcement prospects.

The black market thrives on the wings of vibrant negotiation, yet the law provides few behavioral boundaries in those negotiations. Similarly, international law includes an expectation that parties will negotiate terms of treaties. No consistent, enforceable legal structure exists, however, to give force to any constraints on the negotiating behavior of those states. Finally, in some negotiations, the product of the bargain precludes any obvious remedies—even in cases when one of the parties exceeded expected boundaries of behavior. If two businesses deceive each other in crafting the terms of a joint venture, the law informs how the damage from their conduct may be remedied. If, however, two legislators deceive each other in negotiations over the terms of a new piece of legislation, no obvious bases for legal rescission or damages exist.

In these contexts, the threat of extra-legal penalties (in addition, of course, to personal ethical commitments) may constrain negotiators' behavior. For example, in many of the circumstances described above, an aggrieved negotiator may impose a reputational sanction on the transgressor by revealing the allegedly inappropriate behavior. [Tinsley, et al., *Reputations*] Many parties will behave differently in a bargaining session they believe to be entirely private than in negotiations that take place within the shadow of a threat to disclose. Although the prospect of publicity is different in structure from legal sanction, it nevertheless holds some promise of altering the negotiating behavior of those who are beyond the reach of the formal law of bargaining.

Endnotes

This chapter represents a slightly modified and updated version of an article by the same authors under the same title, appearing at 87 MARQUETTE LAW REVIEW 838 (2004).

[1] *See generally* RESTATEMENT (SECOND) OF TORTS § 525 (1986), RESTATEMENT (SECOND) OF CONTRACTS § 164 (1982).

[2] *See* Royal Bus. Machs., Inc. v. Lorraine Corp., 633 F.2d 34, 42 (7th Cir. 1980) (calling such statements "'puffing' to be expected in any sales transaction").

[3] Nasik Breeding & Research Farm Ltd. v. Merck & Co., 165 F. Supp. 2d 514, 530 (S.D.N.Y. 2001).

[4] *See, e.g.*, Vulcan Metals Co. v. Simmons Mfg. Co., 248 F. 853 (2d Cir. 1918).

[5] *See* Pacesetter Homes v. Brodkin, 85 Cal. Rptr. 39, 43 (Cal. Ct. App. 1970).

[6] *See, e.g.*, In re Trump, 7 F.3d 357, 369 (3d Cir. 1993) (finding that repeated warnings of risk meant that "no reasonable investor could believe anything but that the ... bonds represented a rather risky, speculative investment," despite other optimistic claims about the financial stability of the issuer).

[7] Morta v. Korea Ins. Corp., 840 F.2d 1452, 1456 (9th Cir. 1988).

[8] *See, e.g.*, Kabatchnick v. Hanover-Elm Bldg. Corp., 103 N.E.2d 692 (Mass. 1952) (falsely claiming a "bona fide offer from one Melvin Levine ... of $10,000 per year"); Beavers v. Lamplighters Realty, 556 P.2d 1328 (Okla. 1976) (falsely claiming a prospective buyer was willing to pay the asking price for a house and would be delivering a check that same day).

[9] Laidlaw v. Organ, 15 U.S. (2 Wheat) 178 (1817).

[10] Kannavos v. Annino, 240 N.E.2d 708 (Mass. 1969).

[11] *See, e.g.*, Weintraub v. Krobatsch, 317 A.2d 68 (N.J. 1974) (sellers must disclose known insect infestation of house).

[12] *See* RESTATEMENT (SECOND) OF CONTRACTS § 175(1) (1982).

[13] *See* RUSSELL KOROBKIN, NEGOTIATION THEORY AND STRATEGY 149-175 (2002).

[14] Indelicato v. Provident Life & Accident Ins. Co., 1990 U.S. Dist. LEXIS 12759 (S.D.N.Y. 1990).

[15] First Nat'l Bank of Cincinnati v. Pepper, 547 F.2d 708 (2d. Cir. 1976); The First Nat'l Bank of Cincinnati v. Pepper, 454 F.2d 626 (2d Cir. 1972).

[16] *See, e.g.,* Austin Instruments, Inc. v. Loral Corp., 272 N.E.2d 533 (N.Y. 1971).

[17] *See* RESTATEMENT (SECOND) OF CONTRACTS §177 (1979)

[18] *See* Armendariz v. Foundation Health Psychare Services, 6 P.3d 669 (2000).

[19] Minors and persons suffering from mental incapacity fit into this category. *See, e.g.,* Dengler v. Crisman, 516 A.2d 1231 (Pa. Super. Ct. 1986).

[20] *See* 29 U.S.C. § 158(d) (2003).

[21] N.L.R.B. v. Katz, 369 U.S. 736 (1962).

[22] *See* Homestead Nursing & Rehabilitation Center, 310 N.L.R.B. 678 (1993) (delay, failure to send agent with sufficient authority, and withdrawal of previously tentatively agreed upon provisions are indicia of bad faith); Atlanta Hilton & Towers, 271 N.L.R.B. 1600 (1984) (same, adding refusal to provide relevant information). Regarding take-it-or-leave-it approach to bargaining, compare NLRB v. Gen. Elec., 418 F.2d 736 (2d Cir. 1969) (take-it-or-leave-it approach violates good faith requirement), *with* Logemann Bros., 298 N.L.R.B. 1018 (1990) (take-it-or-leave-it on some provisions does not necessarily constitute bad faith bargaining).

[23] *See, e.g.,* WIS. STAT. § 709 (1995).

[24] *See, e.g.,* Matter of Marriage of Eltzroth, 679 P.2d 1369 (Or. App. 1984) ("the fiduciary duty … imposed as a result of the confidential relationship between the parties … continues while the parties contemplate divorce, as long as the confidential relationship remains intact and the parties are not dealing at arms' length through separate agents or attorneys."); Vai v. Bank of America National Trust & Savings Ass'n, 364 P.2d 247 (1961); Sally B. Sharp, *Fairness Standards and Separation Agreements: A Word of Caution on Contractual Freedom,* 132 UNIVERSITY OF PENNSYLVANIA LAW REVIEW 1399, 1414-24 (1984) (surveying the legal implications of the confidential relationship between spouses).

[25] *See* Castillo v. Spiliada Mar. Corp., 937 F.2d 240, 243 (5th Cir. 1991) ("[S]eamen have enjoyed a special status in our judicial system [because] they occupy a unique position. A seaman isolated on a ship on the high seas is often vulnerable to the exploitation of his employer.").

[26] *See, e.g.,* Drawdy v. Drawdy, 268 S.E.2d 30 (S.C. 1980) ("[I]t is incumbent on the family court … to satisfy itself that the agreement is a fair contractual end of the parties' marital claims.").

[27] *See, e.g.,* Mars Steel Corp. v. Cont'l Ill. Nat'l Bank, 834 F.2d 677 (7th Cir. 1987).

[28] *See, e.g.,* United States v. City of Miami, 614 F.2d 1322, 1331 (5th Cir. 1980).

[29] *See, e.g.,* HAW. REV. STAT. § 481p (2001) (option to cancel telemarketer-induced sales); 16 C.F.R. § 429.1 (2003) (cooling off period for door-to-door sales).

[30] *See, e.g.,* OR. REV. STAT. § 646.315-375 (2001); OHIO REV. CODE ANN. § 1345.71-.78 (Anderson 2001).

[31] MODEL RULES OF PROF'L CONDUCT R. 4.1(a) (2004).

[32] *Id.* at R. 4.1 cmt.2.

[33] A second difference regarding attorneys' bargaining ethics stems from the provisions of Model Rule 8.4, which provides that it is "professional misconduct" for a lawyer to "engage in conduct involving dishonesty, fraud, deceit, or misrepresentation." Although this provision appears to constrain attorneys' behavior extensively, the rule has historically been the subject of only very limited enforcement. *See* Peter Jarvis & Bradley Tellam, *A Negotiation Ethics Primer for Lawyers,* 31 GONZAGA LAW REVIEW 549 (1995).

[34] *See* James Lawrence, *Collaborative Lawyering: A New Development in Conflict Resolution,* 17 OHIO STATE JOURNAL ON DISPUTE RESOLUTION 431 (2002).

❧ 22 ❧

Trust and Distrust

Roy J. Lewicki

Editors' Note: *Can you both trust and distrust the other side? In fact, we often do exactly that. Lewicki provides practical advice on dealing with trust and distrust in each interaction. Of particular importance to negotiators facing troubled relationships, this chapter shows how distrust is not merely a mirror image of trust: it actually works quite differently. Effective negotiators must learn both to build trust and to manage distrust. This chapter should be read in conjunction with Tinsley et al., Reputations.*

Trust indicates a willingness to become vulnerable to another based on confident positive expectations of the other's conduct. It has often been praised as the "glue" that holds relationships together and enables individuals to perform more efficiently and effectively. Trust reduces uncertainty over future outcomes, simplifies decision processes, and provides us with peace of mind. The phenomenon of trust has been extensively explored by a variety of disciplines across the social sciences, including economics, social psychology, and political science.

Trust is critical to negotiation, for several reasons. First, judgments about the other's trustworthiness allow us to begin the negotiation process. If we believed that we could not trust the other, we would probably not want to move toward constructing a deal with them, nor believe what they were telling us during the negotiation process. Thus, trust is essential to both determining the other's credibility in the conversation, and meeting the commitments and promises they make as we move toward agreement. Second, trust enables us to save time and energy in constructing the agreement. If we trust the other, formal agreements can be simpler, shorter and less specific. We do not have to stipulate every possible circumstance in the agreement. Finally, even the most complex and sophisticated formal contract cannot stipulate every detail or possible contingency about the deal; thus, trust enhances the enforcement of deals because each side believes the other will act in the "spirit" rather than the letter of the agreement.

Trust has been defined in many different ways. For example, one commonly accepted definition in the research literature on trust is that "trust is a psychological state comprising the intention to accept vulnerability based upon positive expectations of the intentions or behavior of another."[1] Similarly, others describe trust as "confident positive expectations regarding another's conduct", where confident positive expectations are defined as "a belief in, a propensity to attribute virtuous intentions to, and a willingness to act on the basis of the other's conduct."[2]

The need for trust arises from our *interdependence* with others. We often depend on other people to help us obtain, or at least not to frustrate, the outcomes we value (and they on us). As our interests with others are intertwined, we also must recognize that there is an element of *risk* involved insofar as we often encounter situations in which we cannot compel the cooperation we seek. Therefore, trust can be very valuable in social interactions.

To show how trust is critical to effective negotiation, I will elaborate on our definitions by drawing a distinction between trust and distrust.[3] Contrary to the traditional notion of trust as a unidimensional construct (i.e., that trust and distrust are bipolar opposites), research is shifting to acknowledge that trust and distrust exist along separate dimensions. Whereas trust is seen as the trustor's confident *positive* expectations regarding the trustee's conduct, distrust is defined as the trustor's confident *negative* expectations regarding the trustee's conduct.[4] While both trust and distrust involve movements toward certainty of another's conduct, the nature of that certainty and the emotional and behavioral reactions that come with it will differ considerably. That is, trust evokes a feeling of hope and a demonstrated willingness to become vulnerable to the trustee. Distrust, on the other hand, evokes fear and actions to buffer oneself from the harmful conduct of the other party. I represent this distinction in the figure below.

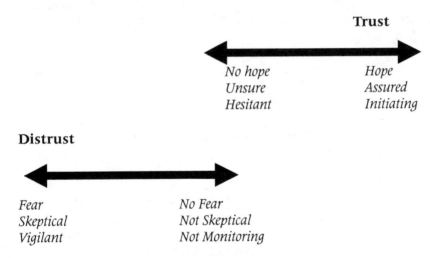

Viewing trust and distrust as existing along separate dimensions also affirms the way we tend to view relationships with others, which is that they are generally complex and multidimensional. We don't completely trust or distrust others; instead, we can both trust *and* distrust another person. In other words, we may trust someone in some contexts, but not in others, and similarly distrust them in some contexts and not others. You may trust another individual to arrive on time for a meeting, but not to complete the required paperwork with the care that must be shown toward it. Said another way, we can consider any complex relationship with another person as multifaceted; each facet of the relationship represents an interaction that provides us with information about the other. The greater the variety of settings and contexts in which we interact with that other person, the more complex and multifaceted the relationship becomes. Within the same relationship, elements of trust and distrust may peacefully coexist because they are related to different experiences with the other or knowledge of the other in different contexts.[5]

Thus, arriving at an overall evaluation of the other party (the trustee) involves a complex assessment that considers *both* trust and distrust. Moreover, this new view of trust stresses that both trust and distrust have a valid role in managing complex relationships: *contrary to traditional, normative views that trust is good and distrust is bad, this new perspective recognizes that trust is valuable insofar as it is appropriate to the context, and that a healthy amount of distrust can protect against the risk of exploitation.* Excessive (blind) distrust, however, is probably as dysfunctional as excessive (blind) trust.

Accordingly, negotiations can be managed most effectively when attention is given to managing the initiation and development of trust, as well as to tempering distrust. In the sections that follow, I describe the origins of trust and distrust and the impact of trust and distrust on negotiations. I articulate strategies for building trust and for managing distrust in a negotiation. Finally, I will suggest several approaches for repairing damaged trust, and conclude by discussing the practical implications of my review for the effective negotiator.

Current Thinking About Trust

Theory on the origins of interpersonal trust has proceeded broadly along three fronts: (1) explaining differences in the individual propensity to trust, (2) understanding dimensions of trustworthy behavior, and (3) suggesting levels of trust development.

Individual Propensity to Trust

Personality theorists have developed one of the oldest theoretical perspectives on trust, and argued that some people are more likely to trust than others.[6] Viewed as a fairly stable trait over time, trust is a generalized expectation that individuals hold, believing that other people will be trustworthy or can be relied upon. This expectation is rather stable within an individual but varies significantly across individuals; it most likely develops and changes as major trusting events have been honored (or violated) in that individual's history of prior social interactions, and may have its most pronounced effect in novel or ambiguous situations. Developmental psychologists have suggested that the development of a generalized expectancy to trust is deeply rooted in early childrearing practices with parents, siblings and significant others.[7] Others have suggested that trust may also be biological. [Yarn & Jones, *Biology*]

Characteristics of Trustworthy People

Our trust in another individual (the trustee) can be grounded in our evaluation of his/her ability, integrity, and benevolence.[8] The more we observe these characteristics in another person, in a given situation, the more likely we will be to trust that person. *Ability* refers to an assessment of the trustee's knowledge, skill, or competency. Trust requires an appraisal that the trustee is able to do a job well, possesses the necessary skills, and will perform in a manner that will meet our expectations. If a person promises to fulfill an obligation or do a job, our judgment of their ability or competence to actually meet the obligation or complete the job will be essential to our willingness to trust them.

Integrity is the degree to which the trustee adheres to principles that are acceptable to the trustor. This dimension leads us to trust another based on the consistency of their past actions with us, the credibility of their communication, their commitment to adhere to reasonable standards of fairness, and the congruence between their words and deeds. Finally, *benevolence* is our assessment that the trusted individual is concerned enough about our welfare to either advance our interests, or at least not impede them. The trustee's perceived intentions or motives are most central. Being supportive of our interests, communicating honestly and openly, and showing willingness to delegate decisions and share power or control with us, are all indicators of one's benevolence.

Although these three dimensions are likely to be linked to each other, they each contribute separately to influence the level of trust in another within a relationship. However, ability and integrity are likely to be most influential early in a relationship, while information about the other's benevolence may need more time to emerge. The effect of benevolence will increase trust as the relationship between the parties grows closer; I discuss this in the next section as I describe two major types of trust.

Two Types of Trust

Recent work on trust has argued that trust and distrust are fundamentally different. In addition, recent studies have shown that there are several different types of trust.[9] Trust in a 'shallow' (more superficial) relationship is probably different from trust in a 'deep' (more close, intense) relationship; we will define these different types of trust as calculus-based trust and identification-based trust.

Calculus-Based Trust

Calculus-based trust (CBT) is concerned with assuring consistent behavior in the other. CBT is grounded in the assumption that the other will do what they say because (a) they are rewarded for keeping their word and preserving the relationship, or (b) they fear the consequences of not doing what they said they would do. Trust is sustained to the degree that the punishment for not trusting is clear, viable, and likely to occur. Thus, the threat of punishment is likely to be as significant, if not more significant, as a motivator to sustain CBT than the promise of reward.

This form of trust is most consistent with relationships that are largely arms-length market transactions, *or* with the early stages of relationships that might become closer and more personal. In these relationships, the trustor (intuitively or explicitly) calculates the value of creating and sustaining trust in the relationship relative to the costs of sustaining or severing the relationship. Compliance with calculus-based trust is often assured both by providing rewards for being trusting (and trustworthy) and by the threat that if trust is violated, one will either directly pay the price for breaking the agreement, or their reputation for being trustworthy will be hurt and will affect future dealings. A parent trusts his son with the keys to the sports car because bringing the car back in good shape will be rewarded with future opportunities to drive it, *and* because the failure to do so will result in significant loss of driving privileges and an unwillingness to trust the son with the keys or other privileges in the future.

Identification-Based Trust

The second type of trust is grounded in identification with the other's desires and intentions. At this level, trust exists because the parties effectively understand and appreciate each other's wants, desires and values; this mutual understanding is developed to the point that each party can effectively act for the other. Identification-based trust (IBT) thus permits a party to serve as the other's agent in interpersonal transactions.[10] The other can be confident that his or her interests will be fully protected, and that no surveillance or monitoring of the actor is necessary. As the parties get to know each other and identification develops, the parties come to understand what they must do to sustain the other's trust. One comes to learn what really matters to the other, and comes to place the same importance on those behaviors, qualities, expectations and standards as the other does. Using the same example, the parent trusts the son because the son clearly understands the responsibility attached to driving a sports car, empathizes with the risk felt by the parent, and visibly treats the car with extra care and caution.

IBT is the type of trust one might expect to see developed in close friendships, partnerships, or long standing business relationships. Parties affirm strong identification-based trust by developing a collective identity (a joint name, title, logo, etc.); co-locating (working together in the same building or neighborhood); creating joint products or goals, such as a new product line or building a new living space together; and committing to commonly shared values, such that the parties are actually committed to the same objectives and can substitute for each other in external transactions. A suitable metaphor for identification-based trust may be a musical one, such as "harmonizing" or "jamming." Great identification-based trust can be seen in all kinds of relationships and teams. When people can anticipate each other's actions and intentions and flawlessly execute a great symphony, a complex surgery, a spectacular touchdown, a flawless relay race handoff, or an alley-oop pass to the basket with one second left on the clock, we see the product of strong, positive identification-based trust.

Current Thinking About Distrust

Distrust is the confident expectation that another individual's motives, intentions, and behaviors are sinister and harmful to one's own interests. In interdependent relationships, this often entails a sense of fear and anticipation of discomfort or danger. Distrust naturally prompts us to take steps that reduce our vulnerability in an attempt to protect our interests. Accordingly, our distrust of others is likely to evoke a competitive (as opposed to cooperative) orientation that can stimulate or exacerbate conflict. A distrusting orientation has also been linked to lower job satisfaction, motivation and workplace commitment.

Causes of Distrust

Distrust may arise due to differences in group membership: individuals identify and are positively attached to their in-groups, yet assign negative *stereotypes* to out-group members and may view them with suspicion and hostility. Distrust can also arise directly as the result of *past personal experiences* among individuals, such as when one person breaks a promise to another. Distrust can also result from knowing another's *reputation*, [Tinsley, et al., *Reputations*] meaning that while there has been no direct personal experience, indirect information may be enough to create distrusting expectations. Finally, distrust is likely to increase with the *magnitude of a past trust violation*, the number of past violations, and the perception that the offender intended to commit the violation.

Some Level of Distrust May be Functional

Although the discussion suggests that distrust can be patently harmful, there are potentially valuable benefits of some distrust. All of us have had experiences where we misjudged another person as credible and trustworthy, only to be exploited. Hence, distrust can be a valuable mechanism that prevents us from falling prey to a naive view of another that allows us to be blind to clues of their untrustworthiness (and thus makes us unwitting co-conspirators to our own exploitation). A certain level of distrust is also vital to preventing excessive group cohesion that precludes sound decision-making (called "groupthink").[11] In addition, a certain amount of distrust allows us to set boundaries around another's behavior in a way that limits their freedom yet permits functional interaction. (So, for example, I might trust my friend to walk my dog, but not trust them with a key to my house that would let them enter any time they choose). Vigilance toward the other, periodic monitoring of their behavior, and formal contracts are all reasonable and appropriate ways to assure compliance. It also may be necessary to strictly compartmentalize and set "appropriate" boundaries in certain relationships, so that we minimize the areas in which one becomes vulnerable to another. In short, it is possible (and even advisable) to have a "healthy dose" of distrust, particularly with people whom we do not know well.

But Too Much Distrust May Be Dysfunctional

However, distrust can lead to adverse effects as well. Once in place, distrust forms a powerful frame on subsequent events in the relationship, such that even good-faith efforts by the offender to restore the relationship are met with skepticism and suspicion. The result is a "self-fulfilling prophecy," where every move the other person makes is interpreted as additional evidence that justifies an initial decision to distrust him/her. This distrust not only inhibits cooperation and successful negotiation, but also may result in retaliation that causes the conflict to escalate. [Coleman, et al., *Dynamical*] Taken to its extreme, distrust can give rise to paranoid cognitions—false or exaggerated cognitions that one is subject to malevolent treatment by others.[12] [Jeglic & Jeglic, *Disordered People*] Such perceptions drive individuals to the point of hypervigilance (excessively trying to make sense of every action the other person takes) and rumination (brooding or "stewing" on the meaning of the other person's behavior and their intentions), resulting in a faulty diagnosis about whether the other can be trusted or not. Distrust leads the parties to reduce their willingness to share information and engage in problem-solving in conflict situations, and hence to be more likely to use distributive bargaining approaches with the other party, an approach that usually overlooks integrative, value-creating opportunities. Distrust can also cause conflicts to escalate, as positions harden and the parties become increasingly reluctant to yield concessions. The negative emotions that emerge with distrust—fear, suspicion and anger—cause the trustor to vilify and demonize the other party. This view becomes especially damaging when the parties use these perspectives of each other to justify retaliatory actions that cause the conflict to escalate out of control.

Two Types of Distrust

Similar to our discussion of calculus- and identification-based levels of trust, we can draw the same distinction between calculus-based distrust (CBD) and identification-based distrust (IBD). CBD is confident *negative* expectations of another's conduct. These expectations are grounded in impersonal, arms-length transactions where the overall costs of maintaining trust are expected to outweigh the benefits of maintaining trust. We expect that in any encounter with the other, the costs will outweigh the benefits. In these relationships, we have two fundamental choices: either choose to *not* deal with this individual, or, if we must deal with them, then construct boundaries that limit the degree of interdependence and vulnerability inherent in the transaction. In addition, we can put into place systems that allow for monitoring and enforcement so as to assure that distrust can be managed in areas where we might be vulnerable (for example, limited access for joint venture research scientists employed by a competitor). It is essential for the parties to try to establish open communication to clarify their objectives, so both sides can try to ascertain the boundaries that merit trust versus distrust. Alternatively, CBD can be managed by cultivating alternative relationships to satisfy one's interests. When one has alternative ways to get one's needs met, the need to trust a specific other decreases. This limits the degree of dependence on someone who may violate the trust.

Identification-based distrust (IBD) is confident negative expectations of another's conduct, grounded in a perceived incompatibility of closely-held values, dissimilar or competing goals, and/or a negative emotional attachment. We expect that we have little in common with the other; in fact, the other may be a committed adversary who is out to do us in. IBD denotes incompatible values and goals, and also a negative emotional attachment to the other. Distrust is felt viscerally (in the "gut") as much as cognitively (in the head). In most cases, we would choose to separate ourselves from people with whom we have strong IBD, and minimize both our interaction with them and our dependence on them. However, there are times when we must continue relationships with these people. There are several ways to cope with this situation. First, our differences with this person may be more imagined than real. Efforts to talk out our differences, often with the help of a third party who can facilitate communications, may help the parties realize possible commonalities (if only there is common distrust that should be managed). However, if this is not effective, the parties will need to identify those specific areas where they need to work together, and "bound" their interactions with each other so that discussions around those issues are careful, controlled, and above board. So, for example, if a colleague and I do not trust each other but have to work together on an important committee, we will limit our interaction to professional work on the committee, but otherwise avoid each other outside those meetings. The parties may also try to work out their differences in other key areas of contention, but if the distrust between them is strong and longstanding, such efforts are unlikely to be productive. Thus, if we cannot learn to live with the distrust we have for each other outside the committee, one of us may have to resign from the committee to keep from impeding its work.

The Impact of Trust on Negotiations

Before discussing the implications of these four forms of trust on a negotiation, we will briefly review the research that has been done on the role of trust in the negotiation process.

Many researchers have explored trust in negotiation.[13] Early studies were often conducted with more primitive conceptualizations of trust than described here, and in reasonably primitive experimental settings, and hence the findings were rather limited in nature. As one might expect, this early research generally showed that higher levels of trust make negotiation easier, while lower levels of trust make negotiation more difficult. Similarly, integrative processes tend to increase trust, while more distributive processes are likely to decrease trust.[14] Recent research on trust has revealed a more complex relationship between trust and negotiation behavior, as follows:

- Many people approach a new relationship with an unknown other party with remarkably high levels of trust. While people in new relationships might be expected to start their trust of the other at "zero," in fact, most of us assume that the other can be trusted and are remarkably willing to trust the other, even with very little information or knowledge about the other.[15]
- Trust tends to cue cooperative behavior. Parties who trust each other approach each other with cooperative dispositions.[16]
- Individual motives also shape both trust and expectations of the other's behavior. Parties who are more cooperatively motivated report higher initial trust of the other party and more positive initial impressions of the other than those who are individually motivated.[17]
- Trustors, and those trusted, may focus on different things as trust is being built. Trustors may focus primarily on the risks of being trusted (e.g. how vulnerable they are), while those being trusted focus on the benefits to be received from the trust. Here we see a negotiator 'framing bias' [Korobkin & Guthrie, *Heuristics*] by the sender and receiver that shapes how trust actions are viewed. From the trustor's perspective, they are more likely to trust when the risk is low, but their willingness to trust does not seem to

depend on the level of benefit received by the person being trusted. However, the receiver is more likely to trust when the benefits to be received
from the trust are high, but their trust does not seem to depend on the
level of vulnerability feared by the trustor. Moreover, each party reported
that they were not particularly sensitive to the factors that affected their
counterpart's decision—that is, each could not or did not put themselves in
the other's shoes and understand how the other would see it.[18] Thus, trust
building might be greatly facilitated if parties can communicate more
clearly about the vulnerabilities to be felt or the benefits to be received, and
how to manage these effectively.

- The nature of the negotiation task (distributive vs. integrative) can shape
how parties judge the trust. In a more distributive context, trustors tend to
focus on the risks they face, while those who are in a position to receive
and then reciprocate the others' trust focus on the benefits that the trustors have provided them. Given the framing biases about risk,[19] however,
neither party tends to consider the other's point of view prior to making a
decision whether to reciprocate the other's trust. As a result, the possibilities for trust to break down, or not be fulfilled, may increase because
neither party truly understands the risks or rewards as perceived by the
other. More reciprocity occurs among individuals who are better at taking
the perspective of the other in a negotiation, and can also be 'coached' by
encouraging a negotiator to consider the views of the other party in their
decision-making. [20]
- Greater expectations of trust between negotiators lead to greater information sharing with the other party;[21] similarly, greater expectations of
distrust lead to less information sharing.[22]
- Greater information sharing tends to enhance effectiveness in achieving a
good negotiation outcome (and less information sharing tends to diminish
effectiveness in achieving a good outcome), although this effectiveness
may *not* necessarily be the result of greater trust.[23]
- Distributive processes lead negotiators to see the negotiation dialogue, and
critical events in the dialogue, as largely about the nature of the negotiation task (i.e. how to divide the pie). Distributive processes also lead people
to judge the other party negatively. Both of these perspectives tend to reduce trust. In contrast, integrative processes lead negotiators to see the
dialogue as largely about interests, relationships, and positive affect, and to
see the other positively; these perspectives tend to increase trust.[24]
- Trust increases the likelihood that negotiation will proceed on a favorable
course over the life of a negotiation. Researchers have begun to examine
key events or 'turning points' in negotiation, i.e. comments or behaviors
that turn the negotiation in a more positive (or more negative) direction.[25]
One study has generally shown that trust increases the likelihood of more
facilitative turning points around interests and the relationship, and decreases the number of inhibitory turning points around discussion of a
distributive task or negative characterization of the other party. These processes subsequently lead to higher levels of trust at the end of the
negotiation, and lower levels of distrust, and the process increases both
calculative-based trust and identification-based trust.[26]
- Face-to-face negotiation encourages greater trust development than negotiating electronically (e.g., on-line). [Bhappu & Barsness, *E-Mail*] There is
evidence that parties anticipating an online negotiation expect less trust
before the negotiations begin, are less satisfied with their negotiation outcomes, are less confident in the quality of their performance during the

negotiation, trust the other less after the negotiation, and have less desire for a future interaction with the other party.[27]

- Negotiators who are representing others' interests, rather than their own interests, tend to behave in a less trusting way (be less trustworthy), and tend to expect that the other will be more trusting. As a result of being less trustworthy, negotiators engage in less "give and take" with the other party, and expect the other to engage in less give and take.[28]

Building Trust and Managing Distrust in Negotiations

Given this review of trust and negotiation research, and the discussion of the four forms of trust (CBT, IBT, CBD and IBD), there are clear action strategies for negotiators who wish to build trust with another party. These strategies are summarized in Table 1. Note that if a negotiator is beginning a relationship with another party, or expects that the relationship with the other party will be no more than a market transaction, then the negotiator need only be concerned about developing and maintaining calculus-based trust (CBT), and managing calculus-based distrust (CBD). However, if the negotiator expects that the relationship could develop into a more intense, deeper, personal relationship, where identification-based trust (IBT) would be more common, then the negotiator should establish calculus-based trust and also work to build identification-based trust. However, this process cannot be rushed, nor can it be one-sided. Trust building is a bilateral process that requires *mutual* commitment and effort, especially when attempting to de-escalate conflict. While one party can initiate actions that may move the trust-development process forward, the strongest trust must be mutually developed, and at a pace acceptable to both parties. Finally, if the negotiator senses that identification-based distrust is building, then he/she should work both to carefully manage the relationship and to minimize contact with the other.

Table 1
Actions to Manage Different Forms of Trust in Negotiations[29]

How to Increase Calculus-Based Trust
1. Perform competently. Show your ability to proficiently perform duties and obligations.
2. Create and meet the other party's expectations. Establish consistency and predictability. Be clear about what you intend to do and then do what you say.
3. Stress the benefits of creating mutual trust. Point out the benefits that can be gained for the other, or both parties, by maintaining such trust. Keep promises.
4. Establish credibility. Make sure your statements are honest and accurate. Tell the truth and keep your word. Communicate accurately, openly and transparently.
5. Show concern for others. Act in a way that respects and protects other people. Show sensitivity to their needs desires and interests.
6. Share and delegate control. Share power and allow the other to have voice and control over the process.
7. Develop a good reputation. Work to have others believe that you are someone who both has, and deserves, a reputation for being trusting and acting trustworthily.

How to Increase Identification-Based Trust
1. Develop similar interests. Try to be interested in the same things.

2. Identify similar goals and objectives. Try to identify and explore similar goals, objectives, scenarios for the future.
3. Act and respond similar to the other. Try to do what you know he or she would do in the same situation.
4. Identify common principles and values (but not at the expense of being insincere or compromising your values).
5. Actively discuss your commonalities, and develop plans to enhance and strengthen them.

How to Manage Calculus-Based Distrust

1. Monitor the other party's actions. Make sure they are doing what they say they would do.
2. Prepare formal agreements (contracts, memoranda of understanding, etc.) that specify what each party has committed to do, and specify the consequences that will occur if each party does not fulfill their obligations.
3. Build in plans for 'inspecting' and verifying the other's commitments. Specify how you will know if the other party is not living up to their agreements, and establish procedures for gathering data to verify their commitments.[30]
4. Develop ways to make sure that the other party cannot take advantage of your trust and good will by 'invading' other parts of your personal space. Be vigilant of the other's actions and constantly monitor your personal boundaries.
5. Use formal legal mechanisms if there are concerns that the other is taking advantage of you.
6. Actively engage third parties (mediators and arbitrators) to assure clear communication and create manageable agreements and boundaries.

How to Manage Identification-Based Distrust

1. Expect that you and the other will regularly disagree, see things differently, take opposing views and stand for different ideals and principles.
2. Assume that the other party will exploit or take advantage of you if he/she has the opportunity. Closely monitor your boundaries with this person regularly.
3. Check out and verify information, commitments and promises made to you by the other party. Never take their word as given.
4. Minimize whatever interdependence you have with this party, and strongly manage the interdependencies that you have to have. Be vigilant of their efforts to take advantage of you or your good will. Be controlled and 'distant' in what you say and how you say it to this person.
5. Minimize personal self-disclosure to this individual, so as to not disclose information that could make you vulnerable. Do not share any confidences or secrets; assume you will be betrayed if you do.
6. Always assume that with this person, you should not let your guard down, and that any vulnerability will be exploited.

Rebuilding Trust

A chapter on trust would be incomplete without giving brief attention to ways to rebuild trust that has been broken. Effective trust repair is often necessary to restart negotiations or move them forward. Although the process is difficult, there are steps the offender can take to enhance the likelihood of stimulating the victim's willingness to reconcile, and further the trust rebuilding process. [Waldman

& Luskin, *Anger & Forgiveness*; Brown & Robbennolt, *Apology*] However, rebuilding trust is a process, not an event. As such, it is likely to consume a lot of time and resources. Actions in the short term may be confined to managing distrust. Nonetheless, here are recommendations for rebuilding trust (mostly focused on CBT actions):

- *Take action immediately after the violation.* Offenders should act quickly to engage in restorative efforts. This communicates sensitivity to the victim and the relationship, and avoids the double-burden the victim has to incur by both suffering the consequences of the violation *and* the embarrassment of confronting the offender with the consequences of his behavior.

- *Provide an apology, and give a thorough account of what happened.* Take responsibility for your actions if you are culpable, and express remorse for the harm created for the victim. Your remorse indicates to the victim that you have also suffered as a result of your actions, and the victim may be less likely to pursue vengeance and escalate the conflict. Also, be sure to carefully explain the circumstances that led to the violation, so the victim can understand the events that led you to your decisions. This will help them see the rationale behind your actions and give them a better sense of the values and parameters that are likely to shape your actions in the future.

- *Be sincere.* The victim is closely scrutinizing your motives and intentions, so it is imperative to sincerely strive to repair the harm from the violation. Take action unilaterally and volitionally, and make every effort to show through your words and actions that you genuinely desire to earn the victim's trust again.

- *Be cognizant of the day-to-day history of the relationship.* If the overall history of the relationship is good, and there are few if any past trust violations, the prospects for trust repair are more promising than in relationships characterized by many trust violations or few trust-confirming events. Make it a priority to honor trust on a daily basis in order to provide a conducive environment for trust repair should the need arise.

- *Provide restitution/penance.* Substantiate your verbal claims with concrete actions that demonstrate a good-faith effort to compensate the victim for the harmful effects of the violation. In CBT relationships, what the victim wants more than your kind words is some tangible aspect of the transaction that he/she was counting on.

- *Restate and renegotiate expectations for the future, and be trustworthy in future interactions.* You are likely to be "on probation" for a period, as the victim tests the waters to see if you actually resume trustworthy behavior. Be sure to take this into account, and take proactive steps to manage the expectations of the victim by specifically articulating what standards should be expected. Then commit to following these standards in the future—and, finally, make good on that commitment.[31]

Endnotes

[1] Denise Rousseau, et al., *Not So Different After All: A Cross-discipline View of Trust*, 23 THE ACADEMY OF MANAGEMENT REVIEW 393, 395(1998).

[2] Roy Lewicki, et al., *Trust and Distrust: New Relationships and Realities*, 23 THE ACADEMY OF MANAGEMENT REVIEW 439 (1998).

[3] Edward Tomlinson & Roy Lewicki, *Managing Interpersonal Trust and Distrust*, in BEYOND INTRACTABILITY (Guy Burgess & Heidi Burgess eds., 2003), *available at* http://www.beyondintractability.org/m/trust_overview.jsp.

[4] *See* Lewicki, et al., *supra*, note 2.

[5] *See* Roy Lewicki & Carolyn Wiethoff, *Trust, Trust Development and Trust Repair, in* THE HAND-BOOK OF CONFLICT RESOLUTION 86 (Morton Deutsch & Peter Coleman eds., 2000).

[6] *See, e.g.,* Julian Rotter, *Generalized Expectancies for Interpersonal Trust*, 26 AMERICAN PSYCHOLO-GIST. 443 (1971).

[7] *See* ERIC ERIKSON, CHILDHOOD AND SOCIETY (1963).

[8] *See* Roger Mayer, et al., *An Intergrative Model of Organizational Trust*, 20 ACADEMY OF MAN-AGEMENT REVIEW 709 (1995).

[9] *See, e.g.,* Roy Lewicki & Barbara Benedict Bunker, *Trust in Relationships: A Model of Development and Decline, in* CONFLICT, COOPERATION, AND JUSTICE: ESSAYS INSPIRED BY THE WORKS OF MORTON DEUTSCH 133 (Barbara Benedict Bunker & Jeffery Z. Rubin eds., 1995); Roy Lewicki & Barbara Benedict Bunker, *Developing and Maintaining Trust in Work Relationships, in* TRUST IN ORGANIZATIONS: FRONTIERS OF THEORY AND RESEARCH 114 (Roderick Kramer & Tom Taylor eds., 2000); Lewicki & Wiethoff, *supra,* note 5.

[10] *See* Morton Deutsch, *Cooperation and Trust: Some Theoretical Notes*, 10 NEBRASKA SYMPOSIUM ON MOTIVATION 275 (1962).

[11] *See, e.g.,* IRVING JANIS, GROUPTHINK: PSYCHOLOGICAL STUDIES OF POLICY DECISIONS AND FIAS-COS (1983).

[12] *See* Roderick Kramer, *The Sinister Attribution Error: Paranoid Cognition and Collective Distrust in Organizations*, 18 MOTIVATION & EMOTION 199 (1994).

[13] *See* Roy Lewicki et al., *Relationships in Negotiation, in* NEGOTIATION Chapter 10 (5th ed. 2005) for a summary of this work.

[14] *See* Mara Olekalns, et al., *Social Value Orientations and Negotiator Outcomes*, 26 EUROPEAN JOURNAL OF SOCIAL PSYCHOLOGY 299 (1996).

[15] *See* Kramer, *supra* note 12; Debra Meyerson, et al., *Swift Trust and Temporary Groups,* in TRUST IN ORGANIZATIONS, *supra,* note 9, at 165.

[16] *See* John K. Butler, *Behaviors, Trust and Goal Achievement in a Win-Win Negotiating Role Play*, 20 GROUP & ORG. MGMT. 486 (1995); John K. Butler, *Trust Expectations, Information Sharing, Climate of Trust, and Negotiation Effectiveness and Efficiently*, 24 GROUP & ORGANIZATION MAN-AGEMENT 217 (1999).

[17] *See* Mara Olekalns, et al., *The Dynamics of Trust in Negotiation* (Melb. Bus. Sch., Working Paper No. 2002-09, 2002).

[18] *See* Deepak Malhotra, *Trust and Reciprocity Decisions: The Differing Perspectives of Trustors and Trusted Parties,* 94 ORGANIZATION BEHAVIOR & HUMAN DECISION PROCESSES 61 (2004).

[19] *See* Deepak Malhotra, Reciprocity in the Context of Trust: The Differing Perspective of Trustors and Trusted Parties (May 2003) (unpublished Ph.D. dissertation, Northwestern University) (on file with author).

[20] *Id.*

[21] *See* Butler, *Trust, Expectations, Information, supra* note 16.

[22] *See* Butler, *Trust and Goal Achievement, supra* note 16.

[23] *See* Butler, *Trust, Expectations, Information, supra* note 16; Olekalns, et al., *supra,* note 17.

[24] *See* Olekalns, et al., *supra,* note 17.

[25] *See* Gillian Greene & Michael Wheeler, *Awareness and Action in Critical Moments*, 20 NEGO-TIATION JOURNAL 349 (2004).

[26] *See* Olekalns, et al. *supra,* note 16.

[27] *See* Charles Naquin & Gaylen Paulson, *Online Bargaining and Interpersonal Trust*, 88 JOURNAL OF APPLIED PSYCHOLOGY 113 (2003).

[28] Fei Song, *Trust and Reciprocity: The Differing Norms of Individuals and Group Representatives* (Sept. 14, 2004) (unpublished paper) (on file with author).

[29] Based on Lewicki and Stevenson, 1997; Lewicki, McAllister and Bies, 1998; Lewicki and Wiethoff, 2000.

[30] The reader will remember the well-known quote, attributed to President Ronald Reagan: "Trust, but verify!"

[31] *See* Lewicki & Wiethoff, *supra* note 5; Edward Tomlinson, et al., *The Road to Reconciliation: Antecedents of Victim Willingness to Reconcile Following a Broken Promise*, 30 JOURNAL OF MAN-AGEMENT 165 (2004).

❧ 23 ❧

Reputations in Negotiation

Catherine H. Tinsley, Jack J. Cambria
& Andrea Kupfer Schneider

Editors' Note: *Time was when a Formica plaque could often be found on the desk of a certain type of negotiator. It said "Yea, when I walk through the Valley of the Shadow of Death I shall fear no evil, for I am the meanest son of a bitch in the valley." Is it really to your advantage to have a reputation as one of the junkyard dogs of negotiation? The authors approach the question from three very different starting points. Tinsley summarizes the research on reputation in controlled settings. Schneider turns to real-life reputations of lawyers in action. Finally, Cambria shows how the life-and-death negotiations which characterize the work of the New York Police Department's Hostage Negotiation Team have led to a new understanding of reputation. This chapter should be read in conjunction with Lewicki on Trust.*

Regard your good name as the richest jewel you can possibly be possessed of....
The way to gain a good reputation is to endeavor to be what you desire to appear.
Socrates (469 BC - 399 BC)

A good reputation is more valuable than money.
Publilius Syrus, Roman poet (~100 BC)

As both the ancient Greeks and Romans observed, reputations are critical assets, which need to be purposefully built and carefully protected. Organizations have been quick to discover the importance of developing and maintaining a favorable reputation or "brand" in the eyes of the public. A recent keyword search on google.com for *brand management* turned up 24.5 million links, such as "how the world's leading companies are managing their brands" and "how brand management builds business and increases sales." A similar search on the more specific *protecting corporate reputation* turned up 769,000 links, which typically cautioned how reputations are a company's most valuable asset. Interestingly, a google.com search with the keywords *protecting negotiator reputation* turned up 25,600 links which is a significant number but only one-thirtieth or 3% of the number of links, found for *protecting corporate reputation*. Yet, of course, there are far more negotiators than corporations. What these searches suggest is that although negotiator reputations are acknowledged to exist, the criticality of building and protecting a negotiation reputation may not yet be fully realized.

In this chapter, we draw from both academic research and professional experience to argue why reputations are critical for negotiators. We explain how reputations influence the negotiation process and hence negotiated outcomes. Moreover, we use theory developed in other domains (game theory and social and cognitive psychology) to help us reason why reputations should influence the negotiation process. We document both micro-individual level studies and macro-market level studies that have demonstrated the influence of reputations on negotiations in the legal and business domains. Then, we turn to the professional experience of the Commanding Officer of the New York Police Department's Hostage Negotiation Team to demonstrate that negotiators' reputations are a critical asset, even in these more unusual, high-stress, singular-round negotiations.

How Reputations Influence Negotiations

Before explaining how reputations influence negotiations we must first explore the meaning of reputation. What is a reputation? In his seminal work on cooperative behavior, Axelrod provides a definition of reputations in a game-theoretic context. Specifically, "a player's reputation is embodied in the beliefs of others about the strategy that player will use."[1] Thus, game theorists tend to define a person's reputation as another's expectation of how that person will behave. Psychologists step further back, suggesting that a reputation is a coherent image of the nature of someone's character which then directs how that person will behave, subject to situational constraints. In other words, reputations not only suggest *how* another party will behave in a situation, but also *why* that party will take certain actions—what the underlying intent is of the actions—due to the nature of that party's character.

For psychologists, this coherent image of the nature of the other party's character is called a person-schema. Schemas are cognitive structures, based on declarative knowledge, which give meaning to environmental stimuli.[2] The importance of identifying reputations as perceptual mechanisms that evoke schema is because of the durable nature of schemas. When parties have an organizing schema from the outset, it influences their interpretation of subsequent information.[3] Specifically, people selectively perceive schema-consistent information (or behavior) from an individual and tend to ignore or discount schema-inconsistent behavior. Moreover, the prejudicial effects of schemas are more powerful if parties have an organizing schema from the outset of an interaction than if the schema is applied afterwards.[4] This explains the "sticky" nature of reputations. A reputation, once developed, is relatively easy to maintain (as in our opening Greek quotation), yet a reputation once tarnished is very difficult to build back again. [Lewicki, *Trust*]

A final important characteristic of reputations is that they emerge over time. Often this time is thought to span across different transactions, so that reputations are a way of linking transactions across time. For example, although one may be currently negotiating a more discrete transaction (e.g., car purchase, raise at work), these discrete transactions will often occur with someone with whom you have previously negotiated (as a repeat customer, when discussing job assignments), or with whom you might expect to negotiate in the future. It is in these repeat-play situations that parties have been advised to be concerned with their reputations,[5] and that parties themselves appear to have an intuitive sense that reputations are important. For example, studies show that parties expecting to interact with each other in the future tend to be more cooperative[6] and less exploitative[7] than parties who expect no future interaction. Yet, as we will show, even parties in one-shot negotiations should be concerned about their reputations and should work towards building the appropriate reputation within the context of that discrete negotiation.

If reputations are perceptual mechanisms that develop over time and evoke person-schemas as to the nature of the other party's character, how do these reputations influence the negotiation process? Although negotiators typically try to maximize their final outcomes, the process by which final outcomes are maximized is "mixed motive" in nature, meaning that in order for negotiators to maximize their own individual outcomes they must both try to cooperate with the other side to create joint value (the strategy also known as integration) and claim individual value (the strategy also known as competition). Given that there are at least two strategic orientations embedded in any negotiated exchange, negotiations are marked by high degrees of uncertainty (as to which strategic orientation the other is using at any one point in time). This uncertainty is where reputations become important.[8]

Uncertainty abounds, in that a negotiator rarely knows for sure what his counterpart cares about, what his alternatives might be, and thus whether his counterpart's behavior is an attempt to create value or claim value. For example, if Negotiator A asks Negotiator B what his or her interests are, is A trying to integrate and create value (meaning that A is asking for B's interests because A is trying to discover and bridge communal interests) or is A trying to distribute and claim value (by discovering information that can later be leveraged for personal gain)? Similarly, if Negotiator A tells B that an issue such as "delivery timing" is important, is A trying to create value (by revealing important priorities that can be traded off) or is A trying to claim value (using a strategy of simply claiming that everything is important)? Because negotiators have incomplete information, B must make judgment calls about A's intentions before deciding how truthfully and completely to respond.

Because reputations provide negotiators with a schema for understanding the counterpart's character, they help a negotiator "identify" or interpret the meaning of a counterpart's action.[9] Returning to our example, if A is known for her ability to craft mutually beneficial deals (i.e., she has an integrative reputation), B will likely interpret A's intent as cooperative, whereas if A is known for her ability to extract deep concessions (i.e., she has a distributive reputation), B will likely ascribe a selfish intent to A. This evaluative consistency has been termed a "halo" effect—once a general image of a person is formed (that is, the distributive negotiator or integrative negotiator schema has been triggered), subsequent actions are interpreted consistently with the prior image.[10] Of course, B's interpretation of A's intentions will influence how truthfully or completely B responds. Hence, reputations affect the quality of outcomes by influencing parties' perceptions of their counterpart's intentions as well as their subsequent behavioral responses.

What Reputation Should One Establish?

If we assume that there are two general strategic orientations one can take in a negotiation—integrative/cooperative or distributive/competitive, there are likewise two general reputations a negotiator can develop—integrative/ cooperative or tough/ competitive.[11] An "integrative" negotiator would be someone who is known for trying to: cooperate, problem-solve, be trustworthy and compassionate, create joint value, or generally get a deal that works for both (or all) parties. A "distributive" negotiator would be someone who is known for trying to: be tough, use power, extract concessions, claim value, or make sure they get a good deal personally.[12] Which is the more desirable reputation?

One argument is that a distributive reputation is most desirable and will help a negotiator by intimidating the other party. For example, a negotiator might purposely delay a negotiation to build a reputation for toughness that can be used to extract concessions from a counterpart;[13] of course this works only if the counterpart has a higher cost for delay. Alternatively, a party might threaten negative consequences to force concessions from her counterpart. In these cases, a negotiator's reputation for being a tough, value claimer might reinforce that her threats are credible and, therefore, effective.[14] It also is possible that a reputation for tough distributive bargaining may be enough to deter others from trying to leverage their power, even in the absence of any power moves. A tough reputation can act as a deterrent—if someone is known for being a tough distributive negotiator, this reputation might deter the other party from entering into a game of "chicken." Hence, when negotiations are more distributive than integrative in nature, parties with a distributive reputation (i.e., those who are generally characterized as being skilled value claimers) could reap significant rewards regardless of whether they actually employ these tactics. It is necessary to note, however, that reputation is a two-edged sword, in which the negotiator's reputation is also known to others who influence the negotiation process, or who may even have direct power over the negotiator. The career of any negotiator employed by Stalin who became perceived at home as what we would today call "integrative" was both unhappy and short.[15] Anecdotally, it appears common among some kinds of negotiators to seek to maintain two conflicting reputations, one (cooperative) for external and the other (hardball player) for internal organizational consumption.

However, when negotiations have a significant integrative potential, as most do, then having a reputation as a skilled distributive negotiator might be a handicap. To achieve a negotiation's integrative potential, negotiators must, among other things, make tradeoffs among issues and add issues that might address the other party's interests.[16] The success of these tactics lies in sharing information to develop an accurate understanding of the parties' interests and priorities.[17] For example, if a party understands what her counterpart cares about, she can propose trades that will meet her counterpart's interests, or she can offer other resources that may not otherwise be considered. An accurate understanding of each other's interests requires negotiators to build rapport and create an environment of trust at the table.[18] Shared trust engenders a cooperative orientation, which encourages parties to share specific information about their interests, preferences, and priorities.[19]

These tactics—building rapport, trust, and sharing information—are likely to be undercut by a negotiator's distributive reputation. A negotiator's distributive reputation would evoke a schema of a typical hard bargainer—singularly focused on maximizing his/her own gain by making extreme offers, conceding little, threatening the other party's resistance point, and employing other tough tactics.[20] Although these hard bargaining tactics can maximize individual profit on distributive issues, they can interfere with issues that provide opportunities for joint gain.[21]

Results From the Lab

In a series of experimental studies, Tinsley and O'Connor found that a distributive reputation hurt a negotiator, whereas an integrative reputation was beneficial to the negotiator.[22] What is remarkable about these studies is that a negotiator's reputation was completely fictional, randomly assigned, and unknown to the individual negotiator. They paired negotiators to negotiate a complex, multi-issue buyer/seller exchange. The negotiation was over the sale of a syndicated TV show, where there was one purely distributive issue (price) and three ways in which joint value could be created: (1) by finding a compatible issue—the sale of a second TV show; (2) by trading off two issues because one was valued more by the buyer and the other valued more by the seller; and (3) by creating a contingency contract that allowed parties to "bet on" their differential projections as to how popular the TV show would be in the upcoming months.[23] [Moffitt, *Contingent Agreements*] Issues in this negotiation each have an economic value that can be scored so that the economic value of the outcome to each party (and hence to the negotiation pair) can be calculated.

In the study on distributive reputations, half the participants were randomly assigned to the "control" condition. Neither party in this condition received any reputation information. The other half of the participants were in the "distributive reputation" condition. Half of those in the distributive reputation condition were then randomly assigned to receive information that their partner had a reputation for being a tough, distributive bargainer. The other half were told nothing. Thus, for each pair of negotiators in the "distributive reputation" condition, one side had information that the counterpart had a distributive reputation, while the other side had no corresponding information about either the first party's reputation or the fact that they themselves had a distributive reputation (to avoid any "stereotype reactance" behavior).

Results showed that when negotiators were given information that their counterpart had a distributive reputation, the negotiators completely shut down their flow of information. They shared significantly less information about their specific interests, needs, and priorities[24]—which is exactly the kind of information necessary to expand joint gain. Moreover, they were significantly more likely to just beat around the bush—making small talk—sharing general information about the negotiation, and essentially wasting time and not sharing anything useful for forming a mutually desirable outcome. As a result, negotiation pairs in the "distributive reputation" condition achieved economically worse outcomes than negotiators in the "control" condition, and negotiators that were randomly labeled as having a distributive reputation did significantly worse than other negotiators.

In a study on integrative reputations, the results were essentially the mirror opposite. Here again, half the participants were randomly assigned to the "control" condition and neither party in this condition received any reputation information. The other half of the participants were in the "integrative reputation" condition, where half of them were randomly assigned to receive information that their partner had a reputation for being a cooperative, integrative bargainer. Again, the other half in this condition were told nothing. Thus, for each pair of negotiators in the "integrative reputation" condition, one side had information that the counterpart had an integrative reputation, while the other side had no corresponding information about either the first party's reputation or the fact that they themselves had an integrative reputation.

In this second study, results showed that when negotiators were given information that their counterpart had an integrative reputation, the negotiators opened up and freely shared what might be sensitive information. They shared significantly more information about their specific interests, needs, and priorities—which is exactly the kind of information necessary to expand joint gain. Moreover, they were significantly less likely to just beat around the bush. As a result, negotiation pairs in the "integrative reputation" condition achieved economically better outcomes than negotiators in the "control" condition. Also, both negotiators in the integrative reputation condition did equally well economically, suggesting that an integrative reputation of *one* negotiator was all that was necessary to set the negotiation on an integrative course. Finally, in this study they tested negotiators' satisfaction with the process and willingness to negotiate in the future, and found that both sides in the "integrative condition" were more satisfied and more willing to negotiate in the future than the negotiators in the control condition.

These results, combined, suggest that in multi-issue business negotiation, having an integrative reputation can help negotiators achieve deals with higher economic value than if they had a reputation as a distributive bargainer. This economic benefit is realized because the average party facing a negotiator with an integrative reputation does not appear to exploit the other's benevolence, but rather tries to use this cooperativeness to fashion high quality deals. In other words, our randomly distributed negotiators who faced a counterpart labeled as 'integrative' did not try to exploit this integrative counterpart, but on the contrary were influenced by this integrative reputation to share sensitive information. (Of course, a negotiator with a well-earned 'distributive' reputation might act differently). Moreover, the negotiators facing the counterparts with the integrative reputation who opened up and shared sensitive information about interests and priorities were not exploited by the counterpart (for recall these "integrative" reputations were fictional and randomly assigned). Rather, this opening up and sharing of information appears to have been treated as a sign of good will, to be repaid in kind. Thus both parties in the "integrative condition" achieved high economic outcomes.

Although these results are compelling, they alone are not definitive in suggesting that integrative reputations are more beneficial to a negotiator than distributive reputations. Does this same pattern extend to non-buyer/seller exchanges? Does this same pattern extend to negotiations outside of a controlled laboratory situation? That is, what is the generalizability of these results?

Results from Surveys of Lawyers About the Real World

In a well-known article, Robert Gilson and Robert Mnookin hypothesize a theory of reputation markets for lawyers.[25] This theory of reputation markets has several components. First, like Axelrod, the theory uses the game theoretic construct of the prisoner's dilemma where lawyers can either choose to cooperate or defect—the same behavioral choice outlined earlier. Gilson and Mnookin hypothesized that reputation markets could alleviate the prisoner's dilemma in litigation by signaling a cooperative or competitive intent to the other side.[26] If a lawyer had a cooperative reputation and the other side knew that, they would be more likely to work together (and save their respective clients time and money). If, however, the lawyer had a distributive reputation and the other side knew that, the other side would respond in kind (by, for example, dragging out discovery). What reputation markets hypothesized, we have already seen proven in the lab studies cited above. So, how do lawyers' reputations actually get measured in reality?

One way of measuring reputation is to see what that reputation is worth in the real world. In the real world, we would see that "worth" through either what clients would pay for that reputation, or how attorneys would assess that reputation. What is the view of attorneys toward each other given that these other attorneys create and measure that reputation? If lawyers value an integrative approach in their colleagues, we would expect them to perceive that as a more effective negotiation approach. Similarly, if lawyers do not find a distributive approach valuable, lawyers would tend to describe this approach as relatively ineffective in negotiations. As we explained earlier, reputations are created over time and through interactions. Therefore, to measure lawyers' reputations, we need to ask lawyers about other lawyers' behaviors.

In a negotiation study conducted in Chicago and Milwaukee, over 700 lawyers (out of 2,500) sent back a mailed questionnaire that asked lawyers to rate their counterpart attorneys using 89 adjectives, 60 negotiation techniques, and 14 goals. The attorneys also rated their counterparts for effectiveness. The studied attorneys were grouped in two, three, and four styles based on statistical analysis.[27] As we would expect given the lab studies, attorneys do value an integrative reputation as measured by its perceived effectiveness. For example (in the four-cluster analysis where attorneys were divided into "true problem-solving," "cautious problem-solving," "ethical adversarial" and "unethical adversarial"), 72% of those attorneys described as true problem-solvers were perceived as effective by their peers (and only 1% of these attorneys were seen as ineffective). In contrast, only 3% of un-ethical adversarial attorneys were perceived as effective, while 75% of unethical adversarial attorneys were perceived as ineffective. (Being ethical adversarial only helped somewhat—only 16% were perceived as effective, with 40% perceived as ineffective).

The theory of reputation markets also hypothesizes that in smaller markets it will be easier to create and maintain an integrative reputation. So, extrapolating from the theory, we would expect to see a "reward" for integrative behavior in smaller markets, and "punishment" for distributive behavior. Similarly, in the lar-ger markets where an integrative reputation is harder to create and maintain, we would expect to see both smaller rewards for integrative behavior and smaller punishments for distributive behavior. Using this study of attorneys, we can see whether there was a difference by geography (small city versus big city) and by practice area. Both the four-cluster analysis and two-cluster analysis (dividing lawyers only into "problem-solving" and "adversarial") showed statistically sig-nificant differences by city and practice area.[28]

Not surprisingly, attorneys were seen as more effective when they displayed problem-solving behaviors in a smaller market. For example, in Milwaukee, prob-lem-solving attorneys (in the two cluster analysis) were found to be 66% effective, whereas in Chicago, 59% of problem-solving attorneys were considered effective. Additionally, in the four-cluster analysis, 74.2% of attorneys categorized as true problem-solvers were rated as effective in Milwaukee compared to 70% of true problem-solvers in Chicago. And the reverse is true as well—lawyers who are ad-versarial are seen as less effective in the smaller market of Milwaukee. For example, there were *no* unethical adversarial attorneys considered effective in Milwaukee compared to 6.1% of unethical adversarial attorneys in Chicago who were considered effective by their counterparts.[29] Finally, as expected, there is less punishment for being adversarial in the bigger market of Chicago. In the two-cluster analysis, adversarial attorneys were considered more effective in Chicago than in Milwaukee: 41% of Chicago adversarial attorneys were reported to be ef-fective versus 34% of adversarial attorneys in Milwaukee.

We would also expect that smaller practice areas would lead to a greater ability to create and benefit from an integrative reputation. When examining the data by practice area, the highest percentage of true problem-solvers amongst the various practice areas was, perhaps surprisingly, in criminal law, with 49.2% of attorneys considered true problem-solvers. While the subject matter of the negotiations in this group (plea bargaining) does not lead immediately to the conclusion that in-tegrative behavior is effective, in fact the repeat-play in criminal law is probably higher than any other practice area (remembering that we are speaking of the lawyers, not their clients). Other studies have found that the impact of repeated interactions among lawyers does lead to higher settlement rates.[30]

The exception to this hypothesis, however, is found in the family law area. Gil-son and Mnookin hypothesized that an integrative reputation would be worthwhile in family practice. And clearly one would expect both from the exten-sive family law literature and from the subject matter that cooperation would be rewarded. However, the family law practice area had only 37.7% true problem-solving attorneys, placing family law fifth amongst the seven practice areas of law. Moreover, family law had the highest percentage of attorneys considered unethical adversarial—14.8% of attorneys. Further work needs to be done to explain these findings, but one could hypothesize that some percentage of clients in the family law area pay for, expect and reward adversarial behavior even more than in other practice areas. This impact of the client on the creation and maintenance of a reputation is another area for further research.

Results From the Field

Thus far we've seen that in both a business domain and a legal domain, in both the lab and with practicing attorneys, a reputation for being cooperative appears superior to a reputation for being tough or distributive. But does this extend even further, to crisis negotiations? Does this extend to barricade situations where a criminal or psychopath has isolated himself, issuing threats and demands and perhaps even holding hostages? In these cases, might force or the threat of force be more appropriate? The answer is yes, the threat of force (on the part of law-enforcement) is important to motivate a dialogue between the perpetrator and the crisis negotiator. But within the negotiation,[31] itself, having a reputation for being cooperative, trustworthy, and honest is critical for successful resolution. This matters in more than just the selected case area of hostage negotiations. [Taylor & Donohue, *Hostage Negotiation*]

Consider the following true (though names are fictitious) story in which several different negotiators, with different reputations, were involved; one proved unsuccessful at achieving resolution and the other proved to be an overwhelming success, with the end result being that a life was saved.

Billy (not his real name) was a 48-year-old male who came to the attention of the police after he called his estranged girlfriend and told her that he was going to kill himself. The girlfriend knew that he was depressed over their recent breakup and was refusing to accept that the relationship was over; she also knew that Billy had a gun. She quickly called the police, which summoned several different units from within the department, including the Emergency Service Unit (ESU), the NYPD's tactical team, and the Hostage Negotiation Team (HNT). The former girlfriend informed the police that Billy had been diagnosed with bipolar disorder. [Jeglic & Jeglic, *Disordered People*] When the negotiators first established contact with him, they quickly learned that he was in his manic stage. He remained that way for the next 50 hours.

This marathon negotiation proved to be difficult and complex, utilizing 17 separate hostage negotiators, and even recycling negotiators back in, before it was finally concluded. In a situation such as this, when an individual is holding himself hostage with a gun, negotiation is the only viable solution. Certainly the police do not want to make a tactical assault and put themselves in a position of having to shoot the individual to keep him from shooting himself.

Billy quickly revealed himself as being extremely intelligent, particularly when it came to holding his own with the negotiators, and at times he even appeared to be negotiating the negotiators. At one point, he cleverly "set up" one of the negotiators by asking if he had a family. The negotiator responded that he had a wife and two children. Billy then asked the negotiator if he looked forward to spending a long life together with them? Again the negotiator responded yes. Billy then retorted, "Well that's wonderful and I respect you for that. So why then, do you assume that I want those same things and why do you not respect my wishes to want to die?" The negotiator had no immediate response.

About 20 hours into the negotiation, a new negotiator, "Paul," was put on the phone. This was a calculated plan, as Paul had a reputation for being able to push negotiations to the limit, in many cases instilling just enough pressure to convince hostage-takers into surrendering. Paul was at times adversarial and confrontational in his approach. In the four hours that Paul spoke, his tactics did not prove effective for this individual. Billy indicated to the next negotiator that he did not like Paul's brash approach, and that Paul was not to speak with him again or he would immediately shoot himself.

It was ultimately another negotiator, named "Rachael," who finally convinced Billy to come out. Rachael had spoken to Billy early on in the negotiations, and Billy recalled during their final negotiation that she had been very compassionate and demonstrated genuine concern for his well-being. Rachael effectively developed a positive and encouraging rapport with Billy, to the point where he was able to trust her enough to finally come out.

What is particularly striking about this story is that a cooperative reputation proved critical even in a situation where there was little chance of any repeat-play. That is, in most business and legal negotiations, negotiators routinely interact with each other over time. Contracts are updated, union-management terms are renegotiated, and attorneys see each other again. As most game theorists would explain, in a repeat-play, mixed-motive game (such as a multi-round prisoners' dilemma), parties are made best off when they can cooperate and trust that the other party will cooperate as well.[32] Hence, as mentioned in the first section, repeat-play encourages an attentiveness to how one is perceived by the other side (i.e., an attentiveness to one's reputation), and an awareness that one wants to be perceived as cooperative rather than exploitative.

What the NYPD Hostage Negotiation Training teaches, however, is each discrete negotiation can be seen as a repeat-play situation. A negotiator's behavior at the beginning of the negotiation has critical implications for a hostage taker's responses to the negotiator at later stages of the negotiation. Indeed, a rule of thumb stipulates that the first 15-45 minutes (of what might be a protracted, multi-day negotiation) are the most critical. In this early window a negotiator must try to begin establishing his or her reputation for trustworthiness, problem-solving, compassion, and cooperation (though of course each situation is different and often the first 45 minutes are just allowing the hostage taker to vent). People are inclined to manage psychological distress by believing in the credibility of those upon whom they must depend to get them through their misfortune. If a crisis negotiator demonstrates a strong and sincere desire to resolve the crisis in a compassionate and cooperative way, then the chances of successful resolution are enhanced.

The negotiator establishes this reputation slowly and by creating "small wins." One common technique is to first ask the hostage taker if he wants the negotiator to tell the truth or not. This does several things. First, it starts a reciprocity process, because when the hostage taker says "yes"[33] and the negotiator agrees, then the negotiator has made a concession of sorts, establishing that the negotiator is willing to work with the hostage taker or problem-solve. Second, when the hostage taker says "yes" the negotiator can then agree and has started to build his or her reputation for honesty. Third, when the hostage taker says "yes" the negotiator can then reply that he will be honest, but the hostage taker must promise to not do any harm if he has a negative reaction to what the negotiator might say. This starts to establish the negotiator's reputation for compassion and problem-solving—that the negotiator wants a good outcome for everyone. It also begins establishing control for the negotiator. Hostage negotiators must convey a cooperative spirit while simultaneously establishing the authority to eventually remove control from the hostage taker. Another common question to ask in this critical early stage is, "How did we get here today and how can we get out of this?" (Sometimes these are asked as separate questions, but always using the negotiator's own phrasing, which may be far less direct than our summary version of these all-important questions). This establishes the negotiator as compassionate. Also, by eliciting ideas from the hostage taker for how to get out of this situation, these questions signal that the negotiator wants to work together with the hostage taker to find a mutually-beneficial solution, reinforcing a reputation for cooperation and problem-solving. Of course, this question also invites the hostage taker to begin telling his story, a critical component of the process we discuss below.

Demands are elicited—"what do you need," "how can we get out of this situation"—as a way of getting at the hostage taker's underlying interests. This again establishes the negotiator as cooperative, a problem-solver. Of course, the negotiator has to be clever in how he or she responds to certain demands. Oftentimes, the negotiator will paraphrase demands, successively lowering their actual content. For example, if a hostage taker asks for $1 million and a jet to Bermuda, the negotiator might paraphrase by replying, "ok, so you want some money and to get out of this safely." In this way, the negotiator is continuing to build a cooperative reputation while simultaneously lowering the expectations or reference points of the hostage taker. The goal is essentially to lower the demands of the hostage taker to a level where the negotiator can agree and resolution can occur.

Another element to this critical opening dialogue is the expression of emotion. Oftentimes the hostage taker will want to vent about the negative events that have brought him to this place. The negotiator can elicit these emotions in a reflective way, saying for example, "You seem angry (sad/upset), can you tell me why?" Reflecting emotions often gets the hostage taker to agree ("You're damn right I'm angry") which starts to build reciprocity as well as the reputation for compassion and cooperation. [Shapiro, *Emotion*] Sometimes the negotiator will then draw upon his or her own life experiences of these angry (sad/upset) emotions to again establish the reputation of compassion and cooperation. This is one reason why selection criteria for crisis negotiators are so demanding. Candidates, for example, typically have at least 12 years NYPD experience, ensuring they have the maturity and life experience to relate to such emotions as love, hurt, success, and perhaps, most importantly, failure. Of course, eliciting these emotions not only builds reciprocity and a favorable reputation but also has the added benefit of allowing the hostage taker to vent his emotions, which often dissipates them, often allowing a more rational and realistic conversation to emerge.

Although crisis negotiations are very personal and each negotiator would have his or her own unique dialogue, commonalities of approach do exist. One fundamental agreement is that negotiators must pay attention to their reputation, even within this one-shot context. Moreover, a reputation for credibility, trustworthiness, cooperation, and compassion (i.e., an integrative reputation) is what a crisis negotiator is trying to build.

Conclusion

Reputation is too important to be left to chance. Negotiators need to understand the impact of their reputation, and must work to maintain that reputation throughout the negotiation. We have argued that an integrative reputation leads to better rapport and information sharing, leading to more creative and more satisfying outcomes. Furthermore, this integrative behavior is perceived as more effective by one's negotiation counterpart. Finally, even under conditions in which repeated interactions are highly unlikely, the ability to create a trustworthy reputation has value even within that single negotiation interaction. Creating and maintaining an integrative reputation can take time and effort, but as Socrates suggests, these are well spent resources for a "jewel" of a reputation, and a reputation once built is cheaper to maintain than to re-gain.

Endnotes

[1] ROBERT AXELROD, THE EVOLUTION OF COOPERATION 150 (1984).

[2] SUSAN T. FISKE & SHELLEY E. TAYLOR, SOCIAL COGNITION (1991); Catherine H. Tinsley & Susan E. Brodt, *Conflict Management in Asia: A Dynamic Framework and Future Directions, in* HANDBOOK OF ASIAN MANAGEMENT (Kwon Leung & Steven White eds., 2004).

[3] FISKE & TAYLOR, *supra* note 2; Justine Owens, Gordon H. Bower, & John B. Black, *The "Soap-Opera" Effect in Story Recall,* 7 MEMORY AND COGNITION 185 (1979).

[4] FISKE & TAYLOR, *supra* note 2.

[5] LEIGH THOMPSON, THE MIND AND HEART OF THE NEGOTIATOR (1998).

[6] Orly Ben-Yoav & Dean G. Pruitt, *Accountability to Constituents: A Two-Edged Sword,* 34 ORGANIZATION BEHAVIOR AND HUMAN PROCESSES 282 (1984).

[7] David Marlow, Kenneth J. Gergen & Anthony Doob, *Opponents' Personality, Expectation of Social Interaction and Interpersonal Bargaining,* 3 JOURNAL OF PERSONALITY AND SOCIAL PSYCHOLOGY 206 (1966).

[8] Indeed, it has been noted that reputations only exist in a world of uncertainty—if actions or outcomes are certain, then reputations become irrelevant.

[9] Robin R. Vallacher & Danial M. Wegner, *Levels of Personal Agency: Individual Variation in Action Identification,* 57 JOURNAL OF PERSONALITY AND SOCIAL PSYCHOLOGY 660 (1989).

[10] *E.g.,* John M. Darley & Paget H. Gross, *A Hypothesis-Confirming Bias in Labeling Effects,* 44 JOURNAL OF PERSONALITY AND SOCIAL PSYCHOLOGY 20 (1983).

[11] Some writers would argue that there are more than two choices of style or that a combination of styles would be most appropriate. For our purposes and for clarity, however, we limit the discussion to these two extremes.

[12] Andrea Kupfer Schneider, *Shattering Negotiation Myths: Empirical Evidence On The Effectiveness Of Negotiation Style,* 7 HARVARD NEGOTIATION LAW REVIEW 143-233 (2002).

[13] Dipankar Ghosh, *Nonstrategic Delay in Bargaining: An Experimental Investigation,* 67 ORGANIZATIONAL BEHAVIOR AND HUMAN DECISION PROCESSES 312 (1996).

[14] ERIC RASMUSEN, GAMES AND INFORMATION: AN INTRODUCTION TO GAME THEORY (1989).

[15] *See* SIMON SEBAG MONTEFIORE, STALIN: THE COURT OF THE RED TSAR (2004).

[16] Laurie R. Weingart, et al., *Tactical Behavior and Negotiation Outcomes,* 1 INTERNATIONAL JOURNAL OF CONFLICT MANAGEMENT 7 (1990); DEAN G. PRUITT & PETER J. CARNEVALE, NEGOTIATION IN SOCIAL CONFLICT (1993).

[17] Leigh L. Thompson, *Information Exchange in Negotiation,* 27 JOURNAL OF EXPERIMENTAL SOCIAL PSYCHOLOGY 161 (1991); Dean G. Pruitt & Steven A. Lewis, *Development of Integrative Solutions in Bilateral Negotiation,* 31 JOURNAL OF PERSONALITY AND SOCIAL PSYCHOLOGY 621 (1975).

[18] THOMPSON, *supra* note 5.

[19] Mara Olekalns & Philip L. Smith, *Social Value Orientations and Strategy Choices in Competitive Negotiations,* 25 PERSONALITY AND SOCIAL PSYCHOLOGY BULLETIN 657 (1999).

[20] ROY J. LEWICKI, DAVID M. SAUNDERS, & JOHN M. MINTON, ESSENTIALS OF NEGOTIATION (1997).

[21] Laurie R. Weingart, Elaine Hyder, & Michael J. Prietula, *Knowledge Matters: The Effect of Tactical Descriptions on Negotiation Behavior Outcome,* 70 JOURNAL OF PERSONALITY AND SOCIAL PSYCHOLOGY 1205 (1996).

[22] Catherine H. Tinsley, et al., *Tough Guys Finish Last: The Perils of a Distributive Reputation,* 88 ORGANIZATIONAL BEHAVIOR AND HUMAN DECISION PROCESSES 621 (2002) [hereinafter Tinsley, *Tough Guys*]; KATHLEEN M. O'CONNOR & CATHERINE H. TINSLEY, LOOKING FOR A STRATEGIC ADVANTAGE AT THE NEGOTIATING TABLE? CULTIVATE A REPUTATION FOR MUTUALLY-BENEFICIAL DEALMAKING (2004) (Unpublished working paper presented at the International Association for Conflict Management annual meetings).

[23] *See* DAVID LAX & JAMES SEBENIUS, THE MANAGER AS NEGOTIATOR (1986) for further discussion of how contingency contracts that trade-off differential projections of the future create joint (integrative) value in a negotiation.

[24] Tinsley, *Tough Guys*, *supra* note 21. "Significantly" here means in the statistical sense, in that ANOVA showed these negotiators were significantly more likely than corresponding negotiators in the control group to act as described.

[25] Ronald J. Gilson & Robert H. Mnookin, *Disputing Through Agents: Cooperation and Conflict Between Lawyers in Litigation*, 94 COLUMBIA LAW REVIEW 509 (1995).

[26] *Id.*

[27] Schneider, *supra* note 12.

[28] *Id.*

[29] *Id.*

[30] *Id. See also* Jason Scott Johnston & Joel Waldfogel, *Does Repeat Play Elicit Cooperation? Evidence from Federal Civil Litigation*, 31 JOURNAL OF LEGAL STUDIES 39 (2002).

[31] In fact, most law-enforcement separates the use of force, which is supplied independently by a tactical unit, from the negotiation, which is an independent unit or team.

[32] AXELROD, *supra* note 1.

[33] HT's always say "yes." "As crazy as hostage takers can be (and they can be very, very crazy), I've never had any of them ever say 'yes, please lie to me'" Hugh McGowan, *in* Jack Cambria et al., *Negotiation Under Extreme Pressure: The "Mouth Marines" and the Hostage Takers*, 18 NEGOTIATION JOURNAL 331 (2002).

‎‎‎‎‎‎‎ 24 ‎

Giving Future Generations a Voice

Kimberly A. Wade-Benzoni

Editors' Note: *Most discussions of negotiation tacitly assume that self-interest is the predominant, or even the only, basis for what is going on. Discussing the fascinating research on intergenerational behavior, Wade-Benzoni explains that many situations actually include an element of "negotiating with the future"—and that in these settings, people may act in unexpected and pro-social ways. This chapter should be read in conjunction with Welsh on Fairness.*

For most of history, we did not have the capacity to break, bankrupt, or obliterate the future. But in the day and age of the atomic bomb, deficit financing, dramatic global-scale environmental change, and genetic engineering, we have unprecedented power to shape the future and, consequently, great responsibility to take into account how our actions might affect future generations. Intergenerational contexts push the boundaries of more traditional conceptions of negotiations to include the reconciliation of conflicting interests between parties who may not exist contemporaneously.

Different generations have profound effects on one another—even in the absence of the opportunity for explicit interaction. The decisions and behaviors of earlier generations shape the options for those in the future, and the mere existence of future generations changes the experience of the present generation. One of the most important aspects of intergenerational relations is the fact that the interests of present and future generations are not always aligned. Cutting taxes while increasing spending, relaxing controls on greenhouse emissions (creating cheaper energy in the short term, but higher costs in the future), and unlimited consumption of non-replenishable resources are examples of behaviors that benefit the present generation while burdening future generations. In such situations, the consequences associated with a decision or action are at least partially decoupled, in that benefits accrue immediately to the present generation while associated burdens are deferred to a later point in time. Intergenerational justice may require a reversal of that pattern, such that it may be necessary for the present generation to make a sacrifice in order to protect the interests of future generations.

In most societies, there is a presumption of a moral obligation toward future generations. People generally value the outcomes to future generations[1] and we tend to agree that fairness in the distribution of resources across generations should be upheld to some degree if societies are to persist and flourish over time. In this chapter, I will discuss some of the psychological barriers to implementing well-intended fairness to future generations, as well as some unexpected social-psychologically based motivators to promoting intergenerational beneficence in situations where it may seem unlikely based on traditional economic thought.

Intergenerational Conflict

At the heart of intergenerational conflict is the need for trade-offs among the interests of different generations. The present generation is faced with a dilemma of whether to incur costs themselves for the benefit of future generations. Intergenerational conflict is further escalated, and decisions further complicated, when the consequences to future generations (whether they are positive or negative) increase over time. In these situations, intergenerational beneficence involves deferring benefits so that they can grow, or addressing burdens to prevent them from mounting in the future. In the case of long-term investments, for example, future generations are expected to experience greater monetary benefits relative to those foregone by earlier generations. Similarly, future generations can experience more serious negative consequences as a result of the present generation leaving burdens for them (such as toxic waste that is buried where it poisons drinking water decades later) than would be experienced by the present generation had they handled the burdens themselves.

In intergenerational contexts where consequences increase over time, the nature of the decision is critically different from more traditional negotiations in that it is not possible for decision-makers to maximize on both the distributive and collective dimensions. Rather, they are faced with a stark choice between the two: increasing the size of the "pie" of resources by deferring escalating benefits (or preventing escalating burdens) for future others requires self-sacrifice on the distributive dimension (i.e., keeping less benefits or taking on more burdens oneself). Since decisions and behaviors that benefit actors in the present translate into more serious downsides for future actors, a self-interested choice is even more selfish than it would be otherwise. This feature further elevates the dilemma that people face when allocating resources to powerless future others, and exacerbates the inherent power asymmetry between present and future generations. The parties who have control over the decision process (present generation) are not the parties with the most at stake (future generations) and thus the dependency of future generations on the present generation is intensified.

Power asymmetry goes hand-in-hand with the fact that future or later generations often do not have the opportunity to reciprocate the behavior or deeds of previous generations. If future generations can speak for themselves and "fight back" if necessary, then the situation starts to resemble more typical, traditional intergroup and negotiation situations. The goal in the empirical work reviewed in this paper has been to examine phenomena that are more uniquely intergenerational and thus has focused on contexts with full power asymmetry and the absence of direct reciprocity. Further, in order to isolate social psychologically based factors motivating intergenerational beneficence and to rule out economically and materially based ones, the research has focused on situations where social actors are removed from the social exchange context after they make intergenerational decisions (and thus cannot be affected themselves by future consequences).

Barriers to Intergenerational Beneficence

Psychological Distance

A central barrier to intergenerational beneficence is the inherent psychological distance between decision-makers and the future consequences of their decisions.

This distance is due to the fact that long-term intergenerational implications of decisions are *both* temporally and personally removed. First, the consequences of intergenerational decisions are removed from the decision-maker through the temporal delay that exists between the decision and the consequences of that decision. Consistent with the findings from the literature on intertemporal choice, prior work in intergenerational contexts indicates that the greater the time delay between an intergenerational decision and the consequences of that decision to future generations, the less people act on the behalf of future generations.[2] People discount the value of commodities that will be consumed in the future, reflecting an inborn impatience and preference for immediate over postponed consumption. As time delay increases, people have greater difficulty fully understanding the consequences of decisions. Beyond these cognitive limitations, however, motivational effects—such as the immediate pain of deferral—also make it difficult for people to delay benefits for the future.

The psychological distance that is already present from the time dimension is compounded in the intergenerational context by the fact that it is *others* (rather than oneself) that will be affected in the future by one's decisions. When making tradeoffs between the well-being of oneself and that of others, there is a tension between self-interest and the desire to benefit others. Although people may care about the outcomes of others, tradeoffs between one's own and others' well-being are typically skewed to the point where very little weight is put on the effect of one's decisions on others.[3] The impact of individuals' decisions on themselves is generally far more immediate than their impact on other parties. In terms of intergenerational sacrifices, the costs of changing one's behavior are more immediate than the future benefits to others, not only in the temporal sense, but also because they affect the decision-maker directly.

Reciprocity

While philosophers and theorists have cited the lack of immediacy of future consequences (i.e., psychological distance) as one reason why people often do not act on the behalf of future generations, they have pointed more strongly to the absence of traditional bonds of reciprocity as a factor thwarting sacrifice for future generations.[4] One generation typically does not benefit from the sacrifices it makes for future generations.

In conventional negotiation contexts, reciprocity takes the form of mutual reinforcement by two parties of each other's actions.[5] In intergenerational contexts, reciprocity takes a more generalized form in which people can "reciprocate" the good or evil left to them by previous generations by behaving similarly to the next generation.[6] In other words, people can pass on benefits (or burdens) to future generations as a matter of retrospective obligation (or retaliation) for the good (or bad) received from past generations. The beneficence of prior generations can create a sense of indebtedness, and thus people want to "pay it forward" by acting generously to the next generation. Thus, intergenerational reciprocity can come into play as either a barrier or a facilitator of intergenerational beneficence depending on the behavior of prior generations.

Ethicists who advocate intergenerational justice focus on the related notion of "moral reciprocity," in which the present generation treats future generations as they would like to have been treated themselves by the preceding generation.[7] The presumption is that everyone would prefer to be treated fairly by others, and so people should treat others fairly as well. Moral reciprocity, or how one *would like* to be treated by others, however, may or may not correspond to how one *is or was* actually treated by others. Empirically, intergenerational research shows that when making decisions affecting outcomes to future generations, individuals may consider how they *would like* to have been treated by previous generations, but behavior appears to be mostly driven by how people *were actually* treated by previous generations.[8] Thus, our intergenerational behavior has more far reaching implications than we may realize. Not only does it affect the next generation directly, but also influences how the next generation will treat subsequent generations.

Egocentrism

Our interpretation of the past and translation to the future, however, is subject to deeply rooted and pervasive biases—especially with respect to fairness judgments. There is a consensus among theorists and a convergence of empirical evidence that fairness judgments are typically biased in a self-serving manner, even though such subjective perceptions can appear objective and unbiased to moral reasoners themselves.[9] Individuals are motivated by self-interest to obtain benefits for and avoid burdens to themselves. They are also motivated to preserve positive self-images that they are concerned about issues of justice and that they have contributed their fair share to others and the common good. Self-serving interpretations of fairness provide a convenient reconciliation of these two apparently conflicting goals. Individuals can have what they want *and* believe their actions are fair.

Research has confirmed the role of egocentric biases in resource allocation contexts including negotiations[10] and social dilemmas.[11] The bias manifests itself as a strong tendency for people to justify allocating more of a limited resource to themselves relative to others on the basis of fairness. Further, this effect has been found to generalize across different cultures[12]—highlighting the pervasiveness of the role of egocentric judgments of fairness in resource allocation decisions.

Self-serving biases in judgments of fairness are also relevant in the intergenerational domain. Individuals' judgments about what is fair for one generation to leave for the next depends on whether the decision-maker is in the generation who is leaving the resources (generation x) or the one for whom the resources are being left (generation x + 1). Specifically, people believe that it is fair for the preceding generation to leave more benefits for the succeeding generation if the individuals making the judgments are the succeeding generation than if the individuals making the judgments are in the preceding generation.[13] This finding helps to explain how intergenerational inequities can occur even when people are explicitly focused on making fair allocations of resources among generations.

Uncertainty

Uncertainty about how future generations will be affected by our actions is fundamental to intergenerational dilemmas, adds non-trivially to moral reasoning when intergenerational allocation decisions are made, and is central to understanding the psychology of intergenerational decisions. Decisions regarding the future inevitably involve uncertainty. Uncertainty about the future is due partly to the actual number of possible events that can happen over time to prevent the occurrence of expected consequences, and partly due to our limited knowledge about the future.[14] The further the consequences of a decision reach in time, the less we are able to anticipate the aftermath of our decisions.[15]

Uncertainty comes into play in intergenerational contexts in many ways. Future consequences of intergenerationally relevant decisions are often not well-determined or even knowable. Damage to future generations might be severe, but the probability of occurrence of such damage is unknown. The consequences of an enhanced greenhouse effect, for example, range from severe global warming to hardly any changes to a cooling down of parts of the globe. Further, the preferences and values of future others might be unknown as well.

Uncertainty operates in conjunction with egocentrism in intergenerational decisions such that when people are assessing the fairness of what *previous* generations have left for them, they focus on the importance of equality between generations. When assessing fairness of what they should leave for the *next* generation, however, they emphasize the uncertainty of the future. Uncertainty gives people an excuse to choose outcomes that favor themselves because they can reason that maybe events will turn out better than predicted. They are able to maintain optimistic biases about how the world will be in the future because there is not yet any data available to disconfirm their beliefs. Thus, when there is greater uncertainty about future consequences, people judge that it is fair to leave less of a beneficial resource for future generations (or alternatively get more from the previous generation) as compared to situations with less uncertainty about the intergenerational consequences of decisions.[16]

Promoting Intergenerational Beneficence
In light of the combination of temporal and interpersonal distance inherent in intergenerational decisions, lack of direct reciprocity between generations, egocentrism, and uncertainty about the future, we might expect the prospects for future generations to be quite grim. Fortunately, alongside the barriers, the research on intergenerational decisions has uncovered a number of factors that can help promote intergenerational beneficence.

Affinity
The psychological distance between oneself and future generations stemming from the interpersonal dimension can be reduced by increasing what has been called "affinity" to future generations. [Guthrie, *Compliance*] Building on earlier work,[17] affinity is conceptualized as a combination of empathy, perspective-taking and perceived oneness. It is a function of the extent to which the present generation feels empathetic toward future generations, is able to visualize future generations, and believes they understand how their actions will affect future generations. Research shows that greater levels of affinity promote more intergenerational beneficence.[18] Similarly, people can gain a sense of vicariously experiencing the benefits and burdens left to future generations if adequate levels of intergenerational identification are present.[19] High affinity and identification with the future generation by definition blurs the distinction between interests of the present generation and those of the future generation.

Further, research shows that people have greater affinity with future generations when they are responsible for creating the benefits and burdens that they are allocating than when they are not responsible for creating those benefits and burdens.[20] Benefits and burdens that are allocated by the present generation to future generations are sometimes inherited (from previous generations or others) and sometimes created by the present generation themselves. When individuals are responsible for creating the benefits and burdens that they are allocating, their decision-making relies on more complex processes that leads to more perspective taking, greater empathy for future others, and ultimately more affinity with them than when they are not responsible for creating the benefits and burdens. Since greater affinity is linked with greater intergenerational beneficence, whether or not the present generation bears the responsibility for creating the benefits and burdens is an important factor in intergenerational allocation decisions.

Benefits Versus Burdens
The majority of research in the negotiation literature has focused on positive or beneficial resources. In allocation contexts (including intergenerational ones),

however, people may be allocating either desirable benefits (e.g., money, natural resources) or undesirable burdens (e.g., debt, hazardous waste). Research has shown that the treatment of benefits and burdens are not psychologically equivalent and produce different decision processes.[21] In negotiation contexts, people consistently exhibit more self-interested behavior in the distribution of burdens as compared to benefits.[22] In contrast, in the intergenerational context, the pattern of behavior is quite the opposite: intergenerational beneficence is greater (i.e., self-interested behavior is lower) in the allocation of burdens as compared to benefits. This phenomenon, which appears to be unique to intergenerational decisions, is robust across multiple studies using different participant populations, experimental designs, and intergenerational contexts.[23]

The difference can be understood by considering the unique features of intergenerational decisions. In traditional negotiation situations, since joint decisions are required, people can expect the other negotiating parties to be concerned with their own interests and thus need not feel solely responsible for others' outcomes. In contrast, in intergenerational contexts where future generations do not have a voice in allocation decisions made in the past, earlier generations cannot expect future generations to defend their own interests. Consequently, decision-makers are responsible for the outcomes to both the present generation (often including themselves) and future others. People hesitate to impose explicitly aversive outcomes on others who have no power to veto the decision and, consequently, intergenerational allocations of burdens create more of an ethical dilemma for decision-makers as compared to benefits. In support of this notion, in the same studies, people reported that ethical considerations came more into play in the intergenerational allocation of burdens than benefits.[24] The pattern of results in this series of experiments on intergenerational allocations of benefits versus burdens highlights the need to consider how and when intergenerational decisions may differ from behavior in other contexts that share some, but not all, of the features that typify intergenerational situations.

Legacies & Immortality Striving

While there is naturally some overlap and consistency with the research on intertemporal choice involving only oneself, and self-other tradeoffs without time delay, the combination of intertemporal and interpersonal dimensions that characterizes intergenerational dilemmas creates its own psychological dynamics that can offer unexpected other-oriented motivation. An important part of the psychology of intergenerational decision-making is rooted in very basic needs and concerns that people have about leaving legacies. The notion of a legacy is a concept that is only meaningful and emergent in a context where a person's behavior has implications for other people in the future. The presence of both the components of "otherness" and "future-ness" is fundamental to the conceptualization of legacies. Leaving a legacy enables people to create something that will outlive themselves and thus provides a symbolic form of immortality.[25] Indeed, older individuals, typically around and after the time of retirement, start to engage in work that will solidify their long-term legacy.[26] Intergenerational altruism can help people to feel a part of something that will outlast their own individual existence. While altruism of any kind has the potential to help people to create their own positive legacy, intergenerational altruism is even more effective at achieving that goal because the temporal aspect increases the likelihood that the social entity receiving the benefit will presumably exist in the future.[27]

This notion highlights how the combination of intertemporal and interpersonal dimensions can actually promote intergenerational beneficence rather than work against it. People need to feel that life is meaningful, they have a sense of purpose, and they have made a useful contribution to the world. Intergenerational altruism can help to fill that need by enabling people to make a connection with an entity that will continue to exist after they are gone. Being able to live on, even if only in impact and memory, is an important motivator of intergenerational beneficence.

Conclusion

When different generations exist contemporaneously, then intergenerational relations look a lot more like traditional intergroup and negotiation situations. In contrast, this chapter considers situations when the present generation is responsible for being the voice of future others. The intergenerational context challenges the boundaries of the traditional negotiation realm by helping us to understand how conflicting interests might be reconciled when other parties who are affected by outcomes are not only not at the table (and thus do not have their own voice), but may not even exist yet. Beyond understanding intergenerational behavior itself, insights from intergenerational research help us to better understand other-oriented behavior in general. Critically, it adds the role of time as we consider the implications of when consequences to others do not materialize immediately, but only after a time delay.

Mere extrapolation of the work from traditional economics, intertemporal choice, negotiations, and egocentrism would lead us to predict that future generations can expect next to nothing. But theoretical and empirical work on intergenerational decisions shows that people do act on behalf of future generations—even when there is nothing in it for them economically or materially. Across more than a dozen studies where people allocate resources between themselves and future generations, people consistently exhibit surprising levels of intergenerational beneficence, and rarely give nothing to future generations. Interestingly, when needy others are not at the table and thus have no voice, the context can elicit stewardship tendencies.

In this chapter, I have outlined the social psychological factors that have been shown to influence the extent to which people will exhibit intergenerational beneficence in recent empirical work on intergenerational decisions. These factors include: time, reciprocity, egocentrism, uncertainty, affinity, responsibility, resource valence, and immortality striving.

In today's world, intergroup conflict transcends time and space as we face problems that affect multiple generations. The goal in the intergenerational justice research has been to understand better the factors that affect decisions with intergenerational implications in order to help us bring our own behaviors more in line with the value we place on fairness to future generations.

Endnotes

[1] WILLETT KEMPTON, JAMES S. BOSTER, & JENNIFER A. HARTLEY, ENVIRONMENTAL VALUES IN AMERICAN CULTURE (1995).

[2] Kimberly A. Wade-Benzoni, Intergenerational Justice: Discounting, Reciprocity, & Fairness as Factors that Influence How Resources are Allocated Across Generations (1996) (unpublished dissertation) (on file with author) [hereinafter Wade-Benzoni, Intergenerational]; KIMBERLY A. WADE-BENZONI, HARRIS SONDAK, & ADAM GALINSKY, LEAVING A LEGACY: THE INTERGENERATIONAL ALLOCATION OF BENEFITS AND BURDENS (2005) [hereinafter WADE-BENZONI, LEAVING].

[3] George Loewenstein, *Behavioral Decision Theory and Business Ethics: Skewed Tradeoffs Between Self and Other, in* CODES OF CONDUCT: BEHAVIORAL RESEARCH INTO BUSINESS ETHICS 214 (D.M. Messick & A.E. Tenbrunsel eds., 1996).

[4] NORMAN S. CARE, *Future Generations, Public Policy, and the Motivation Problem*, ENVIRONMENTAL ETHICS 4 (1982).

[5] TALCOTT PARSONS, THE SOCIAL SYSTEM (1951); ALVIN W. GOULDER, *Reciprocity and Autonomy in Function Theory*, in SYMPOSIUM ON SOCIOLOGICAL THEORY (Llewellyn Gross ed., 1959); ALVIN W. GOULDER, *The Norm of Reciprocity*, 25 AMERICAN SOCIOLOGICAL REVIEW 161 (1960).

[6] Kimberly A. Wade-Benzoni, *A Golden Rule Over Time: Reciprocity in Intergenerational Allocation Decisions*, 45 ACADEMY OF MANAGEMENT JOURNAL 1011(2002) [hereinafter Wade-Benzoni, *Golden*].

[7] JOHN RAWLS, A THEORY OF JUSTICE (1950); D.A.J. RICHARDS, *Contractual Theory, Intergenerational Justice, and Energy Policy*, in ENERGY AND THE FUTURE (D. MacLean & P.G. Brown eds., 1981).

[8] Wade-Benzoni, *Golden, supra* note 6.

[9] Nicholas Epley & Eugene M. Caruso, *Egocentric Ethics*, 25 SOCIAL JUSTICE RESEARCH 171 (2004).

[10] Linda Babock, et al., *Biased Judgements of Fairness in Bargaining*, 85 AMERICAN ECONOMIC REVIEW 1337 (1995); Max Bazerman & Margaret A. Neale, *Improving Negotiation Effectiveness Under Final Offer Arbitration: The Role of Selection and Training*, 67 JOURNAL OF APPLIED PSYCHOLOGY 543 (1982); Margaret A. Neale & Max H. Bazerman, *The Role of Perspective-Taking Ability in Negotiating under Different Forms of Arbitration*, 36 INDUSTRIAL & LABOR RELATIONS REVIEW 378 (1983).

[11] Kimberly A. Wade-Benzoni, et al., *Egocentric Interpretations of Fairness in Asymmetric, Environmental Social Dilemmas: Explaining Harvesting Behavior and the Role of Communication*, 67 ORGANIZATIONAL BEHAVIOR & HUMAN DECISION PROCESSES 111 (1996).

[12] Kimberly A. Wade-Benzoni, et al., *Cognitions and Behavior in Asymmetric Social Dilemmas: A Comparison of Two Cultures*, 87 JOURNAL OF APPLIED PSYCHOLOGY 87 (2002).

[13] Wade-Benzoni, Intergenerational, *supra* note 2; Kimberly A. Wade-Benzoni, et al., Egocentric Interpretations of Fairness in the Allocation of Resources Across Generations (2005) (Duke University, Working Paper) (on file with the author) [hereinafter Wade-Benzoni, Egocentric].

[14] H. Jungerman & F. Fleisher, *As Time Goes by: Psychological Determinants of Time Preferences*, in THE FORMULATION OF TIME PREFERENCE in A MULTIDISCIPLINARY PERSPECTIVE (Guy Kirsch, et al. eds., 1988).

[15] R. Hillerbrand, *The Problem of Uncertainty*, in THEORIES OF INTERGENERATIONAL JUSTICE (Axel Gosseries & Lucas H. Meyer eds., Forthcoming).

[16] Wade-Benzoni, Intergenerational, *supra* note 2; Wade-Benzoni, Egocentric, *supra* note 13.

[17] C. DANIEL BATSON, THE ALTRUISM QUESTION: TOWARD A SOCIAL-PSYCHOLOGICAL ANSWER (1991); Robert Cialdini, et al., *Reinterpreting the Empathy-Altruism Relationship: When One Into One Equals Oneness*, 73 JOURNAL OF PERSONALITY & SOCIAL PSYCHOLOGY 481 (1997).

[18] Wade-Benzoni, Intergenerational, *supra* note 2; WADE-BENZONI, LEAVING, *supra* note 2.

[19] Kimberly A. Wade-Benzoni, *Intergenerational Identification and Cooperation in Organizations and Society*, in 5 RESEARCH ON MANAGMENT GROUPS & TEAMS 257 (Margaret Neale, et al. eds., 2003).

[20] WADE-BENZONI, LEAVING, *supra* note 2.

[21] W.I. Griffith & Jane Sell, *The Effects of Competition on Allocators' Preferences for Contributive and Retributive Justice Rules*, 18 EUROPEAN JOURNAL OF SOCIAL PSYCHOLOGY 443 (1988); Helmut Lamm & Egon Kayser, *The Allocation of Monetary Gain and Loss Following Dyadic Performance: The Weight Given to Effort and Ability Under Conditions of Law and High Intra-Dyadic Attraction* 8 EUROPEAN JOURNAL OF SOCIAL PSYCHOLOGY 275 (1978); Elizabeth A. Mannix, et al., *Equity, Equality, or Need? The Effects of Organizational Culture on the Allocation of Benefits and Burdens*, 63 ORGANIZATIONAL BEHAVIOR & HUMAN DECISION PROCESSES 276 (1995); Gregory B. Northcraft, et al., *Benefits and Burdens: Does It Really What We Allocate?* 9 SOCIAL JUSTICE RESEARCH 27 (1996); Gerardo A. Okhuysen, et al., *Saving the Worst for Last: The Effect of Time Horizon on the Efficiency of Negotiating Benefits and Burdens*, 91 ORGANIZATIONAL BEHAVIOR & HUMAN DECISION PROCESSES 269 (2003); Harris Sondak, et al., *The Negotiated Allocation of Benefits and Burdens: The Impact of Outcome Valence, Contribution, and Relationship*, 64 ORGANIZATIONAL BEHAVIORAL

& HUMAN DECISION PROCESSES 249 (1995); Kjell Y. Törnblom, *Positive and Negative Allocation: A Typology and Model For Conflicting Justice Principles, in* ADVANCES IN GROUP PROCESSES (vol. 5) (Edward Lawler & Barry Markovsky eds., 1988)

[22] Mannix, et al., *supra* note 21; Northcraft, et al., *supra* note 21; Okhuysen, et al., *supra* note 21; Sondak, et al., *supra* note 21.

[23] WADE-BENZONI, LEAVING, *supra* note 2.

[24] *Id.*

[25] Jeff Greenberg, et al., *Terror Management Theory of Self-Esteem and Social Behavior: Empirical Assessments and Conceptual Refinements, in* 29 ADVANCED EXPERIMENTS IN SOCIAL PSYCHOLOGY 61 (M.P. Zanna ed., 1997).

[26] Dan P. McAdams, et al., *Stories of Commitment: The Psychological Construction of Generative Lives*, 72 JOURNAL OF PERSONALITY & SOCIAL PSYCHOLOGY 678 (1997).

[27] Kimberly A. Wade-Benzoni, *Legacies, Immortality, and the Future: The Psychology of Intergenerational Altruism, in* RESEARCH ON MANAGING GROUPS AND TEAMS (vol. 8) (Margaret Neale, et al. eds., Forthcoming).

᎒ 25 ᎒

Identity: More than Meets the "I"

Daniel L. Shapiro

Editors' Note: *How can you expect to get good results in a negotiation if you give little thought to who you really are, and to who your counterpart is? Shapiro analyzes the research on identity, showing how you can predict the likely reactions of your counterpart to some kinds of proposals—as well as your own propensity to avoid some kinds of proposals that might be to your advantage. This chapter should be read in close conjunction with the chapters on internal conflict, psychology and perceptions.*

Three Perspectives on Identity-Based Negotiation Research

As the Berlin Wall came to a crashing fall, so too did the equilibrium of global tensions. The Soviet Union lost its Superpower status; communism lost its reign over much of Europe; and both the United States and the Soviet Union reduced their level of support for proxy states of their Cold War. In many countries, ethnopolitical tensions combusted. The result was an explosion of intrastate violence, refugee transmigration, and political instability.

Amidst this backdrop, many researchers on conflict resolution and negotiation joined a growing research track working to understand *intergroup identity conflict*.[1] Known in short as "identity-based conflict,"[2] this area of study focuses on disagreement or warfare between groups divided along ethnic, political, religious, or cultural lines. Identity is conceived as a set of stable characteristics focused on one's *group* affiliations, beliefs, and shared values.

Meanwhile, other identity-based negotiation research has turned from the group to the individual level, studying *intrapersonal identity*.[3] At this level, identity is understood to be the story you tell yourself about yourself.[4] [Heen & Stone, *Perceptions*] An identity conflict manifests when there is a conflict between your view of yourself and an alternative view of yourself. An associate at a law firm may feel an intrapersonal identity conflict when she sees herself as a loyal associate but decides to switch to a neighboring firm that offers her a higher salary. The associate may wonder: am I a loyal person, or am I willing to betray friends for the right price?

The focus of this essay is on a third level of one's identity that stands at the crossroads between individual and group identity. This research track focuses on *interpersonal identity*, also known as "relational identity."[5] Your relational identity is the way you conceive of yourself in relation to someone else with whom you are interacting. In other words, the way you conceive of yourself is dependent, at least in part, on with whom you interact. In a relationship with one's boss, a person may be obsequious and accommodating. That same person may be assertive and outgoing in his relationship with his children. In either case, the identity of the individual as a servile worker or loving father becomes enwrapped in the quality and type of relationship.

In this brief essay, I describe two mistaken assumptions about identity that can negatively impact the negotiation process and outcome. These two assumptions are that a negotiator's identity is constant across time and across context. [Avruch, *Buyer—Seller*] These assumptions are based on the general idea that a negotiator's identity is an immutable given—that it does not and cannot change.[6] I argue that a better assumption is that a negotiator can choose many elements of his or her identity, which can lead to an improved negotiation process and outcome.

Mistaken Assumptions About Identity

Many negotiators see their identity as fixed. People in individualistic cultures, in particular, may tend to believe in the immutability of relational identity more than those from collectivist cultures. In a collectivist culture, people tend to take on the values of the social groups to which they belong. Changed group membership would constitute a changed sense of relational identity. In contrast, people in an individualistic culture tend to see their identity as consistent whether across time or context, and they view their identity as a constant whether interacting with one group or another. Thus, behavior is seen as an unflappable product of one's unchangeable identity: "I cannot change the way I act, because I cannot change the person I am." This thinking is the result of two assumptions that leave a negotiator frozen in his or her current behavioral regime.

Mistaken Assumption #1: Identity is Constant Across TIME

Negotiators often assume that their identity is constant across time. Two reasons support the partial validity of this assumption. First, for most people, our sense of selfhood *feels* consistent over time. Whether or not we continue to enjoy hopscotch or teddy bears beyond our childhood years, we recognize that we are the only person who experienced personally the multiple stages of our own life; and we still may recall viscerally the emotional wave that accompanied our first kiss, our first day of college, or the moment we learned that someone close to us died. Second, certain elements of our behavior imprint an indelible mark upon our perceived identity. A lawyer who commits an unethical act at work may come to believe that he is a bad person. A negotiator who is never able to assert her own interests may come to see herself as victim to the discretion of others. Such self-conceptions may stay with a person for weeks, years, or a lifetime.

Nevertheless, our identities consist of two basic elements—an "I" and a "me"—and these both change over time.[7] No one is the exact same person he or she was ten years ago.

The "me" is the narrative you tell yourself about yourself. It is your self-concept, a schema about yourself that you build at both a conscious and unconscious level. The "me" is constantly under construction and constantly trying to make sense of the emotions, thoughts, and behavior that you experience. If you excel at swimming, you may begin to think of yourself as a good swimmer. If others laugh at your jokes, you may conceive of yourself (i.e., your "me") as a good joke teller.

If the "me" is the narrative you tell yourself about yourself, then who is the person constructing that story? What is the difference between your self-narrative and "you?" The "I" is a metaphor for the automatic thoughts, feelings, and actions that you experience and that seem outside of your control. It is your experiential self, your unfiltered visceral and cognitive experience of the world as you live it. When you find yourself absorbed by music or work, your "I" dominates your experience. When you are driving on the highway without much effort or thought, you are at the whim of your "I." When you are writing an article and are completely enraptured in the flow of what you are writing,[8] you are in the untainted hands of your "I." Or when "Gone with the Wind" stirs you to tears, that is your "I" in action.

The important point is that the "I" and the "me" each change as you have new experiences, and each influences the other.[9] As you develop a new sense of yourself, a revised "me," your "I" experiences the world in a different light. And revisions of your "I" contribute to a revised sense of your "me." As you react in new and different ways, you tend to construct a modified understanding of "who you are."

Mistaken Assumption #2: Identity is Constant Across CONTEXTS

A second common assumption is that a negotiator's identity is consistent across contexts.[10] This assumption is prevalent in many conflict assessment instruments, which ask a negotiator to assess his or her conflict style. Is a person's conflict style that of avoidance, collaboration, accommodation, compromise, or confrontation? Such instruments assume that negotiator behavior is consistent regardless of context.

This assumption is not wholly invalid. A lawyer who strongly asserts her views with opposing counsel may also strongly assert her views in all other conversations—whether talking with a client, a colleague, a spouse, or a child. Similarly, some people seek actively to avoid any hint of conflict not only with their bosses, but also with everyone else in their lives.

Yet most of the time a negotiator's behavior changes significantly across contexts. Our identity is largely relational.[11] We interact differently with different people. In a relationship with a despised boss, a subordinate may feel tense and resentful, acting in ways that spite the boss. In a relationship with a loving spouse, that same person may feel emotions of tenderness and affection, acting in ways that support the relationship.

In a negotiation, the relational identity that we co-construct as we interact with the other person and the resulting emotional, cognitive, and behavioral consequences on us and on the other do not always serve our negotiating purposes. We may fail to speak up in an interaction with an outgoing counterpart. Or we may be overly assertive with a reserved other, who decides not to negotiate with us in a cooperative manner.

This "relational identity" consists of two main elements: autonomy and affiliation.[12] Autonomy is the freedom to choose your own actions.[13] When the other side's negotiator "tells" you where to meet for lunch or gives you "the final proposal" without first consulting you on it, your autonomy may feel impinged. Affiliation is a sense of interpersonal connection. You may feel closely affiliated to some colleagues, whereas affiliation may be difficult to build with others.

The degree to which a negotiator feels a sense of autonomy and affiliation typically varies with context. A lawyer may feel a great amount of autonomy in advocating for a client's needs. Yet that same lawyer may feel very little autonomy in advocating for her own needs in her relationship with her husband at home. Likewise, a lawyer may feel a great deal of emotional openness and affiliation toward a friendly client, while feeling anxiety about disclosing even trivial personal information with an angry client.

A Better Assumption: Negotiators Can Construct Their Identities

Negotiators often fail to realize that their own assumptions about identity can handicap their behavior. If we assume that identity is rigid and fixed, we may fail to adapt to the dynamic circumstances of which we are a part and end up meeting fewer of our interests than we otherwise could. Conversely, if we assume that identities are fungible, an important consequence is that we can choose how we want to be treated in a negotiation—and how we want to treat others.[14]

Self-awareness is a first step toward choosing alternative ways of acting that enhance our negotiation efficacy. Such awareness can provoke powerful learning about ourselves. Are we more emotionally disclosing with our colleagues than with our spouse? Why? What might we do to change the situation, if so desired? Self-awareness allows the "me" to understand the automatic activity of the "I." The "me" can then rationally think about what activities improve negotiation success and what behaviors constrain behavior. Through this process, we can choose new behaviors that satisfy more of our interests and needs in a negotiation.

Mindfulness is a key skill in becoming more self-aware. Professor Leonard Riskin [Riskin, *Mindfulness*] researches the negotiation power that can be derived from noticing, without judgment, the experiences and feelings that pass through one's awareness.[15] Mindfulness enables a negotiator to become aware of internal thoughts and feelings of ambivalence, strong emotional pulls, and cravings for power. Rather than reacting immediately to those feelings and thoughts, the mindful negotiator can reflect on wise options for behavior.

There are a number of popular activities that help people become more aware of their relational identity in a negotiation. For example, consider the Interpersonal Skills Exercise developed at Harvard Law School for their negotiation workshops.[16] In this exercise, students work in small teams with fellow students, a course instructor, and a family systems psychotherapist. Each student brings to the exercise an interpersonal skill that he or she has difficulty performing, such as saying "no" to requests by a good friend.[17] Through the use of role plays, videotaping, and certain aspects of psychodrama, the student practices the challenging interpersonal skill in a safe, intensive, and interactive environment. Feedback is provided by peers and the course instructor.

In the process of developing a skill set that may be lacking, students often learn that the behavior in which they want to engage does not comport with their own conception of who they are, regardless of with whom they are interacting. This is an intrapersonal identity conflict. However, in many cases, students are faced with the reality that they have a particular skill set but are unable to use it in specific types of relationships. A student may be very assertive when representing her client, but may be unable to assert her own wishes in a negotiation with her spouse or boss. This is the territory of a relational identity conflict.

Through the Interpersonal Skills Exercise, students learn more about the internal, automatic scripts that shape their automated thoughts, feelings, and behavior (i.e., their "I"). They also learn more about their self-conception, their "me." Hence, they are able to recognize interpersonal situations in which they unduly limit or expand their own autonomy or affiliation to their detriment. They might realize that their decision not to ask for a salary raise is based upon an autonomy-limiting assumption that "the boss wouldn't give it to me anyway." Or they might realize that their decision to accommodate to all requests by colleagues is based upon the unrealistic assumption that positive affiliations between people can only be maintained if there is no disagreement between them. As a result of such realizations, students have the empowering opportunity to *choose* whether they want to continue typical patterns of behavior, or to modify their behavior to improve the process and outcome of their negotiation.

Another exercise to help students explore issues of relational identity is the "Relational Identity Exercise" (RIE). A facilitator can run through the steps of the activity with students, having them independently write down their responses during each step:

- Ask students to identify a recent interpersonal conflict in which they did not express themselves as well as they could have (e.g., "I recently got into an argument with my mother about whether to come home for Thanksgiving, and half-way through the conversation, I got so mad that I hung up on her").

- Have students analyze ways in which they unduly limited or expanded their autonomy and affiliation in the situation. For example, did they feel overly constrained in terms of their autonomy to speak back to the other person? Did they feel too affiliated to the other person to raise issues that might upset the other?

- Tell students to imagine that their conflict situation will recur tomorrow. Given their better understanding of their identity-based concerns, have them consider one action they might say or do differently to improve the situation.

- Review the exercise with students, asking questions such as: what did you learn about yourself from this activity? What did you learn about the power of identity in your negotiations?

- Optional: have students write up their discoveries in a confidential journal that they hand in to the professor.

Summary

Many negotiators assume that identity is a fixed, immutable concept. In this essay, I suggest that in most situations, identity is fungible across time and across contexts. Negotiators have the power to construct their identities in ways that improve their negotiation process and outcome. To this end, self-awareness is essential, followed by conscious decisions about how to act in ways that lead to more satisfying outcomes.

Endnotes

The author wishes to express gratitude to Chris Honeyman, Andrea Schneider and Michael Moffitt for feedback on earlier drafts of this essay.

[1] *See* Ronald J. Fisher, *Training as Interactive Conflict Resolution: Characteristics and Challenges*, 2 INTERNATIONAL NEGOTIATION 331 (1997); Herbert Kelman & Nadim Rouhana, *Promoting Joint Thinking in International Conflicts: An Israeli/Palestinian Continuing Workshop*, 50 JOURNAL OF SOCIAL ISSUES 157 (1994); Vamik Volkan, *Transgenerational Transmissions and Chosen Traumas: An Aspect of Large-Group Identity*, 34 GROUP ANALYSIS 79 (2001).

[2] *See* JAY ROTHMAN, RESOLVING IDENTITY-BASED CONFLICT: IN NATIONS, ORGANIZATIONS, AND COMMUNITIES (1997).

[3] *See* WILLIAM WILMOT & JOYCE HOCKER, INTERPERSONAL CONFLICTS (5th ed. 1998).

[4] *See* DOUGLAS STONE, ET AL., DIFFICULT CONVERSATIONS: HOW TO DISCUSS WHAT MATTERS MOST (1999).

[5] *See* Daniel Shapiro, *Negotiating Emotions*, 20 CONFLICT RESOLUTION QUARTERLY 67 (2002).

[6] *See, e.g.,* CULTURE AND NEGOTIATION (Guy Faure & Jeffery Z. Rubin eds., 1993).

[7] *See* PETER HARTLEY, INTERPERSONAL COMMUNICATION (1993); IVANA MARKOVA, HUMAN AWARENESS: ITS SOCIAL DEVELOPMENT (1987); MIND, SELF, AND SOCIETY FROM THE STANDPOINT OF A SOCIAL BEHAVIORIST (George Mead ed., 1934); CARL R. ROGERS, CLIENT-CENTERED THERAPY: ITS CURRENT PRACTICE, IMPLICATIONS, AND THEORY (1951); CARL R. ROGERS, ON BECOMING A PERSON: A THERAPIST'S VIEW OF PSYCHOTHERAPY (1961); CARL R. ROGERS & BARRY STEVENS, PERSON TO PERSON: THE PROBLEM OF BEING HUMAN: A NEW TREND IN PSYCHOLOGY (1967); Daniel Shapiro & Vanessa Liu, *Psychology of a Stable Peace, in* THE PSYCHOLOGY OF RESOLVING GLOBAL CONFLICT: FROM WAR TO PEACE (Mari Fitzduff & Chris Stout eds., 2005).

[8] *See* MIHALY CSIKSZENTMIHALYI, FLOW: THE PSYCHOLOGY OF OPTIMAL EXPERIENCE (1990).

[9] *See* Daniel Shapiro, *Vertigo: The Impact of Strong Emotions on Negotiation* (2004) (Harvard Negotiation Project Working Paper) (on file with author); Shapiro & Lui, *supra,* note 7.

[10] *See* LOUIS KRIESBERG, CONSTRUCTIVE CONFLICTS: FROM ESCALATION TO RESOLUTION (1998).

[11] *See* Shapiro, *supra* note 5.

[12] *See* Shapiro, *supra* notes 5 & 9; Shapiro & Liu, *supra,* note 7.

[13] *See* James Averill & Elma Nunley, Voyages of the Heart: Living an Emotionally Creative Life (1992).

[14] The notion of relational identity has implications for large scale conflicts. Groups involved in an ethnopolitical conflict often view one another as adversaries. They see this relational identity as fixed. The theory of relational identity suggests that, on the contrary, groups can co-construct new ways of interacting with one another that promote cooperative behavior. The transformative process is by no means simple. A chapter by Shapiro and Liu details the application of relational identity to ethnopolitical conflict management. Shapiro & Liu, *supra,* note 7.

[15] Leonard Riskin, *The Contemplative Lawyer: On the Potential Contributions of Mindfulness Mediation to Law Students, Lawyers, and Their Clients,* 7 HARVARD NEGOTIATION LAW REVIEW 1 (2002).

[16] *See* Robert Bordone, *Teaching Interpersonal Skills for Negotiation and for Life,* 16 NEGOTIATION JOURNAL 377 (2000).

[17] *See id.*

☙ 26 ☙

Internal and External Conflict

Morton Deutsch

Editors' Note: *Have you ever been in a negotiation where you (or the other side) seem to be acting instinctively, but perhaps not helpfully? Have you wondered what was going on inside your counterpart? Deutsch summarizes how psychological theory applies to basic negotiation, and explains how negotiators' internal conflicts affect them and everybody else in the room.*

In situations involving interaction between individuals, groups, or nations, the internal state of the individual, group, or nation will often have profound effects on the interactions which take place. The reverse is also true: the interactions that take place will often have profound impact on the internal states of the interacting entities. In this chapter, I shall provide an example of the effects of internal conflicts upon negotiations and consider some ways of managing the difficulties they often create. The example will be of negotiations about conflicts between a husband and wife. Although the example is about interpersonal conflict, I shall draw some general conclusions that may be applicable to intergroup and international conflict.

Before discussing the husband and wife conflict, I briefly consider some relevant aspects of Psychodynamic Theory to provide a framework for understanding such conflicts.

Psychodynamic Theory: The Effect of Internal Conflict Upon External Conflict[1]

Psychodynamic theory, as developed by Freud and other psychoanalytic theorists, emphasizes the role of unconscious internal conflict as critical to the understanding of human development and behaviors. There are seven basic ideas in psychodynamic theory that are relevant to this chapter. They are discussed below.

An Active Unconscious
People actively seek to remain unaware (unconscious) of those of their impulses, thoughts, and actions that make them feel very disturbing emotions (for example, anxiety, guilt, shame).

Internal Conflict

People may have internal conflict between desires and conscience, desires and fears, and what the "good" self wants and what the "bad" self wants; the conflict may occur outside of consciousness.

Control and Defense Mechanisms

People develop tactics and strategies to control their impulses, thoughts, actions, and realities so that they will not feel anxious, guilty, or ashamed. If their controls are ineffective, they develop defense mechanisms to keep from feeling these disturbing emotions.

Stages of Development

From birth on to old age, people go through stages of development. Associated with the stages are normal frustrations, a development crisis, and typical defense mechanisms. Certain forms of psychopathology are likely to develop if severe frustration and crisis face the child during a particular stage, with the result that the child becomes "fixated" at that stage; in addition, some adult character traits are thought to originate in each given stage.

The Layered Personality

How someone has gone through the stages of development determines current personality. One can presumably discover the residue of earlier stages of development in current personality and behavior. Thus, a paranoid/schizoid adult personality supposedly reflects a basic fault in the earliest stage of development in which the infant did not experience the minimal love, care, and nurturance that would enable him to feel basic trust in the world. The concept of layered personality does not imply that earlier faults cannot be repaired. However, it does imply that an adult personality with a repaired fault is not the same as one that did not need repair. Under severe frustration or anxiety, such a personality is apt to regress to an earlier stage.

Conflict with Another Can Lead to Anxiety

People may feel anxious because they sense they are unable to control their destructive or evil impulses toward the other in a heated conflict. Or the conflict may lead to a sense of helplessness and vulnerability if they feel overwhelmed by the power and strength of the other.

Defense Mechanisms

If the anxiety aroused by the conflict with another is intense, the individual may rely on unconscious defense mechanisms to screen it out in an attempt to reduce the anxiety. Anxiety is most apt to be aroused if one's basic security, self-conception, self-worth, or social identity is threatened. Defense mechanisms are pathological or ineffective if they create the conditions that perpetuate the anxiety.

The defense mechanisms that people use are determined in part by their layered personality, which may have given rise to a characterological tendency to employ certain defense mechanisms rather than others, and also in part by the situation they confront. Psychoanalysts have identified many defense mechanisms; they are usually discussed in relation to intrapsychic conflict. We believe that they are also applicable in interpersonal and other external conflict. We have space to discuss only a number of the important ones for understanding conflict with others.

- *Denial* occurs when it is too disturbing to recognize the existence of a conflict (as between husband and wife about their affection toward one another, so they deny it: repressing it, so that it remains unconscious, or suppressing it so they don't think about it).

- *Avoidance* involves not facing the conflict, [Bingham, *Avoiding Negotiating*] even when you are fully aware of it. To support avoidance, you develop ever-changing *rationalizations* for not facing the conflict ("I'm too tired", "This is not the right timing," "She is not ready," "It will not do any good").

- *Projection* allows denial of faults in yourself. It involves projecting or attributing your own faults to the other ("You're too hostile," "You don't trust me," "You're to blame, not me," "I'm attacking to prevent you from attacking me"). Suspicion, hostility, vulnerability, hypervigilance, and helplessness, as well as attacking or withdrawing from the potential attack of the other, are often associated with this defense.

- *Reaction formation* involves taking on the attributes and characteristics of the other with whom you are in conflict. The conflict is masked by agreement with or submission to the other, by flattering and ingratiating yourself with the other. A child who likes to be messy but is very anxious about her mother's angry reactions may become excessively neat and finicky in a way that is annoying to her mother.

- *Displacement* involves changing the topic of conflict or changing the party with whom you engage in conflict. Thus, if it is too painful to express openly your hurt and anger toward your spouse because he is not sufficiently affectionate, you may constantly attack him as being too stingy with money. If it is too dangerous to express your anger toward your exploitative boss, you may direct it at a subordinate who annoys you.

- *Counterphobic* defenses entail denial of anxiety about conflict by aggressively seeking it out by being confrontational, challenging, or having a chip on your shoulder.

- *Escalation of the importance of the conflict* is a complex mechanism that entails narcissistic self-focus on your own needs with inattention to the other's needs, histrionic intensity of emotional expressiveness and calling attention to yourself, and demanding needfulness. The needs involved in the conflict become life-or-death issues, the emotions expressed are very intense, and the other person must give in. The function of this defense is to get the other to feel that your needs are urgent and must have highest priority.

- In *intellectualization and minimization of the importance of the conflict*, you do not feel the intensity of your needs intellectually but instead experience the conflict with little emotion. You focus on details and side issues, making the central issue from your perspective in the conflict seem unimportant to yourself and the other.

The psychoanalytical emphasis on intrapsychic conflict, anxiety, and defense mechanisms highlights the importance of understanding the interplay between internal conflict and the external conflict with another. Thus, if an external conflict elicits anxiety and defensiveness, the anxious party is apt to project onto, transfer, or attribute to the other party characteristics similar to those of internalized significant others who, in the past, elicited similar anxiety in unresolved earlier conflict. Similarly, the anxious party may unconsciously attribute to himself the characteristics he had in the earlier conflict. Thus, if you are made very anxious by a conflict with a supervisor (you feel your basic security is threatened), you may distort your perception of the supervisor and what she is saying so that you unconsciously experience the conflict as similar to unresolved conflict between your mother and yourself as a child.

If you or the other is acting defensively, it is important to understand what is making you or her anxious, what threat is being experienced. The sense of threat, anxiety, and defensiveness hamper developing a productive and cooperative problem-solving orientation toward the conflict. Similarly, transference reactions produce a distorted perception of the other and interfere with realistic, effective problem-solving (for example, reacting to the other as though she were similar to your parent). You can sometimes tell when the other is projecting a false image onto you by your own countertransference reaction: you feel that she is attempting to induce you to enact a role that feels inappropriate in your interactions with her. You can sometimes become aware of projecting a false image onto the other by recognizing that other people don't see her this way, or that you are defensive and anxious in your response to her with no apparent justification.

Negotiations Between Individuals

As a psychologist, I have had the opportunity to do therapeutic work with couples who have been involved in bitter conflicts over issues that they considered non-negotiable. I will briefly describe a young couple who was involved in what I have elsewhere characterized as a "malignant process" of dealing with their conflicts.[2]

The malignancy of their process of dealing with their conflicts was reflected in the tendency for them to escalate a dispute about almost any specific issue (for example, a household chore or their child's bedtime) into a power struggle in which each spouse felt that his or her self-esteem or core identity was at stake. The malignant process resulted in (as well as resulted from) justified mutual suspicion; correctly perceived mutual hostility; a win-lose orientation to conflicts; a tendency for each to act toward the other in a way that would lead the other to respond in a way that would, in turn, confirm the former's worst suspicion about the latter; an inability to understand and empathize with the other's needs and vulnerabilities; and a reluctance—based on stubborn pride, nursed grudges, and fear of humiliation—to initiate or respond to a positive generous action to break out of the escalating vicious cycle in which they were entrapped.

Many couples involved in such malignant conflicts do not seek help; they continue to abuse one another, sometimes violently, or they break up. The couple that I worked with sought help for several reasons. On the one hand, their conflicts were becoming physically violent: this frightened them and it also ran counter to their strongly held intellectual values regarding violence. On the other hand, there were strong constraints making it difficult for them to separate. They felt they would be considerably worse off economically, their child would suffer, and they had mutually congenial intellectual, esthetic, sexual, and recreational interests.

Developing a Readiness to Negotiate

Before I turn to a discussion of the negotiation of a non-negotiable issue, let me briefly discuss the steps involved in getting the couple to the point where they were ready to negotiate. There were two major interrelated steps, each of which involved many substeps. The first entailed helping each spouse to recognize that the present situation of a bitter, stalemated conflict no longer served his or her real interests.[3] The second step involved aiding the couple to become aware of the possibility that each of them could be better off than they currently were if they recognized their conflict as a joint problem, which required creative, joint efforts in order to improve their individual situations. The two steps do not follow one another in neat order: progress in either step facilitates progress in the other.

Irrational Deterrents to Negotiation

There are many reasons why otherwise intelligent and sane individuals may persist in behaviors that perpetuate a destructive conflict harmful to their rational interests. Some of the common reasons are:

- Perpetuating the conflict enables one to blame one's own inadequacies, difficulties, and problems on the other so that one can avoid confronting the necessity of changing oneself. Thus, in the couple I treated, the wife perceived herself to be a victim, and felt that her failure to achieve her professional goals was due to her husband's unfair treatment of her as exemplified by his unwillingness to share responsibilities for the household and child-care. Blaming her husband provided her with a means of avoiding her own apprehensions about whether she personally had the abilities and courage to fulfill her aspirations. Similarly, the husband who provoked continuous criticism from his wife for his domineering, imperious behavior employed criticisms to justify his emotional withdrawal, thus enabling him to avoid dealing with his anxieties about personal intimacy and emotional closeness. Even though the wife's accusations concerning her husband's behavior were largely correct, as were the husband's toward her, each had an investment in maintaining the other's noxious behavior, because of the defensive self-justifications such behavior provided.[4]

- Perpetuating the conflict enables one to maintain and enjoy skills, attitudes, roles, resources, and investments that one has developed and built up during the course of one's history. The wife's role as "victim" and the husband's role as "unappreciated emperor" had long histories. Each had well-honed skills and attitudes in relation to their respective roles that made their roles very familiar and natural to enact in times of stress. Less familiar roles, in which one's skills and attitudes are not well-developed, are often avoided because of the fear of facing the unknown. Analogous to similar social institutions, these personality "institutions" also seek out opportunities for exercise and self-justification, and in so doing help to maintain and perpetuate themselves.

- Perpetuating the conflict enables one to have a sense of excitement, purpose, coherence, and unity which is otherwise lacking in one's life. Some people feel aimless, dissatisfied, at odds with themselves, bored, unfocused, and unenergetic. Conflict, especially if it has dangerous undertones, can serve to counteract these feelings: it can give a heightened sense of purpose as well as unity, and can also be energizing as one mobilizes oneself for struggle against the other. For depressed people who lack self-esteem, conflict can be an addictive stimulant which is sought out to mask an underlying depression.

- Perpetuating the conflict enables one to obtain support and approval from interested third parties. Friends and relatives on each side may buttress the opposing positions of the conflicting parties with moral, material, and ideological support. For the conflicting parties to change their positions and behaviors may entail the dangers of loss of esteem, rejection, and even attack from others who are vitally significant to them.

How does a therapist or other third party help the conflicting parties overcome such deterrents to recognizing that their bitter, stalemated conflict no longer serves their real interests? The general answer, which is quite often difficult to implement in practice, is to help each of the conflicting parties change in such a way that the conflict no longer is maintained by conditions in the parties that are extrinsic to the conflict. In essence, this entails helping each of the conflicting parties to achieve the self-esteem and self-image that would make them no longer need the destructive conflict process as a defense against their sense of personal inadequacy, their fear of taking on new and unfamiliar roles, their feeling of purposelessness and boredom, and their fears of rejection and attack if they act independently of others. Fortunately the strength of the irrational factors binding the conflicting parties to a destructive conflict process is often considerably weaker than the motivation arising from the real havoc and distress resulting from the conflict. Emphasis on this reality, if combined with a sense of hope that the situation can be changed for the better, provides a good basis for negotiation.

Conditions That Foster the Recognition of the Conflict as a Joint Problem Requiring Joint Efforts

What are the conditions that are likely to help conflicting parties become aware of the possibility that each of them could be better off than they currently are if they recognize that their conflict is a joint problem that requires creative, joint efforts in order to improve their individual situations? A number of such conditions are listed below:

- Crucial to this awareness is the recognition that one cannot impose a solution which may be acceptable or satisfactory to oneself upon the other. In other words, there is recognition that a satisfactory solution for oneself requires the other's agreement, and that this is unlikely unless the other is also satisfied with the solution. Such recognition implies an awareness that a mutually acceptable agreement will require at least a minimal degree of cooperation.
- To believe that the other is ready to engage in a joint problem-solving effort, one must believe that the other has also recognized that he or she cannot impose a solution—that is, the other has also recognized that a solution has to be mutually acceptable.
- The conflicting parties must have some hope that a mutually acceptable agreement can be found. This hope may rest upon their own perception of the outlines of a possible fair settlement or it may be based on their confidence in the expertise of third parties, or even on a generalized optimism.
- The conflicting parties must have confidence that if a mutually acceptable agreement is concluded, both will abide by it, or that violations will be detected before the losses to the self and the gains to the other become intolerable. If the other is viewed as unstable, lacking self-control, or untrustworthy, it will be difficult to have confidence in the viability of an agreement unless one has confidence in third parties who are willing and able to guarantee the integrity of an agreement. [Zartman, *Ripeness*]

The foregoing conditions for establishing a basis of initiating the joint work necessary in serious negotiation are much easier to develop when the conflicting parties are part of a strong community in which there are well-developed norms, procedures, professionals, and institutions which encourage and facilitate problem-solving negotiations. [Morash, *Nonevents*] When the encouragements to negotiation do not exist as a result of belonging to a common community, the availability of helpful, skilled, prestigious, and powerful third parties who will use their influence to foster problem-solving negotiations between the conflict parties becomes especially important. [Love & Stulberg, *Mediation*]

Negotiating the Non-Negotiable

Issues that seem vitally important to a person, such as one's identity, security, self-esteem, or reputation, often are experienced as non-negotiable. [Avruch, *Buyer—Seller*] Thus, consider the husband and wife who viewed themselves in conflict over a non-negotiable issue. The wife who worked (and wanted to do so) wanted the husband to share equally in the household and child-care responsibilities; she considered equality between the genders to be one of her core personal values. The husband wanted a traditional marriage with a traditional division of responsibilities, in which he would have primary responsibility for income-producing work outside the home while his wife would have primary responsibility for the work related to the household and child-care. The husband considered household work and child-care as inconsistent with his deeply rooted image of adult masculinity. The conflict seemed non-negotiable to the couple. For the wife it would be a betrayal of her feminist values to accept her husband's terms; for the husband, it would be a violation of his sense of adult masculinity to become deeply involved in housework and child-care.

However, this non-negotiable conflict became negotiable when, with the help of the therapist, the husband and wife were able to listen to and really understand each other's feelings and the ways in which their respective life experiences had led them to the views they each held. Understanding the other's position fully, and the feelings and experiences which are behind them, made them each feel less hurt and humiliated by the other's position and more ready to seek solutions that would accommodate the interests of both. They realized that with their joint incomes they could afford to pay for household and child-care help, which would enable the wife to be considerably less burdened by these responsibilities without increasing the husband's chores in these areas; of course, doing so lessened the amount of money they had available for other purposes.

This solution was not a perfect one for either party. The wife and husband would each have preferred that the other share their own view of what a marriage should be like. However, their deeper understanding of the other's position made them feel less humiliated and threatened by it, and less defensive toward the other. It also enabled them to negotiate a mutually acceptable agreement that lessened the tensions between them despite their continuing differences in basic perspectives. [Heen & Stone, *Perceptions*]

The general conclusions that I draw from this and other experiences with a "non-negotiable" issue is that most such issues *are* negotiable even though the underlying basic differences between the conflicting parties may not be reconcilable. The issues become negotiable when the conflicting parties learn to listen, understand, and empathize with the other party's position, interests, and feelings, providing they are also able to communicate to the other their understanding and empathy. Even though understanding and empathy do not imply agreement with the other's views, they indicate an openness and responsiveness which reduces hostility and defensiveness and which also allows the other to be more open and responsive. Such understanding and empathy help the conflicting parties to reduce their feeling that their self-esteem, security, or identity will be threatened and endangered by recognizing that the other's feelings and interests, as well as one's own, deserve consideration in dealing with the issues of conflict.

"Non-negotiable" issues also become negotiable when the conflicting parties can be shown that their vital interests will be protected or enhanced by negotiation. As Fisher, Ury and Patton have stressed, it is helpful for negotiators to learn the difference between "positions" and "interests."[5] The positions of the conflicting parties may be irreconcilable, but their interests may be concordant. Helping parties in conflict to be fully in touch with their long-term interests may enable them to see beyond their non-negotiable positions to their congruent interests. An atmosphere of mutual understanding and empathy fosters the conditions that permit conflicting parties to get beyond their initial rigid, non-negotiable positions to their underlying interests.

Although this chapter does not have the space to discuss the interaction between intragroup conflict and intergroup conflict, it seems reasonable to hypothesize that inner conflicts within groups that are involved in an intergroup conflict hamper the development of a constructive process of resolving the intergroup conflict, and make it less likely that a sustainable cooperative agreement that improves intergroup relations will be attained. Implicit in our discussion of internal conflict within individuals in an interpersonal conflict are some general principles that may be applicable to the intergroup context. They are simply, in relation to both the intragroup as well as the intergroup conflicts, to: (1) create a safe, congenial context in which the true interest (rather than positions) of the conflicting parties can be mutually understood; (2) work to strengthen their common, cooperative interests and seek to expand them; (3) find ways to weaken and inhibit their destructive interest as well as constructive substitutes to replace them. Obviously, whether all of this can be done or how it can be done will depend upon circumstances that are specific to the particular conflicts.

Endnotes

[1] For a good introduction to psychodynamic theory *see generally* JAY R. GREENBERG & STEPHEN A. MITCHELL, OBJECT RELATIONS IN PSYCHODYNAMIC THEORY (1983); CHARLES RYCROFT, A CRITICAL DICTIONARY OF PSYCHOANALYSIS (1995); DAVID L. SMITH, APPROACHING PSYCHOANALYSIS: AN INTRODUCTORY COURSE (1999).
[2] For a further discussion of malignant conflicts *see* MORTON DEUTSCH, DISTRIBUTIVE JUSTICE: A SOCIAL-PSYCHOLOGICAL PERSPECTIVE pt. 3 at 262-87 (1985).
[3] For more on "mutually hurting stalemates," *see* William Zartman, *Ripeness*, Chapter 17 in this volume.
[4] For more on the differences between the way individuals explain their point of view and the unarticulated and unadmitted "theory-in-use" that is actually guiding them, *see* Scott Peppet and Michael Moffitt, *Learning How to Learn to Negotiate*, Chapter 70 in this volume.
[5] ROGER FISHER, ET AL., GETTING TO YES: NEGOTIATING AGREEMENT WITHOUT GIVING IN (1981).

❧ 27 ❧

Knowing Yourself: Mindfulness

Leonard L. Riskin

Editors' Note: How are you supposed to negotiate effectively if you can't concentrate on the signals your counterpart is giving? How can you look your client in the eye and say you've done your best if you allow that routine mindlessness—to which we're all subject—to occur without even a conscious attempt to fight it? Riskin summarizes years of research on techniques for improving concentration.

A Problem: Mindlessness in Negotiating

It is a fact of the human condition that we are suffused with fears, insecurities, passions, impulses, judgments, rationalizations, assumptions, biases, and the mental shortcuts that some academics call "heuristics." [Korobkin & Guthrie, *Heuristics*] These can be more or less available to our conscious awareness, and we can be more or less able to resist them.

Such mental and emotional influences, of course, help guide us through life and through professional activities, including negotiating and lawyering. The problem is that they also can interfere with our ability to do these activities well. They can, for instance, draw our attention away from where we want it to be. When we want to listen to a client or read a document, we may be distracted by worries about whether the client likes us, or by thoughts (or chains of thoughts) about almost anything—the laundry, whether we made the right career choice, or why we didn't schedule that trip to the Bahamas. The less conscious awareness we have of these impulses, fears, passions, thoughts, and habitual assumptions and behaviors, the more likely we are to succumb to them.

The mind tends to wander, and very often we do not realize where it has gone. Usually it is dwelling in the past or future, keeping us from paying attention to the present moment. Understood in this way, intermittent mindlessness—which, to Harvard psychology professor Ellen Langer, means "the light's on but nobody is at home"[1]—can affect and afflict just about everyone in conducting virtually any activity.

Mindlessness impairs our work as practitioners of dispute resolution in several ways. First, it can stop a negotiator from being "present" with the other participants or with herself, which means she is not fully aware of what is going on. Second, in the grip of mindlessness, we sometimes rely on old habits and assumptions, rather than deciding what behavior is most suitable in the precise circumstances we are encountering. Manifestations of mindlessness, according to Professor Langer, include being "trapped by categories,"[2] "automatic behavior,"[3] and "acting from a single perspective."[4]

This is a special problem for many negotiators who have been trained in law; legal education, and much of law practice is infused with an adversarial perspective, which I have previously called the "Lawyer's Standard Philosophical Map" (LSPM):

> On the lawyer's standard philosophical map ... the client's situation is seen atomistically; many links are not printed. The duty to represent the client zealously within the bounds of the law discourages concern with both the opponents' situation and the overall social effect of a given result.
>
> Moreover, on the lawyer's standard philosophical map, quantities are bright and large while qualities appear dimly or not at all. When one party wins, in this vision, usually the other party loses, and, most often, the victory is reduced to a money judgment. This "reduction" of nonmaterial values—such as honor, respect, dignity, security and love—to amounts of money, can have one of two effects. In some cases, these values are excluded from the decision-makers' considerations, and thus from the consciousness of the lawyers, as irrelevant. In others, they are present but transmuted into something else—a justification for money damages.... The lawyer's standard world view is based upon a cognitive and rational outlook. Lawyers are trained to put people and events into categories that are legally meaningful, to think in terms of rights and duties established by rules, to focus on acts more than persons. This view requires a strong development of cognitive capabilities, which is often attended by the under-cultivation of emotional faculties.[5]

In the negotiation context, the LSPM is expressed in adversarial (as opposed to problem-solving or interest-based) negotiation strategies and tactics. And although most law school courses and CLE programs emphasize problem-solving or interest based approaches to negotiation, in the heat of practice, many lawyers tend to fall back, almost reflexively, on the adversarial. This means, of course, that they sometimes miss opportunities for creating better agreements for their clients and other parties to a dispute, and for gaining as much satisfaction as they might from their work.

In order to make appropriate use of either adversarial or problem-solving strategies and techniques, lawyers need a high degree of awareness about their own habitual reactions, including thoughts, emotions and behaviors—and the distance, discipline, and discernment to decide which of these to follow. But negotiation and mediation instruction—especially that provided to law students and lawyers—does not ordinarily provide such foundational training. Instead, teachers and trainers tend to assume that lawyers and law students already have capabilities of attention and awareness that will enable them not only to understand problem-solving, interest-based approaches but also to implement them, when and as appropriate, in professional practice. Regrettably, this assumption often is invalid.

The next section explains an important method for developing the necessary foundational awareness capacities. In the section after that, I describe a series of specific meditation exercises. The treatment of all the topics is this Chapter is necessarily brief; fuller explanations are available in the sources cited in the endnotes.

A Potential Solution: Mindfulness in Practice and Mindfulness Meditation

Mindfulness, as I use the term, means being aware, moment to moment, without judgment, of one's bodily sensations, thoughts, emotions, and consciousness.[6] It is a systematic strategy for paying attention and for investigating one's own mind, a skill that one cultivates through meditation and then deploys in daily life. The meditation practice begins with developing concentration, usually by focusing on the breath. Next, the mediator learns to direct his attention, one step at a time, to bodily sensations, emotions, and thoughts, then works toward "bare attention," a nonjudgmental moment-to-moment awareness of whatever passes through any of the sense organs or the mind. Mindfulness meditation (also known as insight meditation and vipassana meditation) both requires and produces a measure of equanimity, which reinforces the ability to fix attention where we want it to be (for example, on our client).[7]

The practice has a number of other potential benefits that motivate people to participate. It commonly helps people deal better with stress, develop self-understanding (which helps them clarify their own goals and motivations) and understanding of others, and feel compassion and empathy. Recently scientists have found evidence that mindfulness meditation also can produce brain wave activity that is associated with happiness, apparently shifting a person's disposition, not just her mood.[8] In Buddhist philosophy, mindfulness meditation is an important part of the quest for freedom from the suffering caused by craving and aversion.

It also seems likely to improve performance in virtually any kind of activity; the outcomes it fosters correlate with success in a variety of fields. Daniel Goleman—a psychologist, journalist, and authority on meditation—has articulated the concept of emotional intelligence, which he distinguishes from academic intelligence, the basis for the IQ and most other intelligence tests.[9] This idea of emotional intelligence entails five basic emotional and social competencies: self-awareness, self-regulation, motivation, empathy, and social skills. Goleman argues, marshaling a great deal of empirical evidence, that emotional intelligence is much more important than academic intelligence in predicting success at virtually any occupation or profession—assuming, of course, an adequate level of academic intelligence. Mindfulness meditation can help develop the first four of these emotional intelligence competencies—self-awareness, self-regulation, motivation, and empathy. These, in turn, are likely to help produce the fifth emotional intelligence competency—social skills.

Although mindfulness meditation derives from ancient practices, in recent years it has found employment in a variety of secular settings. In the U.S., for instance, specialized programs have appeared for medical patients in chronic pain; professional basketball players; journalists; undergraduate, nursing, and medical students; corporate and foundation executives; and the Green Berets. Most important for our purposes, extensive meditation instruction has been offered to lawyers in at least three large law firms (the Boston offices of Hale & Dorr and Nutter, McClennan & Fish and the Minneapolis office of Leonard, Street & Deinard) and to persons who work in the criminal justice system. A variety of programs—ranging widely in length, intensity, and scope—have been offered to law students at Cardozo, Columbia, Connecticut, CUNY, Denver, Hamline, Harvard, Hastings, Miami, Missouri-Columbia, North Carolina, Stanford, Suffolk, and Yale. Mindfulness meditation also has been a central focus of many programs for lawyers across the U.S., ranging from five-day retreats to brief introductory sessions, some of which have carried CLE credit. In recent years, mindfulness meditation has appeared in a variety of programs in connection with teaching mediation, negotiation and other lawyering skills at a number of universities, including Harvard Law School,[10] Northwestern University, the University of Missouri-Columbia School of Law, Pepperdine University School of Law and the University of Texas School of Law.[11] These efforts have had a range of focuses, including managing stress, developing spirituality, clarifying motivations, or enhancing skills in law school, law practice, or law teaching.

Mindfulness can help negotiators and lawyers in several ways. As mentioned, it provides methods for calming the mind, concentrating, experiencing compassion and empathy, and achieving an awareness of, and "distance" from, thoughts, emotions, and habitual impulses that can interfere with making good judgments and with building rapport and motivating others. All of these outcomes can help negotiators and lawyers make appropriate strategic decisions, moment to moment. In a negotiation, for instance, when our counterpart issues a threat and we feel an impulse to retaliate, mindfulness helps us to insert a "wedge of awareness,"[12] which allows us to examine that impulse and decide whether retaliation is more appropriate than another move that would more likely foster value creation, understanding, or healing. In addition, there is evidence that a positive mood enhances performance in problem-solving negotiation.[13] And it seems reasonable to suspect that mindfulness could help negotiators be more aware of certain deep assumptions, including those based on ethnicity or culture, and of psychological processes that can interfere with wise decision-making, such as reactive devaluation, optimistic overconfidence, risk aversion, and anchoring. [Korobkin & Guthrie, *Heuristics*; Caton Campbell & Docherty, *Framing*; Goh, *Errors*; Kelly, *Indigenous Experience*; Morash, *Nonevents*; Yarn & Jones, *Biology*; and Shestowsky, *Persuasion*]

Building the Foundation: Meditation Practices

Mindfulness means being aware of, moment to moment and without judgment, whatever passes through the senses and the mind—sounds, sights, smells, other bodily sensations, emotions, and thoughts and images. We aspire to be *aware* that we are hearing while we are hearing; to be aware that we are thinking while we are thinking, and so forth. With such non-judgmental awareness, we gain a kind of freedom. For instance, if, while we are interviewing a client, we become aware that our mind has wandered off to thoughts about next week's football game, we can swiftly bring our attention back to the client. If we become aware of an impulse to get away from our client—manifested, for instance, by feelings of aversion, anxiety or fear and accompanying bodily sensations—we can make a discerning judgment about whether to follow that impulse in light of the circumstances and our obligations as a lawyer.

We cultivate mindfulness through a progression of meditative practices. The most basic of these practices is concentration on the breath. From there we move to bodily sensations, thoughts, emotions, and finally, to choiceless awareness or bare attention, a non-judgmental awareness of whatever arises through any of the sense organs or the mind.[14]

As indicated below, it is helpful to have support for your meditation practice, including individual and group educational activities. However, to give you a sense of meditative practices and an opportunity to practice on your own, I set forth below a series of instructions for the following meditations:

- Awareness of Breath
- Awareness of Bodily Sensations
- Awareness of Thoughts
- Awareness of Emotions
- (Almost) Choiceless Awareness

Awareness of Breath

Basic Meditation on the Breath

Sit comfortably with your back and neck erect—either on a chair with your feet flat on the floor, or on a meditation cushion on the floor with your legs crossed—and your hands on your knees or your thighs.[15] Begin to settle yourself by bringing attention to sound. As best you can, observe sounds as they arise, stay present, and fall away, and do this without worrying about the cause of each sound and without judging the sounds. However, if thoughts about the source of sounds and judgments arise, simply notice them, and return the attention to sound.

After a few minutes, bring your attention to the sensation of your breath at the place where it is easiest for you to notice. This might be at the nostrils, as the air enters and leaves, or in the chest or abdomen, as they rise and fall with inhalations and exhalations. Focus on the sensations of one inhalation at a time, one exhalation at a time. When you notice that your mind has wandered, this is a moment of mindfulness! Gently escort your attention back to the breath. If you have a lot of trouble concentrating on the breath, you might try one of the following: (1) Silently note "rising" and "falling" or "in" and "out" or "up" and "down" with each breath; or (2) Silently count each exhalation until you reach ten; when you reach 10, or go past 10 or lose count, begin again at one. During such activities, the words should be in the background, the sensations in the foreground.

The first time you do this meditation, try it for five minutes. As you become comfortable with it, extend the practice to 15 minutes or more, ideally twice a day. Notice, without judgment, how the mind wanders, and its propensity to latch on to—get carried away with—thoughts, feelings, and sensations.

Extended Meditation on the Breath

When you become comfortable with the Basic Meditation on the breath—which could be a matter of days, weeks, or months—you may want to move to a more extended version of the breath meditation.

Begin with the Basic Meditation on the Breath, as described in the preceding instructions. This time, when you become aware that the mind has wandered, notice where it has gone. Become aware of whether it is in the past or future, and its focus, e.g. on thoughts, bodily sensations, emotions; notice its impermanence, and then gently return the attention to the breath.

Comment on Breath Meditation

These meditations on the breath tend to create a calm state of mind that enables one to perceive and think more clearly. The difference between the Basic and the Extended Awareness of Breath Meditations is what you do when your mind wanders. In the Basic method, when you notice that the mind has wandered from the breath, you simply bring the attention back to the breath; in other words, you are trying to ignore any distractions so that you can be "absorbed" in the breath. In the Extended form, when you observe that the attention has wandered from the breath, you notice where it has gone—momentarily concentrating on that—and then bring the attention back to the breath. This subtle distinction will be clearer after you practice a bit.

How long should you practice? As a general matter, you will get more benefit from more practice. I suggest starting with fifteen minutes twice each day, and gradually increasing the time up to 30 and then 45 minutes. It is especially important to practice every day, even if it is for a very short time.

Meditation on the Body—The Body Scan

It is best to do this for 30-45 minutes, but shorter times can work as well. (I am not suggesting that you do this immediately after the extensive meditation on the breath that I described above. It is more of an alternative to the mindfulness of breath practice, and, as you will see, incorporates elements of that practice). Get into a comfortable position. The ideal position for the body scan is lying on your back on a yoga mat or blanket or soft carpeting, with your feet hanging loosely to the side, arms by your side, and hands palm-up. Sitting in a chair also works, and lessens the chance of falling asleep.

Begin meditating on the breath, as described above. After about three minutes, on an out breath, move the awareness from the breath down the left side of the body to the toes on the left foot. Notice any sensations in the toes—on the skin, in the muscles. If you observe no sensations at all in the toes, that is o.k. After a few moments, on an out breath, move your attention to the bottom of the foot. Gradually, in this manner, move your attention systematically throughout the body, moving, more or less, as follows, noticing, as best you can, any sensations on the skin, in the muscles, in the joints:

- the left ankle, calf, knee, thigh, buttock;
- the right toes, foot, ankle, calf, knee, thigh, buttock;
- the genital area;
- the abdominal area, chest, upper back;
- shoulders, lower back;
- the left upper arm, elbow, lower arm, hand, fingers and thumb (as best you can, moving the attention from one digit to another);
- the right upper arm, elbow, lower arm, hand, fingers and thumb (one digit at a time);
- the neck, front, sides and back;
- the cheeks, chin, lips, mouth (roof, floor, sides, tongue, teeth), eyes, eye lids, ears;
- the head—sides, back, top;
- the entire body, noticing any sensations on the skin, in the tissue, in the bones and joints, as they arise in any part of the body.

As you are moving the attention through the body, here are a few suggestions:

- The attitude here is non-judgmental curiosity. You are trying to observe what's going on in the body, not to judge it. If, however, it turns out that the mind is judging—e.g. if the thought arises, "I wish my hair were thicker"—simply observe that thought, and don't judge yourself harshly for having such a thought, rather than simply observing the scalp.
- You may find it helpful to imagine that you are breathing into and out of the part of the body on which you are focusing.
- When you notice that the mind has wandered away from the part of the body on which you are focusing, that is a moment of mindfulness; simply return the attention to that part of the body.[16]

- If, however, the attention is distracted by a very strong unpleasant sensation, such as a pain or an itch, instead of drawing the attention back to the part of the body on which you are focusing, simply focus on the unpleasant sensation. As best you can, observe it without judgment. But as judgment arises, notice that, too. Observe the changing nature of the physical sensation, and notice the thoughts associated with it. Usually such thoughts relate to wishing the sensation would go away. In this sense, there is a distinction between pain—the physical sensation—and suffering—wishing things were other than the way they are.
- Use the breath as a source of stability. In the same way that a swimmer may occasionally return for temporary support to the side of the pool or a pier in a lake, when you lose track or get stuck in any sounds, bodily sensations or feelings, bring the attention momentarily to the breath, until the attention feels stable enough to return the part of the body on which you are focusing.

Awareness of Thoughts Meditation

To prepare for Awareness of Thoughts Meditation, begin with a brief Extended Awareness of the Breath Meditation, as described above. Once the mind is relatively settled, bring the attention to thoughts and thinking. The idea is to become aware, without judgment, of thoughts as they arise, stay present, and drop out of awareness. For most people, this is more challenging than being aware of the breath and bodily sensations. For that reason, you may find it helpful to silently "label" thoughts as they arise. For instance, you might say, "thinking" when you notice a thought arise.

The main idea here is to be *aware* that you are thinking *while* you are thinking, and to have enough distance from the thinking that you can decide whether that's what you want your mind to be doing.

This meditation is particularly useful in helping us learn to deal with distracting thoughts. In addition, it gives us the opportunity to notice that we have almost no control over what thoughts arise, though we do have choices over how we respond to them. If we have enough presence of mind to be aware of thoughts as they arise, we also have a chance to assess their validity[17] and appreciate the saying, "Don't believe everything you think."

Awareness of Emotions

Prepare for this by meditating on the breath and then doing a brief (say, two-minute) body scan. Once the mind is settled, open the awareness to emotions. Try to notice—again, without judgment—feelings such as fear, sadness, joy, love, revulsion, anxiety. Once again the appropriate attitude is curiosity, mingled with a compassion for self. If you observe carefully, you will see that what we think of as an emotion is closely connected to thoughts and bodily sensations. You may find it helpful to silently label the emotions that you recognize. As in all the meditations in this sequence, you may find it useful to use the breath as a source of stability, returning to it whenever you lose track of where your attention is or should be or when you need a "rest."

(Almost) Choiceless Awareness

Prepare for this by meditating on the breath and then doing a brief body scan. Once the mind is settled, open the awareness to all of the objects that we addressed in the previously-described meditations—sounds, the breath, bodily sensations (this includes sounds and the breath as well as smells), thoughts, and emotions. To help you pay attention, here are a few suggestions. Once again, use the breath as a source of stability.[18] It may be helpful for you to keep in mind categories of experiences and to label experiences accordingly. One device is to focus on the "triangle of awareness"—thoughts, emotions, sensations.[19] It may help you to label your experiences in terms of these three categories and to notice any relationships among them.[20]

Reinforcing the Foundation: Bringing Mindfulness into Daily Life and Negotiation Activities

Meditation is the key to building the foundation for states of concentration and mindfulness. But the impact of meditation can be increased dramatically through regular practice and a variety of supporting activities. These include developing a daily meditation practice; sitting regularly with a group; attending meditation retreats, lectures and workshops—including those that seek to apply mindfulness to negotiation, mediation and law practice; reading about meditation practices; keeping a journal of your meditation experiences and insights; and engaging in other mindfulness-related activities, such as certain forms of yoga, T'ai Chi, and Qi Gong.

Preparing for Activities

I find it very useful to use meditative practices to prepare for various challenging activities, and for transitions between ordinary activities.

In preparing for activities you expect to be challenging, the most appropriate meditative practice to use might vary with your current state of mind and the nature of the prospective activity. Your level of experience with various meditative practices also might have an impact. Here are a few suggestive examples:

Before a Negotiation or a Mediation

A meditation on the breath or on bodily sensations could help calm the mind and body. As you feel more calm, and depending upon your level of experience and comfort with the other meditations, you may wish to extend your focus to thoughts and emotions, and even to the practice of (almost) bare attention. Such awareness could give you insight into particular issues or concerns that might be bothering you. In negotiations, for example, as Roger Fisher and Daniel Shapiro put it, most people have the same "core concerns": appreciation, affiliation, autonomy, status and role.[21] [Shapiro, *Emotions*] Any of these could manifest in thoughts, emotions, and sensations. And, of course, any of these could get in the way of your mindful attention to the task at hand. However, if you can muster moment-to-moment awareness and equanimity about concerns you are experiencing—say a sense of threat to your status—that, in itself, could diminish the power of such concern, and allow you to maintain the appropriate focus. Similarly, such non-judgmental awareness may give you reason to suspect that your negotiation counterpart has similar concerns, and give you the presence of mind to address them. Such meditations also will heighten your general level of awareness, enhancing the likelihood that you will be able to maintain a mindful awareness in the midst of the negotiation.

Antipathy Toward Others

If you are feeling antipathy toward any of the parties or lawyers or insecure about their attitudes toward you, there are a number of steps you can take.

Meditate on the Breath, Body, Emotions, Thoughts. The same meditations as described above may be useful, as they tend to give you some insight about your own thoughts and emotions and to develop empathy as well as compassion for yourself and others. In addition, there are other meditations that are specifically intended to develop positive emotions, such as loving kindness.[22]

Meditate on Your Intentions. It can be very illuminating to observe thoughts and intentions as they arise and to make a discerning choice about whether to actually carry them out. You may notice, for example, negative thoughts about your negotiation counterpart—or about yourself. You also may notice thoughts or impulses about how to negotiate—e.g., to follow adversarial strategies or problem-solving strategies. The mindful, non-judgmental awareness of such thoughts and impulses can allow you to examine them and make a discerning choice about whether and how to follow them. In other words, the non-judgmental awareness provides a degree of freedom from impulsive and habitual patterns of behavior.

Carrying Out Activities

Building the foundation (through a regular meditation practice and related supporting activities) and meditating before particularly challenging events will enhance the likelihood that you will be able to be mindful in everyday life. Such a foundation improves your alertness and skill at noticing when you are *not* mindful—e.g., when you are distracted by strong emotions, self-centered thoughts or other cognitive processes, or strong sensations in the body—and in being able to return your attention to the task at hand. The real challenge to being mindful is in *remembering* to be mindful. Here are a few suggestions for bringing mindful awareness to routine activities of everyday life and particularly challenging professional situations.

Find a Few Routine Activities to do Mindfully

Activities such as walking, waiting for an elevator or a green traffic light, doing the dishes, or answering the phone, as well as transitions between activities, can make good reminders. You could even choose something that you find irritating, maybe a truck horn or alarm.

Drop Your Attention to Your Breath and to Bodily Sensations

When you are feeling agitated, say, during a negotiation, such a shift in focus to awareness can have a calming effect that can enable you to think more clearly. Even when you are not feeling agitated, periodically shifting to such a focus can calm the mind and free you from the constraining effects of strong emotions that might otherwise impair your judgment.

Try the "STOP" Technique

This simple technique, developed and taught by the Stress Reduction Clinic at the University of Massachusetts Medical School, includes the following steps:
- Stop whatever you are doing or thinking
- Take a breath
- Observe and open to the breath, bodily sensations, and emotions. Also observe and open to all the senses and the external environment.
- Proceed.[23]

Notice Distractions to Listening, and Keep Listening

While you are listening to someone speak—in a negotiation, an interview, a conversation, a class—try to really pay attention. To do that you may have to notice when you are *not* listening—e.g., when the mind is distracted by emotions, discursive thought, thinking about what *you* will say next, worries, bodily sensations, desires—and to bring your attention back to the speaker. Also notice any impulses to interrupt the speaker—because of impatience, because you think you know what the speaker will say next, because you have a need to say something—and try resisting that temptation. Use silence, and notice your and the other person's reactions to silence.

Mentally Send Good Wishes to Others

Try sending good wishes to others, mentally. The others could include people you pass on the street, friends, enemies, and the lawyers and clients on the other side of your cases. Observe any resistance you feel to doing this as well as your reactions.

Reflecting Upon or Reviewing Activities

It is especially useful to practice mindfulness meditation during a break or shortly after completing a significant activity, such as a negotiation, for two reasons: first, it can help you in the transition, to decompress or detach, so that you can be present for whatever happens next. Second, sometimes—even if you try to focus on the present moment—your mind will automatically generate insights about what happened or about why you or others did what they did. You may get ideas about what to do next or how to undo mistakes.

In addition to mindfulness practice at such points, some people find it helpful to deliberately reflect on the negotiation activity, calling to mind any discomfort, unease or difficulty that might keep them from being more present.[24] This can produce lots of insight.

Conclusion

I hope this has piqued your interest in knowing more about how awareness skills can help you feel and perform better as a negotiator. In one sense, being mindful is the easiest task in the world. All you need to do is pay attention, and you can do that right now. In another sense, it is the hardest job you will ever undertake. The simplest meditations, such as meditating on the breath, require determination and alertness, so you can know, in each moment, where your mind is. But the effort will be rewarded, and not only in our professional lives. Mindfulness also can help us take part more fully in life, our own and others'.

Endnotes

This draws upon and extends my previous writings on this topic, which present more detail on some of the ideas that appear in this Chapter. LEONARD L. RISKIN, AWARENESS IN LAWYERING: A PRIMER ON PAYING ATTENTION IN THE AFFECTIVE ASSISTANCE OF COUNSEL: PRACTICING LAW AS A HEALING PROFESSION (Marjorie Silver ed., forthcoming 2006); Leonard L. Riskin, *Mindfulness: Foundational Training for Dispute Resolution*, 54 JOURNAL OF LEGAL EDUCATION 79 (2004); Leonard L. Riskin, *The Contemplative Lawyer: On the Potential Benefits of Mindfulness Meditation to Law Students, Lawyers, and Their Clients*, 7 HARVARD NEGOTIATION LAW REVIEW 1 (2002); Leonard L. Riskin, *Paying Attention in Law: The Role of Mindfulness Medita-*

tion, in HEALING AND THE LAW (David Link & Thomas Shaffer eds., forthcoming 2006). Special thanks to Chris Honeyman & Andrea Schneider for "coaxing" this chapter into being.

[1] ELLEN J. LANGER, MINDFULNESS 9 (1983).

[2] *Id.* at 11-12.

[3] *Id.* at 12-16.

[4] *Id.* at 16-18.

[5] Leonard L. Riskin, *Mediation and Lawyers*, 43 OHIO STATE LAW JOURNAL 44-45 (1982). Other limiting mind-sets also contribute to the problems I describe. *See, e.g.,* ROBERT H. MNOOKIN, ET AL., BEYOND WINNING: NEGOTIATING TO CREATE VALUE IN DEALS AND DISPUTES 9-91 (2000) (describing limiting mind-sets associated with client counseling and negotiation).

[6] *See* JON KABAT-ZINN, FULL CATASTROPHE LIVING (1991); JOSEPH GOLDSTEIN, INSIGHT MEDITATION: THE PRACTICE OF FREEDOM (1994).

[7] For distinctions between mindfulness and other forms of meditation, *see* Leonard L. Riskin, *Mindfulness: Foundational Training for Dispute Resolution*, 54 JOURNAL OF LEGAL EDUCATION 79, 83-84 n. 25 (2004).

[8] Richard J. Davidson, et al., *Alterations in Brain and immune Function Produced by Mindfulness Meditation*, 65 PSYCHOSOMATIC MEDICINE 564 (2003). Davidson and his colleagues found that mediators had increased levels of brainwave activity in the left prefrontal cortex (which is known to correlate with the experience of happiness) and decreased activity in the right prefrontal cortex. High activity in the right prefrontal cortex is associated with the experiences of stress and anger. *See also,* Daniel Goldman, *Finding Happiness: Cajole Your Brain to Lean to the Left*, N. Y. TIMES, Feb. 4, 2003, at F5.

[9] DANIEL GOLEMAN, EMOTIONAL INTELLIGENCE: WHY IT CAN MATTER MORE THAN IQ (1995).

[10] *See* HARVARD NEGOTIATION INSIGHT INITIATIVE,
http://www.pon.harvard.edu/research/projects/b_drp.php3.

[11] *See* INITIATIVE ON MINDFULNESS IN LAW AND DISPUTE RESOLUTION,
http://www.law.missouri.edu/csdr/programs/mindfulness; THE CENTER FOR CONTEMPLATIVE MIND IN SOCIETY'S LAW PROGRAM,
http://www.contemplativemind.org/programs/law/about.html; and HARVARD NEGOTIATION INSIGHT INITIATIVE, http://www.pon.harvard.edu/hnii.

[12] MATTHEW FLICKSTEIN, SWALLOWING THE RIVER GANGES: A PRACTICE GUIDE TO THE PATH OF PURIFICATION 28 (2001).

[13] *See* MARTIN E. P. SELIGMAN, AUTHENTIC HAPPINESS: USING THE NEW POSITIVE PSYCHOLOGY TO REALIZE YOUR POTENTIAL FOR LASTING FULFILLMENT 39 (2002). For a more critical—and pessimistic—discussion, *see* Scott Peppet, *Mindfulness in the Law and ADR: Can Saints Negotiate? A Brief Introduction to the Problems of Prefect Ethics in Bargaining*, 7 HARVARD NEGOTIATION LAW REVIEW 83 (2002); *See also,* Van M. Pounds, *Promoting Truthfulness in Negotiations: A Mindful Approach*, 40 WILLAMETTE LAW REVIEW 181 (2004); MAX H. BAZERMAN & MARGARET A. NEALE, NEGOTIATING RATIONALLY 121-22 (1992) (asserting that negotiators in a good mood may be more vulnerable to certain psychological traps, which are known as the framing, escalation of commitment, and availability effects).

[14] Different teachers present these practices in different ways and in various orders and combinations. The meditation instructions that follow are based on my own experience as a student and teacher of meditation. They draw on numerous sources, many of which I can no longer identify. For other instructions and a sense of the variety of practices, *See generally* JOSEPH GOLDSTEIN, THE EXPERIENCE OF INSIGHT (1987); VENERABLE HENEPOLA GUNARATANA, MINDFULNESS IN PLAIN ENGLISH (2002); KABAT-ZINN, *supra* note 6; JON KABAT-ZINN, WHEREVER YOU GO, THERE YOU ARE: MINDFULNESS MEDITATION IN EVERYDAY LIFE (2005); JACK KORNFIELD, A PATH WITH HEART: A GUIDE TO THE PROMISES AND PERILS OF SPIRITUAL LIFE (1993); BREATH SWEEPS MIND: A FIRST GUIDE TO MEDITATION PRACTICE (Jean Smith ed., 1998).

[15] Meditation traditionally has been done sitting, standing or lying down. In addition there are various forms of walking meditation, which are particularly useful in bringing mindfulness into daily life. For further information on walking meditation, which means being

present while walking, *See* GOLDSTEIN, *supra* note 6, at 136-37; FLICKSTEIN, *supra* note 12, at 78-82.

[16] When you become familiar with the body scan, e.g., after you have done it several times, you might address distractions by using the "triangle of awareness"—thoughts, bodily sensations, and emotions (an idea developed at the Stress Redution Clinic at the University of Massachusetts Medical School and used in its teaching programs). For example, when you notice that the mind is distracted by thinking, try also to observe any bodily sensations and emotions that accompany the thoughts.

[17] For an example of how to use this ability to deal with "offensive" comments in a negotiation, *see* Andrea Kupfer Schneider, *Effective Responses to Offensive Comments*, 10 NEGOTIATION JOURNAL 107 (1994).

[18] I call this "(Almost)" Choiceless Awareness, because in Choiceless Awareness (a.k.a. Bare Attention) one does not choose to focus on the breath, or anything else.

[19] *See supra* note 16.

[20] As you may notice, the three factors often are deeply interrelated. Each can cause either of the others.

[21] *See* ROGER FISHER & DANIEL SHAPIRO, BEYOND REASON: USING EMOTIONS AS YOU NEGOTIATE (2005).

[22] *See* SHARON SALZBURG, LOVING-KINDNESS: THE REVOLUTIONARY ART OF HAPPINESS (1997); Leonard L. Riskin, *Awareness in Lawyering: A Primer on Paying Attention*, in THE AFFECTIVE ASSISTANCE OF COUNSEL (Marjorie Silver ed., forthcoming 2006).

[23] For a more extended version of this technique, *see* ZINDEL SEGAL, ET AL., MINDFULNESS-BASED COGNITIVE THERAPY FOR DEPRESSION: A NEW APPROACH TO PREVENTING RELAPSE 173-75 (2002).

[24] I am indebted to Daniel Bowling and Rachel Wohl for this idea.

⁓ 28 ⁓

On Bargaining Power

Russell Korobkin

Editors' Note: *Strip away concepts of power based in your opponent's relative wealth compared to yours, or based on other popular myths, says Korobkin here. What are you going to do if there is no agreement? What is the other party likely to do? Answer those questions, and you will know who really has how much power in this situation. (For counterpoint, read Bernard's Powerlessness.)*

In an ideal world, all negotiators would have what are sometimes called "common interests."[1] The old chandelier that to me is clutter in the basement would be an antique to you, and your pleasure in receiving it would be outweighed only by my joy in getting rid of it. In most bargaining situations, however, negotiators' interests are in conflict. You might like the chandelier more than I do, which makes a mutually advantageous bargain possible, but it is currently lighting my dining room and I would prefer to keep it rather than give it away. You are interested in buying the chandelier from me, but you want to pay a low price. I will consider selling it to you, but I want a high price. In this zero-sum contest, the outcome will most likely depend on the distribution of bargaining power, defined as the ability to convince the other negotiator to give us what we want even when the other would prefer not to do so.

The source of bargaining power is misunderstood by many negotiators, who wrongly assume that the indicia of success in other realms of life are directly related to power at the negotiating table. Wealth, brains, beauty, political connections, prestige, and social influence are nice to have, but none of these items guarantee you the ability to exercise power in any particular negotiation. Bargaining power is situational, not personal. In some labor disputes, unions have more power than management; in others, management has more power than unions. In some merger negotiations, the target company enjoys more power than the suitor; in others, the dynamic is reversed. In some litigation settlement negotiations, the plaintiff has more power than the defendant; in others, the defendant enjoys the advantage. An employee seeking a raise from his boss might enjoy a relative power advantage, or he might not.

In each of these situations, relative bargaining power stems entirely from the negotiator's ability to, explicitly or implicitly, make a single threat credibly: "I will walk away from the negotiating table without agreeing to a deal if you do not give me what I demand." The source of the ability to make such a threat, and therefore the source of bargaining power, is the ability to project that he has a desirable alternative to reaching an agreement, often referred to as a "BATNA."[2] This chapter elaborates on this claim.[3]

BATNA Strength

What you and what your bargaining counterpart will do in case of impasse determines your relative power in the negotiation. In market situations with fungible buyers and sellers, your BATNA is to enter into a similar transaction with someone other than your negotiating counterpart and, thus, your power depends implicitly on the forces of supply and demand. Imagine that you arrive at an automobile dealership hoping to pay "dealer invoice" for the new car of your choice and begin to negotiate with a dealer who hopes to charge the "sticker price." Your BATNA is to buy an identical car from another dealer, and you have no reason to prefer this dealer over his competitors. The dealer's BATNA is to wait for the next customer to enter the showroom and attempt to sell the car to that customer. Just as you don't care from whom you buy the car, the dealer doesn't care about the identity of the purchaser so long as he pays cash or has good credit.

If the model you have selected is in short supply and all of the other dealers in town have a waiting list of purchasers, your BATNA is relatively weak (you will have to wait for a car and probably pay a premium) and the dealer's BATNA is relatively strong (he is confident that another customer will be willing to pay the sticker price). In this situation, the dealer enjoys more bargaining power because he can threaten impasse if you do not agree to pay the sticker price. That threat would be credible because, if you refuse to pay that amount, impasse would be in his best interest. In contrast, if all dealers are overstocked and the new year's models are soon to arrive, you will enjoy a relative power advantage. You can credibly threaten to walk away if the dealer will not agree to a handsome discount, because the chances are good that another dealer, anxious to reduce inventory, would likely agree to a discount. In turn, this means that impasse with this particular dealer would be in your best interest if you do not receive the price that you demand.

Unlike the new car example, many transactions involve goods or services that are somewhat unique, such that they create a degree of bilateral monopoly: that is, identical transactions are unavailable to one or both parties. In this case, each negotiator's BATNA will usually be a substitute transaction that is different in character from the subject of the present negotiation. For example, assume that you are negotiating with a potential employer. You want a high salary; the employer wants to hire you for a low salary and save resources. If impasse results, both parties will enter into similar but not identical transactions. The employer will hire a different person for the job, with similar but somewhat different skills, experiences, and qualifications from yours. You will accept employment with another firm doing somewhat different work.

In this case, the distribution of bargaining power depends on whose alternative is more desirable to him. If you have job offers in hand from many desirable firms offering high salaries, while the employer's second-choice job candidate has substantially worse qualifications than yours, you will have a power advantage and are likely to receive a very attractive offer of compensation. On the other hand, if the economy is sputtering and your only alternative offer is for a substantially less interesting job at a low salary, while the firm has a stack of job applications from other impressive graduates, the firm has relative power and is likely to obtain your services for a relatively low price.

Still other bargaining situations can be characterized as pure bilateral monopolies: that is, no substitute transactions are available to either party. In this case, the consequence of impasse will be that neither party enters into any transaction. Both parties therefore have a BATNA of not transacting at all, and relative bargaining power depends upon which party finds the status quo more acceptable. Litigation bargaining is an example of a pure bilateral monopoly situation. A plaintiff and defendant who fail to reach agreement do not have the option of entering into settlement agreements with other negotiators. Instead, an impasse will mean that litigation continues and the dispute will ultimately be submitted to adjudication.[4]

Bargaining power in this situation depends on whether this course of events is more desirable for the plaintiff or the defendant. If the plaintiff's case is strong on the legal merits and provable damages are high, the plaintiff will enjoy bargaining power because she can credibly threaten to end negotiations and proceed to adjudication if she does not receive the high settlement price that she demands. The defendant, of course, can make the same threat if the plaintiff will not accept a low settlement offer, but the threat would not be credible because it would not be in the defendant's best interest to take a weak case to court and face the likelihood of a large verdict rather than agree to pay a higher settlement price (but one that is still lower than the expected verdict). Similarly, holding constant the quality of the parties' legal cases, a disputant who employs a less expensive or a contingent fee lawyer, or one who has relatively more resources at his disposal, has bargaining power because the expected cost of continued litigation is less painful, making the threat to break off negotiations if his settlement demands are not met more credible.

Perception is Reality

Strictly speaking, it is not the actual, objective quality of the negotiator's BATNA that determines his degree of bargaining power, but what the counterpart believes that the negotiator believes about the quality of his BATNA. For example, if an employee receives a job offer from a competing firm and asks his boss for a raise, the employee's power depends on whether the boss believes that the employee will accept the competing offer if the demand for a raise is not met. The credibility of the employee's threat to walk away from the negotiation is unaffected by the fact that neither the boss nor any of the employees' colleagues would prefer the competing offer to the employee's current job at his current salary. Where power is concerned, the beauty of a BATNA is in the eye of the beholder, and eccentricity is not penalized as long as it is perceived to be genuine.[5] The employee's threat of impasse will be credible to the boss, thus giving the employee power, even if the employee himself actually would not prefer the competing offer, so long as the boss thinks that the employee would prefer that offer.

An objectively strong BATNA is helpful, of course, because a BATNA that *appears* strong renders the negotiator's claim that he believes his BATNA *is* strong more credible. The employee's threat of impasse will more likely translate into bargaining power if his competing job offer is a $300,000 per year CEO position than if it is a $15,000 per year mailroom attendant position. But either a phantom BATNA (i.e., a nonexistent alternative) or a real BATNA with phantom value (i.e., an existent but undesirable alternative) can be a source of power in the hands of a persuasive negotiator.

Because the parties' *perceptions* of their and their counterparts' alternative courses of action are ultimately what determines the allocation of bargaining power, information is critical. A car buyer who knows both the dealer invoice price of the model in which he is interested and that dealers usually sell it for $500 over invoice will enjoy more bargaining power than the buyer who wanders into the dealership without doing research, for two related reasons. First, the informed buyer will know that the dealer's threat to create an impasse if the buyer will not pay the full sticker price is not credible, and thus the buyer will not be tempted to acquiesce to the dealer's demand. Second, if the buyer demonstrates to the dealer that he is so informed, the dealer will be more likely to perceive as credible *his* threat to walk away from the negotiation if the dealer will not agree to sell for $500 over invoice. More generally, when B knows that A knows the precise value of A's BATNA (i.e., buying from another dealer for $500 over invoice), A can credibly threaten not to settle for any deal that is not at least as valuable as his BATNA.

Patience and Power

In many bargaining contexts, especially those involving some degree of bilateral monopoly, the BATNA of both parties, at least in the short term, will be to continue to negotiate, not to pursue a substitute transaction. In this situation, a negotiator's threat not to agree unless her demands are met is in essence a threat of temporary rather than permanent impasse. When both parties have a BATNA of temporary impasse, the negotiator for whom temporary impasse is less costly has the strongest BATNA and thus a relative bargaining power advantage. In this situation, then, the less problematic or costly temporary impasse is for a negotiator, the more power she will enjoy. If we define "patience" in negotiation as the ability to withstand the costs of temporary impasse, it follows that patience translates into bargaining power.

When a union and management meet to attempt to negotiate a settlement of a strike, union members rarely threaten to find substitute employment, and management is precluded by law from firing the striking workers.[6] The union's threat is that if management does not meet its demands, it will continue to strike, extending the impasse. Management's threat is that, if the union does not accede to its terms, it will continue to permit the strike to go on. If the union has a large strike fund and if management cannot fill its orders with the labor of replacement workers, the union can be more patient in reaching an agreement and will consequently enjoy superior bargaining power. In contrast, if the union's strike fund is empty and its members cannot pay their rents while management has a large quantity of inventory in storage, temporary impasse will be relatively more costly to the union, giving management power.

A similar analysis is often useful in the litigation bargaining setting. If the plaintiff and defendant do not reach a settlement, their dispute will ultimately go to court for adjudication. But if the trial date is not imminent, the BATNA of both parties in the short term is to hold out for a better offer from the other side. In this situation, power resides with the party that can be more patient. If the plaintiff needs money to meet his living expenses or has a strong psychological need for closure of the litigation, she might be less patient, giving the defendant a power advantage. On the other hand, if the plaintiff has retained counsel on a contingent fee basis whereas the defendant is paying his lawyer $300 per hour to conduct discovery in preparation for a possible trial and to continue negotiations with the plaintiff's lawyer, the plaintiff might be extremely patient and the defendant less so, giving the plaintiff relative power in the settlement negotiations.

The Risks of Power

In a world in which opposing negotiators had perfect information about the other's alternatives and preferences and both made all negotiating decisions with cold rationality, attempts to exercise bargaining power would never cause impasse. In any situation in which a mutually beneficial agreement were possible, the party with relatively less power would yield to the party with relatively more.[7]

Few negotiations, however, are characterized by perfect information and lack of emotion, and both of these facts mean that attempts to exercise power can easily lead to impasse. If both negotiators believe that they have a strong BATNA but that their counterpart does not, each might try to exercise power while neither yields. Thus, lawsuits go to trial, labor strikes drag on, and ethnic warfare continues,[8] even when agreements that would make both sides better off are feasible, because each party believes his adversary is on the verge of surrender. Alternatively, or in addition, the less powerful party might resent the sense of coercion or inequity inherent in the more powerful negotiator's demands and refuse to yield, even knowing that this course of action will result in a worse outcome for himself, at least objectively speaking, as well as for his bargaining counterpart.[9]

Because negotiators who yield to superior power often feel that they have been ill-treated by their counterpart, a successful exercise of power can have negative relational and reputational consequences. Thus, an employer who succeeds in convincing an employee with a poor BATNA to agree to work for a relatively low salary might find that the short-term savings comes with the baggage of a disaffected worker and difficulty in recruiting employees in the future. A corporate lawyer who uses his client's excellent BATNA as leverage to squeeze every possible concession out of his counterpart in contract negotiations might find that, in the future, other companies call his client to do deals only as a last resort.

These possibilities make the exercise of bargaining power as potentially risky as it is potentially rewarding. Before attempting to employ bargaining power, the negotiator must carefully compare the gains that might be achieved to the increased risk of impasse today and the costs of angering, alienating, or reducing trust among potential future trading partners. A negotiator with good judgment not only knows how to identify and exploit sources of power but also when not to do so.

Endnotes

[1] *See, e.g.*, DAVID A. LAX & JAMES K. SEBENIUS, THE MANAGER AS NEGOTIATOR (1986).

[2] *See* ROGER FISHER, ET AL., GETTING TO YES 100 (2d ed. 1991) (coining the well-known acronym, short for "Best Alternative to a Negotiated Agreement").

[3] For a more elaborate treatment of this subject, *see* RUSSELL KOROBKIN, NEGOTIATION THEORY AND STRATEGY 149-82 (2002).

[4] In the case of a low value claim, the plaintiff's BATNA might be to dismiss the suit. But assuming adjudication dominates dismissal for the plaintiff, adjudication will be the plaintiff's BATNA. Usually, negotiating parties have different BATNAs, but notice that in the litigation context they have the same BATNA, because a plaintiff who opts for adjudication has the legal right to force the defendant to submit to adjudication also. Of course, the fact that the two parties have the same BATNA (submitting to adjudication) does not suggest that this BATNA has the same value to each of them or that they will have the same reservation price. For a more complete discussion, *see* Russell Korobkin, *A Positive Theory of Legal Negotiation*, 88 GEORGETOWN LAW JOURNAL 1789, 1794-97 (2000).

[5] As Thomas Schelling wrote, the person who stands on a stranger's porch and threatens to kill himself if the stranger does not give him $10 is more likely to be paid "if his eyes are bloodshot." THOMAS SCHELLLING, THE STRATEGY OF CONFLICT 22 (1960).

[6] *See* National Labor Relations Act, 29 U.S.C. § 158(a)(1), (3) (2000). Although not important for the analysis here, the law is actually somewhat more complicated than this statement suggests. Management may legally hire "permanent" replacement workers and consequently refuse to give striking workers their jobs back when the strike ends until there are vacancies.

[7] Game theorists have demonstrated that, under these assumptions, negotiators would divide the cooperative surplus to be gained from reaching agreement in proportion to their relative costs of impasse. *See, e.g.,* DOUGLAS G. BAIRD, ET AL., GAME THEORY AND THE LAW 222 (1994).

[8] *Cf.* Russell Korobkin & Jonathan Zasloff, *A Negotiation Theory Perspective on the Israeli-Palestinian Conflict After Yasser Arafat,* 30 YALE JOURNAL OF INTERNATIONAL LAW 1, 38-39 (2005) (arguing that one explanation for the ongoing Middle East conflict is that both sides believe that they can outlast the other).

[9] An excellent example is the "ultimatum game," in which Player A proposes a division of a stake—say $10-and Player B either accepts the proposal, in which case both players receive the allocation proposed by A, or rejects the proposal, in which case both players receive $0. Although Player B maximizes his income by accepting any nonzero offer, research repeatedly demonstrates that experimental subjects in the role of B often reject low (but nonzero) offers, thus making both players worse off. *See, e.g.,* Ernst Fehr & Simon Gachter, *Fairness and Retaliation: The Economics of Reciprocity,* 14 JOURNAL OF ECONOMIC PERSPECTIVE 159 (2000); Werner Guth & Reinhard Tietz, *Ultimatum Bargaining Behavior: A Survey and Comparison of Experimental Results,* 11 JOURNAL OF ECONOMIC PSYCHOLOGY 417 (1990).

℘ 29 ℘

Power, Powerlessness and Process

Phyllis E. Bernard

Editors' Note: *Do you ever feel yourself powerless in negotiation? Are you, perhaps, involved right now in a negotiation in which others feel powerless, and in which their reactions are causing the negotiation to go into a tailspin? Here, Bernard deconstructs the concept of powerlessness, and helps you understand what you can still do in either situation. This chapter should be read in conjunction with Korobkin on Power and Kolb on Moves and Turns.*

The very fact that this book contains chapters on power and powerlessness testifies to the maturation of the negotiation field. In earlier days success was portrayed as depending more upon the skills and willingness of the negotiators than anything else, since the standard negotiation was presumed to take place among relative equals.

More, perhaps, than other topics in this volume, powerlessness and power cannot really be examined within the single process of negotiation: by their nature, they demand evaluation in context with other processes that the powerless might seek to use, or may have imposed on them instead. In the past decade ADR has shifted from a voluntary process entered into by persons of relatively equivalent bargaining power to a *de jure* or *de facto* mandate, for virtually all persons accessing the civil justice system. ADR—beginning with settlement negotiations— has become the gatekeeper to the court house.[1] This raises concerns when the court—replete with judges to enunciate and enforce legal principles and procedures—is the only meaningful, reliable way to rebalance power between the powerful and the powerless.

Professor Owen Fiss' critique of settlement negotiations provided the touchstone, cautioning against replacing the public processes of the court room with the private processes of ADR. Fiss argued that without the transparency and accountability of a formalized justice system, the rights of the powerless could not be protected against abuse by the powerful.[2] Critical race theorists, led by Professor Richard Delgado, took this a step farther, suggesting that minorities should shun ADR proceedings, seeking fairness instead in the court room alone.[3]

The expectation that the powerless can exercise power in the court room is a cherished American ideal. Yet, if power is defined in traditional terms of ethnicity, national origin, gender, social or economic class, one can readily doubt whether the powerless can attain justice through litigation. [Korobkin, *Power*] Undeniably, certain landmark court cases have reshaped the American landscape, leveling the playing field between the powerless and the powerful.[4] Nevertheless, day to day reality shows these shining moments are the exception, rather than the norm.[5]

Almost by definition, the "powerless" usually lack legal counsel in civil cases, because they cannot afford it.[6] They are likely to lack the sophisticated experience, education and rhetorical skills to represent themselves successfully in court. The formalized, linear method of discourse favored by persons of authority (as required by the court room) works against the more flexible and sometimes circular storytelling styles of minorities and women. These differences in communication styles, as much as anything else, can fatally undermine the success of a *pro se* litigant—or an unrepresented party to a negotiation or mediation.[7] Finally, they are likely to stand alone against the powerful, without the leverage of group action.

One of the most intriguing and challenging analyses of power dynamics in ADR comes from Profs. Baruch Bush and Joseph Folger in their exegesis on transformative mediation.[8] The transformative approach challenges the very proposition that anyone—even the "powerless" as traditionally defined in material terms—is truly without power. Bush and Folger define power among parties in non-traditional terms of personal, subjective attributes such as a "sense of self-worth, security, self-determination and autonomy."[9] The transformative approach does not wholly ignore the connection between material resources and material results; but the theory specifically eschews outcome-orientation. This offers a helpful theoretical framework for analysis; but in practice its success may depend upon the presence of a third party neutral, which is absent in dyadic negotiations.

A critical race analysis would ineluctably place primary authority for decision-making in the hands of attorneys and judges since the law itself is seen as the great leveler. By contrast, the transformative analysis places primary authority in the hands of parties, as the only position consistent with the principle of party autonomy and the right of self-determination. In attempting to articulate a canon of negotiation that blends theory about powerlessness with actual practice, we tread a delicate line. Veering too much to one side, we invoke condescension and paternalism towards the powerless. Veering too much toward the other side, we risk the callous libertarianism that "grants to the rich and poor alike the right to sleep under bridges."[10] Neither theoretical construct discussed thus far would propose either extreme. Still, they flag the perils of overextension.

Naturally, the first impulse of a lawyer is to look to the law for guidance. But that impulse should be tempered by an understanding of context. The core ethics rules for American lawyers unblinkingly accept that under the "generally accepted conventions in negotiation," one should expect manipulation and deception.[11] Restated, it is an accepted norm for the party with greater power to say and do almost anything to prevent the party with less power from succeeding. In defining limits upon what a party can say or do, the discussion focuses on degree and duty concerning the statements or omissions made in exercising this power advantage: what were the magnitude and materiality of misstatements or misrepresentations? Did the lawyer fail to disclose material information when obliged to do so as a matter of law?[12] Note that the bottom line for ethical conduct in a negotiation remains *legal* obligations—which typically cannot be enforced without action in a court of law or through a bar disciplinary committee. [Korobkin, et al., *Law of Bargaining*]

When bar associations set ethical boundary lines based on *realpolitik*, one cannot expect much different treatment in the courts themselves. As framed in court, the issue will be whether a powerful party took gross advantage of their position in a negotiation to harm the less powerful party. And if so, should the negotiated agreement be allowed to stand, protected under and enforceable through the law—despite the questionable means by which it was obtained? Curiously, although the signal feature of the law is its capacity to create a more level playing field among parties of greatly disparate power, the law often lacks an adequate vocabulary to address this issue squarely. The concepts of negotiation concerning powerlessness derive from doctrines of contract law; these, again, only have meaning where lawyers and the courts exert a palpable influence.

The legal concepts concerning negotiated settlements begin with the inquiry whether there was a meeting of the minds. This is the testing ground for both described theoretical approaches concerning power dynamics in negotiation. If we assume that every person has power of some sort, and every person has a right of self-determination, then every party has a right to enter into agreements others might not have chosen. This echoes the transformative approach. The issue is whether the parties understood the terms of the negotiated agreement at that time. No more, no less.

The meeting of the minds analysis tiptoes rather clumsily around the central issue: whether the parties had sufficient information in hand to give knowing consent. In a transformative mediation the third party neutral endeavors to assure that the party with less material power has adequate time to consider possible resources and options. This improves the likelihood that the less powerful party does in fact understand the settlement's terms and implications. In direct party to party negotiations there may be no such mechanism to foster knowledgeable consent. This is where critical race theorists (and others) would argue formal litigation is needed to assure fairness.

The next legal concept about negotiation asks whether the party characterized as being more powerful fraudulently withheld information from the less powerful party, or misrepresented material facts where there was a duty to disclose the truth.[13] Note "duty" is defined as a matter of law, not morality alone.

Finally, the third legal concept questions directly the use or misuse of power in negotiation. Powerlessness appears largely in the doctrines of coercion or unconscionability.[14] Courts will intervene if a gross imbalance of information, power, or savvy operated to such a one-sided advantage that it would "shock the conscience" for a civilized legal system to enforce the negotiated agreement.[15]

An evolved canon of negotiation for the new ADR would recognize that the powerless are often *compelled* to negotiate with the powerful. Further, a party may require a solid, material outcome (*viz.*, not to be evicted from their home) despite a paucity of material resources. The potential therapeutic, non-material benefits of a negotiation may be insufficient when confronting such tangible harm.

Thus, the new canon would not encourage persons lacking the traditional attributes of power to negotiate in a structure that presupposes equality. This requires a serious rethinking of the standard negotiation processes as supported by rules of professional ethics and law. A new canon regarding power and powerlessness would reconsider the process itself, seeking a middle way between the poles of unrestrained litigation and purely interest-based negotiation.

The first step in building this new canon is to question the idea that negotiations operate—or ideally should operate—outside the ambit of the law. Especially where negotiation is compelled, coerced or connived in lieu of a meaningful judicial hearing, negotiated agreements between parties of grossly unequal power must track established legal principle. Acceptable norms of negotiation conduct should not be founded upon maneuvers that barely scrape the lowest threshold of ethics, especially when the powerless party is unrepresented by counsel.

This canon does not call for a major departure from current negotiation theory. It merely states that when the power to articulate and effect interests is grossly misaligned there is a preference for principled negotiation—based on articulated shared values or norms—rather than interest-based negotiation—based on each party's individual needs. This may argue in favor of mediation with a third-party neutral, instead of party to party negotiation.

The next step of the new canon does anticipate a different process, focused on the resources surrounding and supporting the negotiation. For years the active involvement of lawyers and judges in negotiations has been characterized as, ideally, something to avoid. However, when the powerless are compelled to negotiate with the powerful and material outcomes are vital, we are not dealing with ideal circumstances. This is the time to call upon the services of lawyers well-versed in non-adversarial, problem-solving methods.[16] [Macfarlane, *New Advocacy*] The court, too, plays an important role to assure some measure of good faith and substantive fairness. Under this new canon the court's participation would not be seen as a failure of ADR; but instead as a guarantee of fairness.

For parties who are not represented by counsel, our society—beginning with the court clerk's office itself—must make available much more guidance.[17] Currently, the bewildered lay person rarely meets success in navigating the labyrinth of civil process. Court personnel are prohibited from giving meaningful assistance, or risk being charged with the unauthorized practice of law. If the legal profession fails to offer services in a manner and at a cost that the poor and working poor can manage, then bar organizations throughout the nation must retreat from challenging non-lawyer practitioners who assist the powerless in negotiations.[18]

A more radical departure from current concepts may be the most important. A new canon of negotiation would recognize that confidentiality—where a deal is made behind the iconic "closed door"—often does not serve the powerless.[19] Neither does confidentiality offer the transparency of public processes necessary to assure our larger system of justice is in sync with reality. Transparency may be essential to assure accountability, not only to the immediate parties, but also to the larger society and the evolution of public values.[20]

Much of confidentiality law and ethics rests upon institutional habits that assume equal bargaining power. This extends to the doctrine that confidentiality must be maintained unless a complaining party can demonstrate that the negotiation or mediation has resulted in a "manifest injustice."[21] Logic should dictate that in a negotiation between the powerless and the powerful, the presumptions should operate in the opposite direction. The gross disparity in power may be—in and of itself—an inchoate injustice. With this presumption in place, the legal burden shifts. The dominant party now would be required to show that the inherent injustice of the negotiation did not manifest in tangible, material harm to the other party. Toward that end, habitual confidentiality protections would be lifted to assist both parties in demonstrating that justice was or was not done. Such transparency can rebalance power.

There is also power in numbers. We may need to think more inclusively about participation; to include as many of the "powerless" as possible in the negotiations.[22] [Mayer, *Allies*] Many persons beyond the named parties in a conflict may have a vital interest not only in the outcome, but in the resolution process itself. Moreover, an expanded model of participation often better suits the cultural expectations of America's increasingly diverse communities,[23] [Kelly, *Indigenous Experience*] and may draw upon the strengths of America's traditional mainstream communities to develop and voluntarily enforce negotiated resolutions.[24]

In the 21st century, the concept of shared values around which communities can cohere—indeed, the very concept of community—is being tested to new limits.[25] Negotiation offers the most promising, pragmatic way to define these new contours. But long-term confidence in the process will turn on whether negotiations are used merely to muffle dissent, or instead to allow individualized justice.

If society wishes to know whether parties emerge from negotiations with a subjective sense that justice has been done, our ADR systems must pose and pursue the question; not sink into complacency because the standard canons of negotiation have been followed. Just as importantly, ADR professionals, attorneys and courts must listen to the answers of parties at greatest risk of injustice, and be prepared to consider new canons of transparency and inclusiveness to rebalance the uneven table.

Endnotes

[1] That the "new ADR" often lacks genuine voluntariness ought to figure prominently in assessing the success of ADR; but this issue of consent versus coercion remains underexamined. *See* Jeffrey W. Stempel, *Reflections on Judicial ADR and the Multi-Door Courthouse at Twenty: Fait Accompli, Failed Overture, or Fledgling Adulthood?*, 11 OHIO STATE JOURNAL ON DISPUTE RESOLUTION 297, 351 (1996).
[2] Owen M. Fiss, *Against Settlement*, 93 YALE LAW JOURNAL 1073 (1984).
[3] Richard Delgado, et al., *Fairness and Formality: Minimizing the Risk of Prejudice in Alternative Dispute Resolution*, 1985 WISCONSIN LAW REVIEW 1359, 1359 (1985). Later, feminist critics would voice their skepticism, particularly with regard to applying ADR to family cases involving domestic violence. *See* Trina Grillo, *The Mediation Alternative: Process Dangers for Women*, 100 YALE LAW JOURNAL 1545 (1991); *see* Penelope E. Bryan, *Killing Us Softly: Divorce Mediation and the Politics of Power*, 40 BUFFALO LAW REVIEW 441 (1992).
[4] Some cases, such as Brown v. Board of Education, 347 U.S. 483 (1954) and 349 U.S. 294 (1955), have had such a profound influence that they evolved into a reference point for society at large. But cases such as this do not arise overnight, nor *sua sponte*. They arise through the sophisticated coordination of legal theory and litigation. The lengthy, expensive court room struggle to rebalance power between the white majority and black minority, climaxing in *Brown*, has been documented in many books, including most recently CHARLES J. OGLETREE, JR., ALL DELIBERATE SPEED: REFLECTIONS ON THE FIRST HALF CENTURY OF BROWN V. BOARD OF EDUCATION (2004).
[5] Landlord-tenant courts throughout the nation open a window to this gritty reality. *See, e.g.*, Barbara Bezdek, *Silence in the Court: Participation and Subordination of Poor Tenants' Voices in Legal Process*, 20 HOFSTRA LAW REVIEW 533, 533-607 (1992).
[6] Prof. Russell Engler's review of party representation showed that from 80% to 90% of the poor and working poor appear without counsel in civil cases. When negotiations occur, they are typically between the attorney representing the powerful against the powerless, who appears *pro se*. Russell Engler, *Out of Sight and Out of Line: The Need for Regulation of Lawyers' Negotiations with Unrepresented Poor Persons*, 85 CALIFORNIA LAW REVIEW 79, 79 (1997).
[7] For fuller discussion of these intertwined themes and their intersection with class, *see* Sherrilyn A. Ifill, *Racial Diversity on the Bench: Beyond Role Models and Public Confidence*, 57 WASHINGTON & LEE LAW REVIEW 405 (2000).
[8] ROBERT A. BARUCH BUSH & JOSEPH D. FOLGER, THE PROMISE OF MEDIATION: RESPONDING TO CONFLICT THROUGH EMPOWERMENT AND RECOGNITION (1994).
[9] *Id.* at 87. Power can take many forms, can be acknowledged and used in many ways. When goals are primarily relational rather than merely material, this reframing of power can be particularly effective. *See* Phyllis E. Bernard, *Mediating with an 800-lb Gorilla: Medicare and ADR*, 60 WASHINGTON & LEE LAW REVIEW 1417, 1438-48, and a description of the empowerment model for patient-physician dialogue at 1450-55.
[10] From ANATOLE FRANCE, LE LYS ROUGE ch. VII (1894), (quoted in Justice Frankfurter's concurrence in Griffin v. Illinois, 351 U.S. 12, 23 (1956) and Heckler v. Ringer, 466 U.S. 602, 646 (1984)).
[11] MODEL RULES OF PROFESSIONAL CONDUCT RULE 4.1, cmt. 2 (2003) (Truthfulness in Statements to Others): "Under generally accepted conventions in negotiation, certain types of statements ordinarily are not taken as statements of material fact."
[12] In *Spaulding v. Zimmerman*, 116 N.W.2d 704 (Minn. 1962), the court found such a serious misalignment of law and social norms that it vacated a negotiated settlement agreement due to lack of disclosure. The court acknowledged that during adversarial negotiations defendant's attorney might have been minimally justified in not disclosing what the defendant knew about the severity of plaintiff's medical condition. Nevertheless, after the adversarial status had ended, disclosure should have been made.
[13] Claims of fraudulent misrepresentation, failure to disclose onerous terms, concealment of interconnecting loan and insurance companies, etc. often plague negotiations between the working poor and consumer loan companies. A balanced, nuanced view of this interplay—both its impact on individuals and the challenges of group action to pursue fairness—can be found in *Smith v. Tower Loan of Miss., Inc.*, 216 Federal Rules Decisions 338 (S.D. Miss. 2003), *affirmed at Smith v. Crystian*, 91 Federal Appx. 952, 2004 U.S. LEXIS 4955 (5th Cir. 2004). The powerless are "generally characterized by low income and marginal credit records," which leaves few options for short-term loans. Small loan companies pre-

sent a more favorable alternative than pawn shops, cash advance and auto credit loans. Still, these "lenders of last resort" may engage in predatory practices that stretch the limits of law and ethics. 216 Federal Rules Decisions at 363. Notwithstanding, many customers could not claim to have been wholly uninformed about the onerous terms of the loan, or about the legal protections available. This information was clearly stated in plain English on the loan agreement, yet the person in need signed the agreement anyway, exercising their right of self-determination.

[14] *See Diamond v. Premier Capital, Inc.*, 346 F.3d 224 (1st Cir. 2003), where a debtor in a voluntary bankruptcy under Chapter 7 was threatened by one unsecured creditor that the creditor would cause his realtor's license to be revoked if he did not agree to the negotiated settlement. The court found the statement of the creditor's attorney may have constituted "coercion or harassment," because it "could reasonably be deemed tantamount to a threat" of immediate action in violation of the Bankruptcy Code. 346 F.3d at 227-229.

[15] Ironically, we see this frequently in mandatory arbitration clauses embedded in commercial contracts under which the less powerful party waives their right to litigate, or even to use in arbitration state law that was enacted specifically to assure substantive fairness. *See Ticknor v. Choice Hotels International, Inc.*, 265 F.3d 931 (9th Cir. 2001); and a contrary result in *Choice Hotels International, Inc. v. Chewl's Hospitality, Inc.*, 91 Fed. Appx. 810, 2003 U.S. App. LEXIS 25441 (4th Cir. 2003). Here, "less powerful" does not mean low income, but recognizes the large disparity in sophistication, resources and information that typically exists between franchisees and franchisors.

[16] The emerging specialties of collaborative and cooperative lawyering offer hopeful examples of this cadre of lawyers. *See* the description and comparison, complete with suggestions on types of cases that would be more or less suitable with different styles of representation: John Lande & Gregg Herman, *Fitting the Forum to the Family Fuss: Choosing Mediation, Collaborative Law, or Cooperative Law for Negotiating Divorce Cases*, 42 FAMILY COURT REVIEW 280 (2004).

[17] Consider the *"pro se* summary process packet" which some states require to be sent to tenants when a landlord files a summons and complaint, as described by Joel Kurtzburg & Jamie Henikoff, *Freeing the Parties From the Law: Designing an Interest and Rights Focused Model of Landlord/Tenant Mediation*, 1997 JOURNAL OF DISPUTE RESOLUTION 53, 115 (1997).

[18] Valid concerns can be raised about the prudence of permitting "legal document services" or limited scope of lawyering ("unbundled" legal services). *See* Juliet L. Kaz, *Note, Legal Document Services: Dangerous Alternatives to Attorneys?*, 2 J. LEGAL ADVOC. & PRAC. 122 (2000); Forrest S. Mosten, *Unbundling of Legal Services and the Family Lawyer*, 28 FAMILY LAW QUARTERLY 421 (1994). Nevertheless, our nation continues to face a serious maldistribution of legal services which remains largely unaddressed.

[19] Granted, without confidentiality protections parties may not offer an apology or other expression of regret or compassion that could promote healing, reconciliation, or even—more pragmatically—a reduced dollar demand for settlement. *See* Jonathan R. Cohen, *Legislating Apology: The Pros and Cons*, 70 UNIVERSITY OF CINCINNATI LAW REVIEW 819 (2002); Gerald R. Williams, *Negotiation as a Healing Process*, 1996 JOURNAL OF DISPUTE RESOLUTION 1 (1996); Jennifer G. Brown and Jennifer Robbennolt, *Apology*, Chapter 49 in this volume.

[20] A decade after Fiss' prescient cautions, Galanter & Cahill offered preliminary observations on the "special and general" effects upon societal behavior when comparing adjudication vs. negotiation; including information sharing as a "public good," "deterrence," "moral education," "mobilizing and demobilizing," and "precedent and patterning." Marc Galanter & Mia Cahill, *"Most Cases Settle": Judicial Promotion and Regulation of Settlements*, 46 STANFORD LAW REVIEW 1339, 1379-87 (July 1994).

[21] For a much fuller exposition of the doctrine of manifest injustice and confidentiality *see* Scott H. Hughes, *The Uniform Mediation Act: To the Spoiled Go the Privileges*, 85 MARQUETTE LAW REVIEW 9, 54-63 (2001).

[22] For example, there may be much merit in offering a voice to non-parties who have been substantially affected by the societal costs of business failure and displacement. Nathalie D. Martin, *Noneconomic Interests in Bankruptcy: Standing on the Outside Looking In*, 59 OHIO STATE LAW JOURNAL 429, 494-96 (1998).

[23] A decade ago the federal government recognized the need to accommodate multicultural differences to secure environmental justice in negotiating permits. *See* John C. Duncan, Jr., *Multicultural Participation in the Public Hearing Process: Some Theoretical, Pragmatized and Analeptical Considerations*, 24 COLUMBIA JOURNAL OF ENVIRONMENTAL LAW 169 (1999). Also note explicitly collective interests and styles of negotiation prevalent in at least some minority cultures, as discussed in Loretta Kelly, *Indigenous Experiences*, Chapter 35 in this volume.

[24] For a description of how the standard U.S. Department of Agriculture farmer-lender mediation could be expanded to include non-party members of the rural community based on adaptations of African tribal peacemaking methods, *see* Phyllis E. Bernard, *The Administrative Law Judge as a Bridge Between Law and Culture*, 23 JOURNAL OF NATIONAL ASSOCIATION ADMINISTRATIVE LAW JUDGES (PEPPERDINE UNIVERSITY SCHOOL OF LAW) 1, 48-54 (2003).

[25] For a brief but potent description of the edges of this tension, *see* Doriane Lambelet Coleman, *Individualizing Justice Through Multiculturalism: The Liberals' Dilemma*, *in* THE CONFLICT AND CULTURE READER 182-190 (Pat K. Chew ed., 2001).

✧ 30 ✧

Untapped Power: Emotions in Negotiation

Daniel L. Shapiro

Editors' Note: *To many negotiators and mediators an "emotional issue" sounds like one with no real substance to it, yet one that's liable to damage the situation at any moment. Shapiro shows how unsophisticated that view is. Emotions, recognized and unrecognized, regularly trap professional negotiators as well as clients, when these emotions can be anticipated and dealt with constructively. Not only that, but there are positive uses of emotion in negotiation.*

We don't experience the world as it is. We experience the world as we are.
Anais Nin

Two lawyers meet for the first time to negotiate a settlement. To the unaware observer, their greeting is perhaps notable for its uneventfulness. They shake hands, sit down, introduce themselves, and begin talking about the concerns of their respective clients. Each wants to negotiate this small case quickly in order to move on to big, lucrative cases waiting in the docket. And each knows that an agreement can easily be created to meet the interests of their current clients.

Under the surface, however, each lawyer experiences a world of emotions. "He's much older than I expected," thinks the one lawyer. She worries that he might try to control the whole negotiation process, and she calls to mind possible statements she could say to assert her professional status in the interaction. Meanwhile, the older lawyer looks at this younger negotiator and recalls an image of his ex-wife. He feels instantly repelled, but feigns cordial professionalism. Not surprisingly, then, neither listens very well to the other during the meeting; neither learns the other's interests nor shares their own; and neither brainstorms options that might lead to mutual gains. They merely haggle over how much money the one client will pay the other. Each side firmly entrenches in a monetary position; and they close the meeting at impasse.

Are emotions a barrier to a wise agreement? Is it best for negotiators like these two lawyers to toss their emotions aside and to focus purely on the "important" substantive matters, like money? In this brief essay, I suggest reasons why emotions constitute a risk to negotiator efficacy. I then explain that emotions are unavoidable in a negotiation and propose ways in which emotions actually can be *helpful* in reaching a wise agreement.

Emotions Can Obstruct a Negotiated Agreement

There are a number of ways in which emotions can hinder the ability of negotiators to reach a wise agreement in a fair and amicable way.[1] First, emotions may divert our attention from substantive matters. If we or others are angry or upset, both of us will have to deal with the hassle of emotions. Whether we decide to yell back, to sit quietly and ignore the outburst, or to storm out of the room, somehow we will need to respond.

Second, revelation of emotions can open us up to being manipulated. If we blush with embarrassment or flinch with surprise, these observable reactions offer the other party hints about our "true" concerns. A careful observer of our emotional reactions may learn which issues we value most and least—and could use that information to try to extract concessions from us.

For example, John and Mary, a husband and wife, shopped for an anniversary ring in New York City. After hours of shopping, they entered a small store with a sign in the window that read, "Lowest price in town." Mary spotted a sapphire ring in the corner of the main display case. She looked at John, looked at the ring, and smiled in excitement. A jeweler approached them and took the ring out of the display case. John inquired about the asking price. The jeweler named his "rock bottom" price. John was surprised, but not only because of its cost. Moments earlier, he had overheard the jeweler offering another couple that same ring for $400 less. John suspected that the jeweler had raised the asking price after seeing Mary's excitement about the ring. The couple decided to buy a ring elsewhere.

Third, thinking may take a subordinate role to feeling. Emotions are desirable for falling in love, but they make it difficult to think precisely in a negotiation. Because we cannot easily quantify or measure emotions, talking about emotions reduces the role of hard data, facts, and logic. It makes little sense to try to negotiate quantitatively over emotions: "I'll give you 10% more respect if you give me 20% less resentment."

Fourth, unless we are careful, emotions will take charge of us. They may cause us to lose our temper, to stumble anxiously over our words, or to sulk uncontrollably in self-pity. We may neglect even our own substantive goals. In anger, we may reject an agreement that is superior to our alternatives.[2] Or we may focus not on our substantive goals at all, but rather on hurting the negotiator whose actions triggered our anger.[3]

Thus, it is not surprising that a negotiator may fear the power of emotions. They are dangerous and can be destructive. However, this analysis is only a partial picture of the role that emotions play in a negotiation.

Get Rid of Emotions?

Folk wisdom offers clear advice about how to deal with emotions in negotiation: do not get emotional. Negotiators commonly are encouraged to "Swallow your pride," "Do not worry," and "Keep a straight face." For a negotiator, emotions are seen as an impediment to avoid at all costs. However, this advice is untenable and often makes things worse.

Emotions are Unavoidable

Human beings are in a state of "perpetual emotion."[4] Whether negotiating with another lawyer or with a friend, we constantly experience affective states of some type or another, such as anger, boredom, nostalgia, or anxiety.[5] Emotions are stimulated by the context surrounding us (e.g., walking into another lawyer's office), by our own actions, feelings, and thoughts (e.g., worrying about one's junior status), and by the actions of the other negotiator toward us (e.g., their demeaning behavior toward us).

Negotiators can be personally affected in many different ways, including by impulses, emotions, moods, and attitudes.[6] An *impulse* is a strong desire to do a particular behavior now, without much thought about possible consequences. If the young lawyer experiences feelings of mistreatment by the older lawyer, she may have an impulse to storm out of the room, ruining the possibility of a negotiated agreement.

Negotiators often feel the more generalized pushes and pulls of *emotions*, which are positive or negative reactions to matters of personal significance. In contrast to impulses, which propel us to do a *particular* behavior now, such as to tear up the "biased" proposal drafted by the other side, emotions motivate us toward general kinds of behavior, such as to attack the other party in *some way* for their self-serving behavior. An important part of most emotions is the action tendency,[7] which is the type of behavioral urge associated with that emotion. In anger, for example, the action tendency is to strike out or attack. In guilt, the action tendency is to repent. Of course, a person may not act upon the action tendency; that is why it is called a tendency and not an actuality.

Moods are low intensity affective states, background music to our thoughts and actions. Whether we experience a positive mood due to our pay raise or a negative mood due to the rainy weather, our moods may have an effect on our negotiating behavior.[8]

Attitudes are positive or negative evaluations of a person, institution, policy, or event.[9] If the young lawyer learns that her counterpart is deceiving her, she may develop a negative attitude toward him.

Suppressing Emotions Can Make Things Worse

It is not possible to suppress one's actual feelings. We feel some particular emotion, and then we come to realize the emotion which we are experiencing. It is possible, however, to suppress the expression of those feelings.[10] A negotiator may feel angry toward another without expressing that anger through words, tone of voice, or body language.

Suppressing resentment, anger, or other strong emotions can debilitate a negotiator's cognitive and behavioral functioning in several ways.[11] First, the negative emotional experience remains, leaving the negotiator in an internal state of tension. This agitated state may motivate us to act in ways that do not serve our short- or long-term interests.[12] A negotiator may hide her anger toward a colleague, then explode weeks later at a trivial behavior conducted by the colleague. Second, the effort to suppress the display of emotions consumes important cognitive energy. People are limited in their cognitive capacity to process information,[13] so additional cognitive tasks decrease a negotiator's ability to think about important substantive or process issues. Third, a negotiator who suppresses his or her emotions may be more likely to stereotype that counterpart as an "adversary," leading to competitive behavior. There is evidence that the act of suppressing emotions increases physiological arousal both personally and in one's negotiating

counterpart.[14] With heightened physiological arousal, each negotiator has a reduced attentional capacity, making stereotypical thinking more likely.[15]

Emotions Can Help You Reach Your Negotiation Goals

Emotions affect our ability to reach negotiation goals. In most negotiations, each
party has two goals: affective satisfaction and instrumental satisfaction.[16] The ability to deal effectively with emotions increases the likelihood of attaining those
goals.

Affective satisfaction is our general level of satisfaction with the emotions we
experienced during an interaction. Affective satisfaction focuses on our feelings
about our feelings—our "meta-emotions" for short.[17] How do we feel about the
feelings we experienced in the negotiation? In reflecting upon our interaction with
the other party, do we generally feel satisfied with our emotional experience, or do
we feel angry, upset, and dissatisfied?

A second goal focuses on instrumental satisfaction, the extent to which substantive work requirements are fulfilled. If two lawyers walk away from a week-
long negotiation with plenty of good feelings but no new ideas about how to deal
effectively with their differences, the meeting might be considered an affective
success but an instrumental failure.

Using Emotions to Move You toward Your Negotiation Goals

Negotiators are not merely victim to the dangers of emotions. In fact, interest-
based negotiators can reap great benefit by understanding the information communicated via emotions and by enlisting positive emotions into their interactions.

Understanding the Information Communicated by Emotions

The emotion theorist Sylvin Tompkins suggested that emotions amplify motivation.[18] They signal the importance of issues to us and let us know about what we
care. They bring personally important goals into the forefront of attention and give
them urgency. The goals may be instrumental or affective in nature.

Hence, awareness of emotions, one's own and those of others, provides a negotiator with an understanding of the importance of each person's interests and
concerns. A negotiator may come to realize the extent to which she wants a particular object (instrumental satisfaction) or a particular kind of treatment and
deference (affective satisfaction). [Schneider, *Aspirations*] With expanded information about the relative importance of interests, parties are more capable of devising
options for mutual gain.

Emotions are not only internal; they have a communicative function.[19] If the
other negotiator says something that offends you, the look on your face may
change. Your eyebrows may furrow and your lips may pucker. Your voice may become deeper, and the rhythm of your speech may turn more abrupt. Through these
behaviors, you are communicating to the other negotiator that you are angry. By
expressing your emotion, you provide the other with important information about
how you want to be treated.

Even if you suppress the expression of your own emotions, they are still communicating information to at least one person: you. The feeling of butterflies in
your stomach signals to you that you may be anxious. The feeling of heaviness
throughout your body signals that you may be disappointed. Although some negotiators are very good at hiding the expression of their "true" feelings from others,
it is much more complicated to hide your own feelings from yourself.

Because emotions communicate information, an observant negotiator may try to exploit that information. Some negotiators try to stimulate an emotion—positive or negative—in others for strategic gain.[20] A car salesperson may try to build a positive affiliation with the customer to encourage the sale of a car on his car lot ("You have kids? Me, too! This car is great for taking the kids on vacation.") [Guthrie, *Compliance*] Or the salesperson may feign surprise at a customer's "outrageously low" asking price for the car.

Does emotional manipulation work? Sometimes. Negotiators may be exploited if they are unaware that their emotions are being manipulated. However, putting aside ethical and moral questions, the exploitive use of emotions is not foolproof.[21] First, negotiators who use exploitive tactics may get caught. A customer may learn that the car salesperson does *not* actually have children and may decide to take her business elsewhere. Second, the tactics of a manipulative negotiator may backfire. A salesperson's feigned surprise at a customer's "outrageously low" asking price may cause the customer *not* to feel ashamed at her asking price, but rather to feel annoyed at the salesperson's comment and to shop elsewhere.

Exploiting emotions runs the additional risk of damaging long-term relationships. Many negotiations involve people who have ongoing relationships with one another and who are in close and consistent contact. Lawyers, politicians, diplomats, and organizational employees tend to interact with a small and stable network of colleagues. Emotional exploitation may work to one negotiator's advantage in the short term, but over the course of time others may become aware of the manipulation, become angry, and subvert the exploitation through overt or covert retaliation.[22] Even in situations of asymmetric power, the less powerful person may use subtle tactics to retaliate against the exploitation. ("Sorry boss, but I forgot to send out the package on time yesterday.")

Negative Emotions Have Downfalls in a Negotiation

Negative emotions are not completely useless in a negotiation. Consider a simple distributive negotiation. If two boys argue over who should get the last cookie in the cookie jar, the child who expresses more anger—yelling louder and making more credible threats to hurt the other—may be at an advantage. The expression of anger communicates a willingness to go to extremes, even if that means getting in trouble or foregoing a better alternative.

Yet negative emotions have serious downfalls in a negotiation. The angry boys do not explore value-creating options, such as asking a parent if they can go to the store to buy more cookies. And once the conflict over the cookie is resolved, emotional residue may become the seeds of future conflict.[23] The boy who did not get the cookie may feel resentment, which easily may fuel future disagreement.

Enlisting Positive Emotions to Motivate Collaboration

A growing body of research suggests that positive emotions increase the likelihood that negotiators will satisfy their instrumental and affective goals. Compared to those in a neutral mood, negotiators in a positive mood achieve more optimally integrative outcomes, use fewer aggressive behaviors, and report higher enjoyment of their interaction.[24] As parties build affiliation with one another and develop fulfilling roles, they become more engaged in their negotiation tasks and experience a state of "flow," a peak motivational experience that is intrinsically and personally rewarding.[25]

Positive emotions contribute to the long-term sustainability of each party's commitments. Negotiators may experience positive emotions toward one another due to joint participation in the negotiation process, joint brainstorming on the agreement, or a positive emotional connection with one another. The power of positive emotions toward the agreement and toward the other can override the temptation for parties to dishonor their commitments.

Positive emotions also foster cognitive expansion. Positive emotions can aid negotiators' attempts to problem-solve creative options to satisfy their interests.[26] Positive emotions trigger the release of a neurochemical called dopamine, which in turn fosters improved cognitive ability for a negotiator to think creatively. These findings are consistent with the research of Barbara Fredrickson,[27] who proposes that certain positive emotions—including joy, interest, contentment, and pride— all share the ability to broaden attentional, cognitive, and behavioral ability. This theory is supported by a tremendous amount of research conducted by Alice Isen and colleagues.[28] Isen's research suggests that people experiencing positive affect demonstrate thinking that is flexible, creative, integrative, and efficient. Each of these characteristics is important for an interest-based negotiator, who is trying to brainstorm creative options that satisfy each party's interests.

Some of the motivational benefit of positive emotions can be reaped whether one is a hard bargainer or interest-based negotiator. In either case, each party needs the other to create a joint agreement. That is the essence of negotiation. Hence, the parties must co-manage the negotiation process, and the collaborative inclinations fostered by positive emotions can improve the efficiency of that process. Even parties in a single, nonrepeat negotiation must co-manage the negotiation process. The stimulation of positive emotions, as well as the consequent eliciting of collaborative behaviors, can facilitate the efficiency of the negotiation.

Conclusion

While it is true that emotions can be a barrier to a value-maximizing agreement, the common advice to "get rid of emotions" is infeasible and unwise. On the contrary, research suggests that negotiators can improve the efficiency and effectiveness of a negotiation by gaining an understanding of the information communicated by emotions, their own and those of others, and enlisting positive emotions into the negotiation.

Endnotes

[1] The ideas in this section are drawn primarily from: ROGER FISHER & DANIEL SHAPIRO, BEYOND REASON: USING EMOTIONS AS YOU NEGOTIATE (2005).
[2] Max Bazerman, et al., *The Death and Rebirth of the Social Psychology of Negotiations*, in BLACKWELL HANDBOOK OF SOCIAL PSYCHOLOGY 196 (Garth Fletcher & Margaret Clark eds., 2000); Modan Pillutla & J. Keith Murnighan, *Unfairness, Anger and Spite: Emotional Rejections of Ultimatum Offers*, 68 ORGANIZATIONAL BEHAVIOR AND HUMAN DECISION PROCESSES 208-24 (1996).
[3] Joseph Daly, *The Effects of Anger on Negotiations Over Mergers and Acquisitions*, 7 NEGOTIATION JOURNAL 31-39 (1991).
[4] DANIEL SHAPIRO, *A Negotiator's Guide to Emotions: Four "Laws" to Effective Practice*, DISPUTE RESOLUTION MAGAZINE, Winter 2001, at 3-8.
[5] David Watson & Lee Anna Clark, *Emotions, Moods, Traits, and Temperaments: Conceptual Distinctions and Empirical Findings*, in THE NATURE OF EMOTIONS: FUNDAMENTAL QUESTIONS 89 (Paul Ekman & Richard Davidson eds., 1994).
[6] Shapiro, *supra* note 4.
[7] NICO FRIJDA, THE EMOTIONS (1986).

[8] Alice Isen, *Positive Affect and Decision Making*, in HANDBOOK OF EMOTIONS 417 (Jeannette Haviland-Jones & Michael Lewis eds., 2000).

[9] ICEK AJZEN, ATTITUDES, PERSONALITY, AND BEHAVIOR (1988).

[10] I do acknowledge evidence suggesting that it may not be possible to suppress the micro-expressions that occur immediately upon experiencing a particular emotion. *See* Mark G. Frank & Paul Ekman, *The Ability to Detect Deceipt Generalizes Across Different Types of Highstake Lies*, 72 JOURNAL OF PERSONALITY AND SOCIAL PSYCHOLOGY 1429 (1997).

[11] James Gross, *Emotion Regulation: Affective, Cognitive, and Social Consequences*, 39 PSYCHO-PHYSIOLOGY 281-91 (2002).

[12] James Averill, *Emotions are Many Splendored Things*, in THE NATURE OF EMOTIONS, *supra* note 5, at 99-102.

[13] SUSAN FISKE & SHELLEY TAYLOR, SOCIAL COGNITION (2d ed. 1991).

[14] Gross, *supra* note 11.

[15] Delroy Paulhus, et al., *Some Effects of Arousal on Sex Stereotyping*, 18 PERSONALITY AND SOCIAL PSYCHOLOGY BULLETIN 325-30 (1992).

[16] DANIEL SHAPIRO, NEGOTIATION RESIDUALS: THE IMPACT OF AFFECTIVE SATISFACTION ON LONG-TERM RELATIONSHIP QUALITY (2000) [hereinafter, SHAPIRO, NEGOTIATION RESIDUALS]; Daniel Shapiro, *Negotiating Emotions*, 20 CONFLICT RESOLUTION QUARTERLY 68 (2002).

[17] JOHN GOTTMAN, ET AL., META-EMOTION: HOW FAMILIES COMMUNICATE EMOTIONALLY (1997).

[18] Silvan Tomkins, *Affect as the Primary Motivational System*, in FEELINGS AND EMOTIONS: THE LOYOLA SYMPOSIUM 101-10 (Magda Arnold ed., 1970).

[19] Robert Levenson, *Human Emotion: A Functional View*, in THE NATURE OF EMOTIONS, *supra* note 5, at 123-26.

[20] Bruce Barry, *The Tactical Use of Emotion in Negotiation*, in RESEARCH ON NEGOTIATION IN OR-GANIZATIONS 93-121 (Robert Bies, et al. eds., 1999).

[21] ROBERT AXELROD, THE EVOLUTION OF COOPERATION (1984).

[22] Keith Allred, et al., *The Influence of Anger and Compassion on Negotiation Performance*, 70 OR-GANIZATIONAL BEHAVIOR AND HUMAN DECISION PROCESSES 175-87 (1997).

[23] SHAPIRO, NEGOTIATION RESIDUALS, *supra* note 16.

[24] Peter Carnevale & Alice Isen, *The Influence of Positive Affect and Visual Access on the Discovery of Integrative Solutions in Bilateral Negotiation*, 37 ORGANIZATIONAL BEHAVIOR AND HUMAN DECI-SION PROCESSES 1, 1-13 (1986).

[25] MIHALY CSIKSZENTMIHALYI, FLOW: THE PSYCHOLOGY OF OPTIMAL EXPERIENCE (1990).

[26] Joseph Forgas, *On Feeling Good and Getting Your Way: Mood Effects on Negotiator Cognition and Bargaining Strategies*, 72 JOURNAL OF PERSONALITY AND SOCIAL PSYCHOLOGY 565-77 (1998); Isen, *supra* note 8.

[27] Barbara Fredrickson, *The Role of Positive Emotions in Positive Psychology: The Broaden-and-Build Theory of Positive Emotions*, 56 AMERICAN PSYCHOLOGIST 218-226 (2001).

[28] Isen, *supra* note 8.

❧ 31 ❧

A spirations

Andrea Kupfer Schneider

Editors' Note: *When you set out to negotiate with someone, how do you evaluate what you're really trying to achieve? Is it an unfocused want, something better than your BATNA, anything you can get that's above your reservation price? Schneider analyzes research showing that a conscious choice of goal helps you come out with more. Four keys to this are "making your reach a little longer than your arm;" setting goals you can justify in public without laughing or lying; making them specific; and paying real attention to goals which can't be expressed in a number.*

You can't always get what you want,
But if you try sometimes,
You just might find,
You get what you need.
Rolling Stones, YOU CAN'T ALWAYS GET WHAT YOU WANT*

Good negotiators spend a lot of time thinking about how to determine their BATNA,[1] and assess their interests, but often may not spend enough time focusing on aspirations. And, as even the Rolling Stones know, unless negotiators actually set a specific goal and try to reach it, they will undoubtedly fall short. Social science research confirms that negotiators with higher aspirations tend to achieve better bargaining results. Yet, once negotiators start to focus more on aspirations, they also need to think about how aspirations should be set, how they are distinguished from a BATNA or the reservation point at which the negotiation should go to her BATNA (which, of course, is not quite the same thing as the reservation point that triggers it) and how negotiators can err in setting overly optimistic aspirations.

Aspirations are the specific goals in a negotiation that a negotiator wishes to achieve as part of an agreement. Aspirations can be monetary, as in, "He doesn't want to pay more than $50,000 to settle this case," or "She'd like to receive $300,000 for this house." Aspirations can also be non-monetary as in "He'd like to feel fairly treated" or "She wants the painting over the fireplace from her grandmother's estate," and they can often be a combination of monetary and non-monetary goals such as "He'd like to receive an apology and $75,000 to cover medical expenses plus pain and suffering." Aspirations are based on the underlying needs and interests of the negotiator, and they are conceptually independent of the negotiator's bottom line. For example, a negotiator might be willing to sell her house for $250,000 if that is the best offer she can expect, while aspiring to receive a sale price of $300,000. This essay addresses prescriptive advice on how negotiators should determine their aspirations. Richard Shell counsels that aspirations should be optimistic, specific, and justifiable.[2] So what does that mean?

Optimistic Aspirations

Negotiators should establish optimistic aspirations because empirical evidence has shown that negotiators with higher aspirations tend to achieve better bargaining results. The classic study demonstrating this proposition was run by psychologists Sidney Siegel and Lawrence Fouraker in 1960.[3] One set of negotiators were given a modest goal of $2.10 profit in a buy-sell negotiation and the other set were given the "high aspirations" of $6.10. Both sets were told that they could keep any profits they made and could qualify for a second, "double-their-money" round if they met or exceeded their specified bargaining goals. The negotiators with the more ambitious $6.10 goal achieved a mean profit of $6.25, far outperforming the median profit of $3.35 achieved by those with the modest $2.10 goal. More recently, Sally Blount White and Margaret Neale set up an experiment in house buying where buyers and sellers were each given reservation prices in addition to aspirational goals for the house price.[4] Again, those buyers with high aspirations (to buy the house at a low price) did better than those buyers with low aspirations (as did the sellers with high aspirations).

There are different explanations for this. First, a negotiator's aspirations help to determine the outer limit of what she will request.[5] Because a negotiator will almost never achieve more than what she asks for, setting relatively high goals is important so that the negotiator makes suitably assertive demands.

Second, optimistic aspirations can cause negotiators to work harder at bargaining to achieve their desirable outcome. Jennifer Brown hypothesizes that when negotiators set an aspiration level, they gain more utility as offers increase toward that level versus the utility gained as offers proceed beyond that level.[6] In other words, the marginal utility associated with each improvement beyond one's aspirations is less than the marginal utility associated with movement toward the aspirations. This theory implies that negotiators will care relatively more about achieving their aspirations than exceeding them.

Russell Korobkin writes that one effect of negotiators working harder is that negotiators with high aspirations will also exhibit more patience at the bargaining table than those with low aspirations.[7] Rather than getting frustrated and either walking away or giving in, the negotiator with high aspirations will be willing to tolerate a longer give-and-take in order to reach her aspirations. As more patient negotiators achieve a greater share of the gains of negotiation than less patient negotiators,[8] high aspirations can lead to better outcomes.

Specific Aspirations

Aspirations should be specific. A general goal of "doing well" or "let's see what they say" is insufficient to trigger the positive behavioral benefits of setting aspirations discussed above.[9] Much in the same way that negotiators learn to define their BATNA and then use it to determine their bottom line, negotiators should take vague aspirations and turn them into specific goals for the negotiation.

In addition, specific goals for the negotiation can keep the negotiator more focused on his or her interests than on the game of negotiation. If a negotiator enters the negotiation with an ambiguous "let's see what happens" agenda, it is far easier to become entangled in debilitating negotiation mistakes such as getting anchored on the counterpart's numbers, assuming a fixed pie, or getting one's ego wrapped up in irrational escalation.[Korobkin & Guthrie, *Heuristics*]

Justifiable Aspirations

While negotiators should set relatively aggressive aspirations, those aspirations should be reasonable enough to be justifiable, for several important reasons. First, negotiators will be more likely to succeed in convincing their adversary to reach an agreement based on their aspiration level if they can argue that such an outcome is derived from objective criteria. [Welsh, *Fairness*] These objective criteria include what a court would decide, standard business practice, fair market value, or other legitimate criteria, such as the painting that a granddaughter wants from her grandmother's estate is one the granddaughter helped pick out at the gallery.

The availability of objective criteria also makes it easier for the negotiator to justify a refusal to make concessions. Demands that are not realistically grounded are harder to hold onto during the bargaining process. Imagine two scenarios— one in which a seller would like to get $500,000 for her house because it is a nice round number and she could use it to buy another house, versus one in which the seller lists her house for $500,000, based on the fair market value of the house in comparison to other houses in the neighborhood. In the latter case, the seller has fair and convincing arguments for why she will not accept less and is less likely to move quickly off her list price.

Demands that lack an objective justification also encourage the opposing negotiator to make unprincipled counter demands. If financial desire is the justification for the seller's list price, then the buyer could just as easily respond with a lowball offer citing their limited ability to get a mortgage. A justifiable list price of $500,000 instead should lead to the more appropriate counteroffer of $450,000 based on the objective criteria that the roof needs to be replaced or that the kitchen should be updated.

An additional reason that aspirations should be justifiable is that overly aggressive aspirations can lead to a negotiation impasse even when mutually beneficial agreements are possible. Korobkin argues that aspirations can act as an "anchor" that skews a negotiator's bottom line.[10] In circumstances in which determining where to set one's bottom line is especially difficult, aggressive aspirations are likely to cause a negotiator to set his bottom line higher than an objective analysis of his alternatives to reaching a negotiated agreement would indicate is appropriate. Thus, aspirations that are too high can indirectly lead the negotiator to reject proposed agreements that are actually within an objectively acceptable range. Korobkin also contends that aspirations can anchor negotiators' views of what agreement is objectively fair: the higher the aspirations, the higher the negotiator's perception of what fairness demands.[11] This additional fairness effect of aspirations can cause negotiators to reject "acceptable" proposals, to the extent that negotiators frequently reject proposed agreements that they perceive as unfair even if the agreement would be superior to their bottom line. [Welsh, *Fairness*]

Why Don't Negotiators Set Appropriately High Aspirations?

Negotiators often fail to follow the "optimistic but justifiable" approach to setting aspirations; instead they set vague goals such as "achieving a good deal" or aspiring to relatively low, easy-to-achieve results. Why? One reason is that specific, optimistic aspirations can result in disappointment when they are not achieved. Setting low or non-specific goals—what Shell calls a "wimp-win" approach[12]— maximizes the likelihood of success and protects self-esteem. If a negotiator sets his goals low, as the seller who advertises "make an offer" in the local paper and is willing to accept the first offer on a piano, this "low aspirations" negotiator is more likely to accomplish his goals. On the other hand, if a negotiator sets his goal high, as in a seller who is aiming to sell the piano for close to the original purchase price, that "high aspirations" negotiator may be disappointed in himself when he can only negotiate a deal at half the original price. The "high aspirations" piano seller may well have received much more than the "low aspirations" piano seller, but he may be more focused on his perceived (aspirations-based) loss. In order to avoid this disappointment, negotiators often set low goals. To make things worse, this disappointment from one negotiation can lead negotiators to set lower goals in future negotiations, again in a self-protective response.

Another reason why negotiators set low aspirations is when the negotiator feels that she lacks enough information about the other side's interests and bottom line to confidently predict what results are possible. A negotiator may assume that she needs the deal more than her counterpart or may not understand why reaching a settlement is important to the other side. Without this information, she may set her goals lower than the goals should be from an objective perspective. For example, if a house seller receives an offer that is $20,000 below the listed price after the house has been on the market for several weeks without any interest, the seller's response could depend on the information the seller has about the buyer. Without any information, the seller might be so excited to get an offer that she accepts the offer immediately. On the other hand, if the seller learns that the buyer needs to move next month or has told his agent that this was his favorite house, the seller may be more willing to hold on to high aspirations. Just as setting aspirations takes preparation and the appropriate criteria, it also requires preparation about the other side.

Finally, a negotiator may set low goals when she is relatively uninterested in the result or wants to avoid conflict with another person. [Bingham, *Avoiding Negotiating*] Of course, these low goals may be appropriate as long as the negotiator makes a rational decision about this.

Subjective and Objective Values

A last note on aspirations concerns subjective goals. Recently, social psychologists have tried to create a measurement for subjective value in negotiation rather than just measurable objective items.[13] According to the theory, subjective value in a negotiation can be an end in itself (I feel good about the outcome); can be seen as intuition about the objective (economic) outcomes; and can also be seen as a predictor for future objective value.

First, feeling good about oneself and the outcome of the negotiation is clearly an important goal that we have seen reflected in literature on fairness, trust and procedural justice. Second, subjective valuation of an outcome may shed light on objective values as well. Since we can never really know how we have done objectively in a real negotiation—negotiators do not usually sit down and exchange information the way we might in class, comparing BATNA's, bargaining ranges, and goals—psychologists argue that negotiator intuition and one's subjective assessment of the outcome is as good as it gets, in terms of assessing motivations and tendencies of negotiators. Finally, the subjective value of the negotiation creates reputations that feed back into future interactions. In other words, if we create subjective value (they feel good) for the other side, he or she is more likely to want to interact with us in the future in a positive way.[14] This reputational value [Tinsley, et al., *Reputations*] can add to one's objective outcomes in the future. Furthermore, this subjective value also makes it more likely that the agreement will actually be implemented.

One interesting tool for measuring subjective value was created by Curhan, et al. and tested over four studies. Their questionnaire (available at www.subjectivevalue.com) asks about four areas: the actual outcome of the negotiation; one's self; the process of the negotiation; and the relationship between the parties. For outcome, subjective value is measured by how satisfied you are with the actual outcome, the balance between your outcome and the other side's outcome, whether you feel you "lost", and whether the outcome is legitimate. In measuring subjective value for self, the questionnaire asks whether you "lost face", whether you behaved appropriately, if the negotiation made you feel more or less competent, and whether you behaved according to your own values. Process questions include whether your counterpart listened to your concerns, whether the process was fair, how satisfied you were with the ease or difficulty in reaching an agreement, and whether your counterpart considered your needs in the negotiation. Finally, the relationship questions ask whether you are satisfied with the relationship, what kind of impression the other side made, whether you trusted your counterpart, and whether the negotiation built a good foundation.

The concept of subjective value can help us think more broadly about our aspirations in negotiation as we go forward to set them optimistically, specifically, and justifiably.

Conclusion

This essay has argued the importance of setting aspirations in negotiation and thinking as carefully about our goals as we negotiators think about our bottom lines. First, this essay discussed why aspirations should be set and should be optimistic. Studies show that negotiators with higher goals accomplish more. Second, this essay examined why aspirations should be specific, in order to trigger the positive behavioral benefits of setting aspirations and to keep negotiators focused. Third, this essay outlined how to set these aspirations based on objective criteria, and explained why aspirations must be justifiable: justifiable aspirations are more persuasive and also help to keep negotiators from making the mistake of setting unrealistic aspirations that cause them to walk away from good agreements. Fourth, this essay examined why negotiators fail to set specific goals— because they want to avoid disappointment or lack information. In the end, while there are some risks of disappointment and unrealized settlements involved in setting optimistic goals, studies demonstrate that setting specific, optimistic and justifiable aspirations results in negotiations that accomplish more of what the negotiator wants. Finally, this essay argued that aspirations should also be broadened to include more subjective measures of success.

Endnotes

* ABKCO 1969

[1] BATNA is "Best Alternative to a Negotiated Agreement." ROGER FISHER, ET AL., GETTING TO YES: NEGOTIATING AGREEMENT WITHOUT GIVING IN (2d ed. 1991).

[2] G. RICHARD SHELL, BARGAINING FOR ADVANTAGE: NEGOTIATION STRATEGIES FOR REASONABLE PEOPLE 30-34 (1999).

[3] *See* SIDNEY SIEGEL & LAWRENCE E. FOURAKER, BARGAINING AND GROUP DECISION MAKING 64 (1960).

[4] *See* Sally Blount White & Margaret A. Neale, *The Role of Negotiator Aspirations and Settlement Expectancies in Bargaining Outcomes*, 57 ORGANIZATIONAL BEHAVIOR & HUMAN DECISION PROCESSES 303, 304-05 (1994).

[5] SHELL, *supra* note 2, at 26. While Shell argues that aspirations actually set the outer limit, it is also quite possible that negotiators will make an opening demand beyond their aspirations knowing that the initial offer will likely come down.

[6] Jennifer Gerarda Brown, *The Role of Hope in Negotiation*, 44 UCLA LAW REVIEW 1661 (1997).

[7] Russell Korobkin, *Aspirations and Settlement*, 88 CORNELL LAW REVIEW 1, 44-48 (2002).

[8] *See, e.g.*, RUSSELL KOROBKIN, NEGOTIATION THEORY AND STRATEGY 171-73 (2002).

[9] SHELL, *supra* note 2, at 33.

[10] Korobkin, *supra* note 8, at 32-33.

[11] *Id.* at 41-44.

[12] SHELL, *supra* note 2, at 32.

[13] Jared Curhan, et al., *What do People Value When They Negotiate? Mapping the Domain of Subjective Value in Negotiation*, JOURNAL OF PERSONALITY AND SOCIAL PSYCHOLOGY (forthcoming); *see also*, Jared Curhan, et al., *The Subjective Value Inventory, at* http://www.subjectivevalue.com/pages/1/index.htm (last visited Feb. 25, 2006).

[14] Psychologists note that future subjective value and short-term objective value can sometimes conflict (I will get more money now if I share very little information but, in the process, create no subjective value in happiness or reputation for the other side, who is now unlikely to want to interact with me in the future).

❧ 32 ❧

Miswanting

Chris Guthrie & David F. Sally

Editors' Note: *If you're assuming that a settlement will make you (or your client) happy, it's time to question that assumption. By explaining the work of positive psychology (or what makes people happy), these authors explore how people often end up misdiagnosing their own goals. But if you understand your own and your client's pressures toward misidentifying what you need out of a negotiation, you are better prepared to set goals that will actually work for you both. This should be read in conjunction with Schneider on Aspirations.*

The defining feature of "principled" or "problem-solving" negotiation is its emphasis on "interests" rather than "positions." In negotiation parlance, positions are what disputants declare they want. Interests, on the other hand, are the "needs, desires, concerns, and fears" that underlie stated positions.[1]

Disputants routinely negotiate over positions. Each party to a negotiation adopts a position, argues for it, and eventually makes concessions (or not) to reach an agreement. Unfortunately, however, agreements based on positions are unlikely to meet the wants and needs that motivated the parties to adopt those positions in the first place.

Proponents of problem-solving negotiation argue that disputants should therefore seek not to assert positions but rather to identify and satisfy their underlying interests. Indeed, according to the proponents of this approach to negotiation, the very "object of a negotiation" is to satisfy "underlying interests."[2] On this view, disputants should try to get what they really want at the bargaining table.

But what if they don't know what they *really* want?

Impact Bias

Researchers from an emerging movement within psychology—labeled "positive psychology" or "hedonic psychology"—have learned a great deal in recent years about what people really want. Of greatest relevance to this Chapter, researchers have discovered that people are often mistaken about what they want or what will make them happy.

It is not that people are entirely unaware of what they want or how they will feel. In fact, people are generally quite skilled at predicting whether they will feel positively or negatively about some event or item.[3] People accurately predict, for example, that they will feel favorably about a promotion and unfavorably about a demotion. Likewise, people are generally pretty good at predicting the specific emotion(s) they

will experience upon obtaining some item or experiencing some event.[4] People anticipate, for instance, that they will feel pride and joy upon being promoted and anger
and embarrassment upon being demoted.

What people struggle with, however, is predicting both the *intensity* and *duration* of
their emotional reactions to an event or outcome. One's sense of well-being turns
significantly on this kind of prediction:

> Often people predict correctly the valence of their emotional reactions
> ("I'll feel good if I get the job") and correctly predict the specific emotions
> they will experience (e.g., joy). Even when achieving such accuracy, how-
> ever, it is important for people to predict what the initial intensity of the
> reaction will be (how much joy they will experience) and the duration of
> that emotion (how long will they feel this way). It is useful to know that
> we will feel happy on our first day at a new job, but better to know how
> happy and how long this feeling will last, before committing ourselves to
> a lifetime of work as a tax attorney. It is helpful to know that it will be
> painful to end a long-term relationship, but better to know how painful
> and whether the pain will last half a second or half a decade.[5]

Unfortunately, people have a tendency to overestimate the impact of future events
on their emotional well-being. Psychologists Daniel Gilbert and Timothy Wilson refer
to this phenomenon as the "impact bias."[6]

Gilbert, Wilson, and other researchers have found that the impact bias influences
reactions to all kinds of life events, including romantic breakups, personal insults,
failed exams, sports victories, electoral defeats, winning prizes, receiving gifts, failing
to lose weight, failing to obtain a promotion, and being diagnosed with a serious illness.[7] With few exceptions, people tend to overestimate the emotional impact such
events will have on their lives.

Researchers are not entirely sure why people have such difficulty assessing the
emotional impact of various life events and outcomes, but they have identified several
potential explanations. First, when predicting reactions to a future event, people tend
to ignore the impact that *other* events are likely to have on their sense of well-being.
Researchers refer to this as "focalism"[8] or a "focusing illusion."[9] Relatedly, when
choosing between items, people tend to ignore the features the items share in common and overestimate the emotional impact that distinct features of the chosen
option will have on their well-being. People are prone, in other words, to an "isolation
effect."[10] Also, people underestimate the extent to which they use "sense-making
processes" to dampen the emotional impact of an experience or outcome.[11] People
"inexorably explain and understand events that were initially surprising and unpredictable, and this process lowers the intensity of emotional reactions to the events."[12]
In advance, however, they fail to appreciate that they are equipped with this "psychological immune system."[13]

Whatever its source, the existence of the impact bias means that people often
"miswant." Writing in a *New York Times Magazine* article, Jon Gertner explains this as
follows:

> [W]e might believe that a new BMW will make life perfect. But it will
> almost certainly be less exciting than we anticipated; nor will it excite us
> for as long as predicted.... Gilbert and his collaborator Tim Wilson call the
> gap between what we predict and what we ultimately experience the 'im-
> pact bias'—'impact' meaning the errors we make in estimating both the
> intensity and duration of our emotions and 'bias' our tendency to err. The
> phrase characterizes how we experience the dimming excitement over not
> just a BMW but also over any object or event that we presume will make
> us happy. Would a 20 percent raise or winning the lottery result in a con-
> tented life? You may predict it will, but almost surely it won't turn out

that way. And a new plasma television? You may have high hopes, but the impact bias suggests that it will almost certainly be less cool, and in a shorter time, than you imagine. Worse, Gilbert has noted that these mistakes of expectation can lead directly to mistakes in choosing what we think will give us pleasure. He calls this 'miswanting.'[14]

"Miswanting" in Negotiation

The potential impact of the impact bias on negotiation is straightforward. If people in general are likely to have difficulty determining what they really want because of a tendency to overestimate how attaining that item will affect their sense of well-being, disputants are likely to have difficulty identifying what they really want in negotiation for the very same reason. Just like the consumer who erroneously believes he will be much happier if he purchases a new BMW, the disputant seeking to obtain money or vindication or whatever else may very well overestimate the impact obtaining it will have on her sense of well-being. Indeed, it seems reasonable to speculate that the added complexity of a negotiation—in particular, the tension and conflict between the parties—will make it even more difficult for disputants to discern what they really want.

This has important implications for lawyers and other agents who represent disputants in negotiation. Under the prevailing model of the lawyer-client relationship—the so-called "client-centered" counseling model—the client is viewed as a fully competent and autonomous actor who retains full decisional authority over her case.[15] The lawyer, by contrast, is a largely passive and objective advisor who strives to avoid encroaching on client autonomy in the decision-making process.[16]

This model of the lawyer-client relationship is arguably embodied in many of the ethical rules that govern lawyer conduct. For example, Rule 1.2 of the Model Rules of Professional Conduct provides that "[a] lawyer shall abide by a client's decisions concerning the objectives of representation," "consult with the client as to the means by which they are pursued," and "abide by a client's decision whether to settle a matter."[17] Likewise, Canon 7-7 of the Model Code of Professional Responsibility provides that "it is for the client to decide whether he will accept a settlement offer,"[18] and Canon 7-8 provides that "the lawyer should always remember that the decision whether to forego legally available objectives or methods because of non-legal factors is ultimately for the client and not for himself."[19]

The client-centered approach to lawyering—both in theory and as reflected in various ethical rules—is both sensible and respectful. After all, the client is the principal, and the lawyer is merely the agent hired by the client. The client "owns" the problem, and she will reap the primary benefit (or bear the primary brunt) of the outcome. Thus, it seems appropriate to vest decision-making power solely in her hands. Research on the impact bias gives one pause, however, because it suggests that clients may have difficulty predicting what they want out of a negotiation. Even given this difficulty, the client will generally know better than anyone else what she wants. But in at least some circumstances, her lawyer may have insight that she does not. Namely, in those cases where the client is a "one-shotter" and the lawyer is a "repeat player" who has represented dozens or even hundreds of similarly situated clients in like cases, it seems *possible* that the lawyer might have a deeper understanding of the client's underlying wants.[20]

Suppose, for example, that a lawyer named "Linda" represents a client named "Clint." Clint used to be an executive with Company X. He enjoyed working at Company X, and several close friends remain there. Unfortunately, Company X fired him a year ago despite good performance evaluations. Clint believes, based on a couple of e-mails his former boss sent to a friend, that he was terminated due to his race. After investigating Clint's claim, Linda filed suit against Company X on Clint's behalf, asserting myriad violations under Title VII, the primary federal employment discrimination law.

Upon receiving a copy of the complaint, the lawyer for Company X indicated that the company would like to meet to discuss settlement of Clint's claim. Linda agreed. Before the settlement talks, she arranged a meeting with Clint to make sure she understood his interests. At this meeting, Clint told Linda he wanted "a lot of money." When pressed to explain why he wanted "a lot of money," Clint told her that he wanted the money to provide a luxurious lifestyle for himself and his family and to provide him with the financial resources that would enable him to retire.

Armed with this information, Linda met with the lawyer from Company X to discuss settlement. After lengthy discussions about the alleged facts, the applicable law, Clint's interests, and Company X's interests, the lawyer for Company X offered to settle the case by paying Clint a modest sum of money reflecting his "back pay" and by re-hiring him at Company X. He also informed Linda that Company X had already fired Clint's former boss.

Linda told him she would discuss the offer with Clint. When she met with Clint, Linda described some of the advantages associated with the offer, and she also acknowledged some of the advantages associated with foregoing settlement and proceeding to trial. Clint told her that he would rather go to trial than accept the offer because he wanted the flexibility, financial security, and lifestyle that a substantial award would bring.

Having represented several similarly situated clients in the past and having familiarized herself with the research on the impact bias, Linda is skeptical that Clint truly understands what he wants. She worries that even if he prevails at trial and recovers a sizeable award, his contentment with that award will be short-lived. She knows, for example, that money (beyond a comfortable, middle-class amount) contributes minimally to happiness.[21] She also knows that friendships and social interaction do increase one's sense of well-being,[22] and Clint has several close friends at Company X with whom he would interact on a much more regular basis if he were to return to work. Finally, she knows that people are happier when they are fully engaged in some productive activity,[23] and Clint seems to have had this kind of engagement at Company X.

So what is Linda to do? She can certainly discuss these issues with Clint by informing him about the impact bias. She could tell him, for example, that people often make poor predictions about what they want and how happy they will feel if they get it. "I think you ought to know, Clint," she could say, "that no matter what they hope for when they buy a ticket, many lottery winners end up being no happier than they were before they won."[24]

But besides providing this information to Clint, how hard can Linda push him to settle the case on these terms? Under the client-centered view of the lawyer's role, and perhaps even under the applicable ethical rules, she probably cannot push too hard. Research drawn from the emerging field of hedonic psychology *suggests*, however, that she should be allowed—and maybe even encouraged—to play a much more active role in Clint's decision-making.

Linda's dilemma is but a microcosm of the broader dilemma faced by policy makers, regulators, and others trying to facilitate efficient decision-making in society. The impact bias and other departures from purely "rational" decision-making may warrant intervention by outsiders or regulation by authorities.[25] Open consideration of paternalism of this sort raises hackles in the legal community at large because it is deemed taboo to impinge on individual autonomy and freedom of choice. But it may be possible to find some middle ground by employing non-coercive interventions—including defaults, framing, and cooling off periods—to assist those who might miswant in negotiation. Linda might use each of these tools to help Clint make a better decision, while leaving both of his options—going to trial with the hope of a large judgment or returning to work with back pay—available.

Default options have real force in choice situations because individuals generally prefer the status quo.[26] For example, companies have raised the savings rates of their employees by changing the default from non-enrollment to automatic participation in company 401(K) plans.[27] Likewise, Linda might suggest to Clint that returning to Company X should be viewed as his default because it restores him to his original position. By shifting Clint's perception of his default to his prior employment with Company X, Linda may be able to influence the way he views his litigation options, placing the power of the status quo and inertia behind the option that seems most likely to promote his well-being.

Individuals are also influenced by the way options are framed, specifically whether the "downsides" or "upsides" are highlighted. For example, when choosing between a sure gain and a probabilistic gain with a comparable expected value, most people will choose the sure thing. In the context of Linda's representation of Clint, Linda might emphasize that settlement reflects a sure gain, while Clint's expected judgment at trial is only a probabilistic gain. With this frame, Linda implicitly invokes "prospect theory"[28] to increase the attractiveness of settlement and decrease the attractiveness of trial.

Cooling-off periods between the presentation of options and the final choice may also promote well-being. In negotiation, making the final decision away from the bargaining table offers two potential benefits. First, it might reduce the cognitive load on the decision-maker at the bargaining table itself, and research suggests that reducing cognitive load can increase the accuracy of individuals' affective forecasts.[29] Second, a "time out" might also enable the decision-maker to manage his emotions more effectively. For example, if Clint's motivation in taking Company X to court was vengeance, he might overvalue his long-term satisfaction from hurting the company, especially when he is in the same room as Company X representatives. Requiring that he wait until he is at a remove might help him make a better decision. Finally, Linda might suggest to Clint that he use the intermission to produce a detailed diary of what his typical day will look like if he takes the company's offer or if he goes to court and wins a big award. How will he fill his day between waking and falling asleep? In other settings, this exercise has helped the diarists counteract the impact bias.[30]

Conclusion

Negotiation scholars and practitioners have long known that disputants may not get what they want at the bargaining table. Perhaps what they want is unreasonable, unavailable, or even unlawful; perhaps they will commit decision errors in the negotiation process due to "heuristics and biases"; [Korobkin & Guthrie, *Heuristics*] perhaps their counterparts will simply "out-negotiate" them using successful "hardball" negotiation tactics or the more subtle but still effective "compliance tactics" employed by advertisers and retailers; [Guthrie, *Compliance*] perhaps other "barriers" might prevent them from getting what they want.[31]

What negotiation scholars and practitioners have generally assumed, however, is that disputants know what they want. The work reported in this Chapter calls this assumption into question. In his *New York Times Magazine* interview, Gilbert explained it this way, "You know, the Stones said, 'You can't always get what you want.' [But] I don't think that's the problem. The problem is you can't always *know* what you want."[32] Likewise, the most significant problem plaguing disputants may very well be that they can't always know what they want.

The dilemma for lawyers (who are susceptible to the impact bias in their own right, of course) is what to do with this insight. In our view, the lawyer who is truly client-centered will neither substitute her judgment for that of her client nor turn a blind eye to the very real possibility that her client is mistaken about what he really wants. Client-centeredness requires her to eschew extreme paternalism on the one hand and extreme anti-paternalism on the other in favor of a more balanced approach to legal counseling.

Endnotes

This Chapter was adapted from Chris Guthrie & David Sally, *The Impact of the Impact Bias on Negotiation*, 87 MARQUETTE LAW REVIEW 817 (2004).

[1] ROGER FISHER, ET AL., GETTING TO YES: NEGOTIATING AGREEMENT WITHOUT GIVING IN 40 (2d ed. 1991).
[2] *Id.*
[3] Timothy D. Wilson & Daniel T. Gilbert, *Affective Forecasting*, 35 ADVANCES IN EXPERIMENTAL SOCIAL PSYCHOLOGY 345, 347 (2003).
[4] *Id.* at 347.
[5] *Id.* at 349.
[6] *Id.* at 351.
[7] *See* Daniel T. Gilbert, et al., *The Trouble with Vronsky: Impact Bias in the Forecasting of Future Affective States, in* THE WISDOM IN FEELING: PSYCHOLOGICAL PROCESSES IN EMOTIONAL INTELLIGENCE 114, 116 (Lisa Feldman Barrett & Peter Salovey eds., 2002).
[8] Wilson & Gilbert, *supra* note 3, at 366.
[9] David A. Schkade & Daniel Kahneman, *Does Living in California Make People Happy? A Focusing Illusion in Judgments of Life Satisfaction*, 9 PSYCHOLOGICAL SCIENCE 340 (1998).
[10] Elizabeth W. Dunn, et al., *Location, Location, Location: The Misprediction of Satisfaction in Housing Lotteries*, 29 PERSONALITY & SOCIAL PSYCHOLOGY BULLETIN 1421, 1422 (2003).
[11] Wilson & Gilbert, *supra* note 3, at 371.
[12] *Id.*
[13] *See* Gilbert, et al., *supra* note 7, at 124-25.
[14] Jon Gertner, *The Futile Pursuit of Happiness*, N.Y. TIMES MAGAZINE, Sept. 7, 2003, at 46.
[15] DAVID A. BINDER, ET AL., LAWYERS AS COUNSELOR 282 (2d ed. 2001).
[16] *Id.* at 288-89.
[17] MODEL RULES OF PROFESSIONAL CONDUCT, Rule 1.2(a) (1999).
[18] MODEL CODE OF PROFESSIONAL RESPONSIBILITY, EC 7-7 (1986).
[19] *Id.* at EC 7-8.
[20] Marc Galanter, *Why the 'Haves' Come Out Ahead: Speculating on the Limits of Legal Change*, 9 LAW & SOCIETY REVIEW 95, 97 (1974).
[21] *See, e.g.*, ROBERT E. LANE, THE LOSS OF HAPPINESS IN MARKET DEMOCRACIES (1996) (demonstrating empirically that increased wealth beyond a poverty level has little to do with a sense of happiness); Mihaly Csikszentmihalyi, *If We Are So Rich, Why Aren't We Happy?*, 54 AMERICAN PSYCHOLOGIST 821, 822-23 (1999) (summarizing studies showing that material wealth has little impact on subjective well-being); David G. Myers, *The Funds, Friends, and Faith of Happy People*, 55 AMERICAN PSYCHOLOGIST 56, 59 (2000) ("Happiness tends to be lower among the very poor. Once comfortable, however, more money provides diminishing returns on happiness.").
[22] *See, e.g.*, LANE, *supra* note 21, at 6 ("[W]e get happiness primarily from people ..."); Myers, *supra* note 21, at 62 (reporting results that "confirm the correlation between social support and well-being").
[23] *See, e.g.*, MIHALY CSIKSZENTMIHALYI, FLOW: THE PSYCHOLOGY OF OPTIMAL EXPERIENCE 3 (1990) ("Contrary to what we usually believe, moments like these, the best moments in our lives, are not the passive, receptive, relaxing times—although such experiences can also be enjoyable, if we have worked hard to attain them. The best moments usually occur when a person's body or mind is stretched to its limits in a voluntary effort to accomplish something difficult and worthwhile.").
[24] *See, e.g.*, Philip Brickman, et al., *Lottery Winners and Accident Victims: Is Happiness Relative?*, 36 JOURNAL OF PERSONALITY & SOCIAL PSYCHOLOGY 917 (1978).
[25] *See, e.g.*, Colin Camerer, et al., *Regulation for Conservatives: Behavioral Economics and the Case for 'Asymmetric Paternalism,'* 151 UNIVERSITY OF PENNSYLVANIA LAW REVIEW 1211 (2003); Cass R. Sunstein & Richard H. Thaler, *Libertarian Paternalism is Not an Oxymoron*, 70 UNIVERSITY OF CHICAGO LAW REVIEW 1159 (2003).
[26] *See* William Samuelson & Robert Zeckhauser, *Status Quo Bias in Decision Making*, 1 JOURNAL OF RISK & UNCERTAINTY 7 (1988).
[27] *See* Brigitte C. Madrian & Dennis F. Shea, *The Power of Suggestion: Inertia in 401(k) Participation and Savings Behavior*, 116 QUARTERLY JOURNAL OF ECONOMICS 1149 (2001).
[28] *See* Daniel Kahneman & Amos Tversky, *Prospect Theory: An Analysis of Decision Under Risk*, 47 ECONOMETRICA 263 (1979).
[29] *See* Daniel T. Gilbert, et al., *The Future is Now: Temporal Correction in Affective Forecasting*, 88 ORGANIZATION OF BEHAVIOR & HUMAN DECISION PROCESSES 430, 434-36 (2002).
[30] *See* Wilson & Gilbert, *supra* note 3.
[31] *See generally* BARRIERS TO CONFLICT RESOLUTION (Kenneth Arrow, et al. eds., 1995).
[32] Gertner, *supra* note 14, at 46 (emphasis in original).

❧ 33 ❦

In Our Bones (Or Brains): Behavioral Biology

Douglas H. Yarn & Gregory Todd Jones

Editors' Note: *Research on our innate responses to conflict, and to different situations that arise in negotiation, has been burgeoning. It's not just a matter of fight-or-flight; it turns out we are programmed in a number of overlapping and sometimes competing ways. And, as Yarn and Jones summarize, the research now suggests that we may be primed to collaborate more than to compete.*

We negotiate to influence the other side's behavior, and to do this effectively, we need a good understanding of people. This understanding often involves some knowledge and appreciation of the personalities, traits, characteristics, and backgrounds of the specific individuals with whom you are negotiating. Obviously, people are different, and many of the authors in this section will discuss recognizing and dealing with such differences, be they cultural, [Kelly, xx; Goh, xx; Avruch, *Buyer—Seller*] gender-based, [Kolb & Putnam, *Gender*] or a consequence of unique developmental and experiential histories. [Deutsch, *Internal Conflict*; Jeglic & Jeglic, *Disordered People*] However, you cannot discuss differences without having some underlying assumptions about commonalities. A good negotiator also understands *how* people *in general* behave and how to use this knowledge to predict and influence behavior. Thus, our starting point for understanding the other side (and ourselves for that matter) should be our "sameness," those behavioral traits we share as human beings, the shared aspects of our human nature. In this chapter, we address the problem of human nature in negotiation by discussing possible contributions behavioral biology may make to the theory and practice of negotiation.[1] We conclude that behavioral biology helps us to predict and influence behavior in negotiation because it reveals more about *why* people behave the way they often do. We also take the opportunity to provide the reader with references to a small part of the vast and rapidly expanding literature in this area, heretofore mostly ignored by the field of conflict resolution.

Why Are Negotiators Seemingly Irrational?

The dominant paradigm of negotiation promoted in most current conflict resolution practice and theory assumes that the negotiators are *homo economicus*, and thus behave and decide in accordance with a model of rational expectations, that is, with fully defined preferences, complete knowledge of available alternatives, and full information shared with other parties. Yet, experienced negotiators and mediators know that this rationality is difficult and most often impossible to achieve. The significant differences between these theoretical expectations and what negotiators actually experience can be traced to the evolution of the human brain.

At its most fundamental level, human behavior is a biological phenomenon, because, ultimately, all theories about human behavior are theories about the brain—an organ operating on physical principles that receives stimuli, makes computations, and directs behavioral outputs. Far from being an all-purpose computer or "blank slate,"[2] the brain has been shaped over millions of years by evolutionary forces producing a *species-typical* brain[3] that produces species-typical behavioral outputs in response to various stimuli. When modern *homo sapiens* appeared, approximately 100,000 years ago, our brains were pretty much as they are now—adapted to meet the challenges of life in an ancestral environment that biologists refer to as the "environment of evolutionary adaptation" (the "EEA"). The EEA was both a physical and social environment the challenges of which might be boiled down to food choice (eating), predator avoidance (survival), and mate selection (reproduction). If it is common for humans to exhibit a given behavior today, then the predisposition to behave that way may have enhanced survival and reproduction over time in the EEA and as a result became "hard-wired" in our brains through natural selection.

While the 100,000 years that have passed since life in the ancestral environment may seem like a long time, in evolutionary terms this is merely a blink of the eye, offering little time for natural selection to evolve our brains further. The environment in which we live, however, has changed dramatically in this time period. In short, we have a Paleolithic mind in a post-modern age, and behavior that seems irrational in the present environment may be perfectly rational when considered in the context of the EEA.[4] This mismatch between our ancestral evolved brains and the present day environment may explain the various heuristics, biases, and emotions [Korobkin & Guthrie, *Heuristics*; Shapiro, *Emotions*] that seem to irrationally depart from the model of *homo economicus* decision-making.

What Underlies Competitive or Cooperative Negotiation Behavior?

Most if not all of these heuristics, biases, and emotions have a biological explanation rooted in the tensions between competitive and cooperative behaviors that are a consequence of our sociality. Overly competitive behaviors are often blamed for negotiation impasses, but from a biological perspective, competitive behavior is hardly surprising, as purely selfish behavior certainly would seem to enhance reproduction and the survivability of one's genes in a world of scarce resources. And yet, we also cooperate, and this too increases reproductive fitness.[5] In the EEA, social group formation was cooperative behavior that improved our ancestors' ability to warn of and fight off predators and to find mates. With social living, however, comes conflict and competition over resources. The adaptive way to deal with conflict with others of one's species and thereby maintain the benefits of social cohesion is essentially to negotiate, to form friendships, alliances, and coalitions, members of which would protect and share resources. Such cooperative, altruistic behavior among kin makes biological sense and is common among animals—the closer the kin, the more shared genes.[6] Altruistic behavior towards non-kin is also common among social animals and has been explained by the notion of direct reciprocity—by helping B today, A expects B to reciprocate tomorrow.[7]

As a social behavior, negotiation involves some degree of cooperation to achieve a mutually-accepted agreement. But there is a critical tension between cooperative, altruistic behavior and competitive behavior—how does A trust B to behave fairly? While it is our nature to cooperate,[8] it is also our nature to "cheat" and take advantage of other's tendencies to cooperate, because the competitive selfish gene[9] tempts B to defect and merely free ride, to gain the benefits of cooperation without the costs.[10] Negotiation engages our unconscious evolved behavioral drives to be both competitive and cooperative.

Some Biological Preferences in Negotiation Behavior

The inherent tension between our behavioral tendencies to compete or cooperate presents the negotiator with some fundamental problems: how do you determine whom to trust, whether you've been treated fairly, and what to do when cheated? To some extent, we may be hard-wired to answer these questions, and in the following subsections, we present some of the emerging research on the sources of emotion surrounding trust, fairness, vengefulness, and forgiveness.

Trust

Should I trust the other side, and how do I get them to trust me? Intuitively, we understand that trust is at the foundation of virtually all social interaction and is crucial to economic, political, and social success.[11] [Lewicki, *Trust*] Of course, some degree of trust is essential for successful negotiations.

Considering its social importance, it is not surprising that scientists are beginning to uncover a biological basis for trust among humans that may be an evolutionary adaptation to promote the benefits of social exchange.[12] Some have found neuro-chemical determinants of trusting behavior, including the neuropeptide oxytocin, which can be stimulated by touch and other social interaction and seems to induce trusting behavior.[13] Others have employed functional magnetic resonance imaging (fMRI) to locate the neural correlates of trust, and have discovered that the "intention to trust" was mirrored by neural activation in the caudate nucleus, an area of the brain associated with reward processing.[14] Interestingly, this area of the brain is also activated when subjects receive money, consume cocaine, or view pictures of loved ones. Thus, trust may offer physiological rewards of its own, and humans may have an inherent "taste" or "preference" to trust or even to be trustworthy.

Although trust among family members and friends may be predictable based upon the experience of repeated cooperative encounters, this taste for trust may help explain why we trust unrelated strangers to the extent that we do.[15] This also makes people potentially vulnerable to being taken advantage of, so our brains have evolved an ability to interpret what others are thinking or intend based on their actions and communication, verbal and non-verbal. This "theory of mind" develops by approximately 4-5 years of age and is evidenced by the ability to attribute independent mental states to others, i.e., to understand that people may hold different perceptions or beliefs than you.[16] [Sally, *Theory of Mind*] This "mentalising" performed by the brain requires the stimulus of social signals, one source of which is the human face.[17] Researchers have found that many facial expressions are universal in meaning[18] and that even the most accomplished "poker face" is incapable of masking some "micro-expressions."[19] We also look for other social information, such as reputation. [Tinsley, et al., *Reputations*] One theory is that humans evolved the linguistic capabilities of the brain for the primary purpose of exchanging information with each other about who to trust.[20] When people talk about you, it gives others clues as to whether or not you are trustworthy.

A Sense of Fairness

In negotiation, a seemingly rational solution is often rejected by the other side as unfair. This has been found in an experimental setting using the simple ultimatum game in which two players are given the opportunity to win a sum of money. [Sally & Jones, *Game Theory*] The proposer suggests how the sum should be split between the two. The responder either accepts or rejects the offer. If accepted, the money is divided accordingly. If rejected, the players receive nothing.[21] Game theory predicts the rational outcome: the proposer will offer the smallest possible share and the responder, believing that something is better than nothing, will accept any positive share.[22] However, in a large number of human experiments, this is not what happens. Most proposers offer a 40 to 50% share and half of the responders reject offers less than 30%.[23] The most frequent outcome is an even split. Most people, it turns out, are strongly motivated by concerns for fairness and reciprocity, even when it is costly.[24] Similar behavior has been observed in nonhuman primates.[25] How might such fairness norms, [Welsh, *Fairness*] often contrary to strict self-interest, have evolved?

Game theoretic models and computer simulations of bargaining tasks have demonstrated that fairness can evolve in ultimatum game contexts where the players can obtain information about deals that have been made in the past—in other words, where players have reputations.[26] Other experimental research shows that when these fairness norms are implemented, intentions matter.[27] Unfair outcomes, when unintended, are not judged as harshly.

The proximate mechanisms of these fairness norms have recently been explored by a team of scientists using functional magnetic resonance imaging (fMRI) to scan the brains of players engaged in an ultimatum game as they responded to fair and unfair offers proffered by both human proposers and computers.[28] The bilateral anterior insula, a brain region often associated with negative emotional states like anger and disgust, showed higher activation for unfair offers, and in fact, the level of activation was correlated with the proportion of rejected offers. On the other hand, the dorsolateral prefrontal cortex, a region linked to cognitive processes such as goal maintenance, also showed higher activation for unfair offers, but was instead correlated with those offers that were ultimately accepted. The subjects seemed to be conflicted between the standard economic solution of accepting any positive amount and the more emotional response associated with unfairness—and this conflict was confirmed by activation in the anterior cingulated cortex, a brain region implicated in the detection of cognitive conflict. By the way, these activations were not as high when the unfair offers came from computer partners. After all, computers can't have intentions. But humans do, and from an evolutionary point of view, this sense of fairness helps one judge the intentions of others, thereby determining who to trust. In addition, it serves as a heuristic to help individuals from being taken advantage of.[29] [Welsh, *Fairness;* Wade-Benzoni, *Future*]

A Taste for Revenge

People do take advantage of others, and at the heart of most disputing is the perception by one or both parties that the other has benefited to their detriment. This sense of being aggrieved poses a huge barrier to negotiating agreement; it is not uncommon to find disputants engaged in litigation even when the costs exceed the rational value of settlement. Such vengeful behavior may be rewarded by the brain. Scientists have scanned subjects' brains using Positron Emission Tomography (PET) while the subjects made the decision whether to punish a person who had abused trust by violating a fairness norm.[30] The study showed that, as with decisions to trust, the caudate nucleus, a reward center, was activated while making the punish decision. These results reflect an expected satisfaction from punishing unfairness that may be an evolutionary adaptation that helped maintain group solidarity and cooperation while allowing the individual to assert a social reputation.[31]

This neurochemistry has evolutionary roots. The kin altruism[32] and reciprocal altruism[33] discussed earlier are not enough to explain the successful operation of reciprocity norms when dealing with strangers; however, if humans generally were known to be willing to punish unfair and non-cooperative behavior even though the punishment is costly and yields no material gain, it would encourage cooperation and discourage subsequent cheating and non-reciprocal behavior. While this may immediately bring to mind the classic "tit-for-tat" strategy,[34] altruistic punishment, also known as strong reciprocity[35] or "moralistic aggression" in animal behavior where it is regularly observed, is truly altruistic, producing public good at significant expense to those who punish. For example, chimps will not tolerate food sharing with, or groom, other chimps that don't share food or help groom.[36] In its extreme, social animals may ostracize repeat offenders, which in the EEA would have likely resulted in death. This selfless policing of social norms is a public good that contributes to social cohesion. It is robust in various behavioral experimental conditions,[37] and strongly reciprocal behaviors are regularly described in human experience.[38] Thus, even in the face of a rational solution, it is not surprising when negotiators get angry, show increasing resistance, or force an impasse if they still hold a grudge from some previous encounter or perceive that the other side is behaving badly or unfairly in the current negotiations.

The Need to Forgive and Apologize

A negotiated solution is hardly possible in the face of on-going vengeful, punishing behavior, but if individuals are interdependent, they will need to resume cooperative interaction at some point. Other social primates engage in conciliatory and consolation behaviors to restore important relationships after fights and other aggression.[39] These may be the evolutionary antecedents of the human behaviors associated with seeking and granting forgiveness. [Waldman & Luskin, *Anger & Forgiveness*] The evolution of such behaviors makes sense. For the person feeling aggrieved, on-going negative reciprocity can prove too costly. In dynamic environments where responses to social norms are in flux, decisions to punish may not only be costly in and of themselves, but may carry steep opportunity costs associated with failing to cooperate with a previous defector who has newly decided to cooperate.[40] Indeed, the human need to forgive is a significant emotion for which scientists are beginning to trace the neural correlates.[41] In turn, targets of moralistic aggression find it advantageous to engage in behavior that hastens forgiveness. A recent body of theoretical scholarship[42] suggests that apologetic behavior evolved for this purpose. Indeed, computational studies recently performed at the Primate Research Institute at Kyoto University in Japan suggest that apology can play a role similar to altruistic punishment as a means of maintaining cooperation, as long as the apology, which signals a willingness to conform to social norms in the future, is sufficiently costly.[43] [Brown & Robbennolt, *Apology*]

Some Cursory Conclusions

So what is a negotiator who can't tell a PET scan from an fMRI image to make of all of this? Our brains and, as a direct consequence, the nature of conflict and cooperation, have been shaped by millions of years of evolution that have encoded specific behaviors in the function of our neuroanatomy. Regions of the negotiator's brain struggle between competing and cooperating, and consequently natural proclivities surrounding trust, fairness, vengefulness, and forgiveness can both impede and facilitate negotiations.

Thanks to our shared anatomy, we are pre-programmed, even addicted in a very real sense, to trust others. A negotiator's natural inclination, particularly when lacking negative experience and social information, will be to trust, and perhaps to be more trustworthy. This inclination can be strengthened by simple preparations that promote production of the appropriate neuropeptides: comfortable surroundings, friendliness, the willingness to extend a hand (touch), and the sharing of food. And over the course of repeated interactions, you can reinforce this inclination further by establishing a reputation for trustworthiness and fairness. The same reputation is likely to become social information that will be exchanged and thereby enhance your ability to influence trusting behavior in negotiations with strangers in the future. Trust, however, is a two-edged sword, and awareness of our tendencies to trust may help us to avoid exploitation.

This offers some prescriptions for successful negotiations. We should give our partners every reason to respond to their natural inclination towards fairness, with appeal to objective standards and with assurances, where possible, that unavoidable negative outcomes were not a product of our intent. And perchance, where we might be perceived as acting unfairly, we should not be surprised if our partner reciprocates with behavior that may be irrational, even extremely costly. Our understanding of this tendency in ourselves as well as in others can help us avoid irrational escalation.

Where trust is breached, we must be aware that the same brain region that gives us a warm glow while viewing pictures of our loved ones also drives us to punish unfairness even when the act of punishment will cost more than we could ever hope to gain. Understanding the power of strong reciprocity can help us to manage the urge within ourselves as well as to be prepared for the reaction in others. If the other side feels we have acted unfairly and breached their trust, we should appeal to their desire to forgive by offering an apology. Often we must be given a reason to forgive, and one effective way to do so is to provide a costly signal that unfair behavior will not be repeated in the future.

The central message is not a particularly astounding one: successful social interaction generally, and negotiation more specifically, requires a finely tuned understanding of other people's intentions and actions. Behavioral biology teaches us that we have evolved brains that are usually pretty accurate in unconsciously making such calculations. Nevertheless, a more conscious understanding of the biology underlying negotiating behaviors may help us anticipate some behaviors and develop strategies to influence cooperative negotiating behaviors. Above all, we should not lose sight of the fact that the neuroanatomy that accounts for adaptive behaviors and emotions involving competition and cooperation has been selected over millions of years with survival of the species as the only objective. Far from being pathological deviations from the traditional model of rational decision-making, these are shared characteristics that account for who we are and define our nature as human beings. As behavioral negotiation theory has begun to mature, *homo economicus* has begun to evolve into *homo sapiens*. That is, human behavior has become more central to negotiation theory.[44] Negotiators should introduce themselves to *homo sapiens* and get to know him well.

Endnotes

[1] For the behavioral biology experts among our readers, we hasten to acknowledge that our treatment of the studies we have chosen to review is far from complete. So much so, that some may argue that our sins of omission have rendered some material inexact. While this is certainly a fair criticism, given length considerations, our choice was to carve out elements of the biology that best illuminated the practice of negotiation. For all of the details, we refer the reader to the generous notes included at the end of the chapter.

[2] STEVEN PINKER, THE BLANK SLATE: THE MODERN DENIAL OF HUMAN NATURE (2002).

[3] JEROME H. BARKOW, ET AL., THE ADAPTED MIND (1992).

[4] Owen Jones, *Time-Shifted Rationality and the Law of Law's Leverage: Behavioral Economics Meets Behavioral Biology,* 95 NORTHWESTERN UNIVERSITY LAW REVIEW 1141 (2001).

[5] In fact, competition and cooperation has been encoded in organisms without brains at all, purely a function of genetics. Social amoeba and other microbes engage in cooperative, altruistic behaviors to enhance survival in resource-poor environments. They also cheat and punish. *See, e.g.,* Michael Travisano & Gregory J. Velicer, *Strategies of Microbial Cheater Control,* 12 TRENDS IN MICROBIOLOGY 72 (2004); Gregory J. Velicer, *Social Strife in the Microbial World,* 11 TRENDS IN MICROBIOLOGY 330 (2003); Richard E. Lenski & Gregory J. Velicer, *Games Microbes Play,* 1 SELECTION 51 (2000); Gregory J. Velicer, et al., *Developmental Cheating in the Social Bacterium Myxococcus Xanthus,* 404 NATURE 598 (2000).

[6] William Hamilton, *The Genetical Evolution of Social Behavior,* 37 JOURNAL OF THEORETICAL BIOLOGY 1 (1964).

[7] Robert Trivers, *The Evolution of Reciprocal Altruism,* 46 QUARTERLY REVIEW OF BIOLOGY 35 (1971).

[8] Functional magnetic resonance imaging (fMRI) reveals areas of the brain associates specifically with cooperative behaviors. James K. Rilling, et al., *A Neural Basis for Social Cooperation,* 35 NEURON 395 (2002).

[9] Indeed, there may be no particular gene specifically associated with competitiveness—although we have yet to see—but the "selfish gene" is a widely used term popularized by Richard Dawkins. *See* RICHARD DAWKINS, THE SELFISH GENE (1990).

[10] Research shows that humans are in essence natural-born liars. David Livingstone Smith, *Natural-Born Liars,* SCIENTIFIC AMERICAN MIND (June 2005).

[11] *See* Gregory Todd Jones, *Trust, Institutionalization, & Corporate Reputations: Public Independent Fact-Finding from a Risk Management Perspective,* 13 UNIVERSITY OF MIAMI BUSINESS LAW REVIEW 121 (2005); Ernst Fehr & John A. List, *The Hidden Costs and Returns of Incentives—Trust and Trustworthiness Among CEOs,* 2 JOURNAL OF THE EUROPEAN ECONOMIC ASSOCIATION 743 (2004); R. William Ide & Douglas H. Yarn, *Public Independent Fact-Finding: A Trust-Generating Institution for an Age of Corporate Illegitimacy and Public Mistrust,* 56 VANDERBILT LAW REVIEW 1113 (2003); Paul J. Zak, *Trust,* 7 JOURNAL OF FINANCIAL TRANSFORMATION 13 (2003); Stephen Knack & Paul J. Zak, *Building Trust: Public Policy, Interpersonal Trust, and Economic Development,* 10 SUPREME COURT ECONOMIC REVIEW 91 (2002); Paul J. Zak & Stephen Knack, *Trust and Growth,* 111 ECONOMIC JOURNAL 295 (2001); Stephen Knack & Phillip Keefer, *Does Social Capital Have an Economic Payoff? A Cross-Country Investigation,* 112 QUARTERLY JOURNAL OF ECONOMICS 1251 (1997); Joyce Berg, et al., *Trust, Reciprocity, and Social History,* 10 GAMES AND ECONOMIC BEHAVIOR 12 (1995); JAMES S. COLEMAN, FOUNDATIONS OF SOCIAL THEORY (1990); Kenneth Arrow, *Gifts and Exchanges,* 1 PHILOSOPHY AND PUBLIC AFFAIRS 343 (1972).

[12] Paul J. Zak, *Trust: A Temporary Human Attachment Facilitated by Oxytocin,* 28 BEHAVIORAL AND BRAIN SCIENCES 368 (2005); Paul J. Zak, et al., *The Neurobiology of Trust,* 1032 ANNALS OF THE ACADEMY OF SCIENCES 224 (2004); Michael Kosfeld, et al., *Oxytocin Increases Trust in Humans,* 435 NATURE 673 (2005); Brooks King-Casas, et al., *Getting to Know You: Reputation and Trust in a Two-Person Economic Exchange,* 308 SCIENCE 78 (2005); Richard A. Depue & Jeannine V. Morrone-Strupinsky, *A Neurobiological Model of Affiliative Bonding: Implications for Conceptualizing a Human Trait of Affiliation,* 28 BEHAVIORAL AND BRAIN SCIENCES 313 (2005); Ernst Fehr, et al., *Neuroeconomic Foundations of Trust and Social Preferences,* AMERICAN ECONOMIC REVIEW (forthcoming); Thomas Insel & Larry Young, *The Neurobiology of Attachment,* 2 NEUROSCIENCE 129 (2001).

[13] Zak, *supra* note 12; Michael Kosfeld, et al., *supra* note 12; Antonio Damasio, *Brain Trust,* 435 NATURE 571 (2005); Paul J. Zak, et al., *supra* note 12.

[14] King-Casas, et al., *supra* note 12.

[15] Zak, *supra* note 12.

[16] Biological evidence of the theory of mind function is provided by studies of people who suffer from schizophrenia, autism, or Asperger's syndrome in whom the attribution of mental states is impaired. Tom F. D. Farrow, et al., *Investigating the Functional Anatomy of Empathy and Forgiveness,* 12 NEUROREPORT 2433 (2001). Sally and Hill investigated the relationship between this "mentalising" and performance in social dilemma games—in

children and adults with and without autistic spectrum disorders. Their results suggest that strategic responses, both in the well-known prisoner's dilemma and in the use of strategically unequal offers in bargaining tasks, are associated with this mentalising ability. Elisabeth Hill & David Sally, *Dilemmas and Bargains: Autism, Theory-of-Mind, Cooperation, and Fairness*, (Inst. of Cognitive Neuroscience, Working Paper 2005) (*available at* http://ssrn.com/abstract=407040). Elisabeth Hill, et al., *Does Mentalising Ability Influence Cooperative Decision-Making in a Social Dilemma? Introspective Evidence from a Study of Adults with Autism Spectrum Disorder*, 11 JOURNAL OF CONSCIOUSNESS STUDIES 144 (2004); David Sally, *Into the Looking Glass: Discerning the Social Mind Through the Mindblind*, 18 ADVANCES IN GROUP PROCESSES 99 (2001). Successful social interaction seems to depend on an ability to get your mind around the minds of others.

[17] Research on canine play-fighting behavior shows the large role of signaling in communicating whether individuals are merely playing or are actually being aggressive, *see* Marc Bekoff, *Play Signals as Punctuation: The Structure of Social Play in Canids*, 132 BEHAVIOUR 419 (1995).

[18] Paul Ekman & Wallace V. Friesen, *Constants Across Cultures in the Face and Emotion*, 17 JOURNAL OF PERSONALITY AND SOCIAL PSYCHOLOGY 124 (1971).

[19] Paul Ekman & Wallace V. Friesen, *Nonverbal Leakage and Clues to Deception*, 32 PSYCHIATRY 88 (1969).

[20] R. DUNBAR, GROOMING, GOSSIP AND THE EVOLUTION OF LANGUAGE (1996).

[21] COLIN CAMERER, ET AL., ADVANCES IN BEHAVIORAL ECONOMICS (2004).

[22] Martin A. Nowak, et al., *Fairness Versus Reason in the Ultimatum Game* 289, SCIENCE 1773 (2000).

[23] Gary Bolton & Rami Zwick, *Anonymity Versus Punishment in Ultimatum Bargaining*, 10 GAMES AND ECONOMIC BEHAVIOR 95 (1995); Werner Güth & Reinhard Tietz, *Ultimatum Bargaining Behavior: A Survey and Comparison of Experimental Results*, 11 JOURNAL OF ECONOMIC PSYCHOLOGY 417 (1990); Richard Thaler, *The Winner's Curse*, 2 JOURNAL OF ECONOMIC PERSPECTIVES 191 (1988); Werner Güth, et al., *An Experimental Analysis of Ultimatum Bargaining*, 3 JOURNAL OF ECONOMIC BEHAVIOR AND ORGANIZATION 367 (1982).

[24] Ernst Fehr & Klaus Schmidt, *Theories of Fairness and Reciprocity—Evidence and Economic Applications* (Institute for Empirical Research in Economics, Working Paper No. 75, 2000) (available at http://www.uibk.ac.at/c/c4/c409/kerschbamer/s05/LS-Fehr-Schmidt-a.pdf).

[25] Sarah F. Brosnan & Frans B.M. de Waal, *Socially Learned Preferences for Differentially Rewarded Tokens in the Brown Capuchin Monkey, Cebus Apella*, 119 JOURNAL OF COMPARATIVE PSYCHOLOGY 133 (2004); Sarah F. Brosnan & Frans B.M. de Waal, *Monkeys Reject Unequal Play*, 425 NATURE 297 (2003).

[26] Gregory T. Jones, *The Social Evolution of Strategic Forgiveness* (unpublished simulation results) (on file with author); IVAR KOLSTAD, THE EVOLUTION OF SOCIAL NORMS (2003); Karl Sigmund, et al., *The Economics of Fair Play*, 286 SCIENTIFIC AMERICAN 83 (2002); Nowak, et al., *supra* note 22; KEN BINMORE, GAME THEORY AND THE SOCIAL CONTRACT: PLAYING FAIR (2000).

[27] Jörg Oechssler, *Intentions Matter: Lessons from Bargaining Experiments*, 159 JOURNAL OF INSTITUTIONAL AND THEORETICAL ECONOMICS 195 (2003); Armin Falk, et al., *On the Nature of Fair Behavior*, 41 ECONOMICS INQUIRY 20 (1999).

[28] Alan Sanfey, et al., *The Neural Basis of Economic Decision-Making in the Ultimatum Game*, 300 SCIENCE 1755 (2003).

[29] In addition to a sense of substantive fairness, humans seem to have a taste for procedural fairness as reflected in the growing body of research around procedural justice. E. ALLAN LIND & TOM TYLER, THE SOCIAL PSYCHOLOGY OF PROCEDURAL JUSTICE (1988); JOHN THIBAUT & LAUREN WALKER, PROCEDURAL JUSTICE (1975). Again, consistent with social evolution theory, the primary concerns of individuals are whether the process signals their inclusion in the social group.

[30] Dominique J.F. de Quervain, et al., *The Neural Basis of Altruistic Punishment*, 305 SCIENCE 1254 (2004); Brian Knutson, *Sweet Revenge*, 305 SCIENCE 1246 (2004).

[31] Alan Sanfey, et al., *The Neural Basis of Economic Decision-Making in the Ultimatum Game*, 300 SCIENCE 1755 (2003).

[32] William D. Hamilton, *The Genetical Evolution of Social Behavior*, 37 JOURNAL OF THEORETICAL BIOLOGY 1 (1964).

[33] Trivers, *supra* note 7.

[34] ROBERT AXELROD, THE EVOLUTION OF COOPERATION (1984).

[35] Herbert Gintis, et al., *Explaining Altruistic Behavior in Humans*, 24 EVOLUTION AND HUMAN BEHAVIOR 153 (2003).

[36] Christophe Boesch, *Cooperative Hunting in Wild Chimpanzees*, 48 ANIMAL BEHAVIOR 653 (1994).

[37] For example, wage decisions are strongly reciprocated with work effort in labor markets, Ernst Fehr, et al., *Gift Exchange and Reciprocity in Competitive Experimental Markets*, 42 EUROPEAN ECONOMIC REVIEW 1 (1998); Ernst Fehr, et al., *Reciprocity as a Contract Enforcement Device: Experimental Evidence*, 65 ECONOMETRICA 833 (1997); Ernst Fehr, et al., *Does Fairness Prevent Market Clearing?* 108 QUARTERLY JOURNAL OF ECONOMICS 437 (1993), altruistic punishment of self-interested behavior is common in the ultimatum game, Colin Camerer & Richard Thaler, *Ultimatums, Dictators, and Manners*, 9 JOURNAL OF ECONOMIC PERSPECTIVES 209 (1995); Alvin E. Roth, et al., *Bargaining and Market Behavior in Jerusalem, Ljubljana, Pittsburgh, and Tokyo: An Experimental Study*, 81 AMERICAN ECONOMIC REVIEW 1068 (1991); Güth & Tietz, *supra* note 23, and costly punishment is doled out to free riders in public goods games; Ernst Fehr & Simon Gächter, *Altruistic Punishment in Humans*, 415 NATURE 137 (2002); Ernst Fehr & Simon Gächter, *Cooperation and Punishment*, 90 AMERICAN ECONOMIC REVIEW 980 (2000); Ernst Fehr & Simon Gächter, *Fairness and Retaliation: The Economics of Reciprocity*, 14 JOURNAL OF ECONOMIC PERSPECTIVES 159 (2000); Simon Gächter & Ernst Fehr, *Collective Action as a Social Exchange*, 39 JOURNAL OF ECONOMIC BEHAVIOR AND ORGANIZATION 341 (1999); Elinor Ostrom, et al., *Covenants With and Without a Sword: Self-Governance Is Possible*, 86 AMERICAN POLITICAL SCIENCE REVIEW 404 (1992); Toshio Yamagishi, *The Provision of a Sanctioning System as a Public Good*, 51 JOURNAL OF PERSONALITY AND SOCIAL PSYCHOLOGY 265 (1986).

[38] Including wage setting by firms, TRUMAN F. BEWLEY, WHY WAGES DON'T FALL DURING A RECESSION (2000), tax compliance, James Andreoni, et al., *Tax Compliance*, 36 JOURNAL OF ECONOMIC LITERATURE 818 (1998), and cooperation in the protection of local environmental public goods. ELINOR OSTROM, GOVERNING THE COMMONS: THE EVOLUTION OF INSTITUTIONS FOR COLLECTIVE ACTION (1990); JAMES ACHESON, THE LOBSTER GANGS OF MAINE (1988).

[39] Frans B.M. de Waal & Jennifer J. Pokorny, *Primate Conflict Resolution and Its Relation to Human Forgiveness*, in HANDBOOK OF FORGIVENESS 17 (Everett L. Worthington, Jr. ed., 2005); FILIPO AURELI & FRANS B.M. DE WAAL, NATURAL CONFLICT RESOLUTION (2000); Frans B.M. de Waal, *Primates: A Natural Heritage of Conflict Resolution*, 289 SCIENCE 586 (2000); Josep F. Call, et al., *Reconciliation Patterns Among Stumptail Macaques: A Multivariate Approach*, 58 ANIMAL BEHAVIOR 165 (1999); Frans B.M. de Waal, *Reconciliation Among Primates: A Review of Empirical Evidence and Unresolved Issues*, in PRIMATE SOCIAL CONFLICT 111 (William A. Mason & Sally P. Mendoza eds., 1993); Frans B.M. de Waal & Angeline van Roosmalen, *Reconciliation and Consolation Among Chimpanzees*, 5 BEHAVIORAL ECOLOGY AND SOCIOBIOLOGY 55 (1979).

[40] Jones, *supra* note 26.

[41] Forgiveness is related to empathy, Tania Singer & Ernst Fehr, *The Neuroeconomics of Mind Reading and Empathy*, (IZA Discussion Paper No. 1647; IEW Working Paper Series No. 222) (July 2005), *available at* http://ssrn.com/abstract=747904; Stephanie D. Preston & Frans B.M. de Waal, *Empathy: Its Ultimate and Proximate Bases*, 25 BEHAVIORAL AND BRAIN SCIENCES 1 (2002); Filipo Aureli & Colleen M. Schaffner, *Empathy as a Special Case of Emotional Mediation of Social Behavior*, 25 BEHAVIORAL AND BRAIN SCIENCES 23 (2002), but recent investigations of the functional anatomy of the two judgments show that they are distinct. Tom F.D. Farrow & Peter W.R. Woodruff, *Neuroimaging of Forgivability*, in HANDBOOK OF FORGIVENESS 259 (Everett L. Worthington, Jr. ed., 2005); Tom F.D. Farrow, et al., *Investigating the Functional Anatomy of Empathy and Forgiveness*, 12 NEUROREPORT 2433 (2001). Researchers in the UK used functional magnetic resonance imaging (fMRI) to examine the neural correlates of making empathic and forgivability judgments. *Id.*. Their results suggest that "attempting to understand others is physiologically distinct from determining the forgivability of their actions." *Id.* at 2435. While the two types of judgments shared activations in some areas of the brain, like the left frontal cortex, activation of the posterior cingulated gyrus was unique to forgiveness judgments. This is a region that with limbic connections has been associated with decision-making, attentional tasks, and problem-solving, including a sort of mental imagery that may extend to that of other people's views. *Id.* There seems to be a biological explanation for why we can put ourselves in another person's shoes without necessarily being able to forgive them.

[42] Erin A. O'Hara, *Apology and Thick Trust: What Spouse Abusers and Negligent Doctors Might Have in Common*, 79 CHICAGO-KENT LAW REVIEW 1055 (2004); Erin A. O'Hara & Douglas H. Yarn, *On Apology and Consilience*, 77 WASHINGTON LAW REVIEW 1121 (2002).

[43] O'Hara & Yarn, *supra* note 42, which shows the biological and economic reasoning. Kyoko Okamoto & Shuichi Matsumura, *The Evolution of Punishment and Apology: An Iterated Prisoner's Dilemma*, 14 EVOLUTIONARY ECOLOGY 703 (2000).

[44] Richard Thaler, *From Homo Economicus to Homo Sapiens*, 14 JOURNAL OF ECONOMIC PERSPECTIVES 133 (2000).

⚛ 34 ⚛

Typical Errors of Westerners

Bee Chen Goh

Editors' Note: *It's no longer rare for negotiators based in a Western culture and instinctively applying Western concepts to find themselves in dealings with people who start from a very different cultural frame of reference. Goh, a Chinese-Malaysian law professor working in Australia, deconstructs the typical errors that negotiators unfamiliar with Chinese culture can be expected to make. This chapter should be read in conjunction with Kelly's chapter on negotiating with indigenous people; together, they can provide you with a fast tour that will provide some hints as to what you might encounter in still other cultures.*

You walk into the boardroom ready to negotiate. You are as prepared as ever. This one is going to be no different. It may be easy; it may be tough. Much depends on the anticipated outcome, and, of course, the personalities of the other side. But, this time around, you find that the rules you are accustomed to do not make any sense of the situation. You are perplexed, frustrated, and helpless. What has gone wrong? You are at a loss.

This chapter essentially deals with cross-cultural pitfalls in communication between the Chinese and Westerners. The use of the term 'Chinese' here is ethnological, referring to a people who share collectivistic habits of behavior with a dominant Confucian heritage. The reference to a 'Westerner' assumes an Anglo-Saxon tending towards individualistic values.

Cross-cultural negotiation can perplex any uninitiated negotiator. The rules of negotiation are different. And, because the rules are largely unspoken and operate in the unconscious, oftentimes, such negotiators have no idea as to what is not right about the whole thing.

Take the value of 'confrontation', for a start. Individualist cultures are accustomed to the idea of confrontation. Confrontation, essentially, is an indispensable component of negotiation in Western cultures. There is nothing strange about it. It operates in the Western unconscious mind and directs communication and behavior accordingly. It is so obvious that it is not even questioned or brought into one's awareness in the typical Western environment. From a young age, children brought up in such a culture are instructed to speak their minds and assert their rights.

In contrast, the word 'negotiation' is foreign and alien to the collectivist world, as exemplified by the Chinese, Japanese and most indigenous communities. Children of such cultures are trained to *hint* to get what they want. The concept of negotiation, in its equivalence, is subtle, implicit and indirect, totally at odds with the idea of confrontation. Little wonder that many untrained cross-cultural negotiators feel disoriented and disheartened.[1] For a Westerner, it is hard to imagine having to wait to be noticed, and to need to decipher the hidden meanings behind words and gestures. This can mean much hard work, and even meaningless. It can also cause a certain amount of trepidation: what if the guess-work is wrong? For the Chinese, on the other hand, it is hard to imagine regularly asserting oneself in a conversation.

Perception is another critical factor in cross-cultural scenarios. Unconsciously or subconsciously, we bring with us our own cultural baggage to the boardroom. Our perception of people and events and things is, in turn, influenced by our underlying assumptions and habits, and frames our reality. It is, therefore, all the more important that we cultivate an awareness of different rules on communication and behavior crucial to a successful untangling of the cross-cultural web.

Take, for instance, the Chinese negotiators who are prone to collectivist patterns of thinking and behavior. Western negotiators who deal with them will be struck by their relational tendencies: a desire for group goals, harmony, cooperation, gift-giving, face-saving, subtle persuasion rather than aggressive confrontation, high-context communicative styles, and, generally, a focus on a person-centred instead of a paper-centred approach. Culture becomes a silent communicator. For the Chinese, generally speaking, relationship-building takes precedence over deal-making. The latter goal is subsumed within the primary goal of establishing friendships. Inter-personal trust is important. (No wonder business relationships are likened to marriages). Because of the importance of inter-personal trust, contracts are not regarded as crucial, in the Western sense. In fact, contracts are antithetical to trust-building. For the Chinese, even if there are contracts governing the parties' transactions, more than likely they are overlooked in times of disputes, and the Chinese party could insist on the principle of reasonableness in the interpretation and implementation of contractual obligations. Such an attitude is concordant with the Chinese long-term view of events and how reciprocity functions. The underlying expectation is that rather than exacting one's pound of flesh (or the modern equivalent, resorting to litigation) it makes better sense to work together and to try to iron out differences. The principle of *rang*, or 'yielding', is a much-cherished Confucian virtue. One who is able to practise *rang*, who learns how to compromise, is regarded as a virtuous and honourable person.[2]

In this respect, Westerners should be aware that Westerners operate from an essentially transactional platform. They value efficiency, pride in competition, and flourish in an environment of direct communication. Contracts are sacrosanct as they act as instruments of reliance (largely in place of interpersonal trust). Their approach is largely paper-centred.

This is not to say that relationships are unimportant in Western cultures. What is highlighted is the fact that relationships, in the business negotiating environment, are subsumed within the primary aim of deal-closing. Transactions, as such, take precedence over relationships. Understanding this crucial difference can help one to resolve many of the perplexing cross-cultural (Sino-Western) communication behavior patterns.

A quick example suffices. It is not uncommon for newly-met negotiating counterparts to be promptly ushered around in local sightseeing tours by the Chinese—while the concerned Westerners feel uneasy, as they are under a deadline pressure and wish to get things over and done with. This is a typical clash between the relational (Chinese approach to forming friendships and getting to know the people involved) and the transactional (Western approach to deal-making and economic efficiency) tendencies.

Below are ten common traps to avoid in Sino-Western negotiations in which cultural ignorance has caused unnecessary misunderstanding.

'Ignorance is Not Bliss'

Cross-cultural mistakes can be very costly, and it does one well to educate oneself and be familiar with another's cultural habits. We can easily draw upon our own individual culture-shock experiences to understand the discomfort and frustration. A globalized negotiator who chooses not to understand another's culture is courting disaster. Ignorance is definitely not bliss. Cross-cultural misunderstandings abound and mistakes can be avoided just by being attentive to the cultural language (both explicit and implicit) of one's negotiating counterpart.

Take, for instance, a simple thing as the exchange of business cards. This can entail both ritual and communication. A Westerner often regards receiving a business card as merely conveying the contact information of the other party and may act in a manner which is somewhat cursory towards its receipt. However, to a collectivist Chinese, the exchange of business cards represents communicative behavior. The information contained immediately alerts the Chinese party as to the order of behavior, in the social hierarchical sense.[3] The status-conscious Chinese will read the contents of the card immediately, and use it to discern the other's position or rank, with immediate consequences for how the interaction unfolds. Among other criteria often used, because Chinese society tends to value education highly, a Westerner's social standing in the eyes of his/her Chinese negotiating counterpart will rise according to the educational qualifications and the prestige of the awarding institutions. For those Westerners anticipating dealing with Chinese, it is therefore often important, though often overlooked by the Westerner, to include one's educational qualifications (if any) in one's business card.

Furthermore, bearing in mind that the Chinese are a relational people, business cards can easily trigger conversational topics by the sharing of common educational backgrounds or some other commonalities. What can appear as small-talk to the Westerner represents part of the relationship-building exercise for the Chinese.

'There is Such a Thing as a Free Lunch'

A meal is the best negotiation facilitator from the Chinese perspective. Meals are fertile grounds for cultivating social ties and deepening inter-personal bonds. Very often, when a Chinese 'invites' a person for a meal in a restaurant, he or she also foots the bill. This practice is often not understood by the Westerner. It is an example of the collectivism-individualism dichotomy. For the collectivist Chinese, group behavior is important and harmony is cherished. It is therefore regarded as proper for the inviter to pay; when one invites, one has taken on an obligation to look after the other members within the group, as it were. For the individualist Westerner, inviting another shows that one seeks the pleasure of the other's company, but there is not necessarily a social need to go the extra mile of footing the 'group' bill, as the individuals often expect to look after themselves individually. Such a social practice has baffled many a Westerner: in fact, a Canadian once remarked to me that he had failed to understand this bill-fighting behavior in

(Japanese, in this case) restaurants when he was on work assignment there, until he heard my explanation.

The significance of meals is in the relationship-building exercise. The Chinese believe that it is easier to get things done when there is an inter-personal association which facilitates more open communication.

'Eat, Eat, and Be Merry and Negotiate'

Westerners tend to think that business and pleasure should not mix. For the Chinese, the contrary is more likely to be true. Much of the deadlock or stalemate in the boardroom can be ironed out or smoothed away in the dining room, in subtle and indirect ways over a meal. Sometimes, the issues addressed this way are relatively minor, but a Shanghai lawyer once solved a major contractual difference between his overseas clients and the local Chinese party just by his hosting a dinner and talking things through during the meal.

In the Chinese context, one could say that eating is a relational tool, subconsciously and firmly embedded in the Chinese culture to serve both physical and communicative functions.

'Do Beat About the Bush'

Generally speaking, the Chinese neither like to give nor take 'No' for an answer. 'No' comes across as a socially offensive word, causing one to lose face. Consequently, ambiguity in communication is favoured. It is challenging for a listener to try to interpret a Chinese 'Maybe' response as a real 'maybe', or a disguised 'no', or simply a 'yes'. The solution is in the use of intermediaries. When the listener is uncertain, rather than press upon the speaker for the real meaning, it is best to turn to an intermediary, for example, the speaker's close friend, secretary or the like. Such a meandering approach may seem time-wasting to an individualist who is focussed on efficiency, but not to a collectivist who is relationship-oriented.

Chen makes the following observation:

Traditional Chinese writing runs from the top of the page to the bottom, while the Western writing system runs from left to right. When Chinese people are reading traditional texts, it looks as though they are nodding their heads and saying "Yes, Yes." When Westerners are reading, they appear to be shaking their heads and saying "No, No."[4]

The Chinese are used to high-context communication wherein the essential message is encoded in the context of the situation rather than expressly articulated. This kind of communication is indirect and can come across as very challenging to a Westerner who is more used to a direct way of communication which is low-context. Again, this divergence in communicative styles appears to serve collectivist and individualist tendencies respectively.

'Beware Not Chinese Bearing Gifts'

The relational nature of the Chinese people necessitates gift-giving behavior. Gift-giving is seen as a gesture of goodwill and facilitates relationship-building in the long term. It also demonstrates one's desire to wish to maintain friendship.

Gift-giving behavior can fall into two categories: expressive or instrumental.[5] In the former, it is nothing more than illustrating the cultural desire for friendship. In the latter, gifts are given for a purpose, what in Western parlance is known as 'bribery'.

Gift-giving is an art. Presenting the 'wrong' gift, i.e. that which is culturally inappropriate, can sour a relationship and cause social offence. For instance, the colour 'white' is associated with mournful events (like funerals). If a Western party gives a bunch of white flowers as a welcome gift to his or her Chinese counterpart, that immediately suggests 'death' to the Chinese recipient! An otherwise happy occasion can turn into the exact opposite. Another example is giving a clock as a gift for a birthday. 'Clock', in Mandarin, is homophonic with 'termination' or 'the end' and is a culturally inappropriate gift for a birthday, which connotes the opposite. These are merely two relatively obvious examples of the situation both necessary, and fraught with possibilities of misunderstanding. This may in turn help to explain the Chinese cultural tendency to give money gifts instead of objects. A sum of money in red packets (called 'ang pow') is not only a gift of convenience, but is also less likely to cause social offence.

Another cultural imperative in gift-giving is the cultivation of '*guan-xi*' between the parties. *Guan-xi* means connections, and these represent very powerful ties. It has even prompted Chen, quoting Eric Tsang, to venture to suggest that Westerners doing business with the Chinese ought to undertake '*guan-xi* audits'.[6] It is likened to the Western concept of 'old boys' network' but is a great deal stronger in the Chinese sense due to the obligations involved. For instance, on the ground of *guan-xi*, a negotiator may take advantage of a situation by calling upon the *guan-xi* network and invoke the obligatory ties owed by the other person in order to achieve one's goals. It would be a tremendous loss of face for one to ignore *guan-xi* obligations.[7] To maintain continuing good '*guan-xi*', gifts are exchanged at festive occasions, of which there are many in Chinese culture, like the Chinese New Year (or Spring Festival), the Moon-cake Festival (or Mid-Autumn Festival), Winter Festival, and other personal occasions such as birthdays and anniversaries.[8]

'Out of Sight, Not Out of Mind'

It may be commonplace for Westerners who are more used to short-term goals to think that once a particular purpose is achieved, the personalities behind it can be forgotten. For the Chinese who believe in long-term goals, relationships are often maintained over a considerable period of time. As such, they deem it very important to keep in contact. Old friends are like vintage wine, better than new.

Business with the Chinese is about relationships. Business partners grow old together, in the Chinese long-term view. Hence, the saying, 'lao pen-yu' meaning 'old friends'. When the friendship bond is strong, the business relationship tends to be more steadfast: conflicts are easier to manage as friends tend to be more forgiving, as compared with one-off dealmakers.

In this day and age when businesses are so globalized, the use of e-mail is a good tool in facilitating such constant communication. This gesture is much appreciated by the relational Chinese people. E-cards for personal occasions are an easy and costless way of keeping one's friendship channels open. [Bhappu & Barsness, *E-mail*]

'Everything Comes to Those Who Wait'

The Chinese, as a general rule, are a patient people. In fact, in the Confucian tradition, perseverance is a highly regarded virtue.

Negotiating with the Chinese can become an exercise in patience. This is what has prompted Pye to remark that, when negotiating in China, you need 'abiding patience.'[9] If Westerners are culturally unaware of this, it can easily frustrate them as Westerners are accustomed to things 'here and now'—as exemplified, perhaps, by the phenomenal rise of fast food.

Admittedly, the decision-making process can come across painfully slow for the Westerner, especially the Western executive who may be empowered to act and decide. This is usually not the case with the collectivist Chinese whose decisions depend, by and large, on group effort. The latter approach is undoubtedly time-consuming. Patience is, therefore, needed.

'You Guard Your Back, We Save Our Face'

Most cultures are used to the idea of face-saving behavior. However, with the Chinese, the concept of 'face' is both other-related and self-related. In fact, it is the former that represents a collectivist trait. A collectivistic Chinese will be inclined towards preserving the face of the other party before his/her own. This is in contrast with a Western party who would be more interested in protecting his/her own face rather than the other person's, again a demonstration of an individualistic value.

In the Chinese sense, the concept of 'face' can bear either of the two connotations: *mien-tze* or *lien*. *Mien'tze* refers to prestige or reputation, which can be added or subtracted. *Lien* implies 'integrity' and can be forfeited in the case of wrongdoing or engaging in conduct which is socially undesirable. However, both *mien-tze* and *lien* mean the physical face; they differ in their respective metaphysical connotations.[10]

At meetings or large group gatherings, one must take care not to say or do anything that may cause a Chinese party to lose face in public. A confrontational encounter, at a board meeting, for instance, where aggressive behavior is displayed and loud voices exchanged, may signal the end of one's business relationship. Oftentimes, this can be irreversible, in the sense that the hurt remains long after the business deal is done; the Chinese party may consider the Western party as a write-off. What is worse, news may spread to associates, and others may refuse future dealings as well.

'You Speak Your Mind, We Mind What We Speak'

The Chinese are highly status-conscious. They are used to a socially hierarchical structure. As a result, there is communication etiquette involved in this form of vertical social structure. This is to be contrasted with the Western horizontal social structure, whereby each person is regarded as equal (within bounds). What immediately comes to mind is the use of the first-name in Western culture. Social equality means that Western people are accustomed to addressing each other on a first-name basis, including children who refer to their elders (like parents and grandparents) comfortably with the latter's first names. In Chinese culture, respect for the elders is paramount. It is unthinkable for young Chinese children to call their parents or grandparents by their first names. In fact, in traditional Chinese society, one does not even call one's elder siblings by first names but would refer to them as 'big sister' (for the eldest girl in the family) and then 'second sister' (for the next born girl) and so on.

In business dealings, the use of title is, in turn, naturally important for the Chinese. It is therefore essential to address one's Chinese counterpart according to the position or rank, e.g. 'President Li', 'Chairman Wong' in order to accord due respect.

'Tradition Dies Hard'

It is important for Westerners to realize that the Chinese are used to long-term views and have experienced a civilization that spans over five millennia. Tradition is highly valued and most of the rituals are preserved. Respecting cultural differences is not merely important, but crucial. Collectivism tends to foster traditional values which, in turn, introduce the element of stability in relationships and the underlying social structure. In contrast, individualism cherishes creativity and freedom, and change, rather than tradition, is treasured. A culturally enlightened Westerner who understands why the Chinese are cultural adherents to ancient customs and traditions will find it a lot easier to negotiate with them and to accommodate such (from the Western point of view) idiosyncratic behavior.

In terms of philosophic influence, it is almost taken for granted that Confucianism plays a pervasive role in shaping Chinese etiquette. The traditionalist Chinese is often a Confucian at heart. Westerners who seek to deal with the Chinese must make the effort to learn about Confucianism in order to understand where their Chinese counterparts are "coming from." The way the Western mindset differs from the Chinese mindset may be attributable to such divergent philosophic leanings, so that some effort given to such background study can pay off when, inevitably, a situation arises that is not treated in the textbooks.

Additionally, much of Chinese culture is also influenced by Taoism, a belief in the way the Universal forces govern humanity's life on earth. There is, as it were, the Trinity of Heaven, Earth and Humanity, closely intertwined in an engaging and mutually influencing relationship. To a Taoist, natural disasters are a result of people being in conflict with one another and living in disharmony. The Taoists principally subscribe to a way of existing which goes with the flow, instead of against it. Harmony is then achieved between persons, events and things. This concept of harmony explains in part why the Chinese cherish inter-personal relationships above profiteering.[11]

Dealing with cultural behavior patterns requires one to engage in generalisations. It is, however, prudent to remind oneself that one must take the negotiator the way one finds him or her. Generally speaking, when Westerners deal with the Confucian Chinese, the former are likely to find the cultural traits highlighted above. Such an understanding can help ease one's frustration and confusion considerably. Like everything else, practice makes perfect; but even a beginning cross-cultural negotiator should always act consciously and be alert to cross-cultural differences that can emerge in a negotiation. After all, our goal as negotiators *is* to enhance human communication in a meaningful way, minimise misunderstandings and manage conflicts.

Endnotes

[1] BEE CHEN GOH, NEGOTIATING WITH THE CHINESE 86 (1996); ROBERT M. MARCH, THE JAPANESE NEGOTIATOR: SUBTLETY AND STRATEGY BEYOND WESTERN LOGIC 15 (1988).

[2] BEE CHEN GOH, LAW WITHOUT LAWYERS, JUSTICE WITHOUT COURTS: ON TRADITIONAL CHINESE MEDIATION 57-58 (1988); MICHAEL J. MOSER, LAW AND SOCIAL CHANGE IN A CHINESE COMMUNITY: A CASE STUDY FROM RURAL TAIWAN 68 (1982).

[3] The questions that may come to the recipient's mind are: 'Where do I fit in?', 'How shall I treat this person?'

[4] MING-JER CHEN, INSIDE CHINESE BUSINESS: A GUIDE FOR MANAGERS WORLDWIDE 121 (2001).

[5] An excellent scholarly study undertaken of Chinese gift-giving behavior can be found in YUNXIANG YAN, THE FLOW OF GIFTS: RECIPROCITY AND SOCIAL NETWORKS IN A CHINESE VILLAGE (1996).

[6] CHEN, *supra* note 4, at 63.

[7] *See also* CHEN, *supra* note 4, at 45-65.

[8] A list of festive events may be found in GOH, *supra* note 1, at 61-69.

[9] LUCIAN W. PYE, CHINESE COMMERCIAL NEGOTIATING STYLE 12 (1982).

[10] GOH, *supra* note 1, at 95-98; *see also,* CHEN, *supra* note 4, at 72-77.

[11] A useful guide to understanding Chinese philosophies can be found in YU-LAN FUNG, A SHORT HISTORY OF CHINESE PHILOSOPHY (1948).

☙ 35 ❧

Indigenous Experiences in Negotiation

Loretta Kelly

Editors' Note: *In a contribution likely to shake many readers' implicit assumptions, an Australian Aboriginal mediator uses a detailed examination of one key type of case to examine how negotiators who make the common Western assumptions can trip over their own feet as soon as they find themselves negotiating with people who operate from totally different cultural assumptions. The lessons from this chapter are relevant even for ordinary negotiators with no plans to go to the outback.*

Negotiating with people from another culture can be awkward and taxing. When the other party is not only from another culture but is a *community* of people,[1] the difficulties are doubled. In this chapter I provide some hints for a 'western' negotiator when tackling such a situation. I write from my perspective as an Australian Aboriginal lawyer and mediator.

Although I have mediated many inter- and intra- cultural disputes,[2] it is my experience in native title negotiations that I draw upon in this chapter. Native title negotiations have become an excellent illustration of the problems that tend to arise in other settings. A little of the legal background, however, is necessary first.

Native title—also known in other Anglophile countries as 'aboriginal title'—is a complex area of property law. It is an attempt to shoe-horn the Indigenous relationship to our land into a new category of Australian common law—native title— first recognized in the Australian High Court case of *Mabo v. Queensland*,[3] and consequently formalized by the Federal Government in statute[4] establishing the National Native Title Tribunal.

In some Australian states and territories, such as New South Wales (NSW), Aboriginal land rights were created prior to the *Mabo* decision. Land rights are purely a creature of statute, and quite distinct from native title. In NSW this form of land tenure was created in 1983 by the *Aboriginal Land Rights Act*. The interplay between title created by Aboriginal land rights legislation,[5] native title, Crown ('state government') title and leasehold title has created the sort of complexity in Australian property law not seen since we switched our system of freehold land tenure from 'old system' title (still prevalent in the United States) to statutory ('Torrens') title more than a century ago.

If we go a little further back in NSW history—to the early part of the 19th century—we see that the emerging law of the new colony of NSW (based entirely on British law) was complicit in, and adapted to suit, the progressive parceling-out of

Indigenous lands (that is, the entire Australian continent and islands) to white 'settlers' without payment to, or treaty with, its Aboriginal and Torres Strait Islander owners. It is the 'remnant' lands—the (at the time) uneconomic land not wanted by either settlers or the government—with which both land rights and native title are principally concerned. These remnant Crown lands—mainly existing in the less populated areas of the country—provide less disputation than the far more contentious 'leasehold lands.' The latter are the vast (mainly) pastoral lands in western NSW, Queensland and Victoria (also northern South Australia and throughout Western Australia), often held under 99-year or perpetual leases. The other ground-breaking native title case, *Wik*,[6] held that native title could survive on leasehold land. The practical import of that decision, however, is the subject of ongoing, often heated, negotiation, mediation and litigation.

This history must be kept in mind when reading the following scenario, for it is only recently that Indigenous tenure of land (the sort of tenure that existed prior to invasion in 1788) has been recognized by the legislature and judiciary of Australia.

The scenario used here for illustration is an agglomeration of facts from the author's experience on the management team of the Gumbaynggirr[7] Nation Aboriginal Corporation (which will hold the title to several small pieces of land on the north coast of NSW, if our native title claims are successful); my interviews conducted as part of an Australian Research Council grant with native title claimants, mediators and professional consultants (such as anthropologists); and my personal contacts with Aboriginal people from central Australia.

The scenario is intended to highlight aspects of negotiation with a non-western people that can easily go awry for a well-meaning 'western' negotiator. But it is not only that we are 'the other' (a non-western people) that makes the negotiation challenging; it is that we have been devastated by colonization, marginalized by dominant institutions, and stripped of dignity. In the midst of a wealthy nation, our people hang on to what little we have. It is no wonder a mindset exists in our community that whatever we have will be taken away.

A Negotiation Scenario

The setting is the board room of an Aboriginal land council in the Northern Territory, Australia. The land council's premises are located in Alice Springs, the major town in central Australia.

A large table separates the two parties. You are the lawyer for a mining company. You are keen to obtain exploration rights for gold over a large tract of land in central Australia. The land concerned is approximately 500km from Alice Springs—at least a day's drive.

There is a (Aboriginal) native title claim over the land: it has not yet been determined by the National Native Title Tribunal, but given the success of a similar claim in nearby South Australia, it is likely to be successful.

The lawyer for the Northern Territory government sits next to you. She is determined to get a good deal for your client as well: the larger the mining operation, the bigger the royalties for the Government.

There are eight native title claimant representatives present. These are all Aboriginal people from the tribe making the native title claim. They have been given authority by the larger claimant group (the tribe) to deal with your application for exploration. Six women sit towards the back, one of them a young woman breastfeeding. Two of them, both men, sit towards the front. One is a young man who is very talkative (he appears to be in his 30s). An older, quiet man (with initiation scars evident through his T-shirt) sits nearby. Your experience with Aboriginal people is that men with initiation scars, especially if they are older, have considerable power in their community. Sitting in between the two Aboriginal men is their lawyer, a young and assertive white man.

You sit opposite these two men with your colleague. You are keen to negotiate directly with the Aboriginal claimants, aware that—based on your previous negotiations with other Aboriginal group—their lawyer will probably try to dominate.

The meeting starts with the introductions. The young Aboriginal man is charismatic; he speaks fluent English and appears to have influence over the other claimants.

The negotiation proceeds quickly. You and your colleague establish a good rapport with the young man; he appears to be friendly with the lawyer and constantly speaks with the other claimants sitting behind him (in their local language). The old man nods and smiles often.

Before you know it, their lawyer says that there is agreement to start exploration immediately. All that is required is that you employ the young man, who will ensure that exploration activities are kept well away from sacred sites. Your company is also required to keep the Aboriginal claimants fully informed of any mineral discoveries on the land.

The Aboriginal claimants' lawyer asks the six women sitting behind: "you understand? Mining company not touch sacred country." Several of the older women nod.

You shake hands with their lawyer, the young man and the older man. As you walk towards the door, you see all the women talking. The young woman who had been breastfeeding comes up to you and says: "you understand this is only 'in principle' agreement—we take this back to community to get approval. You know that fella (she points to the young man) don't know about women's sites—that's where you wanna look for gold, hey?"

This startles you—you thought the lawyer, the young man and the old man represented the interests of all the claimants. Why didn't the women speak up during the negotiation? You thought this group had authority to negotiate for the entire claimant group. And what do you do if the young man doesn't know about the women's sites on the exploration land?

Native Title

In this chapter, I will use Australian native title negotiations as proxy for many other kinds of negotiations in which Indigenous and Western negotiators encounter each other, with frequent incomprehension and just as frequent long-term failure. Often, the failure occurs when, on the surface, a "deal" was reached.

Native title is an Indigenous right to land that has not been extinguished by inconsistent Crown (Government) grants. It arises where there is continuing connection to that land according to traditional (pre-western colonization) Indigenous laws and customs.

Australian courts and commentators have described native title interests as a "bundle of rights." It could just as easily be said that native title interests have given rise to a "bundle of disputes!" The nature of the conflicts resulting from native title claims is multi-faceted in nature, and complex.

In order to process native title claims the Australian (Federal) Government has established a system of determining whether native title exists, and what rights it consists of, through the National Native Title Tribunal and the Federal Court. There is also, within the native title regime, a mechanism that allows for negotiation and mediation, an explicit part of the alternative dispute resolution "spectrum." The primary reason for establishing an alternative dispute resolution process was the ever-present imperative to cut the cost of litigation.

Since the enactment of the Federal *Native Title Act* in 1993, Aboriginal and Torres Strait Islander peoples have been participating in processes of negotiation and mediation regarding native title. Despite the potential of the alternative dispute resolution process, Indigenous people involved in the native title claims process express frustration, disappointment and disillusionment. To an average native title claimant, the native title system has the appearance of a huge, impenetrable, alien edifice that was constructed in order to deliberately complicate and delay. The systemic bias is summed up by the words of Wayne Atkinson, Yorta Yorta claimant:

> Proof requirements in native title claims fall heavily on Indigenous applicants. The non-Indigenous parties, who have usually been the prime beneficiaries of Indigenous land and resources, are not required to prove their identity or connection to the land. Nor, as stated by Yorta Yorta elder Margaret Wirripunda, are they required "to prove by what authority they are on our land."[8]

Aboriginal Decision-Making

The landscape is richly symbolic for Indigenous Australians. Creation stories dictated appropriate modes of behavior, and set standards. Collectively affirmed standards were enforced by applying social pressure to ensure conformity. Children were taught acceptable modes of behavior through stories[9] [Volpe, et al., *Unknown*] and were taught by example rather than by direct instruction.

For these and other reasons, prior to invasion of Australia by the British, there was an egalitarian diffusion of power amongst Aboriginal tribes, rather than a single leader. The British found it hard to deal with this egalitarian system—the lack of Kings and Queens. Early British invaders nominated people within the community to act as representatives of the community, handing out the titles "King" and "Queen" to those they considered to be leaders of their people. These titles ignored the reality of collective Aboriginal decision-making. Such titles were bestowed by white people in positions of authority to make it easier for them to identify Aboriginal leaders with whom they could deal. The consequences of this practice, whether or not intentional, were the mocking of traditional laws and disharmony in the community. This autocratic approach of governing was totally alien to Aboriginal culture. The communal approach to decision-making continues, to the most part, in Aboriginal communities today. As Behrendt argues, the liberal concept of the autonomous self-interested individual is contrary to Aboriginal customs of decision-making through group consensus for the benefit of the community, rather than the individual.[10]

Indigenous Lack of Power

There are many contexts in which power imbalances are so great that parties cannot negotiate on fair grounds. [Bernard, *Powerlessness*] Gender-related inequalities, power differentials caused by political, financial and psychological factors, as well as unequal access to resources (including lawyers), limited educational opportunities, lack of confidence and unfamiliarity with negotiation techniques are some such contexts.[11] Power imbalances between disputants "may be reflected in outcomes, rendering them fundamentally unfair and unreasonable."[12]

Aboriginal people are even more disempowered than the non-English speaking working class; indeed, we are often referred to as the under-class. The systemic and chronic disadvantage suffered by Aboriginal people through over 200 years of oppression, discrimination, violence and attempted genocide means that we display many of the same psychological characteristics as victims of long-term domestic violence.

It is this historical and contemporary disempowerment of Indigenous Australians that impacts on our ability to negotiate in the native title arena. We are the most socio-economically disadvantaged group in Australian society. We fall short on all social and economic indicators compared to non-Indigenous Australians. This lack of social and economic power coupled with the small Aboriginal population (about 2% of the total Australian population) means that our political power within the non-Aboriginal community is minimal, even though our moral persuasiveness and media exposure are greater than our numbers would predict. This lack of political power should be noted in relation to the ability of Aboriginal people to deal with powerful government, mining and pastoral interests. Aboriginal communities do not have the resources available to us that our adversaries do to undertake complex and costly litigation, despite some funding of native title claims with public monies. Nor do we sit down as equals in negotiations or mediations. Native Americans are in a similarly disadvantaged position. If anything, they have even less 'voice' in the US than Indigenous people do in Australia. It is likely that much of my discussion about disempowerment of Indigenous Australians could equally be applied to Indigenous peoples of the Americas, Pacific Islands, New Zealand and Scandinavia.

Over the last 200 years, the lives of Australian Aboriginal people have been controlled and dominated by white people and governments. Yet it is these very government institutions and white powerful companies with whom we are required to negotiate for our native title interests. There are numerous problems facing native title claimants in the native title system; in particular, claimants have identified problems in undertaking negotiations with non-native title claimants. These problems include the lengthy timeframes and stress placed on claimants, the failure of the system to empower claimants, and the dominance of white structures and white people within the system.

Empowerment as the Goal

The core objective of negotiation should be empowerment of the parties. This may be financial, professional, social, emotional, spiritual or even physiological (or a combination of these). However, the perspectives of many native title claimants suggest that this objective is lost in the native title structure.

If Aboriginal people are to achieve empowerment through a process that is designed by—and for—non-Aboriginal people, the 'goal posts' have to be shifted much further than would otherwise be needed in the situation where all parties are westerners. Socio-economic disadvantage, as well as the historical factors of dispossession, means that native title claimants are not able to negotiate on an equal footing. Native title claimants come to the negotiation with a mindset of disempowerment.

In referring to an experience with negotiation, one claimant commented:
Well I've never felt empowered by them (the National Native Title Tribunal). I more or less might have felt intimidated by them. I don't think they empowered me in any way … both sides are trying to win something, and they say it's a win-win situation. The way we've been treated, as I say, is that they want us to give everything. When the minister said he was too busy to see us, and he sent this other government representative, all this person offered was all the welfare things that's normal: "we'll give so much to Aboriginal health; do this and do that." There were no other benefits than what comes from the mainstream welfare anyway. So she wasn't offering nothing. When we went to negotiate with the government, they seemed to try to intimidate you. It seemed to be just the opposite to empowerment.[13]

Structural Empowerment

The intent of the native title alternative dispute resolution (ADR) process has evolved over the past decade to explicitly include 'non-native title outcomes' to try to redress some aspects of these long-term grievances. The reason that the ADR process can work much more effectively than the litigation process is because of its broader objective of empowerment (see my 'core objective' of negotiation, above). Perhaps the power-brokers in native title are beginning to realize that financial and time efficiencies may be the *outcome* of ADR, but should not be the *motive* for preferring ADR.

Yet is this objective of empowerment possible, without mechanisms not provided for in the legislation? I would argue that it is not. In particular, the negotiation process cannot achieve this purpose unless it is reorganized to provide a space for re-empowerment. The representatives of the dominant party need to create a forum where the disempowered feel that we have a legitimate voice; while some might think that the non-dominant party should do this in its own interests, in practice a disempowered party is not in a position to take on this task. Despite all the strategies a good negotiator might use to equalize the power of the parties, the fact is, as Dodson says, "Aboriginal people haven't had much of a chance to get used to having a say in decisions affecting our land."[14] Furthermore, when we do speak about our land:

> Because native title is at the core of Indigenous identity, every native title
> claim will have a complex social dimension and significant social conse-
> quences.[15]

Thus there is no way around the need for structural change: the negotiation model used and the strategies adopted by representatives of both parties need to address the inherent power imbalances, or enduring agreements cannot be reached. In native title negotiations, the need for emotional and spiritual empowerment are perhaps more significant than financial or proprietary restitution. Therefore, a culturally safe space needs to be provided to enable the disadvantaged parties to tell their story. As Dodson says, native title dispute resolution needs:

> [To] become a truly cross-cultural negotiation instead of a coercive and
> predetermined story in which Aboriginal people have their limited role al-
> ready scripted for them.[16]

From an Aboriginal perspective, the negotiation process can seem confrontational. One native title claimant stated: "I don't like talking to white people [seated] all in rows."[17] Although claimants may be wishing to tell their story in a negotiation, the forum can be confrontational and intimidating. Dodson comments:

> In my experience, Aboriginal people do not usually use verbal confronta-
> tions, insults, interruptions, objections, etc as a rhetoric device in
> argument. Lawyers do. Non-Aboriginal people are generally familiar with
> this and understand it as theatrics.[18]

My own experience of inter-cultural negotiation tends to agree with Dodson's observations: non-Aboriginal professionals not only understand the theatrics, but are willing and ready to 'perform' accordingly. Presenting an argument to a group is part of a university education in any of the arts; graduates know that part of their job will more than likely require them to 'perform' a presentation to stakeholders. For Aboriginal people not so educated (in the western sense), it is far more difficult. It is a big personal risk to stand up in front of people to talk about something of great personal significance. Aboriginal people often cannot hide our emotion behind a modernist façade of objectivity—something that lawyers, sociologists, anthropologists, social workers, and so on, are trained to do. In any case, "opening up" emotionally is difficult for any person who has been badly hurt.

There is also an operational risk that conflict will escalate: our social and cultural experience is that verbal confrontation is often a precursor to physical confrontation. Dodson confirms this point: "for Indigenous people, verbal confrontation is often the start of violence."[19]

Lawyers Do Not Empower

One supposed solution to our avoidance of verbal confrontation is for the (white) lawyers to intervene on our behalf: to jump in and "save us;" to "fight our battles." Well-intentioned lawyers can do this without realizing that its effect is further disempowerment. Given that the dynamics of native title negotiation and mediation can result in confrontation, the lawyers (being accustomed to this confrontation) for the claimants often intervene and argue on behalf of the claimants. The dilemma has been described by claimants in their interviews with me. While there is a desire on the part of claimants to articulate their views in the negotiation, the process can be intimidating, particularly when non-claimant groups get confrontational, so "we can tend to hand it over to our lawyer."[20] One claimant stated that she felt so intimidated—because of all the non-Aboriginal parties— that she allowed her lawyer to take control of the negotiations:

> Because, they [the non-claimants] know so much about us—like the land claim and all about us, where we was, you know what I mean—the land claim itself. They needed to know any more, but I couldn't tell em anymore anyhow—told em what I knew—about the land and our place and all that sort of thing—walking and talking. I didn't think I could say anything more to us. But some of those meetings I didn't agree with them— some of them. But I didn't say anything.[21]

This quote raises two important issues. First, the claimant who said this to me was trying to convey her exasperation with the unending need of opposing parties and counsel for information. She told them all the creation stories she knew about her country, but it wasn't enough for them; they wanted more detail, more words, more justification for the claim. Lawyers think that if someone has a plausible and solid claim, then one can submit a plausible and extensive argument to those who dispute the claim. The problem is that the claim of each tribe/nation to their parcel of land ("country") was never in dispute until the British came. It is only recently that we have had to develop an argument about our continuing connection to the land.

Secondly, the solution, clearly, does not lie in our lawyers taking over the process and speaking on our behalf. Again, this ultimately disempowers native title claimants. Yet our lawyers, particularly when the issues are legally technical, will dominate the negotiation process—of course, "in our best interests!" This particular problem extends even beyond Indigenous people. [Nolan-Haley, *Informed Consent*] At one of my own native title meetings, when a report by our solicitor was provided, several claimant group members demanded to know from the lawyers why they were doing the negotiating instead of claimant representatives. The response was that "there were many technical issues that needed to be addressed."[22] One claimant member responded, "we're sick of you whitefella lawyers speaking on our behalf."[23]

It is thus the dispute resolution process itself that needs to change to ensure that claimants are empowered by the process. There are, in fact, some surprisingly simple measures that might be adopted. One is to have the lawyers sitting behind the claimants, to give the claimants a sense of being in charge of the claim (and in charge of the lawyer). In the same vein, the Northern Territory Aboriginal Land Commissioner has an interesting way of breaking up the conventional courtroom setup. He goes and sits right near the Aboriginal witness who is giving evidence. There is no amplification, so anyone who wants to hear has to come around too. This means that the Aboriginal speaker is the center of the process, and the lawyers are marginalized.[24] At the end of this chapter, I will consider some other possibilities.

But without a change in other aspects of the process, including appropriate venues and facilitators, such seating arrangements will not achieve the necessary shift in the power dynamics that is required to see true empowerment of native title claimants.

No Incentive for Good Faith Negotiations

There are several provisions in the *Native Title Act 1993* (NTA) that require parties to negotiate in good faith. But the positions of power that governments and huge companies hold in negotiating with Indigenous parties, leaves the non-Indigenous parties with little incentives to negotiate in good faith. In a recent study,[25] I found that failure on the part of governments to negotiate in good faith was a common concern:

> We tried to get the government to mediate with us to come to some agreement, but with politicians, they always know how to maneuver out of it. The only time they met with us was when we first went into their office. The minister met with us and said he would negotiate native title, but that was the last time we seen him. We repeatedly sent letters to him, but we always got a smart answer. You know how they maneuver out of it? They are spin doctors, that what we call them here—they can spin out of anything. Then the minister sent another person to negotiate with us. She didn't know nothing about native title. And she was more or less just insulting our intelligence ... they claim that for years they've been negotiating with us. But in reality, they've just been evading negotiating with us.[26]

Yet cynicism is an easy answer. With this daunting array of obstacles, there are still some strategies and tactics that might help. The procedurally minor (and economical) matter of who sits where is one example; in the concluding section of this chapter, I will attempt some others, with the "fair warning" that here I am advocating, in part, untested theory.

Some Concrete Suggestions Resulting From the Scenario

What are some of the strategies that you could have adopted to ensure better outcomes in the negotiation scenario presented above?

Choose your negotiating team carefully.

- If you are not from the same cultural/ethnic group as the other party, choose a trusted colleague who is of the same ethnicity as the other party. If there is no-one of the same ethnicity in your organization, contact a consultant from outside your organization who is.
- But be wary of engaging a consultant who is (what we Aboriginal people call) a "big talker" some of our own people who set themselves up as experts or consultants, like the young man in the scenario, are eloquent and

charismatic. But under the slick exterior, they garner far less respect, knowledge and trust than they claim; sometimes they are simply bullies.

- So, not sure who to ask? Why not ask the other party (or other people of their community) whom they would recommend? This demonstrates respect for the integrity of the other party and trust in their character.
- Make sure you match the gender and other demographics of the other party. If your side is currently all male, but theirs includes some females, then you should similarly include women. If they have an older person(s), you should too.

Engage personally in extensive pre-negotiation.

- It is most likely that the other party will be intimidated by you. Look for common areas of interest during pre-negotiation meetings.
- Get to know the other party/ies informally; perhaps share a meal with them. Meet in a place they choose.
- Keep them informed every step of the way; if you are going to be late, phone them. They may not phone you; some of their representatives may not show up; some may even verbally abuse you when things become "emotional"—but you must keep up your standards as a mark of respect for them.
- If you leave them in the dark about anything you're up to, your faithfulness will immediately be doubted.[27]
- Find out who people are, how they're related to each other, and what roles they have in the community. But be careful not to look like you're conducting an investigation. If you're not interested in such relationships (even though it will assist your negotiation)—don't ask.
- Don't talk about 'business' in pre-negotiation—unless they ask you to. Then you should be brief, but open.
- In the scenario above, for example, if the western negotiators had met with the other party beforehand, they would have discovered some key information:
  - That the woman breastfeeding is the grand-daughter of a prominent and respected old man who had recently passed away. She is one of the few in the community to have finished year 12 of school and is studying at university by correspondence.
  - That none of the Aboriginal representatives (other than the young man) have respect for their lawyer, Simon; he was known as "six-month Simon" when he used to work for the Aboriginal legal service. This was because of his propensity to advise his clients to plead guilty (regardless of their actual guilt) to their charges and they would routinely receive a six-month prison sentence. And the Aboriginal representatives had no choice of lawyer—he was appointed to them by their native title representative body.
  - The Government's lawyer—your colleague—had lost all respect from the community; she had (on behalf of the Government) consistently refused a "consent native title determination." As a result, two years ago the claim went to the Federal Court for adjudication, and there is still no determination.
  - That the young Aboriginal man was raised in a (white) foster family in Darwin from the age of seven. He returned home about five years ago, but mainly lives in Alice Springs, where he runs his native title consul-

tancy firm. He has several vehicles on permanent loan to community members, including to the older man sitting next to him—whom he employs as a "consultant" for various projects. The young man is known to "run" the native title claim.

The negotiation should be "owned" by both parties.

- In the stated scenario, you are representing the powerful party. It is important that some of your power is surrendered to the less powerful party.
- Have the negotiations take place in a venue of their choice. In the scenario, the non-Aboriginal parties thought they were being culturally sensitive by holding it in an Aboriginal venue—in the office of the land council. If the Aboriginal party had a choice, most likely they would have preferred to negotiate at home—"on country."
- Make sure that the dates of the negotiation are not at times when large numbers of the community may be absent; for example, during school vacation periods. It is also best to avoid the two days after "pension day" (payment by government of unemployment, old age and disability benefits) for any serious discussions: even if a community member does not drink or gamble, they have to deal with family members who do. Substance abuse, gambling addiction and family violence are serious problems in many Indigenous communities; the negotiating team members may have to take time out to deal with these problems.
- Avoid jargon or technical terms. In the stated scenario, the young man may feel that you are being condescending to him if you explain technical terms that he already understands. Pre-empt this by saying, for example, "I know some of you already know what "future acts" means in native title law. But I want to be sure that everyone understands."
- Make sure everyone has had a feed and there are plenty of refreshments, especially tea and coffee. Allow time to have plenty of breaks—we all like to "caucus" during such moments to check our understandings and argue our viewpoints less formally. Don't try to 'be friendly' by intruding on the informal gatherings of the other party during breaks (unless asked); they need this time to talk frankly or simply to relax.

Ensure you are negotiating with representatives of the other party who have authority not only to make decisions but to make good decisions.

- As implied above, one 'big talker' on the other side can disrupt negotiations. He or she may be unrepresentative of the other party. Worse still, the other party may have no respect for the big talker.
- Don't address your questions to their lawyer. Even if they speak a different language, address the person concerned (not the interpreter) in the first person. [Kaufman, *Interpreter*] Unfortunately, the lawyer for the other party will probably not be Indigenous; most Indigenous law graduates are absorbed by the public service where better conditions of employment are received.
- Even though the representatives of the other party may, in western terms, have authority to make decisions, it is unlikely that they will be comfortable doing so without consulting the rest of the community. Communal decision-making is something that hierarchical cultures have trouble grasping; they are anxious for someone to make a decision. Be patient.

- If the other party agrees to something that is beneficial to you, but detrimental to them, then that is a bad decision for *both* parties. The agreement is unlikely to last and will probably result in litigation.

Active listening is the key to good communication.
- Yes, an obvious principle. But do we practice it? You should be doing a lot of listening and not much talking (but of course you should be open about what your side is offering).
- Ask open questions (as long as it does not intrude on their privacy).
- Make a point of talking to the quiet ones. In the scenario, the women kept quiet (this is not always the case with Aboriginal communities—sometimes we can be the most vocal). Perhaps the women did not speak because they were not asked; maybe they were in fear of the two men. In this scenario, the western negotiators did not know that the older man was a domestic violence perpetrator—one of the six women was his first wife who had been badly injured by him in an assault. In any event, the problem was not their failure to speak, but rather the negotiator's failure to involve them in the process. The knowledge of the women about sacred sites on the prospect land may be one of their few sources of power; they were not going to reveal this readily (and certainly not to any men).
- Allow silence; don't be embarrassed by it and try to "fill" it. In the scenario, the Aboriginal claimants' lawyer liked to take up any silent periods to show off his knowledge of Aboriginal law and culture. Yet he completely misunderstood the reaction of the women to his question: "you understand? Mining company not touch sacred country." The women who nodded thought that he was saying the mining company will not go on to sacred country; that is, that they will not even *explore* it. The non-Aboriginal people understood it as being that the company will not *mine* any sacred sites. The negotiation did not even raise what the women defined as *public* sacred sites versus *secret* sacred sites, or what sort of activities would be involved in exploration

Be aware of non-verbal communication.
- Check your understanding; not just of words, but of tone and body language. For example, in the given scenario, the negotiator could have asked the women, "I notice that you have not said anything yet. Can you help me to understand your point of view?"
- If they dress casually, you should do so as well. But if the other party uses profanities, this is not a signal for you to do likewise; as a "professional," they probably expect higher standards of you.

Monitor yourself.
- your language and tone
- your body language
- your assumptions
- In relation to the latter, be particularly careful about stereotypes. For example, in the stated scenario, the negotiator for the mining company may have assumed that women are not permitted to engage in "business," or that they don't understand what's going on, or that the woman breastfeeding is not interested in the discussion.

- Another common (false) assumption about Aboriginal people is that we don't look you in the eye. In earlier times, non-Aboriginal people thought that this was a sign of our untrustworthiness; later, anthropologists claimed that this is just part of our culture. Wrong. In my experience, it is when an Aboriginal person feels disempowered we will not make eye contact. The other common reason for avoiding eye contact is when we do not respect or trust the other (usually non-Aboriginal) person. An exception: in "traditional" Aboriginal communities (usually in remote Australia), avoidance of eye contact also occurs in the context of "avoidance" relationships, such as between a son and his mother-in-law.
- Be careful of your body language and tone of voice: in "high context" cultures (such as indigenous cultures), it's pretty obvious if you're in a hurry or if you don't want to be there. Be honest; if you cannot stay long, say so—don't try to hide it, because it will show.

Don't try to "push" the negotiation process

- Even in the negotiation, don't be concerned if the discussion moves "off point." The other side is as much aware as you are of the reason you are here: they will come back to "business" when they are ready.
- And don't push for an immediate answer to your proposal. If you do have a commercial deadline, say so early on, and make it clear that it cannot be postponed (if that is true). The more you push, the more you'll encounter resistance.
- If you are personally 'invested' in this negotiation, it simply looks to the other side like another person/company is trying to take advantage of them. This deal may be important for your career, but for them, life will go on just like before if nothing eventuates. For disadvantaged communities, it is sometimes hard to believe that life can get better.

This chapter has really only touched on the nature of negotiation with Indigenous communities. I have used native title negotiations in Australia to illustrate the different approach required by western corporate or government negotiators when the other party is a non-western community that utilizes collective decision-making. But there are "western" communities that emphasize collective decision-making. For example, multiple-occupancy communities—known in our vernacular as "hippy communes"—are collectives with diffuse sources of power. They are critical of modernist liberalism's emphasis on the autonomy of the individual and its belief that self-interest leads to the greatest satisfaction.

Over the past decade (at least in Australia) we have seen conservativism appropriate the terminology of communitarianism, in order to camouflage itself amongst "aspirant" class hopes for a richer-but-still-friendly nation. For example, both sides of politics now refer to "our community" instead of "this society." This has muddied the waters for Aboriginal people; we have to counter the argument from government that their particular proposal is "better for the community," with our argument that *their* community is not *our* community. This use of communitarian language by conservative forces, however, is only a thin veneer over 19th century liberalism, with its emphasis on such things as the ability of any individual to freely negotiate an agreement that is beneficial to them. In native title negotiations this duality from government can be confusing: their rhetoric speaks of group identity and communal interests, but it's a disguise for law and policy that is grounded in laissez-faire economics.

Poor ethnic and indigenous minorities are well aware that we possess very little wealth or power. So when government or corporate Australia comes knocking, we are defensive: "what do they want from me?" rather than optimistic: "could this deal be beneficial to me?" We are so afraid of being tricked or trampled upon that it can be difficult to perceive that the other party is offering something that may result in our empowerment: economists call this "risk-aversion."

I am hesitant to extend my "suggestions" to negotiations with other marginalized ethnic communities, simply because of my lack of experience and research outside of Aboriginal-western ADR processes. But my intuition is that much of this is applicable to negotiations with anyone who comes from shattered communities where trust is crushed. Yet there are people who gain from our remaining like that: our disadvantage supports a vast number of mainly white middle-class professionals: police, lawyers, court staff, juvenile justice officers, corrective services, social and welfare workers, child protection officers, special education teachers, mental health workers, hospital staff, funeral homes (as well as the owners of pubs, liquor shops, casinos, licensed clubs and gambling agencies). So in our dealings with this "helping" class (excluding those mentioned in parentheses), we feel the pull of the undercurrents that are the converse of (but created by) this huge swell of "help:" undercurrents of complacency, condescension and control.

Indigenous communities across the colonized developed world exist in a disadvantaged and disempowered reality. Even when western negotiators adopt the principles and techniques outlined above, they must nevertheless "come to the table with truth, compassion and a commitment to human rights and social justice." [28] Governments and commercial organizations need to commit to the principle that when parties are empowered they are more likely to reach fairer and more reasonable outcomes that will benefit all parties involved.

Endnotes

[1] The community is usually represented by several people in the negotiation process.

[2] I use these terms to mean disputes between: a party who is of the minority culture and a party who is of the majority culture (inter-cultural); and parties who are both of the minority culture.

[3] (No 2) 175 C.L.R. 1 (1992).

[4] *Native Title Act 1993* (Commonwealth of Australia).

[5] Only a few jurisdictions in Australia enacted statutes that gave ownership of land to Indigenous people. The one I am referring to is the New South Wales *Aboriginal Land Rights Act (1983)*.

[6] *Wik Peoples v State of Queensland* 187 C.L.R. 1 (1996).

[7] Pronounced roughly as "goom [as in book]-bayn-gear."

[8] Wayne Atkinson, *Mediating the Mindset of Opposition: The Yorta Yorta Case*, 5(15) INDIGENOUS LAW BULLETIN 8, 9 (Feb./Mar. 2002).

[9] The use of stories transcends culture; note the similarity in the training of hostage negotiators in the New York Police Department, in Maria R. Volpe, Jack J. Cambria, Hugh McGowan and Christopher Honeyman, *Negotiation with the Unknown*, Chapter 74 in this volume.

[10] LARISSA BEHRENDT, ABORIGINAL DISPUTE RESOLUTION 17 (1995).

[11] LAURENCE BOULLE, MEDIATION: PRINCIPLES, PROCESS, PRACTICE 57-58 (1996).

[12] *Id.* at 57.

[13] Anonymous native title claimant 'E', *Interview with Loretta Kelly*, Oct. 2 2003 (location of interview withheld as it may identify the interviewee).

[14] Mick Dodson, *Power and Cultural Differences in Native Title Mediation*, 3(84) ABORIGINAL LAW BULLETIN 8, 9 (Sept. 1996).

[15] *Id.* at 9-10.

[16] *Id.* at 10.

[17] Anonymous native title claimant 'C', *Interview with Loretta Kelly,* May 28, 2003 (location of interview withheld as it may identify the interviewee).

[18] Dodson, *supra* note 14, at 8.

[19] *Id.*

[20] Anonymous native title claimant 'C', *Interview with Loretta Kelly,* May 28, 2003 (location of interview withheld as it may identify the interviewee).

[21] Anonymous native title claimant 'C', *Interview with Loretta Kelly,* May 28, 2003 (location of interview withheld as it may identify the interviewee).

[22] Solicitor for anonymous native title claimant group, North Coast NSW, *Meeting of claimant group attended by Loretta Kelly,* 2004. Location and precise date of meeting withheld, as it may identify the claimant group and their solicitor.

[23] Anonymous native title claimant, North Coast NSW, *Meeting of claimant group attended by Loretta Kelly,* 2004 (location and precise date of meeting withheld, as it may identify the claimant group and individual participants at the meeting).

[24] Dodson, *supra* note 14, at 10.

[25] Note that the main findings of this research, which was funded by the Australian Research Council, are found in the forthcoming Federation Press book by Loretta Kelly and Larissa Behrendt—(working title) *Native Title Mediation and Aboriginal Empowerment.*

[26] Anonymous native title claimant 'E', *Interview with Loretta Kelly,* Oct. 2 2003 (location of interview withheld as it may identify the interviewee).

[27] As in endnote 4 above, this is similar to the advice given to NYPD hostage negotiators.

[28] Tony Lee, *The Natives are Restless: A Personal Reflection on Ten Years of Native Title, in* 23 HISTORY AND NATIVE TITLE: STUDIES IN WESTERN AUSTRALIAN HISTORY 29, 32 (Chistine Choo & Shawn Hollbach eds., 2003).

෪ 36 ෫

Gender is More than Who We Are

Deborah M. Kolb & Linda L. Putnam

Editors' Note: *While many negotiation analysts have observed behavior differences resulting from gender, this chapter takes the issues much further. The authors analyze patterns of thinking and behavior which are central to how we all handle conflict but which often remain obscure to members of the opposite gender, even after a lifetime of close contact.*

After many years of indifference, the study of gender is now an important area of scholarship in negotiation. At the same time as interest has grown, so too have the perspectives on gender and negotiation evolved. Elsewhere, we have suggested that there are three major ways to look at gender.[1] The first, and by far the most common, is to treat gender as differences between men and women. A second approach, an interpretive one, treats gender as being socially constructed. And the third approach, with its roots in postmodern thinking, uses a lens of gender to look at how theory and practice render invisible key elements of the social enactment of negotiation. Our purpose in this paper is to review these different perspectives, but to focus more directly on research based on the interpretive and postmodern approaches. Because most of the gender research occurs in the laboratory, the focus has been primarily on individuals in interaction. To extend our understanding of gender and negotiations, we need to look more closely at organizations as a primary site for the construction of gender identities.[2] In this paper, we will trace the different ways gender has been studied in negotiation and show how a focus on organizations as gendered entities is critical to understanding about the ways gender matters in negotiation.

Gender Equals Difference

As Rubin and Brown noted in 1976, sex is one of the most easily measured variables, so it is not surprising that the question, "Do men and women negotiate differently?" is frequently asked.[3] Recent research suggests that women don't ask, often let opportunities for negotiation slip by, typically set low goals, concede easily, and let their emotions show, among other factors.[4] Although individual studies on sex differences may produce significant findings, cumulative results across studies are often contradictory. Meta-analyses of these studies have shown only small statistically significant differences and on just two dimensions: women tend to be more cooperative than men and tend to receive lower outcomes when money is at issue.[5]

To ask a question about differences between men and women assumes that gender is a stable attribute of individuals. Accounting for these differences requires that there is some basis in biology, socialization, role theory, or entitlements to explain why they exist.[6] The most common argument posits that women emphasize nurturance and support in their relationships because of their social development and the mothering roles they often play (or are expected to play). In contrast, according to this argument, men are groomed for separation and individualism, behaviors presumably more suited to the demands of negotiation.[7] Thus women are more likely to treat a negotiation as an event in a long-term relationship, one linked to a larger social context and concerned with fairness and sensitivity to others, while men see it as a one-time event with no direct consequences for future interactions.[8] Without directly testing for the origins of gender differences, these explanations become tautological and are often marshaled after the fact to account for women's deficiencies when they negotiate. For example, when men outperform women in salary negotiations, the explanations given for these differences are "the problems" that women have in negotiating.[9]

In a field that prides itself on pragmatism, the advice that results from this stream of research is problematic. First, the findings boil down to two points— either women are the same as men or they are different from them (i.e., deficient). So the advice is directed only to women; namely, how can women overcome their deficiencies and better equip themselves to negotiate or how can they strengthen their instrumental orientation to the task.[10] No similar advice exists for men. Second, the advice from this work may itself be gendered and subject to gender stereotypes that people use to judge behavior.[11] Thus, to tell a woman to act in a more self-interested, assertive, or instrumental way assumes that these behaviors are neutral in the sense that men and women can use them with the same effects and same consequences. However, these behaviors when enacted by a woman are likely to be seen differently than they are when men employ them. Assertiveness, self-orientation, and an instrumental focus may backfire against women. This type of asymmetry has created double binds for women in other research arenas.[12] In the leadership field, for example, it has been shown that beliefs about effective leaders, which tend to reflect masculine, agentic qualities, conflict with beliefs about femininity. A double bind test for a woman leader is the question—can she be a leader and a woman too? If she acts decisively and pushes for what she needs—behaviors we might expect from leaders—she may be seen as too pushy. But if she conforms to feminine expectations and consults widely, she is seen as indecisive.[13]

Others value difference—articulating a woman's point of view that brings unnoticed benefits to the negotiation process and the agreements that it produces. From this perspective, a focus on relationships, the skills of empathy, and the ability to manage conflict and competition simultaneously are thought (although not explicitly tested) to be advantageous in negotiations.[14] However, when researchers have tested to see if a "feminine concern" for others is correlated with joint gains, the findings are not encouraging.[15] It is not enough to care about the other party. For women to achieve high joint gains, in this case profit, they need to be primed to pay more attention to their own needs. Further, appreciating the feminine skills that negotiators bring to the table ignores the ways that these skills are not equally valued when compared with the more "masculine" skills basic to claiming behavior in distributive negotiations.

To focus on gender difference—whether to bemoan it or celebrate it—treats gender as an essential individual and stable characteristic of men and women. First, the approach treats men and women as internally homogenous categories, yet we know there is considerable variability within the sexes. Second, it fails to recognize that gender is hierarchically arrayed in society, and so to focus on difference is to accept a false symmetry in which the masculine emerges as the standard and the woman as the other.[16] In the negotiation field, the research and the pragmatic advice derived from the gender difference perspective reinforces masculine attributes; that is, it inadvertently places a premium on enlightened self-interest, analytic rationality, objectivity, and instrumentality.[17] In contrast, those attributes typically labeled as feminine—empathy, concern for relationships, subjectivity, and emotional expressiveness—remain less valued. As Joan Scott points out, what may start out as an explanation of the experiences that lead to differences between women and men, often translates into "women are the way they are because they are women."[18] When we focus on the question—whether men and women negotiate differently—it is the women that emerge as in deficit and in need of "fixing."

Interpretive Perspectives on Gender

Interpretive perspectives shift the focus away from essentialist characteristics of men and women to the negotiation interaction itself. From this perspective, gender is continually socially constructed, produced and reproduced. In other words, we "do gender" rather than have a gender.[19] "Doing gender" means that in the process of enacting a social practice (such as negotiation), individuals are constantly engaged in constructing identities and social situations in gendered ways. In this way, gender is not an individual characteristic, but both a means and an outcome of the ways parties socially construct negotiation. Interpretive perspectives emphasize the fluidity, flexibility, and variability of gender-related behaviors. The challenge is to understand how parties enact negotiation in a particularly gendered way. If the research question from the first perspective is, "Do men and women negotiate differently?" the interactive perspective raises a more useful question, "When and under what conditions does gender shape the course of interactions?[20] Three levels of analysis comprise these conditions—the individual, the interactional and the situational/organizational levels.

Individual Level and Gender Roles

One way gender gets mobilized in negotiations concerns identity and how salient gender is to an individual negotiator. At the individual level, therefore, one can consider the degree to which negotiators identify with the masculine and/or feminine sides of themselves and take up those roles or positions in the process. From this perspective, a man might choose, either consciously or unconsciously, to act in a stereotypically masculine way—shouting, bullying, acting competitively—because he believes that the context prompts him to behave in this way. By the same token, a woman might take up the role of helper or concentrate on the relationship, again because she perceives that the context calls for her to behave in that way. Work by Michele Gelfand and her associates looks at what they call relational self-construal, that is, the degree to which negotiators access a *relational self.*[21] Even though women are more likely to access a relational self-construal, men may also tap into this aspect of their identities. Similarly, Lisa Barron, in her studies of salary negotiation, identifies masculine and feminine orientations that are not necessarily defined by gender.[22] Bargainers, in other words, have some choice as to the degree to which they take on gender roles in a negotiation—that is, they are not doomed by their gender.

Interaction Level and Gender Construction

Gender can also become salient because others expect that and act as if gender matters. Stereotyped expectations that push a woman to assume an accommodative role or a man to be competitive can create a narrow band of gendered behaviors, which in turn reinforce gender identity. Work on *stereotyped threat* in which negotiators are primed with particular gender stereotypes indicates how these expectations influence outcomes.[23] Specifically, when researchers link masculine stereotypes to negotiation effectiveness, men achieve higher payoffs than do women. Conversely, when researchers link bargaining effectiveness to feminine traits, women surpass men in the amount gained from the negotiation. These studies also illustrate that participants are susceptible to enacting negotiation in a gendered way, especially when they are primed to do so. Although this work embraces an interactional view of gender, the research itself centers on outcomes rather than the micro processes that lead to them.

Situational Effects and Gendered Constructions

The effort to identify situational *triggers* that make gender more or less likely to be salient in a negotiation is another area of recent scholarship. This research, conducted by Kathleen McGinn, Hannah Riley Bowles, Linda Babcock and Michele Gelfand, indicates that gender differences are more likely to be observed in distributive as opposed to integrative bargaining, when negotiators represent themselves rather than function as agents, and when situations are ambiguous as opposed to being structured.[24] These effects, observed in the laboratory, are only a partial exploration of the ways that situation and context can impact gender in negotiations.

Organizations and institutions in which negotiations take place are not gender neutral.[25] Their structures, cultures, and norms of operating are often gendered in the sense that they are likely to fit the experiences of men, more than of women. This research in the organizational field focuses on *second generation* gender issues.[26] While first generation gender issues are overt, "second generation" refers to the cultures and work practices that appear gender neutral on the surface but have differential effects on men and women. Second generation issues enacted in organizations define the contexts for negotiations. Consider, for example, the opportunity structure in one organization. Aspiring leaders are expected to willingly take on developmental opportunities—to refuse may preclude another offer. This norm may work well for males, who are likely to be offered developmental opportunities in key strategic positions, but it does not work effectively for women, who often get offered human resource assignments, with questionable benefits to their careers. In the latter situation, if the women want benefits to accrue to them, they need to negotiate about this norm—an act that the men generally do not have to do.

Indeed, around a wide range of issues, women often have to negotiate for things that men generally do not—e.g., work and personal life arrangements, or credit for *invisible work,* the relational, behind the scenes work that women often do.[27] Second generation issues also reflect power relationships and so can create double binds for women. In another organization, women were routinely offered positions with lesser titles than their male counterparts. If they pushed for a comparable title in their promotion negotiations, they were often perceived as 'aggressive' and deemed less suitable for the job. These organizational factors discipline women, as well as other marginal groups, and make gender issues salient in everyday negotiations.[28]

A Gender Lens on Negotiation

Another way to conceptualize gender in negotiation is not about individuals, nor the conditions under which gender becomes mobilized; but rather it focuses on gender as an organizing principle of social life.[29] With its roots in postmodern literatures, this perspective questions the apparent neutrality of what constitutes knowledge in a field, and it shows how power shapes certain truths and taken-for-granted assumptions.[30] Using this perspective, we have examined the gendered nature of negotiation itself by exploring how the theory, research, and norms of practice privilege certain ways of being (that is, masculine) and marginalize others, that is, the feminine. This point underscores the assumption that gender relations are always situated in power. Using this lens, we focus on what is silenced or ignored in the field. In our own work, the first author elaborates on the shadow negotiation rooted in the power and relational dynamics heretofore under-theorized in negotiation.[31] This perspective illuminates three particular areas: the problem of social position; the challenges of maintaining legitimacy in bargaining interactions; and the possibilities of transformative outcomes from negotiations.

Elaborating Social Positioning

Most theory and research in negotiation fails to explore how social positioning in an organization's hierarchy influences choices and imposes constraints on bargainers regardless of gender. The importance of social positioning is illustrated in field studies of employees who are newcomers to management in organizations. In an investigation of salary negotiations, for example, one team of researchers found that prospective minority employees, who had access to organizational social networks, achieved higher salaries than those who were outside the networks, even though both groups had good BATNAs.[32] Thus, people who do not have contacts or friends in organizations are disadvantaged in entry-level salary negotiations. Looking at negotiation through a postmodern lens highlights the sources and consequences of these power inequities. Similar to second generation gender issues, power/structure dimensions in organizations influence the dynamics of negotiations. [Bernard, *Powerlessness*] It suggests that theory and research need to consider the challenges of social positioning, its roots in status and/or identity, and how positioning impacts the process and outcomes of negotiation.[33] By making this shift, research and theory can help other negotiators in disadvantageous positions, as well as women. The framework of strategic moves—making value visible, raising the costs of the status quo, enlisting allies, and managing the process—is one approach that enhances the stances at the table of negotiators who are in disadvantaged positions. [Kolb, *Moves & Turns*]

Elaborating Legitimacy

The power and positioning of a negotiator are not finally established at the outset of the bargaining; but can be continually contested. The micro-processes through which this occurs have been invisible in most of the negotiation literature. Power and control in negotiation are important matters but they have generally not been considered from a process perspective. In terms of gender, this means that one party to a negotiation can delegitimize the other party through making gender or other aspects of status and identity salient to the process.[34] For example, when attention is drawn to physical characteristics of body or appearance, or where a person's style is characterized as too emotional or 'excited,' it can put her in a defensive position where she may find it more difficult to advocate for herself and her ideas. Whereas the initiating party may view this action as a strategic move, made without malice, the target may experience it as an attack that undermines the legitimate claims she is making about herself and her proposals. Delegitimizing one of the parties during a negotiation reduces the likelihood of a mutually beneficial outcome for both bargainers, unless the target is able to resist. Research on the micro-processes of negotiation interaction reveals a number of options for how people can resist these strategic moves through the use of "turns". "Turns" are ways that negotiators can respond to the other party's efforts to discredit or undermine actions by shifting the meaning of those behaviors.[35] [Kolb, *Moves &* *Turns*] Turning the interaction takes place in the "shadow" of a negotiation. These turns are also ways of resisting gender stereotypes as well as responding to moves that can put any negotiator in a disadvantageous position.[36]

Elaborating Interdependence and Transformation

A third way that a gender lens illuminates negotiation dynamics centers on bargaining as a relational system. Rather than valuing a woman's concern for relationships as the perspective of gender difference research does, a gender lens focuses on how a relational orientation might influence theory and practice. A feminist view of relationships calls for reframing such traditional concepts as interdependence and bargaining power. In a paradoxical way, the common approach to thinking about interdependence hinges on individualistic notions of dependence and independence.[37] As parties negotiate issues at the table, they also work out the nature of their dependence on each other. In the traditional literature, bargaining power derives from these perceptions of dependence and independence as a function of each person's Best Alternative to a Negotiated Agreement.[38] [Korobkin, *Power*] As negotiators endeavor to improve their BATNAs, they highlight their independence and minimize their interdependence. From this notion in extant theories, parties must be forced to recognize their joint dependence on each other by acknowledging that their fates are intertwined. In effect, interdependence becomes equated with jointly controlling each other's fate.

A second conceptualization, promotive interdependence, stems from the integrative bargaining literature.[39] Specifically, through problem-solving, parties bargain on issues to meet each other's individual needs and to discover how their interdependence benefits each of them. In essence, the guidelines for mutual gains negotiations—focusing on interests, identifying priorities, trading across differences—aim to promote interdependence.

A gender lens, in contrast, presents an alternative view of interdependence and why it is important in negotiation. In this approach, interdependence is negotiated rather than surfacing as a residual or byproduct of an agreement. Interdependence is created through the way negotiators connect with each other to appreciate and understand how their lives are intertwined. Thus, connecting rather than strategic activity forms the nature of interdependence. Second, interdependence involves change and learning through a stance of curiosity that recognizes that dialogue and mutual inquiry are necessary, even in negotiation, to understand and appreciate the other person. Our own research reveals that asking questions about the context of the situation, listening for silences, and raising hidden agendas not only enable parties to appreciate how they are interdependent, but they also help them to see the dispute in a new light.[40] This new way of understanding the conflict comes, in part, from gaining new insights about the context of the situation.

By working on interdependence, new understandings can transform the very nature of a negotiation. Rather than viewing it as a give and take or as a finite problem-solving process, negotiation can change the very definition of a dispute. Transformation occurs as parties come to see the issues in a different way.[41] This new dimension moves outside of both parties' frames of reference and situates the problem in a new realm. A dispute over resources and turf, for example, might be recast as a structural issue that negatively affects the performance of both parties. Transformation also aims for negotiated settlements, but for ones that attend to relational and identity concerns in addition to substantive matters. Parties to a turf dispute join together to negotiate with others to alter the conditions that created the problem in the first place.

Conclusion

The study of gender and negotiation has evolved from the early days in which scholars wondered if women were more cooperative than men. Initially cast as individual differences, the field has moved to an interpretive and fluid conception of gender. This more recent research, however, is also limited by its failure to include the organizational contexts within which negotiations occur. Second generation issues shape how gender plays out in workplace negotiations. Without attending to these issues, even this contemporary work may reinforce existing stereotypes and practices.

The gender lens perspective, in contrast, asks fundamental questions about the field itself, particularly the positioning of negotiators as advocates and the way that gendered assumptions permeate the bargaining process. Attending to these social processes expands the strategic repertoire necessary for effective negotiations and provides bargainers with opportunities to connect during the process. Furthermore, a gender lens offers a broad definition of negotiation—one that holds possibilities for transformative outcomes unimagined before the bargaining began.

Endnotes

[1] Deborah M. Kolb & Linda L. Putnam, *Through the Looking Glass: Negotiation Theory Refracted Through the Lens of Gender, in* FRONTIERS IN DISPUTE RESOLUTION IN INDUSTRIAL RELATIONS AND HUMAN RESOURCES (Sandra Gleason ed., 1997); Linda L. Putnam & Deborah M. Kolb, *Rethinking Negotiation: Feminist Views of Communication and Exchange, in* RETHINKING ORGANIZATIONAL AND MANGERIAL COMMUNICATION FROM FEMINIST PERSPECTIVES (Patrice M. Buzzanell ed., 2000).
[2] Robin Ely & Irene Padavic, *A Feminist Analysis of Micro Research on Gender in Organizations: Suggestions for Advancing the Field* (Harvard Business School, Working Paper No. 05-040, January 2005).
[3] JEFFREY RUBIN & BERT R. BROWN, THE SOCIAL PSYCHOLOGY OF BARGAINING AND NEGOTIATION (1975).
[4] LINDA BABCOCK & SARA LASCHEVER, WOMEN DON'T ASK: NEGOTIATION AND THE GENDER DIVIDE (2003).
[5] Amy E. Walters, et al., *Gender and Negotiator Competitiveness: A Meta-analysis*, 76 ORGANIZATIONAL BEHAVIOR AND HUMAN DECISION PROCESSES 1 (1998); Alice F. Stuhlmacher & Amy E. Walters, *Gender Differences in Negotiation Outcomes: A Meta-analysis*, 52 PERSONNEL PSYCHOLOGY 653 (1999).
[6] Ely & Padavic, *supra* note 2.
[7] Deborah M. Kolb & Gloria Coolidge, *Her Place at the Table, in* NEGOTIATION THEORY AND PRACTICE (J. William Breslin & Jeffrey Z. Rubin eds., 1991).
[8] Leonard Greenhalgh & Deborah I. Chapman, *Joint Decision-making: The Inseparability of Relationship and Negotiation, in* NEGOTIATION AS A SOCIAL PROCESS (Roderick M. Kramer & David M. Messick eds., 1995); Leonard Greenhalgh & Roderick W. Gilkey, *Our Game, Your Rules: Developing Effective Negotiating Approaches, in* NOT AS FAR AS YOU THINK: THE REALITIES OF WORKING WOMEN (L. Moore ed., 1986); Jennifer J. Halpern & Judi McLean Parks, *Vive la Différence: Differences Between Males and Females in Process and Outcomes in a Low-Conflict Negotiation*, 7 INTERNATIONAL JOURNAL OF CONFLICT MANAGEMENT 45 (1996).

[8] Stuhlmacher & Walters, *supra* note 5.

[9] Debra E. Meyerson & Deborah M. Kolb, *Moving Out of the "Armchair": Developing a Framework to Bridge the Gap Between Feminist Theory and Practice*, 7 ORGANIZATION 589 (2000).

[10] BABCOCK & LASCHEVER, *supra* note 4.

[11] VIRGINIA VALIAN, WHY SO SLOW? THE ADVANCEMENT OF WOMEN (1998).

[12] JOYCE K. FLETCHER, DISAPPEARING ACTS (1999); Julia T. Wood & Charles Conrad, *Paradox in the Experiences of Professional Women*, 47 THE WESTERN JOURNAL OF SPEECH COMMUNICATION 305 (1983).

[13] Alice H. Eagly & Linda Carli, *The Female Leadership Advantage: An Evaluation of the Evidence*, 14 THE LEADERSHIP QUARTERLY 807 (2003); DEBORAH M. KOLB, ET AL., HER PLACE AT THE TABLE: A WOMAN'S GUIDE TO NEGOTIATING FIVE CHALLENGES TO LEADERSHIP SUCCESS (2004).

[14] Kolb & Coolidge, *supra* note 7.

[15] Patrick S. Calhoun & William P. Smith, *Integrative Bargaining: Does Gender Make a Difference?*, 10 INTERNATIONAL JOURNAL OF CONFLICT MANAGEMENT 203 (1999).

[16] IRENE PADAVIC & BARBARA F. RESKIN, WOMEN AND MEN AT WORK (2002); Ely & Padavic, *supra* note 2.

[17] Kolb & Putnam, *supra* note 1.

[18] JOAN WALLACH SCOTT, GENDER AND THE POLITICS OF HISTORY (1988).

[19] JUDITH A. HOWARD & JOCELYN HOLLANDER, GENDERED SITUATIONS, GENDERED SELVES (1997); Candace West & D.H. Zimmerman, *Doing Gender*, 1 GENDER AND SOCIETY 125 (1987).

[20] Kay Deaux & Brenda Major, *A Social Psychological Model of Gender*, in THEORETICAL PERSPECTIVES ON SEXUAL DIFFERENCE (Deborah Rhode ed., 1990).

[21] Michele Gelfand, et al., A Dynamic Theory of Gender in Negotiation (2003) (unpublished paper, on file with University of Maryland).

[22] Lisa Barron, *Ask and You Shall Receive? Gender Differences in Negotiators' Beliefs About Requests for a Higher Salary*, 56 HUMAN RELATIONS 635 (2003).

[23] Laura J. Kray & Leigh Thompson, *Gender Stereotypes and Negotiation Performance*, in RESEARCH IN ORGANIZATIONAL BEHAVIOR (Barry M. Staw & Rod Kramer eds.) (forthcoming 26th vol.); Carol Rose, *Bargaining and Gender: Feminism, Sexual Distinctions, and the Law*, 18 HARVARD JOURNAL OF LAW AND PUBLIC POLICY 547 (1995).

[24] Hannah R. Bowles, et al., Constraints and Triggers: Situational Mechanics of Gender in Negotiation (Harvard University, John F. Kennedy School of Government, Working Paper No. RWP05-051, 2005); Gelfand, et al., *supra* note 21.

[25] Ely & Padavic, *supra* note 2; Karen Lee Ashcraft, *Gender, Discourse, and Organization: Framing a Shifting Relationship*, in THE SAGE HANDBOOK OF ORGANIZATIONAL DISCOURSE (David Grant, et al. eds., 2004).

[26] Susan Sturm, *Second Generation Employment Discrimination: A Structural Approach*, 101 COLUMBIA LAW REVIEW 458 (2001); Deborah E. Meyerson & Deborah M. Kolb, *Moving Out of the Armchair: Developing a Framework to Bridge the Gap Between Feminist Theory and Practice*, 7 ORGANIZATION 589 (2000).

[27] JOYCE K. FLETCHER, DISAPPEARING ACTS (1999).

[28] DEBORAH M. KOLB & JUDITH WILLIAMS, EVERYDAY NEGOTIATIONS: NAVIGATING THE HIDDEN AGENDAS OF BARGAINING (2003); KOLB, ET AL., *supra* note 13.

[29] Joan Acker, *Hierarchies, Jobs, Bodies: A Theory of Genderized Organizations*, 4 GENDER AND SOCIETY 139 (1990); Robin J. Ely, *Feminist Critiques of Research on Gender in Negotiations* (Center for Gender in Organizations, Working Paper No. 6, 1999); FLETCHER, *supra* note 12.

[30] Marta Calas & Linda Smircich, *From a Woman's Point of View: Feminist Approaches to Organization Studies*, in HANDBOOK OF ORGANIZATION STUDIES (Stuart R. Clegg, et al. eds., 1996).

[31] KOLB & WILLIAMS, *supra* note 28.

[32] Mark-David Seidel, et al., *Friends in High Places: The Effects of Social Networks on Salary Negotiations*, 45 ADMINISTRATIVE SCIENCE QUARTERLY 1 (2000).

[33] Deborah M. Kolb & Judith Williams, *Breakthrough Bargaining*, 6080 HARVARD BUSINESS REVIEW 87 (2001).

[34] KOLB & WILLIAMS, *supra* note 28.

[35] Deborah M. Kolb, *Staying in the Game or Changing It: An Analysis of Moves and Turns in Negotiation*, 20 NEGOTIATION JOURNAL 253 (2004).

[36] SYLVIA GHERARDI, GENDER, SYMBOLISM, AND ORGANIZATIONAL CULTURE (1996).

[37] SAMUEL BACHARACH & EDWARD LAWLER, BARGAINING: POWER, TACTICS AND OUTCOMES (1981).

[38] DAVID A. LAX & JAMES K. SEBENIUS, THE MANAGER AS NEGOTIATOR: BARGAINING FOR COOPERATION AND COMPETITIVE GAIN (1986).

[39] RICHARD E. WALTON & ROBERT B. MCKERSIE, A BEHAVIORAL THEORY OF LABOR NEGOTIATIONS: AN ANALYSIS OF A SOCIAL INTERACTION SYSTEM (1965).

[40] Deborah M. Kolb & Linda L. Putnam, Relational Interdependence, Paper Presented at the Annual Meetings of the Academy of Management (Aug. 7-11, 2002); Putnam & Kolb, *supra* note 1.

[41] Linda L. Putnam, *Transformations and Critical Moments in Negotiations*, 20 NEGOTIATION JOURNAL 269 (2004).

ℭ𝔰 37 𝔰ℭ

Religion and Conflict

Jeffrey R. Seul

Editors' Note: *Conflict has long been a preoccupation of each of the world's major religions. Each has its own tradition and its own culture of handling conflict. In many cases, mutual misunderstandings as to what that culture is, or distortions by parties who claim to operate within the traditions of a given religion, have caused more conflict. How should you react when you know that someone you will be negotiating with derives much of their identity from a religious frame? Seul summarizes what is known about each of the major religions and its conflict-handling tradition.*

References to "religious conflict" are commonplace, but those using the term seldom explain what they mean. At a minimum, it signals one's belief that religion plays a central role in a given conflict. That role is often left undefined, however, perhaps because one assumes it is too obvious to merit explanation. Most would agree that broad-scale, institutionally sanctioned, violent religious campaigns like the Crusades are largely a thing of the past. If one defines religious conflict by a situation where the disputants are attempting to achieve religious hegemony, however, then few disputes qualify as "religious conflict." Even those whose actions are explicitly propelled by religious objectives typically are not seeking complete, worldwide religious domination, regardless of cost or consequence.[1]

Short of providing the impetus for the type of organized, violent religious campaigns of past eras, however, religion can influence conflict in myriad ways. Religion is a powerful identity anchor that frequently provides a key fault line along which conflict occurs. Religious perspectives and norms also may define the contours of a party's frame of reference, guiding a party's behavior and decisions in a dispute, whether the dispute is about school prayer or abortion, where religion is overtly implicated, or about drilling for oil in Alaska or a breached contract, where religion's influence may be less evident.

This chapter explores some of the roles religion can play in the generation and resolution of conflict. The first section briefly examines the relationship between religion, individual and group identity construction and maintenance, and conflict. The second (and principal) section of the chapter provides a very general overview of some of the dominant perspectives on conflict within the five largest world religions—Judaism, Christianity, Islam, Hinduism and Buddhism. The final section offers a few tentative ideas about how to utilize religious perspectives and resources in conflict resolution activities.

Before proceeding further, however, a definition of "religion" is in order. All religions, or religious sects, arguably share four key characteristics:

A discourse whose concerns transcend the human, temporal, and contingent, and that claims for itself a similarly transcendent status ... [a] set of practices whose goal is to produce a proper world and/or proper human subjects, as defined by a religious discourse to which these practices are connected ... [a] community whose members construct their identity with reference to a religious discourse and its attendant practices ... [and an] institution that regulates religious discourse, practices, and community, reproducing them over time and modifying them as necessary, while asserting their eternal validity and transcendent value.[2]

Each of the religions discussed in this chapter, or their major branches, conform to this definition (as do many other religious traditions not considered in this chapter).

When talking about the relationship between religion and conflict, especially in a brief and general format like this chapter, two cautions are in order. First, religions are not monolithic. The five major world religions discussed in this chapter are internally diverse, each with numerous strains and sects, as well as perspectives on conflict that have shifted over time in response to the changing contexts in which they were articulated. Second, even within discrete religious sects, perspectives on conflict (and all other matters) typically vary. Each religion has resources that can be used to justify avoiding conflict; engaging in conflict coercively, whether violently or nonviolently; or attempting to resolve conflict consensually. A brief chapter on the relationship between religion and conflict cannot possibly chart this complex terrain with great accuracy or completeness.

Religious Identity and Conflict

A long tradition of research by social psychologists sheds light on the ways in which individual and group efforts to construct and maintain a secure identity contribute to conflict.[3] Most of this research focuses on intergroup conflict, such as conflict among racial groups in the United States, Catholics and Protestants in Northern Ireland, and self-identified political conservatives and liberals. While material resource disparities undoubtedly contribute to much conflict between groups, social scientific research suggests that resource disparities alone do not produce conflict. Persistent conflict between groups arguably occurs only when the groups also compete for enhanced symbolic status vis-à-vis one another (which may, of course, bring material rewards).[4] Investment bankers and artists may, as generalized groups, have greatly disparate resources, but we do not witness violent conflict between them because neither considers the other particularly relevant for purposes of social comparison. Their identities do not intersect in any way that is likely to produce competition for greater social or political status. Intergroup conflict may occur where two or more groups, each of which considers itself to have a distinct social identity (e.g., Greek and Turkish Cypriots or the Tamils and Sinhalese in Sri Lanka), also consider the other group(s) relevant for purposes of assessing their own respective social status.

This insight may help explain why religion and conflict are so frequently intertwined. Individuals and groups strive to establish stable, secure identities, and religions powerfully serve this identity impulse. Religions lend meaning to the broadest possible range of human relationships—to oneself, to groups with which one identifies and those with which one does not identify, to the universe and all that inhabits it, and to God, or that which one considers ultimately real or true.

Religion offers much more to individuals and groups in their effort to construct and maintain secure identities than do most other social institutions, so religion is often at the core of individuals' and groups' conceptions of themselves.[5] Religions support identity development in a wide variety of ways—by situating their adherents within a cosmology and a social worldview, marking time and major life passages with ritual, and supplying leaders and norms that aid decision-making in moments of fear, uncertainty and doubt, to name just a few.

Individual and group identity may be reinforced through conflict, whether it is violent conflict among two or more religious groups (*e.g.*, Roman Catholics, Orthodox Christians, and Muslims in the former Yugoslavia) or nonviolent social conflict between religious persons and those with a more secular orientation (*e.g.*, litigation before the United States Supreme Court regarding the constitutionality of prayer in public schools). The lines of demarcation between groups and the norms and values they embrace may become increasingly clarified through conflict. Even in interpersonal and other dyadic conflicts, conducting oneself according to a religious group's norms may reinforce one's sense of belonging to the group. In sum, the natural human need to establish and maintain a coherent and stable sense of self may at least partially explain why religion so often supplies either the fault line along which conflict occurs or the norms, relationships, and other cultural resources to which people engaged in conflict turn for guidance, justification, or support of their actions.

Religious Perspectives on Conflict and Its Resolution

Conflict is natural and inevitable, of course, and it may be socially beneficial when it is managed well. There are perspectives within each of the world's five largest religious traditions that could justify or inspire a range of responses to actual or threatened insults or injuries that could produce conflict. These responses can be placed along a continuum, with passively nonviolent responses at one end and violent aggression at the other. The major markers along this continuum might be characterized as *nonretaliation* (an inclination to avoid conflict or not to retaliate); *nonviolent action* (attempts to resolve a conflict coercively, but nonviolently); and *violent action*. (Non-retaliation is sometimes also referred to as "absolute pacifism," the view that holds that use of coercive methods, even nonviolent ones like protests, is not pacifistic.[6]) Each of the religions discussed in this chapter provides inspiration for efforts to resolve conflict through negotiation, regardless of whether attempts at negotiation are preceded or accompanied by violent or nonviolent coercive tactics. This section briefly surveys some of the sources and justifications for each of these responses to conflict—nonretaliation, nonviolent action, violent action, and negotiation—within the world's five largest religious traditions. Though many of the perspectives introduced in this section were forged in times of war, their logic often extends easily to the realm of civil disputes.

With the possible exception of Buddhism, there arguably is no single, dominant perspective on conflict in any of these traditions. Rather, there is a wide variety of viewpoints, even among pacifists, on the one hand, and those who accept the use of force, on the other. The best that can be offered in the space permitted is a cursory introduction to the range of perspectives that exist within each religious community. One of the problems with justifications that rest on religious texts or traditions, of course, is the fact that the texts and traditions often provide support for several, quite different courses of action in a given situation. Whatever it ultimately may mean to manage conflict well in a given situation, each of the world's largest religions provide general support (if not always detailed operational guidance) for a range of possible responses.[7]

Judaism

The notion of non-retaliation—choosing not to resist, strike against, or otherwise engage one's antagonist when faced with an affront, injury or threat—finds support in both ancient and contemporary Jewish texts and tradition. As one might expect, the justifications for this ethic of non-retaliation vary, particularly as expressed in early Jewish texts. Some texts that counsel non-retaliation (typically only toward one's cohorts, but not one's clear enemies) premise their advice upon notions of brotherly love, while others ground theirs upon an expectation that God will settle the score.[8] Non-retaliation may not signal a commitment to pacifism; one may choose not to retaliate because one believes God's response will be more potent than one's own.

While it probably is fair to say that "Judaism is not in any sense a pacifist tradition,"[9] there have been a number of prominent Jewish pacifists who have grounded their convictions in their interpretations of the Torah, other Jewish literature, and tradition.[10] The Hebrew Bible foretells a time when the people "shall beat their swords into plowshares,"[11] and the concept of *shalom*, which typically is translated as peace, but which also connotes wholeness and integrity, is central to Jewish tradition. Contemporary Jewish pacifists typically have advocated non-violent resistance, rather than non-resistance.[12]

For most Jews, however, the prospect of peace on earth is a utopian ideal that some (*e.g.*, the Orthodox) associate with the coming of the Messiah. Peace in this sense is not a condition that humankind is capable of producing itself.[13] Jewish teaching generally considers coercive action, including the use of lethal force, to be necessary and justified in some circumstances. Violence in the name of self-defense is not just permitted in the *Mishnah*, a second century Jewish legal treatise, it is advocated.[14] Similarly, the Talmud instructs: "If someone intends to kill you, get in first and kill him."[15]

Themes of forgiveness, charity and moderation do, however, exist alongside more militant perspectives. The least severe alternative should be employed when it will serve one's legitimate purposes as well as more severe alternatives.[16] Peace should be sought before war is declared;[17] when wars must be fought, they should be conducted by ethical means.[18] There is no reason why these same principles could not guide one's conduct in a civil dispute. They suggest that one should not litigate—or resort immediately to scorched earth litigation tactics when one must litigate—where less extreme action may prove effective.

If peace is not conceived in a utopian sense as the absence of conflict, but rather as the constructive management of conflict, then Judaism and the pursuit of peace have a natural resonance. As Rabbi Dan Cohn-Sherbok observes, "Jews relish debate and disagreement."[19] This comfort with debate and disagreement, when juxtaposed with the ethic of *shalom* (pursuit of peace and wholeness), arguably suggests a general leaning toward negotiation as Judaism's preferred approach to conflict resolution. This leaning certainly is evident within the Jewish community itself, which displays a "pattern of unity despite division"[20] across varied strains, sects, and geographies. Some Jewish teachers and texts also explicitly encourage negotiation with one's non-Jewish adversaries.[21] Despite its acceptance of violence whenever necessary and appropriate, constructive transformation of relationships with one's enemies is always to be preferred.[22]

Christianity

The Christian ethic of non-retaliation stems most obviously from a passage in the gospels of Matthew and Luke: "You have heard that it was said, 'An eye for an eye and a tooth for a tooth.' But I say to you, do not resist one who is evil. But if any one strikes you on the right cheek, turn to him the other also."[23] It is developed more fully in the epistles, the letters of encouragement and instruction written by Paul and other early Christian missionaries to members of the fledgling communities they visited, or hoped to visit, during their travels.[24] Members of these communities often were persecuted by their Roman occupiers and other more powerful groups. Non-retaliation is an ethical ideal grounded in the gospels, to be sure, but it could also be considered a strategy for self-preservation and constructive transformation of relationships with non-Christians. As in Judaism, however, the ethic of non-retaliation is probably grounded only partially in notions of brotherly love. Most Christians believe that, ultimately, only God can absolve one's enemies of their offenses. The Christian ethic of non-retaliation is thus premised in equal parts upon humility and subservice to God, on the one hand, and charity toward one's transgressors, on the other.[25]

There is a visible pacifist strain within Christianity that has advocated and practiced various forms of civil disobedience and non-violent resistance to war and perceived social injustice.[26] In some instances, pacifism is institutionalized, as it has been by the so-called Historic Peace Churches: the Quakers, Mennonites, and Brethren. In other instances, pacifism is advocated and practiced by individuals or organized sub-groups within a denomination comprised mainly of non-pacifists. Martin Luther King, Jr. and his followers are perhaps the best known example. The Catholic Worker movement within Roman Catholicism, which has a long history of anti-war protests, is another.

It probably is safe to say that most Christians, like the majority of people everywhere, believe that violence is sometimes justified. The Just War theory evolved over the centuries as Christian leaders and their advisors sought to define those circumstances under which war is morally justified (*Jus ad Bellum*), as well as methods for waging a war commenced with just intentions that will preserve its moral character (*Jus in Bellum*). Just War doctrine holds that the use of lethal force is morally acceptable only when the decision to use it is made by a legitimate authority (*i.e.*, the governor or governing body of an internationally recognized sovereign state), one's cause is just (*e.g.*, self-defense), one's goals are morally worthy (*e.g.*, securing peace), it is the only feasible way to do what is right (the "last resort" criterion), and one has a realistic expectation of success.[27] Furthermore, noncombatants must not be intentionally targeted, and the force used must be both proportionate to the threat and calculated to minimize the possibility of unintended, adverse consequences (*e.g.*, injury to innocent parties).[28] Christianity has thus developed an analytical method for determining when the use of force is justified in conflicts and how to use force with appropriate restraint.

Concern with limits on the use of force suggests a general preference for peaceful resolution of conflict. Indeed, the concept of *shalom* migrated from the Hebrew Bible and Jewish tradition into the Christian scriptures. The word "peace" is used often in the gospels and the other texts of the Christian New Testament—as it is, for example, in Jesus' greetings ("Peace be upon you") and farewells ("Go in peace") and in his praise for those who make peace ("Blessed are the peacemakers"[29]). Jesus encouraged kindness toward and reconciliation with those within and outside one's social group. The Crusades are evidence that Christians have not always adhered to this ideal, but Christian texts and tradition nonetheless are replete with exhortations to manage conflict and difference peacefully and charitably. "If possible, so far as it depends upon you, live peaceably with all," Paul writes to Christians in Rome.[30] Within Christianity, one finds much direct and indirect support for negotiation as an approach to conflict resolution.

Islam

Although the Arabic word Islam is most often translated as "submission," some scholars translate it as "the making of peace"[31]—peace with God and peace with other humans—because of its close relation to *salām*, which means peace. The Qur'an, the Hadiths (writings that transmit the words and deeds of the Prophet Mohammed), and other sources of Islamic authority, tradition and values offer support for Muslims who would respond to conflict without retaliation or through nonviolent forms of resistance. "Break your bows, sever your strings, beat stones on your swords (to break the blades); and when infringed upon by one of the perpetrators, be as the best of Adam's two sons."[32] This is just one of the many recorded sayings of the Prophet that counsel nonviolence. A number of Muslim sects and strains, including the Maziyariyya, the Sufis, and the Ahmadiyya movement, draw inspiration from such sayings as they put principles of nonviolence into practice.

Many of the same texts and other sources of authority, tradition and values that lend support to Muslim pacifists also lend support to those who believe coercive action, including violence, is at times necessary and justified. While Islam often is portrayed as a religion with an overly permissive orientation toward violence,[33] portions of canonical Islamic texts that address the use of force do counsel restraint. Violence is permissible only when one's cause is just. "Nor slay such life as Allah has made sacred," says the Qur'an, "except for just cause."[34] Some scholars discern Islamic equivalents to Just War theory in the Qur'an and other texts, including principles akin to the concept of last resort; declaration of war solely by a legitimate, sovereign authority; and ethical conduct of war.[35]

The term *jihad* deserves special attention. Many associate it with the idea of a holy war, a war fought against infidels to defend or extend the faith. *Jihad* is a deeply ambiguous term, however, and its meanings encompass, but are not limited to, the realm of violent conflict for religious objectives. "In its most general meaning, it refers to the obligations incumbent on all Muslims ... to exert themselves to realize God's will, to lead virtuous lives, and to extend the Islamic community through preaching, education, and so on. [A] related meaning is the struggle for or defense of Islam holy war."[36] The association between *jihad* and armed conflict evolved through centuries of (not always peaceful) interaction between Muslims and non-Muslims, and the two unfortunately have become synonymous among non-Muslims. Most Muslims do not associate the term primarily with armed conflict. Indeed, the Sufis, a sect within Islam, believe "one's battle with oneself (*al-jihad al-akbar*) is more difficult and more compelling than jihad against the enemies of Islam (*al-jihad al-asghar*)."[37]

Muslims also find support for consensual conflict resolution efforts in the Qur'an. "But if the enemy incline towards peace, do thou (also) incline toward peace."[38] As in the early texts of other traditions, however, references to one's enemy typically meant another member of one's community with whom one was engaged in dispute. Some contemporary Muslims are developing theories of religious and cultural inclusivism and pluralism that establish an intellectual foundation for extending traditional Islamic peace building principles beyond the Muslim community.[39]

Hinduism

Hinduism is in significant ways different from the other religions considered in this chapter. Unlike the other religions, in which communities form around a reasonably well defined core set of texts, beliefs and traditions, it sometimes is said that there are as many Hinduisms as there are Hindus.[40] At its most basic level, Hinduism may be loosely defined through its associations with India and the Vedas, a collection of ancient spiritual texts.[41] Beyond that, there is a wide diversity of sometimes mutually exclusive beliefs within contemporary Hinduism (acceptance v. rejection of reincarnation, acceptance v. rejection of the caste structure, etc.). Hinduism (or at least discrete Hindu sects) nonetheless satisfies the definition of religion presented earlier, though it arguably differs from other traditions in that its adherents generally are much freer to construct their own variants of the religion by picking and choosing among the many teachers, texts, sects and other resources that exist within the Hindu universe. To a greater extent than other religions considered in this chapter, Hinduism exists because people of diverse orientations recognize one another as members of a single religion. It should come as no surprise, then, that the same range of perspectives on conflict and its resolution that is evident in other religions also is found in Hinduism.

Non-retaliation and nonviolent resistance in Hinduism are expressions of the concept of *ahimsa*, which typically is translated as nonviolence or non-harmfulness. Although the notion appears in the *Chandogya Upanishad*, an ancient Hindu text, it was Mahatma Gandhi (1869-1948) "more than any other individual who brought ahimsa into the active moral consciousness of Hinduism."[42] According to John Ferguson, Gandhi's nonviolent activism was a departure from prior approaches to the practice of *ahimsa*, which emphasized non-action.[43] A hallmark of Gandhi's approach was "the willingness to suffer without retaliation."[44] In Gandhi's Hinduism (as in other forms of religious pacifism), activist approaches to nonviolence necessarily involve non-resistance to others' violent acts. Indeed, when one talks about nonviolent approaches to conflict management grounded in religious convictions, Gandhi is the quintessential modern example. His life and teachings have deeply influenced the leaders of subsequent nonviolent social movements, including Martin Luther King, Jr.

The legitimization of violence in Hinduism is closely associated with the *Bhagavadgītā*, a poem that is widely regarded as the principal religious text of contemporary Hinduism. The *Bhagavadgītā* originally was part of a much larger work of epic poetry, the *Mahābhārata*. It consists of a dialogue between Lord Krishna, who is God incarnate, and Arjuna, a warrior prince. As the *Bhagavadgītā* opens, Arjuna, who is called to battle, expresses reservations about fighting. Krishna counsels him to engage in battle, in part because it is his duty and destiny as part of the warrior caste (*kshatriya*) and in part because bodily death is not to be feared, as it does not extinguish the soul.[45] Krishna does not deny the virtues of nonviolence, but sees them as the exclusive province of the priestly class (Brahmins).[46] Gandhi read the *Bhagavadgītā* metaphorically—not as a text that sanctions violence, but as an exhortation to purifying, inner struggle, much as Sufis interpret the notion of *jihad*—but many Hindus probably see it, in part, as a text that offers guidance regarding just grounds for, and ethical limits on, the use of force.[47]

Hinduism's inherent pluralism, its capacity for assimilation of disparate perspectives, and the notion of *ahimsa* seem to favor conciliation as the preferred approach to conflict resolution. To the extent contemporary Hindus have faith in the efficacy of negotiation, however, Patrick Olivelle argues that it was not always so, particularly with respect to relations among members of different social groups.[48] The caste structure both assumes and generates social conflict. Contemporary Hindus who see the promise of negotiation as a means for managing and eliminating differences attributable to class, ethnic, and national distinctions arguably are products of Gandhi's influence on Indian politics and culture. Gandhi's strategy for nonviolent political action regarded constitutionalism (which manages disagreement through negotiation) as its first tactic. Other tactics were to be employed only if efforts to resolve conflict consensually failed.[49]

Buddhism

Thanks in part to the Dali Lama, the Vietnamese monk Thich Nhat Hanh, and other highly visible Buddhist proponents of nonviolence, Buddhism currently enjoys a reputation as a religion uniquely conducive to peace. Indeed, the Buddha's example and recorded teachings seem to provide relatively little clear support for resorting to violence. As we shall see, however, some Buddhist rulers, clergy and laypeople nonetheless have pursued their ends through violent means.

The Buddhist ethic of nonviolence is grounded in Buddhism's principal goal, on the one hand, and the ideals and methods by which Buddhists pursue this goal, on the other. At the risk of oversimplification, Buddhists seek to end their own suffering (and to help others end their suffering) by extinguishing the sense of a distinct and permanent self. Buddhism holds that we are unconsciously captive to the illusion of a solid, stable, separate self, and that this is not our true nature. The central idea is that there is no essential "me" that can be isolated from other features of my environment, which is the same from moment to moment and which will survive death. Because the "I" believes there is such a "me," however, I grasp for things (tangible and intangible) that I believe will protect, preserve, and content this separate self. These never quite satisfy, and this endless grasping is the source of our own and others' suffering.

Buddhists pursue the goal of extinguishing the sense of a separate self through practices like meditation (which, among other things, brings the erroneous view of self into consciousness) and through adherence to ideals and precepts for right thought, speech and action. *Ahimsa*, or non-harmfulness, which Hinduism received from Buddhism or Jainism, is one of the central ideals of Buddhism. Other ideals closely associated with nonviolence are loving kindness, sympathy, and compassion.[50] Meditation and the practice of *ahimsa*, loving kindness, sympathy and compassion are viewed as mutually reinforcing. The practice of nonviolence (and the related virtues of loving kindness, sympathy and compassion) is considered both necessary to, and a product of, an ordered mind.[51]

Buddhist scriptures contain numerous explicit injunctions against killing and other forms of violence. "Everyone is afraid of violence; everyone likes life," the Buddha is recorded to have said. "If one compares oneself with others one would never take life or be involved in the taking of life."[52] Or, more pointedly: "Do not kill a living being. You should not kill or condone killing by others. You should abandon the use of violence. You should not use force either against the strong or against the weak."[53] Nonviolence does not imply passivity, however, and both the Buddha[54] and contemporary Buddhists like the Vietnamese monk Thich Nhat Hanh,[55] whom Martin Luther King, Jr. nominated for the Nobel Peace Prize in recognition of the nonviolent protests he led against the Vietnam War, provide examples of constructive, nonviolent responses to conflict.

The emphasis on nonviolence in Buddhist texts and tradition has not always translated into nonviolent relations within Buddhist regions or among Buddhist and non-Buddhist nations. Some Buddhist rulers have tried to legitimize militarism by reference to Buddhist scripture and thought. For example, speaking at his coronation in 1910, King Rama VI of Thailand pointed to the following saying of the Buddha to justify a standing army: "As a town situated on the frontier must be prepared internally and externally, so too should you be prepared."[56] While other scriptural passages that sanction the use of violent force are relatively few, there is enough raw material from which to construct a theory of the legitimate use of force.[57] Many Sinhalese Buddhists in Sri Lanka have effectively embraced a just war theory to legitimize their conduct in their conflict with the Tamils.[58]

Despite these examples, Buddhism has at times had a demonstrably pacifying effect on social and political conflict.[59] The Buddhist notion of no-self does not imply that we do not exist; rather, it suggests that we do not exist as many of us unconsciously believe (and act as if) we do—that is, as ontologically separate beings. Buddhism stresses the interdependence of all things; the radical extent to which we draw sustenance from other beings and elements that co-exist with us. As an approach to conflict resolution, negotiation is highly compatible with Buddhism, because interdependence is an inherent feature of negotiation.

Working with the Religious Dimension of Conflict

How might those involved in a conflict with a discernible religious element, or those who wish to help them, work with this dimension of the conflict, if at all? Should it even be acknowledged and consciously addressed? The following are a few, tentative prescriptions:

- Recognize that religion is central to the identities of some or all of those involved in the conflict. Religion may very well be *the* primary lens through which one sees oneself and the rest of the world, including what is at stake in the conflict. When this is the case, the religious dimension of the conflict must be acknowledged, accepted, and integrated into negotiations and other conflict resolution efforts.

- Recognize that others' beliefs are deeply and sincerely held, regardless of how foreign they may seem from one's own perspective. One is unlikely to persuade another to abandon his or her beliefs (irrespective of the propriety of attempting to do so in the first place).

- Invite religious people involved in the conflict to speak openly about their commitments and the ways in which those commitments influence their perspectives and actions. In social or political conflicts involving multiple stakeholders, invite influential members of all affected religious communities to participate in negotiations and other components of dispute resolution processes.

- Focus on practical opportunities for cooperation, not ideology. Look for ways the parties can cooperate that are consistent with their respective beliefs. For example, pro-life and pro-choice activists may never agree when life begins, but they might be willing to cooperate to develop programs designed to reduce the number of unwanted pregnancies.

- Recognize that the identities of individuals and groups typically are multifaceted, regardless of the salience of any one element, like religion. Look for alternate "points of contact." For instance, two ideological opponents might find a common bond in their respective experiences raising a handicapped child.[60]

- Appeal to the better nature of all those involved in the conflict. Each of the religious traditions considered in this chapter provides support for nonviolent approaches to engaging in conflict and efforts to resolve conflicts consensually. If you are a party to a conflict, focus on these strains within your own tradition and invite others to focus on the complementary strains within their traditions.

Conclusion

Religion can influence conflict in a variety of ways. It may be the defining characteristic of groups that compete for material or social resources, as it is in Northern Ireland; it may be the source of values a party seeks to defend in a dispute, as it is for many in the debate over abortion in the United States; or it may guide a party's conduct in a dispute that superficially seems to have nothing to do with religion. Strains of authority within each of the world's five largest religions provide support for a range of responses to conflict, from conflict avoidance, to nonviolent engagement, to violent confrontation, to efforts to resolve conflict consensually. When there is a clear religious dimension to a conflict, it should be acknowledged, and the parties and those who wish to help them resolve the conflict should attempt to harness its constructive potential.

Endnotes

[1] A number of knowledgeable observers have long argued that even Osama bin Laden, the person who currently is most likely to be identified by westerners as a religious militant, is primarily concerned with driving the United States military and its allies out of Muslim regions such as Iraq, Afghanistan, Saudi Arabia and Palestine rather than converting the world to Islam. *See, e.g.*, Robert A. Pape, *Al Qaeda's Smart Bombs*, N.Y. TIMES, Jul. 9, 2005, at A13; BRUCE LINCOLN, HOLY TERRORS: THINKING ABOUT RELIGION AFTER SEPTEMBER 11 26-27 (2003). Bin Laden himself seems to have confirmed this recently by offering a "long-term truce" if troops are withdrawn from Iraq and Afghanistan. January 2006 bin Laden, transcript *available at* http://news.bbc.co.uk/2/hi/middle_east/4628932.stm (last visited Jan. 21, 2006).

[2] LINCOLN, *supra* note 1, at 5-7.

[3] *See, e.g.*, Henri Tajfel & John C. Turner, *The Society Identity Theory of Intergroup Behavior, in* PSYCHOLOGY OF INTERGROUP RELATIONS 7-24 (Stephen Worchel & William G. Austin eds., 1986).

[4] *Id.*

[5] Jeffrey R. Seul, *Ours is the Way of God: Religion, Identity, and Intergroup Conflict*, 36 JOURNAL OF PEACE RESEARCH 553 (1999).

[6] MOHAMMED ABU-NIMER, NONVIOLENCE AND PEACE BUILDING IN ISLAM: THEORY AND PRACTICE 11 (2003).

[7] Due to space limitations, I have included few quotes from, or references to, primary religious texts. Readers interested in reviewing primary texts where no reference is provided will find references in the secondary sources cited in this chapter.

[8] *See generally* GORDON M. ZERBE, NON-RETALIATION IN EARLY JEWISH AND NEW TESTAMENT TEXTS: ETHICAL THEMES IN SOCIAL CONTEXTS (1993).

[9] Dan Cohn-Sherbok, *War and Peace in Judaism, in* WAR AND PEACE IN WORLD RELIGIONS: THE GERALD WEISFELD LECTURES 2003 81, 89 (Perry Schmidt-Leukel ed., 2003).

[10] *See generally* EVELYN WILCOCK, PACIFISM AND THE JEWS (1994).

[11] *Isaiah* 2:2-4.

[12] *See generally* WILCOCK, *supra* note 10.

[13] *See* JOHN FERGUSON, WAR AND PEACE IN THE WORLD'S RELIGIONS 93 (1993).

[14] *See* Cohn-Sherbok, *supra* note 9, at 88.

[15] *Sanhedrin* 72a.

[16] *Mishneh Torah: Hilchot Rozeach* 1, 13.

[17] FERGUSON, *supra* note 13, at 92-93.

[18] *See* Michael Walzer, *War and Peace in the Jewish Tradition, in* THE ETHICS OF WAR AND PEACE: RELIGIOUS AND SECULAR PERSPECTIVES 95, 106-10 (Terry Nardin ed., 1996).

[19] *See* Cohn-Sherbok, *supra* note 9, at 95.

[20] *See id.*, at 97-98.

[21] *See, e.g., Deut. Rabbah* 5, 14.

[22] *See* FERGUSON, *supra* note 13, at 89.

[23] *Matthew* 5:38-39; *see also Luke* 6:29.

[24] *See generally* ZERBE, *supra* note 8, Chs. 6 and 7.

[25] *See generally id.*

[26] *See generally* Theodore J. Koontz, *Christian Nonviolence: An Interpretation, in* THE ETHICS OF WAR AND PEACE, *supra* note 18, at 169-96.

[27] *See generally* DARRELL COLE, WHEN GOD SAYS WAR IS RIGHT: THE CHRISTIAN'S PERSPECTIVE ON WHEN AND HOW TO FIGHT 77-85 (2002).

[28] *Id.* at 97-101.

[29] *Matthew* 5:9.

[30] *Romans* 12:18

[31] ABU-NIMER, *supra* note 6, at 45.

[32] Abu-Dawud Ibn Sulayman 1998, bd. 35, no. 4246. The reference to "the best of Adam's two sons" is, of course, a reference to Abel, the biblical figure who refused to retaliate against his brother, Cain, and who died.

[33] *See* ABU-NIMER, *supra* note 6, at 25-26 (summarizing recent studies of this nature).

[34] Qur'an 25:68. Self-defense is one clear example of a just cause.

[35] *See, e.g.,* JOHN KELSAY, ISLAM AND WAR: A STUDY IN COMPARATIVE ETHICS (1993). *But see* Bassam Tibi, *War and Peace in Islam, in* THE ETHICS OF WAR AND PEACE, *supra* note 18, at 131 (stating "the Western distinction between just and unjust wars linked to specific grounds for war is unknown in Islam").

[36] JOHN L. ESPOSITO, ISLAM: THE STRAIGHT PATH 93 (1998).

[37] ABU-NIMER, *supra* note 6, at 44-45.

[38] Qur'an 8:61.

[39] *See, e.g.,* ABDULAZIZ SACHEDINA, THE ISLAMIC ROOTS OF DEMOCRATIC PLURALISM (2000).

[40] *See generally* Arvind Sharma, *Hinduism, in* OUR RELIGIONS 1-67 (Arvind Sharma ed., 1993).

[41] *Id.*

[42] FERGUSON, *supra* note 13, at 36.

[43] *Id.*

[44] *Id.*

[45] *Id.* at 30-31.

[46] *Id.* at 31.

[47] Sharma, *supra* note 40, at 56 (drawing a distinction between the warrior tradition in Hinduism, which draws sustenance from the Bhagavadgītā, and contemporary violent Hindu fundamentalism, which he attributes primarily to "the anti-Hindu character of Indian secularism acquired at the hands of the Indian state *after* the martyrdom of Mahatma Gandhi").

[48] Patrick Olivelle, *On Meat-Eaters and Grass Eaters: An Exploration of Human Nature in Katha and Dharma Literature, in* HOLY WAR: VIOLENCE AND THE BHAGAVAD GITA 99-100 (Steven J. Rosen ed., 2002).

[49] FERGUSON, *supra* note 13, at 37.

[50] Perry Schmidt-Leukel, *War and Peace in Buddhism, in* WAR AND PEACE IN WORLD RELIGIONS, *supra* note 9, at 33, 39.

[51] *See* Luis O. Gomez, *Nonviolence and the Self in Early Buddhism, in* INNER PEACE, WORLD PEACE: ESSAYS ON BUDDHISM AND NONVIOLENCE 31, 41 (Kenneth Kraft ed., 1992).

[52] *Dhammapada* 130.

[53] *Suttanipata* 394.

[54] Schmidt-Leukel, *supra* note 50, at 40-41.

[55] *See, e.g.,* THICH NHAT HANH, CREATING TRUE PEACE: ENDING VIOLENCE IN YOURSELF, YOUR FAMILY, YOUR COMMUNITY, AND THE WORLD (2003).

[56] TREVOR LING, BUDDHISM, IMPERIALISM, AND WAR: BURMA AND THAILAND IN MODERN HISTORY 137 (1979).

[57] *See generally* Schmidt-Leukel, *supra* note 50, at 42-53; FERGUSON, *supra* note 13, at 55-56; TESSA J. BARTHOLOMEUSZ, IN DEFENSE OF DHARMA: JUST-WAR IDEOLOGY IN BUDDHIST SRI LANKA (2002).

[58] *See* BARTHOLOMEUSZ, *supra* note 57, at 101-35.

[59] *See* FERGUSON, *supra* note 13, at 51.

[60] According to negotiation scholar Roger Fisher, a pivotal moment in the resolution of one political conflict in which he served as a mediator occurred when two generals, who had been staunch enemies their entire lives, each learned that the other had a handicapped daughter.

෬ 38 ෨

Negotiating with Disordered People

Elizabeth L. Jeglic & Alexander A. Jeglic

Editors' Note: *It's all but routine for a negotiator leaving a meeting to mutter under her breath concerning the perceived mental health issues of someone on the other side. Unfortunately the research now demonstrates that such suspicions may not always be unreasonable. Mental health issues, it turns out, do not prevent people from assuming and holding high status in many kinds of organizations, so you may be negotiating with borderline mentally ill people with some regularity. Furthermore, we know that high-stress situations like death of a family member, divorce or job changes, which often lead to negotiations, can trigger mental illness. Here, a psychologist and a lawyer analyze the most common types of mental illness and tell you what to expect from each of the types you are most likely to encounter in negotiations.*

One assumption that is commonly made when negotiating is that the other negotiator is rational and thus capable of making logical decisions. However, approximately one in five Americans ages 18 and older suffer from a diagnosable mental disorder during the course of any given year.[1] This means that an estimated 44.3 million people in the United States[2] have a diagnosable mental illness that could significantly impair their ability to engage in rational negotiations.

The presence of a mental disorder can cause the person to distort information and facts, process information incorrectly, or be detached from reality. Certain mental disorders can also cause the person to be callous, manipulative or delusional.[3] In addition, we must take into account that individuals with a mental disorder may have limited insight into their disorder, and it is possible that they may be unaware of how the disorder may be impacting their functioning.

To further complicate matters, it may not be immediately obvious that someone has a mental disorder. Unlike a medical disorder, a mental disorder does not have readily identifiable physical symptoms. Therefore, significant negotiations may have already taken place before a red flag is raised and those involved in the negotiations realize that something is amiss. Mental disorders such as major depression, bipolar disorder, anxiety spectrum disorders, psychopathy and psychotic disorders can all impact an individual's ability to engage in rational negotiations. The goal of this essay is to outline some of the effects that mental illness can have on negotiations.

Major Depression

Major depression is one of the most common mental disorders, affecting an estimated 9.5 percent of Americans ages 18 and over in a given year.[4] Based upon the 1998 census residential population estimate, this translates into about 18.8 million people in the United States who are suffering from major depression annually.[5] It is the leading cause of disability in the world,[6] and is characterized by feelings of depression, hopelessness, and a loss of interest and pleasure in daily activities that last for at least two weeks and that interfere with a person's ability to function on a daily basis. Furthermore, depression can cause eating disturbances (eating too much or too little), sleeping disturbances (sleeping too much or too little), a loss of energy, psychomotor agitation or retardation, feelings of guilt or worthlessness, problems concentrating or making decisions, and suicidal thoughts or actions.[7]

According to the cognitive theory of depression, a key feature of the disorder is the depressed individuals' negative view of themselves, their future and the world.[8] These views are maintained by negative mental biases which cause the depressed person to interpret innocuous information in a negative way. For example, depressed individuals are more likely to draw strong negative conclusions without supporting evidence.[9] This type of thinking bias could have a large impact on negotiations as depressed individuals may interpret and distort the information that is presented to them, thus potentially negatively affecting the outcome of the negotiations.

Additionally, depressed people are more likely than non-depressed people to provide irrational explanations. A study by Cook and Peterson[10] compared explanations for negative life events in a sample of depressed and non-depressed individuals. They found that the depressed people offered significantly fewer "rational" or evidence-based explanations for their decisions. This has a direct impact on the process of negotiation as negotiators presuppose that their counterparts are rational and will partake in dialogue based upon logic. However, if negotiators suffer from major depression their ability to think logically may be impaired, thus affecting their ability to adequately represent their cause, or their client's.

Finally, depression is also characterized by concentration difficulties. This can be manifested through difficulty in collecting one's thoughts, trouble focusing on written materials, and difficulty following conversations.[11] In a negotiation, it is vital to be able to think on your feet and respond immediately to situations as they arise. If the negotiator is experiencing depressive symptoms that have impaired his or her concentration, then the individuals' ability to adequately fulfill the ordinary expectations of their negotiating counterpart is put into question.

Bipolar Disorder

Similar to major depression, bipolar disorder (also known as manic depression) is a mood disorder. More than 2 million Americans (approximately 1% of the population) carry this diagnosis.[12] The key diagnostic symptom of bipolar disorder is the dramatic changes in moods: from feelings of being high, elated or irritable to feelings of sadness, despair and hopelessness, with periods of normal moods in between. These periods of highs and lows are referred to as manic and depressive episodes. Along with the changes in mood, individuals with this disorder may also experience significant changes in energy and behavior. These fluctuations in mood are much more severe than just the regular "highs" and "lows" that we all experience. Individuals with bipolar disorder who do not receive treatment have serious impairments in all aspects of their functioning.[13]

The symptoms of an episode of mania include a decreased need for sleep, pressured speech, excessive talking, racing thoughts or flight of ideas, distractibility, increased libido, reckless behavior without regard for consequences, grandiosity (i.e., false conviction of personal wealth, power, inventiveness, and genius, or temporary assumption of a grandiose identity), and severe thought disturbances, which unless treated could result in psychosis.[14]

In contrast, the depressive phase of bipolar disorder is the same as a major depression. During this phase, a person may feel hopeless and lose all interest in other people or usual activities, experience weight fluctuation and feel tired all the time, sleep more than usual or have insomnia, complain of unexplained aches or pains, and have trouble concentrating. A person in the depressive phase is a suicide risk. Individuals with bipolar disorder who are experiencing a depressive episode will have similar thinking impairments to those exhibited by people with major depression including negative biases and irrationality.[15]

Neuropsychological investigations have yielded evidence suggesting that individuals with bipolar disorder may also experience enduring cognitive dysfunction. This dysfunction may best be described as an impairment in the attentional or executive control of action. This includes deficits in skills such as conflict resolution and switching from one task to another. Furthermore, it is suggested that these deficits worsen with the progression and severity of the bipolarity.[16]

Individually, each of these symptoms could impact a person's ability to negotiate rationally. However, when these symptoms are combined during the course of a manic or depressive episode, the consequences can be severe. The impairments experienced by a person with bipolar disorder, especially one who is not participating in treatment, could serve to undermine the negotiation process as their attentional and cognitive processing may be impaired while their thinking may be bordering on psychosis.

Anxiety

In any given year, over 40 million Americans experience an anxiety-related impairment.[17] There are several specific disorders that fall under the broader category of anxiety including panic disorder, social phobia, post traumatic stress disorder (PTSD), generalized anxiety disorder (GAD), and obsessive compulsive disorder (OCD).[18] The lifetime prevalence for a diagnosable anxiety disorder ranges from 1-14% with OCD being the least common and GAD and PTSD being the most common. It should be considered that, although many individuals do not meet the threshold for a diagnosable anxiety, most individuals have experienced some debility from anxiety at some point in their lives.[19]

A recent study[20] found that people diagnosed with an anxiety disorder show neuropsychological impairments compared with people without an anxiety. Overall, the results showed that participants with anxiety disorders were significantly impaired in episodic memory (memory for episodes in your own life) and executive functioning (higher level information processing). When the investigators studied the relation between the type of anxiety and impairment, they found that patients with panic disorder and OCD had impairments in both episodic memory and executive functioning. In contrast, the impairment for patients with social phobia was limited only to their episodic memory. These findings suggest that anxiety disorders have an impact on brain functioning. At present, we do not know if these changes are limited to the course of the anxiety disorder, or if they persist once the disorder has remitted.

Cognitive biases have also been found in patients with anxiety disorders. Patients with anxiety disorders tend to focus more attention on information related to their fears.[21] Therefore, if a fear/anxiety producing stimulus is present, their ability to focus elsewhere can be limited. Research suggests that this bias for stimuli that elicit anxiety is produced without the intervention of conscious strategies, such as focusing attention in the fear producing stimulus.[22]

Psychopathy

Psychopathy (also referred to as sociopathy or antisocial personality disorder) is a personality disorder that is characterized by enduring patterns of perceiving, relating to, and thinking about oneself and the environment in ways that are inconsistent with acceptable social behaviors.[23] Robert Hare, a world-renowned expert in the evaluation of psychopathy, defines psychopathy as a socially devastating disorder characterized by a constellation of affective, interpersonal, and behavioral features. These include egocentricity, impulsivity, irresponsibility, shallow emotions, lack of empathy, guilt, or remorse, pathological lying, manipulativeness, and the persistent violation of social norms and expectations.[24] It is estimated that between 15-20% of the offenders in state and federal prisons are psychopaths.[25] Recently, researchers have focused their attention on the concept of "successful" psychopaths.[26] Lynam and his colleagues[27] define "successful" psychopaths to be individuals who have patterns of psychopathic behavior but who do not have the characteristic arrest and incarceration histories that are found among psychopaths in the prison population. It is estimated that approximately 1% of the general population would meet the diagnostic criteria for psychopathy.

Babiak[28] conducted a series of case studies where he profiled "industrial" or "corporate" psychopaths. These are individuals who meet diagnostic criteria for psychopathy and are found to be working within organizations, often in positions of leadership. As part of his research, Babiak studied a half-dozen unnamed companies. One company was a fast-growing, high-tech firm, while the rest of the companies he profiled were large, multinational organizations that were undergoing dramatic organizational changes. These changes included severe downsizing, restructuring, mergers and acquisitions, and joint ventures. Babiak found that periods of organization instability and change created a favorable environment for the "corporate psychopath," with many actually thriving under such circumstances. The chaotic environment provided the psychopaths with stimulation while affording them ample opportunity to engage in manipulation. The consequences include a disproportionate number of negotiations, and disputes, colored by the personalities of these executives.

It has been suggested by Emmons that psychopaths are frequently driven by the need for power, control, dominance, and prestige. Emmons cites these as characteristics that are valued by corporations, and search committees frequently recruit leaders possessing these traits. These are also qualities that are often cited and singled out for promotion within organizations. Therefore, it has been speculated, by Emmons and others, that many of our top business and political leaders, and perhaps even our negotiating counterparts, may, in fact, be psychopaths.[29]

One reason that these "corporate psychopaths" may go undetected is that they have the ability to present themselves as normal and extremely charming while causing great distress to their co-workers and organizations.[30] Psychopaths have been described as cunning, manipulative, untrustworthy, unethical, parasitic, and utterly remorseless: "There's nothing they won't do, and no one they won't exploit, to get what they want."[31]

In terms of negotiation, psychopaths fall into a completely different category from individuals with other mental disorders. While those with disorders such as depression and anxiety may exhibit impaired functioning, illogical thought processes, and limited rationality, they do not intend their colleagues and counterparts any harm. Psychopaths, on the other hand, are more than willing to wreak havoc in an effort to attain their goals. Psychopaths may appear both logical and rational during the course of a negotiation. But in violation of reasonable expectations of a certain amount of trust and goodwill in a typical negotiation, a psychopath may use whatever means are necessary to achieve what he desires.

Another personality disorder that is commonly associated with psychopathy is narcissism. While diagnostically distinct from psychopathy, narcissism and psychopathy have many overlapping traits. In both cases, these individuals exploit others to meet their own needs and exhibit little or no empathy. However, it is speculated that the key distinction between the two disorders is that psychopaths engage in this type of behavior with malevolent intent, while narcissists do it to compensate for low self esteem.[32]

Narcissism has been defined as a pattern of traits and behaviors that signify infatuation and obsession with one's self to the exclusion of all others and the egotistic and ruthless pursuit of one's gratification, dominance and ambition. Furthermore, narcissistic individuals require constant admiration and adulation, always need to be right, and hold the belief that ordinary people cannot understand them. Since narcissistic individuals are very self involved, this could easily hinder the negotiation as they will be unlikely to view matters from a perspective outside of their own. There is some evidence suggesting that narcissists may become aggressive and violent if their ideas and status are challenged.[33] In the world of negotiations, having one's ideas challenged can be expected, if not guaranteed. Therefore, negotiations with a narcissist may quickly break down.

Psychotic Disorders

Psychotic disorders are characterized by trouble with reality testing—discriminating what is real from what is imagined. Common psychotic symptoms are hallucinations (hearing, seeing, or otherwise sensing the presence of things not actually there) and delusions (false, strongly held beliefs not influenced by logical reasoning or explained by a person's usual cultural concepts). Psychotic disorders include schizophrenia, schizoaffective disorder and delusional disorder. It is estimated that 1% of the population is afflicted with a psychotic disorder.[34]

Psychotic disorders modify a person's ability to think clearly, make good judgments, respond emotionally, communicate effectively, and behave appropriately—all hallmark characteristics of a skilled negotiator. When the psychotic symptoms are severe, people with psychotic disorders often are unable to meet the ordinary demands of daily life.

Unlike many of the other mental disorders whose clinical presentation (or public face) may be more subtle, individuals with schizophrenia and schizoaffective disorder are readily identifiable by their disordered thinking and disorganized behavior. However, it is possible to enter into a negotiation with someone who is suffering from delusional disorder and for the disorder to go undetected. This disorder is characterized by the presence of non-bizarre delusions. These typically are beliefs of something occurring in a person's life which is not out of the realm of possibility (e.g., a spouse is unfaithful, or a friend is a government agent). Unlike the other psychotic disorders, people who have delusional disorder generally don't experience a marked impairment in functioning and their behavior is not noticeably bizarre.[35] It is only if the delusion pertains to the negotiation that the individual's thinking and behavior will be impacted.

Conclusions

It is commonly believed that individuals in positions of authority are psychologically healthier than those who did not achieve such career success. While this may be true, many individuals do not reveal a mental illness, as they fear the stigma and potential fallout. They may struggle to maintain a sheen of normality rather than seek help. Additionally, when one considers the prevalence of mental disorders in our society, there is a reasonable probability that an opposing negotiator or even a colleague may have a diagnosable mental illness. Given the number of impairments that are associated with mental disorders, it is perhaps most logical to enter into a negotiation prepared to face a counterpart that is not rational—with the hope that the evidence will suggest otherwise as the negotiation progresses, but with some forewarning of the likely symptoms if, in fact, you are negotiating with a disordered person.[36]

Endnotes

[1] David A. Regier, et al., *The De Facto US Mental and Addictive Disorders Service System. Epidemiologic Catchment Area Prospective 1-Year Prevalence Rates of Disorders and Services*, 50 ARCHIVES OF GENERAL PSYCHIATRY 85-94 (1993).

[2] William E. Narrow, One-Year Prevalence of Mental Disorders, Excluding Substance Use Disorders, in the U.S.: NIMH ECA Prospective Data, Population Estimates Based on U.S. Census Estimated Residential Population Age 18 and Over (July 1, 1998) (unpublished paper) (on file with author).

[3] AMERICAN PSYCHIATRIC ASSOCIATION: DIAGNOSTIC AND STATISTIC MANUAL OF MENTAL DISORDERS (4th ed., 2000) [hereinafter DSM IV].

[4] Regier, et al., *supra* note 1, at 85-94

[5] Personal communication with William Narrow, Table: One-year Prevalence of Depressive Disorders Among Adults 18 and Over in the U.S.: NIMH ECA Prospective Data. Population Estimates Based on U.S. Census Estimated Residential Population Age and Over (July 1, 1998) (on file with author).

[6] World Health Organization, The World Health Report 2001—Mental Health: New Understanding, New Hope (2001), *available at* http://www.who.int/whr/2001/en/index.html (last visited Apr. 5, 2006).

[7] DSM IV, *supra* note 3.

[8] Aaron T. Beck, *Thinking and Depression: Idiosyncratic Content and Cognitive Distortions*, 9 ARCHIVES OF GENERAL PSYCHIATRY 324-33 (1963). Aaron T. Beck, *Cognitive Models of Depression*, 1 JOURNAL OF COGNITIVE PSYCHOTHERAPY: AN INTERNATIONAL QUARTERLY 5-37 (1987).

[9] David A. Haaga, et al., *Empirical Status of Cognitive Theory of Depression*, 110 PSYCHOLOGICAL. BULLETIN 215-36(1991).

[10] Michele L. Cook & Christopher Peterson, *Depressive Irrationality*, 10 COGNITIVE THERAPY & RESEARCH 293-98 (1986).

[11] *Id.* at 293-98.

[12] Regier, et al., *supra* note 1, at 85-94.

[13] DSM IV, *supra* note 3

[14] *Id.*

[15] *Id.*

[16] I. Nicol Ferrier & Jill M. Thompson, *Cognitive Impairment in Bipolar Affective Disorder: Implications for the Bipolar Diathesis*, 180 BRITISH JOURNAL OF PSYCHIATRY 293(2002).

[17] William E. Narrow, et al., NIMH Epidemiology Note: Prevalence of Anxiety Disorders, One-Year Prevalence Best Estimates Calculated from ECA and NCS Data. Population Estimates Based on U.S. Census Estimated Residential Population Age 18 to 54 (July 1, 1998) (unpublished note) (on file with author) [hereinafter Anxiety Disorders].

[18] DSM IV, *supra* note 3.

[19] Anxiety Disorders, *supra* note 17.

[20] Eija Airaksinen, et al., *Neuropsychological Functions in Anxiety Disorders in Population-Based Samples: Evidence of Episodic Memory Dysfunction*, 39 JOURNAL OF PSYCHIATRIC RESEARCH 207 (2005).

[21] Andrew Mathews & Colin MacLeod, *Selective Processing of Threat Cues in Anxiety States*, 23 BEHAVIOUR RESEARCH & THERAPY 563 (1985).

[22] Colin MacLeod & Elizabeth Rutherford, *Anxiety and the Selective Processing of Emotional Information: Mediating Roles of Awareness, Trait and State Variables, and Personal Relevance of Stimulus Materials*, 30 BEHAVIOUR RESEARCH & THERAPY 479 (1992).

[23] *DSM IV, supra* note 3.

[24] *See generally*, ROBERT D. HARE, WITHOUT CONSCIENCE: THE DISTURBING WORLD OF THE PSYCHOPATHS AMONG US (1999).

[25] Robert D. Hare, *A Research Scale for the Assessment of Psychopathy in Criminal Populations*, 1 PERSONALITY & INDIVIDUAL DIFFERENCES 111(1980).

[26] Paul Babiak, *When Psychopaths Go to Work: A Case Study of an Industrial Psychopath*, 44 APPLIED PSYCHOLOGY: AN INTERNATIONAL REVIEW 171 (1995).

[27] Donald R. Lynam, et al., *Self-Reported Psychopathy: A Validation Study*, 73 JOURNAL OF PERSONALITY ASSESSMENT 110(1999).

[28] Babiak, *supra* note 26, at 171-88.

[29] Robert A. Emmons, *Narcissism: Theory and Measurement*, 52 JOURNAL OF PERSONALITY & SOCIAL PSYCHOLOGY 11 (1987).

[30] *Id.*

[31] HARE, *supra* note 24.

[32] DSM IV, *supra* note 3.

[33] Roy F. Baumeister, et al., *Relation of Threatened Egotism to Violence and Aggression: The Dark Side of High Self-Esteem*, 103 PSYCHOLOGICAL REVIEW 5-33 (1996).

[34] DSM IV, *supra* note 3.

[35] *Id.*

[36] Actual strategies for dealing with disordered individuals are beyond the scope of this chapter. For further discussion, please see MENTAL HEALTH AND PRODUCTIVITY IN THE WORKPLACE: A HANDBOOK FOR ORGANIZATIONS AND CLINICIANS (Jeffrey P. Kahn & Alan M. Langlieb eds., 2003).

☙ 39 ☙

Perceptions and Stories

Sheila Heen & Douglas Stone

Editors' Note: Even when the parties basically recognize the same set of facts, there are often multiple versions of what actually happened. Why is this, and how do these different versions affect negotiations? This chapter demonstrates how each side's version of "the story" in a negotiation needs to be understood, if the other side is to be persuaded to make any significant step toward an agreement.

Eric and Fran are in conflict.

They've always had a hard time working together, but lately the frustration and tension has spilled over to colleagues and family members on each side.

Fran catches you first, her story emerging in messy, manic detail. Eric, she claims, is acting unreasonably. He is incompetent and he is being childish. You know you are only hearing Fran's side of things, but still, you have a hard time imagining how Eric could explain his behavior. It seems inexcusable, and you tell Fran she is right to be so upset.

Eric calls you later that day. He says he doesn't want to speak ill of Fran, but demands that you hear his version of what happened. You listen, as Eric describes what "really happened," and you soon find yourself confused. Eric, it seems, is the real victim here. You try to resist the urge to take Eric's side, but give in: "you are right to be so upset," you tell him.

Moments later, you get an email from a mutual friend, who asks if you know anything about what is going on between Eric and Fran. "I've spoken to both of them," you write, and then realize that you simply haven't figured out how to reconcile what you've heard so far. You know both Fran and Eric well enough to know that neither is lying, or even intentionally shading the truth. And yet their descriptions of the dispute could not be more different.

The Brain as a Story-Based System

What's going on? Artificial intelligence researcher Roger Schank puts it well: "Human memory is story-based."[1] Far from simply reflecting or recording reality, our minds engage in a complex interplay between what we perceive and what we already know, unconsciously adding and deleting information in the service of the story. Disputes occur when the stories we tell about what's happening—who's right, what's fair, who's to blame—diverge. Each side retreats to their own narrative which describes their experience of "reality," and the dispute intensifies.

The mechanics of how divergent stories are generated is the subject of this chapter.

How Stories Take Root and Grow ... in Different Directions

The process is cyclical and self-reinforcing, but let's start with moment to moment perceptions of what's going on. Let's wind the tape back to a crucial point in the dispute between Eric and Fran.

We Observe Different Data

The team has called a meeting to discuss a new project—one that will require Eric and Fran's close cooperation if it is to succeed, and that will affect their reputations, bonuses, and future opportunities. Eric and Fran are sitting side by side at the same meeting, yet they will end up with very different data sets about what happens here.[2]

...Because We Have Access to Different Information

From the moment the meeting starts, Eric and Fran each has access to information that the other person does not. In any organization, where you sit determines what you see. Eric is in sales, so he has a lot of information about the effort it took to bring this client along, the specific demands the client has made, the many terms on which they have managed to hold the line, and the kinds of promises that competitors are making. Eric also knows how frustrated he felt when Fran didn't get back to him last week in a timely fashion with crucial information, and the impact of her neglect on his negotiations with the client to finalize the deal.

Fran is in engineering. As Eric lays out the final agreement with the client, she is instantly aware of the ways in which what Eric has promised cannot be done, and certainly not in the time promised. Her mind flashes on past conversations with Eric and other sales personnel about the hazards of over-promising, and failing to consult adequately with the implementation team prior to closing a deal. She is aware of all the technical and political roadblocks she can expect to encounter in the coming months—spec changes, scope creep, staffing so lean that it will drive her people to their breaking point. Fran also knows what else is on her team's plate right now. She sits silently, but her frustration and sense of being "wronged" mount.

...Because We Select Different Data From The Common Pool

In addition to access to different information, Eric and Fran also have access to common information—what is said at the meeting, the body language of each person, the specs that are handed out—yet they will each pay attention to different data from this common pool.

At any given moment, so much data about the world enters our brains through our senses that paying attention to everything would overwhelm us with stimuli.[3] Hence, ..."[a] key proficiency of consciousness is not the ability to perceive the external world, but rather the ability to shut so much of it out."[4] The Danish writer Tor Norretranders calls this selective attention the "user illusion"—we think we see everything around us, but in fact take in a very small slice of the available information,[5] perhaps as little as one percent of our stimulus field.[6]

So although Fran and Eric will later claim that they "know what happened in the meeting—after all, I was *there!*" in fact, each is able to pay attention only to a thin slice of what happened. Given their differing interests, responsibilities and background, they are likely to collect very different data sets from the meeting itself. In fact, memory researcher Daniel Schacter goes so far as to suggest that "what has happened to us in the past determines what we take out of our daily encounters in life."[7] Eric will report to a colleague that "Fran did not say a positive word about my efforts to land this project." He remembers her saying accusingly, "I'm surprised that you agreed to these deadlines. I'm just really surprised." He does not report, or even remember, Fran saying, "Eric, I know your team has been working really hard on this," nor does he recall much about Fran's presentation on how it might still be possible to bring the project in on deadline.

For her part, Fran will later recall that Eric "made no mention of the fact that I've asked over and over again to be consulted prior to closure," and that "Eric rolled his eyes when I questioned whether the deadlines where realistic." She does not recall Eric saying, "I know these deadlines are incredibly aggressive, and I know that puts pressure on engineering. It was the only way we could win the deal. The client knows we have the best engineers in the world." What each remembers from the meeting is so different, in some sense they attended different meetings.

...And Because Strong Emotions Change How And What We Perceive

To complicate matters, conflict inevitably triggers emotions, which throw their own wrench into these busy brain processes. Chemicals like adrenaline, cortisol, dopamine, serotonin, norepinephrine, and oxytocin[8] create and accompany emotions and profoundly affect our ability to perceive and recall what happens when we are in dispute.

We face conflict when something important to us is threatened: a relationship, our self-image, our well-being. In this state, the memories we retain are much cruder, containing less complexity and specificity, even while they are particularly vivid and deeply encoded. We miss the subtleties or specifics of what is said because our slower, rational mind—housed in the neocortex—is not in charge.[9]

This means that as the conversation in Fran and Eric's meeting becomes heated, their ability to reliably take in complex information or to read subtlety in each others' reactions diminishes. Fran misses Eric's exasperation with her missed call, and Eric doesn't pick up on the question Fran asks about phasing the project. As things escalate, they are more likely to miss data that would offer a way to reconcile.

From Data to Story: Add Meaning

What happens next further polarizes Fran and Eric's perceptions. For we don't simply record the data we observe, like tape recorders or excel spreadsheets. We take the data and interpret what it "means" so that we know how to tell the story that's emerging from our observations.

Frames, Assumptions & Implicit Rules

For instance, Eric doesn't just remember the text of what Fran said. He "remembers" that she was "negative, unappreciative, and oppositional." These are conclusions he reached, perhaps without even being aware that these aspects of his story are his interpretations of her behavior rather than facts.

Our interpretations come from our larger storylines. These are variously referred to in the literature as mental models,[10] heuristics, partisan perceptions,[11] mindsets, schemas, paradigms, or frames.[12] We will use the word frames, because we like the image of someone looking out through the frame of a window—their mind's window—onto the world. Our test for whether something is a frame is a practical one: does knowing someone's frame help explain important aspects of how the person makes sense of the world that would be hard to explain otherwise?

All of us carry assumptions and implicit rules about work, love, friendship, parenting, and the purpose of life. It shouldn't be surprising that they are at the heart of many of our most important conflicts. Deeper understanding of someone's story about a conflict requires learning about the hidden structures that make up their frame on the world, on this conflict and on the conflict's role in the bigger themes of their life.

For instance, here's some data you don't yet know about Fran and Eric. Fran has been in this business for more than thirty years, and is vocal about the increasing pace that technology has encouraged of late. E-mail, voicemail, blackberries … these seem ridiculous to her, as does the expectation that people be on call 24/7 for the smallest issue. "If it's a true emergency, no problem," she says. "But being a professional means being able to prioritize and to respect others' time." She has been outspoken about the importance of work-life balance. She has three teenage children, and also helps to care for her elderly father who suffers from dementia.

Eric is in his late twenties, and comes from a technology start-up. (Your brain, reader, is already busy jumping to a story about the implicit rules and assumptions Eric brings with him about professionalism). "Every voicemail should be returned within three hours," he emphasizes to his new hires. This seems obvious to him.

Yet these frames, as powerful as they are for helping us piece together the data, are usually hidden and rarely discussed. Conflicting frames may be at the heart of a conflict without anyone being aware of either their own frame or the other party's.[13]

Filling in the Gaps

When we encounter new information, we automatically scan our brains for similar or analogous categories in which to file it.[14] This point is crucial: *human beings are not good at remembering isolated "data" or creating unique files in our head. We have to find a way to connect the fragments with stories, and to connect a new story with an existing story already on file.*

Let's imagine you've just met Eric and he mentions to you, "Fran just bumped me in the hall." Without context, you do not know how to make meaning of this information. You look confused, as your brain wonders—do I file this under "accidental bumps" or "narrow halls" or "problematic people" or perhaps even "flirting?" In order to make sense of it, you want to know: who is Fran to Eric? Why did she bump Eric? When and where did this happen? Is this the first time or is it typical of her? Was he on "her side" of the hallway to begin with?

In fact you actually have a little sketch of the tension between Eric and Fran from earlier in this article, and you may have developed a visual image of the "bump" in your mind. Your image is not just pieces of data; you've already linked it to a little story about these clashing coworkers. You the reader, will tell yourself a story about the bumping incident. In your story, Fran may have intentionally bumped Eric, as a way to express her frustration, or perhaps the bump is attached to a larger story about Fran being an extremely difficult person to get along with. Or maybe your story has Eric moving in front of Fran in a threatening way, and Fran refusing to be intimidated. Whatever story you tell, you're *adding* information to the actual data, in order to store the story, as a story, in your mind.

Reinforcing Existing Storylines & Ignoring Disconfirming Data

With no "new file" functions, we have to connect new fragments of data to existing storylines. This means, in turn, that our existing stories influence the new data we select as important, and over time our stories become self-reinforcing. It is those things that are important, meaningful, or familiar to us that automatically attract our attention.[15] Once Fran views Eric as incompetent, she will notice each time Eric acts incompetently (or annoyingly).[16]

She is also more likely to overlook or dismiss disconfirming data—examples of Eric acting competently or kindly, because it does not fit into her story. Or if she does take it in, she might regard it with suspicion ("What does he want?") or as an exception to the way Eric really is ("Look who got lucky today."). This is because our brains work hard to tell simple stories that are consistent with what we already know, and that protect us from the discomfort of ill-fitting data hanging around our memory banks. The cognitive dissonance feels uncomfortable and confusing.[17]

Meaning that Matters: Characters and Causation

Although Eric and Fran's versions of "the truth" about what's happening are quite different, they both involve a predictable pair of story elements that contribute a disproportionate share to the creation of conflict: characters and causation.

The Characters

One of the most common clashes in our stories will be how we describe the characters in them. Our stories about conflict are filled with heroes and villains, victims and oppressors, protector and child, the overbearing and the underappreciated.

Most people have a sympathetic self-story. Fran knows she is doing her best with an overwhelming workload, being straight about what's possible, and acting rationally based on what she knows. Fran, like all of us, casts herself firmly in the role of hero.

Starring: Us as Good Guy Hero

There are a number of reasons we cast ourselves so flatteringly. The first is related to the "private data" we have about ourselves and the accompanying storyline through which we live our lives. Fran knows her own hopes, dreams, problems, feelings, limitations, pressures, coping mechanisms, personal history, and past relationships. She knows the backdrop of larger stories she tells herself about who she is in the world—"this is one more thing for this small town gal to overcome," or "I'm not going to be taken for a sucker *this* time." She knows the ways in which Eric's actions cause her frustration, credibility, confusion, or energy. And she knows her own intentions, why she did what she did given the constraints she was under.

This information—so rich and vivid for Fran—is information that Eric doesn't have.[18] Similarly, Fran has little access to the same information about Eric. If she learns about this at all, it is "second hand," and so the information is bound to be less compelling.[19]

This differential access to information is sometimes called egocentric bias by researchers. It produces couples who each claim to be responsible for 80% of the housework,[20] and only 20% of the arguments. We have lots of information about all we take care of around the house, and of our good intentions and virtuous conduct when it comes to the fights.

In addition to the private data phenomenon, each of us has a self interest in constructing stories that protect our identities as responsible, caring, competent, good people.[21] Eric complains that Fran dropped the ball last week. Fran *knows* this is not true because she knows she is not the kind of person who would drop the ball. Preserving our sense of how we see ourself is crucial; the more another's story challenges how we see ourselves, the less likely it is that we can even hear their perspective.

Against: Them as Bad Guy Villain (or Bumbler at Best)

Once we have snagged the role as hero, this leaves only one role for our counterpart—the villain (aka, "the problem," or "that jerk"). Of course, once we cast the other as overbearing, thoughtless, incompetent, or unkind, we are more likely to notice and encode into memory any new evidence that confirms our view. Called stereotype bias,[22] this tendency can fuel the escalation of a conflict, and means that changing someone's view of the other as villain can be difficult.

This is particularly the case because our story includes not just *what* they are doing, but *why* they're doing it, which makes things worse. Eric's belief that Fran ignored him *on purpose* or because she *don't respect me* causes him to tell a different story about the situation, and his feelings of frustration, hurt, or vindictiveness increase. Incidentally, the more frustrated Eric feels, the more likely he is to describe Fran's actions as intentional.[23] His story is particularly difficult to overturn with disconfirming data, because he does not have access to the private data it turns on—Fran's intentions. Her intentions are invisible to him.

It is a short leap, of course, from "you don't respect me" to "you're a bad person,"—irresponsible, controlling, or at the very least inexcusably thoughtless.[24] I see you as you are—a villain sent straight from central casting.

Of course, during moments of reflection we know it is not so simple as heroes and villains, but in the context of a difficult dispute, such moments are few. We tell positive stories about ourselves, and make negative attributions about others, and before we know it, we are as caught in the flow as the water circling the drain.

Causation and Blame

In a dispute, we do not just want to know *what* went wrong, we want to know *why* it went wrong. You can bet that the stories Fran and Eric tell their friends about the conflict have blame embedded in them. Yet despite our interest in causation, we are strikingly bad at creating accurate explanations that capture what is really going on.

There are two key reasons for this. First, as systems thinker Peter Senge puts it, "The world is made up of circles, but we see straight lines."[25] The second is that it is hard to see causation when we ourselves are participants in the system.

We See Lines Not Circles

Treating causation as a straight line leads to what some theorists have called the "biased punctuation of conflict."[26] Leigh Thompson describes the tendency succinctly:

An actor, A, perceives the history of conflict with another actor, B, as a sequence of B-A, B-A, B-A, in which the initial hostile or aggressive move was made by B, ... causing A to engage in defensive and legitimate retaliatory actions. Actor B punctuates the same history of interaction as A-B, A-B, A-B, however, reversing the roles of aggressor and defender.[27]

Here, Eric complains that Fran is unresponsive and irresponsible. She doesn't return phone calls, and seems impatient when reached. The problem, clearly, is that Fran needs to learn to be a professional—that much is clear, at least to Eric. Actor F causes problem for Actor E.

The true causes of a conflict can more usefully be schematized as a "system" or circle to which where each party contributes. As we wrote in *Difficult Conversations*:

[C]ausation is almost always ... complex. A contribution *system* is present, and that system includes inputs from both people.... Whether the batter strikes out or hits a home run is a result of the interaction between the batter and the pitcher. Depending on your perspective, you might focus on the actions of one or the other, but the actions of both are required for the outcome.[28]

The conceptualization of causation as a circle rather than a line nicely sidesteps the question of whether a conflict started with cause A or cause B. In reality, it may be that A and B were simultaneous, or simply that the inputs from each party are too complex to determine. What we do know is that we are locked into a self-reinforcing system, and once stuck, factors like blame, anger, fear, and image threats set in and make matters worse.[29] The only way out is to uncover the system.

We Don't See Our Own Contribution

A second reason we have trouble with causation is that human beings have a hard time seeing their own contributions to the causation system.

It's difficult for Eric to see how his anxiety, attention to detail, and work style lead him to micro-manage projects. Eric doesn't know how many more calls Fran gets from him than from others.

And it's hard for each of them to see the ways in which their contributions are feeding on themselves, reinforcing the causation loop. When Fran doesn't respond, Eric calls again. This has taught Fran that she doesn't need to pay attention to his first message—if it's important, he'll call again.

And so we can see what neither Eric nor Fran can—that they are each in possession of part of the story, that the caricatures they have constructed of each other are too extreme, and that they are both contributing to the problem. Each side's story blames the other for the problem, and unintentionally, these stories get more and more polarized, perpetuating and escalating the conflict.

Conclusion

Cognitive psychologist Ulrich Neisser observed that "out of a few ... bone chips, we remember a dinosaur."[30] But not just dinosaurs. We construct whole worlds these dinosaurs inhabit, complete with personalities, intentions, histories, and enemies. Our own storylines, themes, metaphors and frames are the lenses through which we make reality into *our* reality.[31]

Helping people understand the differences in their stories, and the frames, implicit assumptions, and biases that contribute to those differences is the path to reconciliation. In the end, we may not always be able to develop a new narrative that works for all parties in a dispute, but we can attempt to follow the simple but elegant advice of poet William Carlos Williams: "Their story, yours, and mine—it's what we all carry with us on this trip we take, and we owe it to each other to respect our stories and learn from them."[32]

Endnotes

[1] ROGER C. SCHANK, TELL ME A STORY: NARRATIVE AND INTELLIGENCE 12 (1990).

[2] Don Schön of MIT and Chris Argyris of Harvard Business School created the *Ladder of Inference*, an analytic tool that illustrates this process by which our brains select data, make inferences from it based on past experiences, and construct conclusions, or stories, about the world.

[3] DANIEL L. SCHACTER, SEARCHING FOR MEMORY: THE BRAIN, THE MIND, AND THE PAST 40 (1996).

[4] STEVEN JOHNSON, MIND WIDE OPEN: YOUR BRAIN AND THE NEUROSCIENCE OF EVERYDAY LIFE 90 (2004).

[5] TOR NORRETRANDERS & JONATHAN SYDENHAM, THE USER ILLUSION: CUTTING CONSCIOUSNESS DOWN TO SIZE 277 (1991).

[6] LEIGH THOMPSON, THE MIND AND HEART OF THE NEGOTIATOR 192 (2005).

[7] SCHACTER, *supra* note 3, at 6.

[8] High status in a group triggers higher serotonin levels (blunting rejection reactions, and creating confidence), and lower cortisol levels (a stress hormone); dopamine is released as a result of something unexpected—positive or negative—and "marks" it in memory as important to learn from; pleasure comes from endorphins and norepinephrine; oxytocin produces relaxation in the face of stress. JOHNSON, *supra* note 4, at 150-57.

[9]This suggests that our brains are wired for "the fear system to take control in threatening situations while preventing the reign of our conscious, deliberate selves." *Id.* at 45-46.

[10] PETER SENGE, THE FIFTH DISCIPLINE 174 (1994).

[11] ROGER FISHER, ET AL., BEYOND MACHIAVELLI: TOOLS FOR COPING WITH CONFLICT 21 (1994).

[12] Erving Goffman offers one of the first definitions of the word frame as used in this context: "I assume that definitions of a situation are built up in accordance with principles of organization which govern events—at least social ones—and our subjective involvement in them; frame is the word I use to refer to such of these basic elements as I am able to identify." ERVING GOFFMAN, FRAME ANALYSIS 11 (1974). Goffman, in turn, borrows his theory of frames from GREGORY BATESON, STEPS TO AN ECOLOGY OF MIND (1972).

[13] Oscar Nudler, *On Conflicts and Metaphors: Toward an Extended Rationality, in* CONFLICT: HUMAN NEEDS THEORY 179 (John Burton ed., 1990).

[14] SCHACTER, *supra* note 3, at 43.

[15] *Id.* at 45-46.

[16] DEAN PRUITT, ET AL., SOCIAL CONFLICT: ESCALATION, STALEMATE, AND SETTLEMENT 102 (2nd ed. 1994).

[17] *See generally* LEON FESTINGER, A THEORY OF COGNITIVE DISSONANCE (1957) for a discussion of cognitive dissonance.

[18] John Gottman argues that familiarity with your spouse's "mental map" or life story is a key to long-term marital happiness. It ensures that you understand the stories your spouse constructs about what happens in your lives, *see* JOHN M. GOTTMAN & NAN SILVER, THE SEVEN PRINCIPLES FOR MAKING MARRIAGE WORK (2000).

[19] DANIEL L. SCHACTER, THE SEVEN SINS OF MEMORY 150-51(2001)

[20] M. Ross & F. Sicoly, *Egocentric biases in Availability and Attribution,* 37 JOURNAL OF PERSONALITY AND SOCIAL PSYCHOLOGY 322 (1979); A. Christensen, et al., *Systematic Error in Behavioral Reports of Dyadic interaction: Egocentric Bias and Content Effects,* 5 BEHAVIORAL ASSESSMENT 129-40 (1983), reported in SCHACTER, *supra* note 19, at 150.

[21] *See generally* DOUGLAS STONE, ET AL., DIFFICULT CONVERSATIONS: HOW TO DISCUSS WHAT MATTERS MOST 111-26 (2000).

[22] SCHACTER, *supra* note 19, at 153-57.

[23] For a helpful discussion of attributions and intentions in conflict settings, *see* Keith Allred, *Anger and Retaliation: The Role of Attribution in Conflict, in* THE HANDBOOK OF CONFLICT RESOLUTION: THEORY AND PRACTICE (Morton Deutsch & Peter T. Coleman eds., 2000).

[24] Whereas I see my own behavior as being embedded in a complex *situational* context and experience myself as being well meaning in light of that context, I don't have access to the context that someone else experiences around themselves, and so I attribute their behavior to simple *character* traits. *See* LEE ROSS & RICHARD E. NISBETT, THE PERSON AND THE SITUATION: PERSPECTIVES OF SOCIAL PSYCHOLOGY 125-39 (1991).

[25] SENGE, *supra* note 10, at 73.

[26] R.L. Kahn and Roderick M. Kramer, *Untying the Knot: De-escalatory processes in International Conflict* (1990), *as cited in* LEIGH THOMPSON, THE MIND AND HEART OF THE NEGOTIATOR 267 (1998).

[27] *Id.; See also,* Keith G. Allred, Kessely Hon & Joseph P. Kalt, *Partisan Misperceptions and Conflict Escalation: Survey From A Tribal/Local Government Conflict* Faculty Research Working Paper Series, JFK School of Government, Harvard University, 2002.

[28] STONE, ET AL., *supra* note 21, at 63-64.

[29] PRUITT, ET AL., *supra* note 16, at 76.

[30] Ulric Neisser, *Cognitive Psychology, in* SCHACTER, *supra* note 19, at 40.

[31] The degree to which our stories can be engaged and changed is an area for future research. Clearly, there are situations that are more and less amenable to "re-storying." The more intense the dispute, the more hardened becomes the narrative, as is the case with trauma or depression, or when there is a threat to a basic human need. Default stories are often highly resistant to change, and more work needs to be done to determine what mediators can do to help parties see the world through frames that are both empowering and that help to manage conflict.

[32] William Carlos Williams, *as quoted in* ROBERT COLES, THE CALL OF STORIES 30 (1989).

❧ 40 ❧

Heuristics and Biases at the Bargaining Table

Russell Korobkin & Chris Guthrie

Editors' Note: So you still think that negotiation is based on "rational" thought? This chapter describes several key aspects of psychology and economics which impact our behavior—whether we like it or not and whether we know it or not. The authors summarize extensive work on how cognitive biases and other "non-rational" decision-making can be recognized, and then used to help reach the agreement you want.

Negotiation is an inherently *interpersonal* activity that nonetheless requires each participant to make *individual* judgments and decisions. Each negotiator must evaluate a proposed agreement, assess its value and the value of alternative courses of action, and ultimately choose whether to accept or reject the proposal.

The interdisciplinary field of "decision theory" offers both a normative account (how individuals *should* act) and descriptive accounts (how individuals *do* act) of decision-making. According to the normative model, negotiators should compare the subjective expected value of an agreement to the subjective expected value of non-agreement, taking into account such factors as risks, differential transaction costs, and reputational and relational consequences of each possible course of action.[1] Once a negotiator has calculated the expected value of each course of action, the negotiator should then select the one that promises the greatest return.[2] [Senger, Risk]

There is less agreement about whether negotiators actually make decisions consistent with this approach. Proponents of descriptive or "positive" models based on "rational choice theory" assume that negotiators will invest optimally in the amount of information needed for decision-making, draw accurate inferences from the information they acquire, and then select the option that maximizes their expected utility. In short, proponents of the rational choice-based models assume that negotiators will make choices consistent with the normative model.

Skeptics of rational choice-based models argue that negotiators rarely behave this "demonically."[3] Instead, negotiators routinely employ more intuitive approaches to judgment and choice that rely on a variety of "heuristics" or mental shortcuts to reduce the complexity and effort involved in the reasoning process.[4] While some researchers believe that negotiators intentionally employ such heuristics to economize on the time and effort required to make decisions, others believe that reliance on heuristics is unconscious. In all likelihood, there is truth in both perspectives; that is, negotiators rely on heuristics intuitively and unconsciously in some circumstances and consciously employ heuristics in others. Either way, negotiators should appreciate the important role that heuristics are likely to play in their decision-making—and in the decision-making of their counterparts—at the bargaining table.

In this chapter, we examine the role of heuristics in negotiation from two vantage points. First, we identify the ways in which some common heuristics are likely to influence the negotiator's decision-making processes. Namely, we discuss anchoring and adjustment, availability, self-serving evaluations, framing, the status quo bias, and contrast effects.[5] Understanding these common heuristics and how they can cause negotiators' judgments and choices to deviate from the normative model can enable negotiators to reorient their behavior so it more closely aligns with the normative model or, alternatively, make informed choices to take advantage of the effort-conserving features of heuristics at the cost of the increased precision that the normative approach offers. Second, we explore how negotiators might capitalize on the knowledge that their counterparts are likely to rely on heuristics in their decision-making processes. We consider, in other words, how negotiators can exploit heuristic reasoning on the part of others for personal gain.

Understanding Negotiator Judgment and Decision-Making

When deciding whether to accept or reject an actual or anticipated set of deal terms, a negotiator must perform two cognitive tasks. First, the negotiator must evaluate the content of the available options, a task we can loosely call "judgment." For example, a negotiator contemplating the purchase of a particular business must try to evaluate the market value of the business's assets, determine what percentage of the business's current clients will be retained in case of a change of ownership, estimate how much profit the business will earn in the future, and evaluate the likelihood that the negotiator would find a similar business to purchase if the negotiator opted not to purchase this one. From this perspective, judgment involves a search for facts about the world.

Second, the negotiator must determine which available option he prefers, a task we can call "choice." For example, would he rather purchase the business under consideration for a specific price or reject such a deal in favor of continuing his search, thus taking a chance that he will find an equally desirable business at a lower price or a more desirable business at the same price?

In performing both of these tasks—i.e., judgment and choice—the rational negotiator *should* evaluate options and make decisions consistent with the normative model of choice. However, both social science research and common experience suggest the negotiator's decision-making processes will often depart from the normative model.

Judgment

Negotiators cannot know the objective values and probabilities of every option they might consider before reaching a negotiated outcome. Thus, to estimate the values and probabilities associated with each option, negotiators are likely to rely on heuristics. Heuristics often enable negotiators to make good judgments in a "fast and frugal" manner.[6] On other occasions, heuristics prove to be poor substitutes for more complex reasoning and result in decisions that fail to best serve the negotiator's interests.

Anchoring and Adjustment

One heuristic approach to judgment that can lead to suboptimal results is known as "anchoring and adjustment." To estimate the value of an option, negotiators are likely to start with the value of a known option, the "anchor," and then adjust to compensate for relevant differences in the character of the known and unknown item.[7]

For example, a negotiator buying a business might estimate its future profits by starting with the known profits recently earned by a similar business and then adjusting his estimate based on the fact that the known business has fewer current clients and higher labor costs than the subject of the negotiation. Alternatively, the negotiator might base his estimate on the profits earned by the business in question the previous year and then adjust his estimate of next year's profits based on changing market conditions or the presence of new competitors. Although adjusting from a known anchor is a useful approach to making a judgment, experimental evidence indicates that people often fail to adjust sufficiently away from the initial "anchor." In other words, negotiators who rely on this heuristic will often undervalue the differences between the known and unknown values.

In addition, especially when numerical estimates are necessary, individuals sometimes anchor on values that are largely, or even completely, irrelevant. In one well-known example, subjects estimated that the average annual temperature in San Francisco was higher after first being asked if it was higher or lower than 558 degrees![8] In an example more obviously relevant to negotiation, we found that the opening offer in a litigation settlement negotiation can affect the recipient's judgment of a subsequent final offer even when the opening offer does not convey relevant information.[9]

Whether a negotiator bases a judgment on an inappropriate anchor or on an appropriate anchor from which he fails to adjust sufficiently, the negotiator's resulting judgment will often be less accurate than it would have been in the absence of that anchor. Returning to our original hypothetical, depending on the anchor consulted, the negotiator could make a suboptimal estimate of the profits the target business is likely to achieve the next year.

Availability

When an option could have a variety of consequences rather than a single certain outcome—for example, if the negotiator enters an agreement to buy the business under consideration, the business might make a large profit or, alternatively, it might go bankrupt—the negotiator will often evaluate the likelihood of the various possible outcomes based on the ease with which they come to mind. Negotiators who make judgments based on how mentally *available* the possible results are, rather than their estimated statistical likelihoods, use a method of judgment known as the "availability" heuristic.[10]

Basing judgment on the availability of outcomes is a reasonable, time-saving device that will often yield acceptable outcomes because availability is often correlated with frequency. But when the available outcomes are not typical, or when there are important differences between the past and future circumstances, the heuristic can lead to flawed predictions. For example, a negotiator evaluating the prospects of entrusting his or her lawsuit to a jury for the purpose of deciding whether to accept a settlement offer might overestimate the likelihood of winning punitive damages at trial if he recalls a recent multi-million dollar verdict in a tobacco lawsuit publicized in the news, because the media exposure afforded to that particular verdict does not reflect how atypical it actually is.[11]

Self-Serving Evaluations

Substantial evidence indicates that individuals are particularly likely to make judgments in ways that confirm pre-existing belief structures,[12] assume high degrees of personal agency in the world,[13] and create a positive presentation of self.[14] This tendency will often result in judgments compromised by what is called the "self-serving" or "egocentric" bias.[15]

A plethora of studies demonstrate that individuals often judge uncertain options as more likely to produce outcomes that are beneficial to them than an objective analysis would suggest.[16] Depending on the specific context, the bias could cause negotiators to overestimate either the likely benefits that would result from reaching a negotiated agreement or the likely benefits that would result from rejecting a proposed agreement and pursuing an alternate course of action. In one study, for example, George Loewenstein and his colleagues assigned some experimental subjects to the role of plaintiff and others to the role of defendant and then asked each to judge the value of the lawsuit based on the very same information.[17] Plaintiff subjects estimated that a judge would award the plaintiff substantially more money should the case go to trial than the defendant subjects estimated, suggesting that, on average, subjects' judgments of the merits of their positions were inflated.[18]

Choice

After judging the objective attributes of available options, negotiators must eventually make a choice between them. Normative models assume that negotiators will make choices based on a comparison of the expected values of each option; the decision theory literature suggests that choices often fail to reflect this reasoning process.

Framing of Risky Choices

When choosing between an option with a known outcome and one with an uncertain outcome, individuals often consider not only the expected value of each choice but also whether the possible outcomes appear to be "gains" or "losses" relative to a reference point.[19] In the standard case, individuals tend to exhibit risk aversion when choosing between an option that promises a certain gain and one that has a chance of resulting in a greater gain but risk-seeking tendencies when choosing between an option associated with a certain loss and one with a probabilistic chance of a larger loss.[20]

These findings suggest that if agreement will generate a certain outcome (such as the settlement of a lawsuit for a fixed sum of money) and non-agreement will leave the negotiator to pursue a risky alternative (such as a trial with a probability of winning a large sum and a probability of winning nothing), the negotiator's choice between agreement and impasse could depend on whether her base of comparison for evaluating the decision options is the status quo or some other reference point, such as a prior state of affairs or her aspiration level. For example, a plaintiff in a lawsuit who believes she has a fifty percent chance of prevailing at trial and can demonstrate damages of $100,000 would probably accept a settlement offer of $50,000 if she evaluates the choice from the perspective of her current financial position, in which she has no money. From this perspective, settlement represents a certain gain and litigation represents a probabilistic but risky chance at achieving a larger gain. However, the same plaintiff would be more likely to reject the settlement if she evaluates her options using the reference point of the $100,000 that she used to have or believes she deserves. From this perspective, a $50,000 settlement represents a certain loss of $50,000, whereas continued litigation offers the risk of a larger loss but the possibility of prevailing and thus avoiding the perceived loss entirely.

The Status Quo Bias

Individuals generally prefer an option if it is consistent with the status quo.[21] Often, we prefer the status quo because we receive more utility from the current state of affairs than we expect to receive from some other state of affairs, suggesting that the status quo bias is consistent with the normative model of choice. In other circumstances, however, reliance on this heuristic can lead decision-makers to make choices that depart from the normative model. The status quo bias suggests that, all other things being equal, negotiators will prefer their initial endowments over endowments they might hope to receive through exchange,[22] that they will favor deal terms that are consistent with legal default rules,[23] and that they will prefer terms of trade that are conventional for the type of bargain that is at issue.[24]

Evidence of the status quo bias suggests that negotiator choice can depend on the negotiator's particular perception of the status quo. Consider, for example, a customer whose car lease is about to expire and who is evaluating the car dealer's offer to sell the car to him for $10,000. The customer's choice between accepting the offer and rejecting the offer (and shopping elsewhere for transportation) could conceivably be effected by whether the customer's perception of the status quo is (a) that he does not own a car or (b) that he operates the leased car. Both descriptions of the world are factually accurate, but the customer is more likely to purchase the car if he focuses on the latter rather than the former because doing so would be consistent with the latter vision of the status quo but not the former.

Contrast Effects

Evidence also suggests that choice can depend on the full range of options available to the decision-maker, even when the normative model suggests that the availability of certain options should be irrelevant. Researchers investigating such "contrast effects"[25] have demonstrated, for example, that individuals are more likely to select an option in the presence of a similar, inferior option than in the absence of the inferior option.[26] In one illustrative experiment, Itamar Simonson and Amos Tversky found that 28% more subjects chose an elegant Cross pen when they were also offered the alternative choices of $6 in cash or an inferior pen than when subjects were offered only the choice between the Cross pen and the $6 in cash. That is, the availability of the inferior pen substantially increased the likelihood that subjects would choose the Cross pen over the $6.[27] The implication is that a negotiator's preference for one agreement possibility over another, or for a proposed agreement over an outside alternative, might depend on whether other options that make the proposed agreement appear desirable in contrast are also considered as part of the calculus.[28]

In some contexts, the presence of a third option, C, could logically affect a decision-maker's preference for A versus B, because C provides information about the quality of A or B. But if C sheds no new light on A or B, any impact it has on the A versus B decision would violate the normative model of choice. As Mark Kelman and his colleagues explain, an individual who prefers chicken to pasta might rationally change her preference to pasta upon learning that veal parmesan is on the menu because "the availability of veal parmesan on the menu might [indicate] that the restaurant specializes in Italian [food]."[29] But "[a] person who prefers chicken over pasta should not change this preference on learning that fish is also available."[30]

Influencing Negotiator Judgment and Decision-Making

Negotiators who recognize that their counterparts are likely to rely on heuristics when making the types of judgments and choices commonly required in bargaining settings can use this knowledge to increase the likelihood both of securing agreements and of securing agreements on highly favorable terms. This section briefly outlines some ways in which a negotiator can make use of heuristic reasoning to influence her counterpart's judgment and choices. We rely heavily on litigation bargaining anecdotes as examples, but the concepts can be employed just as effectively in other negotiation contexts.

Influence Through Anchoring

The anchoring and adjustment heuristic suggests that a negotiator can affect her counterpart's judgment of the quality of a proposed agreement if she can dictate the content of the anchor. In commercial negotiations, where monetary values are usually the bargaining currency, a monetary figure that appears even superficially related to the subject of the negotiation can affect one's counterpart's judgments.

In litigation bargaining, the settlement versus adjudication decision rests in large part on the negotiator's judgment of what a court would award the plaintiff should settlement negotiations fail. Because adjudication results are notoriously difficult to predict, the plaintiff's lawyer has a clear opportunity to improve his chances of convincing the defendant to choose settlement at a favorable price over adjudication (and vice versa for the defendant's lawyer) by manipulating the defendant's evaluation of adjudication. Of course, the plaintiff's lawyer might accomplish this by persuasive argumentation. He might also accomplish this by exposing the defendant to a high anchor—perhaps by making a very high initial settlement demand. Even if the defendant immediately rejects the high demand, the demand could anchor the defendant's prediction of a jury verdict, making that "judgment" higher than it otherwise would be, and thus increasing the likelihood that the defendant would choose a somewhat lower settlement demand over the adjudication alternative.

Several pieces of experimental evidence support this contention. Researchers have found, for instance, that those who open with an extreme demand may be more likely to reach agreement;[31] that those who open with extreme demands may be more likely to receive larger settlements;[32] and that extreme demands are likely to influence mock jurors' assessments of the value of a plaintiff's case.[33]

Influence Through Availability

Recall that the availability heuristic causes probability estimates of outcomes to be influenced by the mental availability of similar prior outcomes. That an outcome's availability is not always highly correlated with its frequency offers an opportunity for exploitation in bargaining. A negotiator can increase the chances that her counterpart will accept a proposed agreement favorable to the negotiator if the negotiator can increase the availability in the counterpart's mind of outcomes that are favorable to the negotiator and unfavorable to the counterpart.

As we identified in the context of the anchoring and adjustment heuristic, the best opportunity to exploit the availability heuristic is when negotiation decision-making requires probabilistic judgments of highly uncertain events, such as outcomes of adjudication. By drawing the defendant's attention to large verdicts in recent cases that bear at least a surface similarity to the case at hand, for example, the plaintiff's lawyer might increase the defendant's prediction of the likelihood that a jury would return a large plaintiff's verdict. This might, in turn, induce the defendant to accept a settlement offer that he would otherwise reject.

Influence Through Framing

The effect of frames on risky choices suggests that a negotiator's choice between a certain option, such as a litigation settlement agreement, and a probabilistic option, such as adjudication, will depend in part on the reference point from which she compares the two options. Assuming that the options have a similar perceived expected value, she is more likely to choose the certain choice if the options appear favorable (i.e., look like gains); if the options appear unfavorable (i.e., look like losses), she is more likely to prefer the risky choice. A negotiator can therefore increase the likelihood that her counterpart will accept a settlement proposal if she can cause the counterpart to select a reference point that makes settlement look positive.

In litigation, for example, a plaintiff is likely to perceive both settlement and the expected value of a judgment at trial as gains relative to the current state of affairs, while a defendant is likely to view both options as losses. Thus, we would predict that a defendant is more likely than a plaintiff to reject a settlement proposal that is roughly equivalent to the expected value of trial.[34] A plaintiff who wishes to maximize the likelihood that the defendant will accept such a proposal, or even one more favorable to the plaintiff, can do so by attempting to reframe the options.

Specifically, the plaintiff might try to induce the defendant to compare his available options not to the status quo but to a different reference point that will make those options seem more attractive. For example, she might try to persuade him to compare his options to a realistic worst-case outcome at trial. Relative to that reference point, a settlement is likely to look like a "gain," which should make the idea of paying the certain settlement appear more attractive.

Influence Through Contrast Effects

A negotiator familiar with contrast effects will recognize that her counterpart is likely to evaluate an option more favorably if a similar but inferior option is available. The negotiator might thus be able to increase the likelihood that her counterpart will select a particular proposal if a similar but inferior proposal is offered in the alternative.

Suppose, for example, that a fired employee files suit against a company for which she used to work, asserting employment discrimination claims under Title VII. Suppose further that the defendant has offered to pay the plaintiff $30,000 cash to settle the case but that the plaintiff is wavering because trial holds some appeal. Assuming that the defendant wants the plaintiff to accept the $30,000 settlement offer, what might defense counsel do to encourage her to accept it?

In lieu of the $30,000 lump sum payment defense counsel might offer to donate $30,000 to the charity of the plaintiff's choice, offer $30,000 in merchandise to the plaintiff, or offer to pay her $10,000 per year for three years. Research on contrast effects suggests that the presence of any of these alternative options should make the $30,000 cash offer seem more attractive by comparison than it would appear standing alone. This, in turn, should increase the likelihood that the plaintiff will choose to accept the settlement proposal and forego trial.

Conclusion

Negotiators often lack control over the identity of their counterparts, the issues under consideration in a negotiation, and the bargaining environment. They do enjoy control over how they make decisions, however. By understanding typical patterns in judgment and choice, the negotiator can exercise that control effectively and even exercise some control over how her counterpart makes decisions as well.

Endnotes

This chapter is adapted from Russell Korobkin & Chris Guthrie, *Heuristics and Biases at the Bargaining Table*, 87 MARQUETTE LAW REVIEW 795 (2004).

[1] *See, e.g.*, RUSSELL KOROBKIN, NEGOTIATION THEORY AND STRATEGY 43-50 (2002).

[2] *See, e.g., id. See also* MAX H. BAZERMAN & MARGARET A. NEALE, NEGOTIATING RATIONALLY 1 (1992). The normative approach, while widely accepted, does have its detractors. *See, e.g.*, Gerd Gigerenzer & Peter M. Todd, *Fast and Frugal Heuristics: The Adaptive Toolbox, in* SIMPLE HEURISTICS THAT MAKE US SMART 3, 5 (Gerd Gigerenzer, et al. eds., 1999) [hereinafter SIMPLE HEURISTICS].

[3] Gigerenzer & Todd, *supra* note 2, at 5.

[4] Amos Tversky and Daniel Kahneman introduced the "heuristics and biases" program into the literature on judgment and decision-making. *See, e.g.*, Thomas Gilovich & Dale Griffin, *Introduction—Heuristics and Biases: Then and Now, in* HEURISTICS AND BIASES 1 (Thomas Gilovich, et al. eds., 2002) [hereinafter HEURISTICS AND BIASES]. In their initial formulation, Tversky and Kahneman explained that "people rely on a limited number of heuristic principles which reduce the complex tasks of assessing probabilities and predicting values to simpler judgmental operations. In general, these heuristics are quite useful, but sometimes they lead to severe and systematic errors." Amos Tversky & Daniel Kahneman, *Judgment Under Uncertainty: Heuristics and Biases,* 185 SCIENCE 1124(1974) [hereinafter Tversky & Kahneman, *Heuristics]*.

[5] In their initial formulation, Tversky and Kahneman identified three basic heuristics—representativeness, availability, and anchoring and adjustment. *See* Tversky & Kahneman, *Heuristics, supra* note 4. More recently, Kahneman and Frederick have argued that the three basic heuristics are representativeness, availability, and the affect heuristic. Daniel Kahneman & Shane Frederick, *Representativeness Revisited: Attribute Substitution in Intuitive Judgment, in* HEURISTICS & BIASES, *supra* note 4, at 53, 56. Nonetheless, most decision researchers use the terms "heuristics and biases" loosely to include several mental shortcuts that decision-makers are likely to make. *See, e.g.*, HEURISTICS AND BIASES, *supra* note 4; JUDGMENT UNDER UNCERTAINTY: HEURISTICS AND BIASES (Daniel Kahneman, Paul Slovic & Amos Tversky eds., 1982).

[6] *See, e.g.*, Jean Czerlinski, et al., *How Good are Simple Heuristics, in* SIMPLE HEURISTICS, *supra* note 2, at 97; Jorg Reiskamp & Ulrich Hoffrage, *When Do People Use Simple Heuristics, and How Can We Tell?, in* SIMPLE HEURISTICS, *supra* note 2, at 141.

[7] *See* Tversky & Kahneman, *Heuristics, supra* note 4.

[8] SCOTT PLOUS, THE PSYCHOLOGY OF JUDGMENT AND DECISION MAKING 146 (1993) (referring to an unpublished study by George Quattrone and colleagues).

[9] *See* Russell Korobkin & Chris Guthrie, *Opening Offers and Out-of-Court Settlement: A Little Moderation May Not Go a Long Way,* 10 OHIO STATE JOURNAL ON DISPUTE RESOLUTION 1, 11-13, 18-19 (1994).

[10] *See* Tversky & Kahneman, *Heuristics, supra* note 4.

[11] The availability heuristic is quite similar to what is sometimes called the "salience" or "vividness" heuristic. *See, e.g.*, RICHARD NISBETT & LEE ROSS, HUMAN INFERENCE: STRATEGIES AND

SHORTCOMINGS OF SOCIAL JUDGMENT 8 (1980).

[12] *See, e.g.,* Charles G. Lord, et al., *Biased Assimilation and Attitude Polarization: The Effects of Prior Theories on Subsequently Considered Evidence,* 37 JOURNAL OF PERSONALITY & SOCIAL PSYCHOLOGY 2098, 2102 (1979).

[13] *See, e.g.,* Neil D. Weinstein, *Unrealistic Optimism About Future Life Events,* 39 JOURNAL OF PERSONALITY & SOCIAL PSYCHOLOGY 806, 814 (1980).

[14] *Id.*

[15] *See, e.g.,* Michael Ross & Fiore Sicoly, *Egocentric Biases in Availability and Attribution,* 37 JOURNAL OF PERSONALITY & SOCIAL PSYCHOLOGY 322 (1979).

[16] *See, e.g.,* Lynn A. Baker & Robert E. Emery, *When Every Relationship Is Above Average: Perceptions and Expectations of Divorce at the Time of Marriage,* 17 LAW & HUMAN BEHAVIOR 439, 441-43 (1993) (finding that recently married couples expect that they will not get divorced, despite knowing the divorce rate); Ross & Sicoly, *supra* note 15, at 324-26 (finding that people overestimate their relative contributions to conversations and their relative contribution to housework); Weinstein, *supra* note 13, at 809-11 (finding that people routinely overestimate how healthy they are relative to others).

[17] *See* George Loewenstein, et al., *Self-Serving Assessments of Fairness and Pretrial Bargaining,* 22 JOURNAL OF LEGAL STUDIES 135 (1993).

[18] *Id.*

[19] This observation is derived from Daniel Kahneman and Amos Tversky's "prospect theory." *See generally* Daniel Kahneman & Amos Tversky, *Prospect Theory: An Analysis of Decision Under Risk,* 47 ECONOMETRICA 263 (1979).

[20] *See* Daniel Kahneman, *Reference Points, Anchors, Norms, and Mixed Feelings,* 51 ORGANIZATIONAL BEHAVIOR & HUMAN DECISION PROCESSES 296 (1992).

[21] *See* Russell Korobkin, *The Endowment Effect and Legal Analysis,* 97 NORTHWESTERN UNIVERSITY LAW REVIEW 1227, 1231-42 (2003).

[22] *See, e.g.,* Daniel Kahneman, et. al., *Experimental Tests of the Endowment Effect and the Coase Theorem,* 98 JOURNAL OF POLITICAL ECONOMICS 1325 (1990).

[23] Russell Korobkin, *The Status Quo Bias and Contract Default Rules,* 83 CORNELL LAW REVIEW 608 (1998).

[24] Russell Korobkin, *Inertia and Preference in Contract Negotiation: The Psychological Power of Default Rules and Form Terms,* 51 VANDERBILT LAW REVIEW 1583 (1998).

[25] *See* Joel Huber, et al., *Adding Asymmetrically Dominated Alternatives: Violations of Regularity and the Similarity Hypothesis,* 9 JOURNAL OF CONSUMER RESEARCH 90 (1982).

[26] *Id.*

[27] Itamar Simonson & Amos Tversky, *Choice in Context: Tradeoff Contrast and Extremeness Aversion,* 29 JOURNAL OF MARKETING RESEARCH 281, 287 (1992).

[28] *See* Chris Guthrie, *Panacea or Pandora's Box?: The Costs of Options in Negotiation,* 88 IOWA LAW REVIEW 601, 617-19 (2003).

[29] Mark Kelman, et al., *Context-Dependence in Legal Decision Making,* 25 JOURNAL OF LEGAL STUDIES 287 n.2 (1996).

[30] *Id.* at 287.

[31] *See* Korobkin & Guthrie, *supra* note 9.

[32] *See* Adam D. Galinsky & Thomas Mussweiler, *First Offers as Anchors: The Role of Perspective-Taking and Negotiator Focus,* 81 JOURNAL OF PERSONALITY & SOCIAL PSYCHOLOGY 657 (2001).

[33] *See, e.g.,* Dale W. Broeder, *The University of Chicago Jury Project,* 38 NEBRASKA LAW REVIEW 744, 756 (1959); Gretchen B. Chapman & Brian H. Bornstein, *The More You Ask For, The More You Get: Anchoring in Personal Injury Verdicts,* 10 APPLIED COGNITIVE PSYCHOLOGY 519, 526-27 (1996).

[34] Jeffrey J. Rachlinski, *Gains, Losses, and the Psychology of Litigation,* 70 SOUTHERN CALIFORNIA LAW REVIEW 113 (1996). This simple analysis is meant only to illustrate the framing issue, not to evaluate the full range of defendants' incentives. Thus, it assumes no transaction costs, no issues involving the time value of money (i.e., the payout would occur at the same time in the event of a trial or a settlement), no difference in reputational consequences between settlement and trial, and no particular desire or reluctance to go to trial beyond the monetary consequences.

❧ 41 ❧

Psychology and Persuasion

Donna Shestowsky

Editors' Note: *We know instinctively that not everyone is persuaded by the same set of facts or the same type of argument. Shestowsky explains the two different types of audiences we typically face in a negotiation, and provides pointers on how to persuade in the way that will be most effective to each audience. This chapter should be read in conjunction with those by Heen & Stone, Guthrie, and Korobkin & Guthrie.*

Persuasion is part art and part science. It is *science* in that many persuasion strategies can be reliably more successful when certain conditions are met or when they are used on a certain type of person. It is *art* in that some negotiators may use the same persuasion strategy more subtly than others or have a knack for quickly and responsively changing strategies when it is called for during a negotiation. Although many lawyers bring an impressive amount of intuitive knowledge of persuasion to negotiations, even the most advanced negotiators may not be aware of the science behind effective persuasion. What are the big lessons stemming from the psychological science of persuasion, and how can lawyers use these findings to maximize their persuasiveness in negotiations? These questions form the basis of this chapter.

Two Routes to Persuasion

Have you ever negotiated with an opposing counsel who failed to be persuaded by the merit of your proposal—even when it was an objectively attractive win-win idea and you made the strongest, most logical arguments to support it? In some instances, of course, your initial view that his resistance stems from his complete irrationality may in fact be correct. [Jeglic & Jeglic, *Disordered People*] More often than not, however, there is another explanation for the resistance: opposing counsel was simply not going to be persuaded by your strong arguments, no matter their validity, but something else just might have done the trick. One important take-away from psychological research is that there are two different ways to persuade—one that relies on argument quality and another that does not. In essence, people can differ in how they process information in ways that have important implications for negotiation and other aspects of lawyering, and different ways of processing create opportunity for different ways to persuade. Understanding this multiple-routes-to-persuasion paradigm and knowing how to use it effectively is key to becoming a more effective negotiator. [1]

According to psychologists, a widely accepted way of understanding the psychology of persuasion stems from the Elaboration Likelihood Model (ELM), which characterizes persuasion as occurring by the relative operation of either of two routes.[2] These two routes are differentiated by the level of cognitive processing (i.e., amount of conscious examination or "elaboration" of the message) that is undertaken by the person exposed to a persuasive communication. As discussed in greater detail below, one route to persuasion, called the "central" route, involves engaging in extensive processing of issue-relevant information in order to make judgments. Negotiators who engage in central processing will carefully consider the merits of your proposals and be persuaded by relevant and logical arguments. By contrast, the other route to persuasion—the "peripheral" route—is marked by a relative lack of effortful processing. Negotiators persuaded by this route will tend to consider your proposals in a more superficial way, and thus will often be swayed by how you "package" or "frame" them rather than by their intrinsic merit.

Whether a negotiator processes your ideas primarily by the central or peripheral route depends on several factors. Some factors are associated with personality (e.g.,. intellectual capacity or motivation). Such elements are obviously outside of your control, but insofar as you can gauge such aspects of opposing counsel before you negotiate, you can maximize your persuasiveness by planning the most well-suited strategy for that "type" of negotiator.[3] More importantly, how a negotiator processes information is also affected by situational factors (e.g., how distracted he is), which you can in fact influence. Better still, you might consider preparing for persuasion by both peripheral and central routes, thereby covering all your bases.

The great lesson of the ELM is that, to be persuasive, you must consider how to communicate messages in the most effective way for your intended audience, not for what seems best to you personally. This lesson is especially critical for lawyers who negotiate with non-lawyers since lawyers often assume that what they happen to find persuasive is also what is likely to persuade others. The kind of training in logic and reasoning that lawyers typically receive in law school and in legal practice can make it challenging for them to truly appreciate that the use of such formal argumentation is but one way to persuade. Lawyers and others who understand the differences between the two routes to persuasion can gain a considerable advantage in negotiations by tailoring persuasive appeals in ways that work effectively for a particular audience, or, conversely, by subtly shaping a particular audience to make a particular strategy more effective. The remainder of this chapter will detail the major differences between the central and peripheral routes to persuasion, describe the circumstances under which a given negotiator is likely to process information via one route versus the other, and offer advice on how to use central and peripheral cues to persuade.

The Central Route to Persuasion

When negotiators think extensively about issue-relevant information in order to evaluate their stance on a given issue, they have processed information via the *central route*. This route to persuasion becomes dominant to the extent that a person's ability and motivation to scrutinize relevant information are both at high levels. Ability involves not only intellectual ability, relating to whether the negotiator can in fact understand your proposals and has the relevant expertise to evaluate them, but situational factors as well—negotiators who are tired, hungry, distracted, or preoccupied by other projects or personal matters are less likely to have the capacity required to think deeply during negotiations.

To process centrally, motivation is also key. Just like for ability, motivation can come from a relatively enduring personality trait, or can be prompted by situational factors (such as when the individual is prompted to regard the issue as highly personally relevant).[4] In terms of personality attributes, some people, quite simply, are more naturally inclined to think deeply than others.[5] These people enjoy thinking and are motivated to do so without any external pressure or reward. Such people are likely to engage in central processing, and will therefore tend to pay careful attention to the content and quality of your arguments when deciding whether to accept your proposals. As discussed below, empirical research has shown that individuals who are not so naturally motivated can often be prompted to engage in similar levels of deep thinking with the right type of encouragement.

Consequences for Persuasion

Not surprisingly, the level of processing in which a negotiator engages has significant consequences for persuasion. When attitudes form or change because information is carefully attended to, understood and evaluated, they tend to be "strong" attitudes. That is, they are much less likely to be affected by the passage of time or the presentation of new information.[6] Importantly, strong attitudes also tend to predict behavior.[7] Thus, when you want an enduring negotiated agreement—one that is unlikely to be revised or subjected to future litigation because the other party subsequently grows dissatisfied and does not want to execute his agreed-upon duties—then persuasion by the central route becomes especially important because it tends to produce strong attitudes that will promote behavioral adherence to the agreement. Persuasion by this route makes the agreement more self-sustaining because the other party will tend to truly believe it is in his best interest to comply with its terms, and the reasons that supported his decision to agree with the terms can serve as a reminder that leads to a process of subtle and continued self-persuasion over time.

Relatedly, when a negotiator thinks deeply about an issue, he is more likely to notice the differences in the quality of the arguments presented to him.[8] He will generally be less persuaded by weak arguments than by strong ones, where arguments categorized as "weak" are simple statements and restatements of belief or appear (to a trained outside observer) to be specious, irrelevant, or illogical, and those categorized as "strong" are ones that offer clear, logical, relevant reasons for the stated position.[9] Thus, when the other party is processing information centrally, your arguments in favor of a given proposal will generally need to be especially strong in order to effectively persuade.

The deep thinking that reflects central processing has also been associated with less persuasion during face-to-face communication. For example, Shestowsky, Wegener and Fabrigar[10] provided research participants with the same facts of a negligence case, but diverging arguments on the issue of negligence, before they were split into pairs for negotiation. Each pair included one person high in motivation to think and the other low, and was asked to discuss the case and negotiate a consensus agreement on liability. The diverging information about the case meant that those in each pair began their discussions disagreeing about the appropriate verdict, much like one would find in plea bargaining or civil settlement negotiations. Shestowsky, et al., expected that those who were highly motivated to think would form opinions of the case that were based on deeper elaboration than their lesser motivated counterparts. Consistent with the idea that high levels of elaboration make attitudes more resistant to persuasion, the pre-negotiation views of highly motivated thinkers better predicted the negotiated outcomes.

Recent research has also found that those who are high in motivation to think tend to lead decision-making in larger groups,[11] which has important implications for people negotiating with an opposing team rather than with a single opposing counterpart. This finding suggests that when the other party to a negotiation is a group, you should focus your presentations on the individual who is most motivated to think, as that person will tend to be the one who brings the others on board when the group convenes to decide whether to accept your proposal. Thankfully, you need not administer a personality scale to the opposing side to determine who is likely to be highly motivated to think—research suggests that they can be identified by noting who tends to talk significantly more than others, and behaves more assertively, during group meetings. Thus, although such behavioral tendencies are not perfect indicators of those who are most likely to process information centrally and persuade their team-mates, they appear to be the *best* subtle indicators that are supported by research.

How You Encourage it in Negotiations
Strategically, you would want the other party to process your proposals centrally only if you truly have something valuable to offer him—where "valuable" is defined as something that you honestly believe might reasonably meet his client's interests. When your proposals have such merit, negotiators who process them centrally are more likely to recognize and accept them on their merits and, consequently, agree to, and abide by, a negotiated outcome that incorporates those proposals. How can you promote persuasion by the central route when this is your strategy? Even if you are negotiating with someone who is not naturally motivated to think, or if you do not know whether they are so inclined, you can nevertheless maximize the likelihood that the other party will think centrally by priming him to consider the negotiation as a "problem" that requires coming up with an objectively reasonable, or accurate, solution (i.e., the best way to satisfy the compatible interests between the two clients, and resolving their competing interests in ways that will make both parties happy with the outcome). Instilling an accuracy motive is one of the most direct means of inducing objectivity in the processing of information.[12] To accomplish this goal, negotiators can attempt to promote a concern for accuracy by asking questions and seeking information, rather than making assertions, requests, threats, and demands.[13] For example, instead of aggressively stating that your small-business client is not willing to give the other party more money in order to settle a personal injury claim because of the consequences it would have on this year's profits, a lawyer-negotiator might frame the same idea in the form of a joint-problem-solving question: "how might we compensate your client without reducing my client's profits this fiscal year, which is a significant concern for my client?" Posing questions, framing the reconciliation of competing interests as a puzzle that requires logical thought, and summarizing arguments in the form of questions rather than as assertions can result in greater thought about a proposal's merits.[14]

    Reducing distractions during negotiations can also promote persuasion via the central route:

> By reducing our critical ability, distractions can decrease the effectiveness of strongly persuasive communications because we are not able to elaborate them favorably. To make matters worse, distraction exerts the opposite effect on weak communications. It makes weak communications more persuasive because it reduces people's cognitive capacity, thereby making it more difficult for them to counter flawed arguments or demolish shaky logic.[15]

Thus, if you can offer cogent arguments to support your proposals, you would benefit from minimizing any distractions opposing counsel might encounter. The stronger the quality of your arguments, the more important it is to provide a quiet, interruption- and distraction-free environment in which your counterpart can carefully consider them.

Conducting negotiations over the phone can also lessen more subtle distractions. When we communicate via technology, we generally attend less to the other person and more to the message they are disseminating.[16] This focus on the message can have potential benefits. For example, in a study comparing negotiations that took place either over the phone or in person,[17] one negotiator in each pair was given a strong case (i.e., a large number of high-quality arguments) to present whereas the other was assigned to present a weak case. The strong case was more successful in the phone condition (where negotiation partners were not visible) than in the face-to-face condition. By contrast, weak arguments were more successful when negotiations took place face-to-face rather than by phone. A clear implication of these findings is that the social constraint of the communication medium can affect the persuasion process that occurs during negotiations. In essence, with the availability of more social cues from a readily visualizable and identifiable counterpart, participants were less affected by the quality of that counterpart's position during the negotiation. Thus, communicating via technology can lead negotiators to focus more on the content and quality of your arguments, rather than being distracted and consequently (mis)led into agreement by more peripheral factors like those made more salient in face-to-face interactions.

Finally, motivation to think can also be enhanced by promoting a sense of individual responsibility for the negotiation outcome. Psychological research has investigated the phenomenon of "social loafing," the tendency for individuals to put less effort into a task when they share responsibility for the outcome as part of a group than when they believe they are individually responsible for the outcome.[18] When negotiating with a group rather than with a single person, you can expect a motivational deficit to result from your fellow negotiators' shared responsibility. Given that such social loafing is associated with less discernment between strong and weak arguments,[19] when you are hoping to persuade by the central route, then you would want to encourage each person in the opposing group to think for himself. You can encourage individual processing by ensuring that each person in the other party participates in the dialogue (e.g., by asking questions of individuals who have been silent, or having a general brainstorming session in which all group members are required to participate).

In sum, persuasion by the central route has significant advantages, especially when an enduring, self-sustaining agreement is sought. Psychological research has helped to clarify the conditions under which negotiators can promote careful thinking, and therefore persuasion, via this route. With some thoughtful planning, you can apply some of the research findings to enhance your persuasiveness in a given negotiation.

The Peripheral Route

Persuasion by the peripheral route is a different creature altogether. In sharp contrast to influence by the central route, persuasion by the peripheral route is marked by a relative lack of deep processing. This route becomes dominant to the extent that a negotiator's motivation or ability to scrutinize attitude-relevant information is lacking. Individuals persuaded by this route tend to be influenced by what psychologists call "peripheral cues"—factors inherent in the persuasion setting that are sufficient to produce attitude change without any active thinking about the idea under consideration.[20] They detect cues like their own emotional state or other cues in the environment such as the opposing negotiator's title or level of attractiveness, and use these cues like heuristics, or mental short cuts, to make decisions without thinking carefully about the relevant information presented to them. For example, negotiators persuaded by this route may agree with someone they believe is an "expert" even if the expert merely supports a given idea or proposal without justifying his position on it.[21] In essence, this expertise heuristic, similar to the authority principle described in Guthrie's article on influence, [Guthrie, *Compliance*] operates as follows: people with excellent credentials typically offer cogent arguments, and because most experts know what they are talking about and have done the thinking for me, I can make decisions simply by relying on theirs.[22] Once they have this kind of mental shortcut in their repertoire, they learn to rely on such shortcuts to make decisions. Some people (e.g., those who lack the capacity to process centrally, and those who are naturally unmotivated to think) might commonly rely such cues. Others may rely on them only when their ability or motivation to process is situationally constrained (e.g., they are tired, hungry, distracted or they believe that someone else on their negotiation team is doing the difficult thinking).

Consequences for Persuasion

When a negotiator is persuaded by the peripheral route, the resulting attitudes tend to be "weaker" as compared to attitudes formed or changed via the deeper thinking and elaboration associated with the central route. That is, they will generally be less persistent (last a shorter period of time), less resistant in the face of counterarguments or new information, and less predictive of behavior.[23] Buyer's remorse is likely to be the product of peripheral strategies. That is, if the buyer was presented with strong arguments regarding the value of the item and purchased it as a result of carefully considering, and being persuaded by, those arguments, then he presumably would be less likely to regret the purchase compared to a situation in which he was influenced by peripheral cues, such as the seller's fast-talking sales pitch or attractiveness. Persuading a negotiator primarily via peripheral cues, therefore, is associated with some risk (though some negotiations may require you to take that risk—sometimes the other party's ability or motivation to think carefully is so constrained that the peripheral route will be the only way you can achieve persuasion). Negotiated agreements are more likely to fall apart if the parties do not truly believe that it is in their self-interest. For an agreement to stand the test of time, you should persuade opposing counsel (and the party they represent) that the settlement is in some sense optimal in terms of satisfying their interests. Simple behavioral compliance with the terms of the settlement, without the private commitment that is the goal of persuasion, all too often means that the settlement will eventually break down and that further conflict will ensue.[24] But in some cases shorter-term acceptance of your proposals may be all that you need—perhaps the goal of the negotiation is to get someone to publicly confess to a crime, or to sign a deed immediately. Research has shown that when a person makes a fairly public (as opposed to private) or written (as opposed to verbal) declaration they are less likely to later renege it, so the route to persuasion may matter less in such instances.[25]

How You Encourage it in Negotiations

The best way to induce persuasion by peripheral cues is to prepare to make such cues subtly available to your opposing party during negotiations. Use of the expertise heuristic, for example, can be prompted in several ways. You can arrange for a powerful member of your firm or organization to conduct the negotiation, emphasize your advanced knowledge-base or accomplishments in an area relevant to the issues, or begin negotiations by summarizing your background in a way that emphasizes your status.[26] In particular, non-lawyers might be swayed by your status as a lawyer when you make a legal argument during the course of a negotiation. Yet another proxy people use for expertise is rapid speech—the confidence that is suggested by rapid message delivery has been shown to have significant persuasive effects.[27]

The mere form of the message can also serve as a heuristic—the sheer number of arguments purported to be contained in a message has been shown to lead to greater persuasion.[28] Thus, starting a presentation during negotiations by stating that there are "ten reasons favoring proposal x" as opposed to "five reasons favoring proposal x" can get the lesser motivated listeners on board, even if you ultimately never describe all of your reasons.[29]

Other cues can also serve as heuristics. Creating positive emotions in the opposing party can be effective in this regard. Positive emotions evoked by an attractive source, good food, or some other cause can contribute to persuasion when people are not processing in depth.[30] In one early study, for example, people snacking on peanuts and soft drinks expressed more agreement with controversial issues than those who were not given such refreshments.[31] Research has also suggested that physically attractive people are generally more persuasive than unattractive ones.[32] Law firms might follow the lead of marketing and sales professionals and use attractive negotiators to make key presentations.

In sum, understanding the role played by cognitive heuristics in persuasion should enable you to include such cues in your messages or in the environments in which your negotiations take place. You can, for example, behave or portray yourself so as to maximize others' perceptions that you are expert (and attractive). They might also create a pleasing, comfortable environment in which to negotiate, perhaps in a boardroom with your firm's credentials and awards on display, and provide refreshments that opposing counsel will find appealing.[33] In addition, you can also build into your persuasion attempt other heuristic cues (such as noting that many more arguments exist in support of your viewpoint than in opposition).

Conclusion: Covering Your Bases

Persuasion skills apply to negotiations in many ways. Litigators routinely try to convince opposing counsel to settle by suggesting that a jury would decide against them if the case proceeds to trial; corporate attorneys and deal-making investment bankers typically try to persuade the other party that the deal they are offering is the best one to meet their needs. Insofar as we would not like others to use social influence principles in improper ways against us, we should be careful to use our knowledge of the principles presented here ethically as well. Surely, the use of advanced persuasion strategies is less objectionable when we are advocating a truly win/win solution to a negotiation problem. Nevertheless, lawyers must balance their mandate to advocate zealously on behalf of the interests of their clients and the ethical rules—both professional and personal—that guide their behavior. Since negotiation and persuasion are almost inseparable ventures, it is important for negotiators to understand the mechanisms of persuasion, both for proactive and defensive reasons. On the proactive front, lawyers and other agents can enhance their persuasiveness when advocating ideas to others on behalf of their clients. On the defensive front, professional negotiators of all kinds can use their knowledge of persuasion to guard against situations in which others may subtly attempt to alter their attitudes or behaviors, and to explain to clients how others might attempt to persuade them against their own best interests. Overall, the ability to recognize and respond intelligently to persuasive attempts can make the difference between being at their mercy and resisting their appeal.

Although, unfortunately, very little psychological research has examined persuasion specifically in the negotiation context, psychology has produced a wealth of research on persuasion more broadly that can serve as a helpful guide. Research supporting the Elaboration Likelihood Model, with its emphasis on two routes to persuasion, suggests that negotiators should consider their audience carefully and prepare persuasion strategies with that audience in mind. When possible, lawyers might also gain some control in this area by selecting their negotiation partner. For example, a lawyer might request a meeting with a particular attorney from the opposing team, whose personality and negotiation style he understands well. If central processing is desired, negotiators can implement any of a number of treatments that can enhance motivation, or capacity, for extensive information processing (e.g., reducing distractions, asking questions to elicit thinking) to make it more likely that strong arguments will be understood and accepted. When peripheral processing is more desirable, negotiators should think carefully how to subtly make such cues available during negotiations. To the extent that the audience's ability or motivation to think is unpredictable or uncertain (which is undoubtedly often the case), negotiators should consider using both central and peripheral strategies to cover both bases, and also apply strategies that promote the careful thinking associated with the central route whenever they offer objectively strong arguments in support of their proposals.[34]

With each new piece of empirical research, the science of persuasion continues to expand. Not all questions that we might have about persuasion have been answered empirically, especially given that the vast majority of persuasion studies have not investigated face-to-face interactions between people who are trying to persuade one another (which is an inherent aspect of most actual negotiations). Many interesting questions await further exploration. For example, we do not have a clear idea how each type of peripheral cue affects persuasion when used simultaneously with many other peripheral cues. We also do not know whether negotiating teams will be more effective persuaders when all team-mates use both central and peripheral strategies or when different strategies are allocated to different negotiators within a team. [Wade, *Tribe*] Research is also silent on many issues concerning agency—for example, if a lawyer negotiating on behalf of a client is persuaded by opposing counsel primarily by way of peripheral cues, does that make the lawyer more likely to use peripheral cues as a persuasive tool when subsequently counseling the client on the advantages of the offer? Until scientific research catches up on these and other important questions, persuasion in the context of negotiation will remain very much an art as well as a science.

Endnotes

The author would like to thank Nathan Sabri and Rebecca Hardberger for their research assistance on this project.

[1] Another recognized dual-process theory is the "heuristic-systematic" model, which also attempts to explain persuasion by contrasting deep processing with more superficial processing. For a thorough application of this model to persuasion in negotiations and conflict situations, *see* Shelly L. Chaiken, et al., *Persuasion in Negotiation and Conflict Situations, in* THE HANDBOOK OF CONFLICT RESOLUTION: THEORY AND PRACTICE 144 (Morton Deutsch & Peter T. Coleman eds., 2000).
[2] RICHARD E. PETTY & JON A. KROSNICK, ATTITUDE STRENGTH: ANTECEDENTS AND CONSEQUENCES (Ohio State University Series on Attitudes and Persuasion, Vol. 4 1995); RICHARD E. PETTY & JOHN T. CACIOPPO, COMMUNICATION AND PERSUASION: CENTRAL AND PERIPHERAL ROUTES TO ATTITUDE CHANGE (1986); Richard E. Petty & John T. Cacioppo, *The Elaboration-Likelihood Model of Persuasion, in* ADVANCES IN EXPERIMENTAL SOCIAL PSYCHOLOGY 123 (Leonard Berkowitz ed., 1986); Richard E. Petty & John T. Cacioppo, *Effects of Forewarning of Persuasive Intent and Involvement on Cognitive Responses and Persuasion*, 5 PERSONALITY & SOCIAL PSYCHOLOGY BULLETIN 173 (1979).

[3] An important caveat about the interpretation of research is in order. When research findings (from psychology, other social sciences, or even medicine for that matter) suggest that there are differences between groups of people who differ according to personality, for example, or exposure to a certain stimulus, these results are based on aggregate data. What is true in the aggregate, in a large sample of people, should not be interpreted as being true of every individual in that sample. Thus, research results reported here can be helpful in *estimating* how a certain type of person might think or behave relative to others, or in light of a given stimulus, but they *cannot* be used to predict with certainty the thoughts or behavior of any *particular* individual.

[4] Richard E. Petty & John T. Cacioppo, *Involvement and Persuasion: Tradition Versus Integration*, 107 PSYCHOLOGY BULLETIN 367 (1990); Richard E. Petty & John T. Cacioppo, *Issue Involvement Can Increase or Decrease Persuasion by Enhancing Message-Relevant Cognitive Responses*, 37 JOURNAL OF PERSONALITY & SOCIAL PSYCHOLOGY 1915 (1979) [hereinafter *Issue Involvement*]; Richard E. Petty & John T. Cacioppo, *Personal Involvement as a Determinant of Argument-based Persuasion*, 41 JOURNAL OF PERSONALITY & SOCIAL PSYCHOLOGY 847 (1981) [hereinafter *Personal Involvement*].

[5] Psychologists refer to these individuals as having a high "need for cognition," or a high intrinsic motivation for, and enjoyment of, effortful thinking. In research, motivation to think is typically measured by the "need for cognition" scale. John T. Cacioppo & Richard E. Petty, *The Need for Cognition*, 42 JOURNAL OF PERSONALITY & SOCIAL PSYCHOLOGY 116 (1982); *see also*, John T. Cacioppo, et al., *Dispositional Differences in Cognitive Motivation: The Life and Times of Individuals Varying in Need for Cognition*, 119 PSYCHOLOGY BULLETIN 197 (1996). High scores on the scale (reflecting a high motivation to think) have been shown to correspond to a tendency to focus on central cues, whereas relatively low scores (reflecting low motivation to think) are generally associated with a tendency to focus on peripheral cues.

[6] *E.g.*, Curtis P. Haugtvedt & Richard E. Petty, *Personality and Persuasion: Need for Cognition Moderates the Persistence and Resistance of Attitude Changes*, 63 JOURNAL OF PERSONALITY & SOCIAL PSYCHOLOGY 308 (1992) (demonstrating that those who are highly motivated to think have more enduring attitudes).

[7] For general discussion *see* Richard E. Petty, et al., *Elaboration as a Determinant of Attitude Strength: Creating Attitudes That are Persistent, Resistant, and Predictive of Behavior, in* ATTITUDE STRENGTH: ANTECEDENTS AND CONSEQUENCES 93 (Richard E. Petty & Jon A. Krosnick eds., 1995).

[8] *Issue Involvement, supra* note 4; *Personal Involvement, supra* note 4. *See also* Richard E. Petty, et al., *Central and Peripheral Routes to Advertising Effectiveness: The Moderating Role of Involvement.* 10 JOURNAL OF CONSUMER RESEARCH 134 (1983) (noting that under conditions of high involvement, higher quality arguments were most effective). This appears to be especially true when communication takes place in written form or when the person is a more passive recipient of your arguments (e.g., merely listening to them without expecting to engage in a discussion about them). In a recent study, people who were high and low in motivation to think interacted one-on-one with a confederate (i.e., a trained actor) who was trained to make either strong or weak arguments opposing the participant's viewpoint on a legal case. Donna Shestowsky & Leonard M. Horowitz, *How the Need for Cognition Scale Predicts Behavior in Mock Jury Deliberations*, 28 LAW & HUMAN BEHAVIOR 305 (2004). In this particular situation, it was those who were not naturally predisposed to think who were more likely to identify the strong arguments as stronger (and the weaker ones as weaker). This phenomenon appears to be related to the fact that those who were more motivated to think felt they made better arguments than the confederate—even when the confederate made strong arguments—thereby making a change in opinion on the case seem less warranted. This finding suggests that, unlike the decades of persuasion research that precede it, when individuals are paired for a negotiation-like task high-NCs may require greater convincing that your arguments are stronger than theirs before they will acknowledge your arguments for their merits.

[9] Robert S. Baron, et al., *Negative Emotion and Message Processing*, 30 JOURNAL OF EXPERIMENTAL SOCIAL PSYCHOLOGY 181 (1994).

[10] Donna Shestowsky, et al., *Need for Cognition and Interpersonal Influence: Individual Differences in Impact on Dyadic Decisions*, 74 JOURNAL OF PERSONALITY & SOCIAL PSYCHOLOGY 1317 (1998).

[11] *See* Shestowsky & Horowitz, *supra* note 8.

[12] Chaiken, *supra* note 1.

[13] *Id.*

[14] *Id. See also*, Richard E. Petty, et al., *To Think or Not to Think: Exploring Two Routes to Persuasion, in* PSYCHOLOGY OF PERSUASION 81-116 (T. C. Brock & S. Shavitt eds., 1994) (reviewing research on methods for encouraging thinking and argument evaluation).

[15] ELIOT R. SMITH & DIANE M. MACKIE, SOCIAL PSYCHOLOGY 287 (2d ed. 2000).

[16] Kimberly Matheson & Mark P. Zanna, *Persuasion as a Function of Self-Awareness in Computer-Mediated Communication*, 4 SOCIAL BEHAVIOR 99 (1989). E-mail adds another dimension, addressed in Anita Bhappu & Zoe Barsness, *Risks of E-Mail*, Chapter 45 in this volume.

[17] IAN E. MORLEY & GEOFFREY M. STEPHENSON, THE SOCIAL PSYCHOLOGY OF BARGAINING (1977).

[18] *See, e.g.,* Bibb Latané, et al. *Many Hands Make Light the Work: The Causes and Consequences of Social Loafing,* 37 JOURNAL OF PERSONALITY & SOCIAL PSYCHOLOGY 822 (1979); Steve J. Karau & Kipling D. Williams, *Social Loafing A Meta-Analytic Review and Theoretical Integration,* 65 JOURNAL OF PERSONALITY & SOCIAL PSYCHOLOGY 681 (1993).

[19] *See* Richard E. Petty, et al., *The Effects of Group Diffusion of Cognitive Effort on Attitudes: An Information Processing View,* 38 JOURNAL OF PERSONALITY & SOCIAL PSYCHOLOGY 81 (1980).

[20] RICHARD E. PETTY & JOHN T. CACIOPPO, ATTITUDES AND PERSUASION: CLASSIC AND CONTEMPORARY APPROACHES 256 (1981).

[21] Richard E. Petty & John T. Cacioppo, *Personal Involvement as a Determinant of Argument-based Persuasion,* 41 JOURNAL OF PERSONALITY & SOCIAL PSYCHOLOGY 847 (1981). *Cf.* Torsten Reimer, et al., *The Use of Heuristics in Persuasion: Deriving Cues on Source Expertise from Argument Quality,* 10 CURRENT RESEARCH OF SOCIAL PSYCHOLOGY 69 (2004) (discussing and offering alternative explanation for Richard E. Petty, et al., *Personal Involvement as a Determinant of Argument-Based Persuasion,* 41 JOURNAL OF PERSONALITY & SOCIAL PSYCHOLOGY 847 (1981).

[22] ELIOT R. SMITH & DIANE M. MACKIE, SOCIAL PSYCHOLOGY 276 (2d ed. 2000).

[23] Persistence, resistance, and attitude-behavior consistency are related (although conceptually distinct) phenomena. An attitude that has changed, for example, has neither resisted persuasion nor persisted successfully over time, and an initial attitude vulnerable to later change will not be likely to predict future related behavior.

[24] *Supra* note 2.

[25] Obtaining an agreement that is public (as opposed to private) and written (as opposed to verbal) can promote compliance. John R Hollenbeck, et al., *An Empirical Examination of the Antecedents of Commitment to. Difficult Goals,* 74 JOURNAL OF APPLIED PSYCHOLOGY 18 (1989) (finding that commitment to difficult goals was higher when goals were made public rather than private); Michael T. Giordano, *Boxing Basinger: Oral Contracts and the Manager's Privilege on the Ropes in Hollywood,* 9 UCLA ENTERTAINMENT LAW REVIEW 285, 299 (2002) (differentiating "promises" from "written contracts" and noting that parties are more likely to follow through with obligations if forced to execute written agreements).

[26] *See* Herbert C. Kelman & Carl I. Hovland, *"Reinstatement" of the Communicator in Delayed Measurement of Opinion Change,* 48 JOURNAL OF ABNORMAL & SOCIAL PSYCHOLOGY 327 (1953).

[27] For a review, *see* Stephen M. Smith & David R. Shaffer, *Speed of Speech and Persuasion: Evidence for Multiple Effects,* 21 PERSONALITY & SOCIAL PSYCHOLOGY BULLETIN 1051 (1995). *See also* W. Gill Woodall & Judee K. Burgoon, *Talking Fast and Changing Attitudes: A Critique and Clarification,* 8 JOURNAL OF NONVERBAL BEHAVIOR 126 (1983) (describing research on the general phenomenon that fast-talkers have a persuasive advantage but reporting results that suggest a more complex relationship between vocal rate, credibility and persuasion than was suggested by previous research).

[28] Shelly Chaiken, *The Heuristic Model of Persuasion, in* 5 SOCIAL INFLUENCE: THE ONTARIO SYMPOSIUM 3-39 (Mark P. Zanna & James M. Olson eds., 1987) (citing research by Chaiken, Axsom, Hicks, Yates, & Wilson).

[29] This finding should not be construed to suggest that negotiators should make as many arguments as possible to support their viewpoint. Research suggests several reasons why more is not necessarily better. For example, people may grow bored or annoyed by extended argumentation, especially if the arguments are repetitive. For a summary of research on this point, *see* RICHARD E. PETTY & JOHN T. CACIOPPO, ATTITUDES AND PERSUASION: CLASSIC AND CONTEMPORARY APPROACHES 70-72 (1981).

[30] These strategies often succeed because of the positive mood they evoke and do not require a cognitive or "thinking" reaction on the part of the individual being persuaded. Pablo Brinol, et al., *Individual Differences in Resistance to Persuasion: The Role of Beliefs and Meta-beliefs, in* RESISTANCE AND PERSUASION (Eric Knowles & Jay A. Linn, eds. 2004) (describing the different effects of mood on persuasion as a function of the level of processing engaged in by the target of the persuasive message).

[31] Irvine L. Janis, et al., *Facilitating Effects of "Eating-While-Reading" on Responsiveness to Persuasive Communications,* 1 JOURNAL OF PERSONALITY & SOCIAL PSYCHOLOGY 181 (1965).

[32] Shelly Chaiken, *Communicator Physical Attractiveness and Persuasion,* 37 JOURNAL OF PERSONALITY & SOCIAL PSYCHOLOGY 1387 (1979); Daniel Linz & Steven Penrod, *Increasing Attorney Persuasiveness in the Courtroom,* 8 LAW & PSYCHOLOGY REVIEW 1, 35-42 (1984) (noting that physically attractive people are typically rated as more persuasive and competent than unattractive individuals); *see also* Alan Feingold, *Good-Looking People Are Not What We Think,* 111 PSYCHOLOGY BULLETIN 304 (1992) (finding that attractive people are perceived as more intelligent and skilled, despite lack of actual significant correlation between these two variables).

[33] Chaiken, *supra* note 1; Richard E. Petty, et al., *Positive Mood and Persuasion: Different Roles for Affect Under High- and Low- Elaboration Conditions,* 64 JOURNAL OF PERSONALITY & SOCIAL PSYCHOLOGY 5 (1993) (noting that positive mood produces more positive attitudes towards advocacy).

[34] Specifically, in the absence of mistrust or other similar barriers, opposing counsel should be persuaded by compelling arguments that demonstrate the proposal is an objectively good one for them, hence framing proposals as win-win can be helpful.

ꝏ 42 ꝏ

Courting Compliance

Chris Guthrie

Editors' Note: *Why is it that attractive or well-liked people tend to do better in negotiation? Guthrie explains the psychology behind six different factors that tend to influence people: liking, authority, reciprocity, scarcity, commitment, and social proof. He offers practical tips, too, exploring how lawyers and other negotiators can use these phenomena to influence their counterparts in negotiation.*

Negotiation is often viewed as an alternative to adjudication. In fact, however, negotiation and adjudication may be more alike than different because each is a process of *persuasion*. Both in the courtroom and at the bargaining table, the lawyer's primary task is to persuade someone other than her own client that her client's positions, interests, and perspectives should be honored.

Despite this apparent similarity, persuasion operates differently in adjudication and negotiation because the lawyer seeks to influence a different party in each process. In adjudication, the lawyer seeks primarily to persuade the judge or jury hearing the case. The judge or jury is empowered to resolve the dispute unilaterally by applying rules of law to the relevant facts of the case. In negotiation, the lawyer seeks to persuade not a judge or jury but rather her counterpart at the bargaining table. One's counterpart in negotiation is free to ignore the law and facts of the case but can only resolve the dispute through bilateral agreement.

The import of these differences is that the lawyer must use different persuasive tactics in each process. In court, the lawyer can use various rhetorical and even dramatic devices to persuade the judge or jury to render a decision under the law that favors her client; in negotiation, the lawyer needs to use a more subtle set of devices to induce her counterpart to agree to enter into a favorable settlement.

Researchers have identified several persuasive devices or compliance tactics that a lawyer can use in negotiation. These compliance tactics operate like "heuristics"[1] or mental shortcuts that individuals employ automatically to make judgments and decisions. When deciding whether to comply with a request, individuals generally look for simple cues—like whether the requester is an authority figure—to help them decide whether to comply. Often, it is sensible for people to behave this way; other times, however, it can induce a "distinct kind of automatic, mindless compliance from people."[2]

Psychologist Robert Cialdini has organized these compliance tactics into six "principles" or "weapons of influence": liking, social proof, commitment and consistency, reciprocity, authority, and scarcity.[3] Each principle can be used to persuade, or as Cialdini puts it, each "can be used like a weapon (of influence) to stimulate people to agree to requests."[4] A lawyer who recognizes that her counterpart is likely to be influenced by these principles may be able to employ them to her client's advantage at the bargaining table. Even those lawyers who would prefer not to employ these techniques will benefit from understanding what they are and how they might be used by their counterparts in negotiation.

Compliance Tactics

The first of these compliance tactics is *liking*. People prefer to comply with requests made by those they know and like.[5] People tend to like those who are physically attractive; those with whom they share something in common; those with whom they are familiar; and those who pay them compliments.[6]

Every lawyer shares something in common with her counterpart—at a bare minimum, both are members of the same profession. Thus, every lawyer can attempt to capitalize on this (and other) similarities at the beginning of the negotiation to try to develop rapport with her counterpart. Empirical evidence suggests that rapport-building can lead to better and faster agreements. In one recent study, Janice Nadler found that law students previously unknown to one another who spent a few minutes chatting on the telephone prior to engaging in an email negotiation obtained better outcomes than did those who did not have a pre-negotiation conversation.[7] Similarly, Jason Johnston and Joel Waldfogel found that lawyers who litigated against each other frequently were more likely than others to settle their cases and to do so more quickly.[8]

The second compliance tactic—*social proof*—rests not on affection but rather on observation. Individuals "view a behavior as correct in a given situation to the degree that we see others performing it."[9] For example, individuals are more likely to laugh when watching situation comedies if the "sitcoms" are accompanied by "laugh tracks."[10] Individuals "use others' laughter"—even canned laughter—"to help decide what is humorous."[11]

Social proof is most likely to prove persuasive under two conditions. First, social proof is more influential under conditions of uncertainty. "In general, when we are unsure of ourselves, when the situation is unclear or ambiguous, when uncertainty reigns, we are most likely to look to and accept the actions of others as correct."[12] Second, social proof is more influential when the observer perceives similarities between herself and the party she is observing. "The principle of social proof operates most powerfully when we are observing the behavior of people just like us. It is the conduct of such people that gives us the greatest insight into what constitutes correct behavior for ourselves."[13]

Thus, social proof might work hand-in-hand with liking to enable one lawyer to persuade the other to behave in the desired manner. For instance, a lawyer who has garnered her counterpart's affection at the outset of the negotiation might exhibit certain behaviors at the bargaining table (e.g., she can attempt to frame the negotiation as a search for jointly desirable outcomes) and thereby "model" that behavior for her counterpart. This, in turn, could induce her counterpart to conduct herself in a similar manner. Likewise, a lawyer might use evidence from similar cases (perhaps drawn from publications containing verdict and settlement data) showing how often—and perhaps even for what amounts—litigants in similar cases have settled. By demonstrating that similarly situated others have settled, the lawyer may be able to persuade her counterpart that settlement is appropriate for her as well.

Drawing largely from research on "cognitive dissonance,"[14] *commitment and consistency* is a third compliance tactic. The basic idea is that "[o]nce we make a choice or take a stand, we will encounter personal and interpersonal pressures to behave consistently with that commitment."[15]

To illustrate, consider the "drive carefully" study.[16] Researchers randomly assigned homeowners in a residential neighborhood to either a control group or an experimental group. A researcher, posing as a "volunteer," asked the homeowners in both groups if they would allow the volunteer to post a gigantic "Drive Carefully" billboard in their front yards. Each homeowner viewed a photo of the billboard demonstrating that it was so large it would almost completely obscure the view of the house from the street. The only difference between the two groups was that two weeks earlier another "volunteer" had asked the homeowners in the experimental group to display a three inch by three inch sign that read "Be a Safe Driver." The subjects in the experimental group, who complied with this seemingly innocuous request, were much more likely to agree to the gigantic billboards in their front yards: 76% of those in the experimental group versus a mere 17% in the control group agreed to do so. "Because they had innocently complied with a trivial safe-driving request a couple of weeks before, those homeowners became remarkably willing to comply with another such request that was massive in size."[17]

Likewise, a lawyer may prosper by encouraging her counterpart to make small commitments early in the negotiation process. Perhaps, for example, she can persuade her counterpart to agree to a minor substantive term such as a confidentiality clause or a no-publicity clause. By inducing one's counterpart to make a small commitment like this, the lawyer may be able to obtain much more substantial agreements later in the process. Her counterpart may simply feel duty bound to comply due to her compliance earlier in the process. This is likely to work particularly well if her counterpart previously agreed to embrace a principle (e.g., equitable division, what a court would do, etc.) and is subsequently asked to agree with the execution of that principle.

Individuals feel obligated not only to behave consistently with prior behavior but also to reciprocate the behavior of others. According to the so-called *reciprocity rule*, we feel we "should try to repay, in kind, what another person has provided us."[18] Because reciprocity appears to be a universal norm, examples of it abound. Consider the following amusing example reported by Cialdini:

> Several years ago, a university professor tried a little experiment. He sent Christmas cards to a sample of perfect strangers. Although he expected some reaction, the response he received was amazing—holiday cards addressed to him came pouring back from people who had never met nor heard of him. The great majority of those who returned cards never inquired into the identity of the unknown professor. They received his holiday greeting card, *click*, and *whirr*, they automatically sent cards in return.[19]

A lawyer can use the reciprocity rule in two ways to persuade her counterpart to make a meaningful concession at the bargaining table. Most obviously, she can make a concession herself, and this can create in her counterpart a sense of obligation to respond similarly.[20] If she started from a more favorable position than her counterpart, the reciprocal concession she induces her counterpart to make is likely to work to her client's advantage in a distributive negotiation.

Less obviously, a lawyer can request a substantial concession, get turned down, and then make a more modest request. In many instances, the lawyer's counterpart will feel obligated to respond to this ostensible "concession." Cialdini calls this the "rejection-then-retreat" strategy and explains it as follows:

> Suppose you want me to agree to a certain request. One way to increase the chances that I will comply is first to make a larger request of me, one that I will most likely turn down. Then, after I have refused, you make the smaller request that you were really interested in all along. Provided that you structured your requests skillfully, I should view your second request as a concession to me and should feel inclined to respond with a concession of my own—compliance with your second request.[21]

The fifth compliance tactic that a lawyer might use to her client's advantage in negotiation is *authority*. Individuals often feel an obligation to comply with those who are in real or perceived authority positions. The most powerful, and troubling, illustration of the power of authority comes from Stanley Milgram's obedience experiments,[22] in which experimental participants inflicted what they thought were dangerous electric shocks on co-participants simply because an authority figure (i.e., the experimenter) instructed them to do so.

The authority principle dictates that individuals often defer to people in positions of apparent authority—leaders, state officials, experimenters in lab coats, etc. Thus, a lawyer routinely tries to invoke the judge as an authority figure and make arguments about what the judge would do in the case to persuade her counterpart to settle. Relatedly, although the authority principle is generally understood to apply to human authorities, it could extend to non-human authority, like the law or legal precedent. Thus, even though lawyers in a settlement negotiation are generally free to disregard applicable legal rules, lawyers appreciate the unique persuasive impact of legal precedent as "authority" and routinely invoke it to persuade counterparts of the merits of some position. (Of course, the counterpart usually arrives armed with legal authority of her own).

Finally, a lawyer might use *scarcity*—the sixth compliance tactic—to her client's advantage in negotiation. Scarcity refers to the idea that "opportunities seem more valuable to us when they are less available."[23] Scarcity induces compliance in large part because it threatens our freedom of choice ("if I don't act now, I will lose the opportunity to do so").

The lawyer who appreciates the impact scarcity is likely to have on her counterpart may try to create the impression in negotiation that opportunities to settle are limited and time is running out. For example, she might extend an offer but give her counterpart a limited window within which to accept it. Likewise, she might make an offer immediately prior to an expected judicial ruling that might be harmful to her counterpart's case, or she might make an offer of judgment under Rule 68 of the Federal Rules of Civil Procedure. In each instance, her counterpart might feel more motivated to settle due to the scarcity principle (and indeed, the scarcity principle undoubtedly helps explain the apparent abundance of settlements on the courthouse steps).

Conclusion

Advertisers, marketers, and salespeople use these compliance tactics to induce consumers to purchase their products. Likewise, a lawyer can use these tactics to induce her counterpart in negotiation to settle on terms that are favorable to her client. Simply because a lawyer *can* use these tactics, however, does not necessarily mean she *should*.

A lawyer should try to obtain the best possible outcome for her client, but she should do so in ways that comport not only with the formal ethical rules but also with her own sense of professional responsibility and personal ethics. (Would I want my mother to know I used that tactic? Would I want my counterpart to use that tactic? How would I feel if the local newspaper ran a story about the negotiation?)

Most lawyers will feel comfortable employing these tactics; indeed, many lawyers already use them, even if they do not apply Cialdini's labels to them. Like other negotiation tactics, these compliance tactics often prove effective and do not automatically run afoul of any formal ethical rules. Other lawyers, however, might feel uncomfortable using at least some of these tactics. For example, a lawyer who attempts to garner his counterpart's affection solely to facilitate agreement, or who attempts to secure a small commitment from his counterpart solely as a way of obtaining a larger one later, might feel as though he is treating his counterpart "as a mere means to one's ends" and is thereby ignoring "general ethical requirements for treating people."[24] The lawyer, as a professional, must decide for him or herself whether, and if so, how, to employ these powerful persuasive devices at the bargaining table.

Endnotes

This chapter is adapted from Chris Guthrie, *Principles of Influence in Negotiation*, 87 MARQUETTE LAW REVIEW 829 (2004).

[1] *See* Amos Tversky & Daniel Kahneman, *Judgment Under Uncertainty: Heuristics and Biases*, 185 SCIENCE 1124 (1974).

[2] ROBERT B. CIALDINI, INFLUENCE: SCIENCE AND PRACTICE x (4th ed. 2001).

[3] *Id.* at ix-x.

[4] *Id.* at 17.

[5] *Id.* at 144.

[6] *Id.* at 148-54.

[7] Janice Nadler, *Legal Negotiation and Communication Technology: How Small Talk Can Facilitate E-Mail Dealmaking*, 9 HARVARD NEGOTIATION LAW REVIEW 225 (2004).

[8] Jason Scott Johnston & Joel Waldfogel, *Does Repeat Play Elicit Cooperation? Evidence from Federal Civil Litigation*, 31 JOURNAL OF LEGAL STUDIES 39 (2002).

[9] CIALDINI, *supra* note 2, at 100.

[10] *Id.* at 99-101 (citing to Raymond G. C. Fuller & Alan Sheehy-Skeffington, *Effects of Group Laughter on Responses to Humorous Materials: A Replication and Extension*, 35 PSYCHOLOGY REPORTS 531 (1974); and Mary M. Smyth & Raymond G. C. Fuller, *Effects of Group Laughter on Responses to Humorous Materials*, 30 PSYCHOLOGY REPORTS 132 (1972). For a different interpretation of the impact of laugh tracks, see Rob Walker, *Making Us Laugh*, N.Y. TIMES MAGAZINE 28 (Dec. 28, 2003) (profiling the inventor of the laugh track and citing psychologist Robert Provine for the proposition that laugh tracks influence us for neurological, not social psychological, reasons).

[11] CIALDINI, *supra* note 2, at 100.

[12] *Id.* at 111.

[13] *Id.* at 119.

[14] *See generally* LEON FESTINGER, A THEORY OF COGNITIVE DISSONANCE (1957).

[15] CIALDINI, *supra* note 2 at 53.

[16] *See* Jonathan L. Freedman & Scott C. Fraser, *Compliance Without Pressure: The Foot-in-the-Door Technique*, 4 JOURNAL OF PERSONALITY & SOCIAL PSYCHOLOGY 195, 199-201 (1966).

[17] CIALDINI, *supra* note 2, at 65.

[18] *Id.* at 20.

[19] *Id.* (citing to a study reported by Kunz & Woolcott).

[20] *See, e.g.*, Paul W. Paese, Ann Marie Schreiber & Adam W. Taylor, *Caught Telling the Truth: Effects of Honesty and Communication Media in Distributive Negotiations*, 12 GROUP DECISION &

NEGOTIATION 537 (2003) (showing that honest disclosures up front induce cooperative behavior from the other party). Note, however, that there is some evidence suggesting that the concessions one makes may be devalued by the recipient due to loss aversion, *see* Daniel Kahneman & Amos Tversky, *Conflict Resolution: A Cognitive Perspective, in* BARRIERS TO CONFLICT RESOLUTION 54 (Kenneth Arrow, et al. eds., 1995), or reactive devaluation. *See* Lee Ross & Constance Stillinger, *Barriers to Conflict Resolution*, 7 NEGOTIATION JOURNAL 389 (1991).

[21] CIALDINI, *supra* note 2, at 38.

[22] For the original study, *see* Stanley Milgram, *Behavioral Study of Obedience*, 67 J. ABNORMAL & SOC. PSYCHOL. 371 (1963). For an overview, *see* STANLEY MILGRAM, OBEDIENCE TO AUTHORITY (1974).

[23] CIALDINI, *supra* note 2, at 205.

[24] Jonathan R. Cohen, *When People Are The Means: Negotiating With Respect*, 14 GEORGETOWN. JOURNAL OF LEGAL ETHICS 739, 743 (2001). Some lawyers might even avoid using these principles—like the authority principle—on the grounds that they might systematically disadvantage members of less powerful groups in society, like members of ethnic minorities, women, and gays and lesbians.

❧ 43 ❧

The Theory of Mind

David F. Sally

Editors' Note: *False beliefs, bluffs and faux pas are the stuff of everyday life in negotiation. The ability to interpret your counterpart's moves as anything other than literal, however, is not innate: it must be learned. And, says Sally, we don't yet quite know how to teach it.*

Our social lives are distinguished by specific maneuvers—the white lie, the bluff, the fantasy, the hint, the apology, the outburst, the ironic remark, the faux pas. Most adults perform, interpret and anticipate these interpersonal maneuvers with such ease that we are rarely cognizant of the underlying, enabling mental capacity, a capacity that has been named *the theory of mind (TOM)*. Those of us with children know, however, that we must be wary of sarcasm for fear of misinterpretation, must be explicit because indirect commands are often ineffectual, must decipher playground episodes or cinematic dramas that seem senseless to young minds, and must muffle the honesty of a toddler when a friend and host who burned the meat and overcooked the vegetables asks, "How's your dinner?" Parental experience coincides with scientific research on TOM that has discovered that this capability normally is innate and develops throughout childhood, and that this developmental path sometimes goes awry and sometimes proceeds faster and farther.

Because social maneuvering is fundamental to most negotiations, researchers in this field should be interested in the advances developmental psychologists, animal behaviorists and cognitive neuroscientists have made in understanding TOM. I will summarize some of these findings here, and my intention, discernable if you apply your TOM, is to intrigue the reader enough that a cross-disciplinary conversation will begin and continue into the foreseeable future.

What Do We Know About TOM?

The theory of mind seems to be a wondrous ability. It seems to be extra-sensory perception (ESP) without the invisible brain waves, communing through the ether without the mysticism, divination without the crystal ball. That we can read the contents of someone's mind—her intentions, emotions, wants, beliefs—with an accuracy significantly greater than guessing is rather remarkable. However, TOM has both mundane cognitive roots and non-human manifestations. In fact, the phrase "theory of mind" was first used in an article describing chimpanzees' abilities to perceive the intentions behind various actions.[1]

One comprehensive model of the mundane roots of TOM is that advanced by Andrew Meltzoff and Alison Gopnik.[2] They suggest that the human brain is endowed with "a fundamental cross-modal representational system that connects self and other."[3] This innate cognitive ability is manifest in an amazing finding: neonates as young as 45 minutes old are able to differentially imitate facial expressions.[4] If you stick your tongue out at them, they will try to razz you back; if you make an "O" mouth at them, they will ogle their lips back at you. Imitation is the cornerstone that supports other developmental milestones: at 9 months, infants point, grunt, scream and generally try to guide the intentions of other people;[5] at 18 months, toddlers understand that other people may want things that they do not;[6] at 24 months, children are pretending, a cognitive activity that calls for multiple mental states;[7] at 30 months, they can take the other's visual perspective, recognizing that an object may be visible to them but hidden from another person in the room.[8]

Finally, by about the age of four, young children can lie![9] Or, at least, they can do the next best thing—pass false belief tests. These tests have become well known as critical assessments of TOM and so, it is worth describing them in more detail.[10] The Sally-Anne tasks and its variants use two dolls to portray a little drama for an audience of one very young participant.[11] The scene opens with Sally and Anne busily playing in a room. Sally has a ball that she places in a nearby basket and covers with a blanket. She skips out of the room. Anne, for whatever nefarious or benevolent reason, gets up and switches the ball from the basket to a box. She recovers the basket, folds closed the flaps of the box and returns to her activity. Sally skips back into the room and the scene freezes. The child is asked, "Where will Sally look for her ball?" Very young children will answer, "the box," but by the age of four, most children will correctly answer, "the basket."

Children three years old and younger have a difficult time distinguishing between what they know to be true and what someone else believes. This fact is supported by another false belief task, this one centered on a brightly colored tin covered with pictures of delicious candy-coated chocolates.[12] The participating child is asked, "What do you think is in here?" and she responds quite naturally with "CANDY!" Much to her disappointment, the child is shown that the tin actually contains pencils. To torment her further, the child is asked, "what did you think was in here?" and "what would another child think is in here?" Little toddlers, but not pre-schoolers, will fail this test as well by replying "pencils" to both questions.

Both of these tasks involve first-order beliefs, i.e., knowing what someone else knows. It is possible to test second-order beliefs as well. For instance, suppose Sally peeked unseen into the room while Anne moved the ball, now where does Anne think that Sally thinks the ball is? Not surprisingly, the four year old mind that can comfortably handle the two tasks above cannot decipher second-order belief situations.[13] In one test, after all age groups succeeded at a first order false belief test, only 71% of six year olds passed a second order false belief test, while 94% of eight year olds and 100% of ten year olds passed.[14] As the presented stories become more complicated (while still remaining true to life), only elementary school children and older can easily decipher tales involving double-bluffs or sarcasm, and only middle school children and older can reliably understand a faux pas.[15]

Autistic children lag behind their normally developing peers to a significant extent with respect to performance on false belief tests.[16] Many scientists now believe that the core deficit of autism is an impaired TOM: in one poignant neologism, the autistic person is "mindblind."[17]

A comparison of the brain scans of "mindseeing" individuals and autistic individuals who viewed a film clip that metaphorically represented social interaction, revealed increased activity in the medial prefrontal cortex and the superior temporal sulcus in the former group.[18] A variety of studies have confirmed that these two regions are critical to the neural network supporting TOM.[19] The medial prefrontal cortex includes areas activated in monitoring the self's inner states. Damage to this area in normal individuals causes both poor performance in false belief tests and behavioral problems akin to those in autism.[20] The second region, the superior temporal sulcus, is associated with the perception and interpretation of movements by living creatures, especially their eyes, hands and mouths.[21] Hence, the neuroscientific evidence is broadly consistent with the TOM developmental story above—that there is an equivalence between the self's inner states and those of the other, and that perceiving and reacting to the face, the eyes and the mouth in particular, are foremost.

What Does TOM Have to Do With Negotiations?

At this point, we might seem very far afield and a reader might legitimately ask me, "What are you thinking?" The connection between TOM and negotiation is, at once, obvious and unspecified. As we have seen, an advanced TOM is necessary to accurately decipher social situations involving false beliefs, bluffs, faux pas, and misrepresentation. What social situation is more rife with these elements than negotiations? TOM must be essential to negotiations, as it is to all normal social interactions. The mindblindness and behavioral problems of autistic individuals reveal what "mindseeing" does for the rest of us:

Autism proves that a theory of mind and the sympathetic process are, simultaneously and inextricably, essential to language, play, interaction, cohesion, imagination and strategy. The choice of an optimal strategy is linked to the sharing of a smile or a touch, and to speaking through hints, metaphors and jokes.[22]

There is an essential thread, then, that connects all social maneuvers, including those in negotiations, and ties them to TOM and its associated neural system.

This deep and broad connection establishes a research agenda that, at the present time, is dormant and unspecified. One can imagine many possible activations:

Do imaging studies confirm that the TOM neural system is active during negotiations? If so, do the patterns of activity vary with the stage of negotiations or with the level of conflict?

Is there a link between TOM capabilities and specific negotiation tactics? For example, one might test whether people who do poorly on a faux pas recognition test are more likely to (1) make a highball or lowball offer to a counterpart with a very strong BATNA;[23] (2) fail to confront and counter an opponent's extreme offer. Are those who are more accurate mindreaders better able to frame their proposals?

Are there tests in other behavioral domains that are predictive of negotiation success? If figurative language relies on TOM, then accuracy in interpreting metaphors might be correlated with negotiation skill. Are fiction readers better negotiators than newspaper readers? How about those who give individualized gifts during the holidays versus those who give cash or gift certificates?

Is there a link between TOM and broad negotiation capabilities? One might imagine that mentalising is more useful in value creation, but a certain social remove is effective in value claiming. However, one could see the relationship going in the other direction, as the next question proposes.

Is TOM responsible for negotiators' emotional entanglements and indirectness about interests and values?

"Normals" have a hair-trigger on their TOMs: they can find intention, emotion, and belief in the casual, chaotic heap of animal entrails, the stochastic, stress-induced sliding of the plates in the Earth's crust, a blinking shadow cast diagonally through the trees by a passing cloud on a moonlit night, or an ant dragging an oversized crumb up and over, up and over, up and over a series of little twigs and stones.[24]

Attributing intentions to every move in a negotiation may be exhausting, frustrating and detrimental. Sometimes, a mistake is just a mistake, a bluff should just be ignored and forgotten, and apologies are just a waste of time.

Just as the very young or autistic viewers imputed to Sally their own knowledge of where her ball was located, a negotiator may know her interests so vividly that she automatically assumes the other side knows. Think about the times you have had a catchy, yet sadly untitled, tune playing in your head. You turn to a significant other and say, "What's the name of that song? You know, the one that goes...," and then you hum or tap a few bars. The other looks at you in puzzlement and you stare in disbelief that he or she cannot recognize it.[25] Autistics certainly are much more literal in their use of language; might this literalness extend into the continuum of TOM capabilities? If so, these people might be much more forthright and direct about their interests in a negotiation, while the rest of us assume that the other side knows what we want.

Is TOM the omitted variable that explains differences in negotiation process and outcomes among different occupations and by gender? Recently, a group of researchers created a self-administered survey that measured the degree to which a normal adult had traits associated with autism, i.e., the person's Autistic-Spectrum Quotient (AQ).[26] When they gave the survey to students at Cambridge University, they found a significant difference between the AQs of those in the sciences, in particular, mathematics, and the AQs of students in the social sciences and humanities. Among all students, men scored slightly, but significantly, higher than women.

These findings might extend into negotiations. Do engineers, mathematicians and scientists negotiate differently than philosophers, poets and marketers? Are gender differences in areas such as initiating negotiations and asking for better offers really being driven by different mentalising capabilities?[27]

Does age improve both TOM and negotiating outcomes? It is clear from our review above that TOM improves throughout childhood. The two published studies that have examined the performance of senior citizens on mentalising tasks contradict each other—one found that 70 year olds were better than 21 year olds, while students outperformed the elderly in the other study.[28] Of course, laboratory-based negotiation research has done a poor job in general of examining bargaining behavior in the years between graduation and the nursing home. Accordingly, analysis of the latter three-quarters of the life span would benefit both fields.

What are the situational influences on TOM? Are normal people occasionally mindblind? It seems possible, for example, that very strong emotions or great social distance might suffice to make the other's mind imperceptible. Our enemies tend to not only be "bad," "strange," and "unlikable," but they seem utterly unfathomable to us as well. One could also imagine that hierarchy might prevent mindseeing both upwards and downwards. If this temporary clouding does occur, the bargaining table is as likely a setting as any other.

It is likely that within the next decade or two cosmetic neurosurgery and advanced neuropharmacology may be able to enhance TOM or correct mentalising deficits. What impact will these interventions have on negotiators and negotiations?

Endnotes

[1] David Premack & Guy Woodruff, *Does the Chimpanzee Have a Theory of Mind?*, 1 BEHAVIORAL AND BRAIN SCIENCES 515 (1978).

[2] ALISON M. GOPNIK & ANDREW N. MELTZOFF, WORDS, THOUGHTS, AND THEORIES (1997).

[3] *Id.* at 129. *See also*, HENRY M. WELLMAN., THE CHILD'S THEORY OF MIND (1990).

[4] Andrew N. Meltzoff & M. Keith Moore, *Imitation of Facial and Manual Gestures by Human Neonates*, 198 SCIENCE 75 (1977); Andrew N. Meltzoff & M. Keith Moore, *Newborn Infants Imitate Adult Facial Gestures*, 54 CHILD DEVELOPMENT 702 (1983); Andrew N. Meltzoff & M. Keith Moore, *Imitation in Newborn Infants: Exploring the Range of Gestures Imitated and the Underlying Mechanisms*, 25 DEVELOPMENTAL PSYCHOLOGY 954 (1989).

[5] ELIZABETH BATES, ET AL., THE EMERGENCE OF SYMBOLS: COGNITION AND COMMUNICATION IN INFANCY (1979).

[6] In one study, babies watched a grown-up point to one of two plates that were piled with crackers or broccoli, and then "mmmm" or "eeewwww." The grown-up would then hold out her hand. Toddlers "gave her broccoli when she had previously expressed a desire for the broccoli and crackers when she expressed a desire for crackers, despite their own unalterable conviction that broccoli is yucky" GOPNIK & MELTZOFF, *supra* note 2, at 150. *See also*, Betty M. Repacholi & Alison Gopnik, *Early Reasoning about Desires: Evidence from 14- and 18-Month Olds*, 33 DEVELOPMENTAL PSYCHOLOGY 12 (1977).

[7] Alan M. Leslie, *Pretense and Representation: The Origins of "Theory of Mind,"* 94 PSYCHOLOGICAL REVIEW 4124 (1987); Peter Carruthers, *Autism as Mind-Blindness: An Elaboration and Partial Defense*, in THEORIES OF THEORIES OF MIND (Peter Carruthers & Peter K. Smith eds., 1996) ("You cannot enjoy supposing or imagining without being conscious of your [mental] activity. In general, enjoying Xing presupposes awareness of Xing—which is why you cannot enjoy digestion, sleepwalking, or subliminal perception." *Id.* at 265) (emphasis in original).

[8] John H. Flavell, et al., *Young Children's Knowledge About Visual Perception: Further Evidence for the Level 1-Level 2 Distinction*, 17 DEVELOPMENTAL PSYCHOLOGY 99 (1981).

[9] Beate Sodian, et al., *Early Deception and the Child's Theory of Mind: False Trails and Genuine Markers*, 62 CHILD DEVELOPMENT 468 (1992).

[10] The test was first invented in Heinz Wimmer & Josef Perner, *Beliefs About Beliefs: Representation and Constraining Function of Wrong Beliefs in Young Children's Understanding of Deception*, 13 COGNITION 103 (1983). A meta-analysis of published false belief tests is contained in Nurit Yirmiya, et al., *Meta-Analyses Comparing Theory of Mind Abilities of Individuals with Autism, Individuals with Mental Retardation, and Normally Developing Individuals*, 124 PSYCHOLOGICAL BULLETIN 283 (1998).

[11] This version is in SIMON BARON-COHEN, MINDBLINDNESS: AN ESSAY ON AUTISM AND THEORY OF MIND (1995).

[12] Josef Perner, et al., *Exploration of the Autistic Child's Theory of Mind: Knowledge, Belief, and Communication*, 60 CHILD DEVELOPMENT 689 (1989).

[13] Kate Sullivan, et al., *Preschoolers Can Attribute Second-Order Beliefs*, 30 DEVELOPMENTAL PSYCHOLOGY 395 (1994).

[14] David F. Sally & Elizabeth L. Hill, *The Development of Interpersonal Strategy: Autism, Theory-of-Mind, Cooperation and Fairness*, 27 JOURNAL OF ECONOMIC PSYCHOLOGY 73 (2006).

[15] For double bluffs, *see* Francesca Happé, *An Advanced Test of Theory of Mind: Understanding of Story Characters' Thoughts and Feelings by Able Autistic, Mentally Handicapped, and Normal Chil-*

dren and Adults, 24 JOURNAL OF AUTISM AND DEVELOPMENTAL DISORDERS 129 (1994). For faux pas, *see* Simon Baron-Cohen, et al., *Recognition of Faux Pas by Normally Developing Children and Children with Asperger Syndrome or High-Functioning Autism*, 29 JOURNAL OF AUTISM AND DEVELOPMENTAL DISORDERS 407 (1999).

[16] *See supra* notes 10 through 15.

[17] BARON-COHEN, *supra* note 11.

[18] Fulvia Castelli, et al., *Autism, Asperger Syndrome and Brain Mechanisms for the Attribution of Mental States to Animated Shapes*, 125 BRAIN 1839 (2002).

[19] Uta Frith & Christopher Frith, *Development and Neurophysiology of Mentalising*, 358 PHILOSOPHICAL TRANSACTIONS OF THE ROYAL SOCIETY B: BIOLOGICAL SCIENCES 459 (2003).

[20] Carol Gregory, et al., *Theory of Mind in Patients with Frontal Variant Frontotemporal Dementia and Alzheimer's Disease: Theoretical and Practical Implications*, 125 BRAIN 752 (2002).

[21] Mark A. Sabbagh & Marjorie Taylor, *Neural Correlates of Theory-of-Mind Reasoning: An Event-Related Potential Study*, 11 PSYCHOLOGICAL SCIENCE 46 (2000); Aina Puce & David Perrett, *Electrophysiology and Brain Imaging of Biological Motion*, 358 PHILOSOPHICAL TRANSACTIONS OF THE ROYAL SOCIETY B: BIOLOGICAL SCIENCES 435 (2003).

[22] David F. Sally, *Into the Looking Glass: Discerning the Social Mind Through the Mindblind*, 18 ADVANCES IN GROUP PROCESSES 99 (2001).

[23] BATNA is "Best Alternative to a Negotiated Agreement." ROGER FISHER, ET AL., GETTING TO YES: NEGOTIATING AGREEMENT WITHOUT GIVING IN (2d ed. 1991).

[24] *Id.* at 110.

[25] Raymond S. Nickerson, *How We Know—and Sometimes Misjudge—What Others Know: Imputing One's Own Knowledge to Others*, 125 PSYCHOLOGICAL BULLETIN 737 (1999).

[26] Simon Baron-Cohen, et al., *The Autism-Spectrum Quotient (AQ): Evidence from Asperger Syndrome/High-Functioning Autism, Males and Females, Scientists and Mathematicians*, 31 JOURNAL OF AUTISM AND DEVELOPMENTAL DISORDERS 5 (2001).

[27] A recent report on gender differences is LINDA BABCOCK & SARA LASCHEVER, WOMEN DON'T ASK: NEGOTIATION AND THE GENDER DIVIDE (2003). The argument that autism reflects broader cognitive divergence between men and women has been made *in* SIMON BARON-COHEN, THE ESSENTIAL DIFFERENCE: THE TRUTH ABOUT THE MALE AND FEMALE BRAIN (2003).

[28] Francesca Happé, et al., *The Getting of Wisdom: Theory of Mind in Old Age*, 34 DEVELOPMENTAL PSYCHOLOGY 358 (1998); Elizabeth A. Maylor, et al., *Does Performance on Theory of Mind Tasks Decline in Old Age?*, 93 BRITISH JOURNAL OF PSYCHOLOGY 465 (2002).

IV. What to Do?

B.   When You're at the Table

❧ 44 ❧

Communication and Interaction Patterns

Linda L. Putnam

Editors' Note: *Certainly you know how to communicate; you're a negotiator, after all. But what if you're trying to decide whether or how to threaten to walk away? How can you communicate to your best possible advantage at some other particularly sensitive moment? Putnam examines three different areas of communications research—negotiation strategies, language analysis and process patterns—to explain that* how *we say things is often as important as* what *we say. This chapter should be read in conjunction with Welsh's on Fairness.*

Negotiation depends on some form of verbal or nonverbal communication. In particular, negotiators use communication to exchange proposals, manage perceived incompatibilities, and work out the nature of a bargaining relationship. Even early studies that employed the Prisoner's Dilemma game relied on a cue system of choices that conveyed implicit messages between negotiators.[1] Scholars who observed actual negotiations recognized the importance of communication and even described types of messages that negotiators exchanged.[2] This early work suggests that communication functions to make bargaining both tacit and explicit. Communication scholars, however, entered the arena of negotiation much later than did social psychologists, legal researchers, and political scientists.[3] During the last twenty-five years, however, scholars have produced a wealth of knowledge about communication processes, knowledge that falls into three broad categories—negotiation strategies and tactics, language and discourse analyses, and process patterns and phases.

These three arenas of research underscore the importance of communication as an impromptu code to signal intentions, respond to the other party's moves, exchange information, coordinate outcomes, and manage the dynamic tensions between cooperation and competition.[4] These dynamic tensions are rooted in mixed-motive interactions in which negotiators often walk tightropes between trust and distrust, escalation and exploitation, and concealing and revealing information. These antithetical poles simultaneously push and pull on the negotiation process. Communication aids in managing the shifts between them; that is, negotiators through their interactions can alter the course of bargaining from an initially cooperative endeavor to a highly competitive one or vice versa. Communication patterns also help negotiators transform their deliberations through redefining the issues, altering interpretations of events, and managing identity and face concerns. In effect, bargainers use social interaction to navigate between extreme opposites, a process that Rubin labels as 'the quintessential illustration of interdependence in negotiation.'[5] Overall, then, communication aids in enacting the very nature of negotiation as an ongoing process rooted in tensions between cooperation and competition.

Studies of communication and negotiation employ a number of research designs that link interaction to bargaining outcomes. In some studies, communication directly influences negotiated outcomes whereas in other research, communication acts as a mediator or moderator of input variables, such as a bargainer's goals, orientations, motivations, gender, and ethnicity.[6] Other investigations, especially ones that examine the development of negotiation over time, treat communication as the bargaining process itself. In like manner, communication research relies on a variety of outcomes, including whether the parties reach an agreement or a stalemate, if they achieve joint or individual gain, and if the negotiation ends up distributive or integrative. Studies of distributive and integrative negotiation also examine the communication strategies or tactics that contribute to these bargaining outcomes.

Negotiation Strategies and Tactics

Early work on communication and negotiation drew from researchers who observed and categorized the frequencies of bargaining strategies and tactics.[7] A negotiation strategy refers to an approach or a broad plan that encompasses a series of moves while tactics are the specific messages that enact the strategies. For example, competitiveness is a strategy often characterized by the use of such tactics as bluffs, exaggerated demands, and commitment statements. The research on negotiation strategies and tactics falls into six arenas: communication styles, distributive and integrative tactics, information management, arguments and reason giving, and generating proposals and concessions.

Communication Styles

Broad negotiation strategies are similar to what communication scholars call styles. However, a style is an automatic or habitual form of behavior while a strategy is often tailored consciously to achieve particular ends. A common style difference in the negotiation literature is tough versus soft bargaining. Tough bargainers open with extreme offers, give few and small concessions, concede slowly, and exaggerate the value of a concession. A meta-analysis of studies that compared these two strategies revealed that tough negotiators received high individual outcomes, but they also increased the likelihood that the negotiation would result in deadlock. Hence, bargainers need to shift from tough to reasonable offers early in a negotiation to avoid potential escalation.[8]

When tough bargaining is treated as a communication style, it resembles aggressiveness or domineering communication. Interestingly, a comparison between cooperative and aggressive negotiators reveals that skills, not styles, predict bargaining effectiveness. Cooperative negotiators who are personable and courteous may be too trusting and critical of their opponent's position while aggressive negotiators may be too demanding. Thus, bargainers should aim to develop the skills of being well prepared, having knowledge of baseline criteria, and being consistent with the facts of a case.[9]

Communication styles also vary in directness. Indirect styles rely on implicit messages and nonverbal cues as opposed to direct persuasion. Negotiators from low-context cultures (typically Western nations) enact direct bargaining styles through using comparisons and contrasts, clear statements of preferences, and reactions to offers; whereas bargainers from high-context countries (typically Eastern cultures) infer a negotiator's priorities and preferences from his or her offers. Indirect styles of inferring preferences are sensitive to tacit cues and demonstrate more flexibility in information sequences than do direct styles. In cross-cultural, cross-context situations, however, bargainers may accommodate each other through using direct styles, frequent questions, and overt problem-solving strategies.[10]

Distributive and Integrative Tactics

Communication strategies are closely tied to distributive and integrative bargaining. Distributive bargaining refers to the goal of maximizing individual gain, claiming value, and engaging in fixed-sum negotiations. Parties who embrace this approach often treat issues and positions as mutually exclusive. In contrast, integrative bargaining emphasizes joint gains, meeting underlying interests, and being flexible in the distribution of resources.[11] Initially, interaction research focused on the communicative tactics that facilitated the use of one approach over the other.[12] For example, studies of labor-management negotiators revealed that frequent use of threats, demands, putdown statements, and irrelevant arguments fostered distributive processes while a reliance on acceptance statements, procedural statements, and making concessions enhanced integrative negotiations. Contentious tactics linked to distributive processes surfaced as powerful, but they did not necessarily lead to higher individual outcomes.[13]

Information Management

Distributive and integrative negotiations also differ in their patterns of information management. Contrary to common beliefs, honest and open information exchange does not necessarily lead to integrative bargaining, as scholars initially predicted. The key point for developing an integrative process is the willingness to exchange particular types of information. Specifically, sharing information about priorities and underlying interests results in high joint gains, but only for bargainers who hold a cooperative orientation. In contrast, parties in distributive negotiations concentrate on exchanging information about positions, talk about their own preferences and priorities, and make more comparisons than do integrative negotiators.[14] Observations of actual bargainers affirm these findings and note that highly skilled negotiators engage in information seeking as a common communication tactic.[15] Seeking information leads to insights about a negotiator's priorities that, in turn, point to integrative outcomes.

Arguments and Reason Giving

In addition to managing information, negotiators make arguments and give reasons for their positions. Argument, in this sense, refers to advocating and refuting positions, not to verbal aggression. Patterns of argument distinguish between skilled and unskilled negotiators as well as integrative and distributive bargaining. Affirming their confidence, skilled negotiators present fewer reasons to support their claims than do unskilled bargainers. Moreover, they avoid diluting their positions by mixing strong and weak arguments, and they use attacking arguments sparingly, only when they want to signal the seriousness of a situation. Successful distributive negotiators reject their opponents' claims and introduce new ideas that favor their own positions. But, recurring use of contentious tactics, especially attacking arguments, often leads to impasse, particularly when bargainers pressure their opponents.[16] Thus, the types of arguments that parties use may influence negotiated outcomes. In some circumstances, arguing about the causes and inherent harms of a problem and the workability of proposals leads to a longer search process that reveals the complexities of an issue and fosters the development of creative solutions. Thus, these patterns of argument promote new understandings that uncover underlying interests to aid in reaching integrative solutions.[17]

Generating Proposals and Concessions

Research on proposal generation parallels studies of arguments. Basically, negotiators who receive high joint gains offer more options than do those who end up with low joint gains. For negotiation pairs that attain integrative settlements, both parties ask for concessions, make frequent offers, and engage in problem-solving. Skilled negotiators, however, do not respond with an immediate counteroffer to their opponents' offers;[18] rather they seek to understand an offer before complicating the discussion with counteroffers. Generating proposals, especially ones that incorporate the needs and interests of both parties, follows a creative process that can arise from shifting arguments over time and working out mismatches in the way parties frame issues. Changing the types of claims that a bargainer makes and adding qualifiers to arguments facilitates proposal generation, while providing additional evidence to a claim stifles proposal development.[19]

The research on communication styles, strategies, and tactics reveals problems with recommending specific behaviors to achieve integrative outcomes. Advising negotiators to share information openly ignores the mixed motive nature of conflict and the fact that bargainers simultaneously reveal and conceal information. Communication styles, whether cooperative or aggressive, or direct or indirect, are not the keys to effective negotiation; it is the particular skills that are effective. Hence, advising negotiators to avoid assertiveness does not necessarily lead to integrative outcomes.

The consequence of using a particular tactic also depends on how it is worded and interpreted. Some tactics, such as putdown statements and attacking the other side, typically foster distributive processes, but using threats can promote integrative bargaining through indicating the seriousness of a position; thus, the same tactic can serve integrative and distributive functions, depending on its position in the overall bargaining.[20]

Finally, argumentation means more than attacking the other party's position. Arguments are grounded in issues, causes for problems, evidence, and claims. Research suggests that discussing the harm and workability of issues fosters proposal development, especially if parties discover different ways to frame their problems. Overall, research on communicative strategies and tactics pushes negotiators to make choices between cooperation and competition or to oscillate back and forth between them. The absence of research on the way tactics are worded, how they occur in sequence, and what they mean contributes to this tendency to align tactics with particular outcomes.

Language and Discourse Analyses

Research on language analysis in negotiation differs from that of strategies and tactics by focusing on the *how* and *why* of talk as opposed to the tactical *functions* of messages. Rather than focusing on broad plans or the way that messages perform bargaining functions, studies of language use focus on the nuances of meaning. Scholars investigate how negotiators use language to signal interpretations of interactions, promote action, and co-develop the bargaining process. Rather than presuming that an activity such as 'making a threat' occurs, researchers examine the discourse that negotiators use to form a threat and how the interpretation of this message ties back to the bargaining context. This work clusters into three broad categories: language as action, communication patterns that manage the process itself, and identity and relational discourses. Each arena focuses on the way that language works within negotiations and how messages evoke diverse interpretations.

Language as Action

Discourse analysts treat language as evoking actions and reactions; thus, to give a threat is to enact a commitment to the other party and to provide an explanation is to produce an account for one's actions. Threats, then, are not simply coercive moves; instead, they evoke different kinds of reactions, depending on the way they are expressed. Ironically, early bargaining scholars recognized variation in the way that language forms bargaining tactics. For example, a firm commitment statement or a forceful threat differs from a flexible one in its finality, specificity, and completeness. A statement such as, "If we do not get a 2% increase on bene-fits by the end of the week, our company will sign with a competitor" includes a specific request, a deadline, and a consequence for noncompliance.[21] A flexible statement, in contrast, employs tentative language, indirect requests, and ambigu-ous wording, e.g., "We need some increases on benefits or we will have to entertain other options."

Threats and commitment statements can compel a negotiator to respond, or they can simply say "no" to the target, thus functioning as a deterrent. These tac-tics are more likely to evoke compliance if the consequence clause is worded positively.[22] For example, the statement, "if you don't perform, I will penalize you" is deemed more credible than, "If you perform well, I will not penalize you." The use of a flexible commitment statement is less likely to escalate a conflict, but it is also less credible than a firm one. In effect, threats and commitment statements are seen as more credible if bargainers use direct language to express them, along with an explicit and direct statement of consequence.[23]

Communication Patterns That Manage the Process

In addition to evoking action, discourse patterns also manage negotiation conver-sations through action-reaction sets of behaviors. Specifically, bargainers who use questions, as opposed to demands, are more likely to elicit responses from their opponents, especially when negotiators know each other and have flexible proce-dures for working together.[24] Imperative statements, such as "Please give me your counteroffer," are commonplace in negotiation, but they are seen as more control-ling than are inquiries. Even though posing questions is a good way to gain insights about an opponent's preferences, the likelihood of a bargainer asking questions relates to his or her role. For example, in transactional negotiations, sellers ask more questions about the buyer's needs, and the buyers make more directional requests such as "can other options be added into the bargaining mix?"[25] Thus, some negotiation roles may be more conducive than others to pos-ing questions. Moreover, some types of inquiries, such as loaded, heated, and trick questions, may generate animosity by making the other party feel uncomfortable. The most effective questions are open-ended, invite the other bargainer to reflect on her thinking, and reveal how both parties are interpreting the issues.[26]

Another way bargainers manage the negotiation process is through the use of procedural and summary statements. These summary statements serve as barome-ters to get readings on the negotiation progress and to chart optional directions.[27] In a similar way, skilled negotiators label or forecast their actions, e.g., "Can I ask you a question?" They also test out interpretations about what a message means, e.g., "You're saying that you would prefer to have the policy spelled out in the con-tract. Am I correct here?" and they express their thoughts and reactions verbally, e.g., "I have mixed feelings about this issue."[28] These discourse patterns, however, are linked to direct styles of expression, ones that may be more common in low-than in high-context cultures.

Identity and Relational Discourse

Language and discourse analysts also examine the identity and relational functions of messages. Taking the lead from early studies on impression management, scholars realized that negotiators have a strong desire to protect their *faces*. A bargainer loses face when some action leads to discrediting his self-image in the eyes of others; hence, negotiators use language to engage in positive and negative facework. Positive face refers to the desire to look credible while negative face stems from the desire for social autonomy. Negotiation research shows that positive face is threatened by the use of criticisms, accusations, and uncooperative behaviors while the use of orders, offers, and threats can threaten negative face and challenge a negotiator's autonomy. Implying that a directive or order should have been done already also threatens the other party's negative face. A negotiator protects the other bargainer's face through using disclaimers, hiding disagreements, and phrasing demands as questions.[29]

Similar to identity messages, bargainers also use discourse to give implicit messages about bargaining relationships and how negotiators see the nature of their interdependence. These relational cues are subtle and often rooted in word choice and language intensity. For instance, bargainers signal how close or formal they want to be with the other party through using particular pronouns, such as *you* versus *person*. Using the term *you* is more informal than employing a third person referent. Moreover, making use of long utterances, compound sentences, and excessive verbs signals formality that expresses a desire to move away from rather than closer to the other party.[30]

Language intensity also conveys messages about bargaining relationships. That is, relationally-oriented negotiators typically avoid the use of rude comments, excessive interruptions of the other party, and deceptive statements.[31] In their desire to preserve relationships, negotiators tone down their language intensity by refraining from the use of colorful adjectives and adverbs, profanity, and innuendos. Skilled versus unskilled negotiators implement this rule by avoiding the use of linguistic 'irritators,' such as, "my *generous* offer to you" or "my *reasonable* response." Even though these nuances of language seem trivial, research shows that they are tied to managing relational tensions, such as struggles between control versus yielding, autonomy versus connectedness, and liking versus disliking that form the negotiation tightrope.[32] Parties work out these tensions through their interactions during a negotiation.

Discourse studies add complexity to research on bargaining tactics. In particular, threats and commitments function as language in action, not simply as power plays. As such, the wording, finality, and completeness of a tactic influence its impact. Discourse that aids in managing the negotiation process contributes to learning about the conflict itself through questions, summary statements, testing interpretations, forecasting, and expressing concerns. Finally, language aids in working out identity and relational concerns. Negotiators actively manage their own and the other party's face through using disclaimers and through qualifying their disagreements. They also manage relationships through monitoring the intensity of their language, using informal pronouns, and discursively working out the dialectics of control and yielding. Overall, discourse studies provide depth and specificity to the ways that tactics are used, what they mean, and how they fit within the negotiation context. They complement both the research on strategies and tactics and the work on process patterns and phases.

Process, Patterns, and Phases

The last area of communication research focuses on how the bargaining develops over time. It examines the actions and reactions of each negotiator that form predictable sequences or patterns over time. This work also uncovers how strategies and tactics cluster together in predictable ways, such as a threat followed by a threat, or followed by another contentious move. Thus, it determines what the patterns are, how they change, and how they relate to negotiated outcomes.

Types of Sequential Patterns

Researchers identify three types of sequential patterns in negotiations—reciprocal, transformational, and complementary.[33] When two negotiators match each other's tactics exactly, a *reciprocal* pattern forms. The most consistent and dominant finding about reciprocal patterns is the development of repetitive conflict cycles in negotiations.[34] Conflict cycles occur when bargainers match each other's use of threats, commitments, or contentious statements in ways that develop a momentum of their own. Once a set of cycles locks into place, it becomes very difficult for negotiators to shift to cooperative interaction.

However, bargainers also reciprocate problem-solving messages, statements of concern, and multiple-issue offers that lead to cooperative interactions. These patterns are more likely to occur when negotiators enter the process with a cooperative orientation and general knowledge of integrative bargaining.[35] Not surprisingly, the development of conflict cycles in negotiations often leads to impasse or to one-sided settlements. In contrast, reciprocating priority information and trade-offs result in high joint profits.[36] One way to prevent a conflict cycle from occurring is to respond with an opposite move that *transforms* the tight reciprocal structure. In particular, giving information, responding with an interest-oriented statement, or making a procedural comment can break up the onset of a conflict cycle and makes it easier for the bargainers to engage in cooperative interaction.

Negotiators also exhibit *complementary* patterns in which they match their opponents by using broadly similar strategies, for example, following a threat with a demand. Labor and management, in particular, engage in a complementary dance in which both sides use clusters of tactics aligned with their respective roles. Assuming an offensive stance, labor responds to management with attacking arguments while management exhibits a defensive role through employing self-supporting arguments and commitment statements. These tactics are broadly similar and become complementary as bargainers balance each other in role specializations. However, if either side shifts to the interaction patterns that typify the other role, conflict spirals are likely to develop.[37] In a similar type of complementary pattern, negotiation dyads that mix cooperative with competitive tactics are likely to reach settlements, whereas dyads that keep the two processes structurally separate are likely to stalemate.[38] For example, negotiators who develop separate stages of competition, e.g., making demands, attacking arguments, and contentious statements followed by discrete stages of cooperation are more likely to stalemate than are those that mix attacking arguments with offers, information exchange, and discussion of procedures. The mixing of different tactics buffers the process from escalation.

Phases of Negotiation Interaction

In lengthy negotiations, sequences of messages layer into each other and reveal phases or constellations of communicative acts that form coherent structures.[39] At one time, theorists believed that distributive and integrative negotiations occurred in distinct stages, often arrayed in three or more developmental periods.[40] Current research, however, suggests that negotiators who begin with distributive processes and move to integrative ones are more likely to reach settlements than are bargainers who begin with integrative interactions and transition to distributive bargaining.[41] Once bargainers enter into a distributive stage, it is more difficult to move back into integrative interactions. Moreover, if bargainers reciprocate information about their priorities in the second stage of a negotiation, they are more likely to reach high joint gains.[42]

The development of negotiations over time also reveals different ways that parties manage issues. Overall, making concessions by combining multiple issues as opposed to trading on a single item one at a time aids in reaching optimal outcomes. Negotiators use logrolling and issue development to reach integrative solutions. Logrolling entails conceding on low priority items to obtain high priority concerns. This approach works effectively when bargainers exchange accurate information about priorities. To reach a resolution, though, negotiators need to unbundle, redefine, and package items differently, not simply increase the number of agenda items on the table.[43]

Issue development focuses on how bargainers discover creative options through reframing or re-evaluating the definition and scope of a problem. These options bridge differences and transform the focus of a conflict as bargainers discover alternatives that were once out of their purview. For example, negotiators might engage in intense arguments on the need to increase management's percent of health care coverage. Employees might contend that health premiums are rising and management needs to cover a greater percentage of these benefits. Management might respond that it is not feasible for them to cover an additional amount of insurance premiums for all employees. After a lengthy deliberation, both sides might reframe the issue, asking 'what is contributing to the rapid rise in health care costs?' rather than 'how do we get management to cover a greater percentage of employees' health benefits?' This reframing comes from splintering and exploring related issues that shift the topic of negotiation, thus producing new options, for example, the alternatives to rebid an insurance carrier or to eliminate optical coverage might reframe the discussion and define the problem as lowering insurance premiums rather than paying a higher percentage of the costs. These alternatives were never on the table until the negotiators reframed the issue and posed a different question. Hence, issue framing derives from the way that agenda items shift during interactions and is a critical aspect of negotiation stage development.[44]

Conclusion

The work on communication and negotiation has evolved considerably since the early days when researchers treated communication as moves in a game. Ironically, communication conveys messages both tacitly and explicitly through negotiation strategies and tactics. These communicative acts do not fit neatly into particular outcomes, since tactics can be worded in a variety of ways and have diverse meanings at different times during a negotiation. Contrary to popular beliefs, selective use of threats can aid in reaching integrative outcomes, if they signal the seriousness of a position or function to prevent an opponent from repeating previously rejected issues. Employing tentative language and using positive wording of consequences also moderates the effects and acceptability of this tactic.

Using contentious tactics is problematic, though, when they occur in a series of reciprocal behaviors that develop into a conflict cycle, often culminating in a deadlock. Hence, negotiators need to buffer these tactics by using transformational or complementary patterns. Asking questions, sharing priority information, making offers, and engaging in problem-solving serve as transformational moves to break a conflict cycle. In like manner, negotiators can counteract the development of conflict cycles through making procedural and summary statements, even suggesting overtly that the negotiation should move in a different direction. Bargainers who label or forecast their actions, avoid linguistic irritators, and attend to the subtle nuances of facework and relational messages are able to traverse the tightrope between cooperation and competition.

Walking this tightrope works best when negotiators embrace both ends of these opposites as legitimate. Cooperation and competition are mutually intertwined in bargaining, as are escalation and exploitation. Communication patterns, such as issue development, that bridge opposites through reframing issues offer the potential to embrace both poles equally.

Endnotes

[1] THOMAS C. SCHELLING, THE STRATEGY OF CONFLICT (1960).
[2] EDWARD PETERS, STRATEGY AND TACTICS IN LABOR NEGOTIATIONS (1955); RICHARD E. WALTON & ROBERT B. MCKERSIE, A BEHAVIORAL THEORY OF LABOR NEGOTIATIONS: AN ANALYSIS OF A SOCIAL INTERACTION SYSTEM (1965); SCHELLING, *supra* note 1.
[3] For early state-of-the-art reviews, *see* Linda L. Putnam & Marshall Scott Poole, *Conflict and Negotiation, in* HANDBOOK OF ORGANIZATIONAL COMMUNICATION 549-99 (Fredric M. Jablin, et al., eds., 1987); Linda L. Putnam & Tricia S. Jones, *The Role of Communication in Bargaining*, 8 HUMAN COMMUNICATION RESEARCH 262-80 (1982).
[4] Jennifer A. Chatman, et al., *Integrating Communication and Negotiation Research*, 3 RESEARCH ON NEGOTIATION IN ORGANIZATIONS (Max. H. Bazerman, et al., eds., 1991).
[5] Jeffrey Z. Rubin, *Negotiation: An Introduction to Some Issues and Themes*, 27 AMERICAN BEHAVIORAL SCIENTIST 135-47 (1983).
[6] Chatman, et al., *Integrating Communication and Negotiation Research, supra* note 4; Laurie R. Weingart, et al., *Conflict Management and Communication Processes, in* THE PSYCHOLOGY OF CONFLICT AND CONFLICT MANAGEMENT IN ORGANIZATIONS, SIOP FRONTIER SERIES (Carsten K. W. De Dreu & Michele J. Gelfand eds., forthcoming).
[7] P. Thomas Hopmann & Clarence Walcott, *The Impact of International Conflict and Détente on Bargaining in Arms Control Negotiations: An Experimental Analysis*, 2 INTERNATIONAL INTERACTIONS 189-206 (1976); Dean G. Pruitt & Steven A. Lewis, *Development of Integrative Solutions in Bilateral Negotiation*, 31 JOURNAL OF PERSONALITY AND SOCIAL PSYCHOLOGY 621 (1975).
[8] W. Clay Hamner & Gary A. Yukl, *The Effectiveness of Different Offer Strategies in Bargaining, in* NEGOTIATIONS: SOCIAL-PSYCHOLOGICAL PERSPECTIVES (Daniel Druckman ed., 1974); Mike Allen, et al., *Comparing Hardline and Softline Bargaining Strategies in Zero-Sum Situations Using Meta-Analysis, in* THEORY AND RESEARCH IN CONFLICT MANAGEMENT (M. Afzalur Rahim ed., 1990).
[9] Gerald R. Williams, *Style and Effectiveness in Negotiation, in* NEGOTIATION: STRATEGIES FOR MUTUAL GAIN (Laura Hall ed., 1993).
[10] Wendy L. Adair, et al., *Negotiation Behavior When Cultures Collide: The U.S. and Japan*, 86 JOURNAL OF APPLIED PSYCHOLOGY 371 (2001); Wendy L. Adair, *Integrative Sequences and Negotiation Outcomes in Same- and Mixed-Culture Negotiations*, 14 INTERNATIONAL JOURNAL OF CONFLICT MANAGEMENT 273 (2003).
[11] WALTON & MCKERSIE, *supra* note 2.
[12] Linda L. Putnam, *Reframing Integrative and Distributive Bargaining: A Process Perspective, in* RESEARCH ON NEGOTIATION IN ORGANIZATIONS (Blair H. Sheppard, et al., eds., 1992).
[13] William A. Donohue, *Analyzing Negotiation Tactics: Development of a Negotiation Interact System*, 7 HUMAN COMMUNICATION RESEARCH 273 (1981); William A. Donohue, *Development of a Model of Rule Use in Negotiation*, 48 COMMUNICATION MONOGRAPHS 106 (1981); Linda L. Putnam & Tricia S. Jones, *Reciprocity in Negotiations: An Analysis of Bargaining Interaction*, 49 COMMUNICATION MONOGRAPHS 171 (1982).
[14] Mara Olekalns & Philip L. Smith, *Social Value Orientations and Strategy Choices in Competitive Negotiations*, 25 PERSONALITY & SOCIAL PSYCHOLOGY BULLETIN 657 (1999); Mara Olekalns & Philip L. Smith, *Negotiating Optimal Outcomes: The Role of Strategic Sequences in Competitive Negotiations*, 24 HUMAN COMMUNICATION RESEARCH 528 (2000); Mara Olekalns & Philip L. Smith, *Testing the Relationships Among Negotiators' Motivational Orientations, Strategy Choices, and Outcomes*, 39 JOURNAL OF EXPERIMENTAL SOCIAL PSYCHOLOGY 101 (2003).
[15] Skilled labor/management negotiators met three criteria: judged effective by both colleagues and opponents, had a strong record of satisfactory settlements, and had low incidence of constituents rejecting negotiated contracts. *See* Neil Rackham & John Carlisle, *The Effective Negotiator—Part I: The Behavior of Successful Negotiators*, 2 JOURNAL OF EUROPEAN

INDUSTRIAL TRAINING 6-10 (1978); *see also*, Frank Tutzauer & Michael E. Roloff, *Communication Processes Leading to Integrative Agreements: Three Paths to Joint Benefits*, 15 COMMUNICATION RESEARCH 360 (1988); Deborah L. Shapiro & Robert J. Bies, *Threats, Bluffs, and Disclaimers in Negotiation*, 60 ORGANIZATIONAL BEHAVIOR AND HUMAN DECISION PROCESSES 14 (1994).

[16] Donohue, *Development of a Model of Rule Use in Negotiation*, supra note 13; Putnam & Jones, supra note 13; Michael E. Roloff, et al., *The Role of Argumentation in Distributive and Integrative Bargaining Contexts: Seeking Relative Advantage But At What Cost?*, in MANAGING CONFLICT: AN INTERDISCIPLINARY APPROACH (M. Afzalur Rahim ed., 1989).

[17] Linda L. Putnam & Steven R. Wilson, *Argumentation and Bargaining Strategies as Discriminators of Integrative Outcomes*, in MANAGING CONFLICT: AN INTERDISCIPLINARY APPROACH (M. Afzalur Rahim ed., Praeger 1989); Linda L. Putnam, et al., *The Evolution of Case Arguments in Teachers' Bargaining*, 23 JOURNAL OF THE AMERICAN FORENSIC ASSOCIATION 63-81 (1986).

[18] Rackham & Carlisle, supra note 15.

[19] Linda L. Putnam & Patricia Geist, *Argument in Bargaining: An Analysis of the Reasoning Process*, 50 SOUTHERN STATES COMMUNICATION JOURNAL 225 (1985); Putnam, et al., supra note 17.

[20] Putnam & Wilson, supra note 17.

[21] WALTON & MCKERSIE, supra note 2.

[22] Pamela Gibbons, et al., *The Role of Language in Negotiations: Threats and Promises*, in COMMUNICATION AND NEGOTIATION (Linda L. Putnam & Michael E. Roloff eds., 1992).

[23] ROY J. LEWICKI, ET AL., NEGOTIATION (3d ed. 1999).

[24] William A. Donohue & Mary E. Diez, *Directive Use in Negotiation Interaction*, 52 COMMUNICATION MONOGRAPHS 305 (1985).

[25] Deborah Cai, et al., *Culture in the Context of Intercultural Negotiation: Individualism-Collectivism and Paths to Integrative Agreements*, 26 HUMAN COMMUNICATION RESEARCH 591-671 (2000).

[26] LEWICKI, ET AL., supra note 23.

[27] Putnam & Jones, supra note 13.

[28] Michael E. Roloff, et al., *Negotiation Skills*, in HANDBOOK OF COMMUNICATION AND SOCIAL INTERACTION SKILLS (John O. Greene & Brant R. Burleson eds., 2003).

[29] Steven R. Wilson, *Face and Facework in Negotiations*, in COMMUNICATION AND NEGOTIATION (Linda L. Putnam & Michael E. Roloff eds., 1992).

[30] William A. Donohue, et al., *Relational Distance in Managing Conflict*, 11 HUMAN COMMUNICATION RESEARCH 387 (1985).

[31] Leonard Greenhalgh & Deborah I. Chapman, *Negotiator Relationships: Construct Measurement and Demonstration of Their Impact on the Process and Outcomes of Negotiations*, 7 GROUP DECISION AND NEGOTIATION 465 (1998); Leonard Greenhalgh & R. W. Gilkey, *The Effect of Relationship Orientation on Negotiator's Cognitions and Tactics*, 2 GROUP DECISION AND NEGOTIATION 103 (1993).

[32] William A. Donohue, *Resolving Relational Paradox: The Language of Conflict in Relationships*, in THE LANGUAGE OF CONFLICT AND RESOLUTION (William F. Eadie & Paul E. Nelson eds., 2003).

[33] Weingart, et al., supra note 6.

[34] Putnam & Jones, *Reciprocity in Negotiations: An Analysis of Bargaining Interaction*, supra note 13.

[35] Laurie R. Weingart, et al., *Knowledge and the Sequential Processes of Negotiation: A Markov Chain Analysis of Response-in-Kind*, 35 JOURNAL OF EXPERIMENTAL SOCIAL PSYCHOLOGY 366 (1999); Laurie R. Weingart, et al., *The Impact of Consideration of Issues and Motivational Orientation on Group Negotiation Process and Outcome*, 78 JOURNAL OF APPLIED PSYCHOLOGY 504 (1993).

[36] Jeanne M. Brett, et al., *Breaking the Bonds of Reciprocity in Negotiations*, 41 ACADEMY OF MANAGEMENT JOURNAL 410 (1998); Olekalns & Smith, *Negotiating Optimal Outcomes*, supra note 14.

[37] Putnam & Jones, supra note 13.

[38] Olekalns & Smith, *Negotiating Optimal Outcomes*, supra note 14.

[39] Michael E. Holmes, *Phase Structures in Negotiation*, in COMMUNICATION AND NEGOTIATION (Linda L. Putnam & Michael E. Roloff eds., 1992).

[40] P. H. GULLIVER, DISPUTES AND NEGOTIATIONS: A CROSS-CULTURAL PERSPECTIVE (1979).

[41] Mara Olekalns, et al., *The Process of Negotiating: Tactics, Phases, and Outcomes*, 67 ORGANIZATIONAL BEHAVIOR AND HUMAN DECISION PROCESSES 68 (1996).

[42] Mara Olekalns, et al., *Phases, Transitions and Interruptions: Modeling Processes in Multi-Party Negotiations*, 14 INTERNATIONAL JOURNAL OF CONFLICT MANAGEMENT 191 (2003).

[43] Leigh Thompson, *Information Exchange in Negotiation*, 27 JOURNAL OF EXPERIMENTAL SOCIAL PSYCHOLOGY 161 (1991); Weingart, et al., *The Impact of Consideration of Issues and Motivational Orientation on Group Negotiation Process and Outcome*, supra note 35.

[44] Linda L. Putnam & Majia Holmer, *Framing, Reframing, and Issue Development*, in COMMUNICATION AND NEGOTIATION (Linda L. Putnam & Michael E. Roloff eds., 1992); Art DeWulf, et al., *How Issues Get Framed and Reframed When Different Communities Meet: A Multi-Level Analysis of a Collaborative Soil Conservation Initiative in the Ecuadorian Andes*, 14 JOURNAL OF COMMUNITY AND APPLIED SOCIAL PSYCHOLOGY 177 (2004).

❧ 45 ❧

Risks of E-Mail

Anita D. Bhappu & Zoe I. Barsness

Editors' Note: *It's increasingly likely that you will find yourself conducting negotiations by e-mail, if only as one aspect of the process. The authors discuss how e-mail changes both what is discussed and how it's discussed, and they have some salutary warnings for you. Using e-mail, it turns out, can distort what you're trying to say, and may also affect your perception of what* they *are trying to say.*

For the first time in human history, mass cooperation across time and space is suddenly economical. "There's a fundamental shift in power happening," says Pierre Omidyar, founder and chairman of the online marketplace eBay Inc. "Everywhere, people are getting together and, using the Internet, disrupting whatever activities they're involved in."*

Negotiations are not immune from the disruptive effects of technology. After all, the communication media that negotiators use can influence not only what information they share and how that information is communicated, but also what information they attend to and how they interpret it. Certain information is easy to communicate face-to-face but difficult to describe in an e-mail. For example, emotional appeals are more challenging to make over e-mail than logical arguments. The exchange of nuanced information can also be constrained by e-mail technology because its structure limits the breadth and depth of information that can be exchanged. Finally, people pay attention to different things and are influenced by different people to varying degrees when using e-mail than face-to-face communication. The social distance imposed by electronic communication may encourage negotiators to engage in more confrontational behavior, or to focus so strongly on their own interests they reduce consideration of the other party's needs. This self-absorption and corresponding lack of other-awareness can make it difficult for electronic negotiators to assess differential preferences and identify potential joint gains. On the other hand, the minimization of status differences that occurs when negotiators communicate electronically may enhance the negotiation process by encouraging lower status negotiators to work harder to achieve their negotiating goals, thus preventing the premature closure of negotiations. In sum, negotiators interacting electronically not only face challenges, they enjoy unique opportunities. In this chapter, we discuss some of the ways in which e-mail alters the information-sharing processes and power dynamics during negotiation that have important ramifications for information exchange and the generation of joint gains. We also discuss useful information-sharing strategies and tactics that negotiators might adopt when interacting electronically to overcome the obstacles and exploit the opportunities that electronic communication presents negotiators.

Lack of Media Richness in E-mail

Media richness is one of two characteristics of e-mail that are particularly relevant to negotiation. Media richness is the capacity of a communication medium to transmit visual and verbal cues, enabling it to support a variety of languages (e.g., body, paralanguage, and natural), provide more immediate feedback, and facilitate communication of personal information.[1] E-mail is considered a lean medium because it transmits neither visual nor verbal cues, whereas face-to-face communication is considered a rich medium because it transmits both. The lack of media richness in electronic communication contexts reduces the social presence of others and increases the perceived social distance among negotiators who are physically separated and communicating by computer.[2] Thus, negotiators' social awareness of each other's personal situation or emotional state, for example, may be seriously diminished. Negotiators may also engage more heavily in self-interested behavior when using e-mail rather than face-to-face communication because they neither see nor hear one another. Furthermore, they may fail to elicit from the other party—or simply ignore—important information about his or her interests and priorities. E-mail usage may, therefore, accentuate a self-interest schema (i.e., the extent to which a negotiator emphasizes his or her own rather than collective interests) and its attendant behaviors.[3]

On the other hand, e-mail usage may limit the leverage of status-based power and encourage more candid information sharing because reduced social cues lower the salience of social group differences and social status. Indeed, the lack of social cues in e-mail causes people to be more direct and confrontational in their communications.[4] Such confrontational behavior can be further exacerbated by the diminished social presence of others and by feelings of anonymity associated with e-mail.[5]

Finally, negotiators are more likely to focus on the content rather than the context of their messages when using e-mail.[6] Given that a significant proportion of a message's meaning comes from its associated visual and verbal cues such as facial expressions, body language, and tone of voice, the inability to transmit these cues when using e-mail may cause negotiators to rely more heavily on logical argumentation and the presentation of facts rather than on emotional or personal appeals. Research suggests, for instance, that communication styles in e-mail are more task-oriented and depersonalized than in face-to-face interactions.[7] Reduced contextual information may, however, impede the negotiator's ability to interpret message meaning. Information exchanged in e-mail tends to be less nuanced than would be information exchanged face-to-face in the same situation because back channel and clarifying information, such as speech acknowledgements (e.g., "mmm" or "huh?") and reactive body language, such as head nods, are reduced.[8] Indeed, much of such clarifying information is simply lost when using e-mail because the information processing costs associated with translating this type of information into purely textual form are significant and sufficiently prohibitive.

In short, e-mail constrains information exchange, diminishing negotiators' ability to accurately assess differential preferences and identify potential joint gains. Indeed, one examination comparing face-to-face and computer-mediated negotiations revealed that negotiators interacting electronically were less accurate in judging the other party's interests.[9] E-mail interaction may also promote the use of distributive tactics exactly because it encourages direct and confrontational communications, leading to conflict spirals that result in lower joint gains or even impasse. Some researchers, for example, have demonstrated a higher incidence of impasse and less integrative outcomes in e-mail than face-to-face negotiations.[10] These findings may reflect the difficulty of establishing rapport when using e-mail because it limits visual access to the nonverbal behavior that enables relational development. The development of rapport has been shown to foster more mutually beneficial settlements, especially in lean media contexts, perhaps because rapport engenders greater social awareness and connection among negotiators.[11]

The effects of electronically mediated communication on negotiation process and outcomes are not entirely detrimental, however. E-mail may facilitate better processing of social conflict exactly because lean media do not transmit visual and verbal cues. The visible presence of others can induce arousal that leads to more aggressive behavioral responses. The absence of visual and verbal cues in e-mail, however, may defuse such triggers.[12] It may also reduce the salience of social group differences, which prevents coalition formation. In addition, because negotiators are physically isolated and the social presence of others is diminished, they can take time to "step out" of the discussion and thoughtfully respond rather than merely react to the other party's behavior, limiting escalation of social conflict even further.[13]

Lastly, e-mail may promote more equal participation among negotiators. The salience of social group differences and social status is reduced in lean media because there are fewer social context cues,[14] encouraging lower status individuals to participate more and reducing social influence bias among negotiators.[15] Rather than discounting or ignoring information provided by lower status individuals, as they might in face-to-face communication, negotiators may be influenced more by this information when using e-mail. Thus, even though less nuanced information is communicated between negotiators, more diverse information may actually be received. Attention to this "new" information may subsequently enable negotiators to identify optimal trades and create more integrative agreements.

Interactivity in E-mail

Interactivity is the other characteristic of e-mail that is particularly relevant to negotiation. Interactivity is the potential of a communication medium to sustain a seamless flow of information between two or more negotiators.[16] Interactivity has two dimensions. The first, a temporal dimension, captures the synchronicity of interactions. Face-to-face communication is synchronous because all negotiators are co-temporal and each party receives an utterance just as it is produced; as a result, speaking turns tend to occur sequentially. E-mail is typically asynchronous because negotiators can read and respond to others' messages whenever they desire and not necessarily sequentially. Parallel processing, the second dimension of interactivity, describes the ability of the medium to enable two or more negotiators to simultaneously submit messages. Parallel processing is common in threaded e-mail discussions such as might occur during a multi-party, online negotiation.

Asynchronous media like e-mail impose high "understanding costs" on negotiators because they provide little "grounding" to participants in the communication exchange.[17] Grounding is the process by which two parties in an interaction develop a shared sense of understanding about a communication and a shared sense of participation in the conversation. Without the clues provided by shared surroundings, nonverbal behavior, tone of voice, or the timing and sequence of the information exchange typically found in face-to-face communication, negotiators may find it challenging to accurately decode the messages that they receive electronically. Information and context are, therefore, parsed differently in asynchronous and synchronous media, which will certainly influence the way that negotiators construct messages as well as their ability to interpret the messages that are sent via e-mail.

Research suggests, for instance, that negotiators using asynchronous e-mail exchange very long comments that include multiple points all in one "bundle."[18] Since the receiver's opportunity to respond to or clarify points that the sender is attempting to make is reduced when using e-mail, the sender is inclined to outline his or her arguments in one e-mail message that is also likely to be more task-oriented and depersonalized.[19] Argument bundling may facilitate the identification of integrative agreements by encouraging negotiators to link issues together and consider them simultaneously rather than sequentially, but such an approach can also place higher demands on the receiver's information processing capabilities.[20] Negotiators may, therefore, have more difficulty establishing meaning and managing feedback in asynchronous e-mail exchanges, further hindering their efforts to successfully elicit and integrate the information that is required to construct a mutually beneficial agreement.

Although asynchronous e-mail exchange is the most common, e-mail can be nearly synchronous if negotiators are all online simultaneously. In this latter case, parallel processing may actually encourage individuals to share more information than in face-to-face communication because it allows negotiators to voice their different perspectives simultaneously.[21] Parallel processing can also undermine existing power dynamics and encourage direct confrontation because it prevents any one individual from suppressing the views of others by seizing control of the discussion.[22] Face-to-face communication, on the other hand, does not support parallel processing and instead constrains negotiators to sequential turn taking. Therefore, the parallel processing dimension of e-mail, which is absent in face-to-face communication, may further support the simultaneous consideration of multiple issues during negotiation. Coupled with the greater diversity of information exchange among parties encouraged by the reduction of power differentials, parallel processing in e-mail is likely to promote the search for joint gains and thus potentially enhance integrative outcomes.

E-mail and Information Exchange

Previous research suggests that at least two distinct information-processing modes are manifest during negotiations: an analytical-rational mode and an intuitive-experiential mode.[23] Individuals who adopt an analytical-rational mode rely more heavily on logic and deductive thinking and their associated tactics (e.g. development of positions and limits, use of logical argumentation, and the presentation of facts), while individuals who adopt an intuitive-experiential mode rely more heavily on intuition and experience and *their* associated tactics (e.g., appeals to emotion, the presentation of concrete personal stories, and the use of metaphors).[24] These two different information-processing styles, however, are not equally suited to the electronic context.

Reduced visual and verbal cues in e-mail may lead negotiators to use more rational-analytical communication tactics (e.g., logical argumentation and the presentation of facts). Such an effect is likely to favor negotiators who value logic and deductive thinking and are more adept at the use of these tactics. Heuristic trial and error search, where negotiators find their way to agreement through the exchange of alternative proposals, is likely to adapt *well* to the e-mail context since it supports issue packaging and argument bundling. However, the intermittent and often overlapping nature of most e-mail exchanges is likely to severely inhibit direct information-sharing approaches that rely on sequential turn-taking and reciprocal question and answer exchange. Negotiators who generally adopt a direct information-sharing strategy may, therefore, find e-mail *ill-suited* to their preferred information-sharing strategy. Indeed, the simultaneous consideration of multiple issues is likely to favor negotiators who rely more heavily on intuitive-experiential thinking styles and tactics.[25] Negotiators with a preference for indirect information-sharing strategies, because they must regularly infer meaning both from what is said (e.g., explicit offers) and what is implied (e.g., proposals entertained), may be more skilled at interpreting the meaning of multi-issue proposals and subsequently more adept at using what they have learned to develop better integrative agreements in e-mail.

Conclusion

People are increasingly relying on e-mail to negotiate deals and transactions, which may save them time, reduce their costs, and increase their convenience. However, the effectiveness of using e-mail to negotiate and the ultimate value that individuals are able to derive from such negotiations depend on communication norms of the negotiators in question. In particular, individuals need to be sensitive to the effects of communication media on social influence and information-sharing processes, which influence information exchange during negotiations. As our discussion suggests, the use of e-mail can both hinder and ameliorate the negotiation process depending on the specific schemas and behaviors enacted by the involved parties. A first step to minimizing the obstacles and enhancing the benefits associated with electronically mediated negotiations is to heighten individuals' awareness of these potential pitfalls and benefits. In doing so, we hope that this discussion will enable negotiators to better manage the negotiation process and reap greater joint gains.

Endnotes

* Robert D. Hof, *The Power of Us: Mass Collaboration on the Internet is Shaking Up Business*, BUSINESS WEEK., JUNE 20, 2005, at 75-82.

[1] Richard L. Daft & Robert H. Lengel, *Information Richness: A New Approach to Managerial Behavior and Organizational Design*, 6 RESEARCH IN ORGANIZATIONAL BEHAVIOR 191 (1984).
[2] JOHN SHORT, ET AL., THE SOCIAL PSYCHOLOGY OF TELECOMMUNICATIONS (1976); Lee Sproull & Sara Kiesler, *Reducing Social Context Clues: Electronic Mail in Organizational Communication*, 32 MANAGEMENT SCIENCE 1492 (1986).
[3] Zoe I. Barsness & Anita D. Bhappu, *At the Crossroads of Technology and Culture: Social Influence, Information Sharing, and Sense-Making Processes During Negotiations*, in NEGOTIATION: THEORETICAL ADVANCES AND CROSS-CULTURAL PERSPECTIVES (Michelle Gelfand & Jeanne Brett eds. 2004).
[4] Sara Kiesler & Lee Sproull, *Group-Decision Making and Communication Technology*, 52 ORGANIZATIONAL BEHAVIOR AND HUMAN DECISION PROCESSES 96 (1992).
[5] Terri L. Griffith & Gregory B. Northcraft, *Distinguishing Between the Forest and the Trees: Media, Features, and Methodology in Electronic Communication Research*, 5 ORGANIZATION SCIENCE 272 (1994).

[6] Rosalie J. Ocker & Gayle J. Yaverbaum, *Asynchronous Computer-Mediated Communication versus Face-to-Face Collaboration: Results on Student Learning, Quality and Satisfaction*, 8 GROUP DECISION AND NEGOTIATIONS 427 (1999).

[7] Nigel J. Kemp & Derek R. Rutter, *Cuelessness and the Content and Style of Conversation*, 21 BRITISH JOURNAL OF SOCIAL PSYCHOLOGY 43 (1982).

[8] Raymond A. Friedman & Steven C. Currall, *Conflict Escalation: Dispute Exacerbating Elements of E-mail Communication*, 56 HUMAN RELATIONS 1325 (2003); Kathleen L. Valley, et al., *"A Matter of Trust:" Effects of Communication on the Efficiency and Distribution of Outcomes*, 34 JOURNAL OF ECONOMIC BEHAVIOR AND ORGANIZATION 211 (1998).

[9] Vairam Arunachalam & William N. Dilla, *Judgment Accuracy and Outcomes in Negotiations: A Causal Modeling Analysis of Decision-Aiding Effects*, 61 ORGANIZATIONAL BEHAVIOR AND HUMAN DECISION PROCESSES 289 (1995).

[10] Rachel Croson, *Look at Me When You Say That: An Electronic Negotiation Simulation*, 30 SIMULATION GAMING 23 (1999); Arunachalam & Dilla, *supra* note 9; Valley, et al., *supra* note 8.

[11] Aimee L. Drolet & Michael W. Morris, *Rapport in Conflict Resolution: Accounting for How Face-to-Face Contact Fosters Mutual Cooperation in Mixed-Motive Conflicts*, 36 JOURNAL OF EXPERIMENTAL SOCIAL PSYCHOLOGY 26 (2000); Don A. Moore, et al., *Long and Short Routes to Success in Electronically Mediated Negotiations: Group Affiliations and Good Vibrations*, 77 ORGANIZATIONAL BEHAVIOR AND HUMAN DECISION PROCESSES 22 (1999).

[12] Peter J. Carnevale, et al., *Looking and Competing: Accountability and Visual Access in Integrative Bargaining*, 40 JOURNAL OF PERSONALITY AND SOCIAL PSYCHOLOGY 111 (1981).

[13] Linda M. Harasim, *Networlds: Networks as a Social Space, in* GLOBAL NETWORKS: COMPUTERS AND INTERNATIONAL COMMUNICATION (1993).

[14] LEE SPROULL & SARA KIESLER, CONNECTIONS: NEW WAYS OF WORKING IN THE NETWORKED ORGANIZATION (1991).

[15] Jane Siegel, et al., *Group Processes in Computer-Mediated Communication*, 37 ORGANIZATIONAL BEHAVIOR AND HUMAN DECISION PROCESSES 157 (1986); Anita D. Bhappu, et al., *Media Effects and Communication Bias in Diverse Groups*, 70 ORGANIZATIONAL BEHAVIOR AND HUMAN DECISION PROCESSES 199 (1997).

[16] Robert E. Kraut, et al., *Task Requirements and Media Choice in Collaborative Writing*, 7 HUMAN COMPUTER INTERACTIONS 375 (1992).

[17] Herbert Clark & Susan Brennan, *Grounding in Communication, in* PERSPECTIVES ON SOCIALLY SHARED COGNITION (Lauren Resnick, et al. eds., 1991); Friedman & Currall, *supra* note 8.

[18] Friedman & Currall, *supra* note 8; Ashley S. Rosette, et al., Paper presented at the Annual Meetings of the International Association for Conflict Management: The Influence of E-Mail on Hong Kong and U.S. Intra-Cultural Negotiations (2001).

[19] Kemp & Rutter, *supra* note 7.

[20] Barsness & Bhappu, *supra* note 3.

[21] Simon S. K. Lam & John Schaubroeck, *Improving Group Decisions by Better Pooling Information: A Comparative Advantage of Group Decision Support Systems*, 85 JOURNAL OF APPLIED PSYCHOLOGY 565-573 (2000).

[22] Jay F. Nunamaker, et al., *Information Technology for Negotiating Groups: Generating Options for Mutual Gain*, 37 MANAGEMENT SCIENCE 1325 (1991).

[23] Seymour Epstein, et al., *Individual Differences in Intuitive-Experimental and Analytical-Rational Thinking Styles*, 71 JOURNAL OF PERSONALITY AND SOCIAL PSYCHOLOGY 390 (1996).

[24] Michelle J. Gelfand & Naomi Dyer, *A Cultural Perspective on Negotiation: Progress, Pitfalls, and Prospects*, 49 APPLIED PSYCHOLOGY: AN INTERNATIONAL REVIEW 62 (2000).

[25] *Id.*

❧ 46 ❧

Strategic Moves and Turns

Deborah M. Kolb

Editors' Note: *In her well-known book on* The Shadow Negotiation, *Kolb focused on the ways in which women are often disadvantaged by the events and patterns that take place out of sight of the negotiating table. Here she has broadened the focus to include others, of any gender and culture, who find themselves "one down" in even trying to begin a serious discussion. If you have found yourself in this situation (and who hasn't?) Kolb has practical advice for you.*

Whenever negotiators bargain over issues—a contract, a budget, a schedule for a product's release, a change in policy—a parallel negotiation unfolds below the surface of the overt negotiation. Yes, people bargain over issues and interests; but they also negotiate how they are going to negotiate. All the time they are working on the issues, they are engaged in a shadow negotiation, in which they work out the terms of their relationship and the expectations they have of each other.[1] Even though the subject seldom comes up directly, they decide between themselves whose interests and needs will hold sway, whose opinions will matter, and how cooperatively they are going to work together.

The shadow negotiation refers to the parallel and complementary dynamic that occurs as parties work on the issues that separate them. It is not that these two processes are separable, but rather that we can look at what is occurring from these two perspectives. We can focus on how parties are dealing with their issues and working (or not) toward agreement. At the same time, we can pay attention to how what they say and what they do also captures a process of positioning (or challenges/acceptance of it).[2] Positioning in the shadow negotiation involves how parties manage impressions of themselves, how they claim and maintain legitimacy and credibility, how they assert what power and influence they have, and how they shape perceptions of what is possible. Central to the shadow negotiation is the idea of strategic moves, and the turns that are used to respond to moves.

Strategic Moves: Power, Process and Appreciative Moves

Strategic moves are actions negotiators take to position themselves (and others) in the negotiation process. There are many situations where negotiators find it difficult to enlist another party to bargain with them. Even when they sit at the same 'table,' it can still be a challenge to get one's ideas heard. Differences in power and position can explain why it may be difficult to get another party to the 'table." Subordinates, for example, must pay acute attention to the demands of a superior and can encounter real difficulty when the time comes to get a boss to listen to their demands. Managers who are in the minority due to their race or gender can find themselves excluded from important networks. [Kolb & Putnam, *Gender*] They may have neither the personal clout and experience nor the organizational standing to convince others that negotiations should start. Further, assumptions about a bargainer's probable behavior can work against her demands and ideas being heard. Someone who is expected to be accommodating, for example, encounters more resistance in bringing others to the table and usually is expected to make more concessions once there.[3]

Strategic moves are intended to bolster perceptions of interdependence so that the other party will rethink their reluctance and start negotiations. In situations where the other party sees no compelling need to negotiate, *power moves* can help bring them to the table. We have identified two major types of power moves: the use of incentives, and raising the costs of the status quo.[4] Incentives emphasize the value proposition—what the other side gets in return, and how negotiating works to its advantage. Raising the costs acts as a pressure lever to underscore the consequences to the other side if it continues to hold out. By enlisting the support of allies the bargainer can further reinforce these incentives or increase the pressure.

In situations where the dynamics of the decision-making process threaten to overpower a negotiator's voice, *process moves* can reshape the negotiation's structure. Process moves, while they do not directly address a bargainer's specific interests, do directly affect the hearing those interests are likely to get. Working behind the scenes, indirectly, to seed ideas or to marshal support before an agenda becomes fixed in anyone's mind can frame the discussion in ways that work to a negotiator's advantage. Process moves, in other words, can influence how receptive others will be to ideas and proposals.

Where talks stall because the other party feels pushed or misunderstandings cloud the issues, *appreciative moves* can foster participation. These moves are appreciative in the sense that they demonstrate that a negotiator accepts that people resist or reject ideas for good strategic reasons from their perspective. The challenge is to understand those reasons. By demonstrating appreciation (authentically), these moves can encourage the other party to engage in a more open dialogue on the issues. Appreciation focuses on face-saving moves, on drawing out and respecting others' perspectives, and on a commitment to keeping dialogue and chains of communication open. Appreciation conveys the importance placed on these perspectives and the opinions, ideas, and feelings that shape them.

Power, process, and appreciative moves are tools bargainers use to manage the shadow negotiation, where the perceptions of relative need and hidden agendas play out. Differences in power and position can put a bargainer in a "one-down" position in the shadow negotiation and make it difficult to engage the other side. Which moves a bargainer employs depends on the particular challenge he or she faces. Most often they are best used in combination and/or sequentially. Power moves encourage the other party to recognize the need to negotiate in the first place. They help bring a reluctant bargainer to the table. Process moves structure the negotiation in ways that create a context in which he or she can be effective— shaping the agenda and the dynamic. Appreciative moves develop openness and trust in the shadow negotiation so that all parties are more likely to want to work together.

Moves and Turns

Negotiators use strategic moves to position themselves to advantage in negotiations. In making these moves, negotiators want to position themselves as competent and legitimate, in order to be credible advocates for themselves and their interests. As such they are part of the normal by-play of negotiations. As parties advocate for themselves in order to create and claim value, their moves can have the effect of putting the other negotiator in a defensive position.[5] From a delegitimated or defensive position, it is then difficult for the other party to advocate for herself in a ways that further the negotiation agenda.[6] That is the risk of using certain strategic moves: in moving to put oneself into a good position, the effect can be to challenge some aspect of the position the other negotiator is claiming. The moves that are of interest are ones that challenge a negotiator's own presentation of self and/or puts him on the defensive so that he finds it hard to advocate credibly. Several of the most common moves—typically, power moves—include:

Challenging Competence or Expertise
With these moves, claims of experience and expertise are called into question. In a contract negotiation, for example, the move—"your fees are way out of line with what you deliver"—calls into question the value of the product/service. The implication is that asking for higher fees is not possible.

Demeaning Ideas
With these moves, the ideas themselves are attacked in ways that give the proponent little room to respond. Saying something like, "you can't be serious about this proposal," makes the idea and the proponent sound ridiculous. Obviously, these moves make it more difficult to argue for what might otherwise be a reasonable idea.

Criticizing Style
Using phrases like "don't get so upset;" "you are so greedy;" "stop being so difficult;" the person—who he/she is, and how he/she acts—becomes the subject of the move. To be challenged as overreacting or inconsiderate positions a negotiator as an irrational person who cannot be reasoned with, or who is selfish or not nice. Theses moves can call forth unfortunate stereotypes such as the hysterical female.[7] They can be unsettling, as few of us think of ourselves as unreasonable, difficult or greedy.

Making Threats
Threats are used to try to force a choice on a negotiator: "Cut your rates or there is no deal." As assertions of power, these moves can back a negotiator into a corner, making it risky to propose some other solution.

Appealing for Sympathy or Flattery
The moves described thus far have been critical of the person and his/her ideas. But in everyday negotiation, operative in the workplace, appeals for sympathy and flattery also can be quite powerful. When people say, "I know you won't let me down" or "I really need your help on this," they are counting on the move to silence, to make it difficult to advocate and press one's ideas.

Strategic moves like these five (and there are likely variants), can be seen as situated exercises of power meant to put a person in his place.[8] In the interactive by-play, these moves effectively position the recipient of the move in a one-down, defensive position. To have one's competence, motives, ideas, legitimacy, and style challenged as the other party presses for advantage not only questions the potential argument or claim a negotiator wants to make, it can also undermine the negotiator's sense of self competence and confidence. In a one-down position, the other negotiator can have the advantage.

Strategic moves present the recipient with a choice. He can make a countermove or he can turn it. Moves are most likely to be responded to with defensive countermoves which are comebacks in kind. For example, when somebody says, "Don't get so upset," a countermove would be, "I am not upset." Similarly, to claim one is not difficult or greedy in response to accusations that one is, tends to reinforce the previous moves. That is, the recipient of the move stays in the original, defensive position. One of the reasons that defensive countermoves are so common is because negotiators do not recognize that a move is being used, so they respond emotionally and defensively.

Strategic moves can also be ignored. For example, in a sales negotiation, when the buyer of advertising from a TV station mentions the poor ratings of a show under discussion, the seller can just ignore the aspersion. Of course the move has been made and it sits there. It is not clear whether the seller agrees or not. When seriously demeaning moves are made about sex or race, to ignore them is potentially to collude in that positioning.[9] Remaining silent implicitly reinforces racist or sexist aspersions.

But moves can be resisted through the use of turns.[10] Turns are intended to change the dynamics of the interactions. First, as responses to moves, turns are moments of potential resistance, where the recipient of the move refuses to take up the defensive position in which she is placed. Second, turns change meaning and so can re-position the person. Turns shift the meaning of the move: they resist the positioning and reframe it. When meanings are unstable, as they are in an unfolding negotiation where two or more interpretations exist at any given moment, these indirect methods or turns can reframe how parties are viewed. A repertoire of turns, such as interrupting the action, naming a challenge, questioning the move, correcting impressions, and diverting to the problem, are means negotiators use to resist the positioning.

Interruption. Interrupting the action disrupts the move. Even the shortest break—getting up from the table, taking a drink of water—shifts the dynamic. People are not in precisely the same position after it.

Naming. To name a move signals recognition of what is occurring. It suggests that the negotiator is not taken in. The turner, in other words, rejects the positioning. To the move, "do not get so upset," a naming turn could be: "I am surprised you said that."

Questioning. Questioning suggests something puzzling about a move. Rather than directly naming a move, to question it is to throw it back to the mover—implying one is not sure what prompted it. "Upset? I am not clear what you mean." would use a question to turn the move.

Correcting. A correcting turn substitutes a different version or motivation to the one the move implied. Rather than just rejecting the positioning, a correcting turn constructs a different positioning for the turner that can neutralize the move. "I always get excited when issues matter to me" would correct the move.

Diverting. A diverting turn shifts the focus to the problem itself. It is a way of ignoring the implication of the move but also has the negotiator take control of the process. "Let's not focus on my emotional state and figure out what we need to do" is a way to divert the move.

Just as strategic moves can be used to bolster one's position vis-à-vis the other party and/or as a means to enlist the other to work together, there are analogous choices in the use of turns.

Equity Turns

Equity turns are used to establish some sense of parity in a negotiation. When competence, ideas, or style are challenged, the negotiator turns the move in order to try to level the playing field. Without a negotiator who is equally able to advocate for herself, there is little incentive for the other party to engage in serious negotiations, particularly the work of mutual gains negotiation. That is, the other party needs a credible advocate, not a defensive wimp, in order to engage. Power moves, which bring people to the table to seriously negotiate, and equity turns are a means to promote interdependence in negotiation. Moves that serve to disempower or put a party on the defensive can be seen as an action by the mover to assert control in the process. These moves signal that the mover sees herself in a one-up position and hence less dependent on the outcome of the negotiation.

What follows is that the target of the move is seen in a one-down position and more dependent. By turning such moves, the target resists this definition. By turning the move, the turner encourages the mover to reconsider; they are more interdependent than the mover might want to acknowledge. In this way, equity turns in the shadow negotiation are one of the ways parties negotiate power and control. Naming and correcting turns are more likely to function in this way and are more common in the earlier stages of a negotiation.[11]

Participative Turns

Just as appreciative moves, like face-saving and drawing out the other's perspective, are used to engage the other parties, so participative turns, in response to moves, can serve a similar function. Whereas equity turns can put the other party on the defensive, participative turns position the other party more as a partner. Turns are participative when they are phrased in such a way that they leave space for the other person to talk from her own legitimate, not defensive, position. These turns acknowledge the problem, but open up the possibility that both can talk about the situation. They can shift the negotiation from blaming and defending to an exploration of what may be possible in the circumstances. Questioning and diverting turns are more likely to accomplish this end.

In an interesting example from the world stage, in trade negotiations between U.S. Trade Representative Charlene Barshefsky and her Chinese counterpart over intellectual property, Barshefsky used interruption and diverting turns *participatively* in response to a threat.

> Menacingly, he (Chinese negotiator) leaned forward across the table toward Barshefsky and said flatly, "It's take it or leave it." Barshefsky, taken aback by the harsh tone, surprised her counterpart by sitting quietly. She waited 30-40 seconds—an eternity given the intensity of the negotiation—and came back with a measured reply: "If the choice is take or leave it, of course I'll leave it. But I can't imagine that's what you meant. I think what you mean is that you'd like me to think over your last offer and that we can continue tomorrow." [12]

Barshefsky's *participative turn* of the threat disrupted it and resulted in a major compromise the next morning. The *interruption* (her silence) was important; it enabled her to reassert control. Further, her *diverting turn* signaled her intention to revise the Chinese negotiator's offer, but did it in a way that gave him space to back down. In this case, her turning a threat signaled that this tactic would not work and pushed the *mover* to reconsider.

Both equity and participative turns have the potential to be critical in shifting a negotiation. Equity turns can involve each party testing the other's mettle. Such posturing can move the negotiations along. Of course, it is also possible that this kind of posturing can result in backlash and impasse. Participative turns seem to be more likely to lead to positive transitions and even the possibility that some forms of transformation might occur.[13]

There's more to negotiation than haggling over issues and working out solutions. The shadow negotiation, though often overlooked, is a critical parallel process to the work negotiators do on their substantive issues. At and away from the bargaining table, negotiators proactively use a range of strategic moves that get negotiations going and moving in a particular direction. Whether a bargainer uses power, process, or appreciative moves in the shadow negotiation depends on the demands of the situation. Power moves encourage another party to recognize the need to negotiate in the first place. [Hawkins, et al., *Access*] Process moves create a context in which a bargainer can shape the negotiation agenda and dynamic so that he or she can be a more effective advocate. Appreciative moves engage the other party in a collaborative exchange by fostering more trust and, possibly, candor in the shadow negotiation. At the same time once into the negotiations, a person can be on the receiving end of strategic moves by the other party(s) that can put her on the defensive. It is difficult to negotiate proactively from a defensive position. Effective negotiators use a range of *turns* to shift the dynamics by leveling the playing field and/or by fostering participation. A consideration of strategic moves, and turns in response to them, opens a window into an often overlooked dimension of negotiations—how parties position themselves relative to each other. This parallel process is worthy of further investigation.

Endnotes

[1] *See* DEBORAH M. KOLB & JUDITH WILLIAMS, EVERYDAY NEGOTIATION (rev. ed. 2003); DEBORAH M. KOLB & JUDITH WILLIAMS, THE SHADOW NEGOTIATION (rev. ed. 2000).

[2] Positioning should not be confused with position. Bronwyn Davies, and Rom Harre, *Positioning: The Discursive Production of Selves*, 1 JOURNAL OF THE THEORY OF SOCIAL BEHAVIOR 43 (1990).

[3] Carol Rose contends, for example, that it does not matter whether women are or are not more inclined to cooperation and accommodation in their negotiations. The assumption that they are makes the job of getting people to the table more difficult and the pressure to make concessions, once there, almost inevitable. Carol Rose, *Bargaining and Gender*, 18 HARVARD JOURNAL OF LAW & PUBLIC POLICY 547 (1995).

[4] *See* Deborah M. Kolb & Judith Williams, *Breakthrough Bargaining*, 2001 HARVARD BUSINESS REVIEW (Feb. 2001).

[5] This notion of strategic moves and their potential effect on negotiators needs to be distinguished from other tactics that appear similar. One type discussed widely in the literature is so called "dirty tricks" where negotiators employ some familiar tactics, such as good cop-bad cop, or blinding light in the eyes in order to throw the other negotiator off. ROGER FISHER, ET AL., GETTING TO YES: NEGOTIATING AGREEMENT WITHOUT GIVING IN 136 (2d ed. 1991). Strategic moves, as we use them here, are not necessarily malicious in intent, nor even intentional, in the sense that they are meant to put off the other party, although they can be. As part of the normal by-play of the negotiations, they occur as one party tries to advocate effectively for himself.

[6] *See* Sara Cobb, *Empowerment and Mediation: A Narrative Perspective*, 9 NEGOTIATION JOURNAL 245 (1993); KOLB & WILLIAMS, EVERYDAY NEGOTIATION, *supra* note 1.

[7] SILVIA GHERARDI, GENDER, SYMBOLISM, AND ORGANIZATIONAL CULTURES (1995).

[8] The focus on the dispersion of power and its multiple modes of functioning has helped scholars focus on the micro processes that construct gender in the workplace. Joanne Martin & Debra Meyerson, *Women and Power: Conformity, Resistance, and Disorganized Coaction*, in POWER AND INFLUENCE IN ORGANIZATIONS (Roderick M. Kramer & Margaret A. Neale eds., 1998); JOYCE K. FLETCHER, DISAPPEARING ACTS: GENDER, POWER, AND RELATIONAL PRACTICE AT WORK (1999). It also serves to empower people in workplace interactions to resist these exercises of power. DEBRA MEYERSON, TEMPERED RADICALS: HOW PEOPLE USE DIFFERENCE TO INSPIRE CHANGE AT WORK (2001).

[9] *See* GHERARDI, *supra* note 7; KOLB & WILLIAMS, EVERYDAY NEGOTIATION, *supra* note 1.

[10] Turns can be seen as exercises of resistance. By recognizing the ways social structures operate through micro processes of power in commonplace interactions, individuals can act individually and collectively to change narratives that position them to disadvantage. PATRICIA EWICK AND SUSAN SILBEY, THE COMMON PLACE OF LAW: STORIES FROM EVERYDAY LIFE (1998).

[11] Deborah M. Kolb, *Staying in the Game or Changing It: An Analysis of* Moves *and* Turns *in Negotiation*, 20 NEGOTIATION JOURNAL 253 (2004).

[12] James K. Sebenius & Rebecca Hulse, *Harvard Business School Case: Charlene Barshefsky (B)* (2001).

[13] It is important to note, that recognizing a move as such and acting to turn it is not always clear cut. I have observed how overtures intended to uncover interests and learn more about a party's situation can often be read as a move. For example, in a buyer-seller negotiation, one can ask about the success of the seller's product or service or what her aspirations are for how it will do in the future. This kind of inquiry can lead to the creation of contingent agreements Max H. Bazerman & James J. Gillespie, *Betting on the Future: The Virtues of Contingent Contracts*, 1999 HARVARD BUSINESS REVIEW 155-60 (Sept. 1999). However, it can also be read as a move to discredit the seller's service. Rather than being forthcoming about aspirations (a good thing), the seller gets into a defensive mode or tries to turn what they misread as a move (a bad thing).

❧ 47 ❧

Creativity and Problem-Solving

Jennifer Gerarda Brown

Editors' Note: *It's routine for people to recognize that negotiations demand creativity. It also seems routine for negotiations to result in rather uncreative solutions, in which many opportunities for a better deal all around were missed. In this chapter, Brown suggests some ways to break out of the predictable—and to get your counterpart to do so too. This chapter should be read in conjunction with the very different forms of creativity discussed in LeBaron & Honeyman on Arts.*

Negotiation experts seem to agree that creative solutions are often the key to reaching value-maximizing outcomes in integrative, interest-based bargaining. Sticking to the problem as it is initially framed and considering only the solutions that most readily present themselves will sometimes yield optimal results, but more often, situations will require the parties and their representatives to think more expansively. This process of thinking more expansively is often referred to as creativity or creative thinking. Some commentators distinguish creative thinking from creativity, arguing that creativity "is more value-laden and tends to be often linked with art (in its broad sense)".[1] Creativity might seem to resemble any other artistic quality, something people lack or possess as much as a matter of genetics as anything else. And yet, like other artistic qualities (observation, hand-eye coordination, vocabulary, or writing skills), creativity may be teachable—or at least, whatever quantity one has as a matter of natural endowment might be enhanced with the right training.[2] On the theory that both creativity and creative thinking can be enhanced with some training and work, this essay will use the terms interchangeably.

The focus of this chapter will be on some methods for teaching and practicing creativity. I discuss the technique most commonly taught in negotiation courses as well as some newer, perhaps more obscure methods. This chapter closes with some questions about the applicability of "creative thinking" to the field of negotiation.

Beyond Brainstorming

Most teachers and trainers of interest-based negotiation will spend some time teaching creative thinking. Following the template set forth in *Getting to Yes*, they will encourage their students to "brainstorm." Brainstorming is a somewhat formalized process in which participants work together to generate ideas. I say that it is formalized because it proceeds according to two important ground rules: participants agree not to evaluate the ideas while they are brainstorming, and they agree not to take "ownership" of the ideas. They strive to generate options and put them on the table, no matter how wacky or far-fetched they may seem. The "no evalua-tion" rule encourages participants to suspend their natural urge to criticize, edit, or censor the ideas. Evaluation can come later, but the notion here is that solutions will flow more easily if people are not assessing them even as they articulate them. The "no ownership" rule also facilitates innovation because participants are en-couraged to feel free to propose an idea or solution without endorsing it—no one can later attribute the idea to the person who proposed it, or try to hold it against that person. People can therefore propose ideas that might actually disadvantage them and benefit their counterparts without conceding that they would actually agree to such proposals in the final analysis.[3] The ground rules for brainstorming constrain the natural inclination to criticize, so that participants are free to imag-ine, envision, and play with ideas, even though these processes come less easily to them.

Why is brainstorming so popular, both in practice and in negotiation training? Perhaps the answer lies not so much in what it activates, but in what it disables. What I mean is that it may be easier to teach people what *not* to do—rather than what to do affirmatively—in order to enhance their creative thinking. We may not know much about how to unleash new sources of creativity for negotiators, but we're pretty sure about some things that impede creative thinking. Theory and practice suggest that creative thinking is difficult when people jump to conclu-sions, close off discussion, or seize upon an answer prematurely. Indeed, the very heuristics that make decision-making possible—those pathways that permit peo-ple to make positive and sometimes normative judgments [Korobkin & Guthrie, *Heuristics*]—can lead people astray. One of the ways they may be led astray is that the heuristic prompts them to decide too quickly what something is or should be. Once judgment has occurred, it is tough to justify the expenditure of additional energy that creative thinking would require. Creativity could be considered the "anti-heuristic"; it keeps multiple pathways of perception and decision-making open, even when people are tempted to choose a single, one-way route to a solu-tion. If we do nothing else, we can attempt to delay this kind of judgment until negotiators have considered multiple options. Brainstorming provides the struc-ture for this kind of delay.

But is brainstorming the only technique for enhancing creativity? The answer would seem to be an easy "no." Psychologists and other specialists in creative thinking have much to teach us beyond brainstorming.[4] In a *Clinical Law Review* article, Janet Weinstein and Linda Morton survey some of the literature on "crea-tive thinking" and suggest "several specific techniques to encourage its inception."[5] Barry Nalebuff and Ian Ayres have similarly proposed specific tech-niques to facilitate creative problem-solving.[6] This section will summarize these suggestions.

Wordplay
Once an issue or problem is articulated, it is possible to play with the words ex-pressing that problem in order to improve understanding and sometimes to yield new solutions.

Shifting Emphasis
To take a fairly simple example, suppose that two neighbors are in a dispute be-cause cigarette butts and other small pieces of trash, deposited by Mr. Smith in his own front yard, are blowing into Mr. Jones's yard, and those that remain in Mr. Smith's yard are detracting from the appearance of the neighborhood (at least as Mr. Jones sees it). Mr. Jones might ask himself (or a mediator at the neighborhood justice center), "How can I get Mr. Smith to stop littering in his yard?" Shifting

the emphasis in this sentence brings into focus various aspects of the problem and suggests possible solutions addressing those specific aspects. Consider the different meanings of the following sentences:

"How can *I* get Mr. Smith to stop littering in his yard?"
"How can I get *Mr. Smith* to stop littering in his yard?"
"How can I get Mr. Smith to stop *littering* in his yard?"
"How can I get Mr. Smith to stop littering in *his* yard?"
"How can I get Mr. Smith to stop littering in his *yard*?"

As the focus of the problem shifts, so too different potential solutions might emerge to address the problem as specifically articulated.[7]

Changing a Word

Sometimes changing a word in the sentence helps to reformulate the problem in a way that suggests new solutions. In the example above, Mr. Jones might change the phrase "littering in his yard" to something else, such as "neglecting his yard" or "hanging out in his yard." It may be that something besides littering lies at the root of the problem, and a solution will be found, for example, not in stopping the littering, but in more regularized yard work.[8]

Deleting a Word

Through word play, parties can delete words or phrases to see whether broadening the statement of the problem more accurately or helpfully captures its essence. Mr. Jones might delete the phrase "Mr. Smith" from his formulation of the problem. He would ask not "How can I get Mr. Smith to stop littering in his yard?" but rather "How can I stop littering [more generally]?" and thereby discover that it is not just Mr. Smith's yard, but the entire street, that is looking bad. Focusing on Mr. Smith as the source of the problem may be counterproductive; Mr. Jones might discover that he needs to organize all of the homeowners on his block to battle littering in order to make a difference. Deleting words sometimes spurs creativity by removing an overly restrictive focus on the issue or problem.[9]

Adding a New Word

A final form of word play that can spur creative thinking is sometimes called "random word association."[10] Through this process, participants choose a word randomly and then think of ways to associate it with the problem. Suppose Mr. Jones and Mr. Smith were given the word "work"[11] and asked how it might relate to their dispute. Here are some possible results:

Work (time, effort): Mr. Smith will try to work harder to keep his yard looking nice, and he'll check Mr. Jones's yard every Saturday to make sure there are no cigarette butts or other pieces of trash in it.

Work (being operational or functional): What the neighborhood needs is a sense of cohesion; Mr. Jones and Mr. Smith will organize a neighborhood beautification project to try to instill a sense of community among their neighbors.

Work (job): Because Mr. Smith's odd working hours sometimes lead him to smoke on his front porch and chat with his friends or family late at night (after Mr. Jones has gone to bed), Mr. Smith will stay in the back of his house after 10 p.m., further from Mr. Jones's bedroom window.

As the different meanings and resulting associations of "work" are explored by the parties, they discover new ways to solve their shared problem. Other seemingly unrelated words might trigger still more associations and more potential solutions.

Adding words can also be helpful if participants insert adjectives that narrow the problem so it appears more manageable. Mr. Jones might ask, "How can I get Mr. Smith to stop littering in his *front* yard?" Narrowing the problem from all of

Mr. Smith's property to the front yard might suggest agreements that could keep Mr. Smith's front yard looking nice but still permit him to use other parts of his property (such as a side or back yard) as he wishes. This approach to word play builds upon the insight that many creative solutions are incremental. The problem will not seem so daunting to the parties when it is narrowed, and they can address the larger issues step by step.[12]

These techniques of word play (especially random word association) are designed to "force the mind to 'jump across' its usual pathways (mental ruts), or make new connections between old pathways in order to create a new idea out of two seemingly disparate ideas."[13] The exercises might feel mechanical to the parties at first, but if adopted with some energy and good faith, they could help the parties to enhance the creativity of their thinking.

Mind-Mapping/Word Clustering

Weinstein and Morton also describe a form of word association called "Word Clustering" or "Mind Mapping," in which participants write the problem out and then write down words that come to mind, randomly, as related to the problem. The words are written without any particular order all over a paper, and once that aspect is completed, lines are drawn connecting the words as connections come to mind.[14]

This technique, they explain, can help participants discover the inner pathways by which their brains are connecting aspects of the problem in hidden ways. These connections can then lead parties to creative ideas about the problem.[15]

De Bono's "Six Hats" Technique

Edward de Bono has proposed a technique he calls "Six Thinking Hats," in which six aspects of a problem are assessed independently. As problem-solvers symbolically don each of six differently colored hats, they focus on an aspect of the problem associated with each color: red for emotions, white for facts, yellow for positive aspects of the situation, green for future implications, black for critique, and blue for process.[16] As Weinstein and Morton point out, the technique of isolating the black/critique hat may be especially important for lawyers, whose tendency to move quickly into a critical mode may prevent them from seeing other important aspects of a problem.[17] If the black hat is worn at or near the end of the process, the Six Hats technique displays a characteristic shared by brainstorming: it delays critique and judgment until other approaches can be tried. And shutting down judgment may enable creativity, as suggested above. By forcing themselves to address separately the emotional, factual, and process issues at stake in a problem, parties may discover room for creative solutions. Creative solutions are sometimes found in the terms of a future relationship between the parties. Wearing the "green hat" may force participants to come to terms with a future they would rather ignore.

The prospect of changing hats, even (perhaps especially) if it is done symbolically, could make some participants uncomfortable. Negotiators and neutrals should bear in mind that age, sex, ethnicity and other cultural specifics may create dignitary interests for some participants that would be threatened or compromised by some techniques for boosting creative thought. Some people would feel embarrassed or humiliated if they were asked to engage in the theatrics required by some of these exercises. For others, the chance to pretend or play might be just the prod they need to open new avenues of thought. In a spirit of flexibility (surely a necessary condition for creativity), therefore, one should be thinking of ways to modify these techniques to fit other needs of the parties. For example, the Six

Hats technique could be transformed into a "Six Flip Charts" exercise using differently colored paper or markers to signal the different focus of each inquiry

Atlas of Approaches

Another technique for stimulating creative ideas about a problem from a variety of perspectives is called the "Atlas of Approaches." Roger Fisher, Elizabeth Kopelman and Andrea Kupfer Schneider propose this approach in *Beyond Machiavelli*, their book on international negotiation.[18] Using the Atlas of Approaches technique, participants adopt the perspectives of professionals from a variety of fields. By asking themselves, for example, "what would a journalist do?", "what would an economist do?", "how would a psychologist view this?", and so on, negotiators are able to form a more interdisciplinary view of their problem. With this more complete picture of the issues and potential outcomes, they might be able to connect disciplines in ways that give rise to creative solutions.

Visualization

When parties use the visualization technique, they take time to imagine the situation they desire, one in which their problem is solved. What do they see? What specific conditions exist, and how might each of those conditions be achieved? Weinstein and Morton suggest that parties can engage in visualization simply by closing their eyes and thinking about the problem in terms that are visual rather than abstract.[19] Another approach is to "look at the problem from above, and see things otherwise invisible."[20] The goal is to deploy a variety of the brain's cognitive pathways (verbal, visual, spatial & abstract), the better to make connections that give rise to creative solutions.

"WWCD": What Would Croesus Do?

This process requires a participant to take the perspective of an unconstrained actor. What solutions suggest themselves if we assume no limit to available money, time, talent, technology, or effort? Nalebuff and Ayres explain: "Croesus (rhymes with Jesus) was the supremely rich king of Lydia (modern Turkey), reigning from 560 to 546 B.C. His wealth came from mining gold.... His lavish gifts and sacrifices made his name synonymous with wealth. Even today we say 'rich as Croesus.'"[21] In some ways, one could think of the WWCD method as a more specific application of brainstorming. As the proponents of brainstorming are quick to point out, creativity and the free flow of ideas can be impeded by criticism or assessment. WWCD takes off the table any assessment based on constraints—financial, technological, etc. If we assume that we can afford and operationalize any solution we can come up with, what might we discover?

A second phase of this approach requires participants to think about the extent to which their unconstrained solution might be modified to make it workable given the existing constraints.[22]

"Feel My Pain"

Sometimes people find creative solutions by focusing sharply on the specific sorts of harm caused by the problem. When one person's decision-making has negative spillover effects on others, economists say that the person's decision or activity is creating "negative externalities."[23] Nalebuff and Ayres argue that "there can be great payoffs to asking whether you're feeling other people's pain," because "[i]gnoring others' interests leads to inefficient decisions."[24] Solutions to this call for the parties to design "incentives so that all parties more fully feel the impacts that their decisions have on each other."[25]

Flipping or Reversal

With this technique, one asks whether flipping or reversing a given situation will work. As Edward de Bono explains,

> In the reversal method, one takes things as they are and then turns them round, inside out, upside down, back to front. Then one sees what happens ... one is not looking for the right answer but for a different arrangement of information which will provoke a different way of looking at the situation.[26]

Chris Honeyman sometimes uses this technique in his work as a neutral when he asks the parties to put forward some really *bad* ideas for resolving the conflict.[27] When people offer ideas in response to a call for "bad" ideas, they may free themselves to offer the ideas they partially or secretly support; again, as in brainstorming, they disclaim ownership of the ideas. It is also possible that the instruction to offer bad ideas stimulates creative thinking because it can seem *funny* to people. Humor is a good stimulant for creativity.[28]

Chris Honeyman's theory is that bad ideas are easy to come by (they can often be found in abundance), and in many bad ideas there resides the kernel of a good idea. Framing them as "bad" ideas effects a sort of reversal or flipping; in de Bono's words, the participants produce a "different arrangement of information."[29] Carrie Menkel-Meadow suggests that negotiators or parties to mediation use another form of reversal when they engage in "perspective-taking" or "role-reversal" exercises.[30]

Most conflicts are multidimensional, giving rise to multiple sites at which elements could be reversed. Once the parties have broken down the situation into component parts, they can try reversing or flipping some elements to see whether this yields superior solutions.

Idea Arbitrage

With idea arbitrage, parties see an existing solution in one context and ask themselves where else it might work.[31] A great example of this from the field of consumer products design is the electric toothbrush with rotating bristles. Nalebuff and Ayres point out that this terrific invention actually grew out of a much more trivial discovery—the rotating lollipop![32] The inventors of the lollipop knew they had a good thing, so they looked for new places to put it to use. Similar stories can be told about Velcro or polycarbonate wheels.[33] This building upon prior discovery is the root of creativity in art and science.[34] With idea arbitrage, the creativity stems from solutions—that is, expanding the problems to which an existing solution may be applied, rather than from a focus on the problems themselves. This approach assumes that there are solutions in search of problems, rather than the other way around.

Toys

A final technique for stimulating creativity would be a no-brainer for anyone under 16 (and for some of us who are considerably older than that): Toys! One former colleague of mine used to bring a Nerf basketball hoop to class occasionally to permit students to take a shot after a particularly insightful answer. I've allowed students to earn extra credit in a professional responsibility course by scripting and performing skits (or "role plays," to use a more methodologically sober term). The students sometimes use costumes and props. Often amusing, these additional objects also seem to stimulate creative thinking in the audience as well as the performers.

Professor Barry Orton uses "Nerf weaponry" when facilitating negotiation of complex telecommunications disputes. He argues that the toys give people a harmless and humorous way to blow off steam and sometimes introduce an element of levity into tense situations.[35] At the conference giving rise to a Marquette Law Review symposium, Professor Andrea Schneider gave each participant a souvenir: a soft foam cube emblazoned with Marquette's logo and the motto "Think Outside the Box." These cubes became creativity-enhancing toys during discussions, as Andrea (and sometimes other participants) would toss them at people who made particularly wacky, off-the-wall, or obnoxious comments. As instruments of mock discipline, the cubes actually lightened the mood and became a kind of trophy (anyone who could say something funny or outrageous enough to deserve a cube toss was raising the creativity bar for everyone else).[36] At a conference designed to stimulate creative, collaborative discussions, the cubes were a fun and effective tool—made all the more so by the spontaneity of Professor Schneider's first toss.

Creative Thinking in Negotiation

I'll close with a few questions about creative thinking. First, can the techniques I've summarized here all find specific application in negotiation? Surely some of them will be less useful than others. WWCD, for example, may have limited use in most conflict situations. Suspending critique during brainstorming is one thing, but many negotiators will be reluctant to assume away *all* constraints. Or they may fear that WWCD discussions will be a waste of time, because once the constraints are again taken into account, the solution will go away entirely.

Idea Arbitrage might also seem to have limited applicability to most negotiations, because the very genesis of the negotiation is a *problem* to be solved, not a solution in search of a problem. On the other hand, Idea Arbitrage may be helpful as a persuasive tool—one that supports creativity. Suppose that a negotiator has come up with a creative solution to a problem, and knows that the solution has been used successfully in another context. Presenting the new, creative solution as an old idea rather than a new one may make it more acceptable to the other side. Lawyers, as we know, love precedent. Idea Arbitrage gives a creative solution a kind of pedigree or set of credentials it might otherwise lack if presented as a brand new idea. Perhaps persuasion is part of creativity—we need tools not only to generate creative thinking, but also to make the results of creative thinking more acceptable to our fellow problem-solvers. [Guthrie, *Compliance*] Thus, all of these techniques belong in the negotiator's toolbox, even if some will have more specialized applicability.

It also seems clear that the nature of the negotiation will strongly determine the kinds of creativity-enhancing techniques that are useful. Not all ideas will work as well in Dispute Settlement Negotiation as they do in Deal Making Negotiation.[37] Our field needs more work on creative thinking specific to the negotiation of disputes in order to improve the representation that clients eventually receive.

This chapter has collected just a few methods that could take negotiators beyond brainstorming when they want to inspire creative thinking. Often moments of inspiration come and go in a flash; we may retain the substantive result of our creativity, but we give little thought to the process—the chain of insights—generating our ideas. The challenge facing negotiation teachers and practitioners is to capture those moments and then analyze the steps (or to use less linear metaphors, the atmosphere or web of connections) that made the creative moments possible. Meeting this challenge requires attention to process as well as product in negotiation. But that is a focus both familiar and customary to negotiation theorists.

Endnotes

[1] Janet Weinstein & Linda Morton, *Stuck in a Rut: The Role of Creative Thinking in Problem Solving and Legal Education*, 9 CLINICAL LAW REVIEW 835, 838 (2003).

[2] *See generally* Carrie Menkel-Meadow, *Aha? Is Creativity Possible in Legal Problem Solving and Teachable in Legal Education*, 6 HARVARD NEGOTIATION LAW REVIEW 97, 122 (2001).

[3] For material on brainstorming, *see* ROGER FISHER, ET AL., GETTING TO YES: NEGOTIATING AGREEMENT WITHOUT GIVING IN 56-62 (2d ed. 1991); ROBERT MNOOKIN, ET AL., BEYOND WINNING: NEGOTIATING TO CREATE VALUE IN DEALS AND DISPUTES 37-39 (2000).

[4] On the other hand, empirical research on enhancing creativity is sparse, and much of what is said about it is probably speculative. Raymond Nickerson, *Enhancing Creativity, in* HANDBOOK OF CREATIVITY 392 (Robert J. Sternberg ed. 1999).

[5] Weinstein & Morton, *supra* note 1, at 837.

[6] BARRY NALEBUFF & IAN AYRES, WHY NOT? HOW TO USE EVERYDAY INGENUITY TO SOLVE PROBLEMS BIG AND SMALL (2003).

[7] *See id.* at 854.

[8] *Id.*

[9] Weinstein & Morton, *supra* note 1, at 854.

[10] *Id.* at 855. *See also,* PAUL E. PLSEK, CREATIVITY, INNOVATION AND QUALITY 42, 247-67 (1997).

[11] I actually chose this word semi-randomly by opening a book, closing my eyes, and pointing to the page. My finger landed on the word "work."

[12] *Supra* note 1, at 855. *See also* Carrie Menkel-Meadow, *The Lawyer as Problem Solver and Third-Party Neutral: Creativity and Non-Partisanship in Lawyering*, 72 TEMPLE LAW REVIEW 785, 798 (1999) (noting the "incremental and recursive" nature of some creativity or invention).

[13] Weinstein &Morton, *supra* note 1, at 856.

[14] *Id.* at 857-58.

[15] *Id. See also* TONY BUZAN, THE MIND MAP (1996); STEVEN EFFERT, CROSS-TRAIN YOUR BRAIN 75 (1999).

[16] EDWARD DE BONO, SIX THINKING HATS (1999).

[17] Weinstein & Morton, *supra* note 1, at 856-57. This is also consistent with the "no evaluation" ground rule in "brainstorming."

[18] ROGER FISHER, ET AL., BEYOND MACHIAVELLI: TOOLS FOR COPING WITH CONFLICT 67 (1996).

[19] Weinstein & Morton, *supra* note 1, at 859.

[20] *Id.*

[21] Nalebuff & Ayres, *supra* note 6, at 16. A more modern form of this question might be, "What Would Bill Gates Do?"

[22] *Id.* at 46.

[23] RICHARD POSNER, ECONOMIC ANALYSIS OF LAW (6th ed. 2002).

[24] NALEBUFF & AYRES, *supra* note 6, at 29.

[25] *Id.*

[26] EDWARD DE BONO, LATERAL THINKING (1977). *See also* NALEBUFF & AYRES, *supra* note 6, at 118.

[27] Telephone conversation with Christopher Honeyman, January 13, 2004.

[28] Clark Freshman, et al., *The Lawyer-Negotiator as Mood Scientist: What We Know and Don't Know about How Mood Relates to Successful Negotiation*, 2002 JOURNAL ON DISPUTE RESOLUTION 1 (2002) ("many studies of psychology and business school students show those in even mildly better moods—after smelling a pleasant scent, or watching a funny five minute video—do better at negotiation"); Roderick Kramer, et al., *Self-enhancement Biases and Negotiator Judgment: Effects of Self-Esteem and Mood*, 56 ORGANIZATION BEHAVIOR & HUMAN DECISION PROCESSES 110 (1993); Alice Isen, et al., *The Influent of Affect on Clinical Problem Solving*, 11 MEDICAL DECISION MAKING 221 (1991).

[29] De Bono, *supra* note 16.

[30] Menkel-Meadow, *supra* note 2, at 122.

[31] NALEBUFF & AYRES, *supra* note 6, at 29.

[32] *See id.* at 31-33 for a great retelling of the story, complete with pictures from the patent application for the lollipop.

[33] *Id.* at 30-31.

[34] Nickerson, *supra* note 4, at 393.

[35] Barry Orton, "Another Alternative Dispute Resolution Tool: Nerf Weaponry", presentation at Wisconsin Association of Mediators "Emerging Issues in Mediation" Conference, Madison, Wisconsin, November 7, 2003.

[36] Clearly, using toys can run into the same cultural/dignitary issues that arise with other forms of dramatic play. *See id.* Part I.C. In some cases the levity would be perceived as disrespect or lack or rigor. Barry Orton argues, however, that these forms of play may be modified for more serious settings. He cites a negotiation in which members of his team carried pens that also served as mini Nerf rocket launchers. By the end of the negotiation, his oh-so-serious counterparts on the other side of the table were asking to trade their matching silver pens for some rocket launchers; Orton declined the silver pens but purchased a set of the launcher-pens for his adversaries. The gift generated a great deal of good will. Orton, *supra* note 35.

[37] Frank E. Sander & Jeffrey Z. Rubin, *The Janus Quality of Negotiations: Dealmaking and Dispute Settlement*, 4 NEGOTIATION LAW JOURNAL 109 (1988).

෴ 48 ෴

Using the Creative Arts

Michelle LeBaron & Christopher Honeyman

Editors' Note: Why should we assume that minds and hearts are changed only at the bargaining table? Among the other settings that influence hearts and minds, the arts deserve a special place. Arts can make human understanding a little easier to achieve, and from a utilitarian perspective, the arts represent a whole series of alternative ways of getting at problems. This chapter uses the experience of a single, unusually arts-oriented city as a framework to examine what is possible.

Nous connaîtrons-nous seulement un peu nous-mêmes sans les arts
(Could we ever know each other in the slightest without the arts?)
—*Gabrielle Roy 1907-1983**

Imagine an airport lounge. Newspapers from around the world occupy stacked slots: together, they are a chorus of defeats and divisions—people fighting, losing, hurting, looking for revenge. These are graphic conflicts, captured in photos that shout desperation and discouragement.

After decades as conflict resolution practitioners and scholars, we know there are other stories, too—stories of hope, connection and human generosity. This chapter is about those stories, and how the creative arts are a resource to motivate, mobilize, and enlarge our perception of what can be done about conflicts. Often, when people think of "the arts," their points of reference are famous painters and sculptors, major museums, world-renowned film directors, and so on. But the arts operate at every level, so their use is within reach of everyday conflict managers. In this chapter, our examples will draw primarily on the local and regional; we have been influenced particularly by experience of Vancouver, Canada,[1] where community arts as ways of bridging differences are especially well-developed.

Einstein famously said that we cannot solve problems using the same thinking that created them;[2] it behooves us to step outside our rationalist logic to consider new uses for approaches that have worked for centuries to bring people together. Creative and community arts have long been resources for resolving conflicts, managing change and supporting community development. From theater, dance and music to commemorative rituals and community celebrations, the creative arts can serve as bridges across differences. They offer holistic ways to know ourselves and others, reconcile paradoxes and stitch torn relations. They may help shift the balance in difficult relationships where the focus is on struggle and reciprocal pain, offering creative and aesthetic pleasure as counterpoints. They arise from traditional wisdom as well as contemporary designs, braiding echoes of familiar identities with new ways forward.

Use of the arts as vehicles for addressing social conflict is as old as human history. Painting, photography, theatre, public rituals and many other forms have sensitized, galvanized, and catalyzed social change. Art often embraces difference and paradox, creating harmony from contrasts. Every mediator has a story of moments when bitter adversaries became, if only for a moment, humanized to each other. Even the most difficult chapters in our histories also contain beauty and moments of kindness. Since beauty and arts are life-affirming and liberating, why would we not see them as essential to our efforts to bridge differences? Artists' attention to expressing things beyond words, and their expertise in combining apparently disparate themes into stirring compositions, are important not only as inspirations for conflict resolution work, but as insights into methodology and approach. After all, what is conflict resolution but the reweaving of strands that seem disconnected—strands of identity, meaning and relationship?

Connecting conflict resolution and the arts is the focus of the *Conflict Resolution, Arts, and iNtercultural Experience* (CRANE) project.[3] Drawing on examples from the project and elsewhere, this chapter illustrates four ways creative arts contribute to conflict resolution across cultural differences. The arts:

- **shift relations**—inspiring audacity, imagination and courage in leaders, interveners and conflict parties;
- **facilitate creativity**—injecting artfulness into stuck places;
- **promote cultural fluency**—giving people ways to relate across diverse worldviews; and
- **offer innovative approaches to conflict**—inspiring holistic, generative ways to encompass paradoxes and differences.

We examine each of these possibilities in turn.

Shifting Relations

Conflict tends to narrow our range of perceptions, and ultimately, possibilities for collaborative engagement. Physiologically, it can trigger a fight-or-flight response that impairs cognitive ability and readies us to avoid or compete with others. [Yarn & Jones, *Biology*] Psychologically, it can reinforce reciprocal images of "the other" as threatening and difficult. Practically, it can lead to barriers rather than bridges. In the midst of escalating conflict across cultures or worldviews, leadership featuring audacity and imagination is sorely needed, yet often lacking.

Theatre and public rituals are powerful ways of uniting people across differences, especially in neighborhoods more often featured on the nightly news as sites of violence than as venues for creative celebrations. The very neighborhoods where many community artists live may feature contested identities, social strife and stretched community resources. Dolly Hopkins, a community arts leader, decided to do something to address divisions in a Vancouver neighborhood.[4] She confronted cultural conflict by working with community members to produce a lantern festival, *Illuminares*. This Trout Lake festival is now an annual event, drawing participants from across the region. Dozens of languages are spoken as people of many generations enjoy making colorful lanterns, then proceeding through a neighborhood where "othering" has given way to shared identities.

In applying the work of Augusto Boal, Hopkins demonstrates the power of theatrical enactments as rehearsals for social engagement. In the hands of the people, Boal argued, even scripted theatre is necessarily radical and political.[5] Headlines Theatre, a Vancouver-based company committed to social justice, uses "forum theater" (described below) to address issues including violence, suicide prevention, racism, youth empowerment, bullying and community development.[6] Theater has also been used as a tool for collaborative policy development, as in the production of *Moby Dick* across Alaska in 2002.[7] The play was staged specifically to begin a dialogue about some of Alaska's most divisive political, social and cultural issues, including subsistence rights and the urban/rural divide in disparate places across the state. Organizers tried several approaches, including Socratic dialogue in Fairbanks and Anchorage, and a culturally-grounded potluck in Barrow. These initiatives led them to conclude that meaningful input into policy is fostered when people share personal stories and connect them to larger narratives.

Of course, the arts—music, visual art, spoken word, film, theater, opera—have not always been used by leaders to unify. Powerful as they are, the arts can be used to manipulate, to amplify nationalism and exclusion. The early Nazi films of Leni Riefenstahl are obvious examples, but there are many others. Audacity, courage and imagination are needed to turn the arts to a focus on peace with justice and rapprochement without indignity or compromise. (Riefenstahl's postwar photographic work with the Nuba[8] can be seen, in fact, as the apologia of an exceptional artist who, in her earlier career, had much to answer for).

Whether used to bring people together or to highlight divisions, the arts open new possibilities and perspectives. They may be indirect in their methods and meanings or explicitly focused on social commentary and increasing possibilities for change. Contemporary art (though tending toward the indirect side of the continuum) is particularly useful in addressing conflict, because it encourages engaging multiple perspectives rather than resting in narrow positions. It can be dramatic and contrary to notions of propriety or expected normalcy. Modern art installations draw our attention to sensory distinctions, exquisite differences, and the continua that encompass fusions of beauty and struggle. These very qualities give the arts a dual function related to intercultural conflict; they are simultaneously inspiration and creative vehicles for shifting stuck relations.

Facilitating Creativity

Conflict resolution practitioners have recently shown increased interest in using creative resources and approaches. [Brown, *Creativity*] In part, this interest stems from awareness that rational, linear approaches to conflict resolution and community building do not completely address some of the challenges facing multicultural communities. It also arises from renewed interest in culturally-based traditions and approaches to conflict that have at least sometimes proven to be effective components in healing difficult conflicts. The arts and other cultural practices are a primary resource for a new edge of practice, offering new modes for engagement and diverse ways of perceiving and addressing divisive conflicts.

By relating in playful ways, sharing something joyful or beautiful, or working collectively to create a piece of art, people can develop a broader base for addressing differences. Music is one medium frequently used to bring people together. The film *Amandla! A Revolution in Four Part Harmony* portrays the role of music in challenging South African apartheid.[9] In communities across South Africa, people of groups kept painfully apart for decades began to sing. They sang their own groups' traditional songs, and unity songs that brought them together as South

Africans. Music was an essential part of the glue that made it possible to paste the pieces of a fractured political and social landscape back together. It was a medium for taking small, incremental steps toward national reconciliation and justice. Music also brought the country of Angola together after civil war when, led by rock musicians from opposite sides of the conflict, the entire country stopped one day at noon and participated in singing a song of peace.[10] In Norway, the Resonant Community project succeeded in reducing interethnic harassment by providing a musical venue for diverse groups to share.[11]

Rena Sharon, in an address to a summit on collaborative governance in the Asia Pacific region, advocated powerfully for music as a metaphor and vehicle for collaboration. She related a conversation with General Roméo d'Allaire, an obviously talented conflict manager,[12] but not an artist, in which he asked about the challenges of interpreting classical chamber music. "What is so complicated?" he asked straightforwardly. "Aren't all the instructions written out? Isn't it all predetermined by the composer?"[13]

D'Allaire's questions prompted Sharon, a professor of collaborative music from the University of British Columbia, to explore the fertility of music as a source of learning about conflict resolution. Drawing an analogy from chamber music performed without either a conductor or an authoritative interpretation from a (usually deceased) composer, she observes that the task of interpretation *"falls to the group of musicians to arrive at an interpretive collective agreement through democratic, non-hierarchical process."*[14] Not only is the process participatory and inclusive, it is subject to dire disagreements, as musicians from diverse backgrounds come carrying different ideas of right tempo, tone and treatment of a given piece of music. Sharon points out that what feels like essential truth to each individual musician will appear to be subjective misapprehension to his collaborative partners: a recipe for intractable conflict. Yet most of us have heard brilliant, fully "resolved" performances that display nothing of any conflict that attended the rehearsals.

One of the CRANE initiatives involves interviewing artists like Sharon about their creative processes. How do they make harmony in the midst of disagreement? How do they use the arts to disturb, yet also offer paths to constructive engagement rather than discouragement and disappointment? How does creativity help them work with paradox, and with each other, when they have different visions and philosophies? How might their artists' sensibilities and attention to what is beneath the surface help in addressing conflict? Which ways do they use to bring disparate, and sometimes contradictory, parts together into wholes?

M.C. Richards, the famous potter, gives us a clue about how one artist might answer these questions, in one of the last pieces she wrote before her death. She connects facility in handling conflict with creativity and inner development, which she says "may be measured by an ability to be peaceably at war, neither victorious nor defeated."[15] Richards goes on to describe the polarities that we must contain internally as well as externally:

> Nature tells us that we are self-directing, self-correcting organisms, who function therefore by a dynamic of polarities: in-breathing and out-breathing, sleeping and waking, expanding and contracting, seeking balance. Our inner development as persons comes about as we are able to bear the wholeness of these opposites, to experience them as mutually completing, as interdependent and interpenetrating, in some sense simultaneous. To see them, in other words, as *alive, moving and interweaving*, like the distinct and yet interflowing rivers that course through the oceans.[16]

As we foster the capacity to contain paradox in ourselves, we become more capable of responding creatively to conflicts, both internal and external. The projection of negative traits onto an "other" may be lessened when we can incorporate contradictions within ourselves. The desire to lash out, inflamed by conflict, may be tempered when we can creatively hold our intense emotions in a place of "witness," recognizing how anger is often escalated when it is an echo of past hurts, personal or collective. Creating art as a response to strong feelings may also help shift stuck dynamics, acting as catharsis and ritual. This account of an improvised dance routine during a large-scale public policy dispute resolution process illustrates the possibilities. Process designer Craig Darling tells how a story in the form of rap music acted as lubricant when a consensus process for making land-use choices across a wide area of Vancouver Island was stuck.

> (In this instance, participants) … had worked over several months to come to consensus about complex issues related to land use planning on the west coast of Canada. The parties felt frustration and discouragement as they came to the difficult issues and choices that confronted them in the final stages of their work. There had been acrimonious exchanges and it seemed possible that the process would break down. The group took a break.
>
> One of the sectors represented at the table was youth. After a break, the youth asked for an opportunity to present something to the group. They situated themselves in the center of the circle, and did a lively rap dance with lyrics addressed to the contentious issues and points of view. It was a stress reliever, an icebreaker and an injection of humor into a day that felt heavy. Participants relaxed. The rap "story" was the catalyst that broke the logjam, and they were able to move forward to resolve the contentious issues dividing them.[17]

Growing recognition of the validity, power and success of arts-based approaches—whether planned or serendipitous—has led to many new creative developments. The proliferation of dialogue-based and storytelling approaches is one example of a family of approaches that are now being used not only to address specific conflicts, but also in decision-making and consultative processes. For example, in Vancouver, storytelling through forum theater has been used to gather public input about homelessness and poverty, yielding a series of recommendations to the city council.[18] In Papua New Guinea, local mediation panels set up in rural areas used dialogue (in this context, the term is used to mean something closer to group storytelling than to negotiation) to resolve differences that threatened to erupt in violence.[19] In Boston, the Public Conversations Project[20] has pioneered creative ways to use metaphors and rituals in helping people dialogue across deep differences, from the ordination of gay community members in churches to conflicts over animal rights and social class.

Promoting Cultural Fluency

In Canada and the United States, conflicts over social issues such as abortion, capital punishment, or the place of gays, lesbians and transgendered people in congregations are not only divisive, but potentially explosive. They have torn communities and families apart, escalated violence, and led to tragic deaths. Cleavages related to class and religion continue to polarize discourse in Europe and elsewhere in the world. While rejecting the claim that we are engaged in a "clash of civilizations,"[21] we still must acknowledge that these social conflicts are carrying considerable ideological, political and emotional freight. Dynamics of power, privilege and uneven access to resources intertwined with stressed political and social systems make the need for civil dialogue more urgent and more challenging.

It is important to acknowledge that cultural or worldview differences are not inevitably the source of social conflicts. These differences shape diverse understandings and ways of communicating, and so may seem to cause conflicts. Cultural fluency—familiarity with ways that cultural understandings and starting points influence what seems "normal" and "natural"—shows us that differences themselves are seldom the source of conflicts. Rather, it is the ways differences are used to create boundaries between "us" and "other" that fuels conflict. Culturally fluent practitioners cultivate awareness of their own cultural lenses and openness to alternative ideas of "common sense." The arts are generative vehicles for this ongoing developmental process.

A recent production of Headlines Theatre in Vancouver illustrates how the arts can help foster cultural fluency. In 2004, several sensational articles in a Vancouver newspaper described problems with violence among Indo-Canadian young men. Generalizations abounded as difficulties were ascribed to the patriarchal nature of the society, intergenerational misunderstandings, and gang activity. David Diamond, the artistic director of the Theatre, engaged with Indo-Canadian community leaders and members, ultimately leading the development and staging of a production called *Here and Now*.

The play used forum theater, an approach that invites audience members to first watch a play, and then view it again, intervening at turning points by temporarily assuming roles in the play from which to try strategies for increasing safety. Through these productions, diverse audience members experienced resonance with the plight of the characters. They left knowing that no one community owns—or should be ascribed as owning—issues related to intergenerational conflict, youth identity struggles, and violence. Though no one named it, they left with increased cultural fluency.

During one recent staging of *Here and Now*, an audience member asked to take over the role of the sister of a boy just beginning to hang out with shady friends. Replacing the character's resignation with determination, she confronted, pleaded and even exposed her own nefarious activities to parents and grandmother in an attempt to change his course. The other members of the cast improvised, responding in character to this new portrayal of the sister/daughter/granddaughter. After letting it run for a few minutes, David Diamond called a pause, asking the characters to reflect on the effects of her intervention. Did it increase safety, or only galvanize the brother's determination to follow his path? Was her confrontational behavior helpful in changing the chain of events that the audience had seen unfold in the first staging of the play, or would it lead to an escalation? Diamond posed questions like these to the characters and the audience, stressing again and again that no one community has clear or uniform answers to these questions.

In the *Here and Now* production, intervention strategies tried by audience members each night of the production are recorded by a community scribe knowledgeable about social services. She gathers the desires and actions tried on the stage by audience members at each performance. These are later collated and analyzed for ideas to enhance existing community programs or inform new initiatives to enhance community safety. In this way, the impact of the production is leveraged far beyond those who actually attend performances.

Another example of the arts as a vehicle for cultural fluency and dialogue comes from a recent class taught by one of the authors in collaboration with Fanchon Silberstein, a docent at the Hirshhorn Museum in Washington, DC. As a learning community, the class identified that one of the most significant barriers to intercommunity and interfaith dialogue is fear. Later that day, we went as a group to the Hirshhorn Museum on the National Mall. On the outside of its concave exterior was a huge banner. Inscribed overhead in over ninety languages was a "global chorus" of the same message: "Don't be afraid."[22] These messages were handwritten by delegates to the United Nations and put onto a banner that stretched 30 feet by 70 feet across the main entrance to the museum. Standing beneath it looking up, class participants had a rich dialogue about its significance on the National Mall. They identified it as an antidote to the fear that suppresses dissent and as a powerful statement in a city that was targeted on September 11, 2001. They spoke of its form as a billboard, garnering attention while advertising a message more essential than the commerce and enterprise generally associated with this form. Dialogue about the stability of the United Nations ensued as we looked at the banner mounted on stone. The beauty of the various hands and scripts led participants to reflect on the rich possibilities when we come together across differences.

As this example illustrates, cultural fluency is best fostered through experience with diversity. It happens less when we are merely in the vicinity of difference, and more when we actually *engage* with people whose identities and ways of making meaning are different from our own. As Jim Hodges, the artist who created "Don't be Afraid" suggests, people and relationships are essential avenues to restoring a world out of control. People can be this avenue when they are open to complexity within and outside themselves, and when they are unafraid. The arts, because they offer pleasurable and non-threatening ways of experiencing differences, are among the most powerful vehicles for shifting conflict.

Offering Innovative Approaches to Conflict

Another aspect of the arts is the process of artistry by which products are created. Artistry connotes graceful invention. In human relations, artistry is the difference between a mechanical process and vibrant, creative engagement. Conflict resolution is increasingly being recognized as a blended art and science. Analysis is important, but without artistry it can become lifeless. When artistry is part of conflict resolution, imagination and intuition are invited into conflict management processes. Creativity is stimulated and celebrated. People find ways to hold the paradoxes of their lives within pictures expansive enough to accommodate seemingly opposed truths, and in a space that allows for exploration of challenging and often difficult realities. The arts are a vehicle for imaginative processes, inviting people to find the seams where the edges of their realities overlap, to explore different ways of seeing the world, and to dialogue with each other across these differences.

Such a dialogue is not easy, of course, nor is it necessarily even particularly direct. See, for example, Andrea Schneider's account of the roiling disputes in 19th-century Paris as the Impressionists' vision asserted itself in competition with the traditional Academy.[23] The disputes were recycled a century later when the Musée d'Orsay was to be established to give the Impressionists a major museum of their own at long last. But both times, these prolonged debates helped update and even redefine France's perception of itself.

The Musée d'Orsay example illustrates both the sizeable interests at stake and the ways in which the arts must integrate with "ordinary" and even "political" concerns. This is a forthright response to a perception, common among North Americans, that the gracefulness and beauty of the arts exist in a separate space from the concerns of daily life—and daily conflict—and are thus irrelevant to the "real business" of conflict. On the contrary: a widely-accepted aspect of mediators' skills is the ability to manage the interaction between the parties—and the ability to *distract* the parties, to offer them a way to recenter their thinking, has long been seen as one key to that management.[24] A direct line can thus be drawn between the functions of gracefulness and beauty and the interaction-management role of the mediator. This is confirmed by the long-standing practice of the highest-level traditional mediators, diplomats in international disputes. Even a cursory review of the typical schedules of many huge diplomatic mediation attempts will confirm that in time-honored and sophisticated multinational practice, business meetings are regularly interspersed with arts-oriented occasions, including opera and ballet performances, visits to cultural displays and of course, large volumes of sophisticated cooking. At a certain level, therefore, the need to integrate beauty and gracefulness into "utilitarian" and often cut-and-thrust conflict management has long been understood.

Conclusion

Creative arts and the process of artistry are important touchstones in conflict resolution practice. They offer windows into worldviews, ushering viewers, readers, or participants in community rituals toward ways of understanding others in context. With stories, colors, vibrancy, and energy, they invite a respite from struggle, even if that respite is temporary. This respite need not involve slapping a veneer of pretty paint over difficult histories. It is not necessarily a balm that answers, or delays answering, key questions in longstanding conflicts. But the arts offer ritual containers through which new aspects of identity can be experienced, and images each side holds of the other made more complex. [Coleman, et al., *Dynamical*] Arts vehicles, adroitly used, may give everyone involved a new picture—if only a picture to hold alongside the well-known experiences of division. The picture at least provides the possibility of a new beginning or a new angle. Creative arts can thus facilitate change in the patterned dances adversaries enact over time.

Endnotes

* This inscription appears on the back of new $20.00 bills in Canada.

[1] Vancouver, and the surrounding region, is gifted with many internationally-known community arts and conflict resolution practitioners whose work brings people together across differences. To help learn from these practitioners, the Faculty of Law at the University of British Columbia, in Vancouver, Canada, through its Program on Dispute Resolution, is undertaking research to examine innovations in the practice of conflict resolution, such as the increased use of storytelling and dialogue.

[2] *See Collected Quotes from Albert Einstein, at*
http://rescomp.stanford.edu/~cheshire/EinsteinQuotes.html (last visited Feb. 9, 2006).

[3] The *Conflict Resolution, Arts, and iNtercultural Experience* (CRANE) project is a three-year project investigating the intersections of creativity, culture and conflict resolution and examining the important role that the arts and creative approaches can play in intercultural community building and conflict resolution. It has brought together mediation practitio-

ners and educators, representatives of community agencies and members of the arts community to develop creative new approaches to cross-cultural conflicts. To date, two key activities of the project have included the development of a *Literature and Resource Review and Annotated Bibliography* and the hosting of a *Moveable Feast* (for a description of this type of meeting, see Christopher Honeyman, *ADR Practitioners and Research in a "Moveable Feast," available at* www.convenor.com/madison/moveable.htm; last visited Feb. 25, 2006). The *Literature and Resource Review* is an ambitious undertaking which explores over 400 sources across the spectrum of academic journals, organizational reports and evaluations, and practitioner websites and other electronic media, which illuminate the use of arts as a resource for conflict resolution. It was developed as a starting point for a much deeper and sustained dialogue on the intersections of arts, culture and conflict resolution and as a practical tool for mediators, facilitators, educators, artists and others involved in working in communities. The complete *Literature and Resource Review* will be available from www.law.ubc.ca/pdr/research/index.html in the spring of 2006. The CRANE project is directed by Michelle LeBaron at the UBC Faculty of Law, Vancouver, BC and funded by the Social Sciences and Humanities Research Council of Canada, 2004-07.

[4] *See* The Public Dreams Society, *at* http://www.publicdreams.org/about.htm (last visited Nov. 14, 2005).

[5] AUGUSTO BOAL, THEATRE OF THE OPPRESSED (2000) (1979).

[6] *See* Headlines Theatre, Theatre for Living, *at* http://www.headlinestheatre.com (last visited Nov. 24, 2005).

[7] JEFFREY HERMANN, ET AL., MOBY DICK CASE STUDY: PERSEVERANCE THEATRE (2002), *at* http://www.americansforthearts.org/AnimatingDemocracy/pdf/labs/moby_dick_case_study.pdf (last visited March 28, 2005).

[8] *See, e.g.,* LENI RIEFENSTAHL, THE LAST OF THE NUBA (1995).

[9] AMANDLA! A REVOLUTION IN FOUR-PART HARMONY (Artisan Entertainment 2002).

[10] *See* Search for Common Ground, *Our Toolbox, at* http://www.sfcg.org/sfcg/sfcg_toolbox.html (last visited Feb. 24, 2006).

[11] KJELL SKYLLSTAD, *Creating a Culture of Peace: The Performing Arts in Interethnic Negotiations*, 4 JOURNAL OF INTERCULTURAL COMMUNICATION (Nov. 2000), *at* http://www.immi.se/intercultural/nr4/skyllstad.htm.

[12] *See* ROMÉO DALLAIRE, SHAKE HANDS WITH THE DEVIL: THE FAILURE OF HUMANITY IN RWANDA (2003).

[13] Rena Sharon, Prof. of Collaborative Music, Univ. of B.C., Address at the Whistler Forum for Dialogue Summit on Citizen Engagement (Nov. 10, 2005).

[14] *Id.*

[15] M.C. Richards, *Separating and Connecting: The Vessel and the Fire, in* THE FABRIC OF THE FUTURE 231, 233 (Mary Jane Ryan ed., 1998).

[16] *Id.*

[17] MICHELLE LEBARON, BRIDGING TROUBLED WATERS: CONFLICT RESOLUTION FROM THE HEART 234 (2002).

[18] Headlines Theatre, *supra* note 6.

[19] Michael Ward, *Cooling Emotions With Money: Compensation Policy Reform in Papua New Guinea*, 15 PACIFIC ECONOMIC BULLETIN 1 (2000), *available at* http://www.peb.any.edu.ua/pdf/PEB15-lward.pdf.

[20] *See* Public Conversations Project, *at* http://www.publicconversations.org/pcp/index.asp (last visited Nov. 24, 2005).

[21] *See* SAMUEL HUNTINGTON, THE CLASH OF CIVILIZATIONS AND THE REMAKING OF WORLD ORDER (1996).

[22] *See Hirshhorn Museum and Sculpture Garden Current Exhibitions, at* http://www.hirshhorn.si.edu/exhibitions/description.asp?ID=33 (last visited Feb. 24, 2006).

[23] ANDREA K. SCHNEIDER, CREATING THE MUSÉE D'ORSAY: THE POLITICS OF CULTURE IN FRANCE (1998).

[24] Christopher Honeyman, *On Evaluating Mediators*, 6 NEGOTIATION JOURNAL 23 (1990).

☙ 49 ❧

Apology in Negotiation

Jennifer Gerarda Brown & Jennifer K. Robbennolt

Editors' Note: *Is "I'm sorry" the hardest phrase to say? Does it matter whether you mean it? This essay examines the critically important issue of apology, and how and when an apology can be helpful or harmful in a negotiation. Reviewing the latest empirical work, the authors discuss the purpose, type and timing of an apology, to ensure that any apology given accomplishes its goals. Note that they find that an apology offered cynically or casually may be worse than none at all. This chapter is linked to Waldman & Luskin.*

One topic that has received increased attention recently is the role that apology might properly play in negotiation and conflict resolution.[1] Whether the number of apologies has increased, as Aaron Lazare argues,[2] or merely the media coverage given to some high profile cases, it is clear that lawyers and their clients are considering apology as a potential element in the resolution of disputes. From a practical perspective, the central goal seems to be identifying the crucial ingredients of an effective apology. But to script an effective apology, one must first consider more theoretical matters, including these important questions:

- What is an apology, and what is the purpose of making one?
- Who should make an apology, and who should receive it?
- When is the optimal time for making an apology?
- What negative consequences (especially legal consequences, such as civil or criminal liability) might flow from the apology, and is it a good thing for the law to eliminate or mitigate these negative consequences?

We will not attempt to answer all of these questions thoroughly within the confines of this brief essay. We will at least touch upon each question, however, and will focus particular attention on the potential purposes of an apology and the qualities that might make it effective, incorporating empirical data where it exists and is relevant.

The Purposes of Apology

Apology has been defined as "an acknowledgment intended as an atonement for some improper or injurious remark or act: an admission to another of a wrong or discourtesy done him accompanied by an expression of regret,"[3] or "[a]n explanation offered to a person affected by one's action that no offence was intended, coupled with the expression of regret for any that may have been given; or, a frank acknowledgment of the offence with expression of regret for it, by way of reparation."[4] As Erving Goffman has explained, apology is a process through which a person symbolically splits "into two parts, the part that is guilty of an offense and the part that dissociates itself from the delict and affirms a belief in the offended rule."[5]

It is significant that Goffman explains apology by reference to its two central purposes, repudiation of wrongful conduct and assent to a different norm. Purposes are important, because the effectiveness of an apology can only be measured with reference to its goals. The purposes of apologies may be as numerous as the people who make them. Deborah Levi has analyzed categories of apology in mediation, and posited four types: "tactical" (acknowledging the victim's suffering in order to gain credibility and influence the victim's bargaining behavior); "explanation" (attempting to excuse the offender's behavior and make the other party understand that behavior); "formalistic" (capitulating to the demand of an authority figure); and "happy-ending" (accepting responsibility and expressing regret for the bad act).[6] Levi's analysis turns upon the words that are said and the specific speech acts that are performed with each type of apology.[7]

Another approach is to tease out the audience for the apology. For the person who is apologizing, whose regard is of central concern? We could think of apology as an essentially self-regarding process. Goffman's description of apology set forth above focuses largely upon the wrongdoer's self-perception or her relationship to the offended rule. Lee Taft articulates a precise formula for this type of apology: "[T]he offender acknowledges through speech the legitimacy of the violated rule, admits fault for its violation, and expresses genuine remorse and regret for the harm caused by his violation."[8] Such apologies can in some ways be viewed as self-serving, not in the sense that they result from selfishness, but that the offender's moral rehabilitation is paramount. The purpose of the apology is to regain moral integrity.

A conception of apology more focused on the recipient is one that strives to console, comfort, or restore dignity. The words spoken might be very much the same as a self-regarding apology, but the primary goal of the speaker is not to affirm his own integrity. Instead, the purpose of accepting blame is primarily to assure the other party of her virtue—that it was the offender (or some other entity), and not the victim, who bore responsibility for the harm that occurred.[9] Also, by sincerely apologizing for the harm caused, the offender recognizes, and, in a sense, empathizes with the victim's pain.

Still another view of apology places third-party effects at the forefront. Here, the primary audience for the apology is not so much the victim of the wrongdoing as it is a third party, often an authority figure. In this case, the obligation to apologize is externally imposed rather than internally driven. Parents of young children may fear that they generate such apologies when they insist that their misbehaving children "say they are sorry," but the instrumental effect can also be seen in adults who hope to reduce criminal sentences by apologizing to their victims.[10]

In addition to the benefits of apology in some criminal law contexts, it is clear that apology can yield advantages in civil lawsuits as well. Sometimes, defendants in civil cases will seek to reduce expected liability by apologizing in mediation or settlement negotiations.[11] Such "tactical" apologies (using Levi's rubric) are self-regarding in the sense that their central aim is defensive, but they are simultaneously attuned to the effect the apology will have on the recipient, for they are at least partially motivated by a desire to elicit specific action (concession) on the part of the other person.

In the broadest sense, the third-party audience for an apology is also the larger community of which both the offender and the victim are a part. The offender's apology may seek to address the loss of dignity that the offense has caused the victim in front of the witnessing community and to convince the witnessing community that the offender's moral integrity has been restored. As Robbennolt and her co-authors have suggested, "[t]he apology ... sends a signal to the offender, the victim, and the community that the victim is a valued and defended member of the community who cannot be treated in a fashion that diminishes her worth."[12]

So far, we have discussed the affirmative goals of apology, and certainly these differences will determine the elements of effective apologies in various contexts (as we shall shortly discuss). But one cannot begin to delineate the characteristics of a good apology without acknowledging the risks of apology. Jonathan Cohen labels these risks "psychological, strategic, void insurance coverage, and legal liability."[13] Theoretical and policy debates have focused on this final category, and explored ways of reducing the risk of liability flowing from apology. State statutes,[14] federal rules of evidence,[15] and other forms of privilege[16] aim to create safe space in which apologies can be made without giving rise to admissions of fault or liability. Scholarly debate has raged about whether apologies made in this safe space can be effective or morally authentic.[17] We do not presume to resolve this debate here, but merely note that any discussion of apology (whether academic or practical) must include apology's downside risks as well as its upside potential.

The Qualities of an Effective Apology

This section will synthesize some of the literature on apology to suggest essential elements of an apology. Not only purpose, as outlined above, but also context (including the prior relationship between the parties)[18] will exert strong influence on the formulation of a good apology.

Legitimate Agents to Deliver and Receive Apologies

There are important questions about legitimacy in those who deliver and receive apologies. When the offense is specific, short-running, or has occurred within the context of a single relationship (or small set of relationships), the answers to these questions will be fairly straightforward. It will not be difficult to identify an offender who might apologize and a victim who might receive the apology. This is not to say that it is always easy to identify victim and offender; in some relationships each person will play both roles. But if the harm has occurred on a small scale or in an interpersonal context, we can usually identify people who, if willing, could legitimately apologize or receive an apology on their own behalf.

When the offense is more complex, more historical, or has occurred on a grander scale, the situation becomes much more difficult. Perhaps it is clear that the Pope can legitimately speak for the Roman Catholic Church and apologize for complicity in the Holocaust,[19] and any living Holocaust survivors are the clear recipients of that apology.[20] But are they the only ones? Can the victims' descendants also be recipients of the apology? Are current-day Roman Catholics, while not perhaps the intended recipients, nonetheless an important audience for this apology? Consider groups that lack a central and authoritative leader such as the Pope. Is it possible for such groups or institutions to apologize authentically?[21]

Introspection and Timing

Almost everyone seems to agree that an apology should be the result of some analysis and introspection on the part of the offender—if it comes too spontaneously or off-the-cuff it loses power and legitimacy. This can create a tension. The offender may need time in order to reflect upon the harm done, form true remorse for the offense, and prepare a heartfelt apology. At the same time, the more an apology is delayed the more profound the offense may seem in the eyes of the victim. This leads some commentators to conclude that a person should apologize as soon as possible (and this folds in the time and introspection that may be necessary to make the apology possible).

Recent empirical research has examined how timing may influence the effectiveness of an apology. Cynthia McPherson Frantz and Courtney Bennigson argue that allowing time for the victim to express his or her concerns and to feel that the offender understands those concerns is central to an effective apology.[22] In one study, Frantz and Bennigson asked participants to recall a recent conflict, to indicate whether and in what order several events had occurred in their conflict, and to answer questions about whether they had been able to voice their concerns and felt understood by the other party to the conflict. Participants also addressed questions about their satisfaction with the resolution of the conflict. Frantz and Bennigson found that apologies that came later in the conflict process were associated with greater satisfaction with the outcome of the conflict than were apologies that were given sooner. This effect was explained by the greater opportunity for voice and understanding experienced by those disputants who received an apology later in the process.[23] In other words, victims valued the chance to tell their stories and *then* receive apologies, rather than just getting quick acknowledgements from offenders.

In a second study, participants were asked to take the role of the injured party in a hypothetical conflict scenario and indicate to what degree they would experience several emotions both before and after a conversation with the offender. In the conversation, the injured party's concerns were voiced and acknowledged by the offender. Participants who received an apology later in this conversation experienced more positive emotional change than did those who received an apology at the beginning of the conversation or those who did not receive an apology in the conversation at all.[24] Frantz and Bennigson conclude that "[a]pologies that are offered too quickly may not be effective, in part because the victim still feels unheard, and is not convinced that the offender knows what he or she did wrong, or why it was hurtful, or how hurtful it was."[25]

Ken Blanchard and Margret McBride outline in great detail the process of introspection that should precede an apology. They urge the reader to ask the following questions in order to discover and acknowledge the wrong that might have occurred:

- What mistakes did I make?
- Did I dismiss another person, their wishes, feelings, or ideas?
- Did I take credit when it was not due?
- Why did I do this?
- Was it an impulsive, thoughtless act?
- Was it calculated?
- Was it a result of my fear, anger, or frustration?
- What was my motivation?
- How long have I let this go on? Is this the first or repeated time? Is this behavior becoming a pattern in my life?

- What is the truth I am not dealing with?
- Am I better than this behavior?[26]

Blanchard and McBride are advising people who might wish to apologize for harm they have caused in business or social contexts; they focus on the emotional, rather than the legal, setting of an apology. Still, their questions might be adapted to a range of situations. The central value here is a guided process of moral inventory—taking stock of one's behavior and the harm that it might have caused.

A Proper Focus and the Question of Responsibility

What comes next seems to be the bone of contention. Does one apologize for the harm that has occurred—the outcome of one's acts—or for the acts themselves? Social scientists distinguish apologies from other types of remedial accounts, such as denials, excuses, or justifications, in that apologies specifically admit responsibility for one's actions.[27] Moreover, Lee Taft and others have argued that in order to be effective, an apology must articulate the norm that has been violated[28] and, in Goffman's terms, "affirm a belief in the offended rule."[29] Sometimes the offended standard is a personal one—a sense of oneself that has been compromised by errant behavior.[30] In other cases, it will be a rule, policy, or social norm of the organization or group of which the offender is a part. In some cases, it will be a legal standard or rule, and it is the breaking of that rule that may give rise to liability.

Others contend that something short of a "full apology" (one that admits fault and expresses regret) can be effective and helpful to the recipient. For example, Jonathan Cohen argues that even though "a full apology will usually be most powerful,"[31] it can also be constructive to simply express sympathy for harm that has occurred, without also taking moral or financial responsibility for that harm.[32]

One of the authors of this chapter conducted a series of experimental studies that explored the effects of whether an offender takes responsibility for his or her actions.[33] Participants read a vignette describing an accident from the perspective of the injured party and evaluated a settlement offer from the other party.[34] Participants who received an apology that accepted responsibility were more likely to accept the settlement offer, thought that the other party was more regretful, more moral, and more likely to act carefully in the future, experienced greater sympathy for the other party, less anger, and more willingness to forgive, and believed that the incident would result in less damage to the parties' relationship than those who did not receive a responsibility-accepting apology.[35] In contrast to apologies that accepted responsibility, apologies that merely expressed sympathy for the victim's injuries did not have the same overall impacts on attributions and appeared to increase participants' uncertainty about whether or not to accept the offer as compared to those who did not receive an apology.[36] Rather, the effects of apologies that only expressed sympathy were more variable and more dependent on the context of the situation, including the severity of the injury or the extent to which the other party was responsible for the harm.[37]

Forbearance/Repair

A final question that emerges is whether the promise to change something in the future is an essential element of an effective apology. The promised change might relate to the offender's own behavior[38] or it could involve promises to repair the harm done. Is an apology complete without this attempt to restore the status quo, where possible?[39]

Forbearance from future offense, in particular, appears to be important to recipients of apologies, and may be inferred even in the absence of an explicit promise. Gregg Gold and Bernard Weiner asked participants to read a scenario describing an incident that was followed by either an expression of remorse or no such expression. They found that offenders who expressed remorse were expected to be less likely to repeat their transgression in the future.[40] We might expect victims who hold such expectations to settle on more favorable terms as a result.

In addition, Steven Scher and John Darley explored the importance of several possible elements of an apology, including promises of forbearance and offers of repair.[41] They found that, while offering any apology provided the most improvement over not offering an apology at all,[42] promises of forbearance and offers of repair each improved the effectiveness of the apology.[43]

For lawyers and other negotiators, the precise wording, timing, and delivery of the apology will depend upon client preferences, the legal context, and the needs of the opposing party.

Implications

The existing literature on apology challenges us to think further about this important moment in conflict. In many disputes, the moments for apology come and go without notice or action, either because lawyers (and other negotiators) do not think to advise their clients on this point, or because aversion to vulnerability (emotional or legal) makes people overly cautious about pursuing this avenue toward resolution. If apology becomes a more accepted point of client counseling and subsequent negotiation, there will be many interesting lines for further inquiry. We will mention two.

First, what responsibilities does an apology create in the receiver? Lee Taft conceives of apology as a necessary link between "an inner urging to repent" and "forgiveness as a moral option for the offended," the "centerpiece in a moral dialectic between sorrow and forgiveness."[44] In addition, some empirical research suggests that an apology script or norm may operate to prescribe that an apology offered by the offender is to be followed by forgiveness of the offender by the recipient. Specifically, Mark Bennett and Christopher Dewberry have explored the constraints that recipients of apologies may face.[45] In one study, they asked participants to judge the recipient of an apology; the recipient either accepted the apology, did not accept the apology, or explicitly rejected the apology. Recipients who explicitly rejected an apology were judged most harshly, while recipients who accepted an apology were judged most favorably.[46] A follow up study found that a recipient who rejected an unconvincing apology[47] was judged just as harshly as the recipient who rejected the apology in the first study, an apology that was presumed to be more convincing.[48] Finally, Bennett and Dewberry asked another set of participants to take on the role of an injured party and to describe their likely response to an unconvincing apology. Despite reporting some desire to reject the apology, participants were highly likely to report that they would accept the apology (either unconditionally or contingent on some condition); no participant reported that he or she would explicitly reject the apology.[49] Thus, even though victims may be able to distinguish among different apologies and behave somewhat differently in response to them, they may feel constrained in their ability to completely reject an apology.

These studies suggest that, having delivered an apology, the offender may expect a positive response from the other party. To what extent can an offender expect that a moral victim will accept the apology and even forgive? If such acceptance and forgiveness are not forthcoming, can the apologizing person somehow be converted into a victim of a new harmful event?

Second, from a policy perspective, what sort(s) of apologies should we be trying to encourage, and how might the law play a role in creating the conditions that will facilitate desired apologies? When we create incentives for people to apologize, do we rob the resulting apologies of their potential power?

This takes us back to the debate concerning "protected apologies." Lee Taft may be correct in finding stronger moral force when an offender apologizes against self-interest, incurring greater vulnerability or exposure. For apologies designed primarily to restore the offender's moral integrity, perhaps some action against self-interest is essential.

But as we explained above, not all apologies are formulated for this purpose. When the primary audience is the victim or a third party, even a "protected" apology may be able to achieve laudable ends. After all, bringing true comfort to a suffering victim is no small matter.

Conclusion

For some victims, words will not be enough. Actions must accompany and give effect to the words if the apology is to have any meaning at all.[50] [Waldman & Luskin, *Anger & Forgiveness*] Sometimes, the follow-on activity will be subject to negotiation. In many cases, an apology will be necessary to make that negotiation possible. The better we understand the potential purposes and formulations of effective apologies, therefore, the richer our understanding of negotiation will be.

Endnotes

Jennifer Gerarda Brown would like to thank Michael Moffitt, Carole Frampton, David Sally, and Ian Ayres for helpful conversations and comments. I also learned a great deal about apology and forgiveness from Jonathan Cohen, Dana Curtis, Fred Luskin, and Lee Taft when they presented a roundtable discussion on the topic as part of the Quinnipiac-Yale Dispute Resolution Workshop, and I thank them for their generosity of mind and spirit.

Jennifer K. Robbennolt would like to thank Brian Bornstein, John Darley, Chris Guthrie, Rob MacCoun, Phil Peters, Len Riskin, Grant Robbennolt, Jean Sternlight, Christina Studebaker, and Chris Wells for a variety of helpful conversations about apologies.

[1] *See, e.g.,* William K. Bartels, *The Stormy Seas of Apologies: California Evidence Code Section 1160 Provides a Safe Harbor for Apologies Made After Accidents*, 28 WESTERN STATE UNIVERSITY LAW REVIEW 141 (2000-01); Max Bolstad, *Learning From Japan: The Case for Increased Use of Apology in Mediation*, 48 CLEVELAND STATE LAW REVIEW 545 (2000); William Bradford, *"With a Very Great Blame on Our Hearts": Reparations, Reconciliation, and an American Indian Plea for Peace with Justice*, 27 AMERICAN INDIAN LAW REVIEW 1 (2002-03); Charles R. Calleros, *Conflict, Apology, and Reconciliation at Arizona State University: A Second Case Study in Hateful Speech*, 27 CUMBERLAND LAW REVIEW 91 (1996-97); Jonathan R. Cohen, *Advising Clients to Apologize*, 72 SOUTHERN CALIFORNIA LAW REVIEW 1009 (1999); Jonathan R. Cohen, *Legislating Apology: The Pros and Cons*, 70 UNIVERSITY OF CINCINNATI LAW REVIEW 819 (2002); Taryn Fuchs-Burnett, *Mass Public Corporate Apology*, DISPUTE RESOLUTION JOURNAL July 2002, at 27; Elizabeth Latif, *Apologetic Justice: Evaluating Apologies Tailored Toward Legal Solutions*, 81 BOSTON UNIVERSITY LAW REVIEW 289 (2001); Erin Ann O'Hara, *Apology and Thick Trust: What Spouse Abusers and Negligent Doctors Might Have in Common*, 79 CHICAGO-KENT LAW REVIEW 1055 (2004); Erin Ann O'Hara & Douglas Yarn, *On Apology and Consilience*, 77 WASHINGTON LAW REVIEW 1121 (2002); Aviva Orenstein, *Apology*

Excepted: Incorporating a Feminist Analysis into Evidence Policy Where You Would Least Expect It, 28 SOUTHWESTERN UNIVERSITY LAW REVIEW 221 (1999); Donna L. Pavlick, *Apology and Mediation: The Horse and Carriage of the Twenty-First Century*, 18 OHIO STATE JOURNAL ON DISPUTE RESOLUTION 829 (2003); Jennifer K. Robbennolt, *Apologies and Legal Settlement: An Empirical Examination*, 102 MICHIGAN LAW REVIEW 460 (2003); Jennifer K. Robbennolt, *What We Know and Don't Know About the Role of Apologies in Resolving Health Care Disputes*, 21 GEORGIA STATE UNIVERSITY LAW REVIEW 1009 (2005); Lee Taft, *Apology Subverted: The Commodification of Apology*, 109 YALE LAW JOURNAL 1135 (2000).

[2] AARON LAZARE, ON APOLOGY 6 (2004).

[3] WEBSTER'S THIRD NEW INTERNATIONAL DICTIONARY (1961).

[4] OXFORD ENGLISH DICTIONARY (2d ed. 1989).

[5] ERVING GOFFMAN, RELATIONS IN PUBLIC 113 (1971).

[6] Deborah L. Levi, *The Role of Apology in Mediation*, 72 NEW YORK UNIVERSITY LAW REVIEW 1165, 1172-75 (1997); *see also* Pavlick, *supra* note 1, at 832 n.8.

[7] Levi, *supra* note 6, at 1178 n.50 (Apologies are words that do not just say something; they "'do something.'") (internal citation omitted).

[8] Taft, *supra* note 1, at 1140 (citing NICHOLAS TAVUCHIS, MEA CULPA 3 (1991)).

[9] For a possible example of such a comforting apology, *see* Jennifer Gerarda Brown, *The Use of Mediation to Resolve Criminal Cases: A Procedural Critique*, 43 EMORY LAW JOURNAL 1247, 1280 (1994) (quoting Attempted Murder: Confrontation (Home Box Office, Final Script 14 1991) (offender says: "See, the reason why I wanted to meet you is because I wanted to tell you it was not your fault. It was not deliberate. Like I said, it was the ghetto. All that stress. And I apologize for doing damage to your life and your family. I apologize.") This provides an example of an apology in which the offender falls somewhat short of taking full responsibility for his actions, but nonetheless attempts to make clear that the victim was not the responsible party. *See also* DOUGLAS STONE, ET AL., DIFFICULT CONVERSATIONS 44 (1999) (because "[i]f someone intended to hurt us, we judge them more harshly than if they hurt us by mistake," it is important to clarify people's intentions when discussing difficult situations).

[10] *See generally* Brown, *supra* note 9. This closely parallels Levi's "formalistic" apology. *See* Levi, *supra* note 5.

[11] Cohen, *Advising Clients to Apologize*, *supra* note 1, at 1066 (People can gain "financial benefits from doing what is ethically right.").

[12] Jennifer K. Robbennolt, et al., *Symbolism and Incommensurability in Civil Sanctioning: Decision Makers as Goal Managers*, 68 BROOKLYN LAW REVIEW 1121, 1147 (2003).

[13] *Id.* at 1023.

[14] MASSACHUSETTS GENERAL LAWS ANNOTATED ch. 233, § 23C (West 2000); *see also* TEXAS CIVIL PRACTICE & REMEDIES CODE ANNOTATED § 18.061 (Vernon 2003).

[15] FEDERAL RULES OF EVIDENCE 408. The rule states in pertinent part: "Evidence of conduct or statements made in compromise negotiations is ... not admissible." *Id.* For a thorough analysis of the rule and its impact on apology, *see* Cohen, *Advising Clients to Apologize*, *supra* note 1, at 1032-36.

[16] *See* UNIF. MEDIATION ACT § 4 (2002) (creating a privilege for mediation communications).

[17] One of the most notable critiques comes from Lee Taft, who argues against such instrumentalism. Apology "offers the offender a vehicle for expressing repentance and the offended an opportunity to forgive," but "'protected' apology" subverts this "moral process." Taft, *supra* note 1, at 1138. *See also* Cohen, *Legislating Apology*, *supra* note 1; Robbennolt, *supra* note 1.

[18] For an analysis of apology in various substantive legal contexts, *see* Cohen, *Advising Clients to Apologize*, *supra* note 1, at 1054-61.

[19] *Pope to Apologize for Sins Committed by Roman Catholics*, available at CNN.Com, http://www.cnn.com/2000/WORLD/europe/03/07/vatican.pardon.02/ (last visited Apr. 12, 2006).

[20] Interestingly, many Jewish leaders found the Pope's statement "disappointing," perhaps because it admitted fault in such a low-key, general way. *See id.*

[21] "National Sorry Day," for example, grew out of frustration with the Australian government's failure to apologize to the Aboriginal people for the forced removal of Aboriginal and Torres Strait Islander children from their families, which the government practiced for 150 years, into the early 1970s. As one organization devoted to planning the day explained:

> Sorry Day will be an important step on the road which all Australians are "walking together." It can help restore the dignity stripped from those affected by removal; and it offers those who carried out the policy—and their successors—a chance to move beyond denial and guilt. It could shape a far more creative partnership between Indigenous and non-Indigenous Australians, with immense benefit to both.

Web site for the Sorry Day Committee, at http://www.austlii.edu.au/au/special/rsjproject/sorry/ (last visited Apr. 12, 2006). The literature on restorative justice and reparations examines these questions in great depth. *See, e.g.,* Bradford, *supra* note 1, at 134-37; JOHN BRAITHWAITE, RESTORATIVE JUSTICE AND RESPONSIVE REGULATION (2002).

[22] Cynthia McPherson Frantz & Courtney Bennigson, *Better Late Than Early: The Influence of Timing on Apology Effectiveness*, 41 JOURNAL OF EXPERIMENTAL SOCIAL PSYCHOLOGY 201 (2005).

[23] *Id.* at 204.

[24] *Id.* at 205.

[25] *Id.* at 202.

[26] KEN BLANCHARD & MARGRET MCBRIDE, THE ONE MINUTE APOLOGY 110 (2003).

[27] *See e.g.,* GOFFMAN, *supra* note 5; Barry R. Schlenker & Bruce W. Darby, *The Use of Apologies in Social Predicaments*, 44 SOCIAL PSYCHOLOGY QUARTERLY 271 (1981); Barry R. Schlenker & Michael F. Weigold, *Interpersonal Processes Involving Impression Regulation and Management*, 43 ANNUAL REVIEW OF PSYCHOLOGY 133 (1992); Marvin B. Scott & Stanford M. Lyman, *Accounts*, 33 AMERICAN SOCIOLOGICAL REVIEW 46 (1968). *See also* MARTHA MINOW, BETWEEN VENGEANCE AND FORGIVENESS 115 (1998) ("Full acceptance of responsibility by the wrongdoer is the hallmark of an apology.").

[28] Taft, *supra* note 1, at 1141 (Nixon's attempted apology in his August 1974 resignation speech failed because he "failed to acknowledge his specific offense, and he failed to identify the norm broken.").

[29] *See* GOFFMAN, *supra* note 5 and accompanying text.

[30] Blanchard and McBride write at some length about this sort of norm. They argue that in order to regain integrity, people must recognize that what they did is inconsistent with who they want to be and reaffirm that they are better than their poor behavior. BLANCHARD & MCBRIDE, *supra* note 27, at 50.

[31] Cohen, *Advising Clients to Apologize, supra* note 1, at 1048.

[32] *Id.* at 1067.

[33] Robbennolt, *supra* note 1.

[34] *Id.* at 484-85.

[35] *Id.* at 487-88.

[36] *Id.* at 496-97.

[37] *Id.* at 498-99.

[38] *See*, for example, the Roman Catholic "Act of Contrition," often spoken as part of the sacrament of reconciliation (or, in pre-Vatican II days, "penance"), which requires a person to articulate a "resolve" to "amend my life."

[39] Some would argue that such restoration is crucial. *See, e.g.,* BLANCHARD & MCBRIDE, *supra* note 27, at 50 (stating that a person who apologizes should "make amends" for harm done, make a commitment to self and others "not to repeat the act, and demonstrate [that] commitment by changing ... behavior").

[40] Gregg J. Gold & Bernard Weiner, *Remorse, Confession, Group Identity, and Expectancies About Repeating a Transgression*, 22 BASIC & APPLIED SOCIAL PSYCHOLOGY 291 (2000). *See also* Randolph B. Pipes & Marci Alessi, *Remorse and a Previously Punished Offense in Assignment of Punishment and Estimated Likelihood of a Repeated Offense*, 85 PSYCHOLOGICAL

REPORT 246 (1999); Dawn T. Robinson, et al., *Heinous Crime or Unfortunate Accident? The Effects of Remorse on Responses to Mock Criminal Confessions*, 73 SOC. FORCES 175 (1994).

[41] Steven J. Scher & John M. Darley, *How Effective Are the Things People Say to Apologize? Effects of the Realization of the Apology Speech Act*, 26 JOURNAL OF PSYCHOLINGUISTIC RESEARCH 127 (1997).

[42] *Id.* at 137.

[43] *Id.* at 133. *See also* Bruce W. Darby & Barry R. Schlenker, *Children's Reactions to Apologies*, 43 JOURNAL OF PERSONALITY & SOCIAL PSYCHOLOGY 742 (1982) (finding more positive reaction to more elaborate apologies than to more perfunctory apologies).

[44] Taft, *supra* note 1, at 1143.

[45] Mark Bennett & Christopher Dewberry, *"I've Said I'm Sorry, Haven't I?" A Study of the Identity Implications and Constraints that Apologies Create for Their Recipients*, 13 CURRENT PSYCHOLOGY 10 (1994).

[46] *Id.* at 14.

[47] Unconvincing given reputation of offender. *Id.* at 16.

[48] *Id.* at 16.

[49] *Id.* at 18-19. 33% reported that they would accept unconditionally; 55% reported that they would accept conditionally. *Id.*

[50] In experimental settings, researchers have found that apologies can be effective in restoring trust and cooperation in simulated negotiation, but not as effective as trustworthy actions. *See* William P. Bottom, et al., *When Talk is Not Cheap: Substantive Penance and Expressions of Intent in Rebuilding Cooperation*, 13 ORGANIZATION SCIENCE 497 (2002); Maurice Schweitzer, et al., *Promises and Lies: Restoring Violated Trust*, at http://opim.wharton.upenn.edu/~schweitz/papers/Promises%20and%20Lies.pdf (last visited May 21, 2003) (Wharton Working Paper) ("[A] 'cheap talk' promise can speed initial trust recovery, but such a promise followed by a series of observed, trustworthy actions is no more effective in restoring long-term trust than a series of trustworthy actions alone.")

∾ 50 ∾

Unforgiven: Anger and Forgiveness

Ellen Waldman & Frederic Luskin

Editors' Note: *How many negotiations are reduced to a numbers game by the un-thinking responses of professional negotiators who don't recognize what is really at stake for their clients? How many negotiators frame what "should" be achieved in the negotiation, conveniently getting around the fact that the agent can't be paid one-third of an apology? Here, a lawyer and a psychologist together examine the evidence that forgiveness may be the single most desirable negotiation outcome in many situations, when measured by physical and mental health of those involved—but that a lockstep push toward forgiveness in all disputes is neither possible, nor desirable. This chapter should be read in conjunction with Brown & Robbennolt on Apology.*

To suffer woes which Hope thinks infinite: / To forgive wrongs darker than death or night; / ... / Neither to change, nor falter, nor repent; / This, like thy glory ... is to be / Good, great and joyous, beautiful and free....
—Percy Bysshe Shelley, Prometheus Unbound, Act IV, 570 (1820).

Forgiveness is not necessary to forge a deal. One can bargain, barter and horse-trade with an unapologetic enemy. One can continue to harbor deep-seated resentments even while signing settlement papers. For this reason, forgiveness and reconciliation have not received extensive treatment in the negotiation literature. But, if the question of whether one can or should forgive one's adversary is not central to the mechanics of getting to yes, it is important in assessing the short and long-term costs of disputing and in developing strategies to minimize those costs.

Attorneys and other third parties involved in heated negotiations regularly work with clients who are deeply angry with those they believe have "done them wrong." Although legal professionals focus on curing the legal problem, frequently this hard fought cure is not sufficient to make clients "feel whole." Clients need an emotional solution as much as a legal one, and the emotional solution frequently calls for forgiveness. Unfortunately, attorneys and other dispute resolution professionals are rarely able to help clients recognize or address that need.

This essay argues that forgiveness promises tangible health benefits and can have transformative effects on individuals locked in intractable conflict. It presents data on embattled individuals whose physical health dramatically improved after participation in forgiveness training and discusses how ongoing enmity triggers the body's biochemical feedback system in maladaptive and destructive ways.

Despite its obvious health benefits, however, forgiveness cannot be prescribed as a universal panacea. Experiments with restorative justice responses to fractured communities suggest that victim forgiveness should only be encouraged after other tangible steps have been taken toward acknowledging victim suffering and healing the victim's physical, psychic, and material wounds. Dispute system designs misperceive the pre-conditions to magnanimity when they assume offender truth-telling or apology will automatically trigger victim forgiveness. True forgiveness can only come from a basic foundation of security. Until victims' basic physical and security needs are met, they cannot and should not be expected to extend grace to their enemies.

The Quality of Mercy

As the world's religious and spiritual literature makes clear, forgiveness[1] is a practice that leads to both emotional healing and spiritual growth. Arguably, learning to forgive is life's most demanding and meaningful task because forgiveness asks the offended person to reappraise both the hurt and its source. This is a significant challenge and, in our adversarial-based legal system, too often ignored.

In the last dozen years, scientific study has uncovered a link between forgiveness and enhanced physical and mental well-being. Unfortunately, even cooperative and settlement-minded disputants seeking to eschew the polarizing rituals of the courtroom are woefully ignorant about how to gain emotional release from their grievances. If the scientific research is to be believed, aggrieved disputants, even if they want to forgive, do not know how. But, forgiveness can be learned.

Forgiveness often begins when disputants recognize that whatever happened to them, while difficult, was not invented by the offending party. In addition, forgiveness comes from an understanding that being hurt or wounded is a difficult, but expected, part of life. In the *Stanford Forgiveness Projects*,[2] forgiveness was taught as one possible response to interpersonal offense—but one that rarely came into play until other responses proved inadequate. Too often, suffering individuals focus repeatedly on their grievances and, as a result, trigger in themselves anger, self-pity and resentment. When individuals are stuck in the cycle of recalled painful experience, finger-pointing and the construction of victim narratives, they put themselves at risk for disease, relationship disruption and emotional distress.

An emerging body of research demonstrates the power of forgiveness to improve physical and emotional well being. *The Stanford Forgiveness Projects* have shown that participants with a diverse array of interpersonal wounds can reduce stress, depression, hurt and anger and increase their sense of optimism. In one controlled and randomized study, 260 participants volunteered to receive nine hours of forgiveness training offered over six weeks. These participants had experienced hurts that ranged from parental neglect to spousal rape to romantic abandonment. After the forgiveness intervention, participants' stress, anger, and optimism levels were measured and compared with a control group who had not received the intervention. Participants in the forgiveness intervention reported that they learned to take their losses less personally and were better able to respond to interpersonal hurt without antagonism. After the nine hour group intervention, participants showed a 50% reduction in hurt, a 10% reduction in long-term anger, a 15% reduction in the experience of stress, a 40% increase in forgiveness, and a 15% decease in the physical symptoms of stress-changes not reported in the control group.[3]

In another series of studies, people from both sides of the conflict in Northern Ireland who had suffered grievous losses were recruited to participate in week-long forgiveness trainings. In the first group were a half-dozen Catholic and Protestant mothers whose sons had been murdered. In the second group were 17 people who had lost an immediate family member to sectarian murder; the third group included a dozen people who both worked in Northern Ireland to promote healing and had suffered personally from the violence in their country. When the mothers were assessed six months after returning to Northern Ireland, they showed a doubling of their willingness to forgive, as well as a 35% reduction in depression, a 25% reduction in anger, and a 50% reduction in stress. The second group, whose losses involved an immediate family member, reported a 35% decline in symptoms of stress (dizziness, headache, stomachache) and a 15% improvement in their experience of physical vitality (which includes energy level, appetite, sleep patterns, and general well-being). In each Northern Ireland group, the participants' rating of the intensity of their hurt declined by over 33%.[4]

Apart from individual functioning, ability to forgive constitutes an important part of maintaining intimate bonds and friendships, and is essential to the repair of relationships after insult or breach. Research suggests that forgiveness has the power to help people heal from infidelity, substance abuse and other relationship wounds.

A focus on the negative, hurtful experiences of one's life has consequences both for mental and physical health. Every time disputants remember a hurt, they release stress chemicals such as epinephrine, norepinephrine and cortisol into their bodies, the purpose of which is to mobilize a fight or flight response. Unfortunately, these chemicals can compromise health and erode the ability to think clearly. For example, these stress chemicals raise blood pressure, reduce aspects of immune functioning and cause muscles to tense. Less well known, and just as problematic, they cause blood to drain away from the higher order thinking centers in the brain while redirecting blood flow to more emotionally reactive parts of the brain. When individuals nurse grievances long after any possible constructive response is possible, the inability to act responsively, concurrent with the painful and health-jeopardizing experience of the stress chemicals, can result in a continual experience of anxiety and victimization.

Forgiveness interrupts this cycle in a number of important ways. When individuals learn to forgive, they are able to manage their own emotional/physical arousal, see the offense with a perspective enlarged by empathy for the offender, change their story of victimization to one of overcoming adversity, or reach, with acceptance, the philosophical conclusion that "into each life some rain must fall."

The Stanford Forgiveness Projects and other research programs show that forgiveness can be successfully taught in a group as well as individual setting, and suggest that forgiveness, when learned, helps to heal not only the individual's specific interpersonal hurt but reduces the tendency to get angry in the future as well.

Forgiveness in Dispute System Design: Recognizing the Necessary Conditions for Amazing Grace

Although attaining forgiveness yields clear physical and psychological benefits, negotiators should not necessarily treat forgiveness as a primary goal in every dispute. Rather, both from the standpoint of individual conflict management and from a larger dispute system design perspective, forgiveness and reconciliation should be viewed as an aspiration to be realized under certain propitious circumstances. Disputants should be encouraged to extend grace toward adversaries in particular contexts, but this magnanimity should not be required as a condition of dispute closure.

It is tempting, when thinking of how to craft the optimally successful dispute resolution process, to build in forgiveness as one stage of the process, coming somewhere after disputant articulation of interests and before the final exchange of offers. Indeed, some theorists have come close to this conceptual model, offering up a theory of third-party assisted negotiation that declares the enhancement of disputant empathy and compassion to be a primary objective.[5] This temptation is even more alluring in the criminal context where traditional retributive approaches overlook forgiveness as a possible palliative for victims, seizing instead on offender punishment as the salve that will calm and heal victim wounds.

Restorative Justice: Trading Vengeance, Gaining Peace?

Alternative restorative approaches reject this retributive account of victim needs. They maintain that a victim's cravings for revenge are regrettable impulses that can be usefully checked in a process that holds out the promise of healing through a victim-offender encounter. A meeting with the offender in which the victim is able to explain the impact of the crime, gain acknowledgement for suffering endured, and learn of the offender's life challenges, is thought to be freeing and empowering. In restorative processes, the victim is said to gain "the public vindication that is achieved through caring and authoritative acknowledgment of their suffering."[6] As one observer of restorative justice has written, "The primary remedies in the restorative medicine cabinet are apology and forgiveness. Restorative justice has tremendous faith that the offender's outward performance of an inner state of contrition will smooth the way to a revival of the victim's sense of honor and well-being, thus releasing the victim into the liberation of forgiveness."[7]

The restorative justice perspective has gained numerous adherents within the conflict resolution community. Its philosophy permeates victim-offender mediation programs, which now number over a thousand throughout the United States, Europe and beyond. But some evidence hints that restorative justice assumptions about the therapeutic value of forgiveness and reconciliation may be inflated: that is, forgiveness and reconciliation may be achievable and therapeutic for some disputants in some circumstances but not for all disputants in all circumstances, as restorativists have been wont to claim.

The data urging restraint in promoting restorative principles comes chiefly from war-torn countries that have eschewed aggressive prosecution of war crimes in favor of more conciliatory approaches. In both South Africa and Rwanda, governments facing a horrific past and an uncertain future gambled that informal procedures focusing on victim story-telling and offender acknowledgement would create greater possibilities for reconciliation than a series of divisive and resource-intensive trials. Both countries set up transitional justice tribunals empowered to award amnesty to, or reduce sentences for, offenders who told the truth about their complicity in domestic and international human rights abuses. Victims in these proceedings were invited to tell their stories and confront their torturers regarding the impact of their crimes. In both Rwanda and South Africa it would appear that "compulsory compassion" receives only mixed reviews.

In Rwanda, a three-month genocidal killing spree in the spring of 1994 left over 800,000 dead. Nearly 130,000 alleged perpetrators behind bars challenged the human rights community to develop mechanisms to cope with the sheer volume of crime to be investigated, evaluated and punished. In tandem with internationally organized prosecutions of the alleged ringleaders, Rwanda implemented a judicial program—Inkiko-Gacaca—drawing on indigenous, pre-colonial traditions of participatory justice. Oriented toward involving communities of victims, offenders and witnesses in the establishment of a communal truth about the massacres, Inkiko-Gacaca sought to heal victims, while encouraging perpetrators to confess their crimes, express remorse, and receive reduced sentences.

Although lay judges were empowered to hand out sentences ranging from community service to extended terms in prison, Inkiko-Gacaca's primary goal was not to deliver punishment. Rather, its primary purpose was to shine a light on the nation's horrors, shame those found to have committed crime, and integrate offenders back into the community with maximal efficiency and community participation. Once victims had the chance to confront offenders, tell their story, and extract an apology, it was thought they would be able to live peacefully in a community with their loved ones' murderers right next door. True to restorativist assumptions, the architects of Inkiko-Gacaca imagined that the construction of a sacred space for victim narrative would restore victim dignity and moral agency in ways that state-inflicted punishment of the offender could not. They assumed that Inkiko-Gacaca potentiates greater healing than does a traditional trial—and so, felt it fair to ask the victim to relinquish some of the sweet satisfactions of revenge in exchange for the more transcendent benefits of the dialogic encounter.[8] "To have your story of unjust suffering entered into a public record and thence into future history—writing is to experience an increment of justice."[9] It would appear, however, that not all victims are ready to make this trade.

In 2002, nearly eight years after the genocide, medical researchers explored the degree of faith and confidence that Rwanda's wounded population held out for inter-ethnic reconciliation, norms of nonviolence, and the restorative justice ideals undergirding the nascent practice of Inkiko-Gacaca.[10] Individuals were surveyed according to their belief in the possibility of establishing mutual ties across ethnic lines, acceptance of social diversity, equality of opportunity and nonviolent alternatives to conflict management. Not surprisingly, individuals' openness to reconciliation was inversely related to levels of experienced trauma. That is, those individuals exposed to high levels of trauma and suffering from higher levels of post-traumatic stress disorder were less likely to believe in the possibility of inter-ethnic cooperation and interdependence than those free of enduring psychological trauma.[11]

Similar results obtain from studies in post-apartheid South Africa. Inquiries into the degree to which that country's Truth and Reconciliation Commission hearings facilitated interracial healing demonstrate that victims must be assured a relatively stable economic and psychological base before they can make moves toward reconciliation. In a series of interviews with victims who had received small sums from the government after establishing that they had been victimized by apartheid's cruelties, it became clear that only those victims whose basic material needs were cared for could muster the "emotional surplus" to extend forgiveness to others.[12] Survivors of abuse in another study also reported that story-telling, confrontation with their offender and public acknowledgment of their suffering was only a partial anodyne; true psychological healing, they reported, could only occur when basic economic and structural change afforded them the necessary materials for a stable existence. The balm of forgiveness, it would seem, could only be conjured once victims had access to the economic goods denied them under apartheid, including ... "affordable housing and health-care, free access to education ..., the provision of special pensions, disability grants, and regular pensions ... and, most importantly ... meaningful training and employment."[13]

This linkage between ability to forgive and economic self-sufficiency can be explained by reference to psychologist Abraham Maslow's hierarchy of needs and theories of self-actualization.[14] Maslow hypothesized that humans were subject to a variety of needs that could be usefully arrayed in the form of a pyramid to reflect their exigency. At the bottom of the pyramid lie the strongest, most urgent needs: the physiological requirements of food, water and air. We can't focus on anything else until these basic needs are satisfied. Next comes the impulse toward safety, security, structure and order, followed by yearnings for love and a sense of belonging. The drive toward community and group identification and acceptance kicks in once the belly is (more or less) full, the body is sheltered and clothed and the immediate threat of physical harm is removed. Once longings for affiliation are satisfied, the drive to attain esteem commands attention. According to Maslow, two forms of esteem-oriented needs exist, one internally directed and the other externally directed. The externally-oriented need focuses on attention and respect garnered from others and manifests itself in concern for status, fame, recognition, reputation, appreciation, and sometimes, dominance. The second, internally-oriented drive corresponds with demands for self-respect. This need is met when one develops confidence and a sense of mastery, achievement and competence in one's ability to navigate the world.

At the apex of Maslow's hierarchy stands the individual who enjoys physical security, love, the esteem of others and self-respect. This individual has now reached the highest level of being—what Maslow terms self-actualization. At the level of self-actualization, an individual's energies are directed toward the fulfillment of his or her human potential. As Maslow explained, to fully self-actualize, the musician must make music, the artist must paint and the poet must write.[15] In addition, while becoming most fully oneself, the self-actualized individual develops a sense of humility and respect toward others and experiences a strong sense of human kinship and compassion.

Forgiveness—the opening of one's heart to those who have trespassed against us—can easily occur once we are at the self-actualizing stage. But, in order for us to extend grace to others, our own needs for food, shelter, safety, security and affiliation must be met. Maslow's schema thus explains why South African Blacks, still at the bottom rung of that nation's economic ladder, have not declared the restorative procedures of the Truth and Reconciliaion Commission an unambiguous success and why supporters and detractors of the Commission's exchange of amnesty for truth tend to stratify along socio-economic lines. Maslow's hierarchy also explains why victims of trauma in Rwanda who had substantially recovered from their abuse were more magnanimous and hopeful about the possibility of inter-ethnic cooperation and non-violence than those who were still suffering from psychic after-shocks.

Applying the Lessons of Restorative Justice: Between Vengeance and Forgiveness in Civil Disputes[16]

Although experiments with restorative justice in the aftermath of mass atrocities in Rwanda and South Africa may seem a long way away from the everyday practices of negotiators in civil disputes, there is reason to believe cautious transfer of the lessons learned is appropriate. The objective disparity between the injuries suffered by victims of genocide and apartheid and those suffered by plaintiffs in civil court may be enormous, but the subjective psychological mechanisms at work in forgiveness and reconciliation remain largely the same. In both contexts, forgiveness requires that the offended person reappraise the injury suffered as well as its source. Maslow's prerequisites for self-actualization do not change according to the degree of harm suffered. The determining factor remains whether the foundational needs of food, safety, security, affiliation and esteem have been satisfied. Because the experience of need, deprivation and satisfaction is inherently subjective, the important measure is the relationship between the litigant's internal expectations and the degree to which those expectations for security, affiliation and respect have been met.

Cautiously transferring the lessons learned from the Truth and Reconciliation Commission and Inkiko-Gacaca to the context of civil litigants implies some basic lessons about forgiveness and reconciliation in dispute resolution. First, we should be wary about making assumptions about what victims or disputants need. Restorative justice assumes that victims need voice, acknowledgment, and participation. Upon receipt of these dignitary goods, victims are expected to eschew revenge and offer up the grace of forgiveness. But a theory of justice that expects or demands forgiveness is likely to fail. Capacity to forgive is predicated on a certain minimal level of well-being. And when restorative processes give victims voice but don't significantly change their desperate material circumstances, the impulse to forgive may shift to bitterness and betrayal.

Similarly, in civil disputes where parties feel wronged, attorneys and third-party neutrals should tread lightly and avoid nudging parties toward forgiveness before they are ready. Party needs for security, affiliation, esteem and self-respect must be met before forgiveness is possible. The negotiation process should be geared first toward these more basic needs—with forgiveness and its attendant goods seen as a more remote, but possible, beneficent outcome.

Conclusion

Forgiveness is a worthy goal in dispute resolution. If disputants can muster the generosity and spiritual calm required to still their vengeful fantasies, they will be rewarded by lower stress levels and enhanced functionality. And yet, we should not assume that if internally-inspired forgiveness is good, externally-required forgiveness is equally so. Dispute resolution systems that expect victims to forgive their oppressors in return for a truthful accounting or apology may be asking too much. Relinquishing the desire for revenge and punishment is a challenging task. It requires high levels of functioning, attainable only at the peak of Maslow's pyramid of needs. Lower-level needs for material security and self-esteem must first be satisfied. Lessons from our forays into restorative justice around the world teach us that, while forgiveness may be divine, basic conditions for human flourishing must be met before we can expect men to act as gods.

Endnotes

[1] A couple of points require elaboration. First, reconciliation is not the same as forgiveness. Reconciliation involves the reestablishment of a relationship, while forgiveness is an emotional and physical experience of making peace. People can reconcile but not forgive, and people can forgive but not ever again participate in a particular relationship. Second, the practice of stress management is essential for calming the body when agitated due to a remembered experience of unkindness. Third, people have a freedom in how they articulate their past that they rarely take advantage of. A simple change in the way one tells a story of how they were hurt has a dramatic effect on emotional and physical well being. Finally, it must be remembered that the goal is not to change the past but to be OK with whatever life we have been given. As the bumper sticker so aptly says, "forgiveness is giving up all hope for a better past."

[2] Fred M. Luskin, *The Art and Science of Forgiveness, in* CONSCIOUSNESS AND HEALING: INTEGRAL APPROACHES TO MIND BODY MEDICINE 335-41 (Marilyn Schlitz, et al., eds. 2004).

[3] Fred M. Luskin, et al., *Effects of Group Forgiveness Intervention on Perceived Stress, State and Trait Anger, Self Reported Health, Symptoms of Stress and Forgiveness*, 7 ALTERNATIVE THERAPIES IN HEALTH AND MEDICINE 106 (2001).

[4] The data collected from casualties of the conflicts in Northern Ireland, though suggestive, does not establish a casual link between learning to forgive and improved physical and mental health. Because these community protocols were not randomized, controlled or blinded, further research with this or similarly devastated populations is necessary to prove that forgiveness is the cause, and not a co-variable, in the steadily improving status of grievously wronged individuals.

[5] ROBERT A. BARUCH BUSH & JOSEPH D. FOLGER, THE PROMISE OF MEDIATION: THE TRANSFORMATIVE APPROACH TO CONFLICT 50 (rev. ed. 2005).

[6] ANNALISE E. ACORN, COMPULSORY COMPASSION: A CRITIQUE OF RESTORATIVE JUSTICE 50 (2004). As one commentator on restorative justice has written, "The victims' authentic longings for justice are better understood in terms of their desire for the experience of affirmation of their worth and secure membership in the community. What victims really want is for the offender to own responsibility for the harm, to shift his or her attitude from disrespect to respect for the victim and the norms of the community, and to feel and express genuine shame, remorse, and contrition...."

[7] *Id.* at 71.

[8] Unlike the Truth and Reconciliation Commission in South Africa, the Rwanda tribunals did not offer complete amnesty in return for truth-telling. Instead, offenders who confess and apologize to victims receive substantially reduced sentences which can be partially satisfied through community service. *See* Maya Goldstein Bolocan, *Rwanda Gacaca: An Experiment in Transitional Justice*, 2004 JOURNAL OF DISPUTE RESOLUTION 355, 385.

[9] Donald Shriver, *Where and When in Political Life is Justice Served by Forgiveness?, in* BURYING THE PAST: MAKING PEACE AND DOING JUSTICE AFTER CIVIL CONFLICT 28 (2001).

[10] Phuong N. Pham, et al., *Trauma and PTSD Symptoms in Rwanda: Implications for Attitudes Toward Justice and Reconciliation*, 292 JOURNAL OF THE AMERICAN MEDICAL ASSOCIATION 602 (Aug. 4, 2004).

[11] *Id.* at 608 ("after controlling for other significant variables, respondents who met the symptom criteria for PTSD were less likely to have positive attitudes toward the Rwanda national trials and were less likely to believe in community and less likely to support interdependence than those who did not meet the PTSD symptom criteria").

[12] Anna Crawford-Pinnerup, *From Rhetoric to Responsibility: Making Reparations to the Survivors of Past Political Violence in South Africa*, CENTRE FOR THE STUDY OF VIOLENCE AND RECONCILIATION (2000), *available at* http://www.csvr.org.za/papers/papr2r6.htm (last visited Feb. 16, 2006).

[13] Christopher J. Colvin, *We Are Still Struggling: Storytelling, Reparations and Reconciliation After the TRC*, CENTRE FOR THE STUDY OF VIOLENCE AND RECONCILIATION (2000), *available at* http://www.csvr.org.za/papers/papcolv.htm (last visited Feb. 16, 2006).

[14] ABRAHAM MASLOW, MOTIVATION AND PERSONALITY (2d ed. 1970).

[15] Maslow elaborated in MOTIVATION AND PERSONALITY "What a man can be, he must be. This is the need we may call self-actualization.... It refers to man's desire for fulfillment, namely to the tendency for him to become actually in what he is potentially: to become everything that one is capable of becoming...." ABRAHAM MASLOW, MOTIVATION AND PERSONALITY (2d ed. 1970).

[16] *See* MARTHA MINOW, BETWEEN VENGEANCE AND FORGIVENESS: FACING HISTORY AFTER GENOCIDE AND MASS VIOLENCE (1999).

IV. What to Do?

C.   When a Deal's in Sight

❧ 51 ❧

Analyzing Risk

Jeffrey M. Senger

Editors' Note: *Should I accept this offer? How can I measure the real value of a settlement offer now, versus the possibility of a much larger verdict years in the future? Here, a highly experienced U.S. Government attorney who has tried many complex cases explains how risk analysis helps us estimate outcomes with more accuracy, and make better decisions.*

Imagine you are the President of the United States, and you are facing a decision on whether to attempt a military mission to rescue Americans trapped in a hostile country. In a meeting in the White House Situation Room, top military advisers describe a possible plan. You ask about the chances of success for the mission. The advisers respond that there are six crucial stages of the plan, and all have to go smoothly in order for the mission to work. They state that the overall chances for the plan are good because each individual stage has an eighty percent chance of success. What would you do?

A field known as "decision analysis" can help answer this type of question and many others in a wide range of situations.[1] When parties understand what their chances of success are for each of several possible choices, they can make better decisions on how to proceed. The tools of decision analysis are particularly useful for negotiators. People who are negotiating need to be able to evaluate what is likely to happen to them if they accept a deal and if they do not.[2]

In the rescue example above, it is easy to see how a President might be tempted to authorize the plan. If the chances of success at each stage of a mission are eighty percent, the chances of success for the overall mission may seem reasonably good. However, decision analysis shows that the mission is much more likely to fail than succeed. The statistical method used to calculate the overall likelihood of success in this situation requires multiplying the chances of success of each individual stage. Thus the President should multiply 0.80 (the chance of succeeding in the first stage) by 0.80 (the chance of the second stage), then multiply this result by 0.80 for the third stage, and so on, all the way through the six stages of the mission. This total, 0.80 x 0.80 x 0.80 x 0.80 x 0.80 x 0.80, (or 0.80 to the sixth power), is 0.26. Thus, the overall chances of success for the mission are only twenty-six percent, or roughly one in four.

Examples of Decision Analysis

The mathematical processes used in risk analysis may be explained further with several examples. Imagine going to a local carnival and approaching a midway booth with a giant "Wheel of Chance." The wheel has many spaces on it, half colored blue and half yellow. The carnival operator tells you that if you spin and the wheel lands on a blue space, you will win $20. If it lands on a yellow space, you win nothing. How much would you pay to play this game?[3]

Many people can answer this question intuitively, without having to use a mathematical analysis. However, examining the mathematics of this example can be helpful to understanding what happens in more complicated situations. Decision analysis principles state that the expected outcome of a situation like this is found by multiplying the probabilities of each possible outcome by the result of that outcome (called the payoff), and then summing these products. In the Wheel of Chance example, the probability of landing on blue is 0.50, and the payoff for landing on blue is $20. Multiplying these numbers yields $10. The probability of landing on yellow is 0.50, the payoff for this is $0, and multiplying these numbers yields $0. Adding these two results, $10 plus $0, gives the expected result of the game: $10.

Figure 1 shows a graphical representation of this situation, which is a simple example of a "decision tree."[4] The trunk of the tree (entitled "Wheel of Chance") breaks off into two branches, representing the two possible outcomes of the game, blue or yellow. This juncture is marked with a circle (called a "chance node"), indicating that the results at this point cannot be controlled. The probabilities of each outcome (0.50) are written below each branch. Each branch ends in a triangle (called a "terminal node"), indicating that the game is over at that point, with payoffs of $20 for blue and $0 for yellow. A computer can be used to "roll back" the tree, which gives the expected value of the tree at the chance node. The box next to the chance node in Figure 1 shows the expected value of $10.

FIGURE 1

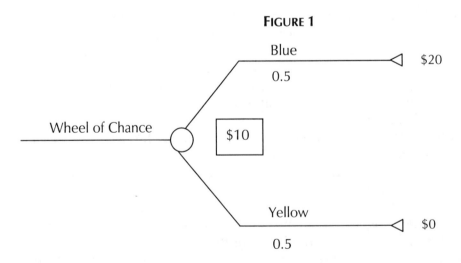

It is worth noting that $10 is not a possible outcome from playing a single game (which yields either $20 or $0). Instead, it is a mathematical construct providing a sense of what the game is worth, in a theoretical sense, to someone who plays it. One way of explaining this is that the expected value represents the average payoff for someone who played the game many times.

Different individuals will have different reactions to this information. People who do not enjoy playing games of chance may be willing to pay only $8 to play the Wheel of Chance (perhaps because they dislike risking money or because they would rather spend their time riding the roller coaster). On the other hand, carnival midways (not to mention Las Vegas casinos) exist because many people are willing to pay considerably more than $10 to play games such as this.[5]

For another example, imagine a slightly different Wheel of Chance. In this game, if the wheel lands on blue you will still win $20, but if it lands on yellow you must pay an additional $10. How much would you pay to play this game? The analytical approach is the same as in the first example: multiply the probabilities by the payoffs and add the results. The probability of landing on blue is 0.50, the payoff for landing on blue is $20, and multiplying these numbers yields $10. The probability of landing on yellow is 0.50, the payoff for this is -$10, and multiplying these numbers yields -$5. Adding these two results, $10 and -$5, gives the expected result of the game: $5. This example is somewhat closer to the realities of litigation, where parties who fail to win lawsuits obtain no damages and must still pay their attorneys. It is shown graphically in Figure 2.

FIGURE 2

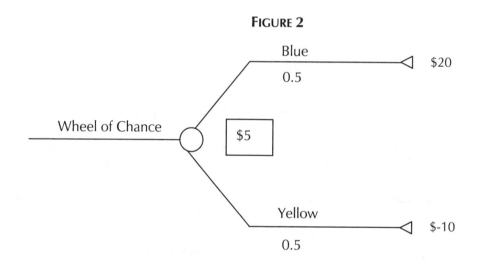

Finally, imagine a high-stakes Wheel of Chance, where the carnival operator will give you $1 million if the wheel lands on blue, but you must pay $400,000 if it lands on yellow. What would you do in this situation? Mathematically, the probability of landing on blue is 0.50, the payoff for landing on blue is $1 million, and multiplying these yields $500,000. The probability of landing on yellow is 0.50, the payoff for this is -$400,000, and multiplying these numbers yields -$200,000. Adding these two results, $500,000 and -$200,000, gives the expected result of the game: $300,000. This is shown in Figure 3 on the next page.

The high-stakes nature of this game introduces another factor into the analysis. Many people could not afford to take a chance of losing $400,000, even though the game as a whole has a highly favorable expected outcome. Similarly, some parties must settle a case in litigation, even when they expect to win, because they cannot afford to take the chance of losing. This provides another way for the rich to get richer—they are able to take favorable risks that others must avoid.

FIGURE 3

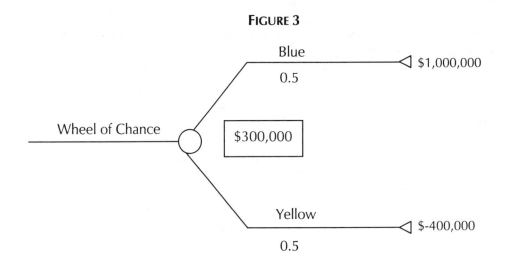

Decision Analysis in Non-Legal Contexts

Decision analysis has wide application outside the legal arena, with interesting implications. In some cases, parties knowingly take significant risks because they determine these risks are necessary in order to achieve important goals. For example, planners know that large public works projects involve substantial risks of bodily injury and even death for workers. With knowledge of the size and nature of the projects, it is even possible to make rough predictions of these events. More than ten people died when the subway system was constructed in Washington, D.C., a result that was reasonably foreseeable when the project began. Nonetheless, projects like this continue to be built because communities (and workers) decide to take risks.[6]

Decision analysis can yield unexpected results. One example is the decision of whether to shop at health food stores. Eating health food from these stores may result in a slightly longer expected lifespan for consumers. On the other hand, because there are relatively fewer health food stores than conventional grocery stores, most people must drive a greater distance to get to one. Driving is a risky endeavor, with a significant risk of bodily injury or death. Some statisticians have speculated that the risks of driving may outweigh any benefits of health food (at least for those who do not live close to a health food store).

Environmental analysts look at these types of calculations as well. Communities have decided to send recycling trucks to pick up materials from homeowners in order to protect the environment. However, for rural areas where citizens are spread widely apart, some have theorized that the pollution created by the trucks, and the gas consumption required for them to make their rounds, may do more harm to the environment than the benefits realized from the newspapers, aluminum cans, and other materials that are recovered.

Supreme Court Justice Stephen Breyer has written about the importance of analyzing risk carefully. He discussed a case over which he presided involving a ten-year effort to force cleanup of a toxic waste dump in New Hampshire:

> The site was mostly cleaned up. All but one of the private parties had settled. The remaining private party litigated the cost of cleaning up the last little bit, a cost of about $9.3 million to remove a small amount of ... [pollutants] by incinerating the dirt. How much extra safety did this $9.3 million buy? The forty-thousand-page record of this ten-year effort indicated (and all the parties seemed to agree) that, without the extra

expenditure, the waste dump was clean enough for children playing on the site to eat small amounts of dirt daily for 70 days each year without significant harm. Burning the soil would have made it clean enough for the children to eat small amounts daily for 245 days per year without significant harm. But there were no dirt-eating children playing in the area, for it was a swamp.[7]

Some may argue that $9.3 million is a small price to pay for protecting the environment, but Breyer responds to that argument as follows:

> The ... reason that it matters whether the nation spends too much to buy a little extra safety is that the resources available to combat health risks are not limitless.... If we take the $9.3 million spent on the New Hampshire waste dump clean-up as an indicator of the general problem of high costs in trying for that "last 10 percent" ($9.3 million times 26,000 toxic waste dumps is $242 billion), we have an answer to the question, "Does it matter if we spend too much over-insuring our safety?" The money is not, or will not be, there to spend, at least not if we want to address more serious environmental or social problems—the need for better prenatal care, vaccinations, and cancer diagnosis, let alone daycare, housing, and education.[8]

Decision Analysis in Legal Negotiation

Moving to the world of negotiation in litigation, imagine you are plaintiff in a lawsuit where the defendant has filed a motion to dismiss the case. You believe you probably will win the motion, and you believe you probably will win the trial as well. The damage award from the trial would be $100,000. The defendant has offered to pay you $40,000 to settle the case. Should you accept the offer?

In order to answer this question, you need to provide a mathematical probability that represents the value of the word "probably." This requires making your best estimate of how likely you are to win the motion and the trial. Assume you decide your chances of winning in each instance are 75%. Would you accept the offer?

In this example, you must prevail in both the motion and the trial in order to win any money. Decision analysis under these circumstances involves multiplying the probability of winning the motion by the probability of winning the trial, 0.75 x 0.75, which is 0.5625. This result is then multiplied by the payoff that results ($100,000), which yields an expected value of $56,250. Under this scenario, the $40,000 offer is too low, and the plaintiff should continue with the lawsuit. This case is represented in Figure 4.

FIGURE 4

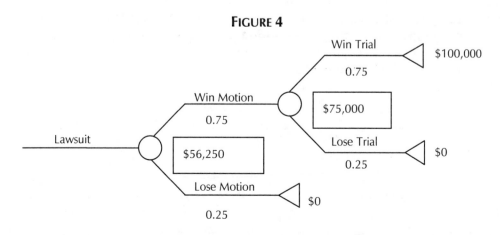

Attorney fees can also affect this analysis. In the example above, the expected out-come of the case is $56,250. Thus, on average, the plaintiff can expect to receive $56,250 from litigation, and the defendant can expect to pay $56,250. However, assume that both sides would face attorney fees of $10,000 if they took the matter all the way through trial. In this case, the expected income from the lawsuit would be only $46,250 for the plaintiff ($56,250 reduced by $10,000 in fees) and the ex-pected cost of the lawsuit would be $66,250 for the defendant ($56,250 in addition to $10,000 in fees).

This difference in expected outcome creates opportunities for the parties to settle. Any settlement amount greater than $46,250 would represent an improve-ment for the plaintiff over litigation, and any settlement amount less than $66,250 is better for the defendant. The $20,000 range between these two numbers is a zone of potential agreement. In this case, it is in the economic best interest of both parties to settle somewhere in that range. Decision analysis can be a valuable tool in this regard to show both parties in a lawsuit how they benefit from reaching a settlement.

Decision analysis can be particularly powerful in complex cases. Consider the multiple stages of proof involved in a Title VII discrimination lawsuit. First, in order to survive a motion for summary judgment, the plaintiff must produce evi-dence sufficient to prevent the defendant from establishing that there is no genuine disputed issue of material fact.[9] At trial, the plaintiff then must establish a prima facie case indicating discrimination.[10] If that burden is met, the defendant must articulate a legitimate, non-discriminatory reason for its actions. In order to prevail, the plaintiff must then establish that this reason is pretextual.

In a hypothetical Title VII case, the plaintiff makes the following estimates: the chance of surviving the motion for summary judgment is 75%, the chance of es-tablishing a prima facie case is 90%, and the chance of establishing that the defendant's explanation is pretextual is 67%. To analyze likely jury awards, the plaintiff estimates that there is a 10% chance that the jury will award $35,000, an 80% chance the jury will award $100,000, and a 10% chance that the jury will award $300,000.[11] This type of calculation is difficult to do by hand and almost impossible to do accurately by means of a hunch. A computer, however, can calcu-late the result in an instant, as shown in Figure 5.

This analysis shows that the expected value of the case at the beginning of liti-gation is $55,853. It also shows how the value of the case changes as litigation proceeds. The second chance node (immediately after the summary judgment stage) has a value of $74,471, indicating that if the plaintiff wins the summary judgment motion, the case rises in worth by almost $20,000. At the final stage (when the jury is deliberating), the case is worth $123,500. This type of analysis can be useful in any negotiation with multiple stages. Even if a party chooses not to settle a case at the beginning, it may prove appropriate to do so later on, de-pending on the values given by the decision analysis.

FIGURE 5

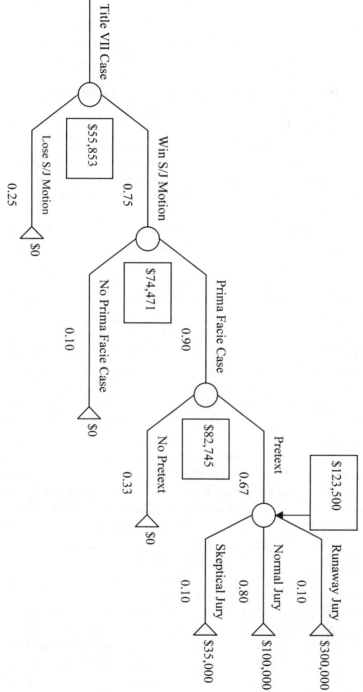

Advantages and Disadvantages of Decision Analysis

Attorneys have not traditionally focused on decision analysis in litigation and negotiation. While business clients are accustomed to looking rigorously at risk and
are trained to do so in M.B.A. programs, lawyers often have little experience with
this mode of analysis and receive no training in the field in law school. Further,
lawyers are sometimes reluctant to broaden the scope of their advice beyond
strictly "legal" problems. A valid decision analysis sometimes should look at a
wider range of issues, including personal risks (individuals can have more at stake
in certain decisions than legal implications alone), business risks (sometimes
companies cannot afford to take a chance on an outcome that would cause bankruptcy, even if the decision analysis shows the odds of it occurring are low) and
community risks (externalities may exist for certain decisions that affect the
community at large more significantly than an individual decision-maker).[12]

Decision analysis is not a perfect tool. The probabilities that parties place on
the likelihood of various events are not magically accurate. The final result of an
analysis is only as reliable as the data that parties use to create it, and the data are
usually uncertain and subjective. Indeed, the figure that results from a decision
analysis can appear artificially precise. Parties must recognize that it represents
only an estimate based on the information available at the time.[13]

Nonetheless, decision analysis can be a valuable tool to enable parties to make
more accurate predictions in negotiation. Assessing future outcomes is uncertain
and subjective no matter what method is used. Predictions based on hunches or
intuition are no more accurate than those based on decision analysis, and they
may be less so. The advantage of decision analysis is that it allows parties to combine several individual hunches in a rigorous mathematical manner. As Professor
Howard Raiffa wrote, "The spirit of decision analysis is divide and conquer: de-
compose a complex problem into simpler problems, get one's thinking straight in
these simpler problems, paste these analyses together with a logical glue, and
come out with a program for action for the complex problem."[14]

Decision analysis can also help parties overcome the human tendency to be
overconfident.[15] The example at the start of this article shows how it is natural to
underestimate the chances for failure in a situation. Looking at the results of a
decision analysis can help bring parties back down to earth. As another example of
this, the author of this chapter is a college football fan who begins every season
with great expectations for his team. One reason for these expectations is that,
over the last thirty years, the probability has been high that the team (the Nebraska Cornhuskers) would win most of its individual games. Statistics professor
(and Nebraska fan) Brad Carlin examined this phenomenon by calculating the
odds of the team winning each of its games. The calculations were done by examining the Sagarin computer rankings of each team, accounting for home field
advantage (typically three or four points), creating an expected margin of victory,
and determining the likelihood of winning based on all of these factors. The probabilities of victory historically have been quite high, as in the following example
from a season several years ago:

Opponent	Likelihood of Victory
Arizona State	92%
Troy State	98%
Utah State	99%
Penn State	74%
Iowa State	83%
McNeese State	99%
Missouri	95%
Oklahoma State	89%
Texas A & M	70%
Texas	73%
Kansas	97%
Kansas State	57%
Colorado	83%

These numbers appear to represent overwhelming odds in favor of victory. Indeed, the team was favored to win every single game, many by more than 90%. However, decision analysis shows that that the likelihood of going undefeated for an entire season is very slim.[16] Calculating the chance of an undefeated season requires multiplying together the chances of winning each individual game (.92 x .98 x .99 x .74, etc.). Using these numbers, the chance of an undefeated regular season is only 11%, or about one in nine. Considering the Big XII championship game and the national championship bowl contest, the odds of winning every game drop to only 3%.

Ultimately, negotiators should use decision analysis as a tool. It can be valuable for parties to use their intuition to make their best estimate of the overall value of a case before beginning any statistical analysis. Once the analysis is complete, parties can then compare their initial estimate with the result generated by the computer. When the results are comparable, parties can have more confidence in their position. If they are significantly different, parties should figure out why. In this way, decision analysis can enable parties to examine their assumptions rigorously and determine the best possible strategy for their negotiations.

Endnotes

This article is based on materials developed by the author for training federal attorneys. The views set forth herein are those of the author and do not necessarily reflect the views of the U.S. Department of Justice or the U.S. Government. An earlier version of this article spears at 87 Marquette law Review 723 (2004). The author wishes to thank Christopher Honeyman, Andrea K. Schneider, Janie Nadler and Jayne Seminare Docherty for their comments.

[1] Readers desiring additional information on the topics covered in this article can consult JEFFREY M. SENGER, FEDERAL DISPUTE RESOLUTION: USING ADR WITH THE UNITED STATES GOVERNMENT 80, 113-15 (2004); Marjorie Corman Aaron, *The Value of Decision Analysis in Mediation Practice*, 11 NEGOTIATION JOURNAL 123 (1995); David P. Hoffer, *Decision Analysis as a Mediator's Tool*, 1 HARVARD NEGOTIATION LAW REVIEW 113 (1996); Marc B. Victor, *The Proper Use of Decision Analysis to Assist Litigation Strategy*, 40 BUSINESS LAWYER 617 (1985).

[2] *See* ROGER FISHER, ET AL., GETTING TO YES: NEGOTIATING AGREEMENT WITHOUT GIVING IN (1981) (describing the importance of analyzing the best alternative to a negotiated agreement, known as "BATNA").

[3] Assume for purposes of the example that the carnival operator has not rigged the wheel to give an unfair result.

[4] Technically, this figure would be called a "chance tree" or an "event tree," because a decision tree would include another branch to indicate the option not to play the game at all.

[5] It is possible to use more advanced decision analysis tools to account for parties' risk preference. These tools can provide more specific information for parties who are inclined either in favor of or against taking risks.

[6] Some government positions include a specific salary component known as "danger pay" to compensate employees for additional risks they face on the job. *See, e.g.,* U.S. Department of State Standardized Regulations 650-57 (2001), *at* www.state.gov/m/a/als/1767.htm.

[7] STEPHEN G. BREYER, BREAKING THE VICIOUS CIRCLE: TOWARD EFFECTIVE RISK REGULATION 11-12 (1993) (internal citations omitted).

[8] *Id.* at 18-19 (internal citations omitted).

[9] Celotex Corp. v. Catrett, 477 U.S. 317, 322-23 (1986).

[10] McDonnell Douglas Corp. v. Green, 411 U.S. 792, 802 (1973).

[11] Jury awards are often estimated with this type of approach, with normal juries being in the middle of the bell curve (because they are more common) and with skeptical juries and runaway juries on either end.

[12] Professor John Wade sets forth a detailed list of reasons lawyers may be reluctant to perform decision analyses in *Systematic Risk Analysis for Negotiators and Litigators: But You Never Told Me It Would Be Like This*, 13 BOND LAW REVIEW 462 (2001).

[13] Parties can perform more complicated calculations, known as "sensitivity analyses," to examine the consequences that result when probability estimates are varied to account for different possible scenarios.

[14] HOWARD RAIFFA, DECISION ANALYSIS: INTRODUCTORY LECTURES ON CHOICES UNDER UNCERTAINTY 271 (1968).

[15] Robert H. Mnookin & Lee Ross, *Introduction, in* BARRIERS TO CONFLICT RESOLUTION 17-18 (Kenneth J. Arrow, et al. eds., 1995).

[16] Fans may also remember that the team lost seven games that year, 2002 (and six in 2004).

C3 52 80

Contingent Agreements

Michael L. Moffitt

Editors' Note: *What if you and the other side have very different views of the future? Should this make it harder to achieve an agreement? In fact, as Moffitt explains, these different views can provide exactly the lubricant needed for the gears to mesh. Contingent agreements can help negotiators move toward an overall agreement, even (or particularly) when they disagree. As one of several chapters discussing particular techniques for use when things get sticky, it should be read in conjunction with Wade's chapter on the Last Gap and Honeyman's on Using Ambiguity.*

"That won't happen." "Yes, it will." "No, it won't." "Will too."

Negotiators generally find no shortage of things about which to disagree. For example, negotiators seeking to resolve a dispute often have sharply differing perceptions of the past. What happened? Whose decisions and actions caused the effects in question? How does their conduct compare with expectations or duties? In some circumstances, settlement is impossible without resolution of these backward-looking questions. Classical dispute resolution theory suggests that one might overcome impasse by shifting the focus of conversations toward the future.[1] Sometimes, however, the shift to a forward-looking exploration merely provides fertile, new grounds for disagreement. Rather than arguing about what happened, the negotiators argue about what will happen. A wholesaler asserts that demand for the product will skyrocket, and the retailer suspects otherwise. A defendant points to the relatively minor and temporary injuries caused in a car crash, but the victim fears that later on, new injuries may manifest themselves. Instinct may suggest that one negotiator will need to persuade the other about the likelihood of future uncertain events. Instead, genuinely held disagreements about the future present an important opportunity for negotiators to discover an attractive exchange. The vehicle for capturing this potential is the contingent agreement.

All contingent agreements share a basic structure: the parties identify the universe of possible future conditions and agree to take on different obligations in each of those conditions. The simplest contingent deals are those in which the future has only two possible relevant conditions. X will happen, or it will not. If X happens, the terms of our deal are ABC; if not, we will do DEF. If I think X is unlikely to happen, I will be happy to give you terms you prefer for ABC, in exchange for terms I favor for DEF. Believing that she will get the work finished on time, an author signs a lucrative book contract with a very harsh penalty for late completion. Buyer loves Seller's house, but really wants a property with off-street parking. Seller firmly expects that the city council will approve a variance required for construction of a new garage, but Buyer is less confident about the likelihood of getting approval. Buyer agrees to purchase the property from Seller at a reduced price, with a substantial additional payment to Seller if the City Council grants a variance within the next twelve months. Negotiators can craft attractive trades by establishing obligations that are contingent on a future uncertain event that affects each side's valuation of the agreement.

Contingent agreements can also include variable terms, pegged to some benchmark to be measured in the future. I think interest rates will increase over the next few months, and you think they will go down. If I am loaning you money today, we will each be happy to agree to a deal with a floating interest rate. A school board is nervous about the future level of state funding available for school districts, while the teachers' union is optimistic. The teachers' union agrees to a wage and benefit increase tied to a particular line item in next year's state budget. The plaintiff believes that he may suffer long-term health effects of exposure to the defendant's product, while the defendant believes no significant health risks exist. The defendant agrees to pay specified medical monitoring expenses for the plaintiff and to assume any future medical costs associated with exposure.[2] Parties to a joint venture agree to final, binding resolution of their intellectual property dispute by an appointed arbitrator.[3] Without the possibility of contingent agreements, uncertainty regarding future conditions can make distributive decisions (for example, who gets how much money) difficult. By linking the allocation of resources to an externally measurable variable, negotiators can sometimes overcome otherwise paralyzing disagreements about the future.

Contingent agreements also present an opportunity to shape the incentives under which one or more of the negotiators will operate going forward. Some negotiated deals involve no future relationship between the negotiators and are self-executing. Buying a trinket in a marketplace involves a simple exchange of money for goods. In more complex circumstances, however, ongoing relationships exist and implementation of the agreement takes place over time. When the negotiated deal involves more than a simple, one-time exchange, parties' behavior after the agreement is relevant. Contingent agreements can help to create incentives for parties to behave well after the terms of the deal are fixed. A company may agree to tie a sales executive's compensation to sales performance, thus promoting sales-maximizing behavior out of the executive after the deal is signed. The health ministry of a developing country approaches a prospective donor, seeking support for particular health sector programs. Both the prospective donor and the developing country want to see multiple sources of funding. They agree to a matching program under which the donor will contribute an amount equal to the funds the ministry secures from other sources, giving the ministry officials added incentive to garner resources. In some contingent deals, one party can affect the likelihood of the contingent trigger—the salesman can make more sales calls, the ministry officials can approach more donors. In these types of deals, contingent agreements can affect parties' behavior after the agreement.

At the same time, precisely because contingent agreements can affect parties' behaviors, some contingent agreements risk creating conditions of moral hazard. Moral hazard is a condition in which one party, under the terms of an agreement, may undetectably or uncontrollably behave in a way that is adverse to the other party.[4] How quickly do you take the speed bumps when you are driving a rental car? Moral hazard suggests that many drivers will drive more cautiously over the bumps if they are driving their own cars because they consider the long-term effects of their driving behavior. Athletes' contracts often contain contingent incentive clauses. If the athlete scores a certain number of points, for example, he or she receives additional money. Such arrangements are a classic example of using contingent agreements to create favorable incentives for the player to perform. Moral hazard arises when, toward the end of the season, a team notices that the athlete is only a few points away from the triggering contingent event. Will the team structure its play to enable the athlete to achieve the statistical goal, or will the prospect of this contingent payment encourage the team's management to focus its efforts on a different player during the remaining games? If a salesperson's contract provides for a thirty percent commission on sales this year, but only a ten percent commission in future years, the salesperson will have an incentive to push deals into the current year—even if the deal he or she could have struck next year would have been on terms more favorable to the company. If a developing country knows that the international community will bail it out if the country's risky currency strategy winds up going poorly, will the country take on an inappropriate risk?[5] Negotiators crafting a contingent agreement should foresee the possibility of moral hazard and, where appropriate, structure incentives and disclosures to minimize the incentive for subsequent adverse behavior.

One challenge in crafting a contingent agreement is identifying the boundaries of future possible conditions with sufficient clarity to know what obligations attach. A married couple might agree, "If the weather is nice tomorrow, we'll hike. Otherwise, we'll go shopping." The next morning, when it is cloudy but not raining, the spouse who wants to hike is likely to declare it "nice," while the person preferring to shop will argue the opposite. Rather than premise future obligations on something difficult to define with precision—the weather, the economy, one's health, political stability—wise contingent deals depend on easily-measured external variables. Did the airport weather station register precipitation in the past twenty-four hours? Did the unemployment rate for the state increase last month? Did the lab results show a drop in the level of "bad" cholesterol in your blood? Did the local elections take place on the pre-specified date? Answering such questions is relatively reliable and low-cost.

Still more complications arise when the contingent variable being measured is under the interpretive control of one party. For example, a mid-level executive may not want to have her bonus tied to the performance of the business unit she oversees if she has concerns that the company may subsequently adopt accounting methods that shift credit from her unit to another unit.[6] Similarly, a screenwriter is more likely to favor a percentage of the box office take over a percentage of the profits a studio reports on a film. Contingent agreements containing unambiguous, external triggers are less likely to produce post-agreement disagreements.

Crafting contingent deals also raises considerable questions about strategic disclosure.[7] Without any disclosure regarding forecasts and preferences, negotiators will not spot the possibility for a contingent agreement. Such disclosures, however, inevitably produce a risk of exploitation. Assume that I am virtually certain that X will happen, and you are virtually certain that X will not happen. If I begin our negotiations by declaring that I am "virtually certain X will happen," you may have an incentive to misstate your actual forecast. Rather than tell me that you are virtually certain of the opposite, you may tell me that you think there is "a decent chance" that X will not happen. You then may have an opportunity to demand a more favorable premium for being the party to take on the apparently greater risk. Contingent agreements are not different from most other aspects of bargaining; this presents opportunities both for mutually beneficial value creation and for one-sided efforts to skew value distribution.

Contingent agreements may affect negotiators' perceptions of "winning" and "losing." Classical negotiation theory counsels negotiators to conceive of negotiations in terms other than win-lose, pointing to the risk that competitive behavior may cloud opportunities for joint gains.[8] In one respect, contingent agreements may present an opportunity for negotiators to avoid the necessity of identifying a winner. Rather than forcing one side to concede on its forecast, contingent agreements permit (in fact, depend on) both sides to maintain their conflicting predictions about the future. At the time of the agreement, therefore, each side can declare "victory," to the extent such a declaration is important.

At the same time, contingent agreements have the nature of a wager. Unless one counts the sheer joy of gambling as a victory, both sides cannot win a wager. The contingent event either happens or it does not. Either way, one side may be disappointed.[9] In some organizational cultures, failure is punished more harshly than success is rewarded. How likely is a mid-level bureaucrat to agree to take on the prospect of a contingent agreement if the unlikely-but-possible "bad" outcome will be attributed to him personally? Even if the contingent agreement is rational from an expected-value perspective, the fear of "losing" the wager involved may lead a negotiator to reject an otherwise elegant contingent arrangement in favor of a non-contingent deal.

Certain contingent structures may help to reduce the risk of visibly "losing." For example, if a plaintiff fears that a jury may award him nothing and a defendant fears a runaway jury award of millions, the two could agree to a small guaranteed recovery in exchange for a cap on the maximum recovery.[10] The losing party at trial will then be grateful to have made the contingent agreement, and the winner's regret will be dampened by having won a favorable verdict.

Given that two people virtually never agree entirely on the likely shape of the future, why aren't all deals contingent? Part of the answer lies in the transaction costs associated with identifying differences and crafting elegant contingent agreements. Two parties crafting the terms of a joint venture cannot imagine that they will plan for every possible contingency. At some point, they will agree to resolve future uncertainties when/if they arise. Even in circumstances without trust or a structural incentive for cooperation, the contingent stakes may simply be too low to justify the effort of crafting and implementing the deal. The costs of crafting a contingent agreement may, in some cases, outweigh the possible benefits of a contingent arrangement.

Another factor dissuading parties from crafting contingent deals is the value some parties place on certainty and finality. Particularly for negotiators embroiled in a dispute, achieving resolution may have an inherent value independent of the terms of the deal. Many disputants find it emotionally costly to carry around uncertainty. A contingent agreement does not represent complete finality, as at least some of the terms are yet to be determined. Uncertainty also can be costly for economic reasons. A company with an uncertain liability or benefit on its books faces considerable challenges in planning appropriate reserves of money, for example. If a company has a large collection of similar contingent agreements, it may be able to spread the risks and allocate money accurately in the aggregate. Similarly, some circumstances may permit parties to manage risks through the use of hedging instruments such as futures or options. Such allocations are not generally available to all individual negotiators, potentially making contingent agreements less attractive. For a contingent agreement to be appropriate in a given context, therefore, the perceived benefit it captures for each negotiator must exceed the transaction costs of discovering and implementing the agreement.

Negotiators arguing about the past sometimes "agree to disagree," preferring instead to focus on what they will do moving forward. Negotiators with differing perceptions of the future should similarly agree to disagree—using contingent agreements to capture the potential benefits of their differences.

Endnotes

[1] *See, e.g.*, JAMES J. ALFINI, ET AL., MEDIATION THEORY AND PRACTICE 128-29 (2001); CARRIE MENKEL-MEADOW, MEDIATION, xxix (2000); JOSEPH STULBERG, TAKING CHARGE: MANAGING CONFLICT 101 (1987).

[2] Such an agreement raises certain risks related to the precision with which the triggering event is defined. Which tests are necessary for monitoring? The plaintiff may want many more tests than the defendant considers appropriate. Even more significantly, who will determine whether the need for particular medical treatment was caused by exposure?

[3] An arbitrator's award is a measurable, external variable to be fixed in the future, on which the parties might agree to base the terms of their agreement. In this sense, arbitration agreements are a form of contingent agreement. *See* Max H. Bazerman & James J. Gillespie, *Betting on the Future: The Virtues of Contingent Contracts*, HARVARD BUSINESS REVIEW, Sept.-Oct. 1999, at 155, 157; DAVID A. LAX & JAMES K. SEBENIUS, THE MANAGER AS NEGOTIATOR 96 (1986). In some sense, parties may also purposefully agree to a currently ambiguous term in a contract, with an understanding that in future conditions a nonparty will interpret the term. *See* Christopher Honeyman, *In Defense of Ambiguity*, 3 NEGOTIATION JOURNAL 81 (1987) (describing the pragmatic considerations of including ambiguous language in agreements—for example, a labor agreement permitting termination only for "just cause").

[4] *See* ROBERT H. MNOOKIN, ET AL., BEYOND WINNING: NEGOTIATING TO CREATE VALUE IN DEALS AND DISPUTES 26 (2000) (defining moral hazard as "[t]he problem created when a contract shifts risk from one party to another party and information asymmetries permit the non-riskbearer to behave adversely under the contract without detection or consequence").

[5] *See* Laura D'Andrea Tyson, *If There Were No IMF, They'd Have to Invent One*, BUSINESS WEEK, Mar. 9, 1998 at 21. ("Without question, the most serious concern about the IMF's intervention is that it contributes to the so-called moral hazard problem, whereby economic actors reap the benefits of their decisions when things go well but are protected when things go poorly. If borrowers and investor do not suffer the costs of bad decisions, won't they be encouraged to make more bad decisions in the future? If the system spares the financial market rod, won't it spoil the financial market child? To some extent, the answer is yes.")

[6] *See also* LAX & SEBENIUS, *supra* note 3, at 97 (describing a union's reluctance to tie wages to a company's profit margin).

[7] For more on strategic disclosure and the tactical considerations raised by information exchange in negotiation, *see* HOWARD RAIFFA, THE ART AND SCIENCE OF NEGOTIATION 44-65 (1982); G. RICHARD SHELL, BARGAINING FOR ADVANTAGE: NEGOTIATION STRATEGIES FOR REASONABLE PEOPLE 132-55 (1999); MNOOKIN, ET AL., *supra* note 4, at 11-43; LAX & SEBENIUS, *supra* note 3, at 29-45.

[8] Perhaps the most widely cited authority for this proposition is in ROGER FISHER, ET AL., GETTING TO YES: NEGOTIATING AGREEMENT WITHOUT GIVING (2d ed. 1991). While the authors of GETTING TO YES do not label it so, many describe a particular stance toward negotiation as "win-win." The label is problematic, but widely recognized.

[9] This assertion is modestly overbroad. Recently, on a business trip with a colleague, we were dashing between gates, trying to make a flight. My colleague expressed confidence that we would make it, while I was convinced we would not. We placed a small wager on our fate. We made the gate with seconds to spare, and as we boarded the plane, I handed over the $1 wager I had lost. I was not in the least disappointed to have been wrong in my prediction. The nature of my position in the wager, however, was uncommon in that I was sure to experience some measure of success in either event.

[10] For more on high-low agreements, *see* Samuel R. Gross & Kent D. Syverud, *Don't Try: Civil Jury Verdicts in a System Geared to Settlement*, 44 UCLA LAW REVIEW 1, 61 (1996); Chris Guthrie, *Better Settle Than Sorry: The Regret Aversion Theory of Litigation Behavior*, 1999 UNIVERSITY OF ILLINOIS LAW REVIEW 43 (1999).

❧ 53 ❧

Using Ambiguity

Christopher Honeyman

Editors' Note: The reality sinks in: everybody's now trying to reach an agreement, but on some fundamental things, the parties really don't agree. Some of those involved see themselves as reasonable people, others are Standing On Principle without any thought of what that will mean in practice. Is there anything you can do to get this dispute over with before it spirals completely out of control? Yes, says Honeyman: you can allow, or even consciously design in, a bit of ambiguity here and there. Doing this knowledgeably can preserve your principles, while allowing for an agreement that works well enough for an imperfect world.

Go to work under any of thousands of labor-management contracts, and you can be fired only for "just cause"—whatever *that* means. A truly vague statement, it's pretty well guaranteed to generate disputes under the contract later, as the parties naturally see a marginal employee differently. So it's a classic example of ambiguity in action. But why on earth would any sane pair of labor and management negotiation teams leave the all-important discharge clause so up-in-the-air?

There is, I think, a very good reason. It starts with the notion that a matter of principle really is often at the root of a dispute—even though experienced negotiators are familiar with the counterpart who takes a strong and seemingly unalterable stand on a point of principle, only to exchange it for money when the price is right. An explicit confrontation over a question of principle can result in a total inability to work out a settlement; so it should not be surprising that negotiators and mediators sometimes paper over these cracks with calculated or innocent ambiguities. This chapter will examine the function of ambiguity in agreements, and defend its deliberate use under certain circumstances.

There will always be those who value the effect of ambiguities on their earnings, such as a full-time labor arbitrator of my acquaintance who once declared happily that "There's no such thing as clear contract language." But most negotiators and mediators seem to have a vague disapproval of ambiguity. This is excusable. Most professional negotiators, most of the time, seek agreements that will be clear, easy to administer, and durable. [Wade & Honeyman, *Lasting Agreement*] A general preference for wrapping up loose ends fits with the notion of "settlement," and a neat and tidy job seems consistent with professionalism.

The principals in many negotiations may bring to bear a different perspective. Even while negotiating an agreement, they are looking down the road to the later interpretation of that agreement; and in the case of permanent relationships like those between labor and management, they are quite likely to be engaged in the arbitration of one dispute, the litigation of another, and the negotiation of a third at the same time.

Much of what happens in complex negotiations can be seen in terms of a struggle between radical and moderate elements within each party. [Bellman, *Team Conflicts* & Matz, *Team Miscommunication*] In a multi-faceted negotiation, the fact that the moderate element on one issue may be the radical element on another obscures, but does not change, the essential relationship between moderate and radical. Bear with me if for simplicity I encapsulate a typical negotiating group as consisting of a radical minority and a moderate majority. (Where the situation is reversed, effective negotiation or mediation is unlikely).

In such a group, the radicals can be expected to emphasize philosophical and ideological purposes, partly out of conviction, but also because this gives them a platform in the continuing attempt to garner public support, and perhaps become the dominant faction. The moderates, meanwhile, are likely to emphasize the practical results of accommodation as opposed to confrontation. I have elsewhere commented [Honeyman, *Understanding Mediators*] that when a mediator is presented with such a situation, the mediator's tendency, or even function, is to help the moderate out-argue the radical within a given party. Mediators, however, are not alone in seeing it as generally preferable to divert an argument over "principle" into a "pragmatic" channel, so that an explicit agreement can be reached. Yet this cannot always be accomplished. The best alternative may sometimes be to leave a deliberate gap or other ambiguity in the agreement: clarity emphasizes the differences, while ambiguity can serve to let each faction maintain its position and self-image in principle, if not necessarily in practice. But does this merely store up trouble for the future? Is it, in some sense, immoral?

The traditional view of ambiguity in an agreement is that it implies either the presence of an unconsidered point, or a deliberate failure to come to grips with the problem. In either case, that view amounts to a belief that where there is ambiguity there is no agreement. A classic example is one presented by Sanda Kaufman. [Kaufman, *Interpreter*] The word *"ceasefire"* carries critically different meanings in Arabic (*hudna*), in Hebrew (*hafsakat esh*) and in English. In English, it means an end to aggressive acts; in Hebrew, *hafsakat esh* means to Israelis that Palestinians must stop all attacks against them, but that if Israel gets wind of a pending terror attack, an anticipatory response is permissible; in Arabic, *hudna* means a temporary scaling down of hostilities, but that a true enemy remains. When any agreement must be rendered in three languages, this particular ambiguity is conspicuously likely to cause trouble.

But I believe there's more to it than that. As every arbitrator knows, agreements are to be read as a whole. And there is a strong impetus on others, as well as arbitrators, to find a way to *interpret* an agreement rather than declare that for the purpose under review, there isn't one—a stance that may be intellectually defensible, but which can have alarming practical results.

The potentially calamitous consequences of an untimely declaration that "Gee, now I look at it closely, there's no agreement after all" can often be predicted by the parties. I take the view that they often *have* predicted such consequences. Parties have impliedly anticipated that agreement-readers will strive to interpret the agreement as a whole to resolve the ambiguity for immediate purposes. In turn, parties have often built in implicit mechanisms for doing so, such that the interpretation of an ambiguity depends partly on the enforcement mechanism specified in the agreement. Suppose, for instance, that you are negotiating two different matters with different parties at the same time. Each party sends you a draft agreement on the same day. In the event of a later dispute over its interpretation, one proposed contract calls for mediation, followed by arbitration if necessary, with both clauses specifying mainstream firms as the neutrals. The other draft contract specifies good-faith negotiations over any differences of interpretation but provides for either party to sue for enforcement at any time. By chance, in another section, both drafts also contain the exact same clause—a rather ambiguous one. But will that clause, in practice, mean the same thing in both contracts?

Every agreement contains at least one express or implied means of securing compliance with its terms. Different mechanisms of enforcement generate different results when exposed to ambiguity, and this can be predicted by anyone who possesses a working knowledge of the several mechanisms. For this reason, an agreement, read as a whole, can in fact provide a functional interpretation to the ambiguity.

A moment's thought about the characteristics of the various enforcement mechanisms will suggest that the choice of negotiation, mediation, arbitration, fact-finding, litigation or unilateral action implies something about the balance of power *within* each party as well as that *between* the parties. Negotiation, for instance, inherently preserves to the parties the power to create something new; but it always requires a backup process, since settlement cannot be guaranteed. Mediation is similar in this respect. But both processes imply more; they anticipate some give-and-take, suggesting that parties specifying these processes are willing to settle for a moderated result in a given case, one that is likely to draw as much from the exigencies of circumstance as from principle. When compared with the rights-only implication of specifying litigation, or the raw power-display of unilateral action (such as, in a labor context, the right to strike over grievances) the expectation of give-and-take is likely to result in significant differences in the practical interpretation of ambiguous language.

Litigation, when selected as the "bottom line" in the event of disagreement over interpretation, implies that the parties have adopted the rules and mores of the society-at-large as their working standards; but because of its expense and the burden of proof, it implies more than that. In ambiguous circumstances, it suggests a larger sphere of unilateral discretion flows to the "acting party," and correspondingly less to the "responding party." And so on. Thus which process, or combination of processes, the parties choose can be an index to the interpretation of other parts of the agreement.

For a couple of illustrations of how this works in practice, I will use labor agreements;[1] not only have they long provided explicit grievance mechanisms for negotiating subsidiary disputes, but they also have a long history of using mediation and arbitration as well, often as steps in the same dispute. Rounding out the menu, labor and management are also no strangers to litigation or to unilateral action. But I will focus on arbitration, because in this context it is particularly revealing. Atypically, in the often-confidential world of ADR, this history is thoroughly documented, with thousands of arbitration awards published and codified, and with many prior grievance settlements discussed in those awards. Also, arbitration alone combines the terminating force of an imposed decision with a value system theoretically drawn from the agreement itself. So it's significant, I think, that almost all of these agreements use arbitration as the final step in subsidiary disputes.

If in fact ambiguity implied the absence of an agreement, the thousands of reported pronouncements of labor arbitrators on ambiguous clauses should reflect that. The fact that they typically do not is instructive as to the underlying intent of the amorphous mass of contending factions often called, in an oversimplification, "the two parties." Meanwhile, labor arbitration proceedings are widely recognized as governed by principles that combine an injunction to the arbitrator to arrive at an award which "draws its essence" from the parties' agreement with an underlying set of nonlegal expectations, expressed in labor cases as "the law of the shop." Labor arbitrators can regularly be heard to denounce the notion that they should apply external law in their decisions, and the system of labor arbitration has continued with surprising stability of attitudes for many years. This is a system that comes as close to pure reliance on the perceived intent of the parties as decision-making systems get. It is significant, therefore, that the bulk of labor arbitration awards concerned with ambiguous contract language in effect apply a general rule that *ambiguity implies moderation.*

To return to the opening example, the common clause in labor contracts, providing that an employee may be discharged (or disciplined) for "just cause," is not ubiquitous. Some parties have been able to agree on a laundry list of circumstances that warrant discharge or don't, and have written that into their agreements. But such an effort generally runs into roadblocks of principle that tend to exacerbate the dispute. Consider, for instance, even so "obvious" a standard for discharge as proven theft: the company says "Theft is theft," the union says "What if it's just a pencil?" Or lateness: the union says "You can't fire someone for being late," the company replies "Then we'll get a few employees who take advantage of that, and we'll be stuck with them for years while they screw up the production schedule any time they feel like it."

In the practical result of countless labor negotiations, the phrase "just cause" is preferred to the divisive thrashing-out of the possible permutations and combinations of circumstance. The phrase is ambiguous, in this instance, because of its vagueness.[2] The company agrees to "just cause" because it is hard to maintain a claim that it should have the right to discharge employees for unjust reasons or no reason at all. The union agrees to it because it is hard to maintain that employees who by definition are getting what they deserve should be kept on the job. Even a cursory review of the vast profusion of cases decided under this standard shows that the awards are generally moderate in tone and fact-driven. And the parties routinely complain about the result, but rarely change the underlying standard.

The long line of subcontracting (or in recent parlance, "outsourcing") cases supplies a second illustration, which draws from a different kind of ambiguity. In theory, nothing could be simpler than for the parties to a labor agreement to write such language as "The employer may subcontract work" or "The company may not subcontract work." However, either phrase will conflict with a basic principle of one of the parties. In the union's case, the principle is that the union represents those who perform certain work, and by strenuous efforts it has managed to raise their wages. The last thing a union can accept is the notion that an employer can, without restriction, give away the employees' work to the cheapest labor it can find through a subcontractor. But at the same time, the question of "make or buy?" is basic to the manufacturing process of any complex product. Industries have a long history, predating any organization of the employees, of routine decision-making as to the best method of obtaining any given component of a product or service. Management therefore finds a principled obstacle to agreeing to give up the right to make such decisions.

Some parties have been able to agree on specific language providing for the right to subcontract under certain circumstances and not under others. But of greater interest here is the plethora of labor agreements which are *silent* as to subcontracting, even though both parties have been aware for decades of the potential or actual issue. These contracts, however, often contain a seniority clause, a recognition clause and a general management rights clause. Typically in subcontracting cases, the union will argue that the recognition clause, combined with language protecting seniority rights and the specified wage scale for the performance of certain work, shows clearly that in the absence of language specifically allowing subcontracting, the agreement must be read as preserving work to the employees represented by the union. The company, in turn, will argue that the management rights clause (generally using a formula something like "the company shall have all rights of management except as limited by this agreement") clearly shows that, since the union has not managed to negotiate language expressly restricting subcontracting, the company has plenary rights to subcontract any work it chooses in the best interest of the business. And then both parties will get down to brass tacks and try their case based on the ambiguity customarily recognized to arise from these conflicting clauses.

The standard desk reference of the labor arbitration trade, universally called *Elkouri*,[3] accurately describes the various tests used by different arbitrators where no specific contract language (or conclusive evidence of bargaining history) exists concerning subcontracting. These general tests, all of which discuss the common clauses favoring the union and favoring the company, are less interesting than the fact that they converge on the same practical considerations. Elkouri summarizes these standards as past practice; justification of the present instance; effect on the union or the bargaining unit; effect on individual employees; the type of work involved and its relation to employees' usual work; whether suitable employees or equipment are available in-house; whether the subcontracting will be regular or long-lasting; and special circumstances, such as an emergency.[4]

What is significant to this discussion is that every one of these standards tends to secure a moderate answer. The resulting fact-driven awards have, of course, regularly prompted the "we was robbed" reaction almost expected of a losing party to a labor arbitration; but in the larger sense, they have found acceptance. This is proven by the simple fact of the longevity of these standards, and by thousands of pairs of parties' bilateral if tacit agreement not to renegotiate the underlying contract language over a long period of time.

In either example, the negotiators who constructed the agreement and the arbitrator who interprets it all show their relationship to the moderate and radical elements on both sides by the practical and predictable result of their actions. The arbitrator in particular—a creature of the agreement and, one hopes, uniquely sensitive to its nuances—serves the moderates' goals by distinguishing between tolerable and intolerable incursions into each party's "principles." The arbitrator couches her decision in terms of the agreement, but strains to avoid using the term "equity" in order to escape the accusation of the radicals on the losing side that the award does not "draw its essence" from the agreement. And in turn, the courts refrain from second-guessing the arbitrator by applying general legal principles, adopting instead the Supreme Court rulings in the "Steelworkers' Trilogy"[5] and related standards for deferral to arbitration's results. At the same time, the "bargaining in the shadow of the arbitrator" that takes place in the earlier stages of grievance processes ensures that the vast majority of grievances are resolved at relatively low transaction costs, preserving to both parties the financial ability to contest a grievance to the point of arbitration when they feel they must. From the point of view of the moderate on either side who desired a workable if not ideal agreement, *the various processes of dispute resolution thus form an intricate ecology, in which each depends on the others for the success of the whole.*

Some may object that the moderating effect I describe is instead an indication of the alleged tendency of arbitrators to compromise.[6] But an award that does not clearly give the whole issue to either party is not proof of the arbitrator's lack of integrity, nor does it demonstrate that the arbitrator was prejudiced. In a "compromise" decision, the arbitrator presumably is motivated by a desire not to offend anyone; but in the awards under discussion here the arbitrators are properly performing their function, which is to interpret conflicting or vague provisions so as to give meaning to the whole agreement.

The net result for negotiators and mediators is that ambiguity can be employed as a tool in achieving an adequate, if imperfect, settlement of a dispute. *Provided that the agreed-on enforcement mechanism is appropriate to this end*, leaving ambiguities can imply that the disposition of subsidiary disputes will be fact-driven and moderate in overall effect. This enables the moderates in either party to compel discourse on terms acceptable to them, and to retain control of their party by avoiding reliance on rhetoric and ideology. A judicious bit of ambiguity therefore becomes a sophisticated means of ensuring that the general philosophy of the party does not have to be compromised explicitly (which would allow radicals to claim that the moderates had "sold them down the river"), while allowing enough putative "wins" by the opposing party to make agreement possible.

Negotiators are employed to create agreements, and should not sneer at an ambiguity when that is a necessary element in obtaining an overall agreement—as long as any subsidiary disputes that result seem likely to be manageable. (A possible exception, beyond the scope of this chapter but worthy of discussion in terms of its ethics, is the situation where a negotiator or mediator suspects that a proposed ambiguity will *not* be interpreted according to the kinds of standards applied above, but will instead be subject to unilateral action. That involves a technically difficult and morally problematic calculation of the "mutual best interest" of conflicting parties.)

But where a "moderating" system obtains for the disposition of subsidiary disputes, there is nothing inherently wrong with gracefully admitting the impossibility of reaching, in every instance, a complete "meeting of the minds." Allowing an ambiguity to pass into the agreement, when there is a reasonable expectation that it will later be interpreted in terms not likely to cause a wider dispute, is just another way to get the agreement done.

Endnotes

This chapter is adapted from the author's *In Defense of Ambiguity*, 3 NEGOTIATION JOURNAL 81 (1987).

[1] This discussion is based on U.S. practice; the underlying legal rights and other expectations of these types of parties vary by country.
[2] WILLIAM EMPSON, SEVEN TYPES OF AMBIGUITY (2d ed., rev. and re-set 1947). Empson distinguished a series of different types of ambiguity, though Empson, who was writing about poetry, identified some types not relevant to disputes. (A "fortunate confusion" is a concept of ambiguity attributable, in the context of an agreement, only to someone who hopes to make a living from it.) Of Empson's list, these seem applicable to disputes: "when a detail is effective several ways at once;" "simultaneous unconnected meanings;" "a contradictory or irrelevant statement, forcing the reader to invent interpretation;" and "full contradiction, marking a division in the author's mind." All of these are consistent with a condition not normally present in poetry—the opposing purposes of plural authors.
[3] FRANK ELKOURI & EDNA ASPER ELKOURI, HOW ARBITRATION WORKS (Alan Miles Ruben ed., 6th ed. 2003).
[4] *Id.* at 748-53.
[5] These three U.S. Supreme Court decisions set the standards for federal courts to use in determining both arbitrability of a given dispute and whether or not an award should be overturned on the merits. *See* United Steelworkers of America v. American Mf. Co., 363 U.S. 564 (1960); United Steelworkers of America v. Enterprise Wheel & Car Corp., 363 U.S. 593 (1960); United Steelworkers of America v. Warrior & Gulf Nav. Co., 363 U.S. 574 (1960).
[6] It is often argued that arbitrators have a tendency to "split the baby" in order to remain acceptable to both sides. I doubt the truth of that assertion, but must note that the fact that it is so often made implies that it is at least widely believed by parties using arbitration. From this, however, it could be inferred that parties holding such suspicions enter into their agreements "knowing," and implicitly tolerating, so widely expected an outcome—also, of course, a form of moderation-by-ambiguity.

❧ 54 ❧

Crossing the Last Gap

John H. Wade

Editors' Note: *It's three o'clock in the morning. You've been negotiating or mediating since 9 a.m. and everybody is exhausted. Each side has made more concessions that it really thinks it should have had to, and the gap between the parties has narrowed to millimeters. But there it has stuck, and will stay stuck unless you do something new. Every sophisticated negotiator or experienced mediator has a personal answer to this problem, a private stock of a few gambits, often tried and sometimes successful. But John Wade has the longest list we have ever seen, 16 techniques in all. Not one of them works all the time, but together they can materially improve your batting average.*

What is the last gap in a negotiation? It is the last step necessary to reach an agreement between the negotiating parties. Often that last gap or last increment emerges after long and exhausting negotiations which have led to agreement on all issues but one. For example, that one issue may be: who gets the grandfather clock? How should the last 10% of the pool of assets be divided? How should the outstanding credit card debt be paid? How to cross the difference of $600 or $1 million in the parties' "final" offers? Will the lease have a five year renewal option attached?

Most lawyers and business people can relate horror stories with humor and/or anguish about clients becoming stuck on the last issue of a lengthy negotiation. Some lawyers can tell how they themselves have offered to write a check to cover the last gap in order to help disputants end the drawn out negotiations, and almost invariably the disputants refuse the offer "as a matter of principle."

The Importance of the Last Gap

Why does the last increment or last issue assume such importance and so often (anecdotally) provide a stumbling block to a negotiated settlement? There are a number of possible explanations, which include:

- The last dance—Negotiations are often compared to a dance, where one or more parties circle each other apparently reluctant to end the process or relationship.
- Unfinished emotional business—Commercial "common sense" sometimes does not prevail at the last gap as one or more parties have a deep hurt or loss which has not been acknowledged or "resolved."

- The last straw—"I have given up so much already"—A common method of negotiation is for each party to open with extreme claims and then gradually make small moves toward a settlement between those extremes. This process often leaves one or both parties with an increasing sense of "loss" and anger.
- Sense of having been tricked—When the last gap is reached, the party who opened with what they perceived to be a "reasonable" offer, often feels tricked as the bargaining range has been dragged towards the person who started with an extreme or "unreasonable" offer. [Schneider, *Aspirations*]
- Skilled helpers attempt to prove worth—Sometimes lawyers (or union officials, etc.) negotiate aggressively about the last gap as a form of theater to justify the fees they will be demanding from their already disappointed clients.
- Recriminations for lost time and money—Sometimes the last gap triggers anger, as the negotiator realizes that he could have settled for the same amount two years earlier. Instead, he has invested two years of time and money to achieve "nothing."

How to Cross the Last Gap in Negotiations

What strategies are available to cross this hurdle in negotiations or mediation? One aspect of an adviser's role is to be an expert in the dynamics of negotiation and to educate the disputants concerning these dynamics. Parties can then have some confidence, even though they may feel in the wilderness, that there are well trodden paths which they have some power to choose between. A negotiator can give information concerning the range of options which are available. What follows is a list of options on how to cross the last gap.

Options for Crossing the Last Gap in Negotiations

The sixteen methods are as follows:

- Talk—Try to convince.
- Split the difference.
- Expanding the pie by subdividing the last gap.
- Expanding the pie by an add-on offer—"What if I moved on.....?"
- Refer to a third party umpire.
- Chance—Flip a coin.
- Chance—Draw gradations from a hat.
- Transfer the last gap to a third party.
- Conditional offers and placating incremental fears—"What if I could convince client to...? How would you respond?"
- Pause—and speak to significant others.
- Pause—and schedule time for a specific offer.
- Defer division of last gap; divide rest.
- Sell last item at auction; split proceeds.
- Pick-a-pile; you cut, I choose.
- Skilled helper has a face-saving tantrum.
- File a (further) court application—pursue pain and hope.

Talk—Try to Convince

A common response at the last one million dollars, $10,000, at the last set of paintings, or the last car, is for one or both disputants to talk—to rehash old arguments in an attempt to convince the other party to give in. These arguments take various forms:

- "I have given up so much in these negotiations; now it's your turn."
- A lengthy filibuster reiterating all the merits of the speaker's claims, and the weaknesses of the agitated or glassy-eyed "listener."
- An angry speech about how the listener's first offer was outrageous, so (s)he should make the last incremental concession "to be fair."
- A lengthy speech about the cost of litigation, the costs already incurred and the likelihood of settlement at the door of the court.
- A detailed historical version of the concessions made to date in the negotiation leading to the predictable conclusion that it is the listener's turn to be reasonable and make the last concession.
- A short but angry speech with express or implied threats of walking out, stonewalling, buying elsewhere, scorched earth, subpoenaing relatives or business associates, or advising the Commissioner of Taxation about unpaid tax of some kind.
- A combination of some or all of these speeches.

Anecdotally, these speeches rarely appear to be directly successful in crossing the last gap. The listeners may become inflamed to hear such a one-sided presentation (yet again) so late in the day and deliver a counter speech, or the speaker may back himself/herself into a positional corner. One negotiator strategy is to interrupt the flow of words with an attempted educational comment, and redirect the disputants to the remaining list of options on the board. "I don't think that these arguments are going to convince any of us as we've all heard them before. The last gap is never crossed by logical argument, so I'm going to ask each of us in turn, which one of the other options on the board you could live with."

Nevertheless, some degree of managed speechmaking at the last gap may serve latent functions of catharsis, boredom, the last dagger, further emotional pain, attempted justification of perceived role and fees of a skilled helper, or the farewell address. A managed last speech may be important given the complex psychological functions which the last gap appears to serve.

Split the Difference

This method is commonly suggested where the last gap consists of money or other divisible items—such as time with a child. It has the merits of simplicity, that both parties "lose" equally and that it is culturally commonplace.

However, given the complex psychological dynamics surrounding the last gap, "splitting the difference" may be seen as too quick, part of an orchestrated plan of attack, or involving another painful "loss."

Double Blind Offer—Split the Difference Via Formulae

This method is used in a number of computer based negotiation programs. Each disputant agrees in writing to make one or more confidential offers to a mediator (or to a computer), on the condition that if the offers are "close" ("close" being agreed upon as a percentage), then the mediator (or computer program) will split the difference and both will be bound.

For example, the parties may be stuck at offers of $300,000 and $200,000 with a gap of $100,000 between them.

They can agree to each make a confidential offer; and that there will be no agreement unless and until one confidential offer is say at least 75% of the other (or perhaps unless and until parties are only $65,000 or less apart).

Thus if each confidentially moves $10,000 and offer $290,000 and $210,000, then there will be no automatic splitting the difference, as $210,000/$290,000 = 72%.

However, if each agrees to another round of confidential offers, and one moves $5,000, and the other moves $10,000, then there is a settlement as $215,000/$280,000 = 77%.

Splitting the difference between $280,000 and $215,000 means that the payout figure is $247,500.

Expanding the Pie By Subdividing the Last Gap

The last increment can sometimes be divided in ways apart from an equal split by dividing the time of use or time of payment. For example, the last $10,000 can be paid over time with or without interest or a painting can be used for alternative months by different parties, with one or the other paying shipping and insurance.

Expanding the Pie by an Add-On Offer

One party can attempt to overcome an impasse on the last increment by re-opening a "decided" issue, or adding another issue to the negotiating table. In these ways, there is an attempt to prevent the "last" issue from being the last. For example:

- "I would be willing to give up my lounge room couch if you return the children's bikes to my house."
- "If that last $10,000 is paid to me, I would be willing to redirect all old customers to you."
- "We have already agreed that you will occupy the house for 3 years, but I'm willing to reconsider that time period if I can have that painting."

Obviously, it is not always easy to re-open or to discover extra value to place on the bargaining table. One of the clear benefits of questioning and listening skills is that a negotiator can develop ideas on the needs, concerns and interests of the other disputant so that extra value can be put on the table. Some negotiators *begin* bargaining with a positional style. When an impasse is reached, they switch (or have a fellow negotiator switch) to an interest-based problem-solving approach.

Refer to a Third Party Umpire

The impasse of the last item can be "resolved" by:

- Agreeing to refer the whole dispute to an arbitrator or judge.
- Agreeing to refer just the issue of crossing the last gap to an arbitrator. A respected expert can be paid for two hours of her time to come to a binding oral or written decision only on the last $20,000, car, Christmas Day or the terms of a leasing option.

In mediation, the disputants may request that a trusted mediator make a *recommendation* or a binding *decision* on how the impasse should be resolved. Most mediators respond to such requests with reluctance and make speeches about neutrality. However, occasionally the parties manage to persuade the mediator to accept one or both of those roles.

Chance—Flip a Coin

Chance provides an important option for deciding who gets the last gap. This is because flipping a coin:

- Is cheap and fast.
- Involves equal chance of winning or losing.
- Avoids loss of face by being "beaten" by other, more personal strategies.
- Is sometimes culturally acceptable in a gambling society.

- Provides a stark visual metaphor of the lottery involved in "going to court," and also reflects the educational conversations of many lawyers and clients.[1]
- Is so abhorrent to some risk-averse disputants that they return to the remaining list of options with enthusiasm!

Chance—Draw From a Range of Solutions

This is an alternative version of chance which avoids the all-or-nothing result of flipping a coin. The disputants agree that several solutions will be written out on slips of paper, placed in a hat, and the one drawn out will prevail.

For example, if the last increment is $20,000, then ten slips of paper can be placed in a hat beginning with "$2000" and ending with "$20,000" with gaps of $2,000 written on each slip of paper. The person drawing the slip receives whatever number is on the drawn piece of paper; the residue of the last gap goes to the other disputant. The writer and some colleagues have used this method successfully on several occasions in business disputes.

Of course, this method can be extended to a range of more complicated alternative solutions.

Transfer the Last Gap to a Third Party

This option involves both parties agreeing to transfer the last gap to a child, a charity, to pay the fees of skilled helpers, such as lawyers or mediators, or to pay for renovating a house or business before a sale.

For example, last increments from the division of a pool of assets in a matrimonial or deceased estate have been transferred:

- To a trust fund to pay for future child support or private school fees.
- In the form of an antique car to a husband on the condition that he bequeath it to his children.
- To pay a mediator's fees.

Such transfers to third parties may have the clear benefits of mutually avoiding a "loss," and of wedding a third party to the solution chosen.

Conditional Offers and Placating the Incremental Fear

Where a pattern of incremental bargaining has been established, each disputant will usually be concerned about the consequences of initiating any offer across the last gap. Why? Because any offer is likely to be whittled away by an incremental counteroffer. For example, if the last gap between A and B is $20,000, and A offers to split the difference ($10,000 to A) how is B likely to respond? B is likely to respond, split the difference again—only $5,000 to A. Thus there is a reluctance to make the first move, and the impasse remains intact.

Accordingly, some negotiators make exploratory conditional offers in an attempt to placate the fear of incremental counteroffers. This works best if there are at least two negotiators (e.g., lawyer and client) on each negotiating team.

Lawyer: What if I could persuade my client to make a split-the-difference offer, would you guarantee that you wouldn't try to cut down her offer?

Opposing Disputant: What do you mean?

Lawyer: Well I'm not willing to put the effort persuading my client against her wishes to modify her position if you're going to try to cut her offer in half. She will then feel betrayed. I'm not willing to put in the work to attempt to persuade her unless I know what your response will be. And there are no guarantees I can persuade her.

Opposing Disputant: "Let me talk to my lawyer about this in private for a moment. We'll be right back".

Obviously, this option can be manipulated by a negotiator attempting to discover the other side's willingness to settle for a hypothesized offer. Moreover, the offeree's response is also clearly conditional ("if your client makes that offer....") and can be withdrawn readily. However, raising any suspicion of reneging will usually be counter-productive at such a late stage of nearly successful negotiations.

Pause—And Speak to Significant Others

The intensity of a negotiation session means that it is easy to become weary, to lose perspective and to make "a mountain out of a molehill." Additionally, some people are cautious and are accustomed to reflecting upon options available before making a commitment.

Accordingly, it is a helpful strategy to suggest a break to consider one or more written options, with a clear appointment to resume negotiations, and with encouragement for each disputant to speak to specified trusted third parties. [Mayer, *Allies*] Where a mediator is being used, it is often helpful for all disputants to make contact with the mediator during the break to clarify, brainstorm and hypothesize on negotiation dynamics (e.g., "What will be the likely response if I make this offer...?")

A skilled "significant other" can also assist an entrenched person to work through a visual risk analysis (again). What are the risks if the gains from the negotiation are "lost" due to a relatively minor last goal or gap?[2] The writer has found that a renewed, visual, and private risk analysis is helpful with parties jammed on the last gap. "What are your goals; what have you gained so far; and what will be lost if you leave here without an agreement?" For example, here is a common "life goal" list prepared by the writer as mediator while sitting with each disputant during family property negotiations which are "jammed" over a last monetary gap.

LIFE GOALS?	THIS OFFER??
To get on with life	
To open a new business	
To invest money	
To stop paying lawyers	
To stay healthy	
To minimize contact with "x"	
To reduce stress on colleagues	
To take a holiday	
To focus on my work	
To avoid becoming bitter	
To regain "control" of my life	
To settle "in the range"	
To reduce risks of paybacks	
To receive [$540,000]—current offer $500,000	
Other??	

Once the goals are visualized and reflected upon, anecdotally most clients are reluctant to lose the 14 dangling gains for the chance of acquiring one missing goal (the last gap).

Pause—And Schedule Time For a Specific Offer

As a variation on the previous procedure, the parties can actually draft a precise or general form of offer before the break is taken. This may, for example, represent a predictable outcome of "splitting the difference" which is too difficult to swallow during the negotiations.

A time and place is then agreed upon for one party to contact the other and make the offer as drafted (e.g., phone on Wednesday night between 6-8 pm). Both agree not to haggle, but either to accept or reject the ritual pre-planned offer and to return to the negotiation/mediation table at a specified time with the result.

This procedure gives a concrete proposal, reduces the fear of incremental haggling during the break, ritualizes conflicted conversations, provides a deadline, and allows the parties to return to the negotiation table knowing what has been decided.

Defer Division of The Last Gap; Divide The Rest

Where parties are in dispute over a pool of assets, it is possible for a portion to be divided as agreed, and for the last gap to be set aside for division at some later time. For example, a wife could take 50%, a husband 40% and the contested gap of 10% be invested in a joint account until the parties are "ready" emotionally or otherwise, to deal with that 10%.

Sell The Last Item at an Auction; Split The Proceeds

This option involves an agreement to sell the last contested item(s) at a without reserve auction, usually with all parties free to bid. The most determined bidder "wins" the item and the net proceeds of the auction are then divided in portions agreed to beforehand.

Recently, the writer was mediating a conflict which jammed on the last gap of who would receive an emotionally important house. The mediator offered to conduct an instant auction, if both parties agreed that the highest bidder would receive the house. They did, and the negotiations concluded successfully.

Pick-A-Pile

Where the last gap consists of a number of items such as "all the furniture," "all the stamp collection," "all the paintings," then the parties can be offered the "pick-a-pile" option, which is well known to family lawyers, and to parents cutting up children's birthday cakes.

One party agrees to divide the chattels into two lists of approximately equal value and submit these lists to the other party by a deadline. The other party then has a specified time in which to choose one list as his/her share.[3]

Like dispute resolution by chance, this pick-a-pile option is so filled with risk and tension that some disputants quickly reject it and return to the list of remaining options with some relief.

Skilled Helper Has a Face-Saving Tantrum

This option is rarely chosen by the disputants. However, some parties comment confidentially during or after a mediation to a mediator, "I wish you would apply more pressure to us both; we are stuck."

Accordingly, when the last gap persists, some mediators, lawyers, or other team members try this option from their box of tools. For example, with varying degrees of simulated anger, the mediator, or other "helper" comments: "I cannot believe it. We have all sat here for three hours and patiently and successfully negotiated through four issues. Now you're about to throw it all away on this miserable pile of furniture. You all really disappoint me. I'm not going to let you out of here until we do the right thing and ...... etc., etc."

This option may cause the tantrum-thrower to lose reputation and clients, or may enable both parties to avoid any loss of face by making the last concession. They can blame the ballistic person for "forcing" the last concession (and rescuing them both from their painted-in corners).

This dramatic option may be particularly successful if the aggressor has gained the respect and trust of all parties (both lawyers and disputants) over a period of time.[4]

File a Court Application—Pursue Pain and Hope

Sometimes, the last gap is too difficult to cross amidst the sense of loss arising from a day or years of concessions. Accordingly, one of the negotiators delivers a mixed message of pain and hope "I believe that this dispute will settle. We have made progress today and, in my opinion, we are not diagnostically in the 1-3% of disputes which need a judicial decision. However we both may need to suffer more pain and expense of filing (further) court applications, open offers, and paying lawyers. Could we now agree to a time to talk over the phone in say 14 days time? etc." (Competent negotiators always organize face-saving methods to re-open negotiations).

Various versions of this pain and hope speech have sometimes led to awkward silences, and then positive responses to the question, "Would you like to take a short break, then try for another 15 minutes to see if this can be concluded today?"

Conclusion

Conflict and transaction managers are becoming more sophisticated in their knowledge of negotiation dynamics. This chapter has attempted to systematically explain some of the reasons for the difficulties experienced in crossing the last gap.

Sixteen ways of crossing the last gap have been described. Visually setting out some or all of these sixteen strategies is a useful addition to a negotiator's repertoire for working with disputants and negotiators to cross the last gap.

Endnotes

See original version of this topic, John H. Wade, *The Last Gap in Negotiations—Why Is It Important? How Can It Be Crossed?*, 6 AUSTRALIAN DISPUTE RESOLUTION JOURNAL 92 (1995).

[1] *See, e.g.,* Austin Sarat & William Felstiner, *Law and Strategy in the Divorce Lawyer's Office,* 20 LAW & SOCIETY REVIEW 93 (1986); Austin Sarat & William Felstiner, *Law and Social Relations: Vocabularies of Motive in Lawyer/Client Interaction,* 22 LAW & SOCIETY REVIEW 737 (1988); John Griffiths, *What do Dutch Lawyers Actually do in Divorce Cases,* 20 LAW & SOCIETY REVIEW 135 (1986); John H. Wade, *The Behaviour of Family Lawyers and the Implications for Legal Education,* 1 LEGAL EDUCATION REVIEW 165 (1989).
[2] *See* John H. Wade, *Systematic Risk Analysis for Negotiators and Litigators: But You Never Told Me It Would Be Like This,* 13 BOND LAW REVIEW 462 (2001).
[3] Precedent clauses for such agreements can be found in AUSTRALIAN FAMILY LAW AND PRACTICE (CCH) at 43-400 and in W and W (1980), FAMILY LAW CASES 90-872 at 75, 531 (Australia).
[4] G. RICHARD SHELL, BARGAINING FOR ADVANTAGE 111-13 (1999); ROBERT B. CIALDINI, INFLUENCE: THE PSYCHOLOGY OF PERSUASION (1984).

✂ 55 ✂

Bargaining in the Shadow of the Tribe

John H. Wade

Editors' Note: *The negotiations have gone on for hours or months or years. A deal is at hand. And now, the other side mentions for the first time that the approval of some previously unrecognized person is required, or there is no deal. Could you have prepared for this? Do you have options at this point? Are you, perhaps, the negotiator making the dread announcement that you must respond to a higher power before a deal's a deal? Here, Wade meticulously deconstructs the circumstances that lead to "shadow of the tribe" negotiations, and suggests what you can do.*

It is rare for an individual present at a negotiation or mediation to have "unlimited" authority to settle or make decisions. Even the most rugged individualist usually has someone looking over his/her shoulder. This may be a spouse, child, business partner, CEO, board of directors, shareholders, head office in Chicago, club or church members. We are all part of some "system" or "network" of influences. These people in the background, sometimes in the shadows, can be described as supporters, influences, bosses, stakeholders, third parties, constituents, outsiders, armchair critics, bush lawyers, sticky beaks, nosey parkers,[1] ratifiers, destabilizers, tribal members, intermeddlers, cheersquads, principals, hawks, doves or moderates.[2] Here in this article, the terminology of "the tribe" will often be used.

The visible negotiator can be labeled an agent, representative, spokesperson, mouth-piece, pawn, victim, channel, or go between.

Christopher Moore characterizes constituent groups as either "bureaucratic" or "horizontal." Bureaucratic constituents are the hierarchy of decision-makers in companies, government agencies, tribes, schools and many other institutions. "Horizontal" constituents are friends, relatives and co-workers whom a disputant feels obliged to consult and listen to.[3] The following case study illustrates the discovery of a powerful horizontal constituent, namely a spouse.

Case Study 1—Ambushed by a Powerful Spouse

A cotton factory owner contracted with an expert factory designer and builder to renovate sections of his mill for $2 million. When the renovations were complete the owner was disappointed as the promised rate of production did not occur until three months thereafter. The new machinery often did not work during the first three months. The factory experienced repetitive "down-time." Accordingly, the factory owner withheld the last payment of $250,000 to the renovator. Incensed, the renovator commenced court action in one state (the state of the contract) to recover the last installment. Predictably, the factory owner cross-claimed, in the state where the factory was actually constructed, for three months of diminished profits, being around $1 million. The entrenched parties and lawyers were required to attend mandatory mediation.

After lengthy and sometimes vitriolic negotiation between the two teams at the table (eleven people in total), the mediator took the two CEOs for a walk down the street. Standing under a tree for an hour with the mediator reframing and asking "what if" questions, led to a settlement between the two CEOs. However, the tough renovator CEO suddenly announced, "Of course I will not be able to settle this today. I will have to run this all past my wife".

The mediator reframed, placated the other irate CEO and retreated with the renovator CEO in order to phone his wife. In a carefully orchestrated conversation, the mediator spoke to the wife (with the husband present) and praised the husband, explained what progress had been made, empathized with her suffering and loss, and brainstormed on the risks of other options. The wife spoke to her renovator husband (with the mediator still present), and in a short time confirmed the grateful husband's decision to settle.

Obviously, some negotiators do not disclose that they will need to convince influential outsiders about any outcome.[4] They lie, or are embarrassed, or overestimate their own influence over their constituents. At a later stage of preparation, or at the joint negotiation meetings, more direct questions may unearth the outsiders in the shadows, ever-present in spirit, though absent in the flesh:

- "How will Mary, the head of your department, feel about that sort of result?"
- "Your wife appears to have suffered a lot as your business struggled. How does she feel about this meeting?"
- "Most insurers I meet have an authorized range, but then need to make phone calls once the recommended result is outside that range. I assume that is also true for you?"
- "You will go through blood, sweat and tears at the negotiation. That will change your perspectives. Are there any club/church/party members sitting calmly back home ready to criticize your efforts?"

Despite all this tactful investigation, no one may know until the fateful request by one party to make a phone call at the "end" of the negotiation. The other negotiators may meanwhile live with ignorance or suspicions.

How to Manage Any Influential Outsiders?

If key tribal members are identified (or suspected) during the routine preparation, or at any subsequent time during a mediation or negotiation, how many ways are there for a negotiator to respond to this information? Set out below are standard responses to add to the toolbox.[5] All have advantages and disadvantages.

- Refuse to negotiate.
- Adjourn until influential figures are "present."
- Carry on regardless.
- Normalize.
- Ask ritualistic "authority" question.
- Insist on written authority within subjective range or objective range of "fairness."
- Agree to use best endeavors to sell the agreement.
- Opinion from an evaluative mediator or expert.
- Consult with the outside authority/influence before negotiation.

- Consult with outside influences before the negotiation and arrange decision-making process.
- Selected "reporting" team members explain settlement and progress to outside authorities before anyone else.
- Warn of dangers of reneging—"What if …?"
- Throw tantrum.

Refuse to Negotiate

The first response to knowledge or suspicion about influential outsiders is to refuse to negotiate or mediate. "I am not willing to waste time and money talking to some middle manager, lackey, puppet, or person without authority to settle." This refusal to negotiate may lead to further conflicts or litigation, subsequent lying about authority to settle, or the emergence of the influencers from the shadows.

Adjourn Until Authority Figures are "Present"

The second response follows normally from the first. That is, one or more disputants may refuse to negotiate or mediate on major questions, unless and until key authority figures are "present" in person or are available on the phone or teleconferencing facility during the mediation or negotiation.

In many conflicts, such brinkmanship is futile as those with persuasive or legal power are too many, too distant, too expensive, or too busy to appear. Nevertheless, many mediations and negotiations are organized creatively to enable:

- An auditorium of constituents and families to be present, witness, speak and vote.
- A CEO from overseas to be "present" via teleconferencing, or telephone.
- Travel of key family or board members to an all day (and sometimes all-night) meeting in a convenient central location.

The presence of numerous influential people creates constant logistical challenges of expense and coordinating calendars. However, once these logistical difficulties are overcome, they provide helpful pressures to "find a solution now that all of us are here." One possible method to manage time is to encourage many people to attend, on the express condition that the number of speakers will be limited to those who are nominated representatives, or to those given the microphone or some other "talking symbol" by a chairperson. This method has been used effectively in large town hall meetings between angry residents and local councils.

Nevertheless, this solution of "adjourn until" will be opposed strongly by middle managers and family members who fear the presence of their own bosses or family during the meeting. These outside authorities may be resentful for the inconvenience of attending; critical of the disputant for "being unable to sort this out by yourself;" and dangerously judgmental of their own tribal representative if too many skeletons come out of the closet during the negotiation.

Additional opposition to this "adjourn until X can be present" option will sometimes come from the *other* disputants. That is, one set of disputants objects to "interference" and "delays" due to the proposed presence of the other disputant's "officious boss," "nosey brother," "pushy husband," "aggressive union member" or "opinionated accountant." These legitimate objections and perceptions can usually be reframed ("So you would like X to work alone/independently?" or "So you are worried about the dynamics if X is present?"). The objector can then be challenged by questions such as: "If Y does not attend, will X ever settle?" "How will you feel if X wants Y to check any deal you reach?" "How can you ensure that the brother/boss/accountant/wife gives an informed opinion, rather than an ignorant reaction?"

The writer as mediator regularly uses similar questions to persuade disputants that they should consent to and welcome the presence of an "appropriate" influential spouse, accountant, or wise friend to "help" another disputant. Despite sometimes initial resistance, the persuasion has always succeeded on the basis that it is "better to have a visible influence, than someone whiteanting[6] in the background." This exercise always involves a further task of trying to find "extra helpers" to equalize numbers present for each faction at the mediation/negotiation.

With a few notable exceptions, the presence of the outside influence has been essential, or at least helpful in order to find a resolution.

Children as Powerful "Outside Influencers"

One common group of powerful influencers who are often not "present" at negotiations and mediations, are children. Parents have legal power to make decisions about their children but sometimes have limited persuasive power, particularly over teenagers in industrialized societies.

Carry on Regardless

The third response to suspicions or knowledge of key influencers, or absence of "complete authority to settle," is to say nothing and continue the process.

Some negotiators may decide that even opening the questions of "Do you both have authority to settle?" or "How shall we identify and manage influential outsiders?" is so inflammatory, complex and time-consuming that it is better not discussed. Arguably, the topic will remain safely buried, either because no substantive resolution is reached or recommended (so no telephone calls need to be made); or the settlement is within the "agent's" range (again, so no telephone calls need to be made); or it is so routine for certain disputants (e.g. middle managers, some insurers) to make phone calls, that it is not necessary to discuss what is normal. Moreover, if a settlement is reached and approval is then sought from an outsider, and this procedural ambush causes offense to the other party, then in those (statistically few?) cases, the negotiations can be "managed" at that stage. Why clumsily anticipate what may not turn into a problem?

Others have seen many negotiations stumble and fail due to the influence of tribal members. These scarred negotiators may be reluctant to "carry on regardless" or "wait and see what happens" in relation to these hovering armchair critics.

Normalize

The fourth response to the perceived pressure from outsiders is for the negotiator to give one or more "normalizing" speeches. The aim of these speeches is to attempt to convince one of the negotiators that the need for outside ratification is "normal;" is not devious; is not normally part of a good cop-bad cop negotiation tactic (though it could be that!); that competent negotiators do not fuss over this procedural step; and that progress can be made despite the need for outside approval. For example, "Jill, in my experience it is normal for middle managers in large businesses or government to seek approval for the agreement you hope to reach today. They cannot risk their jobs by settling without higher level approval. If you insist on them having full authority to settle, their easiest escape is to leave the decision to a judge; then they will avoid being blamed for the outcome."

These kinds of speeches by a team member may assist a disputant to persist with the negotiation/mediation, rather than prematurely choose option one—namely, refuse to negotiate.

Ask Ritualistic "Authority" Question

The fifth possible response to the knowledge or suspicion that one or more of the disputants will need to consult an outsider before signing any settlement, is for the negotiator to ask ritualistically, "Do you have authority to settle this dispute?" This question can be asked in writing in the preparation documents required to be completed by each negotiator. Alternatively, this question can be asked or re-asked at both private and joint meetings. Presumably, some negotiators are hoping for a confident or mumbled "yes" as an answer.

The mumble or the body language may suggest a lie or more complex motives. A more precise and tactical answer could be: "Yes, I have complete authority to negotiate or to settle so long as the outcome is fair/reasonable/in the range. If it is an unusual settlement, or one out of the normal range, then obviously I will have to consult my superiors/constituents/family. I assume that you would have to do likewise if you were in my position."

Whatever answer is given, it leaves the parties with some unresolved tensions. A confident affirmative answer may well be a lie or a mask to complexity; a mumbled affirmative answer will raise suspicions; and a "correct" tactical and qualified affirmative may open a detailed discussion of the meaning of "reasonable"; and a negative answer may lead to option one—a refusal to negotiate.

Insist on Written Authority to Settle Within Subjective Range or Objective Range of "Fairness"

The sixth possible response is for a negotiator to insist that some or all of the negotiators produce a written (and irrevocable) authority to settle. This written step may appear to provide more certainty than the ritualistic oral assurances set out in the previous response.

However, in reality, those who draft such written authorities know that they provide little certainty that the alleged agent will act upon the apparent authority. Why?

This is because an authority can be drafted in one of two ways—subjectively or objectively. A subjective written authority gives the agent the power to enter into such agreement as the agent believes is "reasonable," "fair," "appropriate" or "reflecting common commercial practices." All these words leave the agent with such a broad discretion that if he believes that the outcome is anything other than "advantageous," he may want to consult with the influential constituents anyhow (to protect his/her job or reputation or safety). That is, the representative's broad "legal" authority is qualified by his/her certain knowledge that he has limited "persuasive" authority.

An objective written authority supposedly gives the agent more certainty and less discretion. For example, "My lawyer is hereby given irrevocable authority by me to settle this dispute for an amount not less than $400,000."

However, such an objective authority to settle, is no panacea. First, by defining outcomes only in dollars, it restricts creative packaging. Second, the existence of such a key piece of information, namely the "reservation" or "walk-away," creates the risk that it may be leaked to the other side. Third, the authority may specify a false and flexible figure which can be "accidentally leaked" to the other side. Fourth, the authority does not prevent real or theatrical consultation taking place anyhow.

Agree to Use Best Endeavors

The seventh possible response to the negotiator's knowledge or suspicion that one or more of the negotiators will need to consult with influential outsiders before reaching agreement is to negotiate for the agent to use his/her "best endeavors" to sell the outcome to the constituents.

This option may seem weak. However, the writer and other colleagues have used it successfully on a variety of occasions.

This response anticipates a standard type of conversation between the negotiator (N) and his/her constituents (C) after a mediation or negotiation. For example:

C: "How did the mediation/negotiation go last night?"

N: "Well, we reached agreement. It is not all that you hoped for."

C: "What did you agree to?"

N: "Well, there are four basic provisions as follows ......"

C: "That doesn't seem very fair. Why did we get so little? Are you happy with that outcome?"

N: "Well, I am not happy, but in the circumstances ......"

C: "If you are not happy, why did you agree to it?"

N: "Well, it was the best I (we) could do. The mediator put us under some pressure to be realistic."

C: "We will need some time to reconsider this. It is very disappointing. I certainly will not sign/ratify. They must be laughing about ......"

This standard disclose, disappoint, defend and blame language is clearly foreseeable between some agents and tribes. Many representatives at mediations are in an unenviable position of martyrdom by the awaiting tribal hawks.[7]

This predictable pattern may encourage a wary mediator or negotiator to go through the following steps. First, ask each negotiator (privately and perhaps publicly) "What if you reach an agreement which you believe is satisfactory but which disappoints your constituents/members/family?" Second, the mediator asks "What if the post-settlement conversation with your constituents is as follows..." (mimics the disclose, disappoint, defend and blame language)? In the writer's experience, the representatives tend to nod glumly.

Third, the mediator asks, "Would you (each) be prepared to return to your club/constituents and highly recommend the outcome you reach (tomorrow, next week, next month etc)? There is no point working hard for an agreement if you then allow that routine and undermining conversation to occur. You might as well abandon the meeting now."

The negotiators can usually be persuaded to agree orally or in writing as follows:

"If we reach an agreement after working hard through a range of possibilities, we will not report back to X in a half-hearted fashion. We will unanimously report back to X about the issues and the options. We will unanimously and enthusiastically recommend the outcome we reach as satisfactory, workable, and the best option available. We will endeavor to 'sell' the outcome to our constituents."

Opinion From an Evaluative Mediator or Expert

Following the previous response, there is an eighth method to help the representative save face, job, and safety; and to create doubt for any angry hawks lurking among the constituents.

This involves hiring an evaluative mediator who is respected in the field in which the disputants are negotiating; and/or bringing to the mediation or negotiation an expert in the field as an observer and commentator. An oral or written statement from an attending expert, such as, "This negotiated outcome is, in my opinion, within the range of predictable results in (court/the marketplace)" usually gives the nervous negotiators some welcome ammunition against the outside critics.

Consult with the Outside Authority/Influence Before Negotiation

The ninth possible response of a negotiator to the real or suspected existence of an influential outsider is to consult with that outsider before the joint sessions begin.

The writer uses this method in the majority of his negotiations and mediations. A negotiator asks his/her own constituents, and then secretly or openly any accessible supporters behind the "opposition," a series of routine diagnostic questions about causes of conflict, interventions, glitches, risks if the conflict continues, and possible substantive outcomes. These questions often produce important benefits including new perspectives and hypotheses for both the negotiators and the outsiders, and a sense of inclusion and respect from those constituents,

Consult with Outside Influences Before the Negotiation and Arrange Decision-Making Process

There is a tenth important response which every mediator and negotiator needs to have in his/her conceptual and linguistic repertoire when outside tribal members are obvious or unearthed. This response is to insist upon and organize a "decision rule" within each group of constituents.[8]

> There is a variety of methods by which groups can decide to make decisions. In decision-making groups, the dominant view is to assume that majority rules and at some point take a vote of all members, assuming that any settlement option that receives more than 50 percent of the votes will be the one adopted. Obviously, this is not the only option. Groups can make decisions by dictatorship (one person decides), oligarchy (a small but dominant minority coalition decides), simple majority (one more person than half the group), two-thirds majority, broad consensus (most of the group agrees, and those who dissent agree not to protest or raise objections, and true unanimity (everyone agrees). Understanding what decision rule a group will use before deliberations begin will also significantly affect the group process. For example, if a simple majority will make the decision in a five-person group, then only three people need to agree. Thus, any three people can get together and form a coalition—during the meeting or even prior to the meeting. In contrast, if the rule will be consensus and unanimity, then the group must meet and work hard enough to assure that all parties' interests are raised, discussed, and incorporated into the group decision.[9]

That is, during preparation for negotiation *between* parties, representatives from each group are required to facilitate discussions *within* each of the parties' tribes on the key question—"By what process will the group make a decision?"

For example, a negotiator (or mediator) can typically go through the following steps described below.

Brinkmanship and Doubt Creation

"I am not willing to negotiate unless both groups decide clearly on how they will vote to approve or disapprove their respective representatives' recommendations."

"No group can agree unanimously on what day of the week it is; so don't come back to me with a unanimity rule."

"I am also not willing to accept a 'wait and see' or 'we will work it out later' voting process. That is a recipe for failure and embarrassment for me as your representative. We all know that some of you will be disappointed with the outcome, and some will be able to live with that same outcome."

Facilitate Agreement on Each Group's 'Decision Rule'

"If you wish, I can meet with my group to develop an answer to this key question 'How will we make a decision as a group at the end of the negotiation?'"

"If you wish, I can tell you a range of ways other groups like you have made decisions. You can add those to your list of possibilities before deciding."

Write Out and Publicize the 'Decision Rule' of Each Group Before the Joint Mediation or Negotiation Begins

This third step is helpful as it reduces the chances of a whole group later reneging on their decision rule; and encourages negotiators who can see that the decision-rules may be a way of controlling hawks on their own team, or on the opposition's team. Without a visible decision rule in place, a skilled hawk can exploit the inevitable post-recommendation or post-settlement regrets within a group, and organize rejection of many negotiated or recommended agreements. [Wade & Honeyman, *Lasting Agreement*] The following case example illustrates the use of a pre-determined intra-team decision-making process.

Case Study 2—Face Saving Decision Rule

A mediation occurred between two factions of a church. Both wanted to acquire the church property and exclude the other for a host of alleged miscommunications, misdemeanors and personality defects. Vitriolic litigation had commenced to appoint a trustee for sale of the church.

The two factions were represented at the mediation by 7 and 8 elders respectively. One lawyer took the mediator aside and said that his group of seven could never agree to any outcome as two ("hawks") of the seven had paid all his legal fees; were deeply hurt; and wanted victory as a "matter of principle."

The grateful mediator sent each faction away to determine "How to make a decision at the end of the mediation?" The seven decided upon 5-to-2 majority decision; the 8 upon a 5 to 3 majority decision. This was publicly announced.

Eight hours later, a group of two from each faction reached a recommended outcome which they agreed to "sell" hard to their colleagues. They succeeded. The faction of 7 predictably voted 5-to-2 in favor of the recommended package with the two hawks dissenting.

The pre-existing decision rule then enabled both hawks to make speeches that they did not like the outcome, but they were men of honor, and would comply with the agreed majority vote by their friends.

Selected "Reporting" Team Members Explain Settlement and Progress to Outside Authorities Before Anyone Else

This is another vital response which every negotiator needs to add to his/her toolbox in order to deal with armchair critics who are eagerly awaiting the outcome of a negotiation.

This practice can helpfully complement the previous two responses, namely consulting with outsiders and organizing a decision-rule *before* the negotiation (or mediation). After each negotiation session, an appointed reporting negotiator strives to report to the influential constituents *before* or at the same time as other team members do so. This can be done by phone, fax or email with copies being given simultaneously to the team members on one or both sides. This enables the team of negotiators to build upon the interpretation and language adopted in the report. It will also reduce the predictable dilemma for the other team members of reporting, disappointing, defending, and blaming.

The aims of this response are to:

▪ Protect the negotiating team from hostile outsiders.

- Create doubt for the armchair critics.
- Give the negotiating team and the critics a new set of words, metaphors and expressions to describe the historical events at the negotiation. These words can profoundly influence simmering hostile perceptions and emotions.
- Avoid a defensive negotiator too readily "blaming" another team member, a perceived hawk or dove, or the negotiation process for the outcome.
- Develop further trust in the reporting negotiators who ideally model transparency and problem-solving skills.

The writer uses this practice regularly when organizing negotiations which involve influential outsiders. It sometimes requires persuasion to convince all team members of the potential benefits to them, when a diplomatic "reporting negotiator" provides the first feedback to the waiting constituents. Of course, sometimes hawks break the "reporting" agreement by leaking their own loaded versions about negotiation progress to the press or to their own constituents.

Warn of Dangers of Reneging—"What If …?"

Negotiators usually have a range of phrases to exhort their own team and the other disputants to perform their agreements, despite pressures from outsiders to renege.

These may have the effect of preparing the disputants for such pressures, and giving them a practiced repertoire of language when placed under such pressures to renege. For example:

- "What will you do in the next week when some of our supporters criticize us for reaching this agreement?"
- "How will you respond when some of our fellow committee members say, "You should have obtained a better deal?"
- "Should we practice that speech now so that we gain confidence and consistency?"

This preparation is particularly important in those disputes where there is a necessary gap in time between agreement and ratification of the agreement by constituents or a court. For example, in family, native title, environmental, succession and human rights disputes it is normal for a mediated or negotiated agreement to require court approval before the agreement becomes legally binding. As many lawyers can nervously testify, this pause provides a dangerous gap of days or weeks when one or more parties can be pressured by constituents or self-doubt to renege.

Throw Tantrum

This response involves a mild-mannered negotiator expressing strong and theatrical disapproval when one party suddenly suggests that he needs to consult with an influential outsider. The theatrical negotiator has the goal of pressuring the wavering negotiator into signing immediately, rather than passing responsibility to outsiders.

A negotiator's exhortations might be as follows:

- "I can't believe that at this stage of the meeting, you want to make a phone call! What kind of message will that send to my team? They are likely to walk out angrily and not come back."
- "We have all put in so much work to reach this agreement. And now you want to risk it all with a break so that you can talk to your relatives?"
- "You can't do this Mary! Your reputation as a negotiator will be in tatters. In the future, our firm will insist on negotiating with anyone but you."

The writer has not used the fake tantrum in these circumstances, but has anecdotally heard of others trying this intervention. It obviously has many risks for a negotiator, including allegations of bullying, cultural clumsiness, or ignorance of other more suitable interventions, or a walk-out.

Conclusion

This article has identified and systematized thirteen possible responses to influential tribes and outsiders before, during and after negotiations. There are probably other responses or hybrids which could be added from the repertoires of experienced mediators and negotiators. Obviously, each response has advantages and disadvantages.

In the writer's opinion, this is another common hurdle in negotiations where mediators can add value to "unassisted" negotiations.[10] First, the mediator can question strategically in order to identify influential outsiders; second, pose a neutral problem-solving question (e.g. "how to respond to influential outsiders?"); and third, be aware of and, if possible practiced in, the thirteen responses to this question. These three steps can be mastered by expert negotiators. However, a master negotiator may often (rightly?) be suspected by the opposition of strategic manipulation of the process. Less suspicion of bias may fall upon a respected mediator who is employed by all parties to manage negotiation dynamics including the unruly behavior of hawks, doves and moderates in the background.

This analysis raises challenges for the systematic training of mediators and negotiators: questions for research on the actual behavior of mediators and negotiators in relation to managing the influence of outsiders; questions about the rate of use of each of these responses in different areas of conflict and culture; and questions about what evidence, if any, can be collected to measure and predict the rate of "success" of each response to ubiquitous outside influences.

Endnotes

Adapted from John H. Wade, *Bargaining in the Shadow of the Tribe and Limited Authority to Settle*, 15 BOND LAW REVIEW 115 (2003).

[1] A "sticky beak" is "an inquisitive, prying person;" and a "nosey parker" is "a person who continually pries; a meddler" per THE MACQUARIE DICTIONARY OF AUSTRALIAN COLLOQUIAL-ISMS 220, 299 (1984).
[2] A "hawk" is a competitive member of a group who has a clear solution as a goal which is perceived as "winning", and who is prepared to engage in contentious tactics, sometimes including violence, in order to "win" in the short term. A "dove" is a person whose major goal is peace and non-violence, achieved by peaceful methods including yielding, even if achieved at short-term costs. A "moderate" is a person whose goal is to find a solution acceptable to all disputants and interest groups, by a combination of mild contentious tactics, negotiation, face-saving and compromise.
[3] CHRISTOPHER W. MOORE, THE MEDIATION PROCESS 438-41 (2003).
[4] JOHN H. WADE, REPRESENTING CLIENTS AT MEDIATION AND NEGOTIATION 118-24 (2000). *See* JANET R. JOHNSTON & LINDA E.G. CAMPBELL, IMPASSES OF DIVORCE (1988) (suggesting that pressure from relatives is one of the three primary causes for sustaining conflict between highly-conflicted couples).
[5] *See* John H. Wade, *Tools for a Mediator's Toolbox: Reflections on Matrimonial Property Disputes*, 7 AUSTRALIAN DISPUTE RESOLUTION JOURNAL 93 (1996).
[6] A "whiteant" is a termite which eats timber in houses leaving a veneer of strength, which however collapses under the slightest pressure.
[7] *See* DEAN G. PRUITT & SUNG HEE KIM, SOCIAL CONFLICT-ESCALATION, STALEMATE AND SETTLE-MENT (2003) for an analysis of changes to social structures and psychology which tend to perpetuate conflict.
[8] *See* ROY J. LEWICKI, ET AL., NEGOTIATION (5th ed. 2005).
[9] *Id.* at 367.
[10] For discussions of various standard hurdles: *see id. at* Chapter 17; JOHN S. HAMMOND, ET AL., SMART CHOICES: A PRACTICAL GUIDE TO MAKING BETTER DECISIONS (1999); BARRIERS TO CONFLICT RESOLUTION (Robert Mnookin ed., 1995); and John H. Wade, *The Last Gap in Negotiations—Why Is It Important? How Can It Be Crossed?*, 6 AUSTRALIAN DISPUTE RESOLUTION JOURNAL 93 (1995).

ᖇ 56 ᖾ

A Lasting Agreement

John H. Wade & Christopher Honeyman

Editors' Note: *So, you finally have a deal! How can you make the deal stick? This straightforward chapter provides specific advice on what makes deals fall apart, and what you can do in order to increase the likelihood that your agreement will survive the slings and arrows of outrageous fortune.*

"Peace, peace, they say, when there is no peace"
(Jeremiah, Chapter 8, Verse 11)

It is usually a primary goal of a negotiator not merely to reach an agreement, but also to create an agreement which is durable, along with a mutual sense of commitment to its performance among those signing it.

Agreements which are performed in substance by all parties, which no one walks away from, and which do not require enforcement proceedings can be described as "durable," "final," "stickable" or "committed." We are using this as a working description of a durable agreement in order to sidestep a historic legal debate over whether a contract actually gives each party a choice—to perform the expressed obligations, or to "perform" in a secondary sense, by breaching the contract and paying damages (or accepting other consequences of a breach). This chapter works on the assumption that choosing "secondary" obligations such as damages is not "performance."

What percentage of negotiated agreements in various types of transactions, types of conflict, or in various "cultures," are actually performed as written or promised? For how long do agreements in these varieties of areas "endure" or "stick?" To use more narrow legal language, what percentage of negotiated agreements in these various areas are seriously "breached," or allegedly seriously "breached?"

Various levels of courts ask similar questions about consent or litigated orders. What percentage of judicial orders are complied with, and for how long, in different areas of culture and conflict?

With only anecdotal evidence to rely upon, it is probable that the actual durability rate of agreements varies enormously across class, culture, wealth, and type of transaction or conflict. With extensive research, these patterns of breach could be made visible by "durability graphs" or "performance rates" which may assist to change people's expectations of finality.

For example, low rates of durability (only 10%-20% lasting more than 12 months) would possibly attach to child visitation agreements in certain categories of families. Conversely, high rates of vendor-purchaser durability (85%-90% lasting indefinitely) would possibly attach to house purchases in Australia or America. Purchaser—bank mortgage contracts may also have high rates of performance amongst the middle class, until recession and job losses escalate. Again, such studies of performance and non-performance would assist to modify expectations of "finality" of negotiated agreements.

Many of the factors which hinder *initial* commitment to reaching an agreement also contribute to undermining *ongoing* commitment to performance. Set out below are some of the anecdotal reasons why negotiated agreements are "breached," or are not durable.

Cultural Expectations of Flexibility
In some cultural groups, a written or oral contract is perceived to be only an agreement to work together in the future. It is a symbol of a relationship, not of obligation to perform its detailed terms.[1] [Goh, *Errors*] The agreement has implied terms that if any party has difficulties in performing, then everyone will assemble again and negotiate ways to preserve the relationship, and vary the "obligations."

This interpretation of the impermanence of a contract or agreement may come as a shock to an inexperienced person from a Western or legal culture where legal finality is assumed, and where relationship does not trump commercial certainty.

This leads to the predictable pattern of the economically more powerful party attempting to negotiate that all breaches or variations will be dealt with ultimately by courts or arbitrators from their own culture, and applying their own cultural and legal rules.

Complexity of Ongoing Obligations
The more complex the terms of any negotiated agreement, then the higher the likelihood that various obligations will "break down" with the passage of time and circumstance. The fragility of an agreement increases with multiplication of parties, vague language, period of performance, and number of obligations on human behavior (e.g., "use best endeavors;" "take reasonable steps to refer customers;" "delays caused by inclement weather or unforeseen circumstances").

Of course, many negotiators attempt to reduce ongoing complexity by lengthy definition of vague terms, reference to industry standards, self-enforcing arbitration clauses or decisions by a specified "authority," liquidated damages clauses, and clean-break swaps of money for a defined act.

Shallow Peace
Agreements, treaties or litigation may momentarily provide an outcome, while the underlying causes of conflict remain, together with the emotional and structural changes associated with escalation.[2] The parties achieve shallow "settlement," but not deep "resolution." In those circumstances, the agreement is unlikely to endure. The aggrieved party will find a moral or legal justification to breach it in the next week or decade. Successive agreements may be entered into and breached many times during ongoing family, international or tribal disputes.[3] Eventually, if underlying causes of conflict, emotional and structural changes are addressed satisfactorily, one of these agreements may be substantially performed by all the involved and still surviving parties.

The same reasons which cause conflict also cause the collapse of settlements; it is therefore worth reviewing these reasons here. Christopher Moore has categorized the five causes of conflict as data, interest, structural, value and relationship conflicts.[4] These are represented by the following chart:

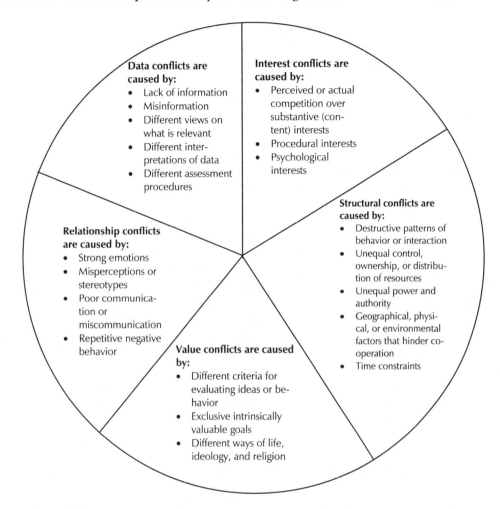

In the comparatively well-researched area of family disputes, many reasons have been identified for the particular difficulties of responding constructively to serious interspousal conflict. Kressel has commented:

Nine shared obstacles to a constructive negotiating experience can be identified:

1. High levels of intraparty conflict
2. Well-established and rigid patterns of destructive interaction
3. Inexperience in the art of negotiating
4. Scarcity of divisible resources
5. Complex issues which threaten loss of face or self-esteem
6. Elevated levels of stress and tension
7. Social norms and institutions for conflict management that are weak or that unintentionally provoke destructive interaction
8. Disparities in the parties' relative power
9. Disparities in the parties' degree of interpersonal sensitivity

The last two of these obstacles are closely associated with the male-female context in which divorce negotiations occur.[5]

Buyer's Remorse

There is a well researched post-agreement emotional state sometimes labeled "buyer's remorse," or "post-settlement blues," or the "winner's curse."[6] This is a state of regret and even depression which strikes many (not all) negotiators who have "lost" an actual or imagined better deal, for a perceived ordinary deal. "What if we had held out for longer, would we have received more?"

This personal sense of loss and regret can be reinforced by armchair critics. [Wade, *Tribe*] Someone experiencing buyer's (or seller's) remorse may refuse to perform the agreement, and can readily create a list of moral and legal justifications for this withdrawal.

Changed Circumstances—"Occupational Morality"

There are some agreements which through custom or market pressure will be re-negotiated regularly because "things change." This is similar to the previous discussion of "cultural expectations of flexibility." However, that heading related to national or regional culture, whereas this category relates to common industrial practices, or common practices of flexibility in particular transactions. One example is an agreement between separated parents about times of access or visitation with their children. A carefully negotiated schedule always is varied/breached/not performed as a child is busy, sick, away on an excursion; or a parent is busy, sick, or sent away by an employer. Another example is employment contracts in research, exporting, military and technological industries. The original "understandings" or contracts for both employer and employee may be subject to constant renegotiation in order to adapt to mandated behavior in competitive fields.

In 1963, a classic study in Wisconsin found firstly that the majority of business "exchanges" were vague and therefore not legally enforceable; and secondly, the majority of business disputes are settled with no reference to the written "contract," much less to lawyers. The study further hypothesized on why the majority of business exchanges are considered by occupational custom and morality to be relatively binding, without being legally contractual.

> Even where agreement can be reached at the negotiation stage, carefully planned arrangements may create undesirable exchange relationships between business units. Some businessmen object that in such a carefully worked out relationship one gets performance only to the letter of the contract. Such planning indicates a lack of trust and blunts the demands of friendship, turning a cooperative venture into an antagonistic horse trade. Yet the greater danger perceived by some businessmen is that one would have to perform his side of the bargain to its letter and thus lose what is called "flexibility." Businessmen may welcome a measure of vagueness in the obligations they assume so that they may negotiate matters in light of the actual circumstances.[7]

Legal Rules Allow Variation Due to Changed Circumstances

Different legal rules exist in every country which enable contracts to be set aside or varied, based on a limited range of events which occur *after* the negotiated agreement.

So the phrase "But I thought we have a concluded agreement," is met by "We did, but we are legally justified in setting it aside because X (a fire, war, death, strike, etc.) has occurred."

The list of legal exceptions to finality of contracts varies from one jurisdiction to another, and is often placed under the label "frustration of contracts." These lists are studied assiduously by national and international lawyers and insurers who are trying to define the risks of nonperformance in each country. Then these lawyers engage in an ongoing industry of drafting standard clauses which narrow or expand those legal loopholes.

The broad cross-cultural legal exceptions to finality based on post-agreement events include:

- The doctrine of frustration.
- Protection of the public purse. For example, child support agreements in some jurisdictions can or must be re-opened once a child is receiving state welfare payments.
- Legislative destabilization based on a new "public policy."

There are many examples where a class of contracts is rendered invalid or unenforceable due to retrospective legislation which is purporting to protect some version of the "public good." For example, legislation invalidating existing contracts with certain classes of people or businesses considered at various times of history to be "the enemy" or "needing protection," such as German, American, Aboriginal, Roman Catholic, Protestant or female, or contracts which involve exportation of diminishing timber stocks, whales, or native animals; or contracts for the sale of newly discovered "dangers"—such as certain drugs, asbestos materials, explosive fertilizers, off-shore tax evasion schemes, or politically incorrect films or literature.

Legal Rules Which Allow for Setting Aside a Contract Due to Pre-Agreement Events

Following the previous legal exceptions to finality based on *post-agreement* events, there are many categories of legal rules (which again vary from country to country) which allow contracts to be challenged based on *pre-agreement* factors.

Once again, these lists of fluctuating rules are studied and systematized daily by armies of lawyers around the planet. [Korobkin, et al., *Law of Bargaining*] These workers are attempting to give some clarity to the loopholes to finality in a wide range of transactions and disputes. These loopholes and attendant risks can then be partly closed by careful drafting of contracts; by insurance; and by adjusting price in favor of the risk-taker. There are some pre-agreement legal loopholes, such as lying, which are difficult to close by drafting or insurance in most countries. For example, a clause which tries to enhance finality by stating to the effect that "one or both parties are free to lie overtly during negotiations with no consequential legal liability" is unlikely to reduce the legal risks attached to overt lying.

Broad cross-cultural legal exceptions to the finality of agreements, based on pre-agreement events, include:

- Innocent, negligent and fraudulent misrepresentation.[8]
- A limited range of mistakes, or unconscionable dealings.
- Non-disclosure of "material" facts in certain classes of agreements such as insurance or family property contracts.
- Entering contracts at a time when such arrangements are illegal by statute (e.g. sale of weapons, drugs, state secrets, or unduly monopolistic sales, as well as sales prejudicing protected farming industries) or against fluctuating public policy at that time.[9]
- Entering negotiations and a resulting contract at a time when one of the parties does not have sufficient *capacity* to consent, due to youthfulness, junior status, depression, undue market pressure, inexperience, lack of in-

formation, lack of independent advice, haste, inappropriate threats, or undue influence.

- Consumer protection laws in some countries give consumers mandatory cooling off periods; warranties which enable return of defective products; independent financial and legal advice; criminal sanctions against marketing tricks such as bait-and-switch advertising; or mandatory disclosures of information.

Efficiency and Accessibility of the Legal "System"

The previous two exceptions to finality of agreements concentrated on legal rules. But rule analysis by itself is unhelpful. It should be complemented by a cultural study of the "law in action." Obviously, access to efficient lawyers, courts and judges differs dramatically across the world, and within countries. There are gradations of expense, uncertainty, delay, and corruption. For example, one yearly study of large international businesses indicates that currently these businesses perceive Finland and New Zealand to have the least corrupt, and China and Indonesia to have substantially more corrupt, court systems and judiciary.[10]

Accordingly, where the legal (as compared to market) enforceability of a contract is unpredictable and/or unavailable, then finality of agreements due to "the law" diminishes.

On a shifting scale, where law enforcement is weak, delayed, uncertain, clumsy, or corrupt, then relationships and market power become more influential in either encouraging or diminishing finality. A subcontractor on a large building site will probably acquiesce when his/her boss reneges on the employment contract, and hope for a job on the next construction site. Even where legal enforceability is accessible, many "innocent" contractors do not bother with the delay and expense of enforcement proceedings. They prefer to invest their time and money in other business ventures, and punish the party allegedly in breach with business isolation.

Nevertheless, it is predictable that China will work hard to improve the image, rule of law, accessibility and independence of its own courts; and that meanwhile foreign businesses will attempt to add legal finality and western values to Chinese trade agreements by negotiating for off-shore arbitration or litigation enforcement clauses.

Lack of Informed Consent

Many agreements, notably settlements at the door of a court, are entered into under pressures of limited time, money, exhaustion, and exhortations to settle from lawyers and some tribal[11] members. [Wade, *Tribe*] Accordingly, some negotiators look back in anger at their confused state, chaotic information, and the pressure-cooker negotiating environment.

This sense of grievance may erupt later in a search for legal or moral justification to "get out of" the deal. For example:

- "My lawyer failed to explain the meaning of that clause."
- "I didn't know that the terms of the agreement were final."
- "I was so confused and distressed on that day that eventually I signed anything put in front of me."
- "My lawyer pressured me into signing by a barrage of threats about court costs and the uncertainty of litigation."

A landmark study in Australia has recorded the early distress of 723 separated spouses. "Property applications can now be made ... during the first year of separation. This may have unfortunate repercussions for those who are so distressed about the event that they can't think rationally, or for those whose animosity towards their spouses or whose guilt influences their decisions." A few of the spouses' comments follow:

> "When the marriage first breaks down, you're not in a proper frame of mind to face the Court etc. One is at a disadvantage. It's not the best time for making decisions." (man)

> "People are so mixed up after separation. The settlement should be decided by independent people." (man)

> "I signed away custody of the children while under stress and medication. I have no chance at present of getting them back." (woman)[12]

These grievances sometimes trigger refusal to comply with the terms of family property settlements. As a matter of legal principle, they rarely are successful as a defense to an enforcement action.[13] But this begs the question whether the "successful" enforcement litigation actually produced promised dollars or performance in the hand.

Judges have consistently taken the view that a client advised by a lawyer is strongly presumed both to have a basic understanding of legal principle, and to have given consent.[14]

In Australia, the most notorious documented "misunderstanding" of family clients occurred in the early 1980's. A survey conducted by the Australian Institute of Family Studies showed that the majority of family clients had settled without a proper understanding of the relevance of superannuation and pension entitlements to the division of property.[15]

All Drafting Has Loopholes

This is particularly apparent where agreements are drafted late at night, or under severe time pressures—smaller time, bigger loopholes. Those professionals who draft agreements regularly know that there are no watertight documents. Even encyclopedic contracts do not allow for every exigency in human affairs, as many words are capable of multiple interpretations. Of course, most negotiators do not have the time, patience, money or inclination to negotiate multi-page documents. They perhaps realistically hope that goodwill, reputation and ("cheap") short documents will encourage performance of 90% of agreements, and tolerate the risk that the other 10% may not be performed when the unexpected occurs.

Fine Tuning "Later"

The dynamics of some negotiations include late night deadlines; presence of tired leaders; hurried general "heads of agreement" drafted and signed, so that important people can go elsewhere; and delegation to lawyers or junior bureaucrats to "fill in the detail" or "complete the technicalities," sometime in the future.

This common and allegedly "efficient" process obviously leads to some almost "finalized" treaties, litigation settlements and commercial leases not actually becoming finalized. This is at least because the devil is in the details, the junior delegates are competitive and fearful for their own reputation, new key unresolved interests arise during drafting, and hawks use the drafting meetings as opportunities to re-open even the "settled" principles.[16]

Any Agreement is Better Than None

Related to the previous point is that sometimes negotiators' goals evolve towards a "quick fix;" or any signed document; or any agreement is better than none. They realize that fine tuning will take too much time; that constituents are becoming restless; that their short-term reputation needs a signed document, even if performance will probably not happen. Managers sometimes sign off on unrealistic agreements with employees as they want to pay attention to other impending crises; peace treaties are often signed even though key clauses are missing, or unrealistic. After the First World War, the Treaty of Versailles was eventually signed in 1919 despite obviously unworkable realignment of borders for many minority groups in Europe and Asia. Signing something was considered essential as negotiators were exhausted, political leaders needed to get home for forthcoming elections, anxious electorates wanted to celebrate "the" peace, militia were engaging in violent self-help, and creating some stable buffers against Bolshevism had become a priority.[17]

Conditional Agreements Subject to State Ratification

Some agreements require ratification, not only by constituents or tribes, but also by the state. This is because government policy or legislation has declared that certain "private ordering" affects important public interests. Therefore a right to veto exists until a public official is convinced that the private agreement has recognized community interests.

Sometimes, this community oversight reduces to a mindless, routine rubber-stamping by a state official or judge. But such low hurdles climb gradually towards expensive, time-consuming and uncertain hearings before an aggressive state judge, tribunal or official who is vigorously protecting actual or perceived public interests. Necessarily, any agreement lives in precarious limbo, subject to buyer's remorse, vengeful hawks, tactical maneuvers, and evidentiary uncertainty while waiting for this second round of public approval.

Examples of private agreements which need court or "official" approval to become relatively "final" or "binding" include:

- Building or forestry contracts which affect the environment.
- Child support agreements which affect the amount of social welfare paid to a custodial parent.
- Media, film, or literature contracts which import racist or pornographic views into the community.
- Private family agreements for the use of finances of a mentally disabled person.
- International treaties entered into by the executive, which legally require ratification by the legislature.
- Family property settlements which intentionally (a "sweetheart deal") or otherwise may result in a spouse becoming dependent on state welfare payments.
- Mergers of large corporations which potentially create monopolies of supply to the public.

Wealth

Wealth of one or both parties may destabilize an agreement. Money and the chance of "success" gives an aggrieved person the capacity and willingness to allege various legal justifications for breach when a future dispute occurs. Among the wealthy, a few years of legal expenses may only represent 1% of the aggrieved person's empire, and the resulting attrition and disparate investment may eventually encourage other parties to renegotiate the now disputed clauses.

Lawyers are instinctively aware of this pattern and that they may also become the target for the subsequent grievance. Accordingly, considerable time and consultation occurs when drafting contracts for the wealthy in order to minimize the chances of a subsequent professional negligence claim (as well as attempting to close loopholes and thereby discourage subsequent legal sorties by an affluent party).

How to Increase the Durability of Negotiated Agreements?

If the above is a catalogue of hypothesized and anecdotally observed reasons for agreements being "breached," or being less than durable, how then to make negotiated agreements more durable?

In simplistic terms, as with the original perceived incentives to *enter* the agreement, *performance* can also be made attractive, and non-performance made unattractive, via economics, emotion, various versions of morality, reputation, legal rules, and accessible, affordable and honest legal enforcement mechanisms applying to the various contracting parties.

If some of the "durability" or "stickability" elements cannot be added to the dynamics of the agreement, then expectations should be lowered. The parties may have achieved one "success" criterion, namely a (signed) agreement. But they may only have a low or moderate chance of another measure of "success," namely performance. Many risk-taking negotiators are willing to buy the chance of performance, and then experience the rollercoaster of performance and breach as the predicted ratio of performed to non-performed agreements is still considered to be a worthwhile investment.

Reversing the above list of factors which encourage breach, the chances of performance of an agreement are enhanced by the following:

- Try to enter contracts with people, groups or nations with whom there are strong long-term relationships. This provides a layer of incentives to perform promises rather than alienate friends and future business.
- When negotiating with cultural groups which perceive an agreement as mainly the beginning of a relationship, be prepared for a lengthy series of rounds of negotiation in exchange for the promise of a long-term relationship.
- Attempt to clarify across cultures whether "yes" means "maybe" or even "no," and whether signed and detailed documents are considered to be "binding," morally, legally, and/or in reputation—or just amount to the declaration that a working relationship now exists, with the actual commitments subject to continuous renegotiation. [Goh, *Errors*]
- Include a serious discussion and contractual clauses (more than boilerplate) on how future misunderstandings and problems will be addressed procedurally and emotionally by skilled people ("dispute resolution" clauses).
- Attempt to agree early on that final determination of any future "problems" with performance will be in an accessible court or arbitration venue which is, first, not corrupt, second, governed by stable and clear legal precedents, and third, that these legal precedents have minimal scope for varying or setting aside the particular type of agreement.
- Where possible, convert a negotiated dispute settlement into a court order so that any breach of the agreement immediately opens additional enforcement mechanisms.
- Draft the agreement in detail, if possible, in accordance with standard industry practices.
- Contract with "stable" countries and people, cultivate back-up suppliers and take out insurance as risk management for non-performance or currency fluctuations.

- Include carefully planned procedures for managing hawks and armchair critics in the background. [Wade, *Tribe*]
- Lower expectations, where there is long-term escalated conflict with some of the emotional and structural changes attached to such entrenched conflict.[18] This particularly applies to tribal conflicts in Northern Ireland, the Balkans, Rwanda, Israel and parts of Africa, but also within many families and businesses. The first year, decade, or century of agreements will undoubtedly not be durable with such dynamics in the background. [Coleman, et al., *Dynamical*]
- Attempt to enter agreements which recognize procedural, emotional and substantive needs of all parties. An aggrieved negotiator at any of those levels will probably be looking for payback or exit at a strategic moment.
- Where a negotiator is on an emotional rollercoaster, try to include his/her long-term friends, doves, moderates, associates, allies or business partners in the negotiations. [Mayer, *Allies*] For years after the initial agreement is signed, they will exert pressure (ongoing negotiations) on the wavering party to "honor his/her commitments," or risk losing their friendship.
- Do not walk close to the line on any of the legal rules, such as duress, deceit, vague terminology or illegality, any of which gives other parties opportunity to allege a loophole to finality.[19]
- Use experienced wordsmiths (a.k.a. lawyers) to include a range of standard clauses which attempt to negate duress, misrepresentation, and/or illegality, and which make specific allowances for future contingencies.
- Try to avoid complex agreements with multiple long-term obligations of performance; try to create "clean-break" obligations where one performance is swapped for another (e.g. bank check upon delivery of goods); try to include self-enforcing clauses so that the transaction costs of enforcement are reduced (e.g. interest of 12% runs on payments in default; security is held by a bank or by one party until performance occurs; payments are released upon progressive certification by an architect; liquidated damages; 1% extra for each day early; 1% less for each day late, etc.).
- Discover and perform an appropriate ritual of commitment—in some places, it is eye contact and a handshake. In others, it may be an alcoholic celebration, or a vow in the presence of a holy book or priest.
- Attempt to reduce buyer's remorse by making congratulatory speeches about the benefits of the agreement; and the list of risks which would follow no agreement; and by never agreeing quickly to any clauses; and by theatrical displays of anguish and pained speeches about the "tough terms," "special deal" or "hard bargain" which is being imposed; and by adding post-agreement gifts and bonuses (corner office, luggage racks, set of steak knives, 12 months' free warranty).
- Publicize the deal by mutual agreement. Then a wider audience places an expectation on all parties that they should perform, or lose face and credibility in future arrangements. Most people have a strong desire to act consistently with their own clear commitments.[20] Thus a media announcement of a treaty, a takeover, or a trade agreement is more than a celebration; it is aimed at moving at least the visible parties from agreement to a deeper level of commitment.

Conclusion

Most negotiators want more than an agreement. They want commitment and performance. It is helpful for negotiators, first, to be aware of the smorgasbord of factors which present warning signs of impending breaches; and second, to be aware of, and skilled at working on, those factors which increase the likelihood of commitment and performance.

Endnotes

[1] ROY J. LEWICKI ET AL., NEGOTIATION (5th ed. 2005).

[2] *See* DEAN G. PRUITT & SUNG HEE KIM, SOCIAL CONFLICT: ESCALATION, STALEMATE AND SETTLEMENT (3rd ed. 2004); CONFLICT: FROM ANALYSIS TO INTERVENTION (Sandra Cheldelin, et al. eds., 2003).

[3] *See, e.g.,* Christopher Honeyman, *The Wrong Mental Image of Settlement*, 17 NEGOTIATION JOURNAL 7 (2001); John H. Wade, *Representing Clients Effectively in Negotiation, Conciliation and Mediation of Family Disputes*, 18 AUSTRALIAN JOURNAL OF FAMILY LAW 283, 299, 302 (2004).

[4] CHRISTOPHER W. MOORE, THE MEDIATION PROCESS: PRACTICAL STRATEGIES FOR RESOLVING CONFLICT 64 (2003).

[5] KENNETH KRESSEL, THE PROCESS OF DIVORCE: HOW PROFESSIONALS AND COUPLES NEGOTIATE SETTLEMENTS 31 (1985); *see also*, JANET R. JOHNSTON & LINDA E.G. CAMPBELL, IMPASSES OF DIVORCE (1988); ELISABETH KUBLER-ROSS, ON DEATH AND DYING (1969); ROBERT S. WEISS, MARITAL SEPARATION (1975); PETER JORDAN, THE EFFECTS OF MARITAL SEPARATION ON MEN (1985).

[6] *See* LEWICKI ET AL., *supra* note 1, at 148.

[7] Stewart Macaulay, *Non-Contractual Relations in Business: A Preliminary Study*, 28 AMERICAN SOCIOLOGICAL REVIEW 55, 64 (1963); *see also*, Stewart Macaulay, *Elegant Models, Empirical Pictures, and the Complexities of Contract*, 11 LAW AND SOCIETY REVIEW 507 (1977).

[8] RUSSELL KOROBKIN, NEGOTIATION THEORY AND STRATEGY 375-416 (2002); NADJA M. SPEGEL ET AL., NEGOTIATION: THEORY AND TECHNIQUES 189-202 (1998).

[9] WILLISTON ON CONTRACTS Vol. 14 (3d ed. 1957); J.W. CARTER & D.J. HARLAND, CONTRACT LAW IN AUSTRALIA 555-641 (4th ed. 2002).

[10] TRANSPARENCY INTERNATIONAL, CORRUPTION PERCEPTIONS INDEX 2004, *at* http://www.transparency.org/policy_and_research/surveys_indices/cpi/2004 (last visited Mar. 8, 2006).

[11] "Tribal" is used here in the sense of relationship to a negotiator's constituents or supporters, not to ethnicity.

[12] SETTLING UP: PROPERTY AND INCOME DISTRIBUTION IN AUSTRALIA 295 (Peter McDonald ed., 1986).

[13] Public Trustee v. Gilbert (1991), 14 FAMILY LAW REPORTS 573 (Australia)

[14] *In Marriage of* Holland (1982), 8 FAMILY LAW REPORTS 233 (Australia); *In Marriage of* Gebert (1990), 14 FAMILY LAW REPORTS 62 (Australia) (husband settled for 10% of assets against his probable entitlement to 40%; court held that there was no miscarriage of justice, as the husband acted freely and was advised to seek legal advice).

[15] SETTLING UP, *supra* note 12, at 199-200; *see also*, John H. Wade, *Deals Which Come Unstuck: Reasons for the Breakdown of Family Settlements*, 9 AUSTRALIAN FAMILY LAWYER 14 (1993).

[16] *See* Honeyman, *supra* note 3.

[17] *See* MARGARET MACMILLAN, PARIS 1919 at 181, 192, 254 (2003).

[18] *See supra* note 2.

[19] Macaulay, *Non-Contractual Relations, supra* note 7, at 62-65 gives various contrary examples, such as where sales staff rely customarily on vague and incomplete terms in order to achieve quick agreements.

[20] *See* G. RICHARD SHELL, BARGAINING FOR ADVANTAGE 196-99 (1999); ROBERT B. CIALDINI, INFLUENCE: SCIENCE AND PRACTICE 52-97 (1st ed. 1984).

V. A Crowd at the Table

A. Enlisting Help

⚜ 57 ⚜

Consequences of Principal and Agent

Jayne Seminare Docherty & Marcia Caton Campbell

Editors' Note: *What's going on away from the negotiating table? How does the relationship between your counterpart and her principals impact you? Docherty and Caton Campbell explain how the structure of the agency relationship, for you and for the other side, can dramatically impact negotiation behaviors and outcomes. This chapter is related to Nolan-Haley's on Informed Consent, but also relates to chapters on team negotiations, particularly Bellman's on internal discord within a team.*

This chapter assumes that becoming a creative, reflective practitioner of negotiation requires more than mastering negotiation techniques or strategies. We think it highly likely that a professional negotiator will encounter negotiation situations where the parties differ in type—e.g., an individual negotiating with a corporation or a corporation negotiating with a local community group. It is also highly likely that a professional negotiator will encounter situations where back table negotiations between the principal party and the agent representing that party disrupt the primary negotiation. There is no way to equip negotiators with a set of discrete skills for managing these kinds of challenges. Instead, negotiators need to understand the structure of the negotiations operating at the same time as the conflicts being addressed by negotiations. This chapter offers some tools for analyzing both the conflict and the negotiation process when it involves agents negotiating on behalf of others.

Negotiation courses usually focus their primary attention on the interactions among the parties involved in the actual negotiation. Such courses also tend either to isolate the negotiation process from the social context within which it is embedded, or to assume that negotiators need only know about one small piece of the social context (e.g., the legal system or the business world). Negotiators should be encouraged to step back from the negotiation process and think more broadly about the social context within which they are operating. To this end, it is useful to consider how the structure of the larger social conflict or social problem affects the negotiation process. Some students of negotiation will protest that they are not dealing with *conflicts*; they are helping people address problems or differences. We would counter that the difference between a conflict and a dispute or "mere problem" can be quite small. It is often a matter of the perceptions of the parties; therefore, it is useful for all students of negotiation to understand the way the nature of the conflict—including its relative intensity—affects a negotiation process.

What do we mean by "social context" and "structure of the larger social conflict?" Negotiation is a process for managing or resolving conflicts that emerge in a particular social context.[1] For example, a negotiation may take place in a corporate setting, in a family, in the legal system, or in an institutional, governmental, or community setting. In each of these cases, the context or setting of the conflict carries certain norms, rules, and expectations—some formal and some informal—about how a negotiation process will be managed. Who needs to be at the table? What kinds of issues are negotiable and what kinds of issues may the parties not even raise in negotiation? How will the parties comport themselves during the negotiation?

Every social conflict, no matter the context within which it emerges, can also be said to have a structure. The structure of a conflict should not be confused with the structure of negotiation, as described by Korobkin,[2] which is also an important issue to be considered in educating negotiators. When we talk about the structure of a conflict, we are referring to features of the conflict such as the number and nature of the parties and the quality of their relationships. This contrasts with the dynamics of a conflict, which looks at changes in the parties' relationships and interactions over time. Think of the "structure of a conflict" as a still photograph of the actors and their relationships taken at a given moment and the "dynamics of a conflict" as a film of their interactions. The structure of a conflict can change as a conflict progresses so structural analysis needs to be done in an iterative manner. Conflict structure includes the *number of parties* involved. Is this a two-party conflict or a multi-party conflict? Structure also includes *the nature of the parties*. Are the parties in the conflict individuals or corporate entities? If they are corporate entities, are they tightly or loosely organized? The number of parties and their nature are only two aspects of conflict structure, but we can use them to illustrate why negotiators should learn to think about the relationship between the structure of a conflict and the negotiation process.

> Negotiation is defined as an interactive communication process by which two or more parties who lack identical interests attempt to find a way to coordinate their behavior or allocate scarce resources in a way that will make them better off than they could be if they were to act alone.[3]

This definition of negotiation references the basic elements of negotiation—parties, issues, goals, and interactions. Like many commonly used definitions of negotiation, it does not address the context of the negotiation encounter, but it is a useful place to start.

When thinking about a negotiation process in the abstract—negotiation as an ideal type—we usually think of two parties even though we know that real life often presents us with multi-party negotiations. We are also inclined to think of parties as negotiating on their own behalf. Again, in real life, we know that parties may be represented by others who negotiate on their behalf. In some contexts, particularly when working with multi-party, community-level negotiations, professionals talk about parties and their representatives. In other settings, particularly law or business, the literature refers to the parties as *principals* and their representatives as *agents*. This chapter will use both sets of terms.

Because negotiation is a process driven by communication, any increase in the number of persons involved—adding more parties or involving agents acting on behalf of principals—complicates the process. We all know what happens in the game of telephone; the more a message gets passed around, the more likely it is to be distorted. When messages must go from principal A to agent A; from agent A to agent B; from agent B to principal B and back again, we have more places where messages can get distorted. If we throw in principal C and agent C, or even more parties and their agents, the communication problems become daunting indeed. Figure 1 diagrams a relatively simple negotiation with two parties represented by agents.[4]

Figure 1: Interconnected or "Embedded" Negotiations

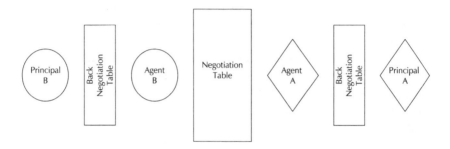

When teaching students the art of negotiating on behalf of others, we can focus on the problems that might arise between agents and principals and give them skills to prevent or overcome those problems. Thus, noting that an agent who does not understand her client's interests and positions might miss opportunities for an integrative agreement, we can make our students practice interviewing skills that will help them uncover the client's interests. Noting the serious problem of poor communication between principal and agent, we can teach active listening, clear presentation, and other communication techniques. We can emphasize the need for establishing informed consent between the negotiator and the client. [Nolan-Haley, *Informed Consent*] Similarly, recognizing that the interests of the agent and the principal sometimes differ, we can familiarize negotiators with the ethical and professional standards regulating their relationship with clients.[5]

These are all valid parts of a good negotiation curriculum, but they are not enough to develop highly skilled reflective practitioners of negotiation. Negotiators also need to learn that introducing principal-agent relationships into a negotiation establishes a set of interconnected negotiations. Principal A and agent A have a set of "back table negotiations" and so do principal B and agent B. The negotiations at the table intersect with and affect the negotiations behind the table and vice versa. Put another way, conflicts between principals and their agents impact the conflicts between the parties to the central conflict and vice versa.

Sometimes agents and their principals use this structure of interconnected negotiations for strategic purposes. Parties can buy time in the primary negotiation by dragging out their back table negotiations. The agent can also use an absent principal as an excuse for taking actions ("my client made me say this") or for declining offers from the other party ("I'm sorry, but my client won't let me accept this offer"). On the other hand, there are times when problems with the back-table negotiations actually jeopardize the central negotiation. [Wade, *Tribe*] Highly skilled negotiators need to understand why this happens and how they can work with these problems.

The back table negotiations are difficult enough when the agent is representing a single individual (say, one spouse in a divorce negotiation). They become extremely complicated when the parties are collective entities (say, corporations, community groups, warring militias, or unions). Yet, efficiency and cost-saving concerns dictate that most negotiations involving collective entities are carried out through representatives.

This is one place it really pays to understand the structure of the larger conflict, because structural factors help determine just how difficult the back table negotiations are likely to become. We have already alluded to the regulatory mechanisms that govern (more or less formally) some principal-agent relationships. However, in many cases these controls do not exist, because representatives of parties are selected through political processes. Their roles as agents in a negotiation are socially and politically negotiated, as is the evaluation of their performance, their ability to continue in the role of agent for a sustained period, and their ability to deliver on any negotiated agreements.

For example, in *What's in a Frame?* in this book, we described a case in which a city proposed a highway extension right through an area considered sacred ground by a local Native American tribe. [Caton Campbell & Docherty, *Framing*] Using the same example here, we might convene a multi-party negotiation involving a coalition of five Native American tribes, elected officials from the city and adjacent counties, developers, a variety of activist groups (including environmentalists, Native American rights groups, and anti-sprawl groups), the state's congressional delegation, and a large federal agency. Obviously, these parties will need to send representatives to negotiate on their behalf, and the negotiation process will need to be designed to accommodate multiple back table negotiations. In a case this complicated, a facilitator or mediator (or a team of facilitators and mediators) may be hired to help manage the negotiation. However, good negotiators should not rely solely on a facilitator or mediator to help them navigate a complex, multi-party negotiation process. Party representatives can be far more effective if they understand why back table negotiations are so important and why those negotiations might stymie the primary negotiation.[6]

Two structural factors can increase or decrease the possibility that conflicts between parties and their representatives will negatively affect the main negotiation. Negotiators should learn to ask the following questions about each representative in a negotiation:

- How formal and structured is the relationship between the principal and the agent?
- How much legitimacy does the agent have?

Some principal-agent relationships are contractual and regulated. An agent is hired to negotiate on behalf of party A. Party A may fire the agent at will, and may also be able to hold the agent accountable for his performance according to the contractual agreement. Party A may also be able to file a complaint against the agent with a professional body, and/or sue the agent. For his part, the agent may quit as representative for party A and may have rights to sue if party A fails to meet contractual obligations. The relationship is professional, not personal; it is contractual, not political. In other words, it is formal and highly structured.

In other cases, however, representatives may be selected through a variety of political processes, ranging in formality from voting to volunteering. A union representative is elected. She must keep a close eye on her constituency lest she not be re-elected, and there are formal mechanisms for recalling her if the rank-and-file members feel that she is not representing their interests. This is a formal and structured process, but it is messier than a contractual relationship. Even less formal and structured are relationships between parties and representatives when the parties are loose coalitions or voluntary membership groups. In these cases, representatives often volunteer to speak for the group or they may be selected based on their personal charisma. If the group is informal and voluntary, the membership of the group may be subject to fluctuations so that the representative may have difficulty presenting a coherent position. Furthermore, there are few if any formal mechanisms for the group to remove a volunteer from the negotiation table.

This leads to the problem of reliability. Can any given agent "deliver" on a negotiated agreement? How accurately is any given agent representing the interests and positions of the parties? Will the back table negotiations—which may take the form of a vote in the case of a union or may be a lot messier and more difficult to track in the case of ad-hoc voluntary organizations—support the agreement reached at the negotiation table? It is usually, but not always, safe to assume that an agent representing a party through a contractual relationship has checked carefully with the party before affirming any agreement. In more political relationships between a party and its representative, it is much harder to predict whether the back table negotiations will support the agreements reached at the main negotiation table.

The more political a relationship is between representative and party, the more others involved in the negotiation need to focus on the question of legitimacy. Legitimacy enters into a negotiation at several points. Each person involved in the negotiation must be seen as a legitimate negotiating partner by the other negotiators, otherwise negotiations cannot proceed. In the case of agents negotiating on behalf of principals, there is an added legitimacy question: does Party A accept the agent representing Party A at the table as a valid representative? Thus, looking at a multi-party negotiation involving representatives of larger parties we can ask: how legitimate is any given representative at any given moment?

Legitimacy or the lack thereof may be related to the way the agent was chosen. If, in the case described above, the Bureau of Indian Affairs appoints representatives for the coalition of five tribes, those representatives will probably have low legitimacy. They may even need to take much more hard-line positions in the negotiation to compensate for their "tainted" appointment. That does not mean we can assume the tribal representatives will have high legitimacy if they are selected from within. Internal conflicts within and among the tribes may distort the selection process. Furthermore, the legitimacy of any representative may change over time and may be affected by the negotiation process. An agent may gain legitimacy by succeeding in the negotiation or lose legitimacy by failing.

Taken together, the formality of the agent-principal relationship and the agent's legitimacy with the party help determine whether agent-principal conflicts (problems with the back table negotiations) are more or less likely to disrupt interparty negotiations. We can use the formality/informality continuum and the low legitimacy/high legitimacy continuum to create a model that illustrates the likelihood that conflicts between a party and its representative will derail a negotiation (Figure 2).

Figure 2: Legitimacy and Formality of Principal-Agent Relationship

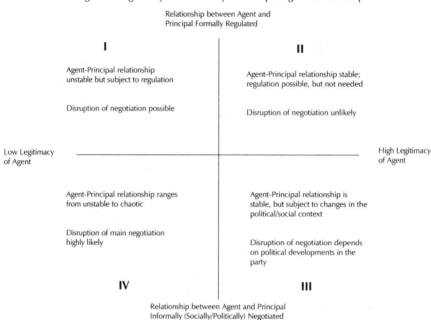

In addition to the legitimacy of other representatives and the formality of their relationship with their respective parties, good negotiators should have some understanding of the way the *nature* of the party impacts their back table negotiations. Some parties can move quickly, while others need significantly more time to validate or reject proposed agreements. This is not *always* a stalling tactic; it may be an honest reflection of the complexity of the party's internal organization, or a reflection of the party's culture. [Kelly, *Indigenous Experience*]

For example, non-native representatives will probably see a Native American representative in our case as potentially able to deliver constituents, but the tribal representative will almost always disavow the ability to speak for anyone but himself as an individual. It is common to hear tribal representatives say something like, "I represent the X people, but I speak only for myself." A tribal representative's ability to deliver constituents depends on extensive and lengthy back table discussions with tribal members, some of which can take months. This is something that non-native negotiators have great difficulty with since temporal efficiency is a hallmark of "good" negotiations in the Western business, legal, and administrative worlds.

Developing a chart such as the following can help a negotiator pay attention to the structural factors that shape back table negotiations between a representative and his party. A blank version of this chart can be filled in for a particular case. The negotiator should also always remember to map her own party on this diagram so that she examines the structural factors that are shaping her own back table negotiation.

Type of Party	Nature of Structure	Speed with which it can act	Coherence of goals
Corporation	Highly organized Hierarchical	Quick—once the necessary component parts become involved	Very coherent—clear, widely shared standards for measuring success (i.e., bottom line)
Government Agency	Hierarchical Organized, but may have some incoherence in the system because of competing mandates and the influence of political actors on policies and Standard Operating Procedures	Slow compared to corporations Quick compared to community organizations and other political groups	May be confused by competing mandates and shifting political scene
Community Organization—e.g., Neighborhood Association	Semi-structured Democratic and therefore open to change	Relatively slow—needs time to build consensus through democratic processes	May not be fully coherent and may lack shared standards for measuring success
Native American Tribe	Frequently subject to internal conflicts between "progressive" and "traditional" factions Culturally more likely to work by consensus rather than majority vote	May be very slow, particularly if tribe works by consensus and deliberation	May be difficult to discern because of internal conflicts

There are many negotiations that do not require the level of analysis outlined in this chapter. However, when faced with a complex negotiation involving different types of parties using representatives, looking at the structure of the larger conflict and the nature of the parties can be a very helpful process. It assists a negotiator in setting realistic expectations about such basic factors as how long a negotiation will probably take and the likelihood of ratification of an agreement reached at the primary negotiation table. A negotiator who understands the pressures and opportunities created by a counterpart's back table negotiations can also craft more creative proposals by incorporating the needs and interests of the agent and her principals into each round of discussion.

Endnotes

[1] Among the contextual features that negotiators should learn to assess is the relative stability or turbulence of the environment in which they are negotiating. For more on this issue *see* JAYNE SEMINARE DOCHERTY, THE LITTLE BOOK OF STRATEGIC NEGOTIATION: NEGOTIATING DURING TURBULENT TIMES (2005).

[2] RUSSELL KOROBKIN, NEGOTIATION THEORY AND STRATEGY 33-220 (2002).

[3] *Id.* at 1.

[4] This diagram and many of the ideas in this chapter were greatly enriched by Jayne Seminare Docherty's conversations with Ron Kraybill (Eastern Mennonite University), Frank Blechman (independent consultant), and Carol Gowler (Conflict Transformation Program, Eastern Mennonite University).

[5] For attorneys, this would include a working knowledge of, among other things, THE MODEL RULES OF PROFESSIONAL CONDUCT (2004).

[6] Multi-party negotiations can be greatly enhanced by the type of pre-negotiation work described in Jayne Seminare Docherty, Negotiation, *One Tool Among Many*, Chapter 65 in this volume. Intervenors may offer parties training in negotiating, as well as engaging in data gathering and fact-finding to help parties arrive at a coherent picture of which issues will be covered in the negotiations and what will not. *Also see* Bernard Mayer, *Allies in Negotiation*, Chapter 69 in this volume.

✿ 58 ✿

Agents and Informed Consent

Jacqueline Nolan-Haley

Editors' Note: *How can you the negotiator ensure that your client is really on board? Nolan-Haley argues that by paying more attention to informed consent not only before, but again at intervals during negotiation, and taking care to reaffirm consent as the process reaches agreement, agents will not only better serve their clients but reach better, more lasting agreements. This chapter should be read in conjunction with Wade's Bargaining in the Shadow of the Tribe.*

In July 2005, the world witnessed an extraordinary negotiation between the Irish Republican Army (IRA) and its allied Sinn Fein Party, and Great Britain, Ireland and the United States. The IRA formally announced the end of its armed conflict and agreed to destroy all of its weapons.[1] Imagine the future consequences if the IRA representatives who negotiated the ceasefire and promised to destroy all weapons had not truly obtained the informed consent of their constituents. In a less dramatic scenario, consider what might happen if a husband, without consulting his wife, offered her services as soccer coach to the town's middle-school team in exchange for the town's commitment to give their child a place on the team. In both cases, the long-term durability of these agreements would be on shaky grounds, because the principal's informed consent is missing.

Negotiating through agents or "representative negotiations" is a commonplace, yet complex and understudied practice. Foremost among the many challenges posed by representative negotiations is loss of control by the principal. Rubin and Sander's classic article on the use of agents in negotiation reinforces the point: "once agents have been introduced the chemistry changes..." and principals may find themselves less in control.[2] Well-known examples of this "chemistry change" arise where the incentives of the principal and agent are not aligned or where the risk preferences of an agent differ from those of the principal.[3] The literature on negotiation labels these challenges as "tensions" and suggests that, if not properly managed, they may result in barriers to negotiated settlements.[4]

How can a principal ensure that an agent serves her interests at the bargaining table? How can she prevent exploitation? Or, guarantee that a durable agreement is reached? Scholars have suggested a number of mechanisms to manage principal-agent tensions that give rise to these questions,[5] but surprisingly little attention has been paid to the concept of informed consent and its potential to act as a corrective. This chapter attempts to fill that void by considering the principle of informed consent in the context of bilateral, representative negotiations.

The Meaning of Informed Consent

Informed consent is an ubiquitous concept that operates in a multitude of different settings, from participatory democracy to international treaties on hazardous chemicals.[6] In the broader political context, the principle of informed consent holds that legitimate government depends upon the informed consent of the governed.[7] This principle has developed into an ethical, moral, and legal concept deeply ingrained in American culture.[8] In those transactions where informed consent is required, the legal doctrine requires that individuals who give consent be competent, informed about the intervention, and consent voluntarily. Informed consent legal analysis, developed largely in medical cases, focuses on the dual requirements of disclosure and consent.

Why Informed Consent Matters When Agents Negotiate

Informed consent is the foundational moral and ethical principle that promotes respect for individual self-determination and honors human dignity. In representative negotiations, the principle of informed consent is not an end in itself but is a means of achieving the fundamental goal of fairness. Fairness requires that principals know what they are doing when they authorize agents to negotiate for them, that they understand the decision-making process, including their right to withdraw consent and discontinue negotiations, and that they understand the outcome reached in negotiation. Toward this end, the principle of informed consent protects the psychological and legal interests associated with the values of autonomy, human dignity and efficiency.

Beyond these aspirational goals, the principle of informed consent has enormous practical significance. Consent is critical to the long-term durability of agreements that agents negotiate on behalf of principals. When a court finds that valid consent is suspect or missing from a negotiated agreement, its life span is short-lived.[9] Likewise, in the realm of international politics, the value of consent in representative negotiations is critical to sustainability. The ongoing conflict between China and Tibet over Chinese occupation of Tibet is illustrative. Despite the "17 Point Agreement" negotiated between the Chinese government and Tibetan representatives in 1951, under which China asserted a claim to rule Tibet, conflict over self-determination of the Tibetan people still persists. Why? Because a substantial segment of the Tibetan population believes that the agreement was signed under coercion by Tibetan representatives who lacked authority.[10]

Apart from its value in promoting fairness and durable agreements, the principle of informed consent is perhaps best understood as the vehicle through which autonomy is measured in decision-making between physicians and patients, and to a lesser degree, between lawyers and clients. It is not possible in this brief essay to consider the broad range of principal-agent relationships where informed consent is a relevant consideration. Thus, my primary focus will be on the attorney-client relationship. I will sketch a framework for informed consent between lawyers and clients that is based on a deliberative process, and identify as questions for future research how informed consent operates in multiparty negotiations and in different cultural settings.

Legal Representative Negotiations

As a matter of general principle, informed consent is an operative rule in legal negotiations.[11] The "law of negotiation" provides remedies and imposes penalties where consent is obtained improperly in negotiation, whether through fraud, coercion, duress or the like. [Korobkin, et al., *Law of Bargaining*] But the question of *how* informed consent operates in representative negotiation settings is an empirical issue about which, in my view, we know very little. How is disclosure provided? What counts as consent?

The informed consent obligations of lawyers acting as agents for clients in negotiations are found in the professional responsibility rules for the legal profession. While the rules provide some conceptual support for the principle of informed consent, they offer little practical guidance to lawyers on how informed consent should operate.[12] The informational requirements for lawyers in Model Rule 1.4, though not as extensive as those imposed upon physicians under tort law, demonstrate a clear mandate for disclosure. Lawyers are required to "explain a matter to the extent reasonably necessary to permit the client to make informed decisions regarding the representation." Regulation of client "consent" rights, on the other hand, is somewhat murky. Model Rule 1.2(a), which governs the allocation of decision-making power in the attorney-client relationship, establishes in effect an "ends/means" approach, in which the client decides the "ends" of a given problem, i.e., whether to accept a particular settlement offer, and the attorney decides the "means." The inherent complexity of determining what constitutes real ends and means has made it difficult to integrate this distinction in legal practice.

The foundational analysis of an informed consent principle in the lawyer-client relationship is rooted in the lawyer's professional obligation to inform clients of relevant information and in the client's autonomy interest in participatory decision-making. The idea of an informed consent principle to govern the attorney-client relationship is of recent origin and compared to the significant interest that the topic has generated in the medical literature, surprisingly little legal literature exists.[13] In general, the notion that lawyers should provide information necessary for clients to become involved in decision-making has met with mixed reaction. Some scholars urge acceptance of the principle, while others argue that based on the difficulty of interpreting this standard in medicine, informed consent is not a desirable standard to govern the attorney-client relationship. At a minimum, however, scholars agree with the philosophy of an informed consent standard to the extent that it pushes lawyers towards making clients real partners in decision-making.[14]

Achieving Informed Consent in Representative Negotiations: A Deliberative Process

How do lawyers gain their clients' informed consent in representative negotiations? In a world of perfect informed consent practice, the transfer of authority from the client-principal to the lawyer-agent would be a relatively straightforward matter. Principals would understand their positions and the underlying interests that support them as well as the opposing principal's positions and underlying interests. They would also understand the range of possible agreements, and their BATNAs (the best outcome they could achieve if no agreement is reached). Likewise, agents would understand their own interests and where they might not be aligned with those of the principal. They would inform principals of their divergent interests, clarify the extent of their authority, and determine whether there were any non-negotiable issues. Principals and agents would then discuss all of these issues, principals would grant authority to agents, and negotiations would proceed.

In the real world, the informed consent process is a much more complicated project. Enter the human factor—the emotions, psychological biases, and different behavioral orientations that affect principals and agents and influence agendas. Mere discussion between principals and agents will be unlikely to create an understanding of the principal and the agent's respective divergent interests. Much more deliberation is required for the kind of understanding between principals and agents that will result in integrative agreements that truly satisfy a principal's interests.

Deliberation honors the reasoning power of clients and lawyers. In the give and take of argument and debate, lawyers and clients gain a better understanding of each other's views. The deliberative process calls for careful calculation and reasoned dialogue.[15] It is a reflective activity that requires active participation by principal and agent.[16] The heart of the deliberative process is the exchange of ideas and debate between principal and agent about ends and means, goals and strategies.

Too often representative negotiations are not preceded by any meaningful deliberation between lawyers and clients. Lawyers do not listen to their clients but presume to know their goals. The methodology of deliberation can improve representative negotiations and foster mutual respect between lawyers and clients. Frank discussions between lawyer and client about the relative merits of particular courses of action can go a long way towards achieving participatory and educated client decision-making, the hallmarks of the informed consent doctrine.[17]

Multiparty Negotiations

Given how little we know about the operational aspects of informed consent in bilateral, representative negotiations, we know even less about how it functions in the multiparty negotiations where the presence of coalitions and shifting nature of BATNAs add layers of complexity to the negotiation process.[18] Whether the framework for a deliberative informed consent process that I have sketched has any traction in the multiparty setting is an empirical question that must take into account two separate issues: (1) the process of identifying the stakeholders whose consent must be obtained and (2) the process that occurs in the shadow or back table negotiations that authorize and give legitimacy to representative agents.

Identifying All Relevant Stakeholders

Who should be included in the group that gives legitimacy to agents? Who decides who speaks for the community? Is there an ideal inclusion process? Our current empirical knowledge base of multiparty negotiations fails to provide meaningful answers to these questions. Yet, we continue in "multiparty process ignorance" at our peril. Failure to identify potential stakeholders and include them in the informed consent process is an invitation to disaster that can completely derail the negotiation process.

Narratives of informed consent "process" disasters can be found in the growing body of literature on the tensions between indigenous communities and national governments over ownership of genetic resources and traditional knowledge.[19] One example, the failure in 2001 of a U.S. sponsored, bioprospecting[20] project in Chiapas, Mexico, demonstrates the perils of an informed consent process that fails to include all relevant stakeholders.[21] In this case, a U.S. government sponsored initiative, the International Cooperative Biodiversity Group (ICBG) funded a project that would produce drugs from plants and microfungi used by the Maya community in Mexico. Under Mexican law a special government permit was required to collect "biotechnological" material in Mexico. The permit would be issued, however, only if the requester had obtained "informed consent" of the owner or legal possessor of the land where the material was located. The communities whose consent was required included about eight thousand villages and about nine hundred thousand Mayan-speaking people. As part of their informed consent efforts, the ICBG team conducted an extensive information campaign in Mayan communities, including public forums, radio spots, distribution of flyers, and a play about the project performed in the native language. After eighteen months, 46 of the 47 visited communities agreed to participate in the project. However, strong opposition from local NGOs who claimed that they had not been given the opportunity to weigh in, doomed the project. Thus, after spending thousands of dollars and almost two years trying to obtain the informed consent of the Mayan communities, the bioprospecting project collapsed.[22]

Shadow Negotiations
Multiparty negotiations do not operate in a vacuum but are part of a larger web of negotiations between constituents and their representatives. We know very little about how the informed consent process works in back table or shadow negotiations. How do agents gain legitimacy? [Docherty & Caton Campbell, *Agency*] How many and which parties need to be in agreement before a decision is binding? How do groups determine what positions their representative agents will take at the primary negotiations? To what extent do shadow negotiations take into account the structure of the larger conflict?[23]

Cultural Considerations
In considering the state of our knowledge about informed consent practice in representative negotiations, we need to learn more about its cultural content. What are the functional equivalents of informed consent, if any, in other cultures and how do they operate? Norms and expectations about informed consent are not universal. We know that as a general matter, not all cultures share the West's reverence for the principle of informed consent or the values that it honors.[24] What implications does this have on representative negotiations in the international arena? When negotiating biodiversity agreements with indigenous peoples?[25] When negotiating multi-lateral nuclear disarmament agreements with North Korea or Iran? When negotiating any agreement with terrorists?

Conclusion
I have suggested that a deliberative informed consent process is an asset in representative negotiations, particularly when lawyers negotiate as agents for clients. The values honored by informed consent as well as its practical benefits can be helpful in managing principal-agent tensions that can act as barriers to the negotiated resolution of disputes. The exchange of ideas and debate between lawyers and clients about ends and means, goals and strategies, enhances understanding of each other's interests and contributes to integrative agreements. The extent to which the deliberative informed consent model would work in other contexts, including multiparty negotiations and different cultural settings, are empirical questions begging for answers.

Endnotes

The author thanks Professor Lela Love for her helpful comments on this draft.

[1] Brian Lavery & Alan Cowell, *I.R.A. Renounces Use of Violence; Vows to Disarm*, N.Y. TIMES, July 29, 2005, at A1.

[2] Jeffery Rubin & Frank Sander, *When Should We Use Agents? Direct vs Representative Negotiation*, 4 NEGOTIATION JOURNAL 400 (1988).

[3] *See* ROBERT H. MNOOKIN, ET AL., BEYOND WINNING: NEGOTIATING TO CREATE VALUES IN DEALS AND DISPUTES 75-76 (2000) [hereinafter MNOOKIN, ET AL.].

[4] Robert H. Mnookin, *Why Negotiations Fail: An Exploration of the Barriers to the Resolution of Conflict*, 8 OHIO STATE JOURNAL ON DISPUTE RESOLUTION 235 (1993).

[5] These include incentive contracts, monitoring systems and bonding, MNOOKIN, ET AL., *supra* note 3 at 76-82, as well as structuring compensation to align the interests of the principal and agent as much as possible. RUSSELL KOROBKIN, NEGOTIATION THEORY AND STRATEGY 321 (2002).

[6] *E.g.*, Rotterdam Convention on the Prior Informed Consent Procedure for Certain Hazardous Chemicals and Pesticides in International Trade, Sept. 11, 1998, 1998 U.S.T. LEXIS 200.

[7] THE DECLARATION OF INDEPENDENCE para. 2 (U.S. 1776).

[8] *See* Jacqueline M. Nolan-Haley, *Informed Consent in Mediation: A Guiding Principle for Truly Educated Decisionmaking*, 74 NOTRE DAME LAW REVIEW 775 (1999).

[9] It should be noted, however, that a lack of informed consent will not necessarily protect a client from the effects of an agreement negotiated by an attorney in mediation. Under traditional agency analysis, a principal is bound by the acts of the agent acting within the scope of her authority. The courts have not been consistent in applying agency analysis to cases involving contested mediation agreements. Nolan-Haley, *supra* note 8 at 809. In some cases, courts appear to strain to find informed consent. *See* Nancy Welsh, *The Thinning Vision of Self-Determination in Court-connected Mediation: The Inevitable Price of Institutionalization*, 6 HARVARD NEGOTIATION LAW REVIEW 1 (2001).

[10] *See* MICHAEL C. VAN WALT VAN PRAAG, THE STATUS OF TIBET: HISTORY, RIGHTS, AND PROSPECTS IN INTERNATIONAL LAW 154-55 (1987); Regina M. Clark, *China's Unlawful Control Over Tibet: The Tibetan People's Entitlement To Self-Determination*, 12 INDIANA INTERNATIONAL & COMPARATIVE LAW REVIEW 293 (2002).

[11] For a discussion of how this principle also operates in the mediation process, *see* Nolan-Haley, *Informed Consent*, *supra* note 8. *See also* John W. Cooley & Lela P. Love, *The Intersection of Evaluation by Mediators and Informed Consent: Warning the Unwary*, 21 OHIO STATE JOURNAL ON DISPUTE RESOLUTION (forthcoming 2006).

[12] Model Rules of Professional Conduct R1.0(e) (2004), defines for lawyers informed consent as "the agreement by a person to a proposed course of conduct after the lawyer has communicated adequate information and explanation about the material risks of and reasonably available alternatives to the proposed course of conduct."

[13] The first significant article urging adoption of an informed consent standard for the legal profession appeared in 1979 with Professor Mark Spiegel's proposal for expanded client decision-making. *See* Mark Spiegel, *Lawyering and Client Decisionmaking: Informed Consent and the Legal Profession*, 128 UNIVERSITY OF PENNSYLVANIA LAW REVIEW 41 (1979).

[14] *See* Nolan-Haley, *supra* note 8 at 787, n.52.

[15] ROBERT H. MNOOKIN & JONATHAN R. COHEN, NEGOTIATING ON BEHALF OF OTHERS 3-6 (Robert H. Mnookin & Lawrence E. Susskind eds., 1999) ("focusing on interests requires richer discussions between principals and agents than commonly occur").

[16] *See* Amy Gutmann, *Can Virtue Be Taught To Lawyers?* 45 STANFORD LAW REVIEW 1759 (1993) (arguing in favor of an obligation of deliberation between lawyers and clients). For a fuller discussion of deliberation between lawyers and clients in mediation see Jacqueline Nolan-Haley, *Lawyers, Clients and Mediation*, 73 NOTRE DAME LAW REVIEW 1369 (1998).

[17] Nolan-Haley, *supra* note 16.

[18] *See, e.g.*, Lawrence Susskind, et al., *What We Have Learned About Teaching Multiparty Negotiation*, 21 NEGOTIATION JOURNAL 395 (2005).

[19] *See, e.g.*, Sara A. Laird & Flavia Noejovich, *Building Equitable Research Relationships with Indigenous Peoples and Local Communities: Prior Informed Consent and Research Agreements in* BIODIVERSITY AND TRADITIONAL KNOWLEDGE: EQUITABLE PARTNERSHIPS IN PRACTICE 187-88 (Sara A. Laird ed., 2002); Laurel A. Firestone, *You Say Yes, I Say No; Defining Community Prior Informed Consent Under the Convention on Biological Diversity*, 16 GEORGETOWN INTERNATIONAL ENVIRONMENTAL LAW REVIEW 171 (2003).

[20] The term "bioprospecting" refers to the collection of biological samples (plants, animals and micro-organisms) and indigenous knowledge to help in discovering genetic resources. The Convention on Biological Diversity (1992) requires that parties engaged in bio-respecting must obtain the informed consent of the source country. *See Bioprospecting*, WIKIPEDIA.ORG, *at* http://en.wikipedia.org/wiki/Bioprospecting (last visited Mar. 7, 2006).

[21] Sabrina Safrin, *Hyperownership in a Time of Biotechnological Promise: The International Conflict to Control the Building Blocks of Life*, 98 AMERICAN JOURNAL OF INTERNATIONAL LAW 641, 655-57 (2004).

[22] For another example of an agreement that failed due to lack of informed consent, *see* Firestone, *supra* note 19, at 207 n.27 (describing an agreement between the Crao and the Federal University of Sao Paulo, Brazil, to study certain medicinal plants used by the tribe and develop medicines that would result in royalties for the tribes. Only 3 out of a total of 17 individual tribes were consulted and included in the contract. As a result, the remaining 14 tribes later sued the university for using the tribes' traditional knowledge without their consent).

[23] The shadow negotiations that took place in Northern Ireland by members of the Northern Ireland Women's Coalition (NIWC) during the negotiations leading to the Good Friday/Belfast Agreement provide an interesting example of how the dynamic of a larger conflict affects both the process and outcome of back table negotiations. *See* Jacqueline Nolan-Haley & Brogna Hinds, *Problem-Solving Negotiation: Northern Ireland's Experience with the Women's Coalition*, 2003 JOURNAL OF DISPUTE RESOLUTION 387. *See generally* Kate Fearon and Monica McWilliams, *The Good Friday Agreement: A Triumph of Substance Over Style*, 22 FORDHAM INTERNATIONAL LAW JOURNAL 1250 (1999).

[24] For example, medical literature reports that in caring for patients from non-western cultures, there is a concern that the formal requirements for obtaining informed consent may impose a western ideal of personal autonomy on some minority patients, especially those who come from cultures that favor what appears to be a family-centered model of decision-making over a more individualistic model. Contrary to the current informed consent standard of full disclosure and patient self-determination, many minority patients may wish to remain uninvolved in the medical decision-making process, and prefer instead to defer to their families or physicians' choices. *See* Robert B. Leflar, *Informed Consent and Patients' Rights in Japan*, 33 HOUSTON LAW REVIEW 1 (1996); Insoo Hyun, *Waiver of Informed Consent, Cultural Sensitivity, and the Problem of Unjust Families*, 32 Hastings Center Report No. 5 14 (2002); Farhat Moazam, *Families, Patients, and Physicians in Medical Decision-making: A Pakistani Perspective*, 30 Hastings Center Report No. 6 28 (2000).

[25] *See* Firestone, *supra* note 19 (describing informed consent requirements in biodiversity agreements). *See also* Nuno Pires de Carvalho, *From the Shaman's Hut to the Patent Office: In Search of a TRIPS-Consistent Requirement to Disclose the Origin of Genetic Resources and Prior Informed Consent*, 17 WASHINGTON UNIVERSITY JOURNAL OF LAW & POLICY 111 (2005). Some scholars claim that by imposing concepts such as informed consent, western intellectual property law is contrary to many important features of indigenous knowledge systems. *See* Laurie Anne Whitt, *Indigenous Peoples, Intellectual Property & the New Imperial Science*, 23 OKLAHOMA CITY UNIVERSITY LAW REVIEW 211, 251 (1998).

❧ 59 ❧

The New Advocacy

Julie Macfarlane

Editors' Note: *This chapter shows how historical notions of the meaning of "zealous advocacy" have evolved into a highly adversarial norm. More and more lawyers, especially those skilled in the use of consensus-building processes such as negotiation and mediation, are finding "zealous advocacy" ineffectual. Macfarlane shows how more sophisticated concepts work to protect clients' interests and get deals done.*

Reclaiming "Advocacy"

In this chapter I shall try to reclaim and redefine what we mean by "advocacy" in conflict resolution in general, and in the practice of negotiation in particular. The term "advocacy" is considered by some to be an ugly or unappealing concept in conflict resolution, incompatible with a problem-solving approach to negotiation. It seems that we have surrendered our populist cultural sense of "advocacy" to an adversarial frame. The traditional selflessness of 18th century conceptions of "advocacy" has long been replaced by aggressively commercial models often characterized by noisy argumentation and table banging—both in the movies and in real-life.

In this chapter, I shall argue that our disassociation of conflict resolution from a populist notion of "advocacy" is less an inevitable consequence of changing social and economic mores than a consequence of our limited imaginations. Part of our collective enchantment with concepts of conflict resolution (peacemaking, consensus-building, interests-based negotiation) rests on their apparent capacity to radically reframe conflict as solvable and to give us new hope. We cannot easily reconcile a philosophical commitment to the service of a single client in a negotiation with a commitment to promoting peace and resolution that meets their interests in a manner acceptable to the other side. Instead we often assume that "standing up for your client" as a negotiation ally is incompatible with, and disables us from, acting as promoters of peace and builders of consensus. We go even further by sometimes equating the much-lauded "paradigm shift" in thinking about conflict with the rejection of any enabling of individual voice or other assertive advocacy.

There are many examples of the power of this assumption in the field of social justice, where activist advocacy is often framed as being at odds with efforts to promote peace and some activists recoil from any appearance of accommodation or reasonableness (suggesting less than complete commitment to their cause). However social justice has most often made tangible gains where strong principles are asserted and mutual understanding sought. Some of the earlier proponents of conflict resolution interventions were themselves operating on an explicitly activist agenda, and saw no practical or ethical contradiction between their commitment to their cause, and their commitment to creative peacemaking.[1] More recent scholarship proposes that an appropriate framing of the third party's role in conflict is as an activist who is committed to finding a politically feasible solution that meets all interests.[2] And contrary to many assumptions about the central role of the third party "neutral", the most important negotiations of our times have been and are conducted by strong advocates seeking peace.[3]

The focus of this chapter will be on the dominant role played by lawyers in many legal, commercial, political and social conflicts. While many conflicts are negotiated by politicians, bureaucrats, technicians, police, activists and others, most significant disputes involve lawyers at some stage in negotiations. When lawyers are involved they expect to assume control of the negotiations—setting the substantive and strategic direction—an expectation which is rarely challenged by non-lawyers.[4] As a result of its social status and power, the legal profession sets a standard and establishes a culture of behaviors that are highly influential in negotiation. The way that the legal profession thinks about its role as a negotiation advocate—and inculcates new entrants with received wisdom—is critical to the currency of what we think of as "advocacy" in the wider conflict resolution field.

We are unaccustomed to thinking "conflict resolution" when we think "lawyers."[5] This is significantly the consequence of a professional legal culture which places a higher value on assertion—sometimes tipping over into aggression—than on persuasion or creativity. We don't naturally associate lawyers with problem-solving and peacemaking in negotiation because of their commitment to the all-important professional norm of "zealous advocacy." This concept takes on an almost religious significance for many lawyers, and drives their assumptions about effective advocacy in negotiations.

The Changing Notion of "Zealous Advocacy"

The description of the lawyer's duty to the client as one of "zealous advocacy" has been the subject of intense debate ever since its original articulation in the American Bar Association's Model Rules of Professional Conduct.[6] The most traditional, literal formulation of zealous advocacy has come to mean doing anything and everything that is lawful in order to advance the client's interests. Described by William Simon as the "Dominant View", this understanding of advocacy assumes that "the only ethical duty distinctive to the lawyer's role is loyalty to the client."[7] The interests of the other side, third parties or the general public are extraneous to this loyalty, and the client's position must be asserted unambiguously.[8] In fact, any sense of these outside interests may distract or undermine the lawyer's focus. This perspective on advocacy also implies that the time for talking is past—there is no suggestion in this model that the lawyer-advocate should be scrutinizing, questioning or reassessing the client's goals or positions, but rather focused on acting as her instrument in furthering these (legal) goals.

In practice, few lawyers would understand their advocacy responsibilities this narrowly. Most lawyers would regard counseling and weighing options as an important part of their role, rather than simply the blind adoption and pursuit of client goals. Practical and effective advocacy must also include information-gathering, appraisal and evaluation, and advice-giving. Nonetheless, the appealing clarity and apparent simplicity of the zealous advocacy model is enormously influential for law students and new entrants to the profession. The emphasis of legal education continues to be on adopting and implementing a single course of action. In the zealous advocacy model, advocacy as implementation represents not only the core of legal representation but the whole of legal advocacy, disregarding the constant need for dialogue with the client, reappraisal and adjustment.

A seductive dimension of the zealous advocacy concept is the idea of aggressive strength it has come to exemplify. Students entering law school are commonly fixated on the idea of acting in this way on behalf of a deserving client, perhaps a vulnerable party facing a wealthy corporation or state authority. In practice, of course, the zealous advocacy principle and the adversarial spirit that is associated with it demands this type of unquestioning commitment to all clients, and not only those that appear "deserving". Furthermore only certain types of clients can afford to finance the full-on efforts of zealous advocacy. Whereas the use of the expression "zealous" was originally be intended to capture the idea of commitment and dedication to the service of one's client, it has increasingly come to be associated with adversarialism—positional arguments, disinterest in the issues raised by the other side, minimal communication, the withholding of any information that may be useful to the other side, and aggressive opening demands in negotiations.

How did the legal profession come to embrace a notion of advocacy that sees justice as so marginal, and adversarial tactics as so normative? The social history of the lawyering profession offers some insights into the evolution of zealous advocacy. The hallowed expert status of the lawyers is derived from 18th century notions of "professionalism" that regarded law as a "gentlemanly" profession, a vocation or higher calling. The apparent selflessness with which the lawyer devotes himself to the client's cause is what legitimizes his unquestioned authority and expertise, and sets him apart from others who sell services with a lower social cachet. The lawyer's own gain or advantage must be secondary to furthering the client's goals. In the words of Lord Brougham,

> An advocate, in the discharge of his duty, knows but one person in all the world, and that person is his client. To save that client by all means and expedients, and at all hazards and costs to other persons, *and amongst them to himself*, is his first and only duty. (emphasis added)[9]

While the vision of the lawyer as the servant of the client provided an original justification for zealous advocacy, the practice of advocacy is significantly changed by the contemporary culture of economic competition and individual wealth-maximization. Competition for clients promotes zealous advocacy which is often more adversarial—and less interested in "justice"—than early 19th century models of legal practice; and probably more adversarial than the original drafters of the Model Rules ever intended. Twenty-first century notions of zealous advocacy can be explained in part by the aspirations and expectations of at least some legal services consumers—those who consider a good part of what they pay for to be the confident assertiveness of an adversarial advocate. It is further established as an appropriate role model by media portrayals of lawyers,[10] and embraced by generations of law students as they focus with intensity on the rite-of-passage experience of competitive mooting.

This approach to legal advocacy inevitably affects attitudes towards negotiating settlement, despite the reality that settlement will almost always be the conclusion of the suit. For a disconcerting number of litigators, settlement is for "wimps." "I would say to the client, if you're interested in settlement, you go and talk to the other side about it, I'm very bad at it. My job is to manage a war, not to manage a peace."[11]

While the complex and diverse culture of legal practice—impacted by numerous factors such as area of practice, size of firm, and the size of the local Bar[12]—makes any generalization about the profession contestable, there is a widespread perception that a culture of adversarialism is on the rise. My own research on commercial litigators found many examples of lawyers who understood their role as highly adversarial. Here is another powerful example,

> I think you can appreciate that what I'm telling you is that litigation is a war ... the objective is to destroy the opponent. If you ever forget that, you are no longer effective. And you have to be sure that the client understands that, that they know that this is a war.[13]

The assumption made by other, perhaps less naturally aggressive, lawyers is that they are expected to behave in an adversarial manner in order to be seen as effective advocates. For example,

> Mainly people come to me because I'm known as a son of bitch. I'm not afraid to go to trial. I won't cave in and go and settle. I have clients who know that and don't mind losing. They want to fight, so they expect me to be a son of a bitch.[14]

> In the construction industry you have to be known to be tough ... [A]ll of the most successful construction firms have good lawyers who fight, and you know if you're going to fool around with these boys, you're going to have to fight.[15]

This expectation extends to relationships with both clients and colleagues. It is probably especially important in shaping relationships with other lawyers in urban centers where there is greater competition for clients, and between lawyers of different levels of experience (for example a new associate dealing with a senior lawyer in another firm). Gaining credibility with another lawyer is associated with adopting the norms of that legal community, which in some instances means adversarial advocacy. One lawyer described the difficulty this presents for communication with other lawyers:

> I mean we're trained as pit bulls, I'm not kidding you, I mean we're trained pit bulls and pit bulls just don't naturally sit down and have a chat with a fellow pit bull, the instinct is to fight and you just get it from the first phone call. I'm bigger and tougher and stronger and better than you are.[16]

Zealous advocacy as it is widely understood and practiced normalizes negotiation behaviors, which in any other frame would be recognized as secretive, uncivil and sometimes unethical. Moreover, this approach to advocacy in negotiations is often highly ineffective in establishing trust, exchanging information about needs and interests, and developing mutually acceptable solutions. The zealous advocacy model, originally framed as the hallmark of client service and commitment to client goals, is often incompatible with contemporary client demands for effective results in negotiation.

Questions That the Zealous Advocacy Model Does Not Answer

Despite its functional efficiency and superficial clarity, there are a number of tensions and strains within the zealous advocacy model. The core concept of lawyer autonomy and objectivity which is part of the exchange transaction between lawyer and client is significantly threatened by the business model of legal practice in which many clients are repeat clients, and where the business of one large client may be fundamental to the economic viability of a practice. The notion that the lawyer will use independent judgment in pursuing the client's goals by best possible means is severely limited by a sense of obligation to a primary client whose business is critical for them to retain. Maintaining lines between zealous and immoral forms of advocacy may be much more difficult with the additional pressure of ensuring that you or your firm retains this client.

The principle of autonomy is also under attack on moral grounds. Murray Schwartz and others[17] have made the observation that lawyers operate under a principle of moral non-accountability in order that they can be unrestrained in the zealous pursuit of their clients' goals. This principle clearly condones and encourages adversarial behavior for its own sake—and that can be highly seductive.

> I come back from court and I say, "I'm a winner! I'm a winner!" or I come back from court saying, "Can you believe what that damn judge did?" It's about winning. And you don't care. I'm a pretty moral person but in the old system you want to win for your client and that's it. So what if the court agreed with your submission that was a little goofy and gives you $2,000 more per month that you shouldn't have gotten? You are a winner, and you did good for your client. So what if you took advantage of some other lawyer's stupidity? I don't care—I'm a winner![18]

For some lawyers, rather than reducing or eliminating tension over moral accountability, the principle of non-accountability raises that tension still further by highlighting the conflict between their own values and those of their client or the adversary system itself. For example,

> My nature, my personality has always been much more collaborative. I struggled to get that adversarial model to begin with. It never felt right. I always felt that I wasn't giving as good service to my clients as I could be giving but I was forced into it because is what the system required.[19]

The assumption of autonomy and the centrality of technical expertise also sits uneasily with a blanket commitment to furthering client wishes. What if the instructions the client gives for negotiation are simply are not in his or her best interests? How does counsel reconcile his commitment with his (sometime) conviction that his client needs to be told what is in his own best interests? Should the lawyer assume that he knows best—he often feels that he does—and persuade his client of this? What should the advocate do where he sees a smarter and more creative way to negotiate, yet his client presses for a more aggressive, unyielding stance? How far should counsel press the client to hold out for a better deal when the client is ready to come to a negotiated settlement?

These and other tensions within the zealous advocacy model also open up the possibility of reclaiming and reframing the notion of advocacy in conflict resolution and negotiations. How can we face these tensions and the other deficiencies within the zealous advocacy model—as well as the reality of a competitive market for clients—and come up with a model of effective advocacy which represents a more intelligent synthesis of strength and persuasion?

An Alternative Model of Advocacy

Just as adversarial advocacy has evolved out of earlier notions of lawyering, we can imagine a new conception of advocacy evolving out of adversarial advocacy in response to the changing conditions of legal practice.[20] I shall call this "advocacy as conflict resolution," although it is misleading to focus on resolution only as a potential outcome. The conflict resolution advocate must also help her client to engage with conflict, offering skills in conflict analysis and the experience of

working continuously with people in conflict. In practical terms, this means working with clients to anticipate, strategize and negotiate—and if possible, implement
outcomes. Before turning to some of the new and discrete skill sets that experienced conflict resolution advocates are beginning to identify, two foundational
points about this alternative model of advocacy need be made.

First, conflict resolution advocacy does not reject all aspects of traditional
rights-based conceptions of advocacy. This is a misconception fostered by some
who advocate new approaches to conflict resolution by promoting a form of religious conversion or "paradigm shift," which mistakenly throws the baby out with
the bathwater.[21] This is far too simplistic. In conflict resolution advocacy, counsel's
loyalty and focus is on achieving the client's best possible outcomes. As one lawyer
committed to collaborative law practice expressed it, "I think, to be honest, it's
natural for an attorney…that my best friend in the room is always going to be my
client…."[22] A contradiction between this loyalty and creative consensus-building
only exists if counsel is convinced that the only and best way to advance the client's wishes is by aggressive positional behaviors. The tensions that may arise—
over when and how to settle, for example—are no different from those that arise
in adversarial advocacy, and have been described above. The difference with conflict resolution advocacy is that these dilemmas can be made explicit and become
resolvable on a clearly principled basis. Whereas adversarial advocacy tends to see
settlement as capitulation, conflict resolution advocacy is committed to evaluating
the pro's, con's and alternatives of any settlement option. This includes evaluation
of legal, cognitive and emotional dimensions, because all of these are part of how
clients appraise settlement.[23] Advocacy as conflict resolution reclaims the constructive and creative promotion of partisan outcomes as a central function of the
advocate's role.

Second, a fundamental tenet of conflict resolution advocacy is that negotiating
on behalf of clients is a critically important skill, and central to the advocate's role.
Studies show consistently that negotiation is a low intensity activity for most lawyers,[24] who spend far more time on the procedural aspects of litigation (drafting
court documents, preparing motions, and conducting discoveries) than they do on
negotiating settlements. Despite the fact that they operate on an often unstated
assumption that they will settle almost all their cases, lawyers do not make negotiations a priority. The settlements appear as if by magic once the parties have
exhausted (and perhaps bankrupted) themselves with the legal process. Researchers have found that most settlements result from one or two exchanges of offers
only. Further, this exchange is usually by arms' length, not by face to face contact—and is almost always a monetarized solution reflecting anticipated likely
legal outcomes (consisting of primarily monetary remedies) rather than creative or
original solutions or outcomes.[25] The client inevitably plays a limited role in any
negotiation which is driven by speculation about legal outcomes—he or she must
defer to the lawyer in matters of legal knowledge.

As a result many lawyers—especially those who have recently entered practice—regard negotiation as a low status and marginal activity, and their level of
negotiation skills as relatively unimportant compared with their technical legal
knowledge. Further, few lawyers are trained or experienced in what it takes to
integrate their clients and their non-legal (personal, business) issues and aspirations into the process of bargaining.

As simple as it sounds, changing the significance attached to negotiating effective and creative settlements would dramatically affect how lawyers train for and
approach this task, and consequently the sophistication of their understanding of

advocacy responsibilities in negotiation. Negotiating on behalf of clients would be turned from something that lawyers do by "going through the motions"—at best unimaginative and perhaps minimally effectual, at worst actually obstructing and delaying settlement—into a dynamic opportunity for creating something of value. Embracing negotiation as a critical strategic play—moving beyond the routine dynamic of exchanging written offers before sawing it off in the middle[26]—and emphasizing the development of more self-conscious and sophisticated negotiation strategies places negotiation clearly in the frame as a valued advocacy skill.

Discrete Skills For Conflict Resolution Advocacy

Counsel experienced in settlement advocacy are able to identify a number of discrete negotiation skills—incorporating cognitive, functional and emotional dimensions—which enable them to be most effective. One observation made frequently by counsel, who invest heavily (in terms of time, continuing education and reflection) in their role as negotiation advocates, is the importance of being able to conceptualize and understand the dispute from the perspective of the other side. This does not mean diluting client loyalty, but it is vital to being able to persuade the other side to settle on your own client's best terms that one understand what they need in order to be able to settle. One lawyer, contrasting this with the traditional litigation approach, found it difficult to do more than identify the entrenched assumption that the other side really didn't matter.

> "You don't worry about the other side as much at a trial because they're the other side. When you're working towards a consensus—then it matters."[27]

Another lawyer identified the difference in a conflict resolution advocacy model as follows:

> "Probably the biggest change I made was really thinking about ... the opposing party's profile and really making an effort to put myself in his/her shoes ... I do that principally as I strategize the case."[28]

Effective negotiators have always operated with an awareness of the other side's interests. These negotiators take the interests of the other side into consideration to enlarge the co-operative space in which negotiations can take place.[29] Beyond the ability to conceptualize the other side's interests and needs, lawyers experienced as conflict resolution advocates also identify the ability to establish a constructive rapport with the other side, including both counsel and client. This requires good interpersonal and communication skills, including the ability to put the other side at ease, demonstrate respect and perhaps even empathy, and most challenging, create a shared sense of trust. Increased use of court-connected mediation can result in the development of stronger and better personal and professional relationships with other lawyers, who find themselves negotiating face-to-face on a regular basis.[30] Collaborative lawyering groups go further in explicitly encouraging strong and trusting professional relationships between lawyers, in order to avoid the "Prisoner's Dilemma" of not knowing what to expect from the other side.[31] In fact, the collegiality of the collaborative lawyering groups is so counter-cultural that it attracts concerns, which range from suspicion over motives to accusations of conniving and cult-like behaviors.

Another critical element of a skill set for conflict resolution advocacy is a quite different approach to fact-gathering and information in the development of a legal case. In a zealous advocacy model, knowledge and information have only one purpose: to advance the client's cause and ultimately, to win. This means that only information that fits the legal argument is either sought or utilized, leaving aside significant information, which may be important to realizing the client's goals. Sharing information is regarded as yet another competitive arena, with information withheld even where it may be of little or no consequence and where it would be beneficial in clarifying the goals of each side.

Reenvisioning the nature and uses of information in conflict resolution advocacy is a radical departure from the zealous advocacy model. First, the type of information that may be important is expanded. The involvement of clients in negotiation and mediation allows for the discussion of different types of information that may have an important impact on the resolution of the conflict, but would not ordinarily be a part of the information discussed between counsel. Also, information may come out in these meetings that neither counsel was previously aware of and may not have thought to ask. Second, understanding information as a shared resource that may advance all party interests requires significant reorientation, both conceptually and collegially. For a less aggressive and more collaborative approach to information sharing to work, lawyers need to be able to build trusting relationships with other counsel and other professionals. There is an obvious need for norms of reciprocity. Such norms have always existed in smaller communities (and also, to a significant degree, in certain forms of practice in larger communities, when lawyers recognize continuing relationships as essential to maintain, such as labor law) where lawyers were accustomed to providing information as requested without forcing their opponent through procedural hoops. In addition, effective conflict resolution advocacy demands that counsel consider not only what information they are willing to provide on request, but also what information would be helpful for the other side to have in order to persuade them that they should settle on their best possible terms.

Finally, conflict resolution advocacy requires counsel to reimagine what they understand as the best outcomes in any case. Traditionally, the best and only outcome was a victory on the legal arguments, which usually means a monetary sum. Experienced counsel are well aware that this is not the only measure of success. Even if "winning" is ultimately achieved, it may not be all that was hoped for. Emotional closure or business viability and recovery is pushed further away in litigation. In civil trials, the process of resolution may be prolonged further by the need for enforcement steps after securing a favorable judgment. This may partly explain why in my 1995 Ontario study, matching a control group of litigants participating in (an advanced stage of) traditional litigation with those who were offered the chance to mediate their dispute, only 8.5% of control group litigants described themselves as completely satisfied with the outcome of their case (either settled between the lawyers or adjudicated). The most frequently given reason for a negative or partly negative assessment of outcome in the remaining 91.5% (including some litigants who won their cases at trial) was the length of time and emotional energy consumed by the process.[32]

Conflict resolution advocacy includes a number of factors besides legal victory in envisioning and evaluating outcomes. Aside from the issue of costs, which all responsible counsel must consider in planning strategy, conflict resolution advocates should also consider how much any one outcome will meet client interests. These could include: recognition and acknowledgement; business expansion or solvency; domestic or commercial future relationships; vindication and justice; and, reputation. These interests have both short-term and long-term elements. They reflect not only outcome goals but also the importance of procedural justice—feeling listened to, taken seriously and fairly treated. In a conflict resolution model of advocacy, it is not only the final deal that matters, but also how the client feels about how it was reached.

Conclusion

Advocates will always be important players in negotiation processes. Often these advocates are lawyers—and where they are not, lay advocates are often hostage to the influence of the populist image of adversarial advocacy. Reclaiming advocacy—and changing historic assumptions, however intellectually questionable, about what makes for effective negotiation advocacy—requires the creation of new meta-principles that transcend the old. Such meta-principles would include a new emphasis on the importance of negotiation in legal practice, a recognition of the potential for interests-based problem-solving, and an acceptance of the value of non-legal solutions.

The promotion of an alternative model of conflict resolution advocacy will also require the thoughtful and skillful development of new behaviors and practices that reflect and enable these meta-principles. Some of these skill sets have been described here, but we have much more work to do on identifying and then teaching these. As ever, the role of the law schools—in encouraging or neglecting the development of these skills—will be critical.

The most significant challenge, however, is a conceptual one. Readjusting our ideas about the role of the advocate in bargaining is complex, and touches on many of our most deeply entrenched assumptions about dispute resolution, both process and outcomes. The development of a credible, coherent and practical alternative to zealous advocacy requires us to be imaginative and flexible in contemplating the extent to which a partisan role can be effective in promoting problem-solving.

Endnotes

[1] *See, e.g.,* Jim Laue & Gerry Cormick, *The Ethics of Intervention in Community Disputes, in* THE ETHICS OF SOCIAL INTERVENTION 205-32 (Gordon Bermant, et al. eds., 1978); JIM LAUE, *Conflict Intervention, in* HANDBOOK OF APPLIED SOCIOLOGY (Marvin Elliott Olsen & Michael Micklin eds., 1981).

[2] *See, e.g.,* JOHN FORESTER, THE DELIBERATIVE PRACTITIONER: ENCOURAGING PARTICIPATORY PLANNING (1999); John Forester & David Stitzel, *Beyond Neutrality: The Possibilities of Activist Mediation in Public Sector Conflicts* 5 NEGOTIATION JOURNAL 251 (1989); John Forester, *Lawrence Susskind: Activist Mediation and Public Disputes, in* WHEN TALK WORKS: PROFILES OF MEDIATORS (Deborah M. Kolb, et al. eds., 1994).

[3] BERNARD S. MAYER, BEYOND NEUTRALITY: CONFRONTING THE CRISIS IN CONFLICT RESOLUTION (2004).

[4] Craig McEwen points out that lawyers appear to be the only profession to have coined a term for those who are not members of that profession—the ubiquitous "non-lawyers."

[5] Asking about the topic of a meeting that day in the hotel conference facility, a waiter commented under his breath "Lawyers and conflict resolution? Huh? I don't usually connect lawyers with conflict resolution" (Vancouver, Delta Hotel March 2002).

[6] *See* MODEL CODE OF PROFESSIONAL CONDUCT Canon 7 (1969); MODEL RULES OF PROFESSIONAL CONDUCT PREAMBLE (2002).

[7] WILLIAM H. SIMON, THE PRACTICE OF JUSTICE: A THEORY OF LAWYER'S ETHICS 8 (1998).

[8] ANTHONY T. KRONMAN, THE LOST LAWYER: FAILING IDEALS OF THE LEGAL PROFESSION 146-48 (1993); SIMON, *supra* note 7, at 68-69.

[9] DAVID LUBAN, *The Fundamental Dilemma of Lawyering: The Ethics of the Hired Gun, in* LAWYERS: A CRITICAL READER 4 (1997) (quoting Lord Henry Brougham from the Trial at large of Her Majesty Queen Caroline Amelia Elizabeth on charges of adulterous intercourse (1821)).

[10] From the growing literature examining media portrayals of lawyer, *see, e.g.,* Michael Asimow, *Bad Lawyers in the Movies*, 24 NOVA LAW REVIEW 533 (2000).

[11] Culture Change Project, Toronto-2, Text Units 50-53 (unpublished data), *available in* Julie Macfarlane, *Culture Change? A Tale of Two Cities and Mandatory Court-Connected Mediation* 2 JOURNAL OF DISPUTE RESOLUTION 241 (2002).

[12] This phenomenon has been described as "communities of practices" (*see* LYNN MATHER, ET AL., DIVORCE LAWYERS AT WORK (2001)) and also as "local legal culture"; *see, e.g.,* Thomas Church, *Examining Local Legal Culture*, 1985 AMERICAN BAR FOUNDATION RESEARCH JOURNAL 449.

[13] Macfarlane, *supra* note 11, at Toronto-2, Text Units 47-50.

[14] *Id.* at Ottawa 6, Text Units 110-13.

[15] *Id.* at Text Units 219-24.

[16] *Id.* at 302, Text Units 52-54.

[17] Murray Schwartz, *The Professionalism and Accountability of Lawyers*, 66 CALIFORNIA LAW REVIEW 669 (1978).

[18] Julie Macfarlane, *Experiences of Collaborative Law: Preliminary Results from the Collaborative Lawyering Research Project* 2004 JOURNAL OF DISPUTE RESOLUTION 179, 203.

[19] Collaborative Law Research Project, Field Visit Lawyer 8, *available in* Macfarlane, *supra* note 18 *and* Julie Macfarlane, *The Emerging Phenomenon of Collaborative Family Law (CFL): A Qualitative Study of CFL Cases* (2005) *available at* http:canada.justice.gc.ca/en/ps/pad/reports/2005-FCY-1) (last visited Mar. 6, 2005).

[20] The most recent (2002) study shows that just 1.8% of filings in the US Federal Court go to a full trial, down from 11.5% in 1962. Marc Galanter, *The Vanishing Trial: An Examination of Trials and Related Matters in Federal and State Courts* 1(3) JOURNAL OF EMPIRICAL LEGAL STUDIES 459 (2004).

[21] Some collaborative family lawyers reject any idea of client advocacy preferring to act "in the interests of the whole family"; and a few reject the role of legal advisor as "contaminating," for example "I give as little legal advice as possible, because there is so much contamination and you are trying to get them focused back on life issues (*Case 16, lawyer 2, entry interview, unit 17*) Macfarlane, *supra* note 19 at §§1(e)(ii) and 3(d).

[22] Macfarlane, *supra* note 18 at 204,Case 11, Lawyer 2.

[23] See the detailed discussion of when and why parties are prepared to settle conflicts in Julie Macfarlane, *Why do People Settle?* 45 MCGILL LAW JOURNAL 663 (2001).

[24] *See* HERB KRITZER, LET'S MAKE A DEAL: UNDERSTANDING THE NEGOTIATION PROCESS IN ORDINARY LITIGATION 49 (1991); HAZEL GENN, HARD BARGAINING: OUT OF COURT SETTLEMENT IN PERSONAL INJURY ACTIONS 105-11 (1987); *see also*, Marc Galanter, *Contracts Symposium: Contract In Court; Or Almost Everything You May Or May Not Want To Know About Contract Litigation*, 2001 WISCONSIN LAW REVIEW 577.

[25] STEVEN H. CLARKE, ET AL., COURT-ORDERED CIVIL CASE MEDIATION IN NORTH CAROLINA: COURT EFFICIENCY AND LITIGANT SATISFACTION (1995).

[26] GENN, *supra* note 24 at 137-38.

[27] Macfarlane, *supra* note 11 at 297, Toronto-14, Text Units 184-185.

[28] *Id.* at 298, Ottawa-3, Text Units 79-81.

[29] The belief that the clients best interests can only be achieved if the interests of the Other Side are taken into account is a central premise of the principled bargaining approach popularized by Fisher and Ury. WILLIAM URY, ET AL., GETTING TO YES (1991).

[30] Macfarlane, *supra* note 11 at 298, Ottawa-13, text Units 519-522; Julie Macfarlane & Michaela Keet, *Learning from Experience: An Evaluation of the Saskatchewan Queens Bench Mediation Program* 2003 SASKATCHEWAN JUSTICE 21; and, Macfarlane, *supra* note 19, at 29.

[31] Macfarlane, *supra* note 19.

[32] Julie Macfarlane, *Court-Based Mediation in Civil Cases: An Evaluation of the Toronto General Division ADR Centre*, 1995 ONTARIO MINISTRY OF THE ATTORNEY-GENERAL, QUEENS PRINTER 22.

⚬ 60 ⚬

Dueling Experts

John H. Wade

Editors' Note: *Your case is complicated; it involves specialized knowledge, and without some help, the judge probably won't understand it and the jury certainly won't. Furthermore, your chances of negotiating a settlement depend on getting some degree of shared understanding with the other side of what the facts are. So you've hired your expert, and the other side has hired its expert—and now the experts themselves are locked in combat. Could you avoid this next time? In the meantime, what do you do now? Wade analyzes your options at every stage, and shows how even when the experts have delivered black-versus-white reports of the facts, you can still salvage the situation.*

A common cause of conflict is missing information or data perceived to be inaccurate. One response to data conflict involves the employment of two or more alleged experts to support the opinions of each party to the conflict. One definition of an "expert" is "a person who has special skill or knowledge in some particular field."[1] These alleged experts may be medical doctors, engineers, lawyers, valuers, builders, accountants or psychologists—to name a few. Experts who are asked to give opinions frequently give diverse opinions on causes, values, and predicted futures.

One positive side of employing experts is that they may be able to reduce data conflicts, such as:

- What caused the concrete to crack?
- What degree of pain the injury will cause in the future?
- How much is the corner store worth?
- What is a judge likely to decide in two years' time?
- How much will the repairs cost?
- How much profit will the business lose over the next ten years due to X?

Many data conflicts are settled due to the dispassionate opinions of one or more alleged experts about history, causation or the future.

But disputants are often astounded to find that two experts can be "so far apart."[2] There is also a darker side to the practice of seeking expert opinions in order to settle conflict.[3] This problematic side often emerges as the conflict escalates. Instead of being part of the solution, the alleged experts become part of the problem for the clients, and for the mediator or facilitators. The writer has labeled this common phenomenon as "dueling 'experts' syndrome."[4] Mediators and professional negotiators become voyeuristic observers of the darker sides of expert assistance.

Dueling Experts' Syndrome

This syndrome involves some or all of the following patterns of behavior: each disputant employs a different expert (ours is the best in the field); each disputant hires an expert who has a reputation for favoring that disputant's preferred outcome (reputational partiality *e.g.*, a plaintiff's doctor); tells different stories to their own expert (garbage in, garbage out); expressly or impliedly hints at the advice she wants from the expert (remember who is paying you). The experts initially do not consult with each other (delusionary isolation); the expert, in order to curry favor and ensure future employment from a repeat player, tells the client in writing what he wants to hear (you get what you pay for); the written over-confident report does not set out either a clear list of factual presumptions made, or the details of the terms of the expert's employment instructions (garbage in, garbage out again), or a clear list of alternative interpretations, or a range from best to worst of alternative "legitimate" views in the field (delusionary certainty); the report is long, rambling and sometimes incomprehensible to the average citizen (mysterious complexity); and each expert is instructed not to show draft reports to the other (no early doubts or compromises).

Once the over-confident (versions of the) expert reports are published, each expert defends his/her version with increasing verbal intensity and insult in order to preserve reputation, ego (now it is personal), future employment and maybe even to settle old scores. Then the expert does what is expected as a snarling Doberman (this is our opening offer). The disputants then invest large amounts of time and money to resolve a personal conflict between the two experts as a prerequisite to resolving their own conflict.

There are other fascinating psychological and economic dynamics to dueling experts' syndrome, particularly when the dueling experts know each other well, enjoy the game, and carry personal baggage from frequent past encounters. More troubling is the repeated pattern whereby many experts, who advocate a particular view, actually begin both to believe in and emotionally support their own view.[5] Wayne Brazil has commented:

> It is commonly believed by many litigators that to simply turn over all the relevant data to a consultant expert is to flirt with disaster: namely, the possibility that your expert will reach a negative conclusion about the role of your client. To reduce the chances of such an eventuality, many litigators carefully control the flow of information to their consultants.... Their hope is that the expert will form a positive opinion, will identify with the attorney's client, and will develop an ego investment in the positive conclusion that the attorney wants reached. Thereafter, the attorney may feed the expert some negative data about the client's conduct in order to prepare the expert to withstand cross-examination. By the time the expert receives the bulk of the negative information (at least so goes the litigator's theory of manipulation), he has so heavily identified with the client's position and has invested so much of his own professional ego in his positive opinion that all his impulses are in the direction of defending rather that reevaluating that opinion. Thus the lawyer hopes to capitalize on the expert's relatively predictable reactions to cognitive dissonance.[6]

The Dynamics of Negotiation and Experts

The normal dynamics of negotiation add additional complexity to, and justification for, dueling experts' syndrome. First, dueling experts know consciously or

subconsciously that they are part of a predictable process. It is well known by negotiation research, anecdote and mythology that vigorous claims usually achieve
better number outcomes than moderate claims. [Schneider, *Aspirations*] Therefore,
if an expert report is both over-confident and near to the "insult zone" (the insult
zone is the number of dollars, acres, rockets, which on current information has no
objective support from the marketplace or from "the going rate"), then it will usually achieve a better outcome for the client than if the report is balanced, qualified
and closer to "the truth" or the settlement zone.[7] Where an expert produces a
"moderate" report, then this shifts the bargaining range considerably in favor of
the other expert who has produced an extreme report.[8]

Second, an enthusiastic dueling expert provides a useful "bad cop" for the
ubiquitous good cop—bad cop negotiation routine. "Deal with the pleasant client,
or else we will have to hand this dispute over to our rabid (lawyers, valuers, psychologists, doctors, engineers, etc)." As one CEO whispered to me during a
mediation, "can we go outside and talk? We will never get anywhere with all those
people arguing their theories" (nodding towards a group of entrenched expert
engineers and lawyers). Whereupon the two CEOs and the mediator went for a
long walk and settled the dispute under a gum tree. In that case, were the dueling
experts helpful to the negotiation or not?

Third, well-known experts who produce long reports may be a useful part of a
strategy of attrition to wear out the other disputants. Those other disputants then
feel obliged to keep spending on opposing, well-known and highly priced experts
in order to create doubt by appearing credible, argumentative, persistent and willing to respond with reactive attrition.

Once again, such apparently dysfunctional routines by dueling experts may
sometimes become functional. These are important negotiation dynamics for negotiators and mediators to recognize and try to respond to constructively, even if
we do not always approve of these sometimes tiresome, expensive, self-serving
and inflammatory routines.[9]

How Can Negotiators and Mediators Respond to Dueling Experts?

Let us assume that the "problem" of dueling experts has already arisen. That is, as
conflict managers we are not here considering the important question of how to
avoid or minimize preemptively the dynamics of dueling experts. That pre-emptive
question will continue to be a major item for law reform agencies and for negotiation tacticians in the future. The writer's preference is for the roadblock of dueling
experts to be anticipated by smart conflict managers. Anticipation can then lead to
a number of preventive tactics.

As the majority of conflicts are settled or abandoned, mediators and lawyers
are often left with the "hard cases," or escalated disputes. This residue often has
attracted the dynamics of dueling experts, such as doctors, lawyers or accountants,
who are "far apart." What can a negotiator, lawyer or mediator do in these cases?

Where a professional negotiator is able to have preparation meetings with individual disputants in person, by email, or over the phone, this provides the ideal
time to identify any dueling experts, define the problem of experts in conflict,
lower expectations, and begin to foreshadow the "normal" range of responses to
dueling experts. Examples of "preparatory" questions by a negotiator might include:

- "So our valuers have come up with preliminary opinions which are miles
  apart? What can we each do about that?"
- "What will we do at the negotiation when predictably one lawyer says 'I'm
  right,' followed by the other lawyer saying, 'No, I'm right'? Will they just

> blah-blah at each other? How much time should be allocated to the 'I'm right, you're wrong' routine?"

- "From what you say, the engineers' initial reports are on different planets? Is that correct? In my experience, we cannot expect one or both to say suddenly 'Oops, I am wrong'."
- "What can you do about the differing medical reports? Flip a coin? Split the difference? I don't want the negotiation meeting to be a waste of time for us all."

More specifically, when confronted with a standard hurdle in negotiations, mediators and negotiators are often taught to go through the following three steps.

Step 1—When in Doubt, Reframe or Summarize

In joint or separate meetings, the first thing that negotiators (and many other skilled helpers) are taught to do is to put a new or old name humbly on what is happening.[10]

"Reframing" is the skill of taking an existing feeling or perspective, and putting this into a new set of words, images or metaphors. Reframing has many potential benefits, including giving new vocabulary, creating doubt and providing a new set of spectacles with which to view an old problem. New perspectives may create changed negotiation behavior.

For example, the problem here might be reframed as, "we both believe that our experts are right, and yet they are so far apart;" "how is it that two experts can come to such different conclusions?;" "our experts seem to have left us with a problem;" "expert one says that the grass is blue, and expert two says that the grass is yellow—is that correct?"

Step 2—Convert the Standard Problem into Standard Problem-Solving Questions

Orthodox problem-solving and decision-making literature emphasizes that "the right question is half the answer."[11]

The standard hurdle of dueling experts can routinely be converted into standard problem-solving questions in emailed agendas, on flip-charts or whiteboards in words such as:

- How to respond to conflicted expert opinions?
- What do others do when confronted by differing experts?
- How to solve our problem of dueling experts?
- What can be done about differing (legal) opinions?
- How can our two experts be so far apart?

Step 3—Brainstorm Non-Judgmentally the (Standard) Range of Options

In the writer's experience as a negotiator and mediator, it is very helpful to disputants to realize that their conflict or "problem" is normal, that thousands before them have experienced the same situation, and that the same thousands of disputants have brainstormed through a list of optional solutions and found one which is at least "satisfactory" to both.

Ideally, this list of options should be extracted slowly and put on a flip chart arising out of the suggestions of the disputants. Visible charts can promote clarity and ownership. Prompts may be used such as:

- "What do we do when two plumbers suggest opposite solutions to a roof leak?"
- "How have other businesses handled such conflicting advice?"

These prompts can become more directive:

- "I'm not suggesting that you should do this, but I have had clients who asked the conflicted experts to write a joint report explaining how two experts could be so far apart. Should I add that to the list of possibilities?"
- "Would you like me to write up some of the 12 ways I have seen clients respond to this common problem? You may have other ideas also."
- "Of the 12 methods we have recorded on the board, which have we seen used most often? If you wish, I can circle the three that I have seen my clients use most often."

The Range of Responses to Dueling Experts

Here are twelve common responses to the problem of dueling experts. It should be emphasized that, in any dispute, several of these responses can be tried. They are not exclusive. Some of these listed solutions will be so unsatisfactory to one or more of the disputants that the range of options may be narrowed quickly.

- Try to convince—"mine is better than yours" or "I'm right, you're wrong."
- Experts jointly explain why differences exist.
- Each expert answers a written list of questions.
- Experts write a jointly signed explanation of differences.
- Third advisory expert attends the mediation or negotiation.
- Third expert writes a non-binding opinion.
- Third expert writes a binding decision.
- Create doubt by introducing new or hypothetical facts.
- Split the difference.
- Trade chips.
- Toss a coin.
- Refer the decision to a judge.

Each of these possible responses will now be considered in more detail, with the advantages and disadvantages of each. Thereby a negotiator, mediator, lawyer or other skilled helper can "add value" to the decision-making process of clients.

Try to Convince—"Mine Is Better Than Yours"

This first predictable response involves the disputants and their respective experts attempting to create doubt for the other side in a joint meeting, perhaps preceded by a written exchange of questions or assertions. Each party orally points out the strengths in their own expert's reports and opinions, and the weaknesses in the others' reports and opinions. The parties can agree upon a structured question and answer time period for each of the experts and/or the disputants. Sometimes the questions can be put in writing by one or more of the parties ahead of the meeting, or asked through the mediator, in order to reduce ambushes and aggressive cross-examination.

This procedure has many potential benefits—clarification, reducing "garbage in, garbage out" decision-making, and witnessing the skills of each expert when questioned. It is a systematic form of creating doubt and new information to assist better decision-making.

However, these debates have the obvious potential to degenerate quickly into attempts to publicly humiliate, and can lead to entrenchment of existing views, hiding information, and expert strutting. Experts, once scarred by such meetings, may be reluctant to face further semi-public batterings unless protected by clear procedures and a strong mediator as chairperson. Some judges, arbitrators and mediators adapt this type of meeting by excluding clients, and just convening a "conference of experts," in the hope of reducing loss of face. Like all interventions, the conference-of-experts has both advantages and disadvantages.

Experts Jointly Explain to the Disputants Why Differences Exist

This second response is different in emphasis than the first. However, both overlap and may happen simultaneously.

The predominant goal is not for each expert to justify why he is "right," and the other is "wrong." Rather, each expert tries to explain visually, orally and in simple language to everyone present, how each conclusion was formed and why they are so different.

Obviously, this has the same potential benefits and detriments as the first response.

The writer has seen this response used effectively where groups of accountants have sat around the table and attempted to explain to everyone present why their valuations of businesses were so disparate. The clients have appreciated having underlying assumptions of each expert clarified, and hearing that valuation methods involve discretionary factors. In this way, posturing certainty was reduced to create realistic uncertainty.

The predictable traps observed at these meetings have been that the experts slide quickly into professional jargon and other forms of insiders' shorthand, and become defensive during questioning. All of these may be remedied by use of visuals, reframing, strategic ignorance, admonitions and triangulation.[12]

Each Expert Answers a List of Written Questions

The third response is to negotiate a procedural agreement whereby each disputant agrees to send a written list of question to the "opponent's" experts, who are instructed to respond with written answers within an agreed time period. The cost of the written answers is usually borne by whoever asks for them.

There are some obvious benefits to this process, including clarification, creating doubt (for all sides), avoidance of hostile public cross-examination, considered responses and saving face. Some of these benefits may be absent in relation to the first two responses.

Experts Write a Jointly Signed Explanation

This fourth response to dueling experts is potentially one of the most helpful. This usually requires pre-mediation or pre-negotiation meetings at which the parties identify the dueling expert hurdle and engage in soft or hard brinkmanship. A negotiator proposing a meeting for that purpose might use phrases like these:

- "I do not want to waste our time and money by convening a meeting where we listen to experts making speeches."
- "Do you predict that either of our experts will back down at a public meeting? How can we help them to save face gently?"
- "I don't know about you, but I cannot understand these 52 pages of contradictory opinions. Who can decipher that maze for us all in words of one syllable?"
- "What if we both instruct your experts to sit in a room together for two hours and write out no more than two pages in point form explaining why their reports are so different?"

If persuaded, the disputants each employ his own expert for a fixed period of time (say 3 hours) to sit in a room with the other expert, and write a "no more than two page document" explaining in simple language why their conclusions are different; most importantly, *both* experts must sign that single explanation. The temptation is always to create two more documents and two new explanations of "why I am right and he is wrong."

This response to dueling experts is also reflected in rules of court in many jurisdictions. Judges as decision-makers, like disputants as decision-makers, want to reduce the confusing garbage in.[13]

If this response is potentially so helpful during negotiations or mediation, then anecdotally why is it apparently so uncommon? Here are some observed and hypothesized reasons for resistance by various parties to the dispute to using this response:

- The joint report may divide the unity of a negotiating team. A key member, namely the expert, may create doubt publicly for his own team.
- An expert who admits to complexity and uncertainty will no longer be an effective "bad cop" in an accepted negotiation routine (and may not be hired again).
- The two (or more) experts may not have the skills to write such a short and simple report.
- The two experts may insist on writing two more reports to prove why their first reports were "correct."
- The joint report costs more money.
- Clients must be assertive in order to make experts (particularly lawyers) do what they want. The experts can legitimately respond: "This process may lead to some dangerous concessions, which will undermine the litigation if we need to proceed to court." (This comment reflects an ongoing and legitimate tension between competition and cooperation in any negotiation or conflict management).
- The jointly signed report may lead to a loss of reputation: "Why didn't you make this clear previously?"

Negotiators need to assist experts to overcome any resistance to revise, with standard comments such as: "Of course, we all know that opinions must be revised as new information emerges;" " I want to hear all the possible bad news early, not in eight months' time;" "We all know that there are legitimate differences of opinion in your fields of expertise, as there are in mine;" "We may have misled you both by feeding different information to you both;" "As you know, a joint report will be ordered by a judge, so let's do it now before our sunk costs escalate." Different cultures have fascinating sentences to help the experts save face.

Third Advisory Expert Attends the Negotiation or Mediation

This response to dueling experts involves both disputants agreeing that they need help, selecting a trusted "extra" expert from a list, or based on a recommendation, and agreeing on how to share payment for this person. Additionally, the parties may agree: that neither disputant will talk to the advisory expert privately; what telephone calls and inquiries can be made, and documents read by the advisory expert; how many meetings will the advisory expert attend; what oral comments are sought from the advisor and whether or not she will write a final report.

The writer has seen this response to dueling experts used very successfully in mediations in a variety of disputes, including renovations of a factory, valuation of superannuation and a business, and dealing with a child's response to a parent moving away.

The advisory expert should normally define her role and limit liability carefully in writing. For example, the written contract could restrict his/her role to that of a "commentator" using "limited" information and state that each party is relying on her own expert's advice. Otherwise, both disputants may turn on the advisor later and declare "but at the mediation/negotiation you told us...."

A skilled and gracious oral commentary by an extra expert, particularly if the commentary suggests "ranges" of possible outcomes, may avoid loss of face for the dueling experts. It is important to discuss whether the extra expert should be a friend, an associate, or a dispassionate stranger. This intervention may also allow the experts to resume bad-cop warfare untouched by diplomacy, if that round of negotiation is unsuccessful.[14]

Third Expert Writes a Non-Binding Opinion

This sixth response to dueling experts is analogous to the previous option, except that the advisory expert is contracted to write a written report, explaining differences and recommending possible solutions.

The disputants usually record in this agreed process that neither will be bound by the opinion, that both are free to produce the opinion in later litigation, and that both are free to rely on their own experts if they wish.

The downsides of this response include increasing costs for the provision of a written report, wariness of professionals about publicly criticizing work of colleagues in documents, numerous reservations in the written report based on the ubiquitous proposition "I do not have all the facts," and the tendency to split the difference between the existing dueling experts' reports.

Third Expert Writes a Binding Decision

This seventh response to dueling experts involves the disputants agreeing to a specified process whereby a named third expert will decide the issue being debated by the dueling experts.

The disputants can each agree to be bound by the expert's decision (e.g. relating to valuation; cause of injury; extent of damages) and thereby create costs and estoppel risks if either tries to relitigate the decided question. (Many third party experts will prefer a form of arbitration as this substantially reduces any risk of liability for professional negligence while making the binding decision.)

Most mediators and negotiators have been involved in successful referrals to binding decisions by third parties. This process has many advantages, including privacy. Arbitration also provides nervous middle managers, CEOs, and governments with a third party to "blame" for the outcome when they are reluctant to take personal responsibility for a negotiated outcome.[15]

However, it should be repeated that this arbitral response to dueling experts also has a litany of well documented disadvantages, such as:

- Loss of control of the outcome.
- Risk of detrimental outcome.
- Delay and expense.
- Cloning the disadvantages of litigation.
- Tendency of arbitrators to split the difference.[16]
- Lengthy negotiation and documentation concerning what is an appropriate arbitral process.[17]

Create Doubt by Introducing New or Hypothetical Facts

This eighth response is common, and is often combined with other responses to dueling experts.

A mediator or negotiator identifies a number of factual, evidentiary or "rule" assumptions which apparently provide the building blocks for each expert's opinion. These foundations may helpfully emerge if and when each expert "attacks" the other's report as "wrong." A mediator or negotiator can then gently and systematically go through this list of assumed facts and ask each expert in turn, first privately and then after rehearsal again in joint sessions—"What if the following new fact was accepted by a judge, would your existing opinions need any updating or variation?"[18]

This process of suggesting new hypothetical facts, has potential benefits of:

- Allowing one or both experts to change their opinions without openly admitting any mistake.
- Demonstrating that expert opinions will need to be updated regularly as new "facts" emerge (i.e. creates doubt).
- Enabling experts to remain aggressively confident of their initial reports "so long as no new facts emerge."
- Echoing the reality that judicial and historical fact-"finding" or fact-"reconstruction" is a hit-and-miss process. In the words of the legal realists, "facts are guesses."[19]

Therefore, hypothesizing new or even surprising "facts" or inferences is not an unrealistic decision-making routine.

Split the Difference

A very common method of managing the real or fake war between dueling experts is to split the difference between those experts. Obviously, this downstream negotiation practice encourages the upstream practice of hiring dueling experts! That is, hiring an extreme expert drags a subsequent split-the-difference outcome in your favor. Phrases a negotiator might use to explore this option include:

- "What if, only for the purposes of today's negotiation, we take the middle figure between the two valuers?"
- "What if we assume for the moment that a judge may award some damages rather than the all or nothing damages predicted by the two lawyers?"

For some disputants, this option of splitting the difference is frustrating as it appears to reward the blatant tactic of generating "false" reports. It also appears to punish further the person who has spent time and money to generate what is perceived to be a more balanced expert report. Nevertheless, the anecdotally frequent use or suggestion of splitting the difference suggests that negotiators need to be ready to manage this frustration.

Splitting the difference between experts is a frequent outcome in certain types of disputes. For example, in the writer's experience in matrimonial property disputes, lawyers routinely prepare for mediations and negotiations a single page summarizing the list of assets and alleged values of each asset. It is common for the right hand side of this summary to have three columns—namely "husband's value," "wife's value," and "mean" or "average value." The average value column gently prophesizes a possible or probable outcome of dueling valuations, at least in poor and middle class families.

Trade Chips

This tenth response to dueling experts is the standard negotiation behavior of trading chips: "If I was prepared to accept (or move towards) your expert's opinion, would you be prepared to give me X?"

Sometimes this strategy may produce a similar substantive result to splitting the difference between the experts. Nevertheless, it may be more psychologically satisfying for one or more disputants who has personal priorities about which element of the packaged outcome is most important. The writer has frequently seen this kind of "trade" eventually take place in matrimonial property negotiations and mediations. A spouse who owns a business often wants his/her dueling expert's valuation of a business to prevail in order to placate business partners, to control future possible tax assessments, or because they have personal insights into the history of the business. Accordingly, the owner eventually is persuaded to make an offer to the other spouse as follows: "If I was prepared to move towards your percentage, would you be prepared to move towards my expert's valuation of the business?"

To which eventually comes the predictable response from the other: "As a matter of principle, yes ... but what do you mean by 'move towards'?"

Toss a Coin

Another possible, and more startling, method to resolve dueling experts is for the disputants to use chance. For example, they can toss a coin and the "winner's" expert prevails.

Ironically, this use of chance has a number of benefits:

- Chance symbolically fulfills the lawyer's comments to their clients that litigation is a "lottery," or "brain surgery with an axe."
- It saves face and egos for the dueling experts.
- Chance provides an instant and cheap outcome.
- Chance avoids the battle of wills and tactics over expert reports whereby one of the disputants feels that (s)he has "lost."
- It enables negotiators to return to head office or to constituents with a definite result, for which, in one sense, the coin is responsible.
- Some negotiators are already accustomed to toss a coin on occasion to resolve other deadlocks, such as the last gap in negotiations. [Wade, *Last Gap*]

Obviously, such an arbitrary and uncontrollable method as coin tossing may be very unattractive to a risk-averse negotiator, or where the experts are far apart. Nevertheless, merely listing "toss a coin" as a possible solution is so shocking to some disputants that they search more diligently for a more acceptable option from the rest of the list.

Refer the Decision to a Judge

The twelfth response to dueling experts is analogous to the previously-mentioned possibility of consensually appointing an arbitrator. However, this twelfth option can be elected consensually or imposed unilaterally when all other options (momentarily) are unacceptable. Additionally, the third person decision-maker is assigned by the state, rather than personally chosen like an arbitrator.

However, judges also may decide to choose one or more of the responses set out above before they accept the buck being passed to them. For example, ordering the experts to confer and submit a single report explaining why they are at odds seems to be an increasingly popular judicial response.

More specifically, there is a large body of rules and policy which judges attempt to balance when deciding which of two or more dueling experts should be given more credibility.[20]

The vastness of the judicial and legislative rules concerning dueling experts is both cause and effect of the uncertainty, expense, and delay attached to this last option—namely "we'll leave it to the judicial lottery;" or "of course, you can always leave it to a judge to decide which parts of each expert's report are acceptable."

Paralysis by Analysis?

As with all problem-solving exercises, this analysis of possible responses to dueling experts may stun and shock inexperienced negotiators. Where "one-shot" negotiators are common, such as in personal injury, family, workplace, discrimination, estate and environmental conflict, the parties' search for "justice," or their slow progress through grief, or the words or silence of their lawyers may not have emotionally prepared them for such a routine and mechanized list of options.

Nevertheless, in the writer's opinion, disputants should be introduced to these realistic options as early as they or their constituents have ears to hear. If professional advisers are concerned about later client recriminations concerning money and time "wasted" on dueling experts and about uninformed consent, then the options should be expressed in writing.[21]

If the preferred versions of "justice" are not available in the vast majority of conflicts, then disputants need to know what lies ahead. They need to be prepared gradually to make wise choices from the routine menus available. Such mechanistic rationality, even when conveyed with skill and compassion, may not be heard, at least the first hundred times.[22]

Conclusion

There are a number of "normal" hurdles which are faced by negotiators and mediators. Dueling experts is one of these. Ideally, wise negotiators, lawyers and conflict managers should anticipate dueling experts syndrome and act preventively. However, it is more likely that mediators and negotiators will be required to react to what has already occurred.

This chapter has attempted to give negotiators and mediators confidence by normalizing this hurdle, reframing, and turning the barrier into a standard problem-solving question such as, "what can be done about the current differing views of the experts?" Finally, twelve possible standard responses to this question have been systematized. No doubt, there are hybrid and other responses which need to be added to this list. Disputants can then discuss which of the twelve standard responses, or hybrids, they prefer, or do not prefer, and in what order of priority. Learning the process and responses can add confidence and tools to the skilled helper's toolbox.

Endnotes

A version of this chapter was originally published in 21 CONFLICT RESOLUTION QUARTERLY 419 (2004).

[1] THE MACQUARIE DICTIONARY 628 (1982).
[2] See, e.g., Crystal Auburn Pty Ltd v. I. L. Wollerman Pty Ltd (2004) 821 Federal Court of Australia (four valuers decided value of a business anywhere between $41,670 to $859,915).
[3] GERARD EGAN, THE SKILLED HELPER (5th ed. 1994) (systematically identifies the "shadow side" of each strategy to "help" clients solve their problems).
[4] JOHN H. WADE, REPRESENTING CLIENTS AT MEDIATION AND NEGOTIATION 3 (2000); See an earlier reference to this term in TRANSFORMATION MANAGEMENT SERVICES, MEDICAL PANELS 39 (1995) (a report for the WorkCover Authority of New South Wales).
[5] See LEON FESTINGER, A THEORY OF COGNITIVE DISSONANCE (1957) (Festinger identified the tendency of most human beings to attempt to bring behavior, emotions and beliefs into a degree of harmony; conversely, to avoid personal "dissonance" or disharmony in these three areas. Lawyers' letters and expert reports are behaviors which tend to drag the writers' emotions and beliefs into line with the rhetoric).
[6] Wayne D. Brazil, The Attorney as Victim: Toward More Candour About the Psychological Price Tag of Litigation Practice, 3 JOURNAL OF THE LEGAL PROFESSION 107, 110 (1978-79).
[7] See ROY J. LEWICKI, ET AL., NEGOTIATION 33-40 (5th ed. 2006). The tradition of beginning negotiations just inside the "insult zone" is being challenged by a variety of legislation. For example, section 198J of the Legal Profession Act 1987 (NSW) imposes a duty upon lawyers not to make a claim or defense of a claim for damages unless these have "reasonable prospects of success." See Nicholas Beaumont, What are "Reasonable Prospects of Success"?, 40

LAW SOCIETY JOURNAL 42 (2002) (Beaumont attempts to interpret "reasonable" as "not fanciful").

[8] LEWICKI, ET AL., *supra* note 7.

[9] Predictably, judges and legislators wrestle continually with these standard tactical uses of "experts." *See* AUSTRALIAN LAW REFORM COMMISSION, REPORT NO. 89, MANAGING JUSTICE: A REVIEW OF THE FEDERAL CIVIL JUSTICE SYSTEM 418-36 (2000); AUSTRALIAN LAW REFORM COMMISSION, DISCUSSION PAPER 62, REVIEW OF THE FEDERAL CIVIL JUSTICE SYSTEM Ch. 13 (1999); Robert E. Cooper, *Federal Court Expert Usage Guidelines*, 16 AUSTRALIAN BAR REVIEW 203 (1998).

[10] LAURENCE BOULLE, MEDIATION SKILLS AND TECHNIQUES 129 (2001).

[11] *See, e.g.,* JOHN S. HAMMOND, ET AL., SMART CHOICES: A PRACTICAL GUIDE TO MAKING BETTER DECISIONS (1999).

[12] One meaning of "triangulation" involves asking or insisting that the disputants speak to the mediator/facilitator/chairperson rather than to each other. The mediator can then summarize or reframe what has been said. This may change the speaker's tone, speed and complexity, especially if the mediator strategically or genuinely alleges ignorance.

[13] AUSTRALIAN LAW REFORM COMMISSION, *supra* note 9, at 424 (critics assert that the present use of expert evidence does not assist judges and other decision-makers to understand, and often clouds issues).

[14] FORREST S. MOSTEN, THE COMPLETE GUIDE TO MEDIATION 296-97 (1997) (describes a "confidential mini-evaluation" which is an oral and confidential opinion on a possible range of outcomes by an expert. This avoids some of the risks of written reports by an expert).

[15] *See* John H. Wade, *Don't Waste My Time on Negotiation and Mediation: This Dispute Needs a Judge*, 18 MEDIATION QUARTERLY 259, 263, 265 (2001).

[16] The tendency of arbitrators to split the difference between experts may be controlled by use of final-offer or "baseball" arbitration. *See* JOHN S. MURRAY, ET AL., ARBITRATION 240-45 (1st ed. 1996).

[17] *See* Wade, *supra* note 15, at 408-09, 432.

[18] The words "what if," "assuming that," or "if" are fundamental for any successful negotiator, mediator, decision-maker or communicator. See the remarkable reference to this in WILLIAM SHAKESPEARE, AS YOU LIKE IT act 5, sc. 4 (1623) ("Your If is the only peacemaker; much virtue in If.").

[19] *E.g.,* JEROME FRANK, COURTS ON TRIAL: MYTH AND REALITY IN AMERICAN JUSTICE 14-36, 80-102 (1949); William Twining, *Taking Facts Seriously*, 34 JOURNAL OF LEGAL EDUCATION 22 (1984).

[20] *See* IAN R. FRECKELTON & HUGH SELBY, EXPERT EVIDENCE: LAW, PRACTICE, PROCEDURE AND ADVOCACY (2d ed. 2002).

[21] *See* John H. Wade, *Systematic Risk Analysis for Negotiators and Litigators: How to Help Clients Make Better Decisions*, 13 BOND LAW REVIEW 462 (2001).

[22] *See, e.g.,* HAMMOND, ET AL., *supra* note 11; AUSTIN SARAT & WILLIAM FELSTINER, DIVORCE LAWYERS AND THEIR CLIENTS (1995) (Sarat and Felstiner recorded many conversations between lawyers and clients whereby lawyers attempt to lower client expectations and teach them by repetitious stories how the legal system "really" operates).

❧ 61 ❧

The Interpreter as Intervener

Sanda Kaufman

Editors' Note: *You're about to start negotiating in a language where you can't even read the alphabet. What to do? This chapter is essential for anyone about to engage in an international negotiation involving multiple languages—which could include many "domestic" negotiations in New York or Chicago or London or Paris. Kaufman explores how translators are neither perfectly neutral third parties, nor part of a team (contrary to common assumptions); shows how they are often powerful and autonomous actors in the negotiation; and demonstrates how important it is to think about the use of interpreters before the day they are hired.*

The most dangerous of all falsehoods is a slightly distorted truth.
G.C. Lichtenberg, physicist (1742-1799)

Any translator who intends to render a work from one language to another
merely by rendering word for word, and slavishly following the order
of the chapters and sentences in the original, will come to grief.
The product of his labor will be unintelligible and ludicrous.
*Maimonides** (1135-1204)

Language Barriers to Negotiations

The word *"ceasefire"* carries critically different meanings in Arabic (*hudna*), in Hebrew (*hafsakat esh*) and English in which negotiations are often conducted in the Israeli-Palestinian conflict. The parties to this conflict also differ over the meaning of *"tahdiah,"* designating in Arabic the period of calm on which sides agreed informally in 2005, in Sharm el Sheik. The "hudna" example led M.D. Halperin to observe that:

> One of the most significant obstacles to be overcome in the Israeli-Palestinian peace process is language. The cultural, conceptual and language barriers that separate the negotiating partners are greater than their negotiation over land and far more difficult to resolve.[1]

UN Resolution 242 (1967) famously carries significantly different meanings in English, Russian, French, and Spanish, hinging on one word—"the"—whose absence in English and Russian leads to the interpretation that Israel should return [some of the] occupied territories, while French and Spanish versions arguably call for a return of [all] *the* occupied territories.[2] Noticed from the outset and neatly lining up with the respective countries' political stands, this discrepancy is only partly intentional since to align up meanings with the English original would have required negotiating additional clarifying words which were not part of the English text.

Anecdotal examples from other places and times abound. For instance, due to a mistranslation, journalists interpreted Pope John Paul II's farewell words to his compatriots in 1999 as an endorsement of Poland's membership in the European Union, instead of the European community he really meant. In 2005, six-party talks regarding North Korea's nuclear program were bogged down by the need to translate to and from English, Russian, Korean, Chinese and Japanese.

Since interpreting is one of the oldest professions, we can find anecdotes going back to the Tower of Babel, itself a metaphor crying out for competent intervention. For example, translation diplomacy was exercised, as was apparently the norm, in rendering to Queen Elizabeth the meaning of a letter from the Sultan of Turkey, in the late 16th century.[3] The Sultan's exhortation to the Queen to demonstrate loyalty and subservience to him was translated in Italian as "sincere friendship." While this may well have been the gist of the formal message, because the Sultan may only have addressed his "friends" in this manner, and while the world may have been well served by the liberty translators took with the original text, we are left to ponder what is preferable in such situations—a literal translation alone, one accompanied by a cultural interpretation, or the one actually favored by diplomats at that time.

Though of lesser global import than negotiations among disputing nations, business negotiations among parties speaking different languages are both increasingly frequent and difficult. For example, at the White House Conference on Trade and Investment in Central and Eastern Europe (held in Cleveland in 1995) I interpreted talks between an American businessman and another country's representatives refusing to pay for services he had delivered. In that situation, by no means uncommon, my choice of words and of what to translate may have affected the outcome. Recognizing a need, how-to negotiation texts[4] have responded with advice to business negotiators on handling such situations. They have warned, for example, that as English is fast becoming lingua franca, English speakers may be at a disadvantage: their counterparts may well be fluent in English and still insist on speaking through interpreters, to gain precious time as they think about their responses.

Communication is the currency of negotiation:[5] "You say what you want, I say what I want and we go back and forth until we find a way to resolve our differences.[6]" Evolutionary psychologists have even argued that language emerged in response to early humans' need to enter into non-aggression or cooperative agreements to avoid mutual destruction through violent acts.[7] Negotiators should, therefore, wish to have full control over the clarity and precision of words they use to convey interests, make offers and promises, persuade, or threaten; for the same reasons, they should also seek to understand precisely what others are telling them.

Ideally, then, negotiations are best conducted in one shared language. Even then, subcultures—geographic, professional, experiential, education- or age-related—yield vocabulary differences that impede communication in obvious and easily correctable ways, as well as in more insidious ways that leave parties unaware of their differences. One consequence is confusion between substantive disagreements and mere vocabulary differences, which may also fool parties into believing they disagree less than in actuality.

However, increasingly negotiators do not even share a language. When they do, their mastery levels may differ, undermining the ability to distinguish nuances, decode metaphors, or decipher cultural subtleties key to understanding the full import of what is said, or avoiding misunderstandings.[8] Getting across exactly what we mean engages our ability to express our ideas in words, but also entails the listener's ability to decode our messages, a challenge that increases as parties communicate across language barriers. What recourse then?

Until electronic devices reach adequate sophistication,[9] interpreters remain the answer. I will discuss the need for interpreters, how they operate, and how they interact with their clients. I will propose that, far from being a passive, inconsequential service, interpreting is active intervention. So it is important for negotiators to recognize it as such and to become aware of all the ways it can affect process and outcomes. Specifically, all involved tend to perceive the interpreters as being partial to, and acting on behalf of, the party whose native language they share. That perception generates a strategic space for interpreters interested in exploiting it—a "dark side" of this service because it is difficult to detect or control. I will also argue that the relationship between negotiators and their interpreters shares some, but not all, the characteristics of principal-agent relationships. Therefore, though it is typically not negotiated, maybe it should be.

Who Needs Interpreters?

The language of negotiations may be English, but each partner in the process thinks in his mother tongue, translates for his citizens in his mother tongue and consciously and subconsciously negotiates through his own cultural bias.
M.D. Halperin, 2003, referring to the Israeli-Palestinian conflict

For simplicity, in what follows I will refer to two negotiators, although the arguments extend to multi-party situations. Even when they do not share a native language, parties may still negotiate directly in a third language, or one of them may negotiate in the other's native language, depending on levels of fluency and comprehension. For example, Indians speaking different languages conduct their affairs in English. So do Palestinians and Israelis. Portuguese negotiators can negotiate in Spanish with Spanish counterparts. Dutch and German negotiators occasionally interact in German.

Typically, people's understanding of a spoken or written foreign language is better than their ability to express themselves in that language (though some instruction methods and some regions of the world do yield better speakers than listeners). Therefore, even when the parties can understand each other in a shared language, they may request an interpreter's assistance especially if the stakes are high and/or if precision is important, as in business negotiations, exchanges among scientists and engineers, conversations across different cultures, or discussions involving legal issues. Note that people's assessment of their own skill level in another language does not necessarily correspond to reality, and is not easily corroborated. Only their responses to direct questions that require precision may reveal misunderstandings. If neither party can understand the other's language or share a third, interpretation is obviously no longer optional.

Language is suffused with metaphors, old and new sayings, and cultural references transparent to native speakers, especially in the absence of geographic, professional or class differences. Some metaphors have become part of the vernacular, while we craft and use others intentionally, to clarify and to persuade, and to enhance the sense of what is shared and induce cooperation. Should we be forced to communicate without these linguistic adornments, we would feel hamstrung and less able to convey precisely what we mean. However, these rich devices are the most difficult to export to another language, and may require interpreter assistance, assuming the latter understands such subtleties. Cultural differences embedded in language may cause misunderstandings even among seasoned professionals. One example is the US-Chinese diplomatic fallout of 2001 surrounding the proper choice of words to express regret for the collision of an American plane with a Chinese one.[10] Although career diplomats share a professional subculture that overrides cultural particularities, languages still trap them in misunderstandings avoidable to some extent through capable interpretation.

The English language has become special in the last decades. People around the world study it in schools and wherever we go we have come to expect that others will understand and respond in English. In one telling example, a ten year-old boy in North Uganda gave an interview in excellent English about the plight of the local population to an NBC journalist.[11] One consequence of the penetration of English in the world's furthest recesses is that native English speakers see little need to become skilled in other languages. As a result, they are possibly disadvantaged in multi-lingual negotiations, needing interpretation while being transparent to their counterparts. It is quite likely that in negotiations involving native English speakers, other negotiators, whether they acknowledge it or not, have weak to excellent understanding and exploit their advantage.

Given their effect on negotiation process and outcomes, it is important to examine how interpreters become messengers, agents, or interveners.

What Do Interpreters Do?

Translation can provide semantic meaning, but not pragmatic meaning. Pragmatic meaning, however, is extremely important in diplomacy. Not being competent in the language of other nations, therefore, severely limits diplomats' and national leaders' ability to understand other nations and accurately predict the behavior of representatives of those nations.
William Gudykunst[12]

Interpretation ranges from literal renditions, which may fail to capture the spirit of what is being said, to conveying the gist and spirit of exchanges, using words that express the sense even if not entirely equivalent to the source.[13] At times, literal translations are explicitly requested, as in US court depositions or appearances of non-English speakers. Sometimes the choice on the continuum between literal and interpretive translation is left to the interpreters, whose preferences are rooted in their professional philosophies.

If they have speaking fluency in one (usually native or strong second) language, interpreters can engage in one-way interpretation, as when simultaneously translating a speech to an audience. For instance, a host of UN interpreters translate simultaneously speeches delivered in one of a small number of official languages. Speaking fluency in two languages allows interpreters to perform two-way, semi-simultaneous (by turns) interpretation among parties. As stakes increase, so does the professional level of interpreters, who have to be fluent in the requisite languages, adhere to interpretation codes of ethics, and have a good grasp of intercultural issues that might crop up during negotiations, to help the parties distinguish between substantive and language differences.

When interpreters are present, it is often unclear whether a negotiator actually understands the other directly, and to what extent. The higher the stakes, the more prudent it is for parties not to negotiate directly in a language not their own, to reduce the risk of misunderstandings. Just as negotiators are well-advised to assume their opponents are at least as smart as they are, they should also assume their counterparts have a working understanding of the language for which they are using interpreters, and never say anything they do not mean others to hear.

Although some professionals and some of their clients believe any mediator is able to intervene in disputes ranging from interpersonal to international, in practice knowledge of content, rules, and practices in specific contexts is necessary. The same holds for interpreters, as language can become quite specialized. Using technically equivalent terms different from those employed in a specific context can detract from negotiations by unnecessarily increasing the time spent on establishing the equivalence. It can also add a layer of misunderstandings in situations that hardly need any more communication obstacles. As well, interpreters' hesitation around choice of words attracts attention to their presence as parties attempt to help clarify context-specific terms. Professional interpreters prepare for assignments by reading their clients' literature and by bringing themselves up-to-date on issues to be discussed, in order to enhance the smoothness of cross-language interactions. It is not uncommon, for the United Nations interpreters for example, to specialize, and be repeatedly assigned to organizations or agencies whose issues and vocabularies they have learned.

Another challenge interpreters encounter as they try to convey the sense, intensity, intent and depth of their clients' conversations is mapping words and expressions from one language into another, while minimizing interference with the process to preserve to the extent possible the feeling of direct communication. In that sense, the more invisible they make themselves to negotiating parties, the more successful they are, not unlike other interveners such as mediators. Many interpreters do succeed in their quest for invisibility, the hallmark of skill, all the more reason for negotiators not to forget their presence or the impact they may have on process and outcomes. The interpreters' "dark side" is their hard-to-control capability of becoming active interveners or agents on one side's behalf, with a point of view on the substance of issues discussed during negotiations.

Interpreters may have no initial stake in the process or outcome of a multilingual exchange. However, if they develop preferences during negotiations, they can exercise them, without necessarily infringing on interpretation ethics. Selecting their location on the literal-interpretive continuum, choosing to render various utterances that may or may not be intended for translation, and conveying at will emotional cues may all predictably affect process and outcomes.

In the business negotiation example mentioned earlier, what the three negotiators were saying to the American businessman and to each other indicated they had no intention to honor their commitment and were not taking his complaint seriously. To convey this to the businessman, I chose a literal extreme, translating flatly everything anyone said. Had they specifically asked me not to translate parts of their conversation not directed at the businessman, I would have had to honor the request. However, as happens in such situations, they wrongly assumed where my loyalties lay,[14] while their lack of knowledge of English robbed them of any measure of control. While partial comprehension of the other's language affords some oversight, it can also mislead. It still leaves room for interpreter discretion, but may cause the negotiator to second-guess and mistrust the interpreter even when this is unwarranted. It is important to note that my choice, as long as uniformly applied, was consistent with interpreter duties, as would have been any other choice along the literal-interpretive continuum, since interpreting means legitimately processing the raw input to render it comprehensible.

My example illustrates one way for interpreters to alter the negotiation outcomes. In general, such actions can affect the tenor of negotiations, mutual trust, good will, and the readiness to share information. While in direct negotiations the parties have some control over their own messages and can interpret in unmediated fashion what they hear, interpreters add noise not unlike "hearsay," whether by design or by the very nature of the activity. They can distort meaning, not translate everything, or explain meanings beyond what a party has actually said or intended to disclose. They can choose to translate side comments or not, to explain or ignore emotional outbursts, and to convey fully or partially the intensity of words (as diplomats did for the Sultan's message to Queen Elizabeth). Importantly, interpreters are fully aware of their power, and often of the effects of their choice of words. They act on others' behalf and reflect on the art, science and ethics of their choices, as suggested by their intense discussions on these subjects at interpreter conferences.

Although generally perceived as having no personal stake in outcomes, interpreters may occasionally feel they do, or they may have an ideologically or identity-driven point of view and inclination to "help" one side. They may feel compelled to put a light finger on the scales, to tip them toward what they perceive as fair, all the while persuading themselves that it is the right thing to do (as I did during the business negotiation), and even part of their job. The more specialized they are, as professional interpreters working in high stakes contexts are, the more knowledgeable of substantive issues they become, and the more able to intervene skillfully enough that their actions are difficult to detect. However, interpreters may also exercise their power when they can persuade themselves that stakes are low enough that their action only matters to their client with no sizeable consequences for others. Instead of regarding interpretation as a neutral service, negotiators should be aware of its "dark side."

Beyond the lack of one-to-one correspondence between languages, interpreters vary in their outlook on their profession, in skill, and in experience in specific contexts, so they are apt to render the same conversation differently. Communicating through interpreters amounts to letting them choose your words, a realization that might, and should, produce anxiety, especially if stakes are high. Both one-way and two-way interpreters are agents whom we entrust with our words while lacking full consent, quality control and trust—typical challenges in principal-agent relationships.[15] I discuss next some aspects and implications of this relationship.

How Do Interpreters Interact With Their Clients?
LANGUAGE, n. The music with which we charm the serpents guarding
another's treasure.
Ambrose Bierce, satirist (1842-1914)[16]

Context matters in the interpreter-client relationship. Even subtle context differences may result in different challenges for the effort to convey meaning. Several situational characteristics shape interpreters' role, including whether each party has its own interpreter, whether power and professionalism are in balance among parties, whether the situation is governed by rules and precedents and defines interpreting tasks precisely, and whether the interpreter is a "natural" stakeholder. Accordingly, interpreters are at times most like advocates, agents or interveners.

Advocate Roles
In situations of power and skill imbalance, the interpreter may end up advocating for the party for whom being misunderstood carries heavy consequences. Non-English-speaking clients may need help in communicating with service providers, to establish entitlements to assistance that hinge on an accurate understanding of needs. Then cultural interpretation is explicitly added to translation, whether volunteered by the interpreter or invited by the parties. The intervener switches then occasionally from translation to advocacy, and adds information to one party that

does not come from the other, but is necessary for clarity. At such times, it helps to ask permission from each party, and explain what information is offered to the other. For example:

Physicians talking to non-English speaking patients must understand their cultural attitudes toward illness or mental and physical handicaps, or risk fatal misunderstandings or a communication shutdown. For instance, to receive medical help, mentally ill patients have to accept it by recognizing their mental illness. I have had to translate physicians' requests for such recognition from people in whose culture this subject is taboo. Unable to bear the shame, one woman preferred to become homeless for two years, rather than agree that she had been mentally ill for years and needed treatment.

In turn, social services providers need interpreters to help educate clients on institutional arrangements, entitlements, and privacy issues. Some business negotiators used to practicing in other environments may have limited understanding of the consequences of misrepresenting the truth. Plaintiffs and defendants have similar difficulties in courts.

Lawyers' clients need assistance to overcome anxieties rooted in past experience, such as fear of authorities or feeling ashamed to find themselves in certain circumstances. One witness to a break-in at her neighbors' house had to explain why she had not called the police. The woman turned to me speechless, hoping I would understand and explain that, where she came from, calling the police was dangerous to the caller, and being seen talking to the police would cover the family in shame.

In many such asymmetrical power situations, interpreters mistakenly become the focus of attention of those with whom they share a native language. Assuming they share more than just language, clients seek and prize interpreters' understanding and approval, and any shame they feel is also relative to the interpreter. Misunderstandings about the interpreter role often crop up: during a deposition in a lawyer's office, a woman became annoyed with my asking her the clarification questions posed by the lawyer about a holiday custom, for which I clearly should have needed no explanation! In municipal court cases of drunk driving or spouse abuse, I am often treated to defendants' detailed disculpatory accounts, meant to improve my opinion of them. Despite my clarifications they often fail to register my role, my obligatory neutrality, the total lack of consequence of my opinions on the court, and the slim chance that we might ever meet again.

Agent and Intervener Roles

One-way interpreters (Figure 1) are comparable to agents, though formally at least, their representation of principals is limited to language and does not extend to interests. Jeswald Salacuse has captured the principal-agent relationship through four key elements:[17] (1) A fiduciary relationship between agent and principal; (2) Control by the principal over the agent; (3) Action by the agent on behalf of the principal; and (4) Consent by both principal and agent to the agency relationship. While element 3 is relatively clear for interpreters and their clients, the fiduciary aspect, the degree of control over agents, and the recognition of agency are problematic.

Two-way interpreters (Figure 1) fit Rubin's definition of a third party: "an individual who is in some way external to a dispute between two other parties, and who interposes (or is interposed) between them."[18] In principle, interpreters should be indifferent among outcomes in a multi-lingual negotiation, especially since evaluation of service quality does not (or should not) hinge on outcome content. This reinforces expectations (though not perceptions) of their neutrality. However, unlike other interveners, they do not participate in process design or management. Their activities match closely those identified by Kaufman and Duncan as central to mediation: information (supply and) transfers.[19]

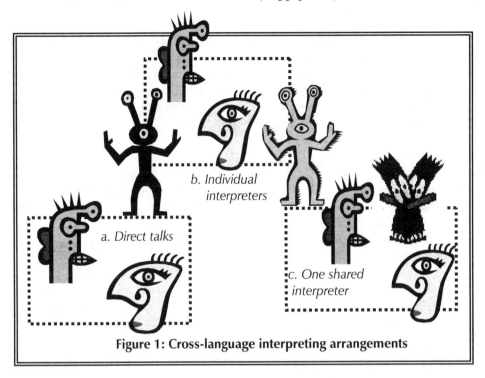

Figure 1: Cross-language interpreting arrangements

a. Direct talks

b. Individual interpreters

c. One shared interpreter

It is noteworthy that neither type of interpreter fits perfectly either the agent or the intervener role: each has both agency and intervention qualities. In general, the one-way interpreters may have no direct interest in outcomes, while the two-way interpreters may alternate as agents of each side.

Table 1 identifies some characteristics in which interpreters, agents, and interveners are comparable, since due to the interpreters' leeway in choosing words on behalf of others the impact of their activities exceeds their seemingly limited role in negotiations. The characteristics interact, so for example, interpreters exercise their power because they can become invisible to the parties, and lack of control over the quality of their work is the source of trust problems. All three modes of intervention operate through language and can exercise more or less directly some form of power over process and outcomes. The extent to which interveners and agents have responsibility for the outcomes of negotiation depends on the specific cases, whereas interpreters are never held responsible for agreements and their content. The "invisible" quality and the neutrality expectation are mostly intervention qualities, whereas the fiduciary responsibility, relationship recognition and client control are mostly agency issues.

Mediators are supposed to feel successful when parties believe they did everything themselves. Ingratitude is a compliment of sorts for the mediator's skill in getting the parties to own their decisions. Interpreters prefer invisibility for a different, though also skill-related reason—creating for the parties the impression of unmediated conversation. In contrast, as stakeholders themselves, agents are neither invisible nor do they seek to be. Invisibility, however, is the interpreters' ticket to their "dark side," as parties may forget they are not really hearing each other's words and are unable to control what the other hears.

Table 1: Comparison Between Interveners, Agents and Interpreters

Mode / Characteristic	Intervention	Agency	Interpretation
Language as key vehicle	Yes	Yes	Yes
Formal responsibility for outcome	Varies	Considerable	None
Power	Some (mainly over process)	Some (over process, content)	Some (over content)
Intervener-like Premium on being "invisible"	Yes	No	Yes
Parties' expectation of neutrality	Yes	No	Yes
Input in process	Yes	Some	No
Agent-like Input in outcome	Indirect	Yes	Indirect
Fiduciary relationship	No	Yes	Partially
Recognition of the relationship	Fully	Fully	Partially
Client ability to control/supervise/evaluate	Strong	Variable	Very weak

Interpreters and interveners are expected to refrain from favoring a party through their actions. However, both negotiators perceive interpreters as having a special relationship with the party with whom they share a native language. Therefore, even in two-way interpretation, one party sees the interpreter as an agent of the other, who also perceives him or her to be "on their side" and to understand that side better. However, this relationship is assumed, rather than explicitly negotiated. The weaker the parties' ability to verify the interpreter's choices, the less wise is this assumption, as my business negotiation example illustrated. One-way situations stand in sharp contrast, because then interpreters can act like the agents they are perceived to be.

Unlike interveners and agents, interpreters do not typically have process input, beyond modest requests about the length of time a party can speak before the interpreter takes a turn. This does not mean their presence does not affect the process. On the contrary, the periodic pauses give the natural flow a choppier quality, but they add to each party's time for reflection. Expression of emotions during negotiation is also impaired or somewhat misinterpreted. For instance, it is not uncommon for English, Americans or Scandinavians to interpret the Mediterranean (rather louder) interaction style as angry and unruly when they do not directly understand the content of exchanges. As the meaning is delayed through interpretation, the impressions linger even after the absence of anger becomes clear.

Interveners' and agents' input in negotiated outcomes is purposeful even when indirect, and it is mostly legitimate and visible to parties who understand the nature of each. Interpretation, on the other hand, is not supposed to affect negotiated outcomes, having a different avowed purpose. Nevertheless, interpreters may affect outcomes by their word choices, either inadvertently, or purposefully, as the translators did for Queen Elizabeth. As in that case, such actions are all the more insidious when consistent with expectations: the Queen had little reason to doubt a sign of friendship she expected. She might have been surprised had she received the original exhortation to subservience.

The fiduciary relationship described by Salacuse[20] as a component of agency also characterizes interpretation. Negotiators do expect their words to be conveyed to the other side. Unlike with agents though, their ability to exert control and evaluate the quality of service received is rather limited, as are their means of inducing alignment of interpreters' interests with their own. More problematic still, perceptions are not necessarily aligned with this reality given both parties' tendency to assume interpreter partiality to the side sharing a native language. Interpreters thus operate in a more weakly controlled space than agents or interveners. They alone have a "dark side"—the capability to give free rein to biases or hidden agendas unless negotiators take steps to protect themselves, especially in high-stakes situations.

Conclusion

> Between two beings there is always the barrier of words. Man has so many
> ears and speaks so many languages. Should it nevertheless be possible to
> understand one another? Is real communication possible if word and
> language betray us every time? Shall, in the end, only the language of
> tanks and guns prevail and not human reason and understanding?
> Joost Merloo, psychiatrist (1903-1976)

Interpreters, with their mixture of agent and intervener attributes, can affect the dynamics and outcomes of cross-language negotiations through communication, the very vehicle through which they are conducted. They alter nuances, tone, emotions, and even content of arguments, adding to, or subtracting from, offers, threats and promises, in amounts and ways that hinge on skill, values, identities, and sometimes interests. Parties can exert only limited control over interpreters, who may be more responsive to their professional peers' evaluations and ethics codes than to the parties.

What is a negotiator to do? Awareness of the nature of interpretation, of its agency and intervention dimensions, of what can and cannot be expected from it, and of some dangers inherent in the activity should help mitigate some of the pitfalls. Rather than viewing interpreting as a neutral, mechanical service, negotiators need to recognize its centrality to negotiations and invest an amount of scrutiny in the selection of interpreters commensurate with their potential impact on process and outcomes. They should also seek to enhance their ability to control quality and neutrality. For example, in high-stakes situations, bi-lingual observers might provide a measure of control and even increased accuracy, given interpreters' sensitivity to peer opinions. Just as they prepare for negotiations, parties may consider preparing for the interpretation: meet with the interpreters before they encounter their counterparts, discuss expectations, process, ways of enhancing precision and reducing ambiguities, and any concerns with the agency aspects of the relationship. Depending on their trust level, negotiators may or may not disclose to interpreters whether they understand the others' language and to what extent. For repeated encounters, negotiators should debrief each session to fine-tune the process and check for any misunderstandings that could not be ironed out in real time. If uncomfortable with service quality or unable to develop a relationship of trust in their agency, negotiators should not hesitate to seek other interpreters even in midstream.

Back to the ceasefire: in English, it means a total end of any act by one party that may be understood as aggressive toward the second party. In Hebrew, *hafsakat esh* means to Israelis that Palestinians must stop all attacks against them, but if Israelis have intelligence of a pending terror attack against them, they can and will act to prevent it. In Arabic, *hudna* means to Palestinians a temporary scaling down of hostilities against a true enemy until one can attack again. These differences are enough to torpedo any agreement after it is signed, and indeed we have already witnessed several rounds of just that. We learn the power and the weakness of words to be vehicles for understanding and barriers to it at the same time. We also learn that people pursue doggedly their own interests rather than the words that represent them, so no unifying words can bridge real and persistent differences. Interpreters can only do so much.

Endnotes

Translation of 1199 text of Maimonides to Shmuel ibn Tibbon, *in* LEO SCHWARTZ, MEMOIRS OF MY PEOPLE (1943).

[1] Micah D. Halperin, 2003.

[2] Shabtai Rosenne, *On Multilingual Interpretation*, 6 ISRAEL LAW REVIEW (1971), *reprinted in* THE ARAB-ISRAELI CONFLICT VOL. II: READINGS (J.N. Moore ed., 1974).

[3] BERNARD LEWIS, FROM BABEL TO DRAGOMANS 28-29 (2004).

[4] *See, e.g.*, TRENHOLME GRIFFIN & W. RUSSELL DAGGATT, THE GLOBAL NEGOTIATOR: BUILDING STRONG BUSINESS RELATIONSHIPS ANYWHERE IN THE WORLD (1990); JEANNE BRETT, NEGOTIATING GLOBALLY: HOW TO NEGOTIATE DEALS, RESOLVE DISPUTES, AND MAKE DECISIONS ACROSS CULTURAL BOUNDARIES (2001).

[5] *See, e.g.*, COMMUNICATION AND NEGOTIATION (Linda Putnam & Michael Roloff eds. 1992); *see also*, Linda Putnam, *Communication and Interaction Patterns*, Chapter 44 in this volume.

[6] ROY LEWICKI, ET AL., THINK BEFORE YOU SPEAK: A COMPLETE GUIDE TO STRATEGIC NEGOTIATION (1996).

[7] STEPHEN PINKER, THE BLANK SLATE (2001).

[8] BRETT, *supra* note 4, at 145-47.

[9] State-of-the-art in machine translations (AltaVista's Babelfish) illustrate this point: The quote from Bismarck "When you say that you agree to a thing in principle, you mean that you have not the slightest intention of carrying it out." translated from English into French and back into English yields: "When you say that you agree in theory on a thing, you want to say that you stripped the lightest intention to carry it outside." Voltaire's "Better is the enemy of good" when translated from English into Russian, comes back into English as: "The more best enemy it is good."

[10] Kevin Avruch, *Culture Apology and International Negotiation: The Case of the Sino-US "Spy Plane" Crisis*, 10 INTERNATIONAL NEGOTIATION 337, 339-41 (220).

[11] *Dateline NBC: Keith Morrison's report on Northern Uganda:* (NBC television broadcast, Aug. 21, 2005).

[12] William Gudykunst, *Diplomacy: A Special Case for Intergroup Communication*, in *Communicating for Peace, Diplomacy and Negotiations*, 14 INTERNATIONAL & INTERCULTURAL COMMUNICATION ANNUAL (1990).

[13] The translations of UN Resolution 242 from English are close to the verbatim end of the range, since the wording had been negotiated. Rendering its sense would have necessitated introducing or eliminating words, requiring further negotiations. The parties chose to allow the ambiguity rather than renew negotiations, with consequences that still impact today's Middle East.

[14] These negotiators perceived me as siding with them, on account of the shared native language. Therefore, they made comments they could not possibly have wanted understood by their American counterpart. For example, at one point they used a derogatory regionalism unfamiliar to me, to convey that their conversation with the American businessman was meant to accomplish nothing more than pass the time. After asking for clarification, I translated it. Having understood the futility of the negotiations, the businessman appealed to then-Secretary of Trade Ron Brown, present at the conference, who intervened successfully on his behalf.

[15] *See* Jeswald Salacuse, *Law and Power in Agency Relationships, in* NEGOTIATING ON BEHALF OF OTHERS: ADVICE TO LAWYERS, BUSINESS EXECUTIVES, SPORTS AGENTS, DIPLOMATS, POLITICIANS, AND EVERYBODY ELSE (Robert Mnookin & Lawrence Susskind eds. 1999); *see also* Jacqueline Nolan-Haley, *Agents and Informed Consent*, Chapter 58 in this volume.

[16] AMBROSE BIERCE, THE DEVIL'S DICTIONARY (1911).

[17] Salacuse, *supra* note 15, at 158.

[18] DYNAMICS OF THIRD PARTY INTERVENTION: KISSINGER IN THE MIDDLE EAST 5 (Jeffery Z. Rubin ed., 1981).

[19] Sanda Kaufman & George T. Duncan, *The Role of Mandates in Third Party Intervention,* 4 NEGOTIATION JOURNAL 403 (1988).

[20] Salacuse, *supra* note 15, at 158.

∝ 62 ∾

Negotiating in Teams

David F. Sally & Kathleen M. O'Connor

Editors' Note: *This chapter, the first of our "teams trilogy," analyzes the research on what individuals accomplish when compared to teams in which the members have differentiated functions. Not surprisingly, the teams turn out to be able to handle more information more accurately more of the time. But of course, that's not the whole story. You will be able to construct a better negotiating team and manage it better if you read this chapter in close conjunction with Bellman's advice on what to do when the team faces disunity, as well as Matz's analysis of how even an extraordinarily sophisticated team can misread its own members' priorities and possibilities.*

Solo advocacy has a mythic prominence in the legal profession. Standing alone before the judge, jury, witness, client or opponent is the central vision of many courtroom dramas, much lawyerly day-dreaming, and, most importantly, almost all legal education. By contrast, managerial education at most business schools these days emphasizes the learning and practice of teamwork and collaboration. This emphasis reflects the realities of work arrangements in modern organizations: whether one considers manufacturing, research and development, banking, consulting, or strategic planning, work is likely to be done by teams rather than through the efforts of a solo employee.[1] This trend is especially true for firms with multiple offices, higher revenues, and more employees.[2] A business student will certainly study teams in a core course on general management and is very likely to find an elective on team dynamics in the school's curriculum.

Not surprisingly, this difference in emphasis is manifest in negotiation research, both its practice and its content. With respect to the former, law school researchers are far more likely to be solo advocates, while their business counterparts utilize a team. One can compare the authorship of articles published in three prominent journals, the *Harvard Negotiation Law Review*, the *Negotiation Journal*, and *Organizational Behavior and Human Decision Processes*, from 1999 to 2004. The first journal features primarily researchers from law schools and the third journal primarily from business schools, while the second is a blend of both. The percentage of articles that were authored by a single person over the last five years is as follows: *Harvard Negotiation Law Review*, 83%; *Negotiation Journal*, 70%; and *Organizational Behavior and Human Decision Processes*, 17%. There are, of course, many factors underlying the dramatic variance in solo authorship, but clearly one essential factor is the cultures of the professions.

In a negotiation, process and content are intimately linked and so it is with the research on negotiations: while the law literature has few examples of work on negotiating teams (a key, somewhat dormant, exception is the work on labor disputes), the organizational behavior literature has recently characterized a number of regularities about teams in negotiations and has concluded that teams and individuals negotiate differently. Hence, the plan and purpose of this chapter: as a team, we will review the most important of these advances in knowledge. Furthermore, because law firms utilize teams as frequently as any other complex, modern organization, we will advocate to our law school colleagues that they attend to these findings, utilize them in the classroom, and contribute to future discoveries about teams and negotiations.

Challenges for Negotiation Teams

Rather than send a solo negotiator to the table, decision-makers may opt to pull together a team to hammer out the terms of a deal. Despite the costs of assigning a deal to a team, there are a number of reasons why this decision can make good sense. Negotiation is cognitively taxing. Parties must continually attend to both their own and the other side's interests and constraints as they work to agree on mutually beneficial terms. Teams allow for a division of labor and a combining of skills that means that N+1 heads are better than one.[3] On a related note, teams are likely to provide functional diversity that can pave the way to better deals. Building a team that includes both process and content experts, strategic as well as tactical thinkers, number crunchers and smooth talkers allows for a range of skills that is likely to outmatch those of any single team member. For political reasons, too, there may be wisdom in picking teammates from different groups. For instance, a local union is likely to select representatives from each of several groups within the bargaining unit to increase the chances that contract terms will be ratified by the unit as a whole. Still, it is not a foregone conclusion that teams should always be chosen over solo negotiators: there are some deep, dangerous pitfalls. Decades of study of groups and teams by social psychologists highlight a fundamental tension experienced by teammates—how to capitalize on the diverse abilities and opinions of members while at the same time acting as a cohesive unit. Scholars have sought answers to these questions by studying the problem from several angles. Questions about the composition of teams continue to attract attention. What are the tradeoffs inherent in assigning teamwork to friends versus strangers?[4] Do the benefits of members with a variety of experiences and skills outweigh the advantages of smooth functioning that are likely to flow from members who are similar to one another?[5]

The short answer to this second question is "yes but." Teamwork presents special challenges in coordination and motivation of members. For instance, groups, especially groups larger than four, can suffer from free rider problems.[6] Rather than adding to the team, the cover afforded by larger groups provides an opportunity for members to reduce their efforts rather than to fully participate in group activities. Even for teammates who are motivated to work hard to serve the team, there are aspects of the process that may interfere with effective decision-making. For instance, people working in teams tend to focus their discussion on facts and opinions that are held in common, leaving unique pieces of information or key bits of data out of the conversation.[7] When these bits of information are critical to the decision, the cost is a low quality outcome.[8] As groups gel and members come to value their cooperative relationships with each other, they can develop an intolerance to dissenting voices, especially when those voices challenge the majority to consider more carefully their own judgments and interpretation of facts.[9] Thus, while there are some advantages to convening a team to carry out work that could be done by a solo, teams need to work hard to ensure the full participation of their members.

Compared to the study of work groups and teams, the literature on negotiation teams is far smaller, making it difficult for scholars to offer many empirically derived recommendations to practitioners. However, one solution to the paucity of empirical evidence is to turn to the wealth of research on work teams for answers. Although this is a reasonable source for insights, it is critical to acknowledge how negotiating teams differ from other kinds of work teams. Social psychologists have made a distinction between purely cooperative teams and purely competitive groups. Cooperative teams have members who share the same motives and incentives and are focused on reaching a common goal. Competitive teams, including those involved in social dilemmas, have members who are motivated to maximize their own gains irrespective of others' outcomes. Negotiating teams face a more complicated set of constraints. When they are working together to draft a plan or marshal support for a set of positions or arguments, members of negotiating teams are engaged in a cooperative task. Yet, if they represent groups with conflicting interests, they have incentives to improve their standing at the expense of their teammates. [Bellman, *Team Conflicts*] Hence, when the team sits down across the table from another team or solo, it is engaged in a mixed-motive task, one that requires the team both to cooperate to reach a mutually beneficial deal and to compete to get the best deal possible for its side. We will consider these unique features of negotiating teams as we review the advantages and liabilities of teamwork at the bargaining table.

The Pros & Cons of Teamwork

A common thread that connects the laboratory studies of negotiating teams is the clear advantage that goes to negotiating teams over solos. Without exception, teams reach deals of better quality than do their solo counterparts.[10] This is true regardless of whether teams negotiate against other teams or against solos, thus it is the team itself that is driving the effect rather than the composition of the other side. There are a number of reasons for this benefit. First, as we noted earlier, negotiating is a complex cognitive task. With every offer and every answer to a question, negotiators are receiving information that may very well yield insights into the other side's priorities, interests, and alternatives. In addition to managing the interpretation of incoming information, negotiators also must craft counteroffers, generate questions, and decide whether and how to answer the other side's questions. Although this is quite a task for a solo negotiator, especially as the complexity of the issues grows and the stakes mount, teams have the option of breaking the task into component parts that can be designated to team members (roles include spokesperson, offer tracker, etc.). [Matz, *Team Miscommunication*] The extra memory capacity and parallel data processing offered by the linked minds of the team may be able to handle complex issues and interests that would overwhelm and "crash" a solo negotiator.

Second, there are tactics available to a team that cannot be implemented by an individual. The most outstanding example is the good cop/bad cop tactic.[11] This tactic depends critically on having two different people perform each role in the proper order (bad cop, then good cop).[12] Another example is the use of an intentionally absent team member who is holding a key resource—projections, budgets, authorization, etc. Note that many solo negotiators use this tactic to transform their side into a team by claiming that any additional offer or concession will have to be approved by the boss.

A third advantage is that with the addition of each new member of the negotiating team, the collective network of colleagues and acquaintances around the team grows. The larger the network, the better the access that the team has to information that can help in its negotiation. For instance, team members may tap into their expanded network, friends of friends and acquaintances of acquaintances, to learn about the other side, their interests, their likely strategy, their outside options. Furthermore, many studies document that when negotiators are able to develop trust, they are able to exchange the information necessary to reach high quality deals.[13] With more members at the table, teams have multiple opportunities either to rely on established relationships or to develop relationships that are likely to be helpful for establishing trust and, therefore, sharing honest and accurate information. This is more than a theoretical possibility that has been confirmed in a field study of labor negotiations.[14]

Particularly when there is potential in the negotiation to make trades among issues or to introduce additional issues, creative thinking can hold the key to mutually beneficial deals. In some cases, the broader the range of talents on the team, the better able the team should be to generate creative solutions. Creativity is threatened when negotiators feel stressed. Thus, to the extent that team membership insulates negotiators from the pressures that solos experience, it is likely to mitigate the stress a negotiator might feel if she or he were handling the negotiation alone. One specific pressure is accountability, namely, representing an outside constituency at the bargaining table. Solo negotiators who are accountable often adopt a rather competitive stance in the negotiation that can limit their ability to build trust, exchange critical information, keep focused on opportunities for joint gains. Teams, however, are insulated from these effects. Even when a team is accountable for its outcomes, the members experience lower accountability pressures than solos, and more importantly, respond less competitively to these pressures. Hence, they are better able to balance a need to get the most out of the deal with an interest in cooperating to ensure that a mutually beneficial deal is reached.[15]

Thus far, we have emphasized the benefits that flow to negotiating teams. Yet, there are downsides to sending teams to the table. The first, and most simple, fact to point out is that teams are costly. Multiple people are being paid to do what one person could conceivably handle. There is a cost/benefit calculation that must ultimately buttress any decision to employ a negotiating team instead of a single bargainer. The same calculation is relevant in determining the size of the team: each new member adds a layer of costs to the deal that will need to be recovered. Also, a member's efforts at this table limit his or her involvement in other productive tasks. Any decision about assigning teams or solos must include some estimate of the costs and a consideration of the likely payouts.

Teams may be self-managing, but they are rarely self-sufficient—an organizational structure and culture supporting teams are necessary to make them effective. One pitfall that decision-makers need to avoid is the "manager's fallacy" or the belief that the key to effective teams is to simply put a group of bright people in a room together and stand back to watch the magic. Difficulties with coordination and motivation that plague some teams need to be understood and steps taken to avoid them before they sabotage any benefits the team could deliver. [Matz, *Team Miscommunication*] In fact, some of the good news about negotiating teams may fail to translate into high quality deals as team size increases beyond the three members that are typically assembled in social psychologists' laboratories. Empirical research on teams and groups working on other kinds of tasks shows that the greater the number of team members, the more anonymous and less accountable any one member may feel. Some members may take this opportunity to scale back their efforts, creating a free rider problem. Assigning people to specific roles and holding them accountable for fulfilling their roles as well as for the team's output is one way to combat this problem on large teams.

Another issue is that because friendship networks are largely based on similarity,[16] a team that arises spontaneously or endogenously across one person's network may be insufficiently diverse for the purpose at hand. Therefore, team oversight might also be necessary to assure that the team is sufficiently heterogeneous. As outlined above, many of the benefits of teams only occur if there are differences in perspectives, information, and histories.

In addition to increasing personnel costs and requiring an active supporting structure, negotiating teams are slow. Coordination becomes a bigger problem as more people are added to the team. Teams need to take steps to ensure that everyone understands his or her role as well as the strategy for the negotiation. It can also be very helpful for the team to establish a mechanism for taking breaks during the negotiation. This can serve two purposes. First, it can help keep the team moving in the same direction as the negotiation unfolds, and second, it gives the teammates a chance to continue to provide unique insights and ideas that can be used to formulate new offers or to readjust strategy. The cost of such breaks is, of course, the protraction of the bargaining sessions.

A lack of coordination can cause teams to fracture, a risk not faced by individual negotiators. As the size of the team grows or as team members become more heterogeneous, the potential for intrateam conflict increases. The intrateam negotiation might end in an impasse as a team struggles to integrate the interests, positions, opinions, and outside options of all its members. It is essential to recognize that this struggle is not all bad: in fact, many intrateam disputes do not block performance.[17] Conflicts that are focused on the task at hand, disagreements over the best strategy, and hashing out whether one set of issues deserves more or less consideration can help the team sort out its priorities, and come to a better outcome than would have been possible had the team avoided the conflict. However, when the conflict becomes personal, the performance of the team is likely to suffer.[18] The possibility of intrateam conflict also implies that teamwork will require time above what solos will need, especially during the critical preparation stage where teammates are getting to know each other and are working to pull together a plan for their negotiation.

The risks from intrateam division can be limited if teams agree to internal decision-making rules (such as "no offers will be accepted at the table" or "every member has veto power") before the negotiation begins. Even if conflicts among teammates over priorities were resolved originally, the team is likely to face considerable difficulties in deciding whether to accept a particular offer, risking impasse or fragmentation in the process. Anticipating difficulties when it comes to making decisions about finalizing deals, it would be helpful to teams to agree on a decision rule. Although unanimity is ideal for satisfying each teammate, the team may be best served by a majority decision rule that ensures that most parties get what they need from the deal.

What We Do Not Know

It should be apparent from our review that management scholars have made only initial forays toward a better understanding of team negotiations. There is a great opportunity for collaboration and teamwork between researchers from management schools and those from law and other schools. Here are a few examples of open questions:

- Do teams enjoy the same advantages over solos in "real world" negotiations that they have in laboratory bargaining sessions? In particular, might law firms be a unique field study site enabling the comparison of the performance of solo advocates and teams of varying sizes?

- How does the culture of the firm or company influence the effectiveness of negotiating teams? Are legal teams, for example, more likely to consolidate multiple roles in one individual? Are there greater problems with information sharing, especially given the various legal rules and norms concerning confidentiality? Are they more likely to implement internal decision rules, and if so, which ones?

- Which specific elements within the negotiation process do teams capitalize upon? Studies could target teams and goal setting, first offers, reciprocal concessions, question asking, information sharing, ultimatums, etc.

- What are the connections among team negotiation, multi-party negotiation, and coalitions? Each of these topics has been pursued individually but few commonalities have been studied. However, it must be true, for example, that some of the techniques that are useful for forming a team are equally useful in solidifying a coalition. A two-party team negotiation can quickly become a much more complicated multi-party situation when one team fractures. [Matz, *Team Miscommunication*]

- Experienced negotiators are more effective in teams than novice negotiators are.[19] But are those who are used to operating in teams more effective in team negotiations than are those who have no team experience? If so, then how significant is the difference? This question is one way to compare the task of negotiation with the other kinds of tasks that have been studied in the small group literature.

Endnotes

[1] JON KATZENBACH & DOUGLAS SMITH, THE WISDOM OF TEAMS: CREATING THE HIGH PERFORMANCE ORGANIZATION (1993).

[2] Dennis J. Devine, et al., *Teams in Organizations: Prevalence, Characteristics, and Effectiveness,* 30(6) SMALL GROUP RESEARCH 678 (1999).

[3] Gayle Hill, *Group Versus Individual Performance: Are N+1 Heads Better Than One?* 91 PSYCHOLOGICAL BULLETIN 517 (1982).

[4] Deborah H. Gruenfeld, et al., *Group Composition and Decision Making: How Member Familiarity and Information Distribution Affect Process and Performance,* 67 ORGANIZATIONAL BEHAVIOR AND HUMAN DECISION PROCESSES 1 (1996); Karen A. Jehn and Priti Pradhan Shah, *Interpersonal Relationships and Task Performance: An Examination of Mediating Processes in Friendship and Acquaintance Groups,* 72 JOURNAL OF PERSONALITY AND SOCIAL PSYCHOLOGY 775 (1997).

[5] Verlin Hinsz, et al., *The Emerging Conceptualization of Groups as Information Processors* 121 PSYCHOLOGICAL BULLETIN 43 (1997).

[6] Bibb Latané, et al., *Many Hands Make Light the Work: The Causes and Consequences of Social Loafing,* 37 JOURNAL OF PERSONALITY AND SOCIAL PSYCHOLOGY 822, 822-32 (1979).

[7] Daniel Gigone and Reid Hastie, *The Common Knowledge Effect: Information Sharing and Group Judgment*, 65 JOURNAL OF PERSONALITY AND SOCIAL PSYCHOLOGY 959 (1992).

[8] Garold Stasser and Dennis D. Stewart, *Discovery of Hidden Profiles by Decision-Making Groups: Solving a Problem versus Making a Judgment*, 63 JOURNAL OF PERSONALITY AND SOCIAL PSYCHOLOGY 426 (1992).

[9] Charlan J. Nemeth, *Differential Contributions of Majority and Minority Influence*, 93 PSYCHOLOGICAL REVIEW 23 (1986).

[10] Jeffery T. Polzer, *Intergroup Negotiations: The Effects of Negotiating Teams*, 40(4) JOURNAL OF CONFLICT RESOLUTION 678 (1996); Leigh Thompson, et al., *Team Negotiation: An Examination of Integrative and Distributive Bargaining*, 70 JOURNAL OF PERSONALITY AND SOCIAL PSYCHOLOGY 66 (1996).

[11] John A. Hilty & Peter J. Carnevale, *"Black-hat/White-hat" Strategy in Bilateral Negotiation*, 55 ORGANIZATIONAL BEHAVIOR AND HUMAN DECISION PROCESSES 444 (1993).

[12] Susan E. Brodt & Marla Tuchinsky, *Working Together but in Opposition: An Examination of the "Good-Cop/Bad-Cop" Negotiating Team Tactic*, 81 ORGANIZATIONAL BEHAVIOR AND HUMAN DECISION PROCESS 155 (2000).

[13] Kathleen Valley, et al., *A Matter of Trust: Effects of Communication on the Efficiency and Distribution of Outcomes*, 34 JOURNAL OF ECONOMIC BEHAVIOR AND ORGANIZATION 211 (1998).

[14] Raymond A. Friedman & Joel Podolny, *Differentiation of Boundary Spanning Roles: Labor Negotiations and Implications for Role Conflict*, 37 ADMINISTRATIVE SCIENCES QUARTERLY 28 (1992).

[15] *See* Kathleen M. O'Connor, *Groups and Solos in Context: The Effects of Accountability on Team Negotiation*, 72 ORGANIZATIONAL BEHAVIOR AND HUMAN DECISION PROCESSES 384 (1997).

[16] David Sally, *A General Theory of Sympathy, Mind-Reading, and Social Interaction, with an Application to the Prisoners' Dilemma*, 39(4) SOCIAL SCIENCE INFORMATION 567, 567-634 (2000).

[17] Allen C. Amason, *Distinguishing the Effects of Functional and Dysfunctional Conflict on Strategic Decision Making: Resolving a Paradox for Top Management Teams*, 39 ACADEMY OF MANAGEMENT JOURNAL 123 (1996).

[18] *Id.*; Karen A. Jehn, *Enhancing Effectiveness: An Investigation of Advantages and Disadvantages of Value-Based Intragroup Conflict*, 5 INTERNATIONAL JOURNAL OF CONFLICT MANAGEMENT 223 (1994).

[19] Jeffrey T. Polzer, *Intergroup Negotiations: The Effects of Negotiating Teams*, 40 JOURNAL OF CONFLICT RESOLUTION 678 (1994).

ೞ 63 ೦೮

Intra-Team Miscommunication

David Matz

Editors' Note: *The second in our trilogy on team negotiations, this chapter uses Matz's interviews of key players in a single, epochal but failed negotiation to ask a key question. Is it possible that team members in even high-level teams, working on really important issues, are subject to pressures which cause them to misread the signals from within their own team as to what is possible? The fact that experienced and savvy negotiators can miss their own team's internal signals has implications for your negotiations too. What can you do, the next time you are working with a team under high pressure and with high stakes, to improve your own communication?*

Most studies of negotiation have looked at the relationship between negotiation sides, and some have looked at the relationship between negotiation and their constituents. Very little study has looked at conflicts inside a negotiating team and the impact of those conflicts on the between-party process. Herewith is a cut at that question.

My examples will all be drawn from Israeli-Arab (mainly Israeli-Palestinian) negotiations. Whether these are typical of team negotiations, or are extreme examples, is a subject for another essay. I will set out first the examples and then draw some schematic inferences from them. I will start with a relatively detailed account of one negotiation (about which I have done substantial research), and then add some sketches of a few others.

From the negotiation at Oslo (1993) to the mediation at Camp David I (2000), the Israeli-Palestinian peace process was marked by month to month zigzags, toward resolution and away. Even so, many thought the process was moving toward the establishment of a Palestinian state and the resolution of the Palestinian refugee question.

This success began to look inevitable when, in 1999, Ehud Barak sought the Israeli prime ministership, declared the goal of a negotiated settlement, won the election decisively, and then, after a good deal of his own zigzagging, sought a summit meeting with PLO Chairman Yasser Arafat for the summer of 2000. Chairman Arafat objected to the summit, calling it premature, but this looked like a negotiating move, a clue only that he would be tough at the summit.

The 13 day negotiation at Camp David, with President Clinton as mediator, ended on July 26 with no agreement. Much very angry and very public finger

pointing followed. Meanwhile, the Israeli settlements on the West Bank continued
to increase, the Palestinian economic situation continued to deteriorate, and in
September, as many had predicted, Intifada II began. Barak's government coalition—already in trouble before Camp David—continued to disintegrate, and in
late 2000 he called for elections to be held on February 6. Ariel Sharon emerged as
Barak's opponent, and the polls showed a substantial and increasing margin of
victory for the challenger. Sharon never varied: were he to win, all of Barak's
commitments to negotiate would be withdrawn. Given Sharon's career-long commitment to military force in relations with the Arabs, his threat was completely
credible and widely believed.

In mid January, three weeks before the Israeli election, the Israelis and the
Palestinians announced that one more negotiation would take place, this one at
Taba, an Egyptian resort. It began on Sunday evening, January 21, and ended on
Saturday afternoon, the 27th. During that week the press reported general mur-
murings of progress. At the closing press conference the parties issued this joint
statement: "The sides declare that they have never been closer to reaching an
agreement and it is thus our shared belief that the remaining gaps could be
bridged with the resumption of negotiations following the Israeli election."

As a longtime student of this particular relationship, I was very confused. The
parties had "never been closer," and with nine days until the election they were
going home because they had run out of time? How could they walk away from a
negotiation of this magnitude with time left to negotiate? Perhaps the cynics were
right: Taba was nothing but a charade, both sides wanting to make Barak look like
a productive negotiator to enhance his chance of re-election. Resume negotiations
after the election? Did they think the vapid optimism of that press statement
could turn around Barak's 18% deficit at the polls? Or did they think that after the
election Sharon would suddenly reveal a new personality and complete the negotiation? What was going on here? What explained what seemed like such bizarre
behavior?

To explain this, I developed a plan to interview the Taba negotiators and to
piece together a picture of what occurred. There were twenty-eight negotiators and
professional staff at Taba; I interviewed seventeen. Neither Prime Minister Barak
nor Chairman Arafat attended any part of the negotiation, though both were in
fairly constant touch with the proceedings. There were about five principal negotiators on each side and each was a significant political player in his own society.
Many of them had ambition for high political office. Though one can identify differences of temperament among these negotiators, all of them had had significant
experience in the peace process and all of them had been identified at one time or
another with major efforts at reaching agreement. In one degree or another they
were all "peaceniks."

Despite these similarities, there was substantial and significant friction among
the players on each side. Each major issue (borders, refugees, Jerusalem, security)
was assigned to a different committee, and there was a constant tension that
committee members were not sharing their work with the rest of their own team.
This tension was fed by and in turn fed suspicions that various players were "giving away the store." Responsibility for on-site leadership of the two teams was not
free of ambiguity, thus inviting a certain jostling for control. Political egos were
sensitive to the favor of the (absent) boss and to their own political futures. Exacerbating these tensions were the highly equivocal mandates under which each set
of negotiators worked: there was no clarity about which concessions would be

accepted by one's own boss, and there were conflicting interpretations within each team about this question.

On one occasion the Israeli foreign minister put a map on the table and Barak's chief of staff declared that no map put forward had any standing until he had approved it. On the Palestinian side, Dajani describes "a fragmented leadership ... consumed by brutal internal struggle over succession and political and economic power.... Sometimes more than one Palestinian claimed to have the authority to negotiate. At other times senior Palestinians would undermine their own official delegation. Anyone who sought to advance the negotiations was soon delegitimized."[1]

Constituencies at home played a role in exacerbating these tensions. There were citizen and government groups on both sides who, as always, saw themselves as smarter and tougher than the negotiators. Those groups were eager to criticize the very act of negotiating, and were especially eager to criticize particular concessions. Many of these groups were important because they would be needed to approve and implement an agreement, and because they were needed by individual negotiators for other purposes. Though the negotiators sought some degree of privacy from the outside world, leaks were inevitable. A concession attributable to one negotiator could easily be converted into a weapon against him.[2] It is one thing to try to persuade groups who were not at the negotiating table to accept a package of concessions that come with a full agreement; it is another to take one concession, and later have to explain why it was acceptable, without the buffering justification of an agreement. Adding a further edge is the vulnerability, inherent in all negotiations and especially potent among Israelis and Palestinians, of being seen as a dupe or a sucker.

While this intra-team friction increased, many of the negotiating committees nonetheless made considerable progress and, had the negotiation not been stopped by Barak (with Arafat's concurrence) several days before it had to be, framework agreements on several key topics were possible.[3] There are many possible explanations for the Barak/Arafat decision to end the negotiation prematurely, but one relevant factor is that, as a result of the intra-team competition and secrecy, *it seems likely that no one on the spot had a clear view of how close many of the negotiators were to agreement and thus did not know the real cost of ending the negotiation at that point.* Understanding this is a clue to the likely missed opportunities for joint gains in other negotiation settings as well: when the various pressures can combine to lead to such apparent misreading of the possibilities on *one's own* side, let alone the opposing side, it becomes more understandable why so many disputes drag on or escalate despite, from the point of view of outside observers, available joint gains.

To shift focus, I want to bring in briefly three other negotiations that provide variations on the intra-team conflict issue. Let's turn first to Camp David I in 1978. On this occasion, President Carter and his mediation team helped Israel and Egypt successfully reach an agreement trading Israeli military withdrawal from the Sinai for Egyptian recognition of Israel. During the mediation Carter grew extremely frustrated with Israeli Prime Minister Begin, primarily over his refusal to remove Israeli settlements from the Sinai. Though both parties had made clear that they wanted an agreement, and though all other major issues had been resolved, Begin had made his position on settlements clear long before the parties began the mediation, and Egyptian President Sadat had made clear that keeping the settlements in the Sinai was a deal breaker. Begin was not alone in the Israeli party in his position, but several important members of his team gave signals that they were more flexible. Thus, one tactic the mediators employed was to support Aharon Barak (then the Attorney General), Ezer Weizman (then defense minister), and Moshe Dayan (then foreign minister) in their efforts in dealing with Begin. Ariel Sharon (then minister of agriculture and not present at Camp David) was enlisted by the Israelis to give Begin further encouragement to remove the settlements, and shortly thereafter Begin found a political path to a breakthrough.

At Camp David II, in 2000, President Clinton and his mediation team saw an analogous difference within the Palestinian team, though not limited to a single issue. Most of the Palestinian negotiating stances, particularly those expressed by Chairman Arafat, showed little flexibility, but conversation with Mohammed Dahlan, chief of security in Gaza, suggested some possibilities. Accordingly Clinton's team appealed to Dahlan to influence Arafat. This had no discernible effect, and after the mediation (which of course produced no agreement) Dahlan and others expressed resentment at the mediator's "interference" with internal team matters. As a leading Palestinian negotiator put it, "There were certain elements in Palestinian politics and Arab politics that went to the Americans and led them to believe that if you present certain ideas, the Palestinians will accept. And the Americans without even bothering to ask those of us who are relevant chose to believe that—especially that Arafat would be satisfied with an office in the Old City—and the Americans locked on this and believed it would be doable. And those of us who said it would not fly became extremists."[4]

A different example of problems caused by intra-team differences also occurred at Camp David II. Yasser Arafat repeated often during the mediation that Palestinian sovereignty over the Temple Mount in Jerusalem was non negotiable. Most memorably he said to Clinton: "I'll send you an invitation to my funeral after my assassination if you insist on this point (negotiability of sovereignty)."[5] More, he never said anything inconsistent with this. Meanwhile, however, several of his top negotiators were, in the finest "problem-solving" tradition, working with Israelis and Americans on various compromises, trying to divide the concept of sovereignty into sharable pieces. One effect of this work by Palestinians, who never suggested what Arafat would do with their work product or even that he approved their doing it, was that the Israelis and the Americans inferred that there was room on the Palestinian side for compromise. But, at the end of the negotiation, Arafat held to his opening "red line:" no compromise. These "mixed signals" from the Palestinian side were part of the stimulus for U.S. and Israeli anger aimed at Arafat during and after the negotiation.

Oslo (1993) presented a different kind of intra-team conflict, one that might be called serial conflict. The Israelis began the process by allowing two academics to meet in secret with high level Palestinians. When those discussions went well, the Israelis substituted a government official (Uri Savir) for the academics, and his redlines differed somewhat from those of the academics. As those discussions went well, the Israelis added an experienced international lawyer (Yoel Singer), but both his style and his frame of reference were radically different from Savir's and sent very different messages to the Palestinians. And, finally, the Israeli foreign minister entered the picture. This left the Palestinians with the task of interpreting each change. Though each new Israeli negotiator represented a step up the bureaucratic and status ladder and thus appealed to the Palestinian need to be taken seriously, the shift in content and tone with each move often left the Palestinians perplexed, skeptical, and worried that they were being toyed with. It also gave ammunition to those on the Palestinian side who interpreted the shifting red lines as evidence that Israel was not serious.

Taking these examples together, one can make the following hypotheses:

- When negotiations are undertaken by teams, conflict within the teams is almost inevitable. Though it is not inevitable that these conflicts will be apparent to the other side, it is common enough that each side, and each mediator, will be on the lookout for such intra-team differences and work to exploit them.

- Conflict within a negotiating team will have many causes, but there will be two probable patterns: there will be those inclined to concilia-tory tactics versus those inclined toward hardnosed tactics; there will be those who interpret moves on the other side as conciliatory and those who interpret the same moves as meaningless or misleading.

- Intra-team conflict will confuse the other side. Are the hints of con-ciliation a representation of the "real intent" of the team, or just the quirks of one member? Are they trial balloons, or a sign that the leader is not really in control? Do the differences represent a battle within the team over what strategy to follow or what its "redlines" should be? Or is one set of messages being sent to make another set look better? (Good cop/bad cop.) Is the leader letting various messages go out as a way to kill time, perhaps waiting until a deadline comes nearer? Or should the messages be read as the acts of semi-autonomous negotia-tors each carrying out his own idea of a good agreement, perhaps appeasing his own constituency outside the negotiating process?

- This confusion can also be a source of intra-team conflict for the other side: those inclined toward conciliation will want to provide positive responses to signs of conciliation from the first side, while those in-clined toward more aggressive negotiating will want to ignore those signs; those inclined to see the first side as a confederation of more or less autonomous actors will want to support those who appear more favorably disposed, while those inclined to see the first side as a coher-ent team will see any schism as part of a threatening plan.

- Intra-team conflict, when known by the other side, can be the basis for a cross-team alliance which then works at some tension with the be-tween-team dynamics.

- The example of Camp David II suggests that a team of mediators be-haves precisely as a team of negotiators: intra-mediation team conflict produces confusion among the negotiators, and intra-negotiation team conflict produces the same confusions and responses from mediators as it does from negotiators.

In sum, when the negotiating or the mediating is done by a team, it is rare that any team speaks with only one voice. The role of such differences will of course vary in different negotiations, but any analysis of a team-conducted negotiation must take account of this dimension of conflict.

Endnotes

[1] Omar M. Dajani, *Surviving Opportunities*, *in* HOW ISRAELIS AND PALESTINIANS NEGOTIATE 72 (Tamara Wittes ed., 2005).

[2] *See* John Wade, *Bargaining in the Shadow of the Tribe*, Chapter 55 in this volume, for a discussion of the risks run by spokespersons even in negotiations that are less fraught.

[3] David Matz, *Why Did Taba End?*, 10 PALESTINE-ISRAEL JOURNAL (2003).

[4] Saeb Erekat quoted in Dajani, *supra* note 1, at 72.

[5] GILEAD SHER, JUST BEYOND REACH 141 (2006).

ಛ 64 ಞ

Internal Conflicts of the Team

Howard S. Bellman

Editors' Note: *The third chapter in our trilogy on teams discusses how, as negotiator or mediator, you may find yourself in a complex dispute in which one of the parties appears to have substantial conflicts within its team. Bellman shows why these conflicts, when they are not amenable to the same techniques the mediator would use for inter-party conflicts, may be resolved by developing an internal mediator within the conflicted team.*

Often the crucial challenges to settlement, and therefore to the mediator, are not between the recognized parties, but within one or more of the parties' teams, or coalitions. Even where there are only two parties to negotiations, a plaintiff and a defendant, or a union and an employer, for example, factions with diverse interests may appear and represent an impediment to resolution. Where there are multiple parties, as in an environmental conflict, some of them may decide to form a coalition of generally like-minded entities, only to find that there are some important differences among them when it comes to specifying settlement terms. This suggests that a mediator will need particular strategies and techniques to address such "internal" challenges.

Here are some very common examples:

- A union represents primary and secondary teachers and art and music specialists. These members have markedly diverse work-days with quite different pupils and schedules and substantive responsibilities. The union may present the interests of all of these teachers and learn that the employer can not be expected to address all of them with improvements due to resource limitations. The union needs to reexamine its aspirations, and the employer needs the union to succeed in that respect so that a settlement may be possible.

- A manufacturing firm is in a contract dispute with a supplier. The firm is represented by individuals from its production and sales departments and a ranking executive with over-all authority. In negotiations to settle pending litigation between the firm and the supplier the sales representatives express far more eagerness to agree with the supplier than the production representatives, as the two departments reflect the desire to remain in the marketplace and the desire to control costs, respectively. The firm must overcome these conflicts and the supplier is eager for them to do so.

- A number of environmental advocacy organizations present themselves as a coalition in negotiations over the remediation and restoration of a contaminated river. When the positions of regulating government agencies and the resources of the responsible industrial parties are revealed it appears that some choices may be necessary between remediation and restoration measures, and between long-term strategies and those that will improve the river in the relative short-run. These differences reflect diverse priorities among the advocacy organizations and must be resolved for settlement, which all of the parties desire, to occur. The agencies and the industrial firms see this internal conflict as consuming valuable time and funds.

No seasoned mediator would find any of the above at all unusual. They are the factional and "personality" conflicts that often explain why mediation has been requested. Of course, they may be seen as indications of inadequate preparation when they are foreseeable. But whether that is the case or not, they represent challenges to the mediator like any other impediment to settlement. But do they require any strategies other than those applied between and among the recognized parties? Is it not enough to simply interpret, translate, instruct, reality-test, examine options, etc, as if the conflict were "external?"

In fact, these familiar mediator tasks and responsibilities do continue to be needed. However, in this "internal" setting, it may be necessary to apply them without the invaluable tactic of the caucus. The mediator should be reluctant to treat the union or the firm, or even the coalition, in a manner that questions its essential assertion of solidarity, or implies that it may not be a well managed entity. There is an embarrassment implicit in this situation that should be addressed sensitively, and probably not by any suggestion that it is substantially the same as the differences among the parties. Divide-and-conquer may be a strategy on the other side of the table of which the factions should be reminded, but it is risky business for the mediator to seem willing to play the factions against one another.

When the mediator is required to address these internal disputes in the presence of all factions, she may remind the strained coalition of the analysis that caused it to form in the first place, i.e., the realities of unequal bargaining power, the politics of a united front, the efficiencies of integrated operations. Perhaps this is just another example of reality-testing. But framed as a reminder of the team's previous analysis, rather than as a revealed flaw in its position, it is less likely to embarrass; and it may yield internal discussions that were needed earlier, but overlooked. As a result, disparate priorities among the negotiating team members may be reexamined and reconciled by, for example, timing settlement terms to provide for a greater array of improvements over a longer period of time so as to control costs.

Another challenge to the mediator in these situations may be continuing to appear impartial in the external negotiations, while providing a near-consultancy to a fractionated party. [Mayer, *Allies*] This assistance, while dedicated to the settlement that all of the parties have engaged the mediator to achieve, may be misunderstood by those who only see a disproportionate amount of attention to another party. It may seem necessary to advise the other parties that settlement prospects seem challenged by internal disagreements. However, that may be nearly impossible without disclosing entrusted confidences. After all, the solidarity that has become problematic was probably a material consideration in all of the parties' highly important strategy calculations. If that solidarity flags, will the union be able to strike successfully, or will the advocacy coalition be able to fund litigation?

On the other hand, a party may learn from the mediator that the party is itself at risk if another's internal disputes are not resolved, and the mediator can assist in that analysis. When that is the case, the party may see that it is in its own interest to revise its proposals to overcome the internal conflicts across the table. The mediator may suggest that presenting such revisions as her own ideas may finesse sensitivities among the factions. Or the mediator, understanding the willingness of the other party to revise, may suggest that the fractionated party propose the revisions. These are useful mediator strategies, but they do not overcome the challenge of the factional dispute that may not be disclosed across the table.

Perhaps, in the final analysis, there is no better strategy than the straightforward assertion that if internal disagreements cannot be disclosed, help with those disagreements will be difficult to elicit; and that if internal disagreements continue to interfere with external discussions, the other party, who may infer their existence anyway, will have no sensible choice but pursue its interests in some other manner.

Another tactic may be worth considering. Sometimes, there is a particular level of trust between the mediator and an individual member of the troubled team or coalition. This may have been achieved during the course of the negotiations at hand, or in past cases. In fact, the troubled team may view this as a valuable factor in the mediation process. In such cases, private conversations between the mediator and that individual may not cause worry or suspicion, and allow the mediator to coach that individual's mediation among her teammates. This approach is particularly promising when the team member, as is not unusual, has a certain inclination to mediate as a general matter. The problem solving capacity of mediation and related methods are not unrecognized within organizations, and individuals with such skills are frequently to be found on negotiating teams.

Where an appropriate individual can be found this strategy of finding an "internal mediator" within the strained coalition may sidestep the impediments of losing the caucus option and appearing to give too much attention to a particular party. Two cautions seem in order. Protecting this individual from being misunderstood by teammates or from being perceived as less than team devoted to his team is a responsibility that he and the mediator should take seriously. Of course, it is not inconceivable that the mediator may be "taken in" by this individual, who may perceive some advantages not intended by the mediator.

To a seasoned mediator it seems too obvious to declare that straight talk, allowed by earned trust and presented with sensitivity, is the mediator's best strategy, whether the challenge at hand is a factional rift or otherwise. When that strategy is underway the need for special tactics for particular situations seems secondary. When that strategy is inhibited by the "politics" within a party, and especially when an internal rift must be confronted early in negotiations, before the mediator has achieved the full confidence of all other participants, the possibility of an "internal mediator" should be considered.

∽ 65 ∾

Negotiation, One Tool Among Many

Jayne Seminare Docherty

Editors' Note: *When setting up for a negotiation, let alone actually in one, it's all too easy to focus on the numerous tasks immediately in front of you. Docherty argues that for many negotiations, the key to unlocking the potential is to think more broadly about how to achieve the overall objectives. What tools are available to supplement the obvious one of sitting down with your counterparts? Should some of these, perhaps, come first? Should some be used simultaneously with negotiation? And should you plan to use still other "away from the table" tools to sustain your agreement?*

Why Negotiation Alone Is Not Enough

In many situations, managing the processes of establishing a bargaining range, reconnoitering the range, and precipitating the decision crisis are no longer sufficient skills for success in negotiation. Negotiators who artificially isolate the process of negotiation from the conflict dynamics that make it necessary are likely to succeed only in carefully defined and delimited dispute domains.[1] [Miller & Dingwall, *Theater*; Docherty, *Models*] Practically speaking, professional negotiators are now expected to understand other conflict intervention tools that can be used to prepare for, support, and sustain a negotiation process. Negotiators may require the services of one or more conflict specialists who can "assist disputants in engaging in conflict throughout its entire course rather than focusing primarily on how to help them move toward resolution." [Mayer, *Allies*]

Negotiators look to other conflict specialists for answers to questions such as: what is adequate informed consent, and how is it shaped by larger political realities? [Wade, *Tribe*] How can we ascertain whether negotiators at the table have gained adequate informed consent from those they represent? [Wade, *Tribe*; Nolan-Haley, *Informed Consent*; Docherty & Caton Campbell, *Agency*] What tools can facilitators use to help parties negotiate their own internal conflicts so that they may participate in negotiations more effectively? [Bellman, *Team Conflicts*] How can we manage the conflicts within negotiation teams? [Sally & O'Connor, *Teams*; Matz, *Team Miscommunication*] When and how can we use allies to help the parties during negotiation? [Mayer, *Allies*] How can we ensure that a negotiated agreement is durable, sustainable, and fair to future generations and other parties not at the table?[2] [Wade-Benzoni, *Future*; Wade & Honeyman, *Lasting Agreement*] How can we craft agreements that are flexible enough to survive the vagaries of a changing political, social, and economic environment? [Moffit, *Contingent Agreements*]

This chapter will identify some of the specific challenges negotiators may face before, during, and after a negotiation, briefly describe other conflict resolution or conflict transformation practices that can be used to support negotiation, and conclude with some general guidelines and practical lessons for mixing negotiation and other conflict processes.

Challenges Before Negotiations Begin

Elsewhere, I have summarized the following prerequisites for negotiation:

- The parties must have a mutually acknowledged relationship.
- The parties must agree that there is a conflict or dispute.
- They must agree that the conflict or dispute is amenable to negotiation.
- Each party must also recognize the other(s) as legitimate negotiation partners.

It also helps greatly if:

- The parties agree about those parts of their context that are most relevant to their negotiations.
- The parties share tacit rules, norms, and expectations about how the negotiation will proceed.[3]

Many things can get in the way of achieving these requirements. For reasons of space, and because other chapters in this book discuss many of these problems in detail, I will simply list here a few of the most common problems.

- The parties do not recognize one another. [Blum & Mnookin, *Not Negotiating*; Bingham, *Avoiding Negotiating*]
- Is this really a conflict? [Morash, *Nonevents*]
- The parties are fighting different battles or playing different games. [Caton Campbell & Docherty, *Framing*]
- The table is uneven or unattractive to some parties. [Bernard, *Powerlessness*]
- Are we negotiating yet? [Goh, *Errors*]

Challenges During Negotiations

Getting to the table does not end the challenges. Many of the previous problems continue to manifest even after the parties get to the table. In addition, other problems can arise. The following list is by no means exhaustive.

- Negotiating through agents.
- Not all of the parties are at the table.
- The parties are forum shopping.
- Implementing the agreement will require resources from others.
- Sustaining an agreement will require political legitimacy.

Challenges After Negotiations Conclude

Concluding a negotiation does not necessarily make the underlying conflict disappear. Difficulties that can arise after negotiations include the following.

- There is no readily available enforcement mechanism or institution.
- The agreement requires ongoing monitoring and evaluation.
- Changes in circumstance create a need to revisit the agreement.

Tools That Can Help

What kinds of tools can help us address these problems? What follows are some very brief descriptions of particular types of interventions or activities. Using these tools requires careful attention to coordination with the negotiation process, and that is a subject too large for this chapter.[4]

Capacity Strengthening

This refers most commonly to the work of non-governmental organizations (NGOs) that work with community members to increase the skills and understanding of individuals, organizations, and institutions to improve their ability to respond to conflicts. The approach relies upon the existence of key members of the community, whether individuals or institutions, who can act as "norm entrepreneurs"[5] to foster the constructive handling of a conflict. [Hauss, *Captive Audience*] Capacity strengthening activities can include *training* and *education* for negotiators so that they can participate in the negotiation process effectively. [Druckman, *Marathon Exercise*] Simply getting to the table is not enough to ensure participation (e.g. after the United Nations mandated that women be included in peace negotiations, we found that Somali warlords were bringing their girlfriends to sit in the room). Education, training, and the cultivation of negotiation skills among women were necessary to give the mandate its desired effect. Capacity strengthening is particularly useful when a low power party is reluctant to come to the table, out of fear they cannot hold their own in the negotiation. However, capacity strengthening is not only for the "weaker" parties. Jointly training all parties in negotiation skills prior to negotiation can help them develop a common approach to negotiation while also improving relationships among the parties.

Developing leadership for the "radical center"[6] can also be a goal of capacity strengthening. In polarized or intractable conflicts,[7] or in conflicts that are prone to polarization, there is often a "moderate middle" group of people open to working together on a problem. They are usually not very organized; it is difficult to whip up passion for moderation and compromise! Capacity strengthening activities with this group can shift the conflict by identifying and empowering parties who are prepared to negotiate and/or put pressure on leaders to moderate their stance and enter into negotiations.

Giving all of the parties involved in a conflict better training in *conflict analysis skills* can also help them decide when to negotiate and when to pursue other options. I have found that a one day training in conflict analysis, delivered to community leaders from all sectors, can transform their understanding of ongoing conflicts, highlight those that can be negotiated, and create positive relationships that support peaceful management of conflicts when they arise.

Conciliation

Long-term, intractable conflicts can create terrible traumas born out of direct violence or long-term injustices. [Coleman, et al., *Dynamical*] Negotiations that are framed in completely rational terms ignore the realities of these old wounds and imperil their own success.[8] Strictly defined, conciliation involves "steps taken by a third party to reduce hostility, lower tension, correct misperceptions, improve communication, and create a favorable climate for negotiation."[9] However, conciliation activities can also include programs that help the parties understand the sources of their trauma so that they can begin a journey of healing that can eventually include making peace with those seen as the source of their trauma.[10] Many practitioners think of conciliation as something that precedes negotiation. We now know, however, that the path of healing is non-linear and that members of a group in a conflict travel the path at different rates. If we had to wait for everyone to be ready to negotiate, we would never be able to negotiate an end to civil violence or long-term conflicts involving issues of structural violence. Furthermore, events outside of the negotiation process can trigger trauma responses in the negotiators and disrupt the negotiations.

It is more useful to see conciliation as a process that accompanies negotiation from the pre-negotiation through the post-negotiation implementation stages. Conciliation activities make room for negotiation, but they may also need to be worked into the negotiation process itself, and they may need to be part of the negotiated solution.[11] This is particularly true when agents are negotiating on be- half of traumatized parties who must then ratify the negotiated agreement. Conciliation is not something that agents can do on behalf of others. The negotia- tors may experience significant personal transformation, and develop good relationships with their counterparts from the other parties. If, however, they emerge from that process announcing to their constituents that peace has come and old wounds have been healed, the people will likely reject their claims and the negotiated agreement.

Conflict Assessment

"A conflict assessment is an information-gathering exercise that produces recom- mendations regarding
- who has a stake in a conflict or proposed consensus building effort;
- what issues are important to those stakeholders;
- whether or not it makes sense to proceed, given the institutions, financial, and other constraints; and
- if so, under what circumstances key parties will agree to participate."[12]

Conflict assessments are critically important for framing a negotiation process that actually addresses complex conflicts. But who should do the assessment, and how should it be done? There are, in fact, different ways to approach this task, and the approach should be appropriate to the context.

A conflict assessment can be done by a hired, neutral outside party, or, in some cases, it can be done by a trusted team of insiders. (See Listening Projects below.) An assessment can be organized in ways that focus primarily on creating an issues matrix for all of the parties.[13] Or, in cases where the conflict is more diffuse and cultural issues are a significant factor, an assessment can use an ethnographic approach to map divergent worldviews as well as issues.[14] Modified approaches to conflict assessment can be used by the negotiators during the negotiation process in order to determine how their constituents and other members of the public are viewing the conflict, the negotiation process, and potential agreements. (See Public Opinion Polling below.)

Confrontation

Not all conflicts are ready for negotiation, but we can help make them ready through other activities, including encouraging or engaging in confrontation. "We often need to help raise the conflict, knowing that this may genuinely exacerbate relationships or the smooth functioning of a group.... Because otherwise we will not be genuinely addressing people's needs; we will instead be contributing to the suppression of issues that will come back in a more serious way later or contribut- ing to the ongoing repression of vulnerable individuals or groups."[15] [Mayer, Allies] This view is based in an understanding that latent conflicts may need to be esca- lated before they are 'ripe' for resolution; and low power parties may need to confront high power parties in order to make the conflict visible.[16] The challenge is to find ways to confront others that do not simultaneously poison relationships, thereby making it more difficult to enter into negotiations. Put bluntly, if you eventually want to get to the negotiation table, it is best not to bash your oppo- nent over the head, assault her identity, demean her, or back her into a corner where fighting is the only option she can see.[17] Allies and conflict coaches can help parties engage in confrontation in ways that leave open the option for negotiation.

Dialogue Processes

Dialogue is a much used and much misused term in the conflict resolution field. Rather than try to catalogue all of the ways people have used dialogue as a conflict intervention, I will just note some different strategies for using 'something called dialogue' and let the reader sort through the different approaches to dialogue. In my opinion, it is helpful to distinguish dialogue from negotiation by saying that dialogues are not expected to result in a negotiated agreement. This differs from the definition used by others in the field. However, I have seen too many instances where participants in a dialogue process had different expectations. Some thought they were negotiating while others thought they were just exploring ideas. If parties are negotiating, they should be clear that they are negotiating. If they are engaging in dialogue in order to build relationships, dispel stereotypes, explore issues and problems in an open manner, and enrich participants' understanding of a difficult situation, that should also be made clear. Dialogue can be used before negotiation to build relationships and a shared understanding of a problem. Dialogue can also be used during negotiation as a way to explore issues with constituents, the general public, or other relevant actors.

Focus Groups

Negotiators can use focus groups to gather input for the negotiation process, determine whether constituents support negotiation, or gather responses to a possible agreement. Used this way, the focus groups are made up of individuals from the same party. By contrast, focus groups involving participants from different stakeholder groups can be used to create a space for dialogue that is informal, natural, and non-threatening. I have used focus groups in this way for conflict assessment of largely latent and non-polarized conflicts, and the experience of hearing others from different groups during my research created a natural impetus for ongoing dialogue groups. Used during negotiation, mixed-party focus groups can also help those not at the table experience some of the relationship building and conciliation that is happening at the table.

Listening Projects

A listening project is more open-ended than most conflict assessments. Rather than craft interview questions that guide respondents to articulate their positions, interests, and needs, a listening project asks respondents more general questions. The result is a data set that can be used to discern issues and conflicts that are not readily apparent at the outset. Listening projects can actually be designed and conducted by the parties themselves, usually with assistance from a research coach. This works particularly well when the questions are framed creatively and in an appreciative manner so that respondents can talk about what is going well and not just what is wrong in a situation. Negotiators can work together in teams to conduct a listening project during a negotiation. This allows them to hear from constituents and others not at the table, and can help keep them grounded in the realities of those who will need to embrace their agreement.

Media Campaigns

Feelings about the media vary wildly among parties in a conflict or a negotiation. Parties often speak of the media as either an asset to be captured and used to one's own advantage, or the tool of the other side and an instigator of unnecessary trouble. "Those involved in consensus building... have mixed feelings about the press. Often, mediators and facilitators seek to avoid press coverage. They worry about inaccurate or biased reporting and the possibility that a news story will inflame an already heated debate."[18] Yet, mediators and negotiators know that news coverage can help a process, too. Except in the shortest of the short-term, there is no avoiding the media, so the key is learning to work with and manage media relationships, so that media coverage advances the negotiation process. How this is done will depend in large measure on the stage of the conflict. Prior to convening a negotiation, media coverage can be used to help educate people about the conflict, the importance of addressing it, and the challenges facing anyone trying to negotiate in this situation. During negotiations, media coverage can keep the public informed about the process, but it is best to negotiate among the parties how they will *jointly* release information to the press. The media can also help publicize events where the negotiators are trying to gather information and input from others. And the media can help prepare the general public for the agreement that is likely to emerge from negotiations. At the end of a process, particularly if the negotiations are only one step in addressing a more complicated conflict, it is critically important that the press not overplay or oversell the agreement. Having the media imply that peace has just broken out does not set the stage for realistic approaches to implementing the agreement. Here, it is particularly helpful to develop an ongoing relationship with the media so that they will continue to take an interest in the implementation phase of the process.

Monitoring, Evaluation and Implementation Committees

Getting agreement may only be the beginning of a larger conflict resolution process. Provisions must be made for actually implementing the agreement. This is the time for negotiators to hand the process off to those who take care of the operational side of things. In many cases, this means the parties must replace policy-level personnel with staff-level personnel. Within each party, the handoff needs to be made clearly; and having an ongoing *implementation working group* or a *governing entity* to manage implementation of an agreement helps the parties stay engaged.[19] These committees or groups should also be tasked with monitoring and evaluating the agreement. It is their job to alert policy personnel when or if it is necessary to reconvene negotiations.

Practical Cooperation Projects

In protracted, intractable conflicts third party intervenors often begin with dialogue processes rather than negotiations. These dialogues may lead to negotiation, or the parties may opt to move to shared action on experimental projects rather than formal negotiations. This can work particularly well when one of the big issues is lack of knowledge. For example, ranchers, environmentalists, and federal agency personnel all committed to making ecosystem management a reality cannot easily negotiate the protocols for ecosystem management, because no one is completely sure what ecosystem management will look like on the ground. So, they agree to set aside a certain area of land, form a working group to manage it for five years using ecosystem management principles (which are being defined as they work), and see what happens. In this case, all they negotiated up front was the parcel of land, the makeup of the teams, some operating guidelines, and the mechanisms for capturing the lessons learned. The rest of the project involves a great many small negotiations. But the key here is the knowledge gained from the project, which will create the basis for a larger policy negotiation. Equipping the working group participants with good negotiation skills will facilitate the project. Knowing when to move from the action project to the policy level negotiation is also important.

Shuttle Diplomacy and Back-Channel Negotiations

Prior to direct negotiation, shuttle diplomacy and back-channel negotiations can be used to promote conciliation, build relationships, and shape an agenda. During negotiations, these same techniques can be used to check in with parties who can't or won't come to the table. These activities can also be used to negotiate with institutions and agencies that will have responsibility for implementing the agreement.

Visioning Processes
Visioning is "a process whereby community members imagine their desired future and set goals for achieving that future. Visioning emphasizes active citizen participation, long-term planning, imagination, a sense of possibility, and common ground."[20] This definition is taken from a resource on resolving public conflicts, but the same approach can be adapted to any level of conflict from interpersonal to organizational to national. Negotiators who are stuck in their bargaining can engage in visioning in order to generate new ideas and possibilities. [Brown, *Creativity*] They can also decide to include a wider audience in the visioning process, which creates buy-in for the negotiation and prepares constituents for change.

How to Make This Work
The keys to mixing negotiation and other processes for handling complex conflicts are ongoing analysis and strategic planning. You need to know where you are in a conflict and what tools will help the parties move to a better place. This requires overall process planning, an understanding of different process options, and a willingness to enlist the help of others.[21] When mixing negotiation with other conflict resolution methods, I find it helpful to use the following general techniques.

Differentiate Processes Clearly
The "script" of negotiation limits the interaction among the parties as they attempt to move negotiation through the requisite phases. Other processes can open up the interactions among participants. However, it is always helpful to be clear with participants when they move from negotiating to other activities. I find that negotiators get the most out of processes such as visioning, brainstorming, dialogue and information gathering when we *mark* the move from one process to another. It is particularly important to declare the other processes "bargaining free zones"—nothing said here will be taken as an offer and no deals will be struck in this space at this time. Moving into a different space with different interaction rules can be facilitated by: moving to another physical location or rearranging the furniture; changing from formal to casual dress; engaging a different facilitator; inviting other participants; or using alternative modes of information processing such as art or drama or storytelling. [LeBaron & Honeyman, *Arts*]

Educate the Parties About Conflict and Conflict Resolution Processes
Facilitators can help negotiators by educating them. Help them understand how to conduct a conflict assessment, how to think analytically about the conflict from multiple perspectives, and how to take the long view. Also, help them make the move from negotiation to other processes and back again by describing the differences between negotiation and visioning and focus groups and conflict assessments. Remind them of the different behavioral and outcome expectations as they move from one process to another.

Change Roles
When negotiators discover they need new information or when they decide they need to test possibilities with constituencies, they may decide to use techniques such as focus groups or listening projects or visioning processes. When doing this, it is helpful if they form themselves into a single team and think of themselves as a learning organization. Instead of trying to gather information to bolster their positions, they can generate a list of questions they *all* need to have answered in order to craft a good agreement. Then they can gather data and analyze it together. Again, it is important to symbolically remind negotiators of the changes as they move from advocates to learning team and back again.

Concluding Thoughts

The chapters in this book offer numerous insights into managing the phases and stages of a negotiation, particularly when we are confronted with a complex reality, difficult problems and unclear dispute domains. Learning to *use well* the multiple approaches to conflict is the work of a lifetime. But understanding the need to use a variety of processes is, at least, a first step on the journey to becoming a well rounded conflict specialist.

Endnotes

[1] "Dispute domains consist of the dominant orientations to the conflict issues at hand in different settings, the conflict resolution options that participants see as available in the settings, and the typical ways that participants interact with each other." In Gale Miller & Robert Dingwall, *When the Play's in the Wrong Theater*, Chapter 6 in this volume; *see also* Jayne Seminare Docherty, *The Unseen Models in our Minds*, Chapter 2 in this volume (rule sets that delimit negotiation in different professional contexts).

[2] JAYNE SEMINARE DOCHERTY, THE LITTLE BOOK OF STRATEGIC NEGOTIATION: NEGOTIATING DURING TURBULENT TIMES (2005).

[3] *Id.* at 20-21.

[4] For further information, *see, e.g.,* CONSENSUS BUILDING HANDBOOK: A COMPREHENSIVE GUIDE TO REACHING AGREEMENT (Lawrence Susskind, et al. eds., 1999); SIMON FISHER, ET AL., WORKING WITH CONFLICT: SKILLS AND STRATEGIES FOR ACTION (2000); LISA SCHIRCH, THE LITTLE BOOK OF STRATEGIC PEACEBUILDING (2004).

[5] *See generally* Christine Ingebritsen, *Norm Entrepreneurs: Scandinavia's Role in World Politics,* 37 COOPERATION & CONFLICT 11 (2002); Lesley Wexler, *The International Deployment of Shame, Second-Best Responses, and Norm Entrepreneurship: The Campaign to Ban Landmines and the Landmine Ban Treaty,* 20 ARIZONA JOURNAL OF INTERNATIONAL & COMPARATIVE LAW 561 (2003).

[6] For an example of the "radical center" in action, *see* Quivira Coalition, *at* http://www.quviracoalition.org (last visited Mar. 6, 2006).

[7] "[I]ntractable conflicts are those that lie at the frontier of the field—the conflicts that stubbornly seem to elude resolution, even when the best available techniques are applied." Beyond Intractability *What Are Intractable Conflicts? at* http://www.beyondintractability.org/essay/meaning_intractability. For a knowledge base dedicated to capturing lessons for dealing with intractable conflicts, *see* Beyond Intractability, *at* http://www.beyondintractability.org/about/overview.jsp (last visited Mar. 6, 2006).

[8] JOHN FORESTER, *On Not Leaving Your Pain at the Door: Political Deliberation, Critical Pragmatism, and Traumatic Histories,* in THE DELIBERATIVE PRACTITIONER: ENCOURAGING PARTICIPATORY PLANNING PROCESSES (1999).

[9] E. FRANKLIN DUKES, RESOLVING PUBLIC CONFLICT: TRANSFORMING COMMUNITY AND GOVERNANCE 188 (1996).

[10] CAROLYN YODER, THE LITTLE BOOK OF TRAUMA HEALING: WHEN VIOLENCE STRIKES AND COMMUNITY SECURITY IS THREATENED (2006).

[11] Truth and Reconciliation Commissions are the most well known processes for achieving this goal. They come in many forms and their effectiveness is still under review.

[12] Lawrence Susskind & Jennifer Thomas-Larmer, *Conducting a Conflict Assessment,* in CONSENSUS BUILDING HANDBOOK, *supra* note 4.

[13] *See id.* at 118.

[14] *See* FISHER, ET AL., *supra* note 4.

[15] BERNARD MAYER, BEYOND NEUTRALITY: CONFRONTING THE CRISIS IN CONFLICT RESOLUTION 119-20 (2004).

[16] *See* ADAM CURLE, MAKING PEACE (1971); JOHN PAUL LEDERACH, BUILDING PEACE: SUSTAINABLE RECONCILIATION IN DIVIDED SOCIETIES (1998).

[17] Hedley Abernethy & Aaron Kishbaugh, Reclaiming Relationship (2005), (unpublished paper) (on file with authors).

[18] James E. Kunde, *Dealing with the Press,* in CONSENSUS BUILDING HANDBOOK, *supra* note 4, at 435-62.

[19] William R. Potapchuk & Jarle Crocker, *Implementing Consensus-Based Agreement,* in CONSENSUS BUILDING HANDBOOK, *supra* note 6 at 527-55.

[20] Dukes, *supra* note 9, at 195.

[21] Susan Carpenter, *Choosing Appropriate Consensus Building Techniques and Strategies,* in CONSENSUS BUILDING HANDBOOK, *supra* note 4, at 61-98; David A. Strauss, *Designing a Consensus Building Process Using a Graphic Road Map,* in CONSENSUS BUILDING HANDBOOK, *supra* note 4, at 137-68.

❦ 66 ❧

The Uses of Mediation

Lela P. Love & Joseph B. Stulberg

Editors' Note: How's your negotiation going? Is it possible you need a mediator? This chapter, the first of our mediation trilogy, uses three different case studies to show why and when mediation can help negotiators reach an agreement. It explains the different types of mediation goals, and how each of those goals can affect the process. This should be read in conjunction with Honeyman on Understanding Mediators and Abramson on the Culturally Suitable Mediator.

Imagine a time you negotiated with someone and it ended in an impasse. You walked away from the discussion even though you sensed that a negotiated outcome was in your best interests. Perhaps you were called a name or accused of something you did not do. Maybe an insulting offer was made. You may have been tired or depressed and working on a "short fuse." Perhaps it was simply too hard to establish a time to meet again with your counterpart. For whichever reason, the negotiation did not succeed. In that same scenario, something different might have happened if you had added a mediator.

Why Add a Mediator to Negotiations?

Negotiations are neither self-generating nor self-sustaining. One party might want to talk, but others refuse to do so. Some talks never start—or collapse—because participants lack effective negotiating skills. Other discussions reach impasse due to misunderstandings, hostile comments or perceived rigidity. These familiar dynamics can disserve parties whose interests lie in resolving their dispute. Understandable—all too human—reasons cause negotiation melt down.

Negotiators can be trapped by other pitfalls. Sometimes parties refuse to initiate direct negotiations (or to request mediation) for fear that their counterpart would interpret that move as a sign of weakness. Some take extreme public positions to protect themselves and their reputations, but in so doing eliminate workable options. Some make inaccurate assumptions about aspects of the situation or their counterpart's motivation. Some fail to determine their priority interests. And some, because of such psychological phenomena as loss aversion or overconfidence in their own judgment, make sub-optimal decisions. [Korobkin & Guthrie, *Heuristics*]

A skilled mediator can defuse or transform these roadblocks into building blocks for movement by promoting constructive participation, minimizing misunderstandings, crystallizing significant interests, framing issues thoughtfully, urging parties to be realistic, and expanding discussion of possible outcomes. How?

What Does a Mediator Do?

A mediator is a neutral intervenor committed to assisting each negotiating party to conduct constructive conversations. She helps structure discussions. She stabilizes dialogue. She injects an attitude of hope and "going the distance." She prods participants to clarify interests, establish priorities and transform rhetoric into proposals. She develops discussion strategies that minimize misunderstandings when tensions run high. She helps parties understand one another when ill-chosen words create bitterness between them. She uses reframing and reality testing to encourage parties to examine and evaluate their assumptions and conclusions. She performs these basic tasks in order to help stakeholders enhance their collective understanding, spark creative problem-solving, and settle their controversy.

A Posture of Optimism

Former Senate Majority Leader, George Mitchell, when referring to his intervention as a mediator in Northern Ireland and the Middle East, states, "Conflicts are created and sustained by human beings. They can be ended by human beings."[1] In mediating the conflict in Northern Ireland, Mitchell describes 700 days of failure followed by one final day of success. Though he became disheartened at times, he did not give up. The mediator is the very last person to give up. Desmond Tutu, the Nobel Peace Laureate who helped negotiate the transition of South Africa from the horrors of apartheid towards black political leadership and racial dignity, concludes that: "no problem anywhere can ever again be considered to be intractable."[2] A mediator is not naïve, but she is persistently optimistic that negotiations—even difficult and stalled negotiations—can be set on course.

Most of us faced with a negotiation that is not working tend to feel that the other person involved is stubborn, selfish, uncooperative, or unreasonable. The presence of an upbeat, optimistic third person can transform the environment of a negotiation. Once the mood is changed, positive momentum can be created.

A Variety of Applications

From disputes on the Internet to controversies erupting on city streets or in school settings to cases filed in court, mediation is increasingly used to address and resolve problems. Situations in very diverse arenas—divorce, labor and employment, construction, landlord-tenant, commercial matters, public policy, and international disputes—all regularly benefit from mediation.

Consider the following:

- A single parent with teenagers moves into an apartment above an elderly couple. The teenagers make noise walking around their apartment, playing loud music and entertaining friends, sometimes late at night. When the downstairs neighbors complain to the teenagers, they respond with crude comments. The elderly couple bangs a broom against the ceiling to signal that the sounds should stop, but this results in the volume increasing. When one of the downstairs neighbors goes upstairs to try to talk with the parent, no one answers the door despite the presence of sounds in the apartment. Vigorous knocking on the door results in a door panel breaking. The upstairs neighbor demands money to replace the door. When the neighbors do talk, conversation results in angry accusations. How will the spiral stop?

- Cheryl is an associate in a large law firm. An African American, she is the only lawyer in the group who is not Caucasian. When other office attorneys socialize, gossip and chat in the corridors, she feels excluded and isolated. She notices that she is not given training opportunities that others are offered and she is not called on in meetings as frequently as others. After her supervising attorney tells her that "B+ work is ok," when an assignment is slightly late, Cheryl believes that she is being set up to fail. When she raises any of these issues, she is given an unsatisfactory explanation. Is her only option to file a racial discrimination complaint against her employer?

- In an Eastern European town, members of the Roma (gypsy) community regularly go through the town dump to scavenge for useable material that has been discarded by others. Various ethnic and religious groups in the town are upset because such scavenging results in the garbage being strewn in disarray, thereby making it impossible for recycling efforts to succeed. Feelings of distrust, hostility, and discrimination create a tinderbox environment capable of exploding instantly into violence. Efforts to identify a Roma group to talk with have proven futile. Is this situation simply a "law enforcement" problem?

For each situation noted, using a mediator would be helpful. How? A short list of negotiating dynamics that result from a mediator's intervention includes:
- The presence of an energizing, yet calming, optimistic intervenor.
- A meeting site and environment that is safe, equitable, comfortable and inspiring for all participants.
- An opportunity for voices to be heard in a respectful way.
- A discussion format and agenda that guides participants to "tell their story" and organizes discussion topics in a clear, targeted manner.
- Procedural and communication tools designed to enhance understanding and movement. Examples of such tools include separate meetings (caucuses) and active listening or reframing.

It is easy to envision how a mediator's attentive presence at a comfortable meeting site would enhance communications between the upstairs and downstairs neighbors. In the second scenario, the mediator transforms an adversarial contest over allegations of racial or gender discrimination into a constructive negotiation discussion by simply and accurately identifying the negotiating issues to include social interaction at the worksite, training opportunities, professional meeting protocols, and performance standards—i.e., items about which the parties can, indeed, bargain. And a mediator's affirmative intervention in the final scenario—often by meeting separately with the various stakeholders to identify the necessary parties to a resolution and explore the concerns that must be addressed to secure stability and respect—can be the first step towards addressing differences. Sometimes such separate meetings provide a constructive "safe haven" through which persons with a history of profound conflict can communicate forcefully with one another without violence erupting.

Different Destinations and Many Paths

In one sense, mediation can be boiled down to a simple target shared by all mediators. Mediators help parties to negotiate more effectively. That often means to help parties communicate more constructively and, in many cases, reach agreements. Beyond that simple target, though, mediators have different goals and different means for achieving them.

What goals—or destinations—do different mediators and different schools of mediation have? Among the most often cited mediation goals are:

- Better understanding for each party of her own goals and interests (empowerment)
- Better understanding among parties (recognition of each other)
- Creative problem-solving and option generation
- Agreements that are durable and optimal
- Settlements acceptable to all parties

One school of mediation only embraces the first two goals (empowerment and recognition). Other mediators only target settlement—an end to the dispute. And others will include all of these goals. Here is a continuum of mediation approaches (above the line) together with a continuum of goals (below the line). The continuum roughly matches mediation approaches or schools with corresponding goals or targets. In real cases, however, it is important to note that any linear depiction is a simplification of a dynamic and complex process.

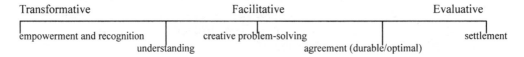

Let's examine these goals.

Empowerment and recognition means that disputing parties come away from mediation stronger in two important respects. They "experience a strengthened awareness of their own self-worth and their own ability to deal with whatever difficulties they face" and they "experience an expanded willingness to acknowledge and be responsive to" the other party.[3] These goals are closely linked to the goal of *understanding* the overall situation better. It is easy to understand how Cheryl, in the employment scenario, imagined she was being excluded. Through mediated discussion about this potentially volatile situation, she can come to realize that others in the office wanted her participation in social life, but her own frequently closed office door deflected attempts to include her. Also, it might be that Cheryl's supervisor's comment about "B+ work" was meant to lessen any pressures Cheryl felt to get things perfect. The supervisor, in turn, might come to understand the adverse impact of his remark. Each party can feel sufficiently safe in mediation to "tell their story"—a more "empowered" state than letting confusion and anger fester. And each can come to understand the other.

The mediator who has *problem-solving* as a goal hopes to engage participants in a forward looking exercise of developing options to address the concerns raised by the parties. Ideally, these options will represent creative—sometimes "out of the box"—solutions to the concerns raised. If the amount of money that a defendant will pay in a personal injury situation is an issue, the mediator might encourage the parties to determine whether there are things the defendant can do for the plaintiff in lieu of money—provide a job, insurance, housing, a vehicle, as a partial or total alternative to an immediate payment or payment over time—that will cost the defendant less and still promote the plaintiff's interests. Or, in the Roma situation described above, perhaps the parties can achieve an arrangement where needy Roma citizens can help the recycling effort while obtaining necessary items for themselves. Any such resolution would build a better relationship and a capacity to engage in future problem-solving should other issues arise.

For many mediators, *agreement* among the parties is a goal of mediation so long as agreement provisions are "reality tested" by the mediator to ensure that commitments are as durable [Wade & Honeyman, *Lasting Agreement*] and optimal as possible. For example, the upstairs and downstairs neighbors might quickly agree to the following terms: "no communication, the upstairs neighbors will wear soft-soled shoes walking around in their apartment, the teenagers will have parties only on Saturday nights, no music after 11 pm, and no banging on the ceiling." Given the parties' proximity as neighbors, some of these proposed arrangements appear implausible (*no* communication between neighbors?), even if well-meaning, so many mediators would want to test these terms for precision (what does "parties" mean?) and workability (will soft-soled shoes alone solve the problem?) and explore a solution that provides the neighbors with some method of communication and constructive interaction.

Other mediators keep a sharp focus on *settlement*—coming to a resolution with respect to contested matters, so long as the settlement is acceptable to all parties. Mediators in pursuit of this goal might use a very forceful style to achieve the goal of settlement. One scholar has described that approach as mediator "trashing" and "bashing."[4] "Trashing" means tearing apart each party's case to encourage them to put realistic numbers on the table.[5] "Bashing" means trying to get parties to move from their entry settlement offers to some mid-point.[6] Settlement-oriented mediators consider the mediation successful if the parties can reach a number they will both endorse.

How Goals are Linked to Process Design

Different mediator strategies and techniques follow from different goals.

- Will the mediator encourage active *participation by the parties*, instead of allowing the lawyer or other professional representatives to dominate the session? If the goal is empowerment and recognition or creative problem-solving, the mediator would want to maximize party participation.
- Will the mediator use the *caucus* (individual meetings with each side)—never, sometimes, or exclusively? If the goal is for the parties to have an enhanced understanding, some schools of mediation encourage no caucus at all.
- What types of *settings* and *time frames* should be employed? In a settlement approach, twenty minutes in the hallway of a courtroom might be deemed an adequate attempt at mediation by mediators who are "trashing and bashing" their way toward a settlement.

What Mediator Should You Add?

You must be clear about your goal before choosing a mediator to help you achieve it. Various benefits outlined above may not be available from all mediators. Some mediators stress stakeholder participation to generate understanding and collaboration, even when hostile responses might jeopardize settlement. Some convert controversies to a discussion of money damages only and try to help parties find an acceptable "number" in a forced march to settlement, thereby minimizing opportunities to enhance understanding and improve relationships.

In addition to inquiring into a particular mediator's approach, other questions should be given consideration. For example, should parties and their representatives select a mediator who is an "expert" in the field? Does the mediator's gender, race or age matter? Is cost a consideration? How does the mediator address the questions of process design? For example, does the mediator discourage "face-to-face" conversation (or joint sessions) in favor of "separate" meetings? Some are comfortable with party representatives assuming a primary role in the discussion while others are not. A careful negotiator can find the type of mediator—and mediation—she wants. [Honeyman, *Understanding Mediators*]

Mediation and Justice

Mediation allows parties to find resolutions that are in keeping with their own preferences and values.

Some mediator approaches—transformative or facilitative—systematically support democratic dialogue and decision-making, improving relations and building communities. Imagine:

- upstairs and downstairs neighbors able to communicate respectfully with one another, developing both an added degree of sensitivity and tolerance;
- an office which can set a precedent for displaying inter-racial and inter-gender cooperation, with Cheryl communicating more clearly her desire for inclusion and training, and a supervisor who comes to understand her perspective; and
- a community where different ethnicities find ways to appreciate their differences and resolve issues that are potentially divisive.

Other approaches to mediation, such as when an evaluative mediator presses parties to settle, are designed to secure speedy and cost-saving closure, thereby advancing the administrative goals of a justice system.

Conclusion—An Experiment Worth Trying

Perhaps the most important thing that negotiators should know about mediation is that it works. Frequently, it brings disputing parties a better understanding of each other and closure to their dispute. Given the emotional and financial costs that conflict can levy, a thoughtful negotiator should not ignore that mediation might provide a promising road out of a dispute.

President Theodore Roosevelt was the first American to be awarded a Nobel Prize for Peace. Like many recipients of the Nobel Peace Prize, he tackled a dispute which seemed intractable and was immensely costly—the war between Russia and Japan at the dawn of the 20th century. Writing to his son in 1905 about his efforts as a mediator, Roosevelt said:

> I have finally gotten the Japanese and Russians to agree to meet to discuss the terms of peace. Whether they will be able to come to agreement or not I can't say. But it is worthwhile to have obtained the chance of peace, and the only possible way to get this chance was to secure such an agreement of the two powers that they would meet and discuss the terms direct. Of course, Japan will want to ask more than she ought to ask, and Russia to give less than she ought to give. Perhaps both sides will prove impracticable. Perhaps one will. But there is a chance that they will prove sensible, and make a peace, which will really be for the interest of each as things are now. At any rate[,] the experiment was worth trying.[7]

Thanks to Roosevelt's persistent efforts, enormous tact, and thoughtful prodding, an agreement was reached that ended the war. As testament to the significance of the accomplishment, the mayor of Portsmouth, New Hampshire, where the treaty was signed, rang the town bells for a full half hour.[8]

While we should not expect town bells to toll when private disputes are resolved, we can nonetheless celebrate the impact on neighbors when a tense and volatile situation—like that of the upstairs and downstairs neighbors—is transformed into a neighborly relationship. We can celebrate the impact on a workplace when employees feel understood, included and supported by their colleagues and supervisors. And, for public disputes, we can celebrate the impact on a community when diverse ethnicities can collaborate with one another to address issues that divide them.

In many scenarios, mediation—a way to generate a possibility for negotiating success—is, as Teddy Roosevelt said, an experiment worth trying.

Endnotes

[1] George Mitchell, *Peace Can Prevail*, DISPUTE RESOLUTION MAGAZINE, Winter 2002 at 4, 6.

[2] Desmond Tutu, *No Future Without Forgiveness*, in THE IMPOSSIBLE WILL TAKE A LITTLE WHILE 396 (Paul Rogat Loeb ed., 2004).

[3] ROBERT A. BARUCH BUSH & JOSEPH P. FOLGER, THE PROMISE OF MEDIATION: RESPONDING TO CONFLICT THROUGH EMPOWERMENT AND RECOGNITION 84-85 (1994).

[4] James Alfini, *Trashing, Bashing and Hashing It Out*, 19 FLORIDA STATE UNIVERSITY LAW REVIEW 47 (1991).

[5] *Id.* at 66.

[6] *Id.* at 69.

[7] Letter from Theodore Roosevelt to Kermit Roosevelt (June 11, 1905), *in* XXI THE WORKS OF THEODORE ROOSEVELT at 595 (Hermann Hagedorn ed., mem'l ed. 1923-1926).

[8] *See* James E. Fender, *Roosevelt, The Mikado and The Czar: Theodore Roosevelt's Mediation of the 1905 Treaty of Portsmouth*, NEW HAMPSHIRE BAR JOURNAL Summer 2005, at 68, 72, (citing Peter E. Randall, *There Are No Victors Here! A Local Perspective on the Treaty of Portsmouth*, 53 PORTSMOUTH MAINE SOCIETY 8 (1985)).

ೞ 67 ೞ

Understanding Mediators

Christopher Honeyman

Editors' Note: *Perhaps you've reached the point in the negotiation where it's time to bring in a third party. This chapter, the second in our mediation trilogy, helps you make wise choices about whom to hire as a mediator. It's designed to help the negotiator understand how mediators actually operate, and to be aware of the skill set and biases within which any given mediator must operate.*

Mediators regularly make claims of neutrality, as well as of quality of service; indeed, neutrality is a foundational claim of the field.[1] Both claims have been opposed before, but generally in terms that are either polemical, or specialized as to subject matter. The notion has been under-explored that there might be limitations on neutrality and on quality of service that on the one hand are generally applicable, and on the other are not, or at least should not be, particularly alarming. This chapter[2] will attempt to pull together and update several previous writings of my own to try to provide an integrated look at some limitations on mediators' quality of performance and neutrality.

Even an experienced negotiator can be rather surprised by the orientations and actions of mediators, particularly when encountering a mediator she has not worked with before. Leonard Riskin's thoughtful series of "grid" explanations[3] has been helpful in explaining the differences, but have concentrated on trying to make clear the nature of the differences themselves, rather than the "why." The simplest way to describe the relationship of this chapter to Riskin's (newest) grids is that the two approaches represent different layers of an overall image of mediation—though the notion of such overlays, admittedly, draws more from graphic arts or Photoshop than from legal or ADR imagery.

Sometimes, the circumstances are such that the canny negotiator would be surprised if there were no surprises in working with a new mediator—e.g., when working in a different culture. [Abramson, *Cross-cultural Mediation*] But unless a negotiator is a "repeat player" with the same pool of mediators, so that individuals become known to each other, sooner or later a surprise is almost inevitable. Many writers have referred to variations among mediators as a matter of "style." That term, however, connotes some kind of choice by the mediator to adopt one style rather than another, and its use is often promptly contradicted by the same writer noting that a mediator usually seems to be unconscious that she has a "style." I believe that term would be better replaced by a matrix of three types of criteria—one conscious, and two, largely unconscious. The variations fall into three main categories: skill differences, which tend to be large in a largely unregulated profession; policies and philosophies, which are generally overt and therefore predictable; and biases, which are often unrecognized by the mediator but correspond to a variety of different kinds of pressures to which the mediator is subject. Using that matrix, this chapter will describe the main variations among mediators, and briefly explain why they occur.

In part, the level of surprise among negotiators is an artifact of mediation's relative novelty in most parts of the negotiation market. In the two negotiation domains that have been using mediators for many decades—labor relations, and traditional diplomacy—such surprise is less common; a definable set of expectations has become part of the culture of each of those fields.[4] Yet even in labor mediation, the supposed autonomy of the practice was one of its most prized attributes. In the mid-1970s, when I first sought employment as a labor mediator, the highly experienced federal mediator who interviewed me remarked (or bragged) that the great thing about working in mediation was that it was the only profession that had no tools, and no rules. The concept was certainly attractive. But was it true?

She Does What She Can: *Skills*

Much has been written about the capabilities of mediators, without great consistency; even within Western culture, the set of skills thought important varies from program to program and setting to setting.[5] But a reasonably "vanilla" set of skill definitions might start with something like the following list, which also includes a sample set of rankings for the first skill:[6]

1. *Manage the Startup*: Effectively begin a productive relationship with the parties.

> 9, 8, or 7 Evidence of pre-planning and "homework done" (where appropriate) was strong. Opening statement was thorough, clear, concise, and set a tone encouraging collaboration.

> 6, 5, or 4 Some evidence of forethought and preparation. Opening statement was adequate but could have been more thorough, clear or concise.

> 3, 2, or 1 Mediator did not appear to have prepared for the case or to have read the file (if applicable). No opening/closing statement, or the explanations given were cursory or inaccurate.

2. *Gather and Comprehend Facts*: Effectively identify and seek out factual information relevant to the case, and sift and organize information that has been gathered.
(Descriptors ranked 9 through 1 for this and remaining characteristics omitted for space reasons. See note 6 above.)

3. *Understand Underlying Positions and Interests*: Draw out and understand the parties' essential concerns and needs, whether or not verbal or articulated in factual information.

4A. *Express Empathy Verbally*: Be consciously aware and considerate of the needs and values of others.

4B. *Express Empathy Nonverbally*: Be conspicuously aware and considerate of the needs and values of others, in body language and other ways not captured by Scale 4A.

5. *Convey Impartiality*: Convey a sense of neutrality to the parties.

6. *Manage the Personalities*: Effectively cope with strong personalities and conflicts between clients and professional representatives.

7A. *Assist Parties in Generating Options*: Pursue collaborative solutions, and assist parties in generating ideas and proposals consistent with the facts and workable for opposing parties.

7B. *Generate Options*: Generate ideas and proposals consistent with the facts and workable for opposing parties.

8A. *Assist Parties in Generating Agreements*: Effectively help the parties move toward finality.

8B. *Generate Agreements*: Effectively move the parties toward finality and "close" an agreement.

9. *Move the Parties Toward an Improved Relationship*: Effectively help the parties move toward better relationships with each other and third parties.

10. *Manage the Interaction and Conclusion*: Effectively manage the concluding process.

Is Anyone Perfect?

It should be immediately apparent that no normal human being has all of these qualities in abundance. In fact, one of the most highly regarded labor mediators in the U.S. studied a similar list (but tailored for labor mediators) and remarked that he thought he could hit the top note on two or three of the scales—on a good day. The top level of description for each of these characteristics thus represents an aspirational ideal for a mediator, not the expected capability of a typical mediator. What is important to the present purpose is that to the best of my knowledge, every mediator ever tested under controlled conditions (several hundred, at least), who was perceived in other ways as good at the work, has been found to score highly on at least one or two of these characteristics, and at least acceptably on the rest. But the exact balance has never been the same twice.

To anticipate what comes next, it is necessary only to reflect on the fact that every professional, in every profession, hopes to achieve something for the clients. If every mediator does what she can, and every mediator has a different balance of skills, the mere exercise of those skills is going to produce different styles of practice, different frames of reference, different options that are open to the mediator (versus those that are effectively closed because of incapability) and most important, *different results for the parties.*

The most obvious example, because it is the subject of vigorous debate within the field as to whether the result should even be called mediation, is that of a mediator whose particular strengths are those articulated in items 7B. and 8B. above. That is an "evaluative" mediator in the making.[7] There are many mediators who combine those qualities with impartiality, high skills at gathering facts, and ability to manage the interaction and close up the case. All of these are skills that are likely to be developed in the course of a judicial career. Among the remainder of the list, however, such skills as empathy, or the ability to guide parties more subtly by assisting them to generate options and agreements rather than taking the lead in that process, are skills some judges have developed, while many others have not. Yet if every mediator seeks to be effective, that pressure to be effective, in some sense, guarantees vigorous use of the skill set already possessed. Thus, it should be no surprise that mediators who possess the skills of evaluation find more moments to call upon those skills than mediators whose skill set is more rounded.

A party whose claims are grounded in arguments based in concepts of societal fairness, and whose proposals for resolution are not easily reduced to numbers (such as dollars) is likely to consider such a mediator biased against it. And this is not an uncommon scenario in major cases, such as where the rights and interests of Native American tribes compete with development interests. [Caton Campbell & Docherty, *Framing*] Conversely, in a case where the parties have different frames, a party which believes its argument is based in black-letter law and its dollar claim is "in the range" is also apt to believe the mediator is not neutral—if it finds itself in the hands of a mediator whose strengths are in empathy and intercultural understanding, and who flatly refuses to provide any hints of how the mediator views "the merits."

A similar problem can arise for any other common combination of skills. I leave it to the reader's imagination (or prejudice) which combination, and what perceptions of failed neutrality, might most logically be expected with a mediator with a background in, say, traditional diplomacy, or engineering, or psychological counseling. The point is that with some knowledge as to the full range of skills that have been found relevant in mediation, and with some forewarning of the likely skill set of the particular mediator you expect to encounter, the reader is in a better position to know what to expect—and also, significantly, to help the mediator perform those functions in which the mediator could use such help.[8]

She Does What She Wants: *Intent*

The reader may have wondered in passing why the list of skills above includes several with "A" and "B" variations. These, the major innovation of the second-generation definitions of a mediator's functions, correspond not merely to differences in skill but also to differences in intent. Up till the mid-1990s, it was widely known among experienced mediators, but not particularly remarked on, that some mediators seemed to have a different orientation to what they were trying to achieve than others.[9] Typically, this revolved around dimensions described as whether the mediator was more concerned with helping the parties to reach an immediate settlement, or to improve their future relationship. This dichotomy was given its sharpest delineation with the publication of an influential book which strongly argued that mediation was best suited for, and should be used primarily towards, generating (or regenerating) parties' respect for each other and ability to cope with disputes with each other and third parties in the future, rather than with settlement of the immediate dispute—a result that was seen as obtainable from other dispute resolution processes.[10]

It is possible, of course, that the choice by a given mediator of what has come to be known as the "transformative" model is not in fact as policy-driven as it would appear, but instead reflects in small or large part the desire for effectiveness already noted. Some combinations of the typical skill set favor effectiveness at transformative approaches, and disfavor venturing far into evaluation, or even into some of the demands of "facilitative" mediation; others, as noted above, favor the reverse. There is thus no bright-line test to be had of whether a transformative, facilitative or evaluative mediator is operating primarily on conviction or on capacity. Furthermore, there is careful research that supports the dismaying finding that all mediators are more evaluative than they think.[11] Nevertheless, the distinction is useful in the attempt to understand what a negotiator is likely to experience, not least because mediators are often quite open about what they regard as deliberate policy choices, even while being guarded about any skill deficiencies—and, frequently, ignorant about their biases.

She Does What She Must: *Bias*

Of course, a deliberate choice in favor of the transformative model, or the evaluative or facilitative, might be described as a bias toward a certain way of operating—with, more to the point, an associated bias towards certain kinds of results. But so openly stated a preference is the least problematic kind of bias, and barely deserves the word. Biases which are unstated or unknown are much more threatening to the negotiator's interests and to the mediator's integrity. There are, unfortunately, a number of them.

Once a mediator undertakes to interrogate parties as to their reasoning or to develop alternative proposals, it is axiomatic that the mediator has a degree of choice over which possibilities will be emphasized and which downplayed. Mediators' claim that "we don't make decisions" is true only to a degree, because often there is more than one set of terms that will make for an acceptable deal, and the mediator can exercise great influence as to which combination of proposals is adopted. In these situations, the sophisticated negotiator demonstrates a practical understanding of how to use knowledge of the pressures on mediators to obtain an advantage. For convenience and without rigidity, biases can be classified into three groups: personal, situational, and structural. Of these, personal bias is by far the most widely recognized form.

Personal Bias

Most people would describe a palpable preference for the negotiator or principals of one party as a personal bias. Also, in disputes where a serious philosophical gulf exists, a mediator may have a propensity to think along the general lines of one of the parties. In addition, past associations or a partisan employment history of the mediator can give the appearance of bias. Apparent bias, though, does not have the same results as actual bias. An axiom, borrowed from an ancient legal principle, states that it is as bad for a mediator to seem biased as it is for an actual bias to exist. But this is not an accurate statement of the effect. Even though it affects the mediator's actions and proposals, an *actual* personal bias may remain unknown to all participants. The *appearance* of personal bias, however, may leave the mediator blissfully ignorant of any problem, while causing one party to act based on its perception that the mediator is biased against it. It is quite common for a party to complain to the mediator's appointing agency, independently seek a different mediator, or return quietly to direct negotiations, without ever confronting the mediator with its suspicions or giving the mediator an opportunity to allay its fears.

It is increasingly accepted practice for a mediator to disclose any known personal conflict, including friendships and past associations. While there is disagreement over what may reasonably constitute a potential conflict, the growing acceptance of the principle of disclosure[12] acts as some reassurance that potentially disadvantaged parties will be given an opportunity to object, or at least investigate further. It also helps the mediator's perceived objectivity, by showing that she has nothing to hide.

Provided that the accepted disclosure rules are applied conscientiously, there is nothing about personal biases which threatens to cause a negotiator general concern, let alone enduring resistance to the use of mediation as a process. That is not the case, however, with the other, more subtle types of bias.

Situational Bias

Situational bias refers to those biases which result from a mediator's source of appointment and obligations to persons or parties other than those immediately involved in the dispute.

Most lay people, if asked, would probably guess that mediators are selected by the parties jointly. In reality, this ideal is rarely achieved, because such a direct mutual selection process calls for a fair degree of mutual trust and willingness to negotiate in the first place. In many types of disputes, the intercession of some organizational third party is necessary to enable the parties to accept a given mediator. Depending on the type of dispute, the appointing or recommending agency may be a court, a nonprofit or for-profit firm that maintains a private roster, a state or federal labor mediation agency, an international body such as the United Nations, or another organization. Although each of these bodies has a pluralistic constituency, none is without an organizational interest of its own. This interest can affect both the mediator's actions and the parties' perceptions, because a mediator with enough of a relationship to an appointing agency to be selected may be presumed to have some degree of fealty to that agency.

Because of universal familiarity, the United Nations is a good example. Suppose that the Secretary-General, upon hearing of a border clash between countries X and Y, fears that a wider war will ensue and wishes to send someone to attempt mediation. Suppose further, in the interest of simplicity, that the major world powers are ignoring the matter, and that both X and Y indicate that mediation would be acceptable. The Secretary-General appoints Ibsen, a recently hired UN civil servant of Swedish extraction. Ibsen has a good reputation, a neutral background as a newspaper editor, and no prior connection with either disputing country.

Can Ibsen be presumed neutral by both parties? Of course, says the observer from a safe distance. But neither President Smith of X nor Prime Minister Jones of Y is quite so sure. Ibsen comes from an organization which has little or no independent military power, and X has lost control of a border village. Smith feels that when push comes to shove the UN will not send troops, and fears that Ibsen may emphasize settlement terms which involve the de facto cession of that village to Y. The capital of Y, meanwhile, is awash in reporters, and it occurs to Jones that Ibsen could easily use his many press contacts to leak information in such a way as to put substantial international pressure on Y to return the village, which Y has considered properly its territory since 1842.

Even ignoring the many other possible complications and the myriad of rumors which attend any serious clash, both Jones and Smith will probably view any discussion with Ibsen regarding the disposition of the village with some misgivings. Is it surprising that neither is willing to trust Ibsen with his innermost thoughts as to what might be a minimally acceptable settlement? And yet in conventional terms Ibsen is as talented, blameless, unbiased and public-spirited a mediator as anyone could want.

In other circumstances, situational bias has an actual, rather than perceived effect. For a wholly innocent example, consider what happens when an attorney, acting as a mediator, realizes that a settlement which is mutually acceptable to the parties is unlawful. An attorney with ethical standards high enough to make her acceptable as a mediator may find it difficult to give herself whole-heartedly to her role as mediator in this situation, even if the impact of the illegality would be minor compared to the result of unsuccessful mediation. (Note, however, that many observers have regarded this type of bias with such equanimity that they advocate the *assumption* of a "public interest" role by the mediator.)

Structural Biases

Structural biases, which stem directly from the nature of mediation, are the most obscure and the least avoidable. There are several of them, so that in given cases they may cancel each other out. They are probably not often conclusive as to the nature of the agreement reached; but that does not mean that they are not real, nor does it mean that a perceptive mediator or negotiator will not notice their subtle effect. Among these biases are tendencies for the process to benefit weaker parties over stronger ones, moderate factions over radical, and negotiators over principals. Another bias, which has no reliable preference for any particular kind of participant, is the tendency for the process to favor a quick or easy way out instead of a real and enduring solution. Finally, the most pernicious problem is that mediation can be an effective tool for a party determined to negotiate in bad faith.

In Joint Gains, the Weaker Party Gains Disproportionately

In any unequal negotiating relationship, the stronger party is in a better position to act unilaterally, while the weaker party seeks to claim some form of perceived equity. [Korobkin, *Power*] An agreement to mediate, however, exposes both parties to some skeptical examination, no matter how polite or restrained, by the mediator. In addition, the agreement to mediate signals an acceptance of the legitimacy of the opposing party's existence, if not of its position. Because a mediator is endowed with a degree of moral authority, no one wants to defend a negotiating position solely on the basis of power; therefore, some claim to law, moral standing or common sense invariably is made. In the process of altering positions (which occurs to some degree even in an unsuccessful mediation attempt), the stronger party is thus led toward positions and proposals based on "defensible" criteria. In other words, the stronger party loses ground because she is led to compete more within the weaker party's frame of reference.

Sensitivity to this tendency seems to vary from place to place, and reduced sensitivity to it may be a mark of greater sophistication among negotiators. In American labor disputes, for example, there has long been a widespread willingness among stronger parties to join in a request for mediation, perhaps on the expectation that the mediator will help knock some sense into the other fellows and make them realize what a poor position they really occupy. By contrast, an official of the British Advisory, Conciliation and Arbitration Service told me, in the mid-1980s, that they found it difficult to get anyone to agree to mediation, since parties felt that to be first to ask for or accede to a mediator's assistance was an admission of weakness. Contemporary practice by attorneys in court-connected mediation seems, fortunately for mediators and parties alike, to be following the American rather than the British labor-management model in this instance.

The Diverse Factions Constituting Each Party Are Not All Treated Equally

In most types of disputes (with the obvious exception of divorces) groups of people are involved on one or both sides. A group may be as small as the tenants of a single building or as large as all consumers of a drug now suspected to have undisclosed side effects; but the interests of all the participants on the same side are never identical. Often the rift between nominally allied factions may be as wide as the gap between the opposing "parties." [Bellman, *Team Conflicts*; Matz, *Team Mis-*

communication; Wade, *Tribe*] Different proposals and trade-offs may benefit these factions disproportionately.

If a given party contains both moderates and radicals, mediation tends to benefit the moderates at the radicals' expense. This is partly because the *process* of mediation, with its emphasis on reasoned dialogue and its implied promise of moderation to all, inherently opposes the radical's prescribed sequence, of disruption followed by massive change. The limited nature of concessions obtainable at any bargaining table, along with mediation's secrecy, apparent legitimacy, and acceptability to the public, work to legitimize the gradualism of the moderate. Therefore, even at the start a mediator is by no means everyone's friend, and no matter how well-meaning her efforts, should not expect to be treated as such.

A parallel tendency is for mediation to submerge minority interests in general. The pressure to obtain an agreement which will get a majority vote within two opposing groups, combined with the customary emphasis on confidentiality, can leave a dissident faction boxed in with little ability to keep effective contact with the opposing party or its own constituency. Sometimes such a faction's first opportunity to affect the outcome occurs when ratification by the entire constituency is required. [Wade & Honeyman, *Lasting Agreement*] By that time, the dissident faction can become militant after being pressured by the mediator and its own "allies," while the majority of the party has become complacent after having prevailed at the bargaining table. The resulting refusal to ratify an agreement has occurred at every level, from local labor unions to the U.S. Senate and the General Assembly of the United Nations.

In Conflicts of Interest Between a Negotiator and the Principals, Mediation Gives the Negotiator an Advantage

Be the negotiator ambassador, lawyer, union business agent or king, there is often some level of conflict of interest with those he represents. In mediation an advantage accrues to the negotiator because he may be able to block a mediator from direct access to his principals, or at least limit that access. [Nolan-Haley, *Informed Consent*] Furthermore, a negotiator often has broader access to sources of information than his principals, and can also communicate with a mediator on a one-to-one basis, out of his principals' hearing. A mediator, on the other hand, may have to bear in mind the likelihood of dealings with a particular negotiator on another day, in another context. These factors enable a negotiator to use a mediator to cloak proposals and deals which support the negotiator's interests as opposed to those of the constituents. This is a particular problem when the "mediator" is appointed by, or is an official of, a powerful third party with favors to bestow.

The First Possible Agreement Is Not Always the Best Possible Agreement

There is almost always more than one set of terms that can make for a mutually acceptable settlement; "give" on one item may compensate for "take" on an apparently unrelated one. However, many mediators are under some degree of time pressure, from the press of other work, the need to show progress to the mediator's appointing agency or peers, and for many other reasons. This pressure encourages a mediator to search for the *first* mutually agreeable settlement package rather than for some conception of the *best* agreement. Often the parties are aware of this. Despite the theoretical existence of an agreement, it is not unusual for negotiators to meet afterwards, with or without the mediator, and modify the original set of terms to their mutual benefit. It is as if these parties needed the mediator's assistance to get within hailing distance of each other, but once that is accomplished, the parties' superior knowledge of their own needs makes direct negotiation fruitful again. Under the same heading, "Never give a mediator your bottom line" is a wise admonition for those who intend to get a better than bottom-line deal if possible. [Schneider, *Aspirations*; Brazil, *Professionalism*]

Mediation Can Actually Abet Bad-Faith Bargaining

The problem of bad-faith bargaining or "playing games" is endemic. Here mediation has two, somewhat contradictory, tendencies. On a personal level, a mediator can conscientiously apply pressure against games-playing, and a searching inquiry into a party's justification for its proposals can be quite effective. However, if a games-player has the power to block a settlement, a mediator may find himself forced to defend and cover for that party rather than expose the bad faith to the full wrath of the opposing party or general public and risk that negotiations will break down entirely. A similar effect may obtain without conscious manipulation by the mediator.[13]

It is natural for mediators (generally optimists by temperament, if not professional requirement) to assume that both parties are acting in good faith, and as already noted, parties usually take care to present some rationale for any position they adopt. Even the most skeptical mediator needs to retain the confidence of both parties, including the games-player, to be effective. In addition, the principle of confidentiality restrains the mediator from attempting to use her influence on public opinion to enforce genuine negotiation. Thus there is, sad to say, at least a degree of potential bias in favor of a party who is negotiating in bad faith.

The upshot of this last set of biases is that any negotiator dealing with a mediator must consider that there is a whole series of possible influences on the mediator which the latter, in maintenance of a self-image of neutrality, may be but dimly aware of.

Conclusion

To say that a profession has biases is not to decry its usefulness. To say that a professional is not superhuman is not to deny her talent or her assiduousness. Both biases, and differences in talents, are facts of life, and those described here should be no more alarming than such legal biases as the presumption of innocence and the burden of proof. The widespread use of mediation, along with its frequent success, shows that the effects of bias are limited, that the talents available are considerable, and that parties can learn to live with imperfection. Through understanding and experience, good negotiators have been able to reduce most of the concerns described here to little more than a *caveat* to be kept in mind when discussing options with a mediator.

But the fact that the biases not only exist, but apply in different ways to mediators with different balances of skills, different personal histories and different sources of appointment, adds to the differing policy choices among even rather competent mediators to produce a truly awe-inspiring range of possible conduct. In the face of so complex a matrix, it might be worth challenging the over-reliance on "neutrality" by asking if any two mediators, assigned identical cases, could ever produce, or should ever have been expected to produce, exactly the same result for the parties.

Since no two real cases are ever identical, we will never know the answer to the "could" question, at least. But while wisely shelving this metaphysical issue, the savvy negotiator might profitably make a mental note to ask lots of other questions of, and about, any new mediator she is considering hiring.

Endnotes

[1] Not untypical is the definition "A mediator is a neutral intervener committed to assist each negotiating party conduct constructive conversations." Lela Love & Joseph B. Stulberg, *The Uses of Mediation*, Chapter 66 in this volume.

[2] A version of this chapter is published in the Penn State Dickinson School of Law symposium issue on mediator neutrality, JOURNAL OF AMERICAN ARBITRATION (VOL. 4, NO. 2, 2005). I would like to thank Penn State law professors Robert Ackerman, Nancy Welsh and Tom Carbonneau for providing me with the opportunity to revisit these issues.

[3] The most recent is Leonard Riskin, *Replacing the Mediator Orientation Grids, Again: Proposing a New New Grid System*, 127 ALTERNATIVES 23 (2005).

[4] It was a surprise to many long-established players when Deborah Kolb—correctly, in my view—defined two quite different cultures of U.S. labor mediation, sharply differentiating practice in the public sector from the private. *See* DEBORAH KOLB, THE MEDIATORS (1984).

[5] *See* Christopher Honeyman, *Five Elements of Mediation*, 4 NEGOTIATION JOURNAL 149 (1988); Christopher Honeyman, *On Evaluating Mediators*, 6 NEGOTIATION JOURNAL 23 (1990); Christopher Honeyman, et al., *Performance-Based Assessment: a Methodology for Use in Selecting, Training and Evaluating Mediators* (1995), *available at* http://www.convenor.com/madison/method.pdf (last visited Apr. 28, 2006). This chapter reconsiders and updates all of these in certain aspects, together with Christopher Honeyman, *Patterns of Bias in Mediation*, 1985 JOURNAL OF DISPUTE RESOLUTION 141 and Christopher Honeyman, *Bias and Mediators' Ethics*, 2 NEGOTIATION JOURNAL 175 (1986).

[6] The list which follows shows the detailed descriptors only for the first item, to save space. This full set of descriptors can be found in Grace G. D'Alo, *Accountability in Special Education Mediation: Many a Slip 'Twixt Vision and Practice?*, 8 HARVARD NEGOTIATION LAW REVIEW 226 (2003). The list was prepared by the author and Grace D'Alo in collaboration with the mediators of a Pennsylvania state agency concerned with mediation of disputes between parents of special needs children, and school boards and officials. It is a "second generation" set of descriptors, which makes a number of distinctions not recognized in the late 1980s, when the initial performance-based selection tests of mediators required development of the skills lists and performance criteria in the articles cited *supra* note 5.

[7] Even some practitioners whose approaches might (rightly or wrongly) be lumped in with this style are diffident about whether it should be considered mediation. *See* Wayne Brazil, *Professionalism and Misguided Negotiating*, Chapter 78 in this volume. This has its ironies, because in all probability mediators (and settlement judges) who have enough sensitivity to be concerned about this also demonstrate that sensitivity in daily practice, which ought to *reduce* the concern that they will rely excessively on the ability to evaluate.

[8] There is reason to believe that many parties, particularly repeat players in complex cases, have in effect internalized this point in the way they structure a case and make available different kinds of experts. *See* Christopher Honeyman, *The Common Core of Mediation*, 8 MEDIATION QUARTERLY 73 (1990).

[9] *See*, for example, the discussion of differing mediators' orientations even within the same program, in Honeyman, *Five Elements of Mediation*, *supra* note 5.

[10] *See generally* ROBERT A. BARUCH BUSH & JOSEPH FOLGER, THE PROMISE OF MEDIATION (2d ed., 2005). In this second edition of the 1995 book, Bush and Folger have significantly refined their concepts, and in the process reduced the starkness of the apparent policy choice. But a choice it remains.

[11] *See* David Greatbatch & Robert Dingwall, *Selective Facilitation: Some Preliminary Observations on a Strategy Used by Divorce Mediators*, 23 LAW & SOCIETY REVIEW 613 (1989). *See also* Sara Cobb & Janet Rifkin, *Practice and Paradox: Deconstructing Neutrality in Mediation*, 16 LAW & SOCIAL INQUIRY 35 (1991).

[12] *See* GEORGETOWN COMMISSION ON ETHICS & STANDARDS OF PRACTICE IN ADR, *Principles for ADR Provider Organizations*, *in* INTERNATIONAL INSTITUTE FOR CONFLICT PREVENTION & RESOLUTION (2002). *See also*, *Patterns of Bias*, & *Bias and Mediators*, *supra* note 5.

[13] In his second autobiography *Ways of Escape*, Graham Greene described the U.N. Middle East mediation machinery as the indirect cause of an hour of shellfire he once endured while traveling along the Suez Canal. In his view, Egypt was using its ready access to mediation to stage brief incidents of shooting which it could terminate through the U.N. before things got out of hand. Greene's description of the use of the ponderous United Nations chain of communication in the hands of a (then) "bad actor" should not be dismissed lightly. GRAHAM GREENE, WAYS OF ESCAPE (1980).

෬ 68 ෭

The Culturally Suitable Mediator

Harold Abramson

Editors' Note: *Often overlooked in the search for a mediator is the need for one whose competence includes cultural awareness. Any ordinary negotiator is more likely than ever before to find herself in a negotiation with a party from another country, or a different culture within the same country. This chapter discusses the most common culture-based differences in mediation styles, and when each might be appropriate. It should be read in conjunction not only with the other chapters on mediation but also with the chapters by Kelly and Goh on negotiating in other cultures.*

Even an adept negotiator can be baffled by cultural differences.[1] When a negotiation reaches an impasse because of an unfamiliar cultural interest or a miscommunication between the parties due to different styles of communicating, negotiating, or decision-making, the negotiator might find it helpful to enlist assistance from a culturally-trained and culturally-appropriate mediator. This chapter considers how such a third party can help you, as a negotiator, bridge cultural differences. It considers when to seek aid from a mediator, what the credentials of the mediator ought to be, and the impact of the mediator's approach on the way you represent your client.

When to Enlist a Mediator?

In a cross-cultural negotiation, a party may need a process that can deal with cultural differences. Parties brought up in dissimilar cultures might require a process that helps them recognize and bridge their different upbringings. They may need a process with a mediator who can help them overcome such cultural gaps as when an Asian or South American party may be more interested in the relationship than the U.S. party who may be more interested in a detailed contract, or when the U.S. party wants extensive discovery while the civil law party sees no need for it. They also may benefit from a mediator who deeply involves the parties, the ones with the greatest knowledge of the dispute, when the negotiation seems to be failing because the cultural practice of one side replaces the principal with her lawyer. By turning to mediation, parties can create a forum in which barriers that parties may not be able to overcome on their own can be addressed.

I recently observed how attorneys can enlist assistance from a mediator when they perceptively engaged in a cross-cultural analysis in a pre-mediation conference. They informed me, as the mediator, that they thought negotiations had failed so far not because they were not on the same page but because one of the parties from a small Western African country could not negotiate with someone whom he thought had acted so unethically. The party said that where he is from, you do not deal with someone like the other party. He would rather take a chance in court and lose (a significant risk according to his own attorney) than settle with someone who acted so unethically. The attorneys indicated that they needed a mediator that could help the parties overcome this impasse.

What Credentials Should The Mediator Possess?

You need a mediator whose training and experience goes beyond the familiar basic credentials. You should expand your standard checklist to include two additional questions that are culturally-related: is the mediator trained to deal with cultural differences? And a second less obvious question, does the mediator approach mediation in a way that fits the cultural needs of the parties? This next section considers these two questions.

Is the Mediator Trained to Deal With Cultural Differences?

A mediator should be trained and experienced in helping parties recognize culturally-shaped interests and overcome culturally-based impasses.

Culturally-Shaped Interests

Your primary purpose in a negotiation, like in any dispute resolution process, is to advance and meet your client's interests, whatever they might be. But what does the term "interests" encompass? Some commentators have suggested that such an inquiry is a narrow cultural one, shaped by western cultural individualism. This narrow view, however, fails to take into account other culturally-driven goals such as interdependence and relatedness.[2] A broad view of interests can capture the full range of cultural needs of clients, leaving to each party's cultural upbringing the content of his or her interests.

Spotting cultural interests can be difficult to do because they can be buried in presenting positions. A dispute that appears to be primarily about money, for instance, might be mostly about protecting a principle, saving face, preserving relationships, or promoting particular community norms and collectivist interests. Although these interests are not unfamiliar in the U.S. culture, these interests can be deeply compelling ones for parties from some non-U.S. cultures.[3]

In collectivist societies such as in China and Japan, parties can have an interest in preserving face, a deeply ingrained personal value that involves being treated with respect and dignity, maintaining positive relationships, and preserving an honorable reputation and social standing in the community. "Face-saving" according to Fisher and Ury, however, "carries a derogatory flavor [in the English language]. People say, 'We are doing that just to let them save face,' implying that a little pretense has been created to allow someone to go along without feeling badly. The tone implies ridicule…. This is a grave misunderstanding of the role and importance of face-saving. Face-saving reflects a person's need to reconcile the stand he takes in a negotiation or an agreement with his principles and with his past words and deeds."[4] [Goh, *Errors*]

When encountering a dispute where these sorts of culturally shaped interests might arise, you may want to select a culturally-trained mediator who can assist parties in recognizing less familiar and yet essential needs that must be met.

Culturally-Shaped Impasses

Disputing parties can encounter impediments due to their different cultural up-bringings that can foster conflicting wants and approaches to the negotiation. Any study of culture reveals numerous examples of behavior common in one culture that could be misinterpreted by someone brought up in another culture, and as result, may produce an impasse. This subject is treated in detail in chapters by Avruch, Goh, and Kelly in this volume, and will not be repeated here. When these cultural differences result in an impasse in a negotiation, you might turn to a cul-turally-trained mediator to help break the impasse. This next section considers the techniques that might be used by a mediator.

Impasse Breaking Techniques

An appropriately trained mediator can help you recognize and overcome cultur-ally-based impasses. The mediator can help you classify an impasse as well as develop a suitable intervention. In a cross-cultural negotiation, a mediator might use the following five steps.[5]

During the first three steps, the mediator prepares for the cross-cultural nego-tiation by mastering a cultural conceptual framework, learning about her own cultural upbringing, and investigating the culture of the other negotiators. The next two steps provide a guide for the mediator as the mediation progresses. The mediator views the negotiating behavior of others with an open mind and then helps parties bridge any differences.

These five steps can be illustrated through the use of a hypothetical. Consider how a U.S. attorney might react when he learns that the other party, an institu-tional client from Japan, will not be represented by someone with substantial settlement authority. Instead, the other side will be represented by a team of nego-tiators who will make decisions by consensus. Furthermore, all the team members cannot be present in the negotiation session. Under these circumstances, the U.S. attorney is likely to suspect that the other side is acting in bad faith. The other side appears to be replacing the person with real settlement authority with an un-wieldy team of negotiators. How might the mediator proceed?

First, the mediator comes to the mediation with a *conceptual framework* that can help her identify and understand cultural characteristics. The mediator must be able to grasp the meaning of "cultural behavior" and how it is different from uni-versal "human behavior." Cultural characteristics have been isolated in numerous studies of culture, including studies relevant to conflict resolution.[6]

The hypothetical implicates a cultural characteristic related to the process of decision-making for each side. This generic characteristic, like virtually all cultural characteristics, encompasses a continuum bound at each end with a value-based pole. At one extreme, societies can be found that are hierarchical, with decisions made by leaders. At the other extreme, societies can be found that are collective, with decisions made by consensus. The actual cultural practice is rarely one ex-treme or the other; it usually falls somewhere between these two end poles of the continuum. Second, the mediator fills in this conceptual framework with a deep understanding of her *own culture or cultures*.[7] A skilled mediator must be cognizant of the degree to which her own behavior is universal or culturally determined, because it is through this personal lens that the mediator observes and assesses the negotiating behavior of others. To reduce distortions, the mediator must learn about her own cultural upbringing in order to appreciate the extent to which her view of other people's behavior may not necessarily reflect a universal view. In the hypothetical, a U.S. mediator should be aware that her possible view that organizations tend to be hierarchical, where decision-making is centralized in "leaders," is not universal organizational behavior. Third, the mediator strengthens her conceptual framework with an understanding of the *culture or cultures of the negotiator(s)*. The mediator should try to identify and research the culture(s) of the clients as well as the attorneys that will be participating in the mediation. In doing so, the mediator should not assume that just because a person was brought up in a clearly identifiable culture, the person will act in accordance with its cultural norms. Furthermore, the mediator should learn as much as possible about the negotiators as individuals, that is learn about their personalities and ways their negotiating behavior may vary from practices of their culture(s). In the hypothetical, the research might reveal that one side is from a society in which organizations typically make decisions based on consensus, but the research may reveal little about their individual personalities.[8]

These first three preparatory steps are relatively easy to complete because they entail collecting mostly accessible information on cultural characteristics. The next two steps, however, are much more difficult to accomplish because they require the mediator to suspend judgment and develop strategies during an intense, dynamic, and fast moving mediation session.

Fourth, the mediator withholds judgments about the parties' negotiating behavior by viewing key behavior with an *open mind*. This mental process requires considerable discipline. It is too easy for a person who routinely judges negotiating behavior to prematurely judge it in a cross-cultural negotiation. In the hypothetical, the mediator should not view one side's collective decision-making process as evidence of good or bad faith; instead she should view this key negotiating behavior as a difference that needs to be addressed.

Fifth and finally, the mediator searches for ways to *bridge* any resulting gap by helping the parties identify the nature of the impasse and by facilitating an intervention. The mediator might facilitate an interest-based negotiation, a compromise, or a decision to defer to one side's practice. In the process of doing so, the parties are likely to learn whether the gap reflects a cultural difference that can be bridged or a strategic ploy (which also could be cultural) that may impede or derail the negotiation.

In the hypothetical, the parties appear to have different views of who with settlement authority must be present in the mediation session. The U.S. party expects the other side to bring a single person with settlement authority, and the other side expects multiple people to sign off and they all cannot be present.

The mediator could facilitate a negotiated solution by resorting to an interest-based approach, where the interests behind the different practices are explicated and respected. In the hypothetical, instead of viewing as bad faith the Japanese party's claim that it cannot agree to anything without a consensus, the mediator might focus on how to respect the Japanese party's need for consensus while still meeting the U.S. party's need for the presence of clients with substantial settlement authority. The parties, for example, could negotiate an arrangement in which the Japanese party brings to the negotiation session all the people who must concur, or at least makes sure the absent people are available by telephone. Then, in the session, the Japanese consensus approach could be respected by giving members of its negotiating team ample time to meet privately.

This calibrated approach can smoke out whether the gap is based on a bridgeable cultural difference or a strategic ploy. This process of negotiation might reveal a difference that reflects an ingrained strategic practice such as haggling with a last minute demand by a senior person that is purposely not at the table.

Sometimes, a gap might be bridged by one side simply deferring to the other side's practice, especially when the other practice is not a deal-breaker or does not implicate core personal values. For instance, the U.S. attorney may defer to the other side's formal practices of carefully using titles and avoiding personal questions about family.

Does the Mediator's Approach Fit the Cultural Needs of the Parties?

Asking whether a mediator's approach fits the cultural needs of the parties can be an unfamiliar but necessary inquiry in order to formulate an effective cross-cultural process. You may want to inquire first what sort of third party assistance the parties and the other attorney are accustomed to. Their cultural experiences can influence the sort of mediator that they will respond to. The problem-solving approach, is not an approach that parties and attorneys readily accept when problem-solving runs counter to their experiences. Under these circumstances, you may need to select a mediator whose approach comports with the cultural upbringing of the other participants in order to create an efficacious process.

This mediator selection method, in which cultural preferences drive formulating the process, is different from the method I have suggested for selecting U.S. mediators in a non-cross-cultural context.[9] In a non-cross-cultural context, parties should select a mediator that will use the approach or mix of approaches that will meet the parties' needs for resolving the dispute. It is a choice driven by an analysis of the advantages and drawbacks of various mediator approaches in view of the parties' needs, including possible cultural ones.

The culturally-driven selection method suggested here, however, may be only a transitional one during this period of movement toward globalization of mediation practices. I recently saw evidence of this movement when participating in a U.S.-Chinese Retreat of dispute resolvers hosted by the CPR Institute.[10] One of the Chinese participants noted that when Chinese companies negotiate with each other and use a mediator, they prefer a more directive approach to mediation (the common Chinese practice) but when Chinese companies use a mediator with non-Chinese businesses, in other words internationally, they use a facilitative approach (a new approach to mediation in China). As the practices across the globe expand to comfortably cover a broader range of mediator approaches, then the emphasis in the mediator selection discussion should shift away from cultural analysis and toward analysis of which approach or mix of approaches is likely to be most effective in resolving a particular dispute.

Before suggesting a culturally nuanced way to classify mediator approaches, the term mediation needs some clarification and definition. There has been much debate over what processes can be legitimately called mediation. It is just too late to justify a favored, circumscribed mediation definition. I prefer a broad, generic definition that has the flexibility of accommodating the diversity of approaches to third party assistance found around the globe. Mediation is simply a negotiation conducted with the assistance of a third party. Instead of focusing on the noun of mediation, you should focus on the adjective in front of the noun. Is the mediation facilitative, evaluative, directive, transformative, some mix, or something else? Any classification system should highlight these different adjectives.

U.S. Problem-Solving and Self-Determination Approach[11]

U.S. practices reflect a culturally shaped view of mediation, a view that is vividly conveyed in the highly regarded U.S. Model Standards of Conduct for Mediators.[12] Although its original mediation definition articulated a problem-solving approach, the recently proposed changes broadens the definition to encompass different "styles" of mediation while only welcoming those styles that comport with the Westernized fundamental principle of party self-determination.

This fundamental policy of party self-determination reflects a distinctively U.S. cultural value that is not given the same sacred regard in more directive practices found in some other areas of the globe, as described below under evaluatively directive and wisely directive mediations.

Although the Model Standards' particular vision of the mediator's role reflects the dominant approach to training mediators in the United States and a widely practiced approach, it is not the exclusive one used. No culture can claim a single, monolithic mediation approach, and the United States is no exception. Two other approaches practiced in the U.S. are transformative and evaluative mediation.

Transformative Mediation

A transformative mediator engages in a mediation practice based on communication and relational theory. Instead of promoting the goal of settlement for the parties, the transformative mediator allows the parties to determine their own direction and supports the parties' own opportunities for perspective-taking, deliberation, and decision-making. The mediator focuses on the parties' interactions and supports their shifts from destructive and alienating interactions to more constructive and open interactions (referred to as empowerment and recognition shifts). In this model, parties are likely to be able to make positive changes in their interactions with each other and, consequently, find acceptable resolution for themselves, where such terms genuinely exist.[13]

Evaluative Mediation

Mediation becomes evaluative when the mediator gives recommendations. The mediator evaluates [Honeyman, *Mediators*] when the mediator offers his or her views of the strengths and weaknesses of the legal case, the reasonableness of particular settlement options, or what might be a reasonable settlement.

The adjective *evaluative* only refers to the power to offer an evaluation, not the power to persuade or pressure the parties to accept the evaluation. However, the mere expression of an evaluation can influence parties, that is assert a directive influence, without the mediator doing anything more than offering the evaluation. Thus, an evaluation is inherently directive and therefore risks diluting the principle of party self-determination. When the mediator goes the next step and assertively persuades and pressures, the mediation moves pass mere evaluation toward more directive forms of mediation.

Evaluatively Directive Mediation

When the mediator evaluates and then pushes his or her evaluation, the mediator shifts into another form of mediation, labeled here as evaluatively directive, an approach that threatens party self-determination. This form of mediation is practiced in the U.S. when mediators implement their evaluative power by either gently encouraging or assertively pressing parties to move toward or adopt their evaluations.

In Continental Europe, the mediator's expected if not preferred role can be influenced by his or her civil law upbringing. In a study that compares mediation practices in Australia, a common law jurisdiction, with Germany, a civil law jurisdiction, Nadja Alexander noted that in Germany: "Like the government legal centres offering conciliation services, most of the dispute resolution processes associated with these conciliation centres [chambers of commerce] do not follow an interest-based mediation model. Rather, the processes offered tend to be directive, interventionist and rights-based in nature."[14]

Wisely Directive Mediation

In some cultures, disputing parties are accustomed to relying on a "wise" third party as a source of the "right" answers who will assertively if not aggressively direct them toward a solution. A wisely directive mediator investigates the dispute, evaluates it, and formulates and promotes solutions based on the wisdom for which he or she was selected. That wisdom could be informed by local cultural norms, religious values, or the mediator's leadership or authoritative position, age, or legal knowledge. Parties expect to receive answers and are receptive to, if not desirous of, adopting them. There seems to be little regard to protecting party self-determination. Therefore, while the role of the wise third party may be to "mediate," the third party effectively functions as a quasi-adjudicator imposing a resolution on the parties. Wisely directive mediators can be found in some Islamic and Chinese cultures, among other places.[15]

Distinguish Wisely Directive Mediation from Other Settlement Processes

Wisely directive is different from evaluative mediation in two primary ways. First, as used in the U.S., evaluative mediation still provides the opportunity for parties to ignore or dismiss the mediator's opinion with minimal consequences, and both the parties and the mediator typically understand this. Second, wisely directive mediation has a different set of assumptions in that both the mediator and the parties expect the mediator to guide them toward a solution parties are prepared to accept.[16] As should be apparent from these descriptions, wisely directive practices is a form of mediation that seems to give the least regard to preserving party self-determination.

This section on various adjectives suggests a continuum of cultural influences and practices around the globe. Any generalizations are risky especially because no country has a monolithic approach. Nevertheless, these generalizations based on likely cultural propensities can at least sensitize attorneys to the range of possible adjectives to look for. A tentative continuum might be constructed with Chinese and Islamic cultures being the most directive, Civil Law cultures less, followed by the U.S. and Australian cultures, with English practices being the most elicitive along with transformative mediation in the U.S. It remains to be seen whether this continuum[17] will withstand the ongoing study of global mediation practices.

This next section considers how a participant's preference point on the elicitive-directive continuum shapes the resulting mediation process.

A Grid of Approaches by Mediators and Parties/Attorneys

As Professor Leonard Riskin emphasized, it takes two to create a mediation process. It is not formulated by the mediator alone or the parties/attorneys alone. Each participant can influence the shape of the resulting mediation process.[18] But, rather than focusing on influence here, I will consider how the cultural preference of each participant, when coalesced in the mediation, produces a distinctive mediation process. Instead of building a grid around each participant's ability to influence the final resulting process, this grid maps each participant's preference.

The grid consists of two axes. The horizontal one maps the mediator's dominant approach to the mediation. It incorporates Riskin's elicitive-directive continuum, a continuum that reflects a range of mediators' approaches found around the globe. Mediators can be highly facilitative, predominately facilitative, facilitative-directive, and varying degrees of directiveness. Riskin carefully defines directiveness broadly to include evaluations and assertive mediator behavior.[19]

The vertical axis maps the cultural preference of the parties/attorneys for third party assistance in resolving disputes.[20] It focuses on their preferred relationship with the mediator. The axis maps a continuum of party/attorney preferences that ranges from preferring elicitive to directive mediators. You would expect parties/attorneys brought up in an individualistic society to lean toward preferring a more elicitive approach and to be less deferential to a mediator's directiveness while a side brought up in a more collectivist society is more likely to prefer a more directive mediator.[21]

Parties/Attorneys' Preference
Prefer Elicitive Approach

A
Problem-Solving

F
Dysfunctional

Mediator's Approach

Elicitive

B
Evaluative

Directive

E
Evaluatively
Directive

D
Dysfunctional

C
Wisely Directive

Prefer Directive Approach

This second axis firmly demonstrates how it takes two to tango—to create the mediation process. A mediator who is directive, even aggressively so, for instance, does not necessarily result in the parties/attorneys being deferential to the mediator's procedural moves or substantive direction. As the second axis clarifies, the parties/attorneys must be willing partners—that is, be receptive to a more directive approach for the resulting process actually to *be* directive.

The grid illustrates the importance of the mediator and parties/attorneys sharing compatible preferences in order for the mediation process to function, and shows how these preferences shape the resulting process. Let's consider several combinations.

If the mediator is extremely elicitive and the parties/attorneys prefer an extremely elicitive approach, then the result can be a classically problem-solving mediation that preserves party self-determination. See point A.

If the mediator is modestly directive and the parties/attorneys prefer a modestly elicitive approach, the result can be a classically evaluative mediation where the mediator offers evaluations and the parties/attorneys give some weight to them. See point B.

If the mediator is extremely directive and the parties/attorneys prefer an extremely directive approach, the result can be a wisely directive mediation. See point C.

If the mediator is extremely elicitive and the parties/attorneys prefer an extremely directive approach, the mediation process may become dysfunctional. The parties/attorneys are likely to become quite frustrated because they are not getting the mediation service that they prefer. See point D.

Within these prototypical results, many gradations can be encountered. For example, if the mediator is evaluative and considerably directive and the parties/attorneys prefer a considerably directive approach, the result is likely to be an evaluatively directive mediation process. See point E. If the mediator is evaluatively directive and the parties/attorneys prefer primarily an elicitive approach, the mediation process also may become dysfunctional because the parties/attorneys are likely to become frustrated with the process. See point F.

In the spirit of Riskin's caveats in his article about his "New New Grid System," this grid hopefully promotes understanding and discussion while avoiding being so complicated that it becomes confusing and unmanageable.[22] The tension between formulating a nuanced grid and one that is easily accessible is inherent in this undertaking. I prefer to err in favor of simplicity in order to present succinctly the encounter between distinctively cultural approaches of mediators and the preferences of parties/attorneys. The resulting grid, however, should not be blindly followed as a confident predictor of the resulting mediation process. Its value is in offering a framework for discerning and selecting the type of mediator who might formulate the sort of mediation process that may be effective with your client and the other side.

Impact of Mediator's Approach on Client Representation

After you select a mediator who is culturally trained and suitable, you need to figure out how to represent your client before that sort of mediator. Knowing that the mediator is *culturally trained* does not impact radically on your approach to representation; it only expands the possibilities of what can be achieved in the mediation. The mediator can assist you in clarifying any culturally-related interests of the parties and overcoming any culturally-related impasses. Selecting a *culturally suitable* mediator, however, can singularly shape your entire representation strategy. Your whole approach to enlisting assistance from the mediator can be shaped by your understanding of how the mediator will approach the process, in other words, your approach will be shaped by the "adjective."[23]

If you select a problem-solving mediator (one that will stay in that mode), you, as the attorney, can advocate as a problem-solver.[24] You have the freedom and security to share information including interests, brainstorm options, recognize weaknesses in your client's legal case, and be open to creative solutions that go beyond the ones in the legal papers. You can feel secure[25] asking the mediator for help—whether to sort out interests, facilitate evaluating the legal case, or develop multiple options. You also have much freedom and security with a transformative mediator, who is trained to support whatever sort of process is structured and implemented by you, your client, and the other side, although you cannot rely on the mediator's expertise or initiatives to create or direct a process, as the transformative mediator is committed to being non-directive.

In contrast, consider the impact of selecting an evaluative (non-directive) mediator on your approach to advocacy. Mediator evaluations can take a variety of forms, including the mediator assessing the reasonableness of various settlement options, assessing the consequences of not settling, or recommending settlement proposals either as the mediation unfolds or as a "mediator's proposal." Knowing that the mediator may formulate one or more of these types of evaluations can induce you to approach the mediation more like an adjudicatory process than a negotiation. Instead of formulating a negotiation strategy based on candid conversations with the mediator and meeting parties' interests, you are apt to return to the traditional adversarial approach, so familiar in the courtroom, in which you withhold unfavorable information, hide any flexibility to avoid implying a lack of confidence in the legal case, and present carefully crafted partisan arguments and positions that are designed to persuade a decision-maker to act favorably.

Alternatively, you might problem-solve, but in a selective way that reduces the risk of an unfavorable assessment by the mediator. In such a constricted problem-solving approach, you still share and advocate your client's interests and engage in such problem-solving moves as brainstorming options and designing creative solutions, but only up to a point. You will avoid sharing information or showing flexibility that may risk a less favorable evaluation from the mediator. This carefully calibrated strategic plan can dilute the potential of a problem-solving process by limiting the ability of parties to uncover optimal solutions. Withholding information may hide valuable matters relevant to devising solutions. Hiding flexibility may cramp the opportunity to search for and devise creative solutions. But, in return, you can secure an evaluation that might spur parties toward settlement.

As a mediator's approach moves further toward the end of the directive continuum, your problem-solving approach will become more constricted until it morphs into a traditional adversarial strategy. When the mediator's approach becomes highly directive, or wisely directive, you are likely to view the mediator as a decision-maker and will advocate accordingly.

Finally, this discussion implies that a mediator will stay within the selected approach throughout the mediation process. But Riskin reminded us that mediation is not a static process. Some, if not many, mediators purposely vary their roles as the mediation progresses by facilitating at one point, evaluating at the point that seems useful, being directive when necessary at another point, and returning to facilitating when it seems appropriate—a practice that they espouse as necessary for resolving disputes.[26] Unfortunately, Riskin omitted assessing the impact of this mediator practice on how attorneys represent their clients. When the mediator freely switches roles, the attorney will likely abandon a nuanced representation approach and adopt the safest mode of client representation, an adversarial one, because the attorney is likely to think that it will provide the best protection against an unfavorable evaluation.

Conclusion

This chapter suggests when a cross-cultural dispute might justify bringing in a mediator. When you decide to do so, you should consider enlisting a third party who is both culturally-trained and culturally-suitable for the dispute. After selecting the mediator, you need to contemplate how to effectively represent your client in the process. There is no one all-purpose strategy that will maximize the opportunities before every sort of mediator. The optimum advocacy approach depends on the sort of mediator selected.

Endnotes

[1] These differences can arise in disputes between parties from different countries as well as between parties within the same country when the parties come from different regions or different religious, ethnic, or professional groups.

[2] *Compare* Amr Abdalla, *Principles of Islamic Interpersonal Conflict Intervention: A Search Within Islam and Western Literature*, 15 JOURNAL OF LAW & RELATIONS 151, 161-62, 165, 176 (2000-2001); ROGER FISHER, ET ALL, GETTING TO YES 41, 48 (2d ed., 1991).

[3] *See* JEANNE M. BRETT, NEGOTIATING GLOBALLY: HOW TO NEGOTIATE DEALS, RESOLVE DISPUTES, AND MAKE DECISIONS ACROSS CULTURAL BOUNDARIES 8-9 (2001).

[4] *See* FISHER, ET AL., *supra* note 2.

[5] Harold Abramson, *International Dispute Resolution: Cross-Cultural Dimensions and Structuring Appropriate Processes*, *in* ALAN RAU, ET AL., PROCESSES OF DISPUTE RESOLUTION 918-21 (3d ed., 2002).

[6] *See, e.g.,* GEERT HOFSTEDE, CULTURE'S CONSEQUENCES (abridged 1980, 1984); GEERT HOFSTEDE, CULTURES AND ORGANIZATIONS: SOFTWARE OF THE MIND (1997); DEAN ALLEN FOSTER, BARGAINING ACROSS BORDERS: HOW TO NEGOTIATE BUSINESS SUCCESSFULLY ANYWHERE IN THE WORLD 264-72 (1992, 1995) (shows how Hofstede's work relates to international negotiations).

[7] For studies of American culture, *see, e.g.,* GARY ALTHEN, AMERICAN WAYS xiii, 4, 8, 9-10, 14, 17, 24-25, 136-37 (1998); EDWARD C. STEWART & MILTON J. BENNETT, AMERICAN CULTURAL PATTERNS: A CROSS-CULTURAL PERSPECTIVE (1991).

[8] *See* Loretta Kelly's description of an Aboriginal Australian representative whose behavior was sharply at variance with those he supposedly represented. Loretta Kelly, *Indigenous Experiences in Negotiation*, Chapter 35 in this volume.

[9] *See* HAROLD ABRAMSON, MEDIATION REPRESENTATION: ADVOCATING IN A PROBLEM-SOLVING PROCESS 133-45 (2004).

[10] The CPR Institute (International Institute for Conflict Prevention & Resolution) conducted this invitation-only one-and-half day retreat at the Mohonk Mountain House in October, 2005.

[11] This section is excerpted and edited from JACQUELINE M. NOLAN-HALEY, ET AL., INTERNATIONAL CONFLICT RESOLUTION: CONSENSUAL ADR PROCESS 123-37 (2005).

[12] The Model Standards were prepared and approved by three leading organizations in the United States dispute resolution field: American Arbitration Association, the Litigation and Dispute Resolution Sections of the American Bar Association, and the Society of Professionals in Dispute Resolution (1992-1994). For a discussion of the Model Standards by the chair of the drafting committee, *see* John Feerick, *Toward Uniform Standards of Conduct for Mediators*, 38 SOUTHERN TEXAS LAW REVIEW 455 (1997). A comprehensive proposal to revise the Model Standards (dated Apr. 10, 2005) is pending before the three sponsoring organizations. *See* MODEL STANDARDS OF CONDUCT FOR MEDIATORS: PROPOSED CHANGES AN REPORTER'S NOTES, *available at* http://moritzlaw.osu.edu/dr/msoc/ (last visited Mar. 14, 2006).

[13] *See* ABRAMSON, supra note 8, at 71-72; *also see* ROBERT A. BARUCH BUSH & JOSEPH P. FOLGER, THE PROMISE OF MEDIATION: RESPONDING TO CONFLICT THROUGH EMPOWERMENT AND RECOGNITION (1994). For an extensive resource list, *see* INSTITUTE FOR THE STUDY OF CONFLICT TRANSFORMATION, INC. *at* http://www.transformativemediation.org (last visited Mar. 14, 2006).

[14] *See* Nadja Alexander, *What's Law Got to Do with It? Mapping Modern Mediation Movements in Civil and Common Law Jurisdictions*, 13 BOND LAW REVIEW 16, 23 (Dec. 2001), *available at* http://www.bond.edu.au/law/blr/vol13-2/Alexander.doc.

[15] *See* George Irani, *Islamic Medication Techniques for Middle East Conflicts*, 3 MIDDLE EASTERN REVIEW OF INTERNATIONAL AFFAIRS 4 (June 1999); John Murray, *The Cairo Stories: Some Reflections on Conflict Resolution in Egypt*, 13 NEGOTIATION JOURNAL 39, 53-54 (1997); Ann Black, *Alternative Dispute Resolution in Brunei Darussalam: The Blending of Imported and Traditional Processes*, 13 BOND LAW REVIEW 16, 26 (Dec. 2001), *available at*

 http://www.bond.edu.au/law/blr/vol13-2/black.doc; SALAH AL-HEJAILAN, MEDIATION AS A MEANS FOR AMICABLE SETTLEMENT DISPUTES IN ARAB COUNTRIES, presented to WIPO Conference on Mediation, Geneva, Switzerland (Mar. 29, 1996), *available at* http://arbiter.wipo.int/events/conferences/1996/hejailan.html; Eric Glassman, *The Function of Mediation in China: Examining the Impact of Regulations Governing the People's Mediation Committees*, 10 UCLA PACIFIC BASIN LAW JOURNAL 460 (1992); Michael T. Colatrella, Jr., *Court-Performed Mediation in the People's Republic of China: A Proposed Model to Improve the United States District Courts' mediation Programs*, 15 OHIO STATE JOURNAL ON DISPUTE RESOLUTION 391, 404-08 (2000); Robert Perkovich, *A Comparative Analysis of Community Mediation in the United States and the People's Republic of China*, 10 TEMPLE INTERNATIONAL & COMPARATIVE LAW JOURNAL 313 (1996).

[16] *See* NOLAN-HALEY, ET AL., *supra* note 6, at 136-37.

[17] Although this analysis concentrates on one prominent feature of mediation, the elicitive-directive continuum along with the corollary party self-determination continuum, a more nuanced analysis of the adjectives would consider other culturally distinguishing features. Mediation processes can be further differentiated based on the degree of impartiality of the mediator and the degree of influence the mediator has over the parties, whether the mediator focuses primarily on process or on process and content, the importance of confidentiality, and whether mediator training is required, among other distinguishing features.

[18] *See* Leonard Riskin, *Decisionmaking in Mediation: The New Old Grid and the New New Grid System*, 79 NOTRE DAME LAW REVIEW 1, 37-46 (2003).

[19] *See id.*

[20] The vertical axis reflects the parties'/attorneys' composite preference for a mediator although the preference of each attorney and each client may differ, especially in a cross-cultural mediation. A separate preference axis can be mapped for each participant. The vertical axis reflects the result negotiated by the participants among themselves regarding the sort of mediator that they want to select. Presumably, it is a result that fits the cultural needs of the parties.

[21] *But see* Christopher Honeyman, et al., *Skill is Not Enough: Seeking Connectedness and Authority in Mediation,* 20 NEGOTIATION JOURNAL 489 (2004) (comparing U.S. practices with community mediations in China and Australia).

[22] *See* Riskin, *supra* note 17, at 50-53.

[23] The following analysis of how the adjective can shape your representation strategy is taken from Harold Abramson, *Problem-Solving Advocacy in Mediations: A Model of Client Representation,* 10 HARVARD NEGOTIATION LAW REVIEW 103, 124-28 (2005).

[24] For a full discussion on how to advocate as a problem-solver, *see* ABRAMSON, *supra* note 8.

[25] *But see* the section on mediation's structural biases in Christopher Honeyman, *Understanding Mediators*, Chapter 67 in the volume.

[26] *See* Riskin, *supra* note 17, at 13-17, 17-21, 28-29 (Riskin further noted how each role can either foster or impair party self-determination).

∞ 69 ∞

Allies in Negotiation

Bernard Mayer

Editors' Note: *In a thought-provoking book, Mayer analyzed new roles that experienced mediators and other neutrals might play. Here, Mayer takes the other side of the coin, and discusses how negotiators could enlist skilled neutrals as allies instead. This could help you to get a complex negotiation framed properly or to approach the other side in ways that will put them in the right frame of mind.*

Since negotiation is a key vehicle for how we handle disputes, a critical question for conflict professionals is how to promote effective negotiations and competent negotiators. Historically, the conflict resolution field has taken three approaches to this. We have provided negotiation training; we have helped design negotiation procedures; and we have provided third parties to conduct negotiation processes. All of these are, of course, valuable contributions—but they are also relatively sparsely used in the universe of significant negotiations. An additional approach to enhancing negotiations is to be found in ally roles. Three questions arise: (1) What competencies can allies provide to assist negotiators? (2) How do allies fit into the negotiation system? (3) How can ally services be made available to negotiators in a practical and acceptable way?

What Are Negotiation Allies?
As with the third party role in conflict, the ally role is one we find wherever there are negotiations. Advocates, lawyers, labor representatives, real estate agents, community organizers, and human resource professionals act as negotiation allies as part of their roles. In this respect, there is nothing particularly new about the concept of a negotiation ally. Since all of these roles, help people get the most out of a negotiation process.

Other approaches assume a different basic purpose and bring a different set of values, skills, and concepts to the ally function. These approaches offer significant additional opportunities to assist negotiators. For the most part, allies focus on assisting in the negotiation process through taking on the lead role in negotiation, through providing substantive expertise, and through helping to enhance the bargaining position of negotiators, primarily by assisting them in developing more powerful alternatives to negotiation (e.g., through developing a strong legal case, political alternatives, or substantive choices). But other significant needs that negotiators have are for assistance in developing their own capacities to be effective and for help in understanding the dynamics of the negotiation process itself.

For example, in many grievance procedures a step involving a direct face-to-face meeting between the grievant and the manager is required. If this does not resolve the dispute, then there are usually later steps involving more formal negotiations, mediation, or arbitration. The focus in most dispute resolution systems is on how to make the latter steps more effective. Usually, very little attention and resources are given to the informal negotiation stage, but these may well provide the best opportunity to resolve the issues involved with a minimum of long-term animosity. The more common negotiation assistance is formal, substantive, and representational, as opposed to informal, procedural, and supportive.

Negotiation allies seldom operate from a conflict paradigm. That is, they do not generally see their role as conflict specialists whose task is to help people engage in conflict productively, creatively, powerfully, and wisely. Their focus is instead on substance, rights, technical issues, or political advice and, as a result, the actual dynamics of the conflict interaction are not dealt with as intentionally or wisely as they might be. While many allies in negotiation are in fact quite experienced in dealing with conflict and often excellent at helping people be effective negotiators, the absence of a conflict perspective means that many potentially useful approaches, analytic and practical, to negotiation are not systematically and consciously brought to the table.

So while negotiation allies are prevalent in most significant negotiation settings, there are a great variety of ways in which this role is perceived, fulfilled, and understood. People in ally roles may view themselves as representatives, advocates, counsel, advisors, organizers, friends, coaches, strategists, substantive experts, supervisors, teachers, or therapists. But what is often missing is a conscious understanding of these roles: a set of conceptual and practical tools that can help them focus on serving to enhance others' negotiating capacity. We can understand the nature of how allies fulfill their roles by considering five variables.

Intentional—De Facto

How aware are allies of the role being played, and how aware are the negotiators of what they are asking from an ally? Further, how aware are allies of the specific approach they are taking to the role, and how aware are negotiators of exactly what they are asking or wanting from an ally? If I am negotiating a salary from a prospective employer, what kind of advice will I seek, how conscious will I even be of asking for advice, and how much do I want advice about what I can realistically expect to get, as opposed to how to conduct the negotiations? When I approach friends, colleagues, or agents, do they see themselves as providing negotiation assistance, or do they see their role in a different light? We have all used allies and we have all been allies in negotiations, but we are not always aware that this is the assistance we are asking for or offering.

Supportive—Directive

Is the assistance offered in the spirit of advice and support for the negotiator, or does the ally take over the negotiation process? [Macfarlane, *New Advocacy*] For example, if I go to a lawyer for assistance with a divorce negotiation, will the lawyer take charge of the negotiation and act primarily as my agent, or will the lawyer act more as my advisor and assistant in conducting the process? To what extent is the ally a partner and co-participant in negotiation, a representative who acts as an agent, or an advisor who assists the party in a supportive way but without actually conducting the negotiation?

Substantive—Procedural

Does the ally offer advice about the substantive elements of the negotiation, e.g., likely outcomes, precedents, options, legal alternatives, etc., or does the ally focus more on the negotiation and communication process itself? Does a seller, for instance, mainly rely on her real estate agent for information about market value and financing or for assistance with setting a reasonable price, deciding when to reject, accept, or make a counteroffer, or when to try to communicate further with the prospective purchaser? If the focus is procedural, what is the lens through which the process is viewed? Does the ally understand negotiation as a communication process, a problem-solving effort, a conflict management procedure, a relationship building effort, all of the above, or none of the above?

Individual—System Focus

Is the commitment, focus, and accountability of the ally to the individual negotiator, to a group, or to a system? As a labor representative in a grievance, one's obligation is to promote the interests of the individual grievant, but it is also to protect the rights of the collective bargaining unit as a whole and to advance the interests of the union as well. In providing advice to someone negotiating a divorce agreement, whether as a lawyer, counselor or friend, one's focus may be on the specific needs of the divorcee, on the needs of the children, or the overall family system.

Tactical—Strategic

Allies are sometimes valuable in helping negotiators see the big picture, but is a given ally's focus more likely to be on specific moves at specific moments in a negotiation? Will an ally focus more on how to frame particular offers, and how to respond to threats or proposals, or will she be more tuned in to the structure of the negotiation and the nature of the relationships among the participants? Will the ally take a short-term view of what can be accomplished in a negotiation, or will she focus on the way a particular negotiation can alter a long-term relationship or open up new opportunities over time?

Of course, in practice, allies act in a variety of ways and do not rigidly adhere to one end of any of these polarities. But we can understand the role of allies in terms of how they operate along each of the continua described by these variables.

What Allies Bring to the Table

Informal, de facto allies are everywhere and are essential players in negotiation. Their role can be both constructive and problematic. Allies can give wise advise about how to pursue a negotiation, or they can project their own needs onto the negotiator in a destructive manner. We have all probably received well intentioned advice on how to handle a conflict that would only have led to an unproductive escalation if we followed it. In fact, one of the key skills of negotiators, and therefore of negotiation allies, is to identify the allies for all participants in the negotiation system, the roles they are playing, and the way they can be used effectively. In this chapter, however, we are most concerned with those allies who function intentionally and supportively, because the conscious use of allies in negotiations has great potential to have a constructive impact on negotiations. What conscious and intentional (and therefore developable) perspectives and skills can allies bring to the table to enhance the negotiation process? Let's focus on several specific perspectives that an ally can add that are essential across a wide range of negotiation settings.

Communication Skills

Communication is at the heart of effective negotiation, and good negotiators are usually good communicators. [Putnam, *Communication*] Allies can help negotiators hone their communication skills, become conscious of how they are communicating and what they are communicating, and become better listeners and observers. Allies also help by providing direct assistance in communicating and by directly observing the communication that occurs during a negotiation. While negotiators can use assistance with a broad range of communication skills, four elements of communication particularly call for the help of allies.

Listening

Allies can help by listening to what is being said in negotiations, by working with the negotiator to understand what is being said by others, by emphasizing the importance of hearing both spoken and unspoken messages, by helping negotiators separate out their reactions to what is being said from the actual message that is being communicated, by encouraging negotiators to provide the time and space in negotiations for listening, and by working with negotiators to develop an atmosphere in which communicating is encouraged and listening is valued.

Framing and Naming

How people present their ideas, thoughts, needs, suggestions, reactions, proposals, information, and arguments in negotiation is a second key communication skill. Very important ideas or proposals are often poorly presented, and this is particularly true when there is a lot of tension or anxiety associated with the communication. Allies can help negotiators frame their comments for maximum constructive effect. Sometimes the most difficult element in framing involves presenting a very hard issue in a way that does not diminish its importance or intensity in any way, but that also does not provoke a defensive reaction, in order to ensure that there is a genuine engagement around it.

Establishing a "Communication Loop"[1]

Effective communication is not about listening and framing as linear and sequential processes. The heart of good communication is the establishment of a *loop* of communication, whereby one is listening while talking and communicating while listening. Sometimes the most important information available to a negotiator can be understood from the reactions of the other party to what the negotiator is saying, while he or she is still saying it; but often we are so focused on what we have to say that we don't notice the reactions of others. Similarly, we often do not understand that how we communicate, especially in the way we listen, is often far more important than what we actually say. These are subtle but ever present dynamics in negotiation that an ally can help the negotiator become more aware of and adept at.

Establishing Systems of Communication

Communication in negotiation is not just about what is directly said at the negotiation table but also establishing a system of communication away from the table.

Paying attention to the totality of the communication system that surrounds a communication is challenging when we are involved in an intense or demanding interaction and is, therefore, one of the ways in which allies can be most helpful.

Integrative—Distributive Wisdom

In one way or another all negotiators must face the essential negotiator's challenge—how to attend to both the distributive and integrative aspects of negotiation,[2] that is how to work effectively for mutual gains while protecting one's own separate interests as well. As Lax and Sebenius have suggested,[3] there are very different tactics that negotiators use when trying to create value and when claiming value, and at times these tactics are contradictory. For example, how much information should one share in the service of exploring the possibility of a creative solution that will be built upon our different needs, knowing that this information can make one more vulnerable?

Negotiators often struggle with how to create the right balance here, [Adler, *Protean*] and there is no one right approach to solving what is sometimes presented as a "prisoner's dilemma." In practice, this means it is hard to know how to pay attention to maintaining good relationships, establishing open communication, sharing information fully, and being willing to discuss a range of proposals while holding firm on key values and concerns, responding to provocative behavior effectively, and defending ourselves against aggressive negotiation tactics. The more intense, complicated, intractable, and long-lasting a conflict is, the more difficult it is to handle this dilemma. This dynamic is present in all difficult negotiations whether interpersonal, inter-organizational or international. For many, the choice feels like it's between acting in a way that violates important values about interpersonal relationships and acting in a way that feels weak and vulnerable. Allies can help negotiators understand the interplay of these dimensions of negotiation, and they can be particularly useful in encouraging people not to act simply and uncritically along either the distributional or integrative dimension but instead to consider how to act wisely along both at the same time.

Emotional Support and Emotional Distance

Significant negotiations can easily stoke up participants' emotions, and emotional exchanges are often key to effective negotiations. The challenge for negotiators is not to suppress their emotions but to use them responsibly and effectively. [Shapiro, *Emotions*] Another challenge is how to stay creative and focused when one is feeling threatened, angry, frustrated, or even excited. Negotiators need both emotional support and perspective. They need allies who will accept their emotions and provide an appropriate expressive outlet, but they also need allies who can maintain some distance from the emotions, to help negotiators see through their feelings to the larger picture. Sometimes those personally closest to the negotiator, such as friends, other team members, or constituents, are the most effective supporters in this regard. But these informal allies, in the name of friendship or because of their own feelings about the negotiation, sometimes reinforce the most reactive, destructive or negative emotions and thereby fail to help the negotiator work through his or her feelings or put them into perspective.

A Process Sense

In most negotiations, the relative amount of time planning and strategizing about substantive issues far outweighs the amount of thought given to procedural issues (if any planning occurs at all). This is true before, during, and after negotiations. If thought is given to process, it is often very limited and tactical in nature. Yet poor or inadequate process may impede negotiations more often than substantive impasse. Maintaining an awareness of process and considering procedural alternatives can be key to moving negotiations forward. Allies with a background in conflict intervention and negotiation can help negotiators consider a whole range of procedural issues such as table formulation, agenda development, in-team processes, information sharing procedures, option generation, incremental exchanges, psychological needs, communication mechanisms, agreement identification and testing, exploring interests at the appropriate level of depth, looking for agreements in principle, and so forth. This is where the availability of allies with experience and training in conflict can be especially valuable.

Understanding Power Dynamics

To some extent, all negotiations involve the application of power. However, what type of power is applied, and how, are critical to how a negotiation unfolds. The crude application of a coercive source of power can lead to an impasse. Good negotiators develop an ability to use their power wisely, subtly, sparingly, and constructively. They also know how to respond effectively to the coercive application of power by others. But in the middle of negotiations, it is easy to get drawn into an unproductive competitive display of power that is neither effective nor actually very powerful. Negotiators often need advice or at least feedback on how to use power in negotiations and how to respond to the power of others, to prevent the interaction devolving into a primitive "tit for tat" sequence of responses. It helps to have some good analytical tools for understanding the sources of power, the nature of its application, and the consequences of different applications.[4] [Korobkin, *Power*; Bernard, *Powerlessness*]

A System Perspective

As discussed above, it is easy for negotiators to lose sight of the system in which a negotiation is embedded and to focus almost exclusively on the specific relationship being played out at the negotiation table. Yet what happens away from the table and the way the negotiation interacts with the larger system of which it is part are critical. This is true whether one is considering the future of the West Bank, a labor management contract, a divorce negotiation, or a commercial dispute. We often do not realize how much our actions and perceptions are governed by the system within which a negotiation is occurring and how limited a set of choices negotiators may actually have. [Miller & Dingwall, *Theater*] An adequate understanding of systems theory, of system maintenance dynamics, and of the way energy travels through systems is not an abstract mental exercise, but an essential aspect of what makes negotiations work. But this is not the natural focus or orientation of most negotiators, and it is another element of the role allies can play in enhancing a negotiator's capacities.

Cultural Awareness

Most negotiations involve issues of diversity and culture. Negotiations usually require working across some cultural boundary such as gender, age, race, ethnicity, religion, geography, organization or profession. As a result, an often hidden but fundamental factor in negotiation involves different norms about communication, problem-solving, face, power, direct dealing, rapport building, time, authority and status.[5] Particularly when negotiating in a new cultural environment or when struggling with how much to try to adapt to another culture or remain within one's own cultural comfort zone, people need assistance in understanding and adapting to the cultural dynamics in a negotiation. [Kelly, *Indigenous Experience*; Goh, *Errors*]

Permission to Settle or Not to Settle

In the end, the decision as to whether to arrive at an agreement or stay in conflict can be a very lonely and frightening moment for negotiators. They often need someone they trust and who they feel has their best interests at heart to talk to at the critical moment when a settlement is in sight. [Wade, *Tribe*] Negotiators often need someone on their side, who they respect and have confidence in, to in effect give them emotional permission to settle, if that is what they choose to do, or to decline to settle. Effective allies don't make this choice for negotiators. They can't—even if they have a lot of influence. They may choose to make a strong recommendation, even to exert considerable amount of pressure, but the wise ally helps negotiators think through their genuine choices, helps them consider alternatives broadly and with a view to the entire system, and helps them think through how to choose the best of all of their alternatives. But at a certain point, allies also provide a kind of psychological reinforcement that can allow a negotiator to make a decision, whatever that may be, with a certain amount of confidence and with a minimum need to second guess. In the role of a mediator, I have seen lawyers provide this function over and over for their clients. An effective advocate helps negotiators develop meaningful and realistic alternatives, helps them assess these alternatives, and then supports them in deciding among the alternatives—including the decision to conclude the negotiation without an agreement.

Alternatives Management

The power of a negotiator is to a great extent defined by the alternatives he or she has. [Korobkin, *Power*] When we have no alternative but to settle, our power is very limited (often dependent on our ability to act as if we have no need for an agreement). So developing effective alternatives to a negotiating agreement or developing realistic alternatives for what we can aim for in negotiation is one of the main ways of increasing our power and flexibility in the negotiation process. Used effectively, this can contribute to a creative and positive negotiation stance. But if negotiators use their alternatives as a bludgeon or in a crude way, they can contribute to the breakdown of the negotiation process. In a way, this is the paradox of whether disputants can (or must) prepare for war and peace at the same time. How negotiators develop, maintain, use and alter their alternatives is therefore key to their ability to participate effectively in negotiations, and an important role of negotiation allies is to help with this.

Using Outside Resources

When people are in the middle of an intense negotiation, it is often hard to think about using outside or unfamiliar resources to assist them. Negotiators may fear a loss of control, may lack confidence in outsiders, or may simply be too wrapped up in the moment to take a step back and think about other resources that may be useful to them. These are reasons why third parties are used relatively infrequently or are not brought in until negotiations have broken down. Other resources are underutilized as well (including a whole range of potential allies). Further, the outside resources that are used may often have a very limited perspective. For example, in serious public disputes, leaders may consult lawyers, political advisors, and sometimes public relations experts. They are less likely to bring in outside technical experts and much less likely to bring in process specialists. Allies can help negotiators think through what other resources they need, how to obtain them, and when to use them. If third parties are brought in, allies can help negotiators work with them effectively.

Attending to Team Dynamics

When negotiations involve teams, as they frequently do, attention needs to be given to team dynamics. Sometimes, an internal facilitator is needed to deal with in-team processes and problems. Whether this particular function is needed or not, however, paying attention to team dynamics, decision-making, communication, and morale is an important and often neglected aspect of effective negotiation. Mediators often find themselves having to try to help a negotiation team work together more effectively, but their role in this is limited by their third party status. Attending to team dynamics is an important potential contribution allies make to the negotiation process.

The Negotiation System

Few significant negotiations occur without the involvement in some way of multiple players. In some way, allies are almost always present. Negotiations often involve bargaining teams. Third parties may have a role, and advocates are often involved as well. The success of a negotiation is often dependent on the cohesiveness and functionality of the whole negotiation system of which allies are only one part. The effectiveness of allies, therefore, is very dependent on how they fit into the whole system, whether they enhance the functionality of a negotiation group or make it more unwieldy, whether their roles are clear or murky, and how they interact with advocates (who are also allies) and third parties.

Role Clarity

Since the ally role is really an amalgam of different possible roles and functions, role clarity is often elusive. The clearer allies are that they are in fact functioning to *support* negotiators and to enable them to be more effective in identifying and meeting their negotiation goals, the more likely it is that they will be able to fit into the negotiation system in a constructive way. The skills that an effective ally brings to the table are in many respects very similar to the skills required for negotiators to be effective. But negotiators are subject to different demands and, in particular, have to be focused on the substance of the negotiation and the decisions that have to be made constantly throughout a negotiation process. If allies are clear that they have a different set of roles and if those roles can be clearly articulated, then they are likely to have an easier time finding a constructive place in the negotiation system.

Some ally roles are easier to define then others. Allies acting as spokespersons, technical or legal consultants, or bargaining agents, may be familiar to negotiators, and their role readily understood. An ally who focuses on communication, process, and systems issues is often playing a less easily defined role. Negotiators may be more comfortable asking for help of a kind that is familiar and easy to define, but the most significant way in which allies can assist with difficult negotiations often lies elsewhere.

Allies and Advocates

Advocates are one important kind of ally, and in its largest sense, advocacy can include a broad range of the ally contributions discussed above. But advocates usually see their role in a more limited way. An advocate's job is in some way to articulate and try to achieve the goals of their client. Advocates usually see their role as trying to get as much as they can for their clients.[6] To some extent, all allies must share the goal of helping negotiators achieve their most essential objectives. But the specific way in which they see themselves doing this and the attention they give to overall system dynamics are different from how traditional advocates do this. Allies do not necessarily represent or speak for the negotiator, but as described here, fulfill a whole series of functions that are intended to assist negotiators to be more effective as their own best advocates. In fact, advocates often need the same kind of assistance from allies that primary negotiators do. Allies with the focus that I have described are not just looking at the particular substance or negotiation interaction but the whole constellation of dynamics that surround it. On the other hand, because their focus is not primarily on the substantive issues per se, allies also have to limit their role in order to be effective.

Allies and Third Parties

The value and potential of allies does not in any way diminish the importance or role that third parties play. As is true with negotiators, the skills of mediators and of effective allies overlap considerably. The need for someone who can facilitate the interaction among the parties to a dispute and help manage the communication and problem-solving process is not always obviated by the presence of effective allies. While needing some of the same skills as third parties, the ally role is fundamentally different. The goal of allies is to help negotiators be more effective and powerful in achieving their interests. When the best way for negotiators to meet their interests is to insure that the others involved in the negotiation also achieve their goals, then the fundamental purpose of the ally and mediator will be similar. But that is not always the best way for negotiators to meet their own interests, and even when it is, that is usually not a reasonable/automatic assumption going into the negotiation. The ally's role is to be part of the negotiator's team in a way that mediators cannot be if they are to maintain their own overall role as facilitators of the negotiation process. [Love & Stulberg, *Mediation*; Honeyman, *Understanding Mediators*]

The dilemma for the mediator is how to maintain everyone's trust and confidence without taking any one party's side or adopting their party's interests in the sense that an ally must. Mediators are trusted because they do *not* take sides—and are mistrusted for the very same reason. Allies face the dilemma of how to stay very clearly on the side and in the corner of the negotiator while always helping the negotiator look at the larger picture. They are trusted because of that commitment, but this also defines the limit of their role.

When third parties are present, allies have a particular role to play in helping negotiators use the third party effectively. They may speak the third party's language, may have worked as third parties themselves, and might find that they can help the interaction between the negotiator and third party. But to remain effective, they must remember that they are allies of the negotiator, not of the third party.

Making Allies Available to Negotiators

Allies in one sense or another are usually present in complicated negotiations, but they are not generally selected with the particular purpose of fulfilling the role as I have described here. Negotiators ask for help, advice, counseling, and advocacy. They do not normally ask for the process oriented systems role that may be the most powerful way conflict specialists can assist with difficult negotiations. But negotiators do ask for allies. Consider these examples of how negotiators have reached out for assistance to just one practitioner group:

- *State agency facing a class action suit.* I was asked to train the negotiation team, help plan negotiation strategy, and offer ongoing consultation as the state and the plaintiffs successfully negotiated a consent decree on child welfare issues.
- *University administration and students.* I provided consultation over several years to university administrators as they considered how to work with student organizations around a number of issues, mostly political in nature.
- *Partnership dissolution negotiation.* A very profitable business partnership was being dissolved and the negotiation was bogging down because of poor interpersonal relationships and high levels of resentment. I worked with one of the parties to help him think through an appropriate approach. He was being advised that he had a strong legal case and should not agree to too great a compromise, but there was a danger that if he discussed his legal case the whole negotiation would immediately break down.
- *Labor union negotiations.* In preparation for a round of collective bargaining, particularly after difficult negotiations, I have been asked on several occasions to work with the management team or with the collective bargaining unit, and sometimes with both, to consider alternative approaches to negotiation.
- *Natural resource dispute.* A coalition of natural resource groups, with significant common goals about biodiversity but with many internal differences, asked for consultation on how to approach negotiations with federal agencies and how to accommodate their own differences in styles.
- *Superfund project manager.* A federal employee managing a Superfund clean-up requested ongoing support in strategizing how to deal with the many different interests and stakeholders. Originally we were asked to facilitate a stakeholder process, but at later stages of the project our work primarily involved coaching the project manager.

None of these involved negotiators specifically asking for negotiation allies, yet that was our role in all of these situations. Sometimes, the initial request was for what appeared to be third party assistance, but it quickly became clear that this was not feasible or optimal, it was just what people knew how to ask for. Many conflict professionals working on large and complex issues find themselves involved mostly in the role of an ally, consultant, strategist, internal facilitator, process consultant or trainer. Often we are asked to play a combination of these roles.

The challenge is how to make negotiation allies more readily useful, credible and available. While some of this may be a marketing challenge, the more profound issue is whether conflict specialists can understand this role thoroughly and can see its potential for themselves. If conflict specialists understand this, if they can look at how often they are asked, in effect if not overtly, to function as advisors or coaches and at how often they may be asked to fulfill other roles where the ally role is what is really needed, then they will increasingly put themselves forward as an ally and will increasingly be utilized as allies.

Another challenge is whether individuals and systems that support and manage negotiations (corporate counsel, labor unions, advocacy groups, human resource departments, equal employment offices, courts, federal agencies, etc.) can see the need for allies and can begin to build more resources and structures to make them available to their constituents or to the parties to the negotiations that they manage. One of the challenges here is to get over a mindset that automatically assumes that the solution to all negotiation problems is to provide either more elaborate "legal" services or some form of third party assistance. [Wade, *Experts*] While these will always be important tools, negotiation managers should also ask—perhaps first—what kinds of allies could be useful and how they might be provided.

Finally, conflict specialists should consider how to work with existing allies, such as advocates, organizers, human resource staff, shop stewards, technical advisers, ombuds offices, corporate counsel, and community leaders. Sometimes the most effective way to contribute to negotiations will not be to work with the negotiators themselves but with their existing allies. If we recognize the general need and general presence of allies in significant conflict, we can work on helping them enhance *their* effectiveness.

Endnotes

[1] *See* BERNARD MAYER, THE DYNAMICS OF CONFLICT RESOLUTION 122-27 (2000).

[2] *See* DAVID LAX & JAMES SEBENIUS, THE MANAGER AS NEGOTIATOR: BARGAINING FOR COOPERATION AND COMPETITIVE GAIN (1986); Kenneth Thomas, *Conflict and Conflict Management, in* HANDBOOK OF INDUSTRIAL AND ORGANIZATIONAL PSYCHOLOGY 889 (Marvin D. Dunnette ed., 1976); ROGER FISHER, ET AL., GETTING TO YES (1991); ROBERT AXELROD, THE EVOLUTION OF COOPERATION (1984).

[3] *See generally*, DAVID LAX & JAMES SEBENIUS, THE MANAGER AS NEGOTIATOR: BARGAINING FOR COOPERATION AND COMPETITIVE GAIN (1986).

[4] *See also,* KENNETH E. BOULDING, CONFLICT AND DEFENSE (1962); Bernard Mayer, *The Dynamics of Power in Mediation and Negotiation,* 16 MEDIATION QUARTERLY 75 (1987); ROBERT AXELROD, EVOLUTION OF COOPERATION (1984).

[5] *See* CHRISTOPHER W. MOORE, THE MEDIATION PROCESS: PRACTICAL STRATEGIES FOR RESOLVING CONFLICT (3d ed. 2003).

[6] c.f., ANTHONY T. KRONMAN, THE LOST LAWYER (1993); JULIE MACFARLANE, THE NEW LAWYER (forthcoming 2007).

❧ 70 ❧

Learning How to Learn to Negotiate

Scott R. Peppet & Michael L. Moffitt

Editors' Note: *This chapter is for everyone who ever wondered if they could really implement all the new negotiation ideas they have read. By analyzing research on how we can learn to learn, the authors of this chapter provide specific advice to negotiators and negotiation trainers. (For those whose students—or colleagues—are more hardheaded than most, this chapter should be read in conjunction with the chapter by Kirschner.)*

All of us negotiate all the time—at work, at home, with colleagues, counterparts, family, and friends. We hope that we learn from these experiences. We imagine that we are building our negotiation skills incrementally, so that over time we are becoming more capable negotiators. But *do* these experiences help us to improve? Unfortunately, an honest assessment suggests that the answer is often "no." Just as reading about negotiation theories is no guarantee of improvement, simply having more experience negotiating does not necessarily make someone a better negotiator. Instead, most of us seem to miss most of the learning opportunities we encounter.

This chapter explores three aspects of learning to negotiate. First, we discuss what it takes for negotiators to learn from their experiences. In particular, we argue that negotiators-in-training need access to valid data about their abilities, their actual practices, and the impact of those practices. Negotiators also need a willingness to explore such data in ways that will expose their implicit, and sometimes unhelpful, action strategies for dealing with conflict or bargaining. Second, we argue that most negotiators do not expose themselves to such learning opportunities—largely for fear of what they might find out about themselves and their abilities. Instead, most of us shield ourselves from real learning, all the while *telling ourselves and others* that we are eager to find ways to learn and improve. Finally, we discuss what negotiators and negotiation teachers can do to overcome some of these barriers to getting better.

As a theoretical foundation for our observations about negotiators' efforts at learning, we draw heavily from the work of Chris Argyris and his colleagues. Argyris uses the umbrella term "Action Science"[1] to describe the process of critically examining one's own behavior in an effort to improve. Much of his work focuses on the learning behaviors of individuals in organizational settings—for example, exploring how managers learn and adapt their managerial practices. Here we apply some of his ideas to the question of how negotiators in all contexts can best learn from their experiences.

What it Takes to Learn to Negotiate (Well)

In the last several decades, negotiation scholars, teachers, and practitioners have developed robust advice on what it takes to negotiate well in varied circumstances. The negotiation literature has moved beyond lists of "dirty tricks" and now incorporates interdisciplinary research from economics, psychology, organizational behavior, and other fields to provide guidance for aspiring students of negotiation. Though not all theories of negotiation articulate advice in the same way, most share some common themes that we will not review in detail in this chapter: search for underlying interests and potentially value-creating trades rather than take arbitrary haggling positions; explore the other side's perspective through listening and empathy even if you discover you disagree with it; build a working relationship with the other side; manage your emotions to engage productively in the conversation rather than suppressing or ignoring feelings, etc. The message in most negotiation courses today is that learning to negotiate requires learning to collaborate and problem-solve with others, despite severe differences. Strategy and self-interest do not disappear, but negotiation students often discover that they can accomplish more, and more easily, by fostering collaboration rather than turning every aspect of every negotiation into a zero-sum, escalatory, or haggling-type experience. In general, the message is that negotiators should be adept at multiple approaches to negotiation. The most skilled negotiators can determine when collaborative approaches make most sense, are able to defend against counterparts who engage in non-collaborative behaviors, and can adopt strategies that produce favorable outcomes even when the other negotiator's competitive approach does not permit collaborative problem-solving. We do not have the space here to review or explain the nuances of all of this advice—we will assume, for our purposes here, that the reader is largely familiar with this canon.

We do not suggest that there is total uniformity in these messages across all negotiation courses, nor that there should be. Collaboration is not always the right approach to every negotiation. Still, among other skills, effective negotiators need the ability to spot opportunities in which collaboration could yield benefits *and* the ability to engage in those collaborative negotiations effectively. We take as our starting point, therefore, that for a student—whether in a corporate or academic setting—to learn to negotiate *well,* that student must learn to collaborate and problem-solve in difficult conflicts.

How can a student of negotiation learn these skills? One aspect of learning to negotiate is simply testing all of this advice against your own experience. For example, if you try to "focus on interests," does it actually help you achieve the results you want? What problems does it create? In what ways must the advice or maxim be modified or tailored to deal with various kinds of circumstances in which it might *not* be helpful?

Testing negotiation advice against your own experiences is an incredibly valuable process—there is a great deal of quality theory about negotiation, and it takes time to absorb and test it. But a negotiator must be careful during this testing process. There is a danger that a negotiator may *mis*interpret her experience, and therefore dismiss valid advice prematurely. If you try to focus on interests and it doesn't seem to help, for example, is that because the advice is bad, or because you implemented the advice poorly? It may be your *skills* that need improvement, not the advice itself.

This brings us to a second, and more challenging, aspect of learning to negotiate: rigorous investigation into one's own actions, skills, and behavioral patterns. If a negotiator is going to construct *valid* tests of different types of negotiation advice, she needs to be able to reflect on her negotiation experiences and really investigate whether those experiences support or discredit the advice. Most negotiation courses, therefore, offer opportunities for students to engage in simulated negotiations, which the students can then review together to compare notes and determine what worked and what didn't.

Really learning from such experiences, however, is much easier said than done. In our experience teaching students in many different organizational and academic contexts, people often do *not* learn much from experience. It is remarkably difficult to change your negotiation habits and techniques—the skills needed to negotiate successfully do not come easily.

Instead, really learning to negotiate requires at least two things that are often missing in negotiation courses (as well as most other educational experiences).[2] First, a negotiator needs high-quality information—or data—about her behavior during these experiences. Without it, she is likely to mislead herself about how she acted, and thus about what her experience means. Second, she needs to engage in high-quality inquiry into her behavior—inquiry that is structured to lead to deep and lasting change in her implicit theories of action. We explore each in turn below.

The Need for High-Quality Information About Your Actions

People rarely act randomly. Instead, we craft our actions through conscious and subconscious choices about how to behave in the circumstances that confront us. Those choices, in turn, are guided by implicit or explicit "rules" that we hold about how the world works, and how to act within it. These rules are theories or hypotheses (e.g., "If someone threatens me, it is best to fight back by..."). In other words, our action choices are guided by "theories of action"—theories about what will be effective in a given circumstance.[3]

Negotiators have no shortage of theories of action. In describing approaches to negotiation, one person may say that she "always looks for common ground." Another says that he "tries to knock the other side off balance." A third insists that she "sticks to her guns," and a fourth says that he "tries to remain open to learning" throughout the conversation with the other side. These examples illustrate explicit or "espoused" theories of action—the action-strategies that we are familiar with and that we try to implement.

We do not, however, always act consistently with our conscious or espoused theories of action. A negotiator says, "It's always best to keep your cool in a negotiation," and then proceeds to explode with emotion during a bargaining session. Afterwards, the negotiator may acknowledge a gap between his espoused theory and his behavior by admitting, "I lost it in there. I really shouldn't have."

To learn to negotiate, we need to examine this gap between how we *advise ourselves* to act in a negotiation and how we *actually* act. You may *think* you are listening, or asking questions, or exploring the other side's interests, but it is quite possible that if you were observing yourself, you would discover the opposite.

There is nothing remarkable about the observation that we do not always do what we set out to do—otherwise we would all be more physically fit! What makes learning difficult, however, is that individuals are very often *unaware* that their actions were inconsistent with their espoused theory of action. For example, a mother describes herself as "completely hands off" vis-à-vis her daughter's wedding, but is actually (according to those around her) quite domineering. A boss says, "my door is always open" but brushes aside most complaints and surrounds herself primarily with people who are not critical of her efforts. A colleague says, "I am *not* shouting" even as his voice gets louder and louder. A student receiving feedback about her performance in a negotiation may tell an observer that she believes constructive criticism is critical to learning. In practice, however, she may shut down, withdraw, or otherwise defend herself when faced with suggestions for improvement.

It is not that we have *no* theory of action at these moments when we act inconsistently with our plan. Again, we rarely act randomly. Instead, our departures from our espoused action-strategies are actually predictable and consistent. The boss continues to brush aside criticism, the colleague's voice almost always rises when the stakes get high, and the student consistently assumes an intellectually defensive stance in a conversation about her performance. These are not isolated events in the lives of these actors. Instead, one can discern a pattern to the governing rules or assumptions driving their behavior, suggesting that they are acting according to *some* theory of action—just not their espoused theories.

Chris Argyris and his colleagues label these implicit patterns or governing rules our "theories-in-use."[4] All of us have implicit rules of action that govern many of our decisions about how to behave. In other words, we have our conscious, explicit set of rules for behavior (our espoused theories of action), and then we have a second set of more implicit rules that actually govern us, particularly in times of stress or conflict. This second set of action-strategies is in some ways invisible to ourselves and others—we may say (and even believe) that we are acting according to our espoused theory of action when in fact we are in the grips of our more implicit theories-in-use.

This underscores our first criterion for learning to negotiate: the need for negotiators-in-training to have access to high-quality data about their own behavior. Only by actually observing yourself can you see whether you acted in keeping with your espoused action-strategy rather than your more default and habitual theories-in-use. Fortunately, students in formalized educational settings may have the opportunity to watch videotape of themselves, to listen to audiotape of their negotiations, or to read transcriptions of such tapes.[5] Some practicing professionals ask (and receive) permission from their negotiating counterparts to record certain interactions, in order to provide the professional with better data on which to base future learning. Even in contexts in which such recording is impossible, a negotiator truly focused on improvement would seek to preserve actual data—for example by inviting in a junior colleague to serve as an observer, with instructions to capture as many specific quotations as possible. High-quality, sustained learning requires that negotiators be able to examine their *actual* behavior (for example, by watching themselves on videotape) rather than rely on their reconstructions of how they *think* they acted.

Often, close examination of such actual data about your behavior can lead to profound discoveries. When you see that you have not acted as you planned—that you have not acted according to your espoused theory of action—and you dig into what set of implicit rules must have taken over to guide you in that instance, it can be a remarkably powerful opportunity to learn. Such learning is possible, however, only with high-quality data with which to confront yourself, so that you do not fool yourself by assuming that you acted as you planned to act.

This is our first criterion for learning to negotiate: access to high-quality information about your own behavior during negotiations.

Inquiry Crafted to Help Question Our Theories-in-Use

Our second criterion, mentioned above, is engaging in high-quality inquiry structured to lead to deep and lasting change in one's implicit theories-in-use. What does that mean?

There are different levels at which we can learn. At one level, when we do something that produces results we dislike, we simply need to figure out a different approach that is more successful. In other words, when we fail, we change course until we succeed. Argyris has called this "single-loop" learning. (See Figure

1.)[6] We "loop" through action strategies, examining the consequences they produce until we find one that gets us the results we want. For example, if we've been avoiding a certain type of conflict, but not getting the results we want, we might adjust our approach and begin to confront such situations more directly (assuming we see that being more direct produces better consequences).

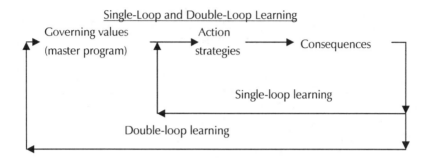

Single-Loop and Double-Loop Learning

We often overlook opportunities to engage in a deeper level of learning, however. "Double-loop" learning involves an honest re-examination of the foundational theories-in-use that led us to choose our default action strategy in the first place. Through careful inquiry, we examine the beliefs, assumptions, and "theories" about the world that originally led us to choose our unsuccessful strategy rather than the more successful approach we discovered through single-loop action-adjustments. Returning to our example, we might ask ourselves why we avoided such conflicts in the first place. What assumptions did we have about the conflict, the players, or ourselves that made us decide that avoiding was best? In what ways were those assumptions misguided—and how must they change if we want to be able to confront such situations consistently and successfully?

Put differently, rather than treat the question of learning as a discrete problem to be solved (e.g., "Should I have made that offer at that time?"), double-loop learning treats learning as a larger enterprise of critical examination. What assumptions was I making about the bargaining process that made me think this was the best approach? What led me to those assumptions? Are they accurate? Are they testable? "[D]ouble-loop learning is not simply a function of how people feel. It is a reflection of how they think—that is, the cognitive rules or reasoning they use to design and implement their actions."[7]

Double-loop learning is critical for sustained behavior change. If a negotiator simply engages in a single-loop process of finding a new strategy that produces better results, she leaves in place the default assumptions and beliefs that led her to choose a different strategy originally. When faced with a similar conflict or circumstance again, those beliefs—or implicit theories-in-use—are likely to re-engage and again lead her to act unproductively. This explains, at least partially, why some negotiation students can consciously adopt a new approach in one negotiation, only to revert to their original approach in subsequent negotiations. Our actions are controlled by our implicit theories-in-use, and without shifting those theories we are unlikely to change our behavior over time.

Negotiators seeking to improve must therefore have two goals. First, they must seek out valid information or data about their behavior, so that they can examine the gap between how they wanted to act and how they actually acted. This will allow the negotiator to successfully engage in a single-loop process of testing different advice, strategies, and tactics to see which produce desired results most consistently. Second, however, the negotiator must inquire into the implicit rules, beliefs, hypotheses, and assumptions that drove her unhelpful actions to start with. What led her to act as she did? What made her choose to stop listening, or take an arbitrary position, or yell irrationally at the other side, or disengage prematurely from a potentially difficult conversation? Without investigating her default theories-in-use, she is unlikely to make real progress.

Why We Don't Learn From Our Experiences

Our twin suggestions may seem easy to implement, but, unfortunately, they are not. Instead, our experience suggests that most negotiators neither seek out valid data about their behavior nor engage in rigorous exploration of their implicit theories-in-use. Here we explore some of the barriers that prevent the kind of learning that leads to sustained improvement.

The primary barrier to learning is behavioral: people often actively seek to *prevent* exposure to the information and inquiry required for learning. How can this be so, particularly in academic and professional settings where students are supposedly committed to improvement? The answers, for most of us, lie in our implicit theories-in-use—our implicit action-strategies.

Research shows that these unarticulated action-strategies are often quite uniform—and quite problematic.[8] According to Argyris, most people have theories-in-use that are governed by four principles or values: (1) achieving our intended purpose, (2) maximizing "winning" and minimizing losing, (3) suppressing negative feelings, and (4) emphasizing rationality.[9] The devilish part is that we often do not *espouse* these values consciously. Indeed, we may espouse shared responsibility, collaboration, finding joint gains, and expressing emotion. Unfortunately, actual observation of most individuals in high-stakes, threatening situations will usually reveal behavior consistent with the four implicit values Argyris identifies. At their core—and despite whatever we might *think* about our openness and commitment to learning—our theories-in-use generally devolve to these four principles in order to help us maintain a sense of *control* over our environment and results.[10]

The way theories-in-use manifest themselves in behavior varies by context, but there are some common themes. These include "making unillustrated attributions and evaluations, advocating courses of action in ways that discourage inquiry, treating one's own views as obviously correct, [and] making covert attributions, evaluations, and face-saving moves such as leaving potentially embarrassing facts unstated."[11] Each of these behaviors helps you to feel in control, even though the behavior may inhibit real learning. A senior account manager tells a younger colleague on their way out of a negotiation that broke down, "You have to play hardball with these guys. I know them, and they're constantly looking for a way to take advantage of others. That's why I had to make the threat. Their hostile reaction just shows that I was onto something." The manager's negotiation strategy assured him of control both in the negotiation and in the post-mortem review with his younger colleague. Furthermore—and most interestingly—the manager's account of the situation after the fact uses evaluative judgment, attribution, and advocacy to maintain a "minimum acceptable level of being in control [or] winning."[12] It is unlikely that the younger colleague will offer observations about the interaction that are inconsistent with the manager's description. As a result, it is unlikely that the manager will learn from this experience. At its worst, the way we typically act produces "defensiveness, misunderstanding, and self-fulfilling and self-sealing processes."[13]

It is important to note that our theories-in-use, though largely or entirely subconscious, are not exactly unskillful. The boss who deflects or avoids criticism is highly skilled—*at avoiding criticism*. She does not wave her hand and tell people not to tell her if anything goes wrong—that would be too obvious, and too explicit. Instead, she asks questions only of those she thinks will tell her un-critical observations. Or she asks the questions in a way that makes it difficult or uncomfortable for a subordinate to raise an issue. Or she emphasizes legitimate examples that support the conclusion that her efforts were successful, rather than inquiring about whether there are any examples to suggest that it was not a complete success. In this way she not only deflects criticism, but *she also manages to deflect criticism about her ability to deflect criticism.* By acting as if (and even saying that) she is open to learning while simultaneously avoiding learning opportunities, the boss skillfully manages to avoid exposure to challenging data that might require real skill-building.

The basic point is that our control-oriented and self-protective implicit theories-in-use make learning difficult. Double-loop learning is not easy, and it is not typical. Individuals and groups are masterful at defending against real examination and testing of underlying values, assumptions, and beliefs. As the gap between our espoused theories and our theories-in-use becomes visible, we tend to run from, rather than embrace, learning about it. Our typical theories-in-use, after all, are about control—and examining their fundamental assumptions requires giving up our understanding of control. This poses true challenges for anyone—including negotiation instructors—hoping to help others with sustainable behavioral change.

Consider the following examples from our own negotiation courses. In keeping with our commitment to provide students with valid information about their behavior, we often try to give our students—whether corporate managers, practicing lawyers, or law students—opportunities to observe their own and others' negotiations either in person or on video. This can take many forms. Sometimes it is as simple as requesting that a student describe her negotiation to others in the class in a way that really allows for testing of the student's assumptions. For example, if a student says "I had no choice in this negotiation—I *had* to start with an outrageous offer or I would've gotten completely taken," we encourage the student to describe the negotiation more concretely so that others in the room can *test* the student's conclusion that "there was no choice, given the circumstances, other than to make an outrageous offer." What did the opposing negotiator say or do, specifically, that led this student to her belief that she had such limited choices? What comments or actions from the opposing negotiator would have led this student to a different conclusion? What had the student herself done that might have contributed to her situation? Does anyone else in the classroom have a suggestion for how she might have reacted differently to the circumstances in which she found herself? Only by giving a more concrete and specific description[14] [Heen & Stone, *Perceptions*] of the circumstances in question can the student provide others in the room with the information *they* need to draw their own conclusions about whether or not her approach was indeed the only one available. In other words, only by really diving into the data of what happened can the student herself create a valid test of her assumptions.

Learning to describe the specific interactions that took place during a negotiation can be surprisingly difficult. Time and time again, students offer vague, general descriptions, and either forget or cannot reconstruct the details of what was actually said or done during their negotiations. Even when asked *before* they negotiate to keep careful notation or to pause and write down actual quotations from the negotiation, most students (like most practitioners) find it difficult.

What makes it so hard to describe negotiations in careful detail? At one level, reconstructing a series of events in this way requires new skills—it can feel clunky and strange. But the instruction "be specific with your descriptions" is not so hard that we would expect rooms full of bright people to fail at it so consistently. In our experience, it often seems as if a more fundamental resistance is taking place. Consciously or subconsciously, students know that providing detailed information (rather than vague generalizations and self-sealing conclusions) opens their assertions about what happened (e.g., "I had no choice") to real testing by others. That vulnerability—that lack of unilateral control over their experience in the class-room—produces anxiety. And as a result, students sometimes work hard *not* to get into the details, even when they understand that avoiding the details will inhibit real learning.

To avoid some of these problems of data reconstruction, we sometimes ask a pair to come forward and negotiate in a "fishbowl" in front of the room, so that they can be observed by others. Sometimes we videotape or audiotape pairs of negotiators and have them review their video or audio either in private, with us, or with others. Sometimes we use the Internet to stream video of pairs of negotiators so that the entire class has access to the video and can watch and learn from all of the captured information about how their classmates negotiated.[15] Sometimes we have them engage in email-only negotiations so that they will have a written tran-script of their entire exchange to review later.

At the risk of falling into our own trap (of staying general and failing to pro-vide you, the reader, with enough detail to draw your own valid conclusions), we can report that students of all types often exhibit a great deal of resistance to en-tering educational experiences that involve real data-capture such as video or audiotaping, review, and analysis. "I don't like seeing myself on video," is the most common plea, followed by "I didn't have a chance to watch it." Even when they have watched the tapes, many students spend considerable energy challenging the validity of the data they see. "The tape didn't capture everything that was going on," or "I wouldn't have handled it this way, if there hadn't been a camera in the room." Both of these critiques are potentially valid, but neither is significant enough that we should completely ignore the data a videotape makes available. Analyzing a tape or transcript of a negotiation is a skill in itself, and one that we have to teach our students to master.[16] More fundamentally, however, we have to teach them to let down their guard and open up to the possibility of learning.

The same is true for negotiation practitioners not engaged in a formal learning environment, but instead trying to learn from their experiences. How often do we seek out opportunities to watch someone else negotiate? How often do we invite others to watch as we negotiate, or ask our counterparts for permission to audio-tape ourselves? If a colleague is planning to observe us in action, do we prepare the colleague to collect useful information (by writing down actual quotations, etc., rather than just saying "Hey, you did great")? And how meaningful is the normal feedback conversation with that colleague? In order to be able to learn from experience, practitioners must learn to learn, and must commit themselves to collecting the information and engaging in the inquiry needed to make learning possible.

Learning to Learn

Learning anything new is difficult—learning to negotiate well is particularly diffi-cult. One of the important reasons lies in the nature of modern negotiation advice. As mentioned above, in the last twenty-five years, most negotiation scholars and teachers have moved away from teaching "dirty tricks" and toward teaching tools for fostering collaboration, joint decision-making, and joint-gain problem-solving.[17] They teach their students to focus on interests rather than take posi-tions, to listen to others' radically different perspectives, to look for creative solutions collaboratively with the other side, to use their emotions during negotia-tions rather than try to suppress them, to work *with* others rather than against them. We are persuaded that many of these developments have been extraordinar-ily helpful, because the underlying advice they seek to impart to students is more robust and more promising than traditional models of negotiation.

To the extent this is good advice, however, it is also very difficult advice to absorb, because *the prevailing negotiation advice emphasizing collaboration runs counter to the implicit theories-in-use that most human beings seem to exhibit when they get into high stakes, high anxiety situations like a negotiation.* We might learn to *espouse* all of this collaborative advice, but if our hidden theories-in-use guide us to actually act in accordance with the four fundamental principles discussed above (e.g., achieving our purpose, winning not losing, suppressing feelings, maintaining the appearance of rationality), our negotiations will only have a false gloss of collaboration layered on top of very traditional, partisan, win-lose behavior.[18]

It is worth pausing here for emphasis, and to highlight our thesis again. We each have espoused theories of action—ways we wish to act. We also have implicit theories-in-use that seem to take over in times of stress, anxiety, or conflict. These theories-in-use, according to Argyris' research and our own experience in helping to coach thousands of negotiators, often revolve around maintaining unilateral control over one's experiences by reverting to win-lose, overly "rational," non-collaborative action-strategies. Such behavior is at odds with the prevailing canons of advice presented to most students of negotiation. In other words, students of negotiation are trying to change in the very ways that are *most difficult* for human beings *to* change.

This gap between our espoused theories and our theories-in-use is *not inevitable*. Theories-in-use need not be about control, and with conscious effort, they *can* change. A negotiator *can* challenge and test her deep assumptions sufficiently to bring her underlying values, beliefs, and behavioral rules in line with collaborative negotiation practices. Practitioners and students *can* shift their theories-in-use to align more closely with productive espoused theories.

Admittedly, making this kind of shift is not easy. Shifting your theory-in-use requires a genuine commitment to (1) capturing and using valid or validatable information, (2) providing yourself and others with the tools and discussion needed to make free and informed choices together about what works and what doesn't, and (3) monitoring over time how well you are implementing your commitment to learning.[19] It is not about *saying* that you want to learn, nor even *meaning* that you want to learn. Shifting a theory-in-use is about actively seeking to create opportunities for you to see actual data about your own practices, to critically examine those data, and to welcome (as part of a healthy learning process) feedback that you are acting inconsistently with your espoused theory of action. Those feedback discussions must combine advocacy and inquiry, link evaluations and attributions to observable data, invite disconfirming data, welcome public testing, and minimize unilateral face-saving. In the beginning, such discussion can feel a little disorienting. Ultimately, however, it is radically liberating.

What might that look like in practice? By engaging with her younger associate, the manager described above may have an opportunity to collect important perspectives on what took place in the room. The manager might discover information that would disconfirm (or confirm) foundational assumptions. The manager might break the chain of self-fulfilling, error-escalating processes.[20] Consider the difference if the manager, rather than immediately "explaining" the negotiation to her junior colleague, instead asked a series of questions like: "What are your reactions to the things you saw in there?" "What specific things did I say that surprised you?" "In what ways do you think my actions contributed to the dynamic that developed?" "What other ways can you imagine someone in my position might have responded?" "Given what you know about my purposes going into this meeting, did any of my behaviors suggest that I changed goals during the conversation?" "What opportunities do you think might have been missed in this interaction?" Notice the role the manager is inviting the younger associate to play, and notice the way she is directing the younger associate to provide specific data that will help the manager to continue the process of testing the utility of her negotiation assumptions and behaviors.

Why don't most managers ask questions like this? If asked, the manager is unlikely to say, "I'm uninterested in learning more" or "The younger associate can offer nothing to my learning experience." Instead, she is likely to say that she does not have the time right now, that her efforts are best focused on helping *the younger associate* to learn, or that asking such pointed questions might make the younger associate uncomfortable. The manager's espoused theory says that learning (among other things) is important. The manager's theories-in-use suggest otherwise. To receive honest and specific answers to the questions listed above deprives the manager of control in the conversation. The data may be unflattering. The manager's behaviors might suggest adherence to an unproductive set of assumptions. The gaps between espoused theories and actual practice are sometimes uncomfortable—uncomfortable enough that many people like this manager skillfully (though perhaps unconsciously) avoid being confronted with these important learning opportunities.

For negotiation instructors, learning to provide opportunities for this level of learning is a lifelong endeavor. Leading groups towards real learning requires a combination of skills and humility that is difficult to achieve and even more difficult to maintain. It requires commitment to collaboration with your students, and enough personal experience, analysis, and awareness to know when you are helping and when you need help. As a preliminary step, it requires thinking through the educational experiences you create—each simulation, each exercise, each class session—to see whether that experience actually provides the students what they need to learn something that can change behavior. Are there opportunities for the student to watch or hear valid information about their behavior during their negotiations? If not, could you work in videotape, audiotape, transcription, or observations so that students have access to such data? Are group discussions designed to help students test what worked and what didn't (single-loop) as well as test why they chose to act in a way that didn't work to begin with (double-loop)? These are all useful questions for course designers to consider.

As a final note, let us say a quick word about safety. Many educators and group facilitators stress the importance of creating a "safe" classroom.[21] If a student's role in a classroom is simply to sit and absorb an instructor's offered wisdom, if a student spends her time in fear that any of her failures will be made public for no apparent reason beyond humiliation, if a student has no say in the structure or content of his learning, one can understand the radical and important proposition that the learning space ought to be made "safe"—that is, free of these arbitrary stresses.

Given the discussion above of the ways in which real learning can provoke anxiety in students, and the ways in which students defend themselves from the information and inquiry needed to learn, we might be expected to champion this approach and vocabulary. Clearly we strive to create physical and emotional safety, in the sense that we do not want our students to be in any danger or suffer pain. We are very cautious, however, about the generalized notion of "safety."

We are strongly committed to *offering* opportunities for real learning to our students, rather than trying to *force* "learning" down their throats. Ultimately, the level of inquiry we engage in must be decided collaboratively, as a group. Just because we are the instructors does not mean that *we* can have delusions of unilateral control either—we must acknowledge and be mindful of the ways in which the group experience is co-created by all the group's members.

At the same time, we think too much focus on "safety" in the classroom is a red herring. Safety often is a camouflage for allowing participants in a group to get away with defensive and unproductive reasoning. It can become the battle cry for those trying to *avoid* learning, rather than for those trying to promote it. At the very least, we must test the notion: what does the group mean by safety? Does each participant experience the same thing as "unsafe"? Are there ways to accommodate individuals' safety concerns without sacrificing the opportunities to learn—without jettisoning videotape altogether, for example, or without simply pretending as if vague descriptions of events are sufficient? We think there are— but the advice often given to instructors and facilitators related to "safety" tilts too much towards self-protection for students and not enough in the direction of learning to learn.

And it is not just concerns about participants' safety that can stand in the way of genuine learning opportunities. Citing participants' safety, some instructors may also mask their own nervousness about exploring the practical application of the theories they are describing. It is much easier to tell a group that negotiators should "focus on interests," for example, than it is to invite the group to watch as someone (perhaps even the instructor) attempts to model the behavior being described. What happens if the student cannot model the behavior well in front of his colleagues? (And what happens if the instructor cannot construct a useful demonstration on the spur of the moment either?) Is the result embarrassing? Threatening? An important learning opportunity for everyone in the group— including the instructor—about the proposed "lesson" about searching for interests? All of the above? Instructors who are able to model the kind of openness to learning we describe in this Chapter may teach their students a lesson even more valuable than the substantive negotiation advice included in that day's lesson plan—they may teach their students how *to learn* to negotiate.

Conclusion

Most of us engage in unconscious, defensive routines that shield us from learning to be better negotiators, even though most of us say that we are open to improvement. As we described above, one of the important contributions of Argyris and his colleagues is the observation that our theories-in-use—the operating assumptions that drive most of our behaviors—tend to emphasize *control*, and thus make us less open to the kind of new information we need to do real, transformative learning.

To be clear, jettisoning control-based theories-in-use does not mean becoming *passive* learners. Truly effective learning about negotiation is a profoundly active enterprise. The negotiator who truly wants to learn must actively seek out valid data about her actual practices. She must inquire into those practices, unearth the operating assumptions that led her to adopt those practices in the first place, examine honestly the impacts of her actions, explore a range of possible alternative actions, and be willing to test the impacts of those alternatives. These behaviors are neither typical nor easy. They are, however, the path to lasting learning and improvement.

Endnotes

This chapter draws heavily on Michael L. Moffitt & Scott R. Peppet, *Action Science & Negotiation*, 87 Marquette Law Review 649 (2004).

[1] The book that captures the bulk of the three theories we describe in this piece is CHRIS ARGYRIS, ET AL., ACTION SCIENCE (1985).
[2] These are necessary, but not sufficient, conditions for learning. Obviously there are many other things a negotiator must have in order to learn—the time to engage in a learning process, sufficient food and water, the ability to communicate, consciousness, etc.
[3] CHRIS ARGYRIS, KNOWLEDGE FOR ACTION 50-51 (1993).

[4] *Id.* at 52.

[5] For more on the use of video in negotiation classes, *see* Scott R. Peppet, *Teaching Negotiating Using Web-Streaming Video*, 18 NEGOTIATION JOURNAL 271 (2002); Michael Moffitt, *Lights, Camera, Begin Final Exam: Testing What We Teach in Negotiation Courses*, 54 JOURNAL OF LEGAL EDUCATION 91 (2004).

[6] This chart is taken from ARGYRIS, *supra* note 3, at 50.

[7] Chris Argyris, *Teaching Smart People How to Learn*, HARVARD BUSINESS REVIEW 99 (May-June 1991).

[8] Based on his studies of thousands of individuals from varied backgrounds, ethnicities, class groups, genders, and nations, Argyris claims that although "espoused theories vary widely, research indicates that there is almost no variance in theory-in-use." ARGYRIS, ET AL., *supra* note 1, at 88-89. *See also* ARGYRIS, *supra* note 3, at 51 ("The behavior of individuals varied widely, but the theory they used to design and implement behavior did not vary.").

[9] ARGYRIS, *supra* note 3, at 52.

[10] Argyris labels the dominant theory-in-use employed by almost all of us, almost all the time, as "Model I behavior." ARGYRIS, ET AL., *supra* note 1, at 88-89.

[11] *Id.* at 89.

[12] ARGYRIS, *supra* note 3, at 52.

[13] *Id.*

[14] The best framework we know for encouraging this particular form of specific description is the Ladder of Inference, an organizing tool originally developed by Chris Argyris and Donald Schon. Summarized briefly, one can chart (on an ascending sequence of inferential steps) the progression individuals make as they select data (from among a universe of observable data), compare those data to existing beliefs, prior experiences, thought processes, etc., and arrive at conclusions about what has happened or what should happen. For a brief description, *see* DOUGLAS STONE, ET AL., DIFFICULT CONVERSATIONS: HOW TO DISCUSS WHAT MATTERS MOST (1999). For an extended view of the utility of the Ladder of Inference in understanding how disputants arrive at differing perceptions and conclusions, *see* Douglas Stone & Sheila Heen, *From Bone Chips to Dinosaurs: Perceptions, Stories, and Conflict in* THE HANDBOOK OF DISPUTE RESOLUTION 150-69 (Michael L. Moffitt & Robert C. Bordone eds., 2005).

[15] *See* Peppet, *supra* note 5.

[16] *See* Moffitt, *supra* note 5, at 106-13.

[17] Many works in this volume articulate aspects of this shift. Among the publications most prominently associated with this focus on joint problem-solving and collaboration are ROGER FISHER & WILLIAM URY, GETTING TO YES (1981); Carrie Menkel-Meadow, *Toward Another View of Legal Negotiation: The Structure of Problem Solving*, 31 UCLA LAW REVIEW 754 (1984); HOWARD RAIFFA, THE ART & SCIENCE OF NEGOTIATION (1982); DAVID LAX & JIM SEBENIUS, THE MANAGER AS NEGOTIATOR (1986), ROBERT MNOOKIN, ET AL., BEYOND WINNING (1999). This list is not exhaustive, of course, as contributions to this understanding of negotiation have come from a broad variety of disciplines.

[18] Some students, of course, are insufficiently assertive and competitive—they tend to try to collaborate *too much*, even in the face of exploitation. Again, we are *not* saying that collaboration and problem-solving are always the right approach, nor that they are all a negotiation instructor should teach her students. Instead, we are noting the difficulties that students experience with learning *any* serious shift in their default assumptions about managing conflict. Throughout this Chapter we have focused on the typical student who is overly competitive, win-lose, and perhaps aggressive, and who will have difficulty really absorbing collaborative strategies because his control-oriented theories-in-use prevent real learning. The same problem exists, however, for a student trying to learn to be *more* assertive and competitive. Often, "overly collaborative" students are simply good at negotiation-ending capitulation. In order to avoid conflict, they simply give up their interests and allow the other side's needs to dominate. *This is still an expression of the same unilateral control theories-in-use.* By avoiding conflict and capitulating, a student can again maintain the semblance of unilateral control. And, again, as the student tries to learn a different approach, he is likely to avoid opportunities to learn because those opportunities create anxiety.

[19] *See* ARGYRIS, ET AL., *supra* note 1, at 98-102.

[20] *See* CHRIS ARGYRIS, FLAWED ADVICE AND THE MANAGEMENT TRAP 52-81 (2000).

[21] *See, e.g.*, JENNY ROGERS, ADULTS LEARNING 15 (3d ed. 1989); Susan Imel, *Guidelines for Working with Adult Learners*, ERIC DIGEST NO. 154 (1994).

⚘ 71 ⚘

Training a Captive Audience

Stuart M. Kirschner

Editors' Note: *Let's say you've finished this book and would like to use some of it. But what about your more hardheaded colleagues, team members or other audiences? Using his experience in training the highly skeptical police officers of the NYPD, psychologist Stuart Kirschner discusses the design of training for a potentially resistant audience.*

The practice of negotiation embeds a great deal of "teaching" activity. In any but the simplest of transactions or disputes, it becomes necessary to inform your counterpart, and your own team (if you work as part of a team), of information and possible new perspectives that you have and they do not have. The fact that you may have a body of knowledge, which you wish to impart to them, may create a trap. Many do not like to be "taught," especially by someone they perceive as an opponent, outsider, or intra-team rival. Even when negotiators or team members clearly recognize the need to gather new perspectives or information, and to adjust their own thinking in relation to either or both, they may resist being given a lecture. Many people who negotiate all the time can be very resistant to changing and/or expanding their thinking.

This chapter discusses the tension which may occur between those who need to transmit information and perspectives, and potentially resistant practitioners. This friction was exemplified when an explicit need arose to create an effective course in negotiation with emotionally disturbed persons for officers of the New York Police Department. The lessons learned from fifteen years of experience in teaching that course may be helpful to other kinds of negotiators (and trainers) as they contemplate how to get their next audience to pay better attention to what they have to say.

Over the past few decades, there has been a dramatic increase in the number of chronically mentally ill people who are treated in the community. This trend has derived from a conscious policy to shift away from inpatient services, with a concomitant downsizing of inpatient facilities for the treatment of psychiatric patients. Deinstitutionalization, changes in the standard for the civil commitment of the mentally ill, and U.S. Supreme Court decisions have all contributed to this shift from inpatient to outpatient treatment.

The rise in numbers of mentally ill people who live in the community has created a number of concerns. The decrease in the number of inpatient beds available for psychiatric patients makes it more difficult for such patients to receive inpatient services when they are in acute crises. In addition, there has been a failure of community-based mental health services to provide adequate out-patient care. One result of these changes is that large numbers of mentally ill people have found themselves among the homeless population. High concentrations of homeless mentally ill have become commonplace in large urban settings throughout the United States. Moreover, there has been a significant increase in the number of mentally ill people in correctional facilities. Estimates indicate that as much as 25% of the inmate population in county, state and federal prisons suffer from a major mental illness. The present trend has been termed the era of the criminalization of the mentally ill. This criminalization has also been considered, by some, to be a direct outgrowth of deinstitutionalization and a failure of the mental health system to provide adequate community-based services to released psychiatric patients.[1]

The presence of significant numbers of the severely and persistently mentally ill in the community poses challenges for the police. Police officers are the first line of intervention for individuals who present an imminent danger to themselves or others (whether they are mentally ill or not). With recent research indicating that a diagnosis of a major mental illness is, in fact, a risk factor for dangerousness,[2] there is clearly a need for police officers to become more proficient in dealing with those who suffer from psychiatric disorders. It is against this backdrop that the training of police to recognize, communicate and intervene with the mentally ill emerges as a major issue in policing. Psychologists can serve a critical function in implementing such training.

The Origin of Emergency Psychological Technician Training
In 1984, Eleanor Bumpers, an elderly and mentally ill woman, was shot and killed by New York City Emergency Service Unit (ESU) police officers as they entered her apartment. The police were unaware of her mental illness and believed they were there to effect what was presumed to be a routine eviction. However, Ms. Bumpers, who was an extremely obese women, was actively psychotic and in an acute paranoid crisis at the time. She charged at the police officers while wielding a knife and, as a result, was shot and killed.

The Eleanor Bumpers incident provided the impetus for the New York City Police Department (NYPD) to change its policy and procedures in regard to dealing with emotionally disturbed people (EDP's). Since then, whenever there is a call to the police and it is confirmed that it involves an EDP, the ESU would be required to respond and, in barricade or hostage situations, the Hostage Negotiation Team (HNT) would send a negotiator to the scene.[3] [Volpe, et al., *Unknown*] In light of this change, a new training program was implemented. The New York City Police Department contracted with John Jay College of Criminal Justice to provide this training.

Structure of the Training Program
The program is referred to as Emergency Psychological Technician (EPT). The five-day, intensive program has evolved since its inception, and includes both experiential and didactic components. During the first half of each day, there are lectures explaining the various types of mental illnesses and personality disorders with

specific emphasis on the signs and symptoms of the various conditions. The second part of each day is devoted to communication skills. Each participant is involved in a role play situation where the officer is required to talk an EDP out from behind a door. The EDP may be barricaded or holding a hostage. (A free standing door is the only prop which is used in the training.) Actor/trainers play the EDP, who manifests a predetermined psychiatric condition (e.g. a person with schizophrenia, bipolar disorder, narcissistic personality disorder, etc.). The actor/trainer has no script and responds, in character, to the officer's verbal interventions. The dialogues are periodically interrupted so that the audience can offer comments and suggestions to the negotiator who is at the door. Thus, these trainings are much like other role-play and fish bowl experiences in other negotiation courses. The participants in the training are mostly police officers who are members of ESU and HNT.

ESU officers of NYPD provide specialized support to all units of the Department. The unit has a number of emergency response vehicles and the officers are highly trained to respond to many types of emergency and catastrophic situations. These situations include such things as construction accidents, water rescue, railway incidents, hazardous material concerns, rope rescue and rappelling, vehicle accidents and bombs. The unit is outfitted with various types of lethal and non-lethal tactical equipment and, while the unit can serve as a S.W.A.T. team, its mission is clearly more than that. The motto for ESU is "When civilians needs help they call the police. When the police need help, they call ESU." ESU officers generally have a number of years of experience on patrol before they will be considered for ESU.

All members of the HNT are ranked as Detective, Detective Sergeant or Detective Lieutenant. To be eligible for selection to this Team, they must have a minimum of twelve years' experience within NYPD and an excellent department record. Higher education is important but not mandatory; the selection of HNT members emphasizes both job and life experiences. While individuals volunteer to become members of ESU or HNT, EPT is a mandatory component of the training they then receive.[4]

Problems and Concerns in Training Police Officers

A number of considerations govern the EPT course, which may provide some context for readers who are grappling with developing formal courses for other kinds of practitioners. Each of these factors constitute important considerations for the training of police officers; however, they are relevant for the training of many types of negotiators, or for that matter, many educators who are faced with "tough" audiences. The following list, while not exhaustive, highlights some of the issues which have been dealt with in developing the course.

The Training Site

The first concern was whether the program would be conducted at an NYPD location (e.g. the Police Academy) or at a facility outside of the Department (e.g. John Jay College of Criminal Justice, which has a long-standing association with the NYPD, but is independent of it). It was concluded that John Jay College would be the training site, for a number of reasons. First, providing an academic atmosphere was thought to facilitate learning. Second, a setting which is not part of the Department gives the participants a sense that there may be something new rather than the usual, routine trainings which are offered by the Department. Third, and significantly for this "student" population, a number of participants have a kind of "institutional paranoia." Training conducted at a Department facility increases the feeling that "the bosses" are overseeing the program and maintaining a watchful eye on all that takes place; using John Jay College offers a sort of sanctuary. Fourth, even though any number of "bosses," (Sergeants, Lieutenants, Captains, and two-star Chiefs), have attended the training sessions, all participants are in civilian clothes. The fact that rank is not obvious to others helps to create a forum which is conducive to freedom of speech.

The Participants

An important feature is the heterogeneity of the group. Participants who are from diverse racial, ethnic, cultural and educational backgrounds bring different perspectives to the group discussions. While most of the participants in EPT are police officers, there are often invited guests in attendance, who may include local, state, federal and foreign law enforcement officers from a variety of jurisdictions and agencies. There are also mental health workers from different disciplines, researchers and academicians frequently in attendance. Moreover, police officers themselves do not constitute a homogenous group of individuals. They bring to the training a wide range of educational backgrounds, interests and personal life experiences. For example, ESU officers are generally multi-talented and have a variety of technical and tactical skills, including some medical training. Some also have Doctorate or Master's degrees, with majors in a wide array of subjects. The heterogeneity of the group works well, allowing the participants to bring in their different views.

Group Size

The size of the group ranges between 25 and 30 participants. Larger groups would not afford an opportunity for every member to practice negotiation skills, and create too much of an impersonal environment. (Smaller groups place too much of a burden on each individual participant, forcing the members to become involved in too many role play situations, which is thought in this context to lead to resistance.) The moderate size of the group allows for better group cohesiveness, a very important aspect of the training. Members get to know each other personally and to work together as a team. It is worth noting that in a Department of forty thousand officers replete with Divisions, Bureaus, Offices and many other organizational subdivisions, the Hostage Negotiation Team is the only unit formally accorded the title "Team."

Duration

The EPT program runs for five consecutive days. A critical part of the training is the experiential component. Each participant takes "center stage" and the group observes and critiques the participant's negotiation skills. The first day is usually the most difficult; at the outset, these individuals are generally reluctant to expose their shortcomings and vulnerabilities. It is the trainer's job to create a safe environment whereby the members of the group feel comfortable so they can candidly engage in the simulated negotiations. Usually, by midway through the second day, participants become relaxed enough to engage in a candid negotiation which is a true representation of how they would behave in an actual situation. Communication skills and negotiation strategies are critiqued in an open forum. The negotiation trainees are also encouraged to critique the exercises and offer suggestions to the trainers (e.g. participants at times have stated that a given simulated situation is too artificial and not "true to life"). This is a conscious departure for much of police training, and helps to set a tone of collegiality—important in the context of the more "pedagogical" part, which follows. By the end of the fifth day, the group has developed an identity of its own and the members have become palpably connected to each other.

The Problem of Standard Pedagogy

While much of the necessary learning is experiential or by demonstration, unfortunately some lecturing is unavoidable. Much of the structure (*e.g.* the split day) can be seen as part of a coordinated plan to help these students to accept the "cod liver oil" part. The remaining risk is that the trainer can easily become too pedantic, leaving the participants with the impression that the material is irrelevant or not applicable to the work that the officer does. Even worse, the material could be presented in a fashion that is only comprehensible to professionals with advanced degrees in psychology. It is the trainer's job to present the material in an interesting and comprehensible fashion, demonstrating how the content is relevant to improving job performance by continuously presenting, throughout the training, how theory is translated into practice. It also underscores the fact that the scenes, which the negotiators have to navigate their way through, must depict actual circumstances or possible scenarios that the officer may encounter at work. But the didactic component must somehow cope with who these officers are. In a nutshell, this is an audience particularly maladapted to sitting in chairs and listening to a lecture.

The Need for Stimulation

The need for stimulation or excitement can lead to risk-taking behavior and is often associated aberrant conduct.[5] However, police officers are also generally people of action.[6] This need to be on the move is one of the major reasons that they entered the profession. The ESU officers, particularly, have this trait in abundance. (Within the police department they are referred to fondly as "The boys with toys.") Because of this they are not often mesmerized by an academic lecture. In addition, frequently an officer's instinctive reaction, to yet another provocative remark by the actor playing an EDP, is to move in tactically, "taking the door" and through the use of other (in normal circumstances, non-lethal) means, getting the EDP into custody. This also reflects the real-world imperfection of negotiation: the trainers must concede that a significant percentage of the cases may, in fact, be resolved in this manner. There is a shared understanding that the ESU officers have a variety of tools, and are proficient in using them. But this training is an exercise in improving verbal communication skills. It is emphasized that, in helping officers to tap and practice these skills, officers are acquiring yet another tool to be placed in their tool box.

It is important that scenes create tension and drama. Intensity can be established only if the scenarios are "true to life." Therefore, scenarios are adapted from actual cases. They often have been modified to better meet the confines of the training situation. The situations are regularly critiqued by the participants so that their suggestions can serve as a guidelines to improve the scenarios. The scenes also must create a dilemma for the officers that makes it extremely difficult for the officers to move in tactically. The situation is such that the officers have little choice but to communicate verbally with the barricade or hostage таker.

The realism of the scenes is reflected by the outpouring of the negotiators' emotions during the exercise. It is obvious that they are involved and focused on the task to the point that officers become oblivious to the presence of an audience. Many officers have completed a negotiation with perspiration visibly soaking through a shirt. The sheer exhaustion has been expressed by many a negotiator who has commented how he or she is "emotionally spent" at the completion of the exercise. Needless to say, the officers' need for stimulation has usually been met.

Credibility of "Didactic" Trainers

What makes and keeps a trainer credible? History, honesty, humility and humor. The psychologist's history and reputation with the Department precedes the individual. Participants in a training generally have some advance knowledge of who the instructor(s) are. In the EPT program, police personnel and the psychologist serve as co-trainers and organizers of the program. The police co-trainers, who have had years of experience in hostage negotiating and working within ESU, are highly respected by their colleagues. As the psychologist in the program, I have developed a close professional alliance and personal friendship with the police co-trainers. My police officer co-trainers often advise the participants that I have a lot to offer. As a result of this advance message to the participants, I have been able to enjoy "instant credibility" or "credibility by association." As an outsider, it is important to develop and maintain such good standing.

An advanced academic degree doesn't necessarily make one credible in every circle. While police officers may respect that one has a degree, they often feel that "the professor" does not understand the world outside of academia, especially from a police officer's perspective. As officers relate their personal experiences, one cannot help being humbled by what they often have encountered while working on the job. It is important for the trainer not to rely merely on academic credentials. On one occasion, a police officer who participated in the training asked me if I knew what Ph.D. stood for. When he told me that it meant "Piled higher and deeper," I immediately adopted the line as my own, and I now introduce myself to the officers with this line.

Police officers often speak about how they ventilate their emotions through humor. Years of working as a cop in New York can make one quite jaded and cynical. Humor often becomes a way of coping with the tragedies and the plight of humanity that they encounter on a daily basis. ESU officers and the seasoned detectives who comprise the HNT have witnessed the worst that life has to offer, and comic relief can be very therapeutic. They have a "gallows humor." While this can be viewed as callousness, it is important to understand this as a coping mechanism. Joining the participants in this type of humor is important way of connecting to the group.

When the trainer is honest and open it sets the tone for the training. Sharing personal experiences helps, especially during the experiential part. The trainer can model how to engage people and develop rapport through the use of one's own humanness. The example that is set by the trainers, in developing a relationship with the group, sets the stage for how the trainees will relate to a barricade or hostage taker. It allows the officer to tap his or her own humanness, an extremely valuable resource.

Work Experience

For the seasoned police officer in New York, there is little that may be new. The breadth and depth of experience is usually great and it is what the officer, in the end, relies on to do his or her job well. It is also a major component of what the officer brings to the negotiation with EDPs. While officers volunteer for ESU and the HNT, and they are usually quite enthusiastic about the new assignment, there is always the concern that some officers may be experiencing "burnout." Disillusionment, depression, anger and apathy are impediments to the negotiation process. These are private feelings which police officers do not readily volunteer. However, within the context of a successful training program, officers often begin to feel comfortable enough to express their discouragement. At times, it enters into their negotiation when they are at the door. As they begin to resolve some of their own feelings about being a police officer, they are at the same time improving their skills as a negotiator.

Anxiety

One can be more critical of people in his or her own profession, in part, because there is the knowledge to do so. I am much more comfortable giving a talk to people who are not psychologists. Psychologists are much more equipped to see flaws in my presentation and to pose questions that I may not be able to answer. In the same way, it is difficult for police officers to expose their knowledge or lack thereof to their fellow officers. Trainers must be sensitive to the fact that the officer, during the simulated negotiations, is performing before his or her peers and is in a position to expose all of his or her shortcomings.

Stereotypes of Trainer

The differences in the way that mental health professionals are trained compared to those who work within the legal system has led to the stereotyping of mental health workers. Due to the fact that psychological theories are generally deterministic in nature, psychologists look for explanations of human behavior. However, within the context of the legal system, this may be viewed as providing excuses for individuals, especially when applied to criminal defendants who enter psychiatric defenses. As a result, psychologists may be viewed as overly paternalistic and "bleeding hearts."[7] This stereotype is often held by police officers whose theoretical perspective is grounded in the legal system, where the assumption is that individuals possess "free will."[8] Their working concept is that people have a choice, and they can choose to be good or bad, even mentally ill or sane. It is important to address one's own philosophy and intrinsic assumptions about personality. To be sure, the way that an officer understands the development of personality and psychiatric disorders directly impacts on the approach that the officer takes to the negotiation.

Conclusion

Teaching police officers how to negotiate with emotionally disturbed persons presents some unique challenges. The nature of this type of negotiation warrants a few considerations:

- In negotiating with a barricaded person or a hostage taker, the communication takes place through a closed door (certainly this is the way the scenes are depicted during the training). I know of no other type of negotiation where this is the case. While other types of negotiation can be done without the use of visual communication (*e.g.* by telephone or e-mail), any agreement which is reached is done without having eye to eye contact. It is certainly important for the police officer to gain a knowledge of various psychiatric conditions, theoretical principles and hostage negotiation strategies; however, the key is for the negotiator to develop good listening skills. Active listening is emphasized throughout the training.

- In some negotiations, the negotiator may be an objective party who serves as a mediator in helping to reconcile differences between other parties. In such negotiations each side maintains a subjective perspective and has a vested interest in the outcome. In negotiating with EDP's, the police officer is involved in a two-party negotiation and while the officer, no doubt, has a vested interest in the outcome, he or she is also obligated to maintain a significant degree of objectivity. The officer must never lose his or her professionalism. In "talking down" an emotionally disturbed barricade or hostage taker the emotional investment and expenditure can be immense. In fact, the negotiation will rarely be successful if the negotiator does not make some emotional investment in the encounter. Yet, at the same time, the negotiator must remain objective and professional. Moreover, the officer must be able to move on to the next job which may be a few minutes away. The officer has to be capable of decathecting (withdrawing this emotional attachment) from what may have been an extremely emotionally exhausting experience.

- In the two-party negotiation between officer and EDP, there is a hierarchical relationship. One clearly can exercise legal power over the other in the performance of a duty. In this sense, the two parties who are involved in the negotiation are not on equal footing. How the officer deals with this inequality and communicates the understanding of his or her role becomes critical in the negotiation process. There is a delicate balance that must be maintained. The officer must be able to confine, contain and control; yet, at the same time, the officer must communicate an understanding of the EDP's distress—without being at all condescending. However, both parties are on equal footing inasmuch as they are humans; and everyone, at some time in their life has been an EDP.[9]

- In the negotiation between officer and EDP, the stakes are as high as they can get. A successful negotiation can preserve life, unsuccessful negotiations can result in death. It is certainly a rare type of negotiation where the failure to resolve the conflict can result in the death of one or more of the parties in conflict or, in fact, an innocent victim (*e.g.* hostage or bystander).

This chapter has addressed some of the issues and concerns relevant to developing a successful program for training police officers to better communicate with emotionally disturbed persons. The conclusion is that, while course content is certainly important, it is often the case that it is not so much *what* is taught but *how* it is taught, and the context in which it is presented. Thus, the process *is* the message:

- The training is presented in an environment which is non-threatening.
- Rapport is established among the participants and between the trainers and the participants. The trust which is an outgrowth of the rapport develops over the course of the training.
- Within the context of a trusting relationship, barriers and defenses are lowered and participants allow themselves to become more vulnerable.

They openly engage in dialogue in the role plays, allowing their true selves to emerge.

- They make mistakes and accept the training as a laboratory where errors can be made without untoward consequences. In effect, the course that the training follows is the same path that a successful negotiation should follow. The officer establishes trust with the EDP by enhancing his own listening skills and making use of his own responsiveness as a human being, allowing the barricader's or hostage taker's "real" needs to become known so that they can then be addressed. As the psychological barriers fall, so do the physical barriers, and ultimately the EDP can safely walk through the door.

The EPT program has proven to be highly successful for the training of police officers; yet there is every reason to believe that the factors which have been addressed and methodology employed in this program would be relevant to the teaching of many difficult-to-reach and resistant students or practitioners.

Endnotes

[1] *See* Stuart Kirschner, *The Mentally Ill in New York City: Treatment and Criminal Justice Management, in* CRIME AND JUSTICE IN NEW YORK CITY, VOL. 1: NEW YORK CITY'S CRIME PROBLEM 156-68 (Andrew Karmen ed., 2001).

[2] *See* CHRISTOPHER D. WEBSTER, ET AL., HCR-20 ASSESSING RISK FOR VIOLENCE (2d ed. 1997). The diagnosis of a definite/serious major mental illness is a risk factor for the re-occurrence of violence.

[3] *See* RAYMOND W. KELLY, NYPD HOSTAGE NEGOTIATIONS ORGANIZATIONAL AND TACTICAL GUIDE

[4] Descriptions of the ESU and HNT provided by Lt. Jack Cambria, Commanding Officer of the NYPD Hostage Negotiation Team and Det. Spec. Anthony Favara, ESU: personal communications.

[5] *See* ROBERT HARE, WITHOUT CONSCIENCE: THE DISTURBING WORLD OF THE PSYCHOPATHS AMONG US (1999). A salient trait of the psychopath is the need for stimulation. Psychopaths become bored easily and seek action. Often the action is antisocial in nature.

[6] *See* DAVID T. LYKKEN, THE ANTISOCIAL PERSONALITIES (1995) (indicating that the same trait for high risk behavior which is often found in criminals can be cultivated to elicit socially appropriate or even heroic behaviors).

[7] *See* GARY B. MELTON, ET AL., PSYCHOLOGICAL EVALUATIONS FOR THE COURTS: A HANDBOOK FOR MENTAL HEALTH PROFESSIONALS AND LAWYERS (1997) (stating that the perceived attitudinal differences between lawyers and mental health professionals may be over-emphasized).

[8] *See* Elizabeth K. White & Audry L. Honig, *The Role of the Police Psychologist in Training, in* POLICE PSYCHOLOGY INTO THE 21ST CENTURY 257-77 (Martin I. Kurke & Ellen M. Scrivner eds., 1995). They state that people in law enforcement generally come in contact with mental health professionals in one of four ways: (1) observing psychologists offer expert testimony in court on behalf of criminals, (2) dealing with psychiatric patients who were inappropriately discharged back into the community by mental health professionals, (3) viewing psychologists provide excuses for malingering police officers who are claiming psychological trauma, and (4) witnessing psychologists evaluate them for fitness for duty or pre-employment screenings. It is because of these types of contacts that many peace officers have little respect for, and a negative view of, psychologists.

[9] In fact, it is regularly emphasized throughout the training that EDP also stands for Every Day People.

❦ 72 ❧

Retraining Ourselves for Conflict Transformation

Charles Hauss

Editors' Note: *As Docherty points out in her introductory chapter on Models, most negotiations take place within an accepted framework of legal and other principles. This chapter describes the real-life experiences of a major NGO working in more politicized kinds of conflict. Hauss forthrightly describes examples from Search for Common Ground, citing failures as well as successes to discuss the larger lessons about conflict handling on a major scale, and in highly politicized environments.*

Many chapters in this book discuss the way we think about negotiation and conflict resolution, from a wide variety of perspectives in the practice, research, and theory of negotiation, mediation, and related conflict resolution techniques.

This chapter will approach the subject from "left field." My task is not to critique what my colleagues have written about, but to expand the discussion of the field in a more "political" direction, using the work we do at Search for Common Ground ("Search") on domestic policy issues in the United States as a jumping off point to make a fairly simple argument. In our work internationally and, now, in the United States we have taken on some of the most divisive political issues facing our country today. That, in turn, has forced us to make our work more explicitly political than that of most other NGOs working in the field. Because our work is so political and requires a long-term commitment and the use of a large "toolbox" of techniques, we need to add to any negotiation canon, the skills of dealing with politics large and small.

Readers who know Search's work will not be surprised because very little of what we do focuses on negotiation, mediation, or arbitration *per se*. Our global staff of about 500 has, for instance, no more than a handful of formally trained mediators and less than a handful of attorneys, none of whom have practiced law in some time. This author is neither, though I should admit that my training as a political scientist gives me even less professional guidance than I would have if I were either an attorney or a mediator. The skills my co-authors have concentrated on are an important component to Search's work, whether it is producing radio and television soap operas, building a women's peace center in Burundi, or conducting consensus building on divisive national public policy issues in the United States. However, as I will argue in the rest of the chapter, the kinds of projects we take on require more than the skills of a negotiator, mediator, or arbitrator. Even though negotiation is always a part of our work, I want to make the case that *political* conflict resolution work requires more of us.

Search for Common Ground: History and Principles

First, Search only gets involved in seemingly intractable conflicts that revolve around race, language, ethnicity, religion, or other emotionally charged "identity based" issues. Whether our goal is to improve relations between the United States and Iran, defuse tensions between ethnic Albanians and Macedonians, or help key stakeholders find ways of expanding health care coverage for the uninsured, we know that there is no single win/win deal that can solve the problem.

These types of conflicts take time—a lot of time. When John Paul Lederach was once asked how long it would take Northern Ireland to truly resolve its conflict, he asked his Catholic questioner when the conflict began and was told: 1690, with the Battle of the Boyne. Lederach's response was that if it took 300 years to create the conflict, it could take that amount of time to reach reconciliation and stable peace. One would hope that Lederach's comment is an overstatement, but there is no doubt that it will take more time than is involved in even a protracted mediation or negotiation to end these types of identity based conflicts.

Second and more important, professionals at Search see our overarching goal as transforming the way people deal with conflict, moving away from adversarial and toward more cooperative approaches. The word "transform" is key here. Our aim is not simply to help people reach agreements, but to use those agreements and the discussions that led to them to reshape profoundly the way people deal with the disputes that are an inevitable and inescapable part of all of our lives.

Third, our work is explicitly political in nature. We are never partisan and rarely could be confused with inside-the-Beltway policy advocates. We try to act as third party neutrals whenever possible. But the conflicts we work on inevitably make our work far more "political" than one would expect in traditional negotiation or mediation.

As a result, our work is based on a few key principles, which we think can help expand the canon as discussed by my fellow authors:

- *Understand the differences, act on the commonalities.* We rely heavily on this statement by General Albert Masondo, who was at one time head of the military wing of the African National Congress, but concluded his career establishing an affirmative action-style program for the South African military. The parties to the disputes we work on have long had their differences *and will continue to do so long after we leave the scene.* However, we have never seen a conflict in which the parties did not have some common goals, values, and interests. We start with those, and keep trying to build on those areas of real and potential agreement.
- *No parachuting.* We rarely get involved in short-term projects in which we are asked to mediate a dispute quickly. There is nothing inherently wrong with that kind of work.[1] Our working assumption, however, has always been that others are already doing that type of mediation and, frankly, can probably do it better than we could. Instead, we go—and we stay. Our projects in the Middle East and Macedonia were started in the early 1990s. We have been in a number of sub-Saharan countries since the middle of that decade. We began working on the abortion issue in the United States at about the same time, a project that we later transformed into a full unit with a mandate to look at all aspects of conflict and politics here.

- *Only go where we are needed.* As the number of chapters in this book suggests, there is no shortage of individuals or organizations doing good work on conflict resolution. Therefore, we have decided not to take on projects where others are already profitably engaged. For instance, we chose not to set up an office in South Africa, even though our Executive Vice President is South African and was an important participant in the transition from apartheid, because there were plenty of NGOs working there already. For similar reasons, we chose to not get involved in Bosnia, but focused on Macedonia, and on Burundi rather than Rwanda. Perhaps most important of all, we knew that when we started our American project in 2000 (and did so with a staff with little experience in the conflict resolution field) we were entering an already "crowded market." We have tried (we think reasonably successfully) not to step on other organizations' toes, and instead to expand the field as a whole.

- *Work with the "other side."* We also only take on projects in which we include all the major stakeholders. Like most conflict resolution NGOs, our staff members tend to be left of center in political affiliation. Those from my generation generally have roots in the peace and other protest movements of the 1960s. But if these are the only people the conflict resolution community reaches, we will be consigned to the political margins.[2] Concretely, that has meant primarily working with political conservatives in the United States, which I will explore in more detail below.

- *Doable, transformable, scalable and fundable.* Search has never tried to develop a methodology to use everywhere or a single theory to underlie our practice. Instead, John Marks, our founder and CEO, likes to quote a statement attributed to Napoléon Bonaparte, *on s'engage, après on voit.* One gets involved then one figures out what is happening.

That said, there is one set of criteria we use in determining whether to undertake a project. Can we complete it successfully given the resources at our disposal? If so, would it lend itself to other, bigger projects later on that will lead to a significant transformation of the relationships among the parties to the dispute? [Coleman, et al., *Dynamical*] Last but by no means least, we can only take on projects that we can fund. We have been relatively successful in raising money from foundations, governments, international organizations, and, now, individual donors. Nonetheless, we simply cannot take on projects that can only be funded out of organizational overhead.

Projects: Search for Common Ground USA

To illustrate these principles, I will next present a series of brief descriptions of what Search does on conflicts within the United States. Before discussing the specific projects, it is important to stress that what we do here in the U.S. is quite different from what our colleagues confront in the rest of the world. There, Search works in countries that have been ripped apart by civil war or other forms of violence. While the United States could hardly be called a non-violent society, we live in a functioning democracy in which our compatriots rarely have to resort to force to work out our political differences.

Search USA was founded in 2000. However, for the seven years before that, we mounted the Common Ground Network on Life and Choice ("the Network"), which was one of the first major attempts to bridge the ideological chasm that exists on abortion and related issues in the United States. The project ran dialogues in twenty cities around the country and held two national conferences. The project, obviously, did not end the controversy about abortion. However, along with a more recent effort by the Public Conversations Project,[3] we were able to help reduce the venom many participants brought to the discussions and help them reach some agreements—such as the need to reduce the rate of teen pregnancy.

More importantly, for the purposes of this chapter, the success of the Network helped convince members of Search's Board to suggest that we create a full division for political work in the United States. After all, if we could get Israelis and Palestinians or Hutus and Tutsis to sit down together, we obviously had some skills that would help out in our increasingly divided country.

One thing became clear almost immediately. It is all but impossible for us to be a neutral third party when we work on controversial issues in our own country. In Burundi or Angola, at least our expatriate staff has little or no vested interest in the conflict itself. That has not been true for us on any of the issues we have worked on in the United States.

As I like to put it, we did not become political eunuchs when we came to work at Search. Instead of claiming some unattainable version of "neutrality," we try to run ideologically *balanced* projects, defined by the range of participants we bring to the table and by our way of operating. If we are facilitating meetings ourselves, we do our best to keep our own political views out of sight—and we succeed most of the time. More importantly, we've discovered in our political as well as our professional lives that there are ways of being a political advocate that can draw someone you disagree with closer to you rather than drive them farther away. For example, in my classrooms, I rarely keep my opinions private nor do I try to make arguments I disagree with—I don't do it very well. Instead, I try to create a "safe space" in which students who disagree with me are comfortable doing so because they know I will listen carefully and take their ideas seriously. We try to create the same kind of atmosphere in the consensus building meetings we facilitate.

Concretely, that has led us to undertake a number of projects at both the national and local levels. Nationally, most of our work has been in trying to help key stakeholders forge consensus on policy issues that could be used as the framework for actual legislation. We were initially inspired by consensus councils and similar institutions that have been established in at least ten states.[4] While the specifics of each council varies, they have one feature in common: trained conflict resolution professionals lead interest group representatives through a consensus building process. Because the major stakeholders are in agreement by the end of the discussions, related legislation is both better designed for a balance of the public's real needs and normally passes in the state houses more easily.

Federal Consensus Efforts

Our first effort was to replicate in Washington what was previously done at the state level, by creating the United States Consensus Council ("USCC"). To launch the project, we recruited former Governor Marc Racicot of Montana (who had been actively involved in Florida for the Bush campaign and then led the president's 2004 reelection campaign) and former Secretary of Agriculture Dan Glickman. Together with them, we assembled a task force that balanced liberals and conservatives, Washingtonians and people from outside the Beltway, and prominent business leaders as well as politicians and conflict resolution experts.

The initial plan was to have Congress create the USCC as a federal agency that would conduct consensus building projects after receiving requests from either the White House or Congress. In fiscal year 2003, an appropriation for the USCC was included in the budget pending authorization by Congress. Unfortunately, the bill needed to be passed under unanimous consent procedures, but one or two senators placed "holds" on the bill, which effectively killed it after it went from committee to the floor. This is not terribly surprising, since it took many years before Congress authorized the United States Institution of Peace ("USIP") in the 1980s—coincidentally with strong support from then House of Representatives member Glickman.

We are in the process of turning the USCC into a project of Search itself until legislation can pass. It will become an organization that promotes the use of consensus building in public policy whether in projects we run ourselves or simply support from the outside.

Since 2001, we have tried to put the underlying principles behind the USCC into practice on a number of policy issues. The first was the highly controversial Faith Based Initiative, which President Bush launched within days of taking office. When it became clear that the Senate would never pass the bill (HR 7) that cleared the House, Senator Rick Santorum and former Senator Harris Wofford (whom he had defeated six years earlier) and Search USA agreed to look for areas of potential agreement.

We convened a group of about thirty leaders from religious and civic groups (e.g., the ACLU, the Assembly of God), which represented all the key groups interested in the initiative. The group itself was chaired by the Rev. Barry Lynn of the Americans United for the Separation of Church and State and the Rev. Ron Sider of Evangelicals for Social Action.

The group met roughly once a month for more than a year. Under Wofford's leadership, the group committed itself to expanding all forms of social service delivery, *whoever* the provider happened to be. We were also able to bring the group close to agreement on almost all of the most controversial issues—including, significantly in the current political climate, a consensus that groups that had a charitable tax status and did not proselytize in their social service work should be eligible to receive federal funds.

We are currently running a similar but even more ambitious project on expanding health care coverage for the uninsured. It is probably more typical of the kind of work we intend to keep doing because (a) widespread agreement already exists that we need to get insurance for as many of the 47 million Americans who lack coverage as soon as possible and (b) there is a political logjam that has blocked progress on the issue for most of the last decade. (That work is ongoing and will not reach any kind of conclusion before this book is published.) In addition to health care, we are currently designing projects to help build consensus, the President's Emergency Plan for AIDS Relief (PEPFAR) that the Administration has provided for HIV/AIDS relief and to help the country determine the right long-term responses to terrorism.

Community Programs

We have also taken on a number of community-based programs, always mindful not to get involved where we might step on existing conflict resolution organizations' political toes.

The most important and most successful of them is a project on prisoner reentry in Philadelphia, which was suggested to us by former Mayor Wilson Goode, who had participated in the Faith Based Initiative consensus group. Philadelphia is unusual in that it has a municipal prison that incarcerates felons as well as "regular" jails for people who commit lesser crimes. The integration of the more than one hundred thousand released offenders, who are often young, poorly educated, and uninvolved fathers, ripples throughout urban society. And while there are not huge ideological divisions on reentry of most kinds of offenders (as there are, for example, on health care or abortion), we quickly discovered that the stakeholders on the issues, ranging from the prosecutors to the ex-offenders themselves, rarely talked to each other.

So, with the help of Goode's organization, Public Private Ventures,[5] we organized a consensus building process which not only brought the stakeholders together but also won a seven figure grant from the "Ready to Work" program of the Department of Labor. The project has not always been an easy one for us to manage, especially because we never expected to become a direct service provider while many of the faith-based organizations we work with in Philadelphia struggle to do their work effectively with limited staffs and budgets. Nonetheless, this is a project that is potentially scalable to other cities (and states) with sizeable prison populations—which means almost everywhere in the United States.

Another project we took on—and one that might teach us more because it was by no means an unqualified success—occurred in Cincinnati. In 2002, a federal lawsuit was filed alleging racial profiling by the local police force. Almost immediately thereafter, a riot broke out right after an(other) African American teenager was killed in circumstances related to that policy.

The federal judge who was assigned the case wisely tried to avoid funneling it into the "default" litigation track. Instead, she hired an experienced mediator, Jay Rothman of the ARIA Group,[6] as a court appointed special master. Rothman brought several thousand Cincinnatians into dialogues, first online and later face-to-face, which eventuated in an agreement that settled the lawsuit. The agreement, notably, was praised both by the head of the ACLU and then Attorney General Ashcroft—public figures who were quite unaccustomed to sharing a "platform," metaphorical or otherwise.

At this juncture, the original mediator went on to other matters. Search decided the ongoing needs played to our strengths, and began to pursue a number of promising opportunities. For instance, just as we began our involvement in the area, a local theater company put on a production of Romeo and Juliet—with a black Romeo and white Juliet. We taped it, interviewed the cast, and held a focus group with people in the audience. We then boiled it down to a one-hour video, and reached—we thought—an agreement with the local PBS station to air it. But that agreement fell apart—as did almost all of the other projects we came up with.

In retrospect, one difference between the Philadelphia and Cincinnati projects is clear. We had, we still believe, good ideas in both places. In fact, those for Cincinnati were probably more far-reaching. What we had in Philadelphia and lacked in Cincinnati, however, was a *local partner* who knew the community and could work effectively in it. Despite all the time we spent in Cincinnati, we were never able to identify such a partner—and the project eventually fell apart. In sum, Search is unlikely to take on a community based project in which it is not clear that there is a local group or, at a minimum, a suitably skilled individual with whom we can work.

Next Steps

As this chapter is written, Search is trying to determine what kinds of issues we should take on in the next two to five years. What we have learned in five years of working at Search-USA and in the broader discussions we have had with colleagues in the field is that negotiation/conflict resolution is at a crossroads. A field dominated by mediators and, perhaps more important, by people (like myself) who are products of the 1960s risks intellectual and political straightjackets, and if not continuously reinvented, is likely to consign itself to a life on the political margins.

In my own work, addressing this means concretely finding ways of working with at least two communities that have not often been approached by the left-of-center.. The first such group consists of Evangelical Christians with an interest in conflict resolution work. Depending on which poll you take seriously, as many as a third of the U.S. population defines itself as Evangelical Christians. In discussions at Wheaton College in Illinois a few years ago, I discovered a whole world of Evangelicals whose conflict resolution work (with Scripture) is coherent with and often similar to the work we do on reconciliation at Search. Yet we did not know each other. The question became, how can we find the common ground that allows us to talk about our field together? Also, how can we then work together to address the culture war issues in this country?

I do not mean to minimize the gap between us. Few of my secular friends even went to see *The Passion of the Christ*, and probably fewer have read any of the *Left Behind* series of novels. But my time at Wheaton and beyond convinced me that we share more than we disagree on.

The other big challenge is to learn to work with the national security and intelligence communities. As I write in mid-2005, Iraq and the war on terrorism are as divisive as any foreign policy issue in recent memory. There is probably even less discussion and dialogue between the conflict resolution community and national security policy makers than there has been between ourselves and the Evangelicals.

I have been fortunate enough to work with serving officers, retirees, and civilian employees at the State Department, the Pentagon, and the CIA. I have been pleasantly surprised by how many of them understand that while they know how to blow things up, they don't have a lot of expertise in rebuilding—and thus need some definition of "us."[7] [Lira, *Military*]

In concluding, let me be as blunt as possible. If we fail to address the issues raised in this chapter, I believe we will limit a larger sense of negotiation and conflict resolution to the margins of political life. The lawyers, other practitioners, and the many scholars who have developed and learned to practice negotiation and other forms of ADR have already endured an era in which the field's skills and knowledge have seemed irrelevant in many of the highest-tension and largest-scale conflicts. The field's new challenge is to scale up, and to modify as necessary, those skills into a metanegotiation of our political life.

Endnotes

[1] *See* Christopher Honeyman & Sandra Cheldelin, *Have Gavel, Will Travel: Dispute Resolution's Innocents Abroad*, 19 DISPUTE RESOLUTION QUARTERLY 363 (2002).

[2] For more on this, see the recent provocative book by BERNARD MAYER, BEYOND NEUTRALITY (2004).

[3] For more information, *see* www.publicconversations.org.

[4] For more information, *see* www.policyconsensus.org.

[5] For more information, *see* www.ppv.org.

[6] For more information, *see* www.ariagroup.com.

[7] To see how far defense intellectuals have come, *see* Thomas M.P. Barnett, THE PENTAGON'S NEW MAP (2004); DEFENSE SCIENCE BOARD, SUMMER STUDY 2004: TRANSITION TO AND FROM HOSTILITIES (Dec. 2004), *available at* http://www.acq.osd.mil/dsb/reports/2004-12-DSB_SS_Report_Final.pdf (discussing how far defense intellectuals have come).

ᙢ 73 ᙣ

Uses of a Marathon Exercise

Daniel Druckman

Editors' Note: *Very few real world negotiations last 45 minutes (with some time left to debrief!) Yet most negotiation simulations used in the classroom operate with just such time and fact constraints. The consequences are naturally rather unrealistic. Druckman challenges the presumed inevitability of such arbitrary or truncated exercises, describing extensive experience in conducting multi-day, multi-stage, research-based negotiation exercises for a variety of clients. If we can't adapt our training models to such realistic approaches, can we seriously argue that we are training people to be real, or even realistic negotiators? Druckman's chapter helps trainers and professors think about changing their simulations.*

The simplicity of many negotiation training exercises stands out as a continuing problem in the field. Often, these either use one-shot deals of minimal complexity, or omit the practical realities of big cases, in which there is always a team involved. For training professionals and others to assume roles in the negotiation of major disputes, it can be helpful to play out an exercise, or linked series of exercises of some complexity, with multiple aspects and stages.

In this chapter, I discuss a series[1] of such exercises. They were developed as part of a project designed to use research findings on negotiation in training. These exercises are preceded by a review of sixteen thematic narratives, focusing attention on the discussion questions accompanying each narrative. They are followed by self-report evaluations. The entire workshop can be implemented in as few as two days or as long as a week. Three days is probably an optimal period, although intensive courses based on this format have been conducted for two weeks. The shorter workshops may forego the role-play; the longer courses usually add coverage of the field, including research on third parties. The discussion is offered not as exemplary, but as a contribution to the mutual learning and search for feedback and correction that have characterized the best of the negotiation field. In this complex series of designs, it will be clear from the overall satisfaction ratings by participants, reported below, that the approach, as it has evolved to date, still can be improved. This is anything but an exercise in complacency.

The project can be thought of as an attempt to bridge theory and research with negotiation practice. It is a contribution to the debate about ways to bring academic and applied cultures into closer contact: these issues are discussed, for example, in the contexts of international negotiation,[2] foreign policy,[3] and conflict resolution.[4] Missing from those discussions, however, is a plan for implementing the connection between these cultures. The project described here is an example of this kind of implementation. It is an extension and update of an earlier publication by Druckman and Robinson.[5]

Bridging Theory to Practice

There are several challenges to implementing a bridging project. One consists of addressing the difference between analytical and political approaches to negotiation. The former strives for precise definition of terms suitable for systematic hypothesis testing. The latter approach prefers vague definitions of terms or positions to retain flexibility in light of changing objectives and strategies. Another challenge is the difference between seeking generalized or contextual/specific knowledge. The former aims to capture similarities in negotiating behavior across a large number of cases, settings, or historical circumstances. The latter emphasizes the importance of the specific settings in which particular negotiations take place. A third challenge is to address the gulf between abstract and experiential knowledge. A theorist generally operates in an abstract world of ideas; practitioners derive insights and lessons from their past negotiating experience. And, a fourth challenge concerns the design of a training environment: how should the relevant research knowledge be communicated? How should the information be used in actual negotiating tasks? What kinds of skills are being developed? This project addresses these challenges.

Differences between theory and practice are bridged here by distinguishing among four functions of negotiation practice: analysis, strategy, performance, and design. Two of these functions, the analyst and strategist, are consulting roles. Analysis refers to the task of providing insights into the link between negotiation process and outcome. Strategy consists of giving advice on approaches for resolving impasses. Performance is the experience of negotiating in a simulation as a team representative. And design is the activity of constructing an exercise for learning about negotiation. Participants become role-players in a sequence of exercises that highlights each of these functions. Research findings are the tools used to analyze actual cases; they are also the tools for developing strategies for resolving impasses. They are utilized in the course of negotiating as representatives of larger parties in a simulated multilateral regional conflict over environmental issues. The simulation experience then sets the stage for a fourth task, in which participants are asked to design a training exercise of their own. The exercises are intended to facilitate participants' learning about concepts from the research literature. But each of these exercises places the findings in a real-world setting.

These exercises depend, for their effectiveness, on the extent to which the concepts are learned. Learning is likely to be enhanced when the material is presented in an appealing, easy-to-comprehend format. An effort was made to accomplish this by organizing the published studies in terms of themes and, then, writing narrative descriptions of the key ideas resulting from the research. To avoid the impression of a fragmented literature, the themes—16 in all—are placed in a framework that shows how pre-conditions, background factors, and conditions impact on the process and outcome of negotiation. Learning aids are also provided in the form of discussion questions, summaries of central points, counter-intuitive insights from the thematic narratives, and advice. Evaluations are conducted to ascertain the learning gains. Each of these parts of the training package is discussed in some detail in the sections to follow.

This chapter is organized into several sections. I begin with a discussion of the thematic narratives, followed by the four role-playing exercises developed to provide opportunities for applying the knowledge from those narratives. Then, I describe the procedures used in a typical training workshop. A tour of the training venues around the world is provided in the next section, along with the results of evaluations. Yet, despite a well-traveled training package, I have discovered some resistances along the way. These barriers to implementation are discussed. The chapter concludes with some lessons learned and avenues for further work, including refining the materials for use in other types of settings.

The Thematic Narratives

A narrative is a short essay that captures key research findings on a theme. In preparing the narratives, I avoid technical jargon and details of methodology but cite the articles that generated the findings. Sixteen narrative topics were identified from a review of the published literature spanning the period from 1965 to 2001. The set of topical narratives is presented in the following sequence and should be familiar to most trainers:

- achieving integrative agreements
- third-party effects on negotiation
- positive and negative affect in negotiation
- culture
- effects of relationship on negotiation
- effects of experience on negotiation
- alternatives to negotiated agreements
- time pressure
- tactics: information exchange
- tactics: presenting two faces in negotiation
- tactics: using rewards in negotiation
- constraints on negotiating flexibility
- the role of power
- gender in negotiation
- representation
- turning points

Several learning aids are included in the training materials with the narratives: discussion/review questions, key points, a set of counter-intuitive insights, and some prescriptions. When the narratives are used for longer courses, a set of hypothetical negotiating dilemmas is presented. Learning is assessed by judging the extent to which the relevant narrative concepts are used to solve each dilemma.[6] A growing literature on negotiation impels me to update some narratives with new findings or to introduce new themes that have emerged from more recent studies.

This set of narratives is based almost entirely on studies published in American journals. For this reason, the knowledge is based on empirical studies, particularly laboratory experiments. This is, however, only one source for knowledge about negotiation. Other sources include negotiating experience, legal, historical, sociological, typological, and philosophical perspectives. These are the approaches favored in the academic cultures of other societies.

An opportunity arose to collaborate with French colleagues on the development of thematic narratives. I encouraged this group, led by Christophe Dupont, to prepare a set of narratives based exclusively on the French negotiation literature. A smaller number of published studies in France resulted in fewer themes than those used to organize the American literature. Five of the nine topics have counterparts in my American-based narratives: *integrative negotiating, emotions, culture, flexibility, and third parties.* Four are not part of the American set, not because of a lack of coverage in the literature but due to limits on our reach with the set compiled to date: *risks, threats and ultimatums, negotiation teams, and trust.* The format is the same for the two sets; the research findings discussed are different. A number of comparisons can be made including similarities and differences in concepts used, advice given, and case studies chosen for exercises.[7] Both sets were used in a recent training that took place in Paris, along with the most recent findings reported in the research literature on several of the narrative topics.

Both sets of narratives consist of "pieces" of negotiation. The impression given by this presentation is that of a fragmented phenomenon; missing is the way that these parts are related to each other. A framework is therefore needed to depict the connections through time. This is done with the format developed originally by Sawyer and Guetzkow.[8] It shows relationships within and between three time periods:

- *antecedent* (preparation, issues, background factors)
- *concurrent* (processes such as bargaining, conditions such as time pressures or external events); and
- *consequent* (including the outcomes and implementation provisions)

When the narrative themes are placed in the boxes of the framework, as shown in Figure 1, the trainee can appreciate a way in which the themes are connected. The framework is thus an organizing device that serves to reduce the impression of a disconnected body of research. This is particularly useful when the narratives are used as tools for analyzing cases. For example, knowing how alternatives (a background factor) and time pressure (a condition) impact on integrative agreements (an outcome) add value to the analysis of a case. Without a framework, the trainee would be limited to a handful of separate concepts that provide snapshots of different aspects of a complex case of negotiation.

Negotiating Functions as Tasks: The Case Studies and Exercises

The narratives and framework provide concepts for understanding negotiation. The next question asks how the concepts can be used in practice. I tackled this question by, first, defining what is meant by "practice." Four tasks performed by practitioners, including those who negotiate and those who support negotiations, were identified. One task consists of analysis and asks about relationships among the various parts of negotiation, such as processes and outcomes. Another is strategy, by which I mean impasse resolution. The question asked is: what strategic recommendations are likely to be most effective in moving the negotiation forward? A third task is referred to as performance. This involves the skills of negotiating, usually in the role of representative of a larger group or nation. A fourth is that of designer. This consists of constructing exercises that can be used for training, often in the form of a role-play. Each of these tasks is implemented with the narratives. They are presented in sequence as consulting roles. Each prior task, such as an analyst, provides an experience that is helpful for doing the next one, such as a strategist.

The analyst and strategist tasks are performed with case studies of actual negotiations. The cases are drawn from the archive of Pew Case Studies in International Affairs held by Georgetown's Institute for the Study of Diplomacy. Seven cases were chosen from an inventory of more than 200. Selection criteria included: (a) a focus primarily on negotiation processes; (b) a detailed description of strategies, moves, proposals, and context; (c) a manageable length for a training session, and, (d) easy-to-find illustrations of concepts from the narratives. Examples of the chosen cases and relevant narratives are the Korean Joggers (emotions, relationships, alternatives, time pressures, rewards, and power), the 1972 Simla Agreement (flexibility, integrative agreements, alternatives, two-faces tactic, power), Panama Canal (alternatives, time pressure, integrative agreements, two-faces tactic, and power), and troop withdrawals from Lebanon (third parties, flexibility, alternatives, emotions, and relationships). Other cases deal with civil wars and multilateral conference diplomacy.

Figure 1. Negotiation Framework with Narrative Themes (in **bold**)

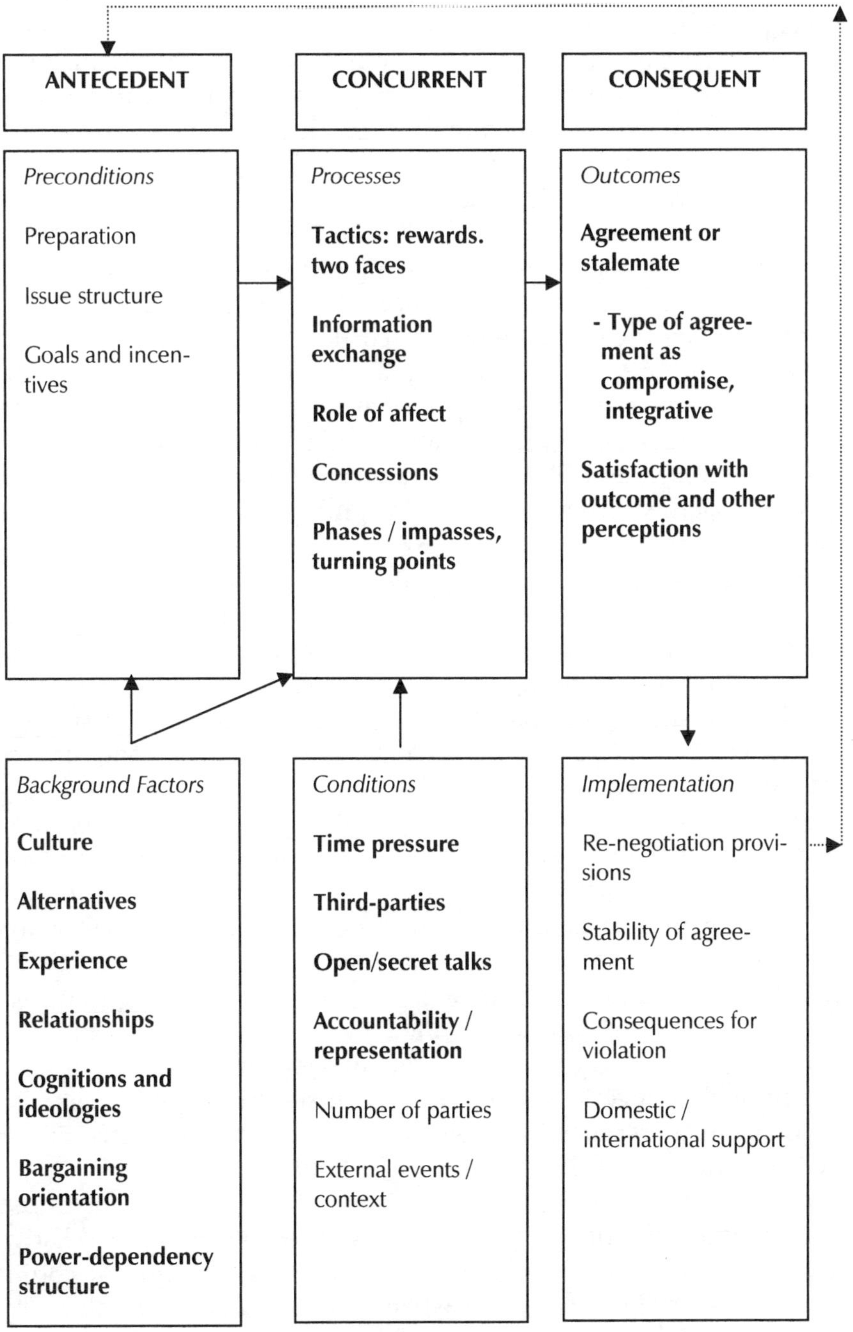

ANTECEDENT	CONCURRENT	CONSEQUENT
Preconditions Preparation Issue structure Goals and incentives	*Processes* **Tactics: rewards. two faces** **Information exchange** **Role of affect** **Concessions** **Phases / impasses, turning points**	*Outcomes* **Agreement or stalemate** **- Type of agreement as compromise, integrative** **Satisfaction with outcome and other perceptions**
Background Factors **Culture** **Alternatives** **Experience** **Relationships** **Cognitions and ideologies** **Bargaining orientation** **Power-dependency structure**	*Conditions* **Time pressure** **Third-parties** **Open/secret talks** **Accountability / representation** Number of parties External events / context	*Implementation* Re-negotiation provisions Stability of agreement Consequences for violation Domestic / international support

To facilitate the tasks of analyst and strategist, study guides were prepared. These come in three parts: the relevant narratives as shown just above, guides for analysis, and guides for strategy. These guides are intended to direct the trainee to aspects of the case that highlight the relevant concepts. An example of an *analysis* guide is as follows:

From *Negotiations on Troop Withdrawals from Lebanon*: on page 12, the author indicates that "all of the parties would be better off with some form of agreement." If, in fact, their alternatives were less attractive than an agreement, explain why a satisfactory agreement did not emerge from the talks.

An example of a *strategy* guide is as follows:

From *Korean Joggers*: suppose that the negotiators refused to adjust their positions to get an agreement. An impasse was caused by Korea's demand of a higher export quota than the U.S. was willing to give. Using the information in the relevant narratives, develop a plan that can be used to advise the respective delegations (either together or separately) on strategies that they might develop to get the talks back on track.

These guides serve to provide a focus for the tasks. The analyst task is usually completed by a three-member team in about an hour and a half. Team members are encouraged to divide their labor by assigning three roles, a case expert, a narrative expert, and an integrator. The product consists of a report that summarizes several ways in which the concepts were used. The strategist role is implemented in about an hour with a similar division of labor among the same team members. This task also produces a summary report that focuses on application of the concepts. Both roles are de-briefed. Each team member participates in a presentation that describes the case, discusses the relevant narrative concepts, and shows how they were used together either to provide insights (analyst task) or to resolve the impasse (strategist task).

The third negotiation function, performance, is implemented with a multilateral simulation. Referred to as the Maun Sea Restoration Project, the exercise consists of six parties who negotiate their different positions on five issues. The parties include four neighboring nations of different size, resources, and regional/global interests, a regional NGO that was formed in response to an environmental crisis in the region, and a coalition of three international organizations (the World Bank, the U.N. Environment Programme, and the U.N. Development Programme) that convened the talks. Each of the six parties can be represented by individuals or small teams depending on the size of a workshop and the number of simulations run. Three or four options (proposed solutions) are defined for each of the issues. Conflict among the parties is created by assigning them different preferences for the issue options. Further, the issues differ in importance for the various parties, allowing for log-rolling or trading on the issues. Certain combinations of options across the issues define solutions that maximize benefits to all the parties; these are integrative agreements. A challenge is to discover them through a negotiation process that mixes plenary meetings (convened by the coalition), bilateral meetings, and caucuses within the teams. The time for this entire simulation ranges from four to eight hours.

Participants are told to keep track of their use of the narrative topics used during the course of negotiating. To aid this task, they are given a check list with the sixteen narrative topics as rows, and time periods as columns. Recordings are made at two times, the half-way point when a break is taken, and the completion when an agreement has been reached or the talks break off. The mid-point reporting reveals themes or ideas regarded as being useful for the earlier formulaic stages of negotiation; the post-negotiation reporting highlights themes seen as being helpful during stages leading to and including the endgame when a decision is needed. Each role-player is asked to check the themes that were used during the negotiation and to write a brief comment about how each was used tactically or to move the talks forward. These data are featured in the de-briefing session and provide feedback to the workshop designers about the contributions of the narrative concepts to performance.

The fourth negotiating function is represented in the designer exercise, which follows the simulation. Participants are asked to construct a simulation that incorporates the ideas from the narratives. The purpose of the exercise is to alert "trainees"—who are often working professionals or experienced diplomats—to aspects of their negotiating behavior that they had been unaware of in their prior experience. To help with this task, six design issues are highlighted:

- Which ideas from the narratives will be incorporated in the simulation?
- What issue will be simulated (e.g., arms control, trade, environment)?
- What kind of party structure will be simulated (e.g., bilateral, trilateral, multilateral)?
- What purpose will be served by the simulation (e.g., general training, specific preparation, hypothesis-testing research)?
- How will context be represented (constituencies, a policy-making process, a marketplace or international system)?
- What kind of information will be collected for evaluation (e.g., self-report questionnaires, taped discussions to evaluate what was learned)?

After deciding on each of the above questions, participants are given a series of steps for developing a scenario: describing the current situation, defining the key roles, describing the issues and positions, and constructing a de-briefing. In their written report, designer teams are encouraged to indicate which narrative concepts were used and how they were incorporated in the simulation. The designs are presented to the other teams during a de-briefing session.

Venues

This training workshop format has traveled far and wide. To date we have conducted workshops on five continents, North and South America,[9] Europe and the Middle East, Asia, and Australia. A variety of groups have experienced the approach, ranging from a one-week class/workshop with 75 students in Cochin, India to a two-day stint with ten executives in Brisbane, Australia. Workshops were conducted with students in law (e.g., Georgetown), business (e.g., Negocia in Paris), and conflict resolution (e.g., Sabanci University in Istanbul, Institute for International Mediation and Conflict Resolution in the Netherlands). A two-week faculty course was organized through the Fulbright senior specialists program in Manila. Seventy members of a Danish labor union (DJOEF) participated in a two-day workshop followed by a one-day training for the labor-union's staff. Other public and private-sector professionals participated in shorter-duration sessions in Peru, Bolivia, and Australia. Our work with the United Nations was the longest relationship that we had with an institution. Funds for this series of workshops were provided by a United States Institute of Peace (USIP) grant and coordinated through the Institute of World Affairs in Washington. These were the most international workshops with almost as many countries represented as there were participants.

These experiences increased my appreciation for the importance of cultural, sectoral, and organizational perspectives in negotiation; they also bolstered my confidence in the broad relevance of social science research. Clearly, negotiation is an essential part of working lives of people in many fields.

Evaluations

Evaluations were conducted at the conclusion of each of these workshops/courses. Forced-choice and open-ended questions were asked about the narratives and three of the roles, analyst, strategist, designer. The results—across the venues— can be summarized.

On the Narratives

The narratives improved understanding of the concepts. Narrative groups performed better than groups given only the themes, but not the content of the narratives.

The narratives were viewed by all participants as providing useful information, relevant, easy to apply to the cases, and helpful in implementing their roles. Prior exposure to negotiation frameworks and an overview of the field enhanced the learning value provided by the set of narratives.

Participants who were experienced members of UN missions indicated that they would consult the narratives for information relevant to work-related issues; when queried several months following the workshop, however, few indicated that they had opportunities to consult the specific narratives to date.

On the Exercises

The three roles (analyst, strategist, designer) were viewed by most participants as being somewhat difficult to execute. Most participants regarded the analyst role as being easier to implement than the strategist and designer roles.

Academic participants rated the three exercises (analyst, strategist, designer) higher than the non-academic (e.g., UN) participants. Diplomats thought that they learned more from the exercises (self reports) than their written reports suggested. Their oral de-briefings were usually better than the written team reports.

Participants thought that analysis was easier for some cases. The "easier" cases, such as the Korean Joggers, were those where the narrative concepts were evident in the description of negotiation dynamics.

Overall Ratings

The highest ratings overall were given by participants in the workshops held in India (one week), Peru (two days), and the Organization of American States (OAS) (two days). However, few mean ratings in any of the sessions were above three (i.e. worse than the mid-point) on a five-step scale ranging from very satisfied (1) to very dissatisfied (5). These ratings are quite positive but also call attention to areas for improvement in the evolving design of this complex series of exercises.

These results suggest that: (a) the narratives work well, (b) learning is enhanced when frameworks and overviews are added, (c) the analyst role may be the easiest to execute by most (but not all) participants, (d) there was a possible illusion of learning by diplomats, and (e) there is long-term interest in using the knowledge. These conclusions are ideas for refining the approach. One idea is to retain the topical narratives format but update each narrative with recent findings and add new topics. Updating was done for the French-English workshop conducted in September, 2005 for four days with recent graduates of Negocia in Paris. Another idea is to include frameworks as part of the training package; this would extend the length of the sessions. A third idea is to determine more specifically how to facilitate the strategist and designer tasks. And, a fourth idea is to encourage refresher training in order to sustain the learning and to develop applications in the workplace.

Implementation Challenges: "Strong" and "Weak" Cultures

Innovative training programs, notably those involving scholarly research, are often difficult to "sell" (figuratively or financially) to potential non-academic clients. Although a longish list of venues in which this material has so far been presented may belie this impression, we have had less success getting our "foot-in-the-door" with some institutions. [Hawkins, et al., *Access*] Reflecting on the difference between those clients who welcomed—and in most cases paid for—our services and those that did not, has led to an insight about types of organizations. The insight turns on a distinction between "strong" and "weak" institutions and cultures. As will be evident, these terms are used here as terms of art, not in their vernacular sense. Institutions with stronger cultures have been less receptive to new training approaches. (This observation is based also on our attempts to offer electronic approaches to mediation.[10])

Differences between the U.S. Department of State (DOS) and the United Nations illuminate this distinction. The DOS is a "strong" institution in the following ways: it has a persistent and slow-to-change organizational culture; low turnover of personnel, many of whom are career foreign or civil service officers; strong conformity (or loyalty) pressures; institutionalized routines; and a mostly centralized structure and leadership. System maintenance seems to be more important than encouraging innovation, with the attendant risks. The UN is a "weak" institution in the following ways: a lack of a persisting organizational culture; high turnover within country missions; diversity of viewpoints is not discouraged; and a decentralized structure and leadership. Innovation is rewarded more than efforts to preserve a system structure and culture.

These features are the sources of varying degrees of inertia within organizations. The strong institutions adapt but slowly to a dynamic external environment, a resistance that would threaten survival in the private and non-profit sectors of many societies, but less problematic for chartered or constitutionally-protected organizations like the DOS. Weaker institutions, however, are more adaptive. This is an eloquent illustration of how a term of art may depart from the vernacular.

This distinction has implications for training programs. Efforts to market our programs at DOS (and the US Department of Defense) were greeted with interest and curiosity, but not adopted. In contrast, the UN was always receptive, inviting us to return several times and noting that the knowledge gained was useful in the workplace. However, receptivity does not insure long-term impacts on negotiating behavior. Refresher training is one solution. Another is to insert the program at regular intervals (annual, semi-annual) for new cohorts, especially in high-turnover organizations like the UN. A third, of course, is continuous redesign to take account of feedback and critiques; see the next section below.

Four implications of the distinction between strong and weak organizations are evident. One is that very strong institutions provide formidable barriers to implementing new ideas, and may be unapproachable. Another is that weaker institutions provide opportunities for innovation from the inside or outside. A third is that most organizations are located between these extremes—as moderately strong or weak. For them, more effort is likely to be needed in developing persuasive arguments of the likely impacts of the training. Fourth, conducting the program is one accomplishment, but institutionalizing the learning is another challenge. Monitoring the learning through time and follow-up refresher training may be helpful.

These implications suggest that the strong-weak distinction (or continuum) may be a useful tool for diagnosing organizations in terms of their receptivity to new ideas. It is also relevant to the prospects for institutional change or transformation. Those prospects are enhanced with certain types of organizations.[11]

Wrapping Up

I have now had many experiences with this approach to learning about negotiation. Three questions are suggested by these experiences. One question of interest is: what have we learned from the workshops conducted to date? Another question is: what changes and additions can be made to improve the package? And, a third question is: what adaptations would be needed for other types of training populations? These questions are addressed in this concluding section of the chapter.

The organization of the narratives suggests that the field breaks down into analytical nuggets. The impression is that we analyze negotiation one variable at a time. This is a bias of an experimental approach which has dominated the American research historically. The approach is less holistic. Yet despite this fragmentation, we have generated a number of interesting insights which are depicted in our package as "counter-intuitives." These insights are also framed as prescriptions or advice. When the insights are used in the strategy and designer exercises, they are regarded as manipulatable features of the negotiation setting. The exercises call attention to levers for changing perceptions and decisions. This is consistent also with findings on impacts of various aspects of the situation.[12] But we need to learn more about the interactions between situational levers and contexts: which features of the situation have the strongest impacts in which settings? The French narratives expand the knowledge base beyond experimental research. They also alert us to cultural influences on the kind of knowledge that we produce and transmit.

The sets of English and French narratives will need to be kept up-to-date and expanded. New findings on such "hot" topics as culture, relationships, and integrative agreements should find their way into the current set.[13] At least a half-dozen new narratives could be written on such themes as conditions for getting to the table (pre-conditions), reputations and attributions (background factors), trust (background factors), number of parties/conference size (conditions), external events/context (conditions), use of warnings, threats, and ultimatums (processes), social motives (pre-conditions), and implementation of agreements.

We have also learned lessons from observing the exercises. Although most participants show (through their products) that they learn how to apply the narratives, the learning may increase with cases that are shorter, less complex, and more transparent in terms of applicability of the narrative concepts. It would be of value to explore these case dimensions systematically and to choose cases for training that meet the criteria. The division of labor among team members—case expert, narrative expert, integrator—seems to work well, but all members should participate in trying to make the connection between narratives and cases. Overall, the designer exercise is viewed as being difficult to execute and as making a smaller contribution to learning the concepts than the other exercises. Yet, this task also produces the most creative de-briefings. We will need to know more about this discrepancy.

Just as we contemplate expanding the set of narratives to other topics, we should consider extending the cases to other settings. Domestic negotiators (and students of domestic negotiations) could benefit from this approach if the applications were familiar to them. This entails adding domestic cases to the package. These may include interpersonal or inter-group disputes as well as those within and between organizations involving employees and employers. A challenge is to locate a clearinghouse of domestic case descriptions with an emphasis on the process. These populations would benefit also from role-plays tailored more closely to their domain of experience. This worked well in one workshop where a familiar conflict involving a labor union was simulated. The designer exercise can then be linked more closely to the role-play by asking participants to design another familiar exercise that highlights the concepts that were particularly salient in the role play just completed. This may enhance the learning benefits from the designer exercise.

We have now conducted the training with participants from a variety of backgrounds. The academic flavor of the approach would seem to make it more conducive to graduate students than to civil servants, private sector professionals, or members of a labor union. Indeed, this may have been the case. However, we were impressed with the effort expended by the non-student populations as well. Many of them regarded the approach as a novel curiosity and were surprised to learn about the volume of research done on this topic. This was a new experience for them and their reactions ranged from mild revelation to child-like enthusiasm. Participants develop an appreciation for the complexity of negotiation—in the form of contingent statements—and would be more skeptical about simple advice such as "develop attractive alternatives to the terms on the table." They now know, for instance, that the power gained from attractive alternatives can also lead to sub-optimal outcomes.

The evaluations showed that learning is enhanced when frameworks are presented prior to the review of narratives. The idea that there are alternative ways of thinking about negotiation is compelling. This is communicated with the help of metaphors, including negotiation as a puzzle, as a game, as organization management, as identity politics, social discourse and so on.[14] [Gadlin, et al., Metaphors] Moving forward, the training challenge is to connect the metaphors with narrative themes and findings. By doing so, participants are provided with various analytical lenses through which to view the cases and role plays. All of this illustrates the heuristic value of the approach, leading us to make refinements that will, we trust, increase its contribution to learning about negotiation and to bridging research with practice.

Endnotes

[1] The exercises are presented in sequence as a theatrical metaphor, a "four-scene performance." The analyst role described below is referred to as "Scene I: The Team Gathers." The strategist role is "Scene II: The World Intrudes." The performer role is "Scene III: Your Turn." And the designer role is presented as "Scene IV: Passing on the Wisdom." Three de-briefings occur, after Scenes II, III, and IV.

[2] Daniel Druckman & P. Terrence Hopmann, Behavioral Aspects of Negotiations on Mutual Security, in BEHAVIOR, SOCIETY, AND NUCLEAR WAR, VOL. 1 (Phillip Tetlock, et al. eds., 1989).

[3] ALEXANDER GEORGE, BRIDGING THE GAP: THEORY AND PRACTICE IN FOREIGN POLICY (1993).

[4] Jacob Bercovitch, et al., *On Bridging the Gap: The Relevance of Theory to the Practice of Conflict Resolution*, 59 AUSTRALIAN JOURNAL OF INTERNATIONAL AFFAIRS 133 (2005).

[5] Daniel Druckman & Victor Robinson, *From Research to Application: Utilizing Research Findings in Negotiation Training Programs*, 3 INTERNATIONAL NEGOTIATION 7 (1998).

[6] *Id.* for an example of a narrative.

[7] A start along these lines is found in Daniel Druckman, et al., *From Research to Application: A Project to Stimulate Training Practitioners to Utilize Research Findings in Negotiation*, paper presented at the First Biennale International Conference on Negotiation, Paris (2003).

[8] Jack Sawyer & Harold Guetzkow, *Bargaining and Negotiation in International Relations*, in INTERNATIONAL BEHAVIOR: A SOCIAL-PSYCHOLOGICAL ANALYSIS (Herbert Kelman ed., 1965).

[9] The entire program is presented in Spanish by Daniel Druckman & Ivan Ormachea, *Negociacion: De La Teoria A La Preactisa* (2003). This publication guides the implementation of the approach in Spanish-language countries.

[10] Daniel Druckman, et al., *E-Mediation: Evaluating the Impacts of an Electronic Mediator on Negotiating Behavior*, 13 GROUP DECISION AND NEGOTIATION 481 (2004).

[11] Kim Cameron & Sarah Freeman, *Cultural Congruence, Strength, and Type: Relationships to Effectiveness*, 5 RESEARCH IN ORGANIZATIONAL CHANGE AND DEVELOPMENT 3 (1991).

[12] Daniel Druckman, *The Situational Levers of Negotiating Flexibility*, 37 JOURNAL OF CONFLICT RESOLUTION 236 (1993); Daniel Druckman, *Situational Levers of Position Change: Further Explorations*, 542 THE ANNALS OF THE AMERICAN ACADEMY OF POLITICAL AND SOCIAL SCIENCE 61 (1995).

[13] An example of a new finding comes from current research on implementation. Malhotra and Ginges found that population (Israeli) support for negotiated agreements increases when the other side (Palestinian) supports the accords as well. The key is the perception of matching: The other side's support is devalued when your side's constituents do not support the agreement. Thus, the unexpected result is that devaluation of the counterpart's view is contingent on the extent to which your own side lines up in support of the negotiated outcome. This finding may be counterintuitive to those who are familiar with the research on reactive devaluation. [Korobkin & Guthrie, *Heuristics and Biases*] But it is consistent with other findings on the importance of synchrony in negotiation, and forms a basis for a new narrative. *See* Deepak Malhotra & Jeremy Ginges, Paper Presented at the Annual Conference of the International Association of Conflict Management, Seville, Spain, *Overcoming Bias in How Negotiated Agreements are Evaluated: A Study of Israeli Attitudes Towards the Geneva Accords* (2005); *see also* Kenneth Arrow et al., BARRIERS TO CONFLICT RESOLUTION (1995); *see also* Daniel Druckman & Richard Harris, *Alternative Models of Responsiveness in International Negotiation*, 34 Journal of Conflict Resolution 234 (1990).

[14] *See* Daniel Druckman, *Negotiating in the International Context*, in PEACEMAKING IN INTERNATIONAL CONFLICT: METHODS AND TECHNIQUES (I. William Zartman & Lewis L. Rasmussan eds., 1997); *see also*, GARETH MORGAN, IMAGES OF ORGANIZATIONS (1997).

❧ 74 ❦

Negotiating with the Unknown

Maria Volpe, Jack J. Cambria,
Hugh McGowan & Christopher Honeyman

Editors' Note: *What happens when all of the classic negotiation advice about preparation goes out the window? Negotiations "on the street" teach us how extensive preparation for the process itself—for teamwork, roles, communication patterns, and trust—is crucial for success when everything you might ordinarily want to know to prepare for a specific case is impossible to find out in time.*

In order to understand the ordinary or near-ordinary, sometimes it pays to study the extreme. This chapter will use the extremely high-tension experiences of hostage negotiators to discuss a few facets of negotiation that are rarely taught to others, but that increasingly seem relevant far beyond their original setting.[1]

Imagine having to negotiate with an unknown entity where, more often than not, the parties have no way of anticipating who they will interact with, or what questions or issues to expect. The parties meet for the first time at a tense scene, with each side typically separated from the other by a closed door. Interested parties tend to be numerous and insistent. Some of these interested parties may be closely associated with the hostages or the hostage taker, such as family, friends, colleagues, neighbors. Some are closely associated with the hostage negotiators, including supervisors and other law enforcement experts. Many others may be strangers to both parties, such as observers, media representatives and politicians. This potentially vast gathering of "significant others" creates what a former commander of the New York Police Department's hostage negotiation team refers to as "negotiations within the negotiation." Moreover, it is not unusual for weapons to be omnipresent on both sides.

Variations on these circumstances describe the "normal" context of the work of police hostage negotiators. They conduct their negotiations wherever and whenever there are highly stressful situations involving individuals being held against their will and where the ongoing communications with the hostage takers are high-stakes, involving potential loss of life. In these encounters, hostage negotiators have one distinct advantage over hostage takers: experience in dealing with such individuals in different situations. Hostage takers have typically never taken hostages before. Hostage negotiators, however, have collectively acquired a wide range of coping skills. These skills, we now believe, are needed in many other set-

658 THE NEGOTIATOR'S FIELDBOOK

tings—settings that do not provide comparable training opportunities. In this chapter, we will discuss several of the most salient.

The reality of police hostage negotiations clashes with conventional wisdom about good negotiation strategy, which emphasizes the need to be prepared. Such preparation normally includes learning as much as one can, not only about one's own position, interests and needs, but as much as one can about the other side, before any meeting takes place. But when a call comes in that triggers a hostage negotiation, this kind of preparation is impossible. On the surface, this inability to prepare for a specific negotiation is unique to hostage situations. But closer examination calls this into question. [Taylor & Donohue, *Hostage Negotiation*] In many ways, hostage negotiation work mirrors the work of a variety of other professions which experience "dealing with the unknown" during the course of their workday. Obvious examples include emergency room doctors, train conductors, and television reporters (each role, of course, has existing training in dealing with forms of "the unknown" *other* than the ones discussed here), but many others find themselves in situations where at least some aspects are unknown enough to fit our premise. The core of our argument here is that it is possible to approach even the unknown as an informed negotiator, albeit in a different sense from the normal usage of that term.

Background: The Emergence of Hostage Negotiations

The deliberate use of police hostage negotiators began in 1973 with the formation of a hostage negotiation team by the New York City Police Department. Created in response to concerns which grew out of the Munich Olympics of 1972, the Attica Prison Riots, the "Dog Day" Brooklyn Bank Robbery and the Williamsburg Sporting Goods Store Robbery, the NYPD Hostage Negotiation Team (HNT), which now has 100 officers, is trained to respond to a variety of situations. As the nation's oldest and largest hostage negotiation team in one of the most diverse and vibrant urban areas in the world, the practice of negotiating with hostage takers has evolved significantly. Central to the NYPD Hostage Negotiation Team's ethos is its motto, "Talk to Me," which is actually more than a motto—it is a working heuristic, guiding the work of the officers. That catchphrase serves as a constant reminder of the need for officers to be good listeners, patient communicators, and articulate team members. Since hostage situations may go on for many hours, both listening to what the hostage takers are really saying and keeping them engaged in dialogue are extremely important.

But it is also important to recognize that when NYPD hostage team officers respond to hostage situations, they are part of a large, complex operation. They are always backed up by the Emergency Service Unit (ESU) officers, commonly known as the tactical team and equipped with shields, shotguns and other weaponry, as well as the Technical Assistance Response Unit (TARU) officers, who provide investigative technical equipment and tactical support. Each of these units has specialized training, and together they function to achieve two common goals: getting the hostages out safely, and getting the hostage taker to "come out"—if possible, safely and voluntarily. Every hostage taker comes out in the end, one way or another, and all of the discussion which follows regarding the need to recognize the hostage takers' humanity is in the context of that fact.

The Elusive Qualifications

Preparation of officers for the hostage negotiation team begins long before an officer is selected. In New York City, hostage negotiators must be sworn police officers who have achieved the rank of Detective with at least 12 years' experience in the Department. Virtually all hostage negotiators are nearly 35 years old when first chosen for the team. This rigorous experience requirement answers the need for officers who will be knowledgeable about police procedures, have achieved stature within the Department as detectives, and are also, simply, old enough to have personally encountered some of life's knocks—love, hurt, disappointment, success, rejection, and most important, failure. Thus when a hostage taker complains about one or another vicissitude of his life, the negotiator can say with credibility "You know what, I know about that too, and we can talk about it." Training in the martial arts is also viewed as an asset, because of its stress on compassion, benevolence, courtesy, sincerity and loyalty—qualities that may seem counterintuitive to those who have no familiarity with martial arts. The real-world criteria for consideration for this team may also be a hint as to the requirements for a successful negotiator in other "no direct preparation possible" environments.

Furthermore, to make meaningful selections from among the 40,000 officers of the NYPD, the hostage negotiation team has developed informal networks of trusted people, often current or former members of the team themselves, who are asked to keep their eyes open for new talent. The team regards with some amusement other organizations' tendency to rely heavily on brief interviews with potential new colleagues, joking that each such candidate tends to show up wearing a "chameleon suit." The better recommendation comes when a known-reliable coworker says "This is just the way this person is. S/he talks to everybody that way; s/he is not putting on an act."

The officers' life experiences and substantive knowledge of police work are supplemented with an intensive two-week training program. Since the hostage team members all have other day-to-day assignments outside the team, and are distributed across many precincts of the sprawling city (in order to ensure that there are always trained negotiators available 24/7 within a reasonable distance of wherever an emergency may take place), they do not necessarily know each other. New HNT officers come together for the first time during the special hostage negotiation training. This training program provides the officers with highly specialized substantive knowledge and process skills, some of which would be familiar to readers of this book from many other fields. The first week consists of selected negotiation theory and practice; the second week consists of Emergency Psychological Training (EPT),[2] [Jeglic & Jeglic, *Disordered People*] where officers are introduced to psychological, mental illness, and drug-related conditions that they will experience during the course of the "jobs." (In HNT usage, a "job" is an individual hostage negotiation case). Proper selection and training of negotiators are vital to future success of the team.

Establishing Respect and Trust

When you cannot prepare for a specific negotiation, the next best thing is to figure out what substitutes may be available. To establish communication with an unknown entity, what needs to be done? The HNT officers need to communicate that they are not going to operate solely from a position of authority and power, with a gun and a badge. Simultaneously they need immediately to demonstrate respect for the person they are talking to, as the beginning of establishing trust. [Lewicki,

Trust] It is important to emphasize that some of the people they are encountering may never have been treated with respect before, by almost anyone they have known. (Hostage takers, naturally, are not a random sample of the population; some have been in trouble at some other point in their lives). There is a duality to this process, however, which must be acknowledged. On one level, the hostage negotiator must "respect people whom no one else may care to respect." On another level, both the respect and the development of trust are limited in scope and serve the overall goal of getting everyone out alive, which must be kept in sight at all times. Treating the other party with respect, however, becomes a very powerful tool toward that goal.

Respect is demonstrated in several ways: greetings, taking the time to make small talk (i.e. schmoozing), articulating ground rules, and clarifying assumptions. Collectively, these techniques "warm up" hostage takers, make them feel more comfortable with continued discussion, and build trust. The specific functions of these techniques are discussed below.

Greetings

At the outset, the officer who is the designated negotiator (i.e. the speaking role in a team that almost always has more than one qualified negotiator) has to figure out how to address the hostage taker. For example, the officer may ask "Mr. Carson, can I call you Mr. Carson?" If the hostage taker responds "no, I want you to call me Superman" (and this has actually occurred), an acknowledgment that the individual has a right to name himself can defuse the tension created by a grandiose claim. Later on, the hostage taker may say "don't call me Superman, my name is Jack"—to which the trained hostage negotiator responds "can I call you Jack?"

Politeness, here, is more than "just politeness." It gives the hostage taker a dignity that he may never have experienced before, or not in a long time—particularly from the police. The politeness takes them back a little bit and the emotional level comes down when that exchange is just the whole dialogue. It is not about getting to the gun or getting the person out, but it is really almost like getting to first base. If the HNT cannot get to first base, it can never get home.

Schmoozing

A subtle and subjective indicator of suitability for the hostage team is an ability to schmooze. In the particular sense in which this term is used within the hostage negotiation team, this is neither a waste of time, nor a phony gambit just to get close to someone or to buy time for setting up some other kind of action. It is, instead, a recognition that the other person, regardless of what they have done, is a human being, and needs some human interaction. (Of course, it also *does* serve to buy time.)

Ground Rules

The hostage negotiator begins the negotiation itself by establishing boundaries for the ensuing exchanges. Hostage negotiators are trained to explain what they are going to do, and explain again when they are doing it. It is a slow process, but a key part of preparing the other party to deal with the officers constructively. If this is skipped, in the interest of "saving time," the hostage taker is likely to get a wrong impression about what the officers intend—starting a slippery slope toward a true disaster.

Clarifying Assumptions

It is easy for hostage negotiators to think that everybody else understands what they are doing. But experience shows that assumptions are dangerous, and can backfire on the hostage negotiators in almost unimaginable ways, leaving the hostage negotiator standing with his/her jaw dropping asking "but didn't you understand what I was trying to do?" The challenge in negotiating with the unknown is to avoid assuming that what you are doing is understood, taking the time to explain your actions even in the midst of a tremendous amount of activity and potential danger. As a result, hostage negotiators always talk about the "drill." This means that the hostage negotiators explain to all of the people involved what the hostage team's role is and what will be done. Part of the drill is to get the on-site negotiation team together in a football-like huddle, so that when others inevitably try to rush them in the negotiation process, the negotiators are ready to respond—by saying, for instance, "here's what we're going to do: we're not going to talk about the gun, we're not going to talk about the fact that that the kids got slapped around. Here's what we're going to do: we're going to—." The hostage taker is thus given a theme. The theme is like a working paper; it is not etched in stone, and it certainly can change. But it has a continuing function; it helps the hostage taker understand that no sudden action, such as a surprise attack, is contemplated, and that also demonstrates to others that the negotiation team has a plan and has the situation under control.

Assumptions are routine and heuristics are not entirely avoidable by anyone who must act in the real world. [Korobkin & Guthrie, *Heuristics*] One purpose of the 12 year minimum of prior experience is to try to ensure that an officer has encountered enough situations in other settings where his or her assumptions turned out to be wrong that the lesson will not have to be learned under life-threatening circumstances.

McGowan has an example from his early career. He was riding with an older officer when they received a stolen-car call, and were dispatched to make out the complaint report. The more experienced officer went up to the person who had called about the car, and was waiting on his porch. The senior officer began by introducing himself, taking his hat off, and starting a general conversation about what kind of car it was. When the man told both officers "It was a '57 Chevy with nice trim on it" the senior officer did not immediately pull out a report pad, but instead recognized that that model was particularly valued by many people, and asked "did it have—(some option or other)?" The owner replied yes, it did have that feature, "it even has an AM/FM radio" (not common on that model.) The two strolled off the porch, out to the front of the house, where there was an empty spot—where the car was supposed to be. They stood in that spot, and simply chatted for a while about the car. After a bit, the senior officer asked the owner "Now, do you have your registration with you?" The man had it—in a piece of plastic, so it didn't get dirty. The officer said "Why don't you give it to this young fellow here and he can start the paperwork?" The man took it out, and gave it to McGowan—who was treated, to his befuddlement, as if he were an assistant. The senior officer and the car owner continued to talk while McGowan recorded all the information.

When McGowan and the senior officer got back in the police car and headed toward the station house, the senior officer realized that McGowan did not understand what he had been doing. The senior officer noted that this car owner had devoted a lot of his time and effort to his car, which was probably one of the most valuable possessions he had. It was obvious that he really took pride in it. The senior officer pointed out that if a police officer had come along and said "Just give me your registration," the rudeness of that interaction would have stayed in the owner's mind as an example of disrespect by the police. What the owner needed from them, the senior officer felt, was a little bit of compassion. The car was still stolen, and given the statistics, the officers probably would not be able to get it back; but at least after the officers left, the taste in the owner's mouth would be a good one as to the attitude of the police toward his loss. McGowan reflects now that working with this partner taught him that a lot of decent police work had to do with the way people are treated—and the story is now used as a reminder to new negotiators about how one makes an entry into a situation. In the negotiation process, the showing of respect comes first; only then can you get to the heart of the matter.

Stories as Context

The use of such stories to teach "negotiating with the unknown" is deliberate. These are not merely stories about how the officers "won out over the other guy;" they are presented to demonstrate how the officers are able to break down resistance by dealing with the emotions in a way that works. The emotions being experienced by the hostage taker may even be the same emotions experienced by the hostage negotiator—a little fear, a little anxiety, a little concern over saying and doing the right thing can be expected on both sides.

One of the key functions of the stories is to help officers get past their official status, because their working experience up to that point has been that official status often functions to ensure compliance. By authorizing officers to give a little bit of themselves, a little bit of their authority to the hostage taker, such as giving the hostage taker the authority to say "No, I want you to call me by my full first name and full last name" or "You got to call me Superman," officers are giving the hostage taker not only respect, but in a small way, power, which may never have been given to them before. This, the team has found, always seems to work to the hostage negotiator's advantage in the end. Since it is counterintuitive to do this, and since officers cannot be taught how to handle every specific situation, the storytelling, which draws on real experiences, validates the use of techniques which often depart radically from standard police training.

The Team's Structure on Site

The use of a team is central to hostage negotiation work. It is designed to help the negotiators concentrate on the process. The "speaking" hostage negotiator is not out there alone; there is a structure. This consists of a primary negotiator; at least one backup coach; a "scribe;" and a coordinator. The role of the coordinator (usually the senior hostage negotiator present) is to bring corporate memory to the situation, provide insights to external police commanders and to the tactical team, and to run interference on behalf of the other negotiators. In this last, critically important function, the coordinator buffers the negotiators from the Chiefs—the term is used here as shorthand for all levels of supervision, described in more detail below—so that the other officers can do their job. Hostage negotiation is far from the only circumstance in which the person responsible for a negotiation must somehow report to difficult supervisors, who may try to micromanage a job and too often do not appreciate the intricacies, the need for patience and the time inevitably involved in making talk work. But in a police department, the hierarchy is overt and often insistent. There could easily be a district commander in the offing, saying "I don't have any time for this, this guy is blocking traffic," or resenting the fact that the case happened on their watch, because there is a meeting to go to, or theater tickets to be considered. Hostage takers, however, cannot be told to come back tomorrow. The role of the coordinator is therefore to handle all of the *external* negotiations that threaten to disrupt the all-important negotiation "at the door." When McGowan was promoted to chief negotiator, he was informed that that did not mean that he got to negotiate any time he wanted. It meant he got to negotiate with the Chief—a significantly less desirable and more challenging honor.

But the other roles played by hostage negotiators such as scribe, coach, etc., are also near-essential in a complex and often fast-moving environment (though it must be admitted that sometimes, despite the desirability of clear role differentiation, shortages of trained personnel on-site mean that someone has to "wear more than one hat"). The team structure is more than just an administrative arrangement; its purpose is to ensure that the negotiator who is doing the talking is not overwhelmed by all of the other tasks that have to be done. This helps both their ability to focus and their ability to keep from rushing into any given phase of the negotiation, unless there is an immediate "Man is holding child out the window" exigency.

Training of Other Officers

It is important to emphasize that "ordinary" police training does not yet contain much of the material developed for hostage negotiators, despite the probability that it would be valuable for every police officer to learn much of it as early as possible in a career. Patrol officers are the first responders to all types of calls made to the police; basic communication and perception skills are central to hostage negotiation work, but perception and communication are also at the heart of any police officer's role. But getting sufficient training time built in continues to be a significant challenge, in police departments as for other organizations where comparable skills are arguably required in order to do the actual job properly. Competing demands for "floor time" in training are a fact of life in large organizations of all kinds.

Still, particularly in terms of police departments' need for constant communication with and the general trust of the public, it is clearly important to reduce the number of rookie mistakes. An example, a telling one precisely because it is far too minor ever to be the subject of corrective discipline, is the thrown-away opportunity when a police officer (usually, one who has little experience, for reasons discussed below) is asked, by a citizen whose stroll has been interrupted by a police barrier, "What's going on?" Often, such an officer will not realize that the citizen is not merely curious, but is concerned about whether there is a problem in his/her neighborhood, whether his/her family is all right, and so on—but has not formulated the question in such a way that this is obvious. An officer who responds with just "Move along!" is throwing away some degree of future potential cooperation of that citizen. An officer who responds with a human level of detail, though, such as "We have a man who is acting a little strange down the block, and has a gun, and we just want to make sure that everything is OK"—which is certainly less detail than the same officer would supply if it was the Mayor's motorcade that was interrupted—is improving the likelihood of some other officer, someday, getting critically important information from that citizen or someone in his/her family.

We believe the operational value of training people in basic human understanding, not just in police departments but in many jobs in society, is underrecognized. But to stick with police departments for now, officers are currently given relatively thorough training in key elements of law. Not yet fully integrated into basic training in police departments, however, are ways to get across the explicit message: "Your career will have more to do with communication than it will have to do with the law. Your career will have more to do with talking to people than with shooting people. Your career is going to have more to do with how you present yourself, so that you are seen by everybody you deal with as recognizing that you represent the entire Department, and that you know they will be dealing with the Department again." We believe the consequences are both serious, and potentially something of which a police department can become convinced: it is part of the folklore of police work that officers who have relatively little time on the job are more vulnerable to civilian complaints. What that means, in a nutshell, is that a key function of training has been deferred, from an organized short training period in a "no harm, no foul" Police Academy environment into what might be years of errant practice, till wisdom catches up with the rookie. How many other kinds of organizations fall prey to this temptation to false economy on basic training is unknown; but we believe the number could be large.

The Limitations of Training

Yet in some ways, we must accept that training is unlikely to carry the emotional-learning effectiveness of actual work experience. Cambria relates a formative moment in his own career, which would be difficult to replicate in formal training. As a young police officer, one day he was coming back from court on the subway. As he got off the train in Brooklyn, the station clerk called over: "Officer, there's a guy who just went under the turnstile, a homeless guy, just went down toward that end of the platform." Cambria did not know what to do with such a minor problem, i.e. whether to issue a summons or not. On balance, he decided the best way to handle it without undue expenditure of time would be simply to tell the homeless man to get out on the street, because obviously people cannot use the subway without paying. Cambria walked all the way down to the end of a long platform, where he saw the homeless man, disheveled, about 50 years old—although he looked older—and with a satchel under his arm. Cambria told him "You didn't pay the fare. You have to leave the subway." Having issued a firm statement, Cambria anticipated some degree of argument, but the man merely said "Okay Officer, I understand." Cambria and the homeless man began walking together back down to the exit, at the other end of the platform. As they were walking, Cambria asked "What do you have in the bag?"

The homeless man replied "Oh, in my bag, Officer, is a screenplay, it's a play I wrote." Cambria was taken aback. Curious, he asked what the play was about. The homeless man replied that the play was titled *Crabs in a Basket*. "If you've ever seen a basketful of crabs, they're all trying to get out. When one finally gets almost to the top of that basket to get out, another crab grabs it and brings it back down, grabs it back down. It's kind of like my life ... it's autobiographical, it's about my life ... every time I get to the top of that basket, some force comes along and grabs me back down."

Cambria describes himself as "blown away." As they approached the exit, he looked again at the homeless man and said "This ride's on me. Have a good day." Cambria told the man he hoped to see the play performed some day. At the cost of irritating the station clerk, Cambria felt he owed the homeless man something, for teaching him an important lesson: he had approached the homeless man with a preconceived notion, and had learned that just because the man was homeless didn't mean he was ignorant, or dangerous. This homeless man was down on his luck, yet he was a human being, with a sense of himself and of his circumstances, and an ability to explain them with eloquence—if given the opportunity. The sense of every individual as a person of worth, deserving of individual and not rule-bound responses, is not easy for a new police officer—or lawyer, or doctor, or other new professional with sudden "status"—to learn. What price do we pay, in our unexpected negotiations, for our failure to incorporate such learning into the training of every such new professional?

The Broader Implications: Other Occupations

We believe there are a variety of other occupations where the skills of a hostage negotiator could be useful to "best practice"—or arguably, essential to avoid mal-practice. Emergency room staff [Morash, *Nonevents*], hospital administrators, utility workers, transit workers, airport employees [Dingwall & Menkel-Meadow, *Last Plane Out*], urban teachers, even the military [Lira, *Military*]: the list goes on and on. Hostage negotiators have frequently encountered social situations in which someone in one of these jobs will ask what they do for a living. When they answer "hostage negotiation," the inquirer replies "Oh, I couldn't do what you do." But in fact, people in these kinds of jobs are involved in unexpected negotia-tions on a daily basis. These jobs are simply unrecognized as involving significant levels of "negotiations with the unknown" except by the most perceptive of their current incumbents. But at least one of the critical elements of hostage negotia-tion training—the officers' need to treat a person who has probably committed a grave offense as a human being—should be, if anything, easier to apply in settings where a violation of criminal law is probably not the presenting issue. Teaching those who must deal with stressed members of the public that treating the person as a human being is the first need, if not the foremost in the end, should not be impossible. Teaching such professionals to be prepared, at a moment's notice, to explain honestly and respectfully what they are doing should not be all that diffi-cult in a country that has been able to build the world's leading higher education system.

Seen this way, the training of police hostage negotiators is no longer so special-ized or so mysterious that others cannot expect to make use of it. Instead, it is surprisingly close to the core of the new conception of a larger context of negotia-tion and conflict management, i.e. the broader notion of negotiation partly as a force for social good and partly as the essential lubricant in the increasingly com-plex machinery of a postmodern society (discussed in the Introduction to this volume). This societal change demands matching changes in ways of relating to other people, as part of basic training in a whole range of professions. The training of hostage negotiators, and their success in practice, shows that it can be done.

Endnotes

[1] For a primer on the life and times of the NYPD's Hostage Negotiation Team, *see* Jack Cambria, et al., *Negotiation Under Extreme Pressure: The "Mouth Marines" and the Hostage Takers*, 18 NEGOTIATION JOURNAL 331 (2002).

[2] The EPT component grew out of the 1984 Eleanor Bumpers case, in which an elderly African-American grandmother was killed by police, when she lunged at them with a knife while they were attempting to follow through on an order to evict her from her Bronx apartment. Although the officer who fired the shotgun was acquitted of criminal wrongdoing, the case led to significant soul-searching as to the level of police understand-ing of mental illness, and the resulting EPT training was made available to ESU officers, and subsequently, to HNT officers.

❦ 75 ❧

Hostage Negotiation Opens Up

Paul J. Taylor & William Donohue

Editors' Note: *The high-stakes world of the hostage negotiator draws instinctive respect from other negotiators. But if you operate in another domain, you could be excused for thinking that hostage negotiation has nothing to do with you. That impression, it turns out, is quite often wrong. Here, two researchers draw parallels to several kinds of business and other disputes in which it often seems that one of the parties acts similarly to a hostage taker. Understanding what hostage negotiators have learned to do in response can be a real asset to a negotiator faced with one of these situations. Read this with Reputations and with Negotiating with the Unknown, and you may find yourself formulating a new idea you can use tomorrow.*

In a typical hostage negotiation situation, a hostage taker threatens to harm himself or another person as a means toward an end. The hostage taker may have been caught robbing a convenience store and taken the hostage as leverage to improve his (nearly all hostage takers are male) situation. Or, he may have some religious, political, or psychological motivation that he hopes to draw attention to by threatening to commit suicide.[1] In hostage scenarios such as these, the police work to end the incident without any loss of life. This is typically achieved by a trained response team that works quickly to contain the scene and create an environment in which the incident commander can employ a number of different strategies. Because of its success as a non-lethal approach, the most common strategy is negotiation.

What makes hostage negotiation unique as a communicative event is the high stakes and heightened ambiguity that underlies the interaction. The hostage taker is negotiating for his life, and the police are negotiating for the lives of the hostages. Such a negotiation is not embedded in the traditional dynamics of normative thinking and good faith, but on the extreme dynamics of emotional arousal and anxiety. The negotiators must listen carefully, resist the temptation to react defensively, and work to build trust and cooperation. The stakes are high, the stress is extreme, and the demands on the negotiators are fierce. When the communication context is stretched in this manner, it opens an important window into the complex dynamics of mixed-motive negotiation.

By the end of this chapter, we hope to give the reader not only an understanding of the dynamics that are important to hostage negotiation, but also some "food for thought" about how best to approach more normative bargaining challenges. While often perceived as unique interactions, hostage negotiations are shaped by a set of dynamics and rules that can inform other negotiation contexts. For example, sales agents are often faced with very hostile buyers who negotiate by giving ultimatums. This form of aggressive, highly distributive bargaining is common in early stages of hostage negotiation, and sales agents can learn many lessons about how to defray these kinds of aggressive strategies. Indeed, many critical features of negotiated interaction have been easier to identify in the hostage context than in its normative counterparts, due to the saliency of interpersonal actions within a high-pressured, crisis context.[2]

The way police negotiators interact with hostage takers may therefore have important lessons for negotiators outside of the hostage context. In this chapter, we explore four aspects of hostage negotiation that are critical to reaching a successful resolution. As it turns out, these facets are equally important lessons for negotiators who want success in a wide range of contexts.

Contain, Contain, Contain!

Experience has taught police teams that it is necessary to contain a hostage taking before engaging in dialogue. Almost without exception, a police team will delay interaction until they are satisfied that they have eliminated routes into and away from the scene, and minimized the ability of the hostage takers to contact third parties. The dangers of not containing a scene are made transparent by incidents in which well-intentioned members of the public are harmed.[3] Equally problematic, and unfortunately more common, are incidents in which information from a third party (e.g., TV coverage) undermines the police negotiator's position.

The availability of information from third parties can dramatically shift the balance of power and undermine a well-crafted persuasive position in many bargaining contexts. Yet, negotiators and scholars outside of the hostage context continue to focus on events at the negotiation table, with only cursory recognition of the "negotiations" that occur away from the table. [Docherty, *Many Tools*] Away from the table, negotiators will often work to manipulate the perceived value of issues, try to gain influence and power, and work to develop and protect their personal identity.[4]

Containment also serves purposes more subtle than minimizing the interference of outside players. For example, the elimination of other opportunities and exit routes is known to have a positive effect on individuals' cooperation within an interaction. Negotiators without alternatives typically show more interdependence, they are more likely to reciprocate concessions, and they achieve higher joint outcomes than negotiators who have alternative options.[5] Police negotiators often refer to this as creating a "we-are-in-it-together" environment, whose rationale centers on the fact that it is more difficult for an individual to withdraw from the negotiating process when they perceive themselves as having a stake in its success.

Beyond helping to influence hostage taker's behavior, containment also plays an important role in police negotiator efforts to present information persuasively. Containment not only allows negotiators to limit a hostage taker's knowledge of what might be available, but it also allows them to distort the value of the alternatives. For example, police negotiators will often remonstrate at length about the difficulty of providing something to the hostage taker. This approach draws on people's typical reaction to scarcity,[6] [Guthrie, *Compliance*] which is to view a resulting offer or concession as considerably more attractive than would otherwise be the case. Similarly, police negotiators will always try to break down any substantive considerations into their constituent parts. Rather than talk about a pizza, they will talk about where the pizza should be bought, what toppings it should have (and whether the police negotiator and hostage taker have common preferences in toppings), what the base should be (and the problems with cold "stuffed crust"), what drink should be included, whether or not there should be any side orders, and so on. A dialogue along these lines might occur as:

"You know Chris, we're trying to help you out. We got you the pizza. We got you the base you wanted, you know that thin crust because I know you hate deep crust. We got you the toppings. what was it? Ham, mushroom and extra pineapple? I'm not sure I could stomach the extra pineapple personally but that's your choice and we got you that. And, we got the pizza from Store A. My boss reckoned we should just go to Store B because it's closer. But I said that's not what Chris wants, he wants a pizza from Store A. So I pulled you in a bit of a favor there by getting the pizza from Store A."

The result is an interaction in which negotiators are able to share a joke over topping preferences, demonstrate concern that the hostage taker also have a drink, concede on providing the desired side order and pizza toppings (which is a concession that deserves reciprocation), and provide the hostage negotiator with needed food. By controlling the presentation, the police negotiator verbally contains the hostage taker by keeping them occupied over the details of the pizza order. They also make clear that they are conciliating on far more than a pizza.

In summary, police negotiators rely on containment to limit the influence of unpredictable outside factors and to allow for some control of how information is fed to the other party. The impact of not containing these factors is very apparent in the high-stakes, uncertain environment of hostage taking, where a mismatch between what negotiators say and what others do or say can critically reshape the conflict, as the end of the Branch Davidian siege at Waco unfortunately testifies.[7] The lesson here, then, is to remember that negotiations are often shaped away from the table, and that individuals' perceptions and beliefs while at the table may be crafted to be very different from the reality away from the table, but only if the negotiation is successfully contained.

Expanding the Emotional Pie

Most negotiation research recognizes the importance of "expanding the pie" and searching for optimal solutions. However, negotiators and negotiation theory have traditionally viewed this integrative strategy as relating to substantive issues. For police negotiators, however, issue exploration comes second to emotional exploration. Recent estimates suggest that nearly 80% of all hostage situations are emotion or relationship driven.[8] For this reason, police negotiators have learned to work quickly to understand and negotiate around expressive aspects of the situation. They seek to reduce the tensions and perceived threats of the context, and they focus early efforts on developing trust and identifying face saving strategies.[9]

What is unique about this perspective is not the recognition that emotive factors play a role in negotiation, since this is now recognized across many disciplines.[10] The unique aspect of this perspective is the way in which emotive concerns are viewed. In many traditional negotiation contexts, relational and identity dynamics continue to be viewed as mediating factors that help or hinder efforts to work towards a substantive agreement. The traditional view is to conceptualize emotion as something that needs to be dealt with before considering instrumental issues,[11] or as something that informs understanding of instrumental positions.[12] In contrast, for the police negotiator, it is as important, if not more important, to search the emotional pie and address emotions as negotiation issues in their own right.

To illustrate this shift in perspective, consider a hypothetical organizational take-over and efforts by the potential buyer to identify what is likely to persuade the organization's board. In all likelihood, a traditional buyer would seek to determine the board's perception of the organization's value by gleaning information about costs and overheads, the value of subsidiary assets, whether money can be saved in staffing, and so on. A police negotiator, however, would seek to determine whether members of the board are concerned for the well-being of their employees, are worried about their personal reputation after the take-over, have a desire to retain influence on the board, and so on. By answering these kinds of emotive questions, a negotiator begins to uncover what might persuade the board members to accept less attractive offers than would rationally be the case when dealing with instrumental factors.

So how do police negotiators expand the emotional pie? There are at least two dimensions to the answer. The first is that police negotiators work proactively to manage a hostage taker's anxieties.[13] Rather than rush to deal with instrumental aspects of the negotiation, police negotiators use techniques such as mirroring, self-disclosure, and paraphrasing to show their interest in the hostage taker's emotive concerns.[14] By coupling this with supportive feedback and non-assumptive questions (e.g., "I've not been in your position, but I guess you must be feeling very lonely"), the negotiator's efforts to show interest encourage the hostage taker to express their concerns while simultaneously venting their emotions. Police negotiators do not try to counter emotionality with rational debate, which is generally ineffective in high-pressure scenarios.[15] Instead, they accept that emotion itself is an important issue of the negotiation, which must be continuously monitored, explored, and addressed. [Shapiro, *Emotions*]

The second is that police negotiators work to identify the hostage taker's main underlying problem or driver. At any one time, a hostage taker will communicate about one particular concern or issue, ranging from concerns about personal identity, to concerns about relational issues such as trust and power, through to concerns about substantive issues.[16] Police negotiators listen carefully to the hostage taker's dialogue, and seek to identify this prevailing issue. They then address it by matching the framing of their own message to the hostage taker's framing. For example, it is not useful to make substantive offers when the hostage taker's real concern is for his personal identity and the shame the incident will bring to his family. By focusing on an inappropriate frame, a negotiator is in danger of making the hostage taker feel misunderstood or unvalued, which may lead to further conflict and heightened emotions. By interpreting the focus of dialogue, negotiators may also act proactively to identify under-explored issues that will expand the emotional pie. For example, by keeping track of changes in dialogue it is possible to gauge how much time has been spent discussing various identity, relational, and substantive issues. If negotiations come to a standstill, negotiators are able to review the motivational focus of previous dialogue and move to an issue that has yet to be covered.

Much of police negotiators' efforts to resolve hostage crises rely on their ability to explore and understand the emotional drivers of the hostage taker. Far from being hindrances or mediating issues in the interaction, emotions are defining points of bargaining that often determine how the interaction unfolds. The lesson for traditional contexts here, then, is that one can never overestimate how beneficial it will be to spend some time exploring aspects of the emotional pie.

Primacy of Relationship

Hostage negotiation revolves around the interplay between demands and issues that both sides must manage. Hostage takers are usually able to articulate their demands. They may want specific, concrete items like money or freedom, or they may make more nebulous demands for revenge. However, they often have difficulty articulating the underlying issues that brought them to this precipice. This negotiation problem, of course, is not unique to hostage takers. [Guthrie & Sally, *Miswanting*] Similarly, police negotiators' demands clearly center on freeing the hostages and ending the incident peacefully. But the process of executing this goal is often driven by various issues that can be difficult to sort through, such as staff fatigue, overtime costs for maintaining the scene, and police jurisdictional and publicity issues.

These demands and issues interact, and the ability of both sides to craft a resolution rests on their ability to transform their relationship into one that can manage the two features. The key transformation involves moving from a highly distributive, competitive relationship to a more collaborative orientation. The route to this transformation begins by providing some time for people to emotionally disengage, after which it becomes possible to slowly exchange relatively low-risk information (e.g., small talk). This helps to build trust, which provides a basis for negotiators to develop a working relationship that can focus on problem-solving. Such problem-solving centers on simple issues such as food and electricity in the beginning, but ultimately the negotiators need to move toward a more engaged collaborative relationship that focuses on underlying issues. When collaborating, the fundamental, underlying basis of the conflict becomes exposed, and personal needs (tied to self concept) emerge, allowing mutually fulfilling outcomes to emerge in turn.

An example might serve to illustrate these points. In an airline hijacking in the early 1970s, a passenger hijacked an airplane bound for Atlanta by packing dynamite under his coat. When negotiations began, he shared demands for many items that included money and fuel to get to Cuba. As the interactions unfolded, the police negotiator learned that the hostage taker hijacked the plane to demonstrate his manhood to his partner, with whom he had fought the night before. This personal issue became a turning point from cooperation (sharing demands and information) to collaboration, in which underlying issues were explored. The resolution called for the hijacker to release the passengers in exchange for a phone to call his partner. The passengers were released, and the phone call was made. (Unfortunately, in this instance, the hijacker committed suicide while on the phone.)

As negotiators manage their issues and demands, both their competitive and collaborative orientations present paradoxical relational challenges. A collaborative relationship is paradoxical because parties like and trust one another, but resist the kind of engagement that would expose them extensively. They are pushing the other away while also pulling them closer. Similarly, a competitive relationship is also paradoxical, since parties do not like and trust one another, but they are highly engaged. They are pulling the other closer in order to defeat or in other ways harm them.

In the opening movements of a hostage negotiation, very competitive relationships tend to dominate. The police negotiator tries to slowly, but deliberately shift away from this approach into more of a time out period characterized by exchanging preliminary information, and moving hostage takers away from demands and threats. Parties explore roles and engage in a great deal of small talk. The goal of the police negotiator is to build sufficient trust to move toward a more cooperative relationship, but without compromising personal credibility. These preliminary discussions often center on such substantive issues as food, heat, light, and logistics as a means of moving the hostage taker into a more cooperative orientation. Once a collaborative orientation starts to emerge, then more substantive issues and demands can be explored. Collaboration is marked by cautious but positive problem-solving for both parties.[17]

The key to moving through these relational frames is to avoid compromising trust and moving in the wrong direction, away from cooperation and back to coexistence. If trust can be established through relatively minor exchanges of food for hostages, then more important demands can follow—but not too rapidly. Thus, police negotiators are keenly aware of how to manage the relational perspectives of hostage takers to build the foundation that allows certain issues and demands to emerge. Without this foundation, executing the substantive goals becomes quite difficult.

The implications of managing relationships effectively are profound. For example, consider the sales agents referred to above. Often they are confronted with hostile buyers who, in a sense, treat these agents like police negotiators, while themselves taking on characteristics of hostage takers. Even if the buyers "must" buy from the sales agent, they often begin by making outrageous demands using the "take-it-or-leave-it" tactic. Thus, the first goal of the agent is to shift the relational frame from competition to coexistence, then to cooperation, and if possible, to collaboration. But the critical shift is the first one, to coexistence or a relational state in which people disengage from the task and simply try to get to know one another. That shift requires at least superficial information sharing, to build trust and affiliation. For example, the agent might ask the buyer to elaborate on his or her demands to uncover a rationale. Then, once the conversation gets rolling, personal topics and affiliative language can be used to move toward more cooperation and greater information exchange.

Going Beyond Yes and Closing the Deal

Generally, once the parties enter at least a moderately collaborative mode, with key issues being exposed and substantive problem-solving holding its course, the parties craft the outline of a deal. At some point, as in the hijacking incident, a deal is struck and both parties say yes. However, one of the most difficult times within hostage taking comes at the end, once an agreement has been reached. At the point of surrender, the hostage taker has lost his leverage, and is very sensitive to any suggestion that he has been tricked, duped, or generally led into a deal that appears different from what he envisaged. To deal with this problem, police negotiators stress the need to move slowly through the surrender sequence, in a very deliberate fashion. Each detail must be carefully orchestrated so that everyone's safety can be maximized.

The lesson for other contexts here is a simple but important one. Aftercare is a big business in negotiation. The goal is not simply to "get to yes," but to close the deal after "yes" has been heard. This closing requires meticulous attention to detail about how the process will unfold, and specific markers of success. [Wade & Honeyman, *Lasting Agreement*]

For example, once the buyer has said yes to the agent about the money part of the deal, then all the process issues kick in. How will the deal be consummated?

Steps 1 through N must be laid out and clearly documented, leading toward the final delivery of the product. The post-yes steps might even include follow-up to ensure customer satisfaction. The key point is that clear steps make the deal work, just as they do in hostage negotiation.

Lessons from Hostage Negotiations

Several lessons about the normative negotiation context can be derived from the crisis context. First, and perhaps most important, the crisis approach to negotiation is very proactive and deliberative. One police negotiator termed it "dynamic inactivity." He meant that hostage negotiation is all about working aggressively behind the scenes to develop strategies and tactics aimed at solving the problem while slowing down a process that might naturally turn frenetic. The goal is to move by "known successful" steps to achieve a successful resolution. For example, police need to contain before negotiating to ensure bargaining in good faith. That rule cannot be compromised except in extreme circumstances. After containment, it is considered critical to explore feelings and emotions while developing the relationship between the hostage taker and negotiator. Negotiators in more normative contexts, such as business, often underestimate the importance and value of being deliberate and thorough and not shortcutting the process.

The second lesson focuses on the need to understand the foundational issues in conflict. Police negotiators cannot deal with superficial treatment of issues because they may not be able to save lives until the hostage taker's deeper issues are at least acknowledged, and probably addressed overtly. The crisis orientation is always focused on uncovering the hostage taker's key drivers. But business negotiators face a similar challenge. In this context, negotiators can get lost in such superficial issues as price and delivery dates, and ignore the larger issues that are really driving the deal. Again, the need to be expedient and take shortcuts often compromises the outcome.

A final lesson that emerges from this analysis is the need to look at a negotiation comprehensively. Crisis negotiation is not a process that is reducible to focusing only on gain or loss frames, or negotiator style, or power differentials. A crisis negotiator has to understand the entire context including constituent relations, events happening external to the scene, and certainly the process of interaction. Of course, the effective business negotiator must take this same broad view. They must also feel their way through a complex web of issues and relationships. Thus we can gain many important insights by exploring the interplay between the normative and crisis negotiation contexts.

Endnotes

[1] Despite the absence of a true hostage, current practice treats these cases similarly, as both the underlying causes and the teams and techniques found useful are similar to those that are effective in a classical hostage scenario.

[2] William Donohue, et al., *Crisis Bargaining in Intense Conflict Situations*, 21 INTERNATIONAL JOURNAL OF GROUP TENSIONS 133 (1991).

[3] MICHAEL MCMAINS & WAYMAN MULLINS, CRISIS NEGOTIATIONS: MANAGING CRITICAL INCIDENTS AND HOSTAGE SITUATIONS IN LAW ENFORCEMENT AND CORRECTIONS (2d ed. 2001).

[4] William Donohue & Gregory Hoobler, *Relational Frames and Their Ethical Implications in International Negotiation, An Analysis Based on the Oslo II Negotiations*, 7 INTERNATIONAL NEGOTIATION 143 (2002); William Donohue & Paul Taylor, *Testing the Role Effect in Terrorist Negotiations*, 8 INTERNATIONAL NEGOTIATION 527 (2003).

[5] Note that in cases of suicide intervention, the police negotiators primary goal remains the same; it is to contain the threat by eliminating the hostage taker's ability to take the alternative option of taking their life. Donohue & Taylor, *supra* note 4; Ellen Giebels, et al., *Interdependence in Negotiation: Effects of Exit Options and Social Motive on Distributive and Integrative Negotiation*, 30 EUROPEAN JOURNAL OF SOCIAL PSYCHOLOGY 255 (2000).

[6] ROBERT B. CIALDINI, INFLUENCE: SCIENCE AND PRACTICE 203 (4th ed. 2000)

[7] Stuart Wright, *A Decade After Waco: Reassessing Crisis Negotiations at Mount Carmel in Light of New Government Disclosures*, 7 NOVA RELIGIO 101, 101-10 (2003).

[8] Vincent Van Hasselt, et al., *Hostage-Taking in the Context of Domestic Violence: Some Case Examples*, 20 JOURNAL OF FAMILY VIOLENCE 21 (2005).

[9] Donohue, et al., *supra* note 2; Paul Taylor, *A Cylindrical Model of Communication Behavior in Crisis Negotiations*, 30 HUMAN COMMUNICATION RESEARCH 7 (2002).

[10] Bruce Barry, *The Tactical Use of Emotion in Negotiation*, *in* RESEARCH ON NEGOTIATION IN ORGANIZATIONS 93-121 (Robert Bies, et al. eds., 1999).

[11] Michael Hammer & Randall Rogan, *Negotiation Models in Crisis Situations: The Value of a Communication-Based Approach*, *in* DYNAMIC PROCESSES OF CRISIS NEGOTIATIONS: THEORY, RESEARCH, AND PRACTICE (Randall Rogan, et al. eds., 1997).

[12] Gerben Van Kleef, et al., *The Interpersonal Effects of Emotions in Negotiations: A Motivated Information Processing Approach*, 87 JOURNAL OF PERSONALITY AND SOCIAL PSYCHOLOGY 510 (2004).

[13] MURRAY MIRON & ARNOLD GOLDSTEIN, HOSTAGE (1979); Gary Noesner & Mike Webster, *Crisis Intervention: Using Active Listening Skills in Negotiations*, 66 FBI LAW ENFORCEMENT BULLETIN 13 (1997).

[14] Hammer & Rogan, *supra* note 11; Noesner & Webster, *supra* note 13; Gregory Vecchi, et al., *Crisis (Hostage) Negotiation: Current Strategies and Issues in High-Risk Conflict Resolution*, 10 AGGRESSION AND VIOLENT BEHAVIOR 533 (2005).

[15] Vecchi, et al., *supra* note 14.

[16] Taylor, *supra* note 9; Paul Taylor & Ian Donald, *The Structure of Communication Behavior in Simulated and Actual Crisis Negotiations*, 30 HUMAN COMMUNICATION RESEARCH 433 (2004).

[17] Note that the police negotiator's frame for problem-solving is a limited one. *See* Jack Cambria, et al., *Negotiation Under Extreme Pressure: The "Mouth Marines" and the Hostage Takers*, 18 NEGOTIATION JOURNAL 331 (2002).

ᜡ 76 ᜡ

The Military Learns to Negotiate

Leonard L. Lira

Editors' Note: *Since as long as anyone can remember, negotiators have used war metaphors as a way to frame what they were thinking, and as an analogy to what might happen if no deal is reached. But the warriors themselves have wised up. In this chapter, U.S. Army Major Leonard Lira shows how the military is beginning to become sophisticated about its own needs for negotiation.*

Negotiations During Military Operations

Conventional wisdom holds that military professionals begin to practice their profession when negotiations, particularly diplomatic negotiations at the state level, have failed. War is the extreme option in conflict, as well as the continuation of politics by violent means. Therefore, it would seem antithetical, according to conventional wisdom, that military professionals would use negotiation skills in military operations bent on destroying the will of the target population. In fact, the American military profession held this view for over 60 years during the Cold War, during which it viewed its sole purpose as to fight and win its nation's wars. During this period, the military viewed as its main objective in war the destruction of the enemy state's combat forces. Military science held, almost as a maxim, that the destruction of an enemy state's military force would lead to the bending of the target population's political will and thus to victory. The military viewed as anathema to this functional imperative any practice that deterred it from using overwhelming violent force with which to accomplish this goal. If negotiations were to occur, they would occur only after the war was won and the fighting done. This view by the military did much to buttress conventional wisdom regarding this issue.

However, recent history of military operations conducted throughout the 1990's and up through the recent Afghanistan and Iraqi campaigns of the early 21st century suggests that military professionals do in fact conduct negotiations within the course of military operations and at all levels. This is due in part to the changing nature of the military professional ethic on the battlefield. It is a change which is profoundly shaping how American armed forces conduct military operations in the 21st century, by transforming the purpose of the American military profession from simply fighting and winning the nation's wars to conducting "total conflict operations."[1] It is also due, in part, to the changing role of the U.S.

military in civil-military relations, which requires the military to participate in the development of the national strategic goals for any given conflict, and by doing so engage in bureaucratic negotiations for changes to its organizational jurisdiction. It is from this context that the constraints in the military's environment, political, operational, and functional manifest themselves.

Therefore, the thesis of this chapter is that, contrary to conventional wisdom, the military profession utilizes negotiation skills at all levels of every military operation as a matter of necessity because of the operating constraints present within its environment, in order to accomplish the overall strategic goals of the nation during conflicts. This chapter will demonstrate this by reviewing the change occurring in the military profession's ethic due to its involvement in the complete spectrum of conflict, and will analyze how at the three levels of military operations (strategic, operational, and tactical) military professionals utilize negotiations to accomplish their goals. Additionally, it will examine within these three levels of analysis the inter-professional analogies across several disciplines that rely on conflict management skills such as negotiation.

The Changing Nature of Military Professional Ethics

The construct of conflict is constant throughout every environment in which the military operates. Nowhere does the military truly operate outside the spectrum of conflict. The military conducts operations either in high intensity conflicts or during low intensity conflicts, but at all times it operates in conflict. It is a misnomer then to use the term "post-conflict" operations to describe military operations after high intensity combat operations diminish but when hostile conflict is still clearly present. A term that better informs the environment that the military operates in after violence de-escalates from the high intensity level is "post-combat" operations. Additionally, the military may desire the continuation of conflict with a different, more positive nature, such as the type of conflict present in economic and political competition. Thereby, the goal of military operations in this phase becomes conflict transformation; changing the environment from war to peace, from violent dissonance to prosperous economic and political competition indicative of social consonance. Only when the military accomplishes this goal can the military force of a liberal democratic society return home with that society's recognition that the military operation was victorious.

This recognition is particularly required with the American military and its client, the American society. Why is this so? Why does the most powerful, most resourced, and best trained military in the history of western civilizations need this domestic endorsement in order to be victorious? The main source of power for the American military comes from a democratic and liberal society, which bases the victory of military operations on the legitimacy of the military's actions in accordance with its own societal values. For example, in the most recent conflicts, non-combatant casualties and the abuse of prisoners in both Iraq and Afghanistan during recent post-combat military operations threaten to undermine citizen support for continued military operations in these countries.[2] This is understandable because in the bipolar world of the Cold War "right" and "wrong" were more clearly spelled out. However, in today's multi-polar world the recent shift in the geopolitical security situation toward multi-level conflicts has left the role of the one remaining superpower appearing morally ambiguous. Thus, society has become more reluctant to confer its endorsement for continued military operations beyond the existence of perceived threats, and this lack of endorsement has caused a reevaluation of the military professional ethic.[3]

The military professional ethic, which once would have been more accepting of non-combatant casualties, even without hesitation due to the primacy of mission accomplishment, is now forced to recognize the moral and legal limitations that shape American society's opinion regarding the application of military force. These constraints impress upon modern military professionals to adopt a "police" model of ethical standards during post-combat and sometimes combat operations in the conflict environment.[4] Both the military and police ethical standards revolve around the question of the amount of force to be used in any given situation. Where the military model focuses on *most force permissible* to use in any given conflict scenario, the police model focuses on the *least force possible*.[5] As such, the change in society's ethical paradigm of conflict discussed above demonstrates that in the modern age of conflict it is incumbent upon the military profession to adopt alternative tools and skills of conflict management, such as negotiation, in addition to the most violent means in order to accomplish its overall goals.

Combat and post-combat operations worldwide have required Army leaders at all levels of military command to participate as U.S representatives in meetings and negotiations with coalition partners, other U.S. Government Agencies and non-government organizations, local leaders, and the local populace.[6] For example, military professionals in Operation Iraqi Freedom, due to their access to and control of the manpower, communications, security forces, and other resources necessary to do anything in Iraq, often found themselves the dominant points of contact for negotiations, whether or not these army professionals were prepared to play that role. The exigencies of war, such as the lack of time, the crisis of impending physical violence, and rationing of resources (manpower, technology, and money) for the primary military objective already make the operating environment of the military professional constrained. The additional complication of political, organizational, and functional constraints on military professionals in the modern conflict environment make it doubly so. There are examples of these constraints at each level of operations that can further demonstrate this point and support this chapter's overall thesis.

The Three Levels of Military Operations[7]

It is important at this point to define the levels of analysis applied in this chapter. The U.S. military practices its profession at three levels of operations: strategic, operational, and tactical. Current military doctrine defines these as levels of war but cautions that they are also applicable to operations other than war.[8] The strategic level is that level of war at which the nation determines national or multinational (alliance or coalition) strategic security objectives. At this level, the President of the United States, through the national security strategy process, develops guidance as to how to use national resources (military, diplomatic, economic, information, and legal) to accomplish these objectives. The National Command Authority (NCA)[9] then develops guidance for the military on the national security objectives, the military missions needed to achieve those objectives, and the allocation of resources required by the military to accomplish its missions. The military's combatant commanders participate in discussions with the NCA through the Chairman of the Joint Chiefs of Staff and with allies and coalition members. Based on these discussions the combatant commanders develop a strategy that relates to both US national strategy and operational activities within the theater of operations. Military strategy, thus derived from policy, provides a framework for conducting operations. It is at this level that the political constraints are best observable.

The second level or operational level links the tactical employment of forces to strategic objectives by focusing on the use of military forces to achieve strategic goals through the design, organization, integration, and conduct of strategies, campaigns, major operations, and battles. It is at this level of analysis that the operational constraints, such as time, manpower, technology, and money become observable.

Current doctrine defines the third level, the tactical level, as the employment of units in combat. It includes the ordered arrangement and maneuver of units in relation to each other and/or to the adversary in order to use their full potential. However, as recent peace and post-combat operational histories indicate and this chapter will show, tactical units conduct far more activities than just combat in conflict environments. Therefore, this level of analysis provides the best observation for the functional constraints of the small unit and the individual military professional.

Negotiations at the Strategic Level of Military Operations

In *The Future of the Army Profession*, Dr. Don Snider and a host of academic and military researchers document two types of political negotiations that military professions encounter at the strategic level. The first type, drawn largely from sociologist Andrew Abbot's study of the *System of Professions*, indicates that the three military professions (maritime, aeronautical, and land) are continuously engaged in fierce bureaucratic competitions with peers, outside agencies, and foreign governments/militaries for control over the situations in which they apply their expertise, i.e. the content of their organizational jurisdiction. This competition manifests itself in ongoing formal negotiations over the effective integration of service capabilities under the combatant and coalition commanders, also known as "roles and missions" debates.[10]

In the second type of negotiations at this level, the military profession engages in negotiation with external constituencies such as the press, the Chief Executive officer and his cabinet, the Congress, international agencies, and ultimately the American people, for control over the boundaries that legitimate the military's jurisdictions within which it applies its expertise. As stated earlier, the strategic leaders of the military profession participate in discussions with the nation's leaders, or leaders of foreign militaries and nations, on how to focus the elements of national power into strategic goals. Those negotiations often take the form of discussions with the nation's leaders over the exact application of the military in specific operations, or as discussions with leaders of foreign militaries and states over the implementation of the strategic goals. These negotiations occur through public relations campaigns, at national security committee meetings, or during Congressional Armed Service Committee hearings.[11]

It is within these two types of discussions at the strategic level that the military profession must address the debate regarding the content and the boundaries of its jurisdiction, and the appropriateness and extent of military involvement throughout the spectrum of conflict. This level of analysis led the researchers of *The Future of the Army Profession* to conclude appropriately "As part of this process, or even separate from it, strategic leaders will find that they need to understand the art of negotiation."[12] This is so that the military profession can navigate successfully past the political constraints presented by the bureaucratic relationship with its competitors and the civil-military relationship with its client.

The politically constrained environment at the strategic level in which the military profession operates is not unlike other executive agencies' political and bureaucratic environments. The diplomatic professionals within the State Department are in constant competition with other executive departments, the United Nations, and international non-governmental organizations for control over the diplomatic content within its jurisdiction and for control over what is or is not within its jurisdictional boundaries. The budgetary fight for resources to conduct diplomatic efforts in conflict situations versus forceful military interventions is an example of the former. The African Crisis Response Initiative (ACRI, now African Contingency Operations Training Assistance, or ACOTA) that was to provide equipment and training to 10,000-12,000 African soldiers before 2002, and which is run by U.S. Special Operations Forces from Central Command and European Command, but actually controlled by the State Department, is an example of the latter. Negotiations at these levels are not new per se, but what is new is the military profession's evolving acceptance of the need for skilled negotiators at this level as well as the operational and tactical level.

Negotiations at the Operational Level of Military Operations

At the operational level, military professionals make decisions on how to use the given tools and resources at the tactical level in order to meet the strategic goals. When the environment calls for less violent measures to achieve mission success, such as in the low intensity level of conflict found in post-combat operations, operational leaders have the opportunity to make decisions and issue guidance that require their subordinate leaders to utilize negotiation skills toward achieving that success. However, the most prominent constraint at this level is the ability to apply resources to match the required course of action. Military organizations, primarily organized for combat operations, have resources and training to conduct one form of conflict management: combat. Operational logistics, subordinate training, and equipment are all constrained resources in that sense if the situation requires less violent forms of conflict management.

Nonetheless, it is also at the operational level where a lack of guidance from both the strategic leaders and the norms of the professional practice, on how military forces should conduct operations in the post-combat phase, provide the greatest opportunity for operational leaders to exercise initiative in deciding the best course to accomplish their mission. Initiatives for alternative courses of action have their best chance for success because the operational leader has the knowledge of the strategic goals and controls the tools to develop actions toward achieving them. The operational leader is also in a position to observe the interests of the population it controls and then to determine the local tribal or community leaders' best alternatives to a negotiated agreement compared to his or her own organization's alternatives. In a new geopolitical multi-polar world, this means that successful negotiations at the operational level will be highly dependant on the operational leaders' ability to exercise initiative in utilizing the given resources in varying and ambiguous operating environments.

A prominent example, cited in numerous news media reports of an operational leader exercising this level of initiative in using alternate conflict management skills (such as negotiation) in Operation Iraqi Freedom, was then Major General David H. Petraeus, commander of the U.S. Army 101st Airborne Division during the combat and post-combat phases of Operation Iraqi Freedom. Shortly after major combat operations ended, General Petraeus took the initiative to begin post-combat operations in order to stabilize his area of responsibility, by reorganizing his division into a stabilization force. A *New York Times* report indicated that one of his first decisions was to have one of his subordinate units begin negotiations with local sheiks and Iraqi customs officials to restore trade with Syria.[13] Additionally, General Petraeus supported agreements negotiated by his subordinate leaders, for instance when he wrote a letter—stamped by the division's notary public—decreeing that the funds be provided to pay government workers, and to negotiate with the strategic leaders of the American forces.

To induce support from the local population, and enhance greater security for his forces, he instituted a policy of "cordon and knock," also called "raid and aid" missions.[14] Further, he negotiated with the Coalition Provincial Authority (CPA), to make a temporary exception to its policy of barring professors of a local university from returning to work because they had been registered Ba'athists under Saddam Hussein. Actions such as these gave General Petraeus enough influence with local leaders that he was able to enter into successful negotiations with the various ethnic groups and tribes to form a local governing council, long before the CPA formed any substantive interim government in Baghdad. The report went on to point out that General Petraeus' willingness to go outside the norm of his profession and embrace the approach of so-called nation building as a central military mission became a major element of success in the northern region of Iraq following the end of combat operations.

The primary skill used in that approach was negotiation. In his negotiation strategy, General Petraeus focused on mutual interests and invented options for mutual gain when he directed his forces to negotiate the opening of the trade route between Iraq and Syria. By negotiating with the CPA to make the exception for the professors, he separated the people within his area of responsibility from the problem of the policies of the old totalitarian regime, which were the major source of contention concerning the CPA. Finally, by using objective criteria for evaluation of where and how to apply limited force, he was able to distinguish between possible insurgents and the non-combatant population of Mosul. From this analysis, two lessons can be drawn. The primary lesson learned from this example is that it is the operational level, the level where the decisions are made on how to implement the tools and resources of the organization, which offers the best opportunity for the initiative to use alternate conflict engagement tools. Leaders at this level have to be willing to make the mental leap outside of the norms of their professional practice in order to seize that initiative.

The constraints at this level are not unlike those presented to any police department around the country. The New York Police Department faces similar constraints of budget, manpower, and training. Due to these constraints, coupled with the threat of lawsuits for over aggressive police action, police professionals recognized the need for alternative forms of conflict management such as negotiation. [Volpe, et al., *Unknown*] As such, the NYPD Hostage Negotiation team was formed. The operational constraints, however, led the operational leaders to decide to organize the team with only one full-time Lieutenant. The rest of the team members are officers trained in negotiation skills but assigned day-to-day to other duties throughout the five boroughs of New York City. Whenever a situation arises where the negotiation team is required, the part-time members are activated and work with the full time Lieutenant to handle the situation. The operational leaders of the NYPD probably underwent a similar type of analysis of their mission and their available resources to accomplish that mission, and like General Petraeus, came to the conclusion that negotiation was a mission-enabling skill that they could apply as a resource. This provides some confirmation to the primary lesson drawn from the military profession that the operational level is where the initiative can be best used in deciding to use negotiation skills. The "take away" from the military and police examples above for professional leaders at the operational level is that leaders at this level need to recognize the need for and their ability to seize the initiative in implementing negotiation skills.

Negotiations at the Tactical Level of Military Operations: "Every Soldier is a Diplomat"[15]

The newest use of negotiation is at the tactical level, where foot soldiers were not previously given the power to negotiate, nor did they have the need to. With the advent of the Afghanistan and Iraq campaigns, soldiers at all levels, including tactical level leaders, have found that they indeed needed to take part in negotiations in the conflict environment in order for the overall military mission to succeed. The constraints at this level are functional and stem from the organizational culture of military professionals as well as the operating environment.

This fact became readily evident to faculty members of the U.S. Military Academy's Department of Social Science when they sent out a survey to tactical level leaders from units re-deploying back from Iraq. Though a low number of individuals replied to the instructors' initial manual survey, those that did indicated that the number one skill required by tactical leaders in post-combat phase of operations was negotiation skills. The respondents provided examples of negotiating construction project contracts, property disputes, pay for former Iraqi government officials, for the establishment of local Iraqi lead governing councils, and for the surrender of insurgents surrounded by military forces in cordoned parts of urban areas.

The functional constraint indicative of organizational training and design in the military became more apparent in a follow up online survey, in which 78% of respondents reported conducting some sort of negotiations in scenarios outside of what they were trained for as military professionals. Soldiers are trained from their first days in the military "to attack, not to comfort" the enemy. They learn a code of professional conduct that espouses a willingness to close with and destroy an enemy through violent combat. This is the warrior ethos inculcated in every U.S. soldier by their basic combat training. Many in the military profession believe this ethos makes soldiers "ill-equipped for non-combat missions and that assigning them to such missions degrades the ethos and compromises soldiers' safety."[16] Other military professionals acknowledge that having soldiers operate in post-combat environments is requisite to conducting combat operations and prerequisite to achieving the military goals that must be accomplished to achieve the political goals. Those same military professionals acknowledge that to operate in this confusing environment, negotiating skills are in fact critical to providing force protection.[17]

Institutionally, the military is starting to recognize this fact. Individual services are adapting their training to meet this new skill requirement. For example, the U.S. Army recognized that there was a discrepancy between doctrine and required practices when it assumed peace operations in Bosnia. To compensate for this the U.S. Army began training in skills such as negotiation to senior leaders in tactical units deploying to Bosnia to conduct peace operations.[18]

Many of the respondents to the survey cited above commented that one of the hardest aspects of negotiating with the indigenous population in every setting was working through interpreters and across cultural divides. [Kaufman, *Interpreter*] Tactical leaders quickly had to become experts in the local cultures, for example understanding the rituals involved during discussions, such as gift giving and the habitual lack of awareness of time. [Goh, *Errors*] More than one respondent stated that learning such cultural customs would have been easier if they had prior train-ing on using interpreters. Tactical leaders had to work through issues of translation and interpreters' attempts to tone down or shape the translation to what they thought the tactical leader wanted to hear. In one example, a tactical leader stated that the interpreter kept trying to answer the leader's questions for the local population without even translating the questions over to the local popu-lation for their reply.

This section makes it clear that military professionals at the tactical level need to understand how to use negotiation skills. Although constraints on their use of those skills such as organizational and cross-ethnical cultural obstacles will exist in the environments in which they will use those skills, military professionals at the tactical level would do well to equip themselves with the basics of "principled negotiations" and inter-cultural communications.

It is important to note that the military, in this respect, is far from the only profession to operate in the "negotiation-constrained" environment in which re-cent thinking has raised the status and visibility of negotiation. An obvious example is the Catholic Church. While their original functions are and will con-tinue to be rather different, the military profession's move to transform conflict in post-combat environments at the tactical level is not unlike that shift that the Catholic Church has recently made toward peacebuilding.[19] Due to the operations of the Church's charitable organizations in post-combat settings, in which violence was prone to erupt among ethnic, religious and cultural groups, it is now taking actions at its version of the tactical level that go beyond its "standard" type of so-cial action, of relief and charity to the poor, and that are more directed toward conflict transformation work.

In fact, Caritas Internationalis published *Peacebuilding: A Caritas Training Manual* in 2002 to assist the confederation of 154 Catholic relief and development agencies in 198 countries to adopt the "new orientation of the transnational Catholic social service apostolate."[20] The handbook advises that indigenous peacebuilders must be developed who can apply "local knowledge" to the task of reconciliation. "Indige-nous peacebuilders" can easily be compared to the "local security force build up" that the tactical military professionals are currently trying to cultivate in Iraq and Afghanistan.

The analogy makes more sense when comparing the reason that this shift is occurring in the church to the reason it occurs at this level of analysis in the mili-tary. The recognition of the organizational and ethnic cultural constraints identified by military professionals is the same for the ecclesiastical profession, at the tactical level. To account for those constraints, in the same manner that the military profession's doctrine addresses them, the Caritas manual recognizes that the church's social service operations cannot continue without its frontline mis-sionaries taking into consideration the communal and cultural issues that led to the conflict in their regions and prevented their church's operational success. Just as the military is slowly recognizing that it can no longer disregard the relation-ship between its function as a just war public agent and the functions of its soldiers as peacemakers in the post-combat environment, the church is finding it cannot continue to disregard the relationship between its function as a faith based nongovernmental organization working toward social and economic justice, and the functions of its missionaries as peacebuilders in the same environment.[21]

Conclusion

This chapter illustrates that, contrary to conventional wisdom, military professionals, like other professionals, utilize alternative conflict management skills,
particularly negotiation, in order to accomplish the goals of their mission. This is
in part due to the changing ethics of the battlefield, where the military ethos of
utilizing belligerent violence is no longer conducive to accomplishing the overall
political goals of society. The practicalities of the post-combat phases indicative of
all military operations conducted by armies from liberal democratic societies will
continue to necessitate the use of negotiation skills.

Military professionals will continue using negotiation skills at the strategic,
operational, and tactical levels of their operating environments. As demonstrated
earlier in this chapter, at the strategic level, military professionals use negotiations
in two settings where the constraints are political and institutional. In the first
setting, they use negotiations in bureaucratic competition to maintain operational
control over the content of their organizational jurisdiction, i.e. what it is that
military professionals can do that other professions may not do. In the second
setting, they use negotiations in the civil-military relationship with the client society to negotiate for control over how the military should implement those
functions within that jurisdiction. At the operational level, military professionals
use their resources available to utilize negotiations in order to accomplish their
mission. The constraints at this level are resource based. Resources may be allocated for one purpose, such as the combat role, but the conditions of the operating
environment may require the operational leader to exercise initiative in re-
allocating those resources. For instance, operational level leaders may utilize military troops in negotiation settings and/or police type operations. This re-allocation
of the role for the soldier has increased the need for new training in negotiation
skills at the tactical level. At this level obstacles inherent to negotiating within
both organizational and cultural environments present functional constraints that
tactical leaders must overcome. These three levels of analysis demonstrate that the
military profession does apply negotiation skills in all aspects of military operations in order to accomplish the overall strategic goals of the nation during
conflicts, and as a matter of necessity due to the operating constraints present at
each level in those operations .

Further, this chapter points to mounting evidence supporting the assertion
that as a profession the military's purpose is transforming from simply fighting
and winning its client's wars, to using all means available to resolve its client's
conflicts. To date, the professional military education (PME) that military professionals receive does not stress this, to my knowledge, as heavily as it should at the
basic through intermediate levels. To remedy this, one recommendation is to include conflict resolution skill building into the core curriculum of all PME levels.
The first skill that should be mandated into PME core curriculum, as indicated by
this chapter, should be negotiation skills training.

Finally, practitioners of every profession can draw analogies from the examples
of military professionals using negotiation skills described in this chapter to apply
to their own professional experiences. A recent commencement speech from LT.
Gen. Ricardo S. Sanchez to the graduates of Texas A&M University makes this
point well:

> Every profession has its battlefields—the courtroom, the classroom, the
> boardroom.... You will immediately find yourself in your chosen profes-
> sion's battlefield facing challenges that parallel what I face as a
> professional warrior—leading units and [individuals] under very tough

conditions to accomplish mission critical to the survival of [your] institution under austere, expeditionary, and uncertain conditions.[22]

Those professions that can skillfully apply the negotiation skill set at every level of their operations will do well in their own battlefields, no matter what level of conflict happens to transpire before them.

Endnotes

The views expressed are those of the author and not necessarily of the Department of the Army, the US Military Academy, or any other agency of the U.S. Government.

[1] Leonard Lira, Major, United States Army, *To Change an Army: Understanding Defense Transformation*, Paper presented at the Annual Joint Conference of the International Security and Arms Control Section—APSA and International Security Section—ISA (Oct. 2004), *available at*
http://www.dean.usma.edu/departments/sosh/research/LiraTo%20change%20an%20Army.pdf.

[2] *See* Tony Pfaff, Military Ethics in Complex Contingencies, *in* FUTURE OF THE ARMY PROFESSION 409-11 (Don M. Snider & Lloyd Matthews eds., 2d ed. 2005) [hereinafter FUTURE]. *See also*, NEWS RELEASE, PEW RESEARCH CENTER, *Iraq Prison Scandal Hits Home, But Most Reject Pullout*, (May 12, 2004), *available at*
http://www.pewtrusts.com/pdf/pew_research_iraq_prison_051204.pdf.

[3] Pfaff, *supra* note 2, at 410.

[4] *Id.* at 411.

[5] *Id.* at 413.

[6] Steven Heidecker & Jon Sowards, *Bilateral Negotiations: The Best Offense is…*, 54(7) ARMY MAGAZINE 50 (July 2004) and DEPARTMENT OF DEFENSE, JOINT TASK FORCE COMMANDER'S HANDBOOK FOR PEACE OPERATIONS DOCTRINE FOR JOINT OPERATIONS, (Washington, D.C.: GPO, June 1997).

[7] For a complete breakdown of size, strength and leadership rank at the strategic, operational and tactical level, *see* U.S. ARMY ORGANIZATION, *at* http://www.army.mil/organization.

[8] DEPARTMENT OF DEFENSE, JOINT PUBLICATION 3-0: DOCTRINE FOR JOINT OPERATIONS (SEPT. 10, 2001), *available at* http://www.dtic.mil/doctrine/jel/new_pubs/jp3_0.pdf.

[9] The President and Secretary of Defense of the United States.

[10] Don Snider, *The U.S. Army as Profession, in* FUTURE, *supra* note 2, at 18-19.

[11] *See also, id. at* 13-15, 131, 225-30, 271-86 and 601-21.

[12] Leonard Wong & Don Snider, *Strategic Leadership of the Army Profession, in* FUTURE, *supra* note 2, at 616.

[13] Michael Gordon, *The Struggle for Iraq: 101st Airborne Scores Success in Northern Iraq*, N.Y. TIMES, Sept. 4, 2003, at A1.

[14] Petraeus stressed the selective use of force. When the units from the division mounted a raid, soldiers did not just burst in. They surrounded the house and then went to the door, knocked and negotiated entry or the surrender of suspected insurgents. Soldiers would then return the next day with funds and humanitarian assistance to repair any damages and improve the neighborhood. "These operations disrupted the enemy, engendered support among the population, and frequently led to additional intelligence." *See* Michael J. Meese and Sean M. Morgan, *New Requirements for Army Expert Knowledge: Afghanistan and Iraq, in* FUTURE, *supra* note 2, at 354.

[15] Lieutenant General David Petraeus, Address to the faculty members of the Department of Social Sciences at the U.S. Military Academy, West Point (Feb. 2004).

[16] Robert Blackstone, *Somalia: Soldiers in SOSO*, MILITARY REVIEW, Mar.-Apr. 2005, at 43.

[17] Quote from a returning U.S. commander from Iraq in an address to the faculty members of the Department of Social Sciences and cadets of USMA, March 30th 2005 and General

Anthony Zinni, USMC (Ret.), as quoted *in* ALLARD, KENNETH. SOMALIA OPERATIONS: LESSONS LEARNED 71 (1995).

[18] Howard Olsen & John Davis, *Training U.S. Army Officers Peace Operations: Lessons from Bosnia*, SPECIAL REPORT 56, (United States Institute of Peace, October 29, 1999), *available at* http://www.usip.org/pubs/specialreports/sr991029.html.

[19] R. Scott Appleby, *Catholic Peacebuilding*, AMERICA: THE CATHOLIC WEEKLY MAGAZINE, Sept. 8, 2003, *available at*

http://www.americamagazine.org/gettext.cfm?articletypeid=1&textID=3145&issueID=449&search=1.

[20] *Id.*

[21] *Id.*

[22] Sam Dillion, *War on Terrorism Dominates Talks Given at Graduations*, N.Y. TIMES June 12, 2005, § 1, at 38 (quoting LTG Ricardo S. Sanchez at Texas A&M University).

❦ 77 ❧

The Last Plane Out...

Robert Dingwall & Carrie Menkel-Meadow

Editors' Note: *If you've always wanted to know what happens when "negotiation experts" actually have to negotiate, this chapter is for you. But it has more to offer than that. Writing about the common negotiation nightmare of a cancelled flight, two scholars draw on many of the field's cultural and other theories to address the very real question: when there's one seat left on the Last Plane Out and many people vying for it, how do you get that seat?*

The Players:

Robert Dingwall, British sociologist and scholar of dispute resolution and other subjects

Carrie Menkel-Meadow, American law professor and scholar of negotiation, mediation, legal ethics and feminist theory

Robert (herein "Bob") Meadow, husband of Carrie and former academic political scientist, now political consultant with millions of miles flown, and years of experience negotiating with thinks-she-knows-it-all above-mentioned negotiation-scholar-wife

Peter, accompanying colleague of Robert

Unnamed French female traveler

Assorted United Airlines gate agents

Extras: About 100 delayed passengers at Denver Airport, June, 1998 (on their way to Aspen, Colorado for a scholarly meeting)

The Time:

June 3, 1998, late at night (important to note this is before September 11, 2001 with relatively flush airlines, little security, a brand new airport in Denver, and no unusually overt hostility between Americans, Brits and French *citizens,* in other words, before cultural name-calling based on different reactions to, and alliances, in the geo-political sphere).

The Place:

Denver International Airport (with pre- and post-action occurrences in other airports)

When scholars write about negotiation, mediation or other forms of conflict resolution, they often display what the great sociologist Erving Goffman once described as a "touching tendency to keep part of the world safe from sociology."[1] If you have read through the contributions to this book, you will have learned a great deal about the theory of negotiation, and about the experience of many accomplished practitioners in observing other people negotiate, in facilitating negotiations, or in doing negotiation as an occupational or professional practice. However, it is easy to forget that all of us are doing negotiation throughout our everyday lives. Like Moliere's M. Jourdain, who discovered that he had been speaking prose for forty years without realizing it, it may pass below our horizon of awareness when and how we are negotiating. [Volpe, et al., *Unknown*] We turn on the theory or the professional skills only when we *knowingly* take on the role of scholar or practitioner. The mundane encounters of our daily existence may remain just that—not explicitly an object of reflection or contemplation. This chapter takes one such encounter, familiar to all modern travelers, and explores the way it was experienced by two negotiation scholars. In doing so, we draw attention to two frequently neglected dimensions of the literature on dispute resolution. In the one, there are some situations in which the outcomes are positional or distributive goods.[2] In the other, sometimes the outcome is affected by backstairs plays that do not form part of the academic script for everything to have an open and acknowledged place in the forum. Positional goods[3] are those that are inherently scarce: only one party can enjoy them at a time so there is no achievable win-win outcome. In other words, sometimes the pie can't be enlarged and can't be divided. Backstairs plays demonstrate the continuing influence of wider social structures of power and influence, beyond the local endowments of negotiators. [Kolb, *Moves & Turns*] We comment here, as well, on two much more frequently discussed negotiation concepts—those of cultural differences and intercultural encounters in negotiation[4] [Goh, *Errors*; Kelly, *Indigenous Experience*] and gender differences in negotiation behaviors or perceptions of those behaviors.[5] [Kolb & Putnam, *Gender*]

In telling our story here we ask you to think about how theory does or does not affect the actual behaviors we choose when negotiating, particularly in less prepared-for, thoughtful, and rational interactions (are any negotiations truly and only "rational?") such as occurs in more crisis-like situations or when the parties are engaged in one-off encounters. In other words, what are our default behaviors in negotiation, when we may not have time to sort through the academic theories or practical "play-books" of our own cognitive models? And what happens when the cognitive models of one party to the negotiation don't match up with those of the other party? Another way of framing this key question might be: how do you get the other side to "play" by your integrative or problem-solving negotiation rules?

Robert's Story

On 3 June 1998, I was on my way to the Law and Society Association (LSA) annual meeting, which was being held at the Snowmass Resort, just outside Aspen, Colorado. This is a rather remote location, served by a small airport only capable of dealing with relatively small incoming planes. From the time of booking, it was clear that the LSA traffic was causing problems for the flight operators in managing the volume of people heading in and out within a short period given their capacity limitations. My routing from the UK involved flight changes at Washington, DC and at Denver. The flight out of DC was delayed by storms in the Midwest, a common event at that time of year, and I finally reached Denver around 8:30 pm, about 27 hours after I got out of bed in Nottingham, UK. I knew that I had actually missed my booked connection for Aspen, so I was prepared for some sort of problem. I was also reunited with a UK colleague, Peter, who had, by chance, been sitting next to me on the Heathrow-Washington leg of the journey.

We joined quite a long line at the United desk, which got considerably longer-maybe 60-80 people in total who were not likely to get out of Denver that night, whether for Aspen or for other points in the Southwest or California. I recognized Carrie Menkel-Meadow just ahead of us.

Carrie's Story

I was traveling to the LSA meeting with my husband (hereinafter "Bob"). When we got to Denver, the Aspen airport had been closed because of poor weather conditions. It turned out that Robert (Dingwall) and I were actually on the same flight from Washington, although we didn't see each other till later in the line—I thought that it was about 100 people, all trying to make arrangements to get out of the airport on the next day. And the Denver to Aspen flights were all on small planes that were totally booked with several hundred people from LSA. So Robert and I were both in the line and we both noticed each other. Although we didn't think about it at the time—Robert was tired and I was furious—it was an extraordinary natural experiment. We had both taught and thought about negotiation and mediation, and we were stuck with the same problem: how were we going to make arrangements for having missed our flight and for getting out the next day?

Robert's Story

Peter and I had probably been in line for 20 minutes or so before we got to the desk. Carrie and her husband were several minutes ahead of us and seemed to have happened on the position being staffed by the supervisor on that shift. We were not really close enough to hear what was going on but clearly Carrie was not making much progress and was getting increasingly animated. However, and I think this may be important, she was not getting angry—the appeals seemed to be to some injustice or unfairness. In other words, it was not "I'm going to sue the pants off you" so much as "this is terribly unfair, the way you are treating me." Carrie's husband did not seem to be saying very much at all, except for an occasional intervention that had more of the tone of a mediation or conciliation. It sounded to me as if he was pitching a line of "Would you believe I have to live with this woman?", where the (male) agent was invited to make Bob's life bearable by reaching some accommodation with Carrie because, as men, we ought to show some solidarity with each other rather than making each other's life more difficult.

Carrie's Story

Here are my reactions as I recall them. Robert has described his perceptions of what he thought I was doing and how he viewed me. I was making appeals to rules, as I understood them (from experience in frequent air travel), and more generalized justice. My perceived-to-be more "quiet" husband, however, is a *very* frequent flyer (with premium status on three different airlines, including United, the airline with whom we were negotiating). So he was letting me make my appeals, that, based on his status, they had to at least get us on the plane the next day. And so I was appealing to rules—their rules for special treatment of frequent flyers and my knowledge of what bad-weather delays require airlines to do. And, I was also appealing the injustice of their initial refusal to do anything or take any responsibility for all of us weary travelers. Quietly, Bob may have been doing those 'do I really have to put up with this crazy woman?' things. But also, he was very quietly asserting that he was an important frequent flyer and they better take care of him because that's what being a frequent flyer is all about. And indeed it was Bob, not me, who asked to see the next level supervisor, and who said, quietly, but firmly, and simply, "I will not move from this line until you or someone with appropriate authority can take care of me." Should this be seen as persistence? Stubbornness? Firmness? Were these expressions experienced differently when made by me vs. by Bob? We all know from our negotiation play books to "ask for the next level" (change negotiators until you get satisfaction, or get someone with authority to make a discretionary and creative decision). At some point we actually did get to a higher level supervisor, who gave us a voucher for a hotel room—but no booking for a flight for the next day. What got to me, however, was my perception that Robert (Dingwall) in the next line, with another agent, was actually being treated differently (and better!).

Robert's Story

I'd been watching Carrie and her husband for a bit, but it seemed to me that she wasn't making a lot of progress. It was obvious this agent was very used to dealing with this line of argument, had a script for it, and wasn't going to depart from that. My colleague was so tired that I got left with the talking. I hadn't taken on board the possibility that United might not acknowledge any responsibility for our predicament, which was part of Carrie's issue. There was some uncertainty as to whether our inability to proceed was due to weather and air traffic control, in which case they weren't necessarily liable to us, or whether it was due to mechanical failure on the scheduled aircraft.

United's line to us was that the delay was due to weather and they had no responsibility to put us up for the night, to give us a meal, or to see that we got out the next day.

But it was rumored in the line that there had been a hard landing that had damaged the landing gear. Anyway, I began to consider other strategies. I have used more confrontational approaches like Carrie's in department stores, to good effect. But these agents were obviously well-trained in strategies for dealing with customers and not giving anything away.[6] (Sales assistants do not always seem to be as well-trained as airline personnel, and stores are often very anxious that noisy arguments with customers will frighten away other trade.) One alternative that I sometimes use is what I call the "poor X" line. This is mainly usable when traveling with a junior colleague, especially if female, or a child, regardless of the gender of the gate agent—"I am not being assertive on my own behalf but we can't possibly treat X like this so let's see what we can work out." However, my sleepy colleague, Peter, looks at least as middle-aged as I do and this wasn't credible. In the end, I chose my default approach—"I have a problem, it's not your fault, but it is your responsibility to work with me to find a solution. The quicker we find it, the quicker we can all go home. Finding a solution is a joint enterprise, I'm not going to make things difficult for you as long as you don't make things difficult for me. You still have another 60 customers behind me in the line to deal with. Let's not worry about the entitlements and the legalities. You've had a hard day and it's going to get harder because those 60 people are going to be even more dissatisfied than me, because they've been waiting longer. What can we do to put a package together?"

I think the strategy was more effective because I was able to play it off a third customer who came to a newly opened position between Carrie and me. From the language she lapsed into when her English failed, I inferred that she was French. She had been hoping to get to Las Vegas but had missed the last flight on any airline. Her immediate tactic was anger. She demanded to see the "executive chief" and kept shouting loudly that United was a "shit airline." The agent who had been dealing with Carrie seemed to have reached the basis of an agreement with her and now began to divide his attention, devoting some to the French woman in support of the more junior agent who was actually dealing with her. However, his line was that he was not required to talk to anyone who was angry and aggressive, that she could either calm down or he would have security escort her to somewhere quiet until she did—which is what happened. It was a very formulaic response and clearly right out of some United manual.

I did flirt with the idea of trying to mediate—her English wasn't brilliant, the agent's French was non-existent, and mine was certainly good enough to perform this task. I am afraid that I concluded that I really wanted to get to bed somewhere, that there was nothing in this for me and that this was not my problem. However, I was able to get into an increasingly collusive relationship with the agent, who was dealing with me on the basis that Brits could be trusted to be stoic, patient, and reasonable, and not cause a lot of trouble, unlike most other "aliens." Much of this was non-verbal and done by mutual gaze shifts, but it did get us fairly rapidly to a conclusion involving hotel rooms and a confirmed flight on the next day, allowing me to thank the agent and to try to make him feel good about having done what was really only what he should have been expected to do. Peter observed the following morning that the French woman had ended up in the same hotel as us (I hadn't noticed) but, given the frequency of the shuttles, she must have been at least 30-45 minutes later arriving.

Carrie's Story

I said to my husband 'you see, if you're a polite British person, that's exactly what you end up with—everything that everyone is supposed to get (but doesn't!)' By "doing" British and being proper and polite—and being male, of course—Robert was making greater progress and his outcomes happened much faster. So there was an efficiency factor, also. And the interesting thing is, though it's just a hypothesis shared between Robert and me, that it was that he was "being British." It could very well have been "the merits," which is that the airline was always going to treat an international traveler, who had been on the road for 27 hours, differently. You could see this as an issue of nationality stereotypes, but anyone could have used the different disputing styles (calm, problem-solving, demanding, angry, emotional, principled or justice seeking). Certainly it was a natural experiment. You could watch the 3 of us—an American argumentative woman lawyer appealing to rules, and justice, accompanied by a white man who was acting a little bit privileged, because of his frequent flyer status; 2 Brits who have had a long night but were being very proper; and an extremely emotional French woman. It would have been fascinating to go back and interview the agents. Just like Robert, I know I was getting back the playbook of how to deal with difficult passengers and what to do with passengers in different circumstances. I was having an argument as you would in a negotiation, on the facts (what caused the flights to be cancelled) and the rules (what duties flowed from what set of facts).

What I knew about the rules (and my husband knew a lot more) was the conditions under which they did have to put us up for the night, give us a meal and book us another flight. We eventually got a room (in a different hotel from Robert)—but the agent would not book us a flight for the next day. What happened then was that my husband got on his cell phone, and called United directly. We got a booking for a flight the next day, from the regular frequent flyer United call-line, away from the gate agent. (So much for the power of "face to face" negotiations!) So, our outcomes were different, too. Eventually the French woman got transported to a hotel, too. And my suspicion was, that of the 100 people standing in line, there were many different outcomes. Some people got their hotels paid for, and meals, and bookings; some people got none of these things. It would have been interesting to be able to gather the complete data sets for this "experiment"—what did each of the 100 passengers ask for and how[7] (their negotiation strategies) and what did they each receive—but alas, even social scientists have to sleep, and I was too exhausted to follow up on my curiosity.

At the gross level of external observation, there were national differences. I do believe that Robert got treated differently, and better, because he was a polite Brit. The hysterical French woman was treated the worst. And I suspect I would not have gotten even my hotel room if my husband hadn't been making his (male) frequent flyer noises. The one appeal that I did make (this is the injustice thing and I don't know if Robert overheard this) was, I really saw myself as a lawyer. I was trying to get something for myself, true—but I also said, "The 65 people behind me all have the same problem, we're all going to the same place, I recognize these people—we're all going to Law and Society. Can we try to figure out whether you can in fact put some extra planes on tomorrow?" I mean I was trying to solve a problem in the way that United management, off the gate, actually eventually solved it (by putting on three more small planes the next morning). And of course in that environment also, it's what is possible in negotiation—that agent had no authority to manage a group problem and make a decision to call up more planes. And I said, "what are you going to do now? You're going to have to say the same thing to 65 people." And so I was then thinking about turning around and attempting some collective action, which was to try to organize everybody.

Discussion

Although this is a single case study, it is of particular interest because of the way that it presents a 'natural experiment' in the use of different negotiation styles under the same environmental conditions. All three travelers, or groups of travelers, had the same goal: to secure a night's food and lodging at the expense of the airline, and then to continue their journey at the earliest opportunity on the following day. Both of these are positional goods: even a major airline hub like Denver has a finite stock of hotel rooms that is put under pressure when there are severe traffic disruptions (or there is at least an incentive to minimize payments for hotel rooms, even if they are available). There is an equally finite supply of seats on next day flights, most of which will already have confirmed travelers on them. There are, of course, certain variations—in the gender and national origin of the participants and in their travel histories in getting to this point—that confer different endowments. Nevertheless, we can use these to explore the implications of the different approaches.

The first item to consider might be the extent to which there are national disputing styles.[8] It is probably of significance here that the agents were US nationals representing a US airline. Any negotiation would need to take account of their cultural expectations and their training. It is certainly arguable, for example, that florid anger might be a more effective strategy with Air France agents. Nevertheless, the United staff clearly had no difficulty in referring to the play book and deeming themselves authorized to refuse service to the French woman. This clearly suggests that angry passengers are not uniquely French. Carrie's strategy struggled because of the way in which she tried to get them to acknowledge an individual problem as a class action. It might well have been more efficient for United to sit everyone for Aspen to one side and give them coffee and doughnuts, so that they could deal with the individual cases for other destinations and then deal with the LSA people as a class. However, this would clearly have required authorization from a management level not available at that time of night (and the food outlets were closed!). It would also have hindered any kind of cost minimization strategy that separated LSA travelers into different classes of entitlement. Robert's position as an international traveler on a through ticket may well have been genuinely different from that of a domestic traveler. However, his strategy, although less altruistic than Carrie's, meshed far better with what the agent could supply as a solution. In effect, he was trying to display empathy with the agent rather than to argue a rational-legal case. Carrie's more lawyerly approach presumed a negotiation partner who would interrupt their focus on line processing—and finishing work for the day—to engage with her intellectually. Robert assumed that the agent was at the end of a long shift and shared his interest in minimizing conflict and getting to bed. It is a textbook observation that negotiation is not a purely rational and cognitive process, so that some measure of emotional engagement, even if in terms of interest, may be necessary to achieve a resolution. [Shapiro, *Emotion*]

To what extent was gender an issue? The key airline staff in this account were all male and there is no doubt that they saw both these women passengers as difficult. The French woman was easy to deal with under their rules of engagement, although her public humiliation also represented a useful opportunity to remind the rest of the line about the behavior expected of them. Both Robert and Carrie's husband, Bob, seemed able to play off this, although there might be an interesting question about whether this tactic would have worked in reverse if the agents had been women. Arguably, though, the real problem was the misfit between the negotiation styles adopted by the two women and the bureaucratic nature of the encounter with the agents.

Raising the emotional tone is not a uniquely female trait. Robert collected a valuable contrast case in summer 2005, while delayed at O'Hare in Chicago. The gate at which he was waiting for a flight to Austin was processing a flight to Minneapolis. A group of passengers arrived just as the aircraft door had closed and the (female) gate agent refused to have it reopened so they could board. An angry male passenger began shouting at her and was sent off to the distant gate where the next flight to Minneapolis was scheduled to leave from. The others shuffled with embarrassment at this behavior and watched him depart before approaching the agent very deferentially to explain that they were rock musicians with a gig in Minneapolis the next day and that it was really important for them to sort out whether they and their luggage could get to that city together in time to set up. The agent immediately opened up the next outgoing flight on her computer and made sure that they all got on it.

Where gender is more of an issue seems to be in the use of another strategy, namely crying. The value of bursting into tears has disconcerted some previous "conference tryout" audiences for this paper, but it is clear that airline staff perceive it as a very different kind of problem. On the way back to the UK from Aspen, Robert was traveling via Chicago. The European flights were heavily booked and Air France capacity had been taken out by a pilots' strike. As a result, there was serious congestion at O'Hare. Another French woman also tried getting angry at the United check-in when told she couldn't be guaranteed a seat (a lot of people, including Robert, were on provisional status until volunteers for re-routing had been taken off their assigned seats). The agents escorted her to a seat in the gate area, refusing to discuss her case until she calmed down. However, she then began to cry, not hysterically but very quietly. This began to attract a lot of passenger attention and a senior manager appeared very rapidly to take her out of the gate area. We have no information on the end of the story but this seems to be a powerful strategy, possibly because a distressed passenger, as opposed to an angry and intemperate one, may have a greater perceived potential for collective mobilization among other passengers. An airline does not look good if it is indifferent to a crying woman, while an angry passenger simply disrupts order at the expense of other passengers who are trying to achieve their goals. Whether different genders of gate agents and travelers respond similarly or differently to each other in these situations would be interesting to study more systematically. Some previous audiences for this paper have suggested that Carrie's efforts to create a group solution or to care about the other passengers in line was a particularly female "caring" approach (somewhat appropriate since Carrie herself has argued for "an ethic of care" in lawyering[9]); though many others have suggested that the class relief approach is more consistent with a lawyer-like (or political activist) approach and is not a gendered response.

Finally, of course, Carrie's eventual resolution depended on resources and networks entirely outside the local negotiation. Her husband, the very frequent flier, did an end-run around the whole arena by calling direct to airline staff at a level that had the discretion to supply solutions that fell outside the powers of local agents.

The Moral of the Story

Being nice to airline staff probably gets you further in the US (but may not elsewhere...). and keeping attached to important social networks (like "privileged" frequent flyer memberships) may signal the ongoing importance of "power" in negotiation settings. More importantly, stories like this illustrate what we actually do in negotiation (as opposed to what we prescribe we should do[10]) or what we think we do. Here we had an opportunity for two negotiation experts to watch each other's negotiation behaviors and how they were perceived and handled by others—and we had, at least in theory, similar bargaining situations. The salient bargaining endowments (nationality, gender, status, professional backgrounds, and knowledge of systems) were varied among us and we had a rare opportunity to compare notes and check our perceptions of what we saw and analyzed with several key participant observers, outside ourselves. Whether our tentative conclusions about the effectiveness or effects of negotiation styles, gender, or nationality are accurate or not, we shared some categories of analysis (that many have written about on the foregoing pages) that enable us to describe, reflect on and analyze what we were doing and what was being "done" to us.

From a scholarly perspective, the moral of this story is that we need more of these stories—with systematic opportunities to put different kinds of people with different kinds of negotiating strategies into similar and experimentally controlled (or real-world) situations to study how these factors influence both process and outcomes—nationality, gender, negotiation styles, culture, power, subject matter expertise or experience, professional backgrounds, etc.

From a practice perspective, we might learn more about the continuing disjuncture between what we think our theories explain and what actually happens in the world. Who we are and who we are negotiating with may often trump the most sophisticated efforts to use "integrative" or problem-solving bargaining strategies. Sadly, even with all our efforts to develop theories and to train all kinds of negotiators to use these theories, good old fashioned power (however, manifested in ascribed or achieved statuses) may still have a large impact on what actually gets done in negotiation. Clearly, context matters a great deal[11] in how negotiations unfold. We would do well to study negotiation variations more systematically in more contexts.

So, we hope you have learned something from the pages in this book and this story, which illustrates how one can analyze a negotiation after the fact (considering endogenous and exogenous influences on the process), ... with the help of a fellow traveler.

Endnotes

[1] ERVING GOFFMAN, ENCOUNTERS: TWO STUDIES IN THE SOCIOLOGY OF INTERACTION 134 (1972).

[2] *But see* Gerald Wetlaufer, *The Limits of Integrative Bargaining*, 85 GEORGETOWN LAW .JOURNAL 369 (1996).

[3] *See* FRED HIRSCH, SOCIAL LIMITS TO GROWTH (rev. ed. 1995).

[4] *See, e.g.*, JEANNE M. BRETT, NEGOTIATING GLOBALLY: HOW TO NEGOTIATE DEALS, RESOLVE DISPUTES, AND MAKE DECISIONS ACROSS CULTURAL BOUNDARIES (2001); JESWALD SALACUSE, MAKING GLOBAL DEALS: WHAT EVERY EXECUTIVE SHOULD KNOW ABOUT NEGOTIATING ABROAD (2002).

[5] *See, e.g.*, DEBORAH M. KOLB & JUDITH WILLIAMS, THE SHADOW NEGOTIATION: HOW WOMEN CAN MASTER THE HIDDEN AGENDAS THAT DETERMINE BARGAINING SUCCESS (2000); Carrie Menkel-Meadow, *Teaching About Gender and Negotiation: Sex, Truths, and Videotape*, 16 NEGOTIATION JOURNAL 357 (2000).

[6] In another airport encounter I (Carrie) once overheard an important Washington official, delayed in his travels, scream at the gate agent "DO YOU KNOW WHO I AM? DO SOMETHING!" To which the gate agent with obvious anger management training simply and calmly said, "Sir, if you don't know who you are, I certainly can't help you!" Since then I have been a vigilant student of the gate agent anger management "playbook," (studying what works and what doesn't).

[7] A recent study concludes that women systematically "ask for" less in negotiations—indeed, they see fewer situations as "negotiable events." LINDA BABCOCK & SARA LASCHEVER, WOMEN DON'T ASK: NEGOTIATION AND THE GENDER DIVIDE (2003).

[8] For one relatively crude attempt to specify national negotiation styles, *see* FRANK L. ACUFF, HOW TO NEGOTIATE ANYTHING WITH ANYONE ANYWHERE AROUND THE WORLD (1997).

[9] Carrie Menkel-Meadow, *Portia in a Different Voice: Some Speculations on a Women's Lawyering Process*, 1 BERKELEY WOMEN'S LAW JOURNAL 39 (1985); Ellen C. DuBois, et al., *Feminist Discourse, Moral Values, and the Law*, 34 BUFFALO LAW REVIEW 11 (1985).

[10] Howard Raiffa originally described the differences in prescription and description in negotiation studies. *See* HOWARD RAIFFA, THE ART AND SCIENCE OF NEGOTIATION: HOW TO RESOLVE CONFLICTS AND GET THE BEST OUT OF BARGAINING (1982), *and* HOWARD RAIFFA, ET AL., NEGOTIATION ANALYSIS: THE SCIENCE AND ART OF COLLABORATIVE DECISION MAKING (2002).

[11] *See* Carrie Menkel-Meadow, *Negotiating with Lawyers, Men and Things: The Contextual Approach Still Matters*, 17 NEGOTIATION JOURNAL 257 (2001); Carrie Menkel-Meadow, *Correspondences and Comparisons in International and Domestic Conflict Resolution*, 18 NEGOTIATION JOURNAL 363 (2002).

ೞ 78 ೞ

Professionalism and Misguided Negotiating

Wayne Brazil

Editors' Note: *A settlement judge is in the unique position of observing lots of high-stakes negotiating every day. Here, one of the U.S. federal courts' most highly regarded settlement judges discusses not only his reactions as a professional to the negotiators who come before him, but the kinds of errors they tend to make. Judges are not the only powerful figures who end up mediating our disputes, so if you expect to be negotiating any kind of case before any kind of powerful player, this chapter is important reading.*

There is more than a little hubris in writing an essay that purports to identify errors that other people make. I am not a social scientist, and I am not an expert in negotiation theory. I am a busy judge who is required to know a little something about a host of different subjects—a fact that precludes depth in any one. I agreed to write this essay because the editors of this volume suggested that a description of typically counterproductive behaviors by lawyers in judicially hosted settlement conferences might be interesting to people who study negotiation systematically—and might help them develop generalizations about negotiation dynamics that would be useful in a wider range of settings. To determine whether any such generalizing might be reliable, however, it is essential to understand the specific context in which I work.

The perspective from which I write is very practical (some would say banal), very context-specific,[1] [Miller & Dingwall, *Theater*] and very subjective. I have neither conducted controlled experiments (even with student guinea pigs) nor systematically collected data to support my points—some (or all) of which may be dead wrong.[2] Moreover, I am fairly confident that my views about what works and what doesn't work have roots, at least in part, in my personal values—in my feelings about what it means to be a good person and to behave in respect-worthy ways.

Because my perceptions likely are influenced by my personal values, [Honeyman, *Understanding Mediators*] I should identify the most apparently relevant of those at the outset. I am a secular moralist, and I am fundamentally unsympathetic with some of the norms that are assumed to inform the traditional version of "the adversary system" of civil litigation. I do not respect efforts, no matter how "skillful," to get more for a client than is deserved under the law and evidence. How people treat one another is very important to me. I rank honesty among the highest of values—perhaps in part because I find dishonesty so threatening. I do not like greed or selfishness. And I am much more comfortable with harmony than with discord. If you wonder about my choice of careers, you are not alone.

Over the years I have hosted some 1,500 settlement conferences and have seen a wide range of approaches by lawyers to settlement negotiations. Many lawyers are good negotiators—and many negotiation breakdowns are attributable not to what a lawyer has done, but to conduct or decisions by a client. [Docherty & Caton Campbell, *Agency*] Some lawyers, however, are not good negotiators, and I have seen a goodly number of behaviors that seem to me to have hurt, needlessly, the prospects of reaching agreement. Having been asked to describe some of those behaviors, this essay focuses on negatives, but there is a positive sub-text that is readily discernible. In many instances, the process of explaining why a particular approach or action is counterproductive necessarily involves pointing to its opposite, i.e., the action or approach that I think is more effective or more likely to advance the negotiation.

The Structure of Settlement Conferences

To reduce the risk of misunderstanding (and of generalizing unreliably to very different settings), I will begin this essay by identifying some of the principal features of the typical negotiation setting in which I work. The negotiations that are the subject of this essay are best understood as triangular.[3] They involve two sides and me. Most of the settlement conferences I host are dominated by private caucusing; group sessions are the exception, not the rule. So the negotiations about which I write are almost always at least in some measure mediated (by a neutral) and indirect.

The way I structure my settlement conferences, and the fact that I am a judge, affect my views about the kinds of behaviors by lawyer-negotiators that are productive and appropriate and the kinds that are not. While not all of my settlement conferences are structured identically, in the most common format I begin the process by making a short 'speech' in which I describe how we will proceed, explain why I organize the proceedings the way I do and what my role will be, and make sure everyone understands the confidentiality rules. I emphasize that one of my goals is to reduce the risk of what I call "false failures," i.e., failures to reach an agreement that are caused by someone making a serious social error that irretrievably contaminates the emotional waters or by our collective failure to guess accurately what terms might be accessible. I explain that the goal of neutralizing these sources of failure underlies my decision to conduct the settlement negotiations primarily through private caucuses and is the main reason that the rules permit me to receive "secrets" from one side at a time.

My speech often has an aggressive moral tone as I emphasize my deep personal and professional commitment to honesty and my refusal to try to pressure or manipulate anyone for any purpose. In part to drive home the point about honesty, I also squarely acknowledge the relative shallowness of my knowledge and the considerable risk of fallibility that would attend any opinions I might offer or any guesses about future events in the case that I might make. By insisting that honoring my oath of office and my commitment to personal integrity is much more important to me than achieving a settlement (or any other end) I hope to encourage the parties to feel my sincerity and to trust me.

Encouraging trust is important in my settlement conference system because I become the primary conduit of communication between the participants in the negotiations. Usually we do not begin with a general session, attended by everyone, in which counsel, in *seriatim* and fairly predictable exercises, would set forth their clients' positions. Instead, after my opening speech (and after answering any questions any participant might have), we most often proceed directly to private caucusing (sometimes in the first round with one lawyer at a time, sometimes in the first round with one side at a time). Informed in each instance by these private meetings, I decide what information will flow from one side to the other. I explain each party's views of the dispute and of the negotiating situation to the other parties. I communicate offers and demands across party lines—or, having been told in "secret" by each party what range or zone of terms might be acceptable, I shuttle back and forth between parties trying to assess whether closure is feasible. [Love & Stulberg, *Mediation*]

Given the role I play, a good lawyer-negotiator understands that it is important to earn my respect and confidence [Lewicki, *Trust*]—so that I do not (subconsciously or otherwise) discount the merits of the negotiator's analysis or the credibility of his representations about his client's situation or positions. As the conduit, I become each party's de facto emissary and spokesperson. It is unwise to have a spokesperson whose confidence in you, or whose trust of you, is compromised.

As the preceding paragraphs make clear, the settlement conference process as I usually manage it bears little resemblance to classic mediation (facilitative or transformative). Structurally (not in fact or philosophically), I am at the center and the parties are not. Instead of the parties assuming the primary roles in the mechanics of the process and accepting primary responsibility for the course, character, and outcome of the proceedings, I take up much of this space. The immediate (but not the ultimate) target of the parties' persuasion efforts is me, not the opposing party. And, in the private caucuses, I talk too soon and too much. I interrupt. I often direct the subject-matter course of the discussions. Sometimes I interact more with the lawyers than with their clients. I do not devote a lot of effort to searching for subtle underlying interests or needs. But I do try to identify what is most important to the parties—which, much more often than not in judicially hosted settlement conferences, is money. And most of the time in our negotiating sessions we are attending to (or at least looking repeatedly over our shoulders at) two 800 pound gorillas: the evidence and the law.

My final cautionary admonition is this: there is an expansive range of approaches to settlement work by judges—so mine cannot be "representative." Some settlement judges do no private caucusing. Some are very assertive; some are passive. Some tend to have considerable confidence in their ability to assess reliably the merits and value of cases, even with the limited information that usually is available to a settlement judge. Others are less confident and more cautious—less likely to feel that they can foretell outcome at trial. Some settlement judges are Social Darwinists; some are social engineers. Because of these and other differences, I suspect there is a fairly wide range of opinion among judges about what kinds of lawyering behaviors are most effective or productive in judicially hosted settlement conferences. So generalizing from what you read here is risky business.

Lawyering Mistakes

The kinds of "mistakes"[4] by lawyers in settlement conferences that I would like to discuss first seem to be rooted in failures to understand (or at least to honor) sub-cultural rules or expectations. In this essay I use the phrase "sub-cultural" to refer to loosely grouped sets of norms and practices that civil litigators in the United States generally have come to share. Some of the norms that help define this subculture are set forth formally in rules promulgated by courts, legislatures, or administrative bodies, e.g., rules of professional responsibility, while others have evolved informally as products of the roles counsel play and the goals they pursue. These norms and ways of interacting with other lawyers and with judges must be learned; for the most part, they are not intuitive. But they are powerful—meaning, among other things, that they are deeply ingrained and that failing to follow them can produce considerable anger and backlash from other civil litigators.

Opening Offers

Norms and behaviors related to negotiating settlements form one important part of the civil litigation subculture. While some of the practices and expectations that litigators generally bring to judicially hosted settlement dances seem morally primitive, at least at first blush, they likely have roots in the need to serve psychologically legitimate ends. For example, in the sub-culture of settlement conferences, it is expected that there will be some space between the first offers or demands that are put on the table and the figures that the clients ultimately might agree to accept. [Schneider, *Aspirations*] By knowingly leaving this kind of gap between first figures and 'bottom lines,' counsel open the way for the negotiations to feel substantial, they create room for at least rough parity of movement between the parties (and thus for a sense of symmetry that can increase prospects for reaching an agreement and improve the likelihood that the agreement will stick) [Wade & Honeyman, *Lasting Agreement*], and they enable their opponent to feel that he has accomplished something (when, at the end of the negotiation day, he has "persuaded" his opponent to move his figure into a more favorable zone). Thus, a lawyer who opens the negotiations by putting a number on the table that is very close to his client's real bottom line makes a mistake that can suck the viscera out of the process.

It also is a mistake, however, to put an opening figure on the table that is out of sub-cultural bounds, i.e., that is transparently extreme. Opening negotiations in a settlement conference with a figure that is outside the zone of sub-cultural plausibility can do considerable harm to a lawyer's effectiveness as a negotiator and to prospects for achieving an agreement. Despite suggestions to the contrary in some of the literature,[5] I have never seen an extreme opening figure "anchor" the negotiations in an unrealistic zone. It is quite unlikely that an extreme offer or demand would succeed in moving the center of gravity of negotiations in a judicially hosted settlement conference into some sphere that unjustifiably favors one party. The judge is not likely to take an extreme number seriously—and is not likely to present it as a serious proposition to the other side (because to do so would undermine the judge's credibility and because judges generally do not like to engage in transparent exercises in gaming).

Instead, an opening offer or demand that is extreme makes the offeror look foolish (or at least naive) and untrustworthy (to both the settlement judge and the other side). An extreme opening offer undermines the offeror's credibility—intensifying the risk that no one will take him seriously later in the negotiations when he puts numbers on the table about which he really is serious.[6]

Moreover, an extreme opening offer or demand discourages engagement by the judge and the other parties—it acts as a disincentive to investing substantial effort in the negotiation process. One important form of "engagement" in a judicially hosted settlement conference is analysis of the legal merits of claims and defenses—critical examination of the evidence and of the play of the pertinent law. By definition, an offer or a demand is "extreme" when it is obvious that there is an unbridgeable distance between it and an arguably plausible assessment of the legal viability and value of the plaintiff's claims. That kind of disconnect gives neither the settlement judge nor opposing counsel any basis for believing that the negotiation could be advanced by a serious examination of the substance of the lawsuit.

By making an offer or demand that does not seem rooted, at least in some measure, in the evidence and law, a negotiator also robs his figure of any semblance of "fairness." And fairness, as a concept and as a feeling, can play a significant role even in negotiations between cynical repeat litigation players. An aura of fairness can enhance the power of both a negotiator and of a settlement position—but a lawyer who opens negotiations with an extreme figure squanders his opportunity to capitalize on that source of power.

Putting an extreme offer or demand on the table also communicates disrespect for the intelligence and the worldliness of both the settlement judge and the other players. When people feel disrespected they may get angry; sometimes they stop thinking; sometimes they leave; and sometimes they look for ways to get revenge. Settlement judges are people. So are other litigants and lawyers. Unnecessarily creating an occasion for any of these kinds of responses to an offer or demand obviously is a mistake.

Misleading Signals

A lawyer who does not understand or accept sub-cultural expectations or rules also can inadvertently mislead (and thereby anger) the settlement judge (and, through her, other parties and their counsel). For example, it can be a mistake for a plaintiff's lawyer to tell the judge in private caucus, *relatively early* in the settlement conference, that her client would consider accepting a figure between $100,000 and $150,000—unless what the lawyer really means to communicate is that her client probably would accept $75,000. Experienced settlement judges hear (understand) things in a specialized context. In some settlement contexts, they don't take lawyers' words literally. Instead, they understand the lawyers' words as signals—as direction indicators. One such context is a private meeting (caucus) early in settlement negotiations. In that context, when the plaintiff's lawyer says his client would take between 100 and 150, the judge hears nothing above 100 and is likely to hear 75. And because settlement judges are in the optimism business, because they get paid to cheerlead, cajole, and hope for movement, they might even hear 65. Generally, the earlier in the settlement process, the lower the figure the settlement judge is likely to "hear" signaled in the number that plaintiff's counsel puts on the table (or, if the number is an offer from a defendant, the higher the judge is likely to understand the figure being signaled). A negotiator who does not understand this runs the risk of inviting the settlement judge to make erroneous assumptions about what the client's real settlement position is. Misplaced expectations (especially in the mind of the settlement judge) can wreak havoc on the negotiation process.

Speeches and Speechifying

I should mention one other kind of mistake that is a product of being out of subcultural synch. Lawyers can do harm to their negotiation cause by the way they make their pitches to the settlement judge during private caucuses. In some state courts, settlement judges can devote only a little time to each settlement conference—and sometimes are required to massage negotiations simultaneously in several cases. In that kind of setting, a lawyer has so little time to try to make an impression that it is not considered inappropriate to deliver to the judge, even in private caucus, a compact version of a closing argument.

But in federal courts judges usually can set aside a substantial block of time for each settlement conference. In that setting, settlement judges expect to engage in a more analytically sophisticated dialogue with counsel—especially when in private caucus. Given that expectation, a lawyer who commences his private caucus interaction with the settlement judge by giving a speech (or any other canned-sounding pitch) makes a bad impression. Judges do not want to hear speeches—except, perhaps, from themselves—especially when they are in a private, one-on-one conversation with a lawyer. Judges want to hear reasoning. And they want the reasoning they hear to be case-specific, or at least specific to the considerations the parties consider most relevant to their settlement decisions. [Welsh, *Fairness*]

Moreover, if the client is present in the private caucus, the settlement judge is likely to discount a "speech" or an emotionally charged position pitch by counsel as little more than an attempt by the lawyer to show off in front of his client. The judge also is likely to worry that a lawyer who makes a speech in the presence of his client in a private caucus is serving his client badly by encouraging false expectations that will make settlement more difficult to reach and, if not achieved, will leave the client feeling disappointed or failed by the system. A lawyer negotiator who provokes such worries in the settlement judge, and who runs such risks with his client, is not doing a good job.

A lawyer who uses her time in private with the judge to make her closing argument also invites the judge to infer that she does not understand or pay attention to the specific context in which he is working—that she assumes (thoughtlessly) that she can transport her behavioral formulas willy-nilly from setting to setting. Such a lawyer seems obtuse and insensitive—or at least lazy. Even more damaging (to her credibility with the judge), however, is the impression that she does not treat each of her cases as *sui generis*—that her mind is satisfied with putting cases in fairly large pigeon-holes and then pushing forward with the litigation under the formula for that category of actions. Experienced judges know, however, that each case really is unique, that viability and value are affected substantially by the specific characteristics of the persons involved and by the specific details in which the particular historical story played out. This is why settlement judges want to hear case-specific facts and case-specific analyses.

It bears emphasis that sometimes the considerations that need to receive the greatest play in the settlement dynamic in litigation have little to do with the merits of the case. For example, in a particular case the factor of greatest consequence in the settlement negotiations might be the imminence of a bankruptcy, or the shelf-life of a product, or the relationship between the parties in some other setting, or a party's need to protect his job or to repair his sense of self. Settlement judges want to help the parties work on the things that matter most—so counsel must tell them (*early* in the settlement conference) when something other than the viability and value of a claim is critical to the negotiations. In my experience, however, much more often than not the settlement of civil lawsuits turns on the legal viability and the economic value of the claim—so it is on those subjects that most of the discussion usually is focused.

This is by no means a necessary feature of negotiation in general—and certainly not of mediation. Rather, the ubiquity of the focus on evidence and law is an artifact of the setting in which I work. Because I am a judge, the parties look to me for expertise in and input about law and evidence. Moreover, because the negotiations I host are about whether and how to settle a specific lawsuit, and because the primary relief for which most plaintiffs in civil litigation pray is monetary, the parties generally expect the negotiations that occur in the courthouse to be centered, at least for some portion of the conference, on the legal merits and the economic value of the case.

The fact that the setting and the parties' expectations tend to push law, evidence, and money to center stage in these negotiations, in combination with the fact that many sitting judges have limited negotiation vision and limited process skills, should lead parties who want their settlement dynamic to be centered around matters other than the legal merits and monetary value of their case to search out a different kind of neutral host and to turn to a process with quite different primary features.

When law, evidence, and monetary value are the primary targets of inquiry, however, settlement judges want to feel that the mind of the lawyer who is sitting across the table from them is careful, balanced, attentive to detail and nuance, and fully cognizant of the ubiquity of indeterminacy in human affairs.[7] [Korobkin & Guthrie, *Heuristics*] It follows that overconfidence and bravado, defensiveness and rigidity, or dogged refusal to acknowledge any merit in any dimension of an opponent's case or settlement proposal, are behaviors that are likely to make the settlement judge question the wisdom or intelligence or good faith of the negotiating lawyer. Settlement judges worry that a lawyer whose approach is infected by any of these behaviors really is unsure of herself or her client's position, or is trying to hide something, or that her mind is insufficiently supple and that her analysis is unrealistic and unreliable. If we have that impression, we are not likely to put much stock in her predictions about liability or her assessments of economic value. That fact is likely to dilute the effect of any analytically premised messages (or offers or demands) that she asks us to take to the other side.

Inexperienced lawyers, in particular, often lack confidence (understandably) in their analysis of the case or in their ability as a negotiator, or both. These circumstances sometimes make inexperienced lawyers more rigid and defensive than their more senior counterparts—a problem that can be exacerbated by a young lawyer's worry that he will be required to explain and justify his decisions to a scrutinizing supervising attorney back at the office. However, an experienced settlement judge often will see through a young lawyer's bravado and perceive it as a mask for professional insecurity or for infirmity of legal position. A lawyer disserves his client's interests if his conduct invites the judge to believe that his positions are more likely the product of anxiety than of solid analysis. A settlement judge is more apt to respond positively to a lawyer who is strong enough to acknowledge areas of uncertainty and to be genuinely interested in using private caucuses with the judge to learn—or at least to consider different perspectives and alternative lines of reasoning.

Credibility

A lawyer's credibility stock with the settlement judge also is likely to drop significantly if she appears arrogant or condescending. Judges distrust a legal mind that thinks it has nothing to learn (even from a judge). Judges with ample egos (of whom there are many) are not likely to respond well to a lawyer who appears to think he is more intelligent and wiser than the judge. Good settlement judges know they do not know everything and are eager to learn—but they have to work harder to remain open to inputs from a lawyer who over-estimates the power of his own intelligence or who is condescending. A natural reaction to being treated with condescension is to want to strike back. Judges have natural reactions. It is unwise, to say the least, to make the judge want to strike back at you.

A good lawyer-negotiator does not try to hide from the fact that life is compli-cated. More than occasionally the same evidence can be understood or interpreted (rationally) in different ways by different people. Litigation is a social process—and social processes are unpredictable (at least under the current limitations of our understanding). So, only fools are positive. All other things being equal, a lawyer who is not perceived by the settlement judge as a fool is likely to be a more effective negotiator. [Tinsley, et al., *Reputations*] The good negotiator's goal should be to project a quiet confidence that (1) is based on careful, objective assessment of all the considerations relevant to settlement, and that (2) was developed in a mind that will take in new information and give it appropriate play in the settle-ment dynamic.

Understand the Judge

These observations lead to a related point. Good lawyer-negotiators try to under-stand not only the opposing lawyer and client, but also the person who will be hosting their settlement conference. [Heen & Stone, *Perceptions*] Understanding their host enables them to tailor their behavior appropriately—to proceed in ways that will earn the judge's confidence and to avoid conduct that is likely to under-mine their credibility or make the judge angry (usually silently).

What the lawyer-negotiator should try to understand, in advance, about the settlement judge has two principal dimensions. First, it is important to understand how the settlement judge will structure the settlement conference and what role she will expect each participant to play during the negotiations. Knowing this enables the lawyer to prepare appropriately. As important, it enables the lawyer to prepare his client for what is likely to occur during the conference. One of the most painful mistakes I have ever seen a lawyer make was a result of his failure to explain to his client, thoroughly and clearly, what to expect during an upcoming settlement conference. In one of the conferences I hosted many years ago I opened the proceedings by describing, perfunctorily, how the session would be structured. I did not bother to explain the rationale for the format we would follow—and did not acknowledge that it might seem disrespectful or rude to the clients. I moved immediately into a series of private meetings with one lawyer at a time. I essen-tially ignored the clients (on both sides) for a fairly substantial period—until, unannounced and uninvited, the CEO of the plaintiff corporation burst into my office, demanded to know why he was being left out, and then aggressively as-sumed control of the rest of the process. His lawyer sat there with his head down, literally, for the bulk of the remainder of the "negotiations"—which turned into a fiasco that yielded nothing but bad feelings all around.

I obviously had made serious mistakes by not describing carefully how the ne-gotiations would be structured, by not explaining why I thought it was best (for the parties) to proceed in the manner I described, and by ignoring the real parties in interest for so long. Equally obviously, I was not the only player in this drama to have made a serious mistake. Plaintiff's counsel should have warned his client, explicitly and well in advance of the session, that judges in our region who host settlement conferences sometimes work extensively with the lawyers before in-volving the clients (even though the judges have ordered the clients to attend the conference in person)—and that the process can seem (and be) rude to the people whose views and decisions matter most (the clients). In addition, plaintiff's coun-sel should have informed me (gently), early in our first private caucus, that his client was a person who was accustomed to being in charge and who likely would not react well to being left "in the hall" for any substantial portion of the negotiations. In combination, these mistakes by me and by plaintiff's counsel resulted in a "negotiation" debacle that inflicted real harm on prospects for a consensual disposition of the case.

One moral of this story is that, before a settlement conference convenes, good lawyers learn as much as they can about how their settlement judge operates and about her values and attitudes—and then take considerable care to teach their clients, in advance, what to expect. How much participation by the client will the judge invite? Will the judge give the client real opportunities to be directly involved? Will she put the client on the spot? Will she pressure the client to participate, to disclose sensitive information, to explain or justify the client's conduct, or to change his settlement position? Will the judge be analytically aggressive and opinionated or essentially passive and gentle? Will she be comfortable or impatient with the feints and dissembling that tend to accompany settlement negotiations? Good lawyers understand that there is a wide range of judicial behavior in these settings—and that a client who is taken by surprise by the process, or by the role or behavior of the judge, can be disoriented into anger, withdrawal, or even excessive malleability. Any such reaction can hurt, needlessly, the client's interest in determining reliably what terms of settlement are appropriate and accessible.

In preparing their clients to participate in settlement conferences it is especially important that counsel do their best to ensure that their clients do not develop unrealistic expectations about what terms might be attainable and what kinds of concessions the other parties might make. It is a serious mistake to be overly optimistic about such matters—and not to discuss them candidly and realistically with the client in advance of the session with the judge.

Gaming

A very different category of mistakes that lawyers sometimes make in judicially hosted settlement conferences can be captured in the word "gaming." As I use the term here, "gaming" does not refer to ideas about negotiation dynamics that have been developed by game theorists, [Sally & Jones, *Game Theory*] but to a loose set of inelegant stratagems that some lawyers use to try to leverage more favorable settlement terms from their opponents. Good lawyer-negotiators understand the difference between "gaming," on the one hand, and, on the other, behaviors that are acceptable (even expected) under widely shared sub-cultural norms about conduct in settlement conferences. [Korobkin, et al., *Law of Bargaining*] Outsiders or newcomers to the subculture are less likely to understand that there is a difference—or where the line separating the two kinds of behaviors is likely to be drawn.

As I noted in an earlier section, lawyers experienced in settlement conference work expect there to be some distance between a party's initial demand and his real bottom line. Even when a plaintiff has decided (secretly) that he would accept a settlement of $70,000, neither an experienced defense lawyer nor an experienced settlement judge will feel deceived when plaintiff's counsel says "My client's demand is $100,000." There is no deception (in our subculture) in making such a demand because these words do not purport to represent the plaintiff's real bottom line and because it is generally understood that, unaccompanied by qualifiers, such a statement reflects only a stage in the process, a position currently taken that is likely subject to downward adjustment.

On the other hand, there are a host of behaviors that clearly fall on the "gaming" side of the line. Some of these behaviors are essentially theatrical: manufactured outrage, inflated despair, melodramatic portrayals of pain and suffering. Others are more akin to playground tactics: bullying, threatening to walk out or to take retaliatory action, and yelling. Another form of gaming consists of bald-faced lying—sometimes about what a client would "never" pay or accept, sometimes about circumstances outside the litigation that are used to try to rationalize unreasonable offers or demands, sometimes about the existence or nonexistence of evidence, sometimes about what the party or lawyer will do next if his offer or demand is not accepted. Thus, "gaming" includes prominent (rather than peripheral) settlement negotiation conduct that is calculated to create artificial (falsely premised) pressures or incentives, or to intentionally deceive an opponent (and/or the settlement judge) about facts or circumstances that clearly are material to settlement decisions. There is a recognized difference, in our sub-culture, between false and artificial inflation of fear, on the one hand, and, on the other, efforts to get an opponent to see the full measure of risks that are rooted in real evidence and law. [Putnam, *Communication*] It is out of sub-cultural bounds to try to capitalize on an opponent's risk aversion by lying about what the material evidence is—or about other factors that play significant roles in the settlement calculus. A lawyer who is caught resorting to such tactics loses the settlement judge as an intermediary. He also risks losing his license.

While there is a range of tolerance for gaming among judges, a lawyer who makes no effort to determine where the host of his settlement conference falls on this spectrum of tolerance risks serious error. Generally, a lawyer-negotiator is likely to do more harm to his client's interests by overestimating a judge's tolerance for gaming than by underestimating that tolerance. Almost regardless of how they practiced before they took the bench, judges tend to lose patience with tactical maneuvering by counsel—in part because it interferes with their ability to do their job, in part because it adds burdens to their already heavy workload, and in part because when they become judges their professional lives are dominated by a new client: justice. That new client changes their perspective and re-arranges their sense of professional self. At the center of that new sense of self there usually is a deep attachment to rationality and fairness—especially procedural fairness. [Welsh, *Fairness*]

A judge who defines herself by how well she promotes these values is not likely to abandon them just because she is hosting a settlement conference. A judge who is hosting a settlement conference is still a judge. Know your host. Because judges care so much about procedural integrity and substantive fairness, and because they are inclined to assume that the way to identify what is fair is to reason carefully and honestly about evidence and law, judges hosting settlement conferences are not likely to respect a lawyer whose approach to negotiations appears to be dominated by tactical maneuvering or pursuit of leverage that has no roots in the relevant facts or legal principles.

Thus, it is a mistake to rush to the numbers—instead of first working through the substantive considerations that should inform the numbers. Similarly, it is a mistake to disclose a real bottom line (in a private caucus) to a settlement judge early in a settlement conference and then ask the judge to try to negotiate an appreciably better deal. And it is a mistake to try to use the judicial host to "nickel and dime" marginally better terms from an opponent.

For similar reasons, a settlement judge is not likely to be impressed by a lawyer-negotiator whose approaches or positions seem excessively reactive—born much more out of response to what the other side does than out of the merits of the underlying dispute (or out of real circumstances outside the litigation that legitimately affect settlement decisions). It is a mistake, for example, for a lawyer-negotiator to let the settlement judge first hear about the most significant weaknesses in his client's case from his opponent. Instead, an effective negotiator in a judicially hosted settlement conference anticipates and acknowledges his opponent's arguments—but makes sure they are considered in full context and that appropriate weight is accorded the strongest counter-arguments.

Trust

One of the goals of a good lawyer-negotiator is to encourage others (the settlement judge, opposing counsel, opposing parties, and his own client) to trust him. Telling even "little" lies can be hazardous. For example, a lawyer takes potentially significant credibility risks if he tells the settlement judge in private caucus that his client's bottom line is X—when it really isn't. That kind of lie risks premature termination of the settlement conference and false failure of the negotiations—and it reduces the likelihood that the settlement judge will believe other assertions made by the lawyer.

A lawyer also can provoke distrust by trying to add components to his client's settlement demand after the parties have worked hard to negotiate an agreement on all the components of the demand that counsel made on behalf of his client at the outset of the negotiations. Belated or *seriatim* addition of conditions, or "necessary" elements of an agreement, can make opposing parties feel abused and manipulated, feelings that can bring the whole settlement edifice down in an irremediable crash.[Wade, *Last Gap*]

Distrust also can be generated by the way counsel talk about other people—even during private caucuses with the judge. It is a mistake to belittle an opponent's abilities or to impugn his professionalism in these settings. A gratuitous *ad hominem* (even in private) shrivels the speaker. And given our sub-cultural commandments about loyalty to clients, a lawyer whose private barbs target his own client is especially likely to be disrespected and distrusted.

A lawyer-negotiator creates an even more fundamental problem for himself if he appears to the settlement judge to elevate his own interests (usually in a fee) over the interests of his client. [Nolan-Haley, *Informed Consent*] This impression can be conveyed, for example, when a lawyer pressures an unsophisticated client to insist on immediate payment of a large settlement (enabling the lawyer to get his full contingency fee right away) instead of establishing a trust fund that would provide a steady stream of income over time while protecting much of the corpus from improvident investment decisions or impulsive expenditures.

A lawyer who intimates (in private caucus) that he is hiding a witness or a document that would be damaging to his client also commits a grievous error[8]—potentially forcing the settlement judge to withdraw from the negotiations, thereby setting off alarm bells for the opposing party.

As some of these observations suggest, how lawyer-negotiators conduct themselves during settlement conferences can affect, sometimes significantly, how the settlement judge spends her time and energy, as well as the character of the role she decides to play in the negotiations. Judges are human beings who have predictable human reactions to the conduct and events they encounter. A settlement judge will react (even if not always visibly) to how others are acting in her presence and to how others treat her. A lawyer whose conduct strays from sub-culturally acceptable paths, or from courses that the judge finds comfortable or constructive, distracts the judge from her primary responsibilities and forces her to spend energy and thought trying to control her reactions and her conduct, energy and thought that she could otherwise spend more productively trying to determine how best to proceed with the negotiations.

Many lawyers don't seem to consider tailoring the way they handle themselves in settlement conferences so as to encourage the settlement judge to move into a mode that best fits the circumstances of the particular case or that would best promote the client's interests. For example, lawyers can steer the judge toward an analytical role by being analytical and seeking analytical feedback. And lawyers can increase the amount of energy and time a judge commits to a settlement conference by making clear their client's interest in trying to settle the case and by giving legs to the process by making concessions or adjustments in their positions at timely junctures.

On the other hand, lawyers whose approach is transparently dominated by tactics, or who seem to be interested only in number swapping, or who insist pugnaciously that their client's position is set in cement, or who are bent on being hard-knuckled and intimidating, are more likely to find that their judicial host is inclined to limit her role—as well as the time she is willing to spend trying to help the parties reach an agreement. So lawyers who really want help from the judge in the settlement process err badly when they adopt an approach that the judge disrespects or that gives her little incentive to commit much of herself to the negotiations.

Emotions

Lawyer-negotiators also can disserve their client's interests by the way they handle their emotions in settlement conferences. While most judges are likely to respect a lawyer who seems genuinely to care about his client and his client's cause, a lawyer who is intensely emotional risks compromising his effectiveness and reducing the likelihood that a settlement conference will be productive. Some settlement judges will be suspicious that a display of emotion from counsel is merely a theatrical device—manufactured to evoke sympathy or to distract attention from substantive weaknesses in a party's position. But even if the lawyer's emotion is perceived as genuine, its presence and prominence can shift the judge's focus away from the activities through which she, as a judge (rather than a therapist or counselor), is best equipped to contribute to the productivity of the settlement dynamic—facilitating careful analysis and clear communication. [Shapiro, *Emotions*]

Moreover, a settlement judge who encounters an intensely emotional lawyer, especially in a private caucus, is likely to fear that the lawyer has fallen victim to ego-blur: that he has become so identified with his client or cause that he has lost his capacity for objective analysis. A judge with such concerns is not likely to be a convincing emissary. And if a lawyer's emotionalism persists it can drive the settlement judge to withdraw completely from the negotiations. Many judges do not trust their ability to deal appropriately with intense emotion, and some will abandon the process because they fear that an intensely emotional lawyer presents an insurmountable barrier to reaching a settlement.

I do not mean to suggest that only robots of rationalism are effective in judicially hosted settlement conferences. Judges understand that people who are involved in litigation, both clients and lawyers, often are accompanied by strong feelings. It is a mistake to ignore or trivialize genuine emotions in these settings. It can be important to acknowledge them—and, sometimes, to give them significant play in a safe environment that is made part of the settlement conference process. But, reasonably or not, settlement judges expect lawyers to think more than feel. So a lawyer whose approach seems dominated by emotion is not likely to enjoy as much credibility with a settlement judge as a lawyer who demonstrates an ability to remain calm and on analytical target. Judges respect a kind of self-control that permits a lawyer to listen—to remain open to new information and lines of reasoning and to incorporate them into a more richly textured understanding of all the circumstances pertinent to the settlement decision. Thus, genuine conviction, strongly felt, is likely to have the most telling effect (on the settlement judge and other parties) when it seems to emerge naturally, in warmth rather than fire, after and as the product of a long dialectical process that has included real consideration of all sides of the matter.

I conclude where I began—emphasizing that these are the observations and opinions of only one judge, a judge who understands that there is a wide range of views on these matters and that the most appropriate and effective approaches to negotiating likely vary, appreciably, with the circumstances and the people involved in any given settlement conference.

Endnotes

[1] The setting in which a negotiation takes place exerts its own power on how that negotiation will play out and on what options even appear tenable to the parties. *See* Gale Miller & Robert Dingwall, *When the Play's in the Wrong Theater*, Chapter 6 in this volume.

[2] *See* Andrea Kupfer Schneider, *Shattering Negotiation Myths: Empirical Evidence On The Effectiveness Of Negotiation Style*, 7 HARVARD NEGOTIATION LAW REVIEW 143 (2002), for empirical support of some of these points.

[3] In a substantial number of my settlement conferences the negotiations have more dimensions than the triangle image captures. Sometimes, for example, there are several parties on one side—and the settlement conference includes some negotiating between parties on that same side. Sometimes a party and its insurer need to engage in negotiations. And sometimes there are differences of view between a party and her lawyer—so the conference includes some negotiating between client and her counsel.

[4] Having made no effort to rank the behaviors that I describe in this essay by how often they occur or how severely they damage negotiations, the sequence in which I discuss them is essentially random.

[5] Citing several studies (empirical or experimental), and data generated by their own experiment, Russell Korobkin and Chris Guthrie assert that "a litigant is likely to achieve a more advantageous settlement if he opens negotiations with an extreme, rather than a moderate, settlement offer." Russell Korobkin & Chris Guthrie, *Opening Offers and Out-of-Court Settlement: A Little Moderation May Not Go a Long Way*, 10 OHIO STATE JOURNAL ON DISPUTE RESOLUTION 1, 4 and n. 18 (1994). I'm not sure what accounts for the apparent difference between this view and my experience. Part of the answer might lie in semantics: perhaps I have become so acculturated that what looks like an "extreme" offer or demand to an outside observer looks perfectly normal (as an opening figure) to me. Another source of the differences between our views may be differences between the settings from which we are trying to draw lessons. The subjects of the experiments that Korobkin and Guthrie conducted were undergraduate college students. They did not engage in negotiations that were interactive or mediated, or that involved more than two offers/demands. The hypotheticals assumed a very short and socially sterilized "negotiation"—and the students were not negotiating with or about anything that was real to them. They faced no real risks and could contemplate no real rewards. In sharp contrast, I host settlement conferences in real litigation that is proceeding in federal court. The participants in my settlement conferences are the parties to the litigation and their lawyers—adults who are

engaged in prolonged and usually expensive struggles over very real money. Moreover, the lawyers are likely to understand that, as an experienced judge, I am not likely to help them try to move the negotiations into an obviously unrealistic (or "unfair") zone. So the active participation of a neutral also is a difference between our data sets that could help explain the differences in our perceptions of settlement dynamics.

[6] Schneider, *supra* note 2 (demonstrating a link between adversarial behavior—like extreme offers—and perceived ineffectiveness).

[7] For a number of reasons researched by social psychologists, such a state of mind is an aspiration often not actually reached at a negotiation table. There are also indications that lawyers in particular wrongly believe their professional training enables them to be fully rational. *See* Jeffrey M. Senger & Christopher Honeyman, *Cracking the Hard-Boiled Student: Some Ways to Turn Research Findings Into Effective Training Exercises*, *in* THE CONFLICT RESOLUTION PRACTITIONER (2001), *available at* http://www.convenor.com/madison/Hard-Boiled%20Student.pdf (last visited May 1, 2006).

[8] Admissions (in private caucus) of this kind of serious misconduct are quite rare.

Ulysses and Business Negotiation

Daniel Rose

Editors' Note: Does Adler's "protean negotiator" really exist, or is this just an ideal type with no real relevance to the hard cold world of business? And does your reputation as someone who cares about the other side help you or hurt you, when it's time to supply the goods and get your price? Here, a businessman with an impeccable reputation makes a radical case: real businesses, which employ real people, must establish and keep a reputation for honesty in their dealings, or they are unlikely to get to be (or remain) big *businesses. The implications are everywhere; just read the newspapers. But people who instinctively believe they should behave well and take the long view in business negotiations have more allies, at the top levels, than they realize.*

Public confidence in individuals, organizations, business and government today is at unprecedented low levels; and that affects attitudes toward how one sees the world. This loss of trust is neither parochial nor national; it is not limited to any one social class, ethnic or religious group or region.

Fidel Castro reports that over half of Cuba's state-controlled petroleum supplies are stolen by Cubans each year; international bankers estimate the billions of dollars donated to Nigeria by the world community are almost exactly equal to the secret deposits in Swiss banks made by Nigerian government officials and their families; the oil-for-food scandals of the U.N. stimulate joking references to "Ali Baba and his 40 diplomats;" Russia's political system has been described as "kleptocracy;" the U.S President's credibility has rarely been so low; in the United States and in Ireland, the Catholic Church is seen as more protective of its priests than of its young male acolytes; and on and on.

In the business world, the scandals of Enron, Tyco and WorldCom were bad enough; even more heartbreaking (and unexpected) was the complicity of the world's leading public accounting firms. And it is a fact of life that, among private individuals, small firms, start-ups and others that feel they are below the radar screen of public awareness, some do anything they like to succeed; their unscrupulous, even blatantly illegal, behavior reflects Immanuel Kant's "crooked timber of humanity from which no straight thing can be made."

At the extreme of the negotiation spectrum is outright fraud, which in law has six characteristics: [Korobkin, et al., *Law of Bargaining*]

- Knowing
- Misrepresentation (of)
- Material
- Facts

- On which the victim reasonably relies
- Resulting in damages

Threats, bribes, kickbacks and other forms of corruption are not unknown. Avoiding negotiations with such perpetrators entirely, if possible, is best. If that is not possible, one should try to enlist the services of experienced third parties, seek independent sources for facts and evaluations, use standardized contract procedures, and carefully check applicable laws and regulations. Verify what you can; get important claims stated precisely and in writing, if possible; request bonds or warranties. So yes, bad adversaries do appear on the scene from time to time.

But fortunately, the vast majority of larger, well-known, highly-regarded business practitioners "march to the beat of a different drummer;" and it is they who set the tone and establish the standards of "what is done" and "what is not done." It is easy to overlook the principle that the larger, the more visible, and more subject to public scrutiny an organization is, the likelier it is to strive for public approbation. Thank heaven for that, for it is those standards that establish the level of trust that a modern society must have to function successfully.

High standards are important in all areas of life, but particularly so in business, because large-scale modern business *requires* public trust for its success. The stakeholders in large-scale modern business organizations—the stock owners, the employees, the suppliers, the customers, the government and the general public—will lower substantially what are called the "transaction costs" of businesses they trust.

Google, Inc., for example, is better able to resist international controls because some three quarters of the American public give Google in particular, but technology firms in general, high ratings for "innovative, reasonably-priced products that enhance their daily lives."

Companies like Johnson & Johnson, Coca-Cola, 3M and Sony have real economic advantages because the public trusts them. Companies like UPS and FedEx are regarded as more reliable than government services; and although the governments may still echo the comment of Herodotus ("Neither snow nor rain nor heat nor gloom of night stays these couriers from the swift completion of their appointed rounds"), the public increasingly puts its trust in, and its cash on, FedEx.

That is negotiation writ large: FedEx and UPS have made promises to the public; the public recognizes by its shift of package business to these firms that the firms generally keep their promises; and millions of transactions a day are the result. (Employees of those companies with "bad press," on the other hand, like Halliburton or Philip Morris, find themselves needing to prove even to their children and their neighbors why they are not to be distrusted.)

In the long run, "accountability" is the key concept of the modern business enterprise. This has been the stated position of business and economic thinkers since Adam Smith, in his *Wealth of Nations* and his *Theory of Moral Sentiments*. But this is not just a matter of theory or principle. It is clearly and demonstrably advantageous for business to operate in a climate of trust; even hard-nosed business schools increasingly emphasize that throughout their curricula.

It is unfortunate that our culture's view of "business" was formulated before the evolution of the modern business enterprise, because moral dealings—ethical negotiations, in other words—for most of these enterprises are necessitated by real-world pressures. Employees want to feel proud of their companies; customer loyalty (acquired by perceptions of reliability and fairness) is "money in the bank"; and public condemnation is likely to be followed in time by public legal regulation. The SEC was established after the 1929 crash, in part, to respond to perceived unethical conduct by big shareholders; Sarbanes-Oxley is a direct result of the Enron and Tyco scandals. The current scandal over CEO salaries may well result in regulation (or at least disclosure requirements.) In modern business, it pays to be, and to be seen to be, on the side of the good guys.

Distrust of business has deep and ancient roots. The warrior class was traditionally ennobled; professionals such as doctors, lawyers, architects and the like were presumed to be motivated by more than self-interest; the clergy were guided by God; the farmer or small artisan earned his bread "by the sweat of his brow,"— a fair exchange. It was the moneychanger, by contrast, who was driven from the Temple. Economic exchange was seen as a "zero sum game," in which one person's gain was at someone else's expense; the modern concept of "value added" was unknown. It is easy to see why, in such a climate, the rich man's chance of Heaven and the camel's of passing through the needle were similar.

Yet even in the ancient world, there were those who thought and acted like modern business leaders. Ulysses, the best example, demonstrated in the *Odyssey* an ability to think creatively with a long-term horizon; to recognize opportunities not seen by others; to listen and to learn, to share knowledge with his team, and to lead by example. He knew that to be trusted he must be trustworthy. Commitment, passion, courage and the ability to negotiate successfully and credibly with an array of stakeholders were Fortune 500 CEO traits which Ulysses in Homer's epic demonstrated two millennia ago. They still work today.

The best modern leaders try to function in a climate of tangible integrity, with "self-interest" seen as "enlightened self-interest." They know that when they fall short, the public is watching. Just as Sarbanes-Oxley regulations—now a major nuisance and significant expense for all business—was the government reaction to public accounting failures, so future abuses will likely lead to additional regulation (and prison terms where indicated).

Every business needs a profitable "bottom line" to justify its existence. Profit, though perhaps not "sufficient," is "necessary;" and transparency and public spiritedness are meaningless for an enterprise in a free market economy that does not give its stockholders an appropriate return on their equity, provide employees with competitive salaries and benefits, and offer its leaders sufficient incentive. The necessary optimizing of income and optimizing of expenses are managements' continuing challenges, if they hope to continue to lead.

To achieve these goals, in some situations management will act like poker or chess players, following the rules but using any permissible strategy to overcome an opponent. In others, they will win by acting like team members with common goals. In some relationships, they act like farmers fattening livestock for the butcher; in others, like farmers nurturing sheep for their wool. But in each case, accountability and enlightened self-interest are what you can expect from the best firms. *Gamesmanship*, Stephen Potter's humorous classic, had as its subtitle, *How to Win Without ACTUALLY Cheating*.[1] Winning by 'gamesmanship' is OK; but cheating is not.

Thus the good negotiators in business—like those in labor disputes, nuclear arms treaty discussions, international trade pacts and the like—do not need to be told to think of themselves as adversaries, but also as colleagues; they already do. [Tinsley, et al., *Reputations*] Their goal is to advance their own interests, of course, but to do so in a context of continuing relationships and an acknowledgment that one's opponent must come away with enough so he will "continue to play the game."

Self-interest is not to be confused with selfishness, as Adam Smith reminds us in perhaps the most famous passage in all economic literature, "It is not from the benevolence of the butcher, the brewer or the baker that we expect our dinner, but from their regard to their own self-interest."[2] *Their* interest, yes, but *our* dinner; and each of us wins.

Good will and a favorable reputation may be intangibles not reflected on corporate ledgers, but their value is indisputable; and every business field has stories of individuals or companies whose actions were above and beyond the call of duty, at short-term expense but of great long-term repayment.

In the New York real estate field, for example, the 9/11 catastrophe provided occasions for the demonstration of company values that were not reported in the press, not conducted with an eye to formal "P.R.," but that engendered trust and loyalty.

In one particular high-rise residential building a few hundred yards from the World Trade Center site, tenants were prevented from returning to their apartments for a number of days, with their dogs and cats and plantings unattended, with some windows left open to the soot and fly ash from the nearby fires. Although senior building personnel too were offered immediate evacuation, they never left the structure, using master keys to enter apartments to feed cats or canaries, walk dogs, water plants, close windows and in some cases to vacuum furniture and wash down soot-covered walls. Tenants in the building were notified by e-mail that no rent would be charged from 9/11 until re-occupancy, and moreover, that anyone wishing an immediate lease cancellation would be accommodated—without the contractual penalty. Key to this story, though, is this: I know for a fact that the staff of that firm never informed its chief officer of these decisions till afterward—simply because they regarded these matters as not calling for any decision up top. That, to me, demonstrates that the ethical culture of dealings was not a matter of a few of the company's executives alone, but was deeply ingrained in the ordinary expectations of their staff. And that's how it should be— and is, throughout the better firms.

The pride that the company's far-flung employees took in those actions, the goodwill and loyalty aroused among tenants in the building, the warm feelings from mortgagees, bankers and professional colleagues (not to mention the profound satisfaction of the company's leaders) are remembered years after the profit and loss statements of 2001 were filed.

Are factors such as pride, reputation and good will important in "negotiations?" I would argue that although they are intangible, they are absolutely real.

In *The Moral Consequences of Economic Growth*, a brilliant new book destined to become a classic, Harvard professor Benjamin Friedman points out that improving economic conditions in a society strengthens democracy and the prospects for freedom, and that the modern business enterprise is the key vehicle to achieve that growth and well-being.[3]

Economically effective and socially responsible business organizations are fundamental parts of modern society. The values they espouse, the standards they set for themselves and the degree to which they implement them have profound ramifications. The aged Ulysses, as portrayed in Tennyson's wonderful poem, would have loved the demanding challenge of running such a corporation.

Endnotes

[1] STEPHEN POTTER, THE THEORY AND PRACTICE OF GAMESMANSHIP: OR THE ART OF WINNING GAMES WITHOUT ACTUALLY CHEATING (1998).
[2] ADAM SMITH, THE WEALTH OF NATIONS 2 (1776, 1937).
[3] BENJAMIN FRIEDMAN, THE MORAL CONSEQUENCES OF ECONOMIC GROWTH (2005).

⠃ 80 ⠆

A New Future For Kashmir?

Ambassador John W. McDonald

Editors' Note: *Only rarely is the public privileged to track a major negotiation and see up close whether the theories actually get put into practice. A multitude of other chapters in the book are implicated here as Ambassador McDonald talks about the prevailing assumptions, the intractable conflict, and a breakthrough move toward progress in the decades-old conflict between India and Pakistan over Kashmir. This chapter stands particularly as a practical illustration, by a consummate practitioner, of the principles explained in the chapters by Coleman et al. and Adler.*

In late November 1995, I was visited in my office in downtown Washington, D.C. by two three-star generals, one from India and the other from Pakistan. Given the animosity between these countries, the mere fact that they would travel across town together for such a visit was itself extraordinary. Within two minutes of their arrival, they asked me to solve the "Kashmir Problem!"

I was honored by their visit and stunned by their request. I laughed unbelievingly at their suggestion and then said "No, I can't do that." But they were very serious career military officers and meant what they asked. We spent the rest of the day talking.

The two Generals told me that they had fought two wars against each other over Kashmir and did not want to fight a third one. I learned they had both recently retired from the military and had been invited by the renowned Stimpson Center to come to Washington, D.C. for six weeks. They had heard about our Institute for Multi-Track Diplomacy (IMTD) from a mutual friend, learned about our systems approach to peace through conflict resolution skill building, and decided to visit us.

They said their two governments were "stuck in time" and did not know what to do. Both governments had repeatedly rejected help from other governments over the issue of Kashmir saying they would resolve the problem themselves. But they had made no progress since 1947, and the problem was just getting worse. It was the Generals' belief that IMTD, being a small, not-for-profit, non-governmental organization (NGO) that would not be seen as a threat to anyone, might have some ideas that could move the two governments to take some positive action, or at least help reduce some of the ongoing violence.

The Province of Jammu and Kashmir has been a thorn in the sides of both Pakistan and India since 1947, when India broke away from the British Empire and the country of Pakistan was created as a new Muslim nation. Even though the Province was 85% Muslim, the then Maharaja decided at the last moment to remain a part of India.

The issue of who "owns" Kashmir became the root cause of the conflict and continues to be so to this day. The nuclear arms issue of recent years has only exacerbated the "Kashmir Problem."

In 1965, after the second Kashmir war, a "Line of Control" ("LoC") was established along the cease-fire line, dividing the province. The six million people in the south of the province are now a part of India and administered by the Indian government. The three million people in the north are a part of Pakistan and administered by that government. The two parts have been totally sealed off from each other since the LoC was created.

The purpose of this chapter is to show how, after many years of thinking not once, but many times, "outside the box," and with patience, perseverance, countless fundraising efforts and cooperation between governments and an NGO, a goal can be achieved that was once thought impossible. I will talk about how IMTD did, after all, get involved in the Kashmir question and how IMTD used a several-pronged approach: utilizing the role of business in peacebuilding; training in negotiation and conflict resolution skills of Azad (Pakistani) Kashmiri; bringing Kashmiri citizens from both sides of the LoC together for training in conflict resolution; and finally, establishing a People's Bus that allows families who were separated from each other for 57 years to come together. Each of these was an essential phase.

IMTD Responds

Two years went by with no action on our part to the Generals' critical invitation to get involved with Kashmir because no one in the funding community was interested. We don't charge for our services overseas so we have to raise funds to carry out the projects requested by the people in a conflict situation. Unfortunately, we could not raise any money for Kashmir.

Suddenly four things happened. In 1997, the McKnight Foundation in Minneapolis and later the Sasakawa Peace Foundation in Tokyo were intrigued about our proposal to involve the business communities in India and Pakistan in a Kashmir peace process and came up with generous funding.

At about the same time, three other things happened. I was visited by the Indian Director of an NGO in Bombay who had done some excellent analysis of the Indian-Kashmir situation. We spoke at length and I put forward my idea of trying to involve some members of the business community in the Kashmir problem. I said there were three power centers in India—the government, the military, and business—and while business did not talk to the other two, they could play a key role in a peace process. I pointed out that in 1988 there were 800,000 visitors to Kashmir and a few months later the number dropped to zero because of fear. The economy collapsed because the conflict had become violent again. If business could take a long-term view of the conflict and become involved they could help reduce the fear, and as tourists returned to the Valley they could invest or re-invest in the region. He liked the idea and invited me to Bombay to meet some business leaders.

The very next day, through the State Department's International Visitors Program, I was visited by a distinguished parliamentary leader from Pakistan who was also a businessman. We had virtually the same conversation, and he invited me to Lahore to meet business leaders there and in Karachi. A week later, I received a letter from an Indian businesswoman who was a consultant to the PHD (Punjab) Chamber of Commerce[1] in New Delhi. She expressed interest in helping develop the role of business and peace and invited me to Delhi.

Dr. Louise Diamond (the co-founder of IMTD) and I talked. She said that in her belief system the coming together of this synergy was a powerful indicator that we should move, and so we started on a journey that continues to this day.

The Role of Business

We had funds on hand to continue our training with the Dalai Lama and the Government of Tibet-in-Exile in Dharamsala, in Northeast India. While we were there we visited New Delhi and Bombay and then Lahore and Karachi over the next several years, in order to build trust relationships with members of the business community in both countries.

IMTD also sent staff members to South Africa, Northern Ireland, Cyprus and Israel-Palestine to develop case studies on the positive role the business community in each of these conflicted areas played in furthering the peace process. In each instance business people, working quietly behind the scenes, away from the press and the TV, put their egos behind them and achieved remarkable changes. These case studies later proved very useful in the discussions with business leaders from India and Pakistan.

In 2001, we held a training session at the PHD Chamber of Commerce for 28 Indian business leaders on their potential role in the Kashmir conflict. A few months later we carried out the same program in Lahore for 50 Pakistani business leaders at LUMS University, which has the most important MBA program in the country. This session was opened by the three-star general from Pakistan who had started me on this path in 1995. He was brilliant in his presentation and totally dedicated to our cause.

We provided all participants with our four case studies to show these business leaders what was possible and to let them see that they were not the first to get involved in a peace process. We also had two distinguished American business leaders as a part of our team for both trainings. Both spoke eloquently about their efforts in the United States to build peaceful communities.

Our long-term plan was to work separately with business leaders and then bring both sides together in addition to working separately with the Kashmiri— and then to bring all four groups together to dialogue. Unfortunately this has not yet come to pass because our two funding organizations had a change of heart. The McKnight Foundation Board decided to support only projects in the State of Minnesota, and the Sasakawa Foundation said "if they stop, we stop." So we had to look elsewhere for resources and continue doing so.

Kashmir—Training for Azad Kashmiri

Pakistan-administered Kashmir, or as they say in Pakistan, Azad Kashmir, which means "Free Kashmir," is a semi-independent, democratic province of Pakistan with its own constitution, parliament, and justice system headed by a Supreme Court, and a multi-party political system with free, non-violent elections and a free press. In fact, two years ago, as a result of a free election, the party in power lost, and there was a peaceful transfer of power to the opposition party.

India-administered Kashmir, however, is another story. Its six million citizens are "protected" by some 700,000 military, police and border guards from the militants across the LoC. Unfortunately, most Indian Kashmiri are quite uninformed about Azad Kashmir and think "they" are all "terrorists over there."

Both the Indian and Pakistan Governments do have one thing in common. For over 55 years neither government had ever asked the citizens of Kashmir what they wanted for their own political future. It seemed as though New Delhi and Islamabad always knew what was best for their Kashmiri. This has now begun to change for the better. I was visited recently by a newly appointed Minister for Kashmir Affairs and Northern Areas from the Government of Pakistan. He was a very personable and impressive individual who was truly concerned about the future of the people living in those areas.

In 1993, while attending an important conference dealing with existing international conflicts sponsored by the United States Institute of Peace in Washington, D.C. I met an exceptional man from Azad Kashmir, Shah Ghulam Qadir, the head of an NGO called the Kashmir Institute of International Relations (KIIR). He was on a panel at that conference talking about Kashmir and got on very well with the Indian panelist who was giving his views of the conflict. The three of us met for coffee afterwards, and I began a friendship with Shah Ghulam Qadir, which has lasted to this day. Shah was the first person I contacted when we decided to take on Kashmir as an IMTD project. He has been a major player in our work ever since as he has dedicated his life to the peaceful resolution of the "Kashmir problem."

In 2000, during one of my trips to the region, Shah asked me if it would be possible for IMTD to train parliamentary leaders from Muzaffarabad, the capital of Azad Kashmir, in negotiation and diplomatic skills. I was delighted at the invitation and asked when he would like us to go to Pakistan to begin the training. He answered "You don't understand. I want the training to take place in Washington D. C. so that we can learn more about the world. We are so isolated in Azad Kashmir."

Since that conversation, we have carried out five week-long training session for some 75 parliamentary leaders, cabinet ministers, members of the opposition party, NGOs, and university professors. We have taken these groups to the State Department, the United States Institute of Peace (USIP), the Federal Mediation Service, and leading NGOs like the Stimpson Center and Center for Strategic and International Studies (CSIS), and time has proven that all parties have greatly benefited from these exchanges of ideas.

Bringing Kashmir Citizens Together in Nepal

Part of my long-term goal was to bring together Kashmiri from both sides of the LoC. After a long struggle, we finally got funds from a private donor and the USIP for a week-long dialogue and training session for ten civil society leaders from Azad Kashmir and ten civil society leaders from Indian Kashmir.

The meeting took place in August 2004 at a peaceful retreat, a lodge in Dhulikhel, an hour outside of the city of Kathmandu, Nepal. We had a great team, with Dr. Eileen Borris, Mr. Ladia Michalcik, IMTD's Program Officer, and me. We chose this resort away from the city because of its beauty, comfort, location and, most importantly, its reasonable cost and the fact that visitors from India did not need a visa to come to Nepal.

This historic coming together of Kashmiri from both sides of the LoC, the first of its kind since separation in 1947, was a great success. Yet some parts of our initiative were difficult to organize.

There was fear and concern on all sides. What finally made it happen, however, was the trust relationships we had built up over the years. Both sides knew we had no hidden agenda and were not pushing any particular "solution" to the Kashmir problem. The Pakistan side was easier for us to organize thanks to our contacts with Shah Qadir. KIIR, with whom we had worked for years, followed our guidelines on the selection of participants and chose all ten Azad Kashmir members.

The Indian side was quite different, and it took time and caused some anguish. There are no NGOs in Indian Kashmir, and we had to ask for recommendations from our many friends in India and Kashmir. We contacted those who were recommended, one by one, over the telephone, to tell them of our plan and convince them it was safe to participate. Our choice of location in Nepal was very helpful in this regard.

With great patience and skill the "Indian Ten" were finally selected. We were pleased that women from both sides of Kashmir signed up to participate. On the Indian side, six of the ten were women, and two were women from Azad Kashmir. This was quite an accomplishment in itself. Interestingly, neither side thought the other would show up in Kathmandu. All 20 participants did arrive, though, and our training began.

We met with each group separately for several hours to get acquainted and explain what we thought the week would be like. Then we all had dinner together. Breaking bread as a group has been a sign of peacebuilding across history. After dinner, we sat together and the trust-building process began. While they all spoke Kashmiri and English, they were separated by history for 57 years and had little accurate information about each other.

One little event really broke the ice and helped the 20 individuals begin to come together. One of the men from Azad Kashmir talked about his sister, who lived in the city of Jammu on the Indian side of Kashmir, and about how angry and frustrated he was because, although he only lived 50 kilometers away, he could never visit her as he could not cross the LoC. One of the Indian women said, "I live in Jammu. Where does your sister live?" He told her, and she said, "Why, that is only ten minutes from where I live. Why don't you write her a letter, and we will take some pictures together. When I get home I will visit your sister and tell her all about our time together and give her the letter and the pictures." That powerful little gesture of friendship changed the atmosphere completely.

At the end of our training session, we all went to the airport together and there were many hugs and some tears. The group had bonded. The promises to keep in touch have been maintained, a web page has been established, and the Indian side is trying to establish their own NGO in Kashmir.

We applied for additional funding to carry out a second "coming together" to build on the first successful approach to bring Kashmiri citizens from both sides of the LoC together. This has now occurred.

The People's Bus

In April 2001, during one of my trips to Azad Kashmir, Shah Qadir asked me if I would like to visit a refugee camp near the capital city of Muzaffarabad. I did not know there was such a camp and agreed to the visit. There were some one thousand people living in the camp, under miserable conditions, all of whom had fled from the Indian side of the LoC in fear of their lives. Many were injured and in poor health. I asked why UN agencies such as UNHCR, UNICEF, UNDP or WFP were not helping out. I was told that this was a delicate issue for the central government in Islamabad which considered this an internal problem. I was shocked—and determined to do something about this very bad situation. After my return to the United States I had several conversations with the UNHCR in Geneva, which confirmed that the Government of Pakistan had, so far, turned down its offer of assistance. I have continued to pursue this matter, most recently with the new Minister for Azad Kashmir, and he has agreed to take a fresh look at the problem.

While at the refugee camp, I was asked to speak to the people in the camp. I started talking about IMTD and the small steps we were taking to reduce conflict in Kashmir; but then, as I was about to lose my audience, I had a great idea that immediately got their attention. I asked if they remembered the "politician's bus" the previous year when the Prime Minister of India took a bus from New Delhi to Lahore, Pakistan, to meet with the Prime Minister of Pakistan. They all said "Yes," because out of that meeting came the Lahore Declaration which had positive language in it about the Kashmir situation. They also knew that Declaration had fallen apart a few months later and that nothing had happened since. I then said "I want to start a 'People's Bus' which will cross the LoC and bring divided families together from both sides of Kashmir for the first time in decades." They all agreed that this was a great idea and cheered me on, recognizing it would be a positive, practical sign of peacebuilding which would allow many of them to finally see their families again.

With their encouragement to follow up on this idea, I returned to Washington, determined to make that "People's Bus" a reality. I did not approach the U.S. Government with this idea. I never wrote a grant proposal. We just got to work at IMTD to find ways to make it happen. The key challenge was to move the idea from Track II (citizen diplomacy) to Track I (government to government diplomacy) because governments were ultimately the only ones capable of taking the political step to open the LoC for this bus exchange.

It was a long three year campaign which involved everyone pushing the idea during repeated calls on the Embassies of Pakistan and India in Washington, D.C., meetings with the press from both countries, and many talks with our friends in both countries. It was a hopeful sign when, as a result of my letter campaign, I actually heard back via the Pakistani Embassy from the President of Pakistan that he liked the idea and would raise it with the Indian Prime Minister when they next met.

The first major breakthrough came from the Indian side, however, when in November 2003 the Indian government proposed half a dozen "Track II" ideas to the Pakistan Government. The third item on the list was the "People's Bus." The Pakistan Government agreed four days later. I was ecstatic, but nothing happened. The two Foreign Ministries got stuck on the details. They could not agree on what kind of documentation for identification was needed for the bus passengers to cross the LoC and return.

In September 2004, after my return from Nepal, I got in the act again by writing both sides and telling them that three of our ten Indian Kashmiri came to Nepal with no passport, only an Indian ID Card. If Nepal would accept this documentation as proof of Kashmir identity, why not try it for the LoC? I was told, "We will handle this;" but they remained stuck. Finally, in December 2004, when the new Prime Minister of India and the President of Pakistan met, their Foreign Ministers were ordered to move the bus project forward. On February 15, 2005, the two Foreign Ministers announced the first bus exchange would take place on April 7, 2005, five years to the day after I had proposed the idea to the people in the refugee camp.

Despite some violence in Indian Kashmir the day before the planned event, the Indian People's Bus did leave on schedule. The high level of visibility given to the new "trust-building measure" between India and Pakistan was further heightened by the fact that the Indian Prime Minister and Mrs. Sonya Gandhi, the head of the Congress Party, the two most powerful people in India, flew to Srinagar, the Indian capital of Kashmir, to wave good-bye to the participants on this historic bus. The Prime Minister of Azad Kashmir in Pakistan, together with huge crowds, welcomed that bus in Mazaffarabad, while the Azad Kashmiri Bus was welcomed on the Indian side with great fanfare.

The high point for me personally was when the mayor of Muzaffarabad telephoned me that same day to thank me and IMTD for our role in making the "People's Bus" a reality.

In the United States this important action of peacebuilding between groups of people, from countries that are strong allies of the United States, was highlighted by the press. In fact, the front page of the *New York Times*, *The Wall Street Journal* and the *Washington Post* carried the same photograph of 20 passengers from Azad Kashmir crossing the recently re-built and re-named "Peace Bridge" and entering Indian Kashmir for a historic first in Indian-Pakistani relations.

Despite this very momentous success, much remains to be done. The impact of the initial exchange of buses continues to be positive and has stimulated several other people exchanges between the two countries. Experts have predicted the bus will eventually become a daily occurrence, and it is expected that truck traffic will start soon. I can only hope that relations will continue to improve. The positive political and economic impact on both sides will not only benefit the region and both countries but also can lead to reducing global tensions.

As a final note, in October 2005, Kashmir was hit by a devastating earthquake which caused much more destruction in Pakistan Kashmir than in Indian Kashmir. Over 80,000 people were killed and it is estimated that three million are homeless. Many countries, including the United States and India, responded quickly to this disaster. Thanks to the ties forged by the People's Bus operations since April 2005, the Indian and Pakistan governments worked closely together, and at least five additional border crossings along the LoC have been opened.

Conclusion

What lessons can be drawn from these different events? There are many, but here are a few of the most essential ones.

There is no such thing as an "intractable" conflict. To obtain positive results, the following are necessary ingredients at the government and citizen levels: building trust, demonstrating goodwill, deploying mutual peacebuilding skills, and having profound dedication to creating peace. Obtaining funds to work in the field of conflict resolution is one of the most difficult factors and can take a long time. Thinking outside the box is key, and risk-taking is also a critical element. Yet, in the end, by instilling hope, each individual and even a small NGO focusing on international peacebuilding can make an impact.

Endnotes

[1] "The Chamber was established in December 1905 as the Punjab Chamber of Commerce and Industry to serve the cause of trade and industry in undivided Punjab. Since then it has traveled a long distance and now serves ten states of Northern Region India, i.e. Punjab, Haryana, Delhi, Uttar Pradesh, Himachal Pradesh, Rajasthan, Jammu & Kashmir, Madhya Pradesh, Chhatisgarh [sic] Uttaranchal and the Union Territory of Chandigarh. The acronym PHD stands for Progress, Harmony, and Development." PHD Chamber of Commerce & Industry, *available at* http://www.phdcci.org/introduction.html (last visited Oct. 31, 2005).

Appendix: An Evolution

This book represents the culmination of an organized effort to combat the trend toward fractionation discussed in the Introduction, and to develop an alternative, more sophisticated, view of negotiation as inherently interdisciplinary. It should be evident from all of the preceding text that an initiative to create even a start toward a true "canon of negotiation" is inherently ambitious on its own terms. Its function as part of a larger strategy, however, is not as obvious. This Appendix places the effort in context. Partly, this is for those general readers who are simply interested. More particularly, the Appendix is offered in the interest of any reader who contemplates some similar action in the future, and who wonders what that might take.

The Origins of This Effort

We would like to acknowledge immediately our great debt to the William and Flora Hewlett Foundation. In a sense, this effort began in the mid-1990s, when the Foundation concluded that despite extraordinary discoveries in how conflict, negotiation, and conflict resolution worked, the nineteen Hewlett Theory Centers, a constellation of research and theory-building groups, had been less successful in communicating these discoveries to practitioners. One of the co-editors of this volume designed the Theory to Practice project in response, and was thereafter funded generously by the Foundation to address that gap (a story told, for its own lessons, in the chapter on Negotiating Access). [Hawkins, et al., *Access*] The Theory to Practice project demonstrated, and made concrete strides to resolve, a pattern in which scholars and practitioners were clearly producing large quantities of new knowledge about human conflict and its resolution, but separately and without effectively integrating theory, research and practice.

Five years' ensuing work made some progress—but also demonstrated that the gap between theorists, researchers and practitioners was just the beginning. Investigation showed that Theory Centers' and others' efforts at bridge-building and collaboration, though numerous, had not kept pace with the burgeoning pressures toward specialization; the field now had so many separations and gaps that it could not properly be called a field at all. In 2002, the Foundation accepted a new proposal, that the "Broad Field" project be chartered specifically to address the reintegration of the many specialties now making up negotiation and conflict resolution. The Broad Field project set out not only to demonstrate the existence of the field's fractionation to the key audience (defined as the field's innovators and "early adopters") but to combat it, by demonstrating the results that could be achieved when sophisticated scholars and practitioners were challenged to work together across the customary boundaries.

The other key purpose of the Broad Field project was the formation of a strong, collaborative, continuing network of scholars and practitioners across academic disciplines and across practice specialties that had mostly ignored each other. Without a sustained such effort throughout the broad field of conflict management, ours can never emerge as a true *field* at all; we believe the consequences, to put it mildly, would be adverse.

These two successive projects, accordingly, have worked with an array of dedicated partner organizations to create a series of new discussions. Each such discussion has had its own immediate purpose; but beyond that, together they have tried to model forms and degrees of interaction that will create a continuing dynamic toward a true cross-fertilization of the field as a whole.[1] To pick one discipline as example, in the series of publications produced in the Broad Field project, various law professors have published co-authored pieces with two social psychologists, a planner, a physicist, a behavioral economist, a conflict transformation specialist, a cognitive psychologist, a professor of management, a hostage negotiator and more. For reasons Docherty discusses early in this book this was not always easy for them. [Docherty, *Models*] But we believe it is essential for our field's future.

The projects have benefited enormously from the enthusiasm of a key group of our colleagues. Promisingly, they come from many domains of expertise. One of the project meetings, for instance, resulted (beyond the directly co-authored pieces) in a coordinated set of publications that brought to bear perspectives from anthropology, mediation and arbitration practice, law teaching, urban planning, conflict studies, family therapy, physics, and Navajo peacemaking (see #2 below). Another resulted in articles from perspectives of law, mediation and arbitration practice, education, government agency administration, sociology, economics, psychology, engineering, ethics, political science, public policy, community relations, court administration, and religious/ethnic conflict (see #3 below). Taken together, our colleagues' efforts are starting to outline how conflict resolution can truly develop into an integrated "broad field."

We have learned a great deal from these academically interdisciplinary and multi-practice-field initiatives. In part the learning has been substantive; the output of the Broad Field project's discussions has included more than 70 articles published to date, not even counting this book. But as noted above, another aspect of that learning has been procedural, in developing a model to make such interdisciplinary efforts less daunting to others than they have been in the past.[2]

In the three-year lifespan of the Broad Field project, four successive topics were chosen for intensive investigation, each in collaboration with one or more academic partners. Each in turn produced a large quantum of new thinking and writing. Each has been far too rich and complex to note here in more than generalities, but it is important at least to do that much, to set the context. They were:

   1. *The need for better feedback from practice experience into theory-building and research design.* Partners with the project in this effort were the Dispute Resolution Consortium of the City University of New York and the Institute for Conflict Analysis and Resolution, George Mason University. Published results included 19 articles in *Negotiation Journal*, Fall 2002 and Winter 2003 (plus another 20 published on the Web).

2. *The truncated and even arbitrary structures of negotiation training*. The project's partner here was the University of New Mexico School of Law. The published results included ten articles in *Conflict Resolution Quarterly*, Spring and Summer 2003.

3. *Threats to the fields of negotiation and alternative dispute resolution arising from increasing routinization of both practice and teaching*. The project's partner was Penn State Dickinson School of Law; published results included 19 articles in the *Penn State Law Review*, Fall 2003 and subsequently.

4. *The need for a truly interdisciplinary "canon of negotiation."* In this, the final and most ambitious phase, the project's institutional partner is the Marquette University School of Law; published results include 25 articles in the *Marquette Law Review*, Spring 2004.

The Existing Common Core of Negotiation

It would be absurd for us to claim to have invented the idea that there is a common core to negotiation, one that transcends practice domain and academic specialty. Others deserve the enormous credit for having broken that ground over the past 25 years. But for reasons described below and in the Introduction, we felt the time had come for a new initiative. In the summer of 2003, we invited an initial group of scholars and practitioners to begin work on developing a "canon of negotiation."

Although we have been fortunate both before and since that occasion to work with some of the best-known and most experienced scholars and practitioners this field has produced, we decided to begin with a population that might seem counterintuitive. We invited leading members of the field's *second* generation to be the first participants. Because they had actually been through the initial courses designed by the first generation of leading scholars, they had read materials in depth and recently. That made for an ideal starting point.

We encountered ready acceptance among this group; it seemed others, too, felt the time was right for this effort. The resulting twenty-five initial essays published in the *Marquette Law Review* became the start toward this book.[3] The scholarly fields we drew from included law, psychology, behavioral economics, cultural studies, urban planning, and philosophy; practice backgrounds included labor mediation and arbitration, ethnic and tribal disputes, and civil and criminal disputes involving the U.S. Department of Justice. In an immediate confirmation of our hypothesis, the group's first day of meetings identified more than two dozen topics that every member agreed *should* be shared across every field in which negotiation was taught, but which currently were not so shared. We estimated that on average, *each of the topics addressed in the first round was substantively known already to no more than half or two-thirds of those present*, despite our having handpicked an exceptionally well-read group. For example, the core concept of interests in a negotiation was reexamined in light of findings from "hedonic psychology" that people don't actually know what it takes to make them happy. These studies should have broad impact across disciplines; but they clearly have not yet had such an impact. [Guthrie & Sally, *Miswanting*.] The two dozen topics identified, moreover, immediately outnumbered those already taught in common across the major disciplines.

Analysis of the field's textbooks across disciplines demonstrated that the list of topics that had developed in one discipline and that had effectively migrated to others remained astonishingly short. As recently as the winter of 2003-2004, we found only six negotiation topics clearly taught in common across business schools, planning schools, law schools and international relations programs—i.e. six subjects which were seen as part of an interdisciplinary canon of negotiation.[4] They were:

- the idea of personal style, strategy or personality (including the concepts of competitive or adversarial v. interest-based or principled or problem-solving);
- the use of communication skills—both listening and talking;
- the concept of integrative v. distributive negotiations;
- the concept of a "bargaining zone" between the parties along with BATNA and reservation prices;
- the use of brainstorming and option creation; and
- the importance of preparation.

All of these, moreover, were found in texts originating in the United States; examining texts in use in the same fields in other countries would probably have narrowed the "in common" group even further.

From First Steps, Toward a "Canon"

It is self-evident that the initial group's 25 identified topics grew to 80 in less than two years. The "how" is discussed briefly below. But we must first emphasize that the "canon" initiative would simply not have been possible without the preceding efforts in this series. These not only demonstrated that it was possible rapidly to develop new working relationships across disciplinary boundaries, and in substantial numbers, but also that it was possible to "produce" dozens of significant new publications on an extremely tight time schedule. The number and reputations of those who have agreed to devote significant effort to one or another of these phases speak for themselves as to the rising confidence of our colleagues that the problems the Broad Field project was chartered to address not only should, but can, be addressed effectively. For us, the result has been an extraordinarily rich series of discussions that have taught us where to look for new knowledge.

A concrete example may be helpful to understanding how an iterative process has worked in practice. In the late stages of the Theory to Practice project, the idea emerged of a single conference session designed to highlight for a cross-section of scholars the extraordinary knowledge base developed by hostage negotiators, particularly within the New York Police Department. Since then, we and our colleagues began to realize just how many aspects of negotiation should be enriched or revised in light of that largely unpublished experience base. The arc of discovery and of collaboration first involved a key partner of the project, CUNY sociologist Maria Volpe, who persuaded two successive retired commanders of the NYPD's Hostage Negotiation Team to speak candidly about their experiences, and to be questioned by two academics in front of a hundred others. Then the current commanding officer agreed to join the discussion and to subject himself to the expected questioning. Finally, his equivalent at the FBI volunteered to join the discussion. The immediate results included a truly eye-opening article, co-authored by them all and also featuring scholars Wallace Warfield of ICAR and Carrie Menkel-Meadow of Georgetown University Law Center. "Negotiation under Extreme Pressure: The Mouth Marines and the Hostage Takers" appeared in *Negotiation Journal*, Fall 2002. But that was just a beginning. Further discussions ensued; for example, organizing a panel at an annual meeting of the International Association for Conflict Management (IACM) led us to two scholars, William Donohue of Michigan State University and Paul Taylor of the University of Liverpool, UK, who had not been part of our own frame of reference before but turned out to have been developing a sophisticated scholarly understanding of hostage negotiation for years.

The upshot (to date) is that a whole series of chapters in this volume has been directly or indirectly influenced by the hostage negotiators. Our understanding of characteristics once thought peculiar to hostage situations but now recognizably part of some business transactions; of the effects of reputation on a negotiator's effectiveness; of the degree to which everyday unexpected negotiations on the street demand some of the knowledge previously available only in hostage nego-tiation training; and of how negotiation works on a multitude of hidden levels within the military, have all benefited markedly from a domain once thought to be so specialized that it was of little relevance to negotiators working in more "nor-mal" circumstances. Similar cross-boundary discoveries and acts of information-sharing can be found throughout this book.

We believe there is already evidence that this approach can work to influence the next round of thinking in the field. Before the first 25 articles resulting from this initiative had even appeared in print, we began to work on the next phase with four key professional organizations (the International Association for Conflict Management, the Law & Society Association, the American Bar Association's Section of Dispute Resolution, and the Association for Conflict Resolution), advis-ing them of the existence of the "canon" initiative, and proposing a series of related sessions for their respective 2004 conferences. All four organizations proved highly cooperative, making significant amounts of conference time avail-able, for which we continue to be grateful. The resulting sixteen sessions, each with three to six different contributors, were all designed to critique what we had already found, and to develop indications as to what was missing. This time, many of the field's leading scholars and practitioners had the opportunity to respond. We taped the sessions at conferences that did not already provide for this, and had transcripts prepared. Subsequently, we combed the transcripts for clues; previous experience had taught us that sometimes a remark that should open up a whole new topic is made off-handedly, and is easily lost. Many times, we ended up call-ing back one of the commentators, and challenging him or her to develop such a half-thought-out "lead" into a serious attempt at formulating a new topic. More than a few chapters in this book, we are gratified to report, reflect their acceptance of such challenges. We believe they, as well as the many other writers recruited by other means, have responded with wisdom and creativity. In this way, we were able to go beyond our original self-imposed charter to find the "important, and known somewhere, but unpublicized," into finding and encouraging truly new contributions to our field.

Since the start of the "canon" initiative in 2003, we have already seen results in recently published textbooks. In part, this comes from the remarkable produc-tivity of the scholars we initially invited to the Marquette symposium. Many of the new textbooks include one or another of the contributing authors to the sympo-sium;[5] also, one of the co-editors of this volume has just published a new negotiation textbook excerpting many of the articles from the symposium.[6] Even more heartening is that academics who were not part of our team have recognized the value of the symposium's approach. The new *Negotiation and Settlement Advocacy* book of readings, for example, includes seven excerpts from the Marquette sympo-sium, more than any other single issue of a journal.[7]

We hope the more complete analysis represented by this book will be seen as helpful by other writers, in turn; but that is for our successors to determine.

Endnotes

[1] The reader can judge the results for herself, based perhaps partly on the caliber and numbers of contributors to this book. The engineering and maintenance of networks in our field is now increasingly recognized as an urgent necessity; this was the subject, for example, of *both* plenary sessions of the November, 2005 special conference on negotiation teaching organized jointly by Harvard's Program on Negotiation and the ESSEC business school in Cergy, France. Because our field has seen so many supposedly collaborative efforts which under the surface embodied strongly hierarchical or ingroup-outgroup notions, it's worth noting that at a certain level, modeling and fostering collaboration has boiled down to a familiar principle: we have at least tried, no doubt imperfectly, to approach our colleagues as we ourselves would wish to be approached. For a close-to-home example, the co-editors agreed at the outset that ours would be an equal partnership; but when we were ready to publish the first series of 25 articles in Marquette's law review, someone's name had to come first. A slightly comic "dispute" ensued, as each of us found reasons to defer to the other. When Andrea insisted, Chris assented—with the proviso that the order would be reversed if there was a second product. There was—this book. That air of "lighthearted seriousness" has been maintained throughout, and proved to be a key asset in attracting many of our contributors. (It's impossible for a group of scholars to take themselves too seriously when the meeting's organizer takes them on a tour of a brewery. Very Milwaukee, that, but it works.)

[2] Readers who are ready to tackle the complexities of interdisciplinary meetings themselves will find much more on this theme in *Engineering broad-based discussions: Engaging multidisciplinary groups to create new ideas in conflict resolution*. This set of critiques of earlier ventures in the Theory to Practice and Broad Field series is published as Monograph #1 of the Research Section, Association for Conflict Resolution (2003); available electronically at www.convenor.com/madison/ACRRS1.htm (last visited Feb. 26, 2006). The Broad Field and Theory to Practice projects also produced a great deal of other material which relates to this theme, much of which has been electronically republished at www.convenor.com.

[3] *Symposium: The Emerging Interdisciplinary Canon of Negotiation*, 87 MARQUETTE LAW REVIEW (2004).

[4] *See e.g.* law textbooks RUSSELL KOROBKIN, NEGOTIATION THEORY AND STRATEGY (2002); STEPHEN B. GOLDBERG, FRANK E.A. SANDER, NANCY H. ROGERS, & SARAH RUDOLPH COLE, DISPUTE RESOLUTION: NEGOTIATION, MEDIATION AND OTHER PROCESSES (2003); business textbooks ROY J. LEWICKI, DAVID M. SAUNDERS & JOHN W. MINTON, ESSENTIALS OF NEGOTIATION (2nd ed. 2001); LEIGH THOMPSON, THE MIND AND HEART OF THE NEGOTIATOR (2nd ed. 2001); environmental and public policy textbook LAWRENCE SUSSKIND AND JEFFREY L. CRUIKSHANK, BREAKING THE IMPASSE: CONSENSUAL APPROACHES TO RESOLVING PUBLIC DISPUTES (1987); conflict studies textbook JOSEPH P. FOLGER, MARSHALL SCOTT POOLE, AND RANDALL K. STUTMAN, WORKING THROUGH CONFLICT: STRATEGIES FOR RELATIONSHIPS, GROUPS, AND ORGANIZATIONS, (4th ed, 2001); social psychology textbook DEAN G. PRUITT AND PETER J. CARNEVALE, NEGOTIATION IN SOCIAL CONFLICT (1993); and communication textbook MICHAEL L. SPANGLE AND MYRA WARREN ISENHART, NEGOTIATION: COMMUNICATION FOR DIVERSE SETTINGS (2003).

[5] For example, Michael Moffitt, Chris Guthrie and Scott Peppet are authors on new editions of ADR texts respectively for PON Books, West and Foundation which used material from the symposium, while Jayne Seminare Docherty has since published *The Little Book of Strategic Negotiation* (2005), also using several kinds of material from the symposium.

[6] CARRIE MENKEL-MEADOW, ET AL., NEGOTIATION PROBLEM-SOLVING AND PROCESSES (2005).

[7] CHARLES B. WIGGINS & L. RANDOLPH LOWRY, NEGOTIATION AND SETTLEMENT ADVOCACY (2005)

Contributors

Hal Abramson is a professor of law at Touro Law Center, NY, where he teaches, trains, and writes on mediation representation and international mediation. He is an experienced mediator of domestic and international business disputes and has mediated disputes involving parties from China, Belgium, Colombia, Egypt, Guinea, India, Israel, Hong Kong, Russia, South Korea, and Venezuela. He recently published two books, *Mediation Representation: Advocating in a Problem-Solving Process* (NITA, Recipient of 2004 Book Award of CPR Dispute Resolution Institute) and *International Conflict Resolution: ADR Consensual Processes* (Co-Authored, West, 2005). His academic degrees are in business administration (B.B.A., University of Michigan), public administration (M.P.A., Harvard University), and law (J.D., Syracuse University and LL.M., Harvard University).

Peter S. Adler, Ph.D. is President of The Keystone Center, which builds applied, consensus-based policy solutions to science-intensive energy, environmental and health-related policy problems. Adler's specialty is multi-party problem-solving. He has extensive experience with water, land use, and business negotiations, and mediates, writes, trains, and teaches in diverse areas of conflict resolution. Prior to his appointment at Keystone, Adler held executive positions with the Hawaii Justice Foundation, the Hawaii Supreme Court, and the Neighborhood Justice Center. He served as President of the Society of Professionals in Dispute Resolution and has authored numerous publications in the field of conflict management.

Kevin Avruch is Professor of Conflict Resolution and Anthropology, Associate Director at the Institute for Conflict Analysis and Resolution, and senior fellow and faculty in the Peace Operations Policy Program, School of Public Policy, at George Mason University. He is the author of numerous articles and essays on culture and conflict analysis and resolution, negotiation, political violence, and ethnonationalism, and the author or editor of five books, most recently *Culture and Conflict Resolution* (1998) and *Information Campaigns for Peace Operations* (2000). He has lectured widely in the United States and abroad. In 1996-1997 he was a senior fellow in the Jennings Randolph Program for International Peace at the United States Institute of Peace.

Zoe I. Barsness is an associate professor of management in the Milgard School of Business at the University of Washington, Tacoma. She earned her Ph.D. in organizational behavior from the Kellogg Graduate School of Management at Northwestern University. Her research focuses on the influence of culture and technologically mediated communication on negotiation processes as well as the impact of recent developments in communications technology, organization structure, and work arrangements on individuals and groups in organizations more generally. Her work has appeared in publications such as *The Academy of Manage-*

ment Journal, Research on Managing Groups and Teams, Research in Organizational Behavior, Social Forces, Social Justice Research, and *Negotiation Journal.*

Howard S. Bellman, over the years since 1965, has mediated in nearly every category of dispute. His work has ranged from the most ordinary civil and labor matters to international diplomacy. A significant portion of his practice has included high-profile, multi-party cases of public concern such as controversial land-use determinations, large-scale environmental remediations, school district desegregation, state-wide education financing litigation, and Indian land claims. Mr. Bellman received B.A. (1959) and Law (1962) degrees from the University of Cincinnati, and an LL.M. (Labor Law, 1963) from New York University. He is a Distinguished Adjunct Professor at Marquette University's Center for Dispute Resolution Education.

Phyllis Bernard is Robert S. Kerr, Jr. Distinguished Professor of Law at Oklahoma City University School of Law and Director of the Center on ADR, including directing the Oklahoma Supreme Court's ADR program in central Oklahoma. In this capacity Bernard initiated flexible models of tribal peacemaking adapted through her work with the ABA Dispute Resolution Section and ABA Africa for use in Nigeria, Rwanda, Liberia, Kenya and the Sudan. Bernard's J.D. is from the University of Pennsylvania Law School. She has served on the governing councils of the ABA Section of Administrative Law and Dispute Resolution Section, where she also was Long-Range Planning Officer; is 2005-2006 Chair, ADR Section, AALS; and is co-editor of the book, *Dispute Resolution Ethics: A Comprehensive Guide* (ABA Books).

Anita D. Bhappu is Assistant Professor of Management and Organizations in the Cox School of Business at Southern Methodist University. She received her Ph.D. in Management from the University of Arizona. Anita studies conflict and communication in diverse work teams, as well as service design and delivery. She is an active member of the Academy of Management and the International Association of Conflict Management. She was recently appointed to the advisory panel of the Innovation and Organizational Change program at the National Science Foundation. Prior to her academic career, Anita was a chemical engineer for the Procter & Gamble Company.

Lisa Blomgren Bingham is the Keller-Runden Professor of Public Service and Director of the Indiana Conflict Resolution Institute (ICRI) at Indiana University's School of Public and Environmental Affairs, Bloomington, Indiana. ICRI conducts field and applied research on conflict resolution and collaborative governance with support from the William and Flora Hewlett Foundation. A graduate of Smith College and the University of Connecticut School of Law, Bingham received the Association for Conflict Resolution's Abner Award for research excellence, and research awards from the American Bar Association Section of Dispute Resolution, International Association for Conflict Management, and Section of Environmental and Natural Resource Administration of the American Society of Public Administration (Best Book, 2005, for *The Promise and Performance of Environmental Conflict Resolution*).

Gabriella Blum is Learned Hand Visiting Assistant Professor at Harvard Law School, teaching and researching International Law and International Negotiations. Blum studied law and economics at Tel-Aviv University, and then served for five years as a Senior Legal Advisor in the International Law Dept., Military Advocate General's Corps, Israel Defense Forces, advising military and other government branches on international legal issues and working on the peace negotiations between Israel and its Arab neighbors. Subsequently, she studied at Harvard for LL.M. and SJ.D. degrees, served another year in the IDF, specializing in counter-terrorism, and was then appointed as Strategic Advisor to the Israeli National Security Council. While at the NSC, she taught negotiation at the College of Management and Tel-Aviv University.

Wayne Brazil has been a United States Magistrate Judge in northern California since 1984. Before joining the court, Judge Brazil was a law professor and a civil litigator. As a magistrate judge, he has handled a wide range of assignments in civil and criminal cases. He has hosted some 1500 settlement conferences. He helped design his court's ADR program and supervises the professional staff that runs it. He has published a number of articles about court sponsorship of ADR programs and two books about judicially hosted settlement processes.

Jennifer Gerarda Brown is Professor of Law and Director, Quinnipiac Center on Dispute Resolution, Quinnipiac University School of Law; Charles Mechem Senior Research Scholar and Director, Program on ADR, Yale Law School. A.B. Bryn Mawr College; J.D. University of Illinois College of Law. Law clerk to the Honorable Harold A. Baker, U.S. District Court for the Central District of Illinois. Litigator with Winston & Strawn, Chicago, Illinois. Bigelow Fellow at University of Chicago Law School; Assistant and Associate Professor at Emory University School of Law. Professor at Quinnipiac since 1995. Teaches Alternative Dispute Resolution, Civil Procedure, and Lawyers' Professional Responsibility; scholarship focuses on these areas as well as gender and sexual orientation.

Lan Bui-Wrzosinska is a faculty member in the Department of Social Psychology of Informatics and Communication at the Warsaw School for Advanced Social Psychology in Poland. She is currently a fellow at the International Center for Cooperation and Conflict Resolution at Teachers College, Columbia University. She has been implementing peer mediation programs in Community Schools in Warsaw and is currently interested in applying the Dynamical Systems theory to conflicts.

Lieutenant Jack J. Cambria is the Commanding Officer of the New York City Police Department's Hostage Negotiation Team. His duties consist of coordinating the efforts of 100 Negotiators, who respond throughout the city to all hostage and related situations. He is responsible for the training and certification of new negotiators and the retraining of current negotiators, and conducts training for many outside law enforcement agencies. He worked with the Emergency Service Unit for the three months following the attack on the World Trade Center, to assist in the rescue and then recovery efforts at Ground Zero.

Marcia Caton Campbell is an assistant professor of urban and regional planning at the University of Wisconsin–Madison. She holds an M.C.R.P. and a Ph.D. in city and regional planning from The Ohio State University, and a B.A. in linguistics from the University of Illinois at Urbana-Champaign. Her research interests include resolution of intractable land use, environmental and public policy disputes; participatory action research directed toward neighborhood- and community-level social change; community-based development planning; and planning for community food systems.

Peter T. Coleman holds a Ph.D. in Social/Organizational Psychology from Teachers College, Columbia University and is Associate Professor of Psychology and Education at Teachers College, where he teaches courses in Conflict Resolution, Social Psychology, and Social Science Research. Dr. Coleman is Director of the International Center for Cooperation and Conflict Resolution (ICCCR) at Teachers College, Columbia University, an innovative Center dedicated to advancing the study and practice of conflict resolution. In 2003, he became the first recipient of the Early Career Award from the American Psychological Association, Division 48: Society for the Study of Peace, Conflict, and Violence. Dr. Coleman co-edited *The Handbook of Conflict Resolution: Theory and Practice* (2000; 2nd edition in press), and has also authored over forty journal articles and chapters.

Morton Deutsch is Professor Emeritus and Director Emeritus of the International Center for Cooperation and Conflict Resolution at Teachers College, Columbia University. He studied with Kurt Lewin at MIT's Research Center for Group Dynamics, where he obtained his Ph.D. in 1948. He is well-known and has been much honored for his pioneering studies in intergroup relations, cooperation-competition, conflict resolution, social conformity, and the social psychology of justice. His 10 books include *The Resolution of Conflict* (1973); *Distributive Justice* (1985); and *The Handbook of Conflict Resolution* (2000, 2006). He has been president of: the Society for the Psychological Study of Social Issues; the International Society of Political Psychology; the Eastern Psychological Association; the New York

State Psychological Association; the Society for the Study of Peace, Conflict and Violence; and several divisions of the American Psychological Association.

Robert Dingwall is Professor and Director of the Institute for the Study of Genetics, Biorisks and Society at the University of Nottingham. He has wide experience of research in the sociologies of medicine, law and science. Disputes and their resolution occur in all these environments. His most substantial contribution to the ADR field, however, rests on a series of studies on language and social interaction in divorce mediation conducted in the UK, including participation in the major evaluation project sponsored by the then Lord Chancellor's Department to investigate the feasibility and acceptability of a national mediation program.

Jayne Seminare Docherty is associate professor of conflict studies at Eastern Mennonite University. She is the author of *Learning Lessons from Waco: When the Parties Bring Their Gods to the Negotiation Table* and *The Little Book of Strategic Negotiation: Negotiating During Turbulent Times* and articles on negotiation and conflict transformation. She has worked with numerous partner organizations to help communities strengthen their capacity to harness the positive energy and minimize the negative consequences of conflict. She is particularly interested in the challenges facing communities and organizations experiencing sudden changes that demand rapid adaptation to new realities, such as a changing population, economic restructuring, changes in laws or regulations, or the losses associated with natural disasters or catastrophic events.

William A. Donohue is Distinguished Professor of Communication at Michigan State University. He received his Ph.D. in 1976 from The Ohio State University in Communication. Bill's work lies primarily in the areas of mediation and crisis negotiation. He has worked extensively with several state and federal agencies in both training and research activities related to violence prevention and hostage negotiation. He has over 70 publications dealing with various communication and conflict issues and has won several awards for his scholarship from national and international professional associations. He is on the editorial board of several journals in the areas of conflict management and communication. Bill also maintains an extensive professional practice in conflict and communication training and intervention.

Daniel Druckman is a professor in the Department of Public and International Affairs at George Mason and in Political Science at the University of Queensland in Brisbane. He has been Vernon M. and Minnie I. Lynch Professor of Conflict Resolution at George Mason and is on the faculty at Sabanci University in Istanbul. He has published widely on negotiating behavior, nationalism, peacekeeping, nonverbal communication, and methodology. His most recent book is *Doing Research: Methods of Inquiry for Conflict Analysis*, published by Sage in 2005. He received the 1995 Otto Klineberg award for Intercultural and International Relations, a Teaching Excellence award in 1998, and an award for the outstanding article published in 2001. He received the 2003 Lifetime Achievement award from the International Association for Conflict Management.

Howard Gadlin has been Ombudsman, and Director of the Center for Cooperative Resolution, at the National Institutes of Health since 1999. Previously he was University Ombudsperson and Adjunct Professor of Education at UCLA, director of the UCLA Conflict Mediation Program and co-director of the Center for the Study and Resolution of Interethnic/Interracial Conflict. Before that Dr. Gadlin was Ombudsperson and Professor of Psychology at the University of Massachusetts, Amherst. Dr. Gadlin is past President of the University and College Ombuds Association and of The Ombudsman Association (TOA), and past Chair of the Coalition of Federal Ombudsmen. He has many years' experience as mediator, trainer and consultant in conflicts related to race, ethnicity and gender, and writes and publishes regularly about these issues.

Kevin Gibson is Associate Professor of Philosophy and Management at Marquette University. He is the director of the Marquette Center for Ethics Studies. He studied with the Harvard Negotiation Project and CDR Associates of Boulder. Dr. Gibson has mediated commercial, environmental, divorce and child custody disputes as well as facilitating a number of settlement conferences. He has worked as a mediator and coach for CDR Associates and the University of Denver Law School. He has a published a number of articles on dispute resolution in journals such as the Negotiation Journal, Mediation Quarterly and the Hastings Center Report. At present, he is a teaching associate with the Marquette Center for Dispute Resolution Education.

Bee Chen Goh, a Malaysian Rhodes Scholar, is Associate Professor of Law at Bond University, Queensland, Australia. Her teaching and research interests are International Law and the Law of Peace, Dispute Resolution (particularly on Chinese, and Cross-cultural Negotiation/Mediation), and Contract Law. Bee Chen has published and presented papers in Australia, New Zealand, the People's Republic of China, Hong Kong, Malaysia and Norway. She is well versed in English, Mandarin, Malay/Indonesian, Hokkien (Taiwanese) and Cantonese. Her major publications include *Negotiating with the Chinese* (1996, Dartmouth), and *Law Without Lawyers, Justice Without Courts: On Traditional Chinese Mediation* (2002, Ashgate). Her current research theme is the idea of peace as a human consciousness movement in the development of contemporary international law.

Chris Guthrie is Associate Dean for Academic Affairs and a Professor of Law at Vanderbilt Law School. A leading dispute resolution and decision-making scholar, Guthrie began his academic career at the University of Missouri and has served as a Visiting Professor at Northwestern, the University of Alabama, and Washington University. He has received multiple prizes for his teaching and research, including the 2001 and 2003 CPR Institute for Dispute Resolution Professional Article prizes.

Charles Hauss wears three professional hats. He works half-time at Search for Common Ground, where he helps develop new projects. He also teaches political science half-time at George Mason University. In his other life, he is also the author of the market leading textbook in comparative politics, and four other books, including two on conflict resolution. He holds a B.A. from Oberlin and an M.A. and Ph.D. from the University of Michigan. He lives in the suburbs of Washington, where he and his wife are working on a book about rethinking national security. Their dog is the world's leading canine expert on conflict resolution since they take her for walks whenever writer's block sets in.

Alexander Hawkins is on the verge of completing his Ph.D. at Cambridge University, where he has also taught criminal justice. His research interests include plea bargaining, and, more generally, the concept of discretionary justice. Now based in Oxford (England), he works as a professional jazz musician.

Sheila Heen is a Managing Partner at Triad Consulting, a Lecturer on Law at Harvard Law School, and a co-author of the *New York Times* Business Bestseller, *Difficult Conversations: How to Discuss What Matters Most* (Penguin 1999). In private practice she helps executives navigate strong disagreement to make tough decisions while preserving relationships with each other, with employees, and with clients. Her public sector work has included work in Barrow, Alaska with the Inupiat Eskimos who own the North Slope, in Cyprus with Greek and Turkish Cypriots, and at The Citadel, as they transition to co-education. She continues to be schooled in negotiation by her six-year-old. She can be reached at heen@post.harvard.edu.

Christopher Honeyman is a consultant, mediator and arbitrator based in Madison, Wisconsin and Washington, DC. He has advised firms, nonprofits, government agencies, universities and foundations throughout the U.S. and in other countries on dispute resolution infrastructure issues, quality control and ethics. His specialty is managing interdisciplinary teams of experts to address complex conflict management problems, and he has led a fifteen-year series of large-scale conflict management research and development projects funded by the Hewlett Foundation. He has served as mediator, arbitrator or in other neutral roles in more than 2,000 cases since the 1970's. Honeyman is also author or co-author of more than 50 articles and book chapters; many have been republished electronically at www.convenor.com

Chris Stern Hyman is a health care lawyer and a mediator. In 1998 she formed Medical Mediation Group LLC with Marc Fleisher, J.D., which provides mediation services and conducts trainings. Chris Hyman has written on state medical boards' pain management policies and on mediation and health care. She received her undergraduate degree from the University of Chicago and her law degree from Brooklyn Law School. Chris Hyman was a co-principal investigator for the Demonstration Mediation and ADR Project of the Project on Medical Liability in Pennsylvania and principal investigator of the New York City Pilot Project for Mediation of Medical Malpractice Claims funded by a grant to Columbia Law School. She can be reached at cshyman@aol.com.

Alexander Jeglic is a lawyer in Washington D.C. working for the Embassy of Australia in the field of International Trade. He has previous experience in dispute resolution with the Chicago International Dispute Resolution Association and the Delegation of the European Commission to the United States Trade Section. He holds a J.D. from Loyola University–Chicago and an LL.M. from George Washington University. He is also a certified member of the Chartered Institute of Arbitrators.

Elizabeth Jeglic is an Assistant Professor of Psychology at the John Jay College of Criminal Justice in New York. She received her doctorate in clinical psychology from Binghamton University and she completed a postdoctoral fellowship at the University of Pennsylvania under the mentorship of Dr. Aaron T. Beck. Dr. Jeglic is an experienced therapist and she has worked with both psychiatric and forensic populations. Her current research interests are the treatment of suicidal behavior and the development of sex offender treatment programs.

Gregory Todd Jones, M.B.A., M.P.A., J.D., Ph.D., is Director of Research at the Interuniversity Consortium on Negotiation and Conflict Resolution and Faculty Research Fellow and Adjunct Professor of Law at Georgia State University College of Law. He directs the Computational Laboratory for Complex Adaptive Systems. During the 2005-06 academic year, Dr. Jones is Visiting Research Scholar at the Max Planck Institute for Research on Collective Goods in Bonn, Germany. Dr. Jones' extensive multi-disciplinary scholarship has appeared in numerous law reviews as well as peer reviewed journals in law, ethics, statistics, and economics.

Sanda Kaufman is Professor of Planning and Public Administration at Cleveland State University's Levin College of Urban Affairs. She holds degrees in architecture, planning (Technion) and public policy analysis (Carnegie Mellon University). Her research spans negotiations, intervention, framing and intractability in public conflicts, participation in public decisions, decision analysis, risk communication, and program evaluation. She has designed and facilitated public meetings, and has trained mediators (United States) and environmental practitioners (Portugal). Her articles have been published in *Negotiation Journal, Conflict Resolution Quarterly, Journal of Conflict Resolution, International Journal for Conflict Management, Environmental Practice, Journal of Planning Education & Research, Journal of Architecture Planning & Research, Fractals, International Journal of Economic Development,* and *Public Works Management and Policy.*

Loretta Kelly is a Gumbaynggirr and Dainggadi woman from the mid-north coast of New South Wales. Loretta was appointed as a lecturer at Southern Cross University in 1999, where she became the first tenured Goori (Aborigine) in an Australian law school. Since completing her B.A. and LL.B. in 1996, she has worked for a number of community and government organizations in dispute resolution and restorative justice. Her passion lies in the development of alternatives to the criminal, civil and family justice systems for her people. Loretta received a Young Australian of the Year Award in Community Service (2000), and has published extensively, trained many Gooris, and mediated countless disputes. But she found her own mediation with *Yuludarra* (the Father) through Christ.

Stuart Kirschner is Associate Professor of Psychology at John Jay College of Criminal Justice. For over a decade he has been principal instructor for the Emergency Psychological Technician (EPT) course, which instructs New York City Police Officers on communication with emotionally disturbed persons. Kirschner received his M.A. from Columbia University and his Ph.D. from the University of North Carolina, Chapel Hill. For 12 years he was an Administrator at Kirby Forensic Psychiatric Center (KFPC), a New York State Office of Mental Health maximum security psychiatric center. Dr. Kirschner has served as expert witness and consultant to defense counsel and prosecutors where psychiatric defenses have been entered, and writes regularly on psychiatric defenses and assessment of dangerousness.

Deborah M. Kolb is the Deloitte Ellen Gabriel Professor for Women and Leadership at Simmons School of Management. From 1991-1994, Kolb was Executive Director of Program on Negotiation at Harvard Law School and is currently co-director of The Negotiations in the Workplace Project. Professor Kolb is the co-author of *Everyday Negotiation: Navigating the Hidden Agendas of Bargaining* and *Her Place at the Table: A Woman's Guide to Negotiating Five Challenges to Leadership Success.* Other books include: *The Mediators, Hidden Conflict In Organizations: Uncovering Behind-The-Scenes Disputes, Making Talk Work* and *Negotiation Eclectic.* Deborah Kolb received her Ph.D. from MIT's Sloan School of Management, her B.A. from Vassar College and an M.B.A. from the University of Colorado.

Russell Korobkin is professor of law at the University of California Los Angeles (UCLA), where he teaches Negotiation and Mediation, Contracts, and Health Care Law. He also conducts negotiation training workshops for lawyers and provides mediation services. Professor Korobkin is the author of the textbook *Negotiation Theory and Strategy* (Aspen Law & Business, 2002), as well as more than 30 scholarly articles on negotiating in the transactional and dispute resolution contexts and other topics that combine law, economics, and psychology. Before entering law teaching, he received his B.A. and J.D. degrees from Stanford University, clerked for the Honorable James L. Buckley of the U.S. Court of Appeals for the District of Columbia Circuit, and worked as an associate at the law firm of Covington and Burling in Washington, D.C.

Michelle LeBaron is Director of the Program on Dispute Resolution and Professor of Law at the University of British Columbia in Vancouver, Canada. Previously, she served as a faculty member at George Mason University in Fairfax, Virginia in Conflict Analysis and Resolution and Women's Studies. She has worked internationally to design and implement culturally fluent conflict management systems in commercial, organizational and family settings. Professor LeBaron's current passion is exploring connections between the arts and cross-cultural conflict resolution. She is the author of *Bridging Troubled Waters: Conflict Resolution from the Heart, Bridging Cultural Conflicts: A New Approach for a Changing World*, and, most recently, *Cross-Cultural Conflict Resolution* (forthcoming from Intercultural Press).

Roy J. Lewicki is the Dean's Distinguished Teaching Professor at the Fisher College of Business, The Ohio State University. He received his Ph.D. in Social Psychology from Teachers College, Columbia University in 1969, and has held faculty positions at Yale, Dartmouth and Duke. He is the author or editor of many research articles and books, including *Negotiation, Negotiation: Readings, Exercises and Cases, Essentials of Negotiation, Making Sense of Intractable Environmental Conflicts,* and *Research on Negotiation in Organizations.* He teaches and consults extensively in the fields of negotiation, conflict management, and executive leadership.

Leonard Lira is a major in the U.S. Army. He is currently a student in the U.S. Army Command and General Staff College. Prior, he served as an assistant professor of political sciences in the Department of Social Sciences at the U.S. Military Academy. While there, he co-authored the department's experimental course: 490B Winning the Peace. Major Lira was commissioned an Armor officer from Sam Houston State University, Huntsville, Texas. He has served in leadership and staff positions at the platoon to division level in the 82d Airborne and 4th Infantry Divisions. He holds a M.P.A., a M.A. in International Relations, and an Advanced Certificate of Studies in International Conflict Resolution and Negotiations from the Maxwell College at Syracuse University.

Lela Porter Love is a professor of law and director of the Kukin Program for Conflict Resolution at Cardozo School of Law. She founded and directs Cardozo's Mediation Clinic, which was among the first clinical programs in the country to train law students to serve as mediators. She serves as a mediator, arbitrator and dispute resolution consultant in community, employment, family, human rights, school-based and commercial cases. Her mediation of a public policy dispute in Glen Cove, NY, brought widespread publicity to the use of mediation in resolving complex litigation. She regularly conducts training programs for mediators and arbitrators in the U.S. and abroad and has authored numerous textbooks, training manuals and articles on dispute resolution.

Frederic Luskin, Ph.D. is the Director of the Stanford University Forgiveness Projects and the author of the best selling book *Forgive for Good: A Proven Prescription for Health and Happiness*. He has conducted 8 successful experiments to validate his forgiveness methodology. He also is the Co-Chair of the Garden of Forgiveness at Ground Zero Project whose goal is adding forgiveness to the menu of responses to the attacks on 9/11. He holds a Ph.D. in Counseling and Health Psychology from Stanford University and is an Associate Professor at the Institute of Transpersonal Psychology.

Julie Macfarlane is Professor at the Faculty of Law of the University of Windsor. She has researched and written extensively on dispute resolution and in particular on the role of lawyers, including a widely used student textbook, many articles in scholarly journals and numerous program evaluations for government. She is presently working on a book, *The New Lawyer*, to be published by the University of British Columbia Press in 2005. She is an active mediator and facilitator.

David Matz is Professor of Dispute Resolution, Director of the Graduate Programs in Dispute Resolution at the University of Massachusetts/Boston, and a partner in The Mediation Group, a Brookline, Mass firm providing mediation, arbitration, training, and consultation services. He has written extensively about mediation and about the negotiations between Israelis and Palestinians, and has lectured widely in the U.S. and Israel on the uses of mediation. He has been adviser to the Israeli Ministry of Justice and to the Israeli High Court on the introduction of mediation into the Israeli judicial system. In 1989 he was Fulbright Professor of Law at the University of Tel Aviv. His mediation work includes commercial transactions, health care, and higher education.

Bernard Mayer (Ph.D.) is a partner at CDR Associates in Boulder, Colorado. Since the late 1970's, Mayer has worked as a mediator, facilitator, trainer, researcher, and dispute systems designer. He has mediated or facilitated the resolution of labor management, public policy, ethnic, business, family, community, and intergovernmental conflicts. Bernie has worked with many international and non-governmental organizations and corporations as well as federal and local government entities in Europe, North America, and Asia. He is the author of many works on conflict resolution, including *The Dynamics of Conflict Resolution: A Practitioners Guide* (Jossey-Bass, 2000) and *Beyond Neutrality: Confronting the Crisis in Conflict Resolution* (Jossey-Bass, 2004).

Ambassador John W. McDonald is a lawyer, diplomat, former international civil servant, development expert, lecturer, and peacebuilder, concerned about global social, economic and ethnic problems. He spent twenty years of his career in Western Europe and the Middle East and worked for sixteen years on United Nations economic and social affairs. He is Chairman and co-founder of the Institute for Multi-Track Diplomacy, in Washington D.C., which focuses on national and international ethnic conflicts. Ambassador McDonald holds a B.A. and a J.D. degree from the University of Illinois, and graduated from the National War College in 1967. He was appointed Ambassador twice by Presidents Carter and Reagan to represent the United States at various UN World Conferences.

Hugh McGowan retired in 2001 from the NYPD after 35 years of service. In his last 13 years with the Department, Lt. McGowan was Commanding Officer and Chief Negotiator of the Hostage Negotiation Team (HNT). He personally responded to and coordinated negotiations at over 1,500 hostage, barricade and suicide incidents. In addition to selecting and training negotiators for the NYPD, he has instructed crisis negotiators from other city, state and Federal agencies and lectured throughout the United States and Australia. Previously, McGowan spent 5 years with the NYPD's Emergency Service Unit. He served 6 years as a Detective Sergeant in the Bomb Squad and is a veteran of the U.S. Army. McGowan has a Ph.D. in Criminal Justice from the CUNY Graduate School.

Carrie Menkel-Meadow is A.B. Chettle, Jr. Professor of Law, Dispute Resolution and Civil Procedure at Georgetown University Law Center and Director of the Georgetown-Hewlett Program in Conflict Resolution and Legal Problem Solving. She is author, co-author or editor of six books on negotiation and conflict resolution and over 100 articles on conflict resolution, civil procedure, negotiation, mediation, legal ethics, jurisprudence, feminist legal theory and legal education. She was among the first to teach Negotiation in an American law school (in the 1970's), has taught at many law schools including Harvard and Stanford, and has trained lawyers, mediators, diplomats and government officials on five continents. She also has extensive practical experience as a mediator and arbitrator in many types of disputes.

Gale Miller is Professor of Sociology and Research Professor of Social and Cultural Sciences, Marquette University. He has longstanding research interests in studying the practical uses of language in social life, particularly how personal troubles and social problems are socially constructed in diverse organizational contexts. He has also worked with practitioners (particularly therapists) in developing the applied aspects of his research findings. Miller's recent research focuses on how families define and cope with divorce and separation, the imprisonment of a family member and other such crises.

Robert H. Mnookin is the Samuel Williston Professor of Law at Harvard Law School, where he chairs the Program on Negotiation and directs the Harvard Negotiation Research Project. He has written or edited numerous scholarly articles and nine books, including *Beyond Winning: Negotiating to Create Value in Deals and Disputes* (with Scott Peppet and Andrew Tulumello) and *Barriers to Conflict Resolution*, a joint project with members and associates of the Stanford Center on Conflict and Negotiation. Professor Mnookin has applied his interdisciplinary approach to negotiation and conflict resolution to a remarkable range of problems, both public and private, as a neutral arbitrator and mediator and as a consultant to governments, international agencies, major corporations and law firms.

Michael Moffitt is an Associate Professor of Law and the Associate Director of the Appropriate Dispute Resolution Program at the University of Oregon. He was formerly a Lecturer on Law at Harvard Law School and served as the Clinical Supervisor of the Harvard Mediation Program. As a mediator, negotiator, and consultant, Professor Moffitt has had clients around the world ranging from senior judges to tribal leaders, from unionized prison guards to accountants, from railroad officials to diplomatic academy trainees. He is the lead editor of *The Handbook of Dispute Resolution*, (Jossey-Bass 2005), and has authored numerous scholarly works. A graduate of Marietta College and Harvard Law School, he served as a law clerk to United States District Judge Ann Aldrich. He is a devoted but mediocre snowboarder and an avid wine taster.

Susan Morash has been a nurse in a variety of settings for 30 years. She currently is Nurse Manager of a general medical unit at Massachusetts General Hospital in Boston, Mass. Previously, Susan worked as a Clinical Nursing Supervisor at MGH for 22 years. In addition to providing administrative and clinical support to the Department of Nursing, she frequently assumed the role of advocate for both patients and staff in the mediation of disputes, customer service issues, and concerns regarding patient care. Susan is also a member of the Massachusetts Victim and Family Support Team in Mass Disasters. She holds an M.A. in Dispute Resolution from the University of Massachusetts, Boston and a B.S. degree in nursing from the University of Massachusetts, Amherst.

Jacqueline Nolan-Haley is a Professor at Fordham University School of Law, where she directs the Conflict Resolution & ADR Program, and the Graduate Studies Program. She teaches courses in International and Interethnic Conflict Resolution, International Organizations, Mediation, and ADR at Fordham Law School and in its Queens University Belfast and University College Dublin Summer Program. Her scholarship focuses on ethical and justice issues related to ADR, and on international conflict resolution. Most recently, she has co-authored *International Conflict Resolution: Consensual ADR Processes* (2005). She consults on several public policy ADR projects and is former Chair of the Alternative Dispute Resolution Section of the Association of American Law Schools and the New York State Bar Association's Alternative Dispute Resolution Committee.

Andrzej Nowak is Director of the Institute of Social Psychology of Informatics and Communications at the Warsaw School for Social Psychology, and Professor of Psychology at University of Warsaw, where he directs the Center for Complex Systems at the Institute for Social Studies. He is also Associate Professor of Psychology, Florida Atlantic University. He has been a Visiting Scholar at the University of North Carolina, Ohio State University, the Netherlands Institute for Advanced Studies, and Vienna's Center for Advanced Studies in the Social Sciences. Using computer simulations (e.g., cellular automata, neural networks), he investigates the dynamism and complexity associated with social influence, social transitions, emotion, and the self. Prof. Nowak has published five books, including two with Robin Vallacher concerning dynamical social psychology.

Kathleen M. O'Connor is an associate professor of management at the Johnson School at Cornell University. She received her doctorate in social and organizational psychology from the University of Illinois, Urbana-Champaign. Professor O'Connor's research and teaching interests center on negotiation. Her recent work examines how negotiators' past experiences affect future deals. One stream looks at negotiators' reputations and how they influence their partners' behavior, as well as the quality of agreements they reach. A second stream follows negotiators over the course of several negotiations to investigate how their past experiences affect future deals. Her work has been published in journals such as *Organizational Behavior and Human Decision Processes, Journal of Experimental Social Psychology,* and *Journal of Applied Psychology.*

Scott R. Peppet is an Associate Professor at the University of Colorado School of Law in Boulder, Colorado, where he teaches Legal Negotiation, Contracts, Legal Ethics, and ADR Ethics. Before moving to Colorado, Scott was a Lecturer on Law at Harvard Law School and a Senior Fellow on Negotiation at the Harvard Negotiation Research Project. He is a graduate of Harvard Law School, where he was an editor of the Harvard Law Review and the co-founder of the Harvard Negotiation Law Review. His is the co-author of an award-winning book titled *Beyond Winning: Negotiating to Create Value in Deals and Disputes* (Harvard University Press, 2000) as well as various academic articles on the subject. In addition to his academic work, he has an active negotiation training and consulting practice.

Linda L. Putnam is the George T. and Gladys H. Abell Professor in the Department of Communication at Texas A & M University. Her current research interests include negotiation, environmental conflict, gender studies, and organizational conflict. She is the co-editor of *The SAGE Handbook of Organizational Discourse* (2004), *The New Handbook of Organizational Communication* (2001), and *Communication and Negotiation* (1992). She is the 1993 recipient of the Charles H. Woolbert Research Award for innovative research in communication, the 1999 Distinguished Scholar Award from the National Communication Association, and the 2005 Steven H. Chaffee Career Productivity Award. She has received funding for her research from the National Science Foundation, the Environmental Protection Agency, and the William and Flora Hewlett Foundation.

Robert Ricigliano is Director of Institute of World Affairs and the Peace Studies Program at the University of Wisconsin–Milwaukee, where he teaches Negotiation and International Mediation. Mr. Ricigliano has worked on peace processes in the Democratic Republic of Congo, Russia, Georgia, Colombia, South Africa, and elsewhere. His recent publications include editing a volume of *Accord* entitled "Choosing to Engage: armed groups and peace processes," Networks of

Effective Action: Implementing a Holistic Approach to Peacebuilding, Cold War, Redux: A Critique of and Alternative to the War on Terrorism, The Choardic Peace Process, and Supporting the Peace Process in the DRC: A Track 1.5 Facilitation Effort. He was Executive Director, Conflict Management Group and Associate Director, Harvard Negotiation Project.

Leonard Riskin is C.A. Leedy Professor of Law and Director of the Center for the Study of Dispute Resolution and the Initiative on Mindfulness in Law and Dispute Resolution at the University of Missouri–Columbia. He earned a J.D. from New York University School of Law and an LL.M. from Yale Law School and served as an attorney with the U.S. Department of Justice. He has taught mediation and mindfulness world-wide to lawyers and law students. Len has published widely on dispute resolution and has written several articles on the potential contributions of mindfulness to law and mediation practice, as well as non-legal writings in popular publications such as the *Atlantic Monthly* and the *New York Times Magazine*.

Jennifer Robbennolt (J.D., Ph.D.) is Professor of Law and Psychology at the University of Illinois. A leading scholar in the areas of psychology and law, torts, and dispute resolution, her research integrates psychology into the study of law and legal institutions, focusing primarily on legal decision-making and the use of empirical research methodology in law. Prior to joining the faculty at the University of Illinois, Professor Robbennolt taught at the University of Missouri School of Law, where she also served as Associate Dean for Faculty Research and Development and continues as a Senior Fellow in the Center for the Study of Dispute Resolution. She has also served as a research associate and lecturer at Princeton University in the Woodrow Wilson School of Public and International Affairs and Department of Psychology.

Daniel Rose is Chairman of Rose Associates, one of New York's oldest and largest real estate organizations managing over 30,000 residential units and millions of square feet of office space. Mr. Rose developed Pentagon City in Arlington, Virginia and the One Financial Center office tower in Boston. His consulting credits include the concept of housing for the performing arts at Manhattan Plaza, New York City. He has a long list of philanthropic undertakings. Among other foreign affairs involvements, Mr. Rose was appointed by President Clinton as Vice Chairman of the Baltic-American Enterprise Fund, which stimulates business activity in Latvia, Lithuania and Estonia. He is a regular participant in Forum, the English-language current events TV program produced from Tehran for an Iranian audience.

Cheyney Ryan is a professor of philosophy at the University of Oregon, where he also teaches in the Law School's masters program on conflict resolution. He has published widely in political philosophy, philosophy of law, and ethics, with a special interest in problems related to war, peace, and the problems of justice and reconciliation. He was named by the *Washington Post* as one of the nation's leading scholars in peace education and has received numerous awards for his writings on peace and justice. Since working with Dorothy Day in the late 1960's, he has had a special interest in religious approaches to peace and non-violence.

David Sally is a behavioral economist whose research has focused on language, cooperation, sympathy, social interaction, fairness and strategy. He is presently a visiting associate professor of business administration at the Tuck School of Business at Dartmouth.

Andrea Kupfer Schneider is a Professor of Law at Marquette University Law School. She has published numerous articles on negotiation and international law, and is a co-author of the recently published *Negotiation: Processes for Problem-Solving, Mediation: Practice, Policy & Ethics,* and *Dispute Resolution: Beyond the Adversarial Model* with Carrie Menkel-Meadow, Lela Love & Jean Sternlight. Her previous books include *Coping with International Conflict* and *Beyond Machiavelli: Tools for Coping with Conflict,* both with Roger Fisher. Andrea is also the author of *Creating the Musée d'Orsay: The Politics of Culture in France.* She received her A.B. from Princeton and her J.D. from Harvard Law School. She also received a Diploma from the Academy of European Law in Florence, Italy.

Jeff Senger is Senior Counsel in the Office of the Associate Attorney General at the United States Department of Justice. He previously served as Senior Counsel in the Office of Dispute Resolution, where he advised and trained federal lawyers around the country in negotiation and alternative dispute resolution. He has also served as a civil rights lawyer, prosecuted felony criminal cases as a Special Assistant United States Attorney, and clerked for a federal judge. He teaches trial techniques at Harvard Law School and is the author of an award-winning book entitled *Federal Dispute Resolution: Using ADR with the United States Government* (Jossey-Bass, 2003.) He is a graduate of Harvard College and Harvard Law School.

Jeff Seul is an attorney and mediator in Boston, Massachusetts. He has taught negotiation and dispute resolution courses as a Lecturer on Law at Harvard Law School since 1998. Jeff was a Senior Associate of the Program on International Conflict Analysis and Resolution at Harvard's Weatherhead Center for International Affairs from 1996 to 2000. He has served as a mediator, facilitator, arbitrator or consultant in a wide range of conflicts and negotiations in both the public and private sectors. His articles on negotiation and conflict resolution have appeared in the *Journal of Peace Research*, the *Ohio State Journal of Dispute Resolution*, *Washington Law Review*, the *Handbook of Dispute Resolution*, and other publications.

Daniel L. Shapiro, Ph.D. is Associate Director of the Harvard Negotiation Project, and is on the faculty at Harvard Law School and in the psychiatry department at Harvard Medical School/McLean Hospital. He specializes in the psychology of negotiation. He co-authored with Roger Fisher the book *Beyond Reason: Using Emotions as You Negotiate* (Viking, 2005). Dr. Shapiro founded and directs the International Negotiation Initiative, a Harvard-based project that develops psychologically focused strategies to reduce ethnopolitical violence. This initiative has advised the International Criminal Court, the U.S. government, and others. Dr. Shapiro's international experience includes training Serbian members of Parliament, Mideast negotiators, Macedonian politicians, and senior U.S. officials. He developed a conflict management program that now reaches nearly one million people across twenty-five countries.

Donna Shestowsky is on the law school faculty at the University of California, Davis. She teaches Alternative Dispute Resolution, Legal Psychology, Negotiation Strategy and Criminal Law. She earned a B.A. and an M.S. (psychology) from Yale University and both a J.D. and a Ph.D. (Psychology) from Stanford University. In 2000, she was a Fellow at the Stanford Center on Conflict and Negotiation. In 2003-2004, she was jointly appointed on the visiting faculty at Northwestern University's School of Law and the Kellogg School of Management and was a Post-Doctoral Fellow at Northwestern University's Dispute Resolution Research Center. Her research appears in leading journals including the *Stanford Law Review*, the *Journal of Social and Personality Psychology* and *Law and Human Behavior*.

Douglas Stone is a Managing Partner at Triad Consulting and a Lecturer on Law at Harvard. He consults for a broad range of organizations, including Merck, Honda, Fidelity, The Citadel, and the W.H.O, and lectures widely on leadership, negotiation, and communication. Doug is co-author of *Difficult Conversations* (Penguin, 2000), which is available in 19 languages and is a *New York Times* Business Bestseller. This book is used as the standard communication text in many business and law schools, and organizations around the world. Doug's articles have appeared in *The New York Times*, the *Boston Globe* and the *Los Angeles Times*. He is a graduate of Brown and Harvard Law School, where he was for many years Associate Director of the Harvard Negotiation Project.

Joseph B. ("Josh") Stulberg is the John W. Bricker Professor of Law at The Ohio State University Moritz College of Law, where he also serves as Associate Dean for Academic Affairs and Faculty Director of the Program on Dispute Resolution. A former Vice President of the American Arbitration Association, Josh regularly conducts mediation training programs for court-annexed programs, government agencies, and professional and community groups throughout the country, and mediates selected employment, commercial, family, and public policy disputes. He has written widely on issues in mediation. Josh is a Fellow in the American College of Civil Trial Mediators. He holds J.D. and Ph.D. degrees and is a member of the New York Bar.

Paul Taylor (Ph.D., University of Liverpool) is a Lecturer in Psychology at The University of Liverpool, UK, and a Research Associate of the Police Research Lab, Carleton University, Canada. His main area of expertise is the analysis of behavior in crisis environments, particularly in relation to negotiation, where his work addresses issues such as effective strategy use and the prediction of future behavior. He has published extensively on hostage negotiation in journals such as *Human Communication Research* and *International Negotiation*, and on police decision strategies in journals including *Applied Cognitive Psychology* and *Criminal Justice and Behavior*. He is frequently asked to represent this research at professional seminars, training courses, and policy development meetings.

Catherine H. Tinsley is an Associate Professor at the McDonough School of Business at Georgetown University, and is Executive Director of the Georgetown University Women's Leadership Initiative. Professor Tinsley is a faculty affiliate at the Center for Peace and Securities Studies, a Zaeslin fellow at the college of Law and Economics, University of Basel, and a CPMR fellow for NASA. She studies how factors such as culture, reputations, and negotiator mobility influence negotiations, as well as how near-miss events bias people's decisions under risk. She has published in numerous peer-reviewed journals and has been on the editorial board of *The Academy of Management Journal*, *International Negotiations: A Journal of Theory and Practice*, and *International Journal of Conflict Management*.

Robin R. Vallacher is Professor of Psychology, Florida Atlantic University, and Research Affiliate at the Center for Complex Systems, Warsaw University. He has been a Visiting Scholar at University of Bern, Switzerland, and the Max Planck Institute for Psychological Research in Munich. Dr. Vallacher's research ranges from social cognition and self-concept to social justice and social change. His current work employs a dynamical systems framework to identify the invariant properties underlying these phenomena. Using experimentation and computer simulations, he and his colleagues are investigating the dynamic underpinnings of self-regulation, social judgment, close relations, inter-group conflict, and the emergence of personality from social interaction. Dr. Vallacher has published five books, including two with Andrzej Nowak that develop the implications of dynamical systems for social psychology.

Maria R. Volpe, Ph.D. is Professor of Sociology, Director of the Dispute Resolution Program at John Jay College of Criminal Justice – City University of New York, and Convener of the CUNY Dispute Resolution Consortium. Dr. Volpe has lectured, researched and written extensively about dispute resolution processes; mediates in educational settings; conducts skills training; facilitates intergroup sessions; administers grant funded projects; serves on editorial boards; and is a Past-President of the Society of Professionals in Dispute Resolution. Her current research focuses on police use of mediation, dispute resolution in educational settings, ADR Responses to 9/11, and barriers to minority participation in dispute resolution. Dr. Volpe received her Ph.D. from New York University, where she was an NIMH Fellow.

John Wade is a professor in the law school at Bond University, Queensland, Australia, and directs its Dispute Resolution Centre. A practicing lawyer, John has had an active mediation practice in organizational, family, and commercial conflicts since 1987. Since 1993 John has taught yearly intensive mediation courses at Pepperdine University in Los Angeles and since 2000 at Southern Methodist University in Texas. He has taught over 150 mediation and negotiation short courses in Hong Kong, New Zealand, London, the U.S. and Australia. John has published over 100 books and articles. His teaching awards include best law teacher at Sydney University (1989); at Bond University (1990); and in Australia (1998). He is editor of the *Bond University Dispute Resolution Newsletter*

(http://www.bond.edu.au/law/centres/drc/newsletter)

Kimberly Wade-Benzoni is an Associate Professor of Management and Center of Leadership and Ethics Scholar at the Fuqua School of Business at Duke University. Her research focuses on intergenerational behavior, conflict management, and interrelationships between societal and organizational interests. Professor Wade-Benzoni's work on intergenerational behavior has been recognized and funded by numerous organizations including the International Association for Conflict Management (Outstanding Dissertation Award, 1999), State Farm Companies Foundation (Dissertation Award in Business, 1995), U.S. Environmental Protection Agency (Graduate Fellowship, 1995-1997), National Science Foundation, Kellogg Environmental Research Center, and Kellogg Dispute Resolution Research Center. She is co-editor of the book, *Environment, Ethics, and Behavior: The Psychology of Environmental Valuation and Degradation* and co-editor of a special issue of *American Behavioral Scientist*.

Ellen Waldman holds a law degree from New York University and an LL.M. in mental health law from the University of Virginia. She directs the mediation program at Thomas Jefferson School of Law and has spearheaded a number of grant projects relating to health care and conflict resolution. She sits on the ethics committees of two local health-care institutions and has served on the mediation rosters of both court and community mediation centers. In the negotiation arena, Professor Waldman writes and speaks on a variety of topics, including bioethics mediation, restorative justice, dispute resolution with high conflict personalities, and therapeutic jurisprudence.

Nancy A. Welsh is Professor of Law at the Dickinson School of Law of The Pennsylvania State University. Her research and writing focuses on the procedural justice provided by court-connected and agency-connected mediation, as well as the effect of institutionalized "alternative" processes on the legitimacy and mission of the courts. Professor Welsh serves on the Mediation Advisory Board for the Federal District Court of the Middle District of Pennsylvania and previously was a member of the Minnesota ADR Review Board, which developed and implemented rules governing the innovative ADR program adopted by the state's courts. She also chairs the Publications Board of the ABA Section of Dispute Resolution.

Douglas Yarn is Executive Director of the Consortium on Negotiation and Conflict Resolution and Professor of Law at Georgia State University. Formerly in-house for the AAA, he is an experienced practitioner and has trained mediators and arbitrators nationwide and designed conflict management systems for private and public entities. His publications include *The Dictionary of Conflict Resolution* (Jossey-Bass 1999), two state practice treatises, and numerous book chapters and articles. He holds degrees from Duke University, University of Georgia, and Cambridge University, England.

I. William Zartman is Jacob Blaustein Distinguished Professor of International Organization and Conflict Resolution at the School of Advanced International Studies of The Johns Hopkins University. He is author of *The Practical Negotiator* (Yale 1982), *Ripe for Resolution* (Oxford 1989), and *Cowardly Lions* (Rienner 2005), and editor of numerous works including *Escalation and Negotiation in International Conflicts* (Cambridge 2005), *Peace vs Justice* (Rowman and Littlefield 2005), *Peacemaking in International Conflict* (USIP 1993, 2006), *Power and Negotiation* (Michigan 2002), *Preventive Negotiation* (Rowman and Littlefield 1995), *Elusive Peace* (Brookings 1995), and *The 50% Solution* (Anchor 1976, Yale 1983). He is a member of the Process of International Negotiation (PIN) Group of the International Institute of Applied Systems Analysis. His doctorate is from Yale and his honorary doctorate is from Louvain.

A

Abusive relationships, 51, 115
Access, negotiation for
  case examples, 133, 134–139
  characteristics of, 140–141
  to clients, 135–137
  to information, 133–135
  phases of, 140, 141
  power relations and, 137, 140
  to scholars, 137–139
  significance of, 133
Access to judicial system, 490
Accountability
  confidentiality and, 260
  importance of, in business sector, 712
  in legal culture, 517
  negotiation allies, 605
  self-interest and, in business sector, 713
Action-strategies, 620
Adversarial stance
  advocacy and, 518
  in legal culture, 240, 514–516
  See also Aggressiveness; Confrontational behavior
Advocacy
  in conflict resolution, 513–514, 517–521
  consensus building and, 640
  in language translation, 540–541
  in legal culture, 514–516, 517
  negative perceptions of, 513–514
  negotiating ally and, 611
  zealousness in, 514–515, 516–517
Affiliation
  context-dependent feelings of, 227–228
  as element of relational identity, 227
  interpersonal identity and, 228–229
Affirmative duties of disclosure, 185, 187
Agency, personal
  agency–structure duality, 7, 8–9, 15
  models of decision making, 13–14
  rational choice theory, 13
  social game theory, 13
Agency relationships
  communication challenges, 498–499
  contractual, 500
  control issues in, 505
  elected representatives, 501
  implications for negotiations, 498–499, 502–504
  informed consent in, 505–508
  interpreter–client relationship and, 541, 542
  legitimacy issues, 501
  mediator bias, 588
  politicized, 501
  source of tension in, 505
  strategic use of, 498–499
  structure of conflict and, 499–500

  volunteer representatives, 501
  See also Outside influences
Aggressiveness
  communication style, 386
  in concept of advocacy, 515
Aging, theory of mind and, 380
Alinsky, Saul, 20
Allies and coalitions
  mediator bias toward factions within, 587–588
  spillover costs of negotiating, 12–13, 106
  valuation of proposals by, 168
  See also Negotiation allies
Alternative dispute resolution
  Australian Aboriginal native title negotiations, 306
  future conceptualization, 4
  as gatekeeper to judicial system, 257
  mandated, 111
  power relations and, 257, 258–261
  role of third party, 94 n32
Altruism
  human nature, 284–285
  intergenerational, 221
  revenge and, 287
Ambiguity
  function of, in agreements, 461–466
  as implied moderation, 464
  in labor dispute grievance mechanisms, 463–464, 465
  power relations between parties in interpretation of, 463
  traditional meaning, 462
American Bar Association, Model Rules of Professional Conduct, 188, 190 n33, 279, 595, 596, 601 n12
Anchoring and adjustment, 353, 356
Anger
  decision-making in, 264
  forgiveness and, 436–437
  negative outcomes, 691, 693
  positive outcomes, 267
  simulated, 115, 473–474
  suppressing, 265
Angola, 97
Antisocial personality disorder, 338
Anxiety and anxiety disorders, 337–338
  confrontational behavior and, 233
  psychodynamic theory, 232, 233–234
Apologies
  for acts vs. harm from acts, 429
  categories, 426
  confidentiality in settlement, 262 n19
  essential elements, 427–430
  evolutionary origins, 287
  forgiveness and, 430–431
  historical basis, 427
  identifying parties to, 427

Coercion
  common law limits, 185–186
  to negotiate, 259, 261 n1
  protected classes, 187
Cognitive dissonance, 373
Cognitive functioning
  advantages of team negotiating, 549
  agency–structure duality, 8–9
  anxiety disorder effects, 338
  benefits of forgiveness, 436–437
  bipolar disorder effects, 336–337
  decision-making models, 351–352
  depression effects, 336
  distortions of, in conflict, 107–111
  evaluation of burdens vs. benefits,
    219–220
  evolutionary model, 284
  excessive distrust, 196
  goal setting, 279–281
  guessing games, 88–89
  interference of internal psychic
    processes, 239–240
  Ladder of Inference, 626 n14
  Lawyer's Standard Philosophical Map,
    240
  making judgments, 352–354
  nature of decision making, 13–15
  open mind toward cultural differences,
    594
  perpetuation of conflict harmful to self
    interest, 235–236
  psychopathy manifestations, 338–339
  in psychotic disorders, 339–340
  reasonableness in, 77–78
  schema model, 204
  self-serving evaluations, 354
  significance of metaphor in, 29
  suppression of emotion and, 265–266
  theories of action, 617–618
  theory of mind, 377–381
  unconscious processes in, 30
  use of heuristics, 351–352
  valuation of alternative information
    sources, 93
  See also Frames; Mindfulness; Rational
    thinking
Cohen, Herb, 178
Coin toss, 470–471, 532
Collaborative law, 12, 16 n16, 17, 162 n17,
    188, 518, 519, 520
Collaborative negotiating
  course of hostage negotiations, 671–672
  positive emotions in, 268
  theories-in-use vs., 623, 626 n18
  training for, 616
Collective bargaining
  avoidance strategies in, 114
  legal limits on, 186–187

Collectivist values
  concept of interest, 592
  face-saving, 298
  perceptions of fairness and, 167
  traditional values, 299
  See also Individualism vs. collectivism
Commitment and consistency, 373
Common law
  on coercion, 185–186
  limits on deception in bargaining,
    183–185
Communication
  in agency relationships, 498–499, 508
  audience considerations, 362
  cultural differences, 295, 296, 306–307,
    311, 386–387
  dialogue vs. negotiation, 568–569
  directness vs. indirectness, 386–387
  distributive, 387
  ethics and language, 180
  evolutionary theory, 285
  expropriation of communitarian
    language, 312
  grounding, 398
  handling concessions, 388
  in hostage negotiations, 659–660
  identity messages, 390
  integrative, 20, 387, 388
  language analysis, 388–390
  loop of, 606
  media interactivity, 397–398
  non-verbal, 311
  parallel processing, 397, 398
  process research, 391–392
  proposal generation, 388
  reason-giving, 387–388
  research trends, 385, 386
  role in negotiations, 385–386
  role of negotiation ally, 606–607
  sequential patterns, 391
  skills training, 136–137
  speechmaking strategy for stuck
    negotiation, 468–469
  strategic and tactical applications,
    386–388
  styles, 386–387, 388
  telecommunications, 365
  through emotions, 266
  tough vs. soft, 386
  transformational moves, 392–393
  See also E-mail communication;
    Language
Communitarian theory, 179
Community programs, 641–642
Compensation, defined, 97
Competition
  for airline resources, 688–695
  assumptions of negotiators, 177–178

latent, 69–71
as obstacle to progress, 65
Structure of negotiation(s)
  agency relationships and, 499–500,
    502–503
  bias in, 587–589
  differentiating negotiation processes,
    571
  as disincentive to negotiate, 118
  dynamical systems approach to change
    in, 68
  empowerment goals, 306–308
  formulation stage, 96–97
  language interpreter's influence, 542
  metaphors as reflective of negotiating
    rules, 32–33
  planning for forgiveness, 438
  settlement conferences, 698–699, 704
  strategic process moves, 402
  strategies for empowerment of
    disadvantaged, 308–313
  structure of conflict vs., 498
  three-dimensional model, 56
Subcontracting, 464–465
Sudan, 149
Sun Tzu, 22
Sympathy, appeals to, 403

T
Take-it-or-leave-it stance, 187, 190 n22,
  405, 672
Tantrums, 473–474, 483–484
Taoism, 299
Team negotiations
  advantages, 549–550
  challenges for, 548–549
  constituent groups, 475
  coordination issues, 551
  cost considerations, 550
  cultural conceptualizations, 593–594
  decision-making rules for, 551
  disadvantages, 550–551
  hidden influences, 475–484
  hostage negotiations, 662–663
  intra-mediation team conflict, 559
  intrateam conflict, 551, 555–559,
    561–563
  mediator bias toward factions within,
    587–588
  persuasion strategy, 365
  rationale, 548
  research, 548, 549
  research needs, 552
  role of negotiating ally, 610
  size of team, 550–551
  target of persuasion in, 363–364
  team diversity, 548, 551
  trends, 548

Telephone or on-line negotiation, 365
  trust development in, 198–199
  See also E-mail communication
Temporal sulcus, 379
Terrorists, negotiating with, 105, 107, 156,
  643
Theater, 416–417, 420
Theory
  agency–structure duality, 8–9
  bridges to practice, 3, 138–139, 646
  buyer-seller model, 81–82
  common features of negotiation theory,
    616
  current trends, 17
  decision theory, 351
  everyday negotiations and, 688,
    694–695
  evolution and, 18
  future prospects, 60
  on influence of procedural fairness
    perceptions, 170
  Protean negotiation, 23–24
  theories-in-use, 620, 621, 623, 626 n18
  theories of action, 617–618
  three-dimensional model, 55–60
  values conflict and, 56, 81
Theory of mind
  autism manifestations, 379
  conceptual models, 377–378
  critical assessments, 378
  definition, 377
  implications for negotiators, 377,
    379–381
  individual development, 377, 378, 380
  neurophysiology, 379
Therapy, psychodynamic, 234
Third-party negotiations
  false claim of offer in, 184–185
  role of negotiating ally, 611
  trust dynamics in, 199
  See also Mediation
Thompson, William Irwin, 25–26
Threats
  language analysis, 388, 389
  participative turn, 405
  perception of, as reality, 253–254
  strategic moves, 403
  tactical use, 392
  of temporary impasse, 254
  See also Coercion
Three-dimensional model of negotiation
  application, 59–60
  context and time factors in, 56–57
  as dynamical system, 57–58
  elements, 55
  future prospects, 60
  rationale, 55–56
Tibet, 506